DAN WAKEFIELD

RALPH WALDO EMERSON

RALPH WALDO EMERSON

ESSAYS & LECTURES

Nature; Addresses, and Lectures
Essays: First and Second Series
Representative Men
English Traits
The Conduct of Life
Uncollected Prose

THE LIBRARY OF AMERICA

Distributed to the trade in the United States
and Canada by the Viking Press.

Published in Great Britain by
the Press Syndicate
of the University of Cambridge
The Pitt Building, Trumpington Street, Cambridge CB2IRP
ISBN O 521 26117 I

Library of Congress Catalog Card Number: 83-5447
For Cataloging in Publication Data, see end of *Notes* section.
ISBN: 0-940450-15-1
───────
First Printing

Manufactured in the United States of America

JOEL PORTE
WROTE THE NOTES AND SELECTED
THE TEXTS FOR THIS VOLUME

Grateful acknowledgement is made to the National Endowment for the Humanities and the Ford Foundation for their generous financial support of this series.

Contents

Each section has its own table of contents

NATURE; ADDRESSES, AND LECTURES

Contents

NATURE

———

A subtle chain of countless rings
The next unto the farthest brings;
The eye reads omens where it goes,
And speaks all languages the rose;
And, striving to be man, the worm
Mounts through all the spires of form.

Introduction

OUR AGE is retrospective. It builds the sepulchres of the fathers. It writes biographies, histories, and criticism. The foregoing generations beheld God and nature face to face; we, through their eyes. Why should not we also enjoy an original relation to the universe? Why should not we have a poetry and philosophy of insight and not of tradition, and a religion by revelation to us, and not the history of theirs? Embosomed for a season in nature, whose floods of life stream around and through us, and invite us by the powers they supply, to action proportioned to nature, why should we grope among the dry bones of the past, or put the living generation into masquerade out of its faded wardrobe? The sun shines to-day also. There is more wool and flax in the fields. There are new lands, new men, new thoughts. Let us demand our own works and laws and worship.

Undoubtedly we have no questions to ask which are unanswerable. We must trust the perfection of the creation so far, as to believe that whatever curiosity the order of things has awakened in our minds, the order of things can satisfy. Every man's condition is a solution in hieroglyphic to those inquiries he would put. He acts it as life, before he apprehends it as truth. In like manner, nature is already, in its forms and tendencies, describing its own design. Let us interrogate the great apparition, that shines so peacefully around us. Let us inquire, to what end is nature?

All science has one aim, namely, to find a theory of nature. We have theories of races and of functions, but scarcely yet a remote approach to an idea of creation. We are now so far from the road to truth, that religious teachers dispute and hate each other, and speculative men are esteemed unsound and frivolous. But to a sound judgment, the most abstract truth is the most practical. Whenever a true theory appears, it will be its own evidence. Its test is, that it will explain all phenomena. Now many are thought not only unexplained but inexplicable; as language, sleep, madness, dreams, beasts, sex.

Philosophically considered, the universe is composed of Nature and the Soul. Strictly speaking, therefore, all that is separate from us, all which Philosophy distinguishes as the NOT ME, that is, both nature and art, all other men and my own body, must be ranked under this name, NATURE. In enumerating the values of nature and casting up their sum, I shall use the word in both senses;—in its common and in its philosophical import. In inquiries so general as our present one, the inaccuracy is not material; no confusion of thought will occur. *Nature*, in the common sense, refers to essences unchanged by man; space, the air, the river, the leaf. *Art* is applied to the mixture of his will with the same things, as in a house, a canal, a statue, a picture. But his operations taken together are so insignificant, a little chipping, baking, patching, and washing, that in an impression so grand as that of the world on the human mind, they do not vary the result.

Chapter I

NATURE

To go into solitude, a man needs to retire as much from his chamber as from society. I am not solitary whilst I read and write, though nobody is with me. But if a man would be alone, let him look at the stars. The rays that come from those heavenly worlds, will separate between him and what he touches. One might think the atmosphere was made transparent with this design, to give man, in the heavenly bodies, the perpetual presence of the sublime. Seen in the streets of cities, how great they are! If the stars should appear one night in a thousand years, how would men believe and adore; and preserve for many generations the remembrance of the city of God which had been shown! But every night come out these envoys of beauty, and light the universe with their admonishing smile.

The stars awaken a certain reverence, because though always present, they are inaccessible; but all natural objects make a kindred impression, when the mind is open to their influence. Nature never wears a mean appearance. Neither does the wisest man extort her secret, and lose his curiosity by finding out all her perfection. Nature never became a toy to a wise spirit. The flowers, the animals, the mountains, reflected the wisdom of his best hour, as much as they had delighted the simplicity of his childhood.

When we speak of nature in this manner, we have a distinct but most poetical sense in the mind. We mean the integrity of impression made by manifold natural objects. It is this which distinguishes the stick of timber of the wood-cutter, from the tree of the poet. The charming landscape which I saw this morning, is indubitably made up of some twenty or thirty farms. Miller owns this field, Locke that, and Manning the woodland beyond. But none of them owns the landscape. There is a property in the horizon which no man has but he whose eye can integrate all the parts, that is, the poet. This is the best part of these men's farms, yet to this their warranty-deeds give no title.

To speak truly, few adult persons can see nature. Most persons do not see the sun. At least they have a very superficial seeing. The sun illuminates only the eye of the man, but shines into the eye and the heart of the child. The lover of nature is he whose inward and outward senses are still truly adjusted to each other; who has retained the spirit of infancy even into the era of manhood. His intercourse with heaven and earth, becomes part of his daily food. In the presence of nature, a wild delight runs through the man, in spite of real sorrows. Nature says,—he is my creature, and maugre all his impertinent griefs, he shall be glad with me. Not the sun or the summer alone, but every hour and season yields its tribute of delight; for every hour and change corresponds to and authorizes a different state of the mind, from breathless noon to grimmest midnight. Nature is a setting that fits equally well a comic or a mourning piece. In good health, the air is a cordial of incredible virtue. Crossing a bare common, in snow puddles, at twilight, under a clouded sky, without having in my thoughts any occurrence of special good fortune, I have enjoyed a perfect exhilaration. I am glad to the brink of fear. In the woods too, a man casts off his years, as the snake his slough, and at what period soever of life, is always a child. In the woods, is perpetual youth. Within these plantations of God, a decorum and sanctity reign, a perennial festival is dressed, and the guest sees not how he should tire of them in a thousand years. In the woods, we return to reason and faith. There I feel that nothing can befall me in life,—no disgrace, no calamity, (leaving me my eyes,) which nature cannot repair. Standing on the bare ground,—my head bathed by the blithe air, and uplifted into infinite space,—all mean egotism vanishes. I become a transparent eye-ball; I am nothing; I see all; the currents of the Universal Being circulate through me; I am part or particle of God. The name of the nearest friend sounds then foreign and accidental: to be brothers, to be acquaintances,—master or servant, is then a trifle and a disturbance. I am the lover of uncontained and immortal beauty. In the wilderness, I find something more dear and connate than in streets or villages. In the tranquil landscape, and especially in the distant line of the horizon, man beholds somewhat as beautiful as his own nature.

The greatest delight which the fields and woods minister, is the suggestion of an occult relation between man and the vegetable. I am not alone and unacknowledged. They nod to me, and I to them. The waving of the boughs in the storm, is new to me and old. It takes me by surprise, and yet is not unknown. Its effect is like that of a higher thought or a better emotion coming over me, when I deemed I was thinking justly or doing right.

Yet it is certain that the power to produce this delight, does not reside in nature, but in man, or in a harmony of both. It is necessary to use these pleasures with great temperance. For, nature is not always tricked in holiday attire, but the same scene which yesterday breathed perfume and glittered as for the frolic of the nymphs, is overspread with melancholy to-day. Nature always wears the colors of the spirit. To a man laboring under calamity, the heat of his own fire hath sadness in it. Then, there is a kind of contempt of the landscape felt by him who has just lost by death a dear friend. The sky is less grand as it shuts down over less worth in the population.

Chapter II

WHOEVER CONSIDERS the final cause of the world, will discern a multitude of uses that enter as parts into that result. They all admit of being thrown into one of the following classes; Commodity; Beauty; Language; and Discipline.

Under the general name of Commodity, I rank all those advantages which our senses owe to nature. This, of course, is a benefit which is temporary and mediate, not ultimate, like its service to the soul. Yet although low, it is perfect in its kind, and is the only use of nature which all men apprehend. The misery of man appears like childish petulance, when we explore the steady and prodigal provision that has been made for his support and delight on this green ball which floats him through the heavens. What angels invented these splendid ornaments, these rich conveniences, this ocean of air above, this ocean of water beneath, this firmament of earth between? this zodiac of lights, this tent of dropping clouds, this striped coat of climates, this fourfold year? Beasts, fire, water, stones, and corn serve him. The field is at once his floor, his work-yard, his play-ground, his garden, and his bed.

> "More servants wait on man
> Than he 'll take notice of."——

Nature, in its ministry to man, is not only the material, but is also the process and the result. All the parts incessantly work into each other's hands for the profit of man. The wind sows the seed; the sun evaporates the sea; the wind blows the vapor to the field; the ice, on the other side of the planet, condenses rain on this; the rain feeds the plant; the plant feeds the animal; and thus the endless circulations of the divine charity nourish man.

The useful arts are reproductions or new combinations by the wit of man, of the same natural benefactors. He no longer waits for favoring gales, but by means of steam, he realizes the fable of Æolus's bag, and carries the two and thirty winds in the boiler of his boat. To diminish friction, he paves the road with iron bars, and, mounting a coach with a ship-load of men, animals, and merchandise behind him, he darts through the country, from town to town, like an eagle or a swallow through the air. By the aggregate of these aids, how is the face of the world changed, from the era of Noah to that of Napoleon! The private poor man hath cities, ships, canals, bridges, built for him. He goes to the post-office, and the human race run on his errands; to the book-shop, and the human race read and write of all that happens, for him; to the court-house, and nations repair his wrongs. He sets his house upon the road, and the human race go forth every morning, and shovel out the snow, and cut a path for him.

But there is no need of specifying particulars in this class of uses. The catalogue is endless, and the examples so obvious, that I shall leave them to the reader's reflection, with the general remark, that this mercenary benefit is one which has respect to a farther good. A man is fed, not that he may be fed, but that he may work.

Chapter III

BEAUTY

A NOBLER WANT of man is served by nature, namely, the love of Beauty.

The ancient Greeks called the world κόσμος, beauty. Such is the constitution of all things, or such the plastic power of the human eye, that the primary forms, as the sky, the mountain, the tree, the animal, give us a delight *in and for themselves*; a pleasure arising from outline, color, motion, and grouping. This seems partly owing to the eye itself. The eye is the best of artists. By the mutual action of its structure and of the laws of light, perspective is produced, which integrates every mass of objects, of what character soever, into a well colored and shaded globe, so that where the particular objects are mean and unaffecting, the landscape which they compose, is round and symmetrical. And as the eye is the best composer, so light is the first of painters. There is no object so foul that intense light will not make beautiful. And the stimulus it affords to the sense, and a sort of infinitude which it hath, like space and time, make all matter gay. Even the corpse has its own beauty. But besides this general grace diffused over nature, almost all the individual forms are agreeable to the eye, as is proved by our endless imitations of some of them, as the acorn, the grape, the pine-cone, the wheat-ear, the egg, the wings and forms of most birds, the lion's claw, the serpent, the butterfly, sea-shells, flames, clouds, buds, leaves, and the forms of many trees, as the palm.

For better consideration, we may distribute the aspects of Beauty in a threefold manner.

1. First, the simple perception of natural forms is a delight. The influence of the forms and actions in nature, is so needful to man, that, in its lowest functions, it seems to lie on the confines of commodity and beauty. To the body and mind which have been cramped by noxious work or company, nature is medicinal and restores their tone. The tradesman, the attorney comes out of the din and craft of the street, and sees the sky and the woods, and is a man again. In their eternal

calm, he finds himself. The health of the eye seems to demand a horizon. We are never tired, so long as we can see far enough.

But in other hours, Nature satisfies by its loveliness, and without any mixture of corporeal benefit. I see the spectacle of morning from the hill-top over against my house, from day-break to sun-rise, with emotions which an angel might share. The long slender bars of cloud float like fishes in the sea of crimson light. From the earth, as a shore, I look out into that silent sea. I seem to partake its rapid transformations: the active enchantment reaches my dust, and I dilate and conspire with the morning wind. How does Nature deify us with a few and cheap elements! Give me health and a day, and I will make the pomp of emperors ridiculous. The dawn is my Assyria; the sun-set and moon-rise my Paphos, and unimaginable realms of faerie; broad noon shall be my England of the senses and the understanding; the night shall be my Germany of mystic philosophy and dreams.

Not less excellent, except for our less susceptibility in the afternoon, was the charm, last evening, of a January sunset. The western clouds divided and subdivided themselves into pink flakes modulated with tints of unspeakable softness; and the air had so much life and sweetness, that it was a pain to come within doors. What was it that nature would say? Was there no meaning in the live repose of the valley behind the mill, and which Homer or Shakspeare could not re-form for me in words? The leafless trees become spires of flame in the sunset, with the blue east for their back-ground, and the stars of the dead calices of flowers, and every withered stem and stubble rimed with frost, contribute something to the mute music.

The inhabitants of cities suppose that the country landscape is pleasant only half the year. I please myself with the graces of the winter scenery, and believe that we are as much touched by it as by the genial influences of summer. To the attentive eye, each moment of the year has its own beauty, and in the same field, it beholds, every hour, a picture which was never seen before, and which shall never be seen again. The heavens change every moment, and reflect their glory or gloom on the plains beneath. The state of the crop in the surrounding farms alters the expression of the earth from week to week. The succession of native plants in the pastures and roadsides, which makes the silent clock by which time tells the summer hours, will make even the divisions of the day sensible to a keen observer. The tribes of birds and insects, like the plants punctual to their time, follow each other, and the year has room for all. By water-courses, the variety is greater. In July, the blue pontederia or pickerel-weed blooms in large beds in the shallow parts of our pleasant river, and swarms with yellow butterflies in continual motion. Art cannot rival this pomp of purple and gold. Indeed the river is a perpetual gala, and boasts each month a new ornament.

But this beauty of Nature which is seen and felt as beauty, is the least part. The shows of day, the dewy morning, the rainbow, mountains, orchards in blossom, stars, moonlight, shadows in still water, and the like, if too eagerly hunted, become shows merely, and mock us with their unreality. Go out of the house to see the moon, and 't is mere tinsel; it will not please as when its light shines upon your necessary journey. The beauty that shimmers in the yellow afternoons of October, who ever could clutch it? Go forth to find it, and it is gone: 't is only a mirage as you look from the windows of diligence.

2. The presence of a higher, namely, of the spiritual element is essential to its perfection. The high and divine beauty which can be loved without effeminacy, is that which is found in combination with the human will. Beauty is the mark God sets upon virtue. Every natural action is graceful. Every heroic act is also decent, and causes the place and the bystanders to shine. We are taught by great actions that the universe is the property of every individual in it. Every rational creature has all nature for his dowry and estate. It is his, if he will. He may divest himself of it; he may creep into a corner, and abdicate his kingdom, as most men do, but he is entitled to the world by his constitution. In proportion to the energy of his thought and will, he takes up the world into himself. "All those things for which men plough, build, or sail, obey virtue;" said Sallust. "The winds and waves," said Gibbon, "are always on the side of the ablest navigators." So are the sun and moon and all the stars of heaven. When a noble act is

done,—perchance in a scene of great natural beauty; when Leonidas and his three hundred martyrs consume one day in dying, and the sun and moon come each and look at them once in the steep defile of Thermopylæ; when Arnold Winkelried, in the high Alps, under the shadow of the avalanche, gathers in his side a sheaf of Austrian spears to break the line for his comrades; are not these heroes entitled to add the beauty of the scene to the beauty of the deed? When the bark of Columbus nears the shore of America;—before it, the beach lined with savages, fleeing out of all their huts of cane; the sea behind; and the purple mountains of the Indian Archipelago around, can we separate the man from the living picture? Does not the New World clothe his form with her palm-groves and savannahs as fit drapery? Ever does natural beauty steal in like air, and envelope great actions. When Sir Harry Vane was dragged up the Tower-hill, sitting on a sled, to suffer death, as the champion of the English laws, one of the multitude cried out to him, "You never sate on so glorious a seat." Charles II., to intimidate the citizens of London, caused the patriot Lord Russel to be drawn in an open coach, through the principal streets of the city, on his way to the scaffold. "But," his biographer says, "the multitude imagined they saw liberty and virtue sitting by his side." In private places, among sordid objects, an act of truth or heroism seems at once to draw to itself the sky as its temple, the sun as its candle. Nature stretcheth out her arms to embrace man, only let his thoughts be of equal greatness. Willingly does she follow his steps with the rose and the violet, and bend her lines of grandeur and grace to the decoration of her darling child. Only let his thoughts be of equal scope, and the frame will suit the picture. A virtuous man is in unison with her works, and makes the central figure of the visible sphere. Homer, Pindar, Socrates, Phocion, associate themselves fitly in our memory with the geography and climate of Greece. The visible heavens and earth sympathize with Jesus. And in common life, whosoever has seen a person of powerful character and happy genius, will have remarked how easily he took all things along with him,—the persons, the opinions, and the day, and nature became ancillary to a man.

3. There is still another aspect under which the beauty of

the world may be viewed, namely, as it becomes an object of the intellect. Beside the relation of things to virtue, they have a relation to thought. The intellect searches out the absolute order of things as they stand in the mind of God, and without the colors of affection. The intellectual and the active powers seem to succeed each other, and the exclusive activity of the one, generates the exclusive activity of the other. There is something unfriendly in each to the other, but they are like the alternate periods of feeding and working in animals; each prepares and will be followed by the other. Therefore does beauty, which, in relation to actions, as we have seen, comes unsought, and comes because it is unsought, remain for the apprehension and pursuit of the intellect; and then again, in its turn, of the active power. Nothing divine dies. All good is eternally reproductive. The beauty of nature reforms itself in the mind, and not for barren contemplation, but for new creation.

All men are in some degree impressed by the face of the world; some men even to delight. This love of beauty is Taste. Others have the same love in such excess, that, not content with admiring, they seek to embody it in new forms. The creation of beauty is Art.

The production of a work of art throws a light upon the mystery of humanity. A work of art is an abstract or epitome of the world. It is the result or expression of nature, in miniature. For, although the works of nature are innumerable and all different, the result or the expression of them all is similar and single. Nature is a sea of forms radically alike and even unique. A leaf, a sun-beam, a landscape, the ocean, make an analogous impression on the mind. What is common to them all,—that perfectness and harmony, is beauty. The standard of beauty is the entire circuit of natural forms,—the totality of nature; which the Italians expressed by defining beauty "il piu nell' uno." Nothing is quite beautiful alone: nothing but is beautiful in the whole. A single object is only so far beautiful as it suggests this universal grace. The poet, the painter, the sculptor, the musician, the architect, seek each to concentrate this radiance of the world on one point, and each in his several work to satisfy the love of beauty which stimulates him to produce. Thus is Art, a nature passed through the alembic of man. Thus in art, does nature work through the will of a man filled with the beauty of her first works.

The world thus exists to the soul to satisfy the desire of beauty. This element I call an ultimate end. No reason can be asked or given why the soul seeks beauty. Beauty, in its largest and profoundest sense, is one expression for the universe. God is the all-fair. Truth, and goodness, and beauty, are but different faces of the same All. But beauty in nature is not ultimate. It is the herald of inward and eternal beauty, and is not alone a solid and satisfactory good. It must stand as a part, and not as yet the last or highest expression of the final cause of Nature.

Chapter IV

LANGUAGE

LANGUAGE is a third use which Nature subserves to man. Nature is the vehicle of thought, and in a simple, double, and threefold degree.

1. Words are signs of natural facts.

2. Particular natural facts are symbols of particular spiritual facts.

3. Nature is the symbol of spirit.

1. Words are signs of natural facts. The use of natural history is to give us aid in supernatural history: the use of the outer creation, to give us language for the beings and changes of the inward creation. Every word which is used to express a moral or intellectual fact, if traced to its root, is found to be borrowed from some material appearance. *Right* means *straight*; *wrong* means *twisted*. *Spirit* primarily means *wind*; *transgression*, the crossing of a *line*; *supercilious*, the *raising of the eyebrow*. We say the *heart* to express emotion, the *head* to denote thought; and *thought* and *emotion* are words borrowed from sensible things, and now appropriated to spiritual nature. Most of the process by which this transformation is made, is hidden from us in the remote time when language was framed; but the same tendency may be daily observed in children. Children and savages use only nouns or names of things, which they convert into verbs, and apply to analogous mental acts.

2. But this origin of all words that convey a spiritual import,—so conspicuous a fact in the history of language,—is our least debt to nature. It is not words only that are emblematic; it is things which are emblematic. Every natural fact is a symbol of some spiritual fact. Every appearance in nature corresponds to some state of the mind, and that state of the mind can only be described by presenting that natural appearance as its picture. An enraged man is a lion, a cunning man is a fox, a firm man is a rock, a learned man is a torch. A lamb is innocence; a snake is subtle spite; flowers express to us the delicate affections. Light and darkness are our familiar expres-

sion for knowledge and ignorance; and heat for love. Visible distance behind and before us, is respectively our image of memory and hope.

Who looks upon a river in a meditative hour, and is not reminded of the flux of all things? Throw a stone into the stream, and the circles that propagate themselves are the beautiful type of all influence. Man is conscious of a universal soul within or behind his individual life, wherein, as in a firmament, the natures of Justice, Truth, Love, Freedom, arise and shine. This universal soul, he calls Reason: it is not mine, or thine, or his, but we are its; we are its property and men. And the blue sky in which the private earth is buried, the sky with its eternal calm, and full of everlasting orbs, is the type of Reason. That which, intellectually considered, we call Reason, considered in relation to nature, we call Spirit. Spirit is the Creator. Spirit hath life in itself. And man in all ages and countries, embodies it in his language, as the FATHER.

It is easily seen that there is nothing lucky or capricious in these analogies, but that they are constant, and pervade nature. These are not the dreams of a few poets, here and there, but man is an analogist, and studies relations in all objects. He is placed in the centre of beings, and a ray of relation passes from every other being to him. And neither can man be understood without these objects, nor these objects without man. All the facts in natural history taken by themselves, have no value, but are barren, like a single sex. But marry it to human history, and it is full of life. Whole Floras, all Linnæus' and Buffon's volumes, are dry catalogues of facts; but the most trivial of these facts, the habit of a plant, the organs, or work, or noise of an insect, applied to the illustration of a fact in intellectual philosophy, or, in any way associated to human nature, affects us in the most lively and agreeable manner. The seed of a plant,—to what affecting analogies in the nature of man, is that little fruit made use of, in all discourse, up to the voice of Paul, who calls the human corpse a seed,—"It is sown a natural body; it is raised a spiritual body." The motion of the earth round its axis, and round the sun, makes the day, and the year. These are certain amounts of brute light and heat. But is there no intent of an analogy between man's life and the seasons? And do the seasons gain no grandeur or pathos from that analogy? The instincts of the ant are very unimportant, considered as the ant's; but the moment a ray of relation is seen to extend from it to man, and the little drudge is seen to be a monitor, a little body with a mighty heart, then all its habits, even that said to be recently observed, that it never sleeps, become sublime.

Because of this radical correspondence between visible things and human thoughts, savages, who have only what is necessary, converse in figures. As we go back in history, language becomes more picturesque, until its infancy, when it is all poetry; or all spiritual facts are represented by natural symbols. The same symbols are found to make the original elements of all languages. It has moreover been observed, that the idioms of all languages approach each other in passages of the greatest eloquence and power. And as this is the first language, so is it the last. This immediate dependence of language upon nature, this conversion of an outward phenomenon into a type of somewhat in human life, never loses its power to affect us. It is this which gives that piquancy to the conversation of a strong-natured farmer or back-woodsman, which all men relish.

A man's power to connect his thought with its proper symbol, and so to utter it, depends on the simplicity of his character, that is, upon his love of truth, and his desire to communicate it without loss. The corruption of man is followed by the corruption of language. When simplicity of character and the sovereignty of ideas is broken up by the prevalence of secondary desires, the desire of riches, of pleasure, of power, and of praise,—and duplicity and falsehood take place of simplicity and truth, the power over nature as an interpreter of the will, is in a degree lost; new imagery ceases to be created, and old words are perverted to stand for things which are not; a paper currency is employed, when there is no bullion in the vaults. In due time, the fraud is manifest, and words lose all power to stimulate the understanding or the affections. Hundreds of writers may be found in every long-civilized nation, who for a short time believe, and make others believe, that they see and utter truths, who do not of themselves clothe one thought in its natural garment, but who feed unconsciously on the language created by the primary writers of the country, those, namely, who hold primarily on nature.

But wise men pierce this rotten diction and fasten words again to visible things; so that picturesque language is at once a commanding certificate that he who employs it, is a man in alliance with truth and God. The moment our discourse rises above the ground line of familiar facts, and is inflamed with passion or exalted by thought, it clothes itself in images. A man conversing in earnest, if he watch his intellectual processes, will find that a material image, more or less luminous, arises in his mind, cotemporaneous with every thought, which furnishes the vestment of the thought. Hence, good writing and brilliant discourse are perpetual allegories. This imagery is spontaneous. It is the blending of experience with the present action of the mind. It is proper creation. It is the working of the Original Cause through the instruments he has already made.

These facts may suggest the advantage which the country-life possesses for a powerful mind, over the artificial and curtailed life of cities. We know more from nature than we can at will communicate. Its light flows into the mind evermore, and we forget its presence. The poet, the orator, bred in the woods, whose senses have been nourished by their fair and appeasing changes, year after year, without design and without heed,—shall not lose their lesson altogether, in the roar of cities or the broil of politics. Long hereafter, amidst agitation and terror in national councils,—in the hour of revolution,—these solemn images shall reappear in their morning lustre, as fit symbols and words of the thoughts which the passing events shall awaken. At the call of a noble sentiment, again the woods wave, the pines murmur, the river rolls and shines, and the cattle low upon the mountains, as he saw and heard them in his infancy. And with these forms, the spells of persuasion, the keys of power are put into his hands.

3. We are thus assisted by natural objects in the expression of particular meanings. But how great a language to convey such pepper-corn informations! Did it need such noble races of creatures, this profusion of forms, this host of orbs in heaven, to furnish man with the dictionary and grammar of his municipal speech? Whilst we use this grand cipher to ex-

pedite the affairs of our pot and kettle, we feel that we have not yet put it to its use, neither are able. We are like travellers using the cinders of a volcano to roast their eggs. Whilst we see that it always stands ready to clothe what we would say, we cannot avoid the question, whether the characters are not significant of themselves. Have mountains, and waves, and skies, no significance but what we consciously give them, when we employ them as emblems of our thoughts? The world is emblematic. Parts of speech are metaphors, because the whole of nature is a metaphor of the human mind. The laws of moral nature answer to those of matter as face to face in a glass. "The visible world and the relation of its parts, is the dial plate of the invisible." The axioms of physics translate the laws of ethics. Thus, "the whole is greater than its part;" "reaction is equal to action;" "the smallest weight may be made to lift the greatest, the difference of weight being com-pensated by time;" and many the like propositions, which have an ethical as well as physical sense. These propositions have a much more extensive and universal sense when applied to human life, than when confined to technical use.

In like manner, the memorable words of history, and the proverbs of nations, consist usually of a natural fact, selected as a picture or parable of a moral truth. Thus; A rolling stone gathers no moss; A bird in the hand is worth two in the bush; A cripple in the right way, will beat a racer in the wrong; Make hay while the sun shines; 'T is hard to carry a full cup even; Vinegar is the son of wine; The last ounce broke the camel's back; Long-lived trees make roots first; — and the like. In their primary sense these are trivial facts, but we repeat them for the value of their analogical import. What is true of proverbs, is true of all fables, parables, and allegories.

This relation between the mind and matter is not fancied by some poet, but stands in the will of God, and so is free to be known by all men. It appears to men, or it does not appear. When in fortunate hours we ponder this miracle, the wise man doubts, if, at all other times, he is not blind and deaf;

> ——"Can these things be,
> And overcome us like a summer's cloud,
> Without our special wonder?"

for the universe becomes transparent, and the light of higher laws than its own, shines through it. It is the standing problem which has exercised the wonder and the study of every fine genius since the world began; from the era of the Egyptians and the Brahmins, to that of Pythagoras, of Plato, of Bacon, of Leibnitz, of Swedenborg. There sits the Sphinx at the road-side, and from age to age, as each prophet comes by, he tries his fortune at reading her riddle. There seems to be a necessity in spirit to manifest itself in material forms; and day and night, river and storm, beast and bird, acid and alkali, preëxist in necessary Ideas in the mind of God, and are what they are by virtue of preceding affections, in the world of spirit. A Fact is the end or last issue of spirit. The visible creation is the terminus or the circumference of the invisible world. "Material objects," said a French philosopher, "are necessarily kinds of *scoriæ* of the substantial thoughts of the Creator, which must always preserve an exact relation to their first origin; in other words, visible nature must have a spiritual and moral side."

This doctrine is abstruse, and though the images of "garment," "scoriæ," "mirror," &c., may stimulate the fancy, we must summon the aid of subtler and more vital expositors to make it plain. "Every scripture is to be interpreted by the same spirit which gave it forth,"—is the fundamental law of criticism. A life in harmony with nature, the love of truth and of virtue, will purge the eyes to understand her text. By degrees we may come to know the primitive sense of the permanent objects of nature, so that the world shall be to us an open book, and every form significant of its hidden life and final cause.

A new interest surprises us, whilst, under the view now suggested, we contemplate the fearful extent and multitude of objects; since "every object rightly seen, unlocks a new faculty of the soul." That which was unconscious truth, becomes, when interpreted and defined in an object, a part of the domain of knowledge,—a new weapon in the magazine of power.

Chapter V

DISCIPLINE

In view of the significance of nature, we arrive at once at a new fact, that nature is a discipline. This use of the world includes the preceding uses, as parts of itself.

Space, time, society, labor, climate, food, locomotion, the animals, the mechanical forces, give us sincerest lessons, day by day, whose meaning is unlimited. They educate both the Understanding and the Reason. Every property of matter is a school for the understanding,—its solidity or resistance, its inertia, its extension, its figure, its divisibility. The understanding adds, divides, combines, measures, and finds nutriment and room for its activity in this worthy scene. Meantime, Reason transfers all these lessons into its own world of thought, by perceiving the analogy that marries Matter and Mind.

1. Nature is a discipline of the understanding in intellectual truths. Our dealing with sensible objects is a constant exercise in the necessary lessons of difference, of likeness, of order, of being and seeming, of progressive arrangement; of ascent from particular to general; of combination to one end of manifold forces. Proportioned to the importance of the organ to be formed, is the extreme care with which its tuition is provided,—a care pretermitted in no single case. What tedious training, day after day, year after year, never ending, to form the common sense; what continual reproduction of annoyances, inconveniences, dilemmas; what rejoicing over us of little men; what disputing of prices, what reckonings of interest,—and all to form the Hand of the mind;—to instruct us that "good thoughts are no better than good dreams, unless they be executed!"

The same good office is performed by Property and its filial systems of debt and credit. Debt, grinding debt, whose iron face the widow, the orphan, and the sons of genius fear and hate;—debt, which consumes so much time, which so cripples and disheartens a great spirit with cares that seem so base, is a preceptor whose lessons cannot be forgone, and is needed most by those who suffer from it most. Moreover, property, which has been well compared to snow,—"if it fall level to-day, it will be blown into drifts to-morrow,"—is the surface action of internal machinery, like the index on the face of a clock. Whilst now it is the gymnastics of the understanding, it is hiving in the foresight of the spirit, experience in profounder laws.

The whole character and fortune of the individual are affected by the least inequalities in the culture of the understanding; for example, in the perception of differences. Therefore is Space, and therefore Time, that man may know that things are not huddled and lumped, but sundered and individual. A bell and a plough have each their use, and neither can do the office of the other. Water is good to drink, coal to burn, wool to wear; but wool cannot be drunk, nor water spun, nor coal eaten. The wise man shows his wisdom in separation, in gradation, and his scale of creatures and of merits is as wide as nature. The foolish have no range in their scale, but suppose every man is as every other man. What is not good they call the worst, and what is not hateful, they call the best.

In like manner, what good heed, nature forms in us! She pardons no mistakes. Her yea is yea, and her nay, nay.

The first steps in Agriculture, Astronomy, Zoölogy, (those first steps which the farmer, the hunter, and the sailor take,) teach that nature's dice are always loaded; that in her heaps and rubbish are concealed sure and useful results.

How calmly and genially the mind apprehends one after another the laws of physics! What noble emotions dilate the mortal as he enters into the counsels of the creation, and feels by knowledge the privilege to BE! His insight refines him. The beauty of nature shines in his own breast. Man is greater that he can see this, and the universe less, because Time and Space relations vanish as laws are known.

Here again we are impressed and even daunted by the immense Universe to be explored. "What we know, is a point to what we do not know." Open any recent journal of science, and weigh the problems suggested concerning Light, Heat, Electricity, Magnetism, Physiology, Geology, and judge whether the interest of natural science is likely to be soon exhausted.

Passing by many particulars of the discipline of nature, we must not omit to specify two.

The exercise of the Will or the lesson of power is taught in every event. From the child's successive possession of his several senses up to the hour when he saith, "Thy will be done!" he is learning the secret, that he can reduce under his will, not only particular events, but great classes, nay the whole series of events, and so conform all facts to his character. Nature is thoroughly mediate. It is made to serve. It receives the dominion of man as meekly as the ass on which the Saviour rode. It offers all its kingdoms to man as the raw material which he may mould into what is useful. Man is never weary of working it up. He forges the subtile and delicate air into wise and melodious words, and gives them wing as angels of persuasion and command. One after another, his victorious thought comes up with and reduces all things, until the world becomes, at last, only a realized will,—the double of the man.

2. Sensible objects conform to the premonitions of Reason and reflect the conscience. All things are moral; and in their boundless changes have an unceasing reference to spiritual nature. Therefore is nature glorious with form, color, and motion, that every globe in the remotest heaven; every chemical change from the rudest crystal up to the laws of life; every change of vegetation from the first principle of growth in the eye of a leaf, to the tropical forest and antediluvian coal-mine; every animal function from the sponge up to Hercules, shall hint or thunder to man the laws of right and wrong, and echo the Ten Commandments. Therefore is nature ever the ally of Religion: lends all her pomp and riches to the religious sentiment. Prophet and priest, David, Isaiah, Jesus, have drawn deeply from this source. This ethical character so penetrates the bone and marrow of nature, as to seem the end for which it was made. Whatever private purpose is answered by any member or part, this is its public and universal function, and is never omitted. Nothing in nature is exhausted in its first use. When a thing has served an end to the uttermost, it is wholly new for an ulterior service. In God, every end is converted into a new means. Thus the use of commodity, re-

garded by itself, is mean and squalid. But it is to the mind an
education in the doctrine of Use, namely, that a thing is
good only so far as it serves; that a conspiring of parts and efforts to the production of an end, is essential to any being.
The first and gross manifestation of this truth, is our inevitable and hated training in values and wants, in corn and
meat.

It has already been illustrated, that every natural process is
a version of a moral sentence. The moral law lies at the centre
of nature and radiates to the circumference. It is the pith and
marrow of every substance, every relation, and every process.
All things with which we deal, preach to us. What is a farm
but a mute gospel? The chaff and the wheat, weeds and
plants, blight, rain, insects, sun,—it is a sacred emblem from
the first furrow of spring to the last stack which the snow of
winter overtakes in the fields. But the sailor, the shepherd,
the miner, the merchant, in their several resorts, have each an
experience precisely parallel, and leading to the same conclusion: because all organizations are radically alike. Nor can it
be doubted that this moral sentiment which thus scents the
air, grows in the grain, and impregnates the waters of the
world, is caught by man and sinks into his soul. The moral
influence of nature upon every individual is that amount of
truth which it illustrates to him. Who can estimate this? Who
can guess how much firmness the sea-beaten rock has taught
the fisherman? how much tranquillity has been reflected to
man from the azure sky, over whose unspotted deeps the
winds forevermore drive flocks of stormy clouds, and leave no
wrinkle or stain? how much industry and providence and affection we have caught from the pantomime of brutes? What
a searching preacher of self-command is the varying phenomenon of Health!

Herein is especially apprehended the unity of Nature,—the
unity in variety,—which meets us everywhere. All the endless
variety of things make an identical impression. Xenophanes
complained in his old age, that, look where he would, all
things hastened back to Unity. He was weary of seeing the
same entity in the tedious variety of forms. The fable of Proteus has a cordial truth. A leaf, a drop, a crystal, a moment of
time is related to the whole, and partakes of the perfection of

the whole. Each particle is a microcosm, and faithfully renders the likeness of the world.

Not only resemblances exist in things whose analogy is obvious, as when we detect the type of the human hand in the flipper of the fossil saurus, but also in objects wherein there is great superficial unlikeness. Thus architecture is called "frozen music," by De Stael and Goethe. Vitruvius thought an architect should be a musician. "A Gothic church," said Coleridge, "is a petrified religion." Michael Angelo maintained, that, to an architect, a knowledge of anatomy is essential. In Haydn's oratorios, the notes present to the imagination not only motions, as, of the snake, the stag, and the elephant, but colors also; as the green grass. The law of harmonic sounds reappears in the harmonic colors. The granite is differenced in its laws only by the more or less of heat, from the river that wears it away. The river, as it flows, resembles the air that flows over it; the air resembles the light which traverses it with more subtile currents; the light resembles the heat which rides with it through Space. Each creature is only a modification of the other; the likeness in them is more than the difference, and their radical law is one and the same. A rule of one art, or a law of one organization, holds true throughout nature. So intimate is this Unity, that, it is easily seen, it lies under the undermost garment of nature, and betrays its source in Universal Spirit. For, it pervades Thought also. Every universal truth which we express in words, implies or supposes every other truth. *Omne verum vero consonat.* It is like a great circle on a sphere, comprising all possible circles; which, however, may be drawn, and comprise it, in like manner. Every such truth is the absolute Ens seen from one side. But it has innumerable sides.

The central Unity is still more conspicuous in actions. Words are finite organs of the infinite mind. They cannot cover the dimensions of what is in truth. They break, chop, and impoverish it. An action is the perfection and publication of thought. A right action seems to fill the eye, and to be related to all nature. "The wise man, in doing one thing, does all; or, in the one thing he does rightly, he sees the likeness of all which is done rightly."

Words and actions are not the attributes of brute nature.

They introduce us to the human form, of which all other organizations appear to be degradations. When this appears among so many that surround it, the spirit prefers it to all others. It says, 'From such as this, have I drawn joy and knowledge; in such as this, have I found and beheld myself; I will speak to it; it can speak again; it can yield me thought already formed and alive.' In fact, the eye,—the mind,—is always accompanied by these forms, male and female; and these are incomparably the richest informations of the power and order that lie at the heart of things. Unfortunately, every one of them bears the marks as of some injury; is marred and superficially defective. Nevertheless, far different from the deaf and dumb nature around them, these all rest like fountain-pipes on the unfathomed sea of thought and virtue whereto they alone, of all organizations, are the entrances.

It were a pleasant inquiry to follow into detail their ministry to our education, but where would it stop? We are associated in adolescent and adult life with some friends, who, like skies and waters, are coextensive with our idea; who, answering each to a certain affection of the soul, satisfy our desire on that side; whom we lack power to put at such focal distance from us, that we can mend or even analyze them. We cannot choose but love them. When much intercourse with a friend has supplied us with a standard of excellence, and has increased our respect for the resources of God who thus sends a real person to outgo our ideal; when he has, moreover, become an object of thought, and, whilst his character retains all its unconscious effect, is converted in the mind into solid and sweet wisdom,—it is a sign to us that his office is closing, and he is commonly withdrawn from our sight in a short time.

Chapter VI

IDEALISM

THUS IS the unspeakable but intelligible and practicable meaning of the world conveyed to man, the immortal pupil, in every object of sense. To this one end of Discipline, all parts of nature conspire.

A noble doubt perpetually suggests itself, whether this end be not the Final Cause of the Universe; and whether nature outwardly exists. It is a sufficient account of that Appearance we call the World, that God will teach a human mind, and so makes it the receiver of a certain number of congruent sensations, which we call sun and moon, man and woman, house and trade. In my utter impotence to test the authenticity of the report of my senses, to know whether the impressions they make on me correspond with outlying objects, what difference does it make, whether Orion is up there in heaven, or some god paints the image in the firmament of the soul? The relations of parts and the end of the whole remaining the same, what is the difference, whether land and sea interact, and worlds revolve and intermingle without number or end,—deep yawning under deep, and galaxy balancing galaxy, throughout absolute space,—or, whether, without relations of time and space, the same appearances are inscribed in the constant faith of man? Whether nature enjoy a substantial existence without, or is only in the apocalypse of the mind, it is alike useful and alike venerable to me. Be it what it may, it is ideal to me, so long as I cannot try the accuracy of my senses.

The frivolous make themselves merry with the Ideal theory, as if its consequences were burlesque; as if it affected the stability of nature. It surely does not. God never jests with us, and will not compromise the end of nature, by permitting any inconsequence in its procession. Any distrust of the permanence of laws, would paralyze the faculties of man. Their permanence is sacredly respected, and his faith therein is perfect. The wheels and springs of man are all set to the hypothesis of the permanence of nature. We are not built like a ship to

be tossed, but like a house to stand. It is a natural consequence of this structure, that, so long as the active powers
predominate over the reflective, we resist with indignation
any hint that nature is more short-lived or mutable than
spirit. The broker, the wheelwright, the carpenter, the toll-
man, are much displeased at the intimation.

But whilst we acquiesce entirely in the permanence of natural laws, the question of the absolute existence of nature still
remains open. It is the uniform effect of culture on the human
mind, not to shake our faith in the stability of particular phenomena, as of heat, water, azote; but to lead us to regard
nature as a phenomenon, not a substance; to attribute necessary existence to spirit; to esteem nature as an accident and
an effect.

To the senses and the unrenewed understanding, belongs a
sort of instinctive belief in the absolute existence of nature. In
their view, man and nature are indissolubly joined. Things are
ultimates, and they never look beyond their sphere. The presence of Reason mars this faith. The first effort of thought
tends to relax this despotism of the senses, which binds us to
nature as if we were a part of it, and shows us nature aloof,
and, as it were, afloat. Until this higher agency intervened,
the animal eye sees, with wonderful accuracy, sharp outlines
and colored surfaces. When the eye of Reason opens, to outline and surface are at once added, grace and expression.
These proceed from imagination and affection, and abate
somewhat of the angular distinctness of objects. If the Reason
be stimulated to more earnest vision, outlines and surfaces
become transparent, and are no longer seen; causes and spirits
are seen through them. The best moments of life are these
delicious awakenings of the higher powers, and the reveren-
tial withdrawing of nature before its God.

Let us proceed to indicate the effects of culture. 1. Our first
institution in the Ideal philosophy is a hint from nature
herself.

Nature is made to conspire with spirit to emancipate us.
Certain mechanical changes, a small alteration in our local position apprizes us of a dualism. We are strangely affected by
seeing the shore from a moving ship, from a balloon, or
through the tints of an unusual sky. The least change in our

point of view, gives the whole world a pictorial air. A man who seldom rides, needs only to get into a coach and traverse his own town, to turn the street into a puppet-show. The men, the women,—talking, running, bartering, fighting,— the earnest mechanic, the lounger, the beggar, the boys, the dogs, are unrealized at once, or, at least, wholly detached from all relation to the observer, and seen as apparent, not substantial beings. What new thoughts are suggested by seeing a face of country quite familiar, in the rapid movement of the rail-road car! Nay, the most wonted objects, (make a very slight change in the point of vision,) please us most. In a camera obscura, the butcher's cart, and the figure of one of our own family amuse us. So a portrait of a well-known face gratifies us. Turn the eyes upside down, by looking at the landscape through your legs, and how agreeable is the picture, though you have seen it any time these twenty years!

In these cases, by mechanical means, is suggested the difference between the observer and the spectacle,—between man and nature. Hence arises a pleasure mixed with awe; I may say, a low degree of the sublime is felt from the fact, probably, that man is hereby apprized, that, whilst the world is a spectacle, something in himself is stable.

2. In a higher manner, the poet communicates the same pleasure. By a few strokes he delineates, as on air, the sun, the mountain, the camp, the city, the hero, the maiden, not different from what we know them, but only lifted from the ground and afloat before the eye. He unfixes the land and the sea, makes them revolve around the axis of his primary thought, and disposes them anew. Possessed himself by a heroic passion, he uses matter as symbols of it. The sensual man conforms thoughts to things; the poet conforms things to his thoughts. The one esteems nature as rooted and fast; the other, as fluid, and impresses his being thereon. To him, the refractory world is ductile and flexible; he invests dust and stones with humanity, and makes them the words of the Reason. The Imagination may be defined to be, the use which the Reason makes of the material world. Shakspeare possesses the power of subordinating nature for the purposes of expression, beyond all poets. His imperial muse tosses the creation like a bauble from hand to hand, and uses it to embody any

caprice of thought that is upper-most in his mind. The remotest spaces of nature are visited, and the farthest sundered things are brought together, by a subtle spiritual connection. We are made aware that magnitude of material things is relative, and all objects shrink and expand to serve the passion of the poet. Thus, in his sonnets, the lays of birds, the scents and dyes of flowers, he finds to be the *shadow* of his beloved; time, which keeps her from him, is his *chest*; the suspicion she has awakened, is her *ornament*;

> The ornament of beauty is Suspect,
> A crow which flies in heaven's sweetest air.

His passion is not the fruit of chance; it swells, as he speaks, to a city, or a state.

> No, it was builded far from accident;
> It suffers not in smiling pomp, nor falls
> Under the brow of thralling discontent;
> It fears not policy, that heretic,
> That works on leases of short numbered hours,
> But all alone stands hugely politic.

In the strength of his constancy, the Pyramids seem to him recent and transitory. The freshness of youth and love dazzles him with its resemblance to morning.

> Take those lips away
> Which so sweetly were forsworn;
> And those eyes,—the break of day,
> Lights that do mislead the morn.

The wild beauty of this hyperbole, I may say, in passing, it would not be easy to match in literature.

This transfiguration which all material objects undergo through the passion of the poet,—this power which he exerts to dwarf the great, to magnify the small,—might be illustrated by a thousand examples from his Plays. I have before me the Tempest, and will cite only these few lines.

> ARIEL. The strong based promontory
> Have I made shake, and by the spurs plucked up
> The pine and cedar.

Prospero calls for music to soothe the frantic Alonzo, and his companions;

> A solemn air, and the best comforter
> To an unsettled fancy, cure thy brains
> Now useless, boiled within thy skull.

Again;

> The charm dissolves apace,
> And, as the morning steals upon the night,
> Melting the darkness, so their rising senses
> Begin to chase the ignorant fumes that mantle
> Their clearer reason.
>   Their understanding
> Begins to swell: and the approaching tide
> Will shortly fill the reasonable shores
> That now lie foul and muddy.

The perception of real affinities between events, (that is to say, of *ideal* affinities, for those only are real,) enables the poet thus to make free with the most imposing forms and phenomena of the world, and to assert the predominance of the soul.

3. Whilst thus the poet animates nature with his own thoughts, he differs from the philosopher only herein, that the one proposes Beauty as his main end; the other Truth. But the philosopher, not less than the poet, postpones the apparent order and relations of things to the empire of thought. "The problem of philosophy," according to Plato, "is, for all that exists conditionally, to find a ground unconditioned and absolute." It proceeds on the faith that a law determines all phenomena, which being known, the phenomena can be predicted. That law, when in the mind, is an idea. Its beauty is infinite. The true philosopher and the true poet are one, and a beauty, which is truth, and a truth, which is beauty, is the aim of both. Is not the charm of one of Plato's or Aristotle's definitions, strictly like that of the Antigone of Sophocles? It is, in both cases, that a spiritual life has been imparted to nature; that the solid seeming block of matter has been pervaded and dissolved by a thought; that this feeble human being has penetrated the vast masses of nature with

an informing soul, and recognised itself in their harmony, that is, seized their law. In physics, when this is attained, the memory disburthens itself of its cumbrous catalogues of particulars, and carries centuries of observation in a single formula.

Thus even in physics, the material is degraded before the spiritual. The astronomer, the geometer, rely on their irrefragable analysis, and disdain the results of observation. The sublime remark of Euler on his law of arches, "This will be found contrary to all experience, yet is true;" had already transferred nature into the mind, and left matter like an outcast corpse.

4. Intellectual science has been observed to beget invariably a doubt of the existence of matter. Turgot said, "He that has never doubted the existence of matter, may be assured he has no aptitude for metaphysical inquiries." It fastens the attention upon immortal necessary uncreated natures, that is, upon Ideas; and in their presence, we feel that the outward circumstance is a dream and a shade. Whilst we wait in this Olympus of gods, we think of nature as an appendix to the soul. We ascend into their region, and know that these are the thoughts of the Supreme Being. "These are they who were set up from everlasting, from the beginning, or ever the earth was. When he prepared the heavens, they were there; when he established the clouds above, when he strengthened the fountains of the deep. Then they were by him, as one brought up with him. Of them took he counsel."

Their influence is proportionate. As objects of science, they are accessible to few men. Yet all men are capable of being raised by piety or by passion, into their region. And no man touches these divine natures, without becoming, in some degree, himself divine. Like a new soul, they renew the body. We become physically nimble and lightsome; we tread on air; life is no longer irksome, and we think it will never be so. No man fears age or misfortune or death, in their serene company, for he is transported out of the district of change. Whilst we behold unveiled the nature of Justice and Truth, we learn the difference between the absolute and the conditional or relative. We apprehend the absolute. As it were, for the first time, *we exist*. We become immortal, for we learn that time and space are relations of matter; that, with a perception of truth, or a virtuous will, they have no affinity.

5. Finally, religion and ethics, which may be fitly called,— the practice of ideas, or the introduction of ideas into life,— have an analogous effect with all lower culture, in degrading nature and suggesting its dependence on spirit. Ethics and religion differ herein; that the one is the system of human duties commencing from man; the other, from God. Religion includes the personality of God; Ethics does not. They are one to our present design. They both put nature under foot. The first and last lesson of religion is, "The things that are seen, are temporal; the things that are unseen, are eternal." It puts an affront upon nature. It does that for the unschooled, which philosophy does for Berkeley and Viasa. The uniform language that may be heard in the churches of the most ignorant sects, is,— "Contemn the unsubstantial shows of the world; they are vanities, dreams, shadows, unrealities; seek the realities of religion." The devotee flouts nature. Some theosophists have arrived at a certain hostility and indignation towards matter, as the Manichean and Plotinus. They distrusted in themselves any looking back to these flesh-pots of Egypt. Plotinus was ashamed of his body. In short, they might all say of matter, what Michael Angelo said of external beauty, "it is the frail and weary weed, in which God dresses the soul, which he has called into time."

It appears that motion, poetry, physical and intellectual science, and religion, all tend to affect our convictions of the reality of the external world. But I own there is something ungrateful in expanding too curiously the particulars of the general proposition, that all culture tends to imbue us with idealism. I have no hostility to nature, but a child's love to it. I expand and live in the warm day like corn and melons. Let us speak her fair. I do not wish to fling stones at my beautiful mother, nor soil my gentle nest. I only wish to indicate the true position of nature in regard to man, wherein to establish man, all right education tends; as the ground which to attain is the object of human life, that is, of man's connection with nature. Culture inverts the vulgar views of nature, and brings the mind to call that apparent, which it uses to call real, and that real, which it uses to call visionary. Children, it is true, believe in the external world. The belief that it appears only, is an afterthought, but with culture, this faith will as surely arise on the mind as did the first.

The advantage of the ideal theory over the popular faith, is this, that it presents the world in precisely that view which is most desirable to the mind. It is, in fact, the view which Reason, both speculative and practical, that is, philosophy and virtue, take. For, seen in the light of thought, the world always is phenomenal; and virtue subordinates it to the mind. Idealism sees the world in God. It beholds the whole circle of persons and things, of actions and events, of country and religion, not as painfully accumulated, atom after atom, act after act, in an aged creeping Past, but as one vast picture, which God paints on the instant eternity, for the contemplation of the soul. Therefore the soul holds itself off from a too trivial and microscopic study of the universal tablet. It respects the end too much, to immerse itself in the means. It sees something more important in Christianity, than the scandals of ecclesiastical history, or the niceties of criticism; and, very incurious concerning persons or miracles, and not at all disturbed by chasms of historical evidence, it accepts from God the phenomenon, as it finds it, as the pure and awful form of religion in the world. It is not hot and passionate at the appearance of what it calls its own good or bad fortune, at the union or opposition of other persons. No man is its enemy. It accepts whatsoever befalls, as part of its lesson. It is a watcher more than a doer, and it is a doer, only that it may the better watch.

Chapter VII

SPIRIT

IT IS ESSENTIAL to a true theory of nature and of man, that it should contain somewhat progressive. Uses that are exhausted or that may be, and facts that end in the statement, cannot be all that is true of this brave lodging wherein man is harbored, and wherein all his faculties find appropriate and endless exercise. And all the uses of nature admit of being summed in one, which yields the activity of man an infinite scope. Through all its kingdoms, to the suburbs and outskirts of things, it is faithful to the cause whence it had its origin. It always speaks of Spirit. It suggests the absolute. It is a perpetual effect. It is a great shadow pointing always to the sun behind us.

The aspect of nature is devout. Like the figure of Jesus, she stands with bended head, and hands folded upon the breast. The happiest man is he who learns from nature the lesson of worship.

Of that ineffable essence which we call Spirit, he that thinks most, will say least. We can foresee God in the coarse, and, as it were, distant phenomena of matter; but when we try to define and describe himself, both language and thought desert us, and we are as helpless as fools and savages. That essence refuses to be recorded in propositions, but when man has worshipped him intellectually, the noblest ministry of nature is to stand as the apparition of God. It is the organ through which the universal spirit speaks to the individual, and strives to lead back the individual to it.

When we consider Spirit, we see that the views already presented do not include the whole circumference of man. We must add some related thoughts.

Three problems are put by nature to the mind; What is matter? Whence is it? and Whereto? The first of these questions only, the ideal theory answers. Idealism saith: matter is a phenomenon, not a substance. Idealism acquaints us with the total disparity between the evidence of our own being, and the evidence of the world's being. The one is perfect; the other, incapable of any assurance; the mind is a part of the nature of things; the world is a divine dream, from which we may presently awake to the glories and certainties of day. Idealism is a hypothesis to account for nature by other principles than those of carpentry and chemistry. Yet, if it only deny the existence of matter, it does not satisfy the demands of the spirit. It leaves God out of me. It leaves me in the splendid labyrinth of my perceptions, to wander without end. Then the heart resists it, because it balks the affections in denying substantive being to men and women. Nature is so pervaded with human life, that there is something of humanity in all, and in every particular. But this theory makes nature foreign to me, and does not account for that consanguinity which we acknowledge to it.

Let it stand, then, in the present state of our knowledge, merely as a useful introductory hypothesis, serving to apprize us of the eternal distinction between the soul and the world.

But when, following the invisible steps of thought, we come to inquire, Whence is matter? and Whereto? many truths arise to us out of the recesses of consciousness. We learn that the highest is present to the soul of man, that the dread universal essence, which is not wisdom, or love, or beauty, or power, but all in one, and each entirely, is that for which all things exist, and that by which they are; that spirit creates; that behind nature, throughout nature, spirit is present; one and not compound, it does not act upon us from without, that is, in space and time, but spiritually, or through ourselves: therefore, that spirit, that is, the Supreme Being, does not build up nature around us, but puts it forth through us, as the life of the tree puts forth new branches and leaves through the pores of the old. As a plant upon the earth, so a man rests upon the bosom of God; he is nourished by unfailing fountains, and draws, at his need, inexhaustible power. Who can set bounds to the possibilities of man? Once inhale the upper air, being admitted to behold the absolute natures of justice and truth, and we learn that man has access to the entire mind of the Creator, is himself the creator in the finite. This view, which admonishes me where the sources of wisdom and power lie, and points to virtue as to

"The golden key
Which opes the palace of eternity,"

carries upon its face the highest certificate of truth, because it
animates me to create my own world through the purification
of my soul.

The world proceeds from the same spirit as the body of
man. It is a remoter and inferior incarnation of God, a projection of God in the unconscious. But it differs from the
body in one important respect. It is not, like that, now subjected to the human will. Its serene order is inviolable by us.
It is, therefore, to us, the present expositor of the divine
mind. It is a fixed point whereby we may measure our departure. As we degenerate, the contrast between us and our
house is more evident. We are as much strangers in nature, as
we are aliens from God. We do not understand the notes of
birds. The fox and the deer run away from us; the bear and
tiger rend us. We do not know the uses of more than a few
plants, as corn and the apple, the potato and the vine. Is not
the landscape, every glimpse of which hath a grandeur, a face
of him? Yet this may show us what discord is between man
and nature, for you cannot freely admire a noble landscape, if
laborers are digging in the field hard by. The poet finds something ridiculous in his delight, until he is out of the sight of
men.

Chapter VIII

PROSPECTS

IN INQUIRIES respecting the laws of the world and the frame of things, the highest reason is always the truest. That which seems faintly possible—it is so refined, is often faint and dim because it is deepest seated in the mind among the eternal verities. Empirical science is apt to cloud the sight, and, by the very knowledge of functions and processes, to bereave the student of the manly contemplation of the whole. The savant becomes unpoetic. But the best read naturalist who lends an entire and devout attention to truth, will see that there remains much to learn of his relation to the world, and that it is not to be learned by any addition or subtraction or other comparison of known quantities, but is arrived at by untaught sallies of the spirit, by a continual self-recovery, and by entire humility. He will perceive that there are far more excellent qualities in the student than preciseness and infallibility; that a guess is often more fruitful than an indisputable affirmation, and that a dream may let us deeper into the secret of nature than a hundred concerted experiments.

For, the problems to be solved are precisely those which the physiologist and the naturalist omit to state. It is not so pertinent to man to know all the individuals of the animal kingdom, as it is to know whence and whereto is this tyrannizing unity in his constitution, which evermore separates and classifies things, endeavoring to reduce the most diverse to one form. When I behold a rich landscape, it is less to my purpose to recite correctly the order and superposition of the strata, than to know why all thought of multitude is lost in a tranquil sense of unity. I cannot greatly honor minuteness in details, so long as there is no hint to explain the relation between things and thoughts; no ray upon the *metaphysics* of conchology, of botany, of the arts, to show the relation of the forms of flowers, shells, animals, architecture, to the mind, and build science upon ideas. In a cabinet of natural history, we become sensible of a certain occult recognition and sympathy in regard to the most unwieldy and eccentric forms of beast, fish, and insect. The American who has been confined, in his own country, to the sight of buildings designed after foreign models, is surprised on entering York Minster or St. Peter's at Rome, by the feeling that these structures are imitations also,—faint copies of an invisible archetype. Nor has science sufficient humanity, so long as the naturalist overlooks that wonderful congruity which subsists between man and the world; of which he is lord, not because he is the most subtile inhabitant, but because he is its head and heart, and finds something of himself in every great and small thing, in every mountain stratum, in every new law of color, fact of astronomy, or atmospheric influence which observation or analysis lay open. A perception of this mystery inspires the muse of George Herbert, the beautiful psalmist of the seventeenth century. The following lines are part of his little poem on Man.

"Man is all symmetry,
Full of proportions, one limb to another,
    And to all the world besides.
    Each part may call the farthest, brother;
For head with foot hath private amity,
    And both with moons and tides.

"Nothing hath got so far
But man hath caught and kept it as his prey;
    His eyes dismount the highest star;
    He is in little all the sphere.
Herbs gladly cure our flesh, because that they
    Find their acquaintance there.

"For us, the winds do blow,
The earth doth rest, heaven move, and fountains flow;
    Nothing we see, but means our good,
    As our delight, or as our treasure;
The whole is either our cupboard of food,
    Or cabinet of pleasure.

"The stars have us to bed:
Night draws the curtain; which the sun withdraws.

Music and light attend our head.
All things unto our flesh are kind,
In their descent and being; to our mind,
In their ascent and cause.

"More servants wait on man
Than he'll take notice of. In every path,
He treads down that which doth befriend him
When sickness makes him pale and wan.
Oh mighty love! Man is one world, and hath
Another to attend him."

The perception of this class of truths makes the attraction which draws men to science, but the end is lost sight of in attention to the means. In view of this half-sight of science, we accept the sentence of Plato, that, "poetry comes nearer to vital truth than history." Every surmise and vaticination of the mind is entitled to a certain respect, and we learn to prefer imperfect theories, and sentences, which contain glimpses of truth, to digested systems which have no one valuable suggestion. A wise writer will feel that the ends of study and composition are best answered by announcing undiscovered regions of thought, and so communicating, through hope, new activity to the torpid spirit.

I shall therefore conclude this essay with some traditions of man and nature, which a certain poet sang to me; and which, as they have always been in the world, and perhaps reappear to every bard, may be both history and prophecy.

'The foundations of man are not in matter, but in spirit. But the element of spirit is eternity. To it, therefore, the longest series of events, the oldest chronologies are young and recent. In the cycle of the universal man, from whom the known individuals proceed, centuries are points, and all history is but the epoch of one degradation.

'We distrust and deny inwardly our sympathy with nature. We own and disown our relation to it, by turns. We are, like Nebuchadnezzar, dethroned, bereft of reason, and eating grass like an ox. But who can set limits to the remedial force of spirit?

'A man is a god in ruins. When men are innocent, life shall

be longer, and shall pass into the immortal, as gently as we awake from dreams. Now, the world would be insane and rabid, if these disorganizations should last for hundreds of years. It is kept in check by death and infancy. Infancy is the perpetual Messiah, which comes into the arms of fallen men, and pleads with them to return to paradise.

'Man is the dwarf of himself. Once he was permeated and dissolved by spirit. He filled nature with his overflowing currents. Out from him sprang the sun and moon; from man, the sun; from woman, the moon. The laws of his mind, the periods of his actions externized themselves into day and night, into the year and the seasons. But, having made for himself this huge shell, his waters retired; he no longer fills the veins and veinlets; he is shrunk to a drop. He sees, that the structure still fits him, but fits him colossally. Say, rather, once it fitted him, now it corresponds to him from far and on high. He adores timidly his own work. Now is man the follower of the sun, and woman the follower of the moon. Yet sometimes he starts in his slumber, and wonders at himself and his house, and muses strangely at the resemblance betwixt him and it. He perceives that if his law is still paramount, if still he have elemental power, if his word is sterling yet in nature, it is not conscious power, it is not inferior but superior to his will. It is Instinct.' Thus my Orphic poet sang.

At present, man applies to nature but half his force. He works on the world with his understanding alone. He lives in it, and masters it by a penny-wisdom; and he that works most in it, is but a half-man, and whilst his arms are strong and his digestion good, his mind is imbruted, and he is a selfish savage. His relation to nature, his power over it, is through the understanding; as by manure; the economic use of fire, wind, water, and the mariner's needle; steam, coal, chemical agriculture; the repairs of the human body by the dentist and the surgeon. This is such a resumption of power, as if a banished king should buy his territories inch by inch, instead of vaulting at once into his throne. Meantime, in the thick darkness, there are not wanting gleams of a better light,—occasional examples of the action of man upon nature with his entire force,—with reason as well as understanding. Such examples are; the traditions of miracles in the earliest antiquity of all

nations; the history of Jesus Christ; the achievements of a
principle, as in religious and political revolutions, and in the
abolition of the Slave-trade; the miracles of enthusiasm, as
those reported of Swedenborg, Hohenlohe, and the Shakers;
many obscure and yet contested facts, now arranged under
the name of Animal Magnetism; prayer; eloquence; self-heal-
ing; and the wisdom of children. These are examples of Reason's momentary grasp of the sceptre; the exertions of a
power which exists not in time or space, but an instantaneous
in-streaming causing power. The difference between the actual and the ideal force of man is happily figured by the
schoolmen, in saying, that the knowledge of man is an evening knowledge, *vespertina cognitio*, but that of God is a
morning knowledge, *matutina cognitio*.

The problem of restoring to the world original and eternal
beauty, is solved by the redemption of the soul. The ruin or
the blank, that we see when we look at nature, is in our own
eye. The axis of vision is not coincident with the axis of
things, and so they appear not transparent but opake. The
reason why the world lacks unity, and lies broken and in
heaps, is, because man is disunited with himself. He cannot
be a naturalist, until he satisfies all the demands of the spirit.
Love is as much its demand, as perception. Indeed, neither
can be perfect without the other. In the uttermost meaning
of the words, thought is devout, and devotion is thought.
Deep calls unto deep. But in actual life, the marriage is not
celebrated. There are innocent men who worship God after
the tradition of their fathers, but their sense of duty has not
yet extended to the use of all their faculties. And there are
patient naturalists, but they freeze their subject under the
wintry light of the understanding. Is not prayer also a study
of truth,—a sally of the soul into the unfound infinite? No
man ever prayed heartily, without learning something. But
when a faithful thinker, resolute to detach every object from
personal relations, and see it in the light of thought, shall, at
the same time, kindle science with the fire of the holiest affections, then will God go forth anew into the creation.

It will not need, when the mind is prepared for study, to
search for objects. The invariable mark of wisdom is to see
the miraculous in the common. What is a day? What is a year?

What is summer? What is woman? What is a child? What is
sleep? To our blindness, these things seem unaffecting. We
make fables to hide the baldness of the fact and conform it,
as we say, to the higher law of the mind. But when the fact
is seen under the light of an idea, the gaudy fable fades and
shrivels. We behold the real higher law. To the wise, therefore, a fact is true poetry, and the most beautiful of fables.
These wonders are brought to our own door. You also are a
man. Man and woman, and their social life, poverty, labor,
sleep, fear, fortune, are known to you. Learn that none of
these things is superficial, but that each phenomenon has its
roots in the faculties and affections of the mind. Whilst the
abstract question occupies your intellect, nature brings it in
the concrete to be solved by your hands. It were a wise inquiry for the closet, to compare, point by point, especially at
remarkable crises in life, our daily history, with the rise and
progress of ideas in the mind.

So shall we come to look at the world with new eyes. It
shall answer the endless inquiry of the intellect,—What is
truth? and of the affections,—What is good? by yielding itself
passive to the educated Will. Then shall come to pass what
my poet said; 'Nature is not fixed but fluid. Spirit alters,
moulds, makes it. The immobility or bruteness of nature, is
the absence of spirit; to pure spirit, it is fluid, it is volatile, it
is obedient. Every spirit builds itself a house; and beyond its
house a world; and beyond its world, a heaven. Know then,
that the world exists for you. For you is the phenomenon
perfect. What we are, that only can we see. All that Adam
had, all that Cæsar could, you have and can do. Adam called
his house, heaven and earth; Cæsar called his house, Rome;
you perhaps call yours, a cobler's trade; a hundred acres of
ploughed land; or a scholar's garret. Yet line for line and
point for point, your dominion is as great as theirs, though
without fine names. Build, therefore, your own world. As fast
as you conform your life to the pure idea in your mind, that
will unfold its great proportions. A correspondent revolution
in things will attend the influx of the spirit. So fast will disagreeable appearances, swine, spiders, snakes, pests, mad-
houses, prisons, enemies, vanish; they are temporary and shall
be no more seen. The sordor and filths of nature, the sun shall

dry up, and the wind exhale. As when the summer comes
from the south; the snow-banks melt, and the face of the
earth becomes green before it, so shall the advancing spirit
create its ornaments along its path, and carry with it the
beauty it visits, and the song which enchants it; it shall draw
beautiful faces, warm hearts, wise discourse, and heroic acts,
around its way, until evil is no more seen. The kingdom of
man over nature, which cometh not with observation,—a dominion such as now is beyond his dream of God,—he shall
enter without more wonder than the blind man feels who is
gradually restored to perfect sight.'

THE AMERICAN SCHOLAR

An Oration delivered before the Phi Beta Kappa Society,
at Cambridge, August 31, 1837

The American Scholar

Mr. President and Gentlemen,

I greet you on the re-commencement of our literary year. Our anniversary is one of hope, and, perhaps, not enough of labor. We do not meet for games of strength or skill, for the recitation of histories, tragedies, and odes, like the ancient Greeks; for parliaments of love and poesy, like the Troubadours; nor for the advancement of science, like our cotemporaries in the British and European capitals. Thus far, our holiday has been simply a friendly sign of the survival of the love of letters amongst a people too busy to give to letters any more. As such, it is precious as the sign of an indestructible instinct. Perhaps the time is already come, when it ought to be, and will be, something else; when the sluggard intellect of this continent will look from under its iron lids, and fill the postponed expectation of the world with something better than the exertions of mechanical skill. Our day of dependence, our long apprenticeship to the learning of other lands, draws to a close. The millions, that around us are rushing into life, cannot always be fed on the sere remains of foreign harvests. Events, actions arise, that must be sung, that will sing themselves. Who can doubt, that poetry will revive and lead in a new age, as the star in the constellation Harp, which now flames in our zenith, astronomers announce, shall one day be the pole-star for a thousand years?

In this hope, I accept the topic which not only usage, but the nature of our association, seem to prescribe to this day,— the American Scholar. Year by year, we come up hither to read one more chapter of his biography. Let us inquire what light new days and events have thrown on his character, and his hopes.

It is one of those fables, which, out of an unknown antiquity, convey an unlooked-for wisdom, that the gods, in the beginning, divided Man into men, that he might be more helpful to himself; just as the hand was divided into fingers, the better to answer its end.

The old fable covers a doctrine ever new and sublime; that there is One Man,—present to all particular men only partially, or through one faculty; and that you must take the whole society to find the whole man. Man is not a farmer, or a professor, or an engineer, but he is all. Man is priest, and scholar, and statesman, and producer, and soldier. In the *divided* or social state, these functions are parcelled out to individuals, each of whom aims to do his stint of the joint work, whilst each other performs his. The fable implies, that the individual, to possess himself, must sometimes return from his own labor to embrace all the other laborers. But unfortunately, this original unit, this fountain of power, has been so distributed to multitudes, has been so minutely subdivided and peddled out, that it is spilled into drops, and cannot be gathered. The state of society is one in which the members have suffered amputation from the trunk, and strut about so many walking monsters,—a good finger, a neck, a stomach, an elbow, but never a man.

Man is thus metamorphosed into a thing, into many things. The planter, who is Man sent out into the field to gather food, is seldom cheered by any idea of the true dignity of his ministry. He sees his bushel and his cart, and nothing beyond, and sinks into the farmer, instead of Man on the farm. The tradesman scarcely ever gives an ideal worth to his work, but is ridden by the routine of his craft, and the soul is subject to dollars. The priest becomes a form; the attorney, a statute-book; the mechanic, a machine; the sailor, a rope of a ship.

In this distribution of functions, the scholar is the delegated intellect. In the right state, he is, *Man Thinking*. In the degenerate state, when the victim of society, he tends to become a mere thinker, or, still worse, the parrot of other men's thinking.

In this view of him, as Man Thinking, the theory of his office is contained. Him nature solicits with all her placid, all her monitory pictures; him the past instructs; him the future invites. Is not, indeed, every man a student, and do not all things exist for the student's behoof? And, finally, is not the true scholar the only true master? But the old oracle said, 'All things have two handles: beware of the wrong one.' In life, too often, the scholar errs with mankind and forfeits his privilege. Let us see him in his school, and consider him in reference to the main influences he receives.

I. The first in time and the first in importance of the influences upon the mind is that of nature. Every day, the sun;
and, after sunset, night and her stars. Ever the winds blow;
ever the grass grows. Every day, men and women, conversing, beholding and beholden. The scholar is he of all men
whom this spectacle most engages. He must settle its value in
his mind. What is nature to him? There is never a beginning,
there is never an end, to the inexplicable continuity of this
web of God, but always circular power returning into itself.
Therein it resembles his own spirit, whose beginning, whose
ending, he never can find,—so entire, so boundless. Far, too,
as her splendors shine, system on system shooting like rays,
upward, downward, without centre, without circumference,—in the mass and in the particle, nature hastens to render account of herself to the mind. Classification begins. To
the young mind, every thing is individual, stands by itself. By
and by, it finds how to join two things, and see in them one
nature; then three, then three thousand; and so, tyrannized
over by its own unifying instinct, it goes on tying things together, diminishing anomalies, discovering roots running under ground, whereby contrary and remote things cohere, and
flower out from one stem. It presently learns, that, since the
dawn of history, there has been a constant accumulation and
classifying of facts. But what is classification but the perceiving that these objects are not chaotic, and are not foreign, but
have a law which is also a law of the human mind? The astronomer discovers that geometry, a pure abstraction of the
human mind, is the measure of planetary motion. The chemist finds proportions and intelligible method throughout matter; and science is nothing but the finding of analogy,
identity, in the most remote parts. The ambitious soul sits
down before each refractory fact; one after another, reduces
all strange constitutions, all new powers, to their class and
their law, and goes on for ever to animate the last fibre of
organization, the outskirts of nature, by insight.

Thus to him, to this school-boy under the bending dome
of day, is suggested, that he and it proceed from one root;
one is leaf and one is flower; relation, sympathy, stirring in
every vein. And what is that Root? Is not that the soul of his
soul?—A thought too bold,—a dream too wild. Yet when

this spiritual light shall have revealed the law of more earthly natures,—when he has learned to worship the soul, and to see that the natural philosophy that now is, is only the first gropings of its gigantic hand, he shall look forward to an ever expanding knowledge as to a becoming creator. He shall see, that nature is the opposite of the soul, answering to it part for part. One is seal, and one is print. Its beauty is the beauty of his own mind. Its laws are the laws of his own mind. Nature then becomes to him the measure of his attainments. So much of nature as he is ignorant of, so much of his own mind does he not yet possess. And, in fine, the ancient precept, "Know thyself," and the modern precept, "Study nature," become at last one maxim.

II. The next great influence into the spirit of the scholar, is, the mind of the Past,—in whatever form, whether of literature, of art, of institutions, that mind is inscribed. Books are the best type of the influence of the past, and perhaps we shall get at the truth,—learn the amount of this influence more conveniently,—by considering their value alone.

The theory of books is noble. The scholar of the first age received into him the world around; brooded thereon; gave it the new arrangement of his own mind, and uttered it again. It came into him, life; it went out from him, truth. It came to him, short-lived actions; it went out from him, immortal thoughts. It came to him, business; it went from him, poetry. It was dead fact; now, it is quick thought. It can stand, and it can go. It now endures, it now flies, it now inspires. Precisely in proportion to the depth of mind from which it issued, so high does it soar, so long does it sing.

Or, I might say, it depends on how far the process had gone, of transmuting life into truth. In proportion to the completeness of the distillation, so will the purity and imperishableness of the product be. But none is quite perfect. As no air-pump can by any means make a perfect vacuum, so neither can any artist entirely exclude the conventional, the local, the perishable from his book, or write a book of pure thought, that shall be as efficient, in all respects, to a remote posterity, as to cotemporaries, or rather to the second age. Each age, it is found, must write its own books; or rather, each generation for the next succeeding. The books of an older period will not fit this.

Yet hence arises a grave mischief. The sacredness which attaches to the act of creation,—the act of thought,—is transferred to the record. The poet chanting, was felt to be a divine man: henceforth the chant is divine also. The writer was a just and wise spirit: henceforward it is settled, the book is perfect; as love of the hero corrupts into worship of his statue. Instantly, the book becomes noxious: the guide is a tyrant. The sluggish and perverted mind of the multitude, slow to open to the incursions of Reason, having once so opened, having once received this book, stands upon it, and makes an outcry, if it is disparaged. Colleges are built on it. Books are written on it by thinkers, not by Man Thinking; by men of talent, that is, who start wrong, who set out from accepted dogmas, not from their own sight of principles. Meek young men grow up in libraries, believing it their duty to accept the views, which Cicero, which Locke, which Bacon, have given, forgetful that Cicero, Locke, and Bacon were only young men in libraries, when they wrote these books.

Hence, instead of Man Thinking, we have the bookworm. Hence, the book-learned class, who value books, as such; not as related to nature and the human constitution, but as making a sort of Third Estate with the world and the soul. Hence, the restorers of readings, the emendators, the bibliomaniacs of all degrees.

Books are the best of things, well used; abused, among the worst. What is the right use? What is the one end, which all means go to effect? They are for nothing but to inspire. I had better never see a book, than to be warped by its attraction clean out of my own orbit, and made a satellite instead of a system. The one thing in the world, of value, is the active soul. This every man is entitled to; this every man contains within him, although, in almost all men, obstructed, and as yet unborn. The soul active sees absolute truth; and utters truth, or creates. In this action, it is genius; not the privilege of here and there a favorite, but the sound estate of every man. In its essence, it is progressive. The book, the college, the school of art, the institution of any kind, stop with some past utterance of genius. This is good, say they,—let us hold by this. They pin me down. They look backward and not forward. But genius looks forward: the eyes of man are set in his forehead, not in his hindhead: man hopes: genius creates. Whatever talents may be, if the man create not, the pure efflux of the Deity is not his;—cinders and smoke there may be, but not yet flame. There are creative manners, there are creative actions, and creative words; manners, actions, words, that is, indicative of no custom or authority, but springing spontaneous from the mind's own sense of good and fair.

On the other part, instead of being its own seer, let it receive from another mind its truth, though it were in torrents of light, without periods of solitude, inquest, and self-recovery, and a fatal disservice is done. Genius is always sufficiently the enemy of genius by over influence. The literature of every nation bear me witness. The English dramatic poets have Shakspearized now for two hundred years.

Undoubtedly there is a right way of reading, so it be sternly subordinated. Man Thinking must not be subdued by his instruments. Books are for the scholar's idle times. When he can read God directly, the hour is too precious to be wasted in other men's transcripts of their readings. But when the intervals of darkness come, as come they must,—when the sun is hid, and the stars withdraw their shining,—we repair to the lamps which were kindled by their ray, to guide our steps to the East again, where the dawn is. We hear, that we may speak. The Arabian proverb says, "A fig tree, looking on a fig tree, becometh fruitful."

It is remarkable, the character of the pleasure we derive from the best books. They impress us with the conviction, that one nature wrote and the same reads. We read the verses of one of the great English poets, of Chaucer, of Marvell, of Dryden, with the most modern joy,—with a pleasure, I mean, which is in great part caused by the abstraction of all *time* from their verses. There is some awe mixed with the joy of our surprise, when this poet, who lived in some past world, two or three hundred years ago, says that which lies close to my own soul, that which I also had wellnigh thought and said. But for the evidence thence afforded to the philosophical doctrine of the identity of all minds, we should suppose some preëstablished harmony, some foresight of souls that were to be, and some preparation of stores for their future wants, like the fact observed in insects, who lay up food before death for the young grub they shall never see.

I would not be hurried by any love of system, by any exaggeration of instincts, to underrate the Book. We all know, that, as the human body can be nourished on any food, though it were boiled grass and the broth of shoes, so the human mind can be fed by any knowledge. And great and heroic men have existed, who had almost no other information than by the printed page. I only would say, that it needs a strong head to bear that diet. One must be an inventor to read well. As the proverb says, "He that would bring home the wealth of the Indies, must carry out the wealth of the Indies." There is then creative reading as well as creative writing. When the mind is braced by labor and invention, the page of whatever book we read becomes luminous with manifold allusion. Every sentence is doubly significant, and the sense of our author is as broad as the world. We then see, what is always true, that, as the seer's hour of vision is short and rare among heavy days and months, so is its record, perchance, the least part of his volume. The discerning will read, in his Plato or Shakspeare, only that least part,—only the authentic utterances of the oracle;—all the rest he rejects, were it never so many times Plato's and Shakspeare's.

Of course, there is a portion of reading quite indispensable to a wise man. History and exact science he must learn by laborious reading. Colleges, in like manner, have their indispensable office,—to teach elements. But they can only highly serve us, when they aim not to drill, but to create; when they gather from far every ray of various genius to their hospitable halls, and, by the concentrated fires, set the hearts of their youth on flame. Thought and knowledge are natures in which apparatus and pretension avail nothing. Gowns, and pecuniary foundations, though of towns of gold, can never countervail the least sentence or syllable of wit. Forget this, and our American colleges will recede in their public importance, whilst they grow richer every year.

III. There goes in the world a notion, that the scholar should be a recluse, a valetudinarian,—as unfit for any handiwork or public labor, as a penknife for an axe. The so-called 'practical men' sneer at speculative men, as if, because they speculate or *see*, they could do nothing. I have heard it said that the clergy,—who are always, more universally than any other class, the scholars of their day,—are addressed as women; that the rough, spontaneous conversation of men they do not hear, but only a mincing and diluted speech. They are often virtually disfranchised; and, indeed, there are advocates for their celibacy. As far as this is true of the studious classes, it is not just and wise. Action is with the scholar subordinate, but it is essential. Without it, he is not yet man. Without it, thought can never ripen into truth. Whilst the world hangs before the eye as a cloud of beauty, we cannot even see its beauty. Inaction is cowardice, but there can be no scholar without the heroic mind. The preamble of thought, the transition through which it passes from the unconscious to the conscious, is action. Only so much do I know, as I have lived. Instantly we know whose words are loaded with life, and whose not.

The world,—this shadow of the soul, or *other me*, lies wide around. Its attractions are the keys which unlock my thoughts and make me acquainted with myself. I run eagerly into this resounding tumult. I grasp the hands of those next me, and take my place in the ring to suffer and to work, taught by an instinct, that so shall the dumb abyss be vocal with speech. I pierce its order; I dissipate its fear; I dispose of it within the circuit of my expanding life. So much only of life as I know by experience, so much of the wilderness have I vanquished and planted, or so far have I extended my being, my dominion. I do not see how any man can afford, for the sake of his nerves and his nap, to spare any action in which he can partake. It is pearls and rubies to his discourse. Drudgery, calamity, exasperation, want, are instructers in eloquence and wisdom. The true scholar grudges every opportunity of action past by, as a loss of power.

It is the raw material out of which the intellect moulds her splendid products. A strange process too, this, by which experience is converted into thought, as a mulberry leaf is converted into satin. The manufacture goes forward at all hours.

The actions and events of our childhood and youth, are

now matters of calmest observation. They lie like fair pictures in the air. Not so with our recent actions,—with the business which we now have in hand. On this we are quite unable to speculate. Our affections as yet circulate through it. We no more feel or know it, than we feel the feet, or the hand, or the brain of our body. The new deed is yet a part of life,— remains for a time immersed in our unconscious life. In some contemplative hour, it detaches itself from the life like a ripe fruit, to become a thought of the mind. Instantly, it is raised, transfigured; the corruptible has put on incorruption. Henceforth it is an object of beauty, however base its origin and neighborhood. Observe, too, the impossibility of antedating this act. In its grub state, it cannot fly, it cannot shine, it is a dull grub. But suddenly, without observation, the selfsame thing unfurls beautiful wings, and is an angel of wisdom. So is there no fact, no event, in our private history, which shall not, sooner or later, lose its adhesive, inert form, and astonish us by soaring from our body into the empyrean. Cradle and infancy, school and playground, the fear of boys, and dogs, and ferules, the love of little maids and berries, and many another fact that once filled the whole sky, are gone already; friend and relative, profession and party, town and country, nation and world, must also soar and sing.

Of course, he who has put forth his total strength in fit actions, has the richest return of wisdom. I will not shut myself out of this globe of action, and transplant an oak into a flower-pot, there to hunger and pine; nor trust the revenue of some single faculty, and exhaust one vein of thought, much like those Savoyards, who, getting their livelihood by carving shepherds, shepherdesses, and smoking Dutchmen, for all Europe, went out one day to the mountain to find stock, and discovered that they had whittled up the last of their pine-trees. Authors we have, in numbers, who have written out their vein, and who, moved by a commendable prudence, sail for Greece or Palestine, follow the trapper into the prairie, or ramble round Algiers, to replenish their merchantable stock.

If it were only for a vocabulary, the scholar would be covetous of action. Life is our dictionary. Years are well spent in country labors; in town,—in the insight into trades and manufactures; in frank intercourse with many men and women;

in science; in art; to the one end of mastering in all their facts a language by which to illustrate and embody our perceptions. I learn immediately from any speaker how much he has already lived, through the poverty or the splendor of his speech. Life lies behind us as the quarry from whence we get tiles and copestones for the masonry of to-day. This is the way to learn grammar. Colleges and books only copy the language which the field and the work-yard made.

But the final value of action, like that of books, and better than books, is, that it is a resource. That great principle of Undulation in nature, that shows itself in the inspiring and expiring of the breath; in desire and satiety; in the ebb and flow of the sea; in day and night; in heat and cold; and as yet more deeply ingrained in every atom and every fluid, is known to us under the name of Polarity,—these "fits of easy transmission and reflection," as Newton called them, are the law of nature because they are the law of spirit.

The mind now thinks; now acts; and each fit reproduces the other. When the artist has exhausted his materials, when the fancy no longer paints, when thoughts are no longer apprehended, and books are a weariness,—he has always the resource *to live*. Character is higher than intellect. Thinking is the function. Living is the functionary. The stream retreats to its source. A great soul will be strong to live, as well as strong to think. Does he lack organ or medium to impart his truths? He can still fall back on this elemental force of living them. This is a total act. Thinking is a partial act. Let the grandeur of justice shine in his affairs. Let the beauty of affection cheer his lowly roof. Those 'far from fame,' who dwell and act with him, will feel the force of his constitution in the doings and passages of the day better than it can be measured by any public and designed display. Time shall teach him, that the scholar loses no hour which the man lives. Herein he unfolds the sacred germ of his instinct, screened from influence. What is lost in seemliness is gained in strength. Not out of those, on whom systems of education have exhausted their culture, comes the helpful giant to destroy the old or to build the new, but out of unhandselled savage nature, out of terrible Druids and Berserkirs, come at last Alfred and Shakspeare.

I hear therefore with joy whatever is beginning to be said

of the dignity and necessity of labor to every citizen. There is virtue yet in the hoe and the spade, for learned as well as for unlearned hands. And labor is everywhere welcome; always we are invited to work; only be this limitation observed, that a man shall not for the sake of wider activity sacrifice any opinion to the popular judgments and modes of action.

I have now spoken of the education of the scholar by nature, by books, and by action. It remains to say somewhat of his duties.

They are such as become Man Thinking. They may all be comprised in self-trust. The office of the scholar is to cheer, to raise, and to guide men by showing them facts amidst appearances. He plies the slow, unhonored, and unpaid task of observation. Flamsteed and Herschel, in their glazed observatories, may catalogue the stars with the praise of all men, and, the results being splendid and useful, honor is sure. But he, in his private observatory, cataloguing obscure and nebulous stars of the human mind, which as yet no man has thought of as such,—watching days and months, sometimes, for a few facts; correcting still his old records;—must relinquish display and immediate fame. In the long period of his preparation, he must betray often an ignorance and shiftlessness in popular arts, incurring the disdain of the able who shoulder him aside. Long he must stammer in his speech; often forego the living for the dead. Worse yet, he must accept,—how often! poverty and solitude. For the ease and pleasure of treading the old road, accepting the fashions, the education, the religion of society, he takes the cross of making his own, and, of course, the self-accusation, the faint heart, the frequent uncertainty and loss of time, which are the nettles and tangling vines in the way of the self-relying and self-directed; and the state of virtual hostility in which he seems to stand to society, and especially to educated society. For all this loss and scorn, what offset? He is to find consolation in exercising the highest functions of human nature. He is one, who raises himself from private considerations, and breathes and lives on public and illustrious thoughts. He is the world's eye. He is the world's heart. He is to resist the vulgar prosperity that retrogrades ever to barbarism, by preserving and communicating heroic sentiments, noble biographies, melodious verse, and the conclusions of history. Whatsoever oracles the human heart, in all emergencies, in all solemn hours, has uttered as its commentary on the world of actions,—these he shall receive and impart. And whatsoever new verdict Reason from her inviolable seat pronounces on the passing men and events of to-day,—this he shall hear and promulgate.

These being his functions, it becomes him to feel all confidence in himself, and to defer never to the popular cry. He and he only knows the world. The world of any moment is the merest appearance. Some great decorum, some fetish of a government, some ephemeral trade, or war, or man, is cried up by half mankind and cried down by the other half, as if all depended on this particular up or down. The odds are that the whole question is not worth the poorest thought which the scholar has lost in listening to the controversy. Let him not quit his belief that a popgun is a popgun, though the ancient and honorable of the earth affirm it to be the crack of doom. In silence, in steadiness, in severe abstraction, let him hold by himself; add observation to observation, patient of neglect, patient of reproach; and bide his own time,—happy enough, if he can satisfy himself alone, that this day he has seen something truly. Success treads on every right step. For the instinct is sure, that prompts him to tell his brother what he thinks. He then learns, that in going down into the secrets of his own mind, he has descended into the secrets of all minds. He learns that he who has mastered any law in his private thoughts, is master to that extent of all men whose language he speaks, and of all into whose language his own can be translated. The poet, in utter solitude remembering his spontaneous thoughts and recording them, is found to have recorded that, which men in crowded cities find true for them also. The orator distrusts at first the fitness of his frank confessions,—his want of knowledge of the persons he addresses,—until he finds that he is the complement of his hearers;—that they drink his words because he fulfils for them their own nature; the deeper he dives into his privatest, secretest presentiment, to his wonder he finds, this is the most acceptable, most public, and universally true. The people delight in it;

the better part of every man feels, This is my music; this is myself.

In self-trust, all the virtues are comprehended. Free should the scholar be,—free and brave. Free even to the definition of freedom, "without any hindrance that does not arise out of his own constitution." Brave; for fear is a thing, which a scholar by his very function puts behind him. Fear always springs from ignorance. It is a shame to him if his tranquillity, amid dangerous times, arise from the presumption, that, like children and women, his is a protected class; or if he seek a temporary peace by the diversion of his thoughts from politics or vexed questions, hiding his head like an ostrich in the flowering bushes, peeping into microscopes, and turning rhymes, as a boy whistles to keep his courage up. So is the danger a danger still; so is the fear worse. Manlike let him turn and face it. Let him look into its eye and search its nature, inspect its origin,—see the whelping of this lion,—which lies no great way back; he will then find in himself a perfect comprehension of its nature and extent; he will have made his hands meet on the other side, and can henceforth defy it, and pass on superior. The world is his, who can see through its pretension. What deafness, what stone-blind custom, what overgrown error you behold, is there only by sufferance,—by your sufferance. See it to be a lie, and you have already dealt it its mortal blow.

Yes, we are the cowed,—we the trustless. It is a mischievous notion that we are come late into nature; that the world was finished a long time ago. As the world was plastic and fluid in the hands of God, so it is ever to so much of his attributes as we bring to it. To ignorance and sin, it is flint. They adapt themselves to it as they may; but in proportion as a man has any thing in him divine, the firmament flows before him and takes his signet and form. Not he is great who can alter matter, but he who can alter my state of mind. They are the kings of the world who give the color of their present thought to all nature and all art, and persuade men by the cheerful serenity of their carrying the matter, that this thing which they do, is the apple which the ages have desired to pluck, now at last ripe, and inviting nations to the harvest. The great man makes the great thing. Wherever Macdonald sits, there is the head of the table. Linnæus makes botany the most alluring of studies, and wins it from the farmer and the herb-woman; Davy, chemistry; and Cuvier, fossils. The day is always his, who works in it with serenity and great aims. The unstable estimates of men crowd to him whose mind is filled with a truth, as the heaped waves of the Atlantic follow the moon.

For this self-trust, the reason is deeper than can be fathomed,—darker than can be enlightened. I might not carry with me the feeling of my audience in stating my own belief. But I have already shown the ground of my hope, in adverting to the doctrine that man is one. I believe man has been wronged; he has wronged himself. He has almost lost the light, that can lead him back to his prerogatives. Men are become of no account. Men in history, men in the world of to-day are bugs, are spawn, and are called 'the mass' and 'the herd.' In a century, in a millennium, one or two men; that is to say,—one or two approximations to the right state of every man. All the rest behold in the hero or the poet their own green and crude being,—ripened; yes, and are content to be less, so *that* may attain to its full stature. What a testimony,—full of grandeur, full of pity, is borne to the demands of his own nature, by the poor clansman, the poor partisan, who rejoices in the glory of his chief. The poor and the low find some amends to their immense moral capacity, for their acquiescence in a political and social inferiority. They are content to be brushed like flies from the path of a great person, so that justice shall be done by him to that common nature which it is the dearest desire of all to see enlarged and glorified. They sun themselves in the great man's light, and feel it to be their own element. They cast the dignity of man from their downtrod selves upon the shoulders of a hero, and will perish to add one drop of blood to make that great heart beat, those giant sinews combat and conquer. He lives for us, and we live in him.

Men such as they are, very naturally seek money or power; and power because it is as good as money,—the "spoils," so called, "of office." And why not? for they aspire to the highest, and this, in their sleep-walking, they dream is highest. Wake them, and they shall quit the false good, and leap to the true, and leave governments to clerks and desks. This revolution is to be wrought by the gradual domestication of the idea of Culture. The main enterprise of the world for splendor, for extent, is the upbuilding of a man. Here are the materials strown along the ground. The private life of one man shall be a more illustrious monarchy,—more formidable to its enemy, more sweet and serene in its influence to its friend, than any kingdom in history. For a man, rightly viewed, comprehendeth the particular natures of all men. Each philosopher, each bard, each actor, has only done for me, as by a delegate, what one day I can do for myself. The books which once we valued more than the apple of the eye, we have quite exhausted. What is that but saying, that we have come up with the point of view which the universal mind took through the eyes of one scribe; we have been that man, and have passed on. First, one; then, another; we drain all cisterns, and, waxing greater by all these supplies, we crave a better and more abundant food. The man has never lived that can feed us ever. The human mind cannot be enshrined in a person, who shall set a barrier on any one side to this unbounded, unboundable empire. It is one central fire, which, flaming now out of the lips of Etna, lightens the capes of Sicily; and, now out of the throat of Vesuvius, illuminates the towers and vineyards of Naples. It is one light which beams out of a thousand stars. It is one soul which animates all men.

But I have dwelt perhaps tediously upon this abstraction of the Scholar. I ought not to delay longer to add what I have to say, of nearer reference to the time and to this country.

Historically, there is thought to be a difference in the ideas which predominate over successive epochs, and there are data for marking the genius of the Classic, of the Romantic, and now of the Reflective or Philosophical age. With the views I have intimated of the oneness or the identity of the mind through all individuals, I do not much dwell on these differences. In fact, I believe each individual passes through all three. The boy is a Greek; the youth, romantic; the adult, reflective. I deny not, however, that a revolution in the leading idea may be distinctly enough traced.

Our age is bewailed as the age of Introversion. Must that

needs be evil? We, it seems, are critical; we are embarrassed with second thoughts; we cannot enjoy any thing for hankering to know whereof the pleasure consists; we are lined with eyes; we see with our feet; the time is infected with Hamlet's unhappiness,—

"Sicklied o'er with the pale cast of thought."

Is it so bad then? Sight is the last thing to be pitied. Would we be blind? Do we fear lest we should outsee nature and God, and drink truth dry? I look upon the discontent of the literary class, as a mere announcement of the fact, that they find themselves not in the state of mind of their fathers, and regret the coming state as untried; as a boy dreads the water before he has learned that he can swim. If there is any period one would desire to be born in,—is it not the age of Revolution; when the old and the new stand side by side, and admit of being compared; when the energies of all men are searched by fear and by hope; when the historic glories of the old, can be compensated by the rich possibilities of the new era? This time, like all times, is a very good one, if we but know what to do with it.

I read with joy some of the auspicious signs of the coming days, as they glimmer already through poetry and art, through philosophy and science, through church and state.

One of these signs is the fact, that the same movement which effected the elevation of what was called the lowest class in the state, assumed in literature a very marked and as benign an aspect. Instead of the sublime and beautiful; the near, the low, the common, was explored and poetized. That, which had been negligently trodden under foot by those who were harnessing and provisioning themselves for long journeys into far countries, is suddenly found to be richer than all foreign parts. The literature of the poor, the feelings of the child, the philosophy of the street, the meaning of household life, are the topics of the time. It is a great stride. It is a sign,—is it not? of new vigor, when the extremities are made active, when currents of warm life run into the hands and the feet. I ask not for the great, the remote, the romantic; what is doing in Italy or Arabia; what is Greek art, or Provençal minstrelsy; I embrace the common, I explore and sit at the feet of the familiar, the low. Give me insight into to-day, and you may have the antique and future worlds. What would we really know the meaning of? The meal in the firkin; the milk in the pan; the ballad in the street; the news of the boat; the glance of the eye; the form and the gait of the body;—show me the ultimate reason of these matters; show me the sublime presence of the highest spiritual cause lurking, as always it does lurk, in these suburbs and extremities of nature; let me see every trifle bristling with the polarity that ranges it instantly on an eternal law; and the shop, the plough, and the leger, referred to the like cause by which light undulates and poets sing;—and the world lies no longer a dull miscellany and lumber-room, but has form and order; there is no trifle; there is no puzzle; but one design unites and animates the farthest pinnacle and the lowest trench.

This idea has inspired the genius of Goldsmith, Burns, Cowper, and, in a newer time, of Goethe, Wordsworth, and Carlyle. This idea they have differently followed and with various success. In contrast with their writing, the style of Pope, of Johnson, of Gibbon, looks cold and pedantic. This writing is blood-warm. Man is surprised to find that things near are not less beautiful and wondrous than things remote. The near explains the far. The drop is a small ocean. A man is related to all nature. This perception of the worth of the vulgar is fruitful in discoveries. Goethe, in this very thing the most modern of the moderns, has shown us, as none ever did, the genius of the ancients.

There is one man of genius, who has done much for this philosophy of life, whose literary value has never yet been rightly estimated;—I mean Emanuel Swedenborg. The most imaginative of men, yet writing with the precision of a mathematician, he endeavored to engraft a purely philosophical Ethics on the popular Christianity of his time. Such an attempt, of course, must have difficulty, which no genius could surmount. But he saw and showed the connection between nature and the affections of the soul. He pierced the emblematic or spiritual character of the visible, audible, tangible world. Especially did his shade-loving muse hover over and interpret the lower parts of nature; he showed the mysterious bond that allies moral evil to the foul material forms, and has given in epical parables a theory of insanity, of beasts, of unclean and fearful things.

Another sign of our times, also marked by an analogous political movement, is, the new importance given to the single person. Every thing that tends to insulate the individual,—to surround him with barriers of natural respect, so that each man shall feel the world is his, and man shall treat with man as a sovereign state with a sovereign state;—tends to true union as well as greatness. "I learned," said the melancholy Pestalozzi, "that no man in God's wide earth is either willing or able to help any other man." Help must come from the bosom alone. The scholar is that man who must take up into himself all the ability of the time, all the contributions of the past, all the hopes of the future. He must be an university of knowledges. If there be one lesson more than another, which should pierce his ear, it is, The world is nothing, the man is all; in yourself is the law of all nature, and you know not yet how a globule of sap ascends; in yourself slumbers the whole of Reason; it is for you to know all, it is for you to dare all. Mr. President and Gentlemen, this confidence in the unsearched might of man belongs, by all motives, by all prophecy, by all preparation, to the American Scholar. We have listened too long to the courtly muses of Europe. The spirit of the American freeman is already suspected to be timid, imitative, tame. Public and private avarice make the air we breathe thick and fat. The scholar is decent, indolent, complaisant. See already the tragic consequence. The mind of this country, taught to aim at low objects, eats upon itself. There is no work for any but the decorous and the complaisant. Young men of the fairest promise, who begin life upon our shores, inflated by the mountain winds, shined upon by all the stars of God, find the earth below not in unison with these,—but are hindered from action by the disgust which the principles on which business is managed inspire, and turn drudges, or die of disgust,—some of them suicides. What is the remedy? They did not yet see, and thousands of young men as hopeful now crowding to the barriers for the career, do not yet see, that, if the single man plant himself indomitably on his instincts, and there abide, the huge world will come round to him. Patience,—patience;—with the shades of all the good and great for company; and for solace, the perspective of your own infinite life; and for work, the study and the communication of principles, the making those instincts prevalent, the conversion of the world. Is it not the chief disgrace in the world, not to be an unit;—not to be reckoned one character;—not to yield that peculiar fruit which each man was created to bear, but to be reckoned in the gross, in the hundred, or the thousand, of the party, the section, to which we belong; and our opinion predicted geographically, as the north, or the south? Not so, brothers and friends,—please God, ours shall not be so. We will walk on our own feet; we will work with our own hands; we will speak our own minds. The study of letters shall be no longer a name for pity, for doubt, and for sensual indulgence. The dread of man and the love of man shall be a wall of defence and a wreath of joy around all. A nation of men will for the first time exist, because each believes himself inspired by the Divine Soul which also inspires all men.

AN ADDRESS

*Delivered before the Senior Class in Divinity College,
Cambridge, Sunday Evening, July 15, 1838*

Address

IN THIS REFULGENT summer, it has been a luxury to draw
the breath of life. The grass grows, the buds burst, the
meadow is spotted with fire and gold in the tint of flowers.
The air is full of birds, and sweet with the breath of the pine,
the balm-of-Gilead, and the new hay. Night brings no gloom
to the heart with its welcome shade. Through the transparent
darkness the stars pour their almost spiritual rays. Man under
them seems a young child, and his huge globe a toy. The cool
night bathes the world as with a river, and prepares his eyes
again for the crimson dawn. The mystery of nature was never
displayed more happily. The corn and the wine have been
freely dealt to all creatures, and the never-broken silence with
which the old bounty goes forward, has not yielded yet one
word of explanation. One is constrained to respect the perfection of this world, in which our senses converse. How wide;
how rich; what invitation from every property it gives to
every faculty of man! In its fruitful soils; in its navigable sea;
in its mountains of metal and stone; in its forests of all
woods; in its animals; in its chemical ingredients; in the powers and path of light, heat, attraction, and life, it is well worth
the pith and heart of great men to subdue and enjoy it. The
planters, the mechanics, the inventors, the astronomers, the
builders of cities, and the captains, history delights to honor.

But when the mind opens, and reveals the laws which traverse the universe, and make things what they are, then
shrinks the great world at once into a mere illustration and
fable of this mind. What am I? and What is? asks the human
spirit with a curiosity new-kindled, but never to be quenched.
Behold these outrunning laws, which our imperfect apprehension can see tend this way and that, but not come full
circle. Behold these infinite relations, so like, so unlike; many,
yet one. I would study, I would know, I would admire forever. These works of thought have been the entertainments
of the human spirit in all ages.

A more secret, sweet, and overpowering beauty appears
to man when his heart and mind open to the sentiment of

virtue. Then he is instructed in what is above him. He learns that his being is without bound; that, to the good, to the perfect, he is born, low as he now lies in evil and weakness. That which he venerates is still his own, though he has not realized it yet. *He ought.* He knows the sense of that grand word, though his analysis fails entirely to render account of it. When in innocency, or when by intellectual perception, he attains to say,—'I love the Right; Truth is beautiful within and without, forevermore. Virtue, I am thine: save me: use me: thee will I serve, day and night, in great, in small, that I may be not virtuous, but virtue;'—then is the end of the creation answered, and God is well pleased.

The sentiment of virtue is a reverence and delight in the presence of certain divine laws. It perceives that this homely game of life we play, covers, under what seem foolish details, principles that astonish. The child amidst his baubles, is learning the action of light, motion, gravity, muscular force; and in the game of human life, love, fear, justice, appetite, man, and God, interact. These laws refuse to be adequately stated. They will not be written out on paper, or spoken by the tongue. They elude our persevering thought; yet we read them hourly in each other's faces, in each other's actions, in our own remorse. The moral traits which are all globed into every virtuous act and thought,—in speech, we must sever, and describe or suggest by painful enumeration of many particulars. Yet, as this sentiment is the essence of all religion, let me guide your eye to the precise objects of the sentiment, by an enumeration of some of those classes of facts in which this element is conspicuous.

The intuition of the moral sentiment is an insight of the perfection of the laws of the soul. These laws execute themselves. They are out of time, out of space, and not subject to circumstance. Thus; in the soul of man there is a justice whose retributions are instant and entire. He who does a good deed, is instantly ennobled. He who does a mean deed, is by the action itself contracted. He who puts off impurity, thereby puts on purity. If a man is at heart just, then in so far is he God; the safety of God, the immortality of God, the majesty of God do enter into that man with justice. If a man dissemble, deceive, he deceives himself, and goes out of acquaintance with his own being. A man in the view of absolute goodness, adores, with total humility. Every step so downward, is a step upward. The man who renounces himself, comes to himself.

See how this rapid intrinsic energy worketh everywhere, righting wrongs, correcting appearances, and bringing up facts to a harmony with thoughts. Its operation in life, though slow to the senses, is, at last, as sure as in the soul. By it, a man is made the Providence to himself, dispensing good to his goodness, and evil to his sin. Character is always known. Thefts never enrich; alms never impoverish; murder will speak out of stone walls. The least admixture of a lie,— for example, the taint of vanity, the least attempt to make a good impression, a favorable appearance,—will instantly vitiate the effect. But speak the truth, and all nature and all spirits help you with unexpected furtherance. Speak the truth, and all things alive or brute are vouchers, and the very roots of the grass underground there, do seem to stir and move to bear you witness. See again the perfection of the Law as it applies itself to the affections, and becomes the law of society. As we are, so we associate. The good, by affinity, seek the good; the vile, by affinity, the vile. Thus of their own volition, souls proceed into heaven, into hell.

These facts have always suggested to man the sublime creed, that the world is not the product of manifold power, but of one will, of one mind; and that one mind is everywhere active, in each ray of the star, in each wavelet of the pool; and whatever opposes that will, is everywhere balked and baffled, because things are made so, and not otherwise. Good is positive. Evil is merely privative, not absolute: it is like cold, which is the privation of heat. All evil is so much death or nonentity. Benevolence is absolute and real. So much benevolence as a man hath, so much life hath he. For all things proceed out of this same spirit, which is differently named love, justice, temperance, in its different applications, just as the ocean receives different names on the several shores which it washes. All things proceed out of the same spirit, and all things conspire with it. Whilst a man seeks good ends, he is strong by the whole strength of nature. In so far as he roves from these ends, he bereaves himself of power, of auxiliaries; his being shrinks out of all remote channels, he becomes less and less, a mote, a point, until absolute badness is absolute death.

The perception of this law of laws awakens in the mind a sentiment which we call the religious sentiment, and which makes our highest happiness. Wonderful is its power to charm and to command. It is a mountain air. It is the embalmer of the world. It is myrrh and storax, and chlorine and rosemary. It makes the sky and the hills sublime, and the silent song of the stars is it. By it, is the universe made safe and habitable, not by science or power. Thought may work cold and intransitive in things, and find no end or unity; but the dawn of the sentiment of virtue on the heart, gives and is the assurance that Law is sovereign over all natures; and the worlds, time, space, eternity, do seem to break out into joy.

This sentiment is divine and deifying. It is the beatitude of man. It makes him illimitable. Through it, the soul first knows itself. It corrects the capital mistake of the infant man, who seeks to be great by following the great, and hopes to derive advantages *from another*,—by showing the fountain of all good to be in himself, and that he, equally with every man, is an inlet into the deeps of Reason. When he says, "I ought;" when love warms him; when he chooses, warned from on high, the good and great deed; then, deep melodies wander through his soul from Supreme Wisdom. Then he can worship, and be enlarged by his worship; for he can never go behind this sentiment. In the sublimest flights of the soul, rectitude is never surmounted, love is never outgrown.

This sentiment lies at the foundation of society, and successively creates all forms of worship. The principle of veneration never dies out. Man fallen into superstition, into sensuality, is never quite without the visions of the moral sentiment. In like manner, all the expressions of this sentiment are sacred and permanent in proportion to their purity. The expressions of this sentiment affect us more than all other compositions. The sentences of the oldest time, which ejaculate this piety, are still fresh and fragrant. This thought dwelled always deepest in the minds of men in the devout and contemplative East; not alone in Palestine, where it reached its purest expression, but in Egypt, in Persia, in India, in China. Europe has always owed to oriental genius, its divine impulses. What these holy bards said, all sane men found agreeable and true. And the unique impression of Jesus upon mankind, whose name is not so much written as ploughed into the history of this world, is proof of the subtle virtue of this infusion.

Meantime, whilst the doors of the temple stand open, night and day, before every man, and the oracles of this truth cease never, it is guarded by one stern condition; this, namely; it is an intuition. It cannot be received at second hand. Truly speaking, it is not instruction, but provocation, that I can receive from another soul. What he announces, I must find true in me, or wholly reject; and on his word, or as his second, be he who he may, I can accept nothing. On the contrary, the absence of this primary faith is the presence of degradation. As is the flood so is the ebb. Let this faith depart, and the very words it spake, and the things it made, become false and hurtful. Then falls the church, the state, art, letters, life. The doctrine of the divine nature being forgotten, a sickness infects and dwarfs the constitution. Once man was all; now he is an appendage, a nuisance. And because the indwelling Supreme Spirit cannot wholly be got rid of, the doctrine of it suffers this perversion, that the divine nature is attributed to one or two persons, and denied to all the rest, and denied with fury. The doctrine of inspiration is lost; the base doctrine of the majority of voices, usurps the place of the doctrine of the soul. Miracles, prophecy, poetry; the ideal life, the holy life, exist as ancient history merely; they are not in the belief, nor in the aspiration of society; but, when suggested, seem ridiculous. Life is comic or pitiful, as soon as the high ends of being fade out of sight, and man becomes nearsighted, and can only attend to what addresses the senses.

These general views, which, whilst they are general, none will contest, find abundant illustration in the history of religion, and especially in the history of the Christian church. In that, all of us have had our birth and nurture. The truth contained in that, you, my young friends, are now setting forth to teach. As the Cultus, or established worship of the civilized world, it has great historical interest for us. Of its blessed words, which have been the consolation of humanity, you need not that I should speak. I shall endeavor to discharge my duty to you, on this occasion, by pointing out two errors in its administration, which daily appear more gross from the point of view we have just now taken.

Jesus Christ belonged to the true race of prophets. He saw with open eye the mystery of the soul. Drawn by its severe harmony, ravished with its beauty, he lived in it, and had his being there. Alone in all history, he estimated the greatness of man. One man was true to what is in you and me. He saw that God incarnates himself in man, and evermore goes forth anew to take possession of his world. He said, in this jubilee of sublime emotion, 'I am divine. Through me, God acts; through me, speaks. Would you see God, see me; or, see thee, when thou also thinkest as I now think.' But what a distortion did his doctrine and memory suffer in the same, in the next, and the following ages! There is no doctrine of the Reason which will bear to be taught by the Understanding. The understanding caught this high chant from the poet's lips, and said, in the next age, 'This was Jehovah come down out of heaven. I will kill you, if you say he was a man.' The idioms of his language, and the figures of his rhetoric, have usurped the place of his truth; and churches are not built on his principles, but on his tropes. Christianity became a Mythus, as the poetic teaching of Greece and of Egypt, before. He spoke of miracles; for he felt that man's life was a miracle, and all that man doth, and he knew that this daily miracle shines, as the character ascends. But the word Miracle, as pronounced by Christian churches, gives a false impression; it is Monster. It is not one with the blowing clover and the falling rain.

He felt respect for Moses and the prophets; but no unfit tenderness at postponing their initial revelations, to the hour and the man that now is; to the eternal revelation in the heart. Thus was he a true man. Having seen that the law in us is commanding, he would not suffer it to be commanded. Boldly, with hand, and heart, and life, he declared it was God. Thus is he, as I think, the only soul in history who has appreciated the worth of a man.

1. In this point of view we become very sensible of the first defect of historical Christianity. Historical Christianity has fallen into the error that corrupts all attempts to communicate

religion. As it appears to us, and as it has appeared for ages, it is not the doctrine of the soul, but an exaggeration of the personal, the positive, the ritual. It has dwelt, it dwells, with noxious exaggeration about the *person* of Jesus. The soul knows no persons. It invites every man to expand to the full circle of the universe, and will have no preferences but those of spontaneous love. But by this eastern monarchy of a Christianity, which indolence and fear have built, the friend of man is made the injurer of man. The manner in which his name is surrounded with expressions, which were once sallies of admiration and love, but are now petrified into official titles, kills all generous sympathy and liking. All who hear me, feel, that the language that describes Christ to Europe and America, is not the style of friendship and enthusiasm to a good and noble heart, but is appropriated and formal,—paints a demigod, as the Orientals or the Greeks would describe Osiris or Apollo. Accept the injurious impositions of our early catachetical instruction, and even honesty and self-denial were but splendid sins, if they did not wear the Christian name. One would rather be

'A pagan, suckled in a creed outworn,'

than to be defrauded of his manly right in coming into nature, and finding not names and places, not land and professions, but even virtue and truth foreclosed and monopolized. You shall not be a man even. You shall not own the world; you shall not dare, and live after the infinite Law that is in you, and in company with the infinite Beauty which heaven and earth reflect to you in all lovely forms; but you must subordinate your nature to Christ's nature; you must accept our interpretations; and take his portrait as the vulgar draw it.

That is always best which gives me to myself. The sublime is excited in me by the great stoical doctrine, Obey thyself. That which shows God in me, fortifies me. That which shows God out of me, makes me a wart and a wen. There is no longer a necessary reason for my being. Already the long shadows of untimely oblivion creep over me, and I shall decease forever.

The divine bards are the friends of my virtue, of my intellect, of my strength. They admonish me, that the gleams which flash across my mind, are not mine, but God's; that they had the like, and were not disobedient to the heavenly vision. So I love them. Noble provocations go out from them, inviting me to resist evil; to subdue the world; and to Be. And thus by his holy thoughts, Jesus serves us, and thus only. To aim to convert a man by miracles, is a profanation of the soul. A true conversion, a true Christ, is now, as always, to be made, by the reception of beautiful sentiments. It is true that a great and rich soul, like his, falling among the simple, does so preponderate, that, as his did, it names the world. The world seems to them to exist for him, and they have not yet drunk so deeply of his sense, as to see that only by coming again to themselves, or to God in themselves, can they grow forevermore. It is a low benefit to give me something; it is a high benefit to enable me to do somewhat of myself. The time is coming when all men will see, that the gift of God to the soul is not a vaunting, overpowering, excluding sanctity, but a sweet, natural goodness, a goodness like thine and mine, and that so invites thine and mine to be and to grow.

The injustice of the vulgar tone of preaching is not less flagrant to Jesus, than to the souls which it profanes. The preachers do not see that they make his gospel not glad, and shear him of the locks of beauty and the attributes of heaven. When I see a majestic Epaminondas, or Washington; when I see among my contemporaries, a true orator, an upright judge, a dear friend; when I vibrate to the melody and fancy of a poem; I see beauty that is to be desired. And so lovely, and with yet more entire consent of my human being, sounds in my ear the severe music of the bards that have sung of the true God in all ages. Now do not degrade the life and dialogues of Christ out of the circle of this charm, by insulation and peculiarity. Let them lie as they befel, alive and warm, part of human life, and of the landscape, and of the cheerful day.

2. The second defect of the traditionary and limited way of using the mind of Christ is a consequence of the first; this, namely; that the Moral Nature, that Law of laws, whose revelations introduce greatness,—yea, God himself, into the

open soul, is not explored as the fountain of the established teaching in society. Men have come to speak of the revelation as somewhat long ago given and done, as if God were dead. The injury to faith throttles the preacher; and the goodliest of institutions becomes an uncertain and inarticulate voice.

It is very certain that it is the effect of conversation with the beauty of the soul, to beget a desire and need to impart to others the same knowledge and love. If utterance is denied, the thought lies like a burden on the man. Always the seer is a sayer. Somehow his dream is told: somehow he publishes it with solemn joy: sometimes with pencil on canvas; sometimes with chisel on stone; sometimes in towers and aisles of granite, his soul's worship is builded; sometimes in anthems of indefinite music; but clearest and most permanent, in words.

The man enamored of this excellency, becomes its priest or poet. The office is coeval with the world. But observe the condition, the spiritual limitation of the office. The spirit only can teach. Not any profane man, not any sensual, not any liar, not any slave can teach, but only he can give, who has; he only can create, who is. The man on whom the soul descends, through whom the soul speaks, alone can teach. Courage, piety, love, wisdom, can teach; and every man can open his door to these angels, and they shall bring him the gift of tongues. But the man who aims to speak as books enable, as synods use, as the fashion guides, and as interest commands, babbles. Let him hush.

To this holy office, you propose to devote yourselves. I wish you may feel your call in throbs of desire and hope. The office is the first in the world. It is of that reality, that it cannot suffer the deduction of any falsehood. And it is my duty to say to you, that the need was never greater of new revelation than now. From the views I have already expressed, you will infer the sad conviction, which I share, I believe, with numbers, of the universal decay and now almost death of faith in society. The soul is not preached. The Church seems to totter to its fall, almost all life extinct. On this occasion, any complaisance would be criminal, which told you, whose hope and commission it is to preach the faith of Christ, that the faith of Christ is preached.

It is time that this ill-suppressed murmur of all thoughtful men against the famine of our churches; this moaning of the heart because it is bereaved of the consolation, the hope, the grandeur, that come alone out of the culture of the moral nature; should be heard through the sleep of indolence, and over the din of routine. This great and perpetual office of the preacher is not discharged. Preaching is the expression of the moral sentiment in application to the duties of life. In how many churches, by how many prophets, tell me, is man made sensible that he is an infinite Soul; that the earth and heavens are passing into his mind; that he is drinking forever the soul of God? Where now sounds the persuasion, that by its very melody imparadises my heart, and so affirms its own origin in heaven? Where shall I hear words such as in elder ages drew men to leave all and follow,—father and mother, house and land, wife and child? Where shall I hear these august laws of moral being so pronounced, as to fill my ear, and I feel ennobled by the offer of my uttermost action and passion? The test of the true faith, certainly, should be its power to charm and command the soul, as the laws of nature control the activity of the hands,—so commanding that we find pleasure and honor in obeying. The faith should blend with the light of rising and of setting suns, with the flying cloud, the singing bird, and the breath of flowers. But now the priest's Sabbath has lost the splendor of nature; it is unlovely; we are glad when it is done; we can make, we do make, even sitting in our pews, a far better, holier, sweeter, for ourselves.

Whenever the pulpit is usurped by a formalist, then is the worshipper defrauded and disconsolate. We shrink as soon as the prayers begin, which do not uplift, but smite and offend us. We are fain to wrap our cloaks about us, and secure, as best we can, a solitude that hears not. I once heard a preacher who sorely tempted me to say, I would go to church no more. Men go, thought I, where they are wont to go, else had no soul entered the temple in the afternoon. A snow storm was falling around us. The snow storm was real; the preacher merely spectral; and the eye felt the sad contrast in looking at him, and then out of the window behind him, into the beautiful meteor of the snow. He had lived in vain. He had no one word intimating that he had laughed or wept, was married or in love, had been commended, or cheated, or chagrined. If he had ever lived and acted, we were none the wiser for it. The capital secret of his profession, namely, to convert life into truth, he had not learned. Not one fact in all his experience, had he yet imported into his doctrine. This man had ploughed, and planted, and talked, and bought, and sold; he had read books; he had eaten and drunken; his head aches; his heart throbs; he smiles and suffers; yet was there not a surmise, a hint, in all the discourse, that he had ever lived at all. Not a line did he draw out of real history. The true preacher can be known by this, that he deals out to the people his life,—life passed through the fire of thought. But of the bad preacher, it could not be told from his sermon, what age of the world he fell in; whether he had a father or a child; whether he was a freeholder or a pauper; whether he was a citizen or a countryman; or any other fact of his biography. It seemed strange that the people should come to church. It seemed as if their houses were very unentertaining, that they should prefer this thoughtless clamor. It shows that there is a commanding attraction in the moral sentiment, that can lend a faint tint of light to dulness and ignorance, coming in its name and place. The good hearer is sure he has been touched sometimes; is sure there is somewhat to be reached, and some word that can reach it. When he listens to these vain words, he comforts himself by their relation to his remembrance of better hours, and so they clatter and echo unchallenged.

I am not ignorant that when we preach unworthily, it is not always quite in vain. There is a good ear, in some men, that draws supplies to virtue out of very indifferent nutriment. There is poetic truth concealed in all the commonplaces of prayer and of sermons, and though foolishly spoken, they may be wisely heard; for, each is some select expression that broke out in a moment of piety from some stricken or jubilant soul, and its excellency made it remembered. The prayers and even the dogmas of our church, are like the zodiac of Denderah, and the astronomical monuments of the Hindoos, wholly insulated from anything now extant in the life and business of the people. They mark the height to which the waters once rose. But this docility is a check upon the mischief from the good and devout. In a large portion of the community, the religious service gives rise to quite other thoughts and emotions. We need not chide the negligent servant. We are struck with pity, rather, at the swift retribution of his sloth. Alas for the unhappy man that is called to stand in the pulpit, and *not* give bread of life. Everything that befalls, accuses him. Would he ask contributions for the missions, foreign or domestic? Instantly his face is suffused with shame, to propose to his parish, that they should send money a hundred or a thousand miles, to furnish such poor fare as they have at home, and would do well to go the hundred or the thousand miles to escape. Would he urge people to a godly way of living;—and can he ask a fellow-creature to come to Sabbath meetings, when he and they all know what is the poor uttermost they can hope for therein? Will he invite them privately to the Lord's Supper? He dares not. If no heart warm this rite, the hollow, dry, creaking formality is too plain, than that he can face a man of wit and energy, and put the invitation without terror. In the street, what has he to say to the bold village blasphemer? The village blasphemer sees fear in the face, form, and gait of the minister.

Let me not taint the sincerity of this plea by any oversight of the claims of good men. I know and honor the purity and strict conscience of numbers of the clergy. What life the public worship retains, it owes to the scattered company of pious men, who minister here and there in the churches, and who, sometimes accepting with too great tenderness the tenet of the elders, have not accepted from others, but from their own heart, the genuine impulses of virtue, and so still command our love and awe, to the sanctity of character. Moreover, the exceptions are not so much to be found in a few eminent preachers, as in the better hours, the truer inspirations of all,—nay, in the sincere moments of every man. But with whatever exception, it is still true, that tradition characterizes the preaching of this country; that it comes out of the memory, and not out of the soul; that it aims at what is usual, and not at what is necessary and eternal; that thus, historical Christianity destroys the power of preaching, by withdrawing it from the exploration of the moral nature of man, where the sublime is, where are the resources of astonishment and power. What a cruel injustice it is to that Law, the joy of the whole earth, which alone can make thought dear and rich; that Law whose fatal sureness the astronomical orbits poorly emulate, that it is travestied and depreciated, that it is behooted and behowled, and not a trait, not a word of it articulated. The pulpit in losing sight of this Law, loses its reason, and gropes after it knows not what. And for want of this culture, the soul of the community is sick and faithless. It wants nothing so much as a stern, high, stoical, Christian discipline, to make it know itself and the divinity that speaks through it. Now man is ashamed of himself; he skulks and sneaks through the world, to be tolerated, to be pitied, and scarcely in a thousand years does any man dare to be wise and good, and so draw after him the tears and blessings of his kind.

Certainly there have been periods when, from the inactivity of the intellect on certain truths, a greater faith was possible in names and persons. The Puritans in England and America, found in the Christ of the Catholic Church, and in the dogmas inherited from Rome, scope for their austere piety, and their longings for civil freedom. But their creed is passing away, and none arises in its room. I think no man can go with his thoughts about him, into one of our churches, without feeling, that what hold the public worship had on men is gone, or going. It has lost its grasp on the affection of the good, and the fear of the bad. In the country, neighborhoods, half parishes are *signing off*,—to use the local term. It is already beginning to indicate character and religion to withdraw from the religious meetings. I have heard a devout person, who prized the Sabbath, say in bitterness of heart, "On Sundays, it seems wicked to go to church." And the motive, that holds the best there, is now only a hope and a waiting. What was once a mere circumstance, that the best and the worst men in the parish, the poor and the rich, the learned and the ignorant, young and old, should meet one day as fellows in one house, in sign of an equal right in the soul,—has come to be a paramount motive for going thither.

My friends, in these two errors, I think, I find the causes of a decaying church and a wasting unbelief. And what greater calamity can fall upon a nation, than the loss of worship? Then all things go to decay. Genius leaves the temple,

to haunt the senate, or the market. Literature becomes frivolous. Science is cold. The eye of youth is not lighted by the
hope of other worlds, and age is without honor. Society lives
to trifles, and when men die, we do not mention them.

And now, my brothers, you will ask, What in these desponding days can be done by us? The remedy is already declared in the ground of our complaint of the Church. We have
contrasted the Church with the Soul. In the soul, then, let the
redemption be sought. Wherever a man comes, there comes
revolution. The old is for slaves. When a man comes, all
books are legible, all things transparent, all religions are
forms. He is religious. Man is the wonderworker. He is seen
amid miracles. All men bless and curse. He saith yea and nay,
only. The stationariness of religion; the assumption that the
age of inspiration is past, that the Bible is closed; the fear of
degrading the character of Jesus by representing him as a
man; indicate with sufficient clearness the falsehood of our
theology. It is the office of a true teacher to show us that God
is, not was; that He speaketh, not spake. The true Christianity,—a faith like Christ's in the infinitude of man,—is lost.
None believeth in the soul of man, but only in some man or
person old and departed. Ah me! no man goeth alone. All
men go in flocks to this saint or that poet, avoiding the God
who seeth in secret. They cannot see in secret; they love to
be blind in public. They think society wiser than their soul,
and know not that one soul, and their soul, is wiser than the
whole world. See how nations and races flit by on the sea of
time, and leave no ripple to tell where they floated or sunk,
and one good soul shall make the name of Moses, or of Zeno,
or of Zoroaster, reverend forever. None assayeth the stern
ambition to be the Self of the nation, and of nature, but each
would be an easy secondary to some Christian scheme, or
sectarian connection, or some eminent man. Once leave your
own knowledge of God, your own sentiment, and take secondary knowledge, as St. Paul's, or George Fox's, or Swedenborg's, and you get wide from God with every year this
secondary form lasts, and if, as now, for centuries,—the
chasm yawns to that breadth, that men can scarcely be convinced there is in them anything divine.

Let me admonish you, first of all, to go alone; to refuse the good models, even those which are sacred in the imagination of men, and dare to love God without mediator or veil. Friends enough you shall find who will hold up to your emulation Wesleys and Oberlins, Saints and Prophets. Thank God for these good men, but say, 'I also am a man.' Imitation cannot go above its model. The imitator dooms himself to hopeless mediocrity. The inventor did it, because it was natural to him, and so in him it has a charm. In the imitator, something else is natural, and he bereaves himself of his own beauty, to come short of another man's.

Yourself a newborn bard of the Holy Ghost,—cast behind you all conformity, and acquaint men at first hand with Deity. Look to it first and only, that fashion, custom, authority, pleasure, and money, are nothing to you,—are not bandages over your eyes, that you cannot see,—but live with the privilege of the immeasurable mind. Not too anxious to visit periodically all families and each family in your parish connection,—when you meet one of these men or women, be to them a divine man; be to them thought and virtue; let their timid aspirations find in you a friend; let their trampled instincts be genially tempted out in your atmosphere; let their doubts know that you have doubted, and their wonder feel *Carl* that you have wondered. By trusting your own heart, you shall gain more confidence in other men. For all our penny-wisdom, for all our soul-destroying slavery to habit, it is not to be doubted, that all men have sublime thoughts; that all men value the few real hours of life; they love to be heard; they love to be caught up into the vision of principles. We mark with light in the memory the few interviews we have had, in the dreary years of routine and of sin, with souls that made our souls wiser; that spoke what we thought; that told us what we knew; that gave us leave to be what we inly were. Discharge to men the priestly office, and, present or absent, you shall be followed with their love as by an angel.

And, to this end, let us not aim at common degrees of merit. Can we not leave, to such as love it, the virtue that glitters for the commendation of society, and ourselves pierce the deep solitudes of absolute ability and worth? We easily come up to the standard of goodness in society. Society's praise can be cheaply secured, and almost all men are content with those easy merits; but the instant effect of conversing with God, will be, to put them away. There are persons who are not actors, not speakers, but influences; persons too great for fame, for display; who disdain eloquence; to whom all we call art and artist, seems too nearly allied to show and by-ends, to the exaggeration of the finite and selfish, and loss of the universal. The orators, the poets, the commanders encroach on us only as fair women do, by our allowance and homage. Slight them by preoccupation of mind, slight them, as you can well afford to do, by high and universal aims, and they instantly feel that you have right, and that it is in lower places that they must shine. They also feel your right; for they with you are open to the influx of the all-knowing Spirit, which annihilates before its broad noon the little shades and gradations of intelligence in the compositions we call wiser and wisest.

In such high communion, let us study the grand strokes of rectitude: a bold benevolence, an independence of friends, so that not the unjust wishes of those who love us, shall impair our freedom, but we shall resist for truth's sake the freest flow of kindness, and appeal to sympathies far in advance; and,— what is the highest form in which we know this beautiful element,—a certain solidity of merit, that has nothing to do with opinion, and which is so essentially and manifestly virtue, that it is taken for granted, that the right, the brave, the generous step will be taken by it, and nobody thinks of commending it. You would compliment a coxcomb doing a good act, but you would not praise an angel. The silence that accepts merit as the most natural thing in the world, is the highest applause. Such souls, when they appear, are the Imperial Guard of Virtue, the perpetual reserve, the dictators of fortune. One needs not praise their courage,—they are the heart and soul of nature. O my friends, there are resources in us on which we have not drawn. There are men who rise refreshed on hearing a threat; men to whom a crisis which intimidates and paralyzes the majority,—demanding not the faculties of prudence and thrift, but comprehension, immovableness, the readiness of sacrifice,—comes graceful and beloved as a bride. Napoleon said of Massena, that he was not himself until the battle began to go against him; then, when the dead began to fall in ranks around him, awoke his powers of combination, and he put on terror and victory as a robe. So it is in rugged crises, in unweariable endurance, and in aims which put sympathy out of question, that the angel is shown. But these are heights that we can scarce remember and look up to, without contrition and shame. Let us thank God that such things exist.

And now let us do what we can to rekindle the smouldering, nigh quenched fire on the altar. The evils of the church that now is are manifest. The question returns, What shall we do? I confess, all attempts to project and establish a Cultus with new rites and forms, seem to me vain. Faith makes us, and not we it, and faith makes its own forms. All attempts to contrive a system are as cold as the new worship introduced by the French to the goddess of Reason,—to-day, pasteboard and fillagree, and ending to-morrow in madness and murder. Rather let the breath of new life be breathed by you through the forms already existing. For, if once you are alive, you shall find they shall become plastic and new. The remedy to their deformity is, first, soul, and second, soul, and evermore, soul. A whole popedom of forms, one pulsation of virtue can uplift and vivify. Two inestimable advantages Christianity has given us; first; the Sabbath, the jubilee of the whole world; whose light dawns welcome alike into the closet of the philosopher, into the garret of toil, and into prison cells, and everywhere suggests, even to the vile, the dignity of spiritual being. Let it stand forevermore, a temple, which new love, new faith, new sight shall restore to more than its first splendor to mankind. And secondly, the institution of preaching,—the speech of man to men,—essentially the most flexible of all organs, of all forms. What hinders that now, everywhere, in pulpits, in lecture-rooms, in houses, in fields, wherever the invitation of men or your own occasions lead you, you speak the very truth, as your life and conscience teach it, and cheer the waiting, fainting hearts of men with new hope and new revelation?

I look for the hour when that supreme Beauty, which ravished the souls of those eastern men, and chiefly of those Hebrews, and through their lips spoke oracles to all time, shall speak in the West also. The Hebrew and Greek Scriptures contain immortal sentences, that have been bread of life to millions. But they have no epical integrity; are fragmentary; are not shown in their order to the intellect. I look for the new Teacher, that shall follow so far those shining laws, that he shall see them come full circle; shall see their rounding complete grace; shall see the world to be the mirror of the soul; shall see the identity of the law of gravitation with purity of heart; and shall show that the Ought, that Duty, is one thing with Science, with Beauty, and with Joy.

LITERARY ETHICS

*An Oration delivered before the Literary Societies
of Dartmouth College, July 24, 1838*

Oration

THE INVITATION to address you this day, with which you have honored me, was a call so welcome, that I made haste to obey it. A summons to celebrate with scholars a literary festival, is so alluring to me, as to overcome the doubts I might well entertain of my ability to bring you any thought worthy of your attention. I have reached the middle age of man; yet I believe I am not less glad or sanguine at the meeting of scholars, than when, a boy, I first saw the graduates of my own College assembled at their anniversary. Neither years nor books have yet availed to extirpate a prejudice then rooted in me, that a scholar is the favorite of Heaven and earth, the excellency of his country, the happiest of men. His duties lead him directly into the holy ground where other men's aspirations only point. His successes are occasions of the purest joy to all men. Eyes is he to the blind; feet is he to the lame. His failures, if he is worthy, are inlets to higher advantages. And because the scholar, by every thought he thinks, extends his dominion into the general mind of men, he is not one, but many. The few scholars in each country, whose genius I know, seem to me not individuals, but societies; and, when events occur of great import, I count over these representatives of opinion, whom they will affect, as if I were counting nations. And, even if his results were incommunicable; if they abode in his own spirit; the intellect hath somewhat so sacred in its possessions, that the fact of his existence and pursuits would be a happy omen.

Meantime I know that a very different estimate of the scholar's profession prevails in this country, and the importunity, with which society presses its claim upon young men, tends to pervert the views of the youth in respect to the culture of the intellect. Hence the historical failure, on which Europe and America have so freely commented. This country has not fulfilled what seemed the reasonable expectation of mankind. Men looked, when all feudal straps and bandages were snapped asunder, that nature, too long the mother of dwarfs, should reimburse itself by a brood of Titans, who should laugh and leap in the continent, and run up the mountains of the West with the errand of genius and of love. But the mark of American merit in painting, in sculpture, in poetry, in fiction, in eloquence, seems to be a certain grace without grandeur, and itself not new but derivative; a vase of fair outline, but empty,—which whoso sees, may fill with what wit and character is in him, but which does not, like the charged cloud, overflow with terrible beauty, and emit lightnings on all beholders.

I will not lose myself in the desultory questions, what are the limitations, and what the causes of the fact. It suffices me to say, in general, that the diffidence of mankind in the soul has crept over the American mind; that men here, as elsewhere, are indisposed to innovation, and prefer any antiquity, any usage, any livery productive of ease or profit, to the unproductive service of thought.

Yet, in every sane hour, the service of thought appears reasonable, the despotism of the senses insane. The scholar may lose himself in schools, in words, and become a pedant; but when he comprehends his duties, he above all men is a realist, and converses with things. For, the scholar is the student of the world, and of what worth the world is, and with what emphasis it accosts the soul of man, such is the worth, such the call of the scholar.

The want of the times, and the propriety of this anniversary, concur to draw attention to the doctrine of Literary Ethics. What I have to say on that doctrine distributes itself under the topics of the resources, the subject, and the discipline of the scholar.

I. The resources of the scholar are proportioned to his confidence in the attributes of the Intellect. The resources of the scholar are co-extensive with nature and truth, yet can never be his, unless claimed by him with an equal greatness of mind. He cannot know them until he has beheld with awe the infinitude and impersonality of the intellectual power. When he has seen, that it is not his, nor any man's, but that it is the soul which made the world, and that it is all accessible to him, he will know that he, as its minister, may rightfully hold all things subordinate and answerable to it. A divine pilgrim in nature, all things attend his steps. Over him stream the flying constellations; over him streams Time, as they, scarcely divided into months and years. He inhales the year as a vapor: its fragrant midsummer breath, its sparkling January heaven. And so pass into his mind, in bright transfiguration, the grand events of history, to take a new order and scale from him. He is the world; and the epochs and heroes of chronology are pictorial images, in which his thoughts are told. There is no event but sprung somewhere from the soul of man; and therefore there is none but the soul of man can interpret. Every presentiment of the mind is executed somewhere in a gigantic fact. What else is Greece, Rome, England, France, St. Helena? What else are churches, literatures, and empires? The new man must feel that he is new, and has not come into the world mortgaged to the opinions and usages of Europe, and Asia, and Egypt. The sense of spiritual independence is like the lovely varnish of the dew, whereby the old, hard, peaked earth, and its old self-same productions, are made new every morning, and shining with the last touch of the artist's hand. A false humility, a complaisance to reigning schools, or to the wisdom of antiquity, must not defraud me of supreme possession of this hour. If any person have less love of liberty, and less jealousy to guard his integrity, shall he therefore dictate to you and me? Say to such doctors, We are thankful to you, as we are to history, to the pyramids, and the authors; but now our day is come; we have been born out of the eternal silence; and now will we live,—live for ourselves,—and not as the pall-bearers of a funeral, but as the upholders and creators of our age; and neither Greece nor Rome, nor the three Unities of Aristotle, nor the three Kings of Cologne, nor the College of the Sorbonne, nor the Edinburgh Review, is to command any longer. Now that we are here, we will put our own interpretation on things, and our own things for interpretation. Please himself with complaisance who will,—for me, things must take my scale, not I theirs. I will say with the warlike king, "God gave me this crown, and the whole world shall not take it away."

The whole value of history, of biography, is to increase my self-trust, by demonstrating what man can be and do. This is the moral of the Plutarchs, the Cudworths, the Tennemanns, who give us the story of men or of opinions. Any history of philosophy fortifies my faith, by showing me, that what high dogmas I had supposed were the rare and late fruit of a cumulative culture, and only now possible to some recent Kant or Fichte,—were the prompt improvisations of the earliest inquirers; of Parmenides, Heraclitus, and Xenophanes. In view of these students, the soul seems to whisper, 'There is a better way than this indolent learning of another. Leave me alone; do not teach me out of Leibnitz or Schelling, and I shall find it all out myself.'

Still more do we owe to biography the fortification of our hope. If you would know the power of character, see how much you would impoverish the world, if you could take clean out of history the lives of Milton, Shakspeare, and Plato,—these three, and cause them not to be. See you not, how much less the power of man would be? I console myself in the poverty of my thoughts; in the paucity of great men, in the malignity and dulness of the nations, by falling back on these sublime recollections, and seeing what the prolific soul could beget on actual nature;—seeing that Plato was, and Shakspeare, and Milton,—three irrefragable facts. Then I dare; I also will essay to be. The humblest, the most hopeless, in view of these radiant facts, may now theorize and hope. In spite of all the rueful abortions that squeak and gibber in the street, in spite of slumber and guilt, in spite of the army, the bar-room, and the jail, *have been* these glorious manifestations of the mind; and I will thank my great brothers so truly for the admonition of their being, as to endeavor also to be just and brave, to aspire and to speak. Plotinus too, and Spinoza, and the immortal bards of philosophy,—that which they have written out with patient courage, makes me bold. No more will I dismiss, with haste, the visions which flash and sparkle across my sky; but observe them, approach them, domesticate them, brood on them, and draw out of the past, genuine life for the present hour.

To feel the full value of these lives, as occasions of hope and provocation, you must come to know, that each admirable genius is but a successful diver in that sea whose floor of pearls is all your own. The impoverishing philosophy of ages has laid stress on the distinctions of the individual, and not on the universal attributes of man. The youth, intoxicated with his admiration of a hero, fails to see, that it is only a projection of his own soul, which he admires. In solitude, in a remote village, the ardent youth loiters and mourns. With inflamed eye, in this sleeping wilderness, he has read the story of the Emperor Charles the Fifth, until his fancy has brought home to the surrounding woods, the faint roar of cannonades in the Milanese, and marches in Germany. He is curious concerning that man's day. What filled it? the crowded orders, the stern decisions, the foreign despatches, the Castilian etiquette? The soul answers—Behold his day here! In the sighing of these woods, in the quiet of these gray fields, in the cool breeze that sings out of these northern mountains; in the workmen, the boys, the maidens, you meet,—in the hopes of the morning, the ennui of noon, and sauntering of the afternoon; in the disquieting comparisons; in the regrets at want of vigor; in the great idea, and the puny execution;—behold Charles the Fifth's day; another, yet the same; behold Chatham's, Hampden's, Bayard's, Alfred's, Scipio's, Pericles's day,—day of all that are born of women. The difference of circumstance is merely costume. I am tasting the self-same life,—its sweetness, its greatness, its pain, which I so admire in other men. Do not foolishly ask of the inscrutable, obliterated past, what it cannot tell,—the details of that nature, of that day, called Byron, or Burke;—but ask it of the enveloping Now; the more quaintly you inspect its evanescent beauties, its wonderful details, its spiritual causes, its astounding whole,—so much the more you master the biography of this hero, and that, and every hero. Be lord of a day, through wisdom and justice, and you can put up your history books.

An intimation of these broad rights is familiar in the sense of injury which men feel in the assumption of any man to limit their possible progress. We resent all criticism, which denies us any thing that lies in our line of advance. Say to the man of letters, that he cannot paint a Transfiguration, or build a steamboat, or be a grand-marshal,—and he will not seem to himself depreciated. But deny to him any quality of literary or metaphysical power, and he is piqued. Concede to him genius, which is a sort of Stoical *plenum* annulling the comparative, and he is content; but concede him talents never so rare, denying him genius, and he is aggrieved. What does this mean? Why simply, that the soul has assurance, by instincts and presentiments, of *all* power in the direction of its ray, as well as of the special skills it has already acquired.

In order to a knowledge of the resources of the scholar, we must not rest in the use of slender accomplishments,—of faculties to do this and that other feat with words; but we must pay our vows to the highest power, and pass, if it be possible, by assiduous love and watching, into the visions of absolute truth. The growth of the intellect is strictly analogous in all individuals. It is larger reception. Able men, in general, have good dispositions, and a respect for justice; because an able man is nothing else than a good, free, vascular organization, whereinto the universal spirit freely flows; so that his fund of justice is not only vast, but infinite. All men, in the abstract, are just and good; what hinders them, in the particular, is, the momentary predominance of the finite and individual over the general truth. The condition of our incarnation in a private self, seems to be, a perpetual tendency to prefer the private law, to obey the private impulse, to the exclusion of the law of universal being. The hero is great by means of the predominance of the universal nature; he has only to open his mouth, and it speaks; he has only to be forced to act, and it acts. All men catch the word, or embrace the deed, with the heart, for it is verily theirs as much as his; but in them this disease of an excess of organization cheats them of equal issues. Nothing is more simple than greatness; indeed, to be simple is to be great. The vision of genius comes by renouncing the too officious activity of the understanding, and giving leave and amplest privilege to the spontaneous sentiment. Out of this must all that is alive and genial in thought go. Men grind and grind in the mill of a truism, and nothing comes out but what was put in. But the moment they desert the tradition for a spontaneous thought, then poetry, wit, hope, virtue, learning, anecdote, all flock to their aid. Observe the phenomenon of extempore debate. A man of cultivated mind, but reserved habits, sitting silent, admires the miracle of free, impassioned, picturesque speech, in the man addressing an assembly;—a state of being and power, how unlike his own! Presently his own emotion rises to his lips, and overflows in speech. He must also rise and say somewhat. Once embarked, once having overcome the novelty of the situation, he finds it just as easy and natural to speak,—to speak with thoughts, with pictures, with rhythmical balance of sentences,—as it was to sit silent; for, it needs not to do, but to suffer; he only adjusts himself to the free spirit which gladly utters itself through him; and motion is as easy as rest.

II. I pass now to consider the task offered to the intellect of this country. The view I have taken of the resources of the scholar, presupposes a subject as broad. We do not seem to have imagined its riches. We have not heeded the invitation it holds out. To be as good a scholar as Englishmen are; to have as much learning as our contemporaries; to have written a book that is read; satisfies us. We assume, that all thought is already long ago adequately set down in books,—all imaginations in poems; and what we say, we only throw in as confirmatory of this supposed complete body of literature. A very shallow assumption. Say rather, all literature is yet to be written. Poetry has scarce chanted its first song. The perpetual admonition of nature to us, is, 'The world is new, untried. Do not believe the past. I give you the universe a virgin to-day.'

By Latin and English poetry, we were born and bred in an oratorio of praises of nature,—flowers, birds, mountains, sun, and moon;—yet the naturalist of this hour finds that he knows nothing, by all their poems, of any of these fine things; that he has conversed with the mere surface and show of them all; and of their essence, or of their history, knows nothing. Further inquiry will discover that nobody,—that not these chanting poets themselves, knew any thing sincere of these handsome natures they so commended; that they contented themselves with the passing chirp of a bird, that they saw one or two mornings, and listlessly looked at sunsets, and repeated idly these few glimpses in their song. But go into the forest, you shall find all new and undescribed. The screaming of the wild geese flying by night; the thin note of the companionable titmouse, in the winter day; the fall of swarms of flies, in autumn, from combats high in the air, pattering down on the leaves like rain; the angry hiss of the wood-birds; the pine throwing out its pollen for the benefit of the next century; the turpentine exuding from the tree;— and, indeed, any vegetation; any animation; any and all, are alike unattempted. The man who stands on the seashore, or who rambles in the woods, seems to be the first man that ever stood on the shore, or entered a grove, his sensations and his world are so novel and strange. Whilst I read the poets, I think that nothing new can be said about morning and evening. But when I see the daybreak, I am not reminded of these Homeric, or Shakspearian, or Miltonic, or Chaucerian pictures. No; but I feel perhaps the pain of an alien world; a world not yet subdued by the thought; or, I am cheered by the moist, warm, glittering, budding, melodious hour, that takes down the narrow walls of my soul, and extends its life and pulsation to the very horizon. *That* is morning, to cease for a bright hour to be a prisoner of this sickly body, and to become as large as nature.

The noonday darkness of the American forest, the deep, echoing, aboriginal woods, where the living columns of the oak and fir tower up from the ruins of the trees of the last millennium; where, from year to year, the eagle and the crow see no intruder; the pines, bearded with savage moss, yet touched with grace by the violets at their feet; the broad, cold lowland, which forms its coat of vapor with the stillness of subterranean crystallization; and where the traveller, amid the repulsive plants that are native in the swamp, thinks with pleasing terror of the distant town; this beauty,—haggard and desert beauty, which the sun and the moon, the snow and the rain, repaint and vary, has never been recorded by art, yet is not indifferent to any passenger. All men are poets at heart. They serve nature for bread, but her loveliness overcomes them sometimes. What mean these journeys to Niagara; these pilgrims to the White Hills? Men believe in the adaptations of utility, always: in the mountains, they may believe in the adaptations of the eye. Undoubtedly, the changes of geology have a relation to the prosperous sprouting of the corn and peas in my kitchen garden; but not less is there a relation of beauty between my soul and the dim crags of Agiocochook up there in the clouds. Every man, when this is told, hearkens with joy, and yet his own conversation with nature is still unsung.

Is it otherwise with civil history? Is it not the lesson of our experience that every man, were life long enough, would write history for himelf? What else do these volumes of extracts and manuscript commentaries, that every scholar writes, indicate? Greek history is one thing to me; another to you. Since the birth of Niebuhr and Wolf, Roman and Greek History have been written anew. Since Carlyle wrote French History, we see that no history, that we have, is safe, but a new classifier shall give it new and more philosophical arrangement. Thucydides, Livy, have only provided materials. The moment a man of genius pronounces the name of the Pelasgi, of Athens, of the Etrurian, of the Roman people, we see their state under a new aspect. As in poetry and history, so in the other departments. There are few masters or none. Religion is yet to be settled on its fast foundations in the breast of man; and politics, and philosophy, and letters, and art. As yet we have nothing but tendency and indication.

This starting, this warping of the best literary works from the adamant of nature, is especially observable in philosophy. Let it take what tone of pretension it will, to this complexion must it come, at last. Take, for example, the French Eclecticism, which Cousin esteems so conclusive; there is an optical illusion in it. It avows great pretensions. It looks as if they had all truth, in taking all the systems, and had nothing to do, but to sift and wash and strain, and the gold and diamonds would remain in the last colander. But, Truth is such a flyaway, such a slyboots, so untransportable and unbarrelable a commodity, that it is as bad to catch as light. Shut the shutters never so quick, to keep all the light in, it is all in vain; it is gone before you can cry, Hold. And so it happens with our philosophy. Translate, collate, distil all the systems, it steads you nothing; for truth will not be compelled, in any mechanical manner. But the first observation you make, in the sincere act of your nature, though on the veriest trifle, may open a new view of nature and of man, that, like a menstruum, shall dissolve all theories in it; shall take up Greece, Rome, Stoicism, Eclecticism, and what not, as mere data and

food for analysis, and dispose of your world-containing system, as a very little unit. A profound thought, anywhere, classifies all things: a profound thought will lift Olympus. The
book of philosophy is only a fact, and no more inspiring fact
than another, and no less; but a wise man will never esteem
it anything final and transcending. Go and talk with a man of
genius, and the first word he utters, sets all your so-called
knowledge afloat and at large. Then Plato, Bacon, Kant, and
the Eclectic Cousin, condescend instantly to be men and mere
facts.

I by no means aim, in these remarks, to disparage the merit
of these or of any existing compositions; I only say that any
particular portraiture does not in any manner exclude or fore-
stall a new attempt, but, when considered by the soul,
warps and shrinks away. The inundation of the spirit sweeps
away before it all our little architecture of wit and memory,
as straws and straw-huts before the torrent. Works of the intellect are great only by comparison with each other; Ivanhoe
and Waverley compared with Castle Radcliffe and the Porter
novels; but nothing is great,—not mighty Homer and Milton,—beside the infinite Reason. It carries them away as a
flood. They are as a sleep.

Thus is justice done to each generation and individual,—
wisdom teaching man that he shall not hate, or fear, or mimic
his ancestors; that he shall not bewail himself, as if the world
was old, and thought was spent, and he was born into the
dotage of things; for, by virtue of the Deity, thought renews
itself inexhaustibly every day, and the thing whereon it shines,
though it were dust and sand, is a new subject with countless
relations.

III. Having thus spoken of the resources and the subject of
the scholar, out of the same faith proceeds also the rule of his
ambition and life. Let him know that the world is his, but he
must possess it by putting himself into harmony with the
constitution of things. He must be a solitary, laborious, modest, and charitable soul.

He must embrace solitude as a bride. He must have his
glees and his glooms alone. His own estimate must be measure enough, his own praise reward enough for him. And

why must the student be solitary and silent? That he may become acquainted with his thoughts. If he pines in a lonely place, hankering for the crowd, for display, he is not in the lonely place; his heart is in the market; he does not see; he does not hear; he does not think. But go cherish your soul; expel companions; set your habits to a life of solitude; then, will the faculties rise fair and full within, like forest trees and field flowers; you will have results, which, when you meet your fellow-men, you can communicate, and they will gladly receive. Do not go into solitude only that you may presently come into public. Such solitude denies itself; is public and stale. The public can get public experience, but they wish the scholar to replace to them those private, sincere, divine experiences, of which they have been defrauded by dwelling in the street. It is the noble, manlike, just thought, which is the superiority demanded of you, and not crowds but solitude confers this elevation. Not insulation of place, but independence of spirit is essential, and it is only as the garden, the cottage, the forest, and the rock, are a sort of mechanical aids to this, that they are of value. Think alone, and all places are friendly and sacred. The poets who have lived in cities have been hermits still. Inspiration makes solitude anywhere. Pindar, Raphael, Angelo, Dryden, De Staël, dwell in crowds, it may be, but the instant thought comes, the crowd grows dim to their eye; their eye fixes on the horizon,—on vacant space; they forget the bystanders; they spurn personal relations; they deal with abstractions, with verities, with ideas. They are alone with the mind.

Of course, I would not have any superstition about solitude. Let the youth study the uses of solitude and of society. Let him use both, not serve either. The reason why an ingenious soul shuns society, is to the end of finding society. It repudiates the false, out of love of the true. You can very soon learn all that society can teach you for one while. Its foolish routine, an indefinite multiplication of balls, concerts, rides, theatres, can teach you no more than a few can. Then accept the hint of shame, of spiritual emptiness and waste, which true nature gives you, and retire, and hide; lock the door; shut the shutters; then welcome falls the imprisoning rain,—dear hermitage of nature. Re-collect the spirits. Have solitary prayer and praise. Digest and correct the past experience; and blend it with the new and divine life.

You will pardon me, Gentlemen, if I say, I think that we have need of a more rigorous scholastic rule; such an asceticism, I mean, as only the hardihood and devotion of the scholar himself can enforce. We live in the sun and on the surface,—a thin, plausible, superficial existence, and talk of muse and prophet, of art and creation. But out of our shallow and frivolous way of life, how can greatness ever grow? Come now, let us go and be dumb. Let us sit with our hands on our mouths, a long, austere, Pythagorean lustrum. Let us live in corners, and do chores, and suffer, and weep, and drudge, with eyes and hearts that love the Lord. Silence, seclusion, austerity, may pierce deep into the grandeur and secret of our being, and so diving, bring up out of secular darkness, the sublimities of the moral constitution. How mean to go blazing, a gaudy butterfly, in fashionable or political saloons, the fool of society, the fool of notoriety, a topic for newspapers, a piece of the street, and forfeiting the real prerogative of the russet coat, the privacy, and the true and warm heart of the citizen!

Fatal to the man of letters, fatal to man, is the lust of display, the seeming that unmakes our being. A mistake of the main end to which they labor, is incident to literary men, who, dealing with the organ of language,—the subtlest, strongest, and longest-lived of man's creations, and only fitly used as the weapon of thought and of justice,—learn to enjoy the pride of playing with this splendid engine, but rob it of its almightiness by failing to work with it. Extricating themselves from the tasks of the world, the world revenges itself by exposing, at every turn, the folly of these incomplete, pedantic, useless, ghostly creatures. The scholar will feel, that the richest romance,—the noblest fiction that was ever woven,—the heart and soul of beauty,—lies enclosed in human life. Itself of surpassing value, it is also the richest material for his creations. How shall he know its secrets of tenderness, of terror, of will, and of fate? How can he catch and keep the strain of upper music that peals from it? Its laws are concealed under the details of daily action. All action is an experiment upon them. He must bear his share of the common load. He must work with men in houses, and not with their names in books. His needs, appetites, talents, affections, accomplishments, are keys that open to him the beautiful museum of human life. Why should he read it as an Arabian tale, and not know, in his own beating bosom, its sweet and smart? Out of love and hatred, out of earnings, and borrowings, and lendings, and losses; out of sickness and pain; out of wooing and worshipping; out of travelling, and voting, and watching, and caring; out of disgrace and contempt, comes our tuition in the serene and beautiful laws. Let him not slur his lesson; let him learn it by heart. Let him endeavor exactly, bravely, and cheerfully, to solve the problem of that life which is set before *him*. And this, by punctual action, and not by promises or dreams. Believing, as in God, in the presence and favor of the grandest influences, let him deserve that favor, and learn how to receive and use it, by fidelity also to the lower observances.

This lesson is taught with emphasis in the life of the great actor of this age, and affords the explanation of his success. Bonaparte represents truly a great recent revolution, which we in this country, please God, shall carry to its farthest consummation. Not the least instructive passage in modern history, seems to me a trait of Napoleon, exhibited to the English when he became their prisoner. On coming on board the Bellerophon, a file of English soldiers drawn up on deck, gave him a military salute. Napoleon observed, that their manner of handling their arms differed from the French exercise, and, putting aside the guns of those nearest him, walked up to a soldier, took his gun, and himself went through the motion in the French mode. The English officers and men looked on with astonishment, and inquired if such familiarity was usual with the Emperor.

In this instance, as always, that man, with whatever defects or vices, represented performance in lieu of pretension. Feudalism and Orientalism had long enough thought it majestic to do nothing; the modern majesty consists in work. He belonged to a class, fast growing in the world, who think, that what a man can do is his greatest ornament, and that he always consults his dignity by doing it. He was not a believer in luck; he had a faith, like sight, in the application of means to ends. Means to ends, is the motto of all his behavior. He believed that the great captains of antiquity performed their exploits only by correct combinations, and by justly comparing the relation between means and consequences; efforts and obstacles. The vulgar call good fortune that which really is produced by the calculations of genius. But Napoleon, thus faithful to facts, had also this crowning merit; that, whilst he believed in number and weight, and omitted no part of prudence, he believed also in the freedom and quite incalculable force of the soul. A man of infinite caution, he neglected never the least particular of preparation, of patient adaptation; yet nevertheless he had a sublime confidence, as in his all, in the sallies of the courage, and the faith in his destiny, which, at the right moment, repaired all losses, and demolished cavalry, infantry, king, and kaisar, as with irresistible thunderbolts. As they say the bough of the tree has the character of the leaf, and the whole tree of the bough, so, it is curious to remark, Bonaparte's army partook of this double strength of the captain; for, whilst strictly supplied in all its appointments, and everything expected from the valor and discipline of every platoon, in flank and centre, yet always remained his total trust in the prodigious revolutions of fortune, which his reserved Imperial Guard were capable of working, if, in all else, the day was lost. Here he was sublime. He no longer calculated the chance of the cannon-ball. He was faithful to tactics to the uttermost,—and when all tactics had come to an end, then, he dilated, and availed himself of the mighty saltations of the most formidable soldiers in nature.

Let the scholar appreciate this combination of gifts, which, applied to better purpose, make true wisdom. He is a revealer of things. Let him first learn the things. Let him not, too eager to grasp some badge of reward, omit the work to be done. Let him know, that, though the success of the market is in the reward, true success is the doing; that, in the private obedience to his mind; in the sedulous inquiry, day after day, year after year, to know how the thing stands; in the use of all means, and most in the reverence of the humble commerce and humble needs of life,—to hearken what *they* say, and so, by mutual reaction of thought and life, to make thought solid, and life wise; and in a contempt for the gabble of to-day's opinions, the secret of the world is to be learned, and the skill truly to unfold it is acquired. Or, rather, is it not, that, by this discipline, the usurpation of the senses is over-come, and the lower faculties of man are subdued to docility; through which, as an unobstructed channel, the soul now eas-ily and gladly flows?

The good scholar will not refuse to bear the yoke in his youth; to know, if he can, the uttermost secret of toil and endurance; to make his own hands acquainted with the soil by which he is fed, and the sweat that goes before comfort and luxury. Let him pay his tithe, and serve the world as a true and noble man; never forgetting to worship the immor-tal divinities, who whisper to the poet, and make him the utterer of melodies that pierce the ear of eternal time. If he have this twofold goodness,—the drill and the inspiration,— then he has health; then he is a whole, and not a fragment; and the perfection of his endowment will appear in his com-positions. Indeed, this twofold merit characterizes ever the productions of great masters. The man of genius should oc-cupy the whole space between God or pure mind, and the multitude of uneducated men. He must draw from the infi-nite Reason, on one side; and he must penetrate into the heart and sense of the crowd, on the other. From one, he must draw his strength; to the other, he must owe his aim. The one yokes him to the real; the other, to the apparent. At one pole, is Reason; at the other, Common Sense. If he be defective at either extreme of the scale, his philosophy will seem low and utilitarian; or it will appear too vague and in-definite for the uses of life.

The student, as we all along insist, is great only by being passive to the superincumbent spirit. Let this faith, then, dic-tate all his action. Snares and bribes abound to mislead him; let him be true nevertheless. His success has its perils too. There is somewhat inconvenient and injurious in his position. They whom his thoughts have entertained or inflamed, seek him before yet they have learned the hard conditions of thought. They seek him, that he may turn his lamp on the dark riddles whose solution they think is inscribed on the walls of their being. They find that he is a poor, ignorant man, in a white-seamed, rusty coat, like themselves, no wise emitting a continuous stream of light, but now and then a jet of luminous thought, followed by total darkness; moreover, that he cannot make of his infrequent illumination a portable taper to carry whither he would, and explain now this dark riddle, now that. Sorrow ensues. The scholar regrets to damp the hope of ingenuous boys; and the youth has lost a star out of his new flaming firmament. Hence the temptation to the scholar to mystify; to hear the question; to sit upon it; to make an answer of words, in lack of the oracle of things. Not the less let him be cold and true, and wait in patience, knowing that truth can make even silence eloquent and memorable. Truth shall be policy enough for him. Let him open his breast to all honest inquiry, and be an artist superior to tricks of art. Show frankly as a saint would do, your experience, methods, tools, and means. Welcome all comers to the freest use of the same. And out of this superior frankness and charity, you shall learn higher secrets of your nature, which gods will bend and aid you to communicate.

If, with a high trust, he can thus submit himself, he will find that ample returns are poured into his bosom, out of what seemed hours of obstruction and loss. Let him not grieve too much on account of unfit associates. When he sees how much thought he owes to the disagreeable antagonism of various persons who pass and cross him, he can easily think that in a society of perfect sympathy, no word, no act, no record, would be. He will learn, that it is not much matter what he reads, what he does. Be a scholar, and he shall have the scholar's part of every thing. As, in the counting-room, the merchant cares little whether the cargo be hides or barilla; the transaction, a letter of credit or a transfer of stocks; be it what it may, his commission comes gently out of it; so you shall get your lesson out of the hour, and the object, whether it be a concentrated or a wasteful employment, even in reading a dull book, or working off a stint of mechanical day labor, which your necessities or the necessities of others impose.

Gentlemen, I have ventured to offer you these considerations upon the scholar's place, and hope, because I thought, that, standing, as many of you now do, on the threshold of this College, girt and ready to go and assume tasks, public and private, in your country, you would not be sorry to be admonished of those primary duties of the intellect, whereof you will seldom hear from the lips of your new companions. You will hear every day the maxims of a low prudence. You will hear, that the first duty is to get land and money, place and name. 'What is this Truth you seek? what is this Beauty?' men will ask, with derision. If, nevertheless, God have called any of you to explore truth and beauty, be bold, be firm, be true. When you shall say, 'As others do, so will I: I renounce, I am sorry for it, my early visions; I must eat the good of the land, and let learning and romantic expectations go, until a more convenient season;'—then dies the man in you; then once more perish the buds of art, and poetry, and science, as they have died already in a thousand thousand men. The hour of that choice is the crisis of your history; and see that you hold yourself fast by the intellect. It is this domineering temper of the sensual world, that creates the extreme need of the priests of science; and it is the office and right of the intellect to make and not take its estimate. Bend to the persuasion which is flowing to you from every object in nature, to be its tongue to the heart of man, and to show the besotted world how passing fair is wisdom. Forewarned that the vice of the times and the country is an excessive pretension, let us seek the shade, and find wisdom in neglect. Be content with a little light, so it be your own. Explore, and explore. Be neither chided nor flattered out of your position of perpetual inquiry. Neither dogmatize, nor accept another's dogmatism. Why should you renounce your right to traverse the star-lit deserts of truth, for the premature comforts of an acre, house, and barn? Truth also has its roof, and bed, and board. Make yourself necessary to the world, and mankind will give you bread, and if not store of it, yet such as shall not take away your property in all men's possessions, in all men's affections, in art, in nature, and in hope.

You will not fear, that I am enjoining too stern an asceticism. Ask not, Of what use is a scholarship that systematically retreats? or, Who is the better for the philosopher who conceals his accomplishments, and hides his thoughts from the waiting world? Hides his thoughts! Hide the sun and moon. Thought is all light, and publishes itself to the universe. It will speak, though you were dumb, by its own miraculous organ. It will flow out of your actions, your manners, and your face. It will bring you friendships. It will impledge you to truth by the love and expectation of generous minds. By virtue of the laws of that Nature, which is one and perfect, it shall yield every sincere good that is in the soul, to the scholar beloved of earth and heaven.

The Method of Nature

GENTLEMEN,

LET US EXCHANGE congratulations on the enjoyments and the promises of this literary anniversary. The land we live in has no interest so dear, if it knew its want, as the fit consecration of days of reason and thought. Where there is no vision, the people perish. The scholars are the priests of that thought which establishes the foundations of the earth. No matter what is their special work or profession, they stand for the spiritual interest of the world, and it is a common calamity if they neglect their post in a country where the material interest is so predominant as it is in America. We hear something too much of the results of machinery, commerce, and the useful arts. We are a puny and a fickle folk. Avarice, hesitation, and following, are our diseases. The rapid wealth which hundreds in the community acquire in trade, or by the incessant expansions of our population and arts, enchants the eyes of all the rest; the luck of one is the hope of thousands, and the bribe acts like the neighborhood of a gold mine to impoverish the farm, the school, the church, the house, and the very body and feature of man.

I do not wish to look with sour aspect at the industrious manufacturing village, or the mart of commerce. I love the music of the water-wheel; I value the railway; I feel the pride which the sight of a ship inspires; I look on trade and every mechanical craft as education also. But let me discriminate what is precious herein. There is in each of these works an act of invention, an intellectual step, or short series of steps taken; that act or step is the spiritual act; all the rest is mere repetition of the same a thousand times. And I will not be deceived into admiring the routine of handicrafts and mechanics, how splendid soever the result, any more than I admire the routine of the scholars or clerical class. That splendid results ensue from the labors of stupid men, is the fruit of higher laws than their will, and the routine is not to be praised for it. I would not have the laborer sacrificed to the result,—I would not have the laborer sacrificed to my convenience and pride, nor to that of a great class of such as me.

Let there be worse cotton and better men. The weaver should not be bereaved of his superiority to his work, and his knowledge that the product or the skill is of no value, except so far as it embodies his spiritual prerogatives. If I see nothing to admire in the unit, shall I admire a million units? Men stand in awe of the city, but do not honor any individual citizen; and are continually yielding to this dazzling result of numbers, that which they would never yield to the solitary example of any one.

Whilst the multitude of men degrade each other, and give currency to desponding doctrines, the scholar must be a bringer of hope, and must reinforce man against himself. I sometimes believe that our literary anniversaries will presently assume a greater importance, as the eyes of men open to their capabilities. Here, a new set of distinctions, a new order of ideas, prevail. Here, we set a bound to the respectability of wealth, and a bound to the pretensions of the law and the church. The bigot must cease to be a bigot to-day. Into our charmed circle, power cannot enter; and the sturdiest defender of existing institutions feels the terrific inflammability of this air which condenses heat in every corner that may restore to the elements the fabrics of ages. Nothing solid is secure; every thing tilts and rocks. Even the scholar is not safe; he too is searched and revised. Is his learning dead? Is he living in his memory? The power of mind is not mortification, but life. But come forth, thou curious child! hither, thou loving, all-hoping poet! hither, thou tender, doubting heart, who hast not yet found any place in the world's market fit for thee; any wares which thou couldst buy or sell,—so large is thy love and ambition,—thine and not theirs is the hour. Smooth thy brow, and hope and love on, for the kind heaven justifies thee, and the whole world feels that thou art in the right.

We ought to celebrate this hour by expressions of manly joy. Not thanks, not prayer seem quite the highest or truest name for our communication with the infinite,—but glad and conspiring reception,—reception that becomes giving in its turn, as the receiver is only the All-Giver in part and in infancy. I cannot,—nor can any man,—speak precisely of things so sublime, but it seems to me, the wit of man, his

THE METHOD OF NATURE

*An Oration delivered before the Society of the Adelphi,
in Waterville College, Maine, August 11, 1841*

strength, his grace, his tendency, his art, is the grace and the presence of God. It is beyond explanation. When all is said and done, the rapt saint is found the only logician. Not exhortation, not argument becomes our lips, but pæans of joy and praise. But not of adulation: we are too nearly related in the deep of the mind to that we honor. It is God in us which checks the language of petition by a grander thought. In the bottom of the heart, it is said; 'I am, and by me, O child! this fair body and world of thine stands and grows. I am; all things are mine: and all mine are thine.'

The festival of the intellect, and the return to its source, cast a strong light on the always interesting topics of Man and Nature. We are forcibly reminded of the old want. There is no man; there hath never been. The Intellect still asks that a man may be born. The flame of life flickers feebly in human breasts. We demand of men a richness and universality we do not find. Great men do not content us. It is their solitude, not their force, that makes them conspicuous. There is somewhat indigent and tedious about them. They are poorly tied to one thought. If they are prophets, they are egotists; if polite and various, they are shallow. How tardily men arrive at any result! how tardily they pass from it to another! The crystal sphere of thought is as concentrical as the geological structure of the globe. As our soils and rocks lie in strata, concentric strata, so do all men's thinkings run laterally, never vertically. Here comes by a great inquisitor with auger and plumb-line, and will bore an Artesian well through our conventions and theories, and pierce to the core of things. But as soon as he probes the crust, behold gimlet, plumb-line, and philosopher take a lateral direction, in spite of all resistance, as if some strong wind took everything off its feet, and if you come month after month to see what progress our reformer has made,—not an inch has he pierced,—you still find him with new words in the old place, floating about in new parts of the same old vein or crust. The new book says, 'I will give you the key to nature,' and we expect to go like a thunderbolt to the centre. But the thunder is a surface phenomenon, makes a skin-deep cut, and so does the sage. The wedge turns out to be a rocket. Thus a man lasts but a very little while, for his monomania becomes insupportably tedious in a few months. It is so with every book and person: and yet—and yet—we do not take up a new book, or meet a new man, without a pulse-beat of expectation. And this invincible hope of a more adequate interpreter is the sure prediction of his advent.

In the absence of man, we turn to nature, which stands next. In the divine order, intellect is primary; nature, secondary; it is the memory of the mind. That which once existed in intellect as pure law, has now taken body as Nature. It existed already in the mind in solution; now, it has been precipitated, and the bright sediment is the world. We can never be quite strangers or inferiors in nature. It is flesh of our flesh, and bone of our bone. But we no longer hold it by the hand; we have lost our miraculous power; our arm is no more as strong as the frost; nor our will equivalent to gravity and the elective attractions. Yet we can use nature as a convenient standard, and the meter of our rise and fall. It has this advantage as a witness, it cannot be debauched. When man curses, nature still testifies to truth and love. We may, therefore, safely study the mind in nature, because we cannot steadily gaze on it in mind; as we explore the face of the sun in a pool, when our eyes cannot brook his direct splendors.

It seems to me, therefore, that it were some suitable pæan, if we should piously celebrate this hour by exploring the *method of nature*. Let us see *that*, as nearly as we can, and try how far it is transferable to the literary life. Every earnest glance we give to the realities around us, with intent to learn, proceeds from a holy impulse, and is really songs of praise. What difference can it make whether it take the shape of exhortation, or of passionate exclamation, or of scientific statement? These are forms merely. Through them we express, at last, the fact, that God has done thus or thus.

In treating a subject so large, in which we must necessarily appeal to the intuition, and aim much more to suggest, than to describe, I know it is not easy to speak with the precision attainable on topics of less scope. I do not wish in attempting to paint a man, to describe an air-fed, unimpassioned, impossible ghost. My eyes and ears are revolted by any neglect of the physical facts, the limitations of man. And yet one who conceives the true order of nature, and beholds the visible as proceeding from the invisible, cannot state his thought, without seeming to those who study the physical laws, to do them some injustice. There is an intrinsic defect in the organ. Language overstates. Statements of the infinite are usually felt to be unjust to the finite, and blasphemous. Empedocles undoubtedly spoke a truth of thought, when he said, "I am God;" but the moment it was out of his mouth, it became a lie to the ear; and the world revenged itself for the seeming arrogance, by the good story about his shoe. How can I hope for better hap in my attempts to enunciate spirtual facts? Yet let us hope, that as far as we receive the truth, so far shall we be felt by every true person to say what is just.

The method of nature: who could ever analyze it? That rushing stream will not stop to be observed. We can never surprise nature in a corner; never find the end of a thread; never tell where to set the first stone. The bird hastens to lay her egg: the egg hastens to be a bird. The wholeness we admire in the order of the world, is the result of infinite distribution. Its smoothness is the smoothness of the pitch of the cataract. Its permanence is a perpetual inchoation. Every natural fact is an emanation, and that from which it emanates is an emanation also, and from every emanation is a new emanation. If anything could stand still, it would be crushed and dissipated by the torrent it resisted, and if it were a mind, would be crazed; as insane persons are those who hold fast to one thought, and do not flow with the course of nature. Not the cause, but an ever novel effect, nature descends always from above. It is unbroken obedience. The beauty of these fair objects is imported into them from a metaphysical and eternal spring. In all animal and vegetable forms, the physiologist concedes that no chemistry, no mechanics, can account for the facts, but a mysterious principle of life must be assumed, which not only inhabits the organ, but makes the organ.

How silent, how spacious, what room for all, yet without place to insert an atom,—in graceful succession, in equal fulness, in balanced beauty, the dance of the hours goes forward still. Like an odor of incense, like a strain of music, like a sleep, it is inexact and boundless. It will not be dissected, nor unravelled, nor shown. Away profane philosopher! seekest thou in nature the cause? This refers to that, and that to the next, and the next to the third, and everything refers. Thou must ask in another mood, thou must feel it and love it, thou must behold it in a spirit as grand as that by which it exists, ere thou canst know the law. Known it will not be, but gladly beloved and enjoyed.

The simultaneous life throughout the whole body, the equal serving of innumerable ends without the least emphasis or preference to any, but the steady degradation of each to the success of all, allows the understanding no place to work. Nature can only be conceived as existing to a universal and not to a particular end, to a universe of ends, and not to one,—a work of *ecstasy*, to be represented by a circular movement, as intention might be signified by a straight line of definite length. Each effect strengthens every other. There is no revolt in all the kingdoms from the commonweal: no detachment of an individual. Hence the catholic character which makes every leaf an exponent of the world. When we behold the landscape in a poetic spirit, we do not reckon individuals. Nature knows neither palm nor oak, but only vegetable life, which sprouts into forests, and festoons the globe with a garland of grasses and vines.

That no single end may be selected, and nature judged thereby, appears from this, that if man himself be considered as the end, and it be assumed that the final cause of the world is to make holy or wise or beautiful men, we see that it has not succeeded. Read alternately in natural and in civil history, a treatise of astronomy, for example, with a volume of French *Memoires pour servir*. When we have spent our wonder in computing this wasteful hospitality with which boon nature turns off new firmaments without end into her wide common, as fast as the madrepores make coral,—suns and planets hospitable to souls,—and then shorten the sight to look into this court of Louis Quatorze, and see the game that is played there,—duke and marshal, abbé and madame,—a gambling table where each is laying traps for the other, where the end is ever by some lie or fetch to outwit your rival and ruin him with this solemn fop in wig and stars,—the king; one can hardly help asking if this planet is a fair specimen of the so generous astronomy, and if so, whether the experiment have not failed, and whether it be quite worth while to make more, and glut the innocent space with so poor an article.

I think we feel not much otherwise if, instead of beholding foolish nations, we take the great and wise men, the eminent souls, and narrowly inspect their biography. None of them seen by himself—and his performance compared with his promise or idea, will justify the cost of that enormous apparatus of means by which this spotted and defective person was at last procured.

To questions of this sort, nature replies, 'I grow.' All is nascent, infant. When we are dizzied with the arithmetic of the savant toiling to compute the length of her line, the return of her curve, we are steadied by the perception that a great deal is doing; that all seems just begun; remote aims are in active accomplishment. We can point nowhere to anything final; but tendency appears on all hands: planet, system, constellation, total nature is growing like a field of maize in July; is becoming somewhat else; is in rapid metamorphosis. The embryo does not more strive to be man, than yonder burr of light we call a nebula tends to be a ring, a comet, a globe, and parent of new stars. Why should not then these messieurs of Versailles strut and plot for tabourets and ribbons, for a season, without prejudice to their faculty to run on better errands by and by?

But nature seems further to reply, 'I have ventured so great a stake as my success, in no single creature. I have not yet arrived at any end. The gardener aims to produce a fine peach or pear, but my aim is the health of the whole tree,—root, stem, leaf, flower, and seed,—and by no means the pampering of a monstrous pericarp at the expense of all the other functions.'

In short, the spirit and peculiarity of that impression nature makes on us, is this, that it does not exist to any one or to any number of particular ends, but to numberless and endless benefit; that there is in it no private will, no rebel leaf or limb, but the whole is oppressed by one superincumbent tendency, obeys that redundancy or excess of life which in conscious beings we call *ecstasy*.

With this conception of the genius or method of nature, let us go back to man. It is true, he pretends to give account of himself to himself, but, at last, what has he to recite but the fact that there is a Life not to be described or known otherwise than by possession? What account can he give of his essence more than *so it was to be*? The *royal* reason, the Grace of God seems the only description of our multiform but ever identical fact. There is virtue, there is genius, there is success, or there is not. There is the incoming or the receding of God: that is all we can affirm; and we can show neither how nor why. Self-accusation, remorse, and the didactic morals of self-denial and strife with sin, is a view we are constrained by our constitution to take of the fact seen from the platform of action; but seen from the platform of intellection, there is nothing for us but praise and wonder.

The termination of the world in a man, appears to be the last victory of intelligence. The universal does not attract us until housed in an individual. Who heeds the waste abyss of possibility? The ocean is everywhere the same, but it has no character until seen with the shore or the ship. Who would value any number of miles of Atlantic brine bounded by lines of latitude and longitude? Confine it by granite rocks, let it wash a shore where wise men dwell, and it is filled with expression; and the point of greatest interest is where the land and water meet. So must we admire in man, the form of the formless, the concentration of the vast, the house of reason, the cave of memory. See the play of thoughts! what nimble gigantic creatures are these! what saurians, what palaiotheria shall be named with these agile movers? The great Pan of old, who was clothed in a leopard skin to signify the beautiful variety of things, and the firmament, his coat of stars,—was but the representative of thee, O rich and various Man! thou palace of sight and sound, carrying in thy senses the morning and the night and the unfathomable galaxy; in thy brain, the geometry of the City of God; in thy heart, the bower of love and the realms of right and wrong. An individual man is a fruit which it cost all the foregoing ages to form and ripen. The history of the genesis or the old mythology repeats itself in the experience of every child. He too is a demon or god thrown into a particular chaos, where he strives ever to lead things from disorder into order. Each individual soul is such, in virtue of its being a power to translate the world into some particular language of its own; if not into a picture, a statue, or a dance,—why, then, into a trade, an art, a science, a mode of living, a conversation, a character, an influence. You admire pictures, but it is as impossible for you to paint a right picture, as for grass to bear apples. But when the genius comes, it makes fingers: it is pliancy, and the power of transferring the affair in the street into oils and colors. Raphael must be born, and Salvator must be born.

There is no attractiveness like that of a new man. The sleepy nations are occupied with their political routine. England, France and America read Parliamentary Debates, which no high genius now enlivens; and nobody will read them who trusts his own eye: only they who are deceived by the popular repetition of distinguished names. But when Napoleon unrolls his map, the eye is commanded by original power. When Chatham leads the debate, men may well listen, because they must listen. A man, a personal ascendency is the only great phenomenon. When nature has work to be done, she creates a genius to do it. Follow the great man, and you shall see what the world has at heart in these ages. There is no omen like that.

But what strikes us in the fine genius is that which belongs of right to every one. A man should know himself for a necessary actor. A link was wanting between two craving parts of nature, and he was hurled into being as the bridge over that yawning need, the mediator betwixt two else unmarriageable facts. His two parents held each of one of the wants, and the union of foreign constitutions in him enables him to do gladly and gracefully what the assembled human race could not have sufficed to do. He knows his materials; he applies himself to his work; he cannot read, or think, or look, but he unites the hitherto separated strands into a perfect cord. The thoughts he delights to utter are the reason of his incarnation. Is it for him to account himself cheap and superfluous, or to linger by the wayside for opportunities? Did he not come into being because something must be done which he and no other is and does? If only he *sees*, the world will be visible enough. He need not study where to stand, nor to put things in favorable lights; in him is the light, from him all things are illuminated, to their centre. What patron shall he ask for employment and reward? Hereto was he born, to deliver the thought of his heart from the universe to the universe, to do an office which nature could not forego, nor he be discharged from rendering, and then immerge again into the holy silence and eternity out of which as a man he arose. God is rich, and many more men than one he harbors in his bosom, biding their time and the needs and the beauty of all. Is not this the theory of every man's genius or faculty? Why then goest thou as some Boswell or listening worshipper to this saint or to that? That is the only lese-majesty. Here art thou with whom so long the universe travailed in labor; darest thou think meanly of thyself whom the stalwart Fate brought forth to unite his ragged sides, to shoot the gulf, to reconcile the irreconcilable?

Whilst a necessity so great caused the man to exist, his health and erectness consist in the fidelity with which he transmits influences from the vast and universal to the point on which his genius can act. The ends are momentary: they are vents for the current of inward life which increases as it is spent. A man's wisdom is to know that all ends are momentary, that the best end must be superseded by a better. But there is a mischievous tendency in him to transfer his thought from the life to the ends, to quit his agency and rest in his acts: the tools run away with the workman, the human with the divine. I conceive a man as always spoken to from behind, and unable to turn his head and see the speaker. In all the millions who have heard the voice, none ever saw the face. As children in their play run behind each other, and seize one by the ears and make him walk before them, so is the spirit our unseen pilot. That well-known voice speaks in all languages, governs all men, and none ever caught a glimpse of its form. If the man will exactly obey it, it will adopt him, so that he shall not any longer separate it from himself in his thought, he shall seem to be it, he shall be it. If he listen with insatiable ears, richer and greater wisdom is taught him, the sound swells to a ravishing music, he is borne away as with a flood, he becomes careless of his food and of his house, he is the fool of ideas, and leads a heavenly life. But if his eye is set on the things to be done, and not on the truth that is still taught, and for the sake of which the things are to be done, then the voice grows faint, and at last is but a humming in his ears. His health and greatness consist in his being the channel through which heaven flows to earth, in short, in the fulness in which an ecstatical state takes place in him. It is pitiful to be an artist, when, by forbearing to be artists, we might be vessels filled with the divine overflowings, enriched by the circulations of omniscience and omnipresence. Are there not moments in the history of heaven when the human race was not counted by individuals, but was only the Influenced, was God in distribution, God rushing into multiform benefit? It is sublime to receive, sublime to love, but this lust of imparting as from *us*, this desire to be loved, the wish to be recognized as individuals,—is finite, comes of a lower strain.

Shall I say, then, that, as far as we can trace the natural history of the soul, its health consists in the fulness of its reception,—call it piety, call it veneration—in the fact, that enthusiasm is organized therein. What is best in any work of art, but that part which the work itself seems to require and do; that which the man cannot do again, that which flows from the hour and the occasion, like the eloquence of men in a tumultuous debate? It was always the theory of literature, that the word of a poet was authoritative and final. He was supposed to be the mouth of a divine wisdom. We rather envied his circumstance than his talent. We too could have gladly prophesied standing in that place. We so quote our Scriptures; and the Greeks so quoted Homer, Theognis, Pindar, and the rest. If the theory has receded out of modern criticism, it is because we have not had poets. Whenever they appear, they will redeem their own credit.

This ecstatical state seems to direct a regard to the whole and not to the parts; to the cause and not to the ends; to the tendency, and not to the act. It respects genius and not talent; hope, and not possession: the anticipation of all things by the intellect, and not the history itself; art, and not works of art; poetry, and not experiment; virtue, and not duties.

There is no office or function of man but is rightly discharged by this divine method, and nothing that is not noxious to him if detached from its universal relations. Is it his work in the world to study nature, or the laws of the world? Let him beware of proposing to himself any end. Is it for use?

nature is debased, as if one looking at the ocean can remember only the price of fish. Or is it for pleasure? he is mocked: there is a certain infatuating air in woods and mountains which draws on the idler to want and misery. There is something social and intrusive in the nature of all things; they seek to penetrate and overpower, each the nature of every other creature, and itself alone in all modes and throughout space and spirit to prevail and possess. Every star in heaven is discontented and insatiable. Gravitation and chemistry cannot content them. Ever they woo and court the eye of every beholder. Every man who comes into the world they seek to fascinate and possess, to pass into his mind, for they desire to republish themselves in a more delicate world than that they occupy. It is not enough that they are Jove, Mars, Orion, and the North Star, in the gravitating firmament: they would have such poets as Newton, Herschel and Laplace, that they may re-exist and re-appear in the finer world of rational souls, and fill that realm with their fame. So is it with all immaterial objects. These beautiful basilisks set their brute, glorious eyes on the eye of every child, and, if they can, cause their nature to pass through his wondering eyes into him, and so all things are mixed.

Therefore man must be on his guard against this cup of enchantments, and must look at nature with a supernatural eye. By piety alone, by conversing with the cause of nature, is he safe and commands it. And because all knowledge is assimilation to the object of knowledge, as the power or genius of nature is ecstatic, so must its science or the description of it be. The poet must be a rhapsodist: his inspiration a sort of bright casualty: his will in it only the surrender of will to the Universal Power, which will not be seen face to face, but must be received and sympathetically known. It is remarkable that we have out of the deeps of antiquity in the oracles ascribed to the half fabulous Zoroaster, a statement of this fact, which every lover and seeker of truth will recognize. "It is not proper," said Zoroaster, "to understand the Intelligible with vehemence, but if you incline your mind, you will apprehend it: not too earnestly, but bringing a pure and inquiring eye. You will not understand it as when understanding some particular thing, but with the flower of the mind. Things divine are not attainable by mortals who understand sensual things, but only the light-armed arrive at the summit."

And because ecstasy is the law and cause of nature, therefore you cannot interpret it in too high and deep a sense. Nature represents the best meaning of the wisest man. Does the sunset landscape seem to you the palace of Friendship,—those purple skies and lovely waters the amphitheatre dressed and garnished only for the exchange of thought and love of the purest souls? It is that. All other meanings which base men have put on it are conjectural and false. You cannot bathe twice in the same river, said Heraclitus; and I add, a man never sees the same object twice: with his own enlargement the object acquires new aspects.

Does not the same law hold for virtue? It is vitiated by too much will. He who aims at progress, should aim at an infinite, not at a special benefit. The reforms whose fame now fills the land with Temperance, Anti-Slavery, Non-Resistance, No Government, Equal Labor, fair and generous as each appears, are poor bitter things when prosecuted for themselves as an end. To every reform, in proportion to its energy, early disgusts are incident, so that the disciple is surprised at the very hour of his first triumphs, with chagrins, and sickness, and a general distrust: so that he shuns his associates, hates the enterprise which lately seemed so fair, and meditates to cast himself into the arms of that society and manner of life which he had newly abandoned with so much pride and hope. Is it that he attached the value of virtue to some particular practices, as, the denial of certain appetites in certain specified indulgences, and, afterward, found himself still as wicked and as far from happiness in that abstinence, as he had been in the abuse? But the soul can be appeased not by a deed but by a tendency. It is in a hope that she feels her wings. You shall love rectitude and not the disuse of money or the avoidance of trade: an unimpeded mind, and not a monkish diet; sympathy and usefulness, and not hoeing or coopering. Tell me not how great your project is, the civil liberation of the world, its conversion into a Christian church, the establishment of public education, cleaner diet, a new division of labor and of land, laws of love for laws of property;—I say to you plainly there is no end to which your practical faculty can aim, so sacred or so large, that, if pursued for itself, will not at last become carrion and an offence to the nostril. The imaginative faculty of the soul must be fed with objects immense and eternal. Your end should be one inapprehensible to the senses: then will it be a god always approached,— never touched; always giving health. A man adorns himself with prayer and love, as an aim adorns an action. What is strong but goodness, and what is energetic but the presence of a brave man? The doctrine in vegetable physiology of the *presence*, or the general influence of any substance over and above its chemical influence, as of an alkali or a living plant, is more predicable of man. You need not speak to me, I need not go where you are, that you should exert magnetism on me. Be you only whole and sufficient, and I shall feel you in every part of my life and fortune, and I can as easily dodge the gravitation of the globe as escape your influence.

But there are other examples of this total and supreme influence, besides Nature and the conscience. "From the poisonous tree, the world," say the Brahmins, "two species of fruit are produced, sweet as the waters of life, Love or the society of beautiful souls, and Poetry, whose taste is like the immortal juice of Vishnu." What is Love, and why is it the chief good, but because it is an overpowering enthusiasm? Never self-possessed or prudent, it is all abandonment. Is it not a certain admirable wisdom, preferable to all other advantages, and whereof all others are only secondaries and indemnities, because this is that in which the individual is no longer his own foolish master, but inhales an odorous and celestial air, is wrapped round with awe of the object, blending for the time that object with the real and only good, and consults every omen in nature with tremulous interest. When we speak truly,—is not he only unhappy who is not in love? his fancied freedom and self-rule—is it not so much death? He who is in love is wise and is becoming wiser, sees newly every time he looks at the object beloved, drawing from it with his eyes and his mind those virtues which it possesses. Therefore if the object be not itself a living and expanding soul, he presently exhausts it. But the love remains in his mind, and the wisdom it brought him; and it craves a new and higher object. And the reason why all men honor love, is because it looks up and not down; aspires and not despairs.

And what is Genius but finer love, a love impersonal, a love of the flower and perfection of things, and a desire to draw a new picture or copy of the same? It looks to the cause and life: it proceeds from within outward, whilst Talent goes from without inward. Talent finds its models, methods, and ends, in society, exists for exhibition, and goes to the soul only for power to work. Genius is its own end, and draws its means and the style of its architecture from within, going abroad only for audience, and spectator, as we adapt our voice and phrase to the distance and character of the ear we speak to. All your learning of all literatures would never enable you to anticipate one of its thoughts or expressions, and yet each is natural and familiar as household words. Here about us coils forever the ancient enigma, so old and so unutterable. Behold! there is the sun, and the rain, and the rocks: the old sun, the old stones. How easy were it to describe all this fitly; yet no word can pass. Nature is a mute, and man, her articulate speaking brother, lo! he also is a mute. Yet when Genius arrives, its speech is like a river; it has no straining to describe, more than there is straining in nature to exist. When thought is best, there is most of it. Genius sheds wisdom like perfume, and advertises us that it flows out of a deeper source than the foregoing silence, that it knows so deeply and speaks so musically, because it is itself a mutation of the thing it describes. It is sun and moon and wave and fire in music, as astronomy is thought and harmony in masses of matter.

What is all history but the work of ideas, a record of the incomputable energy which his infinite aspirations infuse into man? Has any thing grand and lasting been done? Who did it? Plainly not any man, but all men: it was the prevalence and inundation of an idea. What brought the pilgrims here? One man says, civil liberty; another, the desire of founding a church; and a third, discovers that the motive force was plantation and trade. But if the Puritans could rise from the dust, they could not answer. It is to be seen in what they were, and not in what they designed; it was the growth and expansion of the human race, and resembled herein the sequent Revolution, which was not begun in Concord, or Lexington, or Virginia, but was the overflowing of the sense of natural right in every clear and active spirit of the period. Is a man boastful and knowing, and his own master?—we turn from him without hope: but let him be filled with awe and dread before the Vast and the Divine, which uses him glad to be used, and our eye is riveted to the chain of events. What a debt is ours to that old religion which, in the childhood of most of us, still dwelt like a sabbath morning in the country of New England, teaching privation, self-denial and sorrow! A man was born not for prosperity, but to suffer for the benefit of others, like the noble rock-maple which all around our villages bleeds for the service of man. Not praise, not men's acceptance of our doing, but the spirit's holy errand through us absorbed the thought. How dignified was this! How all that is called talents and success, in our noisy capitals, becomes buzz and din before this man-worthiness! How our friendships and the complaisances we use, shame us now! Shall we not quit our companions, as if they were thieves and pot-companions, and betake ourselves to some desert cliff of mount Katahdin, some unvisited recess in Moosehead Lake, to bewail our innocency and to recover it, and with it the power to communicate again with these sharers of a more sacred idea?

And what is to replace for us the piety of that race? We cannot have theirs: it glides away from us day by day, but we also can bask in the great morning which rises forever out of the eastern sea, and be ourselves the children of the light. I stand here to say, Let us worship the mighty and transcendent Soul. It is the office, I doubt not, of this age to annul that adulterous divorce which the superstition of many ages has effected between the intellect and holiness. The lovers of goodness have been one class, the students of wisdom another, as if either could exist in any purity without the other. Truth is always holy, holiness always wise. I will that we keep terms with sin, and a sinful literature and society, no longer, but live a life of discovery and performance. Accept the intellect, and it will accept us. Be the lowly ministers of that pure omniscience, and deny it not before men. It will burn up all profane literature, all base current opinions, all the false powers of the world, as in a moment of time. I draw from nature the lesson of an intimate divinity. Our health and reason as men needs our respect to this fact, against the heedlessness

and against the contradiction of society. The sanity of man
needs the poise of this immanent force. His nobility needs the
assurance of this inexhaustible reserved power. How great
soever have been its bounties, they are a drop to the sea
whence they flow. If you say, 'the acceptance of the vision is
also the act of God:'—I shall not seek to penetrate the mystery, I admit the force of what you say. If you ask, 'How can
any rules be given for the attainment of gifts so sublime?' I
shall only remark that the solicitations of this spirit, as long
as there is life, are never forborne. Tenderly, tenderly, they
woo and court us from every object in nature, from every fact
in life, from every thought in the mind. The one condition
coupled with the gift of truth is its use. That man shall be
learned who reduceth his learning to practice. Emanuel Swedenborg affirmed that it was opened to him, "that the spirits
who knew truth in this life, but did it not, at death shall lose
their knowledge." "If knowledge," said Ali the Caliph, "call-
eth unto practice, well; if not, it goeth away." The only way
into nature is to enact our best insight. Instantly we are
higher poets, and can speak a deeper law. Do what you know,
and perception is converted into character, as islands and continents were built by invisible infusories, or, as these forest
leaves absorb light, electricity, and volatile gases, and the
gnarled oak to live a thousand years is the arrest and fixation
of the most volatile and ethereal currents. The doctrine of this
Supreme Presence is a cry of joy and exultation. Who shall
dare think he has come late into nature, or has missed anything excellent in the past, who seeth the admirable stars of
possibility, and the yet untouched continent of hope glittering with all its mountains in the vast West? I praise with wonder this great reality, which seems to drown all things in the
deluge of its light. What man seeing this, can lose it from his
thoughts, or entertain a meaner subject? The entrance of this
into his mind seems to be the birth of man. We cannot describe the natural history of the soul, but we know that it is
divine. I cannot tell if these wonderful qualities which house
to-day in this mortal frame, shall ever re-assemble in equal
activity in a similar frame, or whether they have before had a
natural history like that of this body you see before you; but
this one thing I know, that these qualities did not now begin

to exist, cannot be sick with my sickness, nor buried in any grave; but that they circulate through the Universe: before the world was, they were. Nothing can bar them out, or shut them in, but they penetrate the ocean and land, space and time, form and essence, and hold the key to universal nature. I draw from this faith courage and hope. All things are known to the soul. It is not to be surprised by any communication. Nothing can be greater than it. Let those fear and those fawn who will. The soul is in her native realm, and it is wider than space, older than time, wide as hope, rich as love. Pusillanimity and fear she refuses with a beautiful scorn: they are not for her who putteth on her coronation robes, and goes out through universal love to universal power.

MAN THE REFORMER

A Lecture read before the Mechanics' Apprentices'
Library Association, Boston, January 25, 1841

Man the Reformer

I wish to offer to your consideration some thoughts on the particular and general relations of man as a reformer. I shall assume that the aim of each young man in this association is the very highest that belongs to a rational mind. Let it be granted, that our life, as we lead it, is common and mean; that some of those offices and functions for which we were mainly created are grown so rare in society, that the memory of them is only kept alive in old books and in dim traditions; that prophets and poets, that beautiful and perfect men, we are not now, no, nor have even seen such; that some sources of human instruction are almost unnamed and unknown among us; that the community in which we live will hardly bear to be told that every man should be open to ecstasy or a divine illumination, and his daily walk elevated by intercourse with the spiritual world. Grant all this, as we must, yet I suppose none of my auditors will deny that we ought to seek to establish ourselves in such disciplines and courses as will deserve that guidance and clearer communication with the spiritual nature. And further, I will not dissemble my hope, that each person whom I address has felt his own call to cast aside all evil customs, timidities, and limitations, and to be in his place a free and helpful man, a reformer, a benefactor, not content to slip along through the world like a footman or a spy, escaping by his nimbleness and apologies as many knocks as he can, but a brave and upright man, who must find or cut a straight road to everything excellent in the earth, and not only go honorably himself, but make it easier for all who follow him, to go in honor and with benefit.

In the history of the world the doctrine of Reform had never such scope as at the present hour. Lutherans, Hernhutters, Jesuits, Monks, Quakers, Knox, Wesley, Swedenborg, Bentham, in their accusations of society, all respected something,—church or state, literature or history, domestic usages, the market town, the dinner table, coined money. But now all these and all things else hear the trumpet, and must rush to judgment,—Christianity, the laws, commerce, schools, the farm, the laboratory; and not a kingdom, town, statute, rite, calling, man, or woman, but is threatened by the new spirit.

What if some of the objections whereby our institutions are assailed are extreme and speculative, and the reformers tend to idealism; that only shows the extravagance of the abuses which have driven the mind into the opposite extreme. It is when your facts and persons grow unreal and fantastic by too much falsehood, that the scholar flies for refuge to the world of ideas, and aims to recruit and replenish nature from that source. Let ideas establish their legitimate sway again in society, let life be fair and poetic, and the scholars will gladly be lovers, citizens, and philanthropists.

It will afford no security from the new ideas, that the old nations, the laws of centuries, the property and institutions of a hundred cities, are built on other foundations. The demon of reform has a secret door into the heart of every lawmaker, of every inhabitant of every city. The fact, that a new thought and hope have dawned in your breast, should apprize you that in the same hour a new light broke in upon a thousand private hearts. That secret which you would fain keep,—as soon as you go abroad, lo! there is one standing on the doorstep, to tell you the same. There is not the most bronzed and sharpened money-catcher, who does not, to your consternation, almost, quail and shake the moment he hears a question prompted by the new ideas. We thought he had some semblance of ground to stand upon, that such as he at least would die hard; but he trembles and flees. Then the scholar says, 'Cities and coaches shall never impose on me again; for, behold every solitary dream of mine is rushing to fulfilment. That fancy I had, and hesitated to utter because you would laugh,—the broker, the attorney, the market-man are saying the same thing. Had I waited a day longer to speak, I had been too late. Behold, State Street thinks, and Wall Street doubts, and begins to prophesy!'

It cannot be wondered at, that this general inquest into abuses should arise in the bosom of society, when one considers the practical impediments that stand in the way of virtuous young men. The young man, on entering life, finds the way to lucrative employments blocked with abuses. The ways of trade are grown selfish to the borders of theft, and supple to the borders (if not beyond the borders) of fraud. The employments of commerce are not intrinsically unfit for a man, or less genial to his faculties, but these are now in their general course so vitiated by derelictions and abuses at which all connive, that it requires more vigor and resources than can be expected of every young man, to right himself in them; he is lost in them; he cannot move hand or foot in them. Has he genius and virtue? the less does he find them fit for him to grow in, and if he would thrive in them, he must sacrifice all the brilliant dreams of boyhood and youth as dreams; he must forget the prayers of his childhood; and must take on him the harness of routine and obsequiousness. If not so minded, nothing is left him but to begin the world anew, as he does who puts the spade into the ground for food. We are all implicated, of course, in this charge; it is only necessary to ask a few questions as to the progress of the articles of commerce from the fields where they grew, to our houses, to become aware that we eat and drink and wear perjury and fraud in a hundred commodities. How many articles of daily consumption are furnished us from the West Indies; yet it is said, that, in the Spanish islands, the venality of the officers of the government has passed into usage, and that no article passes into our ships which has not been fraudulently cheapened. In the Spanish islands, every agent or factor of the Americans, unless he be a consul, has taken oath that he is a Catholic, or has caused a priest to make that declaration for him. The abolitionist has shown us our dreadful debt to the southern negro. In the island of Cuba, in addition to the ordinary abominations of slavery, it appears, only men are bought for the plantations, and one dies in ten every year, of these miserable bachelors, to yield us sugar. I leave for those who have the knowledge the part of sifting the oaths of our customhouses; I will not inquire into the oppression of the sailors; I will not pry into the usages of our retail trade. I content myself with the fact, that the general system of our trade, (apart from the blacker traits, which, I hope, are exceptions denounced and unshared by all reputable men,) is a system of selfishness; is not dictated by the high sentiments of human nature; is not measured by the exact law of reciprocity; much less by the sentiments of love and heroism, but is a system of distrust, of concealment, of superior keenness, not of giving but of taking advantage. It is not that which a man delights to unlock to a noble friend; which he meditates on with joy and self-approval in his hour of love and aspiration; but rather what he then puts out of sight, only showing the brilliant result, and atoning for the manner of acquiring, by the manner of expending it. I do not charge the merchant or the manufacturer. The sins of our trade belong to no class, to no individual. One plucks, one distributes, one eats. Every body partakes, every body confesses,—with cap and knee volunteers his confession, yet none feels himself accountable. He did not create the abuse; he cannot alter it. What is he? an obscure private person who must get his bread. That is the vice,—that no one feels himself called to act for man, but only as a fraction of man. It happens therefore that all such ingenuous souls as feel within themselves the irrepressible strivings of a noble aim, who by the law of their nature must act simply, find these ways of trade unfit for them, and they come forth from it. Such cases are becoming more numerous every year.

But by coming out of trade you have not cleared yourself. The trail of the serpent reaches into all the lucrative professions and practices of man. Each has its own wrongs. Each finds a tender and very intelligent conscience a disqualification for success. Each requires of the practitioner a certain shutting of the eyes, a certain dapperness and compliance, an acceptance of customs, a sequestration from the sentiments of generosity and love, a compromise of private opinion and lofty integrity. Nay, the evil custom reaches into the whole institution of property, until our laws which establish and protect it, seem not to be the issue of love and reason, but of selfishness. Suppose a man is so unhappy as to be born a saint, with keen perceptions, but with the conscience and love of an angel, and he is to get his living in the world; he finds himself excluded from all lucrative works; he has no farm, and he cannot get one; for, to earn money enough to buy one, requires a sort of concentration toward money, which is the selling himself for a number of years, and to him the present hour is as sacred and inviolable as any future hour. Of course, whilst another man has no land, my title to mine, your title to yours, is at once vitiated. Inextricable seem to be the twinings and tendrils of this evil, and we all involve ourselves in it the deeper by forming connections, by wives and children, by benefits and debts.

Considerations of this kind have turned the attention of many philanthropic and intelligent persons to the claims of manual labor, as a part of the education of every young man. If the accumulated wealth of the past generations is thus tainted,—no matter how much of it is offered to us,—we must begin to consider if it were not the nobler part to renounce it, and to put ourselves into primary relations with the soil and nature, and abstaining from whatever is dishonest and unclean, to take each of us bravely his part, with his own hands, in the manual labor of the world.

But it is said, 'What! will you give up the immense advantages reaped from the division of labor, and set every man to make his own shoes, bureau, knife, wagon, sails, and needle? This would be to put men back into barbarism by their own act.' I see no instant prospect of a virtuous revolution; yet I confess, I should not be pained at a change which threatened a loss of some of the luxuries or conveniences of society, if it proceeded from a preference of the agricultural life out of the belief, that our primary duties as men could be better discharged in that calling. Who could regret to see a high conscience and a purer taste exercising a sensible effect on young men in their choice of occupation, and thinning the ranks of competition in the labors of commerce, of law, and of state? It is easy to see that the inconvenience would last but a short time. This would be great action, which always opens the eyes of men. When many persons shall have done this, when the majority shall admit the necessity of reform in all these institutions, their abuses will be redressed, and the way will be open again to the advantages which arise from the division of labor, and a man may select the fittest employment for his peculiar talent again, without compromise.

But quite apart from the emphasis which the times give to the doctrine, that the manual labor of society ought to be shared among all the members, there are reasons proper to every individual, why he should not be deprived of it. The use of manual labor is one which never grows obsolete, and which is inapplicable to no person. A man should have a farm or a mechanical craft for his culture. We must have a basis for our higher accomplishments, our delicate entertainments of poetry and philosophy, in the work of our hands. We must have an antagonism in the tough world for all the variety of our spiritual faculties, or they will not be born. Manual labor is the study of the external world. The advantage of riches remains with him who procured them, not with the heir. When I go into my garden with a spade, and dig a bed, I feel such an exhilaration and health, that I discover that I have been defrauding myself all this time in letting others do for me what I should have done with my own hands. But not only health, but education is in the work. Is it possible that I who get indefinite quantities of sugar, hominy, cotton, buckets, crockery ware, and letter paper, by simply signing my name once in three months to a cheque in favor of John Smith and Co. traders, get the fair share of exercise to my faculties by that act, which nature intended for me in making all these far-fetched matters important to my comfort? It is Smith himself, and his carriers, and dealers, and manufacturers, it is the sailor, the hidedrogher, the butcher, the negro, the hunter, and the planter, who have intercepted the sugar of the sugar, and the cotton of the cotton. They have got the education, I only the commodity. This were all very well if I were necessarily absent, being detained by work of my own, like theirs, work of the same faculties; then should I be sure of my hands and feet, but now I feel some shame before my wood-chopper, my ploughman, and my cook, for they have some sort of self-sufficiency, they can contrive without my aid to bring the day and year round, but I depend on them, and have not earned by use a right to my arms and feet.

Consider further the difference between the first and second owner of property. Every species of property is preyed on by its own enemies, as iron by rust; timber by rot; cloth by moths; provisions by mould, putridity, or vermin; money by thieves; an orchard by insects; a planted field by weeds and the inroad of cattle; a stock of cattle by hunger; a road by rain and frost; a bridge by freshets. And whoever takes any of these things into his possession, takes the charge of defending

them from this troop of enemies, or of keeping them in repair. A man who supplies his own want, who builds a raft or
a boat to go a fishing, finds it easy to caulk it, or put in a
thole-pin, or mend the rudder. What he gets only as fast as
he wants for his own ends, does not embarrass him, or take
away his sleep with looking after. But when he comes to give
all the goods he has year after year collected, in one estate to
his son, house, orchard, ploughed land, cattle, bridges, hard-
ware, wooden-ware, carpets, cloths, provisions, books,
money, and cannot give him the skill and experience which
made or collected these, and the method and place they have
in his own life, the son finds his hands full,—not to use these
things,—but to look after them and defend them from their
natural enemies. To him they are not means, but masters.
Their enemies will not remit; rust, mould, vermin, rain, sun,
freshet, fire, all seize their own, fill him with vexation, and he
is converted from the owner into a watchman or a watch-dog
to this magazine of old and new chattels. What a change!
Instead of the masterly good humor, and sense of power, and
fertility of resource in himself; instead of those strong and
learned hands, those piercing and learned eyes, that supple
body, and that mighty and prevailing heart, which the father
had, whom nature loved and feared, whom snow and rain,
water and land, beast and fish seemed all to know and to
serve, we have now a puny, protected person, guarded by
walls and curtains, stoves and down beds, coaches, and men-
servants and women-servants from the earth and the sky, and
who, bred to depend on all these, is made anxious by all that
endangers those possessions, and is forced to spend so much
time in guarding them, that he has quite lost sight of their
original use, namely, to help him to his ends,—to the prose-
cution of his love; to the helping of his friend, to the worship
of his God, to the enlargement of his knowledge, to the serving of his country, to the indulgence of his sentiment, and he
is now what is called a rich man,—the menial and runner of
his riches.

Hence it happens that the whole interest of history lies in
the fortunes of the poor. Knowledge, Virtue, Power are the
victories of man over his necessities, his march to the dominion of the world. Every man ought to have this opportunity

to conquer the world for himself. Only such persons interest us, Spartans, Romans, Saracens, English, Americans,
who have stood in the jaws of need, and have by their
own wit and might extricated themselves, and made man victorious.

I do not wish to overstate this doctrine of labor, or insist
that every man should be a farmer, any more than that every
man should be a lexicographer. In general, one may say, that
the husbandman's is the oldest, and most universal profession, and that where a man does not yet discover in himself
any fitness for one work more than another, this may be preferred. But the doctrine of the Farm is merely this, that every
man ought to stand in primary relations with the work of the
world, ought to do it himself, and not to suffer the accident
of his having a purse in his pocket, or his having been bred
to some dishonorable and injurious craft, to sever him from
those duties; and for this reason, that labor is God's education; that he only is a sincere learner, he only can become a
master, who learns the secrets of labor, and who by real cunning extorts from nature its sceptre.

Neither would I shut my ears to the plea of the learned
professions, of the poet, the priest, the lawgiver, and men of
study generally; namely, that in the experience of all men of
that class, the amount of manual labor which is necessary to
the maintenance of a family, indisposes and disqualifies for
intellectual exertion. I know, it often, perhaps usually, happens, that where there is a fine organization apt for poetry
and philosophy, that individual finds himself compelled to
wait on his thoughts, to waste several days that he may enhance and glorify one; and is better taught by a moderate and
dainty exercise, such as rambling in the fields, rowing, skating, hunting, than by the downright drudgery of the farmer
and the smith. I would not quite forget the venerable counsel
of the Egyptian mysteries, which declared that "there were
two pairs of eyes in man, and it is requisite that the pair
which are beneath should be closed, when the pair that are
above them perceive, and that when the pair above are closed,
those which are beneath should be opened." Yet I will suggest
that no separation from labor can be without some loss of
power and of truth to the seer himself; that, I doubt not, the

faults and vices of our literature and philosophy, their too great fineness, effeminacy, and melancholy, are attributable to the enervated and sickly habits of the literary class. Better that the book should not be quite so good, and the bookmaker abler and better, and not himself often a ludicrous contrast to all that he has written.

But granting that for ends so sacred and dear, some relaxation must be had, I think, that if a man find in himself any strong bias to poetry, to art, to the contemplative life, drawing him to these things with a devotion incompatible with good husbandry, that man ought to reckon early with himself, and, respecting the compensations of the Universe, ought to ransom himself from the duties of economy, by a certain rigor and privation in his habits. For privileges so rare and grand, let him not stint to pay a great tax. Let him be a cænobite, a pauper, and if need be, celibate also. Let him learn to eat his meals standing, and to relish the taste of fair water and black bread. He may leave to others the costly conveniences of housekeeping, and large hospitality, and the possession of works of art. Let him feel that genius is a hospitality, and that he who can create works of art needs not collect them. He must live in a chamber, and postpone his self-indulgence, forewarned and forearmed against that frequent misfortune of men of genius,—the taste for luxury. This is the tragedy of genius,—attempting to drive along the ecliptic with one horse of the heavens and one horse of the earth, there is only discord and ruin and downfall to chariot and charioteer.

The duty that every man should assume his own vows, should call the institutions of society to account, and examine their fitness to him, gains in emphasis, if we look at our modes of living. Is our housekeeping sacred and honorable? Does it raise and inspire us, or does it cripple us instead? I ought to be armed by every part and function of my household, by all my social function, by my economy, by my feasting, by my voting, by my traffic. Yet I am almost no party to any of these things. Custom does it for me, gives me no power therefrom, and runs me in debt to boot. We spend our incomes for paint and paper, for a hundred trifles, I know not what, and not for the things of a man. Our expense is almost all for conformity. It is for cake that we run in debt; 't is not the intellect, not the heart, not beauty, not worship, that costs so much. Why needs any man be rich? Why must he have horses, fine garments, handsome apartments, access to public houses, and places of amusement? Only for want of thought. Give his mind a new image, and he flees into a solitary garden or garret to enjoy it, and is richer with that dream, than the fee of a county could make him. But we are first thoughtless, and then find that we are moneyless. We are first sensual, and then must be rich. We dare not trust our wit for making our house pleasant to our friend, and so we buy ice-creams. He is accustomed to carpets, and we have not sufficient character to put floor-cloths out of his mind whilst he stays in the house, and so we pile the floor with carpets. Let the house rather be a temple of the Furies of Lacedæmon, formidable and holy to all, which none but a Spartan may enter or so much as behold. As soon as there is faith, as soon as there is society, comfits and cushions will be left to slaves. Expense will be inventive and heroic. We shall eat hard and lie hard, we shall dwell like the ancient Romans in narrow tenements, whilst our public edifices, like theirs, will be worthy for their proportion of the landscape in which we set them, for conversation, for art, for music, for worship. We shall be rich to great purposes; poor only for selfish ones.

Now what help for these evils? How can the man who has learned but one art, procure all the conveniences of life honestly? Shall we say all we think?—Perhaps with his own hands. Suppose he collects or makes them ill;—yet he has learned their lesson. If he cannot do that.—Then perhaps he can go without. Immense wisdom and riches are in that. It is better to go without, than to have them at too great a cost. Let us learn the meaning of economy. Economy is a high, humane office, a sacrament, when its aim is grand; when it is the prudence of simple tastes, when it is practised for freedom, or love, or devotion. Much of the economy which we see in houses, is of a base origin, and is best kept out of sight. Parched corn eaten to-day that I may have roast fowl to my dinner on Sunday, is a baseness; but parched corn and a house with one apartment, that I may be free of all perturbations, that I may be serene and docile to what the mind shall speak, and girt and road-ready for the lowest mission of knowledge or goodwill, is frugality for gods and heroes.

Can we not learn the lesson of self-help? Society is full of infirm people, who incessantly summon others to serve them. They contrive everywhere to exhaust for their single comfort the entire means and appliances of that luxury to which our invention has yet attained. Sofas, ottomans, stoves, wine, game-fowl, spices, perfumes, rides, the theatre, entertainments,—all these they want, they need, and whatever can be suggested more than these, they crave also, as if it was the bread which should keep them from starving; and if they miss any one, they represent themselves as the most wronged and most wretched persons on earth. One must have been born and bred with them to know how to prepare a meal for their learned stomach. Meantime, they never bestir themselves to serve another person; not they! they have a great deal more to do for themselves than they can possibly perform, nor do they once perceive the cruel joke of their lives, but the more odious they grow, the sharper is the tone of their complaining and craving. Can anything be so elegant as to have few wants and to serve them one's self, so as to have somewhat left to give, instead of being always prompt to grab? It is more elegant to answer one's own needs, than to be richly served; inelegant perhaps it may look to-day, and to a few, but it is an elegance forever and to all.

I do not wish to be absurd and pedantic in reform. I do not wish to push my criticism on the state of things around me to that extravagant mark, that shall compel me to suicide, or to an absolute isolation from the advantages of civil society. If we suddenly plant our foot, and say,—I will neither eat nor drink nor wear nor touch any food or fabric which I do not know to be innocent, or deal with any person whose whole manner of life is not clear and rational, we shall stand still. Whose is so? Not mine; not thine; not his. But I think we must clear ourselves each one by the interrogation, whether we have earned our bread to-day by the hearty contribution of our energies to the common benefit? and we must not cease to *tend* to the correction of these flagrant wrongs, by laying one stone aright every day.

But the idea which now begins to agitate society has a

wider scope than our daily employments, our households, and the institutions of property. We are to revise the whole of our social structure, the state, the school, religion, marriage, trade, science, and explore their foundations in our own nature; we are to see that the world not only fitted the former men, but fits us, and to clear ourselves of every usage which has not its roots in our own mind. What is a man born for but to be a Reformer, a Re-maker of what man has made; a renouncer of lies; a restorer of truth and good, imitating that great Nature which embosoms us all, and which sleeps no moment on an old past, but every hour repairs herself, yielding us every morning a new day, and with every pulsation a new life? Let him renounce everything which is not true to him, and put all his practices back on their first thoughts, and do nothing for which he has not the whole world for his reason. If there are inconveniences, and what is called ruin in the way, because we have so enervated and maimed ourselves, yet it would be like dying of perfumes to sink in the effort to reattach the deeds of every day to the holy and mysterious recesses of life.

The power, which is at once spring and regulator in all efforts of reform, is the conviction that there is an infinite worthiness in man which will appear at the call of worth, and that all particular reforms are the removing of some impediment. Is it not the highest duty that man should be honored in us? I ought not to allow any man, because he has broad lands, to feel that he is rich in my presence. I ought to make him feel that I can do without his riches, that I cannot be bought,—neither by comfort, neither by pride,—and though I be utterly penniless, and receiving bread from him, that he is the poor man beside me. And if, at the same time, a woman or a child discovers a sentiment of piety, or a juster way of thinking than mine, I ought to confess it by my respect and obedience, though it go to alter my whole way of life.

The Americans have many virtues, but they have not Faith and Hope. I know no two words whose meaning is more lost sight of. We use these words as if they were as obsolete as Selah and Amen. And yet they have the broadest meaning, and the most cogent application to Boston in 1841. The Americans have no faith. They rely on the power of a dollar; they are deaf to a sentiment. They think you may talk the north wind down as easily as raise society; and no class more faithless than the scholars or intellectual men. Now if I talk with a sincere wise man, and my friend, with a poet, with a conscientious youth who is still under the dominion of his own wild thoughts, and not yet harnessed in the team of society to drag with us all in the ruts of custom, I see at once how paltry is all this generation of unbelievers, and what a house of cards their institutions are, and I see what one brave man, what one great thought executed might effect. I see that the reason of the distrust of the practical man in all theory, is his inability to perceive the means whereby we work. Look, he says, at the tools with which this world of yours is to be built. As we cannot make a planet, with atmosphere, rivers, and forests, by means of the best carpenters' or engineers' tools, with chemist's laboratory and smith's forge to boot, — so neither can we ever construct that heavenly society you prate of, out of foolish, sick, selfish men and women, such as we know them to be. But the believer not only beholds his heaven to be possible, but already to begin to exist, — not by the men or materials the statesman uses, but by men transfigured and raised above themselves by the power of principles. To principles something else is possible that transcends all the power of expedients.

Every great and commanding moment in the annals of the world is the triumph of some enthusiasm. The victories of the Arabs after Mahomet, who, in a few years, from a small and mean beginning, established a larger empire than that of Rome, is an example. They did they knew not what. The naked Derar, horsed on an idea, was found an overmatch for a troop of Roman cavalry. The women fought like men, and conquered the Roman men. They were miserably equipped, miserably fed. They were Temperance troops. There was neither brandy nor flesh needed to feed them. They conquered Asia, and Africa, and Spain, on barley. The Caliph Omar's walking stick struck more terror into those who saw it, than another man's sword. His diet was barley bread; his sauce was salt; and oftentimes by way of abstinence he ate his bread without salt. His drink was water. His palace was built of mud; and when he left Medina to go to the conquest of

Jerusalem, he rode on a red camel, with a wooden platter hanging at his saddle, with a bottle of water and two sacks, one holding barley, and the other dried fruits.

But there will dawn ere long on our politics, on our modes of living, a nobler morning than that Arabian faith, in the sentiment of love. This is the one remedy for all ills, the panacea of nature. We must be lovers, and at once the impossible becomes possible. Our age and history, for these thousand years, has not been the history of kindness, but of selfishness. Our distrust is very expensive. The money we spend for courts and prisons is very ill laid out. We make, by distrust, the thief, and burglar, and incendiary, and by our court and jail we keep him so. An acceptance of the sentiment of love throughout Christendom for a season, would bring the felon and the outcast to our side in tears, with the devotion of his faculties to our service. See this wide society of laboring men and women. We allow ourselves to be served by them, we live apart from them, and meet them without a salute in the streets. We do not greet their talents, nor rejoice in their good fortune, nor foster their hopes, nor in the assembly of the people vote for what is dear to them. Thus we enact the part of the selfish noble and king from the foundation of the world. See, this tree always bears one fruit. In every household, the peace of a pair is poisoned by the malice, slyness, indolence, and alienation of domestics. Let any two matrons meet, and observe how soon their conversation turns on the troubles from their "*help*," as our phrase is. In every knot of laborers, the rich man does not feel himself among his friends, — and at the polls he finds them arrayed in a mass in distinct opposition to him. We complain that the politics of masses of the people are controlled by designing men, and led in opposition to manifest justice and the common weal, and to their own interest. But the people do not wish to be represented or ruled by the ignorant and base. They only vote for these, because they were asked with the voice and semblance of kindness. They will not vote for them long. They inevitably prefer wit and probity. To use an Egyptian metaphor, it is not their will for any long time "to raise the nails of wild beasts, and to depress the heads of the sacred birds." Let our affection flow out to our fellows; it would operate in a day the greatest of all revolutions. It is better to work on institutions by the sun than by the wind. The state must consider the poor man, and all voices must speak for him. Every child that is born must have a just chance for his bread. Let the amelioration in our laws of property proceed from the concession of the rich, not from the grasping of the poor. Let us begin by habitual imparting. Let us understand that the equitable rule is, that no one should take more than his share, let him be ever so rich. Let me feel that I am to be a lover. I am to see to it that the world is the better for me, and to find my reward in the act. Love would put a new face on this weary old world in which we dwell as pagans and enemies too long, and it would warm the heart to see how fast the vain diplomacy of statesmen, the impotence of armies, and navies, and lines of defence, would be superseded by this unarmed child. Love will creep where it cannot go, will accomplish that by imperceptible methods,—being its own lever, fulcrum, and power,—which force could never achieve. Have you not seen in the woods, in a late autumn morning, a poor fungus or mushroom,—a plant without any solidity, nay, that seemed nothing but a soft mush or jelly,—by its constant, total, and inconceivably gentle pushing, manage to break its way up through the frosty ground, and actually to lift a hard crust on its head? It is the symbol of the power of kindness. The virtue of this principle in human society in application to great interests is obsolete and forgotten. Once or twice in history it has been tried in illustrious instances, with signal success. This great, overgrown, dead Christendom of ours still keeps alive at least the name of a lover of mankind. But one day all men will be lovers; and every calamity will be dissolved in the universal sunshine.

Will you suffer me to add one trait more to this portrait of man the reformer? The mediator between the spiritual and the actual world should have a great prospective prudence. An Arabian poet describes his hero by saying,

> "Sunshine was he
> In the winter day;
> And in the midsummer
> Coolness and shade."

He who would help himself and others, should not be a subject of irregular and interrupted impulses of virtue, but a continent, persisting, immovable person,—such as we have seen
a few scattered up and down in time for the blessing of the
world; men who have in the gravity of their nature a quality
which answers to the fly-wheel in a mill, which distributes the
motion equably over all the wheels, and hinders it from falling unequally and suddenly in destructive shocks. It is better
that joy should be spread over all the day in the form of
strength, than that it should be concentrated into ecstasies,
full of danger and followed by reactions. There is a sublime
prudence, which is the very highest that we know of man,
which, believing in a vast future,—sure of more to come than
is yet seen,—postpones always the present hour to the whole
life; postpones talent to genius, and special results to character. As the merchant gladly takes money from his income to
add to his capital, so is the great man very willing to lose
particular powers and talents, so that he gain in the elevation
of his life. The opening of the spiritual senses disposes men
ever to greater sacrifices, to leave their signal talents, their best
means and skill of procuring a present success, their power
and their fame,—to cast all things behind, in the insatiable
thirst for divine communications. A purer fame, a greater
power rewards the sacrifice. It is the conversion of our harvest
into seed. As the farmer casts into the ground the finest ears
of his grain, the time will come when we too shall hold nothing back, but shall eagerly convert more than we now possess
into means and powers, when we shall be willing to sow the
sun and the moon for seeds.

LECTURE ON THE TIMES

Read at the Masonic Temple, Boston,
December 2, 1841

Lecture on the Times

THE TIMES, as we say—or the present aspects of our social state, the Laws, Divinity, Natural Science, Agriculture, Art, Trade, Letters, have their root in an invisible spiritual reality. To appear in these aspects, they must first exist, or have some necessary foundation. Beside all the small reasons we assign, there is a great reason for the existence of every extant fact; a reason which lies grand and immovable, often unsuspected behind it in silence. The Times are the masquerade of the eternities; trivial to the dull, tokens of noble and majestic agents to the wise; the receptacle in which the Past leaves its history; the quarry out of which the genius of today is building up the Future. The Times—the nations, manners, institutions, opinions, votes, are to be studied as omens, as sacred leaves, whereon a weighty sense is inscribed, if we have the wit and the love to search it out. Nature itself seems to propound to us this topic, and to invite us to explore the meaning of the conspicuous facts of the day. Everything that is popular, it has been said, deserves the attention of the philosopher: and this for the obvious reason, that although it may not be of any worth in itself, yet it characterizes the people.

Here is very good matter to be handled, if we are skilful; an abundance of important practical questions which it behoves us to understand. Let us examine the pretensions of the attacking and defending parties. Here is this great fact of Conservatism, entrenched in its immense redoubts, with Himmaleh for its front, and Atlas for its flank, and Andes for its rear, and the Atlantic and Pacific seas for its ditches and trenches, which has planted its crosses, and crescents, and stars and stripes, and various signs and badges of possession, over every rood of the planet, and says, 'I will hold fast; and to whom I will, will I give; and whom I will, will I exclude and starve:' so says Conservatism; and all the children of men attack the colossus in their youth, and all, or all but a few, bow before it when they are old. A necessity not yet commanded, a negative imposed on the will of man by his condition, a deficiency in his force, is the foundation on which it rests. Let this side be fairly stated. Meantime, on the other part, arises Reform, and offers the sentiment of Love as an overmatch to this material might. I wish to consider well this affirmative side, which has a loftier port and reason than heretofore, which encroaches on the other every day, puts it out of countenance, out of reason, and out of temper, and leaves it nothing but silence and possession.

The fact of aristocracy, with its two weapons of wealth and manners, is as commanding a feature of the nineteenth century, and the American republic, as of old Rome, or modern England. The reason and influence of wealth, the aspect of philosophy and religion, and the tendencies which have acquired the name of Transcendentalism in Old and New England; the aspect of poetry, as the exponent and interpretation of these things; the fuller development and the freer play of Character as a social and political agent;—these and other related topics will in turn come to be considered.

But the subject of the Times is not an abstract question. We talk of the world, but we mean a few men and women. If you speak of the age, you mean your own platoon of people, as Milton and Dante painted in colossal their platoons, and called them Heaven and Hell. In our idea of progress, we do not go out of this personal picture. We do not think the sky will be bluer, or honey sweeter, or our climate more temperate, but only that our relation to our fellows will be simpler and happier. What is the reason to be given for this extreme attraction which *persons* have for us, but that they are the Age? they are the results of the Past; they are the heralds of the Future. They indicate,—these witty, suffering, blushing, intimidating figures of the only race in which there are individuals or changes, how far on the Fate has gone, and what it drives at. As trees make scenery, and constitute the hospitality of the landscape, so persons are the world to persons. A cunning mystery by which the Great Desart of thoughts and of planets takes this engaging form, to bring, as it would seem, its meanings nearer to the mind. Thoughts walk and speak, and look with eyes at me, and transport me into new and magnificent scenes. These are the pungent instructors who thrill the heart of each of us, and make all other teaching

formal and cold. How I follow them with aching heart, with
pining desire! I count myself nothing before them. I would
die for them with joy. They can do what they will with me.
How they lash us with those tongues! How they make the
tears start, make us blush and turn pale, and lap us in Elysium
to soothing dreams, and castles in the air! By tones of
triumph; of dear love; by threats; by pride that freezes; these
have the skill to make the world look bleak and inhospitable,
or seem the nest of tenderness and joy. I do not wonder at
the miracles which poetry attributes to the music of Orpheus,
when I remember what I have experienced from the varied
notes of the human voice. They are an incalculable energy
which countervails all other forces in nature, because they are
the channel of supernatural powers. There is no interest or
institution so poor and withered, but if a new strong man
could be born into it, he would immediately redeem and replace it. A personal ascendency,—that is the only fact much
worth considering. I remember, some years ago, somebody
shocked a circle of friends of order here in Boston, who supposed that our people were identified with their religious de-
nominations, by declaring that an eloquent man,—let him be
of what sect soever,—would be ordained at once in one of
our metropolitan churches. To be sure he would; and not
only in ours, but in any church, mosque, or temple, on the
planet; but he must be eloquent, able to supplant our method
and classification, by the superior beauty of his own. Every
fact we have was brought here by some person; and there is
none that will not change and pass away before a person,
whose nature is broader than the person which the fact in
question represents. And so I find the Age walking about in
happy and hopeful natures, in strong eyes, and pleasant
thoughts, and think I read it nearer and truer so, than in the
statute-book, or in the investments of capital, which rather
celebrate with mournful music the obsequies of the last age.
In the brain of a fanatic; in the wild hope of a mountain boy,
called by city boys very ignorant, because they do not know
what his hope has certainly apprised him shall be; in the love-
glance of a girl; in the hair-splitting conscientiousness of
some eccentric person, who has found some new scruple to
embarrass himself and his neighbors withal; is to be found

that which shall constitute the times to come, more than in the now organized and accredited oracles. For, whatever is affirmative and now advancing, contains it. I think that only is real, which men love and rejoice in; not what they tolerate, but what they choose; what they embrace and avow, and not the things which chill, benumb, and terrify them.

And so why not draw for these times a portrait gallery? Let us paint the painters. Whilst the Daguerreotypist, with camera-obscura and silver plate, begins now to traverse the land, let us set up our Camera also, and let the sun paint the people. Let us paint the agitator, and the man of the old school, and the member of Congress, and the college-professor, the formidable editor, the priest, and reformer, the contemplative girl, and the fair aspirant for fashion and opportunities, the woman of the world who has tried and knows;—let us examine how well she knows. Could we indicate the indicators, indicate those who most accurately represent every good and evil tendency of the general mind, in the just order which they take on this canvass of Time; so that all witnesses should recognise a spiritual law, as each well known form flitted for a moment across the wall, we should have a series of sketches which would report to the next ages the color and quality of ours.

Certainly, I think, if this were done, there would be much to admire as well as to condemn; souls of as lofty a port, as any in Greek or Roman fame, might appear; men of great heart, of strong hand, and of persuasive speech; subtle thinkers, and men of wide sympathy, and an apprehension which looks over all history, and everywhere recognises its own. To be sure, there will be fragments and hints of men, more than enough: bloated promises, which end in nothing or little. And then truly great men, but with some defect in their composition, which neutralizes their whole force. Here is a Damascus blade, such as you may search through nature in vain to parallel, laid up on the shelf in some village to rust and ruin. And how many seem not quite available for that idea which they represent! Now and then comes a bolder spirit, I should rather say, a more surrendered soul, more informed and led by God, which is much in advance of the rest, quite beyond their sympathy, but predicts what shall soon be the general fulness; as when we stand by the seashore, whilst the tide is coming in, a wave comes up the beach far higher than any foregoing one, and recedes; and for a long while none comes up to that mark; but after some time the whole sea is there and beyond it.

But we are not permitted to stand as spectators of the pageant which the times exhibit: we are parties also, and have a responsibility which is not to be declined. A little while this interval of wonder and comparison is permitted us, but to the end that we shall play a manly part. As the solar system moves forward in the heavens, certain stars open before us, and certain stars close up behind us; so is man's life. The reputations that were great and inaccessible change and tarnish. How great were once Lord Bacon's dimensions! he is now reduced almost to the middle height; and many another star has turned out to be a planet or an asteroid: only a few are the fixed stars which have no parallax, or none for us. The change and decline of old reputations are the gracious marks of our own growth. Slowly, like light of morning, it steals on us, the new fact, that we, who were pupils or aspirants, are now society: do compose a portion of that head and heart we are wont to think worthy of all reverence and heed. We are the representatives of religion and intellect, and stand in the light of Ideas, whose rays stream through us to those younger and more in the dark. What further relations we sustain, what new lodges we are entering, is now unknown. To-day is a king in disguise. To-day always looks mean to the thoughtless, in the face of an uniform experience, that all good and great and happy actions are made up precisely of these blank to-days. Let us not be so deceived. Let us unmask the king as he passes. Let us not inhabit times of wonderful and various promise without divining their tendency. Let us not see the foundations of nations, and of a new and better order of things laid, with roving eyes, and an attention preoccupied with trifles.

The two omnipresent parties of History, the party of the Past and the party of the Future, divide society to-day as of old. Here is the innumerable multitude of those who accept the state and the church from the last generation, and stand on no argument but possession. They have reason also, and, as I think, better reason than is commonly stated. No Burke, no Metternich has yet done full justice to the side of conservatism. But this class, however large, relying not on the intellect but on instinct, blends itself with the brute forces of nature, is respectable only as nature is, but the individuals have no attraction for us. It is the dissenter, the theorist, the aspirant, who is quitting this ancient domain to embark on seas of adventure, who engages our interest. Omitting then for the present all notice of the stationary class, we shall find that the movement party divides itself into two classes, the actors, and the students.

The actors constitute that great army of martyrs who, at least in America, by their conscience and philanthropy, occupy the ground which Calvinism occupied in the last age, and compose the visible church of the existing generation. The present age will be marked by its harvest of projects for the reform of domestic, civil, literary, and ecclesiastical institutions. The leaders of the crusades against War, Negro slavery, Intemperance, Government based on force, Usages of trade, Court and Custom-house Oaths, and so on to the agitators on the system of Education and the laws of Property, are the right successors of Luther, Knox, Robinson, Fox, Penn, Wesley, and Whitfield. They have the same virtues and vices; the same noble impulse, and the same bigotry. These movements are on all accounts important; they not only check the special abuses, but they educate the conscience and the intellect of the people. How can such a question as the Slave trade be agitated for forty years by all the Christian nations, without throwing great light on ethics into the general mind? The fury, with which the slave-trader defends every inch of his bloody deck, and his howling auction-platform, is a trumpet to alarm the ear of mankind, to wake the dull, and drive all neutrals to take sides, and to listen to the argument and the verdict. The Temperance-question, which rides the conversation of ten thousand circles, and is tacitly recalled at every public and at every private table, drawing with it all the curious ethics of the Pledge, of the Wine-question, of the equity of the manufacture and the trade, is a gymnastic training to the casuistry and conscience of the time. Antimasonry had a deep right and wrong, which gradually emerged to sight out of the turbid controversy. The political questions touching the Banks; the Tariff; the limits of the executive power; the right of the constituent to instruct the representative; the treatment of the Indians; the Boundary wars; the Congress of nations; are all pregnant with ethical conclusions; and it is well if government and our social order can extricate themselves from these alembics, and find themselves still government and social order. The student of history will hereafter compute the singular value of our endless discussion of questions, to the mind of the period.

Whilst each of these aspirations and attempts of the people for the Better is magnified by the natural exaggeration of its advocates, until it excludes the others from sight, and repels discreet persons by the unfairness of the plea, the movements are in reality all parts of one movement. There is a perfect chain,—see it, or see it not,—of reforms emerging from the surrounding darkness, each cherishing some part of the general idea, and all must be seen, in order to do justice to any one. Seen in this their natural connection, they are sublime. The conscience of the Age demonstrates itself in this effort to raise the life of man by putting it in harmony with his idea of the Beautiful and the Just. The history of reform is always identical; it is the comparison of the idea with the fact. Our modes of living are not agreeable to our imagination. We suspect they are unworthy. We arraign our daily employments. They appear to us unfit, unworthy of the faculties we spend on them. In conversation with a wise man, we find ourselves apologizing for our employments; we speak of them with shame. Nature, literature, science, childhood, appear to us beautiful; but not our own daily work, not the ripe fruit and considered labors of man. This beauty which the fancy finds in everything else, certainly accuses that manner of life we lead. Why should it be hateful? Why should it contrast thus with all natural beauty? Why should it not be poetic, and invite and raise us? Is there a necessity that the works of man should be sordid? Perhaps not.—Out of this fair Idea in the mind springs the effort at the Perfect. It is the interior testimony to a fairer possibility of life and manners, which agitates society every day with the offer of some new amendment. If we would make more strict inquiry concerning its origin, we find ourselves rapidly approaching the inner boundaries of thought, that term where speech becomes silence, and science conscience. For the origin of all reform is in that mysterious fountain of the moral sentiment in man, which, amidst the natural, ever contains the supernatural for men. That is new and creative. That is alive. That alone can make a man other than he is. Here or nowhere resides unbounded energy, unbounded power.

The new voices in the wilderness crying "Repent," have revived a hope, which had well nigh perished out of the world, that the thoughts of the mind may yet, in some distant age, in some happy hour, be executed by the hands. That is the hope, of which all other hopes are parts. For some ages, these ideas have been consigned to the poet and musical composer, to the prayers and the sermons of churches; but the thought, that they can ever have any footing in real life, seems long since to have been exploded by all judicious persons. Milton, in his best tract, describes a relation between religion and the daily occupations, which is true until this time.

"A wealthy man, addicted to his pleasure and to his profits, finds religion to be a traffic so entangled, and of so many piddling accounts, that of all mysteries he cannot skill to keep a stock going upon that trade. What should he do? Fain he would have the name to be religious; fain he would bear up with his neighbors in that. What does he, therefore, but resolve to give over toiling, and to find himself out some factor, to whose care and credit he may commit the whole managing of his religious affairs; some divine of note and estimation that must be. To him he adheres, resigns the whole warehouse of his religion, with all the locks and keys, into his custody; and indeed makes the very person of that man his religion; esteems his associating with him a sufficient evidence and commendatory of his own piety. So that a man may say, his religion is now no more within himself, but is become a dividual moveable, and goes and comes near him, according as that good man frequents the house. He entertains him, gives him gifts, feasts him, lodges him; his religion comes home at night, prays, is liberally supped, and sumptuously laid to sleep, rises, is saluted, and after the malmsey, or some well spiced beverage, and better breakfasted than he whose morning appetite would have gladly fed on green figs between Bethany and Jerusalem, his religion walks abroad at eight, and leaves his kind entertainer in the shop, trading all day without his religion."

This picture would serve for our times. Religion was not invited to eat or drink or sleep with us, or to make or divide an estate, but was a holiday guest. Such omissions judge the church; as the compromise made with the slaveholder, not much noticed at first, every day appears more flagrant mischief to the American constitution. But now the purists are looking into all these matters. The more intelligent are growing uneasy on the subject of Marriage. They wish to see the character represented also in that covenant. There shall be nothing brutal in it, but it shall honor the man and the woman, as much as the most diffusive and universal action. Grimly the same spirit looks into the law of Property, and accuses men of driving a trade in the great boundless providence which had given the air, the water, and the land to men, to use and not to fence in and monopolize. It casts its eye on Trade, and Day Labor, and so it goes up and down, paving the earth with eyes, destroying privacy, and making thorough-lights. Is all this for nothing? Do you suppose that the reforms, which are preparing, will be as superficial as those we know?

By the books it reads and translates, judge what books it will presently print. A great deal of the profoundest thinking of antiquity, which had become as good as obsolete for us, is now re-appearing in extracts and allusions, and in twenty years will get all printed anew. See how daring is the reading, the speculation, the experimenting of the time. If now some genius shall arise who could unite these scattered rays! And always such a genius does embody the ideas of each time. Here is great variety and richness of mysticism, each part of which now only disgusts, whilst it forms the sole thought of some poor Perfectionist or "Comer out," yet, when it shall be taken up as the garniture of some profound and all-reconciling thinker, will appear the rich and appropriate decoration of his robes.

These reforms are our contemporaries; they are ourselves; our own light, and sight, and conscience; they only name the relation which subsists between us and the vicious institutions which they go to rectify. They are the simplest statements of man in these matters; the plain right and wrong. I cannot choose but allow and honor them. The impulse is good, and the theory; the practice is less beautiful. The Reformers affirm the inward life, but they do not trust it, but use outward and vulgar means. They do not rely on precisely that strength which wins me to their cause; not on love, not on a principle, but on men, on multitudes, on circumstances, on money, on party; that is, on fear, on wrath, and pride. The love which lifted men to the sight of these better ends, was the true and best distinction of this time, the disposition to trust a principle more than a material force. I think *that* the soul of reform; the conviction, that not sensualism, not slavery, not war, not imprisonment, not even government, are needed, — but in lieu of them all, reliance on the sentiment of man, which will work best the more it is trusted; not reliance on numbers, but, contrariwise, distrust of numbers, and the feeling that then are we strongest, when most private and alone. The young men, who have been vexing society for these last years with regenerative methods, seem to have made this mistake; they all exaggerated some special means, and all failed to see that the Reform of Reforms must be accomplished without means.

The Reforms have their high origin in an ideal justice, but they do not retain the purity of an idea. They are quickly organized in some low, inadequate form, and present no more poetic image to the mind, than the evil tradition which they reprobated. They mix the fire of the moral sentiment with personal and party heats, with measureless exaggerations, and the blindness that prefers some darling measure to justice and truth. Those, who are urging with most ardor what are called the greatest benefits of mankind, are narrow, self-pleasing, conceited men, and affect us as the insane do. They bite us, and we run mad also. I think the work of the reformer as innocent as other work that is done around him; but when I have seen it near, I do not like it better. It is done in the same way, it is done profanely, not piously; by management, by tactics, and clamor. It is a buzz in the ear. I cannot feel any pleasure in sacrifices which display to me such partiality of character. We do not want actions, but men; not a chemical drop of water, but rain; the spirit that sheds and showers actions, countless, endless actions. You have on some occasion played a bold part. You have set your heart and face against society, when you thought it wrong, and returned it frown for frown. Excellent: now can you afford to forget it, reckoning all your action no more than the passing of your hand through the air, or a little breath of your mouth? The world leaves no track in space, and the greatest action of man no mark in the vast idea. To the youth diffident of his ability, and full of compunction at his unprofitable existence, the temptation is always great to lend himself to public movements, and as one of a party accomplish what he cannot hope to effect alone. But he must resist the degradation of a man to a measure. I must act with truth, though I should never come to act, as you call it, with effect. I must consent to inaction. A patience which is grand; a brave and cold neglect of the offices which prudence exacts, so it be done in a deep, upper piety; a consent to solitude and inaction, which proceeds out of an unwillingness to violate character, is the century which makes the gem. Whilst therefore I desire to express the respect and joy I feel before this sublime connection of reforms, now in their infancy around us, I urge the more earnestly the paramount duties of self-reliance. I cannot find language of sufficient energy to convey my sense of the sacredness of private integrity. All men, all things, the state, the church, yea the friends of the heart are phantasms and unreal beside the sanctuary of the heart. With so much awe, with so much fear, let it be respected.

The great majority of men, unable to judge of any principle until its light falls on a fact, are not aware of the evil that is around them, until they see it in some gross form, as in a class of intemperate men, or slaveholders, or soldiers, or fraudulent persons. Then they are greatly moved; and magnifying the importance of that wrong, they fancy that if that abuse were redressed, all would go well, and they fill the land with clamor to correct it. Hence the missionary and other religious efforts. If every island and every house had a Bible, if every child was brought into the Sunday School, would the wounds of the world heal, and man be upright?

But the man of ideas, accounting the circumstance nothing, judges of the commonwealth from the state of his own mind. 'If,' he says, 'I am selfish, then is there slavery, or the effort to establish it, wherever I go. But if I am just, then is there no slavery, let the laws say what they will. For if I treat all men as gods, how to me can there be such a thing as a slave?' But how frivolous is your war against circumstances. This denouncing philanthropist is himself a slaveholder in every word and look. Does he free me? Does he cheer me? He is the state of Georgia, or Alabama, with their sanguinary slave-laws walking here on our north-eastern shores. We are all thankful he has no more political power, as we are fond of liberty ourselves. I am afraid our virtue is a little geographical. I am not mortified by our vice; that is obduracy; it colors and palters, it curses and swears, and I can see to the end of it; but, I own, our virtue makes me ashamed; so sour and narrow, so thin and blind, virtue so vice-like. Then again, how trivial seem the contests of the abolitionist, whilst he aims merely at the circumstance of the slave. Give the slave the least elevation of religious sentiment, and he is no slave: you are the slave: he not only in his humility feels his superiority, feels that much deplored condition of his to be a fading trifle, but he makes you feel it too. He is the master. The exaggeration, which our young people make of his wrongs, characterizes themselves. What are no trifles to them, they naturally think are no trifles to Pompey.

We say, then, that the reforming movement is sacred in its origin; in its management and details timid and profane. These benefactors hope to raise man by improving his circumstances: by combination of that which is dead, they hope to make something alive. In vain. By new infusions alone of the spirit by which he is made and directed, can he be remade and reinforced. The sad Pestalozzi, who shared with all ardent spirits the hope of Europe on the outbreak of the French Revolution, after witnessing its sequel, recorded his conviction, that "the amelioration of outward circumstances will be the effect, but can never be the means of mental and moral improvement." Quitting now the class of actors, let us turn to see how it stands with the other class of which we spoke, namely, the students.

A new disease has fallen on the life of man. Every Age, like every human body, has its own distemper. Other times have had war, or famine, or a barbarism domestic or bordering, as their antagonism. Our forefathers walked in the world and went to their graves, tormented with the fear of Sin, and the terror of the Day of Judgment. These terrors have lost their force, and our torment is Unbelief, the Uncertainty as to what we ought to do; the distrust of the value of what we do, and the distrust that the Necessity (which we all at last believe in) is fair and beneficent. Our Religion assumes the negative form of rejection. Out of love of the true, we repudiate the false: and the Religion is an abolishing criticism. A great perplexity hangs like a cloud on the brow of all cultivated persons, a certain imbecility in the best spirits, which distinguishes the period. We do not find the same trait in the Arabian, in the Hebrew, in Greek, Roman, Norman, English periods; no, but in other men a natural firmness. The men did not see beyond the need of the hour. They planted their foot strong, and doubted nothing. We mistrust every step we take. We find it the worst thing about time, that we know not what to do with it. We are so sharp-sighted that we can neither work nor think, neither read Plato nor not read him.

Then there is what is called a too intellectual tendency. Can there be too much intellect? We have never met with any such excess. But the criticism, which is levelled at the laws and manners, ends in thought, without causing a new method of life. The genius of the day does not incline to a deed, but to a beholding. It is not that men do not wish to act; they pine to be employed, but are paralyzed by the uncertainty what they should do. The inadequacy of the work to the faculties, is the painful perception which keeps them still. This happens to the best. Then, talents bring their usual temptations, and the current literature and poetry with perverse ingenuity draw us away from life to solitude and meditation. This could well be borne, if it were great and involuntary; if the men were ravished by their thought, and hurried into ascetic extravagances. Society could then manage to release their shoulder from its wheel, and grant them for a time this privilege of sabbath. But they are not so. Thinking, which was a rage, is become an art. The thinker gives me results, and never invites me to be present with him at his invocation of truth, and to enjoy with him its proceeding into his mind.

So little action amidst such audacious and yet sincere profession, that we begin to doubt if that great revolution in the art of war, which has made it a game of posts instead of a game of battles, has not operated on Reform; whether this be not also a war of posts, a paper blockade, in which each party is to display the utmost resources of his spirit and belief, and no conflict occur; but the world shall take that course which the demonstration of the truth shall indicate.

But we must pay for being too intellectual, as they call it. People are not as light-hearted for it. I think men never loved life less. I question if care and doubt ever wrote their names so legibly on the faces of any population. This *Ennui*, for which we Saxons had no name, this word of France has got a terrific significance. It shortens life, and bereaves the day of its light. Old age begins in the nursery, and before the young American is put into jacket and trowsers, he says, 'I want something which I never saw before;' and 'I wish I was not I.' I have seen the same gloom on the brow even of those adventurers from the intellectual class, who had dived deepest and with most success into active life. I have seen the authentic sign of anxiety and perplexity on the greatest forehead of the state. The canker worms have crawled to the topmost bough of the wild elm, and swing down from that. Is there less oxygen in the atmosphere? What has checked in this age the animal spirits which gave to our forefathers their bounding pulse?

But have a little patience with this melancholy humor. Their unbelief arises out of a greater Belief; their inaction out of a scorn of inadequate action. By the side of these men, the hot agitators have a certain cheap and ridiculous air; they even look smaller than the others. Of the two, I own, I like the speculators best. They have some piety which looks with faith to a fair Future, unprofaned by rash and unequal attempts to realize it. And truly we shall find much to console us, when we consider the cause of their uneasiness. It is the love of greatness, it is the need of harmony, the contrast of the dwarfish Actual with the exorbitant Idea. No man can compare the ideas and aspirations of the innovators of the present day, with those of former periods, without feeling how great and high this criticism is. The revolutions that impend over society are not now from ambition and rapacity, from impatience of one or another form of government, but from new modes of thinking, which shall recompose society after a new order, which shall animate labor by love and science, which shall destroy the value of many kinds of property, and replace all property within the dominion of reason and equity. There was never so great a thought laboring in the breasts of men, as now. It almost seems as if what was aforetime spoken fabulously and hieroglyphically, was now spoken plainly, the doctrine, namely, of the indwelling of the Creator in man. The spiritualist wishes this only, that the spiritual principle should be suffered to demonstrate itself to the end, in all possible applications to the state of man, without the admission of anything unspiritual, that is, anything positive, dogmatic, or personal. The excellence of this class consists in this, that they have believed; that, affirming the need of new and higher modes of living and action, they have abstained from the recommendation of low methods. Their fault is that they have stopped at the intellectual perception; that their will is not yet inspired from the Fountain of Love. But whose fault is this? and what a fault, and to what inquiry does it lead! We have come to that which is the spring of all power, of beauty and virtue, of art and poetry; and who shall tell us according to what law its inspirations and its informations are given or withholden?

I do not wish to be guilty of the narrowness and pedantry of inferring the tendency and genius of the Age from a few and insufficient facts or persons. Every age has a thousand sides and signs and tendencies; and it is only when surveyed from inferior points of view, that great varieties of character appear. Our time too is full of activity and performance. Is there not something comprehensive in the grasp of a society which to great mechanical invention, and the best institutions of property, adds the most daring theories; which explores the subtlest and most universal problems? At the manifest risk of repeating what every other Age has thought of itself, we might say, we think the Genius of this Age more philosophical than any other has been, righter in its aims, truer, with less fear, less fable, less mixture of any sort.

But turn it how we will, as we ponder this meaning of the times, every new thought drives us to the deep fact, that the Time is the child of the Eternity. The main interest which any aspects of the Times can have for us, is the great spirit which gazes through them, the light which they can shed on the wonderful questions, What we are? and Whither we tend? We do not wish to be deceived. Here we drift, like white sail across the wild ocean, now bright on the wave, now darkling in the trough of the sea;—but from what port did we sail? Who knows? Or to what port are we bound? Who knows? There is no one to tell us but such poor weather-tossed mariners as ourselves, whom we speak as we pass, or who have hoisted some signal, or floated to us some letter in a bottle from far. But what know they more than we? They also found themselves on this wondrous sea. No; from the older sailors, nothing. Over all their speaking-trumpets, the gray sea and the loud winds answer, Not in us; not in Time. Where then but in Ourselves, where but in that Thought through which we communicate with absolute nature, and are made aware that, whilst we shed the dust of which we are built, grain by grain, till it is all gone, the law which clothes us with humanity remains new? where, but in the intuitions which are vouchsafed us from within, shall we learn the Truth? Faithless, faithless, we fancy that with the dust we depart and are not; and do not know that the law and the perception of the law are at last one; that only as much as the law enters us, becomes us, we are living men,—immortal with the immortality of this law. Underneath all these appearances, lies that which is, that which lives, that which causes. This ever renewing generation of appearances rests on a reality, and a reality that is alive.

To a true scholar the attraction of the aspects of nature, the departments of life, and the passages of his experience, is simply the information they yield him of this supreme nature which lurks within all. That reality, that causing force is moral. The Moral Sentiment is but its other name. It makes by its presence or absence right and wrong, beauty and ugliness, genius or depravation. As the granite comes to the sur-

face, and towers into the highest mountains, and, if we dig
down, we find it below the superficial strata, so in all the
details of our domestic or civil life, is hidden the elemental
reality, which ever and anon comes to the surface, and forms
the grand men, who are the leaders and examples, rather than
the companions of the race. The granite is curiously concealed
under a thousand formations and surfaces, under fertile soils,
and grasses, and flowers, under well-manured, arable fields,
and large towns and cities, but it makes the foundation of
these, and is always indicating its presence by slight but sure
signs. So is it with the Life of our life; so close does that also
hide. I read it in glad and in weeping eyes: I read it in the
pride and in the humility of people: it is recognized in every
bargain and in every complaisance, in every criticism, and in
all praise: it is voted for at elections; it wins the cause with
juries; it rides the stormy eloquence of the senate, sole victor;
histories are written of it, holidays decreed to it; statues,
tombs, churches, built to its honor; yet men seem to fear and
to shun it, when it comes barely to view in our immediate
neighborhood.

For that reality let us stand: that let us serve, and for that
speak. Only as far as *that* shines through them, are these
times or any times worth consideration. I wish to speak of
the politics, education, business, and religion around us,
without ceremony or false deference. You will absolve me
from the charge of flippancy, or malignity, or the desire to
say smart things at the expense of whomsoever, when you see
that reality is all we prize, and that we are bound on our
entrance into nature to speak for that. Let it not be recorded
in our own memories, that in this moment of the Eternity,
when we who were named by our names, flitted across the
light, we were afraid of any fact, or disgraced the fair Day by
a pusillanimous preference of our bread to our freedom.
What is the scholar, what is the man *for*, but for hospitality
to every new thought of his time? Have you leisure, power,
property, friends? you shall be the asylum and patron of every
new thought, every unproven opinion, every untried project,
which proceeds out of good will and honest seeking. All the
newspapers, all the tongues of to-day will of course at first
defame what is noble; but you who hold not of to-day, not

of the times, but of the Everlasting, are to stand for it: and the highest compliment man ever receives from heaven, is the sending to him its disguised and discredited angels.

THE CONSERVATIVE

*A Lecture delivered at the Masonic Temple,
Boston, December 9, 1841*

The Conservative

THE TWO PARTIES which divide the state, the party of Conservatism and that of Innovation, are very old, and have disputed the possession of the world ever since it was made. This quarrel is the subject of civil history. The conservative party established the reverend hierarchies and monarchies of the most ancient world. The battle of patrician and plebeian, of parent state and colony, of old usage and accommodation to new facts, of the rich and the poor, reappears in all countries and times. The war rages not only in battle-fields, in national councils, and ecclesiastical synods, but agitates every man's bosom with opposing advantages every hour. On rolls the old world meantime, and now one, now the other gets the day, and still the fight renews itself as if for the first time, under new names and hot personalities.

Such an irreconcilable antagonism, of course, must have a correspondent depth of seat in the human constitution. It is the opposition of Past and Future, of Memory and Hope, of the Understanding and the Reason. It is the primal antagonism, the appearance in trifles of the two poles of nature.

There is a fragment of old fable which seems somehow to have been dropped from the current mythologies, which may deserve attention, as it appears to relate to this subject.

Saturn grew weary of sitting alone, or with none but the great Uranus or Heaven beholding him, and he created an oyster. Then he would act again, but he made nothing more, but went on creating the race of oysters. Then Uranus cried, 'a new work, O Saturn! the old is not good again.'

Saturn replied. 'I fear. There is not only the alternative of making and not making, but also of unmaking. Seest thou the great sea, how it ebbs and flows? so is it with me; my power ebbs; and if I put forth my hands, I shall not do, but undo. Therefore I do what I have done; I hold what I have got; and so I resist Night and Chaos.'

'O Saturn,' replied Uranus, 'thou canst not hold thine own, but by making more. Thy oysters are barnacles and cockles, and with the next flowing of the tide, they will be pebbles and sea-foam.'

'I see,' rejoins Saturn, 'thou art in league with Night, thou art become an evil eye; thou spakest from love; now thy words smite me with hatred. I appeal to Fate, must there not be rest?'—'I appeal to Fate also,' said Uranus, 'must there not be motion?'—But Saturn was silent, and went on making oysters for a thousand years.

After that, the word of Uranus came into his mind like a ray of the sun, and he made Jupiter; and then he feared again; and nature froze, the things that were made went backward, and, to save the world, Jupiter slew his father Saturn.

This may stand for the earliest account of a conversation on politics between a Conservative and a Radical, which has come down to us. It is ever thus. It is the counteraction of the centripetal and the centrifugal forces. Innovation is the salient energy; Conservatism the pause on the last movement. 'That which is was made by God,' saith Conservatism. 'He is leaving that, he is entering this other;' rejoins Innovation.

There is always a certain meanness in the argument of conservatism, joined with a certain superiority in its fact. It affirms because it holds. Its fingers clutch the fact, and it will not open its eyes to see a better fact. The castle, which conservatism is set to defend, is the actual state of things, good and bad. The project of innovation is the best possible state of things. Of course, conservatism always has the worst of the argument, is always apologizing, pleading a necessity, pleading that to change would be to deteriorate; it must saddle itself with the mountainous load of the violence and vice of society, must deny the possibility of good, deny ideas, and suspect and stone the prophet; whilst innovation is always in the right, triumphant, attacking, and sure of final success. Conservatism stands on man's confessed limitations; reform on his indisputable infinitude; conservatism on circumstance; liberalism on power; one goes to make an adroit member of the social frame; the other to postpone all things to the man himself; conservatism is debonnair and social; reform is individual and imperious. We are reformers in spring and summer; in autumn and winter, we stand by the old; reformers in the morning, conservers at night. Reform is affirmative, conservatism negative; conservatism goes for comfort, reform for truth. Conservatism is more candid to behold another's worth; reform more disposed to maintain and increase its own. Conservatism makes no poetry, breathes no prayer, has no invention; it is all memory. Reform has no gratitude, no prudence, no husbandry. It makes a great difference to your figure and to your thought, whether your foot is advancing or receding. Conservatism never puts the foot forward; in the hour when it does that, it is not establishment, but reform. Conservatism tends to universal seeming and treachery, believes in a negative fate; believes that men's temper governs them; that for me, it avails not to trust in principles; they will fail me; I must bend a little; it distrusts nature; it thinks there is a general law without a particular application,—law for all that does not include any one. Reform in its antagonism inclines to asinine resistance, to kick with hoofs; it runs to egotism and bloated self-conceit; it runs to a bodiless pretension, to unnatural refining and elevation, which ends in hypocrisy and sensual reaction.

And so whilst we do not go beyond general statements, it may be safely affirmed of these two metaphysical antagonists, that each is a good half, but an impossible whole. Each exposes the abuses of the other, but in a true society, in a true man, both must combine. Nature does not give the crown of its approbation, namely, beauty, to any action or emblem or actor, but to one which combines both these elements; not to the rock which resists the waves from age to age, nor to the wave which lashes incessantly the rock, but the superior beauty is with the oak which stands with its hundred arms against the storms of a century, and grows every year like a sapling; or the river which ever flowing, yet is found in the same bed from age to age; or, greatest of all, the man who has subsisted for years amid the changes of nature, yet has distanced himself, so that when you remember what he was, and see what he is, you say, what strides! what a disparity is here!

Throughout nature the past combines in every creature with the present. Each of the convolutions of the sea-shell, each node and spine marks one year of the fish's life, what was the mouth of the shell for one season, with the addition of new matter by the growth of the animal, becoming an ornamental node. The leaves and a shell of soft wood are all that the vegetation of this summer has made, but the solid columnar stem, which lifts that bank of foliage into the air to draw the eye and to cool us with its shade, is the gift and legacy of dead and buried years.

In nature, each of these elements being always present, each theory has a natural support. As we take our stand on Necessity, or on Ethics, shall we go for the conservative, or for the reformer. If we read the world historically, we shall say, Of all the ages, the present hour and circumstance is the cumulative result; this is the best throw of the dice of nature that has yet been, or that is yet possible. If we see it from the side of Will, or the Moral Sentiment, we shall accuse the Past and the Present, and require the impossible of the Future.

But although this bifold fact lies thus united in real nature, and so united that no man can continue to exist in whom both these elements do not work, yet men are not philosophers, but are rather very foolish children, who, by reason of their partiality, see everything in the most absurd manner, and are the victims at all times of the nearest object. There is even no philosopher who is a philosopher at all times. Our experience, our perception is conditioned by the need to acquire in parts and in succession, that is, with every truth a certain falsehood. As this is the invariable method of our training, we must give it allowance, and suffer men to learn as they have done for six millenniums, a word at a time, to pair off into insane parties, and learn the amount of truth each knows, by the denial of an equal amount of truth. For the present, then, to come at what sum is attainable to us, we must even hear the parties plead as parties.

That which is best about conservatism, that which, though it cannot be expressed in detail, inspires reverence in all, is the Inevitable. There is the question not only, what the conservative says for himself? but, why must he say it? What insurmountable fact binds him to that side? Here is the fact which men call Fate, and fate in dread degrees, fate behind fate, not to be disposed of by the consideration that the Conscience commands this or that, but necessitating the question, whether the faculties of man will play him true in resisting the facts of universal experience? For although the commands of the Conscience are *essentially* absolute, they are *historically* limitary. Wisdom does not seek a literal rectitude, but an useful, that is, a conditioned one, such a one as the faculties of man and the constitution of things will warrant. The reformer, the partisan loses himself in driving to the utmost some specialty of right conduct, until his own nature and all nature resist him; but Wisdom attempts nothing enormous and disproportioned to its powers, nothing which it cannot perform or nearly perform. We have all a certain intellection or presentiment of reform existing in the mind, which does not yet descend into the character, and those who throw themselves blindly on this lose themselves. Whatever they attempt in that direction, fails, and reacts suicidally on the actor himself. This is the penalty of having transcended nature. For the existing world is not a dream, and cannot with impunity be treated as a dream; neither is it a disease; but it is the ground on which you stand, it is the mother of whom you were born. Reform converses with possibilities, perchance with impossibilities; but here is sacred fact. This also was true, or it could not be: it had life in it, or it could not have existed; it has life in it, or it could not continue. Your schemes may be feasible, or may not be, but this has the endorsement of nature and a long friendship and cohabitation with the powers of nature. This will stand until a better cast of the dice is made. The contest between the Future and the Past is one between Divinity entering, and Divinity departing. You are welcome to try your experiments, and, if you can, to displace the actual order by that ideal republic you announce, for nothing but God will expel God. But plainly the burden of proof must lie with the projector. We hold to this, until you can demonstrate something better.

The system of property and law goes back for its origin to barbarous and sacred times; it is the fruit of the same mysterious cause as the mineral or animal world. There is a natural sentiment and prepossession in favor of age, of ancestors, of barbarous and aboriginal usages, which is a homage to the element of necessity and divinity which is in them. The respect for the old names of places, of mountains, and streams, is universal. The Indian and barbarous name can never be supplanted without loss. The ancients tell us that the gods loved the Ethiopians for their stable customs; and the Egyptians and Chaldeans, whose origin could not be explored, passed among the junior tribes of Greece and Italy for sacred nations.

Moreover, so deep is the foundation of the existing social system, that it leaves no one out of it. We may be partial, but Fate is not. All men have their root in it. You who quarrel with the arrangements of society, and are willing to embroil all, and risk the indisputable good that exists, for the chance of better, live, move, and have your being in this, and your deeds contradict your words every day. For as you cannot jump from the ground without using the resistance of the ground, nor put out the boat to sea, without shoving from the shore, nor attain liberty without rejecting obligation, so you are under the necessity of using the Actual order of things, in order to disuse it; to live by it, whilst you wish to take away its life. The past has baked your loaf, and in the strength of its bread you would break up the oven. But you are betrayed by your own nature. You also are conservatives. However men please to style themselves, I see no other than a conservative party. You are not only identical with us in your needs, but also in your methods and aims. You quarrel with my conservatism, but it is to build up one of your own; it will have a new beginning, but the same course and end, the same trials, the same passions; among the lovers of the new I observe that there is a jealousy of the newest, and that the seceder from the seceder is as damnable as the pope himself.

On these and the like grounds of general statement, conservatism plants itself without danger of being displaced. Especially before this *personal* appeal, the innovator must confess his weakness, must confess that no man is to be found good enough to be entitled to stand champion for the principle. But when this great tendency comes to practical encounters, and is challenged by young men, to whom it is no abstraction, but a fact of hunger, distress, and exclusion from opportunities, it must needs seem injurious. The youth, of course, is an innovator by the fact of his birth. There he stands, newly born on the planet, a universal beggar, with all the reason of

things, one would say, on his side. In his first consideration
how to feed, clothe, and warm himself, he is met by warnings
on every hand, that this thing and that thing have owners,
and he must go elsewhere. Then he says; If I am born into
the earth, where is my part? have the goodness, gentlemen of
this world, to show me my wood-lot, where I may fell my
wood, my field where to plant my corn, my pleasant ground
where to build my cabin.

'Touch any wood, or field, or house-lot, on your peril,' cry
all the gentlemen of this world; 'but you may come and work
in ours, for us, and we will give you a piece of bread.'

And what is that peril?

Knives and muskets, if we meet you in the act; imprisonment, if we find you afterward.

And by what authority, kind gentlemen?

By our law.

And your law,—is it just?

As just for you as it was for us. We wrought for others
under this law, and got our lands so.

I repeat the question, Is your law just?

Not quite just, but necessary. Moreover, it is juster now
than it was when we were born; we have made it milder and
more equal.

I will none of your law, returns the youth; it encumbers
me. I cannot understand, or so much as spare time to read
that needless library of your laws. Nature has sufficiently provided me with rewards and sharp penalties, to bind me not
to transgress. Like the Persian noble of old, I ask "that I may
neither command nor obey." I do not wish to enter into your
complex social system. I shall serve those whom I can, and
they who can will serve me. I shall seek those whom I love,
and shun those whom I love not, and what more can all your
laws render me?

With equal earnestness and good faith, replies to this plaintiff an upholder of the establishment, a man of many virtues:

Your opposition is feather-brained and overfine. Young
man, I have no skill to talk with you, but look at me; I have
risen early and sat late, and toiled honestly, and painfully for
very many years. I never dreamed about methods; I laid my
bones to, and drudged for the good I possess; it was not got

by fraud, nor by luck, but by work, and you must show me a warrant like these stubborn facts in your own fidelity and labor, before I suffer you, on the faith of a few fine words, to ride into my estate, and claim to scatter it as your own.

Now you touch the heart of the matter, replies the reformer. To that fidelity and labor, I pay homage. I am unworthy to arraign your manner of living, until I too have been tried. But I should be more unworthy, if I did not tell you why I cannot walk in your steps. I find this vast network, which you call property, extended over the whole planet. I cannot occupy the bleakest crag of the White Hills or the Alleghany Range, but some man or corporation steps up to me to show me that it is his. Now, though I am very peaceable, and on my private account could well enough die, since it appears there was some mistake in my creation, and that I have been *mis*sent to this earth, where all the seats were already taken,—yet I feel called upon in behalf of rational nature, which I represent, to declare to you my opinion, that, if the Earth is yours, so also is it mine. All your aggregate existences are less to me a fact than is my own; as I am born to the earth, so the Earth is given to me, what I want of it to till and to plant; nor could I, without pusillanimity, omit to claim so much. I must not only have a name to live, I must live. My genius leads me to build a different manner of life from any of yours. I cannot then spare you the whole world. I love you better. I must tell you the truth practically; and take that which you call yours. It is God's world and mine; yours as much as you want, mine as much as I want. Besides, I know your ways; I know the symptoms of the disease. To the end of your power, you will serve this lie which cheats you. Your want is a gulf which the possession of the broad earth would not fill. Yonder sun in heaven you would pluck down from shining on the universe, and make him a property and privacy, if you could; and the moon and the north star you would quickly have occasion for in your closet and bedchamber. What you do not want for use, you crave for ornament, and what your convenience could spare, your pride cannot.

On the other hand, precisely the defence which was set up for the British Constitution, namely, that with all its admitted defects, rotten boroughs and monopolies, it worked well, and substantial justice was somehow done; the wisdom and the worth did get into parliament, and every interest did by right, or might, or sleight, get represented;—the same defence is set up for the existing institutions. They are not the best; they are not just; and in respect to you, personally, O brave young man! they cannot be justified. They have, it is most true, left you no acre for your own, and no law but our law, to the ordaining of which, you were no party. But they do answer the end, they are really friendly to the good; unfriendly to the bad; they second the industrious, and the kind; they foster genius. They really have so much flexibility as to afford your talent and character, on the whole, the same chance of demonstration and success which they might have, if there was no law and no property.

It is trivial and merely superstitious to say that nothing is given you, no outfit, no exhibition; for in this institution of *credit*, which is as universal as honesty and promise in the human countenance, always some neighbor stands ready to be bread and land and tools and stock to the young adventurer. And if in any one respect they have come short, see what ample retribution of good they have made. They have lost no time and spared no expense to collect libraries, museums, galleries, colleges, palaces, hospitals, observatories, cities. The ages have not been idle, nor kings slack, nor the rich niggardly. Have we not atoned for this small offence (which we could not help) of leaving you no right in the soil, by this splendid indemnity of ancestral and national wealth? Would you have been born like a gipsy in a hedge, and preferred your freedom on a heath, and the range of a planet which had no shed or boscage to cover you from sun and wind,—to this towered and citied world? to this world of Rome, and Memphis, and Constantinople, and Vienna, and Paris, and London, and New York? For thee Naples, Florence, and Venice, for thee the fair Mediterranean, the sunny Adriatic; for thee both Indies smile; for thee the hospitable North opens its heated palaces under the polar circle; for thee roads have been cut in every direction across the land, and fleets of floating palaces with every security for strength, and provision for luxury, swim by sail and by steam through all the waters of this world. Every island for thee has a town; every town a hotel. Though thou wast born landless, yet to thy industry and thrift and small condescension to the established usage,—scores of servants are swarming in every strange place with cap and knee to thy command, scores, nay hundreds and thousands, for thy wardrobe, thy table, thy chamber, thy library, thy leisure; and every whim is anticipated and served by the best ability of the whole population of each country. The king on the throne governs for thee, and the judge judges; the barrister pleads, the farmer tills, the joiner hammers, the postman rides. Is it not exaggerating a trifle to insist on a formal acknowledgment of your claims, when these substantial advantages have been secured to you? Now can your children be educated, your labor turned to their advantage, and its fruits secured to them after your death. It is frivolous to say, you have no acre, because you have not a mathematically measured piece of land. Providence takes care that you shall have a place, that you are waited for, and come accredited; and, as soon as you put your gift to use, you shall have acre or acre's worth according to your exhibition of desert,—acre, if you need land;—acre's worth, if you prefer to draw, or carve, or make shoes, or wheels, to the tilling of the soil.

Besides, it might temper your indignation at the supposed wrong which society has done you, to keep the question before you, how society got into this predicament? Who put things on this false basis? No single man, but all men. No man voluntarily and knowingly; but it is the result of that degree of culture there is in the planet. The order of things is as good as the character of the population permits. Consider it as the work of a great and beneficent and progressive necessity, which, from the first pulsation of the first animal life, up to the present high culture of the best nations, has advanced thus far. Thank the rude fostermother though she has taught you a better wisdom than her own, and has set hopes in your heart which shall be history in the next ages. You are yourself the result of this manner of living, this foul compromise, this vituperated Sodom. It nourished you with care and love on its breast, as it had nourished many a lover of the right, and many a poet, and prophet, and teacher of men. Is it so irremediably bad? Then again, if the mitigations are considered, do not all the mischiefs virtually vanish? The form is bad, but see you not how every personal character reacts on the form, and makes it new? A strong person makes the law and custom null before his own will. Then the principle of love and truth reappears in the strictest courts of fashion and property. Under the richest robes, in the darlings of the selectest circles of European or American aristocracy, the strong heart will beat with love of mankind, with impatience of accidental distinctions, with the desire to achieve its own fate, and make every ornament it wears authentic and real.

Moreover, as we have already shown that there is no pure reformer, so it is to be considered that there is no pure conservative, no man who from the beginning to the end of his life maintains the defective institutions; but he who sets his face like a flint against every novelty, when approached in the confidence of conversation, in the presence of friendly and generous persons, has also his gracious and relenting motions, and espouses for the time the cause of man; and even if this be a shortlived emotion, yet the remembrance of it in private hours mitigates his selfishness and compliance with custom.

The Friar Bernard lamented in his cell on Mount Cenis the crimes of mankind, and rising one morning before day from his bed of moss and dry leaves, he gnawed his roots and berries, drank of the spring, and set forth to go to Rome to reform the corruption of mankind. On his way he encountered many travellers who greeted him courteously; and the cabins of the peasants and the castles of the lords supplied his few wants. When he came at last to Rome, his piety and good will easily introduced him to many families of the rich, and on the first day he saw and talked with gentle mothers with their babes at their breasts, who told him how much love they bore their children, and how they were perplexed in their daily walk lest they should fail in their duty to them. 'What!' he said, 'and this on rich embroidered carpets, on marble floors, with cunning sculpture, and carved wood, and rich pictures, and piles of books about you?'—'Look at our pictures and books,' they said, 'and we will tell you, good Father, how we spent the last evening. These are stories of godly children and holy families and romantic sacrifices made in old or in recent times by great and not mean persons; and last evening, our family was collected, and our husbands and brothers discoursed sadly on what we could save and give in the hard times.' Then came in the men, and they said, 'What cheer, brother? Does thy convent want gifts?' Then the friar Bernard went home swiftly with other thoughts than he brought, saying, 'This way of life is wrong, yet these Romans, whom I prayed God to destroy, are lovers, they are lovers; what can I do?'

The reformer concedes that these mitigations exist, and that, if he proposed comfort, he should take sides with the establishment. Your words are excellent, but they do not tell the whole. Conservatism is affluent and openhanded, but there is a cunning juggle in riches. I observe that they take somewhat for everything they give. I look bigger, but am less; I have more clothes, but am not so warm; more armor, but less courage; more books, but less wit. What you say of your planted, builded and decorated world, is true enough, and I gladly avail myself of its convenience; yet I have remarked that what holds in particular, holds in general, that the plant Man does not require for his most glorious flowering this pomp of preparation and convenience, but the thoughts of some beggarly Homer who strolled, God knows when, in the infancy and barbarism of the old world; the gravity and sense of some slave Moses who leads away his fellow slaves from their masters; the contemplation of some Scythian Anacharsis; the erect, formidable valor of some Dorian townsmen in the town of Sparta; the vigor of Clovis the Frank, and Alfred the Saxon, and Alaric the Goth, and Mahomet, Ali, and Omar the Arabians, Saladin the Curd, and Othman the Turk, sufficed to build what you call society, on the spot and in the instant when the sound mind in a sound body appeared. Rich and fine is your dress, O conservatism! your horses are of the best blood; your roads are well cut and well paved; your pantry is full of meats and your cellar of wines, and a very good state and condition are you for gentlemen and ladies to live under; but every one of these goods steals away a drop of my blood. I want the necessity of supplying my own wants. All this costly culture of yours is not necessary. Greatness does not need it. Yonder peasant, who sits neglected there in a corner, carries a whole revolution of man and nature in his head, which shall be a sacred history to some future ages. For man is the end of nature; nothing so easily organizes itself in every part of the universe as he; no moss, no lichen is so easily born; and he takes along with him and puts out from himself the whole apparatus of society and condition *extempore*, as an army encamps in a desert, and where all was just now blowing sand, creates a white city in an hour, a government, a market, a place for feasting, for conversation, and for love.

These considerations, urged by those whose characters and whose fortunes are yet to be formed, must needs command the sympathy of all reasonable persons. But beside that charity which should make all adult persons interested for the youth, and engage them to see that he has a free field and fair play on his entrance into life, we are bound to see that the society, of which we compose a part, does not permit the formation or continuance of views and practices injurious to the honor and welfare of mankind. The objection to conservatism, when embodied in a party, is, that in its love of acts, it hates principles; it lives in the senses, not in truth; it sacrifices to despair; it goes for availableness in its candidate, not for worth; and for expediency in its measures, and not for the right. Under pretence of allowing for friction, it makes so many additions and supplements to the machine of society, that it will play smoothly and softly, but will no longer grind any grist.

The conservative party in the universe concedes that the radical would talk sufficiently to the purpose, if we were still in the garden of Eden; he legislates for man as he ought to be; his theory is right, but he makes no allowance for friction; and this omission makes his whole doctrine false. The idealist retorts, that the conservative falls into a far more noxious error in the other extreme. The conservative assumes sickness as a necessity, and his social frame is a hospital, his total legislation is for the present distress, a universe in slippers and flannels, with bib and papspoon, swallowing pills and herb-tea. Sickness gets organized as well as health, the vice as well as the virtue. Now that a vicious system of trade has existed so long, it has stereotyped itself in the human generation, and misers are born. And now that sickness has got such a foothold, leprosy has grown cunning, has got into the ballot-box; the lepers outvote the clean; society has resolved itself into a Hospital Committee, and all its laws are quarantine. If any man resist, and set up a foolish hope he has entertained as good against the general despair, society frowns on him, shuts him out of her opportunities, her granaries, her refectories, her water and bread, and will serve him a sexton's turn. Conservatism takes as low a view of every part of human action and passion. Its religion is just as bad; a lozenge for the sick; a dolorous tune to beguile the distemper; mitigations of pain by pillows and anodynes; always mitigations, never remedies; pardons for sin, funeral honors,—never self-help, renovation, and virtue. Its social and political action has no better aim; to keep out wind and weather, to bring the day and year about, and make the world last our day; not to sit on the world and steer it; not to sink the memory of the past in the glory of a new and more excellent creation; a timid cobbler and patcher, it degrades whatever it touches. The cause of education is urged in this country with the utmost earnestness,—on what ground? why on this, that the people have the power, and if they are not instructed to sympathize with the intelligent, reading, trading, and governing class, inspired with a taste for the same competitions and prizes, they will upset the fair pageant of Judicature, and perhaps lay a hand on the sacred muniments of wealth itself, and new distribute the land. Religion is taught in the same spirit. The contractors who were building a road out of Baltimore, some years ago, found the Irish laborers quarrelsome and refractory, to a degree that embarrassed the agents, and seriously interrupted the progress of the work. The corporation were advised to call off the police, and build a Catholic chapel; which they did; the priest presently restored order, and the work went on prosperously. Such hints, be sure, are too valuable to be lost. If you do not value the Sabbath, or other religious institutions, give yourself no concern about maintaining them. They have already acquired a market value as conservators of property; and if priest and church-member should fail, the chambers of commerce and the presidents of the Banks, the very innholders and landlords of the county would muster with fury to their support.

Of course, religion in such hands loses its essence. Instead of that reliance, which the soul suggests on the eternity of truth and duty, men are misled into a reliance on institutions, which, the moment they cease to be the instantaneous creations of the devout sentiment, are worthless. Religion among the low becomes low. As it loses its truth, it loses credit with the sagacious. They detect the falsehood of the preaching, but when they say so, all good citizens cry, Hush; do not weaken the state, do not take off the strait jacket from dangerous persons. Every honest fellow must keep up the hoax the best he can; must patronize providence and piety, and wherever he sees anything that will keep men amused, schools or churches or poetry, or picture-galleries or music, or what not, he must cry "Hist-a-boy," and urge the game on. What a compliment we pay to the good SPIRIT with our superserviceable zeal!

But not to balance reasons for and against the establishment any longer, and if it still be asked in this necessity of partial organization, which party on the whole has the highest claims on our sympathy? I bring it home to the private heart, where all such questions must have their final arbitrement. How will every strong and generous mind choose its ground,—with the defenders of the old? or with the seekers of the new? Which is that state which promises to edify a great, brave, and beneficent man; to throw him on his resources, and tax the strength of his character? On which part will each of us find himself in the hour of health and of aspiration?

I understand well the respect of mankind for war, because that breaks up the Chinese stagnation of society, and demonstrates the personal merits of all men. A state of war or anarchy, in which law has little force, is so far valuable, that it puts every man on trial. The man of principle is known as such, and even in the fury of faction is respected. In the civil wars of France, Montaigne alone, among all the French gentry, kept his castle gates unbarred, and made his personal integrity as good at least as a regiment. The man of courage and resources is shown, and the effeminate and base person. Those who rise above war, and those who fall below it, it easily discriminates, as well as those, who, accepting its rude conditions, keep their own head by their own sword.

But in peace and a commercial state we depend, not as we ought, on our knowledge and all men's knowledge that we are honest men, but we cowardly lean on the virtue of others. For it is always at last the virtue of some men in the society, which keeps the law in any reverence and power. Is there not something shameful that I should owe my peaceful occupancy of my house and field, not to the knowledge of my countrymen that I am useful, but to their respect for sundry other reputable persons, I know not whom, whose joint virtues still keep the law in good odor?

It will never make any difference to a hero what the laws are. His greatness will shine and accomplish itself unto the end, whether they second him or not. If he have earned his bread by drudgery, and in the narrow and crooked ways which were all an evil law had left him, he will make it at least honorable by his expenditure. Of the past he will take no heed; for its wrongs he will not hold himself responsible: he will say, all the meanness of my progenitors shall not bereave me of the power to make this hour and company fair and fortunate. Whatsoever streams of power and commodity flow to me, shall of me acquire healing virtue, and become fountains of safety. Cannot I too descend a Redeemer into nature? Whosoever hereafter shall name my name, shall not record a malefactor, but a benefactor in the earth. If there be power in good intention, in fidelity, and in toil, the north wind shall be purer, the stars in heaven shall glow with a kindlier beam, that I have lived. I am primarily engaged to myself to be a public servant of all the gods, to demonstrate to all men that there is intelligence and good will at the heart of things, and ever higher and yet higher leadings. These are my engagements; how can your law further or hinder me in what I shall do to men? On the other hand, these dispositions establish their relations to me. Wherever there is worth, I shall be greeted. Wherever there are men, are the objects of my study and love. Sooner or later all men will be my friends, and will testify in all methods the energy of their regard. I cannot thank your law for my protection. I protect it. It is not in its power to protect me. It is my business to make myself revered. I depend on my honor, my labor, and my dispositions, for my place in the affections of mankind, and not on any conventions or parchments of yours.

But if I allow myself in derelictions, and become idle and dissolute, I quickly come to love the protection of a strong law, because I feel no title in myself to my advantages. To the intemperate and covetous person no love flows; to him mankind would pay no rent, no dividend, if force were once relaxed; nay, if they could give their verdict, they would say, that his self-indulgence and his oppression deserved punishment from society, and not that rich board and lodging he now enjoys. The law acts then as a screen of his unworthiness, and makes him worse the longer it protects him.

In conclusion, to return from this alternation of partial views, to the high platform of universal and necessary history, it is a happiness for mankind that innovation has got on so far, and has so free a field before it. The boldness of the hope men entertain transcends all former experience. It calms and cheers them with the picture of a simple and equal life of truth and piety. And this hope flowered on what tree? It was not imported from the stock of some celestial plant, but grew here on the wild crab of conservatism. It is much that this old and vituperated system of things has borne so fair a child. It predicts that amidst a planet peopled with conservatives, one Reformer may yet be born.

THE TRANSCENDENTALIST

*A Lecture read at the Masonic Temple, Boston,
January, 1842*

The Transcendentalist

THE FIRST THING we have to say respecting what are called *new views* here in New England, at the present time, is, that they are not new, but the very oldest of thoughts cast into the mould of these new times. The light is always identical in its composition, but it falls on a great variety of objects, and by so falling is first revealed to us, not in its own form, for it is formless, but in theirs; in like manner, thought only appears in the objects it classifies. What is popularly called Transcendentalism among us, is Idealism; Idealism as it appears in 1842. As thinkers, mankind have ever divided into two sects, Materialists and Idealists; the first class founding on experience, the second on consciousness; the first class beginning to think from the data of the senses, the second class perceive that the senses are not final, and say, the senses give us representations of things, but what are the things themselves, they cannot tell. The materialist insists on facts, on history, on the force of circumstances, and the animal wants of man; the idealist on the power of Thought and of Will, on inspiration, on miracle, on individual culture. These two modes of thinking are both natural, but the idealist contends that his way of thinking is in higher nature. He concedes all that the other affirms, admits the impressions of sense, admits their coherency, their use and beauty, and then asks the materialist for his grounds of assurance that things are as his senses represent them. But I, he says, affirm facts not affected by the illusions of sense, facts which are of the same nature as the faculty which reports them, and not liable to doubt; facts which in their first appearance to us assume a native superiority to material facts, degrading these into a language by which the first are to be spoken; facts which it only needs a retirement from the senses to discern. Every materialist will be an idealist; but an idealist can never go backward to be a materialist.

The idealist, in speaking of events, sees them as spirits. He does not deny the sensuous fact: by no means; but he will not see that alone. He does not deny the presence of this table, this chair, and the walls of this room, but he looks at these things as the reverse side of the tapestry, as the *other end*, each being a sequel or completion of a spiritual fact which nearly concerns him. This manner of looking at things, transfers every object in nature from an independent and anomalous position without there, into the consciousness. Even the materialist Condillac, perhaps the most logical expounder of materialism, was constrained to say, "Though we should soar into the heavens, though we should sink into the abyss, we never go out of ourselves; it is always our own thought that we perceive." What more could an idealist say?

The materialist, secure in the certainty of sensation, mocks at fine-spun theories, at star-gazers and dreamers, and believes that his life is solid, that he at least takes nothing for granted, but knows where he stands, and what he does. Yet how easy it is to show him, that he also is a phantom walking and working amid phantoms, and that he need only ask a question or two beyond his daily questions, to find his solid universe growing dim and impalpable before his sense. The sturdy capitalist, no matter how deep and square on blocks of Quincy granite he lays the foundations of his banking-house or Exchange, must set it, at last, not on a cube corresponding to the angles of his structure, but on a mass of unknown materials and solidity, red-hot or white-hot, perhaps at the core, which rounds off to an almost perfect sphericity, and lies floating in soft air, and goes spinning away, dragging bank and banker with it at a rate of thousands of miles the hour, he knows not whither,—a bit of bullet, now glimmering, now darkling through a small cubic space on the edge of an unimaginable pit of emptiness. And this wild balloon, in which his whole venture is embarked, is a just symbol of his whole state and faculty. One thing, at least, he says is certain, and does not give me the headache, that figures do not lie; the multiplication table has been hitherto found unimpeachable truth; and, moreover, if I put a gold eagle in my safe, I find it again to-morrow;—but for these thoughts, I know not whence they are. They change and pass away. But ask him why he believes that an uniform experience will continue uniform, or on what grounds he founds his faith in his figures, and he will perceive that his mental fabric is built up on just as strange and quaking foundations as his proud edifice of stone.

In the order of thought, the materialist takes his departure from the external world, and esteems a man as one product of that. The idealist takes his departure from his consciousness, and reckons the world an appearance. The materialist respects sensible masses, Society, Government, social art, and luxury, every establishment, every mass, whether majority of numbers, or extent of space, or amount of objects, every social action. The idealist has another measure, which is metaphysical, namely, the *rank* which things themselves take in his consciousness; not at all, the size or appearance. Mind is the only reality, of which men and all other natures are better or worse reflectors. Nature, literature, history, are only subjective phenomena. Although in his action overpowered by the laws of action, and so, warmly coöperating with men, even preferring them to himself, yet when he speaks scientifically, or after the order of thought, he is constrained to degrade persons into representatives of truths. He does not respect labor, or the products of labor, namely, property, otherwise than as a manifold symbol, illustrating with wonderful fidelity of details the laws of being; he does not respect government, except as far as it reiterates the law of his mind; nor the church; nor charities; nor arts, for themselves; but hears, as at a vast distance, what they say, as if his consciousness would speak to him through a pantomimic scene. His thought,— that is the Universe. His experience inclines him to behold the procession of facts you call the world, as flowing perpetually outward from an invisible, unsounded centre in himself, centre alike of him and of them, and necessitating him to regard all things as having a subjective or relative existence, relative to that aforesaid Unknown Centre of him.

From this transfer of the world into the consciousness, this beholding of all things in the mind, follow easily his whole ethics. It is simpler to be self-dependent. The height, the deity of man is, to be self-sustained, to need no gift, no foreign force. Society is good when it does not violate me; but best when it is likest to solitude. Everything real is self-existent. Everything divine shares the self-existence of Deity. All that you call the world is the shadow of that substance which you are, the perpetual creation of the powers of thought, of those that are dependent and of those that are independent of your will. Do not cumber yourself with fruitless pains to mend and remedy remote effects; let the soul be erect, and all things will go well. You think me the child of my circumstances: I make my circumstance. Let any thought or motive of mine be different from that they are, the difference will transform my condition and economy. I—this thought which is called I,— is the mould into which the world is poured like melted wax. The mould is invisible, but the world betrays the shape of the mould. You call it the power of circumstance, but it is the power of me. Am I in harmony with myself? my position will seem to you just and commanding. Am I vicious and insane? my fortunes will seem to you obscure and descending. As I am, so shall I associate, and, so shall I act; Cæsar's history will paint out Cæsar. Jesus acted so, because he thought so. I do not wish to overlook or to gainsay any reality; I say, I make my circumstance: but if you ask me, Whence am I? I feel like other men my relation to that Fact which cannot be spoken, or defined, nor even thought, but which exists, and will exist.

The Transcendentalist adopts the whole connection of spiritual doctrine. He believes in miracle, in the perpetual openness of the human mind to new influx of light and power; he believes in inspiration, and in ecstasy. He wishes that the spiritual principle should be suffered to demonstrate itself to the end, in all possible applications to the state of man, without the admission of anything unspiritual; that is, anything positive, dogmatic, personal. Thus, the spiritual measure of inspiration is the depth of the thought, and never, who said it? And so he resists all attempts to palm other rules and measures on the spirit than its own.

In action, he easily incurs the charge of antinomianism by his avowal that he, who has the Lawgiver, may with safety not only neglect, but even contravene every written commandment. In the play of Othello, the expiring Desdemona absolves her husband of the murder, to her attendant Emilia. Afterwards, when Emilia charges him with the crime, Othello exclaims,

"You heard her say herself it was not I."

Emilia replies,

"The more angel she, and thou the blacker devil."

Of this fine incident, Jacobi, the Transcendental moralist, makes use, with other parallel instances, in his reply to Fichte. Jacobi, refusing all measure of right and wrong except the determinations of the private spirit, remarks that there is no crime but has sometimes been a virtue. "I," he says, "am that atheist, that godless person who, in opposition to an imaginary doctrine of calculation, would lie as the dying Desdemona lied; would lie and deceive, as Pylades when he personated Orestes; would assassinate like Timoleon; would perjure myself like Epaminondas, and John de Witt; I would resolve on suicide like Cato; I would commit sacrilege with David; yea, and pluck ears of corn on the Sabbath, for no other reason than that I was fainting for lack of food. For, I have assurance in myself, that, in pardoning these faults according to the letter, man exerts the sovereign right which the majesty of his being confers on him; he sets the seal of his divine nature to the grace he accords."*

In like manner, if there is anything grand and daring in human thought or virtue, any reliance on the vast, the unknown; any presentiment; any extravagance of faith, the spiritualist adopts it as most in nature. The oriental mind has always tended to this largeness. Buddhism is an expression of it. The Buddhist who thanks no man, who says, "do not flatter your benefactors," but who, in his conviction that every good deed can by no possibility escape its reward, will not deceive the benefactor by pretending that he has done more than he should, is a Transcendentalist.

You will see by this sketch that there is no such thing as a Transcendental party; that there is no pure Transcendentalist; that we know of none but prophets and heralds of such a philosophy; that all who by strong bias of nature have leaned to the spiritual side in doctrine, have stopped short of their goal. We have had many harbingers and forerunners; but of a purely spiritual life, history has afforded no example. I mean, we have yet no man who has leaned entirely on his character, and eaten angels' food; who, trusting to his sentiments, found

*Coleridge's Translation.

life made of miracles; who, working for universal aims, found himself fed, he knew not how; clothed, sheltered, and weaponed, he knew not how, and yet it was done by his own hands. Only in the instinct of the lower animals, we find the suggestion of the methods of it, and something higher than our understanding. The squirrel hoards nuts, and the bee gathers honey, without knowing what they do, and they are thus provided for without selfishness or disgrace.

Shall we say, then, that Transcendentalism is the Saturnalia or excess of Faith; the presentiment of a faith proper to man in his integrity, excessive only when his imperfect obedience hinders the satisfaction of his wish. Nature is transcendental, exists primarily, necessarily, ever works and advances, yet takes no thought for the morrow. Man owns the dignity of the life which throbs around him in chemistry, and tree, and animal, and in the involuntary functions of his own body; yet he is balked when he tries to fling himself into this enchanted circle, where all is done without degradation. Yet genius and virtue predict in man the same absence of private ends, and of condescension to circumstances, united with every trait and talent of beauty and power.

This way of thinking, falling on Roman times, made Stoic philosophers; falling on despotic times, made patriot Catos and Brutuses; falling on superstitious times, made prophets and apostles; on popish times, made protestants and ascetic monks, preachers of Faith against the preachers of Works; on prelatical times, made Puritans and Quakers; and falling on Unitarian and commercial times, makes the peculiar shades of Idealism which we know.

It is well known to most of my audience, that the Idealism of the present day acquired the name of Transcendental, from the use of that term by Immanuel Kant, of Konigsberg, who replied to the skeptical philosophy of Locke, which insisted that there was nothing in the intellect which was not previously in the experience of the senses, by showing that there was a very important class of ideas, or imperative forms, which did not come by experience, but through which experience was acquired; that these were intuitions of the mind itself; and he denominated them *Transcendental* forms. The extraordinary profoundness and precision of that man's thinking have given vogue to his nomenclature, in Europe and America, to that extent, that whatever belongs to the class of intuitive thought, is popularly called at the present day *Transcendental.*

Although, as we have said, there is no pure Transcendentalist, yet the tendency to respect the intuitions, and to give them, at least in our creed, all authority over our experience, has deeply colored the conversation and poetry of the present day; and the history of genius and of religion in these times, though impure, and as yet not incarnated in any powerful individual, will be the history of this tendency.

It is a sign of our times, conspicuous to the coarsest observer, that many intelligent and religious persons withdraw themselves from the common labors and competitions of the market and the caucus, and betake themselves to a certain solitary and critical way of living, from which no solid fruit has yet appeared to justify their separation. They hold themselves aloof: they feel the disproportion between their faculties and the work offered them, and they prefer to ramble in the country and perish of ennui, to the degradation of such charities and such ambitions as the city can propose to them. They are striking work, and crying out for somewhat worthy to do! What they do, is done only because they are overpowered by the humanities that speak on all sides; and they consent to such labor as is open to them, though to their lofty dream the writing of Iliads or Hamlets, or the building of cities or empires seems drudgery.

Now every one must do after his kind, be he asp or angel, and these must. The question, which a wise man and a student of modern history will ask, is, what that kind is? And truly, as in ecclesiastical history we take so much pains to know what the Gnostics, what the Essenes, what the Manichees, and what the Reformers believed, it would not misbecome us to inquire nearer home, what these companions and contemporaries of ours think and do, at least so far as these thoughts and actions appear to be not accidental and personal, but common to many, and the inevitable flower of the Tree of Time. Our American literature and spiritual history are, we confess, in the optative mood; but whoso knows these seething brains, these admirable radicals, these unsocial worshippers, these talkers who talk the sun and moon away, will believe that this heresy cannot pass away without leaving its mark.

They are lonely; the spirit of their writing and conversation is lonely; they repel influences; they shun general society; they incline to shut themselves in their chamber in the house, to live in the country rather than in the town, and to find their tasks and amusements in solitude. Society, to be sure, does not like this very well; it saith, Whoso goes to walk alone, accuses the whole world; he declareth all to be unfit to be his companions; it is very uncivil, nay, insulting; Society will retaliate. Meantime, this retirement does not proceed from any whim on the part of these separators; but if any one will take pains to talk with them, he will find that this part is chosen both from temperament and from principle; with some unwillingness, too, and as a choice of the less of two evils; for these persons are not by nature melancholy, sour, and unsocial,—they are not stockish or brute,—but joyous; susceptible, affectionate; they have even more than others a great wish to be loved. Like the young Mozart, they are rather ready to cry ten times a day, "But are you sure you love me?" Nay, if they tell you their whole thought, they will own that love seems to them the last and highest gift of nature; that there are persons whom in their hearts they daily thank for existing,—persons whose faces are perhaps unknown to them, but whose fame and spirit have penetrated their solitude,—and for whose sake they wish to exist. To behold the beauty of another character, which inspires a new interest in our own; to behold the beauty lodged in a human being, with such vivacity of apprehension, that I am instantly forced home to inquire if I am not deformity itself: to behold in another the expression of a love so high that it assures itself,—assures itself also to me against every possible casualty except my unworthiness;—these are degrees on the scale of human happiness, to which they have ascended; and it is a fidelity to this sentiment which has made common association distasteful to them. They wish a just and even fellowship, or none. They cannot gossip with you, and they do not wish, as they are sincere and religious, to gratify any mere curiosity which you may entertain. Like fairies, they do not wish to be spoken of. Love me, they say, but do not ask who is my cousin and my uncle. If you do not need to hear my thought, because you can read it in my face and behavior, then I will tell it you from sunrise to sunset. If you cannot divine it, you would not understand what I say. I will not molest myself for you. I do not wish to be profaned.

And yet, it seems as if this loneliness, and not this love, would prevail in their circumstances, because of the extravagant demand they make on human nature. That, indeed, constitutes a new feature in their portrait, that they are the most exacting and extortionate critics. Their quarrel with every man they meet, is not with his kind, but with his degree. There is not enough of him,—that is the only fault. They prolong their privilege of childhood in this wise, of doing nothing,—but making immense demands on all the gladiators in the lists of action and fame. They make us feel the strange disappointment which overcasts every human youth. So many promising youths, and never a finished man! The profound nature will have a savage rudeness; the delicate one will be shallow, or the victim of sensibility; the richly accomplished will have some capital absurdity; and so every piece has a crack. 'T is strange, but this masterpiece is a result of such an extreme delicacy, that the most unobserved flaw in the boy will neutralize the most aspiring genius, and spoil the work. Talk with a seaman of the hazards to life in his profession, and he will ask you, "Where are the old sailors? do you not see that all are young men?" And we, on this sea of human thought, in like manner inquire, Where are the old idealists? where are they who represented to the last generation that extravagant hope, which a few happy aspirants suggest to ours? In looking at the class of counsel, and power, and wealth, and at the matronage of the land, amidst all the prudence and all the triviality, one asks, Where are they who represented genius, virtue, the invisible and heavenly world, to these? Are they dead,—taken in early ripeness to the gods,— as ancient wisdom foretold their fate? Or did the high idea die out of them, and leave their unperfumed body as its tomb and tablet, announcing to all that the celestial inhabitant, who once gave them beauty, had departed? Will it be better with the new generation? We easily predict a fair future to each new candidate who enters the lists, but we are frivolous and volatile, and by low aims and ill example do what we can to defeat this hope. Then these youths bring us a rough but effectual aid. By their unconcealed dissatisfaction, they expose our poverty, and the insignificance of man to man. A man is a poor limitary benefactor. He ought to be a shower of benefits—a great influence, which should never let his brother go, but should refresh old merits continually with new ones; so that, though absent, he should never be out of my mind, his name never far from my lips; but if the earth should open at my side, or my last hour were come, his name should be the prayer I should utter to the Universe. But in our experience, man is cheap, and friendship wants its deep sense. We affect to dwell with our friends in their absence, but we do not; when deed, word, or letter comes not, they let us go. These exacting children advertise us of our wants. There is no compliment, no smooth speech with them; they pay you only this one compliment, of insatiable expectation; they aspire, they severely exact, and if they only stand fast in this watchtower, and persist in demanding unto the end, and without end, then are they terrible friends, whereof poet and priest cannot choose but stand in awe; and what if they eat clouds, and drink wind, they have not been without service to the race of man.

With this passion for what is great and extraordinary, it cannot be wondered at, that they are repelled by vulgarity and frivolity in people. They say to themselves, It is better to be alone than in bad company. And it is really a wish to be met,—the wish to find society for their hope and religion,—which prompts them to shun what is called society. They feel that they are never so fit for friendship, as when they have quitted mankind, and taken themselves to friend. A picture, a book, a favorite spot in the hills or the woods, which they can people with the fair and worthy creation of the fancy, can give them often forms so vivid, that these for the time shall seem real, and society the illusion.

But their solitary and fastidious manners not only withdraw them from the conversation, but from the labors of the world; they are not good citizens, not good members of society; unwillingly they bear their part of the public and private burdens; they do not willingly share in the public charities, in the public religious rites, in the enterprises of education, of missions foreign or domestic, in the abolition of the slave-trade, or in the temperance society. They do not even like to vote. The philanthropists inquire whether Transcendentalism does not mean sloth: they had as lief hear that their friend is dead, as that he is a Transcendentalist; for then is he paralyzed, and can never do anything for humanity. What right, cries the good world, has the man of genius to retreat from work, and indulge himself? The popular literary creed seems to be, 'I am a sublime genius; I ought not therefore to labor.' But genius is the power to labor better and more availably. Deserve thy genius: exalt it. The good, the illuminated, sit apart from the rest, censuring their dulness and vices, as if they thought that, by sitting very grand in their chairs, the very brokers, attorneys, and congressmen would see the error of their ways, and flock to them. But the good and wise must learn to act, and carry salvation to the combatants and demagogues in the dusty arena below.

On the part of these children, it is replied, that life and their faculty seem to them gifts too rich to be squandered on such trifles as you propose to them. What you call your fundamental institutions, your great and holy causes, seem to them great abuses, and, when nearly seen, paltry matters. Each 'Cause,' as it is called, — say Abolition, Temperance, say Calvinism, or Unitarianism, — becomes speedily a little shop, where the article, let it have been at first never so subtle and ethereal, is now made up into portable and convenient cakes, and retailed in small quantities to suit purchasers. You make very free use of these words 'great' and 'holy,' but few things appear to them such. Few persons have any magnificence of nature to inspire enthusiasm, and the philanthropies and charities have a certain air of quackery. As to the general course of living, and the daily employments of men, they cannot see much virtue in these, since they are parts of this vicious circle; and, as no great ends are answered by the men, there is nothing noble in the arts by which they are maintained. Nay, they have made the experiment, and found that, from the liberal professions to the coarsest manual labor, and from the courtesies of the academy and the college to the conventions of the cotillon-room and the morning call, there is a spirit of cowardly compromise and seeming, which intimates a frightful skepticism, a life without love, and an activity without an aim.

Unless the action is necessary, unless it is adequate, I do not wish to perform it. I do not wish to do one thing but once. I do not love routine. Once possessed of the principle, it is equally easy to make four or forty thousand applications of it. A great man will be content to have indicated in any the slightest manner his perception of the reigning Idea of his time, and will leave to those who like it the multiplication of examples. When he has hit the white, the rest may shatter the target. Every thing admonishes us how needlessly long life is. Every moment of a hero so raises and cheers us, that a twelvemonth is an age. All that the brave Xanthus brings home from his wars, is the recollection that, at the storming of Samos, "in the heat of the battle, Pericles smiled on me, and passed on to another detachment." It is the quality of the moment, not the number of days, of events, or of actors, that imports.

New, we confess, and by no means happy, is our condition: if you want the aid of our labor, we ourselves stand in greater want of the labor. We are miserable with inaction. We perish of rest and rust: but we do not like your work.

'Then,' says the world, 'show me your own.'

'We have none.'

'What will you do, then?' cries the world.

'We will wait.'

'How long?'

'Until the Universe rises up and calls us to work.'

'But whilst you wait, you grow old and useless.'

'Be it so: I can sit in a corner and *perish*, (as you call it,) but I will not move until I have the highest command. If no call should come for years, for centuries, then I know that the want of the Universe is the attestation of faith by my abstinence. Your virtuous projects, so called, do not cheer me. I know that which shall come will cheer me. If I cannot work, at least I need not lie. All that is clearly due to-day is not to lie. In other places, other men have encountered sharp trials, and have behaved themselves well. The martyrs were sawn asunder, or hung alive on meat-hooks. Cannot we screw our courage to patience and truth, and without complaint, or even with good-humor, await our turn of action in the Infinite Counsels?'

But, to come a little closer to the secret of these persons, we must say, that to them it seems a very easy matter to answer the objections of the man of the world, but not so easy to dispose of the doubts and objections that occur to themselves. They are exercised in their own spirit with queries, which acquaint them with all adversity, and with the trials of the bravest heroes. When I asked them concerning their private experience, they answered somewhat in this wise: It is not to be denied that there must be some wide difference between my faith and other faith; and mine is a certain brief experience, which surprised me in the highway or in the market, in some place, at some time,—whether in the body or out of the body, God knoweth,—and made me aware that I had played the fool with fools all this time, but that law existed for me and for all; that to me belonged trust, a child's trust and obedience, and the worship of ideas, and I should never be fool more. Well, in the space of an hour, probably, I was let down from this height; I was at my old tricks, the selfish member of a selfish society. My life is superficial, takes no root in the deep world; I ask, When shall I die, and be relieved of the responsibility of seeing an Universe which I do not use? I wish to exchange this flash-of-lightning faith for continuous daylight, this fever-glow for a benign climate.

These two states of thought diverge every moment, and stand in wild contrast. To him who looks at his life from these moments of illumination, it will seem that he skulks and plays a mean, shiftless, and subaltern part in the world. That is to be done which he has not skill to do, or to be said which others can say better, and he lies by, or occupies his hands with some plaything, until his hour comes again. Much of our reading, much of our labor, seems mere waiting: it was not that we were born for. Any other could do it as well, or better. So little skill enters into these works, so little do they mix with the divine life, that it really signifies little what we do, whether we turn a grindstone, or ride, or run, or make fortunes, or govern the state. The worst feature of this double consciousness is, that the two lives, of the understanding and of the soul, which we lead, really show very little relation to each other, never meet and measure each other: one prevails now, all buzz and din; and the other prevails then, all infinitude and paradise; and, with the progress of life, the two discover no greater disposition to reconcile themselves. Yet, what is my faith? What am I? What but a thought of serenity and independence, an abode in the deep blue sky? Presently the clouds shut down again; yet we retain the belief that this petty web we weave will at last be overshot and reticulated with veins of the blue, and that the moments will characterize the days. Patience, then, is for us, is it not? Patience, and still patience. When we pass, as presently we shall, into some new infinitude, out of this Iceland of negations, it will please us to reflect that, though we had few virtues or consolations, we bore with our indigence, nor once strove to repair it with hypocrisy or false heat of any kind.

But this class are not sufficiently characterized, if we omit to add that they are lovers and worshippers of Beauty. In the eternal trinity of Truth, Goodness, and Beauty, each in its perfection including the three, they prefer to make Beauty the sign and head. Something of the same taste is observable in all the moral movements of the time, in the religious and benevolent enterprises. They have a liberal, even an æsthetic spirit. A reference to Beauty in action sounds, to be sure, a little hollow and ridiculous in the ears of the old church. In politics, it has often sufficed, when they treated of justice, if they kept the bounds of selfish calculation. If they granted restitution, it was prudence which granted it. But the justice which is now claimed for the black, and the pauper, and the drunkard is for Beauty,—is for a necessity to the soul of the agent, not of the beneficiary. I say, this is the tendency, not yet the realization. Our virtue totters and trips, does not yet walk firmly. Its representatives are austere; they preach and denounce; their rectitude is not yet a grace. They are still liable to that slight taint of burlesque which, in our strange world, attaches to the zealot. A saint should be as dear as the apple of the eye. Yet we are tempted to smile, and we flee from the working to the speculative reformer, to escape that same slight ridicule. Alas for these days of derision and criticism! We call the Beautiful the highest, because it appears to us the golden mean, escaping the dowdiness of the good, and the heartlessness of the true.—They are lovers of nature also, and find an indemnity in the inviolable order of the world for the violated order and grace of man.

There is, no doubt, a great deal of well-founded objection to be spoken or felt against the sayings and doings of this class, some of whose traits we have selected; no doubt, they will lay themselves open to criticism and to lampoons, and as ridiculous stories will be to be told of them as of any. There will be cant and pretension; there will be subtilty and moonshine. These persons are of unequal strength, and do not all prosper. They complain that everything around them must be denied; and if feeble, it takes all their strength to deny, before they can begin to lead their own life. Grave seniors insist on their respect to this institution, and that usage; to an obsolete history; to some vocation, or college, or etiquette, or beneficiary, or charity, or morning or evening call, which they resist, as what does not concern them. But it costs such sleepless nights, alienations and misgivings,—they have so many moods about it;—these old guardians never change *their* minds; they have but one mood on the subject, namely, that Antony is very perverse,—that it is quite as much as Antony can do, to assert his rights, abstain from what he thinks foolish, and keep his temper. He cannot help the reaction of this injustice in his own mind. He is braced-up and stilted; all freedom and flowing genius, all sallies of wit and frolic nature are quite out of the question; it is well if he can keep from lying, injustice, and suicide. This is no time for gaiety and grace. His strength and spirits are wasted in rejection. But the strong spirits overpower those around them without effort. Their thought and emotion comes in like a flood, quite withdraws them from all notice of these carping critics; they surrender themselves with glad heart to the heavenly guide, and only by implication reject the clamorous nonsense of the hour. Grave seniors talk to the deaf,—church and old book mumble and ritualize to an unheeding, preöccupied and advancing mind, and thus they by happiness of greater momentum lose no time, but take the right road at first.

But all these of whom I speak are not proficients; they are novices; they only show the road in which man should travel, when the soul has greater health and prowess. Yet let them feel the dignity of their charge, and deserve a larger power. Their heart is the ark in which the fire is concealed, which shall burn in a broader and universal flame. Let them obey the Genius then most when his impulse is wildest; then most when he seems to lead to uninhabitable desarts of thought and life; for the path which the hero travels alone is the highway of health and benefit to mankind. What is the privilege and nobility of our nature, but its persistency, through its power to attach itself to what is permanent?

Society also has its duties in reference to this class, and must behold them with what charity it can. Possibly some benefit may yet accrue from them to the state. In our Mechanics' Fair, there must be not only bridges, ploughs, carpenters' planes, and baking troughs, but also some few finer instruments,—raingauges, thermometers, and telescopes; and in society, besides farmers, sailors, and weavers, there must be a few persons of purer fire kept specially as gauges and meters of character; persons of a fine, detecting instinct, who betray the smallest accumulations of wit and feeling in the bystander. Perhaps too there might be room for the exciters and monitors; collectors of the heavenly spark with power to convey the electricity to others. Or, as the storm-tossed vessel at sea speaks the frigate or 'line packet' to learn its longitude, so it may not be without its advantage that we should now and then encounter rare and gifted men, to compare the points of our spiritual compass, and verify our bearings from superior chronometers.

Amidst the downward tendency and proneness of things, when every voice is raised for a new road or another statute, or a subscription of stock, for an improvement in dress, or in dentistry, for a new house or a larger business, for a political party, or the division of an estate,—will you not tolerate one or two solitary voices in the land, speaking for thoughts and principles not marketable or perishable? Soon these improvements and mechanical inventions will be superseded; these modes of living lost out of memory; these cities rotted, ruined by war, by new inventions, by new seats of trade, or the geologic changes:—all gone, like the shells which sprinkle the seabeach with a white colony to-day, forever renewed to be forever destroyed. But the thoughts which these few hermits strove to proclaim by silence, as well as by speech, not only by what they did, but by what they forbore to do, shall abide in beauty and strength, to reorganize themselves in nature, to invest themselves anew in other, perhaps higher endowed and happier mixed clay than ours, in fuller union with the surrounding system.

THE YOUNG AMERICAN

A Lecture read before the Mercantile Library Association,
Boston, February 7, 1844

The Young American

IT IS REMARKABLE, that our people have their intellectual culture from one country, and their duties from another. This false state of things is newly in a way to be corrected. America is beginning to assert itself to the senses and to the imagination of her children, and Europe is receding in the same degree. This their reaction on education gives a new importance to the internal improvements and to the politics of the country. Who has not been stimulated to reflection by the facilities now in progress of construction for travel and the transportation of goods in the United States?

This rage for road building is beneficent for America, where vast distance is so main a consideration in our domestic politics and trade, inasmuch as the great political promise of the invention is to hold the Union staunch, whose days seemed already numbered by the mere inconvenience of transporting representatives, judges, and officers across such tedious distances of land and water. Not only is distance annihilated, but when, as now, the locomotive and the steamboat, like enormous shuttles, shoot every day across the thousand various threads of national descent and employment, and bind them fast in one web, an hourly assimilation goes forward, and there is no danger that local peculiarities and hostilities should be preserved.

1. But I hasten to speak of the utility of these improvements in creating an American sentiment. An unlooked for consequence of the railroad, is the increased acquaintance it has given the American people with the boundless resources of their own soil. If this invention has reduced England to a third of its size, by bringing people so much nearer, in this country it has given a new celerity to *time*, or anticipated by fifty years the planting of tracts of land, the choice of water privileges, the working of mines, and other natural advantages. Railroad iron is a magician's rod, in its power to evoke the sleeping energies of land and water.

The railroad is but one arrow in our quiver, though it has great value as a sort of yard-stick, and surveyor's line. The bountiful continent is ours, state on state, and territory on territory, to the waves of the Pacific sea;

> "Our garden is the immeasurable earth,
> The heaven's blue pillars are Medea's house."

The task of surveying, planting, and building upon this immense tract, requires an education and a sentiment commensurate thereto. A consciousness of this fact, is beginning to take the place of the purely trading spirit and education which sprang up whilst all the population lived on the fringe of sea-coast. And even on the coast, prudent men have begun to see that every American should be educated with a view to the values of land. The arts of engineering and of architecture are studied; scientific agriculture is an object of growing attention; the mineral riches are explored; limestone, coal, slate, and iron; and the value of timber-lands is enhanced.

Columbus alleged as a reason for seeking a continent in the West, that the harmony of nature required a great tract of land in the western hemisphere, to balance the known extent of land in the eastern; and it now appears that we must estimate the native values of this broad region to redress the balance of our own judgments, and appreciate the advantages opened to the human race in this country, which is our fortunate home. The land is the appointed remedy for whatever is false and fantastic in our culture. The continent we inhabit is to be physic and food for our mind, as well as our body. The land, with its tranquilizing, sanative influences, is to repair the errors of a scholastic and traditional education, and bring us into just relations with men and things.

The habit of living in the presence of these invitations of natural wealth is not inoperative; and this habit, combined with the moral sentiment which, in the recent years, has interrogated every institution, usage, and law, has, naturally, given a strong direction to the wishes and aims of active young men to withdraw from cities, and cultivate the soil. This inclination has appeared in the most unlooked for quarters, in men supposed to be absorbed in business, and in those connected with the liberal professions. And, since the walks of trade were crowded, whilst that of agriculture cannot easily be, inasmuch as the farmer who is not wanted by others can yet grow his own bread, whilst the manufacturer or the trader, who is not wanted, cannot,—this seemed a happy tendency. For, beside all the moral benefit which we may expect from the farmer's profession, when a man enters it considerately, this promised the conquering of the soil, plenty, and beyond this, the adorning of the country with every advantage and ornament which labor, ingenuity, and affection for a man's home, could suggest.

Meantime, with cheap land, and the pacific disposition of the people, every thing invites to the arts of agriculture, of gardening, and domestic architecture. Public gardens, on the scale of such plantations in Europe and Asia, are now unknown to us. There is no feature of the old countries that strikes an American with more agreeable surprise than the beautiful gardens of Europe; such as the Boboli in Florence, the Villa Borghese in Rome, the Villa d'Este in Tivoli, the gardens at Munich, and at Frankfort on the Maine: works easily imitated here, and which might well make the land dear to the citizen, and inflame patriotism. It is the fine art which is left for us, now that sculpture, painting, and religious and civil architecture have become effete, and have passed into second childhood. We have twenty degrees of latitude wherein to choose a seat, and the new modes of travelling enlarge the opportunity of selection, by making it easy to cultivate very distant tracts, and yet remain in strict intercourse with the centres of trade and population. And the whole force of all the arts goes to facilitate the decoration of lands and dwellings. A garden has this advantage, that it makes it indifferent where you live. A well-laid garden makes the face of the country of no account; let that be low or high, grand or mean, you have made a beautiful abode worthy of man. If the landscape is pleasing, the garden shows it,—if tame, it excludes it. A little grove, which any farmer can find, or cause to grow near his house, will, in a few years, make cataracts and chains of mountains quite unnecessary to his scenery; and he is so contented with his alleys, woodlands, orchards, and river, that Niagara, and the Notch of the White Hills, and Nantasket Beach, are superfluities. And yet the selection of a fit houselot has the same advantage over an indifferent one, as the selection to a given employment of a man who has a genius for that work. In the last case, the culture of years will never make the most painstaking apprentice his equal: no more will gardening give the advantage of a happy site to a house in a hole or on a pinnacle. In America, we have hitherto little to boast in this kind. The cities drain the country of the best part of its population: the flower of the youth, of both sexes, goes into the towns, and the country is cultivated by a so much inferior class. The land,—travel a whole day together,—looks poverty-stricken, and the buildings plain and poor. In Europe, where society has an aristocratic structure, the land is full of men of the best stock, and the best culture, whose interest and pride it is to remain half the year on their estates, and to fill them with every convenience and ornament. Of course, these make model farms, and model architecture, and are a constant education to the eye of the surrounding population. Whatever events in progress shall go to disgust men with cities, and infuse into them the passion for country life, and country pleasures, will render a service to the whole face of this continent, and will further the most poetic of all the occupations of real life, the bringing out by art the native but hidden graces of the landscape.

I look on such improvements, also, as directly tending to endear the land to the inhabitant. Any relation to the land, the habit of tilling it, or mining it, or even hunting on it, generates the feeling of patriotism. He who keeps shop on it, or he who merely uses it as a support to his desk and ledger, or to his manufactory, values it less. The vast majority of the people of this country live by the land, and carry its quality in their manners and opinions. We in the Atlantic states, by position, have been commercial, and have, as I said, imbibed easily an European culture. Luckily for us, now that steam has narrowed the Atlantic to a strait, the nervous, rocky West is intruding a new and continental element into the national mind, and we shall yet have an American genius. How much better when the whole land is a garden, and the people have grown up in the bowers of a paradise. Without looking, then, to those extraordinary social influences which are now acting in precisely this direction, but only at what is inevitably doing around us, I think we must regard the *land* as a commanding and increasing power on the citizen, the sanative and Americanizing influence, which promises to disclose new virtues for ages to come.

2. In the second place, the uprise and culmination of the new and anti-feudal power of Commerce, is the political fact of most significance to the American at this hour.

We cannot look on the freedom of this country, in connexion with its youth, without a presentiment that here shall laws and institutions exist on some scale of proportion to the majesty of nature. To men legislating for the area betwixt the two oceans, betwixt the snows and the tropics, somewhat of the gravity of nature will infuse itself into the code. A heterogeneous population crowding on all ships from all corners of the world to the great gates of North America, namely, Boston, New York, and New Orleans, and thence proceeding inward to the prairie and the mountains, and quickly contributing their private thought to the public opinion, their toll to the treasury, and their vote to the election, it cannot be doubted that the legislation of this country should become more catholic and cosmopolitan than that of any other. It seems so easy for America to inspire and express the most expansive and humane spirit; new-born, free, healthful, strong, the land of the laborer, of the democrat, of the philanthropist, of the believer, of the saint, she should speak for the human race. It is the country of the Future. From Washington, proverbially 'the city of magnificent distances,' through all its cities, states, and territories, it is a country of beginnings, of projects, of designs, and expectations.

Gentlemen, there is a sublime and friendly Destiny by which the human race is guided,—the race never dying, the individual never spared,—to results affecting masses and ages. Men are narrow and selfish, but the Genius or Destiny is not narrow, but beneficent. It is not discovered in their calculated and voluntary activity, but in what befalls, with or without their design. Only what is inevitable interests us, and it turns out that love and good are inevitable, and in the course of things. That Genius has infused itself into nature. It indicates itself by a small excess of good, a small balance in brute facts always favorable to the side of reason. All the facts in any part of nature shall be tabulated, and the results shall indicate the same security and benefit; so slight as to be hardly observable, and yet it is there. The sphere is flattened at the poles, and swelled at the equator; a form flowing necessarily from the fluid state, yet *the* form, the mathematician assures us, required to prevent the protuberances of the continent, or even of lesser mountains cast up at any time by earthquakes, from continually deranging the axis of the earth. The census of the population is found to keep an invariable equality in the sexes, with a trifling predominance in favor of the male, as if to counterbalance the necessarily increased exposure of male life in war, navigation, and other accidents. Remark the unceasing effort throughout nature at somewhat better than the actual creatures: *amelioration in nature*, which alone permits and authorizes amelioration in mankind. The population of the world is a conditional population; these are not the best, but the best that could live in the existing state of soils, gases, animals, and morals: the best that could *yet* live; there shall be a better, please God. This Genius, or Destiny, is of the sternest administration, though rumors exist of its secret tenderness. It may be styled a cruel kindness, serving the whole even to the ruin of the member; a terrible communist, reserving all profits to the community, without dividend to individuals. Its law is, you shall have everything as a member, nothing to yourself. For Nature is the noblest engineer, yet uses a grinding economy, working up all that is wasted to-day into to-morrow's creation; — not a superfluous grain of sand, for all the ostentation she makes of expense and public works. It is because Nature thus saves and uses, laboring for the general, that we poor particulars are so crushed and straitened, and find it so hard to live. She flung us out in her plenty, but we cannot shed a hair, or a paring of a nail, but instantly she snatches at the shred, and appropriates it to the general stock. Our condition is like that of the poor wolves: if one of the flock wound himself, or so much as limp, the rest eat him up incontinently.

That serene Power interposes the check upon the caprices and officiousness of our wills. Its charity is not our charity. One of its agents is our will, but that which expresses itself in our will, is stronger than our will. We are very forward to help it, but it will not be accelerated. It resists our meddling, eleemosynary contrivances. We devise sumptuary and relief laws, but the principle of population is always reducing wages to the lowest pittance on which human life can be sustained. We legislate against forestalling and monopoly; we would have a common granary for the poor; but the selfishness which hoards the corn for high prices, is the preventive of famine; and the law of self-preservation is surer policy than any legislation can be. We concoct eleemosynary systems, and it turns out that our charity increases pauperism. We inflate our paper currency, we repair commerce with unlimited credit, and are presently visited with unlimited bankruptcy.

It is easy to see that the existing generation are conspiring with a beneficence, which, in its working for coming generations, sacrifices the passing one, which infatuates the most selfish men to act against their private interest for the public welfare. We build railroads, we know not for what or for whom; but one thing is certain, that we who build will receive the very smallest share of benefit. Benefit will accrue; they are essential to the country, but that will be felt not until we are no longer countrymen. We do the like in all matters:—

> "Man's heart the Almighty to the Future set
> By secret and inviolable springs."

We plant trees, we build stone houses, we redeem the waste, we make prospective laws, we found colleges and hospitals, for remote generations. We should be mortified to learn that the little benefit we chanced in our own persons to receive was the utmost they would yield.

The history of commerce, is the record of this beneficent tendency. The patriarchal form of government readily becomes despotic, as each person may see in his own family. Fathers wish to be the fathers of the minds of their children, and behold with impatience a new character and way of thinking presuming to show itself in their own son or daughter. This feeling, which all their love and pride in the powers of their children cannot subdue, becomes petulance and tyranny when the head of the clan, the emperor of an empire, deals with the same difference of opinion in his subjects. Difference of opinion is the one crime which kings never forgive. An empire is an immense egotism. "I am the State," said the French Louis. When a French ambassador mentioned to Paul of Russia, that a man of consequence in St. Petersburg was interesting himself in some matter, the Czar interrupted him,—"There is no man of consequence in this empire, but he with whom I am actually speaking; and so long only as I am speaking to him, is he of any consequence." And Nicholas, the present emperor, is reported to have said to his council, "The age is embarrassed with new opinions; rely on me, gentlemen, I shall oppose an iron will to the progress of liberal opinions."

It is easy to see that this patriarchal or family management gets to be rather troublesome to all but the papa; the sceptre comes to be a crowbar. And this unpleasant egotism, Feudalism opposes, and finally destroys. The king is compelled to call in the aid of his brothers and cousins, and remote relations, to help him keep his overgrown house in order; and this club of noblemen always come at last to have a will of their own; they combine to brave the sovereign, and call in the aid of the people. Each chief attaches as many followers as he can, by kindness, maintenance, and gifts; and as long as war lasts, the nobles, who must be soldiers, rule very well. But when peace comes, the nobles prove very whimsical and uncomfortable masters; their frolics turn out to be insulting and degrading to the commoner. Feudalism grew to be a bandit and brigand.

Meantime Trade had begun to appear: Trade, a plant which grows wherever there is peace, as soon as there is peace, and as long as there is peace. The luxury and necessity of the noble fostered it. And as quickly as men go to foreign parts, in ships or caravans, a new order of things springs up; new command takes place, new servants and new masters. Their information, their wealth, their correspondence, have made them quite other men than left their native shore. *They* are nobles now, and by another patent than the king's. Feudalism had been good, had broken the power of the kings, and had some good traits of its own; but it had grown mischievous, it was time for it to die, and, as they say of dying people, all its faults came out. Trade was the strong man that broke it down, and raised a new and unknown power in its place. It is a new agent in the world, and one of great function; it is a very intellectual force. This displaces physical strength, and instals computation, combination, information, science, in its room. It calls out all force of a certain kind that slumbered in the former dynasties. It is now in the midst of its career. Feudalism is not ended yet. Our governments still partake largely of that element. Trade goes to make the governments insignificant, and to bring every kind of faculty of every individual that can in any manner serve any person, *on sale.* Instead of a huge Army and Navy, and Executive Departments, it converts Government into an Intelligence-Office, where every man may find what he wishes to buy, and expose what he has to sell, not only produce and manufactures, but art, skill, and intellectual and moral values. This is the good and this the evil of trade, that it would put everything into market, talent, beauty, virtue, and man himself.

By this means, however, it has done its work. It has its faults, and will come to an end, as the others do. The philosopher and lover of man have much harm to say of trade; but the historian will see that trade was the principle of Liberty; that trade planted America and destroyed Feudalism; that it makes peace and keeps peace, and it will abolish slavery. We complain of its oppression of the poor, and of its building up a new aristocracy on the ruins of the aristocracy it destroyed. But the aristocracy of trade has no permanence, is not entailed, was the result of toil and talent, the result of merit of some kind, and is continually falling, like the waves of the sea, before new claims of the same sort. Trade is an instrument in the hands of that friendly Power which works for us in our own despite. We design it thus and thus; it turns out otherwise and far better. This beneficent tendency, omnipotent without violence, exists and works. Every line of history inspires a confidence that we shall not go far wrong; that things mend. That is the moral of all we learn, that it warrants Hope, the prolific mother of reforms. Our part is plainly not to throw ourselves across the track, to block improvement, and sit till we are stone, but to watch the uprise of successive mornings, and to conspire with the new works of new days. Government has been a fossil; it should be a plant. I conceive that the office of statute law should be to express, and not to impede the mind of mankind. New thoughts, new things. Trade was one instrument, but Trade is also but for a time, and must give way to somewhat broader and better, whose signs are already dawning in the sky.

3. I pass to speak of the signs of that which is the sequel of trade.

In consequence of the revolution in the state of society wrought by trade, Government in our times is beginning to wear a clumsy and cumbrous appearance. We have already seen our way to shorter methods. The time is full of good signs. Some of them shall ripen to fruit. All this beneficent socialism is a friendly omen, and the swelling cry of voices for the education of the people, indicates that Government has other offices than those of banker and executioner. Witness the new movements in the civilized world, the Communism of France, Germany, and Switzerland; the Trades' Unions; the English League against the Corn Laws; and the whole *Industrial Statistics*, so called. In Paris, the blouse, the badge of the operative, has begun to make its appearance in the saloons. Witness, too, the spectacle of three Communities which have within a very short time sprung up within this Commonwealth, besides several others undertaken by citizens of Massachusetts within the territory of other States. These proceeded from a variety of motives, from an impatience of many usages in common life, from a wish for greater freedom than the manners and opinions of society permitted, but in great part from a feeling that the true offices of the State, the State had let fall to the ground; that in the scramble of parties for the public purse, the main duties of government were omitted,—the duty to instruct the ignorant, to supply the poor with work and with good guidance. These communists preferred the agricultural life as the most favorable condition for human culture; but they thought that the farm, as we manage it, did not satisfy the right ambition of man. The farmer after sacrificing pleasure, taste, freedom, thought, love, to his work, turns out often a bankrupt, like the merchant. This result might well seem astounding. All this drudgery, from cockcrowing to starlight, for all these years, to end in mortgages and the auctioneer's flag, and removing from bad to worse. It is time to have the thing looked into, and with a sifting criticism ascertained who is the fool. It seemed a great deal worse, because the farmer is living in the same town with men who pretend to know exactly what he wants. On one side, is agricultural chemistry, coolly exposing the nonsense of our spendthrift agriculture and ruinous expense of manures, and offering, by means of a teaspoonful of artificial guano, to turn a sandbank into corn; and, on the other, the farmer, not only eager for the information, but with bad crops and in debt and bankruptcy, for want of it. Here are Etzlers and mechanical projectors, who, with the Fourierists, undoubtingly affirm that the smallest union would make every man rich;—and, on the other side, a multitude of poor men and women seeking work, and who cannot find enough to pay their board. The science is confident, and surely the poverty is real. If any means could be found to bring these two together!

This was one design of the projectors of the Associations which are now making their first feeble experiments. They were founded in love, and in labor. They proposed, as you know, that all men should take a part in the manual toil, and proposed to amend the condition of men, by substituting harmonious for hostile industry. It was a noble thought of Fourier, which gives a favorable idea of his system, to distinguish in his Phalanx a class as the Sacred Band, by whom whatever duties were disagreeable, and likely to be omitted, were to be assumed.

At least, an economical success seemed certain for the enterprise, and that agricultural association must, sooner or later, fix the price of bread, and drive single farmers into association, in self-defence; as the great commercial and manufacturing companies had already done. The Community is only the continuation of the same movement which made the joint-stock companies for manufactures, mining, insurance, banking, and so forth. It has turned out cheaper to make calico by companies; and it is proposed to plant corn, and to bake bread by companies.

Undoubtedly, abundant mistakes will be made by these first adventurers, which will draw ridicule on their schemes. I think, for example, that they exaggerate the importance of a favorite project of theirs, that of paying talent and labor at one rate, paying all sorts of service at one rate, say ten cents the hour. They have paid it so; but not an instant would a dime remain a dime. In one hand it became an eagle as it fell, and in another hand a copper cent. For the whole value of the dime is in knowing what to do with it. One man buys with it a land-title of an Indian, and makes his posterity princes; or buys corn enough to feed the world; or pen, ink, and paper, or a painter's brush, by which he can communicate himself to the human race as if he were fire; and the other buys barley candy. Money is of no value; it cannot spend itself. All depends on the skill of the spender. Whether, too, the objection almost universally felt by such women in the community as were mothers, to an associate life, to a common table, and a common nursery, &c., setting a higher value on the private family with poverty, than on an association with wealth, will not prove insuperable, remains to be determined.

But the Communities aimed at a higher success in securing to all their members an equal and thorough education. And on the whole, one may say, that aims so generous, and so forced on them by the times, will not be relinquished, even if these attempts fail, but will be prosecuted until they succeed.

This is the value of the Communities; not what they have done, but the revolution which they indicate as on the way. Yes, Government must educate the poor man. Look across the country from any hill-side around us, and the landscape seems to crave Government. The actual differences of men must be acknowledged, and met with love and wisdom. These rising grounds which command the champaign below, seem to ask for lords, true lords, *land*-lords, who understand the land and its uses, and the applicabilities of men, and whose government would be what it should, namely, mediation between want and supply. How gladly would each citizen pay a commission for the support and continuation of good guidance. None should be a governor who has not a talent for governing. Now many people have a native skill for carving out business for many hands; a genius for the disposition of affairs; and are never happier than when difficult practical questions, which embarrass other men, are to be solved. All lies in light before them; they are in their element. Could any means be contrived to appoint only these! There really seems a progress towards such a state of things, in which this work shall be done by these natural workmen; and this, not certainly through any increased discretion shown by the citizens at elections, but by the gradual contempt into which official government falls, and the increasing disposition of private adventurers to assume its fallen functions. Thus the costly Post Office is likely to go into disuse before the private transportation-shop of Harnden and his competitors. The currency threatens to fall entirely into private hands. Justice is continually administered more and more by private reference, and not by litigation. We have feudal governments in a commercial age. It would be but an easy extension of our commercial system, to pay a private emperor a fee for services, as we pay an architect, an engineer, or a lawyer. If any man has a talent for righting wrong, for administering difficult affairs, for counselling poor farmers how to turn their estates to good husbandry, for combining a hundred private enterprises to a general benefit, let him in the county-town, or in Court-street, put up his sign-board, Mr. Smith, *Governor*, Mr. Johnson, *Working king*.

How can our young men complain of the poverty of things in New England, and not feel that poverty as a demand on their charity to make New England rich? Where is he who seeing a thousand men useless and unhappy, and making the whole region forlorn by their inaction, and conscious himself of possessing the faculty they want, does not hear his call to go and be their king?

We must have kings, and we must have nobles. Nature provides such in every society,—only let us have the real instead of the titular. Let us have our leading and our inspiration from the best. In every society some men are born to rule, and some to advise. Let the powers be well directed, directed by love, and they would everywhere be greeted with joy and honor. The chief is the chief all the world over, only not his cap and his plume. It is only their dislike of the pretender, which makes men sometimes unjust to the accomplished man. If society were transparent, the noble would everywhere be gladly received and accredited, and would not be asked for his day's work, but would be felt as benefit, inasmuch as he was noble. That were his duty and stint,—to keep himself pure and purifying, the leaven of his nation. I think I see place and duties for a nobleman in every society; but it is not to drink wine and ride in a fine coach, but to guide and adorn life for the multitude by forethought, by elegant studies, by perseverance, self-devotion, and the remembrance of the humble old friend, by making his life secretly beautiful.

I call upon you, young men, to obey your heart, and be the nobility of this land. In every age of the world, there has been a leading nation, one of a more generous sentiment, whose eminent citizens were willing to stand for the interests of general justice and humanity, at the risk of being called, by the men of the moment, chimerical and fantastic. Which should be that nation but these States? Which should lead that movement, if not New England? Who should lead the leaders, but the Young American? The people, and the world, is now suffering from the want of religion and honor in its public mind. In America, out of doors all seems a market; in doors, an air-tight stove of conventionalism. Every body who comes into our houses savors of these habits; the men, of the market; the women, of the custom. I find no expression in our state papers or legislative debate, in our lyceums or churches, specially in our newspapers, of a high national feeling, no lofty counsels that rightfully stir the blood. I speak of those organs which can be presumed to speak a popular sense. They recommend conventional virtues, whatever will earn and preserve property; always the capitalist; the college, the church, the hospital, the theatre, the hotel, the road, the ship, of the capitalist,—whatever goes to secure, adorn, enlarge these, is good; what jeopardizes any of these, is damnable. The 'opposition' papers, so called, are on the same side. They attack the great capitalist, but with the aim to make a capitalist of the poor man. The opposition is against those who have money, from those who wish to have money. But who announces to us in journal, or in pulpit, or in the street, the secret of heroism,

> "Man alone
> Can perform the impossible?"

I shall not need to go into an enumeration of our national defects and vices which require this Order of Censors in the state. I might not set down our most proclaimed offences as the worst. It is not often the worst trait that occasions the loudest outcry. Men complain of their suffering, and not of the crime. I fear little from the bad effect of Repudiation; I do not fear that it will spread. Stealing is a suicidal business; you cannot repudiate but once. But the bold face and tardy repentance permitted to this local mischief, reveal a public mind so preoccupied with the love of gain, that the common sentiment of indignation at fraud does not act with its natural force. The more need of a withdrawal from the crowd, and a resort to the fountain of right, by the brave. The timidity of our public opinion, is our disease, or, shall I say, the publicness of opinion, the absence of private opinion. Good-nature is plentiful, but we want justice, with heart of steel, to fight down the proud. The private mind has the access to the totality of goodness and truth, that it may be a balance to a corrupt society; and to stand for the private verdict against popular clamor, is the office of the noble. If a humane measure is propounded in behalf of the slave, or of the Irishman, or the Catholic, or for the succor of the poor, that sentiment, that project, will have the homage of the hero. That is his nobility, his oath of knighthood, to succor the helpless and oppressed; always to throw himself on the side of weakness, of youth, of hope, on the liberal, on the expansive side, never on the defensive, the conserving, the timorous, the lock and bolt system. More than our good-will we may not be able to give. We have our own affairs, our own genius, which chains us to our proper work. We cannot give our life to the cause of the debtor, of the slave, or the pauper, as another is doing; but to one thing we are bound, not to blaspheme the sentiment and the work of that man, not to throw stumbling-blocks in the way of the abolitionist, the philanthropist, as the organs of influence and opinion are swift to do. It is for us to confide in the beneficent Supreme Power, and not to rely on our money, and on the state because it is the guard of money. At this moment, the terror of old people and of vicious people, is lest the Union of these States be destroyed: as if the Union had any other real basis than the good pleasure of a majority of the citizens to be united. But the wise and just man will always feel that he stands on his own feet; that he imparts strength to the state, not receives security from it; and that if all went down, he and such as he would quite easily combine in a new and better constitution. Every great and memorable community has consisted of formidable individuals, who, like the Roman or the Spartan, lent his own spirit to the state and made it great. Yet only by the supernatural is a man strong; nothing is so weak as an egotist. Nothing is mightier than we, when we are vehicles of a truth before which the state and the individual are alike ephemeral.

Gentlemen, the development of our American internal resources, the extension to the utmost of the commercial system, and the appearance of new moral causes which are to modify the state, are giving an aspect of greatness to the Future, which the imagination fears to open. One thing is plain for all men of common sense and common conscience, that here, here in America, is the home of man. After all the deductions which are to be made for our pitiful politics, which stake every gravest national question on the silly die, whether James or whether Jonathan shall sit in the chair and hold the purse; after all the deduction is made for our frivolities and insanities, there still remains an organic simplicity and liberty, which, when it loses its balance, redresses itself presently, which offers opportunity to the human mind not known in any other region.

It is true, the public mind wants self-respect. We are full of vanity, of which the most signal proof is our sensitiveness to foreign and especially English censure. One cause of this is our immense reading, and that reading chiefly confined to the productions of the English press. It is also true, that, to imaginative persons in this country, there is somewhat bare and bald in our short history, and unsettled wilderness. They ask, who would live in a new country, that can live in an old? and it is not strange that our youths and maidens should burn to see the picturesque extremes of an antiquated country. But it is one thing to visit the pyramids, and another to wish to live there. Would they like tithes to the clergy, and sevenths to the government, and horse-guards, and licensed press, and grief when a child is born, and threatening, starved weavers, and a pauperism now constituting one-thirteenth of the population? Instead of the open future expanding here before the eye of every boy to vastness, would they like the closing in of the future to a narrow slit of sky, and that fast contracting to be no future? One thing, for instance, the beauties of aristocracy, we commend to the study of the travelling American. The English, the most conservative people this side of India, are not sensible of the restraint, but an American would seriously resent it. The aristocracy, incorporated by law and education, degrades life for the unprivileged classes. It is a questionable compensation to the embittered feeling of a proud commoner, the reflection that a fop, who, by the magic of title, paralyzes his arm, and plucks from him half the graces and rights of a man, is himself also an aspirant excluded with the same ruthlessness from higher circles, since there is no end to the wheels within wheels of this spiral heaven. Something may be pardoned to the spirit of loyalty when it becomes fantastic; and something to the imagination, for the baldest life is symbolic. Philip II. of Spain rated his ambassador for neglecting serious affairs in Italy, whilst he debated some point of honor with the French ambassador; "You have left a business of importance for a ceremony." The ambassador replied, "Your majesty's self is but a ceremony." In the East, where the religious sentiment comes in to the support of the aristocracy, and in the Romish church also, there is a grain of sweetness in the tyranny; but in England, the fact seems to me intolerable, what is commonly affirmed, that such is the transcendent honor accorded to wealth and birth, that no man of letters, be his eminence what it may, is received into the best society, except as a lion and a show. The English have many virtues, many advantages, and the proudest history of the world; but they need all, and more than all the resources of the past to indemnify a heroic gentleman in that country for the mortifications prepared for him by the system of society, and which seem to impose the alternative to resist or to avoid it. That there are mitigations and practical alleviations to this rigor, is not an excuse for the rule. Commanding worth, and personal power, must sit crowned in all companies, nor will extraordinary persons be slighted or affronted in any company of civilized men. But the system is an invasion of the sentiment of justice and the native rights of men, which, however decorated, must lessen the value of English citizenship. It is for Englishmen to consider, not for us; we only say, let us live in America, too thankful for our want of feudal institutions. Our houses and towns are like mosses and lichens, so slight and new; but youth is a fault of which we shall daily mend. This land, too, is as old as the Flood, and wants no ornament or privilege which nature could bestow. Here stars, here woods, here hills, here animals, here men abound, and the vast tendencies concur of a new order. If only the men are employed in conspiring with the designs of the Spirit who led us hither, and is leading us still, we shall quickly enough advance out of all hearing of other's censures, out of all regrets of our own, into a new and more excellent social state than history has recorded.

ESSAYS

First Series

Contents

HISTORY

———

There is no great and no small
To the Soul that maketh all:
And where it cometh, all things are;
And it cometh everywhere.

I am owner of the sphere,
Of the seven stars and the solar year,
Of Cæsar's hand, and Plato's brain,
Of Lord Christ's heart, and Shakspeare's strain.

ESSAY I

History

THERE IS ONE MIND common to all individual men. Every man is an inlet to the same and to all of the same. He that is once admitted to the right of reason is made a freeman of the whole estate. What Plato has thought, he may think; what a saint has felt, he may feel; what at any time has befallen any man, he can understand. Who hath access to this universal mind is a party to all that is or can be done, for this is the only and sovereign agent.

Of the works of this mind history is the record. Its genius is illustrated by the entire series of days. Man is explicable by nothing less than all his history. Without hurry, without rest, the human spirit goes forth from the beginning to embody every faculty, every thought, every emotion, which belongs to it in appropriate events. But the thought is always prior to the fact; all the facts of history preëxist in the mind as laws. Each law in turn is made by circumstances predominant, and the limits of nature give power to but one at a time. A man is the whole encyclopædia of facts. The creation of a thousand forests is in one acorn, and Egypt, Greece, Rome, Gaul, Britain, America, lie folded already in the first man. Epoch after epoch, camp, kingdom, empire, republic, democracy, are merely the application of his manifold spirit to the manifold world.

This human mind wrote history, and this must read it. The Sphinx must solve her own riddle. If the whole of history is in one man, it is all to be explained from individual experience. There is a relation between the hours of our life and the centuries of time. As the air I breathe is drawn from the great repositories of nature, as the light on my book is yielded by a star a hundred millions of miles distant, as the poise of my body depends on the equilibrium of centrifugal and centripetal forces, so the hours should be instructed by the ages, and the ages explained by the hours. Of the universal mind each individual man is one more incarnation. All its properties consist in him. Each new fact in his private experience flashes a light on what great bodies of men have done, and the crises of his life refer to national crises. Every revolution was first a thought in one man's mind, and when the same thought occurs to another man, it is the key to that era. Every reform was once a private opinion, and when it shall be a private opinion again, it will solve the problem of the age. The fact narrated must correspond to something in me to be credible or intelligible. We as we read must become Greeks, Romans, Turks, priest and king, martyr and executioner, must fasten these images to some reality in our secret experience, or we shall learn nothing rightly. What befell Asdrubal or Cæsar Borgia is as much an illustration of the mind's powers and depravations as what has befallen us. Each new law and political movement has meaning for you. Stand before each of its tablets and say, 'Under this mask did my Proteus nature hide itself.' This remedies the defect of our too great nearness to ourselves. This throws our actions into perspective: and as crabs, goats, scorpions, the balance, and the waterpot lose their meanness when hung as signs in the zodiac, so I can see my own vices without heat in the distant persons of Solomon, Alcibiades, and Catiline.

It is the universal nature which gives worth to particular men and things. Human life as containing this is mysterious and inviolable, and we hedge it round with penalties and laws. All laws derive hence their ultimate reason; all express more or less distinctly some command of this supreme, illimitable essence. Property also holds of the soul, covers great spiritual facts, and instinctively we at first hold to it with swords and laws, and wide and complex combinations. The obscure consciousness of this fact is the light of all our day, the claim of claims; the plea for education, for justice, for charity, the foundation of friendship and love, and of the heroism and grandeur which belong to acts of self-reliance. It is remarkable that involuntarily we always read as superior beings. Universal history, the poets, the romancers, do not in their stateliest pictures—in the sacerdotal, the imperial palaces, in the triumphs of will or of genius—anywhere lose our ear, anywhere make us feel that we intrude, that this is for better men; but rather is it true, that in their grandest strokes we feel most at home. All that Shakspeare says of the king, yonder slip of a boy that reads in the corner feels to be true of himself. We sympathize in the great moments of history, in the great discoveries, the great resistances, the great prosperities of men;—because there law was enacted, the sea was searched, the land was found, or the blow was struck *for us*, as we ourselves in that place would have done or applauded.

We have the same interest in condition and character. We honor the rich, because they have externally the freedom, power, and grace which we feel to be proper to man, proper to us. So all that is said of the wise man by Stoic, or oriental or modern essayist, describes to each reader his own idea, describes his unattained but attainable self. All literature writes the character of the wise man. Books, monuments, pictures, conversation, are portraits in which he finds the lineaments he is forming. The silent and the eloquent praise him and accost him, and he is stimulated wherever he moves as by personal allusions. A true aspirant, therefore, never needs look for allusions personal and laudatory in discourse. He hears the commendation, not of himself, but more sweet, of that character he seeks, in every word that is said concerning character, yea, further, in every fact and circumstance,—in the running river and the rustling corn. Praise is looked, homage tendered, love flows from mute nature, from the mountains and the lights of the firmament.

These hints, dropped as it were from sleep and night, let us use in broad day. The student is to read history actively and not passively; to esteem his own life the text, and books the commentary. Thus compelled, the Muse of history will utter oracles, as never to those who do not respect themselves. I have no expectation that any man will read history aright, who thinks that what was done in a remote age, by men whose names have resounded far, has any deeper sense than what he is doing to-day.

The world exists for the education of each man. There is no age or state of society or mode of action in history, to which there is not somewhat corresponding in his life. Every thing tends in a wonderful manner to abbreviate itself and yield its own virtue to him. He should see that he can live all history in his own person. He must sit solidly at home, and not suffer himself to be bullied by kings or empires, but know that he is greater than all the geography and all the government of the world; he must transfer the point of view from which history is commonly read, from Rome and Athens and London to himself, and not deny his conviction that he is the court, and if England or Egypt have any thing to say to him, he will try the case; if not, let them for ever be silent. He must attain and maintain that lofty sight where facts yield their secret sense, and poetry and annals are alike. The instinct of the mind, the purpose of nature, betrays itself in the use we make of the signal narrations of history. Time dissipates to shining ether the solid angularity of facts. No anchor, no cable, no fences, avail to keep a fact a fact. Babylon, Troy, Tyre, Palestine, and even early Rome, are passing already into fiction. The Garden of Eden, the sun standing still in Gibeon, is poetry thenceforward to all nations. Who cares what the fact was, when we have made a constellation of it to hang in heaven an immortal sign? London and Paris and New York must go the same way. "What is History," said Napoleon, "but a fable agreed upon?" This life of ours is stuck round with Egypt, Greece, Gaul, England, War, Colonization, Church, Court, and Commerce, as with so many flowers and wild ornaments grave and gay. I will not make more account of them. I believe in Eternity. I can find Greece, Asia, Italy, Spain, and the Islands,—the genius and creative principle of each and of all eras in my own mind.

We are always coming up with the emphatic facts of history in our private experience, and verifying them here. All history becomes subjective; in other words, there is properly no history; only biography. Every mind must know the whole lesson for itself,—must go over the whole ground. What it does not see, what it does not live, it will not know. What the former age has epitomized into a formula or rule for manipular convenience, it will lose all the good of verifying for itself, by means of the wall of that rule. Somewhere, sometime, it will demand and find compensation for that loss by doing the work itself. Ferguson discovered many things in astronomy which had long been known. The better for him.

History must be this or it is nothing. Every law which the state enacts indicates a fact in human nature; that is all. We must in ourselves see the necessary reason of every fact,—see how it could and must be. So stand before every public and private work; before an oration of Burke, before a victory of Napoleon, before a martyrdom of Sir Thomas More, of Sidney, of Marmaduke Robinson, before a French Reign of Terror, and a Salem hanging of witches, before a fanatic Revival, and the Animal Magnetism in Paris, or in Providence. We assume that we under like influence should be alike affected, and should achieve the like; and we aim to master intellectually the steps, and reach the same height or the same degradation, that our fellow, our proxy, has done.

All inquiry into antiquity,—all curiosity respecting the Pyramids, the excavated cities, Stonehenge, the Ohio Circles, Mexico, Memphis,—is the desire to do away this wild, savage, and preposterous There or Then, and introduce in its place the Here and the Now. Belzoni digs and measures in the mummy-pits and pyramids of Thebes, until he can see the end of the difference between the monstrous work and himself. When he has satisfied himself, in general and in detail, that it was made by such a person as he, so armed and so motived, and to ends to which he himself should also have worked, the problem is solved; his thought lives along the whole line of temples and sphinxes and catacombs, passes through them all with satisfaction, and they live again to the mind, or are *now*.

A Gothic cathedral affirms that it was done by us, and not done by us. Surely it was by man, but we find it not in our man. But we apply ourselves to the history of its production. We put ourselves into the place and state of the builder. We remember the forest-dwellers, the first temples, the adherence to the first type, and the decoration of it as the wealth of the nation increased; the value which is given to wood by carving led to the carving over the whole mountain of stone of a cathedral. When we have gone through this process, and added thereto the Catholic Church, its cross, its music, its processions, its Saints' days and image-worship, we have, as it were, been the man that made the minster; we have seen how it could and must be. We have the sufficient reason.

The difference between men is in their principle of association. Some men classify objects by color and size and other accidents of appearance; others by intrinsic likeness, or by the relation of cause and effect. The progress of the intellect is to the clearer vision of causes, which neglects surface differences. To the poet, to the philosopher, to the saint, all things are friendly and sacred, all events profitable, all days holy, all men divine. For the eye is fastened on the life, and slights the circumstance. Every chemical substance, every plant, every animal in its growth, teaches the unity of cause, the variety of appearance.

Upborne and surrounded as we are by this all-creating nature, soft and fluid as a cloud or the air, why should we be such hard pedants, and magnify a few forms? Why should we make account of time, or of magnitude, or of figure? The soul knows them not, and genius, obeying its law, knows how to play with them as a young child plays with graybeards and in churches. Genius studies the causal thought, and, far back in the womb of things, sees the rays parting from one orb, that diverge ere they fall by infinite diameters. Genius watches the monad through all his masks as he performs the metempsychosis of nature. Genius detects through the fly, through the caterpillar, through the grub, through the egg, the constant individual; through countless individuals, the fixed species; through many species, the genus; through all genera, the steadfast type; through all the kingdoms of organized life, the eternal unity. Nature is a mutable cloud, which is always and never the same. She casts the same thought into troops of forms, as a poet makes twenty fables with one moral. Through the bruteness and toughness of matter, a subtle spirit bends all things to its own will. The adamant streams into soft but precise form before it, and, whilst I look at it, its outline and texture are changed again. Nothing is so fleeting as form; yet never does it quite deny itself. In man we still trace the remains or hints of all that we esteem badges of servitude in the lower races; yet in him they enhance his nobleness and grace; as Io, in Æschylus, transformed to a cow, offends the imagination; but how changed, when as Isis in Egypt she meets Osiris-Jove, a beautiful woman, with nothing of the metamorphosis left but the lunar horns as the splendid ornament of her brows!

The identity of history is equally intrinsic, the diversity equally obvious. There is at the surface infinite variety of things; at the centre there is simplicity of cause. How many are the acts of one man in which we recognize the same char-

acter! Observe the sources of our information in respect to
the Greek genius. We have the *civil history* of that people, as
Herodotus, Thucydides, Xenophon, and Plutarch have given
it; a very sufficient account of what manner of persons they
were, and what they did. We have the same national mind
expressed for us again in their *literature*, in epic and lyric
poems, drama, and philosophy; a very complete form. Then
we have it once more in their *architecture*, a beauty as of temperance itself, limited to the straight line and the square,—a
builded geometry. Then we have it once again in *sculpture*,
the "tongue on the balance of expression," a multitude of
forms in the utmost freedom of action, and never transgress-
ing the ideal serenity; like votaries performing some religious
dance before the gods, and, though in convulsive pain or
mortal combat, never daring to break the figure and decorum
of their dance. Thus, of the genius of one remarkable people,
we have a fourfold representation: and to the senses what
more unlike than an ode of Pindar, a marble centaur, the peri-
style of the Parthenon, and the last actions of Phocion?

Every one must have observed faces and forms which,
without any resembling feature, make a like impression on the
beholder. A particular picture or copy of verses, if it do not
awaken the same train of images, will yet superinduce the
same sentiment as some wild mountain walk, although the
resemblance is nowise obvious to the senses, but is occult and
out of the reach of the understanding. Nature is an endless
combination and repetition of a very few laws. She hums the
old well-known air through innumerable variations.

Nature is full of a sublime family likeness throughout her
works; and delights in startling us with resemblances in the
most unexpected quarters. I have seen the head of an old
sachem of the forest, which at once reminded the eye of a
bald mountain summit, and the furrows of the brow suggested the strata of the rock. There are men whose manners
have the same essential splendor as the simple and awful
sculpture on the friezes of the Parthenon, and the remains of
the earliest Greek art. And there are compositions of the same
strain to be found in the books of all ages. What is Guido's
Rospigliosi Aurora but a morning thought, as the horses in
it are only a morning cloud. If any one will but take pains to

observe the variety of actions to which he is equally inclined in certain moods of mind, and those to which he is averse, he will see how deep is the chain of affinity.

A painter told me that nobody could draw a tree without in some sort becoming a tree; or draw a child by studying the outlines of its form merely,—but, by watching for a time his motions and plays, the painter enters into his nature, and can then draw him at will in every attitude. So Roos "entered into the inmost nature of a sheep." I knew a draughtsman employed in a public survey, who found that he could not sketch the rocks until their geological structure was first explained to him. In a certain state of thought is the common origin of very diverse works. It is the spirit and not the fact that is identical. By a deeper apprehension, and not primarily by a painful acquisition of many manual skills, the artist attains the power of awakening other souls to a given activity.

It has been said, that "common souls pay with what they do; nobler souls with that which they are." And why? Because a profound nature awakens in us by its actions and words, by its very looks and manners, the same power and beauty that a gallery of sculpture, or of pictures, addresses.

Civil and natural history, the history of art and of literature, must be explained from individual history, or must remain words. There is nothing but is related to us, nothing that does not interest us,—kingdom, college, tree, horse, or iron shoe, the roots of all things are in man. Santa Croce and the Dome of St. Peter's are lame copies after a divine model. Strasburg Cathedral is a material counterpart of the soul of Erwin of Steinbach. The true poem is the poet's mind; the true ship is the ship-builder. In the man, could we lay him open, we should see the reason for the last flourish and tendril of his work; as every spine and tint in the sea-shell preëxist in the secreting organs of the fish. The whole of heraldry and of chivalry is in courtesy. A man of fine manners shall pronounce your name with all the ornament that titles of nobility could ever add.

The trivial experience of every day is always verifying some old prediction to us, and converting into things the words and signs which we had heard and seen without heed. A lady, with whom I was riding in the forest, said to me, that the

woods always seemed to her *to wait*, as if the genii who inhabit them suspended their deeds until the wayfarer has
passed onward: a thought which poetry has celebrated in the
dance of the fairies, which breaks off on the approach of human feet. The man who has seen the rising moon break out of
the clouds at midnight has been present like an archangel at the
creation of light and of the world. I remember one summer day,
in the fields, my companion pointed out to me a broad cloud,
which might extend a quarter of a mile parallel to the horizon,
quite accurately in the form of a cherub as painted over
churches,—a round block in the centre, which it was easy to
animate with eyes and mouth, supported on either side by
wide-stretched symmetrical wings. What appears once in the
atmosphere may appear often, and it was undoubtedly the
archetype of that familiar ornament. I have seen in the sky a
chain of summer lightning which at once showed to me that
the Greeks drew from nature when they painted the thunderbolt in the hand of Jove. I have seen a snow-drift along the
sides of the stone wall which obviously gave the idea of the
common architectural scroll to abut a tower.

By surrounding ourselves with the original circumstances,
we invent anew the orders and the ornaments of architecture,
as we see how each people merely decorated its primitive
abodes. The Doric temple preserves the semblance of the
wooden cabin in which the Dorian dwelt. The Chinese pa-
goda is plainly a Tartar tent. The Indian and Egyptian temples
still betray the mounds and subterranean houses of their forefathers. "The custom of making houses and tombs in the living rock," says Heeren, in his Researches on the Ethiopians,
"determined very naturally the principal character of the Nu-
bian Egyptian architecture to the colossal form which it assumed. In these caverns, already prepared by nature, the eye
was accustomed to dwell on huge shapes and masses, so that,
when art came to the assistance of nature, it could not move
on a small scale without degrading itself. What would statues
of the usual size, or neat porches and wings, have been, associated with those gigantic halls before which only Colossi
could sit as watchmen, or lean on the pillars of the interior?"

The Gothic church plainly originated in a rude adaptation
of the forest trees with all their boughs to a festal or solemn

arcade, as the bands about the cleft pillars still indicate the green withes that tied them. No one can walk in a road cut through pine woods, without being struck with the architectural appearance of the grove, especially in winter, when the bareness of all other trees shows the low arch of the Saxons. In the woods in a winter afternoon one will see as readily the origin of the stained glass window, with which the Gothic cathedrals are adorned, in the colors of the western sky seen through the bare and crossing branches of the forest. Nor can any lover of nature enter the old piles of Oxford and the English cathedrals, without feeling that the forest overpowered the mind of the builder, and that his chisel, his saw, and plane still reproduced its ferns, its spikes of flowers, its locust, elm, oak, pine, fir, and spruce.

The Gothic cathedral is a blossoming in stone subdued by the insatiable demand of harmony in man. The mountain of granite blooms into an eternal flower, with the lightness and delicate finish, as well as the aerial proportions and perspective, of vegetable beauty.

In like manner, all public facts are to be individualized, all private facts are to be generalized. Then at once History becomes fluid and true, and Biography deep and sublime. As the Persian imitated in the slender shafts and capitals of his architecture the stem and flower of the lotus and palm, so the Persian court in its magnificent era never gave over the nomadism of its barbarous tribes, but travelled from Ecbatana, where the spring was spent, to Susa in summer, and to Babylon for the winter.

In the early history of Asia and Africa, Nomadism and Agriculture are the two antagonist facts. The geography of Asia and of Africa necessitated a nomadic life. But the nomads were the terror of all those whom the soil, or the advantages of a market, had induced to build towns. Agriculture, therefore, was a religious injunction, because of the perils of the state from nomadism. And in these late and civil countries of England and America, these propensities still fight out the old battle in the nation and in the individual. The nomads of Africa were constrained to wander by the attacks of the gad-fly, which drives the cattle mad, and so compels the tribe to emigrate in the rainy season, and to drive off the cattle to the higher sandy regions. The nomads of Asia follow the pasturage from month to month. In America and Europe, the nomadism is of trade and curiosity; a progress, certainly, from the gad-fly of Astaboras to the Anglo and Italo-mania of Boston Bay. Sacred cities, to which a periodical religious pilgrimage was enjoined, or stringent laws and customs, tending to invigorate the national bond, were the check on the old rovers; and the cumulative values of long residence are the restraints on the itineracy of the present day. The antagonism of the two tendencies is not less active in individuals, as the love of adventure or the love of repose happens to predominate. A man of rude health and flowing spirits has the faculty of rapid domestication, lives in his wagon, and roams through all latitudes as easily as a Calmuc. At sea, or in the forest, or in the snow, he sleeps as warm, dines with as good appetite, and associates as happily, as beside his own chimneys. Or perhaps his facility is deeper seated, in the increased range of his faculties of observation, which yield him points of interest wherever fresh objects meet his eyes. The pastoral nations were needy and hungry to desperation; and this intellectual nomadism, in its excess, bankrupts the mind, through the dissipation of power on a miscellany of objects. The home-keeping wit, on the other hand, is that continence or content which finds all the elements of life in its own soil; and which has its own perils of monotony and deterioration, if not stimulated by foreign infusions.

Every thing the individual sees without him corresponds to his states of mind, and every thing is in turn intelligible to him, as his onward thinking leads him into the truth to which that fact or series belongs.

The primeval world,—the Fore-World, as the Germans say,—I can dive to it in myself as well as grope for it with researching fingers in catacombs, libraries, and the broken reliefs and torsos of ruined villas.

What is the foundation of that interest all men feel in Greek history, letters, art, and poetry, in all its periods, from the Heroic or Homeric age down to the domestic life of the Athenians and Spartans, four or five centuries later? What but this, that every man passes personally through a Grecian period. The Grecian state is the era of the bodily nature, the perfection of the senses,—of the spiritual nature unfolded in strict unity with the body. In it existed those human forms which supplied the sculptor with his models of Hercules, Phœbus, and Jove; not like the forms abounding in the streets of modern cities, wherein the face is a confused blur of features, but composed of incorrupt, sharply defined, and symmetrical features, whose eye-sockets are so formed that it would be impossible for such eyes to squint, and take furtive glances on this side and on that, but they must turn the whole head. The manners of that period are plain and fierce. The reverence exhibited is for personal qualities, courage, address, self-command, justice, strength, swiftness, a loud voice, a broad chest. Luxury and elegance are not known. A sparse population and want make every man his own valet, cook, butcher, and soldier, and the habit of supplying his own needs educates the body to wonderful performances. Such are the Agamemnon and Diomed of Homer, and not far different is the picture Xenophon gives of himself and his compatriots in the Retreat of the Ten Thousand. "After the army had crossed the river Teleboas in Armenia, there fell much snow, and the troops lay miserably on the ground covered with it. But Xenophon arose naked, and, taking an axe, began to split wood; whereupon others rose and did the like." Throughout his army exists a boundless liberty of speech. They quarrel for plunder, they wrangle with the generals on each new order, and Xenophon is as sharp-tongued as any, and sharper-tongued than most, and so gives as good as he gets. Who does not see that this is a gang of great boys, with such a code of honor and such lax discipline as great boys have?

The costly charm of the ancient tragedy, and indeed of all the old literature, is, that the persons speak simply,—speak as persons who have great good sense without knowing it, before yet the reflective habit has become the predominant habit of the mind. Our admiration of the antique is not admiration of the old, but of the natural. The Greeks are not reflective, but perfect in their senses and in their health, with the finest physical organization in the world. Adults acted with the simplicity and grace of children. They made vases, tragedies, and statues, such as healthy senses should,—that is, in good taste. Such things have continued to be made in all ages, and are now, wherever a healthy physique exists; but, as a class, from their superior organization, they have surpassed all. They combine the energy of manhood with the engaging unconsciousness of childhood. The attraction of these manners is that they belong to man, and are known to every man in virtue of his being once a child; besides that there are always individuals who retain these characteristics. A person of child-like genius and inborn energy is still a Greek, and revives our love of the Muse of Hellas. I admire the love of nature in the Philoctetes. In reading those fine apostrophes to sleep, to the stars, rocks, mountains, and waves, I feel time passing away as an ebbing sea. I feel the eternity of man, the identity of his thought. The Greek had, it seems, the same fellow-beings as I. The sun and moon, water and fire, met his heart precisely as they meet mine. Then the vaunted distinction between Greek and English, between Classic and Romantic schools, seems superficial and pedantic. When a thought of Plato becomes a thought to me, — when a truth that fired the soul of Pindar fires mine, time is no more. When I feel that we two meet in a perception, that our two souls are tinged with the same hue, and do, as it were, run into one, why should I measure degrees of latitude, why should I count Egyptian years?

The student interprets the age of chivalry by his own age of chivalry, and the days of maritime adventure and circumnavigation by quite parallel miniature experiences of his own. To the sacred history of the world, he has the same key. When the voice of a prophet out of the deeps of antiquity merely echoes to him a sentiment of his infancy, a prayer of his youth, he then pierces to the truth through all the confusion of tradition and the caricature of institutions.

Rare, extravagant spirits come by us at intervals, who disclose to us new facts in nature. I see that men of God have, from time to time, walked among men and made their commission felt in the heart and soul of the commonest hearer. Hence, evidently, the tripod, the priest, the priestess inspired by the divine afflatus.

Jesus astonishes and overpowers sensual people. They cannot unite him to history, or reconcile him with themselves. As they come to revere their intuitions and aspire to live holily, their own piety explains every fact, every word.

How easily these old worships of Moses, of Zoroaster, of Menu, of Socrates, domesticate themselves in the mind. I cannot find any antiquity in them. They are mine as much as theirs.

I have seen the first monks and anchorets without crossing seas or centuries. More than once some individual has appeared to me with such negligence of labor and such commanding contemplation, a haughty beneficiary, begging in the name of God, as made good to the nineteenth century Simeon the Stylite, the Thebais, and the first Capuchins.

The priestcraft of the East and West, of the Magian, Brahmin, Druid, and Inca, is expounded in the individual's private life. The cramping influence of a hard formalist on a young child in repressing his spirits and courage, paralyzing the understanding, and that without producing indignation, but only fear and obedience, and even much sympathy with the tyranny,—is a familiar fact explained to the child when he becomes a man, only by seeing that the oppressor of his youth is himself a child tyrannized over by those names and words and forms, of whose influence he was merely the organ to the youth. The fact teaches him how Belus was worshipped, and how the Pyramids were built, better than the discovery by Champollion of the names of all the workmen and the cost of every tile. He finds Assyria and the Mounds of Cholula at his door, and himself has laid the courses.

Again, in that protest which each considerate person makes against the superstition of his times, he repeats step for step the part of old reformers, and in the search after truth finds like them new perils to virtue. He learns again what moral vigor is needed to supply the girdle of a superstition. A great licentiousness treads on the heels of a reformation. How many times in the history of the world has the Luther of the day had to lament the decay of piety in his own household! "Doctor," said his wife to Martin Luther, one day, "how is it that, whilst subject to papacy, we prayed so often and with such fervor, whilst now we pray with the utmost coldness and very seldom?"

The advancing man discovers how deep a property he has in literature,—in all fable as well as in all history. He finds that the poet was no odd fellow who described strange and impossible situations, but that universal man wrote by his pen a confession true for one and true for all. His own secret biography he finds in lines wonderfully intelligible to him, dotted down before he was born. One after another he comes up in his private adventures with every fable of Æsop, of Homer, of Hafiz, of Ariosto, of Chaucer, of Scott, and verifies them with his own head and hands.

The beautiful fables of the Greeks, being proper creations of the imagination and not of the fancy, are universal verities. What a range of meanings and what perpetual pertinence has the story of Prometheus! Beside its primary value as the first chapter of the history of Europe, (the mythology thinly veiling authentic facts, the invention of the mechanic arts, and the migration of colonies,) it gives the history of religion with some closeness to the faith of later ages. Prometheus is the Jesus of the old mythology. He is the friend of man; stands between the unjust "justice" of the Eternal Father and the race of mortals, and readily suffers all things on their account. But where it departs from the Calvinistic Christianity, and exhibits him as the defier of Jove, it represents a state of mind which readily appears wherever the doctrine of Theism is taught in a crude, objective form, and which seems the self-defence of man against this untruth, namely, a discontent with the believed fact that a God exists, and a feeling that the obligation of reverence is onerous. It would steal, if it could, the fire of the Creator, and live apart from him, and independent of him. The Prometheus Vinctus is the romance of skepticism. Not less true to all time are the details of that stately apologue. Apollo kept the flocks of Admetus, said the poets. When the gods come among men, they are not known. Jesus was not; Socrates and Shakspeare were not. Antæus was suffocated by the gripe of Hercules, but every time he touched his mother earth, his strength was renewed. Man is the broken giant, and, in all his weakness, both his body and his mind are invigorated by habits of conversation with nature. The power of music, the power of poetry to unfix, and, as it were, clap wings to solid nature, interprets the riddle of Orpheus. The philosophical perception of identity through endless mutations of form makes him know the Proteus. What else am I who laughed or wept yesterday, who slept last night like a corpse, and this morning stood and ran? And what see

I on any side but the transmigrations of Proteus? I can symbolize my thought by using the name of any creature, of any fact, because every creature is man agent or patient. Tantalus is but a name for you and me. Tantalus means the impossibility of drinking the waters of thought which are always gleaming and waving within sight of the soul. The transmigration of souls is no fable. I would it were; but men and women are only half human. Every animal of the barn-yard, the field, and the forest, of the earth and of the waters that are under the earth, has contrived to get a footing and to leave the print of its features and form in some one or other of these upright, heaven-facing speakers. Ah! brother, stop the ebb of thy soul,—ebbing downward into the forms into whose habits thou hast now for many years slid. As near and proper to us is also that old fable of the Sphinx, who was said to sit in the road-side and put riddles to every passenger. If the man could not answer, she swallowed him alive. If he could solve the riddle, the Sphinx was slain. What is our life but an endless flight of winged facts or events! In splendid variety these changes come, all putting questions to the human spirit. Those men who cannot answer by a superior wisdom these facts or questions of time, serve them. Facts encumber them, tyrannize over them, and make the men of routine the men of *sense*, in whom a literal obedience to facts has extinguished every spark of that light by which man is truly man. But if the man is true to his better instincts or sentiments, and refuses the dominion of facts, as one that comes of a higher race, remains fast by the soul and sees the principle, then the facts fall aptly and supple into their places; they know their master, and the meanest of them glorifies him.

See in Goethe's Helena the same desire that every word should be a thing. These figures, he would say, these Chirons, Griffins, Phorkyas, Helen, and Leda, are somewhat, and do exert a specific influence on the mind. So far then are they eternal entities, as real to-day as in the first Olympiad. Much revolving them, he writes out freely his humor, and gives them body to his own imagination. And although that poem be as vague and fantastic as a dream, yet is it much more attractive than the more regular dramatic pieces of the same author, for the reason that it operates a wonderful relief to the mind from

the routine of customary images,—awakens the reader's invention and fancy by the wild freedom of the design, and by the
unceasing succession of brisk shocks of surprise.

The universal nature, too strong for the petty nature of the
bard, sits on his neck and writes through his hand; so that
when he seems to vent a mere caprice and wild romance, the
issue is an exact allegory. Hence Plato said that "poets utter
great and wise things which they do not themselves understand." All the fictions of the Middle Age explain themselves
as a masked or frolic expression of that which in grave earnest
the mind of that period toiled to achieve. Magic, and all that
is ascribed to it, is a deep presentiment of the powers of science. The shoes of swiftness, the sword of sharpness, the
power of subduing the elements, of using the secret virtues of
minerals, of understanding the voices of birds, are the obscure
efforts of the mind in a right direction. The preternatural
prowess of the hero, the gift of perpetual youth, and the like,
are alike the endeavour of the human spirit "to bend the
shows of things to the desires of the mind."

In Perceforest and Amadis de Gaul, a garland and a rose
bloom on the head of her who is faithful, and fade on the
brow of the inconstant. In the story of the Boy and the Man-
tle, even a mature reader may be surprised with a glow of
virtuous pleasure at the triumph of the gentle Genelas; and,
indeed, all the postulates of elfin annals,—that the fairies do
not like to be named; that their gifts are capricious and not
to be trusted; that who seeks a treasure must not speak; and
the like,—I find true in Concord, however they might be in
Cornwall or Bretagne.

Is it otherwise in the newest romance? I read the Bride of
Lammermoor. Sir William Ashton is a mask for a vulgar
temptation, Ravenswood Castle a fine name for proud poverty, and the foreign mission of state only a Bunyan disguise
for honest industry. We may all shoot a wild bull that would
toss the good and beautiful, by fighting down the unjust and
sensual. Lucy Ashton is another name for fidelity, which is
always beautiful and always liable to calamity in this world.

But along with the civil and metaphysical history of man,
another history goes daily forward,—that of the external

world,—in which he is not less strictly implicated. He is the compend of time; he is also the correlative of nature. His power consists in the multitude of his affinities, in the fact that his life is intertwined with the whole chain of organic and inorganic being. In old Rome the public roads beginning at the Forum proceeded north, south, east, west, to the centre of every province of the empire, making each market-town of Persia, Spain, and Britain pervious to the soldiers of the capital: so out of the human heart go, as it were, highways to the heart of every object in nature, to reduce it under the dominion of man. A man is a bundle of relations, a knot of roots, whose flower and fruitage is the world. His faculties refer to natures out of him, and predict the world he is to inhabit, as the fins of the fish foreshow that water exists, or the wings of an eagle in the egg presuppose air. He cannot live without a world. Put Napoleon in an island prison, let his faculties find no men to act on, no Alps to climb, no stake to play for, and he would beat the air and appear stupid. Transport him to large countries, dense population, complex interests, and antagonist power, and you shall see that the man Napoleon, bounded, that is, by such a profile and outline, is not the virtual Napoleon. This is but Talbot's shadow;

> "His substance is not here:
> For what you see is but the smallest part
> And least proportion of humanity;
> But were the whole frame here,
> It is of such a spacious, lofty pitch,
> Your roof were not sufficient to contain it."
>
> *Henry VI.*

Columbus needs a planet to shape his course upon. Newton and Laplace need myriads of ages and thick-strewn celestial areas. One may say a gravitating solar system is already prophesied in the nature of Newton's mind. Not less does the brain of Davy or of Gay-Lussac, from childhood exploring the affinities and repulsions of particles, anticipate the laws of organization. Does not the eye of the human embryo predict the light? the ear of Handel predict the witchcraft of harmonic sound? Do not the constructive fingers of Watt, Fulton, Whittemore, Arkwright, predict the fusible, hard, and temperable texture of metals, the properties of stone, water, and wood? Do not the lovely attributes of the maiden child predict the refinements and decorations of civil society? Here also we are reminded of the action of man on man. A mind might ponder its thought for ages, and not gain so much self-knowledge as the passion of love shall teach it in a day. Who knows himself before he has been thrilled with indignation at an outrage, or has heard an eloquent tongue, or has shared the throb of thousands in a national exultation or alarm? No man can antedate his experience, or guess what faculty or feeling a new object shall unlock, any more than he can draw to-day the face of a person whom he shall see to-morrow for the first time.

I will not now go behind the general statement to explore the reason of this correspondency. Let it suffice that in the light of these two facts, namely, that the mind is One, and that nature is its correlative, history is to be read and written.

Thus in all ways does the soul concentrate and reproduce its treasures for each pupil. He, too, shall pass through the whole cycle of experience. He shall collect into a focus the rays of nature. History no longer shall be a dull book. It shall walk incarnate in every just and wise man. You shall not tell me by languages and titles a catalogue of the volumes you have read. You shall make me feel what periods you have lived. A man shall be the Temple of Fame. He shall walk, as the poets have described that goddess, in a robe painted all over with wonderful events and experiences;—his own form and features by their exalted intelligence shall be that variegated vest. I shall find in him the Foreworld; in his childhood the Age of Gold; the Apples of Knowledge; the Argonautic Expedition; the calling of Abraham; the building of the Temple; the Advent of Christ; Dark Ages; the Revival of Letters; the Reformation; the discovery of new lands; the opening of new sciences, and new regions in man. He shall be the priest of Pan, and bring with him into humble cottages the blessing of the morning stars and all the recorded benefits of heaven and earth.

Is there somewhat overweening in this claim? Then I reject all I have written, for what is the use of pretending to know what we know not? But it is the fault of our rhetoric that we cannot strongly state one fact without seeming to belie some other. I hold our actual knowledge very cheap. Hear the rats in the wall, see the lizard on the fence, the fungus under foot, the lichen on the log. What do I know sympathetically, morally, of either of these worlds of life? As old as the Caucasian man,—perhaps older,—these creatures have kept their counsel beside him, and there is no record of any word or sign that has passed from one to the other. What connection do the books show between the fifty or sixty chemical elements, and the historical eras? Nay, what does history yet record of the metaphysical annals of man? What light does it shed on those mysteries which we hide under the names Death and Immortality? Yet every history should be written in a wisdom which divined the range of our affinities and looked at facts as symbols. I am ashamed to see what a shallow village tale our so-called History is. How many times we must say Rome, and Paris, and Constantinople! What does Rome know of rat and lizard? What are Olympiads and Consulates to these neighbouring systems of being? Nay, what food or experience or succour have they for the Esquimaux seal-hunter, for the Kanàka in his canoe, for the fisherman, the stevedore, the porter?

Broader and deeper we must write our annals,—from an ethical reformation, from an influx of the ever new, ever sanative conscience,—if we would trulier express our central and wide-related nature, instead of this old chronology of selfishness and pride to which we have too long lent our eyes. Already that day exists for us, shines in on us at unawares, but the path of science and of letters is not the way into nature. The idiot, the Indian, the child, and unschooled farmer's boy, stand nearer to the light by which nature is to be read, than the dissector or the antiquary.

SELF-RELIANCE

———

"Ne te quæsiveris extra."

———

"Man is his own star; and the soul that can
  Render an honest and a perfect man,
  Commands all light, all influence, all fate;
  Nothing to him falls early or too late.
  Our acts our angels are, or good or ill,
  Our fatal shadows that walk by us still."
    Epilogue to Beaumont and Fletcher's
    Honest Man's Fortune

Cast the bantling on the rocks,
Suckle him with the she-wolf's teat;
Wintered with the hawk and fox,
Power and speed be hands and feet.

Self-Reliance

I READ the other day some verses written by an eminent painter which were original and not conventional. The soul always hears an admonition in such lines, let the subject be what it may. The sentiment they instil is of more value than any thought they may contain. To believe your own thought, to believe that what is true for you in your private heart is true for all men,—that is genius. Speak your latent conviction, and it shall be the universal sense; for the inmost in due time becomes the outmost,—and our first thought is rendered back to us by the trumpets of the Last Judgment. Familiar as the voice of the mind is to each, the highest merit we ascribe to Moses, Plato, and Milton is, that they set at naught books and traditions, and spoke not what men but what they thought. A man should learn to detect and watch that gleam of light which flashes across his mind from within, more than the lustre of the firmament of bards and sages. Yet he dismisses without notice his thought, because it is his. In every work of genius we recognize our own rejected thoughts: they come back to us with a certain alienated majesty. Great works of art have no more affecting lesson for us than this. They teach us to abide by our spontaneous impression with good-humored inflexibility then most when the whole cry of voices is on the other side. Else, to-morrow a stranger will say with masterly good sense precisely what we have thought and felt all the time, and we shall be forced to take with shame our own opinion from another.

There is a time in every man's education when he arrives at the conviction that envy is ignorance; that imitation is suicide; that he must take himself for better, for worse, as his portion; that though the wide universe is full of good, no kernel of nourishing corn can come to him but through his toil bestowed on that plot of ground which is given to him to till. The power which resides in him is new in nature, and none but he knows what that is which he can do, nor does he know until he has tried. Not for nothing one face, one character, one fact, makes much impression on him, and another none. This sculpture in the memory is not without preëstablished harmony. The eye was placed where one ray should fall, that it might testify of that particular ray. We but half express ourselves, and are ashamed of that divine idea which each of us represents. It may be safely trusted as proportionate and of good issues, so it be faithfully imparted, but God will not have his work made manifest by cowards. A man is relieved and gay when he has put his heart into his work and done his best; but what he has said or done otherwise, shall give him no peace. It is a deliverance which does not deliver. In the attempt his genius deserts him; no muse befriends; no invention, no hope.

Trust thyself: every heart vibrates to that iron string. Accept the place the divine providence has found for you, the society of your contemporaries, the connection of events. Great men have always done so, and confided themselves childlike to the genius of their age, betraying their perception that the absolutely trustworthy was seated at their heart, working through their hands, predominating in all their being. And we are now men, and must accept in the highest mind the same transcendent destiny; and not minors and invalids in a protected corner, not cowards fleeing before a revolution, but guides, redeemers, and benefactors, obeying the Almighty effort, and advancing on Chaos and the Dark.

What pretty oracles nature yields us on this text, in the face and behaviour of children, babes, and even brutes! That divided and rebel mind, that distrust of a sentiment because our arithmetic has computed the strength and means opposed to our purpose, these have not. Their mind being whole, their eye is as yet unconquered, and when we look in their faces, we are disconcerted. Infancy conforms to nobody: all conform to it, so that one babe commonly makes four or five out of the adults who prattle and play to it. So God has armed youth and puberty and manhood no less with its own piquancy and charm, and made it enviable and gracious and its claims not to be put by, if it will stand by itself. Do not think the youth has no force, because he cannot speak to you and me. Hark! in the next room his voice is sufficiently clear and emphatic. It seems he knows how to speak to his contemporaries. Bashful or bold, then, he will know how to make us seniors very unnecessary.

The nonchalance of boys who are sure of a dinner, and would disdain as much as a lord to do or say aught to conciliate one, is the healthy attitude of human nature. A boy is in the parlour what the pit is in the playhouse; independent, irresponsible, looking out from his corner on such people and facts as pass by, he tries and sentences them on their merits, in the swift, summary way of boys, as good, bad, interesting, silly, eloquent, troublesome. He cumbers himself never about consequences, about interests: he gives an independent, genuine verdict. You must court him: he does not court you. But the man is, as it were, clapped into jail by his consciousness. As soon as he has once acted or spoken with eclat, he is a committed person, watched by the sympathy or the hatred of hundreds, whose affections must now enter into his account. There is no Lethe for this. Ah, that he could pass again into his neutrality! Who can thus avoid all pledges, and having observed, observe again from the same unaffected, unbiased, unbribable, unaffrighted innocence, must always be formidable. He would utter opinions on all passing affairs, which being seen to be not private, but necessary, would sink like darts into the ear of men, and put them in fear.

These are the voices which we hear in solitude, but they grow faint and inaudible as we enter into the world. Society everywhere is in conspiracy against the manhood of every one of its members. Society is a joint-stock company, in which the members agree, for the better securing of his bread to each shareholder, to surrender the liberty and culture of the eater. The virtue in most request is conformity. Self-reliance is its aversion. It loves not realities and creators, but names and customs.

Whoso would be a man must be a nonconformist. He who would gather immortal palms must not be hindered by the name of goodness, but must explore if it be goodness. Nothing is at last sacred but the integrity of your own mind. Absolve you to yourself, and you shall have the suffrage of the world. I remember an answer which when quite young I was prompted to make to a valued adviser, who was wont to importune me with the dear old doctrines of the church. On my saying, What have I to do with the sacredness of traditions, if I live wholly from within? my friend suggested,—"But these impulses may be from below, not from above." I replied, "They do not seem to me to be such; but if I am the Devil's child, I will live then from the Devil." No law can be sacred to me but that of my nature. Good and bad are but names very readily transferable to that or this; the only right is what is after my constitution, the only wrong what is against it. A man is to carry himself in the presence of all opposition, as if every thing were titular and ephemeral but he. I am ashamed to think how easily we capitulate to badges and names, to large societies and dead institutions. Every decent and well-spoken individual affects and sways me more than is right. I ought to go upright and vital, and speak the rude truth in all ways. If malice and vanity wear the coat of philanthropy, shall that pass? If an angry bigot assumes this bountiful cause of Abolition, and comes to me with his last news from Barbadoes, why should I not say to him, 'Go love thy infant; love thy wood-chopper: be good-natured and modest: have that grace; and never varnish your hard, uncharitable ambition with this incredible tenderness for black folk a thousand miles off. Thy love afar is spite at home.' Rough and graceless would be such greeting, but truth is handsomer than the affectation of love. Your goodness must have some edge to it,—else it is none. The doctrine of hatred must be preached as the counteraction of the doctrine of love when that pules and whines. I shun father and mother and wife and brother, when my genius calls me. I would write on the lintels of the door-post, *Whim*. I hope it is somewhat better than whim at last, but we cannot spend the day in explanation. Expect me not to show cause why I seek or why I exclude company. Then, again, do not tell me, as a good man did to-day, of my obligation to put all poor men in good situations. Are they *my* poor? I tell thee, thou foolish philanthropist, that I grudge the dollar, the dime, the cent, I give to such men as do not belong to me and to whom I do not belong. There is a class of persons to whom by all spiritual affinity I am bought and sold; for them I will go to prison, if need be; but your miscellaneous popular charities; the education at college of fools; the building of meeting-houses to the vain end to which many now stand; alms to sots; and the thousandfold Relief Societies;—though I confess with shame I sometimes succumb and give the dollar, it is a wicked dollar which by and by I shall have the manhood to withhold.

Virtues are, in the popular estimate, rather the exception than the rule. There is the man *and* his virtues. Men do what is called a good action, as some piece of courage or charity, much as they would pay a fine in expiation of daily non-appearance on parade. Their works are done as an apology or extenuation of their living in the world,—as invalids and the insane pay a high board. Their virtues are penances. I do not wish to expiate, but to live. My life is for itself and not for a spectacle. I much prefer that it should be of a lower strain, so it be genuine and equal, than that it should be glittering and unsteady. I wish it to be sound and sweet, and not to need diet and bleeding. I ask primary evidence that you are a man, and refuse this appeal from the man to his actions. I know that for myself it makes no difference whether I do or forbear those actions which are reckoned excellent. I cannot consent to pay for a privilege where I have intrinsic right. Few and mean as my gifts may be, I actually am, and do not need for my own assurance or the assurance of my fellows any secondary testimony.

What I must do is all that concerns me, not what the people think. This rule, equally arduous in actual and in intellectual life, may serve for the whole distinction between greatness and meanness. It is the harder, because you will always find those who think they know what is your duty better than you know it. It is easy in the world to live after the world's opinion; it is easy in solitude to live after our own; but the great man is he who in the midst of the crowd keeps with perfect sweetness the independence of solitude.

The objection to conforming to usages that have become dead to you is, that it scatters your force. It loses your time and blurs the impression of your character. If you maintain a dead church, contribute to a dead Bible-society, vote with a great party either for the government or against it, spread your table like base housekeepers,—under all these screens I have difficulty to detect the precise man you are. And, of course, so much force is withdrawn from your proper life.

But do your work, and I shall know you. Do your work, and you shall reinforce yourself. A man must consider what a blindman's-buff is this game of conformity. If I know your sect, I anticipate your argument. I hear a preacher announce for his text and topic the expediency of one of the institutions of his church. Do I not know beforehand that not possibly can he say a new and spontaneous word? Do I not know that, with all this ostentation of examining the grounds of the institution, he will do no such thing? Do I not know that he is pledged to himself not to look but at one side,—the permitted side, not as a man, but as a parish minister? He is a retained attorney, and these airs of the bench are the emptiest affectation. Well, most men have bound their eyes with one or another handkerchief, and attached themselves to some one of these communities of opinion. This conformity makes them not false in a few particulars, authors of a few lies, but false in all particulars. Their every truth is not quite true. Their two is not the real two, their four not the real four; so that every word they say chagrins us, and we know not where to begin to set them right. Meantime nature is not slow to equip us in the prison-uniform of the party to which we adhere. We come to wear one cut of face and figure, and acquire by degrees the gentlest asinine expression. There is a mortifying experience in particular, which does not fail to wreak itself also in the general history; I mean "the foolish face of praise," the forced smile which we put on in company where we do not feel at ease in answer to conversation which does not interest us. The muscles, not spontaneously moved, but moved by a low usurping wilfulness, grow tight about the outline of the face with the most disagreeable sensation.

For nonconformity the world whips you with its displeasure. And therefore a man must know how to estimate a sour face. The by-standers look askance on him in the public street or in the friend's parlour. If this aversation had its origin in contempt and resistance like his own, he might well go home with a sad countenance; but the sour faces of the multitude, like their sweet faces, have no deep cause, but are put on and off as the wind blows and a newspaper directs. Yet is the discontent of the multitude more formidable than that of the senate and the college. It is easy enough for a firm man who knows the world to brook the rage of the cultivated classes. Their rage is decorous and prudent, for they are timid as being very vulnerable themselves. But when to their feminine rage the indignation of the people is added, when the ignorant and the poor are aroused, when the unintelligent brute force that lies at the bottom of society is made to growl and mow, it needs the habit of magnanimity and religion to treat it godlike as a trifle of no concernment.

The other terror that scares us from self-trust is our consistency; a reverence for our past act or word, because the eyes of others have no other data for computing our orbit than our past acts, and we are loath to disappoint them.

But why should you keep your head over your shoulder? Why drag about this corpse of your memory, lest you contradict somewhat you have stated in this or that public place? Suppose you should contradict yourself; what then? It seems to be a rule of wisdom never to rely on your memory alone, scarcely even in acts of pure memory, but to bring the past for judgment into the thousand-eyed present, and live ever in a new day. In your metaphysics you have denied personality to the Deity: yet when the devout motions of the soul come, yield to them heart and life, though they should clothe God with shape and color. Leave your theory, as Joseph his coat in the hand of the harlot, and flee.

A foolish consistency is the hobgoblin of little minds, adored by little statesmen and philosophers and divines. With consistency a great soul has simply nothing to do. He may as well concern himself with his shadow on the wall. Speak what you think now in hard words, and to-morrow speak what to-morrow thinks in hard words again, though it contradict every thing you said to-day.—'Ah, so you shall be sure to be misunderstood.'—Is it so bad, then, to be misunderstood? Pythagoras was misunderstood, and Socrates, and Jesus, and Luther, and Copernicus, and Galileo, and Newton, and every pure and wise spirit that ever took flesh. To be great is to be misunderstood.

I suppose no man can violate his nature. All the sallies of his will are rounded in by the law of his being, as the inequalities of Andes and Himmaleh are insignificant in the curve of the sphere. Nor does it matter how you gauge and try him.

A character is like an acrostic or Alexandrian stanza;—read it forward, backward, or across, it still spells the same thing. In this pleasing, contrite wood-life which God allows me, let me record day by day my honest thought without prospect or retrospect, and, I cannot doubt, it will be found symmetrical, though I mean it not, and see it not. My book should smell of pines and resound with the hum of insects. The swallow over my window should interweave that thread or straw he carries in his bill into my web also. We pass for what we are. Character teaches above our wills. Men imagine that they communicate their virtue or vice only by overt actions, and do not see that virtue or vice emit a breath every moment.

There will be an agreement in whatever variety of actions, so they be each honest and natural in their hour. For of one will, the actions will be harmonious, however unlike they seem. These varieties are lost sight of at a little distance, at a little height of thought. One tendency unites them all. The voyage of the best ship is a zigzag line of a hundred tacks. See the line from a sufficient distance, and it straightens itself to the average tendency. Your genuine action will explain itself, and will explain your other genuine actions. Your conformity explains nothing. Act singly, and what you have already done singly will justify you now. Greatness appeals to the future. If I can be firm enough to-day to do right, and scorn eyes, I must have done so much right before as to defend me now. Be it how it will, do right now. Always scorn appearances, and you always may. The force of character is cumulative. All the foregone days of virtue work their health into this. What makes the majesty of the heroes of the senate and the field, which so fills the imagination? The consciousness of a train of great days and victories behind. They shed an united light on the advancing actor. He is attended as by a visible escort of angels. That is it which throws thunder into Chatham's voice, and dignity into Washington's port, and America into Adams's eye. Honor is venerable to us because it is no ephemeris. It is always ancient virtue. We worship it to-day because it is not of to-day. We love it and pay it homage, because it is not a trap for our love and homage, but is self-dependent, self-derived, and therefore of an old immaculate pedigree, even if shown in a young person.

I hope in these days we have heard the last of conformity and consistency. Let the words be gazetted and ridiculous henceforward. Instead of the gong for dinner, let us hear a whistle from the Spartan fife. Let us never bow and apologize more. A great man is coming to eat at my house. I do not wish to please him; I wish that he should wish to please me. I will stand here for humanity, and though I would make it kind, I would make it true. Let us affront and reprimand the smooth mediocrity and squalid contentment of the times, and hurl in the face of custom, and trade, and office, the fact which is the upshot of all history, that there is a great responsible Thinker and Actor working wherever a man works; that a true man belongs to no other time or place, but is the centre of things. Where he is, there is nature. He measures you, and all men, and all events. Ordinarily, every body in society reminds us of somewhat else, or of some other person. Character, reality, reminds you of nothing else; it takes place of the whole creation. The man must be so much, that he must make all circumstances indifferent. Every true man is a cause, a country, and an age; requires infinite spaces and numbers and time fully to accomplish his design;—and posterity seem to follow his steps as a train of clients. A man Cæsar is born, and for ages after we have a Roman Empire. Christ is born, and millions of minds so grow and cleave to his genius, that he is confounded with virtue and the possible of man. An institution is the lengthened shadow of one man; as, Monachism, of the Hermit Antony; the Reformation, of Luther; Quakerism, of Fox; Methodism, of Wesley; Abolition, of Clarkson. Scipio, Milton called "the height of Rome"; and all history resolves itself very easily into the biography of a few stout and earnest persons.

Let a man then know his worth, and keep things under his feet. Let him not peep or steal, or skulk up and down with the air of a charity-boy, a bastard, or an interloper, in the world which exists for him. But the man in the street, finding no worth in himself which corresponds to the force which built a tower or sculptured a marble god, feels poor when he looks on these. To him a palace, a statue, or a costly book have an alien and forbidding air, much like a gay equipage, and seem to say like that, 'Who are you, Sir?' Yet they all are his, suitors for his notice, petitioners to his faculties that they will come out and take possession. The picture waits for my verdict: it is not to command me, but I am to settle its claims to praise. That popular fable of the sot who was picked up dead drunk in the street, carried to the duke's house, washed and dressed and laid in the duke's bed, and, on his waking, treated with all obsequious ceremony like the duke, and assured that he had been insane, owes its popularity to the fact, that it symbolizes so well the state of man, who is in the world a sort of sot, but now and then wakes up, exercises his reason, and finds himself a true prince.

Our reading is mendicant and sycophantic. In history, our imagination plays us false. Kingdom and lordship, power and estate, are a gaudier vocabulary than private John and Edward in a small house and common day's work; but the things of life are the same to both; the sum total of both is the same. Why all this deference to Alfred, and Scanderbeg, and Gustavus? Suppose they were virtuous; did they wear out virtue? As great a stake depends on your private act to-day, as followed their public and renowned steps. When private men shall act with original views, the lustre will be transferred from the actions of kings to those of gentlemen.

The world has been instructed by its kings, who have so magnetized the eyes of nations. It has been taught by this colossal symbol the mutual reverence that is due from man to man. The joyful loyalty with which men have everywhere suffered the king, the noble, or the great proprietor to walk among them by a law of his own, make his own scale of men and things, and reverse theirs, pay for benefits not with money but with honor, and represent the law in his person, was the hieroglyphic by which they obscurely signified their consciousness of their own right and comeliness, the right of every man.

The magnetism which all original action exerts is explained when we inquire the reason of self-trust. Who is the Trustee? What is the aboriginal Self, on which a universal reliance may be grounded? What is the nature and power of that science-baffling star, without parallax, without calculable elements, which shoots a ray of beauty even into trivial and impure actions, if the least mark of independence appear? The inquiry

leads us to that source, at once the essence of genius, of virtue, and of life, which we call Spontaneity or Instinct. We
denote this primary wisdom as Intuition, whilst all later
teachings are tuitions. In that deep force, the last fact behind
which analysis cannot go, all things find their common origin.
For, the sense of being which in calm hours rises, we know
not how, in the soul, is not diverse from things, from space,
from light, from time, from man, but one with them, and
proceeds obviously from the same source whence their life
and being also proceed. We first share the life by which things
exist, and afterwards see them as appearances in nature, and
forget that we have shared their cause. Here is the fountain
of action and of thought. Here are the lungs of that inspiration which giveth man wisdom, and which cannot be denied
without impiety and atheism. We lie in the lap of immense
intelligence, which makes us receivers of its truth and organs
of its activity. When we discern justice, when we discern
truth, we do nothing of ourselves, but allow a passage to its
beams. If we ask whence this comes, if we seek to pry into
the soul that causes, all philosophy is at fault. Its presence or
its absence is all we can affirm. Every man discriminates between the voluntary acts of his mind, and his involuntary perceptions, and knows that to his involuntary perceptions a
perfect faith is due. He may err in the expression of them, but
he knows that these things are so, like day and night, not to
be disputed. My wilful actions and acquisitions are but roving;—the idlest reverie, the faintest native emotion, command my curiosity and respect. Thoughtless people contradict
as readily the statement of perceptions as of opinions, or
rather much more readily; for, they do not distinguish between perception and notion. They fancy that I choose to see
this or that thing. But perception is not whimsical, but fatal.
If I see a trait, my children will see it after me, and in course
of time, all mankind,—although it may chance that no one
has seen it before me. For my perception of it is as much a
fact as the sun.

The relations of the soul to the divine spirit are so pure,
that it is profane to seek to interpose helps. It must be that
when God speaketh he should communicate, not one thing,
but all things; should fill the world with his voice; should

scatter forth light, nature, time, souls, from the centre of the present thought; and new date and new create the whole. Whenever a mind is simple, and receives a divine wisdom, old things pass away,—means, teachers, texts, temples fall; it lives now, and absorbs past and future into the present hour. All things are made sacred by relation to it,—one as much as another. All things are dissolved to their centre by their cause, and, in the universal miracle, petty and particular miracles disappear. If, therefore, a man claims to know and speak of God, and carries you backward to the phraseology of some old mouldered nation in another country, in another world, believe him not. Is the acorn better than the oak which is its fulness and completion? Is the parent better than the child into whom he has cast his ripened being? Whence, then, this worship of the past? The centuries are conspirators against the sanity and authority of the soul. Time and space are but physiological colors which the eye makes, but the soul is light; where it is, is day; where it was, is night; and history is an impertinence and an injury, if it be any thing more than a cheerful apologue or parable of my being and becoming.

Man is timid and apologetic; he is no longer upright; he dares not say 'I think,' 'I am,' but quotes some saint or sage. He is ashamed before the blade of grass or the blowing rose. These roses under my window make no reference to former roses or to better ones; they are for what they are; they exist with God to-day. There is no time to them. There is simply the rose; it is perfect in every moment of its existence. Before a leaf-bud has burst, its whole life acts; in the full-blown flower there is no more; in the leafless root there is no less. Its nature is satisfied, and it satisfies nature, in all moments alike. But man postpones or remembers; he does not live in the present, but with reverted eye laments the past, or, heedless of the riches that surround him, stands on tiptoe to foresee the future. He cannot be happy and strong until he too lives with nature in the present, above time.

This should be plain enough. Yet see what strong intellects dare not yet hear God himself, unless he speak the phraseology of I know not what David, or Jeremiah, or Paul. We shall not always set so great a price on a few texts, on a few lives. We are like children who repeat by rote the sentences of gran-

dames and tutors, and, as they grow older, of the men of
talents and character they chance to see,—painfully recollecting the exact words they spoke; afterwards, when they come
into the point of view which those had who uttered these
sayings, they understand them, and are willing to let the
words go; for, at any time, they can use words as good when
occasion comes. If we live truly, we shall see truly. It is as
easy for the strong man to be strong, as it is for the weak to
be weak. When we have new perception, we shall gladly dis-
burden the memory of its hoarded treasures as old rubbish.
When a man lives with God, his voice shall be as sweet as the
murmur of the brook and the rustle of the corn.

And now at last the highest truth on this subject remains
unsaid; probably cannot be said; for all that we say is the far-
off remembering of the intuition. That thought, by what I
can now nearest approach to say it, is this. When good is near
you, when you have life in yourself, it is not by any known
or accustomed way; you shall not discern the foot-prints of
any other; you shall not see the face of man; you shall not
hear any name;—the way, the thought, the good, shall be
wholly strange and new. It shall exclude example and experience. You take the way from man, not to man. All persons
that ever existed are its forgotten ministers. Fear and hope are
alike beneath it. There is somewhat low even in hope. In the
hour of vision, there is nothing that can be called gratitude,
nor properly joy. The soul raised over passion beholds identity and eternal causation, perceives the self-existence of Truth
and Right, and calms itself with knowing that all things go
well. Vast spaces of nature, the Atlantic Ocean, the South
Sea,—long intervals of time, years, centuries,—are of no account. This which I think and feel underlay every former state
of life and circumstances, as it does underlie my present, and
what is called life, and what is called death.

Life only avails, not the having lived. Power ceases in the
instant of repose; it resides in the moment of transition from
a past to a new state, in the shooting of the gulf, in the dart-
ing to an aim. This one fact the world hates, that the soul
becomes; for that for ever degrades the past, turns all riches to
poverty, all reputation to a shame, confounds the saint with
the rogue, shoves Jesus and Judas equally aside. Why, then,

do we prate of self-reliance? Inasmuch as the soul is present, there will be power not confident but agent. To talk of reliance is a poor external way of speaking. Speak rather of that which relies, because it works and is. Who has more obedience than I masters me, though he should not raise his finger. Round him I must revolve by the gravitation of spirits. We fancy it rhetoric, when we speak of eminent virtue. We do not yet see that virtue is Height, and that a man or a company of men, plastic and permeable to principles, by the law of nature must overpower and ride all cities, nations, kings, rich men, poets, who are not.

This is the ultimate fact which we so quickly reach on this, as on every topic, the resolution of all into the ever-blessed ONE. Self-existence is the attribute of the Supreme Cause, and it constitutes the measure of good by the degree in which it enters into all lower forms. All things real are so by so much virtue as they contain. Commerce, husbandry, hunting, whaling, war, eloquence, personal weight, are somewhat, and engage my respect as examples of its presence and impure action. I see the same law working in nature for conservation and growth. Power is in nature the essential measure of right. Nature suffers nothing to remain in her kingdoms which cannot help itself. The genesis and maturation of a planet, its poise and orbit, the bended tree recovering itself from the strong wind, the vital resources of every animal and vegetable, are demonstrations of the self-sufficing, and therefore self-relying soul.

Thus all concentrates: let us not rove; let us sit at home with the cause. Let us stun and astonish the intruding rabble of men and books and institutions, by a simple declaration of the divine fact. Bid the invaders take the shoes from off their feet, for God is here within. Let our simplicity judge them, and our docility to our own law demonstrate the poverty of nature and fortune beside our native riches.

But now we are a mob. Man does not stand in awe of man, nor is his genius admonished to stay at home, to put itself in communication with the internal ocean, but it goes abroad to beg a cup of water of the urns of other men. We must go alone. I like the silent church before the service begins, better than any preaching. How far off, how cool, how chaste the persons look, begirt each one with a precinct or sanctuary! So let us always sit. Why should we assume the faults of our friend, or wife, or father, or child, because they sit around our hearth, or are said to have the same blood? All men have my blood, and I have all men's. Not for that will I adopt their petulance or folly, even to the extent of being ashamed of it. But your isolation must not be mechanical, but spiritual, that is, must be elevation. At times the whole world seems to be in conspiracy to importune you with emphatic trifles. Friend, client, child, sickness, fear, want, charity, all knock at once at thy closet door, and say,—'Come out unto us.' But keep thy state; come not into their confusion. The power men possess to annoy me, I give them by a weak curiosity. No man can come near me but through my act. "What we love that we have, but by desire we bereave ourselves of the love."

If we cannot at once rise to the sanctities of obedience and faith, let us at least resist our temptations; let us enter into the state of war, and wake Thor and Woden, courage and constancy, in our Saxon breasts. This is to be done in our smooth times by speaking the truth. Check this lying hospitality and lying affection. Live no longer to the expectation of these deceived and deceiving people with whom we converse. Say to them, O father, O mother, O wife, O brother, O friend, I have lived with you after appearances hitherto. Henceforward I am the truth's. Be it known unto you that henceforward I obey no law less than the eternal law. I will have no covenants but proximities. I shall endeavour to nourish my parents, to support my family, to be the chaste husband of one wife,—but these relations I must fill after a new and unprecedented way. I appeal from your customs. I must be myself. I cannot break myself any longer for you, or you. If you can love me for what I am, we shall be the happier. If you cannot, I will still seek to deserve that you should. I will not hide my tastes or aversions. I will so trust that what is deep is holy, that I will do strongly before the sun and moon whatever inly rejoices me, and the heart appoints. If you are noble, I will love you; if you are not, I will not hurt you and myself by hypocritical attentions. If you are true, but not in the same truth with me, cleave to your companions; I will seek my own. I do this not selfishly, but humbly and truly. It is alike your interest, and mine, and all men's, however long we have dwelt in lies, to live in truth. Does this sound harsh to-day? You will soon love what is dictated by your nature as well as mine, and, if we follow the truth, it will bring us out safe at last.—But so you may give these friends pain. Yes, but I cannot sell my liberty and my power, to save their sensibility. Besides, all persons have their moments of reason, when they look out into the region of absolute truth; then will they justify me, and do the same thing.

The populace think that your rejection of popular standards is a rejection of all standard, and mere antinomianism; and the bold sensualist will use the name of philosophy to gild his crimes. But the law of consciousness abides. There are two confessionals, in one or the other of which we must be shriven. You may fulfil your round of duties by clearing yourself in the *direct*, or in the *reflex* way. Consider whether you have satisfied your relations to father, mother, cousin, neighbour, town, cat, and dog; whether any of these can upbraid you. But I may also neglect this reflex standard, and absolve me to myself. I have my own stern claims and perfect circle. It denies the name of duty to many offices that are called duties. But if I can discharge its debts, it enables me to dispense with the popular code. If any one imagines that this law is lax, let him keep its commandment one day.

And truly it demands something godlike in him who has cast off the common motives of humanity, and has ventured to trust himself for a taskmaster. High be his heart, faithful his will, clear his sight, that he may in good earnest be doctrine, society, law, to himself, that a simple purpose may be to him as strong as iron necessity is to others!

If any man consider the present aspects of what is called by distinction *society*, he will see the need of these ethics. The sinew and heart of man seem to be drawn out, and we are become timorous, desponding whimperers. We are afraid of truth, afraid of fortune, afraid of death, and afraid of each other. Our age yields no great and perfect persons. We want men and women who shall renovate life and our social state, but we see that most natures are insolvent, cannot satisfy their own wants, have an ambition out of all proportion to their practical force, and do lean and beg day and night continually. Our housekeeping is mendicant, our arts, our occupations, our marriages, our religion, we have not chosen, but society has chosen for us. We are parlour soldiers. We shun the rugged battle of fate, where strength is born.

If our young men miscarry in their first enterprises, they lose all heart. If the young merchant fails, men say he is *ruined*. If the finest genius studies at one of our colleges, and is not installed in an office within one year afterwards in the cities or suburbs of Boston or New York, it seems to his friends and to himself that he is right in being disheartened, and in complaining the rest of his life. A sturdy lad from New Hampshire or Vermont, who in turn tries all the professions, who *teams it, farms it, peddles*, keeps a school, preaches, edits a newspaper, goes to Congress, buys a township, and so forth, in successive years, and always, like a cat, falls on his feet, is worth a hundred of these city dolls. He walks abreast with his days, and feels no shame in not 'studying a profession,' for he does not postpone his life, but lives already. He has not one chance, but a hundred chances. Let a Stoic open the resources of man, and tell men they are not leaning willows, but can and must detach themselves; that with the exercise of self-trust, new powers shall appear; that a man is the word made flesh, born to shed healing to the nations, that he should be ashamed of our compassion, and that the moment he acts from himself, tossing the laws, the books, idolatries, and customs out of the window, we pity him no more, but thank and revere him,—and that teacher shall restore the life of man to splendor, and make his name dear to all history.

It is easy to see that a greater self-reliance must work a revolution in all the offices and relations of men; in their religion; in their education; in their pursuits; their modes of living; their association; in their property; in their speculative views.

1. In what prayers do men allow themselves! That which they call a holy office is not so much as brave and manly. Prayer looks abroad and asks for some foreign addition to come through some foreign virtue, and loses itself in endless mazes of natural and supernatural, and mediatorial and miraculous. Prayer that craves a particular commodity,—any thing less than all good,—is vicious. Prayer is the contemplation of

the facts of life from the highest point of view. It is the soliloquy of a beholding and jubilant soul. It is the spirit of God
pronouncing his works good. But prayer as a means to effect
a private end is meanness and theft. It supposes dualism and
not unity in nature and consciousness. As soon as the man is
at one with God, he will not beg. He will then see prayer in
all action. The prayer of the farmer kneeling in his field to
weed it, the prayer of the rower kneeling with the stroke of
his oar, are true prayers heard throughout nature, though for
cheap ends. Caratach, in Fletcher's Bonduca, when admonished to inquire the mind of the god Audate, replies,—

> "His hidden meaning lies in our endeavours;
> Our valors are our best gods."

Another sort of false prayers are our regrets. Discontent is
the want of self-reliance: it is infirmity of will. Regret calamities, if you can thereby help the sufferer; if not, attend your
own work, and already the evil begins to be repaired. Our
sympathy is just as base. We come to them who weep foolishly, and sit down and cry for company, instead of imparting
to them truth and health in rough electric shocks, putting
them once more in communication with their own reason.
The secret of fortune is joy in our hands. Welcome evermore
to gods and men is the self-helping man. For him all doors
are flung wide: him all tongues greet, all honors crown, all
eyes follow with desire. Our love goes out to him and embraces him, because he did not need it. We solicitously and
apologetically caress and celebrate him, because he held on his
way and scorned our disapprobation. The gods love him
because men hated him. "To the persevering mortal," said
Zoroaster, "the blessed Immortals are swift."

As men's prayers are a disease of the will, so are their creeds
a disease of the intellect. They say with those foolish Israel-
ites, 'Let not God speak to us, lest we die. Speak thou, speak
any man with us, and we will obey.' Everywhere I am hindered of meeting God in my brother, because he has shut his
own temple doors, and recites fables merely of his brother's,
or his brother's brother's God. Every new mind is a new
classification. If it prove a mind of uncommon activity and
power, a Locke, a Lavoisier, a Hutton, a Bentham, a Fourier,

it imposes its classification on other men, and lo! a new system. In proportion to the depth of the thought, and so to the number of the objects it touches and brings within reach of the pupil, is his complacency. But chiefly is this apparent in creeds and churches, which are also classifications of some powerful mind acting on the elemental thought of duty, and man's relation to the Highest. Such is Calvinism, Quakerism, Swedenborgism. The pupil takes the same delight in subordinating every thing to the new terminology, as a girl who has just learned botany in seeing a new earth and new seasons thereby. It will happen for a time, that the pupil will find his intellectual power has grown by the study of his master's mind. But in all unbalanced minds, the classification is idolized, passes for the end, and not for a speedily exhaustible means, so that the walls of the system blend to their eye in the remote horizon with the walls of the universe; the luminaries of heaven seem to them hung on the arch their master built. They cannot imagine how you aliens have any right to see,—how you can see; 'It must be somehow that you stole the light from us.' They do not yet perceive, that light, unsystematic, indomitable, will break into any cabin, even into theirs. Let them chirp awhile and call it their own. If they are honest and do well, presently their neat new pinfold will be too strait and low, will crack, will lean, will rot and vanish, and the immortal light, all young and joyful, million-orbed, million-colored, will beam over the universe as on the first morning.

2. It is for want of self-culture that the superstition of Travelling, whose idols are Italy, England, Egypt, retains its fascination for all educated Americans. They who made England, Italy, or Greece venerable in the imagination did so by sticking fast where they were, like an axis of the earth. In manly hours, we feel that duty is our place. The soul is no traveller; the wise man stays at home, and when his necessities, his duties, on any occasion call him from his house, or into foreign lands, he is at home still, and shall make men sensible by the expression of his countenance, that he goes the missionary of wisdom and virtue, and visits cities and men like a sovereign, and not like an interloper or a valet.

I have no churlish objection to the circumnavigation of the

globe, for the purposes of art, of study, and benevolence, so that the man is first domesticated, or does not go abroad with the hope of finding somewhat greater than he knows. He who travels to be amused, or to get somewhat which he does not carry, travels away from himself, and grows old even in youth among old things. In Thebes, in Palmyra, his will and mind have become old and dilapidated as they. He carries ruins to ruins.

Travelling is a fool's paradise. Our first journeys discover to us the indifference of places. At home I dream that at Naples, at Rome, I can be intoxicated with beauty, and lose my sadness. I pack my trunk, embrace my friends, embark on the sea, and at last wake up in Naples, and there beside me is the stern fact, the sad self, unrelenting, identical, that I fled from. I seek the Vatican, and the palaces. I affect to be intoxicated with sights and suggestions, but I am not intoxicated. My giant goes with me wherever I go.

3. But the rage of travelling is a symptom of a deeper unsoundness affecting the whole intellectual action. The intellect is vagabond, and our system of education fosters restlessness. Our minds travel when our bodies are forced to stay at home. We imitate; and what is imitation but the travelling of the mind? Our houses are built with foreign taste; our shelves are garnished with foreign ornaments; our opinions, our tastes, our faculties, lean, and follow the Past and the Distant. The soul created the arts wherever they have flourished. It was in his own mind that the artist sought his model. It was an application of his own thought to the thing to be done and the conditions to be observed. And why need we copy the Doric or the Gothic model? Beauty, convenience, grandeur of thought, and quaint expression are as near to us as to any, and if the American artist will study with hope and love the precise thing to be done by him, considering the climate, the soil, the length of the day, the wants of the people, the habit and form of the government, he will create a house in which all these will find themselves fitted, and taste and sentiment will be satisfied also.

Insist on yourself; never imitate. Your own gift you can present every moment with the cumulative force of a whole life's cultivation; but of the adopted talent of another, you have only an extemporaneous, half possession. That which each can do best, none but his Maker can teach him. No man yet knows what it is, nor can, till that person has exhibited it. Where is the master who could have taught Shakspeare? Where is the master who could have instructed Franklin, or Washington, or Bacon, or Newton? Every great man is a unique. The Scipionism of Scipio is precisely that part he could not borrow. Shakspeare will never be made by the study of Shakspeare. Do that which is assigned you, and you cannot hope too much or dare too much. There is at this moment for you an utterance brave and grand as that of the colossal chisel of Phidias, or trowel of the Egyptians, or the pen of Moses, or Dante, but different from all these. Not possibly will the soul all rich, all eloquent, with thousand-cloven tongue, deign to repeat itself; but if you can hear what these patriarchs say, surely you can reply to them in the same pitch of voice; for the ear and the tongue are two organs of one nature. Abide in the simple and noble regions of thy life, obey thy heart, and thou shalt reproduce the Foreworld again.

4. As our Religion, our Education, our Art look abroad, so does our spirit of society. All men plume themselves on the improvement of society, and no man improves.

Society never advances. It recedes as fast on one side as it gains on the other. It undergoes continual changes; it is barbarous, it is civilized, it is christianized, it is rich, it is scientific; but this change is not amelioration. For every thing that is given, something is taken. Society acquires new arts, and loses old instincts. What a contrast between the well-clad, reading, writing, thinking American, with a watch, a pencil, and a bill of exchange in his pocket, and the naked New Zealander, whose property is a club, a spear, a mat, and an undivided twentieth of a shed to sleep under! But compare the health of the two men, and you shall see that the white man has lost his aboriginal strength. If the traveller tell us truly, strike the savage with a broad axe, and in a day or two the flesh shall unite and heal as if you struck the blow into soft pitch, and the same blow shall send the white to his grave.

The civilized man has built a coach, but has lost the use of his feet. He is supported on crutches, but lacks so much support of muscle. He has a fine Geneva watch, but he fails of the skill to tell the hour by the sun. A Greenwich nautical almanac he has, and so being sure of the information when he wants it, the man in the street does not know a star in the sky. The solstice he does not observe; the equinox he knows as little; and the whole bright calendar of the year is without a dial in his mind. His note-books impair his memory; his libraries overload his wit; the insurance-office increases the number of accidents; and it may be a question whether machinery does not encumber; whether we have not lost by refinement some energy, by a Christianity entrenched in establishments and forms, some vigor of wild virtue. For every Stoic was a Stoic; but in Christendom where is the Christian?

There is no more deviation in the moral standard than in the standard of height or bulk. No greater men are now than ever were. A singular equality may be observed between the great men of the first and of the last ages; nor can all the science, art, religion, and philosophy of the nineteenth century avail to educate greater men than Plutarch's heroes, three or four and twenty centuries ago. Not in time is the race progressive. Phocion, Socrates, Anaxagoras, Diogenes, are great men, but they leave no class. He who is really of their class will not be called by their name, but will be his own man, and, in his turn, the founder of a sect. The arts and inventions of each period are only its costume, and do not invigorate men. The harm of the improved machinery may compensate its good. Hudson and Behring accomplished so much in their fishing-boats, as to astonish Parry and Franklin, whose equipment exhausted the resources of science and art. Galileo, with an opera-glass, discovered a more splendid series of celestial phenomena than any one since. Columbus found the New World in an undecked boat. It is curious to see the periodical disuse and perishing of means and machinery, which were introduced with loud laudation a few years or centuries before. The great genius returns to essential man. We reckoned the improvements of the art of war among the triumphs of science, and yet Napoleon conquered Europe by the bivouac, which consisted of falling back on naked valor, and disencumbering it of all aids. The Emperor held it impossible to make a perfect army, says Las Casas, "without abolishing our arms, magazines, commissaries, and carriages, until, in imitation of the Roman custom, the soldier should receive his supply of corn, grind it in his hand-mill, and bake his bread himself."

Society is a wave. The wave moves onward, but the water of which it is composed does not. The same particle does not rise from the valley to the ridge. Its unity is only phenomenal. The persons who make up a nation to-day, next year die, and their experience with them.

And so the reliance on Property, including the reliance on governments which protect it, is the want of self-reliance. Men have looked away from themselves and at things so long, that they have come to esteem the religious, learned, and civil institutions as guards of property, and they deprecate assaults on these, because they feel them to be assaults on property. They measure their esteem of each other by what each has, and not by what each is. But a cultivated man becomes ashamed of his property, out of new respect for his nature. Especially he hates what he has, if he see that it is accidental,—came to him by inheritance, or gift, or crime; then he feels that it is not having; it does not belong to him, has no root in him, and merely lies there, because no revolution or no robber takes it away. But that which a man is does always by necessity acquire, and what the man acquires is living property, which does not wait the beck of rulers, or mobs, or revolutions, or fire, or storm, or bankruptcies, but perpetually renews itself wherever the man breathes. "Thy lot or portion of life," said the Caliph Ali, "is seeking after thee; therefore be at rest from seeking after it." Our dependence on these foreign goods leads us to our slavish respect for numbers. The political parties meet in numerous conventions; the greater the concourse, and with each new uproar of announcement, The delegation from Essex! The Democrats from New Hampshire! The Whigs of Maine! the young patriot feels himself stronger than before by a new thousand of eyes and arms. In like manner the reformers summon conventions, and vote and resolve in multitude. Not so, O friends! will the God deign to enter and inhabit you, but by a method precisely the reverse. It is only as a man puts off all foreign support, and stands alone, that I see him to be strong and to prevail. He is weaker by every recruit to his banner. Is not a man better than a town? Ask nothing of men, and in the endless mutation, thou only firm column must presently appear the upholder of all that surrounds thee. He who knows that power is inborn, that he is weak because he has looked for good out of him and elsewhere, and so perceiving, throws himself unhesitatingly on his thought, instantly rights himself, stands in the erect position, commands his limbs, works miracles; just as a man who stands on his feet is stronger than a man who stands on his head.

So use all that is called Fortune. Most men gamble with her, and gain all, and lose all, as her wheel rolls. But do thou leave as unlawful these winnings, and deal with Cause and Effect, the chancellors of God. In the Will work and acquire, and thou hast chained the wheel of Chance, and shalt sit hereafter out of fear from her rotations. A political victory, a rise of rents, the recovery of your sick, or the return of your absent friend, or some other favorable event, raises your spirits, and you think good days are preparing for you. Do not believe it. Nothing can bring you peace but yourself. Nothing can bring you peace but the triumph of principles.

COMPENSATION

The wings of Time are black and white,
Pied with morning and with night.
Mountain tall and ocean deep
Trembling balance duly keep.
In changing moon, in tidal wave,
Glows the feud of Want and Have.
Gauge of more and less through space
Electric star and pencil plays.
The lonely Earth amid the balls
That hurry through the eternal halls,
A makeweight flying to the void,
Supplemental asteroid,
Or compensatory spark,
Shoots across the neutral Dark.

Man's the elm, and Wealth the vine;
Stanch and strong the tendrils twine:
Though the frail ringlets thee deceive,
None from its stock that vine can reave.
Fear not, then, thou child infirm,
There's no god dare wrong a worm.
Laurel crowns cleave to deserts,
And power to him who power exerts;
Hast not thy share? On winged feet,
Lo! it rushes thee to meet;
And all that Nature made thy own,
Floating in air or pent in stone,
Will rive the hills and swim the sea,
And, like thy shadow, follow thee.

Compensation

EVER SINCE I was a boy, I have wished to write a discourse on Compensation: for it seemed to me when very young, that on this subject life was ahead of theology, and the people knew more than the preachers taught. The documents, too, from which the doctrine is to be drawn, charmed my fancy by their endless variety, and lay always before me, even in sleep; for they are the tools in our hands, the bread in our basket, the transactions of the street, the farm, and the dwelling-house, greetings, relations, debts and credits, the influence of character, the nature and endowment of all men. It seemed to me, also, that in it might be shown men a ray of divinity, the present action of the soul of this world, clean from all vestige of tradition, and so the heart of man might be bathed by an inundation of eternal love, conversing with that which he knows was always and always must be, because it really is now. It appeared, moreover, that if this doctrine could be stated in terms with any resemblance to those bright intuitions in which this truth is sometimes revealed to us, it would be a star in many dark hours and crooked passages in our journey that would not suffer us to lose our way.

I was lately confirmed in these desires by hearing a sermon at church. The preacher, a man esteemed for his orthodoxy, unfolded in the ordinary manner the doctrine of the Last Judgment. He assumed, that judgment is not executed in this world; that the wicked are successful; that the good are miserable; and then urged from reason and from Scripture a compensation to be made to both parties in the next life. No offence appeared to be taken by the congregation at this doctrine. As far as I could observe, when the meeting broke up, they separated without remark on the sermon.

Yet what was the import of this teaching? What did the preacher mean by saying that the good are miserable in the present life? Was it that houses and lands, offices, wine, horses, dress, luxury, are had by unprincipled men, whilst the saints are poor and despised; and that a compensation is to

be made to these last hereafter, by giving them the like gratifications another day,—bank-stock and doubloons, venison
and champagne? This must be the compensation intended;
for what else? Is it that they are to have leave to pray and
praise? to love and serve men? Why, that they can do now.
The legitimate inference the disciple would draw was,—'We
are to have *such* a good time as the sinners have now';—or,
to push it to its extreme import,—'You sin now; we shall sin
by and by; we would sin now, if we could; not being successful, we expect our revenge to-morrow.'

The fallacy lay in the immense concession, that the bad are
successful; that justice is not done now. The blindness of the
preacher consisted in deferring to the base estimate of the
market of what constitutes a manly success, instead of confronting and convicting the world from the truth; announcing the presence of the soul; the omnipotence of the will: and
so establishing the standard of good and ill, of success and
falsehood.

I find a similar base tone in the popular religious works of
the day, and the same doctrines assumed by the literary men
when occasionally they treat the related topics. I think that our
popular theology has gained in decorum, and not in principle,
over the superstitions it has displaced. But men are better than
this theology. Their daily life gives it the lie. Every ingenuous
and aspiring soul leaves the doctrine behind him in his own
experience; and all men feel sometimes the falsehood which
they cannot demonstrate. For men are wiser than they know.
That which they hear in schools and pulpits without afterthought, if said in conversation, would probably be questioned
in silence. If a man dogmatize in a mixed company on Providence and the divine laws, he is answered by a silence which
conveys well enough to an observer the dissatisfaction of the
hearer, but his incapacity to make his own statement.

I shall attempt in this and the following chapter to record
some facts that indicate the path of the law of Compensation;
happy beyond my expectation, if I shall truly draw the smallest arc of this circle.

POLARITY, or action and reaction, we meet in every part of
nature; in darkness and light; in heat and cold; in the ebb and

flow of waters; in male and female; in the inspiration and expiration of plants and animals; in the equation of quantity and quality in the fluids of the animal body; in the systole and diastole of the heart; in the undulations of fluids, and of sound; in the centrifugal and centripetal gravity; in electricity, galvanism, and chemical affinity. Superinduce magnetism at one end of a needle; the opposite magnetism takes place at the other end. If the south attracts, the north repels. To empty here, you must condense there. An inevitable dualism bisects nature, so that each thing is a half, and suggests another thing to make it whole; as, spirit, matter; man, woman; odd, even; subjective, objective; in, out; upper, under; motion, rest; yea, nay.

Whilst the world is thus dual, so is every one of its parts. The entire system of things gets represented in every particle. There is somewhat that resembles the ebb and flow of the sea, day and night, man and woman, in a single needle of the pine, in a kernel of corn, in each individual of every animal tribe. The reaction, so grand in the elements, is repeated within these small boundaries. For example, in the animal kingdom the physiologist has observed that no creatures are favorites, but a certain compensation balances every gift and every defect. A surplusage given to one part is paid out of a reduction from another part of the same creature. If the head and neck are enlarged, the trunk and extremities are cut short.

The theory of the mechanic forces is another example. What we gain in power is lost in time; and the converse. The periodic or compensating errors of the planets is another instance. The influences of climate and soil in political history are another. The cold climate invigorates. The barren soil does not breed fevers, crocodiles, tigers, or scorpions.

The same dualism underlies the nature and condition of man. Every excess causes a defect; every defect an excess. Every sweet hath its sour; every evil its good. Every faculty which is a receiver of pleasure has an equal penalty put on its abuse. It is to answer for its moderation with its life. For every grain of wit there is a grain of folly. For every thing you have missed, you have gained something else; and for every thing you gain, you lose something. If riches increase, they are increased that use them. If the gatherer gathers too much, nature takes out of the man what she puts into his

chest; swells the estate, but kills the owner. Nature hates monopolies and exceptions. The waves of the sea do not more
speedily seek a level from their loftiest tossing, than the varieties of condition tend to equalize themselves. There is always
some levelling circumstance that puts down the overbearing,
the strong, the rich, the fortunate, substantially on the same
ground with all others. Is a man too strong and fierce for
society, and by temper and position a bad citizen,—a morose
ruffian, with a dash of the pirate in him;—nature sends him
a troop of pretty sons and daughters, who are getting along
in the dame's classes at the village school, and love and fear
for them smooths his grim scowl to courtesy. Thus she contrives to intenerate the granite and felspar, takes the boar out
and puts the lamb in, and keeps her balance true.

The farmer imagines power and place are fine things. But
the President has paid dear for his White House. It has commonly cost him all his peace, and the best of his manly attributes. To preserve for a short time so conspicuous an
appearance before the world, he is content to eat dust before
the real masters who stand erect behind the throne. Or, do
men desire the more substantial and permanent grandeur of
genius? Neither has this an immunity. He who by force of
will or of thought is great, and overlooks thousands, has the
charges of that eminence. With every influx of light comes
new danger. Has he light? he must bear witness to the light,
and always outrun that sympathy which gives him such keen
satisfaction, by his fidelity to new revelations of the incessant
soul. He must hate father and mother, wife and child. Has he
all that the world loves and admires and covets?—he must
cast behind him their admiration, and afflict them by faithful-
ness to his truth, and become a byword and a hissing.

This law writes the laws of cities and nations. It is in vain
to build or plot or combine against it. Things refuse to be
mismanaged long. *Res nolunt diu male administrari.* Though
no checks to a new evil appear, the checks exist, and will appear. If the government is cruel, the governor's life is not
safe. If you tax too high, the revenue will yield nothing. If
you make the criminal code sanguinary, juries will not con-
vict. If the law is too mild, private vengeance comes in. If the
government is a terrific democracy, the pressure is resisted by

an overcharge of energy in the citizen, and life glows with a
fiercer flame. The true life and satisfactions of man seem to
elude the utmost rigors or felicities of condition, and to establish themselves with great indifference under all varieties of
circumstances. Under all governments the influence of character remains the same,—in Turkey and in New England
about alike. Under the primeval despots of Egypt, history
honestly confesses that man must have been as free as culture
could make him.

These appearances indicate the fact that the universe is represented in every one of its particles. Every thing in nature
contains all the powers of nature. Every thing is made of one
hidden stuff; as the naturalist sees one type under every metamorphosis, and regards a horse as a running man, a fish as a
swimming man, a bird as a flying man, a tree as a rooted man.
Each new form repeats not only the main character of the
type, but part for part all the details, all the aims, further-
ances, hindrances, energies, and whole system of every other.
Every occupation, trade, art, transaction, is a compend of the
world, and a correlative of every other. Each one is an entire
emblem of human life; of its good and ill, its trials, its enemies, its course and its end. And each one must somehow
accommodate the whole man, and recite all his destiny.

The world globes itself in a drop of dew. The microscope
cannot find the animalcule which is less perfect for being little. Eyes, ears, taste, smell, motion, resistance, appetite, and
organs of reproduction that take hold on eternity,—all find
room to consist in the small creature. So do we put our life
into every act. The true doctrine of omnipresence is, that God
reappears with all his parts in every moss and cobweb. The
value of the universe contrives to throw itself into every
point. If the good is there, so is the evil; if the affinity, so the
repulsion; if the force, so the limitation.

Thus is the universe alive. All things are moral. That soul,
which within us is a sentiment, outside of us is a law. We feel
its inspiration; out there in history we can see its fatal
strength. "It is in the world, and the world was made by it."
Justice is not postponed. A perfect equity adjusts its balance
in all parts of life. Οἱ χύβοι Διὸς ἀεὶ εὐπίπτουσι,—
The dice of God are always loaded. The world looks like a

multiplication-table, or a mathematical equation, which, turn it how you will, balances itself. Take what figure you will, its exact value, nor more nor less, still returns to you. Every secret is told, every crime is punished, every virtue rewarded, every wrong redressed, in silence and certainty. What we call retribution is the universal necessity by which the whole appears wherever a part appears. If you see smoke, there must be fire. If you see a hand or a limb, you know that the trunk to which it belongs is there behind.

Every act rewards itself, or, in other words, integrates itself, in a twofold manner; first, in the thing, or in real nature; and secondly, in the circumstance, or in apparent nature. Men call the circumstance the retribution. The causal retribution is in the thing, and is seen by the soul. The retribution in the circumstance is seen by the understanding; it is inseparable from the thing, but is often spread over a long time, and so does not become distinct until after many years. The specific stripes may follow late after the offence, but they follow because they accompany it. Crime and punishment grow out of one stem. Punishment is a fruit that unsuspected ripens within the flower of the pleasure which concealed it. Cause and effect, means and ends, seed and fruit, cannot be severed; for the effect already blooms in the cause, the end preëxists in the means, the fruit in the seed.

Whilst thus the world will be whole, and refuses to be disparted, we seek to act partially, to sunder, to appropriate; for example,—to gratify the senses, we sever the pleasure of the senses from the needs of the character. The ingenuity of man has always been dedicated to the solution of one problem,—how to detach the sensual sweet, the sensual strong, the sensual bright, &c., from the moral sweet, the moral deep, the moral fair; that is, again, to contrive to cut clean off this upper surface so thin as to leave it bottomless; to get a *one end*, without an *other end*. The soul says, Eat; the body would feast. The soul says, The man and woman shall be one flesh and one soul; the body would join the flesh only. The soul says, Have dominion over all things to the ends of virtue; the body would have the power over things to its own ends.

The soul strives amain to live and work through all things. It would be the only fact. All things shall be added unto it,—

power, pleasure, knowledge, beauty. The particular man aims
to be somebody; to set up for himself; to truck and higgle for
a private good; and, in particulars, to ride, that he may ride;
to dress, that he may be dressed; to eat, that he may eat; and
to govern, that he may be seen. Men seek to be great; they
would have offices, wealth, power, and fame. They think that
to be great is to possess one one side of nature,—the sweet, without the other side,—the bitter.

This dividing and detaching is steadily counteracted. Up to
this day, it must be owned, no projector has had the smallest
success. The parted water reunites behind our hand. Pleasure
is taken out of pleasant things, profit out of profitable things,
power out of strong things, as soon as we seek to separate
them from the whole. We can no more halve things and get
the sensual good, by itself, than we can get an inside that shall
have no outside, or a light without a shadow. "Drive out nature with a fork, she comes running back."

Life invests itself with inevitable conditions, which the unwise seek to dodge, which one and another brags that he does
not know; that they do not touch him;—but the brag is on
his lips, the conditions are in his soul. If he escapes them in
one part, they attack him in another more vital part. If he has
escaped them in form, and in the appearance, it is because he
has resisted his life, and fled from himself, and the retribution
is so much death. So signal is the failure of all attempts to
make this separation of the good from the tax, that the experiment would not be tried,—since to try it is to be mad,—but
for the circumstance, that when the disease began in the will,
of rebellion and separation, the intellect is at once infected, so
that the man ceases to see God whole in each object, but is
able to see the sensual allurement of an object, and not see
the sensual hurt; he sees the mermaid's head, but not the
dragon's tail; and thinks he can cut off that which he would
have, from that which he would not have. "How secret art
thou who dwellest in the highest heavens in silence, O thou
only great God, sprinkling with an unwearied Providence certain penal blindnesses upon such as have unbridled desires!"*

The human soul is true to these facts in the painting of

*St. Augustine, Confessions, B. I.

fable, of history, of law, of proverbs, of conversation. It finds a tongue in literature unawares. Thus the Greeks called Jupiter, Supreme Mind; but having traditionally ascribed to him many base actions, they involuntarily made amends to reason, by tying up the hands of so bad a god. He is made as helpless as a king of England. Prometheus knows one secret which Jove must bargain for; Minerva, another. He cannot get his own thunders; Minerva keeps the key of them.

> "Of all the gods, I only know the keys
> That ope the solid doors within whose vaults
> His thunders sleep."

A plain confession of the in-working of the All, and of its moral aim. The Indian mythology ends in the same ethics; and it would seem impossible for any fable to be invented and get any currency which was not moral. Aurora forgot to ask youth for her lover, and though Tithonus is immortal, he is old. Achilles is not quite invulnerable; the sacred waters did not wash the heel by which Thetis held him. Siegfried, in the Nibelungen, is not quite immortal, for a leaf fell on his back whilst he was bathing in the dragon's blood, and that spot which it covered is mortal. And so it must be. There is a crack in every thing God has made. It would seem, there is always this vindictive circumstance stealing in at unawares, even into the wild poesy in which the human fancy attempted to make bold holiday, and to shake itself free of the old laws,—this back-stroke, this kick of the gun, certifying that the law is fatal; that in nature nothing can be given, all things are sold.

This is that ancient doctrine of Nemesis, who keeps watch in the universe, and lets no offence go unchastised. The Furies, they said, are attendants on justice, and if the sun in heaven should transgress his path, they would punish him. The poets related that stone walls, and iron swords, and leathern thongs had an occult sympathy with the wrongs of their owners; that the belt which Ajax gave Hector dragged the Trojan hero over the field at the wheels of the car of Achilles, and the sword which Hector gave Ajax was that on whose point Ajax fell. They recorded, that when the Thasians erected a statue to Theagenes, a victor in the games, one of his rivals went to it by night, and endeavoured to throw it down by repeated blows, until at last he moved it from its pedestal, and was crushed to death beneath its fall.

This voice of fable has in it somewhat divine. It came from thought above the will of the writer. That is the best part of each writer, which has nothing private in it; that which he does not know; that which flowed out of his constitution, and not from his too active invention; that which in the study of a single artist you might not easily find, but in the study of many, you would abstract as the spirit of them all. Phidias it is not, but the work of man in that early Hellenic world, that I would know. The name and circumstance of Phidias, however convenient for history, embarrass when we come to the highest criticism. We are to see that which man was tending to do in a given period, and was hindered, or, if you will, modified in doing, by the interfering volitions of Phidias, of Dante, of Shakspeare, the organ whereby man at the moment wrought.

Still more striking is the expression of this fact in the proverbs of all nations, which are always the literature of reason, or the statements of an absolute truth, without qualification. Proverbs, like the sacred books of each nation, are the sanctuary of the intuitions. That which the droning world, chained to appearances, will not allow the realist to say in his own words, it will suffer him to say in proverbs without contradiction. And this law of laws which the pulpit, the senate, and the college deny, is hourly preached in all markets and workshops by flights of proverbs, whose teaching is as true and as omnipresent as that of birds and flies.

All things are double, one against another.—Tit for tat; an eye for an eye; a tooth for a tooth; blood for blood; measure for measure; love for love.—Give and it shall be given you.—He that watereth shall be watered himself.—What will you have? quoth God; pay for it and take it.—Nothing venture, nothing have.—Thou shalt be paid exactly for what thou hast done, no more, no less.—Who doth not work shall not eat.—Harm watch, harm catch.—Curses always recoil on the head of him who imprecates them.—If you put a chain around the neck of a slave, the other end fastens itself around your own.—Bad counsel confounds the adviser.—The Devil is an ass.

It is thus written, because it is thus in life. Our action is overmastered and characterized above our will by the law of nature. We aim at a petty end quite aside from the public good, but our act arranges itself by irresistible magnetism in a line with the poles of the world.

A man cannot speak but he judges himself. With his will, or against his will, he draws his portrait to the eye of his companions by every word. Every opinion reacts on him who utters it. It is a thread-ball thrown at a mark, but the other end remains in the thrower's bag. Or, rather, it is a harpoon hurled at the whale, unwinding, as it flies, a coil of cord in the boat, and if the harpoon is not good, or not well thrown, it will go nigh to cut the steersman in twain, or to sink the boat.

You cannot do wrong without suffering wrong. "No man had ever a point of pride that was not injurious to him," said Burke. The exclusive in fashionable life does not see that he excludes himself from enjoyment, in the attempt to appropriate it. The exclusionist in religion does not see that he shuts the door of heaven on himself, in striving to shut out others. Treat men as pawns and ninepins, and you shall suffer as well as they. If you leave out their heart, you shall lose your own. The senses would make things of all persons; of women, of children, of the poor. The vulgar proverb, "I will get it from his purse or get it from his skin," is sound philosophy.

All infractions of love and equity in our social relations are speedily punished. They are punished by fear. Whilst I stand in simple relations to my fellow-man, I have no displeasure in meeting him. We meet as water meets water, or as two currents of air mix, with perfect diffusion and interpenetration of nature. But as soon as there is any departure from simplicity, and attempt at halfness, or good for me that is not good for him, my neighbour feels the wrong; he shrinks from me as far as I have shrunk from him; his eyes no longer seek mine; there is war between us; there is hate in him and fear in me.

All the old abuses in society, universal and particular, all unjust accumulations of property and power, are avenged in the same manner. Fear is an instructer of great sagacity, and the herald of all revolutions. One thing he teaches, that there is rottenness where he appears. He is a carrion crow, and though you see not well what he hovers for, there is death somewhere. Our property is timid, our laws are timid, our cultivated classes are timid. Fear for ages has boded and mowed and gibbered over government and property. That obscene bird is not there for nothing. He indicates great wrongs which must be revised.

Of the like nature is that expectation of change which instantly follows the suspension of our voluntary activity. The terror of cloudless noon, the emerald of Polycrates, the awe of prosperity, the instinct which leads every generous soul to impose on itself tasks of a noble asceticism and vicarious virtue, are the tremblings of the balance of justice through the heart and mind of man.

Experienced men of the world know very well that it is best to pay scot and lot as they go along, and that a man often pays dear for a small frugality. The borrower runs in his own debt. Has a man gained any thing who has received a hundred favors and rendered none? Has he gained by borrowing, through indolence or cunning, his neighbour's wares, or horses, or money? There arises on the deed the instant acknowledgment of benefit on the one part, and of debt on the other; that is, of superiority and inferiority. The transaction remains in the memory of himself and his neighbour; and every new transaction alters, according to its nature, their relation to each other. He may soon come to see that he had better have broken his own bones than to have ridden in his neighbour's coach, and that "the highest price he can pay for a thing is to ask for it."

A wise man will extend this lesson to all parts of life, and know that it is the part of prudence to face every claimant, and pay every just demand on your time, your talents, or your heart. Always pay; for, first or last, you must pay your entire debt. Persons and events may stand for a time between you and justice, but it is only a postponement. You must pay at last your own debt. If you are wise, you will dread a prosperity which only loads you with more. Benefit is the end of nature. But for every benefit which you receive, a tax is levied. He is great who confers the most benefits. He is base—and that is the one base thing in the universe—to receive favors and render none. In the order of nature we cannot render benefits to those from whom we receive them, or only sel-

dom. But the benefit we receive must be rendered again, line
for line, deed for deed, cent for cent, to somebody. Beware
of too much good staying in your hand. It will fast corrupt
and worm worms. Pay it away quickly in some sort.

Labor is watched over by the same pitiless laws. Cheapest,
say the prudent, is the dearest labor. What we buy in a
broom, a mat, a wagon, a knife, is some application of good
sense to a common want. It is best to pay in your land a
skilful gardener, or to buy good sense applied to gardening;
in your sailor, good sense applied to navigation; in the house,
good sense applied to cooking, sewing, serving; in your
agent, good sense applied to accounts and affairs. So do you
multiply your presence, or spread yourself throughout your
estate. But because of the dual constitution of things, in labor
as in life there can be no cheating. The thief steals from himself. The swindler swindles himself. For the real price of labor
is knowledge and virtue, whereof wealth and credit are signs.
These signs, like paper money, may be counterfeited or stolen, but that which they represent, namely, knowledge and
virtue, cannot be counterfeited or stolen. These ends of labor
cannot be answered but by real exertions of the mind, and in
obedience to pure motives. The cheat, the defaulter, the gam-
bler, cannot extort the knowledge of material and moral nature which his honest care and pains yield to the operative.
The law of nature is, Do the thing, and you shall have the
power: but they who do not the thing have not the power.

Human labor, through all its forms, from the sharpening
of a stake to the construction of a city or an epic, is one immense illustration of the perfect compensation of the universe. The absolute balance of Give and Take, the doctrine
that every thing has its price,—and if that price is not paid,
not that thing but something else is obtained, and that it is
impossible to get any thing without its price,—is not less
sublime in the columns of a leger than in the budgets of
states, in the laws of light and darkness, in all the action and
reaction of nature. I cannot doubt that the high laws which
each man sees implicated in those processes with which he is
conversant, the stern ethics which sparkle on his chisel-edge,
which are measured out by his plumb and foot-rule, which
stand as manifest in the footing of the shop-bill as in the his-

tory of a state,—do recommend to him his trade, and though seldom named, exalt his business to his imagination.

The league between virtue and nature engages all things to assume a hostile front to vice. The beautiful laws and substances of the world persecute and whip the traitor. He finds that things are arranged for truth and benefit, but there is no den in the wide world to hide a rogue. Commit a crime, and the earth is made of glass. Commit a crime, and it seems as if a coat of snow fell on the ground, such as reveals in the woods the track of every partridge and fox and squirrel and mole. You cannot recall the spoken word, you cannot wipe out the foot-track, you cannot draw up the ladder, so as to leave no inlet or clew. Some damning circumstance always transpires. The laws and substances of nature—water, snow, wind, gravitation—become penalties to the thief.

On the other hand, the law holds with equal sureness for all right action. Love, and you shall be loved. All love is mathematically just, as much as the two sides of an algebraic equation. The good man has absolute good, which like fire turns every thing to its own nature, so that you cannot do him any harm; but as the royal armies sent against Napoleon, when he approached, cast down their colors and from enemies became friends, so disasters of all kinds, as sickness, offence, poverty, prove benefactors:—

> "Winds blow and waters roll
> Strength to the brave, and power and deity,
> Yet in themselves are nothing."

The good are befriended even by weakness and defect. As no man had ever a point of pride that was not injurious to him, so no man had ever a defect that was not somewhere made useful to him. The stag in the fable admired his horns and blamed his feet, but when the hunter came, his feet saved him, and afterwards, caught in the thicket, his horns destroyed him. Every man in his lifetime needs to thank his faults. As no man thoroughly understands a truth until he has contended against it, so no man has a thorough acquaintance with the hindrances or talents of men, until he has suffered from the one, and seen the triumph of the other over his own want of the same. Has he a defect of temper that unfits him to live in society? Thereby he is driven to entertain himself alone, and acquire habits of self-help; and thus, like the wounded oyster, he mends his shell with pearl.

Our strength grows out of our weakness. The indignation which arms itself with secret forces does not awaken until we are pricked and stung and sorely assailed. A great man is always willing to be little. Whilst he sits on the cushion of advantages, he goes to sleep. When he is pushed, tormented, defeated, he has a chance to learn something; he has been put on his wits, on his manhood; he has gained facts; learns his ignorance; is cured of the insanity of conceit; has got moderation and real skill. The wise man throws himself on the side of his assailants. It is more his interest than it is theirs to find his weak point. The wound cicatrizes and falls off from him like a dead skin, and when they would triumph, lo! he has passed on invulnerable. Blame is safer than praise. I hate to be defended in a newspaper. As long as all that is said is said against me, I feel a certain assurance of success. But as soon as honeyed words of praise are spoken for me, I feel as one that lies unprotected before his enemies. In general, every evil to which we do not succumb is a benefactor. As the Sandwich Islander believes that the strength and valor of the enemy he kills passes into himself, so we gain the strength of the temptation we resist.

The same guards which protect us from disaster, defect, and enmity, defend us, if we will, from selfishness and fraud. Bolts and bars are not the best of our institutions, nor is shrewdness in trade a mark of wisdom. Men suffer all their life long, under the foolish superstition that they can be cheated. But it is as impossible for a man to be cheated by any one but himself, as for a thing to be and not to be at the same time. There is a third silent party to all our bargains. The nature and soul of things takes on itself the guaranty of the fulfilment of every contract, so that honest service cannot come to loss. If you serve an ungrateful master, serve him the more. Put God in your debt. Every stroke shall be repaid. The longer the payment is withholden, the better for you; for compound interest on compound interest is the rate and usage of this exchequer.

The history of persecution is a history of endeavours to

cheat nature, to make water run up hill, to twist a rope of sand. It makes no difference whether the actors be many or one, a tyrant or a mob. A mob is a society of bodies voluntarily bereaving themselves of reason, and traversing its work. The mob is man voluntarily descending to the nature of the beast. Its fit hour of activity is night. Its actions are insane like its whole constitution. It persecutes a principle; it would whip a right; it would tar and feather justice, by inflicting fire and outrage upon the houses and persons of those who have these. It resembles the prank of boys, who run with fire-engines to put out the ruddy aurora streaming to the stars. The inviolate spirit turns their spite against the wrongdoers. The martyr cannot be dishonored. Every lash inflicted is a tongue of fame; every prison, a more illustrious abode; every burned book or house enlightens the world; every suppressed or expunged word reverberates through the earth from side to side. Hours of sanity and consideration are always arriving to communities, as to individuals, when the truth is seen, and the martyrs are justified.

Thus do all things preach the indifferency of circumstances. The man is all. Every thing has two sides, a good and an evil. Every advantage has its tax. I learn to be content. But the doctrine of compensation is not the doctrine of indifferency. The thoughtless say, on hearing these representations,— What boots it to do well? there is one event to good and evil; if I gain any good, I must pay for it; if I lose any good, I gain some other; all actions are indifferent.

There is a deeper fact in the soul than compensation, to wit, its own nature. The soul is not a compensation, but a life. The soul *is*. Under all this running sea of circumstance, whose waters ebb and flow with perfect balance, lies the aboriginal abyss of real Being. Essence, or God, is not a relation, or a part, but the whole. Being is the vast affirmative, excluding negation, self-balanced, and swallowing up all relations, parts, and times within itself. Nature, truth, virtue, are the influx from thence. Vice is the absence or departure of the same. Nothing, Falsehood, may indeed stand as the great Night or shade, on which, as a background, the living universe paints itself forth; but no fact is begotten by it; it cannot work; for

it is not. It cannot work any good; it cannot work any harm.
It is harm inasmuch as it is worse not to be than to be.

We feel defrauded of the retribution due to evil acts, because the criminal adheres to his vice and contumacy, and
does not come to a crisis or judgment anywhere in visible
nature. There is no stunning confutation of his nonsense before men and angels. Has he therefore outwitted the law? Inasmuch as he carries the malignity and the lie with him, he so
far deceases from nature. In some manner there will be a
demonstration of the wrong to the understanding also; but
should we not see it, this deadly deduction makes square the
eternal account.

Neither can it be said, on the other hand, that the gain of
rectitude must be bought by any loss. There is no penalty to
virtue; no penalty to wisdom; they are proper additions of
being. In a virtuous action, I properly *am*; in a virtuous act,
I add to the world; I plant into deserts conquered from Chaos
and Nothing, and see the darkness receding on the limits of
the horizon. There can be no excess to love; none to knowledge; none to beauty, when these attributes are considered in
the purest sense. The soul refuses limits, and always affirms
an Optimism, never a Pessimism.

His life is a progress, and not a station. His instinct is trust.
Our instinct uses "more" and "less" in application to man, of
the *presence of the soul*, and not of its absence; the brave man
is greater than the coward; the true, the benevolent, the wise,
is more a man, and not less, than the fool and knave. There
is no tax on the good of virtue; for that is the incoming of
God himself, or absolute existence, without any comparative.
Material good has its tax, and if it came without desert or
sweat, has no root in me, and the next wind will blow it
away. But all the good of nature is the soul's, and may be
had, if paid for in nature's lawful coin, that is, by labor which
the heart and the head allow. I no longer wish to meet a good
I do not earn, for example, to find a pot of buried gold,
knowing that it brings with it new burdens. I do not wish
more external goods,—neither possessions, nor honors, nor
powers, nor persons. The gain is apparent; the tax is certain.
But there is no tax on the knowledge that the compensation
exists, and that it is not desirable to dig up treasure. Herein I

rejoice with a serene eternal peace. I contract the boundaries of possible mischief. I learn the wisdom of St. Bernard,— "Nothing can work me damage except myself; the harm that I sustain I carry about with me, and never am a real sufferer but by my own fault."

In the nature of the soul is the compensation for the inequalities of condition. The radical tragedy of nature seems to be the distinction of More and Less. How can Less not feel the pain; how not feel indignation or malevolence towards More? Look at those who have less faculty, and one feels sad, and knows not well what to make of it. He almost shuns their eye; he fears they will upbraid God. What should they do? It seems a great injustice. But see the facts nearly, and these mountainous inequalities vanish. Love reduces them, as the sun melts the iceberg in the sea. The heart and soul of all men being one, this bitterness of *His* and *Mine* ceases. His is mine. I am my brother, and my brother is me. If I feel overshadowed and outdone by great neighbours, I can yet love; I can still receive; and he that loveth maketh his own the grandeur he loves. Thereby I make the discovery that my brother is my guardian, acting for me with the friendliest designs, and the estate I so admired and envied is my own. It is the nature of the soul to appropriate all things. Jesus and Shakspeare are fragments of the soul, and by love I conquer and incorporate them in my own conscious domain. His virtue,—is not that mine? His wit,—if it cannot be made mine, it is not wit.

Such, also, is the natural history of calamity. The changes which break up at short intervals the prosperity of men are advertisements of a nature whose law is growth. Every soul is by this intrinsic necessity quitting its whole system of things, its friends, and home, and laws, and faith, as the shell-fish crawls out of its beautiful but stony case, because it no longer admits of its growth, and slowly forms a new house. In proportion to the vigor of the individual, these revolutions are frequent, until in some happier mind they are incessant, and all worldly relations hang very loosely about him, becoming, as it were, a transparent fluid membrane through which the living form is seen, and not, as in most men, an indurated heterogeneous fabric of many dates, and of no settled character, in which the man is imprisoned. Then there can be enlargement, and the man of to-day scarcely recognizes the man of yesterday. And such should be the outward biography of man in time, a putting off of dead circumstances day by day, as he renews his raiment day by day. But to us, in our lapsed estate, resting, not advancing, resisting, not coöperating with the divine expansion, this growth comes by shocks.

We cannot part with our friends. We cannot let our angels go. We do not see that they only go out, that archangels may come in. We are idolaters of the old. We do not believe in the riches of the soul, in its proper eternity and omnipresence. We do not believe there is any force in to-day to rival or re-create that beautiful yesterday. We linger in the ruins of the old tent, where once we had bread and shelter and organs, nor believe that the spirit can feed, cover, and nerve us again. We cannot again find aught so dear, so sweet, so graceful. But we sit and weep in vain. The voice of the Almighty saith, 'Up and onward for evermore!' We cannot stay amid the ruins. Neither will we rely on the new; and so we walk ever with reverted eyes, like those monsters who look backwards.

And yet the compensations of calamity are made apparent to the understanding also, after long intervals of time. A fever, a mutilation, a cruel disappointment, a loss of wealth, a loss of friends, seems at the moment unpaid loss, and unpayable. But the sure years reveal the deep remedial force that underlies all facts. The death of a dear friend, wife, brother, lover, which seemed nothing but privation, somewhat later assumes the aspect of a guide or genius; for it commonly operates revolutions in our way of life, terminates an epoch of infancy or of youth which was waiting to be closed, breaks up a wonted occupation, or a household, or style of living, and allows the formation of new ones more friendly to the growth of character. It permits or constrains the formation of new acquaintances, and the reception of new influences that prove of the first importance to the next years; and the man or woman who would have remained a sunny garden-flower, with no room for its roots and too much sunshine for its head, by the falling of the walls and the neglect of the gardener, is made the banian of the forest, yielding shade and fruit to wide neighbourhoods of men.

SPIRITUAL LAWS

———

The living Heaven thy prayers respect,
House at once and architect,
Quarrying man's rejected hours,
Builds therewith eternal towers;
Sole and self-commanded works,
Fears not undermining days,
Grows by decays,
And, by the famous might that lurks
In reaction and recoil,
Makes flame to freeze, and ice to boil;
Forging, through swart arms of Offence,
The silver seat of Innocence.

Spiritual Laws

WHEN THE ACT of reflection takes place in the mind, when we look at ourselves in the light of thought, we discover that our life is embosomed in beauty. Behind us, as we go, all things assume pleasing forms, as clouds do far off. Not only things familiar and stale, but even the tragic and terrible, are comely, as they take their place in the pictures of memory. The river-bank, the weed at the water-side, the old house, the foolish person,—however neglected in the passing,—have a grace in the past. Even the corpse that has lain in the chambers has added a solemn ornament to the house. The soul will not know either deformity or pain. If, in the hours of clear reason, we should speak the severest truth, we should say, that we had never made a sacrifice. In these hours the mind seems so great, that nothing can be taken from us that seems much. All loss, all pain, is particular; the universe remains to the heart unhurt. Neither vexations nor calamities abate our trust. No man ever stated his griefs as lightly as he might. Allow for exaggeration in the most patient and sorely ridden hack that ever was driven. For it is only the finite that has wrought and suffered; the infinite lies stretched in smiling repose.

The intellectual life may be kept clean and healthful, if man will live the life of nature, and not import into his mind difficulties which are none of his. No man need be perplexed in his speculations. Let him do and say what strictly belongs to him, and, though very ignorant of books, his nature shall not yield him any intellectual obstructions and doubts. Our young people are diseased with the theological problems of original sin, origin of evil, predestination, and the like. These never presented a practical difficulty to any man,—never darkened across any man's road, who did not go out of his way to seek them. These are the soul's mumps, and measles, and whooping-coughs, and those who have not caught them cannot describe their health or prescribe the cure. A simple mind will not know these enemies. It is quite another thing that he should be able to give account of his faith, and expound to another the theory of his self-union and freedom. This requires rare gifts. Yet, without this self-knowledge, there may be a sylvan strength and integrity in that which he is. "A few strong instincts and a few plain rules" suffice us.

My will never gave the images in my mind the rank they now take. The regular course of studies, the years of academical and professional education, have not yielded me better facts than some idle books under the bench at the Latin School. What we do not call education is more precious than that which we call so. We form no guess, at the time of receiving a thought, of its comparative value. And education often wastes its effort in attempts to thwart and balk this natural magnetism, which is sure to select what belongs to it.

In like manner, our moral nature is vitiated by any interference of our will. People represent virtue as a struggle, and take to themselves great airs upon their attainments, and the question is everywhere vexed, when a noble nature is commended, whether the man is not better who strives with temptation. But there is no merit in the matter. Either God is there, or he is not there. We love characters in proportion as they are impulsive and spontaneous. The less a man thinks or knows about his virtues, the better we like him. Timoleon's victories are the best victories; which ran and flowed like Homer's verses, Plutarch said. When we see a soul whose acts are all regal, graceful, and pleasant as roses, we must thank God that such things can be and are, and not turn sourly on the angel, and say, 'Crump is a better man with his grunting resistance to all his native devils.'

Not less conspicuous is the preponderance of nature over will in all practical life. There is less intention in history than we ascribe to it. We impute deep-laid, far-sighted plans to Cæsar and Napoleon; but the best of their power was in nature, not in them. Men of an extraordinary success, in their honest moments, have always sung, 'Not unto us, not unto us.' According to the faith of their times, they have built altars to Fortune, or to Destiny, or to St. Julian. Their success lay in their parallelism to the course of thought, which found in them an unobstructed channel; and the wonders of which they were the visible conductors seemed to the eye their deed.

Did the wires generate the galvanism? It is even true that there was less in them on which they could reflect, than in another; as the virtue of a pipe is to be smooth and hollow. That which externally seemed will and immovableness was willingness and self-annihilation. Could Shakspeare give a theory of Shakspeare? Could ever a man of prodigious mathematical genius convey to others any insight into his methods? If he could communicate that secret, it would instantly lose its exaggerated value, blending with the daylight and the vital energy the power to stand and to go.

The lesson is forcibly taught by these observations, that our life might be much easier and simpler than we make it; that the world might be a happier place than it is; that there is no need of struggles, convulsions, and despairs, of the wringing of the hands and the gnashing of the teeth; that we miscreate our own evils. We interfere with the optimism of nature; for, whenever we get this vantage-ground of the past, or of a wiser mind in the present, we are able to discern that we are begirt with laws which execute themselves.

The face of external nature teaches the same lesson. Nature will not have us fret and fume. She does not like our benevolence or our learning much better than she likes our frauds and wars. When we come out of the caucus, or the bank, or the Abolition-convention, or the Temperance-meeting, or the Transcendental club, into the fields and woods, she says to us, 'So hot? my little Sir.'

We are full of mechanical actions. We must needs intermeddle, and have things in our own way, until the sacrifices and virtues of society are odious. Love should make joy; but our benevolence is unhappy. Our Sunday-schools, and churches, and pauper-societies are yokes to the neck. We pain ourselves to please nobody. There are natural ways of arriving at the same ends at which these aim, but do not arrive. Why should all virtue work in one and the same way? Why should all give dollars? It is very inconvenient to us country folk, and we do not think any good will come of it. We have not dollars; merchants have; let them give them. Farmers will give corn; poets will sing; women will sew; laborers will lend a hand; the children will bring flowers. And why drag this dead weight of a Sunday-school over the whole Christendom? It is natural and beautiful that childhood should inquire, and maturity should teach; but it is time enough to answer questions when they are asked. Do not shut up the young people against their will in a pew, and force the children to ask them questions for an hour against their will.

If we look wider, things are all alike; laws, and letters, and creeds, and modes of living, seem a travestie of truth. Our society is encumbered by ponderous machinery, which resembles the endless aqueducts which the Romans built over hill and dale, and which are superseded by the discovery of the law that water rises to the level of its source. It is a Chinese wall which any nimble Tartar can leap over. It is a standing army, not so good as a peace. It is a graduated, titled, richly appointed empire, quite superfluous when town-meetings are found to answer just as well.

Let us draw a lesson from nature, which always works by short ways. When the fruit is ripe, it falls. When the fruit is despatched, the leaf falls. The circuit of the waters is mere falling. The walking of man and all animals is a falling forward. All our manual labor and works of strength, as prying, splitting, digging, rowing, and so forth, are done by dint of continual falling, and the globe, earth, moon, comet, sun, star, fall for ever and ever.

The simplicity of the universe is very different from the simplicity of a machine. He who sees moral nature out and out, and thoroughly knows how knowledge is acquired and character formed, is a pedant. The simplicity of nature is not that which may easily be read, but is inexhaustible. The last analysis can no wise be made. We judge of a man's wisdom by his hope, knowing that the perception of the inexhaustibleness of nature is an immortal youth. The wild fertility of nature is felt in comparing our rigid names and reputations with our fluid consciousness. We pass in the world for sects and schools, for erudition and piety, and we are all the time jejune babes. One sees very well how Pyrrhonism grew up. Every man sees that he is that middle point, whereof every thing may be affirmed and denied with equal reason. He is old, he is young, he is very wise, he is altogether ignorant. He hears and feels what you say of the seraphim, and of the tin-pedler. There is no permanent wise man, except in the figment of the Stoics. We side with the hero, as we read or paint, against the coward and the robber; but we have been ourselves that coward and robber, and shall be again, not in the low circumstance, but in comparison with the grandeurs possible to the soul.

A little consideration of what takes place around us every day would show us, that a higher law than that of our will regulates events; that our painful labors are unnecessary, and fruitless; that only in our easy, simple, spontaneous action are we strong, and by contenting ourselves with obedience we become divine. Belief and love, — a believing love will relieve us of a vast load of care. O my brothers, God exists. There is a soul at the centre of nature, and over the will of every man, so that none of us can wrong the universe. It has so infused its strong enchantment into nature, that we prosper when we accept its advice, and when we struggle to wound its creatures, our hands are glued to our sides, or they beat our own breasts. The whole course of things goes to teach us faith. We need only obey. There is guidance for each of us, and by lowly listening we shall hear the right word. Why need you choose so painfully your place, and occupation, and associates, and modes of action, and of entertainment? Certainly there is a possible right for you that precludes the need of balance and wilful election. For you there is a reality, a fit place and congenial duties. Place yourself in the middle of the stream of power and wisdom which animates all whom it floats, and you are without effort impelled to truth, to right, and a perfect contentment. Then you put all gainsayers in the wrong. Then you are the world, the measure of right, of truth, of beauty. If we will not be mar-plots with our miserable interferences, the work, the society, letters, arts, science, religion of men would go on far better than now, and the heaven predicted from the beginning of the world, and still predicted from the bottom of the heart, would organize itself, as do now the rose, and the air, and the sun.

I say, *do not choose*; but that is a figure of speech by which I would distinguish what is commonly called *choice* among men, and which is a partial act, the choice of the hands, of the eyes, of the appetites, and not a whole act of the man. But that which I call right or goodness is the choice of my

constitution; and that which I call heaven, and inwardly aspire after, is the state or circumstance desirable to my constitution; and the action which I in all my years tend to do, is
the work for my faculties. We must hold a man amenable to
reason for the choice of his daily craft or profession. It is not
an excuse any longer for his deeds, that they are the custom
of his trade. What business has he with an evil trade? Has he
not a *calling* in his character.

Each man has his own vocation. The talent is the call.
There is one direction in which all space is open to him. He
has faculties silently inviting him thither to endless exertion.
He is like a ship in a river; he runs against obstructions on
every side but one; on that side all obstruction is taken away,
and he sweeps serenely over a deepening channel into an infinite sea. This talent and this call depend on his organization,
or the mode in which the general soul incarnates itself in him.
He inclines to do something which is easy to him, and good
when it is done, but which no other man can do. He has no
rival. For the more truly he consults his own powers, the
more difference will his work exhibit from the work of any
other. His ambition is exactly proportioned to his powers.
The height of the pinnacle is determined by the breadth of
the base. Every man has this call of the power to do somewhat unique, and no man has any other call. The pretence
that he has another call, a summons by name and personal
election and outward "signs that mark him extraordinary, and
not in the roll of common men," is fanaticism, and betrays
obtuseness to perceive that there is one mind in all the individuals, and no respect of persons therein.

By doing his work, he makes the need felt which he can
supply, and creates the taste by which he is enjoyed. By doing
his own work, he unfolds himself. It is the vice of our public
speaking that it has not abandonment. Somewhere, not only
every orator but every man should let out all the length of all
the reins; should find or make a frank and hearty expression
of what force and meaning is in him. The common experience
is, that the man fits himself as well as he can to the customary
details of that work or trade he falls into, and tends it as a
dog turns a spit. Then is he a part of the machine he moves;
the man is lost. Until he can manage to communicate himself

to others in his full stature and proportion, he does not yet find his vocation. He must find in that an outlet for his character, so that he may justify his work to their eyes. If the labor is mean, let him by his thinking and character make it liberal. Whatever he knows and thinks, whatever in his apprehension is worth doing, that let him communicate, or men will never know and honor him aright. Foolish, whenever you take the meanness and formality of that thing you do, instead of converting it into the obedient spiracle of your character and aims.

We like only such actions as have already long had the praise of men, and do not perceive that any thing man can do may be divinely done. We think greatness entailed or organized in some places or duties, in certain offices or occasions, and do not see that Paganini can extract rapture from a catgut, and Eulenstein from a jews-harp, and a nimble-fingered lad out of shreds of paper with his scissors, and Landseer out of swine, and the hero out of the pitiful habitation and company in which he was hidden. What we call obscure condition or vulgar society is that condition and society whose poetry is not yet written, but which you shall presently make as enviable and renowned as any. In our estimates, let us take a lesson from kings. The parts of hospitality, the connection of families, the impressiveness of death, and a thousand other things, royalty makes its own estimate of, and a royal mind will. To make habitually a new estimate,—that is elevation.

What a man does, that he has. What has he to do with hope or fear? In himself is his might. Let him regard no good as solid, but that which is in his nature, and which must grow out of him as long as he exists. The goods of fortune may come and go like summer leaves; let him scatter them on every wind as the momentary signs of his infinite productiveness.

He may have his own. A man's genius, the quality that differences him from every other, the susceptibility to one class of influences, the selection of what is fit for him, the rejection of what is unfit, determines for him the character of the universe. A man is a method, a progressive arrangement; a selecting principle, gathering his like to him, wherever he goes. He takes only his own out of the multiplicity that sweeps and circles round him. He is like one of those booms which are set out from the shore on rivers to catch drift-wood, or like the loadstone amongst splinters of steel. Those facts, words, persons, which dwell in his memory without his being able to say why, remain, because they have a relation to him not less real for being as yet unapprehended. They are symbols of value to him, as they can interpret parts of his consciousness which he would vainly seek words for in the conventional images of books and other minds. What attracts my attention shall have it, as I will go to the man who knocks at my door, whilst a thousand persons, as worthy, go by it, to whom I give no regard. It is enough that these particulars speak to me. A few anecdotes, a few traits of character, man-ners, face, a few incidents, have an emphasis in your memory out of all proportion to their apparent significance, if you measure them by the ordinary standards. They relate to your gift. Let them have their weight, and do not reject them, and cast about for illustration and facts more usual in literature. What your heart thinks great is great. The soul's emphasis is always right.

Over all things that are agreeable to his nature and genius, the man has the highest right. Everywhere he may take what belongs to his spiritual estate, nor can he take any thing else, though all doors were open, nor can all the force of men hin-der him from taking so much. It is vain to attempt to keep a secret from one who has a right to know it. It will tell itself. That mood into which a friend can bring us is his dominion over us. To the thoughts of that state of mind he has a right. All the secrets of that state of mind he can compel. This is a law which statesmen use in practice. All the terrors of the French Republic, which held Austria in awe, were unable to command her diplomacy. But Napoleon sent to Vienna M. de Narbonne, one of the old noblesse, with the morals, man-ners, and name of that interest, saying, that it was indispens-able to send to the old aristocracy of Europe men of the same connection, which, in fact, constitutes a sort of free-masonry. M. de Narbonne, in less than a fortnight, penetrated all the secrets of the imperial cabinet.

Nothing seems so easy as to speak and to be understood. Yet a man may come to find *that* the strongest of defences and of ties,—that he has been understood; and he who has received an opinion may come to find it the most inconvenient of bonds.

If a teacher have any opinion which he wishes to conceal, his pupils will become as fully indoctrinated into that as into any which he publishes. If you pour water into a vessel twisted into coils and angles, it is vain to say, I will pour it only into this or that;—it will find its level in all. Men feel and act the consequences of your doctrine, without being able to show how they follow. Show us an arc of the curve, and a good mathematician will find out the whole figure. We are always reasoning from the seen to the unseen. Hence the perfect intelligence that subsists between wise men of remote ages. A man cannot bury his meanings so deep in his book, but time and like-minded men will find them. Plato had a secret doctrine, had he? What secret can he conceal from the eyes of Bacon? of Montaigne? of Kant? Therefore, Aristotle said of his works, "They are published and not published."

No man can learn what he has not preparation for learning, however near to his eyes is the object. A chemist may tell his most precious secrets to a carpenter, and he shall be never the wiser,—the secrets he would not utter to a chemist for an estate. God screens us evermore from premature ideas. Our eyes are holden that we cannot see things that stare us in the face, until the hour arrives when the mind is ripened; then we behold them, and the time when we saw them not is like a dream.

Not in nature but in man is all the beauty and worth he sees. The world is very empty, and is indebted to this gilding, exalting soul for all its pride. "Earth fills her lap with splendors" *not her own.* The vale of Tempe, Tivoli, and Rome are earth and water, rocks and sky. There are as good earth and water in a thousand places, yet how unaffecting!

People are not the better for the sun and moon, the horizon and the trees; as it is not observed that the keepers of Roman galleries, or the valets of painters, have any elevation of thought, or that librarians are wiser men than others. There are graces in the demeanour of a polished and noble person, which are lost upon the eye of a churl. These are like the stars whose light has not yet reached us.

He may see what he maketh. Our dreams are the sequel of our waking knowledge. The visions of the night bear some proportion to the visions of the day. Hideous dreams are exaggerations of the sins of the day. We see our evil affections embodied in bad physiognomies. On the Alps, the traveller sometimes beholds his own shadow magnified to a giant, so that every gesture of his hand is terrific. "My children," said an old man to his boys scared by a figure in the dark entry, "my children, you will never see any thing worse than yourselves." As in dreams, so in the scarcely less fluid events of the world, every man sees himself in colossal, without knowing that it is himself. The good, compared to the evil which he sees, is as his own good to his own evil. Every quality of his mind is magnified in some one acquaintance, and every emotion of his heart in some one. He is like a quincunx of trees, which counts five, east, west, north, or south; or, an initial, medial, and terminal acrostic. And why not? He cleaves to one person, and avoids another, according to their likeness or unlikeness to himself, truly seeking himself in his associates, and moreover in his trade, and habits, and gestures, and meats, and drinks; and comes at last to be faithfully represented by every view you take of his circumstances.

He may read what he writes. What can we see or acquire, but what we are? You have observed a skilful man reading Virgil. Well, that author is a thousand books to a thousand persons. Take the book into your two hands, and read your eyes out; you will never find what I find. If any ingenious reader would have a monopoly of the wisdom or delight he gets, he is as secure now the book is Englished, as if it were imprisoned in the Pelews' tongue. It is with a good book as it is with good company. Introduce a base person among gentlemen; it is all to no purpose; he is not their fellow. Every society protects itself. The company is perfectly safe, and he is not one of them, though his body is in the room.

What avails it to fight with the eternal laws of mind, which adjust the relation of all persons to each other, by the mathematical measure of their havings and beings? Gertrude is enamoured of Guy; how high, how aristocratic, how Roman his mien and manners! to live with him were life indeed, and no purchase is too great; and heaven and earth are moved to that end. Well, Gertrude has Guy; but what now avails how high, how aristocratic, how Roman his mien and manners, if his heart and aims are in the senate, in the theatre, and in the billiard-room, and she has no aims, no conversation, that can enchant her graceful lord?

He shall have his own society. We can love nothing but nature. The most wonderful talents, the most meritorious exertions, really avail very little with us; but nearness or likeness of nature,—how beautiful is the ease of its victory! Persons approach us famous for their beauty, for their accomplishments, worthy of all wonder for their charms and gifts; they dedicate their whole skill to the hour and the company, with very imperfect result. To be sure, it would be ungrateful in us not to praise them loudly. Then, when all is done, a person of related mind, a brother or sister by nature, comes to us so softly and easily, so nearly and intimately, as if it were the blood in our proper veins, that we feel as if some one was gone, instead of another having come; we are utterly relieved and refreshed; it is a sort of joyful solitude. We foolishly think in our days of sin, that we must court friends by compliance to the customs of society, to its dress, its breeding, and its estimates. But only that soul can be my friend which I encounter on the line of my own march, that soul to which I do not decline, and which does not decline to me, but, native of the same celestial latitude, repeats in its own all my experience. The scholar forgets himself, and apes the customs and costumes of the man of the world, to deserve the smile of beauty, and follows some giddy girl, not yet taught by religious passion to know the noble woman with all that is serene, oracular, and beautiful in her soul. Let him be great, and love shall follow him. Nothing is more deeply punished than the neglect of the affinities by which alone society should be formed, and the insane levity of choosing associates by others' eyes.

He may set his own rate. It is a maxim worthy of all acceptation, that a man may have that allowance he takes. Take the place and attitude which belong to you, and all men acquiesce. The world must be just. It leaves every man, with profound unconcern, to set his own rate. Hero or driveller, it meddles not in the matter. It will certainly accept your own measure of your doing and being, whether you sneak about and deny your own name, or whether you see your work produced to the concave sphere of the heavens, one with the revolution of the stars.

The same reality pervades all teaching. The man may teach by doing, and not otherwise. If he can communicate himself, he can teach, but not by words. He teaches who gives, and he learns who receives. There is no teaching until the pupil is brought into the same state or principle in which you are; a transfusion takes place; he is you, and you are he; then is a teaching; and by no unfriendly chance or bad company can he ever quite lose the benefit. But your propositions run out of one ear as they ran in at the other. We see it advertised that Mr. Grand will deliver an oration on the Fourth of July, and Mr. Hand before the Mechanics' Association, and we do not go thither, because we know that these gentlemen will not communicate their own character and experience to the company. If we had reason to expect such a confidence, we should go through all inconvenience and opposition. The sick would be carried in litters. But a public oration is an escapade, a non-committal, an apology, a gag, and not a communication, not a speech, not a man.

A like Nemesis presides over all intellectual works. We have yet to learn, that the thing uttered in words is not therefore affirmed. It must affirm itself, or no forms of logic or of oath can give it evidence. The sentence must also contain its own apology for being spoken.

The effect of any writing on the public mind is mathematically measurable by its depth of thought. How much water does it draw? If it awaken you to think, if it lift you from your feet with the great voice of eloquence, then the effect is to be wide, slow, permanent, over the minds of men; if the pages instruct you not, they will die like flies in the hour. The way to speak and write what shall not go out of fashion is, to speak and write sincerely. The argument which has not power to reach my own practice, I may well doubt, will fail to reach yours. But take Sidney's maxim:—"Look in thy heart, and write." He that writes to himself writes to an eternal public. That statement only is fit to be made public, which you have come at in attempting to satisfy your own curiosity. The writer who takes his subject from his ear, and not from his heart, should know that he has lost as much as he seems to have gained, and when the empty book has gathered all its praise, and half the people say, 'What poetry! what genius!' it still needs fuel to make fire. That only profits which is profitable. Life alone can impart life; and though we should burst, we can only be valued as we make ourselves valuable. There is no luck in literary reputation. They who make up the final verdict upon every book are not the partial and noisy readers of the hour when it appears; but a court as of angels, a public not to be bribed, not to be entreated, and not to be overawed, decides upon every man's title to fame. Only those books come down which deserve to last. Gilt edges, vellum, and morocco, and presentation-copies to all the libraries, will not preserve a book in circulation beyond its intrinsic date. It must go with all Walpole's Noble and Royal Authors to its fate. Blackmore, Kotzebue, or Pollok may endure for a night, but Moses and Homer stand for ever. There are not in the world at any one time more than a dozen persons who read and understand Plato:—never enough to pay for an edition of his works; yet to every generation these come duly down, for the sake of those few persons, as if God brought them in his hand. "No book," said Bentley, "was ever written down by any but itself." The permanence of all books is fixed by no effort friendly or hostile, but by their own specific gravity, or the intrinsic importance of their contents to the constant mind of man. "Do not trouble yourself too much about the light on your statue," said Michel Angelo to the young sculptor; "the light of the public square will test its value."

In like manner the effect of every action is measured by the depth of the sentiment from which it proceeds. The great man knew not that he was great. It took a century or two for that fact to appear. What he did, he did because he must; it was the most natural thing in the world, and grew out of the circumstances of the moment. But now, every thing he did, even to the lifting of his finger or the eating of bread, looks large, all-related, and is called an institution.

These are the demonstrations in a few particulars of the genius of nature; they show the direction of the stream. But the stream is blood; every drop is alive. Truth has not single victories; all things are its organs,—not only dust and stones, but errors and lies. The laws of disease, physicians say, are as beautiful as the laws of health. Our philosophy is affirmative, and readily accepts the testimony of negative facts, as every shadow points to the sun. By a divine necessity, every fact in nature is constrained to offer its testimony.

Human character evermore publishes itself. The most fugitive deed and word, the mere air of doing a thing, the intimated purpose, expresses character. If you act, you show character; if you sit still, if you sleep, you show it. You think, because you have spoken nothing when others spoke, and have given no opinion on the times, on the church, on slavery, on marriage, on socialism, on secret societies, on the college, on parties and persons, that your verdict is still expected with curiosity as a reserved wisdom. Far otherwise; your silence answers very loud. You have no oracle to utter, and your fellow-men have learned that you cannot help them; for, oracles speak. Doth not wisdom cry, and understanding put forth her voice?

Dreadful limits are set in nature to the powers of dissimulation. Truth tyrannizes over the unwilling members of the body. Faces never lie, it is said. No man need be deceived, who will study the changes of expression. When a man speaks the truth in the spirit of truth, his eye is as clear as the heavens. When he has base ends, and speaks falsely, the eye is muddy and sometimes asquint.

I have heard an experienced counsellor say, that he never feared the effect upon a jury of a lawyer who does not believe in his heart that his client ought to have a verdict. If he does not believe it, his unbelief will appear to the jury, despite all his protestations, and will become their unbelief. This is that law whereby a work of art, of whatever kind, sets us in the same state of mind wherein the artist was when he made it. That which we do not believe, we cannot adequately say, though we may repeat the words never so often. It was this conviction which Swedenborg expressed, when he described a group of persons in the spiritual world endeavouring in vain to articulate a proposition which they did not believe; but they could not, though they twisted and folded their lips even to indignation.

A man passes for that he is worth. Very idle is all curiosity concerning other people's estimate of us, and all fear of remaining unknown is not less so. If a man know that he can do any thing,—that he can do it better than any one else,—he has a pledge of the acknowledgment of that fact by all persons. The world is full of judgment-days, and into every assembly that a man enters, in every action he attempts, he is gauged and stamped. In every troop of boys that whoop and run in each yard and square, a new-comer is as well and accurately weighed in the course of a few days, and stamped with his right number, as if he had undergone a formal trial of his strength, speed, and temper. A stranger comes from a distant school, with better dress, with trinkets in his pockets, with airs and pretensions: an older boy says to himself, 'It 's of no use; we shall find him out to-morrow.' 'What has he done?' is the divine question which searches men, and transpierces every false reputation. A fop may sit in any chair of the world, nor be distinguished for his hour from Homer and Washington; but there need never be any doubt concerning the respective ability of human beings. Pretension may sit still, but cannot act. Pretension never feigned an act of real greatness. Pretension never wrote an Iliad, nor drove back Xerxes, nor christianized the world, nor abolished slavery.

As much virtue as there is, so much appears; as much goodness as there is, so much reverence it commands. All the devils respect virtue. The high, the generous, the self-devoted sect will always instruct and command mankind. Never was a sincere word utterly lost. Never a magnanimity fell to the ground, but there is some heart to greet and accept it unexpectedly. A man passes for that he is worth. What he is engraves itself on his face, on his form, on his fortunes, in letters of light. Concealment avails him nothing; boasting nothing. There is confession in the glances of our eyes; in our smiles; in salutations; and the grasp of hands. His sin bedaubs him, mars all his good impression. Men know not why they do not trust him; but they do not trust him. His vice glasses his eye, cuts lines of mean expression in his cheek, pinches the nose, sets the mark of the beast on the back of the head, and writes O fool! fool! on the forehead of a king.

If you would not be known to do any thing, never do it. A man may play the fool in the drifts of a desert, but every grain of sand shall seem to see. He may be a solitary eater, but he cannot keep his foolish counsel. A broken complexion, a swinish look, ungenerous acts, and the want of due knowledge,—all blab. Can a cook, a Chiffinch, an Iachimo be mistaken for Zeno or Paul? Confucius exclaimed,—"How can a man be concealed! How can a man be concealed!"

On the other hand, the hero fears not, that, if he withhold the avowal of a just and brave act, it will go unwitnessed and unloved. One knows it,—himself,—and is pledged by it to sweetness of peace, and to nobleness of aim, which will prove in the end a better proclamation of it than the relating of the incident. Virtue is the adherence in action to the nature of things, and the nature of things makes it prevalent. It consists in a perpetual substitution of being for seeming, and with sublime propriety God is described as saying, I AM.

The lesson which these observations convey is, Be, and not seem. Let us acquiesce. Let us take our bloated nothingness out of the path of the divine circuits. Let us unlearn our wisdom of the world. Let us lie low in the Lord's power, and learn that truth alone makes rich and great.

If you visit your friend, why need you apologize for not having visited him, and waste his time and deface your own act? Visit him now. Let him feel that the highest love has come to see him, in thee, its lowest organ. Or why need you torment yourself and friend by secret self-reproaches that you have not assisted him or complimented him with gifts and salutations heretofore? Be a gift and a benediction. Shine with real light, and not with the borrowed reflection of gifts. Common men are apologies for men; they bow the head, excuse themselves with prolix reasons, and accumulate appearances, because the substance is not.

We are full of these superstitions of sense, the worship of magnitude. We call the poet inactive, because he is not a president, a merchant, or a porter. We adore an institution, and do not see that it is founded on a thought which we have. But real action is in silent moments. The epochs of our life are not in the visible facts of our choice of a calling, our marriage, our acquisition of an office, and the like, but in a silent

thought by the way-side as we walk; in a thought which re-
vises our entire manner of life, and says,—'Thus hast thou
done, but it were better thus.' And all our after years, like
menials, serve and wait on this, and, according to their ability, execute its will. This revisal or correction is a constant
force, which, as a tendency, reaches through our lifetime. The
object of the man, the aim of these moments, is to make daylight shine through him, to suffer the law to traverse his
whole being without obstruction, so that, on what point
soever of his doing your eye falls, it shall report truly of his
character, whether it be his diet, his house, his religious
forms, his society, his mirth, his vote, his opposition. Now
he is not homogeneous, but heterogeneous, and the ray does
not traverse; there are no thorough lights: but the eye of the
beholder is puzzled, detecting many unlike tendencies, and a
life not yet at one.

Why should we make it a point with our false modesty to
disparage that man we are, and that form of being assigned
to us? A good man is contented. I love and honor Epaminondas, but I do not wish to be Epaminondas. I hold it more
just to love the world of this hour, than the world of his
hour. Nor can you, if I am true, excite me to the least uneasiness by saying, 'He acted, and thou sittest still.' I see action
to be good, when the need is, and sitting still to be also good.
Epaminondas, if he was the man I take him for, would have
sat still with joy and peace, if his lot had been mine. Heaven
is large, and affords space for all modes of love and fortitude.
Why should we be busybodies and superserviceable? Action
and inaction are alike to the true. One piece of the tree is cut
for a weathercock, and one for the sleeper of a bridge; the
virtue of the wood is apparent in both.

I desire not to disgrace the soul. The fact that I am here
certainly shows me that the soul had need of an organ here.
Shall I not assume the post? Shall I skulk and dodge and duck
with my unseasonable apologies and vain modesty, and imagine my being here impertinent? less pertinent than Epaminondas or Homer being there? and that the soul did not know its
own needs? Besides, without any reasoning on the matter, I
have no discontent. The good soul nourishes me, and unlocks
new magazines of power and enjoyment to me every day. I

will not meanly decline the immensity of good, because I have heard that it has come to others in another shape.

Besides, why should we be cowed by the name of Action? 'T is a trick of the senses,—no more. We know that the ancestor of every action is a thought. The poor mind does not seem to itself to be any thing, unless it have an outside badge,—some Gentoo diet, or Quaker coat, or Calvinistic prayer-meeting, or philanthropic society, or a great donation, or a high office, or, any how, some wild contrasting action to testify that it is somewhat. The rich mind lies in the sun and sleeps, and is Nature. To think is to act.

Let us, if we must have great actions, make our own so. All action is of an infinite elasticity, and the least admits of being inflated with the celestial air until it eclipses the sun and moon. Let us seek *one* peace by fidelity. Let me heed my duties. Why need I go gadding into the scenes and philosophy of Greek and Italian history, before I have justified myself to my benefactors? How dare I read Washington's campaigns, when I have not answered the letters of my own correspondents? Is not that a just objection to much of our reading? It is a pusillanimous desertion of our work to gaze after our neighbours. It is peeping. Byron says of Jack Bunting,—

> "He knew not what to say, and so he swore."

I may say it of our preposterous use of books,—He knew not what to do, and so *he read.* I can think of nothing to fill my time with, and I find the Life of Brant. It is a very extravagant compliment to pay to Brant, or to General Schuyler, or to General Washington. My time should be as good as their time,—my facts, my net of relations, as good as theirs, or either of theirs. Rather let me do my work so well that other idlers, if they choose, may compare my texture with the texture of these and find it identical with the best.

This over-estimate of the possibilities of Paul and Pericles, this under-estimate of our own, comes from a neglect of the fact of an identical nature. Bonaparte knew but one merit, and rewarded in one and the same way the good soldier, the good astronomer, the good poet, the good player. The poet uses the names of Cæsar, of Tamerlane, of Bonduca, of Belisarius; the painter uses the conventional story of the Virgin

Mary, of Paul, of Peter. He does not, therefore, defer to the nature of these accidental men, of these stock heroes. If the poet write a true drama, then he is Cæsar, and not the player of Cæsar; then the selfsame strain of thought, emotion as pure, wit as subtle, motions as swift, mounting, extravagant, and a heart as great, self-sufficing, dauntless, which on the waves of its love and hope can uplift all that is reckoned solid and precious in the world,—palaces, gardens, money, navies, kingdoms,—marking its own incomparable worth by the slight it casts on these gauds of men,—these all are his, and by the power of these he rouses the nations. Let a man believe in God, and not in names and places and persons. Let the great soul incarnated in some woman's form, poor and sad and single, in some Dolly or Joan, go out to service, and sweep chambers and scour floors, and its effulgent daybeams cannot be muffled or hid, but to sweep and scour will instantly appear supreme and beautiful actions, the top and radiance of human life, and all people will get mops and brooms; until, lo! suddenly the great soul has enshrined itself in some other form, and done some other deed, and that is now the flower and head of all living nature.

We are the photometers, we the irritable goldleaf and tinfoil that measure the accumulations of the subtle element. We know the authentic effects of the true fire through every one of its million disguises.

LOVE

"I was as a gem concealed;
Me my burning ray revealed."
Koran

Love

EVERY PROMISE of the soul has innumerable fulfilments; each of its joys ripens into a new want. Nature, uncontainable, flowing, forelooking, in the first sentiment of kindness anticipates already a benevolence which shall lose all particular regards in its general light. The introduction to this felicity is in a private and tender relation of one to one, which is the enchantment of human life; which, like a certain divine rage and enthusiasm, seizes on man at one period, and works a revolution in his mind and body; unites him to his race, pledges him to the domestic and civic relations, carries him with new sympathy into nature, enhances the power of the senses, opens the imagination, adds to his character heroic and sacred attributes, establishes marriage, and gives permanence to human society.

The natural association of the sentiment of love with the heyday of the blood seems to require, that in order to portray it in vivid tints, which every youth and maid should confess to be true to their throbbing experience, one must not be too old. The delicious fancies of youth reject the least savour of a mature philosophy, as chilling with age and pedantry their purple bloom. And, therefore, I know I incur the imputation of unnecessary hardness and stoicism from those who compose the Court and Parliament of Love. But from these formidable censors I shall appeal to my seniors. For it is to be considered that this passion of which we speak, though it begin with the young, yet forsakes not the old, or rather suffers no one who is truly its servant to grow old, but makes the aged participators of it, not less than the tender maiden, though in a different and nobler sort. For it is a fire that, kindling its first embers in the narrow nook of a private bosom, caught from a wandering spark out of another private heart, glows and enlarges until it warms and beams upon multitudes of men and women, upon the universal heart of all, and so lights up the whole world and all nature with its generous flames. It matters not, therefore, whether we attempt to describe the passion at twenty, at thirty, or at eighty years. He who paints it at the first period will lose some of its later, he who paints it at the last, some of its earlier traits. Only it is to be hoped that, by patience and the Muses' aid, we may attain to that inward view of the law, which shall describe a truth ever young and beautiful, so central that it shall commend itself to the eye, at whatever angle beholden.

And the first condition is, that we must leave a too close and lingering adherence to facts, and study the sentiment as it appeared in hope and not in history. For each man sees his own life defaced and disfigured, as the life of man is not, to his imagination. Each man sees over his own experience a certain stain of error, whilst that of other men looks fair and ideal. Let any man go back to those delicious relations which make the beauty of his life, which have given him sincerest instruction and nourishment, he will shrink and moan. Alas! I know not why, but infinite compunctions embitter in mature life the remembrances of budding joy, and cover every beloved name. Every thing is beautiful seen from the point of the intellect, or as truth. But all is sour, if seen as experience. Details are melancholy; the plan is seemly and noble. In the actual world—the painful kingdom of time and place—dwell care, and canker, and fear. With thought, with the ideal, is immortal hilarity, the rose of joy. Round it all the Muses sing. But grief cleaves to names, and persons, and the partial interests of to-day and yesterday.

The strong bent of nature is seen in the proportion which this topic of personal relations usurps in the conversation of society. What do we wish to know of any worthy person so much, as how he has sped in the history of this sentiment? What books in the circulating libraries circulate? How we glow over these novels of passion, when the story is told with any spark of truth and nature! And what fastens attention, in the intercourse of life, like any passage betraying affection between two parties? Perhaps we never saw them before, and never shall meet them again. But we see them exchange a glance, or betray a deep emotion, and we are no longer strangers. We understand them, and take the warmest interest in the development of the romance. All mankind love a lover. The earliest demonstrations of complacency and kindness are nature's most winning pictures. It is the dawn of civility and grace in the coarse and rustic. The rude village boy teases the girls about the school-house door;—but to-day he comes running into the entry, and meets one fair child disposing her satchel; he holds her books to help her, and instantly it seems to him as if she removed herself from him infinitely, and was a sacred precinct. Among the throng of girls he runs rudely enough, but one alone distances him; and these two little neighbours, that were so close just now, have learned to respect each other's personality. Or who can avert his eyes from the engaging, half-artful, half-artless ways of school-girls who go into the country shops to buy a skein of silk or a sheet of paper, and talk half an hour about nothing with the broad-faced, good-natured shop-boy. In the village they are on a perfect equality, which love delights in, and without any coquetry the happy, affectionate nature of woman flows out in this pretty gossip. The girls may have little beauty, yet plainly do they establish between them and the good boy the most agreeable, confiding relations, what with their fun and their earnest, about Edgar, and Jonas, and Almira, and who was invited to the party, and who danced at the dancing-school, and when the singing-school would begin, and other nothings concerning which the parties cooed. By and by that boy wants a wife, and very truly and heartily will he know where to find a sincere and sweet mate, without any risk such as Milton deplores as incident to scholars and great men.

I have been told, that in some public discourses of mine my reverence for the intellect has made me unjustly cold to the personal relations. But now I almost shrink at the remembrance of such disparaging words. For persons are love's world, and the coldest philosopher cannot recount the debt of the young soul wandering here in nature to the power of love, without being tempted to unsay, as treasonable to nature, aught derogatory to the social instincts. For, though the celestial rapture falling out of heaven seizes only upon those of tender age, and although a beauty overpowering all analysis or comparison, and putting us quite beside ourselves, we can seldom see after thirty years, yet the remembrance of these visions outlasts all other remembrances, and is a wreath of flowers on the oldest brows. But here is a strange fact; it may seem to many men, in revising their experience, that they have no fairer page in their life's book than the delicious memory of some passages wherein affection contrived to give a witchcraft surpassing the deep attraction of its own truth to a parcel of accidental and trivial circumstances. In looking backward, they may find that several things which were not the charm have more reality to this groping memory than the charm itself which embalmed them. But be our experience in particulars what it may, no man ever forgot the visitations of that power to his heart and brain, which created all things new; which was the dawn in him of music, poetry, and art; which made the face of nature radiant with purple light, the morning and the night varied enchantments; when a single tone of one voice could make the heart bound, and the most trivial circumstance associated with one form is put in the amber of memory; when he became all eye when one was present, and all memory when one was gone; when the youth becomes a watcher of windows, and studious of a glove, a veil, a ribbon, or the wheels of a carriage; when no place is too solitary, and none too silent, for him who has richer company and sweeter conversation in his new thoughts, than any old friends, though best and purest, can give him; for the figures, the motions, the words of the beloved object are not like other images written in water, but, as Plutarch said, "enamelled in fire," and make the study of midnight.

> "Thou art not gone being gone, where'er thou art,
>   Thou leav'st in him thy watchful eyes, in him thy
>   loving heart."

In the noon and the afternoon of life we still throb at the recollection of days when happiness was not happy enough, but must be drugged with the relish of pain and fear; for he touched the secret of the matter, who said of love,—

> "All other pleasures are not worth its pains";

and when the day was not long enough, but the night, too, must be consumed in keen recollections; when the head boiled all night on the pillow with the generous deed it resolved on; when the moonlight was a pleasing fever, and the stars were letters, and the flowers ciphers, and the air was coined into song; when all business seemed an impertinence, and all the men and women running to and fro in the streets, mere pictures.

The passion rebuilds the world for the youth. It makes all things alive and significant. Nature grows conscious. Every bird on the boughs of the tree sings now to his heart and soul. The notes are almost articulate. The clouds have faces as he looks on them. The trees of the forest, the waving grass, and the peeping flowers have grown intelligent; and he almost fears to trust them with the secret which they seem to invite. Yet nature soothes and sympathizes. In the green solitude he finds a dearer home than with men.

> "Fountain-heads and pathless groves,
> Places which pale passion loves,
> Moonlight walks, when all the fowls
> Are safely housed, save bats and owls,
> A midnight bell, a passing groan,—
> These are the sounds we feed upon."

Behold there in the wood the fine madman! He is a palace of sweet sounds and sights; he dilates; he is twice a man; he walks with arms akimbo; he soliloquizes; he accosts the grass and the trees; he feels the blood of the violet, the clover, and the lily in his veins; and he talks with the brook that wets his foot.

The heats that have opened his perceptions of natural beauty have made him love music and verse. It is a fact often observed, that men have written good verses under the inspiration of passion, who cannot write well under any other circumstances.

The like force has the passion over all his nature. It expands the sentiment; it makes the clown gentle, and gives the coward heart. Into the most pitiful and abject it will infuse a heart and courage to defy the world, so only it have the countenance of the beloved object. In giving him to another, it still more gives him to himself. He is a new man, with new perceptions, new and keener purposes, and a religious solemnity of character and aims. He does not longer appertain to his family and society; *he* is somewhat; *he* is a person; *he* is a soul.

And here let us examine a little nearer the nature of that influence which is thus potent over the human youth. Beauty, whose revelation to man we now celebrate, welcome as the sun wherever it pleases to shine, which pleases everybody with it and with themselves, seems sufficient to itself. The lover cannot paint his maiden to his fancy poor and solitary. Like a tree in flower, so much soft, budding, informing loveliness is society for itself, and she teaches his eye why Beauty was pictured with Loves and Graces attending her steps. Her existence makes the world rich. Though she extrudes all other persons from his attention as cheap and unworthy, she indemnifies him by carrying out her own being into somewhat impersonal, large, mundane, so that the maiden stands to him for a representative of all select things and virtues. For that reason, the lover never sees personal resemblances in his mistress to her kindred or to others. His friends find in her a likeness to her mother, or her sisters, or to persons not of her blood. The lover sees no resemblance except to summer evenings and diamond mornings, to rainbows and the song of birds.

The ancients called beauty the flowering of virtue. Who can analyze the nameless charm which glances from one and another face and form? We are touched with emotions of tenderness and complacency, but we cannot find whereat this dainty emotion, this wandering gleam, points. It is destroyed for the imagination by any attempt to refer it to organization. Nor does it point to any relations of friendship or love known and described in society, but, as it seems to me, to a quite other and unattainable sphere, to relations of transcendent delicacy and sweetness, to what roses and violets hint and foreshow. We cannot approach beauty. Its nature is like opaline doves'-neck lustres, hovering and evanescent. Herein it resembles the most excellent things, which all have this rainbow character, defying all attempts at appropriation and use. What else did Jean Paul Richter signify, when he said to music, "Away! away! thou speakest to me of things which in all my endless life I have not found, and shall not find." The same fluency may be observed in every work of the plastic arts. The statue is then beautiful when it begins to be incomprehensible, when it is passing out of criticism, and can no longer be defined by compass and measuring-wand, but demands an active imagination to go with it, and to say what it is in the act of doing. The god or hero of the sculptor is always represented in a transition *from* that which is representable to the senses, *to* that which is not. Then first it ceases to be a stone. The same remark holds of painting. And of poetry, the success is not attained when it lulls and satisfies, but when it astonishes and fires us with new endeavours after the unattainable. Concerning it, Landor inquires "whether it is not to be referred to some purer state of sensation and existence."

In like manner, personal beauty is then first charming and itself, when it dissatisfies us with any end; when it becomes a story without an end; when it suggests gleams and visions, and not earthly satisfactions; when it makes the beholder feel his unworthiness; when he cannot feel his right to it, though he were Cæsar; he cannot feel more right to it than to the firmament and the splendors of a sunset.

Hence arose the saying, "If I love you, what is that to you?" We say so, because we feel that what we love is not in your will, but above it. It is not you, but your radiance. It is that which you know not in yourself, and can never know.

This agrees well with that high philosophy of Beauty which the ancient writers delighted in; for they said that the soul of man, embodied here on earth, went roaming up and down in quest of that other world of its own, out of which it came into this, but was soon stupefied by the light of the natural sun, and unable to see any other objects than those of this world, which are but shadows of real things. Therefore, the Deity sends the glory of youth before the soul, that it may avail itself of beautiful bodies as aids to its recollection of the celestial good and fair; and the man beholding such a person in the female sex runs to her, and finds the highest joy in contemplating the form, movement, and intelligence of this person, because it suggests to him the presence of that which indeed is within the beauty, and the cause of the beauty.

If, however, from too much conversing with material objects, the soul was gross, and misplaced its satisfaction in the body, it reaped nothing but sorrow; body being unable to fulfil the promise which beauty holds out; but if, accepting the hint of these visions and suggestions which beauty makes to his mind, the soul passes through the body, and falls to admire strokes of character, and the lovers contemplate one another in their discourses and their actions, then they pass to the true palace of beauty, more and more inflame their love of it, and by this love extinguishing the base affection, as the sun puts out the fire by shining on the hearth, they become pure and hallowed. By conversation with that which is in itself excellent, magnanimous, lowly, and just, the lover comes to a warmer love of these nobilities, and a quicker apprehension of them. Then he passes from loving them in one to loving them in all, and so is the one beautiful soul only the door through which he enters to the society of all true and pure souls. In the particular society of his mate, he attains a clearer sight of any spot, any taint, which her beauty has contracted from this world, and is able to point it out, and this with mutual joy that they are now able, without offence, to indicate blemishes and hindrances in each other, and give to each all help and comfort in curing the same. And, beholding in many souls the traits of the divine beauty, and separating in each soul that which is divine from the taint which it has contracted in the world, the lover ascends to the highest beauty, to the love and knowledge of the Divinity, by steps on this ladder of created souls.

Somewhat like this have the truly wise told us of love in all ages. The doctrine is not old, nor is it new. If Plato, Plutarch, and Apuleius taught it, so have Petrarch, Angelo, and Milton. It awaits a truer unfolding in opposition and rebuke to that subterranean prudence which presides at marriages with words that take hold of the upper world, whilst one eye is prowling in the cellar, so that its gravest discourse has a savor of hams and powdering-tubs. Worst, when this sensualism intrudes into the education of young women, and withers the hope and affection of human nature, by teaching that marriage signifies nothing but a housewife's thrift, and that woman's life has no other aim.

But this dream of love, though beautiful, is only one scene in our play. In the procession of the soul from within outward, it enlarges its circles ever, like the pebble thrown into the pond, or the light proceeding from an orb. The rays of the soul alight first on things nearest, on every utensil and toy, on nurses and domestics, on the house, and yard, and passengers, on the circle of household acquaintance, on politics, and geography, and history. But things are ever grouping themselves according to higher or more interior laws. Neighbourhood, size, numbers, habits, persons, lose by degrees their power over us. Cause and effect, real affinities, the longing for harmony between the soul and the circumstance, the progressive, idealizing instinct, predominate later, and the step backward from the higher to the lower relations is impossible. Thus even love, which is the deification of persons, must become more impersonal every day. Of this at first it gives no hint. Little think the youth and maiden who are glancing at each other across crowded rooms, with eyes so full of mutual intelligence, of the precious fruit long hereafter to proceed from this new, quite external stimulus. The work of vegetation begins first in the irritability of the bark and leaf-buds. From exchanging glances, they advance to acts of courtesy, of gallantry, then to fiery passion, to plighting troth, and marriage. Passion beholds its object as a perfect unit. The soul is wholly embodied, and the body is wholly ensouled.

> "Her pure and eloquent blood
>   Spoke in her cheeks, and so distinctly wrought,
>   That one might almost say her body thought."

Romeo, if dead, should be cut up into little stars to make the heavens fine. Life, with this pair, has no other aim, asks no more, than Juliet,—than Romeo. Night, day, studies, talents, kingdoms, religion, are all contained in this form full of soul, in this soul which is all form. The lovers delight in endearments, in avowals of love, in comparisons of their regards. When alone, they solace themselves with the remembered image of the other. Does that other see the same star, the same melting cloud, read the same book, feel the same emotion, that now delight me? They try and weigh their affection, and, adding up costly advantages, friends, opportunities, properties, exult in discovering that willingly, joyfully, they would give all as a ransom for the beautiful, the beloved head, not one hair of which shall be harmed. But the lot of humanity is on these children. Danger, sorrow, and pain arrive to them, as to all. Love prays. It makes covenants with Eternal Power in behalf of this dear mate. The union which is thus effected, and which adds a new value to every atom in nature, for it transmutes every thread throughout the whole web of relation into a golden ray, and bathes the soul in a new and sweeter element, is yet a temporary state. Not always can flowers, pearls, poetry, protestations, nor even home in another heart, content the awful soul that dwells in clay. It arouses itself at last from these endearments, as toys, and puts on the harness, and aspires to vast and universal aims. The soul which is in the soul of each, craving a perfect beatitude, detects incongruities, defects, and disproportion in the behaviour of the other. Hence arise surprise, expostulation, and pain. Yet that which drew them to each other was signs of loveliness, signs of virtue; and these virtues are there, however eclipsed. They appear and reappear, and continue to attract; but the regard changes, quits the sign, and attaches to the substance. This repairs the wounded affection. Meantime, as life wears on, it proves a game of permutation and combination of all possible positions of the parties, to employ all the resources of each, and acquaint each with the strength and weakness of the other. For it is the nature and end of this relation, that they should represent the human race to each other. All that is in the world, which is or ought to be known, is cunningly wrought into the texture of man, of woman.

> "The person love does to us fit,
>   Like manna, has the taste of all in it."

The world rolls; the circumstances vary every hour. The angels that inhabit this temple of the body appear at the windows, and the gnomes and vices also. By all the virtues they are united. If there be virtue, all the vices are known as such; they confess and flee. Their once flaming regard is sobered by time in either breast, and, losing in violence what it gains in extent, it becomes a thorough good understanding. They resign each other, without complaint, to the good offices which man and woman are severally appointed to discharge in time, and exchange the passion which once could not lose sight of its object, for a cheerful, disengaged furtherance, whether present or absent, of each other's designs. At last they discover that all which at first drew them together,—those once sacred features, that magical play of charms,—was deciduous, had a prospective end, like the scaffolding by which the house was built; and the purification of the intellect and the heart, from year to year, is the real marriage, foreseen and prepared from the first, and wholly above their consciousness. Looking at these aims with which two persons, a man and a woman, so variously and correlatively gifted, are shut up in one house to spend in the nuptial society forty or fifty years, I do not wonder at the emphasis with which the heart prophesies this crisis from early infancy, at the profuse beauty with which the instincts deck the nuptial bower, and nature, and intellect, and art emulate each other in the gifts and the melody they bring to the epithalamium.

Thus are we put in training for a love which knows not sex, nor person, nor partiality, but which seeks virtue and wisdom everywhere, to the end of increasing virtue and wisdom. We are by nature observers, and thereby learners. That is our permanent state. But we are often made to feel that our affections are but tents of a night. Though slowly and with pain, the objects of the affections change, as the objects of thought do. There are moments when the affections rule and absorb the man, and make his happiness dependent on a person or persons. But in health the mind is presently seen again,—its overarching vault, bright with galaxies of immutable lights, and the warm loves and fears that swept over us as clouds, must lose their finite character and blend with God, to attain their own perfection. But we need not fear that we can lose any thing by the progress of the soul. The soul may be trusted to the end. That which is so beautiful and attractive as these relations must be succeeded and supplanted only by what is more beautiful, and so on for ever.

FRIENDSHIP

A ruddy drop of manly blood
The surging sea outweighs,
The world uncertain comes and goes,
The lover rooted stays.
I fancied he was fled,
And, after many a year,
Glowed unexhausted kindliness
Like daily sunrise there.
My careful heart was free again,—
O friend, my bosom said,
Through thee alone the sky is arched,
Through thee the rose is red,
All things through thee take nobler form,
And look beyond the earth,
And is the mill-round of our fate
A sun-path in thy worth.
Me too thy nobleness has taught
To master my despair;
The fountains of my hidden life
Are through thy friendship fair.

ESSAY VI
Friendship

W E HAVE a great deal more kindness than is ever spoken. Maugre all the selfishness that chills like east winds the world, the whole human family is bathed with an element of love like a fine ether. How many persons we meet in houses, whom we scarcely speak to, whom yet we honor, and who honor us! How many we see in the street, or sit with in church, whom, though silently, we warmly rejoice to be with! Read the language of these wandering eye-beams. The heart knoweth.

The effect of the indulgence of this human affection is a certain cordial exhilaration. In poetry, and in common speech, the emotions of benevolence and complacency which are felt towards others are likened to the material effects of fire; so swift, or much more swift, more active, more cheering, are these fine inward irradiations. From the highest degree of passionate love, to the lowest degree of good-will, they make the sweetness of life.

Our intellectual and active powers increase with our affection. The scholar sits down to write, and all his years of meditation do not furnish him with one good thought or happy expression; but it is necessary to write a letter to a friend, — and, forthwith, troops of gentle thoughts invest themselves, on every hand, with chosen words. See, in any house where virtue and self-respect abide, the palpitation which the approach of a stranger causes. A commended stranger is expected and announced, and an uneasiness betwixt pleasure and pain invades all the hearts of a household. His arrival almost brings fear to the good hearts that would welcome him. The house is dusted, all things fly into their places, the old coat is exchanged for the new, and they must get up a dinner if they can. Of a commended stranger, only the good report is told by others, only the good and new is heard by us. He stands to us for humanity. He is what we wish. Having imagined and invested him, we ask how we should stand related in conversation and action with such a man, and are uneasy with fear. The same idea exalts conversation with him. We talk better than we are wont. We have the nimblest fancy, a richer memory, and our dumb devil has taken leave for the time. For long hours we can continue a series of sincere, graceful, rich communications, drawn from the oldest, secretest experience, so that they who sit by, of our own kinsfolk and acquaintance, shall feel a lively surprise at our unusual powers. But as soon as the stranger begins to intrude his partialities, his definitions, his defects, into the conversation, it is all over. He has heard the first, the last and best he will ever hear from us. He is no stranger now. Vulgarity, ignorance, misapprehension are old acquaintances. Now, when he comes, he may get the order, the dress, and the dinner,—but the throbbing of the heart, and the communications of the soul, no more.

What is so pleasant as these jets of affection which make a young world for me again? What so delicious as a just and firm encounter of two, in a thought, in a feeling? How beautiful, on their approach to this beating heart, the steps and forms of the gifted and the true! The moment we indulge our affections, the earth is metamorphosed; there is no winter, and no night; all tragedies, all ennuis, vanish,— all duties even; nothing fills the proceeding eternity but the forms all radiant of beloved persons. Let the soul be assured that somewhere in the universe it should rejoin its friend, and it would be content and cheerful alone for a thousand years.

I awoke this morning with devout thanksgiving for my friends, the old and the new. Shall I not call God the Beautiful, who daily showeth himself so to me in his gifts? I chide society, I embrace solitude, and yet I am not so ungrateful as not to see the wise, the lovely, and the noble-minded, as from time to time they pass my gate. Who hears me, who understands me, becomes mine,—a possession for all time. Nor is nature so poor but she gives me this joy several times, and thus we weave social threads of our own, a new web of relations; and, as many thoughts in succession substantiate themselves, we shall by and by stand in a new world of our own creation, and no longer strangers and pilgrims in a traditionary globe. My friends have come to me unsought.

The great God gave them to me. By oldest right, by the divine affinity of virtue with itself, I find them, or rather not I, but the Deity in me and in them derides and cancels the thick walls of individual character, relation, age, sex, circumstance, at which he usually connives, and now makes many one. High thanks I owe you, excellent lovers, who carry out the world for me to new and noble depths, and enlarge the meaning of all my thoughts. These are new poetry of the first Bard,—poetry without stop,—hymn, ode, and epic, poetry still flowing, Apollo and the Muses chanting still. Will these, too, separate themselves from me again, or some of them? I know not, but I fear it not; for my relation to them is so pure, that we hold by simple affinity, and the Genius of my life being thus social, the same affinity will exert its energy on whomsoever is as noble as these men and women, wherever I may be.

I confess to an extreme tenderness of nature on this point. It is almost dangerous to me to "crush the sweet poison of misused wine" of the affections. A new person is to me a great event, and hinders me from sleep. I have often had fine fancies about persons which have given me delicious hours; but the joy ends in the day; it yields no fruit. Thought is not born of it; my action is very little modified. I must feel pride in my friend's accomplishments as if they were mine,—and a property in his virtues. I feel as warmly when he is praised, as the lover when he hears applause of his engaged maiden. We over-estimate the conscience of our friend. His goodness seems better than our goodness, his nature finer, his temptations less. Every thing that is his,—his name, his form, his dress, books, and instruments,—fancy enhances. Our own thought sounds new and larger from his mouth.

Yet the systole and diastole of the heart are not without their analogy in the ebb and flow of love. Friendship, like the immortality of the soul, is too good to be believed. The lover, beholding his maiden, half knows that she is not verily that which he worships; and in the golden hour of friendship, we are surprised with shades of suspicion and unbelief. We doubt that we bestow on our hero the virtues in which he shines, and afterwards worship the form to which we have ascribed this divine inhabitation. In strictness, the soul does not re-

spect men as it respects itself. In strict science all persons underlie the same condition of an infinite remoteness. Shall we
fear to cool our love by mining for the metaphysical foundation of this Elysian temple? Shall I not be as real as the things
I see? If I am, I shall not fear to know them for what they
are. Their essence is not less beautiful than their appearance,
though it needs finer organs for its apprehension. The root of
the plant is not unsightly to science, though for chaplets and
festoons we cut the stem short. And I must hazard the production of the bald fact amidst these pleasing reveries, though
it should prove an Egyptian skull at our banquet. A man who
stands united with his thought conceives magnificently of
himself. He is conscious of a universal success, even though
bought by uniform particular failures. No advantages, no
powers, no gold or force, can be any match for him. I cannot
choose but rely on my own poverty more than on your
wealth. I cannot make your consciousness tantamount to
mine. Only the star dazzles; the planet has a faint, moon-like
ray. I hear what you say of the admirable parts and tried temper of the party you praise, but I see well that for all his purple
cloaks I shall not like him, unless he is at last a poor Greek like
me. I cannot deny it, O friend, that the vast shadow of the Phenomenal includes thee also in its pied and painted immensity,—thee, also, compared with whom all else is shadow. Thou
art not Being, as Truth is, as Justice is,—thou art not my soul,
but a picture and effigy of that. Thou hast come to me lately,
and already thou art seizing thy hat and cloak. Is it not that the
soul puts forth friends as the tree puts forth leaves, and presently, by the germination of new buds, extrudes the old leaf?
The law of nature is alternation for evermore. Each electrical
state superinduces the opposite. The soul environs itself with
friends, that it may enter into a grander self-acquaintance or
solitude; and it goes alone for a season, that it may exalt its
conversation or society. This method betrays itself along the
whole history of our personal relations. The instinct of affection revives the hope of union with our mates, and the returning sense of insulation recalls us from the chase. Thus every
man passes his life in the search after friendship, and if he
should record his true sentiment, he might write a letter like
this to each new candidate for his love.

DEAR FRIEND: —

If I was sure of thee, sure of thy capacity, sure to match my mood with thine, I should never think again of trifles in relation to thy comings and goings. I am not very wise; my moods are quite attainable; and I respect thy genius; it is to me as yet unfathomed; yet dare I not presume in thee a perfect intelligence of me, and so thou art to me a delicious torment. Thine ever, or never.

Yet these uneasy pleasures and fine pains are for curiosity, and not for life. They are not to be indulged. This is to weave cobweb, and not cloth. Our friendships hurry to short and poor conclusions, because we have made them a texture of wine and dreams, instead of the tough fibre of the human heart. The laws of friendship are austere and eternal, of one web with the laws of nature and of morals. But we have aimed at a swift and petty benefit, to suck a sudden sweetness. We snatch at the slowest fruit in the whole garden of God, which many summers and many winters must ripen. We seek our friend not sacredly, but with an adulterate passion which would appropriate him to ourselves. In vain. We are armed all over with subtle antagonisms, which, as soon as we meet, begin to play, and translate all poetry into stale prose. Almost all people descend to meet. All association must be a compromise, and, what is worst, the very flower and aroma of the flower of each of the beautiful natures disappears as they approach each other. What a perpetual disappointment is actual society, even of the virtuous and gifted! After interviews have been compassed with long foresight, we must be tormented presently by baffled blows, by sudden, unseasonable apathies, by epilepsies of wit and of animal spirits, in the heyday of friendship and thought. Our faculties do not play us true, and both parties are relieved by solitude.

I ought to be equal to every relation. It makes no difference how many friends I have, and what content I can find in conversing with each, if there be one to whom I am not equal. If I have shrunk unequal from one contest, the joy I find in all the rest becomes mean and cowardly. I should hate myself, if then I made my other friends my asylum.

"The valiant warrior famoused for fight,
After a hundred victories, once foiled,
Is from the book of honor razed quite,
And all the rest forgot for which he toiled."

Our impatience is thus sharply rebuked. Bashfulness and apathy are a tough husk, in which a delicate organization is protected from premature ripening. It would be lost if it knew itself before any of the best souls were yet ripe enough to know and own it. Respect the *naturlangsamkeit* which hardens the ruby in a million years, and works in duration, in which Alps and Andes come and go as rainbows. The good spirit of our life has no heaven which is the price of rashness. Love, which is the essence of God, is not for levity, but for the total worth of man. Let us not have this childish luxury in our regards, but the austerest worth; let us approach our friend with an audacious trust in the truth of his heart, in the breadth, impossible to be overturned, of his foundations.

The attractions of this subject are not to be resisted, and I leave, for the time, all account of subordinate social benefit, to speak of that select and sacred relation which is a kind of absolute, and which even leaves the language of love suspicious and common, so much is this purer, and nothing is so much divine.

I do not wish to treat friendships daintily, but with roughest courage. When they are real, they are not glass threads or frostwork, but the solidest thing we know. For now, after so many ages of experience, what do we know of nature, or of ourselves? Not one step has man taken toward the solution of the problem of his destiny. In one condemnation of folly stand the whole universe of men. But the sweet sincerity of joy and peace, which I draw from this alliance with my brother's soul, is the nut itself, whereof all nature and all thought is but the husk and shell. Happy is the house that shelters a friend! It might well be built, like a festal bower or arch, to entertain him a single day. Happier, if he know the solemnity of that relation, and honor its law! He who offers himself a candidate for that covenant comes up, like an Olympian, to the great games, where the first-born of the world are the competitors. He proposes himself for contests where Time,

Want, Danger, are in the lists, and he alone is victor who has truth enough in his constitution to preserve the delicacy of his beauty from the wear and tear of all these. The gifts of fortune may be present or absent, but all the speed in that contest depends on intrinsic nobleness, and the contempt of trifles. There are two elements that go to the composition of friendship, each so sovereign that I can detect no superiority in either, no reason why either should be first named. One is Truth. A friend is a person with whom I may be sincere. Before him I may think aloud. I am arrived at last in the presence of a man so real and equal, that I may drop even those undermost garments of dissimulation, courtesy, and second thought, which men never put off, and may deal with him with the simplicity and wholeness with which one chemical atom meets another. Sincerity is the luxury allowed, like diadems and authority, only to the highest rank, *that* being permitted to speak truth, as having none above it to court or conform unto. Every man alone is sincere. At the entrance of a second person, hypocrisy begins. We parry and fend the approach of our fellow-man by compliments, by gossip, by amusements, by affairs. We cover up our thought from him under a hundred folds. I knew a man, who, under a certain religious frenzy, cast off this drapery, and, omitting all compliment and commonplace, spoke to the conscience of every person he encountered, and that with great insight and beauty. At first he was resisted, and all men agreed he was mad. But persisting, as indeed he could not help doing, for some time in this course, he attained to the advantage of bringing every man of his acquaintance into true relations with him. No man would think of speaking falsely with him, or of putting him off with any chat of markets or reading-rooms. But every man was constrained by so much sincerity to the like plaindealing, and what love of nature, what poetry, what symbol of truth he had, he did certainly show him. But to most of us society shows not its face and eye, but its side and its back. To stand in true relations with men in a false age is worth a fit of insanity, is it not? We can seldom go erect. Almost every man we meet requires some civility,—requires to be humored; he has some fame, some talent, some whim of religion or philanthropy in his head that is not to be questioned, and which spoils all conversation with him. But a friend is a sane man who exercises not my ingenuity, but me. My friend gives me entertainment without requiring any stipulation on my part. A friend, therefore, is a sort of paradox in nature. I who alone am, I who see nothing in nature whose existence I can affirm with equal evidence to my own, behold now the semblance of my being, in all its height, variety, and curiosity, reiterated in a foreign form; so that a friend may well be reckoned the masterpiece of nature.

The other element of friendship is tenderness. We are holden to men by every sort of tie, by blood, by pride, by fear, by hope, by lucre, by lust, by hate, by admiration, by every circumstance and badge and trifle, but we can scarce believe that so much character can subsist in another as to draw us by love. Can another be so blessed, and we so pure, that we can offer him tenderness? When a man becomes dear to me, I have touched the goal of fortune. I find very little written directly to the heart of this matter in books. And yet I have one text which I cannot choose but remember. My author says, — "I offer myself faintly and bluntly to those whose I effectually am, and tender myself least to him to whom I am the most devoted." I wish that friendship should have feet, as well as eyes and eloquence. It must plant itself on the ground, before it vaults over the moon. I wish it to be a little of a citizen, before it is quite a cherub. We chide the citizen because he makes love a commodity. It is an exchange of gifts, of useful loans; it is good neighbourhood; it watches with the sick; it holds the pall at the funeral; and quite loses sight of the delicacies and nobility of the relation. But though we cannot find the god under this disguise of a sutler, yet, on the other hand, we cannot forgive the poet if he spins his thread too fine, and does not substantiate his romance by the municipal virtues of justice, punctuality, fidelity, and pity. I hate the prostitution of the name of friendship to signify modish and worldly alliances. I much prefer the company of ploughboys and tin-peddlers, to the silken and perfumed amity which celebrates its days of encounter by a frivolous display, by rides in a curricle, and dinners at the best taverns. The end of friendship is a commerce the most strict and homely that can be joined; more strict than any of which we have experience. It is for aid and comfort through all the relations and passages of life and death. It is fit for serene days, and graceful gifts, and country rambles, but also for rough roads and hard fare, shipwreck, poverty, and persecution. It keeps company with the sallies of the wit and the trances of religion. We are to dignify to each other the daily needs and offices of man's life, and embellish it by courage, wisdom, and unity. It should never fall into something usual and settled, but should be alert and inventive, and add rhyme and reason to what was drudgery.

Friendship may be said to require natures so rare and costly, each so well tempered and so happily adapted, and withal so circumstanced, (for even in that particular, a poet says, love demands that the parties be altogether paired,) that its satisfaction can very seldom be assured. It cannot subsist in its perfection, say some of those who are learned in this warm lore of the heart, betwixt more than two. I am not quite so strict in my terms, perhaps because I have never known so high a fellowship as others. I please my imagination more with a circle of godlike men and women variously related to each other, and between whom subsists a lofty intelligence. But I find this law of *one to one* peremptory for conversation, which is the practice and consummation of friendship. Do not mix waters too much. The best mix as ill as good and bad. You shall have very useful and cheering discourse at several times with two several men, but let all three of you come together, and you shall not have one new and hearty word. Two may talk and one may hear, but three cannot take part in a conversation of the most sincere and searching sort. In good company there is never such discourse between two, across the table, as takes place when you leave them alone. In good company, the individuals merge their egotism into a social soul exactly co-extensive with the several consciousnesses there present. No partialities of friend to friend, no fondnesses of brother to sister, of wife to husband, are there pertinent, but quite otherwise. Only he may then speak who can sail on the common thought of the party, and not poorly limited to his own. Now this convention, which good sense demands, destroys the high freedom of great conversation, which requires an absolute running of two souls into one.

No two men but, being left alone with each other, enter into simpler relations. Yet it is affinity that determines *which* two shall converse. Unrelated men give little joy to each other; will never suspect the latent powers of each. We talk sometimes of a great talent for conversation, as if it were a permanent property in some individuals. Conversation is an evanescent relation,—no more. A man is reputed to have thought and eloquence; he cannot, for all that, say a word to his cousin or his uncle. They accuse his silence with as much reason as they would blame the insignificance of a dial in the shade. In the sun it will mark the hour. Among those who enjoy his thought, he will regain his tongue.

Friendship requires that rare mean betwixt likeness and unlikeness, that piques each with the presence of power and of consent in the other party. Let me be alone to the end of the world, rather than that my friend should overstep, by a word or a look, his real sympathy. I am equally balked by antagonism and by compliance. Let him not cease an instant to be himself. The only joy I have in his being mine, is that the *not mine* is *mine*. I hate, where I looked for a manly furtherance, or at least a manly resistance, to find a mush of concession. Better be a nettle in the side of your friend than his echo. The condition which high friendship demands is ability to do without it. That high office requires great and sublime parts. There must be very two, before there can be very one. Let it be an alliance of two large, formidable natures, mutually beheld, mutually feared, before yet they recognize the deep identity which beneath these disparities unites them.

He only is fit for this society who is magnanimous; who is sure that greatness and goodness are always economy; who is not swift to intermeddle with his fortunes. Let him not intermeddle with this. Leave to the diamond its ages to grow, nor expect to accelerate the births of the eternal. Friendship demands a religious treatment. We talk of choosing our friends, but friends are self-elected. Reverence is a great part of it. Treat your friend as a spectacle. Of course he has merits that are not yours, and that you cannot honor, if you must needs hold him close to your person. Stand aside; give those merits room; let them mount and expand. Are you the friend of your friend's buttons, or of his thought? To a great heart he will still be a stranger in a thousand particulars, that he may come near in the holiest ground. Leave it to girls and boys to regard a friend as property, and to suck a short and all-confounding pleasure, instead of the noblest benefit.

Let us buy our entrance to this guild by a long probation. Why should we desecrate noble and beautiful souls by intruding on them? Why insist on rash personal relations with your friend? Why go to his house, or know his mother and brother and sisters? Why be visited by him at your own? Are these things material to our covenant? Leave this touching and clawing. Let him be to me a spirit. A message, a thought, a sincerity, a glance from him, I want, but not news, nor pottage. I can get politics, and chat, and neighbourly conveniences from cheaper companions. Should not the society of my friend be to me poetic, pure, universal, and great as nature itself? Ought I to feel that our tie is profane in comparison with yonder bar of cloud that sleeps on the horizon, or that clump of waving grass that divides the brook? Let us not vilify, but raise it to that standard. That great, defying eye, that scornful beauty of his mien and action, do not pique yourself on reducing, but rather fortify and enhance. Worship his superiorities; wish him not less by a thought, but hoard and tell them all. Guard him as thy counterpart. Let him be to thee for ever a sort of beautiful enemy, untamable, devoutly revered, and not a trivial conveniency to be soon outgrown and cast aside. The hues of the opal, the light of the diamond, are not to be seen, if the eye is too near. To my friend I write a letter, and from him I receive a letter. That seems to you a little. It suffices me. It is a spiritual gift worthy of him to give, and of me to receive. It profanes nobody. In these warm lines the heart will trust itself, as it will not to the tongue, and pour out the prophecy of a godlier existence than all the annals of heroism have yet made good.

Respect so far the holy laws of this fellowship as not to prejudice its perfect flower by your impatience for its opening. We must be our own before we can be another's. There is at least this satisfaction in crime, according to the Latin proverb;—you can speak to your accomplice on even terms. *Crimen quos inquinat, æquat.* To those whom we admire and love, at first we cannot. Yet the least defect of self-possession vitiates, in my judgment, the entire relation. There can never be deep peace between two spirits, never mutual respect, until, in their dialogue, each stands for the whole world.

What is so great as friendship, let us carry with what grandeur of spirit we can. Let us be silent,—so we may hear the whisper of the gods. Let us not interfere. Who set you to cast about what you should say to the select souls, or how to say any thing to such? No matter how ingenious, no matter how graceful and bland. There are innumerable degrees of folly and wisdom, and for you to say aught is to be frivolous. Wait, and thy heart shall speak. Wait until the necessary and everlasting overpowers you, until day and night avail themselves of your lips. The only reward of virtue is virtue; the only way to have a friend is to be one. You shall not come nearer a man by getting into his house. If unlike, his soul only flees the faster from you, and you shall never catch a true glance of his eye. We see the noble afar off, and they repel us; why should we intrude? Late,—very late,—we perceive that no arrangements, no introductions, no consuetudes or habits of society, would be of any avail to establish us in such relations with them as we desire,—but solely the uprise of nature in us to the same degree it is in them; then shall we meet as water with water; and if we should not meet them then, we shall not want them, for we are already they. In the last analysis, love is only the reflection of a man's own worthiness from other men. Men have sometimes exchanged names with their friends, as if they would signify that in their friend each loved his own soul.

The higher the style we demand of friendship, of course the less easy to establish it with flesh and blood. We walk alone in the world. Friends, such as we desire, are dreams and fables. But a sublime hope cheers ever the faithful heart, that elsewhere, in other regions of the universal power, souls are now acting, enduring, and daring, which can love us, and which we can love. We may congratulate ourselves that the period of nonage, of follies, of blunders, and of shame, is passed in solitude, and when we are finished men, we shall grasp heroic hands in heroic hands. Only be admonished by what you already see, not to strike leagues of friendship with cheap persons, where no friendship can be. Our impatience betrays us into rash and foolish alliances which no God attends. By persisting in your path, though you forfeit the little you gain the great. You demonstrate yourself, so as to put yourself out of the reach of false relations, and you draw to you the first-born of the world,—those rare pilgrims whereof only one or two wander in nature at once, and before whom the vulgar great show as spectres and shadows merely.

It is foolish to be afraid of making our ties too spiritual, as if so we could lose any genuine love. Whatever correction of our popular views we make from insight, nature will be sure to bear us out in, and though it seem to rob us of some joy, will repay us with a greater. Let us feel, if we will, the absolute insulation of man. We are sure that we have all in us. We go to Europe, or we pursue persons, or we read books, in the instinctive faith that these will call it out and reveal us to ourselves. Beggars all. The persons are such as we; the Europe an old faded garment of dead persons; the books their ghosts. Let us drop this idolatry. Let us give over this mendicancy. Let us even bid our dearest friends farewell, and defy them, saying, 'Who are you? Unhand me: I will be dependent no more.' Ah! seest thou not, O brother, that thus we part only to meet again on a higher platform, and only be more each other's, because we are more our own? A friend is Janus-faced: he looks to the past and the future. He is the child of all my foregoing hours, the prophet of those to come, and the harbinger of a greater friend.

I do then with my friends as I do with my books. I would have them where I can find them, but I seldom use them. We must have society on our own terms, and admit or exclude it on the slightest cause. I cannot afford to speak much with my friend. If he is great, he makes me so great that I cannot descend to converse. In the great days, presentiments hover before me in the firmament. I ought then to dedicate myself to them. I go in that I may seize them, I go out that I may seize them. I fear only that I may lose them receding into the sky in which now they are only a patch of brighter light. Then, though I prize my friends, I cannot afford to talk with them and study their visions, lest I lose my own. It would indeed give me a certain household joy to quit this lofty seeking, this spiritual astronomy, or search of stars, and come down to warm sympathies with you; but then I know well I shall mourn always the vanishing of my mighty gods. It is true, next week I shall have languid moods, when I can well afford to occupy myself with foreign objects; then I shall regret the lost literature of your mind, and wish you were by my side again. But if you come, perhaps you will fill my mind only with new visions, not with yourself but with your lustres, and I shall not be able any more than now to converse with you. So I will owe to my friends this evanescent intercourse. I will receive from them, not what they have, but what they are. They shall give me that which properly they cannot give, but which emanates from them. But they shall not hold me by any relations less subtile and pure. We will meet as though we met not, and part as though we parted not.

It has seemed to me lately more possible than I knew, to carry a friendship greatly, on one side, without due correspondence on the other. Why should I cumber myself with regrets that the receiver is not capacious? It never troubles the sun that some of his rays fall wide and vain into ungrateful space, and only a small part on the reflecting planet. Let your greatness educate the crude and cold companion. If he is unequal, he will presently pass away; but thou art enlarged by thy own shining, and, no longer a mate for frogs and worms, dost soar and burn with the gods of the empyrean. It is thought a disgrace to love unrequited. But the great will see that true love cannot be unrequited. True love transcends the unworthy object, and dwells and broods on the eternal, and when the poor interposed mask crumbles, it is not sad, but feels rid of so much earth, and feels its independency the surer. Yet these things may hardly be said without a sort of treachery to the relation. The essence of friendship is entireness, a total magnanimity and trust. It must not surmise or provide for infirmity. It treats its object as a god, that it may deify both.

PRUDENCE

———

Theme no poet gladly sung,
Fair to old and foul to young,
Scorn not thou the love of parts,
And the articles of arts.
Grandeur of the perfect sphere
Thanks the atoms that cohere.

Prudence

WHAT RIGHT have I to write on Prudence, whereof I have little, and that of the negative sort? My prudence consists in avoiding and going without, not in the inventing of means and methods, not in adroit steering, not in gentle repairing. I have no skill to make money spend well, no genius in my economy, and whoever sees my garden discovers that I must have some other garden. Yet I love facts, and hate lubricity, and people without perception. Then I have the same title to write on prudence, that I have to write on poetry or holiness. We write from aspiration and antagonism, as well as from experience. We paint those qualities which we do not possess. The poet admires the man of energy and tactics; the merchant breeds his son for the church or the bar: and where a man is not vain and egotistic, you shall find what he has not by his praise. Moreover, it would be hardly honest in me not to balance these fine lyric words of Love and Friendship with words of coarser sound, and, whilst my debt to my senses is real and constant, not to own it in passing.

Prudence is the virtue of the senses. It is the science of appearances. It is the outmost action of the inward life. It is God taking thought for oxen. It moves matter after the laws of matter. It is content to seek health of body by complying with physical conditions, and health of mind by the laws of the intellect.

The world of the senses is a world of shows; it does not exist for itself, but has a symbolic character; and a true prudence or law of shows recognizes the co-presence of other laws, and knows that its own office is subaltern; knows that it is surface and not centre where it works. Prudence is false when detached. It is legitimate when it is the Natural History of the soul incarnate; when it unfolds the beauty of laws within the narrow scope of the senses.

There are all degrees of proficiency in knowledge of the world. It is sufficient, to our present purpose, to indicate three. One class live to the utility of the symbol; esteeming health and wealth a final good. Another class live above this mark to the beauty of the symbol; as the poet, and artist, and the naturalist, and man of science. A third class live above the beauty of the symbol to the beauty of the thing signified; these are wise men. The first class have common sense; the second, taste; and the third, spiritual perception. Once in a long time, a man traverses the whole scale, and sees and enjoys the symbol solidly; then also has a clear eye for its beauty, and, lastly, whilst he pitches his tent on this sacred volcanic isle of nature, does not offer to build houses and barns thereon, reverencing the splendor of the God which he sees bursting through each chink and cranny.

The world is filled with the proverbs and acts and winkings of a base prudence, which is a devotion to matter, as if we possessed no other faculties than the palate, the nose, the touch, the eye and ear; a prudence which adores the Rule of Three, which never subscribes, which never gives, which seldom lends, and asks but one question of any project,—Will it bake bread? This is a disease like a thickening of the skin until the vital organs are destroyed. But culture, revealing the high origin of the apparent world, and aiming at the perfection of the man as the end, degrades every thing else, as health and bodily life, into means. It sees prudence not to be a several faculty, but a name for wisdom and virtue conversing with the body and its wants. Cultivated men always feel and speak so, as if a great fortune, the achievement of a civil or social measure, great personal influence, a graceful and commanding address, had their value as proofs of the energy of the spirit. If a man lose his balance, and immerse himself in any trades or pleasures for their own sake, he may be a good wheel or pin, but he is not a cultivated man.

The spurious prudence, making the senses final, is the god of sots and cowards, and is the subject of all comedy. It is nature's joke, and therefore literature's. The true prudence limits this sensualism by admitting the knowledge of an internal and real world. This recognition once made,—the order of the world and the distribution of affairs and times being studied with the co-perception of their subordinate place, will reward any degree of attention. For our existence, thus apparently attached in nature to the sun and the returning moon

and the periods which they mark,—so susceptible to climate
and to country, so alive to social good and evil, so fond of
splendor, and so tender to hunger and cold and debt,—reads
all its primary lessons out of these books.

Prudence does not go behind nature, and ask whence it is.
It takes the laws of the world, whereby man's being is conditioned, as they are, and keeps these laws, that it may enjoy
their proper good. It respects space and time, climate, want,
sleep, the law of polarity, growth, and death. There revolve
to give bound and period to his being, on all sides, the sun
and moon, the great formalists in the sky: here lies stubborn
matter, and will not swerve from its chemical routine. Here
is a planted globe, pierced and belted with natural laws, and
fenced and distributed externally with civil partitions and
properties which impose new restraints on the young inhabitant.

We eat of the bread which grows in the field. We live by
the air which blows around us, and we are poisoned by the
air that is too cold or too hot, too dry or too wet. Time,
which shows so vacant, indivisible, and divine in its coming,
is slit and peddled into trifles and tatters. A door is to be
painted, a lock to be repaired. I want wood, or oil, or meal,
or salt; the house smokes, or I have a headache; then the tax;
and an affair to be transacted with a man without heart or
brains; and the stinging recollection of an injurious or very
awkward word,—these eat up the hours. Do what we can,
summer will have its flies: if we walk in the woods, we must
feed mosquitos: if we go a-fishing, we must expect a wet coat.
Then climate is a great impediment to idle persons: we often
resolve to give up the care of the weather, but still we regard
the clouds and the rain.

We are instructed by these petty experiences which usurp
the hours and years. The hard soil and four months of snow
make the inhabitant of the northern temperate zone wiser and
abler than his fellow who enjoys the fixed smile of the tropics.
The islander may ramble all day at will. At night, he may
sleep on a mat under the moon, and wherever a wild date-
tree grows, nature has, without a prayer even, spread a table
for his morning meal. The northerner is perforce a householder. He must brew, bake, salt, and preserve his food, and

pile wood and coal. But as it happens that not one stroke can labor lay to, without some new acquaintance with nature; and as nature is inexhaustibly significant, the inhabitants of these climates have always excelled the southerner in force. Such is the value of these matters, that a man who knows other things can never know too much of these. Let him have accurate perceptions. Let him, if he have hands, handle; if eyes, measure and discriminate; let him accept and hive every fact of chemistry, natural history, and economics; the more he has, the less is he willing to spare any one. Time is always bringing the occasions that disclose their value. Some wisdom comes out of every natural and innocent action. The domestic man, who loves no music so well as his kitchen clock, and the airs which the logs sing to him as they burn on the hearth, has solaces which others never dream of. The application of means to ends insures victory and the songs of victory, not less in a farm or a shop than in the tactics of party or of war. The good husband finds method as efficient in the packing of fire-wood in a shed, or in the harvesting of fruits in the cellar, as in Peninsular campaigns or the files of the Department of State. In the rainy day, he builds a work-bench, or gets his tool-box set in the corner of the barn-chamber, and stored with nails, gimlet, pincers, screwdriver, and chisel. Herein he tastes an old joy of youth and childhood, the cat-like love of garrets, presses, and corn-chambers, and of the conveniences of long housekeeping. His garden or his poultry-yard tells him many pleasant anecdotes. One might find argument for optimism in the abundant flow of this saccharine element of pleasure in every suburb and extremity of the good world. Let a man keep the law,—any law,—and his way will be strown with satisfactions. There is more difference in the quality of our pleasures than in the amount.

On the other hand, nature punishes any neglect of prudence. If you think the senses final, obey their law. If you believe in the soul, do not clutch at sensual sweetness before it is ripe on the slow tree of cause and effect. It is vinegar to the eyes, to deal with men of loose and imperfect perception. Dr. Johnson is reported to have said,—"If the child says he looked out of this window, when he looked out of that,—

whip him." Our American character is marked by a more than average delight in accurate perception, which is shown by the currency of the byword, "No mistake." But the discomfort of unpunctuality, of confusion of thought about facts, of inattention to the wants of to-morrow, is of no nation. The beautiful laws of time and space, once dislocated by our inaptitude, are holes and dens. If the hive be disturbed by rash and stupid hands, instead of honey, it will yield us bees. Our words and actions to be fair must be timely. A gay and pleasant sound is the whetting of the scythe in the mornings of June; yet what is more lonesome and sad than the sound of a whetstone or mower's rifle, when it is too late in the season to make hay? Scatter-brained and "afternoon men" spoil much more than their own affair, in spoiling the temper of those who deal with them. I have seen a criticism on some paintings, of which I am reminded when I see the shiftless and unhappy men who are not true to their senses. The last Grand Duke of Weimar, a man of superior understanding, said:—"I have sometimes remarked in the presence of great works of art, and just now especially, in Dresden, how much a certain property contributes to the effect which gives life to the figures, and to the life an irresistible truth. This property is the hitting, in all the figures we draw, the right centre of gravity. I mean, the placing the figures firm upon their feet, making the hands grasp, and fastening the eyes on the spot where they should look. Even lifeless figures, as vessels and stools,—let them be drawn ever so correctly,—lose all effect so soon as they lack the resting upon their centre of gravity, and have a certain swimming and oscillating appearance. The Raphael, in the Dresden gallery, (the only greatly affecting picture which I have seen,) is the quietest and most passion-less piece you can imagine; a couple of saints who worship the Virgin and Child. Nevertheless, it awakens a deeper impression than the contortions of ten crucified martyrs. For, beside all the resistless beauty of form, it possesses in the highest degree the property of the perpendicularity of all the figures." This perpendicularity we demand of all the figures in this picture of life. Let them stand on their feet, and not float and swing. Let us know where to find them. Let them discriminate between what they remember and what they dreamed, call a spade a spade, give us facts, and honor their own senses with trust.

But what man shall dare tax another with imprudence? Who is prudent? The men we call greatest are least in this kingdom. There is a certain fatal dislocation in our relation to nature, distorting our modes of living, and making every law our enemy, which seems at last to have aroused all the wit and virtue in the world to ponder the question of Reform. We must call the highest prudence to counsel, and ask why health and beauty and genius should now be the exception, rather than the rule, of human nature? We do not know the properties of plants and animals and the laws of nature through our sympathy with the same; but this remains the dream of poets. Poetry and prudence should be coincident. Poets should be lawgivers; that is, the boldest lyric inspiration should not chide and insult, but should announce and lead, the civil code, and the day's work. But now the two things seem irreconcilably parted. We have violated law upon law, until we stand amidst ruins, and when by chance we espy a coincidence between reason and the phenomena, we are surprised. Beauty should be the dowry of every man and woman, as invariably as sensation; but it is rare. Health or sound organization should be universal. Genius should be the child of genius, and every child should be inspired; but now it is not to be predicted of any child, and nowhere is it pure. We call partial half-lights, by courtesy, genius; talent which converts itself to money; talent which glitters to-day, that it may dine and sleep well to-morrow; and society is officered by *men of parts*, as they are properly called, and not by divine men. These use their gifts to refine luxury, not to abolish it. Genius is always ascetic; and piety and love. Appetite shows to the finer souls as a disease, and they find beauty in rites and bounds that resist it.

We have found out fine names to cover our sensuality withal, but no gifts can raise intemperance. The man of talent affects to call his transgressions of the laws of the senses trivial, and to count them nothing considered with his devotion to his art. His art never taught him lewdness, nor the love of wine, nor the wish to reap where he had not sowed. His art is less for every deduction from his holiness, and less for every defect of common sense. On him who scorned the world, as he said, the scorned world wreaks its revenge. He that despiseth small things will perish by little and little. Goethe's Tasso is very likely to be a pretty fair historical portrait, and that is true tragedy. It does not seem to me so genuine grief when some tyrannous Richard the Third oppresses and slays a score of innocent persons, as when Antonio and Tasso, both apparently right, wrong each other. One living after the maxims of this world, and consistent and true to them, the other fired with all divine sentiments, yet grasping also at the pleasures of sense, without submitting to their law. That is a grief we all feel, a knot we cannot untie. Tasso's is no infrequent case in modern biography. A man of genius, of an ardent temperament, reckless of physical laws, self-indulgent, becomes presently unfortunate, querulous, a "discomfortable cousin," a thorn to himself and to others.

The scholar shames us by his bifold life. Whilst something higher than prudence is active, he is admirable; when common sense is wanted, he is an encumbrance. Yesterday, Cæsar was not so great; to-day, the felon at the gallows' foot is not more miserable. Yesterday, radiant with the light of an ideal world, in which he lives, the first of men; and now oppressed by wants and by sickness, for which he must thank himself. He resembles the pitiful drivellers, whom travellers describe as frequenting the bazaars of Constantinople, who skulk about all day, yellow, emaciated, ragged, sneaking; and at evening, when the bazaars are open, slink to the opium-shop, swallow their morsel, and become tranquil and glorified seers. And who has not seen the tragedy of imprudent genius, struggling for years with paltry pecuniary difficulties, at last sinking, chilled, exhausted, and fruitless, like a giant slaughtered by pins?

Is it not better that a man should accept the first pains and mortifications of this sort, which nature is not slack in sending him, as hints that he must expect no other good than the just fruit of his own labor and self-denial? Health, bread, climate, social position, have their importance, and he will give them their due. Let him esteem Nature a perpetual counsellor, and her perfections the exact measure of our deviations.

Let him make the night night, and the day day. Let him control the habit of expense. Let him see that as much wisdom may be expended on a private economy as on an empire, and as much wisdom may be drawn from it. The laws of the world are written out for him on every piece of money in his hand. There is nothing he will not be the better for knowing, were it only the wisdom of Poor Richard; or the State-Street prudence of buying by the acre to sell by the foot; or the thrift of the agriculturist, to stick a tree between whiles, because it will grow whilst he sleeps; or the prudence which consists in husbanding little strokes of the tool, little portions of time, particles of stock, and small gains. The eye of prudence may never shut. Iron, if kept at the ironmonger's, will rust; beer, if not brewed in the right state of the atmosphere, will sour; timber of ships will rot at sea, or, if laid up high and dry, will strain, warp, and dry-rot; money, if kept by us, yields no rent, and is liable to loss; if invested, is liable to depreciation of the particular kind of stock. Strike, says the smith, the iron is white; keep the rake, says the haymaker, as nigh the scythe as you can, and the cart as nigh the rake. Our Yankee trade is reputed to be very much on the extreme of this prudence. It takes bank-notes,—good, bad, clean, ragged,—and saves itself by the speed with which it passes them off. Iron cannot rust, nor beer sour, nor timber rot, nor calicoes go out of fashion, nor money stocks depreciate, in the few swift moments in which the Yankee suffers any one of them to remain in his possession. In skating over thin ice, our safety is in our speed.

Let him learn a prudence of a higher strain. Let him learn that every thing in nature, even motes and feathers, go by law and not by luck, and that what he sows he reaps. By diligence and self-command, let him put the bread he eats at his own disposal, that he may not stand in bitter and false relations to other men; for the best good of wealth is freedom. Let him practise the minor virtues. How much of human life is lost in waiting! let him not make his fellow-creatures wait. How many words and promises are promises of conversation! let his be words of fate. When he sees a folded and sealed scrap of paper float round the globe in a pine ship, and come safe to the eye for which it was writ-

ten, amidst a swarming population, let him likewise feel the
admonition to integrate his being across all these distracting
forces, and keep a slender human word among the storms,
distances, and accidents that drive us hither and thither,
and, by persistency, make the paltry force of one man reappear to redeem its pledge, after months and years, in the
most distant climates.

We must not try to write the laws of any one virtue, looking at that only. Human nature loves no contradictions, but
is symmetrical. The prudence which secures an outward well-
being is not to be studied by one set of men, whilst heroism
and holiness are studied by another, but they are reconcilable.
Prudence concerns the present time, persons, property, and
existing forms. But as every fact hath its roots in the soul,
and, if the soul were changed, would cease to be, or would
become some other thing, the proper administration of outward things will always rest on a just apprehension of their
cause and origin, that is, the good man will be the wise man,
and the single-hearted, the politic man. Every violation of
truth is not only a sort of suicide in the liar, but is a stab at
the health of human society. On the most profitable lie, the
course of events presently lays a destructive tax; whilst frankness invites frankness, puts the parties on a convenient footing, and makes their business a friendship. Trust men, and
they will be true to you; treat them greatly, and they will
show themselves great, though they make an exception in
your favor to all their rules of trade.

So, in regard to disagreeable and formidable things, prudence does not consist in evasion, or in flight, but in courage.
He who wishes to walk in the most peaceful parts of life with
any serenity must screw himself up to resolution. Let him
front the object of his worst apprehension, and his stoutness
will commonly make his fear groundless. The Latin proverb
says, that "in battles the eye is first overcome." Entire self-
possession may make a battle very little more dangerous to
life than a match at foils or at football. Examples are cited by
soldiers, of men who have seen the cannon pointed, and the
fire given to it, and who have stepped aside from the path of
the ball. The terrors of the storm are chiefly confined to the
parlour and the cabin. The drover, the sailor, buffets it all

day, and his health renews itself at as vigorous a pulse under the sleet, as under the sun of June.

In the occurrence of unpleasant things among neighbours, fear comes readily to heart, and magnifies the consequence of the other party; but it is a bad counsellor. Every man is actually weak, and apparently strong. To himself, he seems weak; to others, formidable. You are afraid of Grim; but Grim also is afraid of you. You are solicitous of the good-will of the meanest person, uneasy at his ill-will. But the sturdiest offender of your peace and of the neighbourhood, if you rip up *his* claims, is as thin and timid as any; and the peace of society is often kept, because, as children say, one is afraid, and the other dares not. Far off, men swell, bully, and threaten; bring them hand to hand, and they are a feeble folk.

It is a proverb, that 'courtesy costs nothing'; but calculation might come to value love for its profit. Love is fabled to be blind; but kindness is necessary to perception; love is not a hood, but an eye-water. If you meet a sectary, or a hostile partisan, never recognize the dividing lines; but meet on what common ground remains,—if only that the sun shines, and the rain rains for both; the area will widen very fast, and ere you know it the boundary mountains, on which the eye had fastened, have melted into air. If they set out to contend, Saint Paul will lie, and Saint John will hate. What low, poor, paltry, hypocritical people an argument on religion will make of the pure and chosen souls! They will shuffle, and crow, crook, and hide, feign to confess here, only that they may brag and conquer there, and not a thought has enriched either party, and not an emotion of bravery, modesty, or hope. So neither should you put yourself in a false position with your contemporaries, by indulging a vein of hostility and bitterness. Though your views are in straight antagonism to theirs, assume an identity of sentiment, assume that you are saying precisely that which all think, and in the flow of wit and love roll out your paradoxes in solid column, with not the infirmity of a doubt. So at least shall you get an adequate deliverance. The natural motions of the soul are so much better than the voluntary ones, that you will never do yourself justice in dispute. The thought is not then taken hold of by the right handle, does not show itself proportioned, and in its true bearings, but bears extorted, hoarse, and half witness. But assume a consent, and it shall presently be granted, since, really, and underneath their external diversities, all men are of one heart and mind.

Wisdom will never let us stand with any man or men on an unfriendly footing. We refuse sympathy and intimacy with people, as if we waited for some better sympathy and intimacy to come. But whence and when? To-morrow will be like to-day. Life wastes itself whilst we are preparing to live. Our friends and fellow-workers die off from us. Scarcely can we say, we see new men, new women, approaching us. We are too old to regard fashion, too old to expect patronage of any greater or more powerful. Let us suck the sweetness of those affections and consuetudes that grow near us. These old shoes are easy to the feet. Undoubtedly, we can easily pick faults in our company, can easily whisper names prouder, and that tickle the fancy more. Every man's imagination hath its friends; and life would be dearer with such companions. But, if you cannot have them on good mutual terms, you cannot have them. If not the Deity, but our ambition, hews and shapes the new relations, their virtue escapes, as strawberries lose their flavor in garden-beds.

Thus truth, frankness, courage, love, humility, and all the virtues, range themselves on the side of prudence, or the art of securing a present well-being. I do not know if all matter will be found to be made of one element, as oxygen or hydrogen, at last, but the world of manners and actions is wrought of one stuff, and, begin where we will, we are pretty sure in a short space to be mumbling our ten commandments.

HEROISM

———

"Paradise is under the shadow of swords."
Mahomet

———

Ruby wine is drunk by knaves,
Sugar spends to fatten slaves,
Rose and vine-leaf deck buffoons;
Thunderclouds are Jove's festoons,
Drooping oft in wreaths of dread
Lightning-knotted round his head;
The hero is not fed on sweets,
Daily his own heart he eats;
Chambers of the great are jails,
And head-winds right for royal sails.

Heroism

IN THE ELDER English dramatists, and mainly in the plays of Beaumont and Fletcher, there is a constant recognition of gentility, as if a noble behaviour were as easily marked in the society of their age, as color is in our American population. When any Rodrigo, Pedro, or Valerio enters, though he be a stranger, the duke or governor exclaims, This is a gentleman,—and proffers civilities without end; but all the rest are slag and refuse. In harmony with this delight in personal advantages, there is in their plays a certain heroic cast of character and dialogue,—as in Bonduca, Sophocles, the Mad Lover, the Double Marriage,—wherein the speaker is so earnest and cordial, and on such deep grounds of character, that the dialogue, on the slightest additional incident in the plot, rises naturally into poetry. Among many texts, take the following. The Roman Martius has conquered Athens,—all but the invincible spirits of Sophocles, the duke of Athens, and Dorigen, his wife. The beauty of the latter inflames Martius, and he seeks to save her husband; but Sophocles will not ask his life, although assured that a word will save him, and the execution of both proceeds.

"*Valerius.* Bid thy wife farewell.

Soph. No, I will take no leave. My Dorigen,
Yonder, above, 'bout Ariadne's crown,
My spirit shall hover for thee. Prithee, haste.

Dor. Stay, Sophocles,—with this tie up my sight;
Let not soft nature so transformed be,
And lose her gentler sexed humanity,
To make me see my lord bleed. So, 't is well;
Never one object underneath the sun
Will I behold before my Sophocles:
Farewell; now teach the Romans how to die.

Mar. Dost know what 't is to die?

Soph. Thou dost not, Martius,
And, therefore, not what 't is to live; to die
Is to begin to live. It is to end

371

An old, stale, weary work, and to commence
A newer and a better. 'T is to leave
Deceitful knaves for the society
Of gods and goodness. Thou thyself must part
At last from all thy garlands, pleasures, triumphs,
And prove thy fortitude what then 't will do.
    Val. But art not grieved nor vexed to leave thy life thus?
    Soph. Why should I grieve or vex for being sent
To them I ever loved best? Now I 'll kneel,
But with my back toward thee; 't is the last duty
This trunk can do the gods.
    Mar. Strike, strike, Valerius,
Or Martius' heart will leap out at his mouth:
This is a man, a woman! Kiss thy lord,
And live with all the freedom you were wont.
O love! thou doubly hast afflicted me
With virtue and with beauty. Treacherous heart,
My hand shall cast thee quick into my urn,
Ere thou transgress this knot of piety.
    Val. What ails my brother?
    Soph. Martius, O Martius,
Thou now hast found a way to conquer me.
    Dor. O star of Rome! what gratitude can speak
Fit words to follow such a deed as this?
    Mar. This admirable duke, Valerius,
With his disdain of fortune and of death,
Captived himself, has captivated me,
And though my arm hath ta'en his body here,
His soul hath subjugated Martius' soul.
By Romulus, he is all soul, I think;
He hath no flesh, and spirit cannot be gyved;
Then we have vanquished nothing; he is free,
And Martius walks now in captivity."

    I do not readily remember any poem, play, sermon, novel,
or oration, that our press vents in the last few years, which
goes to the same tune. We have a great many flutes and fla-
geolets, but not often the sound of any fife. Yet, Wordsworth's Laodamia, and the ode of "Dion," and some sonnets,
have a certain noble music; and Scott will sometimes draw a

stroke like the protrait of Lord Evandale, given by Balfour of
Burley. Thomas Carlyle, with his natural taste for what is
manly and daring in character, has suffered no heroic trait in
his favorites to drop from his biographical and historical pictures. Earlier, Robert Burns has given us a song or two. In
the Harleian Miscellanies, there is an account of the battle of
Lutzen, which deserves to be read. And Simon Ockley's History of the Saracens recounts the prodigies of individual valor
with admiration, all the more evident on the part of the nar-
rator, that he seems to think that his place in Christian Oxford requires of him some proper protestations of abhorrence.
But, if we explore the literature of Heroism, we shall quickly
come to Plutarch, who is its Doctor and historian. To him we
owe the Brasidas, the Dion, the Epaminondas, the Scipio of
old, and I must think we are more deeply indebted to him
than to all the ancient writers. Each of his "Lives" is a refu-
tation to the despondency and cowardice of our religious and
political theorists. A wild courage, a Stoicism not of the
schools, but of the blood, shines in every anecdote, and has
given that book its immense fame.

We need books of this tart cathartic virtue, more than
books of political science, or of private economy. Life is a
festival only to the wise. Seen from the nook and chimney-
side of prudence, it wears a ragged and dangerous front. The
violations of the laws of nature by our predecessors and our
contemporaries are punished in us also. The disease and deformity around us certify the infraction of natural, intellectual, and moral laws, and often violation on violation to breed
such compound misery. A lock-jaw that bends a man's head
back to his heels, hydrophobia, that makes him bark at his
wife and babes, insanity, that makes him eat grass; war,
plague, cholera, famine, indicate a certain ferocity in nature,
which, as it had its inlet by human crime, must have its outlet
by human suffering. Unhappily, no man exists who has not
in his own person become, to some amount, a stockholder in
the sin, and so made himself liable to a share in the expiation.

Our culture, therefore, must not omit the arming of the
man. Let him hear in season, that he is born into the state of
war, and that the commonwealth and his own well-being require that he should not go dancing in the weeds of peace,

but warned, self-collected, and neither defying nor dreading the thunder, let him take both reputation and life in his hand, and, with perfect urbanity, dare the gibbet and the mob by the absolute truth of his speech, and the rectitude of his behaviour.

Towards all this external evil, the man within the breast assumes a warlike attitude, and affirms his ability to cope single-handed with the infinite army of enemies. To this military attitude of the soul we give the name of Heroism. Its rudest form is the contempt for safety and ease, which makes the attractiveness of war. It is a self-trust which slights the restraints of prudence, in the plenitude of its energy and power to repair the harms it may suffer. The hero is a mind of such balance that no disturbances can shake his will, but pleasantly, and, as it were, merrily, he advances to his own music, alike in frightful alarms and in the tipsy mirth of universal dissoluteness. There is somewhat not philosophical in heroism; there is somewhat not holy in it; it seems not to know that other souls are of one texture with it; it has pride; it is the extreme of individual nature. Nevertheless, we must profoundly revere it. There is somewhat in great actions, which does not allow us to go behind them. Heroism feels and never reasons, and therefore is always right; and although a different breeding, different religion, and greater intellectual activity would have modified or even reversed the particular action, yet for the hero that thing he does is the highest deed, and is not open to the censure of philosophers or divines. It is the avowal of the unschooled man, that he finds a quality in him that is negligent of expense, of health, of life, of danger, of hatred, of reproach, and knows that his will is higher and more excellent than all actual and all possible antagonists.

Heroism works in contradiction to the voice of mankind, and in contradiction, for a time, to the voice of the great and good. Heroism is an obedience to a secret impulse of an individual's character. Now to no other man can its wisdom appear as it does to him, for every man must be supposed to see a little farther on his own proper path than any one else. Therefore, just and wise men take umbrage at his act, until after some little time be past: then they see it to be in unison with their acts. All prudent men see that the action is clean contrary to a sensual prosperity; for every heroic act measures itself by its contempt of some external good. But it finds its own success at last, and then the prudent also extol.

Self-trust is the essence of heroism. It is the state of the soul at war, and its ultimate objects are the last defiance of falsehood and wrong, and the power to bear all that can be inflicted by evil agents. It speaks the truth, and it is just, generous, hospitable, temperate, scornful of petty calculations, and scornful of being scorned. It persists; it is of an undaunted boldness, and of a fortitude not to be wearied out. Its jest is the littleness of common life. That false prudence which dotes on health and wealth is the butt and merriment of heroism. Heroism, like Plotinus, is almost ashamed of its body. What shall it say, then, to the sugar-plums and cats'-cradles, to the toilet, compliments, quarrels, cards, and custard, which rack the wit of all society. What joys has kind nature provided for us dear creatures! There seems to be no interval between greatness and meanness. When the spirit is not master of the world, then it is its dupe. Yet the little man takes the great hoax so innocently, works in it so headlong and believing, is born red, and dies gray, arranging his toilet, attending on his own health, laying traps for sweet food and strong wine, setting his heart on a horse or a rifle, made happy with a little gossip or a little praise, that the great soul cannot choose but laugh at such earnest nonsense. "Indeed, these humble considerations make me out of love with greatness. What a disgrace is it to me to take note how many pairs of silk stockings thou hast, namely, these and those that were the peach-colored ones; or to bear the inventory of thy shirts, as one for superfluity, and one other for use!"

Citizens, thinking after the laws of arithmetic, consider the inconvenience of receiving strangers at their fireside, reckon narrowly the loss of time and the unusual display: the soul of a better quality thrusts back the unseasonable economy into the vaults of life, and says, I will obey the God, and the sacrifice and the fire he will provide. Ibn Haukal, the Arabian geographer, describes a heroic extreme in the hospitality of Sogd, in Bukharia. "When I was in Sogd, I saw a great building, like a palace, the gates of which were open and fixed back to the wall with large nails. I asked the reason, and was told that the house had not been shut, night or day, for a hundred years. Strangers may present themselves at any hour, and in whatever number; the master has amply provided for the reception of the men and their animals, and is never happier than when they tarry for some time. Nothing of the kind have I seen in any other country." The magnanimous know very well that they who give time, or money, or shelter, to the stranger—so it be done for love, and not for ostentation—do, as it were, put God under obligation to them, so perfect are the compensations of the universe. In some way the time they seem to lose is redeemed, and the pains they seem to take remunerate themselves. These men fan the flame of human love, and raise the standard of civil virtue among mankind. But hospitality must be for service, and not for show, or it pulls down the host. The brave soul rates itself too high to value itself by the splendor of its table and draperies. It gives what it hath, and all it hath, but its own majesty can lend a better grace to bannocks and fair water than belong to city feasts.

The temperance of the hero proceeds from the same wish to do no dishonor to the worthiness he has. But he loves it for its elegancy, not for its austerity. It seems not worth his while to be solemn, and denounce with bitterness flesh-eating or wine-drinking, the use of tobacco, or opium, or tea, or silk, or gold. A great man scarcely knows how he dines, how he dresses; but without railing or precision, his living is natural and poetic. John Eliot, the Indian Apostle, drank water, and said of wine,—"It is a noble, generous liquor, and we should be humbly thankful for it, but, as I remember, water was made before it." Better still is the temperance of King David, who poured out on the ground unto the Lord the water which three of his warriors had brought him to drink, at the peril of their lives.

It is told of Brutus, that when he fell on his sword, after the battle of Philippi, he quoted a line of Euripides,—"O virtue! I have followed thee through life, and I find thee at last but a shade." I doubt not the hero is slandered by this report. The heroic soul does not sell its justice and its nobleness. It does not ask to dine nicely, and to sleep warm. The essence of greatness is the perception that virtue is enough.

Poverty is its ornament. It does not need plenty, and can very well abide its loss.

But that which takes my fancy most, in the heroic class, is the good-humor and hilarity they exhibit. It is a height to which common duty can very well attain, to suffer and to dare with solemnity. But these rare souls set opinion, success, and life, at so cheap a rate, that they will not soothe their enemies by petitions, or the show of sorrow, but wear their own habitual greatness. Scipio, charged with peculation, refuses to do himself so great a disgrace as to wait for justification, though he had the scroll of his accounts in his hands, but tears it to pieces before the tribunes. Socrates's condemnation of himself to be maintained in all honor in the Prytaneum, during his life, and Sir Thomas More's playfulness at the scaffold, are of the same strain. In Beaumont and Fletcher's "Sea Voyage," Juletta tells the stout captain and his company, —

> "*Jul.* Why, slaves, 't is in our power to hang ye.
> *Master.* Very likely,
> 'T is in our powers, then, to be hanged, and scorn ye."

These replies are sound and whole. Sport is the bloom and glow of a perfect health. The great will not condescend to take any thing seriously; all must be as gay as the song of a canary, though it were the building of cities, or the eradication of old and foolish churches and nations, which have cumbered the earth long thousands of years. Simple hearts put all the history and customs of this world behind them, and play their own game in innocent defiance of the Blue-Laws of the world; and such would appear, could we see the human race assembled in vision, like little children frolicking together; though, to the eyes of mankind at large, they wear a stately and solemn garb of works and influences.

The interest these fine stories have for us, the power of a romance over the boy who grasps the forbidden book under his bench at school, our delight in the hero, is the main fact to our purpose. All these great and transcendent properties are ours. If we dilate in beholding the Greek energy, the Roman pride, it is that we are already domesticating the same sentiment. Let us find room for this great guest in our small houses. The first step of worthiness will be to disabuse us of our superstitious associations with places and times, with number and size. Why should these words, Athenian, Roman, Asia, and England, so tingle in the ear? Where the heart is, there the muses, there the gods sojourn, and not in any geography of fame. Massachusetts, Connecticut River, and Boston Bay, you think paltry places, and the ear loves names of foreign and classic topography. But here we are; and, if we will tarry a little, we may come to learn that here is best. See to it, only, that thyself is here;—and art and nature, hope and fate, friends, angels, and the Supreme Being, shall not be absent from the chamber where thou sittest. Epaminondas, brave and affectionate, does not seem to us to need Olympus to die upon, nor the Syrian sunshine. He lies very well where he is. The Jerseys were handsome ground enough for Washington to tread, and London streets for the feet of Milton. A great man makes his climate genial in the imagination of men, and its air the beloved element of all delicate spirits. That country is the fairest, which is inhabited by the noblest minds. The pictures which fill the imagination in reading the actions of Pericles, Xenophon, Columbus, Bayard, Sidney, Hampden, teach us how needlessly mean our life is, that we, by the depth of our living, should deck it with more than regal or national splendor, and act on principles that should interest man and nature in the length of our days.

We have seen or heard of many extraordinary young men, who never ripened, or whose performance in actual life was not extraordinary. When we see their air and mien, when we hear them speak of society, of books, of religion, we admire their superiority, they seem to throw contempt on our entire polity and social state; theirs is the tone of a youthful giant, who is sent to work revolutions. But they enter an active profession, and the forming Colossus shrinks to the common size of man. The magic they used was the ideal tendencies, which always make the Actual ridiculous; but the tough world had its revenge the moment they put their horses of the sun to plough in its furrow. They found no example and no companion, and their heart fainted. What then? The lesson they gave in their first aspirations is yet true; and a better valor and a purer truth shall one day organize their belief. Or why should a woman liken herself to any historical woman, and think, because Sappho, or Sévigné, or De Staël, or the cloistered souls who have had genius and cultivation, do not satisfy the imagination and the serene Themis, none can,— certainly not she. Why not? She has a new and unattempted problem to solve, perchance that of the happiest nature that ever bloomed. Let the maiden, with erect soul, walk serenely on her way, accept the hint of each new experience, search in turn all the objects that solicit her eye, that she may learn the power and the charm of her new-born being, which is the kindling of a new dawn in the recesses of space. The fair girl, who repels interference by a decided and proud choice of influences, so careless of pleasing, so wilful and lofty, inspires every beholder with somewhat of her own nobleness. The silent heart encourages her; O friend, never strike sail to a fear! Come into port greatly, or sail with God the seas. Not in vain you live, for every passing eye is cheered and refined by the vision.

The characteristic of heroism is its persistency. All men have wandering impulses, fits, and starts of generosity. But when you have chosen your part, abide by it, and do not weakly try to reconcile yourself with the world. The heroic cannot be the common, nor the common the heroic. Yet we have the weakness to expect the sympathy of people in those actions whose excellence is that they outrun sympathy, and appeal to a tardy justice. If you would serve your brother, because it is fit for you to serve him, do not take back your words when you find that prudent people do not commend you. Adhere to your own act, and congratulate yourself if you have done something strange and extravagant, and broken the monotony of a decorous age. It was a high counsel that I once heard given to a young person,—"Always do what you are afraid to do." A simple, manly character need never make an apology, but should regard its past action with the calmness of Phocion, when he admitted that the event of the battle was happy, yet did not regret his dissuasion from the battle.

There is no weakness or exposure for which we cannot find consolation in the thought,—this is a part of my constitution, part of my relation and office to my fellow-creature. Has nature covenanted with me that I should never appear to disadvantage, never make a ridiculous figure? Let us be generous of our dignity, as well as of our money. Greatness once and for ever has done with opinion. We tell our charities, not because we wish to be praised for them, not because we think they have great merit, but for our justification. It is a capital blunder; as you discover, when another man recites his charities.

To speak the truth, even with some austerity, to live with some rigor of temperance, or some extremes of generosity, seems to be an asceticism which common good-nature would appoint to those who are at ease and in plenty, in sign that they feel a brotherhood with the great multitude of suffering men. And not only need we breathe and exercise the soul by assuming the penalties of abstinence, of debt, of solitude, of unpopularity, but it behooves the wise man to look with a bold eye into those rarer dangers which sometimes invade men, and to familiarize himself with disgusting forms of disease, with sounds of execration, and the vision of violent death.

Times of heroism are generally times of terror, but the day never shines in which this element may not work. The circumstances of man, we say, are historically somewhat better in this country, and at this hour, than perhaps ever before. More freedom exists for culture. It will not now run against an axe at the first step out of the beaten track of opinion. But whoso is heroic will always find crises to try his edge. Human virtue demands her champions and martyrs, and the trial of persecution always proceeds. It is but the other day that the brave Lovejoy gave his breast to the bullets of a mob, for the rights of free speech and opinion, and died when it was better not to live.

I see not any road of perfect peace which a man can walk, but after the counsel of his own bosom. Let him quit too much association, let him go home much, and stablish himself in those courses he approves. The unremitting retention of simple and high sentiments in obscure duties is hardening the character to that temper which will work with honor, if need be, in the tumult, or on the scaffold. Whatever outrages have happened to men may befall a man again; and very easily in a republic, if there appear any signs of a decay of religion. Coarse slander, fire, tar and feathers, and the gibbet, the youth may freely bring home to his mind, and with what sweetness of temper he can, and inquire how fast he can fix his sense of duty, braving such penalties, whenever it may please the next newspaper and a sufficient number of his neighbours to pronounce his opinions incendiary.

It may calm the apprehension of calamity in the most susceptible heart to see how quick a bound nature has set to the utmost infliction of malice. We rapidly approach a brink over which no enemy can follow us.

> "Let them rave:
> Thou art quiet in thy grave."

In the gloom of our ignorance of what shall be, in the hour when we are deaf to the higher voices, who does not envy those who have seen safely to an end their manful endeavour? Who that sees the meanness of our politics, but inly congratulates Washington that he is long already wrapped in his shroud, and for ever safe; that he was laid sweet in his grave, the hope of humanity not yet subjugated in him? Who does not sometimes envy the good and brave, who are no more to suffer from the tumults of the natural world, and await with curious complacency the speedy term of his own conversation with finite nature? And yet the love that will be annihilated sooner than treacherous has already made death impossible, and affirms itself no mortal, but a native of the deeps of absolute and inextinguishable being.

THE OVER-SOUL

———

"But souls that of his own good life partake,
He loves as his own self; dear as his eye
They are to Him: He 'll never them forsake:
When they shall die, then God himself shall die:
They live, they live in blest eternity."

Henry More

———

Space is ample, east and west,
But two cannot go abreast,
Cannot travel in it two:
Yonder masterful cuckoo
Crowds every egg out of the nest,
Quick or dead, except its own;
A spell is laid on sod and stone,
Night and Day 've been tampered with,
Every quality and pith
Surcharged and sultry with a power
That works its will on age and hour.

The Over-Soul

THERE is a difference between one and another hour of
life, in their authority and subsequent effect. Our faith
comes in moments; our vice is habitual. Yet there is a depth
in those brief moments which constrains us to ascribe more
reality to them than to all other experiences. For this reason,
the argument which is always forthcoming to silence those
who conceive extraordinary hopes of man, namely, the appeal
to experience, is for ever invalid and vain. We give up the past
to the objector, and yet we hope. He must explain this hope.
We grant that human life is mean; but how did we find out
that it was mean? What is the ground of this uneasiness of
ours; of this old discontent? What is the universal sense of
want and ignorance, but the fine inuendo by which the soul
makes its enormous claim? Why do men feel that the natural
history of man has never been written, but he is always leaving behind what you have said of him, and it becomes old,
and books of metaphysics worthless? The philosophy of six
thousand years has not searched the chambers and magazines
of the soul. In its experiments there has always remained, in
the last analysis, a residuum it could not resolve. Man is a
stream whose source is hidden. Our being is descending into
us from we know not whence. The most exact calculator has
no prescience that somewhat incalculable may not balk the
very next moment. I am constrained every moment to acknowledge a higher origin for events than the will I call mine.

As with events, so is it with thoughts. When I watch that
flowing river, which, out of regions I see not, pours for a
season its streams into me, I see that I am a pensioner; not a
cause, but a surprised spectator of this ethereal water; that I
desire and look up, and put myself in the attitude of reception, but from some alien energy the visions come.

The Supreme Critic on the errors of the past and the present, and the only prophet of that which must be, is that great
nature in which we rest, as the earth lies in the soft arms of the atmosphere; that Unity, that Over-soul, within which every man's

particular being is contained and made one with all other; that common heart, of which all sincere conversation is the worship, to which all right action is submission; that overpowering reality which confutes our tricks and talents, and constrains every one to pass for what he is, and to speak from his character, and not from his tongue, and which evermore tends to pass into our thought and hand, and become wisdom, and virtue, and power, and beauty. We live in succession, in division, in parts, in particles. Meantime within man is the soul of the whole; the wise silence; the universal beauty, to which every part and particle is equally related; the eternal ONE. And this deep power in which we exist, and whose beatitude is all accessible to us, is not only self-sufficing and perfect in every hour, but the act of seeing and the thing seen, the seer and the spectacle, the subject and the object, are one. We see the world piece by piece, as the sun, the moon, the animal, the tree; but the whole, of which these are the shining parts, is the soul. Only by the vision of that Wisdom can the horoscope of the ages be read, and by falling back on our better thoughts, by yielding to the spirit of prophecy which is innate in every man, we can know what it saith. Every man's words, who speaks from that life, must sound vain to those who do not dwell in the same thought on their own part. I dare not speak for it. My words do not carry its august sense; they fall short and cold. Only itself can inspire whom it will, and behold! their speech shall be lyrical, and sweet, and universal as the rising of the wind. Yet I desire, even by profane words, if I may not use sacred, to indicate the heaven of this deity, and to report what hints I have collected of the transcendent simplicity and energy of the Highest Law.

If we consider what happens in conversation, in reveries, in remorse, in times of passion, in surprises, in the instructions of dreams, wherein often we see ourselves in masquerade,— the droll disguises only magnifying and enhancing a real element, and forcing it on our distinct notice,—we shall catch many hints that will broaden and lighten into knowledge of the secret of nature. All goes to show that the soul in man is not an organ, but animates and exercises all the organs; is not a function, like the power of memory, of calculation, of comparison, but uses these as hands and feet; is not a faculty, but a light; is not the intellect or the will, but the master of the intellect and the will; is the background of our being, in which they lie,—an immensity not possessed and that cannot be possessed. From within or from behind, a light shines through us upon things, and makes us aware that we are nothing, but the light is all. A man is the façade of a temple wherein all wisdom and all good abide. What we commonly call man, the eating, drinking, planting, counting man, does not, as we know him, represent himself, but misrepresents himself. Him we do not respect, but the soul, whose organ he is, would he let it appear through his action, would make our knees bend. When it breathes through his intellect, it is genius; when it breathes through his will, it is virtue; when it flows through his affection, it is love. And the blindness of the intellect begins, when it would be something of itself. The weakness of the will begins, when the individual would be something of himself. All reform aims, in some one particular, to let the soul have its way through us; in other words, to engage us to obey.

Of this pure nature every man is at some time sensible. Language cannot paint it with his colors. It is too subtile. It is undefinable, unmeasurable, but we know that it pervades and contains us. We know that all spiritual being is in man. A wise old proverb says, "God comes to see us without bell"; that is, as there is no screen or ceiling between our heads and the infinite heavens, so is there no bar or wall in the soul where man, the effect, ceases, and God, the cause, begins. The walls are taken away. We lie open on one side to the deeps of spiritual nature, to the attributes of God. Justice we see and know, Love, Freedom, Power. These natures no man ever got above, but they tower over us, and most in the moment when our interests tempt us to wound them.

The sovereignty of this nature whereof we speak is made known by its independency of those limitations which circumscribe us on every hand. The soul circumscribes all things. As I have said, it contradicts all experience. In like manner it abolishes time and space. The influence of the senses has, in most men, overpowered the mind to that degree, that the walls of time and space have come to look real and insurmountable; and to speak with levity of these limits is, in the world, the sign of insanity. Yet time and space are but inverse measures of the force of the soul. The spirit sports with time, —

> "Can crowd eternity into an hour,
> Or stretch an hour to eternity."

We are often made to feel that there is another youth and age than that which is measured from the year of our natural birth. Some thoughts always find us young, and keep us so. Such a thought is the love of the universal and eternal beauty. Every man parts from that contemplation with the feeling that it rather belongs to ages than to mortal life. The least activity of the intellectual powers redeems us in a degree from the conditions of time. In sickness, in languor, give us a strain of poetry, or a profound sentence, and we are refreshed; or produce a volume of Plato, or Shakspeare, or remind us of their names, and instantly we come into a feeling of longevity. See how the deep, divine thought reduces centuries, and millenniums, and makes itself present through all ages. Is the teaching of Christ less effective now than it was when first his mouth was opened? The emphasis of facts and persons in my thought has nothing to do with time. And so, always, the soul's scale is one; the scale of the senses and the understanding is another. Before the revelations of the soul, Time, Space, and Nature shrink away. In common speech, we refer all things to time, as we habitually refer the immensely sundered stars to one concave sphere. And so we say that the Judgment is distant or near, that the Millennium approaches, that a day of certain political, moral, social reforms is at hand, and the like, when we mean, that, in the nature of things, one of the facts we contemplate is external and fugitive, and the other is permanent and connate with the soul. The things we now esteem fixed shall, one by one, detach themselves, like ripe fruit, from our experience, and fall. The wind shall blow them none knows whither. The landscape, the figures, Boston, London, are facts as fugitive as any institution past, or any whiff of mist or smoke, and so is society, and so is the world. The soul looketh steadily forwards, creating a world before her, leaving worlds behind her. She has no dates, nor rites, nor persons, nor specialties, nor men. The soul knows only the soul; the web of events is the flowing robe in which she is clothed.

After its own law and not by arithmetic is the rate of its progress to be computed. The soul's advances are not made by gradation, such as can be represented by motion in a straight line; but rather by ascension of state, such as can be represented by metamorphosis,—from the egg to the worm, from the worm to the fly. The growths of genius are of a certain *total* character, that does not advance the elect individual first over John, then Adam, then Richard, and give to each the pain of discovered inferiority, but by every throe of growth the man expands there where he works, passing, at each pulsation, classes, populations, of men. With each divine impulse the mind rends the thin rinds of the visible and finite, and comes out into eternity, and inspires and expires its air. It converses with truths that have always been spoken in the world, and becomes conscious of a closer sympathy with Zeno and Arrian, than with persons in the house.

This is the law of moral and of mental gain. The simple rise as by specific levity, not into a particular virtue, but into the region of all the virtues. They are in the spirit which contains them all. The soul requires purity, but purity is not it; requires justice, but justice is not that; requires beneficence, but is somewhat better; so that there is a kind of descent and accommodation felt when we leave speaking of moral nature, to urge a virtue which it enjoins. To the well-born child, all the virtues are natural, and not painfully acquired. Speak to his heart, and the man becomes suddenly virtuous.

Within the same sentiment is the germ of intellectual growth, which obeys the same law. Those who are capable of humility, of justice, of love, of aspiration, stand already on a platform that commands the sciences and arts, speech and poetry, action and grace. For whoso dwells in this moral beatitude already anticipates those special powers which men prize so highly. The lover has no talent, no skill, which passes for quite nothing with his enamoured maiden, however little she may possess of related faculty; and the heart which abandons itself to the Supreme Mind finds itself related to all its works, and will travel a royal road to particular knowledges and powers. In ascending to this primary and aboriginal sentiment, we have come from our remote station on the circumference instantaneously to the centre of the world, where, as in the closet of God, we see causes, and anticipate the universe, which is but a slow effect.

One mode of the divine teaching is the incarnation of the spirit in a form,—in forms, like my own. I live in society; with persons who answer to thoughts in my own mind, or express a certain obedience to the great instincts to which I live. I see its presence to them. I am certified of a common nature; and these other souls, these separated selves, draw me as nothing else can. They stir in me the new emotions we call passion; of love, hatred, fear, admiration, pity; thence comes conversation, competition, persuasion, cities, and war. Persons are supplementary to the primary teaching of the soul. In youth we are mad for persons. Childhood and youth see all the world in them. But the larger experience of man discovers the identical nature appearing through them all. Persons themselves acquaint us with the impersonal. In all conversation between two persons, tacit reference is made, as to a third party, to a common nature. That third party or common nature is not social; it is impersonal; is God. And so in groups where debate is earnest, and especially on high questions, the company become aware that the thought rises to an equal level in all bosoms, that all have a spiritual property in what was said, as well as the sayer. They all become wiser than they were. It arches over them like a temple, this unity of thought, in which every heart beats with nobler sense of power and duty, and thinks and acts with unusual solemnity. All are conscious of attaining to a higher self-possession. It shines for all. There is a certain wisdom of humanity which is common to the greatest men with the lowest, and which our ordinary education often labors to silence and obstruct. The mind is one, and the best minds, who love truth for its own sake, think much less of property in truth. They accept it thankfully everywhere, and do not label or stamp it with any man's name, for it is theirs long beforehand, and from eternity. The learned and the studious of thought have no monopoly of wisdom. Their violence of direction in some degree disqualifies them to think truly. We owe many valuable observations to people who are not very acute or profound, and who say the thing without effort, which we want and have long been hunting in vain. The action of the soul is oftener in that which is felt and left unsaid, than in that which is said in any conversation. It broods over every society, and they unconsciously seek for it in each other. We know better than we do. We do not yet possess ourselves, and we know at the same time that we are much more. I feel the same truth how often in my trivial conversation with my neighbours, that somewhat higher in each of us overlooks this by-play, and Jove nods to Jove from behind each of us.

Men descend to meet. In their habitual and mean service to the world, for which they forsake their native nobleness, they resemble those Arabian sheiks, who dwell in mean houses, and affect an external poverty, to escape the rapacity of the Pacha, and reserve all their display of wealth for their interior and guarded retirements.

As it is present in all persons, so it is in every period of life. It is adult already in the infant man. In my dealing with my child, my Latin and Greek, my accomplishments and my money stead me nothing; but as much soul as I have avails. If I am wilful, he sets his will against mine, one for one, and leaves me, if I please, the degradation of beating him by my superiority of strength. But if I renounce my will, and act for the soul, setting that up as umpire between us two, out of his young eyes looks the same soul; he reveres and loves with me.

The soul is the perceiver and revealer of truth. We know truth when we see it, let skeptic and scoffer say what they choose. Foolish people ask you, when you have spoken what they do not wish to hear, 'How do you know it is truth, and not an error of your own?' We know truth when we see it, from opinion, as we know when we are awake that we are awake. It was a grand sentence of Emanuel Swedenborg, which would alone indicate the greatness of that man's perception,—"It is no proof of a man's understanding to be able to confirm whatever he pleases; but to be able to discern that what is true is true, and that what is false is false, this is the mark and character of intelligence." In the book I read, the good thought returns to me, as every truth will, the image of the whole soul. To the bad thought which I find in it, the same soul becomes a discerning, separating sword, and lops it away. We are wiser than we know. If we will not interfere with our thought, but will act entirely, or see how the thing stands in God, we know the particular thing, and every thing, and every man. For the Maker of all things and all persons stands behind us, and casts his dread omniscience through us over things.

But beyond this recognition of its own in particular passages of the individual's experience, it also reveals truth. And here we should seek to reinforce ourselves by its very presence, and to speak with a worthier, loftier strain of that advent. For the soul's communication of truth is the highest event in nature, since it then does not give somewhat from itself, but it gives itself, or passes into and becomes that man whom it enlightens; or, in proportion to that truth he receives, it takes him to itself.

We distinguish the announcements of the soul, its manifestations of its own nature, by the term *Revelation*. These are always attended by the emotion of the sublime. For this communication is an influx of the Divine mind into our mind. It is an ebb of the individual rivulet before the flowing surges of the sea of life. Every distinct apprehension of this central commandment agitates men with awe and delight. A thrill passes through all men at the reception of new truth, or at the performance of a great action, which comes out of the heart of nature. In these communications, the power to see is not separated from the will to do, but the insight proceeds from obedience, and the obedience proceeds from a joyful perception. Every moment when the individual feels himself invaded by it is memorable. By the necessity of our constitution, a certain enthusiasm attends the individual's consciousness of that divine presence. The character and duration of this enthusiasm varies with the state of the individual, from an ecstasy and trance and prophetic inspiration,—which is its rarer appearance,—to the faintest glow of virtuous emotion, in which form it warms, like our household fires, all the families and associations of men, and makes society possible. A certain tendency to insanity has always attended the opening of the religious sense in men, as if they had been "blasted with excess of light." The trances of Socrates, the "union" of Plotinus, the vision of Porphyry, the conversion of Paul, the aurora of Behmen, the convulsions of George Fox and his Quakers, the illumination of Swedenborg, are of this kind.

What was in the case of these remarkable persons a ravishment has, in innumerable instances in common life, been exhibited in less striking manner. Everywhere the history of religion betrays a tendency to enthusiasm. The rapture of the Moravian and Quietist; the opening of the internal sense of the Word, in the language of the New Jerusalem Church; the *revival* of the Calvinistic churches; the *experiences* of the Methodists, are varying forms of that shudder of awe and delight with which the individual soul always mingles with the universal soul.

The nature of these revelations is the same; they are perceptions of the absolute law. They are solutions of the soul's own questions. They do not answer the questions which the understanding asks. The soul answers never by words, but by the thing itself that is inquired after.

Revelation is the disclosure of the soul. The popular notion of a revelation is, that it is a telling of fortunes. In past oracles of the soul, the understanding seeks to find answers to sensual questions, and undertakes to tell from God how long men shall exist, what their hands shall do, and who shall be their company, adding names, and dates, and places. But we must pick no locks. We must check this low curiosity. An answer in words is delusive; it is really no answer to the questions you ask. Do not require a description of the countries towards which you sail. The description does not describe them to you, and to-morrow you arrive there, and know them by inhabiting them. Men ask concerning the immortality of the soul, the employments of heaven, the state of the sinner, and so forth. They even dream that Jesus has left replies to precisely these interrogatories. Never a moment did that sublime spirit speak in their *patois*. To truth, justice, love, the attributes of the soul, the idea of immutableness is essentially associated. Jesus, living in these moral sentiments, heedless of sensual fortunes, heeding only the manifestations of these, never made the separation of the idea of duration from the essence of these attributes, nor uttered a syllable concerning the duration of the soul. It was left to his disciples to sever duration from the moral elements, and to teach the immortality of the soul as a doctrine, and maintain it by evidences. The moment the doctrine of the immortality is separately taught, man is already fallen. In the flowing of love, in the adoration of humility, there is no question of continuance. No inspired man ever asks this question, or condescends to these evidences. For the soul is true to itself, and the man in whom it is shed abroad cannot wander from the present, which is infinite, to a future which would be finite.

These questions which we lust to ask about the future are a confession of sin. God has no answer for them. No answer in words can reply to a question of things. It is not in an arbitrary "decree of God," but in the nature of man, that a veil shuts down on the facts of to-morrow; for the soul will not have us read any other cipher than that of cause and effect. By this veil, which curtains events, it instructs the children of men to live in to-day. The only mode of obtaining an answer to these questions of the senses is to forego all low curiosity, and, accepting the tide of being which floats us into the secret of nature, work and live, work and live, and all unawares the advancing soul has built and forged for itself a new condition, and the question and the answer are one.

By the same fire, vital, consecrating, celestial, which burns until it shall dissolve all things into the waves and surges of an ocean of light, we see and know each other, and what spirit each is of. Who can tell the grounds of his knowledge of the character of the several individuals in his circle of friends? No man. Yet their acts and words do not disappoint him. In that man, though he knew no ill of him, he put no trust. In that other, though they had seldom met, authentic signs had yet passed, to signify that he might be trusted as one who had an interest in his own character. We know each other very well,—which of us has been just to himself, and whether that which we teach or behold is only an aspiration, or is our honest effort also.

We are all discerners of spirits. That diagnosis lies aloft in our life or unconscious power. The intercourse of society,— its trade, its religion, its friendships, its quarrels,—is one wide, judicial investigation of character. In full court, or in small committee, or confronted face to face, accuser and accused, men offer themselves to be judged. Against their will they exhibit those decisive trifles by which character is read. But who judges? and what? Not our understanding. We do not read them by learning or craft. No; the wisdom of the wise man consists herein, that he does not judge them; he lets them judge themselves, and merely reads and records their own verdict.

By virtue of this inevitable nature, private will is overpowered, and, maugre our efforts or our imperfections, your genius will speak from you, and mine from me. That which we are, we shall teach, not voluntarily, but involuntarily. Thoughts come into our minds by avenues which we never left open, and thoughts go out of our minds through avenues which we never voluntarily opened. Character teaches over our head. The infallible index of true progress is found in the tone the man takes. Neither his age, nor his breeding, nor company, nor books, nor actions, nor talents, nor all together, can hinder him from being deferential to a higher spirit than his own. If he have not found his home in God, his manners, his forms of speech, the turn of his sentences, the build, shall I say, of all his opinions, will involuntarily confess it, let him brave it out how he will. If he have found his centre, the Deity will shine through him, through all the disguises of ignorance, of ungenial temperament, of unfavorable circumstance. The tone of seeking is one, and the tone of having is another.

The great distinction between teachers sacred or literary,— between poets like Herbert, and poets like Pope,— between philosophers like Spinoza, Kant, and Coleridge, and philosophers like Locke, Paley, Mackintosh, and Stewart,— between men of the world, who are reckoned accomplished talkers, and here and there a fervent mystic, prophesying, half insane under the infinitude of his thought,— is, that one class speak *from within*, or from experience, as parties and possessors of the fact; and the other class, *from without*, as spectators merely, or perhaps as acquainted with the fact on the evidence of third persons. It is of no use to preach to me from without. I can do that too easily myself. Jesus speaks always from within, and in a degree that transcends all others. In that is the miracle. I believe beforehand that it ought so to be. All men stand continually in the expectation of the appearance of such a teacher. But if a man do not speak from within the veil, where the word is one with that it tells of, let him lowly confess it.

The same Omniscience flows into the intellect, and makes what we call genius. Much of the wisdom of the world is not wisdom, and the most illuminated class of men are no doubt superior to literary fame, and are not writers. Among the multitude of scholars and authors, we feel no hallowing presence; we are sensible of a knack and skill rather than of inspiration; they have a light, and know not whence it comes, and call it their own; their talent is some exaggerated faculty, some overgrown member, so that their strength is a disease. In these instances the intellectual gifts do not make the impression of virtue, but almost of vice; and we feel that a man's talents stand in the way of his advancement in truth. But genius is religious. It is a larger imbibing of the common heart. It is not anomalous, but more like, and not less like other men. There is, in all great poets, a wisdom of humanity which is superior to any talents they exercise. The author, the wit, the partisan, the fine gentleman, does not take place of the man. Humanity shines in Homer, in Chaucer, in Spenser, in Shakspeare, in Milton. They are content with truth. They use the positive degree. They seem frigid and phlegmatic to those who have been spiced with the frantic passion and violent coloring of inferior, but popular writers. For they are poets by the free course which they allow to the informing soul, which through their eyes beholds again, and blesses the things which it hath made. The soul is superior to its knowledge; wiser than any of its works. The great poet makes us feel our own wealth, and then we think less of his compositions. His best communication to our mind is to teach us to despise all he has done. Shakspeare carries us to such a lofty strain of intelligent activity, as to suggest a wealth which beggars his own; and we then feel that the splendid works which he has created, and which in other hours we extol as a sort of self-existent poetry, take no stronger hold of real nature than the shadow of a passing traveller on the rock. The inspiration which uttered itself in Hamlet and Lear could utter things as good from day to day, for ever. Why, then, should I make account of Hamlet and Lear, as if we had not the soul from which they fell as syllables from the tongue?

This energy does not descend into individual life on any other condition than entire possession. It comes to the lowly and simple; it comes to whomsoever will put off what is foreign and proud; it comes as insight; it comes as serenity and grandeur. When we see those whom it inhabits, we are apprized of new degrees of greatness. From that inspiration the man comes back with a changed tone. He does not talk with men with an eye to their opinion. He tries them. It requires of us to be plain and true. The vain traveller attempts to embellish his life by quoting my lord, and the prince, and the countess, who thus said or did to *him*. The ambitious vulgar show you their spoons, and brooches, and rings, and preserve their cards and compliments. The more cultivated, in their account of their own experience, cull out the pleasing, poetic circumstance,—the visit to Rome, the man of genius they saw, the brilliant friend they know; still further on, perhaps, the gorgeous landscape, the mountain lights, the mountain thoughts, they enjoyed yesterday,—and so seek to throw a romantic color over their life. But the soul that ascends to worship the great God is plain and true; has no rose-color, no fine friends, no chivalry, no adventures; does not want admiration; dwells in the hour that now is, in the earnest experience of the common day,—by reason of the present moment and the mere trifle having become porous to thought, and bibulous of the sea of light.

Converse with a mind that is grandly simple, and literature looks like word-catching. The simplest utterances are worthiest to be written, yet are they so cheap, and so things of course, that, in the infinite riches of the soul, it is like gathering a few pebbles off the ground, or bottling a little air in a phial, when the whole earth and the whole atmosphere are ours. Nothing can pass there, or make you one of the circle, but the casting aside your trappings, and dealing man to man in naked truth, plain confession, and omniscient affirmation.

Souls such as these treat you as gods would; walk as gods in the earth, accepting without any admiration your wit, your bounty, your virtue even,—say rather your act of duty, for your virtue they own as their proper blood, royal as themselves, and over-royal, and the father of the gods. But what rebuke their plain fraternal bearing casts on the mutual flattery with which authors solace each other and wound themselves! These flatter not. I do not wonder that these men go to see Cromwell, and Christina, and Charles the Second, and James the First, and the Grand Turk. For they are, in their own elevation, the fellows of kings, and must feel the servile tone of conversation in the world. They must always be a godsend to princes, for they confront them, a king to a king, without ducking or concession, and give a high nature the refreshment and satisfaction of resistance, of plain humanity, of even companionship, and of new ideas. They leave them wiser and superior men. Souls like these make us feel that sincerity is more excellent than flattery. Deal so plainly with man and woman, as to constrain the utmost sincerity, and destroy all hope of trifling with you. It is the highest compliment you can pay. Their "highest praising," said Milton, "is not flattery, and their plainest advice is a kind of praising."

Ineffable is the union of man and God in every act of the soul. The simplest person, who in his integrity worships God, becomes God; yet for ever and ever the influx of this better and universal self is new and unsearchable. It inspires awe and astonishment. How dear, how soothing to man, arises the idea of God, peopling the lonely place, effacing the scars of our mistakes and disappointments! When we have broken our god of tradition, and ceased from our god of rhetoric, then may God fire the heart with his presence. It is the doubling of the heart itself, nay, the infinite enlargement of the heart with a power of growth to a new infinity on every side. It inspires in man an infallible trust. He has not the conviction, but the sight, that the best is the true, and may in that thought easily dismiss all particular uncertainties and fears, and adjourn to the sure revelation of time, the solution of his private riddles. He is sure that his welfare is dear to the heart of being. In the presence of law to his mind, he is overflowed with a reliance so universal, that it sweeps away all cherished hopes and the most stable projects of mortal condition in its flood. He believes that he cannot escape from his good. The things that are really for thee gravitate to thee. You are running to seek your friend. Let your feet run, but your mind need not. If you do not find him, will you not acquiesce that it is best you should not find him? for there is a power, which, as it is in you, is in him also, and could therefore very well bring you together, if it were for the best. You are preparing with eagerness to go and render a service to which your talent and your taste invite you, the love of men and the hope of fame. Has it not occurred to you, that you have no right to go, unless you are equally willing to be prevented from going? O, believe, as thou livest, that every sound that is spoken over the round world, which thou oughtest to hear, will vibrate on thine ear! Every proverb, every book, every byword that belongs to thee for aid or comfort, shall surely come home through open or winding passages. Every friend whom not thy fantastic will, but the great and tender heart in thee craveth, shall lock thee in his embrace. And this, because the heart in thee is the heart of all; not a valve, not a wall, not an intersection is there anywhere in nature, but one blood rolls uninterruptedly an endless circulation through all men, as the water of the globe is all one sea, and, truly seen, its tide is one.

Let man, then, learn the revelation of all nature and all thought to his heart; this, namely; that the Highest dwells with him; that the sources of nature are in his own mind, if the sentiment of duty is there. But if he would know what the great God speaketh, he must 'go into his closet and shut the door,' as Jesus said. God will not make himself manifest to cowards. He must greatly listen to himself, withdrawing himself from all the accents of other men's devotion. Even their prayers are hurtful to him, until he have made his own. Our religion vulgarly stands on numbers of believers. Whenever the appeal is made—no matter how indirectly—to numbers, proclamation is then and there made, that religion is not. He that finds God a sweet, enveloping thought to him never counts his company. When I sit in that presence, who shall dare to come in? When I rest in perfect humility, when I burn with pure love, what can Calvin or Swedenborg say?

It makes no difference whether the appeal is to numbers or to one. The faith that stands on authority is not faith. The reliance on authority measures the decline of religion, the withdrawal of the soul. The position men have given to Jesus, now for many centuries of history, is a position of authority. It characterizes themselves. It cannot alter the eternal facts. Great is the soul, and plain. It is no flatterer, it is no follower; it never appeals from itself. It believes in itself. Before the immense possibilities of man, all mere experience, all past biography, however spotless and sainted, shrinks away. Before that heaven which our presentiments foreshow us, we cannot easily praise any form of life we have seen or read of. We not only affirm that we have few great men, but, absolutely speaking, that we have none; that we have no history, no record of any character or mode of living, that entirely contents us. The saints and demigods whom history worships we are constrained to accept with a grain of allowance. Though in our lonely hours we draw a new strength out of their memory, yet, pressed on our attention, as they are by the thoughtless and customary, they fatigue and invade. The soul gives itself, alone, original, and pure, to the Lonely, Original, and Pure, who, on that condition, gladly inhabits, leads, and speaks through it. Then is it glad, young, and nimble. It is not wise, but it sees through all things. It is not called religious, but it is innocent. It calls the light its own, and feels that the grass grows and the stone falls by a law inferior to, and dependent on, its nature. Behold, it saith, I am born into the great, the universal mind. I, the imperfect, adore my own Perfect. I am somehow receptive of the great soul, and thereby I do overlook the sun and the stars, and feel them to be the fair accidents and effects which change and pass. More and more the surges of everlasting nature enter into me, and I become public and human in my regards and actions. So come I to live in thoughts, and act with energies, which are immortal. Thus revering the soul, and learning, as the ancient said, that "its beauty is immense," man will come to see that the world is the perennial miracle which the soul worketh, and be less astonished at particular wonders; he will learn that there is no profane history; that all history is sacred; that the universe is represented in an atom, in a moment of time. He will weave no longer a spotted life of shreds and patches, but he will live with a divine unity. He will cease from what is base and frivolous in his life, and be content with all places and with any service he can render. He will calmly front the morrow in the negligency of that trust which carries God with it, and so hath already the whole future in the bottom of the heart.

CIRCLES

Nature centres into balls,
And her proud ephemerals,
Fast to surface and outside,
Scan the profile of the sphere;
Knew they what that signified,
A new genesis were here.

Circles

THE EYE is the first circle; the horizon which it forms is the second; and throughout nature this primary figure is repeated without end. It is the highest emblem in the cipher of the world. St. Augustine described the nature of God as a circle whose centre was everywhere, and its circumference nowhere. We are all our lifetime reading the copious sense of this first of forms. One moral we have already deduced, in considering the circular or compensatory character of every human action. Another analogy we shall now trace; that every action admits of being outdone. Our life is an apprenticeship to the truth, that around every circle another can be drawn; that there is no end in nature, but every end is a beginning; that there is always another dawn risen on mid-noon, and under every deep a lower deep opens.

This fact, as far as it symbolizes the moral fact of the Unattainable, the flying Perfect, around which the hands of man can never meet, at once the inspirer and the condemner of every success, may conveniently serve us to connect many illustrations of human power in every department.

There are no fixtures in nature. The universe is fluid and volatile. Permanence is but a word of degrees. Our globe seen by God is a transparent law, not a mass of facts. The law dissolves the fact and holds it fluid. Our culture is the predominance of an idea which draws after it this train of cities and institutions. Let us rise into another idea: they will disappear. The Greek sculpture is all melted away, as if it had been statues of ice; here and there a solitary figure or fragment remaining, as we see flecks and scraps of snow left in cold dells and mountain clefts, in June and July. For the genius that created it creates now somewhat else. The Greek letters last a little longer, but are already passing under the same sentence, and tumbling into the inevitable pit which the creation of new thought opens for all that is old. The new continents are built out of the ruins of an old planet; the new races fed out of the decomposition of the foregoing. New arts destroy the old. See the investment of capital in aqueducts made useless by hydraulics; fortifications, by gunpowder; roads and canals, by railways; sails, by steam; steam by electricity.

You admire this tower of granite, weathering the hurts of so many ages. Yet a little waving hand built this huge wall, and that which builds is better than that which is built. The hand that built can topple it down much faster. Better than the hand, and nimbler, was the invisible thought which wrought through it; and thus ever, behind the coarse effect, is a fine cause, which, being narrowly seen, is itself the effect of a finer cause. Every thing looks permanent until its secret is known. A rich estate appears to women a firm and lasting fact; to a merchant, one easily created out of any materials, and easily lost. An orchard, good tillage, good grounds, seem a fixture, like a gold mine, or a river, to a citizen; but to a large farmer, not much more fixed than the state of the crop. Nature looks provokingly stable and secular, but it has a cause like all the rest; and when once I comprehend that, will these fields stretch so immovably wide, these leaves hang so individually considerable? Permanence is a word of degrees. Every thing is medial. Moons are no more bounds to spiritual power than bat-balls.

The key to every man is his thought. Sturdy and defying though he look, he has a helm which he obeys, which is the idea after which all his facts are classified. He can only be reformed by showing him a new idea which commands his own. The life of man is a self-evolving circle, which, from a ring imperceptibly small, rushes on all sides outwards to new and larger circles, and that without end. The extent to which this generation of circles, wheel without wheel, will go, depends on the force or truth of the individual soul. For it is the inert effort of each thought, having formed itself into a circular wave of circumstance,—as, for instance, an empire, rules of an art, a local usage, a religious rite,—to heap itself on that ridge, and to solidify and hem in the life. But if the soul is quick and strong, it bursts over that boundary on all sides, and expands another orbit on the great deep, which also runs up into a high wave, with attempt again to stop and to bind. But the heart refuses to be imprisoned; in its first and narrowest pulses, it already tends outward with a vast force, and to immense and innumerable expansions.

Every ultimate fact is only the first of a new series. Every general law only a particular fact of some more general law presently to disclose itself. There is no outside, no inclosing wall, no circumference to us. The man finishes his story,— how good! how final! how it puts a new face on all things! He fills the sky. Lo! on the other side rises also a man, and draws a circle around the circle we had just pronounced the outline of the sphere. Then already is our first speaker not man, but only a first speaker. His only redress is forthwith to draw a circle outside of his antagonist. And so men do by themselves. The result of to-day, which haunts the mind and cannot be escaped, will presently be abridged into a word, and the principle that seemed to explain nature will itself be included as one example of a bolder generalization. In the thought of to-morrow there is a power to upheave all thy creed, all the creeds, all the literatures, of the nations, and marshal thee to a heaven which no epic dream has yet depicted. Every man is not so much a workman in the world, as he is a suggestion of that he should be. Men walk as prophecies of the next age.

Step by step we scale this mysterious ladder: the steps are actions; the new prospect is power. Every several result is threatened and judged by that which follows. Every one seems to be contradicted by the new; it is only limited by the new. The new statement is always hated by the old, and, to those dwelling in the old, comes like an abyss of skepticism. But the eye soon gets wonted to it, for the eye and it are effects of one cause; then its innocency and benefit appear, and presently, all its energy spent, it pales and dwindles before the revelation of the new hour.

Fear not the new generalization. Does the fact look crass and material, threatening to degrade thy theory of spirit? Resist it not; it goes to refine and raise thy theory of matter just as much.

There are no fixtures to men, if we appeal to consciousness. Every man supposes himself not to be fully understood; and if there is any truth in him, if he rests at last on the divine soul, I see not how it can be otherwise. The last chamber, the last closet, he must feel, was never opened; there is always a residuum unknown, unanalyzable. That is, every man believes that he has a greater possibility.

Our moods do not believe in each other. To-day I am full of thoughts, and can write what I please. I see no reason why I should not have the same thought, the same power of expression, to-morrow. What I write, whilst I write it, seems the most natural thing in the world; but yesterday I saw a dreary vacuity in this direction in which now I see so much; and a month hence, I doubt not, I shall wonder who he was that wrote so many continuous pages. Alas for this infirm faith, this will not strenuous, this vast ebb of a vast flow! I am God in nature; I am a weed by the wall.

The continual effort to raise himself above himself, to work a pitch above his last height, betrays itself in a man's relations. We thirst for approbation, yet cannot forgive the approver. The sweet of nature is love; yet, if I have a friend, I am tormented by my imperfections. The love of me accuses the other party. If he were high enough to slight me, then could I love him, and rise by my affection to new heights. A man's growth is seen in the successive choirs of his friends. For every friend whom he loses for truth, he gains a better. I thought, as I walked in the woods and mused on my friends, why should I play with them this game of idolatry? I know and see too well, when not voluntarily blind, the speedy limits of persons called high and worthy. Rich, noble, and great they are by the liberality of our speech, but truth is sad. O blessed Spirit, whom I forsake for these, they are not thou! Every personal consideration that we allow costs us heavenly state. We sell the thrones of angels for a short and turbulent pleasure.

How often must we learn this lesson? Men cease to interest us when we find their limitations. The only sin is limitation. As soon as you once come up with a man's limitations, it is all over with him. Has he talents? has he enterprise? has he knowledge? it boots not. Infinitely alluring and attractive was he to you yesterday, a great hope, a sea to swim in; now, you have found his shores, found it a pond, and you care not if you never see it again.

Each new step we take in thought reconciles twenty seem-

ingly discordant facts, as expressions of one law. Aristotle and
Plato are reckoned the respective heads of two schools. A
wise man will see that Aristotle Platonizes. By going one step
farther back in thought, discordant opinions are reconciled,
by being seen to be two extremes of one principle, and we
can never go so far back as to preclude a still higher vision.

Beware when the great God lets loose a thinker on this
planet. Then all things are at risk. It is as when a conflagration has broken out in a great city, and no man knows what
is safe, or where it will end. There is not a piece of science,
but its flank may be turned to-morrow; there is not any literary reputation, not the so-called eternal names of fame, that
may not be revised and condemned. The very hopes of man,
the thoughts of his heart, the religion of nations, the manners
and morals of mankind, are all at the mercy of a new generalization. Generalization is always a new influx of the divinity
into the mind. Hence the thrill that attends it.

Valor consists in the power of self-recovery, so that a man
cannot have his flank turned, cannot be out-generalled, but
put him where you will, he stands. This can only be by his
preferring truth to his past apprehension of truth; and his
alert acceptance of it, from whatever quarter; the intrepid
conviction that his laws, his relations to society, his Christianity, his world, may at any time be superseded and decease.

There are degrees in idealism. We learn first to play with it
academically, as the magnet was once a toy. Then we see in
the heyday of youth and poetry that it may be true, that it is
true in gleams and fragments. Then, its countenance waxes
stern and grand, and we see that it must be true. It now
shows itself ethical and practical. We learn that God is; that
he is in me; and that all things are shadows of him. The idealism of Berkeley is only a crude statement of the idealism of
Jesus, and that again is a crude statement of the fact, that all
nature is the rapid efflux of goodness executing and organiz-
ing itself. Much more obviously is history and the state of the
world at any one time directly dependent on the intellectual
classification then existing in the minds of men. The things
which are dear to men at this hour are so on account of the
ideas which have emerged on their mental horizon, and
which cause the present order of things as a tree bears its

apples. A new degree of culture would instantly revolutionize the entire system of human pursuits.

Conversation is a game of circles. In conversation we pluck up the *termini* which bound the common of silence on every side. The parties are not to be judged by the spirit they partake and even express under this Pentecost. To-morrow they will have receded from this high-water mark. To-morrow you shall find them stooping under the old pack-saddles. Yet let us enjoy the cloven flame whilst it glows on our walls. When each new speaker strikes a new light, emancipates us from the oppression of the last speaker, to oppress us with the greatness and exclusiveness of his own thought, then yields us to another redeemer, we seem to recover our rights, to become men. O, what truths profound and executable only in ages and orbs are supposed in the announcement of every truth! In common hours, society sits cold and statuesque. We all stand waiting, empty,—knowing, possibly, that we can be full, surrounded by mighty symbols which are not symbols to us, but prose and trivial toys. Then cometh the god, and converts the statues into fiery men, and by a flash of his eye burns up the veil which shrouded all things, and the meaning of the very furniture, of cup and saucer, of chair and clock and tester, is manifest. The facts which loomed so large in the fogs of yesterday,—property, climate, breeding, personal beauty, and the like, have strangely changed their proportions. All that we reckoned settled shakes and rattles; and literatures, cities, climates, religions, leave their foundations, and dance before our eyes. And yet here again see the swift circumspection! Good as is discourse, silence is better, and shames it. The length of the discourse indicates the distance of thought betwixt the speaker and the hearer. If they were at a perfect understanding in any part, no words would be necessary thereon. If at one in all parts, no words would be suffered.

Literature is a point outside of our hodiernal circle, through which a new one may be described. The use of literature is to afford us a platform whence we may command a view of our present life, a purchase by which we may move it. We fill ourselves with ancient learning, install ourselves the best we can in Greek, in Punic, in Roman houses, only that we may wiselier see French, English, and American houses and modes of living. In like manner, we see literature best from the midst of wild nature, or from the din of affairs, or from a high religion. The field cannot be well seen from within the field. The astronomer must have his diameter of the earth's orbit as a base to find the parallax of any star.

Therefore we value the poet. All the argument and all the wisdom is not in the encyclopædia, or the treatise on metaphysics, or the Body of Divinity, but in the sonnet or the play. In my daily work I incline to repeat my old steps, and do not believe in remedial force, in the power of change and reform. But some Petrarch or Ariosto, filled with the new wine of his imagination, writes me an ode or a brisk romance, full of daring thought and action. He smites and arouses me with his shrill tones, breaks up my whole chain of habits, and I open my eye on my own possibilities. He claps wings to the sides of all the solid old lumber of the world, and I am capable once more of choosing a straight path in theory and practice.

We have the same need to command a view of the religion of the world. We can never see Christianity from the catechism:—from the pastures, from a boat in the pond, from amidst the songs of wood-birds, we possibly may. Cleansed by the elemental light and wind, steeped in the sea of beautiful forms which the field offers us, we may chance to cast a right glance back upon biography. Christianity is rightly dear to the best of mankind; yet was there never a young philosopher whose breeding had fallen into the Christian church, by whom that brave text of Paul's was not specially prized:— "Then shall also the Son be subject unto Him who put all things under him, that God may be all in all." Let the claims and virtues of persons be never so great and welcome, the instinct of man presses eagerly onward to the impersonal and illimitable, and gladly arms itself against the dogmatism of bigots with this generous word out of the book itself.

The natural world may be conceived of as a system of concentric circles, and we now and then detect in nature slight dislocations, which apprize us that this surface on which we now stand is not fixed, but sliding. These manifold tenacious qualities, this chemistry and vegetation, these metals and animals, which seem to stand there for their own sake, are means

and methods only,—are words of God, and as fugitive as
other words. Has the naturalist or chemist learned his craft,
who has explored the gravity of atoms and the elective affinities, who has not yet discerned the deeper law whereof this is
only a partial or approximate statement, namely, that like
draws to like; and that the goods which belong to you gravitate to you, and need not be pursued with pains and cost?
Yet is that statement approximate also, and not final. Omnipresence is a higher fact. Not through subtle, subterranean
channels need friend and fact be drawn to their counterpart,
but, rightly considered, these things proceed from the eternal
generation of the soul. Cause and effect are two sides of one
fact.

The same law of eternal procession ranges all that we call
the virtues, and extinguishes each in the light of a better. The
great man will not be prudent in the popular sense; all his
prudence will be so much deduction from his grandeur. But
it behooves each to see, when he sacrifices prudence, to what
god he devotes it; if to ease and pleasure, he had better be
prudent still; if to a great trust, he can well spare his mule
and panniers who has a winged chariot instead. Geoffrey
draws on his boots to go through the woods, that his feet
may be safer from the bite of snakes; Aaron never thinks of
such a peril. In many years neither is harmed by such an accident. Yet it seems to me, that, with every precaution you
take against such an evil, you put yourself into the power of
the evil. I suppose that the highest prudence is the lowest
prudence. Is this too sudden a rushing from the centre to the
verge of our orbit? Think how many times we shall fall back
into pitiful calculations before we take up our rest in the great
sentiment, or make the verge of to-day the new centre. Besides, your bravest sentiment is familiar to the humblest men.
The poor and the low have their way of expressing the last
facts of philosophy as well as you. "Blessed be nothing," and
"the worse things are, the better they are," are proverbs which
express the transcendentalism of common life.

One man's justice is another's injustice; one man's beauty,
another's ugliness; one man's wisdom, another's folly; as one
beholds the same objects from a higher point. One man
thinks justice consists in paying debts, and has no measure in

his abhorrence of another who is very remiss in this duty, and makes the creditor wait tediously. But that second man has his own way of looking at things; asks himself which debt must I pay first, the debt to the rich, or the debt to the poor? the debt of money, or the debt of thought to mankind, of genius to nature? For you, O broker! there is no other principle but arithmetic. For me, commerce is of trivial import; love, faith, truth of character, the aspiration of man, these are sacred; nor can I detach one duty, like you, from all other duties, and concentrate my forces mechanically on the payment of moneys. Let me live onward; you shall find that, though slower, the progress of my character will liquidate all these debts without injustice to higher claims. If a man should dedicate himself to the payment of notes, would not this be injustice? Does he owe no debt but money? And are all claims on him to be postponed to a landlord's or a banker's?

There is no virtue which is final; all are initial. The virtues of society are vices of the saint. The terror of reform is the discovery that we must cast away our virtues, or what we have always esteemed such, into the same pit that has consumed our grosser vices.

> "Forgive his crimes, forgive his virtues too,
> Those smaller faults, half converts to the right."

It is the highest power of divine moments that they abolish our contritions also. I accuse myself of sloth and unprofitableness day by day; but when these waves of God flow into me, I no longer reckon lost time. I no longer poorly compute my possible achievement by what remains to me of the month or the year; for these moments confer a sort of omnipresence and omnipotence which asks nothing of duration, but sees that the energy of the mind is commensurate with the work to be done, without time.

And thus, O circular philosopher, I hear some reader exclaim, you have arrived at a fine Pyrrhonism, at an equivalence and indifference of all actions, and would fain teach us that, *if we are true*, forsooth, our crimes may be lively stones out of which we shall construct the temple of the true God!

I am not careful to justify myself. I own I am gladdened by

seeing the predominance of the saccharine principle through-out vegetable nature, and not less by beholding in morals that unrestrained inundation of the principle of good into every chink and hole that selfishness has left open, yea, into selfish-ness and sin itself; so that no evil is pure, nor hell itself with-out its extreme satisfactions. But lest I should mislead any when I have my own head and obey my whims, let me re-mind the reader that I am only an experimenter. Do not set the least value on what I do, or the least discredit on what I do not, as if I pretended to settle any thing as true or false. I unsettle all things. No facts are to me sacred; none are pro-fane; I simply experiment, an endless seeker, with no Past at my back.

Yet this incessant movement and progression which all things partake could never become sensible to us but by con-trast to some principle of fixture or stability in the soul. Whilst the eternal generation of circles proceeds, the eternal generator abides. That central life is somewhat superior to creation, superior to knowledge and thought, and contains all its circles. For ever it labors to create a life and thought as large and excellent as itself; but in vain; for that which is made instructs how to make a better.

Thus there is no sleep, no pause, no preservation, but all things renew, germinate, and spring. Why should we import rags and relics into the new hour? Nature abhors the old, and old age seems the only disease; all others run into this one. We call it by many names,—fever, intemperance, insanity, stupidity, and crime; they are all forms of old age; they are rest, conservatism, appropriation, inertia, not newness, not the way onward. We grizzle every day. I see no need of it. Whilst we converse with what is above us, we do not grow old, but grow young. Infancy, youth, receptive, aspiring, with religious eye looking upward, counts itself nothing, and aban-dons itself to the instruction flowing from all sides. But the man and woman of seventy assume to know all, they have outlived their hope, they renounce aspiration, accept the ac-tual for the necessary, and talk down to the young. Let them, then, become organs of the Holy Ghost; let them be lovers; let them behold truth; and their eyes are uplifted, their wrin-kles smoothed, they are perfumed again with hope and power. This old age ought not to creep on a human mind. In nature every moment is new; the past is always swallowed and forgotten; the coming only is sacred. Nothing is secure but life, transition, the energizing spirit. No love can be bound by oath or covenant to secure it against a higher love. No truth so sublime but it may be trivial to-morrow in the light of new thoughts. People wish to be settled; only as far as they are unsettled is there any hope for them.

Life is a series of surprises. We do not guess to-day the mood, the pleasure, the power of to-morrow, when we are building up our being. Of lower states,—of acts of routine and sense,—we can tell somewhat; but the masterpieces of God, the total growths and universal movements of the soul, he hideth; they are incalculable. I can know that truth is divine and helpful; but how it shall help me I can have no guess, for *so to be* is the sole inlet of *so to know*. The new position of the advancing man has all the powers of the old, yet has them all new. It carries in its bosom all the energies of the past, yet is itself an exhalation of the morning. I cast away in this new moment all my once hoarded knowledge, as vacant and vain. Now, for the first time, seem I to know any thing rightly. The simplest words,—we do not know what they mean, except when we love and aspire.

The difference between talents and character is adroitness to keep the old and trodden round, and power and courage to make a new road to new and better goals. Character makes an overpowering present; a cheerful, determined hour, which fortifies all the company, by making them see that much is possible and excellent that was not thought of. Character dulls the impression of particular events. When we see the conqueror, we do not think much of any one battle or success. We see that we had exaggerated the difficulty. It was easy to him. The great man is not convulsible or tormentable; events pass over him without much impression. People say sometimes, 'See what I have overcome; see how cheerful I am; see how completely I have triumphed over these black events.' Not if they still remind me of the black event. True conquest is the causing the calamity to fade and disappear, as an early cloud of insignificant result in a history so large and advancing.

The one thing which we seek with insatiable desire is to forget ourselves, to be surprised out of our propriety, to lose our sempiternal memory, and to do something without knowing how or why; in short, to draw a new circle. Nothing great was ever achieved without enthusiasm. The way of life is wonderful: it is by abandonment. The great moments of history are the facilities of performance through the strength of ideas, as the works of genius and religion. "A man," said Oliver Cromwell, "never rises so high as when he knows not whither he is going." Dreams and drunkenness, the use of opium and alcohol are the semblance and counterfeit of this oracular genius, and hence their dangerous attraction for men. For the like reason, they ask the aid of wild passions, as in gaming and war, to ape in some manner these flames and generosities of the heart.

INTELLECT

Go, speed the stars of Thought
On to their shining goals;—
The sower scatters broad his seed,
The wheat thou strew'st be souls.

Intellect

EVERY SUBSTANCE is negatively electric to that which stands above it in the chemical tables, positively to that which stands below it. Water dissolves wood, and iron, and salt; air dissolves water; electric fire dissolves air, but the intellect dissolves fire, gravity, laws, method, and the subtlest unnamed relations of nature, in its resistless menstruum. Intellect lies behind genius, which is intellect constructive. Intellect is the simple power anterior to all action or construction. Gladly would I unfold in calm degrees a natural history of the intellect, but what man has yet been able to mark the steps and boundaries of that transparent essence? The first questions are always to be asked, and the wisest doctor is gravelled by the inquisitiveness of a child. How can we speak of the action of the mind under any divisions, as of its knowledge, of its ethics, of its works, and so forth, since it melts will into perception, knowledge into act? Each becomes the other. Itself alone is. Its vision is not like the vision of the eye, but is union with the things known.

Intellect and intellection signify to the common ear consideration of abstract truth. The considerations of time and place, of you and me, of profit and hurt, tyrannize over most men's minds. Intellect separates the fact considered from *you*, from all local and personal reference, and discerns it as if it existed for its own sake. Heraclitus looked upon the affections as dense and colored mists. In the fog of good and evil affections, it is hard for man to walk forward in a straight line. Intellect is void of affection, and sees an object as it stands in the light of science, cool and disengaged. The intellect goes out of the individual, floats over its own personality, and regards it as a fact, and not as *I* and *mine*. He who is immersed in what concerns person or place cannot see the problem of existence. This the intellect always ponders. Nature shows all things formed and bound. The intellect pierces the form, overleaps the wall, detects intrinsic likeness between remote things, and reduces all things into a few principles.

The making a fact the subject of thought raises it. All that mass of mental and moral phenomena, which we do not make objects of voluntary thought, come within the power of fortune; they constitute the circumstance of daily life; they are subject to change, to fear, and hope. Every man beholds his human condition with a degree of melancholy. As a ship aground is battered by the waves, so man, imprisoned in mortal life, lies open to the mercy of coming events. But a truth, separated by the intellect, is no longer a subject of destiny. We behold it as a god upraised above care and fear. And so any fact in our life, or any record of our fancies or reflections, disentangled from the web of our unconsciousness, becomes an object impersonal and immortal. It is the past restored, but embalmed. A better art than that of Egypt has taken fear and corruption out of it. It is eviscerated of care. It is offered for science. What is addressed to us for contemplation does not threaten us, but makes us intellectual beings.

The growth of the intellect is spontaneous in every expansion. The mind that grows could not predict the times, the means, the mode of that spontaneity. God enters by a private door into every individual. Long prior to the age of reflection is the thinking of the mind. Out of darkness, it came insensibly into the marvellous light of to-day. In the period of infancy it accepted and disposed of all impressions from the surrounding creation after its own way. Whatever any mind doth or saith is after a law; and this native law remains over it after it has come to reflection or conscious thought. In the most worn, pedantic, introverted self-tormenter's life, the greatest part is incalculable by him, unforeseen, unimaginable, and must be, until he can take himself up by his own ears. What am I? What has my will done to make me that I am? Nothing. I have been floated into this thought, this hour, this connection of events, by secret currents of might and mind, and my ingenuity and wilfulness have not thwarted, have not aided to an appreciable degree.

Our spontaneous action is always the best. You cannot, with your best deliberation and heed, come so close to any question as your spontaneous glance shall bring you, whilst you rise from your bed, or walk abroad in the morning after meditating the matter before sleep on the previous night. Our thinking is a pious reception. Our truth of thought is therefore vitiated as much by too violent direction given by our will, as by too great negligence. We do not determine what we will think. We only open our senses, clear away, as we can, all obstruction from the fact, and suffer the intellect to see. We have little control over our thoughts. We are the prisoners of ideas. They catch us up for moments into their heaven, and so fully engage us, that we take no thought for the morrow, gaze like children, without an effort to make them our own. By and by we fall out of that rapture, bethink us where we have been, what we have seen, and repeat, as truly as we can, what we have beheld. As far as we can recall these ecstasies, we carry away in the ineffaceable memory the result, and all men and all the ages confirm it. It is called Truth. But the moment we cease to report, and attempt to correct and contrive, it is not truth.

If we consider what persons have stimulated and profited us, we shall perceive the superiority of the spontaneous or intuitive principle over the arithmetical or logical. The first contains the second, but virtual and latent. We want, in every man, a long logic; we cannot pardon the absence of it, but it must not be spoken. Logic is the procession or proportionate unfolding of the intuition; but its virtue is as silent method; the moment it would appear as propositions, and have a separate value, it is worthless.

In every man's mind, some images, words, and facts remain, without effort on his part to imprint them, which others forget, and afterwards these illustrate to him important laws. All our progress is an unfolding, like the vegetable bud. You have first an instinct, then an opinion, then a knowledge, as the plant has root, bud, and fruit. Trust the instinct to the end, though you can render no reason. It is vain to hurry it. By trusting it to the end, it shall ripen into truth, and you shall know why you believe.

Each mind has its own method. A true man never acquires after college rules. What you have aggregated in a natural manner surprises and delights when it is produced. For we cannot oversee each other's secret. And hence the differences between men in natural endowment are insignificant in comparison with their common wealth. Do you think the porter

and the cook have no anecdotes, no experiences, no wonders
for you? Every body knows as much as the savant. The walls
of rude minds are scrawled all over with facts, with thoughts.
They shall one day bring a lantern and read the inscriptions.
Every man, in the degree in which he has wit and culture,
finds his curiosity inflamed concerning the modes of living
and thinking of other men, and especially of those classes
whose minds have not been subdued by the drill of school
education.

This instinctive action never ceases in a healthy mind, but
becomes richer and more frequent in its informations through
all states of culture. At last comes the era of reflection, when
we not only observe, but take pains to observe; when we of
set purpose sit down to consider an abstract truth; when we
keep the mind's eye open, whilst we converse, whilst we read,
whilst we act, intent to learn the secret law of some class of
facts.

What is the hardest task in the world? To think. I would
put myself in the attitude to look in the eye an abstract truth,
and I cannot. I blench and withdraw on this side and on that.
I seem to know what he meant who said, No man can see
God face to face and live. For example, a man explores the
basis of civil government. Let him intend his mind without
respite, without rest, in one direction. His best heed long
time avails him nothing. Yet thoughts are flitting before him.
We all but apprehend, we dimly forebode the truth. We say,
I will walk abroad, and the truth will take form and clearness
to me. We go forth, but cannot find it. It seems as if we
needed only the stillness and composed attitude of the library
to seize the thought. But we come in, and are as far from it
as at first. Then, in a moment, and unannounced, the truth
appears. A certain, wandering light appears, and is the distinction, the principle, we wanted. But the oracle comes, because we had previously laid siege to the shrine. It seems as if
the law of the intellect resembled that law of nature by which
we now inspire, now expire the breath; by which the heart
now draws in, then hurls out the blood,—the law of undulation. So now you must labor with your brains, and now
you must forbear your activity, and see what the great Soul
showeth.

The immortality of man is as legitimately preached from the intellections as from the moral volitions. Every intellection is mainly prospective. Its present value is its least. Inspect what delights you in Plutarch, in Shakspeare, in Cervantes. Each truth that a writer acquires is a lantern, which he turns full on what facts and thoughts lay already in his mind, and behold, all the mats and rubbish which had littered his garret become precious. Every trivial fact in his private biography becomes an illustration of this new principle, revisits the day, and delights all men by its piquancy and new charm. Men say, Where did he get this? and think there was something divine in his life. But no; they have myriads of facts just as good, would they only get a lamp to ransack their attics withal.

We are all wise. The difference between persons is not in wisdom but in art. I knew, in an academical club, a person who always deferred to me, who, seeing my whim for writing, fancied that my experiences had somewhat superior; whilst I saw that his experiences were as good as mine. Give them to me, and I would make the same use of them. He held the old; he holds the new; I had the habit of tacking together the old and the new, which he did not use to exercise. This may hold in the great examples. Perhaps if we should meet Shakspeare, we should not be conscious of any steep inferiority; no: but of a great equality,—only that he possessed a strange skill of using, of classifying, his facts, which we lacked. For, notwithstanding our utter incapacity to produce any thing like Hamlet and Othello, see the perfect reception this wit, and immense knowledge of life, and liquid eloquence find in us all.

If you gather apples in the sunshine, or make hay, or hoe corn, and then retire within doors, and shut your eyes, and press them with your hand, you shall still see apples hanging in the bright light, with boughs and leaves thereto, or the tasselled grass, or the corn-flags, and this for five or six hours afterwards. There lie the impressions on the retentive organ, though you knew it not. So lies the whole series of natural images with which your life has made you acquainted in your memory, though you know it not, and a thrill of passion flashes light on their dark chamber, and the active power seizes instantly the fit image, as the word of its momentary thought.

It is long ere we discover how rich we are. Our history, we are sure, is quite tame: we have nothing to write, nothing to infer. But our wiser years still run back to the despised recollections of childhood, and always we are fishing up some wonderful article out of that pond; until, by and by, we begin to suspect that the biography of the one foolish person we know is, in reality, nothing less than the miniature paraphrase of the hundred volumes of the Universal History.

In the intellect constructive, which we popularly designate by the word Genius, we observe the same balance of two elements as in intellect receptive. The constructive intellect produces thoughts, sentences, poems, plans, designs, systems. It is the generation of the mind, the marriage of thought with nature. To genius must always go two gifts, the thought and the publication. The first is revelation, always a miracle, which no frequency of occurrence or incessant study can ever familiarize, but which must always leave the inquirer stupid with wonder. It is the advent of truth into the world, a form of thought now, for the first time, bursting into the universe, a child of the old eternal soul, a piece of genuine and immeasurable greatness. It seems, for the time, to inherit all that has yet existed, and to dictate to the unborn. It affects every thought of man, and goes to fashion every institution. But to make it available, it needs a vehicle or art by which it is conveyed to men. To be communicable, it must become picture or sensible object. We must learn the language of facts. The most wonderful inspirations die with their subject, if he has no hand to paint them to the senses. The ray of light passes invisible through space, and only when it falls on an object is it seen. When the spiritual energy is directed on something outward, then it is a thought. The relation between it and you first makes you, the value of you, apparent to me. The rich, inventive genius of the painter must be smothered and lost for want of the power of drawing, and in our happy hours we should be inexhaustible poets, if once we could break through the silence into adequate rhyme. As all men have some access to primary truth, so all have some art or power of communication in their head, but only in the artist does it descend into the hand. There is an inequality, whose laws we do not yet know, between two men and between two moments of the same man, in respect to this faculty. In common hours, we have the same facts as in the uncommon or inspired, but they do not sit for their portraits; they are not detached, but lie in a web. The thought of genius is spontaneous; but the power of picture or expression, in the most enriched and flowing nature, implies a mixture of will, a certain control over the spontaneous states, without which no production is possible. It is a conversion of all nature into the rhetoric of thought, under the eye of judgment, with a strenuous exercise of choice. And yet the imaginative vocabulary seems to be spontaneous also. It does not flow from experience only or mainly, but from a richer source. Not by any conscious imitation of particular forms are the grand strokes of the painter executed, but by repairing to the fountain-head of all forms in his mind. Who is the first drawing-master? Without instruction we know very well the ideal of the human form. A child knows if an arm or a leg be distorted in a picture, if the attitude be natural or grand, or mean, though he has never received any instruction in drawing, or heard any conversation on the subject, nor can himself draw with correctness a single feature. A good form strikes all eyes pleasantly, long before they have any science on the subject, and a beautiful face sets twenty hearts in palpitation, prior to all consideration of the mechanical proportions of the features and head. We may owe to dreams some light on the fountain of this skill; for, as soon as we let our will go, and let the unconscious states ensue, see what cunning draughtsmen we are! We entertain ourselves with wonderful forms of men, of women, of animals, of gardens, of woods, and of monsters, and the mystic pencil wherewith we then draw has no awkwardness or inexperience, no meagreness or poverty; it can design well, and group well; its composition is full of art, its colors are well laid on, and the whole canvas which it paints is life-like, and apt to touch us with terror, with tenderness, with desire, and with grief. Neither are the artist's copies from experience ever mere copies, but always touched and softened by tints from this ideal domain.

The conditions essential to a constructive mind do not ap-

pear to be so often combined but that a good sentence or
verse remains fresh and memorable for a long time. Yet when
we write with ease, and come out into the free air of thought,
we seem to be assured that nothing is easier than to continue
this communication at pleasure. Up, down, around, the kingdom of thought has no inclosures, but the Muse makes us
free of her city. Well, the world has a million writers. One
would think, then, that good thought would be as familiar as
air and water, and the gifts of each new hour would exclude
the last. Yet we can count all our good books; nay, I remember any beautiful verse for twenty years. It is true that the
discerning intellect of the world is always much in advance of
the creative, so that there are many competent judges of the
best book, and few writers of the best books. But some of the
conditions of intellectual construction are of rare occurrence.
The intellect is a whole, and demands integrity in every work.
This is resisted equally by a man's devotion to a single
thought, and by his ambition to combine too many.

Truth is our element of life, yet if a man fasten his attention
on a single aspect of truth, and apply himself to that alone for
a long time, the truth becomes distorted and not itself, but
falsehood; herein resembling the air, which is our natural element, and the breath of our nostrils, but if a stream of the
same be directed on the body for a time, it causes cold, fever,
and even death. How wearisome the grammarian, the phrenologist, the political or religious fanatic, or indeed any possessed mortal whose balance is lost by the exaggeration of a
single topic. It is incipient insanity. Every thought is a prison
also. I cannot see what you see, because I am caught up by a
strong wind, and blown so far in one direction that I am out
of the hoop of your horizon.

Is it any better, if the student, to avoid this offence, and to
liberalize himself, aims to make a mechanical whole of history, or science, or philosophy, by a numerical addition of all
the facts that fall within his vision? The world refuses to be
analyzed by addition and subtraction. When we are young,
we spend much time and pains in filling our note-books with
all definitions of Religion, Love, Poetry, Politics, Art, in the
hope that, in the course of a few years, we shall have condensed into our encyclopædia the net value of all the theories

at which the world has yet arrived. But year after year our tables get no completeness, and at last we discover that our curve is a parabola, whose arcs will never meet.

Neither by detachment, neither by aggregation, is the integrity of the intellect transmitted to its works, but by a vigilance which brings the intellect in its greatness and best state to operate every moment. It must have the same wholeness which nature has. Although no diligence can rebuild the universe in a model, by the best accumulation or disposition of details, yet does the world reappear in miniature in every event, so that all the laws of nature may be read in the smallest fact. The intellect must have the like perfection in its apprehension and in its works. For this reason, an index or mercury of intellectual proficiency is the perception of identity. We talk with accomplished persons who appear to be strangers in nature. The cloud, the tree, the turf, the bird are not theirs, have nothing of them: the world is only their lodging and table. But the poet, whose verses are to be spheral and complete, is one whom Nature cannot deceive, whatsoever face of strangeness she may put on. He feels a strict consanguinity, and detects more likeness than variety in all her changes. We are stung by the desire for new thought; but when we receive a new thought, it is only the old thought with a new face, and though we make it our own, we instantly crave another; we are not really enriched. For the truth was in us before it was reflected to us from natural objects; and the profound genius will cast the likeness of all creatures into every product of his wit.

But if the constructive powers are rare, and it is given to few men to be poets, yet every man is a receiver of this descending holy ghost, and may well study the laws of its influx. Exactly parallel is the whole rule of intellectual duty to the rule of moral duty. A self-denial, no less austere than the saint's, is demanded of the scholar. He must worship truth, and forego all things for that, and choose defeat and pain, so that his treasure in thought is thereby augmented.

God offers to every mind its choice between truth and repose. Take which you please,—you can never have both. Between these, as a pendulum, man oscillates. He in whom the love of repose predominates will accept the first creed, the first philosophy, the first political party he meets,—most likely his father's. He gets rest, commodity, and reputation; but he shuts the door of truth. He in whom the love of truth predominates will keep himself aloof from all moorings, and afloat. He will abstain from dogmatism, and recognize all the opposite negations, between which, as walls, his being is swung. He submits to the inconvenience of suspense and imperfect opinion, but he is a candidate for truth, as the other is not, and respects the highest law of his being.

The circle of the green earth he must measure with his shoes, to find the man who can yield him truth. He shall then know that there is somewhat more blessed and great in hearing than in speaking. Happy is the hearing man; unhappy the speaking man. As long as I hear truth, I am bathed by a beautiful element, and am not conscious of any limits to my nature. The suggestions are thousandfold that I hear and see. The waters of the great deep have ingress and egress to the soul. But if I speak, I define, I confine, and am less. When Socrates speaks, Lysis and Menexenus are afflicted by no shame that they do not speak. They also are good. He likewise defers to them, loves them, whilst he speaks. Because a true and natural man contains and is the same truth which an eloquent man articulates: but in the eloquent man, because he can articulate it, it seems something the less to reside, and he turns to these silent beautiful with the more inclination and respect. The ancient sentence said, Let us be silent, for so are the gods. Silence is a solvent that destroys personality, and gives us leave to be great and universal. Every man's progress is through a succession of teachers, each of whom seems at the time to have a superlative influence, but it at last gives place to a new. Frankly let him accept it all. Jesus says, Leave father, mother, house and lands, and follow me. Who leaves all, receives more. This is as true intellectually as morally. Each new mind we approach seems to require an abdication of all our past and present possessions. A new doctrine seems, at first, a subversion of all our opinions, tastes, and manner of living. Such has Swedenborg, such has Kant, such has Coleridge, such has Hegel or his interpreter Cousin, seemed to many young men in this country. Take thankfully and heartily all they can give. Exhaust them, wrestle with them, let them not go until their blessing be won, and, after a short season, the dismay will be overpast, the excess of influence withdrawn, and they will be no longer an alarming meteor, but one more bright star shining serenely in your heaven, and blending its light with all your day.

But whilst he gives himself up unreservedly to that which draws him, because that is his own, he is to refuse himself to that which draws him not, whatsoever fame and authority may attend it, because it is not his own. Entire self-reliance belongs to the intellect. One soul is a counterpoise of all souls, as a capillary column of water is a balance for the sea. It must treat things, and books, and sovereign genius, as itself also a sovereign. If Æschylus be that man he is taken for, he has not yet done his office, when he has educated the learned of Europe for a thousand years. He is now to approve himself a master of delight to me also. If he cannot do that, all his fame shall avail him nothing with me. I were a fool not to sacrifice a thousand Æschyluses to my intellectual integrity. Especially take the same ground in regard to abstract truth, the science of the mind. The Bacon, the Spinoza, the Hume, Schelling, Kant, or whosoever propounds to you a philosophy of the mind, is only a more or less awkward translator of things in your consciousness, which you have also your way of seeing, perhaps of denominating. Say, then, instead of too timidly poring into his obscure sense, that he has not succeeded in rendering back to you your consciousness. He has not succeeded; now let another try. If Plato cannot, perhaps Spinoza will. If Spinoza cannot, then perhaps Kant. Anyhow, when at last it is done, you will find it is no recondite, but a simple, natural, common state, which the writer restores to you.

But let us end these didactics. I will not, though the subject might provoke it, speak to the open question between Truth and Love. I shall not presume to interfere in the old politics of the skies;—"The cherubim know most; the seraphim love most." The gods shall settle their own quarrels. But I cannot recite, even thus rudely, laws of the intellect, without remembering that lofty and sequestered class of men who have been its prophets and oracles, the high-priesthood of the pure reason, the *Trismegisti*, the expounders of the principles of thought from age to age. When, at long intervals, we turn over their abstruse pages, wonderful seems the calm and grand air of these few, these great spiritual lords, who have walked in the world,—these of the old religion,—dwelling in a worship which makes the sanctities of Christianity look *parvenues* and popular; for "persuasion is in soul, but necessity is in intellect." This band of grandees, Hermes, Heraclitus, Empedocles, Plato, Plotinus, Olympiodorus, Proclus, Synesius, and the rest, have somewhat so vast in their logic, so primary in their thinking, that it seems antecedent to all the ordinary distinctions of rhetoric and literature, and to be at once poetry, and music, and dancing, and astronomy, and mathematics. I am present at the sowing of the seed of the world. With a geometry of sunbeams, the soul lays the foundations of nature. The truth and grandeur of their thought is proved by its scope and applicability, for it commands the entire schedule and inventory of things for its illustration. But what marks its elevation, and has even a comic look to us, is the innocent serenity with which these babe-like Jupiters sit in their clouds, and from age to age prattle to each other, and to no contemporary. Well assured that their speech is intelligible, and the most natural thing in the world, they add thesis to thesis, without a moment's heed of the universal astonishment of the human race below, who do not comprehend their plainest argument; nor do they ever relent so much as to insert a popular or explaining sentence; nor testify the least displeasure or petulance at the dulness of their amazed auditory. The angels are so enamoured of the language that is spoken in heaven, that they will not distort their lips with the hissing and unmusical dialects of men, but speak their own, whether there be any who understand it or not.

ART

Give to barrows, trays, and pans
Grace and glimmer of romance;
Bring the moonlight into noon
Hid in gleaming piles of stone;
On the city's paved street
Plant gardens lined with lilac sweet;
Let spouting fountains cool the air,
Singing in the sun-baked square;
Let statue, picture, park, and hall,
Ballad, flag, and festival,
The past restore, the day adorn,
And make each morrow a new morn.
So shall the drudge in dusty frock
Spy behind the city clock
Retinues of airy kings,
Skirts of angels, starry wings,
His fathers shining in bright fables,
His children fed at heavenly tables.
'T is the privilege of Art
Thus to play its cheerful part,
Man in Earth to acclimate,
And bend the exile to his fate,
And, moulded of one element
With the days and firmament,
Teach him on these as stairs to climb,
And live on even terms with Time;
Whilst upper life the slender rill
Of human sense doth overfill.

Art

BECAUSE THE SOUL is progressive, it never quite repeats itself, but in every act attempts the production of a new and fairer whole. This appears in works both of the useful and the fine arts, if we employ the popular distinction of works according to their aim, either at use or beauty. Thus in our fine arts, not imitation, but creation is the aim. In landscapes, the painter should give the suggestion of a fairer creation than we know. The details, the prose of nature he should omit, and give us only the spirit and splendor. He should know that the landscape has beauty for his eye, because it expresses a thought which is to him good: and this, because the same power which sees through his eyes, is seen in that spectacle; and he will come to value the expression of nature, and not nature itself, and so exalt in his copy, the features that please him. He will give the gloom of gloom, and the sunshine of sunshine. In a portrait, he must inscribe the character, and not the features, and must esteem the man who sits to him as himself only an imperfect picture or likeness of the aspiring original within.

What is that abridgment and selection we observe in all spiritual activity, but itself the creative impulse? for it is the inlet of that higher illumination which teaches to convey a larger sense by simpler symbols. What is a man but nature's finer success in self-explication? What is a man but a finer and compacter landscape than the horizon figures,—nature's eclecticism? and what is his speech, his love of painting, love of nature, but a still finer success? all the weary miles and tons of space and bulk left out, and the spirit or moral of it contracted into a musical word, or the most cunning stroke of the pencil?

But the artist must employ the symbols in use in his day and nation, to convey his enlarged sense to his fellow-men. Thus the new in art is always formed out of the old. The Genius of the Hour sets his ineffaceable seal on the work, and gives it an inexpressible charm for the imagination. As far as the spiritual character of the period overpowers the artist, and finds expression in his work, so far it will retain a certain grandeur, and will represent to future beholders the Unknown, the Inevitable, the Divine. No man can quite exclude this element of Necessity from his labor. No man can quite emancipate himself from his age and country, or produce a model in which the education, the religion, the politics, usages, and arts, of his times shall have no share. Though he were never so original, never so wilful and fantastic, he cannot wipe out of his work every trace of the thoughts amidst which it grew. The very avoidance betrays the usage he avoids. Above his will, and out of his sight, he is necessitated, by the air he breathes, and the idea on which he and his contemporaries live and toil, to share the manner of his times, without knowing what that manner is. Now that which is inevitable in the work has a higher charm than individual talent can ever give, inasmuch as the artist's pen or chisel seems to have been held and guided by a gigantic hand to inscribe a line in the history of the human race. This circumstance gives a value to the Egyptian hieroglyphics, to the Indian, Chinese, and Mexican idols, however gross and shapeless. They denote the height of the human soul in that hour, and were not fantastic, but sprung from a necessity as deep as the world. Shall I now add, that the whole extant product of the plastic arts has herein its highest value, *as history*; as a stroke drawn in the portrait of that fate, perfect and beautiful, according to whose ordinations all beings advance to their beatitude?

Thus, historically viewed, it has been the office of art to educate the perception of beauty. We are immersed in beauty, but our eyes have no clear vision. It needs, by the exhibition of single traits, to assist and lead the dormant taste. We carve and paint, or we behold what is carved and painted, as students of the mystery of Form. The virtue of art lies in detachment, in sequestering one object from the embarrassing variety. Until one thing comes out from the connection of things, there can be enjoyment, contemplation, but no thought. Our happiness and unhappiness are unproductive. The infant lies in a pleasing trance, but his individual character and his practical power depend on his daily progress in the separation of things, and dealing with one at a time. Love and all the passions concentrate all existence around a single form. It is the habit of certain minds to give an all-excluding fulness to the object, the thought, the word, they alight upon, and to make that for the time the deputy of the world. These are the artists, the orators, the leaders of society. The power to detach, and to magnify by detaching, is the essence of rhetoric in the hands of the orator and the poet. This rhetoric, or power to fix the momentary eminency of an object,—so remarkable in Burke, in Byron, in Carlyle,—the painter and sculptor exhibit in color and in stone. The power depends on the depth of the artist's insight of that object he contemplates. For every object has its roots in central nature, and may of course be so exhibited to us as to represent the world. Therefore, each work of genius is the tyrant of the hour, and concentrates attention on itself. For the time, it is the only thing worth naming to do that,—be it a sonnet, an opera, a landscape, a statue, an oration, the plan of a temple, of a campaign, or of a voyage of discovery. Presently we pass to some other object, which rounds itself into a whole, as did the first; for example, a well-laid garden: and nothing seems worth doing but the laying out of gardens. I should think fire the best thing in the world, if I were not acquainted with air, and water, and earth. For it is the right and property of all natural objects, of all genuine talents, of all native properties whatsoever, to be for their moment the top of the world. A squirrel leaping from bough to bough, and making the wood but one wide tree for his pleasure, fills the eye not less than a lion,—is beautiful, self-sufficing, and stands then and there for nature. A good ballad draws my ear and heart whilst I listen, as much as an epic has done before. A dog, drawn by a master, or a litter of pigs, satisfies, and is a reality not less than the frescoes of Angelo. From this succession of excellent objects, we learn at last the immensity of the world, the opulence of human nature, which can run out to infinitude in any direction. But I also learn that what astonished and fascinated me in the first work astonished me in the second work also; that excellence of all things is one.

The office of painting and sculpture seems to be merely initial. The best pictures can easily tell us their last secret. The best pictures are rude draughts of a few of the miraculous dots and lines and dyes which make up the ever-changing "landscape with figures" amidst which we dwell. Painting seems to be to the eye what dancing is to the limbs. When that has educated the frame to self-possession, to nimbleness, to grace, the steps of the dancing-master are better forgotten; so painting teaches me the splendor of color and the expression of form, and, as I see many pictures and higher genius in the art, I see the boundless opulence of the pencil, the indifferency in which the artist stands free to choose out of the possible forms. If he can draw every thing, why draw any thing? and then is my eye opened to the eternal picture which nature paints in the street with moving men and children, beggars, and fine ladies, draped in red, and green, and blue, and gray; long-haired, grizzled, white-faced, black-faced, wrinkled, giant, dwarf, expanded, elfish,—capped and based by heaven, earth, and sea.

A gallery of sculpture teaches more austerely the same lesson. As picture teaches the coloring, so sculpture the anatomy of form. When I have seen fine statues, and afterwards enter a public assembly, I understand well what he meant who said, "When I have been reading Homer, all men look like giants." I too see that painting and sculpture are gymnastics of the eye, its training to the niceties and curiosities of its function. There is no statue like this living man, with his infinite advantage over all ideal sculpture, of perpetual variety. What a gallery of art have I here! No mannerist made these varied groups and diverse original single figures. Here is the artist himself improvising, grim and glad, at his block. Now one thought strikes him, now another, and with each moment he alters the whole air, attitude, and expression of his clay. Away with your nonsense of oil and easels, of marble and chisels: except to open your eyes to the masteries of eternal art, they are hypocritical rubbish.

The reference of all production at last to an aboriginal Power explains the traits common to all works of the highest art,—that they are universally intelligible; that they restore to us the simplest states of mind; and are religious. Since what skill is therein shown is the reappearance of the original soul, a jet of pure light, it should produce a similar impression to that made by natural objects. In happy hours, nature appears to us one with art; art perfected,—the work of genius. And the individual, in whom simple tastes and susceptibility to all the great human influences overpower the accidents of a local and special culture, is the best critic of art. Though we travel the world over to find the beautiful, we must carry it with us, or we find it not. The best of beauty is a finer charm than skill in surfaces, in outlines, or rules of art can ever teach, namely, a radiation from the work of art of human character,—a wonderful expression through stone, or canvas, or musical sound, of the deepest and simplest attributes of our nature, and therefore most intelligible at last to those souls which have these attributes. In the sculptures of the Greeks, in the masonry of the Romans, and in the pictures of the Tuscan and Venetian masters, the highest charm is the universal language they speak. A confession of moral nature, of purity, love, and hope, breathes from them all. That which we carry to them, the same we bring back more fairly illustrated in the memory. The traveller who visits the Vatican, and passes from chamber to chamber through galleries of statues, vases, sarcophagi, and candelabra, through all forms of beauty, cut in the richest materials, is in danger of forgetting the simplicity of the principles out of which they all sprung, and that they had their origin from thoughts and laws in his own breast. He studies the technical rules on these wonderful remains, but forgets that these works were not always thus constellated; that they are the contributions of many ages and many countries; that each came out of the solitary workshop of one artist, who toiled perhaps in ignorance of the existence of other sculpture, created his work without other model, save life, household life, and the sweet and smart of personal relations, of beating hearts, and meeting eyes, of poverty, and necessity, and hope, and fear. These were his inspirations, and these are the effects he carries home to your heart and mind. In proportion to his force, the artist will find in his work an outlet for his proper character. He must not be in any manner pinched or hindered by his material, but through his necessity of imparting himself the adamant will be wax in his hands, and will allow an adequate communication of himself, in his full stature and proportion. He need not cumber himself with a conventional nature and culture, nor ask what is the mode in Rome or in Paris, but that house, and weather, and manner of living which poverty and the fate of birth have made at once so odious and so dear, in the gray, unpainted wood cabin, on the corner of a New Hampshire farm, or in the log-hut of the backwoods, or in the narrow lodging where he has endured the constraints and seeming of a city poverty, will serve as well as any other condition as the symbol of a thought which pours itself indifferently through all.

I remember, when in my younger days I had heard of the wonders of Italian painting, I fancied the great pictures would be great strangers; some surprising combination of color and form; a foreign wonder, barbaric pearl and gold, like the spontoons and standards of the militia, which play such pranks in the eyes and imaginations of school-boys. I was to see and acquire I knew not what. When I came at last to Rome, and saw with eyes the pictures, I found that genius left to novices the gay and fantastic and ostentatious, and it-self pierced directly to the simple and true; that it was familiar and sincere; that it was the old, eternal fact I had met already in so many forms,—unto which I lived; that it was the plain *you and me* I knew so well,—had left at home in so many conversations. I had the same experience already in a church at Naples. There I saw that nothing was changed with me but the place, and said to myself,—'Thou foolish child, hast thou come out hither, over four thousand miles of salt water, to find that which was perfect to thee there at home?'—that fact I saw again in the Academmia at Naples, in the chambers of sculpture, and yet again when I came to Rome, and to the paintings of Raphael, Angelo, Sacchi, Titian, and Leonardo da Vinci. "What, old mole! workest thou in the earth so fast?" It had travelled by my side: that which I fancied I had left in Boston was here in the Vatican, and again at Milan, and at Paris, and made all travelling ridiculous as a treadmill. I now require this of all pictures, that they domesticate me, not that they dazzle me. Pictures must not be too picturesque. Nothing astonishes men so much as common-sense and plain dealing. All great actions have been simple, and all great pic-tures are.

The Transfiguration, by Raphael, is an eminent example of

this peculiar merit. A calm, benignant beauty shines over all this picture, and goes directly to the heart. It seems almost to call you by name. The sweet and sublime face of Jesus is beyond praise, yet how it disappoints all florid expectations! This familiar, simple, home-speaking countenance is as if one should meet a friend. The knowledge of picture-dealers has its value, but listen not to their criticism when your heart is touched by genius. It was not painted for them, it was painted for you; for such as had eyes capable of being touched by simplicity and lofty emotions.

Yet when we have said all our fine things about the arts, we must end with a frank confession, that the arts, as we know them, are but initial. Our best praise is given to what they aimed and promised, not to the actual result. He has conceived meanly of the resources of man, who believes that the best age of production is past. The real value of the Iliad, or the Transfiguration, is as signs of power; billows or ripples they are of the stream of tendency; tokens of the everlasting effort to produce, which even in its worst estate the soul betrays. Art has not yet come to its maturity, if it do not put itself abreast with the most potent influences of the world, if it is not practical and moral, if it do not stand in connection with the conscience, if it do not make the poor and uncultivated feel that it addresses them with a voice of lofty cheer. There is higher work for Art than the arts. They are abortive births of an imperfect or vitiated instinct. Art is the need to create; but in its essence, immense and universal, it is impatient of working with lame or tied hands, and of making cripples and monsters, such as all pictures and statues are. Nothing less than the creation of man and nature is its end. A man should find in it an outlet for his whole energy. He may paint and carve only as long as he can do that. Art should exhilarate, and throw down the walls of circumstance on every side, awakening in the beholder the same sense of universal relation and power which the work evinced in the artist, and its highest effect is to make new artists.

Already History is old enough to witness the old age and disappearance of particular arts. The art of sculpture is long ago perished to any real effect. It was originally a useful art, a mode of writing, a savage's record of gratitude or devotion, and among a people possessed of a wonderful perception of form this childish carving was refined to the utmost splendor of effect. But it is the game of a rude and youthful people, and not the manly labor of a wise and spiritual nation. Under an oak-tree loaded with leaves and nuts, under a sky full of eternal eyes, I stand in a thoroughfare; but in the works of our plastic arts, and especially of sculpture, creation is driven into a corner. I cannot hide from myself that there is a certain appearance of paltriness, as of toys, and the trumpery of a theatre, in sculpture. Nature transcends all our moods of thought, and its secret we do not yet find. But the gallery stands at the mercy of our moods, and there is a moment when it becomes frivolous. I do not wonder that Newton, with an attention habitually engaged on the paths of planets and suns, should have wondered what the Earl of Pembroke found to admire in "stone dolls." Sculpture may serve to teach the pupil how deep is the secret of form, how purely the spirit can translate its meanings into that eloquent dialect. But the statue will look cold and false before that new activity which needs to roll through all things, and is impatient of counterfeits, and things not alive. Picture and sculpture are the celebrations and festivities of form. But true art is never fixed, but always flowing. The sweetest music is not in the oratorio, but in the human voice when it speaks from its instant life tones of tenderness, truth, or courage. The oratorio has already lost its relation to the morning, to the sun, and the earth, but that persuading voice is in tune with these. All works of art should not be detached, but extempore performances. A great man is a new statue in every attitude and action. A beautiful woman is a picture which drives all beholders nobly mad. Life may be lyric or epic, as well as a poem or a romance.

A true announcement of the law of creation, if a man were found worthy to declare it, would carry art up into the kingdom of nature, and destroy its separate and contrasted existence. The fountains of invention and beauty in modern society are all but dried up. A popular novel, a theatre, or a ball-room makes us feel that we are all paupers in the almshouse of this world, without dignity, without skill, or industry. Art is as poor and low. The old tragic Necessity, which lowers on the brows even of the Venuses and the Cupids of the antique, and furnishes the sole apology for the intrusion of such anomalous figures into nature,—namely, that they were inevitable; that the artist was drunk with a passion for form which he could not resist, and which vented itself in these fine extravagances,—no longer dignifies the chisel or the pencil. But the artist and the connoisseur now seek in art the exhibition of their talent, or an asylum from the evils of life. Men are not well pleased with the figure they make in their own imaginations, and they flee to art, and convey their better sense in an oratorio, a statue, or a picture. Art makes the same effort which a sensual prosperity makes; namely, to detach the beautiful from the useful, to do up the work as unavoidable, and, hating it, pass on to enjoyment. These solaces and compensations, this division of beauty from use, the laws of nature do not permit. As soon as beauty is sought, not from religion and love, but for pleasure, it degrades the seeker. High beauty is no longer attainable by him in canvas or in stone, in sound, or in lyrical construction; an effeminate, prudent, sickly beauty, which is not beauty, is all that can be formed; for the hand can never execute any thing higher than the character can inspire.

The art that thus separates is itself first separated. Art must not be a superficial talent, but must begin farther back in man. Now men do not see nature to be beautiful, and they go to make a statue which shall be. They abhor men as tasteless, dull, and inconvertible, and console themselves with color-bags, and blocks of marble. They reject life as prosaic, and create a death which they call poetic. They despatch the day's weary chores, and fly to voluptuous reveries. They eat and drink, that they may afterwards execute the ideal. Thus is art vilified; the name conveys to the mind its secondary and bad senses; it stands in the imagination as somewhat contrary to nature, and struck with death from the first. Would it not be better to begin higher up,—to serve the ideal before they eat and drink; to serve the ideal in eating and drinking, in drawing the breath, and in the functions of life? Beauty must come back to the useful arts, and the distinction between the fine and the useful arts be forgotten. If history were truly told, if life were nobly spent, it would be no longer easy or possible to distinguish the one from the other. In nature, all is useful, all is beautiful. It is therefore beautiful, because it is alive, moving, reproductive; it is therefore useful, because it is symmetrical and fair. Beauty will not come at the call of a legislature, nor will it repeat in England or America its history in Greece. It will come, as always, unannounced, and spring up between the feet of brave and earnest men. It is in vain that we look for genius to reiterate its miracles in the old arts; it is its instinct to find beauty and holiness in new and necessary facts, in the field and road-side, in the shop and mill. Proceeding from a religious heart it will raise to a divine use the railroad, the insurance office, the joint-stock company, our law, our primary assemblies, our commerce, the galvanic battery, the electric jar, the prism, and the chemist's retort, in which we seek now only an economical use. Is not the selfish and even cruel aspect which belongs to our great mechanical works,—to mills, railways, and machinery,—the effect of the mercenary impulses which these works obey? When its errands are noble and adequate, a steamboat bridging the Atlantic between Old and New England, and arriving at its ports with the punctuality of a planet, is a step of man into harmony with nature. The boat at St. Petersburgh, which plies along the Lena by magnetism, needs little to make it sublime. When science is learned in love, and its powers are wielded by love, they will appear the supplements and continuations of the material creation.

ESSAYS

Second Series

Contents

THE POET

A moody child and wildly wise
Pursued the game with joyful eyes,
Which chose, like meteors, their way,
And rived the dark with private ray:
They overleapt the horizon's edge,
Searched with Apollo's privilege;
Through man, and woman, and sea, and star,
Saw the dance of nature forward far;
Through worlds, and races, and terms, and times,
Saw musical order, and pairing rhymes.

Olympian bards who sung
　　Divine ideas below,
Which always find us young,
　　And always keep us so.

The Poet

THOSE who are esteemed umpires of taste, are often persons who have acquired some knowledge of admired pictures or sculptures, and have an inclination for whatever is elegant; but if you inquire whether they are beautiful souls, and whether their own acts are like fair pictures, you learn that they are selfish and sensual. Their cultivation is local, as if you should rub a log of dry wood in one spot to produce fire, all the rest remaining cold. Their knowledge of the fine arts is some study of rules and particulars, or some limited judgment of color or form, which is exercised for amusement or for show. It is a proof of the shallowness of the doctrine of beauty, as it lies in the minds of our amateurs, that men seem to have lost the perception of the instant dependence of form upon soul. There is no doctrine of forms in our philosophy. We were put into our bodies, as fire is put into a pan, to be carried about; but there is no accurate adjustment between the spirit and the organ, much less is the latter the germination of the former. So in regard to other forms, the intellectual men do not believe in any essential dependence of the material world on thought and volition. Theologians think it a pretty air-castle to talk of the spiritual meaning of a ship or a cloud, of a city or a contract, but they prefer to come again to the solid ground of historical evidence; and even the poets are contented with a civil and conformed manner of living, and to write poems from the fancy, at a safe distance from their own experience. But the highest minds of the world have never ceased to explore the double meaning, or, shall I say, the quadruple, or the centuple, or much more manifold meaning, of every sensuous fact: Orpheus, Empedocles, Heraclitus, Plato, Plutarch, Dante, Swedenborg, and the masters of sculpture, picture, and poetry. For we are not pans and barrows, nor even porters of the fire and torch-bearers, but children of the fire, made of it, and only the same divinity transmuted, and at two or three removes, when we know least about it. And this hidden truth, that the fountains whence all this river of Time, and its creatures, floweth, are intrinsically ideal and beautiful, draws us to the consideration of the nature and functions of the Poet, or the man of Beauty, to the means and materials he uses, and to the general aspect of the art in the present time.

The breadth of the problem is great, for the poet is representative. He stands among partial men for the complete man, and apprises us not of his wealth, but of the commonwealth. The young man reveres men of genius, because, to speak truly, they are more himself than he is. They receive of the soul as he also receives, but they more. Nature enhances her beauty, to the eye of loving men, from their belief that the poet is beholding her shows at the same time. He is isolated among his contemporaries, by truth and by his art, but with this consolation in his pursuits, that they will draw all men sooner or later. For all men live by truth, and stand in need of expression. In love, in art, in avarice, in politics, in labor, in games, we study to utter our painful secret. The man is only half himself, the other half is his expression.

Notwithstanding this necessity to be published, adequate expression is rare. I know not how it is that we need an interpreter; but the great majority of men seem to be minors, who have not yet come into possession of their own, or mutes, who cannot report the conversation they have had with nature. There is no man who does not anticipate a supersensual utility in the sun, and stars, earth, and water. These stand and wait to render him a peculiar service. But there is some obstruction, or some excess of phlegm in our constitution, which does not suffer them to yield the due effect. Too feeble fall the impressions of nature on us to make us artists. Every touch should thrill. Every man should be so much an artist, that he could report in conversation what had befallen him. Yet, in our experience, the rays or appulses have sufficient force to arrive at the senses, but not enough to reach the quick, and compel the reproduction of themselves in speech. The poet is the person in whom these powers are in balance, the man without impediment, who sees and handles that which others dream of, traverses the whole scale of experience, and its representative of man, in virtue of being the largest power to receive and to impart.

For the Universe has three children, born at one time, which reappear, under different names, in every system of thought, whether they be called cause, operation, and effect; or, more poetically, Jove, Pluto, Neptune; or, theologically, the Father, the Spirit, and the Son; but which we will call here, the Knower, the Doer, and the Sayer. These stand respectively for the love of truth, for the love of good, and for the love of beauty. These three are equal. Each is that which he is essentially, so that he cannot be surmounted or analyzed, and each of these three has the power of the others latent in him, and his own patent.

The poet is the sayer, the namer, and represents beauty. He is a sovereign, and stands on the centre. For the world is not painted, or adorned, but is from the beginning beautiful; and God has not made some beautiful things, but Beauty is the creator of the universe. Therefore the poet is not any permissive potentate, but is emperor in his own right. Criticism is infested with a cant of materialism, which assumes that manual skill and activity is the first merit of all men, and disparages such as say and do not, overlooking the fact, that some men, namely, poets, are natural sayers, sent into the world to the end of expression, and confounds them with those whose province is action, but who quit it to imitate the sayers. But Homer's words are as costly and admirable to Homer, as Agamemnon's victories are to Agamemnon. The poet does not wait for the hero or the sage, but, as they act and think primarily, so he writes primarily what will and must be spoken, reckoning the others, though primaries also, yet, in respect to him, secondaries and servants; as sitters or models in the studio of a painter, or as assistants who bring building materials to an architect.

For poetry was all written before time was, and whenever we are so finely organized that we can penetrate into that region where the air is music, we hear those primal warblings, and attempt to write them down, but we lose ever and anon a word, or a verse, and substitute something of our own, and thus miswrite the poem. The men of more delicate ear write down these cadences more faithfully, and these transcripts, though imperfect, become the songs of the nations. For nature is as truly beautiful as it is good, or as it is reasonable, and must as much appear, as it must be done, or be known. Words and deeds are quite indifferent modes of the divine energy. Words are also actions, and actions are a kind of words.

The sign and credentials of the poet are, that he announces that which no man foretold. He is the true and only doctor; he knows and tells; he is the only teller of news, for he was present and privy to the appearance which he describes. He is a beholder of ideas, and an utterer of the necessary and causal. For we do not speak now of men of poetical talents, or of industry and skill in metre, but of the true poet. I took part in a conversation the other day, concerning a recent writer of lyrics, a man of subtle mind, whose head appeared to be a music-box of delicate tunes and rhythms, and whose skill, and command of language, we could not sufficiently praise. But when the question arose, whether he was not only a lyrist, but a poet, we were obliged to confess that he is plainly a contemporary, not an eternal man. He does not stand out of our low limitations, like a Chimborazo under the line, running up from the torrid base through all the climates of the globe, with belts of the herbage of every latitude on its high and mottled sides; but this genius is the landscape-garden of a modern house, adorned with fountains and statues, with well-bred men and women standing and sitting in the walks and terraces. We hear, through all the varied music, the ground-tone of conventional life. Our poets are men of talents who sing, and not the children of music. The argument is secondary, the finish of the verses is primary.

For it is not metres, but a metre-making argument, that makes a poem,—a thought so passionate and alive, that, like the spirit of a plant or an animal, it has an architecture of its own, and adorns nature with a new thing. The thought and the form are equal in the order of time, but in the order of genesis the thought is prior to the form. The poet has a new thought: he has a whole new experience to unfold; he will tell us how it was with him, and all men will be the richer in his fortune. For, the experience of each new age requires a new confession, and the world seems always waiting for its poet. I remember, when I was young, how much I was moved one morning by tidings that genius had appeared in a youth who sat near me at table. He had left his work, and gone rambling none knew whither, and had written hundreds of lines, but could not tell whether that which was in him was therein told: he could tell nothing but that all was changed,—man, beast, heaven, earth, and sea. How gladly we listened! how credulous! Society seemed to be compromised. We sat in the aurora of a sunrise which was to put out all the stars. Boston seemed to be at twice the distance it had the night before, or was much farther than that. Rome,—what was Rome? Plutarch and Shakspeare were in the yellow leaf, and Homer no more should be heard of. It is much to know that poetry has been written this very day, under this very roof, by your side. What! that wonderful spirit has not expired! these stony moments are still sparkling and animated! I had fancied that the oracles were all silent, and nature had spent her fires, and behold! all night, from every pore, these fine auroras have been streaming. Every one has some interest in the advent of the poet, and no one knows how much it may concern him. We know that the secret of the world is profound, but who or what shall be our interpreter, we know not. A mountain ramble, a new style of face, a new person, may put the key into our hands. Of course, the value of genius to us is in the veracity of its report. Talent may frolic and juggle; genius realizes and adds. Mankind, in good earnest, have availed so far in understanding themselves and their work, that the foremost watchman on the peak announces his news. It is the truest word ever spoken, and the phrase will be the fittest, most musical, and the unerring voice of the world for that time.

All that we call sacred history attests that the birth of a poet is the principal event in chronology. Man, never so often deceived, still watches for the arrival of a brother who can hold him steady to a truth, until he has made it his own. With what joy I begin to read a poem, which I confide in as an inspiration! And now my chains are to be broken; I shall mount above these clouds and opaque airs in which I live,— opaque, though they seem transparent,—and from the heaven of truth I shall see and comprehend my relations. That will reconcile me to life, and renovate nature, to see trifles animated by a tendency, and to know what I am doing. Life will no more be a noise; now I shall see men and women, and know the signs by which they may be discerned from fools and satans. This day shall be better than my birth-day: then I became an animal: now I am invited into the science of the real. Such is the hope, but the fruition is postponed. Oftener it falls, that this winged man, who will carry me into the heaven, whirls me into the clouds, then leaps and frisks about with me from cloud to cloud, still affirming that he is bound heavenward; and I, being myself a novice, am slow in perceiving that he does not know the way into the heavens, and is merely bent that I should admire his skill to rise, like a fowl or a flying fish, a little way from the ground or the water; but the all-piercing, all-feeding, and ocular air of heaven, that man shall never inhabit. I tumble down again soon into my old nooks, and lead the life of exaggerations as before, and have lost my faith in the possibility of any guide who can lead me thither where I would be.

But leaving these victims of vanity, let us, with new hope, observe how nature, by worthier impulses, has ensured the poet's fidelity to his office of announcement and affirming, namely, by the beauty of things, which becomes a new, and higher beauty, when expressed. Nature offers all her creatures to him as a picture-language. Being used as a type, a second wonderful value appears in the object, far better than its old value, as the carpenter's stretched cord, if you hold your ear close enough, is musical in the breeze. "Things more excellent than every image," says Jamblichus, "are expressed through images." Things admit of being used as symbols, because nature is a symbol, in the whole, and in every part. Every line we can draw in the sand, has expression; and there is no body without its spirit or genius. All form is an effect of character; all condition, of the quality of the life; all harmony, of health; (and, for this reason, a perception of beauty should be sympathetic, or proper only to the good.) The beautiful rests on the foundations of the necessary. The soul makes the body, as the wise Spenser teaches:—

> "So every spirit, as it is most pure,
> And hath in it the more of heavenly light,
> So it the fairer body doth procure

To habit in, and it more fairly dight,
With cheerful grace and amiable sight.
For, of the soul, the body form doth take,
For soul is form, and doth the body make."

Here we find ourselves, suddenly, not in a critical speculation,
but in a holy place, and should go very warily and reverently.
We stand before the secret of the world, there where Being
passes into Appearance, and Unity into Variety.

The Universe is the externisation of the soul. Wherever the
life is, that bursts into appearance around it. Our science is
sensual, and therefore superficial. The earth, and the heavenly
bodies, physics, and chemistry, we sensually treat, as if they
were self-existent; but these are the retinue of that Being we
have. "The mighty heaven," said Proclus, "exhibits, in its
transfigurations, clear images of the splendor of intellectual
perceptions; being moved in conjunction with the unapparent
periods of intellectual natures." Therefore, science always goes
abreast with the just elevation of the man, keeping step with
religion and metaphysics; or, the state of science is an index
of our self-knowledge. Since everything in nature answers to
a moral power, if any phenomenon remains brute and dark,
it is that the corresponding faculty in the observer is not yet
active.

No wonder, then, if these waters be so deep, that we hover
over them with a religious regard. The beauty of the fable
proves the importance of the sense; to the poet, and to all
others; or, if you please, every man is so far a poet as to be
susceptible of these enchantments of nature: for all men have
the thoughts whereof the universe is the celebration. I find
that the fascination resides in the symbol. Who loves nature?
Who does not? Is it only poets, and men of leisure and cultivation, who live with her? No; but also hunters, farmers,
grooms, and butchers, though they express their affection in
their choice of life, and not in their choice of words. The
writer wonders what the coachman or the hunter values in
riding, in horses, and dogs. It is not superficial qualities.
When you talk with him, he holds these at as slight a rate as
you. His worship is sympathetic; he has no definitions, but
he is commanded in nature, by the living power which he

feels to be there present. No imitation, or playing of these things, would content him; he loves the earnest of the north-wind, of rain, of stone, and wood, and iron. A beauty not explicable, is dearer than a beauty which we can see to the end of. It is nature the symbol, nature certifying the super-natural, body overflowed by life, which he worships, with coarse, but sincere rites.

The inwardness, and mystery, of this attachment, drives men of every class to the use of emblems. The schools of poets, and philosophers, are not more intoxicated with their symbols, than the populace with theirs. In our political par-ties, compute the power of badges and emblems. See the great ball which they roll from Baltimore to Bunker hill! In the political processions, Lowell goes in a loom, and Lynn in a shoe, and Salem in a ship. Witness the cider-barrel, the log-cabin, the hickory-stick, the palmetto, and all the cognizances of party. See the power of national emblems. Some stars, lilies, leopards, a crescent, a lion, an eagle, or other figure, which came into credit God knows how, on an old rag of bunting, blowing in the wind, on a fort, at the ends of the earth, shall make the blood tingle under the rudest, or the most conventional exterior. The people fancy they hate poetry, and they are all poets and mystics!

Beyond this universality of the symbolic language, we are apprised of the divineness of this superior use of things, whereby the world is a temple, whose walls are covered with emblems, pictures, and commandments of the Deity, in this, that there is no fact in nature which does not carry the whole sense of nature; and the distinctions which we make in events, and in affairs, of low and high, honest and base, disappear when nature is used as a symbol. Thought makes every thing fit for use. The vocabulary of an omniscient man would em-brace words and images excluded from polite conversation. What would be base, or even obscene, to the obscene, be-comes illustrious, spoken in a new connexion of thought. The piety of the Hebrew prophets purges their grossness. The cir-cumcision is an example of the power of poetry to raise the low and offensive. Small and mean things serve as well as great symbols. The meaner the type by which a law is ex-pressed, the more pungent it is, and the more lasting in the memories of men: just as we choose the smallest box, or case, in which any needful utensil can be carried. Bare lists of words are found suggestive, to an imaginative and excited mind; as it is related of Lord Chatham, that he was accustomed to read in Bailey's Dictionary, when he was preparing to speak in Parliament. The poorest experience is rich enough for all the purposes of expressing thought. Why covet a knowledge of new facts? Day and night, house and garden, a few books, a few actions, serve us as well as would all trades and all spectacles. We are far from having exhausted the significance of the few symbols we use. We can come to use them yet with a terrible simplicity. It does not need that a poem should be long. Every word was once a poem. Every new relation is a new word. Also, we use defects and deformities to a sacred purpose, so expressing our sense that the evils of the world are such only to the evil eye. In the old mythology, mythologists observe, defects are ascribed to divine natures, as lameness to Vulcan, blindness to Cupid, and the like, to signify exuberances.

For, as it is dislocation and detachment from the life of God, that makes things ugly, the poet, who re-attaches things to nature and the Whole,—re-attaching even artificial things, and violations of nature, to nature, by a deeper insight,—disposes very easily of the most disagreeable facts. Readers of poetry see the factory-village, and the railway, and fancy that the poetry of the landscape is broken up by these; for these works of art are not yet consecrated in their reading; but the poet sees them fall within the great Order not less than the bee-hive, or the spider's geometrical web. Nature adopts them very fast into her vital circles, and the gliding train of cars she loves like her own. Besides, in a centred mind, it signifies nothing how many mechanical inventions you exhibit. Though you add millions, and never so surprising, the fact of mechanics has not gained a grain's weight. The spiritual fact remains unalterable, by many or by few particulars; as no mountain is of any appreciable height to break the curve of the sphere. A shrewd country-boy goes to the city for the first time, and the complacent citizen is not satisfied with his little wonder. It is not that he does not see all the fine houses, and know that he never saw such before, but he disposes of them as easily as the poet finds place for the railway. The chief value of the new fact, is to enhance the great and constant fact of Life, which can dwarf any and every circumstance, and to which the belt of wampum, and the commerce of America, are alike.

The world being thus put under the mind for verb and noun, the poet is he who can articulate it. For, though life is great, and fascinates, and absorbs,—and though all men are intelligent of the symbols through which it is named,—yet they cannot originally use them. We are symbols, and inhabit symbols; workman, work, and tools, words and things, birth and death, all are emblems; but we sympathize with the symbols, and, being infatuated with the economical uses of things, we do not know that they are thoughts. The poet, by an ulterior intellectual perception, gives them a power which makes their old use forgotten, and puts eyes, and a tongue, into every dumb and inanimate object. He perceives the independence of the thought on the symbol, the stability of the thought, the accidency and fugacity of the symbol. As the eyes of Lyncæus were said to see through the earth, so the poet turns the world to glass, and shows us all things in their right series and procession. For, through that better perception, he stands one step nearer to things, and sees the flowing or metamorphosis; perceives that thought is multiform; that within the form of every creature is a force impelling it to ascend into a higher form; and, following with his eyes the life, uses the forms which express that life, and so his speech flows with the flowing of nature. All the facts of the animal economy, sex, nutriment, gestation, birth, growth, are symbols of the passage of the world into the soul of man, to suffer there a change, and reappear a new and higher fact. He uses forms according to the life, and not according to the form. This is true science. The poet alone knows astronomy, chemistry, vegetation, and animation, for he does not stop at these facts, but employs them as signs. He knows why the plain, or meadow of space, was strown with these flowers we call suns, and moons, and stars; why the great deep is adorned with animals, with men, and gods; for, in every word he speaks he rides on them as the horses of thought.

By virtue of this science the poet is the Namer, or Language-maker, naming things sometimes after their appearance, sometimes after their essence, and giving to every one its own name and not another's, thereby rejoicing the intellect, which delights in detachment or boundary. The poets made all the words, and therefore language is the archives of history, and, if we must say it, a sort of tomb of the muses. For, though the origin of most of our words is forgotten, each word was at first a stroke of genius, and obtained currency, because for the moment it symbolized the world to the first speaker and to the hearer. The etymologist finds the deadest word to have been once a brilliant picture. Language is fossil poetry. As the limestone of the continent consists of infinite masses of the shells of animalcules, so language is made up of images, or tropes, which now, in their secondary use, have long ceased to remind us of their poetic origin. But the poet names the thing because he sees it, or comes one step nearer to it than any other. This expression, or naming, is not art, but a second nature, grown out of the first, as a leaf out of a tree. What we call nature, is a certain self-regulated motion, or change; and nature does all things by her own hands, and does not leave another to baptise her, but baptises herself; and this through the metamorphosis again. I remember that a certain poet described it to me thus:

Genius is the activity which repairs the decays of things, whether wholly or partly of a material and finite kind. Nature, through all her kingdoms, insures herself. Nobody cares for planting the poor fungus: so she shakes down from the gills of one agaric countless spores, any one of which, being preserved, transmits new billions of spores to-morrow or next day. The new agaric of this hour has a chance which the old one had not. This atom of seed is thrown into a new place, not subject to the accidents which destroyed its parent two rods off. She makes a man; and having brought him to ripe age, she will no longer run the risk of losing this wonder at a blow, but she detaches from him a new self, that the kind may be safe from accidents to which the individual is exposed. So when the soul of the poet has come to ripeness of thought, she detaches and sends away from it its poems or songs,—a fearless, sleepless, deathless progeny, which is not exposed to the accidents of the weary kingdom of time: a fearless, vivacious offspring, clad with wings (such was the virtue of the soul out of which they came), which carry them fast and far, and infix them irrecoverably into the hearts of men. These wings are the beauty of the poet's soul. The songs, thus flying immortal from their mortal parent, are pursued by clamorous flights of censures, which swarm in far greater numbers, and threaten to devour them; but these last are not winged. At the end of a very short leap they fall plump down, and rot, having received from the souls out of which they came no beautiful wings. But the melodies of the poet ascend, and leap, and pierce into the deeps of infinite time.

So far the bard taught me, using his freer speech. But nature has a higher end, in the production of new individuals, than security, namely, *ascension*, or, the passage of the soul into higher forms. I knew, in my younger days, the sculptor who made the statue of the youth which stands in the public garden. He was, as I remember, unable to tell directly, what made him happy, or unhappy, but by wonderful indirections he could tell. He rose one day, according to his habit, before the dawn, and saw the morning break, grand as the eternity out of which it came, and, for many days after, he strove to express this tranquillity, and, lo! his chisel had fashioned out of marble the form of a beautiful youth, Phosphorus, whose aspect is such, that, it is said, all persons who look on it become silent. The poet also resigns himself to his mood, and that thought which agitated him is expressed, but *alter idem*, in a manner totally new. The expression is organic, or, the new type which things themselves take when liberated. As, in the sun, objects paint their images on the retina of the eye, so they, sharing the aspiration of the whole universe, tend to paint a far more delicate copy of their essence in his mind. Like the metamorphosis of things into higher organic forms, is their change into melodies. Over everything stands its dæmon, or soul, and, as the form of the thing is reflected by the eye, so the soul of the thing is reflected by a melody. The sea, the mountain-ridge, Niagara, and every flower-bed, pre-exist, or super-exist, in pre-cantations, which sail like odors in the air, and when any man goes by with an ear sufficiently fine, he overhears them, and endeavors to write down the notes, without diluting or depraving them. And herein is the legitimation of criticism, in the mind's faith, that the poems are a corrupt version of some text in nature, with which they ought to be made to tally. A rhyme in one of our sonnets should not be less pleasing than the iterated nodes of a sea-shell, or the resembling difference of a group of flowers. The pairing of the birds is an idyl, not tedious as our idyls are; a tempest is a rough ode, without falsehood or rant: a summer, with its harvest sown, reaped, and stored, is an epic song, subordinating how many admirably executed parts. Why should not the symmetry and truth that modulate these, glide into our spirits, and we participate the invention of nature?

This insight, which expresses itself by what is called Imagination, is a very high sort of seeing, which does not come by study, but by the intellect being where and what it sees, by sharing the path, or circuit of things through forms, and so making them translucid to others. The path of things is silent. Will they suffer a speaker to go with them? A spy they will not suffer; a lover, a poet, is the transcendency of their own nature,—him they will suffer. The condition of true naming, on the poet's part, is his resigning himself to the divine *aura* which breathes through forms, and accompanying that.

It is a secret which every intellectual man quickly learns, that, beyond the energy of his possessed and conscious intellect, he is capable of a new energy (as of an intellect doubled on itself), by abandonment to the nature of things; that, beside his privacy of power as an individual man, there is a great public power, on which he can draw, by unlocking, at all risks, his human doors, and suffering the ethereal tides to roll and circulate through him: then he is caught up into the life of the Universe, his speech is thunder, his thought is law, and his words are universally intelligible as the plants and animals. The poet knows that he speaks adequately, then, only when he speaks somewhat wildly, or, "with the flower of the mind;" not with the intellect, used as an organ, but with the intellect released from all service, and suffered to take its direction from its celestial life; or, as the ancients were wont to express themselves, not with intellect alone, but with the in-

tellect inebriated by nectar. As the traveller who has lost his
way, throws his reins on his horse's neck, and trusts to the
instinct of the animal to find his road, so must we do with
the divine animal who carries us through this world. For if in
any manner we can stimulate this instinct, new passages
are opened for us into nature, the mind flows into and
through things hardest and highest, and the metamorphosis
is possible.

This is the reason why bards love wine, mead, narcotics,
coffee, tea, opium, the fumes of sandal-wood and tobacco, or
whatever other species of animal exhilaration. All men avail
themselves of such means as they can, to add this extraordinary power to their normal powers; and to this end they prize
conversation, music, pictures, sculpture, dancing, theatres,
travelling, war, mobs, fires, gaming, politics, or love, or science, or animal intoxication, which are several coarser or finer
quasi-mechanical substitutes for the true nectar, which is the
ravishment of the intellect by coming nearer to the fact. These
are auxiliaries to the centrifugal tendency of a man, to his
passage out into free space, and they help him to escape the
custody of that body in which he is pent up, and of that jail-
yard of individual relations in which he is enclosed. Hence a
great number of such as were professionally expressors of
Beauty, as painters, poets, musicians, and actors, have been
more than others wont to lead a life of pleasure and indulgence; all but the few who received the true nectar; and, as it
was a spurious mode of attaining freedom, as it was an emancipation not into the heavens, but into the freedom of baser
places, they were punished for that advantage they won, by a
dissipation and deterioration. But never can any advantage be
taken of nature by a trick. The spirit of the world, the great
calm presence of the creator, comes not forth to the sorceries
of opium or of wine. The sublime vision comes to the pure
and simple soul in a clean and chaste body. That is not an
inspiration which we owe to narcotics, but some counterfeit
excitement and fury. Milton says, that the lyric poet may
drink wine and live generously, but the epic poet, he who
shall sing of the gods, and their descent unto men, must drink
water out of a wooden bowl. For poetry is not 'Devil's wine,'
but God's wine. It is with this as it is with toys. We fill the

hands and nurseries of our children with all manner of dolls, drums, and horses, withdrawing their eyes from the plain face and sufficing objects of nature, the sun, and moon, the animals, the water, and stones, which should be their toys. So the poet's habit of living should be set on a key so low and plain, that the common influences should delight him. His cheerfulness should be the gift of the sunlight; the air should suffice for his inspiration, and he should be tipsy with water. That spirit which suffices quiet hearts, which seems to come forth to such from every dry knoll of sere grass, from every pine-stump, and half-imbedded stone, on which the dull March sun shines, comes forth to the poor and hungry, and such as are of simple taste. If thou fill thy brain with Boston and New York, with fashion and covetousness, and wilt stimulate thy jaded senses with wine and French coffee, thou shalt find no radiance of wisdom in the lonely waste of the pine-woods.

If the imagination intoxicates the poet, it is not inactive in other men. The metamorphosis excites in the beholder an emotion of joy. The use of symbols has a certain power of emancipation and exhilaration for all men. We seem to be touched by a wand, which makes us dance and run about happily, like children. We are like persons who come out of a cave or cellar into the open air. This is the effect on us of tropes, fables, oracles, and all poetic forms. Poets are thus liberating gods. Men have really got a new sense, and found within their world, another world, or nest of worlds; for, the metamorphosis once seen, we divine that it does not stop. I will not now consider how much this makes the charm of algebra and the mathematics, which also have their tropes, but it is felt in every definition; as, when Aristotle defines *space* to be an immovable vessel, in which things are contained;—or, when Plato defines a *line* to be a flowing point; or, *figure* to be a bound of solid; and many the like. What a joyful sense of freedom we have, when Vitruvius announces the old opinion of artists, that no architect can build any house well, who does not know something of anatomy. When Socrates, in Charmides, tells us that the soul is cured of its maladies by certain incantations, and that these incantations are beautiful reasons, from which temperance is generated in souls; when Plato calls the world an animal; and Timæus affirms that the plants also are animals; or affirms a man to be a heavenly tree, growing with his root, which is his head, upward; and, as George Chapman, following him, writes,—

> "So in our tree of man, whose nervie root
>   Springs in his top;"

when Orpheus speaks of hoariness as "that white flower which marks extreme old age;" when Proclus calls the universe the statue of the intellect; when Chaucer, in his praise of 'Gentilesse,' compares good blood in mean condition to fire, which, though carried to the darkest house betwixt this and the mount of Caucasus, will yet hold its natural office, and burn as bright as if twenty thousand men did it behold; when John saw, in the apocalypse, the ruin of the world through evil, and the stars fall from heaven, as the figtree casteth her untimely fruit; when Æsop reports the whole catalogue of common daily relations through the masquerade of birds and beasts;—we take the cheerful hint of the immortality of our essence, and its versatile habit and escapes, as when the gypsies say, "it is in vain to hang them, they cannot die."

The poets are thus liberating gods. The ancient British bards had for the title of their order, "Those who are free throughout the world." They are free, and they make free. An imaginative book renders us much more service at first, by stimulating us through its tropes, than afterward, when we arrive at the precise sense of the author. I think nothing is of any value in books, excepting the transcendental and extraordinary. If a man is inflamed and carried away by his thought, to that degree that he forgets the authors and the public, and heeds only this one dream, which holds him like an insanity, let me read his paper, and you may have all the arguments and histories and criticism. All the value which attaches to Pythagoras, Paracelsus, Cornelius Agrippa, Cardan, Kepler, Swedenborg, Schelling, Oken, or any other who introduces questionable facts into his cosmogony, as angels, devils, magic, astrology, palmistry, mesmerism, and so on, is the certificate we have of departure from routine, and that here is a new witness. That also is the best success in conversation, the magic of liberty, which puts the world, like a ball, in our hands. How cheap even the liberty then seems; how mean to study, when an emotion communicates to the intellect the power to sap and upheave nature: how great the perspective! nations, times, systems, enter and disappear, like threads in tapestry of large figure and many colors; dream delivers us to dream, and, while the drunkenness lasts, we will sell our bed, our philosophy, our religion, in our opulence.

There is good reason why we should prize this liberation. The fate of the poor shepherd, who, blinded and lost in the snow-storm, perishes in a drift within a few feet of his cottage door, is an emblem of the state of man. On the brink of the waters of life and truth, we are miserably dying. The inaccessibleness of every thought but that we are in, is wonderful. What if you come near to it,—you are as remote, when you are nearest, as when you are farthest. Every thought is also a prison; every heaven is also a prison. Therefore we love the poet, the inventor, who in any form, whether in an ode, or in an action, or in looks and behavior, has yielded us a new thought. He unlocks our chains, and admits us to a new scene.

This emancipation is dear to all men, and the power to impart it, as it must come from greater depth and scope of thought, is a measure of intellect. Therefore all books of the imagination endure, all which ascend to that truth, that the writer sees nature beneath him, and uses it as his exponent. Every verse or sentence, possessing this virtue, will take care of its own immortality. The religions of the world are the ejaculations of a few imaginative men.

But the quality of the imagination is to flow, and not to freeze. The poet did not stop at the color, or the form, but read their meaning; neither may he rest in this meaning, but he makes the same objects exponents of his new thought. Here is the difference betwixt the poet and the mystic, that the last nails a symbol to one sense, which was a true sense for a moment, but soon becomes old and false. For all symbols are fluxional; all language is vehicular and transitive, and is good, as ferries and horses are, for conveyance, not as farms and houses are, for homestead. Mysticism consists in the mistake of an accidental and individual symbol for an universal one. The morning-redness happens to be the favorite meteor to the eyes of Jacob Behmen, and comes to stand to him for truth and faith; and he believes should stand for the same realities to every reader. But the first reader prefers as naturally the symbol of a mother and child, or a gardener and his bulb, or a jeweller polishing a gem. Either of these, or of a myriad more, are equally good to the person to whom they are significant. Only they must be held lightly, and be very willingly translated into the equivalent terms which others use. And the mystic must be steadily told,—All that you say is just as true without the tedious use of that symbol as with it. Let us have a little algebra, instead of this trite rhetoric,— universal signs, instead of these village symbols,—and we shall both be gainers. The history of hierarchies seems to show, that all religious error consisted in making the symbol too stark and solid, and, at last, nothing but an excess of the organ of language.

Swedenborg, of all men in the recent ages, stands eminently for the translator of nature into thought. I do not know the man in history to whom things stood so uniformly for words. Before him the metamorphosis continually plays. Everything on which his eye rests, obeys the impulses of moral nature. The figs become grapes whilst he eats them. When some of his angels affirmed a truth, the laurel twig which they held blossomed in their hands. The noise which, at a distance, appeared like gnashing and thumping, on coming nearer was found to be the voice of disputants. The men, in one of his visions, seen in heavenly light, appeared like dragons, and seemed in darkness: but, to each other, they appeared as men, and, when the light from heaven shone into their cabin, they complained of the darkness, and were compelled to shut the window that they might see.

There was this perception in him, which makes the poet or seer, an object of awe and terror, namely, that the same man, or society of men, may wear one aspect to themselves and their companions, and a different aspect to higher intelligences. Certain priests, whom he describes as conversing very learnedly together, appeared to the children, who were at some distance, like dead horses: and many the like misappearances. And instantly the mind inquires, whether these fishes under the bridge, yonder oxen in the pasture, those dogs in the yard, are immutably fishes, oxen, and dogs, or only so appear to me, and perchance to themselves appear upright men; and whether I appear as a man to all eyes. The Bramins and Pythagoras propounded the same question, and if any poet has witnessed the transformation, he doubtless found it in harmony with various experiences. We have all seen changes as considerable in wheat and caterpillars. He is the poet, and shall draw us with love and terror, who sees, through the flowing vest, the firm nature, and can declare it.

I look in vain for the poet whom I describe. We do not, with sufficient plainness, or sufficient profoundness, address ourselves to life, nor dare we chaunt our own times and social circumstance. If we filled the day with bravery, we should not shrink from celebrating it. Time and nature yield us many gifts, but not yet the timely man, the new religion, the reconciler, whom all things await. Dante's praise is, that he dared to write his autobiography in colossal cipher, or into universality. We have yet had no genius in America, with tyrannous eye, which knew the value of our incomparable materials, and saw, in the barbarism and materialism of the times, another carnival of the same gods whose picture he so much admires in Homer; then in the middle age; then in Calvinism. Banks and tariffs, the newspaper and caucus, methodism and unitarianism, are flat and dull to dull people, but rest on the same foundations of wonder as the town of Troy, and the temple of Delphos, and are as swiftly passing away. Our logrolling, our stumps and their politics, our fisheries, our Negroes, and Indians, our boasts, and our repudiations, the wrath of rogues, and the pusillanimity of honest men, the northern trade, the southern planting, the western clearing, Oregon, and Texas, are yet unsung. Yet America is a poem in our eyes; its ample geography dazzles the imagination, and it will not wait long for metres. If I have not found that excellent combination of gifts in my countrymen which I seek, neither could I aid myself to fix the idea of the poet by reading now and then in Chalmers's collection of five centuries of English poets. These are wits, more than poets, though there have been poets among them. But when we adhere to the ideal of the poet, we have our difficulties even with Milton and Homer. Milton is too literary, and Homer too literal and historical.

But I am not wise enough for a national criticism, and must use the old largeness a little longer, to discharge my errand from the muse to the poet concerning his art.

Art is the path of the creator to his work. The paths, or methods, are ideal and eternal, though few men ever see them, not the artist himself for years, or for a lifetime, unless he come into the conditions. The painter, the sculptor, the composer, the epic rhapsodist, the orator, all partake one desire, namely, to express themselves symmetrically and abundantly, not dwarfishly and fragmentarily. They found or put themselves in certain conditions, as, the painter and sculptor before some impressive human figures; the orator, into the assembly of the people; and the others, in such scenes as each has found exciting to his intellect; and each presently feels the new desire. He hears a voice, he sees a beckoning. Then he is apprised, with wonder, what herds of dæmons hem him in. He can no more rest; he says, with the old painter, "By God, it is in me, and must go forth of me." He pursues a beauty, half seen, which flies before him. The poet pours out verses in every solitude. Most of the things he says are conventional, no doubt; but by and by he says something which is original and beautiful. That charms him. He would say nothing else but such things. In our way of talking, we say, 'That is yours, this is mine;' but the poet knows well that it is not his; that it is as strange and beautiful to him as to you; he would fain hear the like eloquence at length. Once having tasted this immortal ichor, he cannot have enough of it, and, as an admirable creative power exists in these intellections, it is of the last importance that these things get spoken. What a little of all we know is said! What drops of all the sea of our science are baled up! and by what accident it is that these are exposed, when so many secrets sleep in nature! Hence the necessity of speech and song; hence these throbs and heart-beatings in the orator, at the door of the assembly, to the end, namely, that thought may be ejaculated as Logos, or Word.

Doubt not, O poet, but persist. Say, 'It is in me, and shall out.' Stand there, baulked and dumb, stuttering and stammering, hissed and hooted, stand and strive, until, at last, rage draw out of thee that *dream*-power which every night shows thee is thine own; a power transcending all limit and privacy, and by virtue of which a man is the conductor of the whole river of electricity. Nothing walks, or creeps, or grows, or exists, which must not in turn arise and walk before him as exponent of his meaning. Comes he to that power, his genius is no longer exhaustible. All the creatures, by pairs and by tribes, pour into his mind as into a Noah's ark, to come forth again to people a new world. This is like the stock of air for our respiration, or for the combustion of our fireplace, not a measure of gallons, but the entire atmosphere if wanted. And therefore the rich poets, as Homer, Chaucer, Shakspeare, and Raphael, have obviously no limits to their works, except the limits of their lifetime, and resemble a mirror carried through the street, ready to render an image of every created thing.

O poet! a new nobility is conferred in groves and pastures, and not in castles, or by the sword-blade, any longer. The conditions are hard, but equal. Thou shalt leave the world, and know the muse only. Thou shalt not know any longer the times, customs, graces, politics, or opinions of men, but shalt take all from the muse. For the time of towns is tolled from the world by funereal chimes, but in nature the universal hours are counted by succeeding tribes of animals and plants, and by growth of joy on joy. God wills also that thou abdicate a manifold and duplex life, and that thou be content that others speak for thee. Others shall be thy gentlemen, and shall represent all courtesy and worldly life for thee; others shall do the great and resounding actions also. Thou shalt lie close hid with nature, and canst not be afforded to the Capitol or the Exchange. The world is full of renunciations and apprenticeships, and this is thine: thou must pass for a fool and a churl for a long season. This is the screen and sheath in which Pan has protected his well-beloved flower, and thou shalt be known only to thine own, and they shall console thee with tenderest love. And thou shalt not be able to rehearse the names of thy friends in thy verse, for an old shame before the holy ideal. And this is the reward: that the ideal shall be real to thee, and the impressions of the actual world shall fall like summer rain, copious, but not troublesome, to thy invulnerable essence. Thou shalt have the whole land for thy park and manor, the sea for thy bath and navigation, without tax and without envy; the woods and the rivers thou shalt own; and thou shalt possess that wherein others are only tenants and boarders. Thou true land-lord! sea-lord! air-lord! Wherever snow falls, or water flows, or birds fly, wherever day and night meet in twilight, wherever the blue heaven is hung by clouds, or sown with stars, wherever are forms with transparent boundaries, wherever are outlets into celestial space, wherever is danger, and awe, and love, there is Beauty, plenteous as rain, shed for thee, and though thou shouldest walk the world over, thou shalt not be able to find a condition inopportune or ignoble.

EXPERIENCE

———

THE lords of life, the lords of life,—
I saw them pass,
In their own guise,
Like and unlike,
Portly and grim,
Use and Surprise,
Surface and Dream,
Succession swift, and spectral Wrong,
Temperament without a tongue,
And the inventor of the game
Omnipresent without name;—
Some to see, some to be guessed,
They marched from east to west:
Little man, least of all,
Among the legs of his guardians tall,
Walked about with puzzled look:—
Him by the hand dear nature took;
Dearest nature, strong and kind,
Whispered, 'Darling, never mind!
Tomorrow they will wear another face,
The founder thou! these are thy race!'

Experience

WHERE do we find ourselves? In a series of which we do not know the extremes, and believe that it has none. We wake and find ourselves on a stair; there are stairs below us, which we seem to have ascended; there are stairs above us, many a one, which go upward and out of sight. But the Genius which, according to the old belief, stands at the door by which we enter, and gives us the lethe to drink, that we may tell no tales, mixed the cup too strongly, and we cannot shake off the lethargy now at noonday. Sleep lingers all our lifetime about our eyes, as night hovers all day in the boughs of the fir-tree. All things swim and glitter. Our life is not so much threatened as our perception. Ghostlike we glide through nature, and should not know our place again. Did our birth fall in some fit of indigence and frugality in nature, that she was so sparing of her fire and so liberal of her earth, that it appears to us that we lack the affirmative principle, and though we have health and reason, yet we have no superfluity of spirit for new creation? We have enough to live and bring the year about, but not an ounce to impart or to invest. Ah that our Genius were a little more of a genius! We are like millers on the lower levels of a stream, when the factories above them have exhausted the water. We too fancy that the upper people must have raised their dams.

If any of us knew what we were doing, or where we are going, then when we think we best know! We do not know today whether we are busy or idle. In times when we thought ourselves indolent, we have afterwards discovered, that much was accomplished, and much was begun in us. All our days are so unprofitable while they pass, that 'tis wonderful where or when we ever got anything of this which we call wisdom, poetry, virtue. We never got it on any dated calendar day. Some heavenly days must have been intercalated somewhere, like those that Hermes won with dice of the Moon, that Osiris might be born. It is said, all martyrdoms looked mean when they were suffered. Every ship is a romantic object, except that we sail in. Embark, and the romance quits our vessel, and hangs on every other sail in the horizon. Our life looks trivial, and we shun to record it. Men seem to have learned of the horizon the art of perpetual retreating and reference. 'Yonder uplands are rich pasturage, and my neighbor has fertile meadow, but my field,' says the querulous farmer, 'only holds the world together.' I quote another man's saying; unluckily, that other withdraws himself in the same way, and quotes me. 'Tis the trick of nature thus to degrade today; a good deal of buzz, and somewhere a result slipped magically in. Every roof is agreeable to the eye, until it is lifted; then we find tragedy and moaning women, and hard-eyed husbands, and deluges of lethe, and the men ask, 'What's the news?' as if the old were so bad. How many individuals can we count in society? how many actions? how many opinions? So much of our time is preparation, so much is routine, and so much retrospect, that the pith of each man's genius contracts itself to a very few hours. The history of literature — take the net result of Tiraboschi, Warton, or Schlegel, — is a sum of very few ideas, and of very few original tales, — all the rest being variation of these. So in this great society wide lying around us, a critical analysis would find very few spontaneous actions. It is almost all custom and gross sense. There are even few opinions, and these seem organic in the speakers, and do not disturb the universal necessity.

What opium is instilled into all disaster! It shows formidable as we approach it, but there is at last no rough rasping friction, but the most slippery sliding surfaces. We fall soft on a thought. *Ate Dea* is gentle,

> "Over men's heads walking aloft,
> With tender feet treading so soft."

People give and bemoan themselves, but it is not half so bad with them as they say. There are moods in which we court suffering, in the hope that here, at least, we shall find reality, sharp peaks and edges of truth. But it turns out to be scene-painting and counterfeit. The only thing grief has taught me, is to know how shallow it is. That, like all the rest, plays about the surface, and never introduces me into the reality, for contact with which, we would even pay the costly price of sons and lovers. Was it Boscovich who found out that bodies never come in contact? Well, souls never touch their objects. An innavigable sea washes with silent waves between us and the things we aim at and converse with. Grief too will make us idealists. In the death of my son, now more than two years ago, I seem to have lost a beautiful estate,—no more. I cannot get it nearer to me. If tomorrow I should be informed of the bankruptcy of my principal debtors, the loss of my property would be a great inconvenience to me, perhaps, for many years; but it would leave me as it found me,—neither better nor worse. So is it with this calamity: it does not touch me: some thing which I fancied was a part of me, which could not be torn away without tearing me, nor enlarged without enriching me, falls off from me, and leaves no scar. It was caducous. I grieve that grief can teach me nothing, nor carry me one step into real nature. The Indian who was laid under a curse, that the wind should not blow on him, nor water flow to him, nor fire burn him, is a type of us all. The dearest events are summer-rain, and we the Para coats that shed every drop. Nothing is left us now but death. We look to that with a grim satisfaction, saying, there at least is reality that will not dodge us.

I take this evanescence and lubricity of all objects, which lets them slip through our fingers then when we clutch hardest, to be the most unhandsome part of our condition. Nature does not like to be observed, and likes that we should be her fools and playmates. We may have the sphere for our cricket-ball, but not a berry for our philosophy. Direct strokes she never gave us power to make; all our blows glance, all our hits are accidents. Our relations to each other are oblique and casual.

Dream delivers us to dream, and there is no end to illusion. Life is a train of moods like a string of beads, and, as we pass through them, they prove to be many-colored lenses which paint the world their own hue, and each shows only what lies in its focus. From the mountain you see the mountain. We animate what we can, and we see only what we animate. Nature and books belong to the eyes that see them. It depends on the mood of the man, whether he shall see the sunset or the fine poem. There are always sunsets, and there is always genius; but only a few hours so serene that we can relish nature or criticism. The more or less depends on structure or temperament. Temperament is the iron wire on which the beads are strung. Of what use is fortune or talent to a cold and defective nature? Who cares what sensibility or discrimination a man has at some time shown, if he falls asleep in his chair? or if he laugh and giggle? or if he apologize? or is affected with egotism? or thinks of his dollar? or cannot go by food? or has gotten a child in his boyhood? Of what use is genius, if the organ is too convex or too concave, and cannot find a focal distance within the actual horizon of human life? Of what use, if the brain is too cold or too hot, and the man does not care enough for results, to stimulate him to experiment, and hold him up in it? or if the web is too finely woven, too irritable by pleasure and pain, so that life stagnates from too much reception, without due outlet? Of what use to make heroic vows of amendment, if the same old lawbreaker is to keep them? What cheer can the religious sentiment yield, when that is suspected to be secretly dependent on the seasons of the year, and the state of the blood? I knew a witty physician who found theology in the biliary duct, and used to affirm that if there was disease in the liver, the man became a Calvinist, and if that organ was sound, he became a Unitarian. Very mortifying is the reluctant experience that some unfriendly excess or imbecility neutralizes the promise of genius. We see young men who owe us a new world, so readily and lavishly they promise, but they never acquit the debt; they die young and dodge the account: or if they live, they lose themselves in the crowd.

Temperament also enters fully into the system of illusions, and shuts us in a prison of glass which we cannot see. There is an optical illusion about every person we meet. In truth, they are all creatures of given temperament, which will appear in a given character, whose boundaries they will never pass: but we look at them, they seem alive, and we presume there is impulse in them. In the moment it seems impulse; in the year, in the lifetime, it turns out to be a certain uniform tune which the revolving barrel of the music-box must play. Men resist the conclusion in the morning, but adopt it as the evening wears on, that temper prevails over everything of time, place, and condition, and is inconsumable in the flames of religion. Some modifications the moral sentiment avails to impose, but the individual texture holds its dominion, if not to bias the moral judgments, yet to fix the measure of activity and of enjoyment.

I thus express the law as it is read from the platform of ordinary life, but must not leave it without noticing the capital exception. For temperament is a power which no man willingly hears any one praise but himself. On the platform of physics, we cannot resist the contracting influences of so-called science. Temperament puts all divinity to rout. I know the mental proclivity of physicians. I hear the chuckle of the phrenologists. Theoretic kidnappers and slave-drivers, they esteem each man the victim of another, who winds him round his finger by knowing the law of his being, and by such cheap signboards as the color of his beard, or the slope of his occiput, reads the inventory of his fortunes and character. The grossest ignorance does not disgust like this impudent knowingness. The physicians say, they are not materialists; but they are:—Spirit is matter reduced to an extreme thinness: O *so* thin!—But the definition of *spiritual* should be, *that which is its own evidence.* What notions do they attach to love! what to religion! One would not willingly pronounce these words in their hearing, and give them the occasion to profane them. I saw a gracious gentleman who adapts his conversation to the form of the head of the man he talks with! I had fancied that the value of life lay in its inscrutable possibilities; in the fact that I never know, in addressing myself to a new individual, what may befall me. I carry the keys of my castle in my hand, ready to throw them at the feet of my lord, whenever and in what disguise soever he shall appear. I know he is in the neighborhood hidden among vagabonds. Shall I preclude my future, by taking a high seat, and kindly adapting my conversation to the shape of heads? When I come to that, the doctors shall buy me for a cent.——'But, sir, medical history; the report to the Institute; the proven facts!'—I distrust the facts and the inferences. Temperament is the veto or limitation-power in the constitution, very justly applied to restrain an opposite excess in the constitution, but absurdly offered as

a bar to original equity. When virtue is in presence, all subordinate powers sleep. On its own level, or in view of nature,
temperament is final. I see not, if one be once caught in this
trap of so-called sciences, any escape for the man from the
links of the chain of physical necessity. Given such an embryo,
such a history must follow. On this platform, one lives in a
sty of sensualism, and would soon come to suicide. But it is
impossible that the creative power should exclude itself. Into
every intelligence there is a door which is never closed,
through which the creator passes. The intellect, seeker of absolute truth, or the heart, lover of absolute good, intervenes
for our succor, and at one whisper of these high powers, we
awake from ineffectual struggles with this nightmare. We hurl
it into its own hell, and cannot again contract ourselves to so
base a state.

The secret of the illusoriness is in the necessity of a succession of moods or objects. Gladly we would anchor, but the
anchorage is quicksand. This onward trick of nature is too
strong for us: *Pero si muove*. When, at night, I look at the
moon and stars, I seem stationary, and they to hurry. Our
love of the real draws us to permanence, but health of body
consists in circulation, and sanity of mind in variety or facility
of association. We need change of objects. Dedication to one
thought is quickly odious. We house with the insane, and
must humor them; then conversation dies out. Once I took
such delight in Montaigne, that I thought I should not need
any other book; before that, in Shakspeare; then in Plutarch;
then in Plotinus; at one time in Bacon; afterwards in Goethe;
even in Bettine; but now I turn the pages of either of them
languidly, whilst I still cherish their genius. So with pictures;
each will bear an emphasis of attention once, which it cannot
retain, though we fain would continue to be pleased in that
manner. How strongly I have felt of pictures, that when you
have seen one well, you must take your leave of it; you shall
never see it again. I have had good lessons from pictures,
which I have since seen without emotion or remark. A deduction must be made from the opinion, which even the wise
express of a new book or occurrence. Their opinion gives me
tidings of their mood, and some vague guess at the new fact,

but is nowise to be trusted as the lasting relation between that intellect and that thing. The child asks, 'Mamma, why don't I like the story as well as when you told it me yesterday?' Alas, child, it is even so with the oldest cherubim of knowledge. But will it answer thy question to say, Because thou wert born to a whole, and this story is a particular? The reason of the pain this discovery causes us (and we make it late in respect to works of art and intellect), is the plaint of tragedy which murmurs from it in regard to persons, to friendship and love.

That immobility and absence of elasticity which we find in the arts, we find with more pain in the artist. There is no power of expansion in men. Our friends early appear to us as representatives of certain ideas, which they never pass or exceed. They stand on the brink of the ocean of thought and power, but they never take the single step that would bring them there. A man is like a bit of Labrador spar, which has no lustre as you turn it in your hand, until you come to a particular angle; then it shows deep and beautiful colors. There is no adaptation or universal applicability in men, but each has his special talent, and the mastery of successful men consists in adroitly keeping themselves where and when that turn shall be oftenest to be practised. We do what we must, and call it by the best names we can, and would fain have the praise of having intended the result which ensues. I cannot recall any form of man who is not superfluous sometimes. But is not this pitiful? Life is not worth the taking, to do tricks in.

Of course, it needs the whole society, to give the symmetry we seek. The parti-colored wheel must revolve very fast to appear white. Something is learned too by conversing with so much folly and defect. In fine, whoever loses, we are always of the gaining party. Divinity is behind our failures and follies also. The plays of children are nonsense, but very educative nonsense. So it is with the largest and solemnest things, with commerce, government, church, marriage, and so with the history of every man's bread, and the ways by which he is to come by it. Like a bird which alights nowhere, but hops perpetually from bough to bough, is the Power which abides in no man and in no woman, but for a moment speaks from this one, and for another moment from that one.

*   *   *

But what help from these fineries or pedantries? What help from thought? Life is not dialectics. We, I think, in these times, have had lessons enough of the futility of criticism. Our young people have thought and written much on labor and reform, and for all that they have written, neither the world nor themselves have got on a step. Intellectual tasting of life will not supersede muscular activity. If a man should consider the nicety of the passage of a piece of bread down his throat, he would starve. At Education-Farm, the noblest theory of life sat on the noblest figures of young men and maidens, quite powerless and melancholy. It would not rake or pitch a ton of hay; it would not rub down a horse; and the men and maidens it left pale and hungry. A political orator wittily compared our party promises to western roads, which opened stately enough, with planted trees on either side, to tempt the traveller, but soon became narrow and narrower, and ended in a squirrel-track, and ran up a tree. So does culture with us; it ends in head-ache. Unspeakably sad and barren does life look to those, who a few months ago were dazzled with the splendor of the promise of the times. "There is now no longer any right course of action, nor any self-devotion left among the Iranis." Objections and criticism we have had our fill of. There are objections to every course of life and action, and the practical wisdom infers an indifferency, from the omnipresence of objection. The whole frame of things preaches indifferency. Do not craze yourself with thinking, but go about your business anywhere. Life is not intellectual or critical, but sturdy. Its chief good is for well-mixed people who can enjoy what they find, without question. Nature hates peeping, and our mothers speak her very sense when they say, "Children, eat your victuals, and say no more of it." To fill the hour,—that is happiness; to fill the hour, and leave no crevice for a repentance or an approval. We live amid surfaces, and the true art of life is to skate well on them. Under the oldest mouldiest conventions, a man of native force prospers just as well as in the newest world, and that by skill of handling and treatment. He can take hold anywhere. Life itself is a mixture of power and form, and will not bear the least excess of either. To finish the moment, to find the journey's end in every step of the road, to live the greatest number of good hours, is wisdom. It is not the part of men, but of fanatics, or of mathematicians, if you will, to say, that, the shortness of life considered, it is not worth caring whether for so short a duration we were sprawling in want, or sitting high. Since our office is with moments, let us husband them. Five minutes of today are worth as much to me, as five minutes in the next millennium. Let us be poised, and wise, and our own, today. Let us treat the men and women well: treat them as if they were real: perhaps they are. Men live in their fancy, like drunkards whose hands are too soft and tremulous for successful labor. It is a tempest of fancies, and the only ballast I know, is a respect to the present hour. Without any shadow of doubt, amidst this vertigo of shows and politics, I settle myself ever the firmer in the creed, that we should not postpone and refer and wish, but do broad justice where we are, by whomsoever we deal with, accepting our actual companions and circumstances, however humble or odious, as the mystic officials to whom the universe has delegated its whole pleasure for us. If these are mean and malignant, their contentment, which is the last victory of justice, is a more satisfying echo to the heart, than the voice of poets and the casual sympathy of admirable persons. I think that however a thoughtful man may suffer from the defects and absurdities of his company, he cannot without affectation deny to any set of men and women, a sensibility to extraordinary merit. The coarse and frivolous have an instinct of superiority, if they have not a sympathy, and honor it in their blind capricious way with sincere homage.

The fine young people despise life, but in me, and in such as with me are free from dyspepsia, and to whom a day is a sound and solid good, it is a great excess of politeness to look scornful and to cry for company. I am grown by sympathy a little eager and sentimental, but leave me alone, and I should relish every hour and what it brought me, the pot-luck of the day, as heartily as the oldest gossip in the bar-room. I am thankful for small mercies. I compared notes with one of my friends who expects everything of the universe, and is disappointed when anything is less than the best, and I found that I begin at the other extreme, expecting nothing, and am always full of thanks for moderate goods. I accept the clangor and jangle of contrary tendencies. I find my account in sots and bores also. They give a reality to the circumjacent picture, which such a vanishing meteorous appearance can ill spare. In the morning I awake, and find the old world, wife, babes, and mother, Concord and Boston, the dear old spiritual world, and even the dear old devil not far off. If we will take the good we find, asking no questions, we shall have heaping measures. The great gifts are not got by analysis. Everything good is on the highway. The middle region of our being is the temperate zone. We may climb into the thin and cold realm of pure geometry and lifeless science, or sink into that of sensation. Between these extremes is the equator of life, of thought, of spirit, of poetry,—a narrow belt. Moreover, in popular experience, everything good is on the highway. A collector peeps into all the picture-shops of Europe, for a landscape of Poussin, a crayon-sketch of Salvator; but the Transfiguration, the Last Judgment, the Communion of St. Jerome, and what are as transcendent as these, are on the walls of the Vatican, the Uffizii, or the Louvre, where every footman may see them; to say nothing of nature's pictures in every street, of sunsets and sunrises every day, and the sculpture of the human body never absent. A collector recently bought at public auction, in London, for one hundred and fifty-seven guineas, an autograph of Shakspeare: but for nothing a school-boy can read Hamlet, and can detect secrets of highest concernment yet unpublished therein. I think I will never read any but the commonest books,—the Bible, Homer, Dante, Shakspeare, and Milton. Then we are impatient of so public a life and planet, and run hither and thither for nooks and secrets. The imagination delights in the wood-craft of Indians, trappers, and bee-hunters. We fancy that we are strangers, and not so intimately domesticated in the planet as the wild man, and the wild beast and bird. But the exclusion reaches them also; reaches the climbing, flying, gliding, feathered and four-footed man. Fox and woodchuck, hawk and snipe, and bittern, when nearly seen, have no more root in the deep world than man, and are just such superficial tenants of the globe. Then the new molecular philosophy shows astronomical interspaces betwixt atom and atom, shows that the world is all outside: it has no inside.

The mid-world is best. Nature, as we know her, is no saint. The lights of the church, the ascetics, Gentoos and Grahamites, she does not distinguish by any favor. She comes eating and drinking and sinning. Her darlings, the great, the strong, the beautiful, are not children of our law, do not come out of the Sunday School, nor weigh their food, nor punctually keep the commandments. If we will be strong with her strength, we must not harbor such disconsolate consciences, borrowed too from the consciences of other nations. We must set up the strong present tense against all the rumors of wrath, past or to come. So many things are unsettled which it is of the first importance to settle,—and, pending their settlement, we will do as we do. Whilst the debate goes forward on the equity of commerce, and will not be closed for a century or two, New and Old England may keep shop. Law of copyright and international copyright is to be discussed, and, in the interim, we will sell our books for the most we can. Expediency of literature, reason of literature, lawfulness of writing down a thought, is questioned; much is to say on both sides, and, while the fight waxes hot, thou, dearest scholar, stick to thy foolish task, add a line every hour, and between whiles add a line. Right to hold land, right of property, is disputed, and the conventions convene, and before the vote is taken, dig away in your garden, and spend your earnings as a waif or godsend to all serene and beautiful purposes. Life itself is a bubble and a skepticism, and a sleep within a sleep. Grant it, and as much more as they will,—but thou, God's darling! heed thy private dream: thou wilt not be missed in the scorning and skepticism: there are enough of them: stay there in thy closet, and toil, until the rest are agreed what to do about it. Thy sickness, they say, and thy puny habit, require that thou do this or avoid that, but know that thy life is a flitting state, a tent for a night, and do thou, sick or well, finish that stint. Thou art sick, but shalt not be worse, and the universe, which holds thee dear, shall be the better.

Human life is made up of the two elements, power and form, and the proportion must be invariably kept, if we would have it sweet and sound. Each of these elements in excess makes a mischief as hurtful as its defect. Everything runs to excess: every good quality is noxious, if unmixed, and, to carry the danger to the edge of ruin, nature causes each man's peculiarity to superabound. Here, among the farms, we adduce the scholars as examples of this treachery. They are nature's victims of expression. You who see the artist, the orator, the poet, too near, and find their life no more excellent than that of mechanics or farmers, and themselves victims of partiality, very hollow and haggard, and pronounce them failures,—not heroes, but quacks,—conclude very reasonably, that these arts are not for man, but are disease. Yet nature will not bear you out. Irresistible nature made men such, and makes legions more of such, every day. You love the boy reading in a book, gazing at a drawing, or a cast: yet what are these millions who read and behold, but incipient writers and sculptors? Add a little more of that quality which now reads and sees, and they will seize the pen and chisel. And if one remembers how innocently he began to be an artist, he perceives that nature joined with his enemy. A man is a golden impossibility. The line he must walk is a hair's breadth. The wise through excess of wisdom is made a fool.

How easily, if fate would suffer it, we might keep forever these beautiful limits, and adjust ourselves, once for all, to the perfect calculation of the kingdom of known cause and effect. In the street and in the newspapers, life appears so plain a business, that manly resolution and adherence to the multiplication-table through all weathers, will insure success. But ah! presently comes a day, or is it only a half-hour, with its angel-whispering,—which discomfits the conclusions of nations and of years! Tomorrow again, everything looks real and angular, the habitual standards are reinstated, common sense is as rare as genius,—is the basis of genius, and experience is hands and feet to every enterprise;—and yet, he who should do his business on this understanding, would be quickly bankrupt. Power keeps quite another road than the turnpikes of choice and will, namely, the subterranean and invisible tunnels and channels of life. It is ridiculous that we are diplomatists, and doctors, and considerate people: there are no dupes like these. Life is a series of surprises, and would not be worth taking or keeping, if it were not. God delights to isolate us every day, and hide from us the past and the future. We would look about us, but with grand politeness he draws down before us an impenetrable screen of purest sky, and another behind us of purest sky. 'You will not remember,' he seems to say, 'and you will not expect.' All good conversation, manners, and action, come from a spontaneity which forgets usages, and makes the moment great. Nature hates calculators; her methods are saltatory and impulsive. Man lives by pulses; our organic movements are such; and the chemical and ethereal agents are undulatory and alternate; and the mind goes antagonizing on, and never prospers but by fits. We thrive by casualties. Our chief experiences have been casual. The most attractive class of people are those who are powerful obliquely, and not by the direct stroke: men of genius, but not yet accredited: one gets the cheer of their light, without paying too great a tax. Theirs is the beauty of the bird, or the morning light, and not of art. In the thought of genius there is always a surprise; and the moral sentiment is well called "the newness," for it is never other; as new to the oldest intelligence as to the young child,—"the kingdom that cometh without observation." In like manner, for practical success, there must not be too much design. A man will not be observed in doing that which he can do best. There is a certain magic about his properest action, which stupefies your powers of observation, so that though it is done before you, you wist not of it. The art of life has a pudency, and will not be exposed. Every man is an impossibility, until he is born; every thing impossible, until we see a success. The ardors of piety agree at last with the coldest skepticism,—that nothing is of us or our works,—that all is of God. Nature will not spare us the smallest leaf of laurel. All writing comes by the grace of God, and all doing and having. I would gladly be moral, and keep due metes and bounds, which I dearly love, and allow the most to the will of man, but I have set my heart on honesty in this chapter, and I can see nothing at last, in success or failure, than more or less of vital force supplied from the Eternal. The results of life are uncalculated and uncalculable. The years teach much which the days never know.

The persons who compose our company, converse, and come and go, and design and execute many things, and somewhat comes of it all, but an unlooked for result. The individual is always mistaken. He designed many things, and drew in other persons as coadjutors, quarrelled with some or all, blundered much, and something is done; all are a little advanced, but the individual is always mistaken. It turns out somewhat new, and very unlike what he promised himself.

The ancients, struck with this irreducibleness of the elements of human life to calculation, exalted Chance into a divinity, but that is to stay too long at the spark,—which glitters truly at one point,—but the universe is warm with the latency of the same fire. The miracle of life which will not be expounded, but will remain a miracle, introduces a new element. In the growth of the embryo, Sir Everard Home, I think, noticed that the evolution was not from one central point, but co-active from three or more points. Life has no memory. That which proceeds in succession might be remembered, but that which is coexistent, or ejaculated from a deeper cause, as yet far from being conscious, knows not its own tendency. So is it with us, now skeptical, or without unity, because immersed in forms and effects all seeming to be of equal yet hostile value, and now religious, whilst in the reception of spiritual law. Bear with these distractions, with this coetaneous growth of the parts: they will one day be *members*, and obey one will. On that one will, on that secret cause, they nail our attention and hope. Life is hereby melted into an expectation or a religion. Underneath the inharmonious and trivial particulars, is a musical perfection, the Ideal journeying always with us, the heaven without rent or seam. Do but observe the mode of our illumination. When I converse with a profound mind, or if at any time being alone I have good thoughts, I do not at once arrive at satisfactions, as when, being thirsty, I drink water, or go to the fire, being cold: no! but I am at first apprised of my vicinity to a new and excellent region of life. By persisting to read or to think, this region gives further sign of itself, as it were in flashes of light, in sudden discoveries of its profound beauty and repose, as if the clouds that covered it parted at intervals, and showed the approaching traveller the inland mountains, with the tranquil eternal meadows spread at their base, whereon flocks graze, and shepherds pipe and dance. But every insight from this realm of thought is felt as initial, and promises a sequel. I do not make it; I arrive there, and behold what was there already. I make! O no! I clap my hands in infantine joy and amazement, before the first opening to me of this august magnificence, old with the love and homage of innumerable ages, young with the life of life, the sunbright Mecca of the desert. And what a future it opens! I feel a new heart beating with the love of the new beauty. I am ready to die out of nature, and be born again into this new yet unapproachable America I have found in the West.

> "Since neither now nor yesterday began
>   These thoughts, which have been ever, nor yet can
>   A man be found who their first entrance knew."

If I have described life as a flux of moods, I must now add, that there is that in us which changes not, and which ranks all sensations and states of mind. The consciousness in each man is a sliding scale, which identifies him now with the First Cause, and now with the flesh of his body; life above life, in infinite degrees. The sentiment from which it sprung determines the dignity of any deed, and the question ever is, not, what you have done or forborne, but, at whose command you have done or forborne it.

Fortune, Minerva, Muse, Holy Ghost,—these are quaint names, too narrow to cover this unbounded substance. The baffled intellect must still kneel before this cause, which refuses to be named,—ineffable cause, which every fine genius has essayed to represent by some emphatic symbol, as, Thales by water, Anaximenes by air, Anaxagoras by (Νους) thought, Zoroaster by fire, Jesus and the moderns by love: and the metaphor of each has become a national religion. The Chinese Mencius has not been the least successful in his generalization. "I fully understand language," he said, "and nourish well my vast-flowing vigor."—"I beg to ask what you call vast-flowing vigor?"—said his companion. "The explanation," replied Mencius, "is difficult. This vigor is supremely great, and in the highest degree unbending. Nourish it cor-

rectly, and do it no injury, and it will fill up the vacancy between heaven and earth. This vigor accords with and assists
justice and reason, and leaves no hunger."—In our more correct writing, we give to this generalization the name of Being,
and thereby confess that we have arrived as far as we can go.
Suffice it for the joy of the universe, that we have not arrived
at a wall, but at interminable oceans. Our life seems not present, so much as prospective; not for the affairs on which it is
wasted, but as a hint of this vast-flowing vigor. Most of life
seems to be mere advertisement of faculty: information is
given us not to sell ourselves cheap; that we are very great.
So, in particulars, our greatness is always in a tendency or
direction, not in an action. It is for us to believe in the rule,
not in the exception. The noble are thus known from the ignoble. So in accepting the leading of the sentiments, it is not
what we believe concerning the immortality of the soul, or
the like, but *the universal impulse to believe*, that is the material
circumstance, and is the principal fact in the history of the
globe. Shall we describe this cause as that which works directly? The spirit is not helpless or needful of mediate organs.
It has plentiful powers and direct effects. I am explained without explaining, I am felt without acting, and where I am not.
Therefore all just persons are satisfied with their own praise.
They refuse to explain themselves, and are content that new
actions should do them that office. They believe that we communicate without speech, and above speech, and that no right
action of ours is quite unaffecting to our friends, at whatever
distance; for the influence of action is not to be measured by
miles. Why should I fret myself, because a circumstance has
occurred, which hinders my presence where I was expected?
If I am not at the meeting, my presence where I am, should
be as useful to the commonwealth of friendship and wisdom,
as would be my presence in that place. I exert the same quality of power in all places. Thus journeys the mighty Ideal
before us; it never was known to fall into the rear. No man
ever came to an experience which was satiating, but his good
is tidings of a better. Onward and onward! In liberated moments, we know that a new picture of life and duty is already
possible; the elements already exist in many minds around
you, of a doctrine of life which shall transcend any written

record we have. The new statement will comprise the skepticisms, as well as the faiths of society, and out of unbeliefs a creed shall be formed. For, skepticisms are not gratuitous or lawless, but are limitations of the affirmative statement, and the new philosophy must take them in, and make affirmations outside of them, just as much as it must include the oldest beliefs.

It is very unhappy, but too late to be helped, the discovery we have made, that we exist. That discovery is called the Fall of Man. Ever afterwards, we suspect our instruments. We have learned that we do not see directly, but mediately, and that we have no means of correcting these colored and distorting lenses which we are, or of computing the amount of their errors. Perhaps these subject-lenses have a creative power; perhaps there are no objects. Once we lived in what we saw; now, the rapaciousness of this new power, which threatens to absorb all things, engages us. Nature, art, persons, letters, religions,—objects, successively tumble in, and God is but one of its ideas. Nature and literature are subjective phenomena; every evil and every good thing is a shadow which we cast. The street is full of humiliations to the proud. As the fop contrived to dress his bailiffs in his livery, and make them wait on his guests at table, so the chagrins which the bad heart gives off as bubbles, at once take form as ladies and gentlemen in the street, shopmen or barkeepers in hotels, and threaten or insult whatever is threatenable and insultable in us. 'Tis the same with our idolatries. People forget that it is the eye which makes the horizon, and the rounding mind's eye which makes this or that man a type or representative of humanity with the name of hero or saint. Jesus the "providential man," is a good man on whom many people are agreed that these optical laws shall take effect. By love on one part, and by forbearance to press objection on the other part, it is for a time settled, that we will look at him in the centre of the horizon, and ascribe to him the properties that will attach to any man so seen. But the longest love or aversion has a speedy term. The great and crescive self, rooted in absolute nature, supplants all relative existence, and ruins the kingdom of mortal friendship and love. Marriage (in what is called the spiritual world) is impossible, because of the inequality be-

tween every subject and every object. The subject is the receiver of Godhead, and at every comparison must feel his
being enhanced by that cryptic might. Though not in energy,
yet by presence, this magazine of substance cannot be otherwise than felt: nor can any force of intellect attribute to the
object the proper deity which sleeps or wakes forever in every
subject. Never can love make consciousness and ascription
equal in force. There will be the same gulf between every me
and thee, as between the original and the picture. The universe is the bride of the soul. All private sympathy is partial.
Two human beings are like globes, which can touch only in
a point, and, whilst they remain in contact, all other points of
each of the spheres are inert; their turn must also come, and
the longer a particular union lasts, the more energy of appe-
tency the parts not in union acquire.

Life will be imaged, but cannot be divided nor doubled.
Any invasion of its unity would be chaos. The soul is not
twin-born, but the only begotten, and though revealing itself
as child in time, child in appearance, is of a fatal and universal
power, admitting no co-life. Every day, every act betrays the
ill-concealed deity. We believe in ourselves, as we do not believe in others. We permit all things to ourselves, and that
which we call sin in others, is experiment for us. It is an instance of our faith in ourselves, that men never speak of crime
as lightly as they think: or, every man thinks a latitude safe
for himself, which is nowise to be indulged to another. The
act looks very differently on the inside, and on the outside; in
its quality, and in its consequences. Murder in the murderer
is no such ruinous thought as poets and romancers will have
it; it does not unsettle him, or fright him from his ordinary
notice of trifles: it is an act quite easy to be contemplated, but
in its sequel, it turns out to be a horrible jangle and confounding of all relations. Especially the crimes that spring
from love, seem right and fair from the actor's point of view,
but, when acted, are found destructive of society. No man at
last believes that he can be lost, nor that the crime in him is
as black as in the felon. Because the intellect qualifies in our
own case the moral judgments. For there is no crime to the
intellect. That is antinomian or hypernomian, and judges law
as well as fact. "It is worse than a crime, it is a blunder," said

Napoleon, speaking the language of the intellect. To it, the world is a problem in mathematics or the science of quantity, and it leaves out praise and blame, and all weak emotions. All stealing is comparative. If you come to absolutes, pray who does not steal? Saints are sad, because they behold sin, (even when they speculate,) from the point of view of the conscience, and not of the intellect; a confusion of thought. Sin seen from the thought, is a diminution or *less*: seen from the conscience or will, it is pravity or *bad*. The intellect names it shade, absence of light, and no essence. The conscience must feel it as essence, essential evil. This it is not: it has an objective existence, but no subjective.

Thus inevitably does the universe wear our color, and every object fall successively into the subject itself. The subject exists, the subject enlarges; all things sooner or later fall into place. As I am, so I see; use what language we will, we can never say anything but what we are; Hermes, Cadmus, Columbus, Newton, Buonaparte, are the mind's ministers. Instead of feeling a poverty when we encounter a great man, let us treat the new comer like a travelling geologist, who passes through our estate, and shows us good slate, or limestone, or anthracite, in our brush pasture. The partial action of each strong mind in one direction, is a telescope for the objects on which it is pointed. But every other part of knowledge is to be pushed to the same extravagance, ere the soul attains her due sphericity. Do you see that kitten chasing so prettily her own tail? If you could look with her eyes, you might see her surrounded with hundreds of figures performing complex dramas, with tragic and comic issues, long conversations, many characters, many ups and downs of fate,—and meantime it is only puss and her tail. How long before our masquerade will end its noise of tamborines, laughter, and shouting, and we shall find it was a solitary performance?—A subject and an object,—it takes so much to make the galvanic circuit complete, but magnitude adds nothing. What imports it whether it is Kepler and the sphere; Columbus and America; a reader and his book; or puss with her tail?

It is true that all the muses and love and religion hate these developments, and will find a way to punish the chemist, who publishes in the parlor the secrets of the laboratory. And we cannot say too little of our constitutional necessity of seeing things under private aspects, or saturated with our humors. And yet is the God the native of these bleak rocks. That need makes in morals the capital virtue of self-trust. We must hold hard to this poverty, however scandalous, and by more vigorous self-recoveries, after the sallies of action, possess our axis more firmly. The life of truth is cold, and so far mournful; but it is not the slave of tears, contritions, and perturbations. It does not attempt another's work, nor adopt another's facts. It is a main lesson of wisdom to know your own from another's. I have learned that I cannot dispose of other people's facts; but I possess such a key to my own, as persuades me against all their denials, that they also have a key to theirs. A sympathetic person is placed in the dilemma of a swimmer among drowning men, who all catch at him, and if he give so much as a leg or a finger, they will drown him. They wish to be saved from the mischiefs of their vices, but not from their vices. Charity would be wasted on this poor waiting on the symptoms. A wise and hardy physician will say, *Come out of that*, as the first condition of advice.

In this our talking America, we are ruined by our good nature and listening on all sides. This compliance takes away the power of being greatly useful. A man should not be able to look other than directly and forthright. A preoccupied attention is the only answer to the importunate frivolity of other people: an attention, and to an aim which makes their wants frivolous. This is a divine answer, and leaves no appeal, and no hard thoughts. In Flaxman's drawing of the Eumenides of Æschylus, Orestes supplicates Apollo, whilst the Furies sleep on the threshold. The face of the god expresses a shade of regret and compassion, but calm with the conviction of the irreconcilableness of the two spheres. He is born into other politics, into the eternal and beautiful. The man at his feet asks for his interest in turmoils of the earth, into which his nature cannot enter. And the Eumenides there lying express pictorially this disparity. The god is surcharged with his divine destiny.

Illusion, Temperament, Succession, Surface, Surprise, Reality, Subjectiveness,—these are threads on the loom of time, these are the lords of life. I dare not assume to give their order, but I name them as I find them in my way. I know better than to claim any completeness for my picture. I am a fragment, and this is a fragment of me. I can very confidently announce one or another law, which throws itself into relief and form, but I am too young yet by some ages to compile a code. I gossip for my hour concerning the eternal politics. I have seen many fair pictures not in vain. A wonderful time I have lived in. I am not the novice I was fourteen, nor yet seven years ago. Let who will ask, where is the fruit? I find a private fruit sufficient. This is a fruit,—that I should not ask for a rash effect from meditations, counsels, and the hiving of truths. I should feel it pitiful to demand a result on this town and county, an overt effect on the instant month and year. The effect is deep and secular as the cause. It works on periods in which mortal lifetime is lost. All I know is reception; I am and I have: but I do not get, and when I have fancied I had gotten anything, I found I did not. I worship with wonder the great Fortune. My reception has been so large, that I am not annoyed by receiving this or that superabundantly. I say to the Genius, if he will pardon the proverb, *In for a mill, in for a million*. When I receive a new gift, I do not macerate my body to make the account square, for, if I should die, I could not make the account square. The benefit overran the merit the first day, and has overran the merit ever since. The merit itself, so-called, I reckon part of the receiving.

Also, that hankering after an overt or practical effect seems to me an apostasy. In good earnest, I am willing to spare this most unnecessary deal of doing. Life wears to me a visionary face. Hardest, roughest action is visionary also. It is but a choice between soft and turbulent dreams. People disparage knowing and the intellectual life, and urge doing. I am very content with knowing, if only I could know. That is an august entertainment, and would suffice me a great while. To know a little, would be worth the expense of this world. I hear always the law of Adrastia, "that every soul which had acquired any truth, should be safe from harm until another period."

I know that the world I converse with in the city and in the farms, is not the world I *think*. I observe that difference, and shall observe it. One day, I shall know the value and law of this discrepance. But I have not found that much was gained by manipular attempts to realize the world of thought. Many eager persons successively make an experiment in this way, and make themselves ridiculous. They acquire democratic manners, they foam at the mouth, they hate and deny. Worse, I observe, that, in the history of mankind, there is never a solitary example of success,—taking their own tests of success. I say this polemically, or in reply to the inquiry, why not realize your world? But far be from me the despair which prejudges the law by a paltry empiricism,—since there never was a right endeavor, but it succeeded. Patience and patience, we shall win at the last. We must be very suspicious of the deceptions of the element of time. It takes a good deal of time to eat or to sleep, or to earn a hundred dollars, and a very little time to entertain a hope and an insight which becomes the light of our life. We dress our garden, eat our dinners, discuss the household with our wives, and these things make no impression, are forgotten next week; but in the solitude to which every man is always returning, he has a sanity and revelations, which in his passage into new worlds he will carry with him. Never mind the ridicule, never mind the defeat: up again, old heart!—it seems to say,—there is victory yet for all justice; and the true romance which the world exists to realize, will be the transformation of genius into practical power.

CHARACTER

The sun set; but set not his hope:
Stars rose; his faith was earlier up:
Fixed on the enormous galaxy,
Deeper and older seemed his eye:
And matched his sufferance sublime
The taciturnity of time.
He spoke, and words more soft than rain
Brought the Age of Gold again:
His action won such reverence sweet,
As hid all measure of the feat.

Work of his hand
He nor commends nor grieves:
Pleads for itself the fact;
As unrepenting Nature leaves
Her every act.

Character

I HAVE READ that those who listened to Lord Chatham felt that there was something finer in the man, than anything which he said. It has been complained of our brilliant English historian of the French Revolution, that when he has told all his facts about Mirabeau, they do not justify his estimate of his genius. The Gracchi, Agis, Cleomenes, and others of Plutarch's heroes, do not in the record of facts equal their own fame. Sir Philip Sidney, the Earl of Essex, Sir Walter Raleigh, are men of great figure, and of few deeds. We cannot find the smallest part of the personal weight of Washington, in the narrative of his exploits. The authority of the name of Schiller is too great for his books. This inequality of the reputation to the works or the anecdotes, is not accounted for by saying that the reverberation is longer than the thunder-clap; but somewhat resided in these men which begot an expectation that outran all their performance. The largest part of their power was latent. This is that which we call Character,—a reserved force which acts directly by presence, and without means. It is conceived of as a certain undemonstrable force, a Familiar or Genius, by whose impulses the man is guided, but whose counsels he cannot impart; which is company for him, so that such men are often solitary, or if they chance to be social, do not need society, but can entertain themselves very well alone. The purest literary talent appears at one time great, at another time small, but character is of a stellar and undiminishable greatness. What others effect by talent or by eloquence, this man accomplishes by some magnetism. "Half his strength he put not forth." His victories are by demonstration of superiority, and not by crossing of bayonets. He conquers, because his arrival alters the face of affairs. ' "O Iole! how did you know that Hercules was a god?" "Because," answered Iole, "I was content the moment my eyes fell on him. When I beheld Theseus, I desired that I might see him offer battle, or at least guide his horses in the chariot-race; but Hercules did not wait for a contest; he conquered whether he stood, or walked, or sat, or whatever thing he did." ' Man, ordinarily a pendant to events, only half attached, and that awkwardly, to the world he lives in, in these examples appears to share the life of things, and to be an expression of the same laws which control the tides and the sun, numbers and quantities.

But to use a more modest illustration, and nearer home, I observe, that in our political elections, where this element, if it appears at all, can only occur in its coarsest form, we sufficiently understand its incomparable rate. The people know that they need in their representative much more than talent, namely, the power to make his talent trusted. They cannot come at their ends by sending to Congress a learned, acute, and fluent speaker, if he be not one, who, before he was appointed by the people to represent them, was appointed by Almighty God to stand for a fact,—invincibly persuaded of that fact in himself,—so that the most confident and the most violent persons learn that here is resistance on which both impudence and terror are wasted, namely, faith in a fact. The men who carry their points do not need to inquire of their constituents what they should say, but are themselves the country which they represent: nowhere are its emotions or opinions so instant and true as in them; nowhere so pure from a selfish infusion. The constituency at home hearkens to their words, watches the color of their cheek, and therein, as in a glass, dresses its own. Our public assemblies are pretty good tests of manly force. Our frank countrymen of the west and south have a taste for character, and like to know whether the New Englander is a substantial man, or whether the hand can pass through him.

The same motive force appears in trade. There are geniuses in trade, as well as in war, or the state, or letters; and the reason why this or that man is fortunate, is not to be told. It lies in the man: that is all anybody can tell you about it. See him, and you will know as easily why he succeeds, as, if you see Napoleon, you would comprehend his fortune. In the new objects we recognize the old game, the habit of fronting the fact, and not dealing with it at second hand, through the perceptions of somebody else. Nature seems to authorize trade, as soon as you see the natural merchant, who appears not so much a private agent, as her factor and Minister of Commerce. His natural probity combines with his insight into the fabric of society, to put him above tricks, and he communicates to all his own faith, that contracts are of no private interpretation. The habit of his mind is a reference to standards of natural equity and public advantage; and he inspires respect, and the wish to deal with him, both for the quiet spirit of honor which attends him, and for the intellectual pastime which the spectacle of so much ability affords. This immensely stretched trade, which makes the capes of the Southern Ocean his wharves, and the Atlantic Sea his familiar port, centres in his brain only; and nobody in the universe can make his place good. In his parlor, I see very well that he has been at hard work this morning, with that knitted brow, and that settled humor, which all his desire to be courteous cannot shake off. I see plainly how many firm acts have been done; how many valiant *noes* have this day been spoken, when others would have uttered ruinous *yeas*. I see, with the pride of art, and skill of masterly arithmetic and power of remote combination, the consciousness of being an agent and playfellow of the original laws of the world. He too believes that none can supply him, and that a man must be born to trade, or he cannot learn it.

This virtue draws the mind more, when it appears in action to ends not so mixed. It works with most energy in the smallest companies and in private relations. In all cases, it is an extraordinary and incomputable agent. The excess of physical strength is paralyzed by it. Higher natures overpower lower ones by affecting them with a certain sleep. The faculties are locked up, and offer no resistance. Perhaps that is the universal law. When the high cannot bring up the low to itself, it benumbs it, as man charms down the resistance of the lower animals. Men exert on each other a similar occult power. How often has the influence of a true master realized all the tales of magic! A river of command seemed to run down from his eyes into all those who beheld him, a torrent of strong sad light, like an Ohio or Danube, which pervaded them with his thoughts, and colored all events with the hue of his mind. "What means did you employ?" was the question asked of the wife of Concini, in regard to her treatment of Mary of

Medici; and the answer was, "Only that influence which every strong mind has over a weak one." Cannot Cæsar in irons shuffle off the irons, and transfer them to the person of Hippo or Thraso the turnkey? Is an iron handcuff so immutable a bond? Suppose a slaver on the coast of Guinea should take on board a gang of negroes, which should contain persons of the stamp of Toussaint L'Ouverture: or, let us fancy, under these swarthy masks he has a gang of Washingtons in chains. When they arrive at Cuba, will the relative order of the ship's company be the same? Is there nothing but rope and iron? Is there no love, no reverence? Is there never a glimpse of right in a poor slave-captain's mind; and cannot these be supposed available to break, or elude, or in any manner overmatch the tension of an inch or two of iron ring?

This is a natural power, like light and heat, and all nature coöperates with it. The reason why we feel one man's presence, and do not feel another's, is as simple as gravity. Truth is the summit of being: justice is the application of it to affairs. All individual natures stand in a scale, according to the purity of this element in them. The will of the pure runs down from them into other natures, as water runs down from a higher into a lower vessel. This natural force is no more to be withstood, than any other natural force. We can drive a stone upward for a moment into the air, but it is yet true that all stones will forever fall; and whatever instances can be quoted of unpunished theft, or of a lie which somebody credited, justice must prevail, and it is the privilege of truth to make itself believed. Character is this moral order seen through the medium of an individual nature. An individual is an encloser. Time and space, liberty and necessity, truth and thought, are left at large no longer. Now, the universe is a close or pound. All things exist in the man tinged with the manners of his soul. With what quality is in him, he infuses all nature that he can reach; nor does he tend to lose himself in vastness, but, at how long a curve soever, all his regards return into his own good at last. He animates all he can, and he sees only what he animates. He encloses the world, as the patriot does his country, as a material basis for his character, and a theatre for action. A healthy soul stands united with the Just and the True, as the magnet arranges itself with the pole, so that he stands to all beholders like a transparent object betwixt them and the sun, and whoso journeys towards the sun, journeys towards that person. He is thus the medium of the highest influence to all who are not on the same level. Thus, men of character are the conscience of the society to which they belong.

The natural measure of this power is the resistance of circumstances. Impure men consider life as it is reflected in opinions, events, and persons. They cannot see the action, until it is done. Yet its moral element pre-existed in the actor, and its quality as right or wrong, it was easy to predict. Everything in nature is bipolar, or has a positive and negative pole. There is a male and a female, a spirit and a fact, a north and a south. Spirit is the positive, the event is the negative. Will is the north, action the south pole. Character may be ranked as having its natural place in the north. It shares the magnetic currents of the system. The feeble souls are drawn to the south or negative pole. They look at the profit or hurt of the action. They never behold a principle until it is lodged in a person. They do not wish to be lovely, but to be loved. The class of character like to hear of their faults: the other class do not like to hear of faults; they worship events; secure to them a fact, a connexion, a certain chain of circumstances, and they will ask no more. The hero sees that the event is ancillary: it must follow *him*. A given order of events has no power to secure to him the satisfaction which the imagination attaches to it; the soul of goodness escapes from any set of circumstances, whilst prosperity belongs to a certain mind, and will introduce that power and victory which is its natural fruit, into any order of events. No change of circumstances can repair a defect of character. We boast our emancipation from many superstitions; but if we have broken any idols, it is through a transfer of the idolatry. What have I gained, that I no longer immolate a bull to Jove, or to Neptune, or a mouse to Hecate; that I do not tremble before the Eumenides, or the Catholic Purgatory, or the Calvinistic Judgment-day,—if I quake at opinion, the public opinion, as we call it; or at the threat of assault, or contumely, or bad neighbors, or poverty, or mutilation, or at the rumor of revolution, or of murder? If I quake, what matters it what I quake at? Our proper vice takes form in one or another shape, according to the sex, age, or temperament of the person, and, if we are capable of fear, will readily find terrors. The covetousness or the malignity which saddens me, when I ascribe it to society, is my own. I am always environed by myself. On the other part, rectitude is a perpetual victory, celebrated not by cries of joy, but by serenity, which is joy fixed or habitual. It is disgraceful to fly to events for confirmation of our truth and worth. The capitalist does not run every hour to the broker, to coin his advantages into current money of the realm; he is satisfied to read in the quotations of the market, that his stocks have risen. The same transport which the occurrence of the best events in the best order would occasion me, I must learn to taste purer in the perception that my position is every hour meliorated, and does already command those events I desire. That exultation is only to be checked by the foresight of an order of things so excellent, as to throw all our prosperities into the deepest shade.

The face which character wears to me is self-sufficingness. I revere the person who is riches; so that I cannot think of him as alone, or poor, or exiled, or unhappy, or a client, but as perpetual patron, benefactor, and beatified man. Character is centrality, the impossibility of being displaced or overset. A man should give us a sense of mass. Society is frivolous, and shreds its day into scraps, its conversation into ceremonies and escapes. But if I go to see an ingenious man, I shall think myself poorly entertained if he give me nimble pieces of benevolence and etiquette; rather he shall stand stoutly in his place, and let me apprehend, if it were only his resistance; know that I have encountered a new and positive quality;— great refreshment for both of us. It is much, that he does not accept the conventional opinions and practices. That nonconformity will remain a goad and remembrancer, and every inquirer will have to dispose of him, in the first place. There is nothing real or useful that is not a seat of war. Our houses ring with laughter and personal and critical gossip, but it helps little. But the uncivil, unavailable man, who is a problem and a threat to society, whom it cannot let pass in silence, but must either worship or hate,—and to whom all parties feel related, both the leaders of opinion, and the obscure and eccentric,—he helps; he puts America and Europe in the wrong, and destroys the skepticism which says, 'man is a doll, let us eat and drink, 'tis the best we can do,' by illuminating the untried and unknown. Acquiescence in the establishment, and appeal to the public, indicate infirm faith, heads which are not clear, and which must see a house built, before they can comprehend the plan of it. The wise man not only leaves out of his thought the many, but leaves out the few. Fountains, fountains, the self-moved, the absorbed, the commander because he is commanded, the assured, the primary,—they are good; for these announce the instant presence of supreme power.

Our action should rest mathematically on our substance. In nature, there are no false valuations. A pound of water in the ocean-tempest has no more gravity than in a midsummer pond. All things work exactly according to their quality, and according to their quantity; attempt nothing they cannot do, except man only. He has pretension: he wishes and attempts things beyond his force. I read in a book of English memoirs, "Mr. Fox (afterwards Lord Holland) said, he must have the Treasury; he had served up to it, and would have it."—Xenophon and his Ten Thousand were quite equal to what they attempted, and did it; so equal, that it was not suspected to be a grand and inimitable exploit. Yet there stands that fact unrepeated, a high-water-mark in military history. Many have attempted it since, and not been equal to it. It is only on reality, that any power of action can be based. No institution will be better than the institutor. I knew an amiable and accomplished person who undertook a practical reform, yet I was never able to find in him the enterprise of love he took in hand. He adopted it by ear and by the understanding from the books he had been reading. All his action was tentative, a piece of the city carried out into the fields, and was the city still, and no new fact, and could not inspire enthusiasm. Had there been something latent in the man, a terrible undemonstrated genius agitating and embarrassing his demeanor, we had watched for its advent. It is not enough that the intellect should see the evils, and their remedy. We shall still postpone our existence, nor take the ground to which we are entitled, whilst it is only a thought, and not a spirit that incites us. We have not yet served up to it.

These are properties of life, and another trait is the notice of incessant growth. Men should be intelligent and earnest. They must also make us feel, that they have a controlling happy future, opening before them, which sheds a splendor on the passing hour. The hero is misconceived and misreported: he cannot therefore wait to unravel any man's blunders: he is again on his road, adding new powers and honors to his domain, and new claims on your heart, which will bankrupt you, if you have loitered about the old things, and have not kept your relation to him, by adding to your wealth. New actions are the only apologies and explanations of old ones, which the noble can bear to offer or to receive. If your friend has displeased you, you shall not sit down to consider it, for he has already lost all memory of the passage, and has doubled his power to serve you, and, ere you can rise up again, will burden you with blessings.

We have no pleasure in thinking of a benevolence that is only measured by its works. Love is inexhaustible, and if its estate is wasted, its granary emptied, still cheers and enriches, and the man, though he sleep, seems to purify the air, and his house to adorn the landscape and strengthen the laws. People always recognize this difference. We know who is benevolent, by quite other means than the amount of subscription to soup-societies. It is only low merits that can be enumerated. Fear, when your friends say to you what you have done well, and say it through; but when they stand with uncertain timid looks of respect and half-dislike, and must suspend their judgment for years to come, you may begin to hope. Those who live to the future must always appear selfish to those who live to the present. Therefore it was droll in the good Riemer, who has written memoirs of Goethe, to make out a list of his donations and good deeds, as, so many hundred thalers given to Stilling, to Hegel, to Tischbein: a lucrative place found for Professor Voss, a post under the Grand Duke for Herder, a pension for Meyer, two professors recommended to foreign universities, &c. &c. The longest list of specifications of benefit, would look very short. A man is a poor creature, if he is to be measured so. For, all these, of course, are exceptions; and the rule and hodiernal life of a good man is benefaction. The true charity of Goethe is to be inferred from the account he gave Dr. Eckermann, of the way in which he had spent his fortune. "Each bon-mot of mine has cost a purse of gold. Half a million of my own money, the fortune I inherited, my salary, and the large income derived from my writings for fifty years back, have been expended to instruct me in what I now know. I have besides seen," &c.

I own it is but poor chat and gossip to go to enumerate traits of this simple and rapid power, and we are painting the lightning with charcoal; but in these long nights and vacations, I like to console myself so. Nothing but itself can copy it. A word warm from the heart enriches me. I surrender at discretion. How death-cold is literary genius before this fire of life! These are the touches that reanimate my heavy soul, and give it eyes to pierce the dark of nature. I find, where I thought myself poor, there was I most rich. Thence comes a new intellectual exaltation, to be again rebuked by some new exhibition of character. Strange alternation of attraction and repulsion! Character repudiates intellect, yet excites it; and character passes into thought, is published so, and then is ashamed before new flashes of moral worth.

Character is nature in the highest form. It is of no use to ape it, or to contend with it. Somewhat is possible of resistance, and of persistence, and of creation, to this power, which will foil all emulation.

This masterpiece is best where no hands but nature's have been laid on it. Care is taken that the greatly-destined shall slip up into life in the shade, with no thousand-eyed Athens to watch and blazon every new thought, every blushing emotion of young genius. Two persons lately,—very young children of the most high God,—have given me occasion for thought. When I explored the source of their sanctity, and charm for the imagination, it seemed as if each answered, 'From my non-conformity: I never listened to your people's law, or to what they call their gospel, and wasted my time. I was content with the simple rural poverty of my own: hence this sweetness: my work never reminds you of that;—is pure of that.' And nature advertises me in such persons, that, in democratic America, she will not be democratized. How cloistered and constitutionally sequestered from the market and from scandal! It was only this morning, that I sent away some wild flowers of these wood-gods. They are a relief from literature,—these fresh draughts from the sources of thought and sentiment; as we read, in an age of polish and criticism, the first lines of written prose and verse of a nation. How captivating is their devotion to their favorite books, whether Æschylus, Dante, Shakspeare, or Scott, as feeling that they have a stake in that book: who touches that, touches them;—and especially the total solitude of the critic, the Patmos of thought from which he writes, in unconsciousness of any eyes that shall ever read this writing. Could they dream on still, as angels, and not wake to comparisons, and to be flattered! Yet some natures are too good to be spoiled by praise, and wherever the vein of thought reaches down into the profound, there is no danger from vanity. Solemn friends will warn them of the danger of the head's being turned by the flourish of trumpets, but they can afford to smile. I remember the indignation of an eloquent Methodist at the kind admonitions of a Doctor of Divinity,—'My friend, a man can neither be praised nor insulted.' But forgive the counsels; they are very natural. I remember the thought which occurred to me when some ingenious and spiritual foreigners came to America, was, Have you been victimized in being brought hither?—or, prior to that, answer me this, 'Are you victimizable?'

As I have said, nature keeps these sovereignties in her own hands, and however pertly our sermons and disciplines would divide some share of credit, and teach that the laws fashion the citizen, she goes her own gait, and puts the wisest in the wrong. She makes very light of gospels and prophets, as one who has a great many more to produce, and no excess of time to spare on any one. There is a class of men, individuals of which appear at long intervals, so eminently endowed with insight and virtue, that they have been unanimously saluted as *divine*, and who seem to be an accumulation of that power we consider. Divine persons are character born, or, to borrow a phrase from Napoleon, they are victory organized. They are usually received with ill-will, because they are new, and because they set a bound to the exaggeration that has been made of the personality of the last divine person. Nature never rhymes her children, nor makes two men alike. When we see a great man, we fancy a resemblance to some historical person, and predict the sequel of his character and fortune, a result which he is sure to disappoint. None will ever solve the problem of his character according to our prejudice, but only in his own high unprecedented way. Character wants room; must not be crowded on by persons, nor be judged from glimpses got in the press of affairs or on few occasions. It needs perspective, as a great building. It may not, probably does not, form relations rapidly; and we should not require rash explanation, either on the popular ethics, or on our own, of its action.

I look on Sculpture as history. I do not think the Apollo and the Jove impossible in flesh and blood. Every trait which the artist recorded in stone, he had seen in life, and better than his copy. We have seen many counterfeits, but we are born believers in great men. How easily we read in old books, when men were few, of the smallest action of the patriarchs. We require that a man should be so large and columnar in the landscape, that it should deserve to be recorded, that he arose, and girded up his loins, and departed to such a place. The most credible pictures are those of majestic men who prevailed at their entrance, and convinced the senses; as happened to the eastern magian who was sent to test the merits of Zertusht or Zoroaster. When the Yunani sage arrived at Balkh, the Persians tell us, Gushtasp appointed a day on which the Mobeds of every country should assemble, and a golden chair was placed for the Yunani sage. Then the beloved of Yezdam, the prophet Zertusht, advanced into the midst of the assembly. The Yunani sage, on seeing that chief, said, "This form and this gait cannot lie, and nothing but truth can proceed from them." Plato said, it was impossible not to believe in the children of the gods, "though they should speak without probable or necessary arguments." I should think myself very unhappy in my associates, if I could not credit the best things in history. "John Bradshaw," says Milton, "appears like a consul, from whom the fasces are not to depart with the year; so that not on the tribunal only, but throughout his life, you would regard him as sitting in judgment upon kings." I find it more credible, since it is anterior information, that one man should *know heaven*, as the Chinese say, than that so many men should know the world. "The virtuous prince confronts the gods, without any misgiving. He waits a hundred ages till a sage comes, and does not doubt. He who confronts the gods, without any misgiving, knows heaven; he who waits a hundred ages until a sage comes, without doubting, knows men. Hence the virtuous prince moves, and for ages shows empire the way." But there is no need to seek remote examples. He is a dull observer whose experience has not taught him the reality and force of magic, as well as of chemistry. The coldest precisian cannot go abroad without encountering inexplicable influences. One man fastens an eye on him, and the graves of the memory render up their dead; the secrets that make him wretched either to keep or to betray, must be yielded;—another, and he cannot speak, and the bones of his body seem to lose their cartilages; the entrance of a friend adds grace, boldness, and eloquence to him; and there are persons, he cannot choose but remember, who gave a transcendant expansion to his thought, and kindled another life in his bosom.

What is so excellent as strict relations of amity, when they spring from this deep root? The sufficient reply to the skeptic, who doubts the power and the furniture of man, is in that possibility of joyful intercourse with persons, which makes the faith and practice of all reasonable men. I know nothing which life has to offer so satisfying as the profound good understanding, which can subsist, after much exchange of good offices, between two virtuous men, each of whom is sure of himself, and sure of his friend. It is a happiness which postpones all other gratifications, and makes politics, and commerce, and churches, cheap. For, when men shall meet as they ought, each a benefactor, a shower of stars, clothed with thoughts, with deeds, with accomplishments, it should be the festival of nature which all things announce. Of such friendship, love in the sexes is the first symbol, as all other things are symbols of love. Those relations to the best men, which, at one time, we reckoned the romances of youth, become, in the progress of the character, the most solid enjoyment.

If it were possible to live in right relations with men!—if we could abstain from asking anything of them, from asking their praise, or help, or pity, and content us with compelling them through the virtue of the eldest laws! Could we not deal with a few persons,—with one person,—after the unwritten statutes, and make an experiment of their efficacy? Could we not pay our friend the compliment of truth, of silence, of forbearing? Need we be so eager to seek him? If we are related, we shall meet. It was a tradition of the ancient world, that no metamorphosis could hide a god from a god; and there is a Greek verse which runs,

"The Gods are to each other not unknown."

Friends also follow the laws of divine necessity; they gravitate to each other, and cannot otherwise:—

When each the other shall avoid,
Shall each by each be most enjoyed.

Their relation is not made, but allowed. The gods must seat themselves without seneschal in our Olympus, and as they can instal themselves by seniority divine. Society is spoiled, if pains are taken, if the associates are brought a mile to meet. And if it be not society, it is a mischievous, low, degrading jangle, though made up of the best. All the greatness of each is kept back, and every foible in painful activity, as if the Olympians should meet to exchange snuff-boxes.

Life goes headlong. We chase some flying scheme, or we are hunted by some fear or command behind us. But if suddenly we encounter a friend, we pause; our heat and hurry look foolish enough; now pause, now possession, is required, and the power to swell the moment from the resources of the heart. The moment is all, in all noble relations.

A divine person is the prophecy of the mind; a friend is the hope of the heart. Our beatitude waits for the fulfilment of these two in one. The ages are opening this moral force. All force is the shadow or symbol of that. Poetry is joyful and strong, as it draws its inspiration thence. Men write their names on the world, as they are filled with this. History has been mean; our nations have been mobs; we have never seen a man: that divine form we do not yet know, but only the dream and prophecy of such: we do not know the majestic manners which belong to him, which appease and exalt the beholder. We shall one day see that the most private is the most public energy, that quality atones for quantity, and grandeur of character acts in the dark, and succors them who never saw it. What greatness has yet appeared, is beginnings and encouragements to us in this direction. The history of those gods and saints which the world has written, and then worshipped, are documents of character. The ages have ex-ulted in the manners of a youth who owed nothing to for-tune, and who was hanged at the Tyburn of his nation, who, by the pure quality of his nature, shed an epic splendor around the facts of his death, which has transfigured every particular into an universal symbol for the eyes of mankind. This great defeat is hitherto our highest fact. But the mind requires a victory to the senses, a force of character which will convert judge, jury, soldier, and king; which will rule animal and mineral virtues, and blend with the courses of sap, of rivers, of winds, of stars, and of moral agents.

If we cannot attain at a bound to these grandeurs, at least, let us do them homage. In society, high advantages are set down to the possessor, as disadvantages. It requires the more wariness in our private estimates. I do not forgive in my friends the failure to know a fine character, and to entertain it with thankful hospitality. When, at last, that which we have always longed for, is arrived, and shines on us with glad rays out of that far celestial land, then to be coarse, then to be critical, and treat such a visitant with the jabber and suspicion of the streets, argues a vulgarity that seems to shut the doors of heaven. This is confusion, this the right insanity, when the soul no longer knows its own, nor where its allegiance, its religion, are due. Is there any religion but this, to know, that, wherever in the wide desert of being, the holy sentiment we cherish has opened into a flower, it blooms for me? if none sees it, I see it; I am aware, if I alone, of the greatness of the fact. Whilst it blooms, I will keep sabbath or holy time, and suspend my gloom, and my folly and jokes. Nature is in-dulged by the presence of this guest. There are many eyes that can detect and honor the prudent and household virtues; there are many that can discern Genius on his starry track, though the mob is incapable; but when that love which is all-suffering, all-abstaining, all-aspiring, which has vowed to it-self, that it will be a wretch and also a fool in this world, sooner than soil its white hands by any compliances, comes into our streets and houses,—only the pure and aspiring can know its face, and the only compliment they can pay it, is to own it.

MANNERS

"How near to good is what is fair!
Which we no sooner see,
But with the lines and outward air
Our senses taken be.

Again yourselves compose,
And now put all the aptness on
Of Figure, that Proportion
Or Color can disclose;
That if those silent arts were lost,
Design and Picture, they might boast
From you a newer ground,
Instructed by the heightening sense
Of dignity and reverence
In their true motions found."

BEN JONSON

Manners

HALF THE WORLD, it is said, knows not how the other half live. Our Exploring Expedition saw the Feejee islanders getting their dinner off human bones; and they are said to eat their own wives and children. The husbandry of the modern inhabitants of Gournou (west of old Thebes) is philosophical to a fault. To set up their housekeeping, nothing is requisite but two or three earthern pots, a stone to grind meal, and a mat which is the bed. The house, namely, a tomb, is ready without rent or taxes. No rain can pass through the roof, and there is no door, for there is no want of one, as there is nothing to lose. If the house do not please them, they walk out and enter another, as there are several hundreds at their command. "It is somewhat singular," adds Belzoni, to whom we owe this account, "to talk of happiness among people who live in sepulchres, among the corpses and rags of an ancient nation which they know nothing of." In the deserts of Borgoo, the rock-Tibboos still dwell in caves, like cliff-swallows, and the language of these negroes is compared by their neighbors to the shrieking of bats, and to the whistling of birds. Again, the Bornoos have no proper names; individuals are called after their height, thickness, or other accidental quality, and have nicknames merely. But the salt, the dates, the ivory, and the gold, for which these horrible regions are visited, find their way into countries, where the purchaser and consumer can hardly be ranked in one race with these cannibals and man-stealers; countries where man serves himself with metals, wood, stone, glass, gum, cotton, silk, and wool; honors himself with architecture; writes laws, and contrives to execute his will through the hands of many nations; and, especially, establishes a select society, running through all the countries of intelligent men, a self-constituted aristocracy, or fraternity of the best, which, without written law or exact usage of any kind, perpetuates itself, colonizes every new-planted island, and adopts and makes its own whatever personal beauty or extraordinary native endowment anywhere appears.

What fact more conspicuous in modern history, than the creation of the gentleman? Chivalry is that, and loyalty is that, and, in English literature, half the drama, and all the novels, from Sir Philip Sidney to Sir Walter Scott, paint this figure. The word *gentleman*, which, like the word Christian, must hereafter characterize the present and the few preceding centuries, by the importance attached to it, is a homage to personal and incommunicable properties. Frivolous and fantastic additions have got associated with the name, but the steady interest of mankind in it must be attributed to the valuable properties which it designates. An element which unites all the most forcible persons of every country; makes them intelligible and agreeable to each other, and is somewhat so precise, that it is at once felt if an individual lack the masonic sign, cannot be any casual product, but must be an average result of the character and faculties universally found in men. It seems a certain permanent average; as the atmosphere is a permanent composition, whilst so many gases are combined only to be decompounded. *Comme il faut*, is the Frenchman's description of good society, *as we must be*. It is a spontaneous fruit of talents and feelings of precisely that class who have most vigor, who take the lead in the world of this hour, and, though far from pure, far from constituting the gladdest and highest tone of human feeling, is as good as the whole society permits it to be. It is made of the spirit, more than of the talent of men, and is a compound result, into which every great force enters as an ingredient, namely, virtue, wit, beauty, wealth, and power.

There is something equivocal in all the words in use to express the excellence of manners and social cultivation, because the quantities are fluxional, and the last effect is assumed by the senses as the cause. The word *gentleman* has not any correlative abstract to express the quality. *Gentility* is mean, and *gentilesse* is obsolete. But we must keep alive in the vernacular, the distinction between *fashion*, a word of narrow and often sinister meaning, and the heroic character which the gentleman imports. The usual words, however, must be respected: they will be found to contain the root of the matter. The point of distinction in all this class of names, as cour-

tesy, chivalry, fashion, and the like, is, that the flower and
fruit, not the grain of the tree, are contemplated. It is beauty
which is the aim this time, and not worth. The result is now
in question, although our words intimate well enough the
popular feeling, that the appearance supposes a substance.
The gentleman is a man of truth, lord of his own actions, and
expressing that lordship in his behavior, not in any manner
dependent and servile either on persons, or opinions, or possessions. Beyond this fact of truth and real force, the word
denotes good-nature or benevolence: manhood first, and then
gentleness. The popular notion certainly adds a condition of
ease and fortune; but that is a natural result of personal force
and love, that they should possess and dispense the goods of
the world. In times of violence, every eminent person must
fall in with many opportunities to approve his stoutness and
worth; therefore every man's name that emerged at all from
the mass in the feudal ages, rattles in our ear like a flourish of
trumpets. But personal force never goes out of fashion. That
is still paramount today, and, in the moving crowd of good
society, the men of valor and reality are known, and rise to
their natural place. The competition is transferred from war
to politics and trade, but the personal force appears readily
enough in these new arenas.

Power first, or no leading class. In politics and in trade,
bruisers and pirates are of better promise than talkers and
clerks. God knows that all sorts of gentlemen knock at the
door; but whenever used in strictness, and with any emphasis,
the name will be found to point at original energy. It describes a man standing in his own right, and working after
untaught methods. In a good lord, there must first be a good
animal, at least to the extent of yielding the incomparable advantage of animal spirits. The ruling class must have more,
but they must have these, giving in every company the sense
of power, which makes things easy to be done which daunt
the wise. The society of the energetic class, in their friendly
and festive meetings, is full of courage, and of attempts,
which intimidate the pale scholar. The courage which girls
exhibit is like a battle of Lundy's Lane, or a sea-fight. The
intellect relies on memory to make some supplies to face these

extemporaneous squadrons. But memory is a base mendicant with basket and badge, in the presence of these sudden masters. The rulers of society must be up to the work of the world, and equal to their versatile office: men of the right Cæsarian pattern, who have great range of affinity. I am far from believing the timid maxim of Lord Falkland, ("that for ceremony there must go two to it; since a bold fellow will go through the cunningest forms,") and am of opinion that the gentleman is the bold fellow whose forms are not to be broken through; and only that plenteous nature is rightful master, which is the complement of whatever person it converses with. My gentleman gives the law where he is; he will outpray saints in chapel, outgeneral veterans in the field, and outshine all courtesy in the hall. He is good company for pirates, and good with academicians; so that it is useless to fortify yourself against him; he has the private entrance to all minds, and I could as easily exclude myself, as him. The famous gentlemen of Asia and Europe have been of this strong type: Saladin, Sapor, the Cid, Julius Cæsar, Scipio, Alexander, Pericles, and the lordliest personages. They sat very carelessly in their chairs, and were too excellent themselves, to value any condition at a high rate.

A plentiful fortune is reckoned necessary, in the popular judgment, to the completion of this man of the world: and it is a material deputy which walks through the dance which the first has led. Money is not essential, but this wide affinity is, which transcends the habits of clique and caste, and makes itself felt by men of all classes. If the aristocrat is only valid in fashionable circles, and not with truckmen, he will never be a leader in fashion; and if the man of the people cannot speak on equal terms with the gentleman, so that the gentleman shall perceive that he is already really of his own order, he is not to be feared. Diogenes, Socrates, and Epaminondas, are gentlemen of the best blood, who have chosen the condition of poverty, when that of wealth was equally open to them. I use these old names, but the men I speak of are my contemporaries. Fortune will not supply to every generation one of these well-appointed knights, but every collection of men furnishes some example of the class: and the politics of this country, and the trade of every town, are controlled by these hardy and irresponsible doers, who have invention to take the lead, and a broad sympathy which puts them in fellowship with crowds, and makes their action popular.

The manners of this class are observed and caught with devotion by men of taste. The association of these masters with each other, and with men intelligent of their merits, is mutually agreeable and stimulating. The good forms, the happiest expressions of each, are repeated and adopted. By swift consent, everything superfluous is dropped, everything graceful is renewed. Fine manners show themselves formidable to the uncultivated man. They are a subtler science of defence to parry and intimidate; but once matched by the skill of the other party, they drop the point of the sword,—points and fences disappear, and the youth finds himself in a more transparent atmosphere, wherein life is a less troublesome game, and not a misunderstanding rises between the players. Manners aim to facilitate life, to get rid of impediments, and bring the man pure to energize. They aid our dealing and conversation, as a railway aids travelling, by getting rid of all avoidable obstructions of the road, and leaving nothing to be conquered but pure space. These forms very soon become fixed, and a fine sense of propriety is cultivated with the more heed, that it becomes a badge of social and civil distinctions. Thus grows up Fashion, an equivocal semblance, the most puissant, the most fantastic and frivolous, the most feared and followed, and which morals and violence assault in vain.

There exists a strict relation between the class of power, and the exclusive and polished circles. The last are always filled or filling from the first. The strong men usually give some allowance even to the petulances of fashion, for that affinity they find in it. Napoleon, child of the revolution, destroyer of the old noblesse, never ceased to court the Faubourg St. Germain: doubtless with the feeling, that fashion is a homage to men of his stamp. Fashion, though in a strange way, represents all manly virtue. It is virtue gone to seed: it is a kind of posthumous honor. It does not often caress the great, but the children of the great: it is a hall of the Past. It usually sets its face against the great of this hour. Great men are not commonly in its halls: they are absent in the field: they are working, not triumphing. Fashion is made up of their children; of those, who, through the value and virtue of somebody, have acquired lustre to their name, marks of distinction, means of cultivation and generosity, and, in their physical organization, a certain health and excellence, which secures to them, if not the highest power to work, yet high power to enjoy. The class of power, the working heroes, the Cortez, the Nelson, the Napoleon, see that this is the festivity and permanent celebration of such as they; that fashion is funded talent; is Mexico, Marengo, and Trafalgar beaten out thin; that the brilliant names of fashion run back to just such busy names as their own, fifty or sixty years ago. They are the sowers, their sons shall be the reapers, and *their* sons, in the ordinary course of things, must yield the possession of the harvest to new competitors with keener eyes and stronger frames. The city is recruited from the country. In the year 1805, it is said, every legitimate monarch in Europe was imbecile. The city would have died out, rotted, and exploded, long ago, but that it was reinforced from the fields. It is only country which came to town day before yesterday, that is city and court today.

Aristocracy and fashion are certain inevitable results. These mutual selections are indestructible. If they provoke anger in the least favored class, and the excluded majority revenge themselves on the excluding minority, by the strong hand, and kill them, at once a new class finds itself at the top, as certainly as cream rises in a bowl of milk: and if the people should destroy class after class, until two men only were left, one of these would be the leader, and would be involuntarily served and copied by the other. You may keep this minority out of sight and out of mind, but it is tenacious of life, and is one of the estates of the realm. I am the more struck with this tenacity, when I see its work. It respects the administration of such unimportant matters, that we should not look for any durability in its rule. We sometimes meet men under some strong moral influence, as, a patriotic, a literary, a religious movement, and feel that the moral sentiment rules man and nature. We think all other distinctions and ties will be slight and fugitive, this of caste or fashion, for example; yet come from year to year, and see how permanent that is, in this Boston or New York life of man, where, too, it has not the least countenance from the law of the land. Not in Egypt or in India a firmer or more impassable line. Here are associations whose ties go over, and under, and through it, a meeting of merchants, a military corps, a college-class, a fire-club, a professional association, a political, a religious convention;—the persons seem to draw inseparably near; yet, that assembly once dispersed, its members will not in the year meet again. Each returns to his degree in the scale of good society, porcelain remains porcelain, and earthen earthen. The objects of fashion may be frivolous, or fashion may be objectless, but the nature of this union and selection can be neither frivolous nor accidental. Each man's rank in that perfect graduation depends on some symmetry in his structure, or some agreement in his structure to the symmetry of society. Its doors unbar instantaneously to a natural claim of their own kind. A natural gentleman finds his way in, and will keep the oldest patrician out, who has lost his intrinsic rank. Fashion understands itself; good-breeding and personal superiority of whatever country readily fraternize with those of every other. The chiefs of savage tribes have distinguished themselves in London and Paris, by the purity of their tournure.

To say what good of fashion we can,—it rests on reality, and hates nothing so much as pretenders;—to exclude and mystify pretenders, and send them into everlasting 'Coventry,' is its delight. We contemn, in turn, every other gift of men of the world; but the habit even in little and the least matters, of not appealing to any but our own sense of propriety, constitutes the foundation of all chivalry. There is almost no kind of self-reliance, so it be sane and proportioned, which fashion does not occasionally adopt, and give it the freedom of its saloons. A sainted soul is always elegant, and, if it will, passes unchallenged into the most guarded ring. But so will Jock the teamster pass, in some crisis that brings him thither, and find favor, as long as his head is not giddy with the new circumstance, and the iron shoes do not wish to dance in waltzes and cotillons. For there is nothing settled in manners, but the laws of behavior yield to the energy of the individual. The maiden at her first ball, the country-man at a city dinner, believes that there is a ritual according to which every act and compliment must be performed, or the failing party must be cast out of this presence. Later, they learn that good sense and character make their own forms every moment, and speak or abstain, take wine or refuse it, stay or go, sit in a chair or sprawl with children on the floor, or stand on their head, or what else soever, in a new and aboriginal way: and that strong will is always in fashion, let who will be unfashionable. All that fashion demands is composure, and self-content. A circle of men perfectly well-bred would be a company of sensible persons, in which every man's native manners and character appeared. If the fashionist have not this quality, he is nothing. We are such lovers of self-reliance, that we excuse in a man many sins, if he will show us a complete satisfaction in his position, which asks no leave to be, of mine, or any man's good opinion. But any deference to some eminent man or woman of the world, forfeits all privilege of nobility. He is an underling: I have nothing to do with him; I will speak with his master. A man should not go where he cannot carry his whole sphere or society with him,—not bodily, the whole circle of his friends, but atmospherically. He should preserve in a new company the same attitude of mind and reality of relation, which his daily associates draw him to, else he is shorn of his best beams, and will be an orphan in the merriest club. "If you could see Vich Ian Vohr with his tail on!——" But Vich Ian Vohr must always carry his belongings in some fashion, if not added as honor, then severed as disgrace.

There will always be in society certain persons who are mercuries of its approbation, and whose glance will at any time determine for the curious their standing in the world. These are the chamberlains of the lesser gods. Accept their coldness as an omen of grace with the loftier deities, and allow them all their privilege. They are clear in their office, nor could they be thus formidable, without their own merits. But do not measure the importance of this class by their pretension, or imagine that a fop can be the dispenser of honor and shame. They pass also at their just rate; for how can they otherwise, in circles which exist as a sort of herald's office for the sifting of character?

As the first thing man requires of man, is reality, so, that appears in all the forms of society. We pointedly, and by name, introduce the parties to each other. Know you before all heaven and earth, that this is Andrew, and this is Gregory;—they look each other in the eye; they grasp each other's hand, to identify and signalize each other. It is a great satisfaction. A gentleman never dodges: his eyes look straight forward, and he assures the other party, first of all, that he has been met. For what is it that we seek, in so many visits and hospitalities? Is it your draperies, pictures, and decorations? Or, do we not insatiably ask, Was a man in the house? I may easily go into a great household where there is much substance, excellent provision for comfort, luxury, and taste, and yet not encounter there any Amphitryon, who shall subordinate these appendages. I may go into a cottage, and find a farmer who feels that he is the man I have come to see, and fronts me accordingly. It was therefore a very natural point of old feudal etiquette, that a gentleman who received a visit, though it were of his sovereign, should not leave his roof, but should wait his arrival at the door of his house. No house, though it were the Thuilleries, or the Escurial, is good for anything without a master. And yet we are not often gratified by this hospitality. Every body we know surrounds himself with a fine house, fine books, conservatory, gardens, equipage, and all manner of toys, as screens to interpose between himself and his guest. Does it not seem as if man was of a very sly, elusive nature, and dreaded nothing so much as a full rencontre front to front with his fellow? It were unmerciful, I know, quite to abolish the use of these screens, which are of eminent convenience, whether the guest is too great, or too little. We call together many friends who keep each other in play, or, by luxuries and ornaments we amuse the young people, and guard our retirement. Or if, perchance, a searching realist comes to our gate, before whose eye we have no care to stand, then again we run to our curtain, and hide ourselves as Adam at the voice of the Lord God in the garden. Cardinal Caprara, the Pope's legate at Paris, defended himself from the glances of Napoleon, by an immense pair of green spectacles. Napoleon remarked them, and speedily managed to rally them off: and yet Napoleon, in his turn, was not great enough with eight hundred thousand troops at his back, to face a pair of freeborn eyes, but fenced himself with etiquette, and within triple barriers of reserve: and, as all the world knows from Madame de Stael, was wont, when he found himself observed, to discharge his face of all expression. But emperors and rich men are by no means the most skilful masters of good manners. No rentroll nor army-list can dignify skulking and dissimulation: and the first point of courtesy must always be truth, as really all the forms of good-breeding point that way.

I have just been reading, in Mr. Hazlitt's translation, Montaigne's account of his journey into Italy, and am struck with nothing more agreeably than the self-respecting fashions of the time. His arrival in each place, the arrival of a gentleman of France, is an event of some consequence. Wherever he goes, he pays a visit to whatever prince or gentleman of note resides upon his road, as a duty to himself and to civilization. When he leaves any house in which he has lodged for a few weeks, he causes his arms to be painted and hung up as a perpetual sign to the house, as was the custom of gentlemen.

The complement of this graceful self-respect, and that of all the points of good breeding I most require and insist upon, is deference. I like that every chair should be a throne, and hold a king. I prefer a tendency to stateliness, to an excess of fellowship. Let the incommunicable objects of nature and the metaphysical isolation of man teach us independence. Let us not be too much acquainted. I would have a man enter his house through a hall filled with heroic and sacred sculptures, that he might not want the hint of tranquillity and self-poise. We should meet each morning, as from foreign countries, and spending the day together, should depart at night, as into foreign countries. In all things I would have the island of a man inviolate. Let us sit apart as the gods, talking from peak to peak all round Olympus. No degree of affection need invade this religion. This is myrrh and rosemary to keep the other sweet. Lovers should guard their strangeness. If they forgive too much, all slides into confusion and meanness. It is easy to push this deference to a Chinese etiquette; but coolness and absence of heat and haste indicate fine qualities. A gentleman makes no noise: a lady is serene. Proportionate is our disgust at those invaders who fill a studious house with blast and running, to secure some paltry convenience. Not less I dislike a low sympathy of each with his neighbor's needs. Must we have a good understanding with one another's palates? as foolish people who have lived long together, know when each wants salt or sugar. I pray my companion, if he wishes for bread, to ask me for bread, and if he wishes for sassafras or arsenic, to ask me for them, and not to hold out his plate, as if I knew already. Every natural function can be dignified by deliberation and privacy. Let us leave hurry to slaves. The compliments and ceremonies of our breeding should signify, however remotely, the recollection of the grandeur of our destiny.

The flower of courtesy does not very well bide handling, but if we dare to open another leaf, and explore what parts go to its conformation, we shall find also an intellectual quality. To the leaders of men, the brain as well as the flesh and the heart must furnish a proportion. Defect in manners is usually the defect of fine perceptions. Men are too coarsely made for the delicacy of beautiful carriage and customs. It is not quite sufficient to good-breeding, a union of kindness and independence. We imperatively require a perception of, and a homage to beauty in our companions. Other virtues are in request in the field and workyard, but a certain degree of taste is not to be spared in those we sit with. I could better eat with one who did not respect the truth or the laws, than with a sloven and unpresentable person. Moral qualities rule the world, but at short distances, the senses are despotic. The same discrimination of fit and fair runs out, if with less rigor, into all parts of life. The average spirit of the energetic class is good sense, acting under certain limitations and to certain ends. It entertains every natural gift. Social in its nature, it respects everything which tends to unite men. It delights in measure. The love of beauty is mainly the love of measure or proportion. The person who screams, or uses the superlative degree, or converses with heat, puts whole drawing-rooms to flight. If you wish to be loved, love measure. You must have genius, or a prodigious usefulness, if you will hide the want of measure. This perception comes in to polish and perfect the parts of the social instrument. Society will pardon much to genius and special gifts, but, being in its nature a convention, it loves what is conventional, or what belongs to coming together. That makes the good and bad of manners, namely, what helps or hinders fellowship. For, fashion is not good sense absolute, but relative; not good sense private, but good sense entertaining company. It hates corners and sharp points of character, hates quarrelsome, egotistical, solitary, and gloomy people; hates whatever can interfere with total blending of parties; whilst it values all peculiarities as in the highest degree refreshing, which can consist with good fellowship. And besides the general infusion of wit to heighten civility, the direct splendor of intellectual power is ever welcome in fine society as the costliest addition to its rule and its credit.

The dry light must shine in to adorn our festival, but it must be tempered and shaded, or that will also offend. Accuracy is essential to beauty, and quick perceptions to politeness, but not too quick perceptions. One may be too punctual and too precise. He must leave the omniscience of business at the door, when he comes into the palace of beauty. Society loves creole natures, and sleepy, languishing manners, so that they cover sense, grace, and good-will; the air of drowsy strength, which disarms criticism; perhaps, because such a person seems to reserve himself for the best of the game, and not spend himself on surfaces; an ignoring eye, which does not see the annoyances, shifts, and inconveniences, that cloud the brow and smother the voice of the sensitive.

Therefore, besides personal force and so much perception as constitutes unerring taste, society demands in its patrician class, another element already intimated, which it significantly terms good-nature, expressing all degrees of generosity, from the lowest willingness and faculty to oblige, up to the heights of magnanimity and love. Insight we must have, or we shall run against one another, and miss the way to our food; but intellect is selfish and barren. The secret of success in society, is a certain heartiness and sympathy. A man who is not happy in the company, cannot find any word in his memory that will fit the occasion. All his information is a little impertinent. A man who is happy there, finds in every turn of the conversation equally lucky occasions for the introduction of that which he has to say. The favorites of society, and what it calls *whole souls*, are able men, and of more spirit than wit, who have no uncomfortable egotism, but who exactly fill the hour and the company, contented and contenting, at a marriage or a funeral, a ball or a jury, a water-party or a shooting-match. England, which is rich in gentlemen, furnished, in the beginning of the present century, a good model of that genius which the world loves, in Mr. Fox, who added to his great abilities the most social disposition, and real love of men. Parliamentary history has few better passages than the debate, in which Burke and Fox separated in the House of Commons; when Fox urged on his old friend the claims of old friendship with such tenderness, that the house was moved to tears. Another anecdote is so close to my matter, that I must hazard the story. A tradesman who had long dunned him for a note of three hundred guineas, found him one day counting gold, and demanded payment: "No," said Fox, "I owe this money to Sheridan: it is a debt of honor: if an accident should happen to me, he has nothing to show." "Then," said the creditor, "I change my debt into a debt of honor," and tore the note in pieces. Fox thanked the man for his confidence, and paid him, saying, "his debt was of older standing, and Sheridan must wait." Lover of liberty, friend of the Hindoo, friend of the African slave, he possessed a great personal popularity; and Napoleon said of him on the occasion of his visit to Paris, in 1805, "Mr. Fox will always hold the first place in an assembly at the Thuilleries."

We may easily seem ridiculous in our eulogy of courtesy, whenever we insist on benevolence as its foundation. The painted phantasm Fashion rises to cast a species of derision on what we say. But I will neither be driven from some allowance to Fashion as a symbolic institution, nor from the belief that love is the basis of courtesy. We must obtain *that*, if we can; but by all means we must affirm *this*. Life owes much of its spirit to these sharp contrasts. Fashion which affects to be honor, is often, in all men's experience, only a ballroom-code. Yet, so long as it is the highest circle, in the imagination of the best heads on the planet, there is something necessary and excellent in it; for it is not to be supposed that men have agreed to be the dupes of anything preposterous; and the re-

spect which these mysteries inspire in the most rude and sylvan characters, and the curiosity with which details of high
life are read, betray the universality of the love of cultivated
manners. I know that a comic disparity would be felt, if we
should enter the acknowledged 'first circles,' and apply these
terrific standards of justice, beauty, and benefit, to the individuals actually found there. Monarchs and heroes, sages and
lovers, these gallants are not. Fashion has many classes and
many rules of probation and admission; and not the best
alone. There is not only the right of conquest, which genius
pretends,—the individual, demonstrating his natural aristocracy best of the best;—but less claims will pass for the time;
for Fashion loves lions, and points, like Circe, to her horned
company. This gentleman is this afternoon arrived from Denmark; and that is my Lord Ride, who came yesterday from
Bagdat; here is Captain Friese, from Cape Turnagain; and
Captain Symmes, from the interior of the earth; and Monsieur Jovaire, who came down this morning in a balloon; Mr.
Hobnail, the reformer; and Reverend Jul Bat, who has converted the whole torrid zone in his Sunday school; and Si-
gnor Torre del Greco, who extinguished Vesuvius by pouring
into it the Bay of Naples; Spahi, the Persian ambassador; and
Tul Wil Shan, the exiled nabob of Nepaul, whose saddle is
the new moon.—But these are monsters of one day, and to-
morrow will be dismissed to their holes and dens; for, in
these rooms, every chair is waited for. The artist, the scholar,
and, in general, the clerisy, wins its way up into these places,
and gets represented here, somewhat on this footing of conquest. Another mode is to pass through all the degrees,
spending a year and a day in St. Michael's Square, being
steeped in Cologne water, and perfumed, and dined, and introduced, and properly grounded in all the biography, and
politics, and anecdotes of the boudoirs.

Yet these fineries may have grace and wit. Let there be gro-
tesque sculpture about the gates and offices of temples. Let
the creed and commandments even have the saucy homage of
parody. The forms of politeness universally express benevolence in superlative degrees. What if they are in the mouths
of selfish men, and used as means of selfishness? What if the
false gentleman almost bows the true out of the world? What

if the false gentleman contrives so to address his companion, as civilly to exclude all others from his discourse, and also to make them feel excluded? Real service will not lose its nobleness. All generosity is not merely French and sentimental; nor is it to be concealed, that living blood and a passion of kindness does at last distinguish God's gentleman from Fashion's. The epitaph of Sir Jenkin Grout is not wholly unintelligible to the present age. "Here lies Sir Jenkin Grout, who loved his friend, and persuaded his enemy: what his mouth ate, his hand paid for: what his servants robbed, he restored: if a woman gave him pleasure, he supported her in pain: he never forgot his children: and whoso touched his finger, drew after it his whole body." Even the line of heroes is not utterly extinct. There is still ever some admirable person in plain clothes, standing on the wharf, who jumps in to rescue a drowning man; there is still some absurd inventor of charities; some guide and comforter of runaway slaves; some friend of Poland; some Philhellene; some fanatic who plants shade-trees for the second and third generation, and orchards when he is grown old; some well-concealed piety; some just man happy in an ill-fame; some youth ashamed of the favors of fortune, and impatiently casting them on other shoulders. And these are the centres of society, on which it returns for fresh impulses. These are the creators of Fashion, which is an attempt to organize beauty of behavior. The beautiful and the generous are, in the theory, the doctors and apostles of this church: Scipio, and the Cid, and Sir Philip Sidney, and Washington, and every pure and valiant heart, who worshipped Beauty by word and by deed. The persons who constitute the natural aristocracy, are not found in the actual aristocracy, or, only on its edge; as the chemical energy of the spectrum is found to be greatest just outside of the spectrum. Yet that is the infirmity of the seneschals, who do not know their sovereign, when he appears. The theory of society supposes the existence and sovereignty of these. It divines afar off their coming. It says with the elder gods,—

"As Heaven and Earth are fairer far
Than Chaos and blank Darkness, though once chiefs;
And as we show beyond that Heaven and Earth,

In form and shape compact and beautiful;
So, on our heels a fresh perfection treads;
A power, more strong in beauty, born of us,
And fated to excel us, as we pass
In glory that old Darkness:
———— for, 't is the eternal law,
That first in beauty shall be first in might."

Therefore, within the ethnical circle of good society, there is a narrower and higher circle, concentration of its light, and flower of courtesy, to which there is always a tacit appeal of pride and reference, as to its inner and imperial court, the parliament of love and chivalry. And this is constituted of those persons in whom heroic dispositions are native, with the love of beauty, the delight in society, and the power to embellish the passing day. If the individuals who compose the purest circles of aristocracy in Europe, the guarded blood of centuries, should pass in review, in such manner as that we could, at leisure, and critically inspect their behavior, we might find no gentleman, and no lady; for, although excellent specimens of courtesy and high-breeding would gratify us in the assemblage, in the particulars, we should detect offence. Because, elegance comes of no breeding, but of birth. There must be romance of character, or the most fastidious exclusion of impertinencies will not avail. It must be genius which takes that direction: it must be not courteous, but courtesy. High behavior is as rare in fiction, as it is in fact. Scott is praised for the fidelity with which he painted the demeanor and conversation of the superior classes. Certainly, kings and queens, nobles and great ladies, had some right to complain of the absurdity that had been put in their mouths, before the days of Waverley; but neither does Scott's dialogue bear criticism. His lords brave each other in smart epigramatic speeches, but the dialogue is in costume, and does not please on the second reading: it is not warm with life. In Shakspeare alone, the speakers do not strut and bridle, the dialogue is easily great, and he adds to so many titles that of being the best-bred man in England, and in Christendom. Once or twice in a lifetime we are permitted to enjoy the charm of noble manners, in the presence of a man or woman

who have no bar in their nature, but whose character emanates freely in their word and gesture. A beautiful form is
better than a beautiful face; a beautiful behavior is better than
a beautiful form: it gives a higher pleasure than statues or
pictures; it is the finest of the fine arts. A man is but a little
thing in the midst of the objects of nature, yet, by the moral
quality radiating from his countenance, he may abolish all
considerations of magnitude, and in his manners equal
the majesty of the world. I have seen an individual, whose
manners, though wholly within the conventions of elegant
society, were never learned there, but were original and
commanding, and held out protection and prosperity; one
who did not need the aid of a court-suit, but carried the holiday in his eye; who exhilarated the fancy by flinging wide the
doors of new modes of existence; who shook off the captivity
of etiquette, with happy, spirited bearing, good-natured and
free as Robin Hood; yet with the port of an emperor,—if
need be, calm, serious, and fit to stand the gaze of millions.

The open air and the fields, the street and public chambers,
are the places where Man executes his will; let him yield or
divide the sceptre at the door of the house. Woman, with her
instinct of behavior, instantly detects in man a love of trifles,
any coldness or imbecility, or, in short, any want of that large,
flowing, and magnanimous deportment, which is indispensable as an exterior in the hall. Our American institutions have
been friendly to her, and at this moment, I esteem it a chief
felicity of this country, that it excels in women. A certain awkward consciousness of inferiority in the men, may give rise to
the new chivalry in behalf of Woman's Rights. Certainly, let
her be as much better placed in the laws and in social forms,
as the most zealous reformer can ask, but I confide so entirely
in her inspiring and musical nature, that I believe only herself
can show us how she shall be served. The wonderful generosity of her sentiments raises her at times into heroical and
godlike regions, and verifies the pictures of Minerva, Juno, or
Polymnia; and, by the firmness with which she treads her upward path, she convinces the coarsest calculators that another
road exists, than that which their feet know. But besides those
who make good in our imagination the place of muses and of
Delphic Sibyls, are there not women who fill our vase with

wine and roses to the brim, so that the wine runs over and fills the house with perfume; who inspire us with courtesy; who unloose our tongues, and we speak; who anoint our eyes, and we see? We say things we never thought to have said; for once, our walls of habitual reserve vanished, and left us at large; we were children playing with children in a wide field of flowers. Steep us, we cried, in these influences, for days, for weeks, and we shall be sunny poets, and will write out in many-colored words the romance that you are. Was it Hafiz or Firdousi that said of his Persian Lilla, She was an elemental force, and astonished me by her amount of life, when I saw her day after day radiating, every instant, redundant joy and grace on all around her. She was a solvent powerful to reconcile all heterogeneous persons into one society: like air or water, an element of such a great range of affinities, that it combines readily with a thousand substances. Where she is present, all others will be more than they are wont. She was a unit and whole, so that whatsoever she did, became her. She had too much sympathy and desire to please, than that you could say, her manners were marked with dignity, yet no princess could surpass her clear and erect demeanor on each occasion. She did not study the Persian grammar, nor the books of the seven poets, but all the poems of the seven seemed to be written upon her. For, though the bias of her nature was not to thought, but to sympathy, yet was she so perfect in her own nature, as to meet intellectual persons by the fulness of her heart, warming them by her sentiments; believing, as she did, that by dealing nobly with all, all would show themselves noble.

I know that this Byzantine pile of chivalry or Fashion, which seems so fair and picturesque to those who look at the contemporary facts for science or for entertainment, is not equally pleasant to all spectators. The constitution of our society makes it a giant's castle to the ambitious youth who have not found their names enrolled in its Golden Book, and whom it has excluded from its coveted honors and privileges. They have yet to learn that its seeming grandeur is shadowy and relative: it is great by their allowance: its proudest gates will fly open at the approach of their courage and virtue. For the present distress, however, of those who are predisposed to suffer from the tyrannies of this caprice, there are easy remedies. To remove your residence a couple of miles, or at most four, will commonly relieve the most extreme susceptibility. For, the advantages which fashion values, are plants which thrive in very confined localities, in a few streets, namely. Out of this precinct, they go for nothing; are of no use in the farm, in the forest, in the market, in war, in the nuptial society, in the literary or scientific circle, at sea, in friendship, in the heaven of thought or virtue.

But we have lingered long enough in these painted courts. The worth of the thing signified must vindicate our taste for the emblem. Everything that is called fashion and courtesy humbles itself before the cause and fountain of honor, creator of titles and dignities, namely, the heart of love. This is the royal blood, this the fire, which, in all countries and contingencies, will work after its kind, and conquer and expand all that approaches it. This gives new meanings to every fact. This impoverishes the rich, suffering no grandeur but its own. What *is* rich? Are you rich enough to help anybody? to succor the unfashionable and the eccentric? rich enough to make the Canadian in his wagon, the itinerant with his consul's paper which commends him "To the charitable," the swarthy Italian with his few broken words of English, the lame pauper hunted by overseers from town to town, even the poor insane or besotted wreck of man or woman, feel the noble exception of your presence and your house, from the general bleakness and stoniness; to make such feel that they were greeted with a voice which made them both remember and hope? What is vulgar, but to refuse the claim on acute and conclusive reasons? What is gentle, but to allow it, and give their heart and yours one holiday from the national caution? Without the rich heart, wealth is an ugly beggar. The king of Schiraz could not afford to be so bountiful as the poor Osman who dwelt at his gate. Osman had a humanity so broad and deep, that although his speech was so bold and free with the Koran, as to disgust all the dervishes, yet was there never a poor outcast, eccentric, or insane man, some fool who had cut off his beard, or who had been mutilated under a vow, or had a pet madness in his brain, but fled at once to him,—that great heart lay there so sunny and hospitable in the centre of the country,—that it seemed as if the instinct of all sufferers drew them to his side. And the madness which he harbored, he did not share. Is not this to be rich? this only to be rightly rich?

But I shall hear without pain, that I play the courtier very ill, and talk of that which I do not well understand. It is easy to see, that what is called by distinction society and fashion, has good laws as well as bad, has much that is necessary, and much that is absurd. Too good for banning, and too bad for blessing, it reminds us of a tradition of the pagan mythology, in any attempt to settle its character. 'I overheard Jove, one day,' said Silenus, 'talking of destroying the earth; he said, it had failed; they were all rogues and vixens, who went from bad to worse, as fast as the days succeeded each other. Minerva said, she hoped not; they were only ridiculous little creatures, with this odd circumstance, that they had a blur, or indeterminate aspect, seen far or seen near; if you called them bad, they would appear so; if you called them good, they would appear so; and there was no one person or action among them, which would not puzzle her owl, much more all Olympus, to know whether it was fundamentally bad or good.'

GIFTS

―――

Gifts of one who loved me,—
'T was high time they came;
When he ceased to love me,
Time they stopped for shame.

Gifts

IT IS SAID that the world is in a state of bankruptcy, that the world owes the world more than the world can pay, and ought to go into chancery, and be sold. I do not think this general insolvency, which involves in some sort all the population, to be the reason of the difficulty experienced at Christmas and New Year, and other times, in bestowing gifts; since it is always so pleasant to be generous, though very vexatious to pay debts. But the impediment lies in the choosing. If, at any time, it comes into my head, that a present is due from me to somebody, I am puzzled what to give, until the opportunity is gone. Flowers and fruits are always fit presents; flowers, because they are a proud assertion that a ray of beauty outvalues all the utilities of the world. These gay natures contrast with the somewhat stern countenance of ordinary nature: they are like music heard out of a work-house. Nature does not cocker us: we are children, not pets: she is not fond: everything is dealt to us without fear or favor, after severe universal laws. Yet these delicate flowers look like the frolic and interference of love and beauty. Men use to tell us that we love flattery, even though we are not deceived by it, because it shows that we are of importance enough to be courted. Something like that pleasure, the flowers give us: what am I to whom these sweet hints are addressed? Fruits are acceptable gifts, because they are the flower of commodities, and admit of fantastic values being attached to them. If a man should send to me to come a hundred miles to visit him, and should set before me a basket of fine summer-fruit, I should think there was some proportion between the labor and the reward.

For common gifts, necessity makes pertinences and beauty every day, and one is glad when an imperative leaves him no option, since if the man at the door have no shoes, you have not to consider whether you could procure him a paint-box. And as it is always pleasing to see a man eat bread, or drink water, in the house or out of doors, so it is always a great satisfaction to supply these first wants. Necessity does everything well. In our condition of universal dependence, it seems heroic to let the petitioner be the judge of his necessity, and to give all that is asked, though at great inconvenience. If it be a fantastic desire, it is better to leave to others the office of punishing him. I can think of many parts I should prefer playing to that of the Furies. Next to things of necessity, the rule for a gift, which one of my friends prescribed, is, that we might convey to some person that which properly belonged to his character, and was easily associated with him in thought. But our tokens of compliment and love are for the most part barbarous. Rings and other jewels are not gifts, but apologies for gifts. The only gift is a portion of thyself. Thou must bleed for me. Therefore the poet brings his poem; the shepherd, his lamb; the farmer, corn; the miner, a gem; the sailor, coral and shells; the painter, his picture; the girl, a handkerchief of her own sewing. This is right and pleasing, for it restores society in so far to its primary basis, when a man's biography is conveyed in his gift, and every man's wealth is an index of his merit. But it is a cold, lifeless business when you go to the shops to buy me something, which does not represent your life and talent, but a goldsmith's. This is fit for kings, and rich men who represent kings, and a false state of property, to make presents of gold and silver stuffs, as a kind of symbolical sin-offering, or payment of black-mail.

The law of benefits is a difficult channel, which requires careful sailing, or rude boats. It is not the office of a man to receive gifts. How dare you give them? We wish to be self-sustained. We do not quite forgive a giver. The hand that feeds us is in some danger of being bitten. We can receive anything from love, for that is a way of receiving it from ourselves; but not from any one who assumes to bestow. We sometimes hate the meat which we eat, because there seems something of degrading dependence in living by it.

"Brother, if Jove to thee a present make,
Take heed that from his hands thou nothing take."

We ask the whole. Nothing less will content us. We arraign society, if it do not give us besides earth, and fire, and water, opportunity, love, reverence, and objects of veneration.

He is a good man, who can receive a gift well. We are either glad or sorry at a gift, and both emotions are unbecoming. Some violence, I think, is done, some degradation borne, when I rejoice or grieve at a gift. I am sorry when my independence is invaded, or when a gift comes from such as do not know my spirit, and so the act is not supported; and if the gift pleases me overmuch, then I should be ashamed that the donor should read my heart, and see that I love his commodity, and not him. The gift, to be true, must be the flowing of the giver unto me, correspondent to my flowing unto him. When the waters are at level, then my goods pass to him, and his to me. All his are mine, all mine his. I say to him, How can you give me this pot of oil, or this flagon of wine, when all your oil and wine is mine, which belief of mine this gift seems to deny? Hence the fitness of beautiful, not useful things for gifts. This giving is flat usurpation, and therefore when the beneficiary is ungrateful, as all beneficiaries hate all Timons, not at all considering the value of the gift, but looking back to the greater store it was taken from, I rather sympathize with the beneficiary, than with the anger of my lord Timon. For, the expectation of gratitude is mean, and is continually punished by the total insensibility of the obliged person. It is a great happiness to get off without injury and heart-burning, from one who has had the ill luck to be served by you. It is a very onerous business, this of being served, and the debtor naturally wishes to give you a slap. A golden text for these gentlemen is that which I so admire in the Buddhist, who never thanks, and who says, "Do not flatter your benefactors."

The reason of these discords I conceive to be, that there is no commensurability between a man and any gift. You cannot give anything to a magnanimous person. After you have served him, he at once puts you in debt by his magnanimity. The service a man renders his friend is trivial and selfish, compared with the service he knows his friend stood in readiness to yield him, alike before he had begun to serve his friend, and now also. Compared with that good-will I bear my friend, the benefit it is in my power to render him seems small. Besides, our action on each other, good as well as evil, is so incidental and at random, that we can seldom hear the acknowledgments of any person who would thank us for a benefit, without some shame and humiliation. We can rarely strike a direct stroke, but must be content with an oblique one; we seldom have the satisfaction of yielding a direct benefit, which is directly received. But rectitude scatters favors on every side without knowing it, and receives with wonder the thanks of all people.

I fear to breathe any treason against the majesty of love, which is the genius and god of gifts, and to whom we must not affect to prescribe. Let him give kingdoms or flower-leaves indifferently. There are persons, from whom we always expect fairy tokens; let us not cease to expect them. This is prerogative, and not to be limited by our municipal rules. For the rest, I like to see that we cannot be bought and sold. The best of hospitality and of generosity is also not in the will, but in fate. I find that I am not much to you; you do not need me; you do not feel me; then am I thrust out of doors, though you proffer me house and lands. No services are of any value, but only likeness. When I have attempted to join myself to others by services, it proved an intellectual trick,— no more. They eat your service like apples, and leave you out. But love them, and they feel you, and delight in you all the time.

NATURE

The rounded world is fair to see,
Nine times folded in mystery:
Though baffled seers cannot impart
The secret of its laboring heart,
Throb thine with Nature's throbbing breast,
And all is clear from east to west.
Spirit that lurks each form within
Beckons to spirit of its kin;
Self-kindled every atom glows,
And hints the future which it owes.

Nature

THERE ARE days which occur in this climate, at almost any season of the year, wherein the world reaches its perfection, when the air, the heavenly bodies, and the earth, make a harmony, as if nature would indulge her offspring; when, in these bleak upper sides of the planet, nothing is to desire that we have heard of the happiest latitudes, and we bask in the shining hours of Florida and Cuba; when everything that has life gives sign of satisfaction, and the cattle that lie on the ground seem to have great and tranquil thoughts. These halcyons may be looked for with a little more assurance in that pure October weather, which we distinguish by the name of the Indian Summer. The day, immeasurably long, sleeps over the broad hills and warm wide fields. To have lived through all its sunny hours, seems longevity enough. The solitary places do not seem quite lonely. At the gates of the forest, the surprised man of the world is forced to leave his city estimates of great and small, wise and foolish. The knapsack of custom falls off his back with the first step he makes into these precincts. Here is sanctity which shames our religions, and reality which discredits our heroes. Here we find nature to be the circumstance which dwarfs every other circumstance, and judges like a god all men that come to her. We have crept out of our close and crowded houses into the night and morning, and we see what majestic beauties daily wrap us in their bosom. How willingly we would escape the barriers which render them comparatively impotent, escape the sophistication and second thought, and suffer nature to intrance us. The tempered light of the woods is like a perpetual morning, and is stimulating and heroic. The anciently reported spells of these places creep on us. The stems of pines, hemlocks, and oaks, almost gleam like iron on the excited eye. The incommunicable trees begin to persuade us to live with them, and quit our life of solemn trifles. Here no history, or church, or state, is interpolated on the divine sky and the immortal year. How easily we might walk onward into the opening landscape, absorbed by new pictures, and by thoughts fast succeeding each other, until by degrees the recollection of home was crowded out of the mind, all memory obliterated by the tyranny of the present, and we were led in triumph by nature.

These enchantments are medicinal, they sober and heal us. These are plain pleasures, kindly and native to us. We come to our own, and make friends with matter, which the ambitious chatter of the schools would persuade us to despise. We never can part with it; the mind loves its old home: as water to our thirst, so is the rock, the ground, to our eyes, and hands, and feet. It is firm water: it is cold flame: what health, what affinity! Ever an old friend, ever like a dear friend and brother, when we chat affectedly with strangers, comes in this honest face, and takes a grave liberty with us, and shames us out of our nonsense. Cities give not the human senses room enough. We go out daily and nightly to feed the eyes on the horizon, and require so much scope, just as we need water for our bath. There are all degrees of natural influence, from these quarantine powers of nature, up to her dearest and gravest ministrations to the imagination and the soul. There is the bucket of cold water from the spring, the wood-fire to which the chilled traveller rushes for safety,—and there is the sublime moral of autumn and of noon. We nestle in nature, and draw our living as parasites from her roots and grains, and we receive glances from the heavenly bodies, which call us to solitude, and foretell the remotest future. The blue zenith is the point in which romance and reality meet. I think, if we should be rapt away into all that we dream of heaven, and should converse with Gabriel and Uriel, the upper sky would be all that would remain of our furniture.

It seems as if the day was not wholly profane, in which we have given heed to some natural object. The fall of snowflakes in a still air, preserving to each crystal its perfect form; the blowing of sleet over a wide sheet of water, and over plains, the waving rye-field, the mimic waving of acres of houstonia, whose innumerable florets whiten and ripple before the eye; the reflections of trees and flowers in glassy lakes; the musical steaming odorous south wind, which converts all trees to windharps; the crackling and spurting of hemlock in the flames; or of pine logs, which yield glory to the walls and faces in the sittingroom,—these are the music and pictures of the most ancient religion. My house stands in low land, with limited outlook, and on the skirt of the village. But I go with my friend to the shore of our little river, and with one stroke of the paddle, I leave the village politics and personalities, yes, and the world of villages and personalities behind, and pass into a delicate realm of sunset and moonlight, too bright almost for spotted man to enter without noviciate and probation. We penetrate bodily this incredible beauty; we dip our hands in this painted element: our eyes are bathed in these lights and forms. A holiday, a villeggiatura, a royal revel, the proudest, most heart-rejoicing festival that valor and beauty, power and taste, ever decked and enjoyed, establishes itself on the instant. These sunset clouds, these delicately emerging stars, with their private and ineffable glances, signify it and proffer it. I am taught the poorness of our invention, the ugliness of towns and palaces. Art and luxury have early learned that they must work as enhancement and sequel to this original beauty. I am over-instructed for my return. Henceforth I shall be hard to please. I cannot go back to toys. I am grown expensive and sophisticated. I can no longer live without elegance: but a countryman shall be my master of revels. He who knows the most, he who knows what sweets and virtues are in the ground, the waters, the plants, the heavens, and how to come at these enchantments, is the rich and royal man. Only as far as the masters of the world have called in nature to their aid, can they reach the height of magnificence. This is the meaning of their hanging-gardens, villas, garden-houses, islands, parks, and preserves, to back their faulty personality with these strong accessories. I do not wonder that the landed interest should be invincible in the state with these dangerous auxiliaries. These bribe and invite; not kings, not palaces, not men, not women, but these tender and poetic stars, eloquent of secret promises. We heard what the rich man said, we knew of his villa, his grove, his wine, and his company, but the provocation and point of the invitation came out of these beguiling stars. In their soft glances, I see what men strove to realize in some Versailles, or Paphos, or Ctesiphon. Indeed, it is the magical lights of the horizon, and the blue sky for the background, which save all our works of art, which were otherwise bawbles. When the rich tax the poor with servility and obsequiousness, they should consider the effect of men reputed to be the possessors of nature, on imaginative minds. Ah! if the rich were rich as the poor fancy riches! A boy hears a military band play on the field at night, and he has kings and queens, and famous chivalry palpably before him. He hears the echoes of a horn in a hill country, in the Notch Mountains, for example, which converts the mountains into an Æolian harp, and this supernatural *tiralira* restores to him the Dorian mythology, Apollo, Diana, and all divine hunters and huntresses. Can a musical note be so lofty, so haughtily beautiful! To the poor young poet, thus fabulous is his picture of society; he is loyal; he respects the rich; they are rich for the sake of his imagination; how poor his fancy would be, if they were not rich! That they have some high-fenced grove, which they call a park; that they live in larger and better-garnished saloons than he has visited, and go in coaches, keeping only the society of the elegant, to watering-places, and to distant cities, are the groundwork from which he has delineated estates of romance, compared with which their actual possessions are shanties and paddocks. The muse herself betrays her son, and enhances the gifts of wealth and well-born beauty, by a radiation out of the air, and clouds, and forests that skirt the road,—a certain haughty favor, as if from patrician genii to patricians, a kind of aristocracy in nature, a prince of the power of the air.

The moral sensibility which makes Edens and Tempes so easily, may not be always found, but the material landscape is never far off. We can find these enchantments without visiting the Como Lake, or the Madeira Islands. We exaggerate the praises of local scenery. In every landscape, the point of aston-ishment is the meeting of the sky and the earth, and that is seen from the first hillock as well as from the top of the Al-leghanies. The stars at night stoop down over the brownest, homeliest common, with all the spiritual magnificence which they shed on the Campagna, or on the marble deserts of Egypt. The uprolled clouds and the colors of morning and evening, will transfigure maples and alders. The difference be-tween landscape and landscape is small, but there is great difference in the beholders. There is nothing so wonderful in any particular landscape, as the necessity of being beautiful under which every landscape lies. Nature cannot be surprised in undress. Beauty breaks in everywhere.

But it is very easy to outrun the sympathy of readers on this topic, which schoolmen called *natura naturata*, or nature passive. One can hardly speak directly of it without excess. It is as easy to broach in mixed companies what is called "the subject of religion." A susceptible person does not like to indulge his tastes in this kind, without the apology of some trivial necessity: he goes to see a wood-lot, or to look at the crops, or to fetch a plant or a mineral from a remote locality, or he carries a fowling piece, or a fishing-rod. I suppose this shame must have a good reason. A dilettantism in nature is barren and unworthy. The fop of fields is no better than his brother of Broadway. Men are naturally hunters and inquisitive of wood-craft, and I suppose that such a gazetteer as wood-cutters and Indians should furnish facts for, would take place in the most sumptuous drawingrooms of all the "Wreaths" and "Flora's chaplets" of the bookshops; yet ordinarily, whether we are too clumsy for so subtle a topic, or from whatever cause, as soon as men begin to write on nature, they fall into euphuism. Frivolity is a most unfit tribute to Pan, who ought to be represented in the mythology as the most continent of gods. I would not be frivolous before the admirable reserve and prudence of time, yet I cannot renounce the right of returning often to this old topic. The multitude of false churches accredits the true religion. Literature, poetry, science, are the homage of man to this unfathomed secret, concerning which no sane man can affect an indifference or incuriosity. Nature is loved by what is best in us. It is loved as the city of God, although, or rather because there is no citizen. The sunset is unlike anything that is underneath it: it wants men. And the beauty of nature must always seem unreal and mocking, until the landscape has human figures, that are as good as itself. If there were good men, there would never be this rapture in nature. If the king is in the palace, nobody looks at the walls. It is when he is gone, and the house is filled with grooms and gazers, that we turn from the people, to find relief in the majestic men that are suggested by the pictures and the architecture. The critics who complain of the sickly separation of the beauty of nature from the thing to be done, must consider that our hunting of the picturesque is inseparable from our protest against false society. Man is fallen; nature is erect, and serves as a differential thermometer, detecting the presence or absence of the divine sentiment in man. By fault of our dulness and selfishness, we are looking up to nature, but when we are convalescent, nature will look up to us. We see the foaming brook with compunction: if our own life flowed with the right energy, we should shame the brook. The stream of zeal sparkles with real fire, and not with reflex rays of sun and moon. Nature may be as selfishly studied as trade. Astronomy to the selfish becomes astrology; psychology, mesmerism (with intent to show where our spoons are gone); and anatomy and physiology, become phrenology and palmistry.

But taking timely warning, and leaving many things unsaid on this topic, let us not longer omit our homage to the Efficient Nature, *natura naturans*, the quick cause, before which all forms flee as the driven snows, itself secret, its works driven before it in flocks and multitudes, (as the ancient represented nature by Proteus, a shepherd,) and in undescribable variety. It publishes itself in creatures, reaching from particles and spicula, through transformation on transformation to the highest symmetries, arriving at consummate results without a shock or a leap. A little heat, that is, a little motion, is all that differences the bald, dazzling white, and deadly cold poles of the earth from the prolific tropical climates. All changes pass without violence, by reason of the two cardinal conditions of boundless space and boundless time. Geology has initiated us into the secularity of nature, and taught us to disuse our dame-school measures, and exchange our Mosaic and Ptolemaic schemes for her large style. We knew nothing rightly, for want of perspective. Now we learn what patient periods must round themselves before the rock is formed, then before the rock is broken, and the first lichen race has disintegrated the thinnest external plate into soil, and opened the door for the remote Flora, Fauna, Ceres, and Pomona, to come in. How far off yet is the trilobite! how far the quadruped! how inconceivably remote is man! All duly arrive, and then race after race of men. It is a long way from granite to the oyster; farther yet to Plato, and the preaching of the immortality of the soul. Yet all must come, as surely as the first atom has two sides.

Motion or change, and identity or rest, are the first and second secrets of nature: Motion and Rest. The whole code of her laws may be written on the thumbnail, or the signet of a ring. The whirling bubble on the surface of a brook, admits us to the secret of the mechanics of the sky. Every shell on the beach is a key to it. A little water made to rotate in a cup explains the formation of the simpler shells; the addition of matter from year to year, arrives at last at the most complex forms; and yet so poor is nature with all her craft, that, from the beginning to the end of the universe, she has but one stuff,—but one stuff with its two ends, to serve up all her dream-like variety. Compound it how she will, star, sand, fire, water, tree, man, it is still one stuff, and betrays the same properties.

Nature is always consistent, though she feigns to contravene her own laws. She keeps her laws, and seems to transcend them. She arms and equips an animal to find its place and living in the earth, and, at the same time, she arms and equips another animal to destroy it. Space exists to divide creatures; but by clothing the sides of a bird with a few feathers, she gives him a petty omnipresence. The direction is forever onward, but the artist still goes back for materials, and begins again with the first elements on the most advanced stage: otherwise, all goes to ruin. If we look at her work, we seem to catch a glance of a system in transition. Plants are the young of the world, vessels of health and vigor; but they grope ever upward towards consciousness; the trees are imperfect men, and seem to bemoan their imprisonment, rooted in the ground. The animal is the novice and probationer of a more advanced order. The men, though young, having tasted the first drop from the cup of thought, are already dissipated: the maples and ferns are still uncorrupt; yet no doubt, when they come to consciousness, they too will curse and swear. Flowers so strictly belong to youth, that we adult men soon come to feel, that their beautiful generations concern not us: we have had our day; now let the children have theirs. The flowers jilt us, and we are old bachelors with our ridiculous tenderness.

Things are so strictly related, that according to the skill of the eye, from any one object the parts and properties of any other may be predicted. If we had eyes to see it, a bit of stone from the city wall would certify us of the necessity that man must exist, as readily as the city. That identity makes us all one, and reduces to nothing great intervals on our customary scale. We talk of deviations from natural life, as if artificial life were not also natural. The smoothest curled courtier in the boudoirs of a palace has an animal nature, rude and aboriginal as a white bear, omnipotent to its own ends, and is directly related, there amid essences and billetsdoux, to Himmaleh mountain-chains, and the axis of the globe. If we consider how much we are nature's, we need not be superstitious about towns, as if that terrific or benefic force did not find us there also, and fashion cities. Nature who made the mason, made the house. We may easily hear too much of rural influences. The cool disengaged air of natural objects, makes them enviable to us, chafed and irritable creatures with red faces, and we think we shall be as grand as they, if we camp out and eat roots; but let us be men instead of woodchucks, and the oak and the elm shall gladly serve us, though we sit in chairs of ivory on carpets of silk.

This guiding identity runs through all the surprises and contrasts of the piece, and characterizes every law. Man carries the world in his head, the whole astronomy and chemistry suspended in a thought. Because the history of nature is charactered in his brain, therefore is he the prophet and discoverer of her secrets. Every known fact in natural science was divined by the presentiment of somebody, before it was actually verified. A man does not tie his shoe without recognising laws which bind the farthest regions of nature: moon, plant, gas, crystal, are concrete geometry and numbers. Common sense knows its own, and recognises the fact at first sight in chemical experiment. The common sense of Franklin, Dalton, Davy, and Black, is the same common sense which made the arrangements which now it discovers.

If the identity expresses organized rest, the counter action runs also into organization. The astronomers said, 'Give us matter, and a little motion, and we will construct the universe. It is not enough that we should have matter, we must also have a single impulse, one shove to launch the mass, and generate the harmony of the centrifugal and centripetal forces. Once heave the ball from the hand, and we can show how all this mighty order grew.'—'A very unreasonable postulate,' said the metaphysicians, 'and a plain begging of the question. Could you not prevail to know the genesis of projection, as well as the continuation of it?' Nature, meanwhile, had not waited for the discussion, but, right or wrong, bestowed the impulse, and the balls rolled. It was no great affair, a mere push, but the astronomers were right in making much of it, for there is no end to the consequences of the act. That famous aboriginal push propagates itself through all the balls of the system, and through every atom of every ball, through all the races of creatures, and through the history and performances of every individual. Exaggeration is in the course of things. Nature sends no creature, no man into the world, without adding a small excess of his proper quality. Given the planet, it is still necessary to add the impulse; so, to every creature nature added a little violence of direction in its proper path, a shove to put it on its way; in every instance, a slight generosity, a drop too much. Without electricity the air would rot, and without this violence of direction, which men and women have, without a spice of bigot and fanatic, no excitement, no efficiency. We aim above the mark, to hit the mark. Every act hath some falsehood of exaggeration in it. And when now and then comes along some sad, sharp-eyed man, who sees how paltry a game is played, and refuses to play, but blabs the secret;—how then? is the bird flown? O no, the wary Nature sends a new troop of fairer forms, of lordlier youths, with a little more excess of direction to hold them fast to their several aim; makes them a little wrong-headed in that direction in which they are rightest, and on goes the game again with new whirl, for a generation or two more. The child with his sweet pranks, the fool of his senses, commanded by every sight and sound, without any power to compare and rank his sensations, abandoned to a whistle or a painted chip, to a lead dragoon, or a gingerbread-dog, individualizing everything, generalizing nothing, delighted with every new thing, lies down at night overpowered by the fatigue, which this day of continual pretty madness has incurred. But Nature has answered her purpose with the curly, dimpled lunatic. She has tasked every faculty, and has secured the symmetrical growth of the bodily frame, by all these attitudes and exertions,—an end of the first importance, which could not be trusted to any care less perfect than her own. This glitter, this opaline lustre plays round the top of every toy to his eye, to ensure his fidelity, and he is deceived to his good. We are made alive and kept alive by the same arts. Let the stoics say what they please, we do not eat for the good of living, but because the meat is savory and the appetite is keen. The vegetable life does not content itself with casting from the flower or the tree a single seed, but it fills the air and earth with a prodigality of seeds, that, if thousands perish, thousands may plant themselves, that hundreds may come up, that tens may live to maturity, that, at least, one may replace the parent. All things betray the same calculated profusion. The excess of fear with which the animal frame is hedged round, shrinking from cold, starting at sight of a snake, or at a sudden noise, protects us, through a multitude of groundless alarms, from some one real danger at last. The lover seeks in marriage his private felicity and perfection, with no prospective end; and nature hides in his happiness her own end, namely, progeny, or the perpetuity of the race.

But the craft with which the world is made, runs also into the mind and character of men. No man is quite sane; each has a vein of folly in his composition, a slight determination of blood to the head, to make sure of holding him hard to some one point which nature had taken to heart. Great causes are never tried on their merits; but the cause is reduced to particulars to suit the size of the partizans, and the contention is ever hottest on minor matters. Not less remarkable is the overfaith of each man in the importance of what he has to do or say. The poet, the prophet, has a higher value for what he utters than any hearer, and therefore it gets spoken. The strong, self-complacent Luther declares with an emphasis, not to be mistaken, that "God himself cannot do without wise men." Jacob Behmen and George Fox betray their egotism in the pertinacity of their controversial tracts, and James Naylor once suffered himself to be worshipped as the Christ. Each prophet comes presently to identify himself with his thought, and to esteem his hat and shoes sacred. However this may discredit such persons with the judicious, it helps them with the people, as it gives heat, pungency, and publicity to their words. A similar experience is not infrequent in private life. Each young and ardent person writes a diary, in which, when the hours of prayer and penitence arrive, he inscribes his soul. The pages thus written are, to him, burning and fragrant: he reads them on his knees by midnight and by the morning star; he wets them with his tears: they are sacred; too good for the world, and hardly yet to be shown to the dearest friend. This is the man-child that is born to the soul, and her life still circulates in the babe. The umbilical cord has not yet been cut. After some time has elapsed, he begins to wish to admit his friend to this hallowed experience, and with hesitation, yet with firmness, exposes the pages to his eye. Will they not burn his eyes? The friend coldly turns them over, and passes from the writing to conversation, with easy transition, which strikes the other party with astonishment and vexation. He cannot suspect the writing itself. Days and nights of fervid life, of communion with angels of darkness and of light, have engraved their shadowy characters on that tear-stained book. He suspects the intelligence or the heart of his friend. Is there then no friend? He cannot yet credit that one may have impressive experience, and yet may not know how to put his private fact into literature; and perhaps the discovery that wisdom has other tongues and ministers than we, that though we should hold our peace, the truth would not the less be spoken, might check injuriously the flames of our zeal. A man can only speak, so long as he does not feel his speech to be partial and inadequate. It is partial, but he does not see it to be so, whilst he utters it. As soon as he is released from the instinctive and particular, and sees its partiality, he shuts his mouth in disgust. For, no man can write anything, who does not think that what he writes is for the time the history of the world; or do anything well, who does not esteem his work to be of importance. My work may be of none, but I must not think it of none, or I shall not do it with impunity.

In like manner, there is throughout nature something

mocking, something that leads us on and on, but arrives no-where, keeps no faith with us. All promise outruns the performance. We live in a system of approximations. Every end is prospective of some other end, which is also temporary; a round and final success nowhere. We are encamped in nature, not domesticated. Hunger and thirst lead us on to eat and to drink; but bread and wine, mix and cook them how you will, leave us hungry and thirsty, after the stomach is full. It is the same with all our arts and performances. Our music, our poetry, our language itself are not satisfactions, but suggestions. The hunger for wealth, which reduces the planet to a garden, fools the eager pursuer. What is the end sought? Plainly to secure the ends of good sense and beauty, from the intrusion of deformity or vulgarity of any kind. But what an operose method! What a train of means to secure a little conversation! This palace of brick and stone, these servants, this kitchen, these stables, horses and equipage, this bank-stock, and file of mortgages; trade to all the world, country-house and cottage by the waterside, all for a little conversation, high, clear, and spiritual! Could it not be had as well by beggars on the highway? No, all these things came from successive efforts of these beggars to remove friction from the wheels of life, and give opportunity. Conversation, character, were the avowed ends; wealth was good as it appeased the animal cravings, cured the smoky chimney, silenced the creaking door, brought friends together in a warm and quiet room, and kept the children and the dinner-table in a different apartment. Thought, virtue, beauty, were the ends; but it was known that men of thought and virtue sometimes had the head-ache, or wet feet, or could lose good time whilst the room was getting warm in winter days. Unluckily, in the exertions necessary to remove these inconveniences, the main attention has been diverted to this object; the old aims have been lost sight of, and to remove friction has come to be the end. That is the ridicule of rich men, and Boston, London, Vienna, and now the governments generally of the world, are cities and governments of the rich, and the masses are not men, but *poor men*, that is, men who would be rich; this is the ridicule of the class, that they arrive with pains and sweat and fury nowhere; when all is done, it is for nothing. They are like one who has interrupted the conversation of a company to make his speech, and now has forgotten what he went to say. The appearance strikes the eye everywhere of an aimless society, of aimless nations. Were the ends of nature so great and cogent, as to exact this immense sacrifice of men?

Quite analogous to the deceits in life, there is, as might be expected, a similar effect on the eye from the face of external nature. There is in woods and waters a certain enticement and flattery, together with a failure to yield a present satisfaction. This disappointment is felt in every landscape. I have seen the softness and beauty of the summer-clouds floating feathery overhead, enjoying, as it seemed, their height and privilege of motion, whilst yet they appeared not so much the drapery of this place and hour, as forelooking to some pavilions and gardens of festivity beyond. It is an odd jealousy: but the poet finds himself not near enough to his object. The pine-tree, the river, the bank of flowers before him, does not seem to be nature. Nature is still elsewhere. This or this is but outskirt and far-off reflection and echo of the triumph that has passed by, and is now at its glancing splendor and heyday, perchance in the neighboring fields, or, if you stand in the field, then in the adjacent woods. The present object shall give you this sense of stillness that follows a pageant which has just gone by. What splendid distance, what recesses of ineffable pomp and loveliness in the sunset! But who can go where they are, or lay his hand or plant his foot thereon? Off they fall from the round world forever and ever. It is the same among the men and women, as among the silent trees; always a referred existence, an absence, never a presence and satisfaction. Is it, that beauty can never be grasped? in persons and in landscape is equally inaccessible? The accepted and betrothed lover has lost the wildest charm of his maiden in her acceptance of him. She was heaven whilst he pursued her as a star: she cannot be heaven, if she stoops to such a one as he.

What shall we say of this omnipresent appearance of that first projectile impulse, of this flattery and baulking of so many well-meaning creatures? Must we not suppose somewhere in the universe a slight treachery and derision? Are we not engaged to a serious resentment of this use that is made of us? Are we tickled trout, and fools of nature? One look at the face of heaven and earth lays all petulance at rest, and soothes us to wiser convictions. To the intelligent, nature converts itself into a vast promise, and will not be rashly explained. Her secret is untold. Many and many an Œdipus arrives: he has the whole mystery teeming in his brain. Alas! the same sorcery has spoiled his skill; no syllable can he shape on his lips. Her mighty orbit vaults like the fresh rainbow into the deep, but no archangel's wing was yet strong enough to follow it, and report of the return of the curve. But it also appears, that our actions are seconded and disposed to greater conclusions than we designed. We are escorted on every hand through life by spiritual agents, and a beneficent purpose lies in wait for us. We cannot bandy words with nature, or deal with her as we deal with persons. If we measure our individual forces against hers, we may easily feel as if we were the sport of an insuperable destiny. But if, instead of identifying ourselves with the work, we feel that the soul of the workman streams through us, we shall find the peace of the morning dwelling first in our hearts, and the fathomless powers of gravity and chemistry, and, over them, of life, preëxisting within us in their highest form.

The uneasiness which the thought of our helplessness in the chain of causes occasions us, results from looking too much at one condition of nature, namely, Motion. But the drag is never taken from the wheel. Wherever the impulse exceeds, the Rest or Identity insinuates its compensation. All over the wide fields of earth grows the prunella or self-heal. After every foolish day we sleep off the fumes and furies of its hours; and though we are always engaged with particulars, and often enslaved to them, we bring with us to every experiment the innate universal laws. These, while they exist in the mind as ideas, stand around us in nature forever embodied, a present sanity to expose and cure the insanity of men. Our servitude to particulars betrays into a hundred foolish expectations. We anticipate a new era from the invention of a locomotive, or a balloon; the new engine brings with it the old checks. They say that by electro-magnetism, your sallad shall be grown from the seed, whilst your fowl is roasting for dinner: it is a symbol of our modern aims and endeavors,—of our condensation and acceleration of objects: but nothing is gained: nature cannot be cheated: man's life is but seventy sallads long, grow they swift or grow they slow. In these checks and impossibilities, however, we find our advantage, not less than in the impulses. Let the victory fall where it will, we are on that side. And the knowledge that we traverse the whole scale of being, from the centre to the poles of nature, and have some stake in every possibility, lends that sublime lustre to death, which philosophy and religion have too outwardly and literally striven to express in the popular doctrine of the immortality of the soul. The reality is more excellent than the report. Here is no ruin, no discontinuity, no spent ball. The divine circulations never rest nor linger. Nature is the incarnation of a thought, and turns to a thought again, as ice becomes water and gas. The world is mind precipitated, and the volatile essence is forever escaping again into the state of free thought. Hence the virtue and pungency of the influence on the mind, of natural objects, whether inorganic or organized. Man imprisoned, man crystallized, man vegetative, speaks to man impersonated. That power which does not respect quantity, which makes the whole and the particle its equal channel, delegates its smile to the morning, and distils its essence into every drop of rain. Every moment instructs, and every object: for wisdom is infused into every form. It has been poured into us as blood; it convulsed us as pain; it slid into us as pleasure; it enveloped us in dull, melancholy days, or in days of cheerful labor; we did not guess its essence, until after a long time.

POLICY

Gold and iron are good
To buy iron and gold;
All earth's fleece and food
For their like are sold.
Boded Merlin wise,
Proved Napoleon great,—
Nor kind nor coinage buys
Aught above its rate.
Fear, Craft, and Avarice
Cannot rear a State.
Out of dust to build
What is more than dust,—
Walls Amphion piled
Phœbus stablish must.
When the Muses nine
With the Virtues meet,
Find to their design
An Atlantic seat,
By green orchard boughs
Fended from the heat,
Where the statesman ploughs
Furrow for the wheat;
When the Church is social worth,
When the state-house is the hearth,
Then the perfect State is come,
The republican at home.

Politics

IN DEALING with the State, we ought to remember that its institutions are not aboriginal, though they existed before we were born: that they are not superior to the citizen: that every one of them was once the act of a single man: every law and usage was a man's expedient to meet a particular case: that they all are imitable, all alterable; we may make as good; we may make better. Society is an illusion to the young citizen. It lies before him in rigid repose, with certain names, men, and institutions, rooted like oak-trees to the centre, round which all arrange themselves the best they can. But the old statesman knows that society is fluid; there are no such roots and centres; but any particle may suddenly become the centre of the movement, and compel the system to gyrate round it, as every man of strong will, like Pisistratus, or Cromwell, does for a time, and every man of truth, like Plato, or Paul, does forever. But politics rest on necessary foundations, and cannot be treated with levity. Republics abound in young civilians, who believe that the laws make the city, that grave modifications of the policy and modes of living, and employments of the population, that commerce, education, and religion, may be voted in or out; and that any measure, though it were absurd, may be imposed on a people, if only you can get sufficient voices to make it a law. But the wise know that foolish legislation is a rope of sand, which perishes in the twisting; that the State must follow, and not lead the character and progress of the citizen; the strongest usurper is quickly got rid of; and they only who build on Ideas, build for eternity; and that the form of government which prevails, is the expression of what cultivation exists in the population which permits it. The law is only a memorandum. We are superstitious, and esteem the statute somewhat: so much life as it has in the character of living men, is its force. The statute stands there to say, yesterday we agreed so and so, but how feel ye this article today? Our statute is a currency, which we stamp with our own portrait: it soon becomes unrecognizable, and in process of time will return to the mint. Nature is not democratic, nor limited-monarchical, but despotic, and will not be fooled or abated of any jot of her authority, by the pertest of her sons: and as fast as the public mind is opened to more intelligence, the code is seen to be brute and stammering. It speaks not articulately, and must be made to. Meantime the education of the general mind never stops. The reveries of the true and simple are prophetic. What the tender poetic youth dreams, and prays, and paints today, but shuns the ridicule of saying aloud, shall presently be the resolutions of public bodies, then shall be carried as grievance and bill of rights through conflict and war, and then shall be triumphant law and establishment for a hundred years, until it gives place, in turn, to new prayers and pictures. The history of the State sketches in coarse outline the progress of thought, and follows at a distance the delicacy of culture and of aspiration.

The theory of politics, which has possessed the mind of men, and which they have expressed the best they could in their laws and in their revolutions, considers persons and property as the two objects for whose protection government exists. Of persons, all have equal rights, in virtue of being identical in nature. This interest, of course, with its whole power demands a democracy. Whilst the rights of all as persons are equal, in virtue of their access to reason, their rights in property are very unequal. One man owns his clothes, and another owns a county. This accident, depending, primarily, on the skill and virtue of the parties, of which there is every degree, and, secondarily, on patrimony, falls unequally, and its rights, of course, are unequal. Personal rights, universally the same, demand a government framed on the ratio of the census: property demands a government framed on the ratio of owners and of owning. Laban, who has flocks and herds, wishes them looked after by an officer on the frontiers, lest the Midianites shall drive them off, and pays a tax to that end. Jacob has no flocks or herds, and no fear of the Midianites, and pays no tax to the officer. It seemed fit that Laban and Jacob should have equal rights to elect the officer, who is to defend their persons, but that Laban, and not Jacob, should elect the officer who is to guard the sheep and cattle. And, if question arise whether additional officers or watch-towers should be provided, must not Laban and Isaac, and those who must sell part of their herds to buy protection for the rest, judge better of this, and with more right, than Jacob, who, because he is a youth and a traveller, eats their bread and not his own.

In the earliest society the proprietors made their own wealth, and so long as it comes to the owners in the direct way, no other opinion would arise in any equitable community, than that property should make the law for property, and persons the law for persons.

But property passes through donation or inheritance to those who do not create it. Gift, in one case, makes it as really the new owner's, as labor made it the first owner's: in the other case, of patrimony, the law makes an ownership, which will be valid in each man's view according to the estimate which he sets on the public tranquillity.

It was not, however, found easy to embody the readily admitted principle, that property should make law for property, and persons for persons: since persons and property mixed themselves in every transaction. At last it seemed settled, that the rightful distinction was, that the proprietors should have more elective franchise than non-proprietors, on the Spartan principle of "calling that which is just, equal; not that which is equal, just."

That principle no longer looks so self-evident as it appeared in former times, partly, because doubts have arisen whether too much weight had not been allowed in the laws, to property, and such a structure given to our usages, as allowed the rich to encroach on the poor, and to keep them poor; but mainly, because there is an instinctive sense, however obscure and yet inarticulate, that the whole constitution of property, on its present tenures, is injurious, and its influence on persons deteriorating and degrading; that truly, the only interest for the consideration of the State, is persons: that property will always follow persons; that the highest end of government is the culture of men: and if men can be educated, the institutions will share their improvement, and the moral sentiment will write the law of the land.

If it be not easy to settle the equity of this question, the peril is less when we take note of our natural defences. We are kept by better guards than the vigilance of such magistrates as we commonly elect. Society always consists, in greatest part, of young and foolish persons. The old, who have seen through the hypocrisy of courts and statesmen, die, and leave no wisdom to their sons. They believe their own newspaper, as their fathers did at their age. With such an ignorant and deceivable majority, States would soon run to ruin, but that there are limitations, beyond which the folly and ambition of governors cannot go. Things have their laws, as well as men; and things refuse to be trifled with. Property will be protected. Corn will not grow, unless it is planted and manured; but the farmer will not plant or hoe it, unless the chances are a hundred to one, that he will cut and harvest it. Under any forms, persons and property must and will have their just sway. They exert their power, as steadily as matter its attraction. Cover up a pound of earth never so cunningly, divide and subdivide it; melt it to liquid, convert it to gas; it will always weigh a pound: it will always attract and resist other matter, by the full virtue of one pound weight;—and the attributes of a person, his wit and his moral energy, will exercise, under any law or extinguishing tyranny, their proper force,—if not overtly, then covertly; if not for the law, then against it; with right, or by might.

The boundaries of personal influence it is impossible to fix, as persons are organs of moral or supernatural force. Under the dominion of an idea, which possesses the minds of multitudes, as civil freedom, or the religious sentiment, the powers of persons are no longer subjects of calculation. A nation of men unanimously bent on freedom, or conquest, can easily confound the arithmetic of statists, and achieve extravagant actions, out of all proportion to their means; as, the Greeks, the Saracens, the Swiss, the Americans, and the French have done.

In like manner, to every particle of property belongs its own attraction. A cent is the representative of a certain quantity of corn or other commodity. Its value is in the necessities of the animal man. It is so much warmth, so much bread, so much water, so much land. The law may do what it will with the owner of property, its just power will still attach to the cent. The law may in a mad freak say, that all shall have power except the owners of property: they shall have no vote. Nevertheless, by a higher law, the property will, year after year, write every statute that respects property. The non-proprietor will be the scribe of the proprietor. What the owners wish to do, the whole power of property will do, either through the law, or else in defiance of it. Of course, I speak of all the property, not merely of the great estates. When the rich are outvoted, as frequently happens, it is the joint treasury of the poor which exceeds their accumulations. Every man owns something, if it is only a cow, or a wheelbarrow, or his arms, and so has that property to dispose of.

The same necessity which secures the rights of person and property against the malignity or folly of the magistrate, determines the form and methods of governing, which are proper to each nation, and to its habit of thought, and nowise transferable to other states of society. In this country, we are very vain of our political institutions, which are singular in this, that they sprung, within the memory of living men, from the character and condition of the people, which they still express with sufficient fidelity,—and we ostentatiously prefer them to any other in history. They are not better, but only fitter for us. We may be wise in asserting the advantage in modern times of the democratic form, but to other states of society, in which religion consecrated the monarchical, that and not this was expedient. Democracy is better for us, because the religious sentiment of the present time accords better with it. Born democrats, we are nowise qualified to judge of monarchy, which, to our fathers living in the monarchical idea, was also relatively right. But our institutions, though in coincidence with the spirit of the age, have not any exemption from the practical defects which have discredited other forms. Every actual State is corrupt. Good men must not obey the laws too well. What satire on government can equal the severity of censure conveyed in the word *politic*, which now for ages has signified *cunning*, intimating that the State is a trick?

The same benign necessity and the same practical abuse appear in the parties into which each State divides itself, of opponents and defenders of the administration of the government. Parties are also founded on instincts, and have better guides to their own humble aims than the sagacity of

their leaders. They have nothing perverse in their origin, but
rudely mark some real and lasting relation. We might as wisely
reprove the east wind, or the frost, as a political party, whose
members, for the most part, could give no account of their
position, but stand for the defence of those interests in which
they find themselves. Our quarrel with them begins, when
they quit this deep natural ground at the bidding of some
leader, and, obeying personal considerations, throw themselves into the maintenance and defence of points, nowise belonging to their system. A party is perpetually corrupted by
personality. Whilst we absolve the association from dishon-
esty, we cannot extend the same charity to their leaders. They
reap the rewards of the docility and zeal of the masses which
they direct. Ordinarily, our parties are parties of circumstance,
and not of principle; as, the planting interest in conflict with
the commercial; the party of capitalists, and that of operatives; parties which are identical in their moral character, and
which can easily change ground with each other, in the support of many of their measures. Parties of principle, as, religious sects, or the party of free-trade, of universal suffrage, of
abolition of slavery, of abolition of capital punishment, degenerate into personalities, or would inspire enthusiasm. The
vice of our leading parties in this country (which may be cited
as a fair specimen of these societies of opinion) is, that they
do not plant themselves on the deep and necessary grounds
to which they are respectively entitled, but lash themselves to
fury in the carrying of some local and momentary measure,
nowise useful to the commonwealth. Of the two great parties,
which, at this hour, almost share the nation between them, I
should say, that, one has the best cause, and the other contains the best men. The philosopher, the poet, or the religious
man, will, of course, wish to cast his vote with the democrat,
for free-trade, for wide suffrage, for the abolition of legal
cruelties in the penal code, and for facilitating in every manner the access of the young and the poor to the sources of
wealth and power. But he can rarely accept the persons whom
the so-called popular party propose to him as representatives
of these liberalities. They have not at heart the ends which
give to the name of democracy what hope and virtue are in
it. The spirit of our American radicalism is destructive and

aimless: it is not loving; it has no ulterior and divine ends; but is destructive only out of hatred and selfishness. On the other side, the conservative party, composed of the most moderate, able, and cultivated part of the population, is timid, and merely defensive of property. It vindicates no right, it aspires to no real good, it brands no crime, it proposes no generous policy, it does not build, nor write, nor cherish the arts, nor foster religion, nor establish schools, nor encourage science, nor emancipate the slave, nor befriend the poor, or the Indian, or the immigrant. From neither party, when in power, has the world any benefit to expect in science, art, or humanity, at all commensurate with the resources of the nation.

I do not for these defects despair of our republic. We are not at the mercy of any waves of chance. In the strife of ferocious parties, human nature always finds itself cherished, as the children of the convicts at Botany Bay are found to have as healthy a moral sentiment as other children. Citizens of feudal states are alarmed at our democratic institutions lapsing into anarchy; and the older and more cautious among ourselves are learning from Europeans to look with some terror at our turbulent freedom. It is said that in our license of construing the Constitution, and in the despotism of public opinion, we have no anchor; and one foreign observer thinks he has found the safeguard in the sanctity of Marriage among us; and another thinks he has found it in our Calvinism. Fisher Ames expressed the popular security more wisely, when he compared a monarchy and a republic, saying, "that a monarchy is a merchantman, which sails well, but will sometimes strike on a rock, and go to the bottom; whilst a republic is a raft, which would never sink, but then your feet are always in water." No forms can have any dangerous importance, whilst we are befriended by the laws of things. It makes no difference how many tons weight of atmosphere presses on our heads, so long as the same pressure resists it within the lungs. Augment the mass a thousand fold, it cannot begin to crush us, as long as reaction is equal to action. The fact of two poles, of two forces, centripetal and centrifugal, is universal, and each force by its own activity develops the other. Wild liberty develops iron conscience. Want of liberty, by strengthening law and decorum, stupefies conscience. 'Lynch-law' prevails only where there is greater hardihood and self-subsistency in the leaders. A mob cannot be a permanency: everybody's interest requires that it should not exist, and only justice satisfies all.

We must trust infinitely to the beneficent necessity which shines through all laws. Human nature expresses itself in them as characteristically as in statues, or songs, or railroads, and an abstract of the codes of nations would be a transcript of the common conscience. Governments have their origin in the moral identity of men. Reason for one is seen to be reason for another, and for every other. There is a middle measure which satisfies all parties, be they never so many, or so resolute for their own. Every man finds a sanction for his simplest claims and deeds in decisions of his own mind, which he calls Truth and Holiness. In these decisions all the citizens find a perfect agreement, and only in these; not in what is good to eat, good to wear, good use of time, or what amount of land, or of public aid, each is entitled to claim. This truth and justice men presently endeavor to make application of, to the measuring of land, the apportionment of service, the protection of life and property. Their first endeavors, no doubt, are very awkward. Yet absolute right is the first governor; or, every government is an impure theocracy. The idea, after which each community is aiming to make and mend its law, is, the will of the wise man. The wise man, it cannot find in nature, and it makes awkward but earnest efforts to secure his government by contrivance; as, by causing the entire people to give their voices on every measure; or, by a double choice to get the representation of the whole; or, by a selection of the best citizens; or, to secure the advantages of efficiency and internal peace, by confiding the government to one, who may himself select his agents. All forms of government symbolize an immortal government, common to all dynasties and independent of numbers, perfect where two men exist, perfect where there is only one man.

Every man's nature is a sufficient advertisement to him of the character of his fellows. My right and my wrong, is their right and their wrong. Whilst I do what is fit for me, and abstain from what is unfit, my neighbor and I shall often agree in our means, and work together for a time to one end. But whenever I find my dominion over myself not sufficient for me, and undertake the direction of him also, I overstep the truth, and come into false relations to him. I may have so much more skill or strength than he, that he cannot express adequately his sense of wrong, but it is a lie, and hurts like a lie both him and me. Love and nature cannot maintain the assumption: it must be executed by a practical lie, namely, by force. This undertaking for another, is the blunder which stands in colossal ugliness in the governments of the world. It is the same thing in numbers, as in a pair, only not quite so intelligible. I can see well enough a great difference between my setting myself down to a self-control, and my going to make somebody else act after my views: but when a quarter of the human race assume to tell me what I must do, I may be too much disturbed by the circumstances to see so clearly the absurdity of their command. Therefore, all public ends look vague and quixotic beside private ones. For, any laws but those which men make for themselves, are laughable. If I put myself in the place of my child, and we stand in one thought, and see that things are thus or thus, that perception is law for him and me. We are both there, both act. But if, without carrying him into the thought, I look over into his plot, and, guessing how it is with him, ordain this or that, he will never obey me. This is the history of governments,—one man does something which is to bind another. A man who cannot be acquainted with me, taxes me; looking from afar at me, ordains that a part of my labor shall go to this or that whimsical end, not as I, but as he happens to fancy. Behold the consequence. Of all debts, men are least willing to pay the taxes. What a satire is this on government! Everywhere they think they get their money's worth, except for these.

Hence, the less government we have, the better,—the fewer laws, and the less confided power. The antidote to this abuse of formal Government, is, the influence of private character, the growth of the Individual; the appearance of the principal to supersede the proxy; the appearance of the wise man, of whom the existing government, is, it must be owned, but a shabby imitation. That which all things tend to educe, which freedom, cultivation, intercourse, revolutions, go to form and deliver, is character; that is the end of nature, to reach unto this coronation of her king. To educate the wise man, the State exists; and with the appearance of the wise man, the State expires. The appearance of character makes the State unnecessary. The wise man is the State. He needs no army, fort, or navy,—he loves men too well; no bribe, or feast, or palace, to draw friends to him; no vantage ground, no favorable circumstance. He needs no library, for he has not done thinking; no church, for he is a prophet; no statute book, for he has the lawgiver; no money, for he is value; no road, for he is at home where he is; no experience, for the life of the creator shoots through him, and looks from his eyes. He has no personal friends, for he who has the spell to draw the prayer and piety of all men unto him, needs not husband and educate a few, to share with him a select and poetic life. His relation to men is angelic; his memory is myrrh to them; his presence, frankincense and flowers.

We think our civilization near its meridian, but we are yet only at the cock-crowing and the morning star. In our barbarous society the influence of character is in its infancy. As a political power, as the rightful lord who is to tumble all rulers from their chairs, its presence is hardly yet suspected. Malthus and Ricardo quite omit it; the Annual Register is silent; in the Conversations' Lexicon, it is not set down; the President's Message, the Queen's Speech, have not mentioned it; and yet it is never nothing. Every thought which genius and piety throw into the world, alters the world. The gladiators in the lists of power feel, through all their frocks of force and simulation, the presence of worth. I think the very strife of trade and ambition are confession of this divinity; and successes in those fields are the poor amends, the fig-leaf with which the shamed soul attempts to hide its nakedness. I find the like unwilling homage in all quarters. It is because we know how much is due from us, that we are impatient to show some petty talent as a substitute for worth. We are haunted by a conscience of this right to grandeur of character, and are false to it. But each of us has some talent, can do somewhat useful, or graceful, or formidable, or amusing, or lucrative. That we do, as an apology to others and to ourselves, for not reaching the mark of a good and equal life. But it does not satisfy *us*, whilst we thrust it on the notice of our companions. It may throw dust in their eyes, but does not smooth our own brow, or give us the tranquillity of the strong when we walk abroad. We do penance as we go. Our talent is a sort of expiation, and we are constrained to reflect on our splendid moment, with a certain humiliation, as somewhat too fine, and not as one act of many acts, a fair expression of our permanent energy. Most persons of ability meet in society with a kind of tacit appeal. Each seems to say, 'I am not all here.' Senators and presidents have climbed so high with pain enough, not because they think the place specially agreeable, but as an apology for real worth, and to vindicate their manhood in our eyes. This conspicuous chair is their compensation to themselves for being of a poor, cold, hard nature. They must do what they can. Like one class of forest animals, they have nothing but a prehensile tail: climb they must, or crawl. If a man found himself so rich-natured that he could enter into strict relations with the best persons, and make life serene around him by the dignity and sweetness of his behavior, could he afford to circumvent the favor of the caucus and the press, and covet relations so hollow and pompous, as those of a politician? Surely nobody would be a charlatan, who could afford to be sincere.

The tendencies of the times favor the idea of self-government, and leave the individual, for all code, to the rewards and penalties of his own constitution, which work with more energy than we believe, whilst we depend on artificial restraints. The movement in this direction has been very marked in modern history. Much has been blind and discreditable, but the nature of the revolution is not affected by the vices of the revolters; for this is a purely moral force. It was never adopted by any party in history, neither can be. It separates the individual from all party, and unites him, at the same time, to the race. It promises a recognition of higher rights than those of personal freedom, or the security of property. A man has a right to be employed, to be trusted, to be loved, to be revered. The power of love, as the basis of a State, has never been tried. We must not imagine that all things are lapsing into confusion, if every tender protestant be not compelled to bear his part in certain social conventions: nor doubt that roads can be built, letters carried, and the fruit of labor secured, when the government of force is at an end. Are our methods now so excellent that all competition is hopeless? Could not a nation of friends even devise better ways? On the other hand, let not the most conservative and timid fear anything from a premature surrender of the bayonet, and the system of force. For, according to the order of nature, which is quite superior to our will, it stands thus; there will always be a government of force, where men are selfish; and when they are pure enough to abjure the code of force, they will be wise enough to see how these public ends of the post-office, of the highway, of commerce, and the exchange of property, of museums and libraries, of institutions of art and science, can be answered.

We live in a very low state of the world, and pay unwilling tribute to governments founded on force. There is not, among the most religious and instructed men of the most religious and civil nations, a reliance on the moral sentiment, and a sufficient belief in the unity of things to persuade them that society can be maintained without artificial restraints, as well as the solar system; or that the private citizen might be reasonable, and a good neighbor, without the hint of a jail or a confiscation. What is strange too, there never was in any man sufficient faith in the power of rectitude, to inspire him with the broad design of renovating the State on the principle of right and love. All those who have pretended this design, have been partial reformers, and have admitted in some manner the supremacy of the bad State. I do not call to mind a single human being who has steadily denied the authority of the laws, on the simple ground of his own moral nature. Such designs, full of genius and full of fate as they are, are not entertained except avowedly as air-pictures. If the individual who exhibits them, dare to think them practicable, he disgusts scholars and churchmen; and men of talent, and women of superior sentiments, cannot hide their contempt. Not the less does nature continue to fill the heart of youth with suggestions of this enthusiasm, and there are now men,—if indeed I can speak in the plural number,—more exactly, I will say, I have just been conversing with one man, to whom no weight of adverse experience will make it for a moment appear im-

possible, that thousands of human beings might exercise towards each other the grandest and simplest sentiments, as
well as a knot of friends, or a pair of lovers.

NOMINALIST AND REALIST

———

In countless upward-striving waves
The moon-drawn tide-wave strives;
In thousand far-transplanted grafts
The parent fruit survives;
So, in the new-born millions,
The perfect Adam lives.
Not less are summer-mornings dear
To every child they wake,
And each with novel life his sphere
Fills for his proper sake.

Nominalist and Realist

I CANNOT often enough say, that a man is only a relative and representative nature. Each is a hint of the truth, but far enough from being that truth, which yet he quite newly and inevitably suggests to us. If I seek it in him, I shall not find it. Could any man conduct into me the pure stream of that which he pretends to be! Long afterwards, I find that quality elsewhere which he promised me. The genius of the Platonists, is intoxicating to the student, yet how few particulars of it can I detach from all their books. The man momentarily stands for the thought, but will not bear examination; and a society of men will cursorily represent well enough a certain quality and culture, for example, chivalry or beauty of manners, but separate them, and there is no gentleman and no lady in the group. The least hint sets us on the pursuit of a character, which no man realizes. We have such exorbitant eyes, that on seeing the smallest arc, we complete the curve, and when the curtain is lifted from the diagram which it seemed to veil, we are vexed to find that no more was drawn, than just that fragment of an arc which we first beheld. We are greatly too liberal in our construction of each other's faculty and promise. Exactly what the parties have already done, they shall do again; but that which we inferred from their nature and inception, they will not do. That is in nature, but not in them. That happens in the world, which we often witness in a public debate. Each of the speakers expresses himself imperfectly: no one of them hears much that another says, such is the preoccupation of mind of each; and the audience, who have only to hear and not to speak, judge very wisely and superiorly how wrongheaded and unskilful is each of the debaters to his own affair. Great men or men of great gifts you shall easily find, but symmetrical men never. When I meet a pure intellectual force, or a generosity of affection, I believe, here then is man; and am presently mortified by the discovery, that this individual is no more available to his own or to the general ends, than his companions; because the power

which drew my respect, is not supported by the total sym-
phony of his talents. All persons exist to society by some shining trait of beauty or utility, which they have. We borrow the
proportions of the man from that one fine feature, and finish
the portrait symmetrically; which is false; for the rest of his
body is small or deformed. I observe a person who makes a
good public appearance, and conclude thence the perfection
of his private character, on which this is based; but he has no
private character. He is a graceful cloak or lay-figure for holidays. All our poets, heroes, and saints, fail utterly in some
one or in many parts to satisfy our idea, fail to draw our
spontaneous interest, and so leave us without any hope of
realization but in our own future. Our exaggeration of all fine
characters arises from the fact, that we identify each in turn
with the soul. But there are no such men as we fable; no
Jesus, nor Pericles, nor Cæsar, nor Angelo, nor Washington,
such as we have made. We consecrate a great deal of nonsense, because it was allowed by great men. There is none
without his foible. I verily believe if an angel should come to
chaunt the chorus of the moral law, he would eat too much
gingerbread, or take liberties with private letters, or do some
precious atrocity. It is bad enough, that our geniuses cannot
do anything useful, but it is worse that no man is fit for society, who has fine traits. He is admired at a distance, but he
cannot come near without appearing a cripple. The men of
fine parts protect themselves by solitude, or by courtesy, or
by satire, or by an acid worldly manner, each concealing, as
he best can, his incapacity for useful association, but they
want either love or self-reliance.

Our native love of reality joins with this experience to teach
us a little reserve, and to dissuade a too sudden surrender to
the brilliant qualities of persons. Young people admire talents
or particular excellences; as we grow older, we value total
powers and effects, as, the impression, the quality, the spirit
of men and things. The genius is all. The man,—it is his
system: we do not try a solitary word or act, but his habit.
The acts which you praise, I praise not, since they are departures from his faith, and are mere compliances. The magnetism which arranges tribes and races in one polarity, is alone
to be respected; the men are steel-filings. Yet we unjustly se-

lect a particle, and say, 'O steel-filing number one! what heart-drawings I feel to thee! what prodigious virtues are these of thine! how constitutional to thee, and incommunicable.' Whilst we speak, the loadstone is withdrawn; down falls our filing in a heap with the rest, and we continue our mummery to the wretched shaving. Let us go for universals; for the magnetism, not for the needles. Human life and its persons are poor empirical pretensions. A personal influence is an *ignis fatuus*. If they say, it is great, it is great; if they say, it is small, it is small; you see it, and you see it not, by turns; it borrows all its size from the momentary estimation of the speakers: the Will-of-the-wisp vanishes, if you go too near, vanishes if you go too far, and only blazes at one angle. Who can tell if Washington be a great man, or no? Who can tell if Franklin be? Yes, or any but the twelve, or six, or three great gods of fame? And they, too, loom and fade before the eternal.

We are amphibious creatures, weaponed for two elements, having two sets of faculties, the particular and the catholic. We adjust our instrument for general observation, and sweep the heavens as easily as we pick out a single figure in the terrestrial landscape. We are practically skilful in detecting elements, for which we have no place in our theory, and no name. Thus we are very sensible of an atmospheric influence in men and in bodies of men, not accounted for in an arithmetical addition of all their measurable properties. There is a genius of a nation, which is not to be found in the numerical citizens, but which characterizes the society. England, strong, punctual, practical, well-spoken England, I should not find, if I should go to the island to seek it. In the parliament, in the playhouse, at dinner-tables, I might see a great number of rich, ignorant, book-read, conventional, proud men,—many old women,—and not anywhere the Englishman who made the good speeches, combined the accurate engines, and did the bold and nervous deeds. It is even worse in America, where, from the intellectual quickness of the race, the genius of the country is more splendid in its promise, and more slight in its performance. Webster cannot do the work of Webster. We conceive distinctly enough the French, the Spanish, the German genius, and it is not the less real, that perhaps we should not meet in either of those nations, a single individual who corresponded with the type. We infer the spirit of the nation in great measure from the language, which is a sort of monument, to which each forcible individual in a course of many hundred years has contributed a stone. And, universally, a good example of this social force, is the veracity of language, which cannot be debauched. In any controversy concerning morals, an appeal may be made with safety to the sentiments, which the language of the people expresses. Proverbs, words, and grammar inflections convey the public sense with more purity and precision, than the wisest individual.

In the famous dispute with the Nominalists, the Realists had a good deal of reason. General ideas are essences. They are our gods: they round and ennoble the most partial and sordid way of living. Our proclivity to details cannot quite degrade our life, and divest it of poetry. The day-laborer is reckoned as standing at the foot of the social scale, yet he is saturated with the laws of the world. His measures are the hours; morning and night, solstice and equinox, geometry, astronomy, and all the lovely accidents of nature play through his mind. Money, which represents the prose of life, and which is hardly spoken of in parlors without an apology, is, in its effects and laws, as beautiful as roses. Property keeps the accounts of the world, and is always moral. The property will be found where the labor, the wisdom, and the virtue have been in nations, in classes, and (the whole life-time considered, with the compensations) in the individual also. How wise the world appears, when the laws and usages of nations are largely detailed, and the completeness of the municipal system is considered! Nothing is left out. If you go into the markets, and the custom-houses, the insurers' and notaries' offices, the offices of sealers of weights and measures, of inspection of provisions,—it will appear as if one man had made it all. Wherever you go, a wit like your own has been before you, and has realized its thought. The Eleusinian mysteries, the Egyptian architecture, the Indian astronomy, the Greek sculpture, show that there always were seeing and knowing men in the planet. The world is full of masonic ties, of guilds, of secret and public legions of honor; that of scholars, for example; and that of gentlemen fraternizing with the upper class of every country and every culture.

I am very much struck in literature by the appearance, that one person wrote all the books; as if the editor of a journal planted his body of reporters in different parts of the field of action, and relieved some by others from time to time; but there is such equality and identity both of judgment and point of view in the narrative, that it is plainly the work of one all-seeing, all-hearing gentleman. I looked into Pope's Odyssey yesterday: it is as correct and elegant after our canon of today, as if it were newly written. The modernness of all good books seems to give me an existence as wide as man. What is well done, I feel as if I did; what is ill-done, I reck not of. Shakspeare's passages of passion (for example, in Lear and Hamlet) are in the very dialect of the present year. I am faithful again to the whole over the members in my use of books. I find the most pleasure in reading a book in a manner least flattering to the author. I read Proclus, and sometimes Plato, as I might read a dictionary, for a mechanical help to the fancy and the imagination. I read for the lustres, as if one should use a fine picture in a chromatic experiment, for its rich colors. 'Tis not Proclus, but a piece of nature and fate that I explore. It is a greater joy to see the author's author, than himself. A higher pleasure of the same kind I found lately at a concert, where I went to hear Handel's Messiah. As the master overpowered the littleness and incapableness of the performers, and made them conductors of his electricity, so it was easy to observe what efforts nature was making through so many hoarse, wooden, and imperfect persons, to produce beautiful voices, fluid and soul-guided men and women. The genius of nature was paramount at the oratorio.

This preference of the genius to the parts is the secret of that deification of art, which is found in all superior minds. Art, in the artist, is proportion, or, a habitual respect to the whole by an eye loving beauty in details. And the wonder and charm of it is the sanity in insanity which it denotes. Proportion is almost impossible to human beings. There is no one who does not exaggerate. In conversation, men are encumbered with personality, and talk too much. In modern sculpture, picture, and poetry, the beauty is miscellaneous; the artist works here and there, and at all points, adding and adding, instead of unfolding the unit of his thought. Beautiful details we must have, or no artist: but they must be means and never other. The eye must not lose sight for a moment of the purpose. Lively boys write to their ear and eye, and the cool reader finds nothing but sweet jingles in it. When they grow older, they respect the argument.

We obey the same intellectual integrity, when we study in exceptions the law of the world. Anomalous facts, as the never quite obsolete rumors of magic and demonology, and the new allegations of phrenologists and neurologists, are of ideal use. They are good indications. Homœopathy is insignificant as an art of healing, but of great value as criticism on the hygeia or medical practice of the time. So with Mesmerism, Swedenborgism, Fourierism, and the Millennial Church; they are poor pretensions enough, but good criticism on the science, philosophy, and preaching of the day. For these abnormal insights of the adepts, ought to be normal, and things of course.

All things show us, that on every side we are very near to the best. It seems not worth while to execute with too much pains some one intellectual, or æsthetical, or civil feat, when presently the dream will scatter, and we shall burst into universal power. The reason of idleness and of crime is the deferring of our hopes. Whilst we are waiting, we beguile the time with jokes, with sleep, with eating, and with crimes.

Thus we settle it in our cool libraries, that all the agents with which we deal are subalterns, which we can well afford to let pass, and life will be simpler when we live at the centre, and flout the surfaces. I wish to speak with all respect of persons, but sometimes I must pinch myself to keep awake, and preserve the due decorum. They melt so fast into each other, that they are like grass and trees, and it needs an effort to treat them as individuals. Though the uninspired man certainly finds persons a conveniency in household matters, the divine man does not respect them: he sees them as a rack of clouds, or a fleet of ripples which the wind drives over the surface of the water. But this is flat rebellion. Nature will not be Buddhist: she resents generalizing, and insults the philosopher in every moment with a million of fresh particulars. It is all idle talking: as much as a man is a whole, so is he also a part; and it were partial not to see it. What you say in your pompous distribution only distributes you into your class and section. You have not got rid of parts by denying them, but are the more partial. You are one thing, but nature is *one thing and the other thing*, in the same moment. She will not remain orbed in a thought, but rushes into persons; and when each person, inflamed to a fury of personality, would conquer all things to his poor crotchet, she raises up against him another person, and by many persons incarnates again a sort of whole. She will have all. Nick Bottom cannot play all the parts, work it how he may: there will be somebody else, and the world will be round. Everything must have its flower or effort at the beautiful, coarser or finer according to its stuff. They relieve and recommend each other, and the sanity of society is a balance of a thousand insanities. She punishes abstractionists, and will only forgive an induction which is rare and casual. We like to come to a height of land and see the landscape, just as we value a general remark in conversation. But it is not the intention of nature that we should live by general views. We fetch fire and water, run about all day among the shops and markets, and get our clothes and shoes made and mended, and are the victims of these details, and once in a fortnight we arrive perhaps at a rational moment. If we were not thus infatuated, if we saw the real from hour to hour, we should not be here to write and to read, but should have been burned or frozen long ago. She would never get anything done, if she suffered admirable Crichtons, and universal geniuses. She loves better a wheelwright who dreams all night of wheels, and a groom who is part of his horse: for she is full of work, and these are her hands. As the frugal farmer takes care that his cattle shall eat down the rowan, and swine shall eat the waste of his house, and poultry shall pick the crumbs, so our economical mother despatches a new genius and habit of mind into every district and condition of existence, plants an eye wherever a new ray of light can fall, and gathering up into some man every property in the universe, establishes thousandfold occult mutual attractions among her offspring, that all this wash and waste of power may be imparted and exchanged.

Great dangers undoubtedly accrue from this incarnation and distribution of the godhead, and hence nature has her maligners, as if she were Circe; and Alphonso of Castille fancied he could have given useful advice. But she does not go unprovided; she has hellebore at the bottom of the cup. Solitude would ripen a plentiful crop of despots. The recluse thinks of men as having his manner, or as not having his manner; and as having degrees of it, more and less. But when he comes into a public assembly, he sees that men have very different manners from his own, and in their way admirable. In his childhood and youth, he has had many checks and censures, and thinks modestly enough of his own endowment. When afterwards he comes to unfold it in propitious circumstance, it seems the only talent: he is delighted with his success, and accounts himself already the fellow of the great. But he goes into a mob, into a banking-house, into a mechanic's shop, into a mill, into a laboratory, into a ship, into a camp, and in each new place he is no better than an idiot: other talents take place, and rule the hour. The rotation which whirls every leaf and pebble to the meridian, reaches to every gift of man, and we all take turns at the top.

For nature, who abhors mannerism, has set her heart on breaking up all styles and tricks, and it is so much easier to do what one has done before, than to do a new thing, that there is a perpetual tendency to a set mode. In every conversation, even the highest, there is a certain trick, which may be soon learned by an acute person, and then that particular style continued indefinitely. Each man, too, is a tyrant in tendency, because he would impose his idea on others; and their trick is their natural defence. Jesus would absorb the race; but Tom Paine or the coarsest blasphemer helps humanity by resisting this exuberance of power. Hence the immense benefit of party in politics, as it reveals faults of character in a chief, which the intellectual force of the persons, with ordinary opportunity, and not hurled into aphelion by hatred, could not have seen. Since we are all so stupid, what benefit that there should be two stupidities! It is like that brute advantage so essential to astronomy, of having the diameter of the earth's orbit for a base of its triangles. Democracy is morose, and runs to anarchy, but in the state, and in the schools, it is indispensable to resist the consolidation of all men into a few men. If John was perfect, why are you and I alive? As long as any man exists, there is some need of him; let him fight for his own. A new poet has appeared; a new character approached us; why should we refuse to eat bread, until we have found his regiment and section in our old army-files? Why not a new man? Here is a new enterprise of Brook Farm, of Skeneateles, of Northampton: why so impatient to baptise them Essenes, or Port-Royalists, or Shakers, or by any known and effete name? Let it be a new way of living. Why have only two or three ways of life, and not thousands? Every man is wanted, and no man is wanted much. We came this time for condiments, not for corn. We want the great genius only for joy; for one star more in our constellation, for one tree more in our grove. But he thinks we wish to belong to him, as he wishes to occupy us. He greatly mistakes us. I think I have done well, if I have acquired a new word from a good author; and my business with him is to find my own, though it were only to melt him down into an epithet or an image for daily use.

"Into paint will I grind thee, my bride!"

To embroil the confusion, and make it impossible to arrive at any general statement, when we have insisted on the imperfection of individuals, our affections and our experience urge that every individual is entitled to honor, and a very generous treatment is sure to be repaid. A recluse sees only two or three persons, and allows them all their room; they spread themselves at large. The man of state looks at many, and compares the few habitually with others, and these look less. Yet are they not entitled to this generosity of reception? and is not munificence the means of insight? For though gamesters say, that the cards beat all the players, though they were never so skilful, yet in the contest we are now considering, the players are also the game, and share the power of the cards. If you criticise a fine genius, the odds are that you are out of your reckoning, and, instead of the poet, are censuring your own caricature of him. For there is somewhat spheral and infinite in every man, especially in every genius, which, if you can come very near him, sports with all your limitations. For, rightly, every man is a channel through which heaven floweth, and, whilst I fancied I was criticising him, I was censuring or rather terminating my own soul. After taxing Goethe as a courtier, artificial, unbelieving, worldly,—I took up this book of Helena, and found him an Indian of the wilderness, a piece of pure nature like an apple or an oak, large as morning or night, and virtuous as a briar-rose.

But care is taken that the whole tune shall be played. If we were not kept among surfaces, every thing would be large and universal: now the excluded attributes burst in on us with the more brightness, that they have been excluded. "Your turn now, my turn next," is the rule of the game. The universality being hindered in its primary form, comes in the secondary form of *all sides*: the points come in succession to the meridian, and by the speed of rotation, a new whole is formed. Nature keeps herself whole, and her representation complete in the experience of each mind. She suffers no seat to be vacant in her college. It is the secret of the world that all things subsist, and do not die, but only retire a little from sight, and afterwards return again. Whatever does not concern us, is concealed from us. As soon as a person is no longer related to our present well-being, he is concealed, or *dies*, as we say. Really, all things and persons are related to us, but according to our nature, they act on us not at once, but in succession, and we are made aware of their presence one at a time. All persons, all things which we have known, are here present, and many more than we see; the world is full. As the ancient said, the world is a *plenum* or solid; and if we saw all things that really surround us, we should be imprisoned and unable to move. For, though nothing is impassable to the soul, but all things are pervious to it, and like highways, yet this is only whilst the soul does not see them. As soon as the soul sees any object, it stops before that object. Therefore, the divine Providence, which keeps the universe open in every direction to the soul, conceals all the furniture and all the persons that do not concern a particular soul, from the senses of that individual. Through solidest eternal things, the man finds his road, as if they did not subsist, and does not once suspect their being. As soon as he needs a new object, suddenly he beholds it, and no longer attempts to pass through it, but takes another way. When he has exhausted for the time the nourishment to be drawn from any one person or thing, that object is withdrawn from his observation, and though still in his immediate neighborhood, he does not suspect its presence.

Nothing is dead: men feign themselves dead, and endure mock funerals and mournful obituaries, and there they stand looking out of the window, sound and well, in some new and strange disguise. Jesus is not dead: he is very well alive: nor John, nor Paul, nor Mahomet, nor Aristotle; at times we believe we have seen them all, and could easily tell the names under which they go.

If we cannot make voluntary and conscious steps in the admirable science of universals, let us see the parts wisely, and infer the genius of nature from the best particulars with a becoming charity. What is best in each kind is an index of what should be the average of that thing. Love shows me the opulence of nature, by disclosing to me in my friend a hidden wealth, and I infer an equal depth of good in every other direction. It is commonly said by farmers, that a good pear or apple costs no more time or pains to rear, than a poor one; so I would have no work of art, no speech, or action, or thought, or friend, but the best.

The end and the means, the gamester and the game,—life is made up of the intermixture and reaction of these two amicable powers, whose marriage appears beforehand monstrous, as each denies and tends to abolish the other. We must reconcile the contradictions as we can, but their discord and their concord introduce wild absurdities into our thinking and speech. No sentence will hold the whole truth, and the only way in which we can be just, is by giving ourselves the lie; Speech is better than silence; silence is better than speech;—All things are in contact; every atom has a sphere of repulsion;—Things are, and are not, at the same time;—and the like. All the universe over, there is but one thing, this old Two-Face, creator-creature, mind-matter, right-wrong, of which any proposition may be affirmed or denied. Very fitly, therefore, I assert, that every man is a partialist, that nature secures him as an instrument by self-conceit, preventing the tendencies to religion and science; and now further assert, that, each man's genius being nearly and affectionately explored, he is justified in his individuality, as his nature is found to be immense; and now I add, that every man is a universalist also, and, as our earth, whilst it spins on its own axis, spins all the time around the sun through the celestial spaces, so the least of its rational children, the most dedicated to his private affair, works out, though as it were under a disguise, the universal problem. We fancy men are individuals; so are pumpkins; but every pumpkin in the field, goes through every point of pumpkin history. The rabid democrat, as soon as he is senator and rich man, has ripened beyond possibility of sincere radicalism, and unless he can resist the sun, he must be conservative the remainder of his days. Lord Eldon said in his old age, "that, if he were to begin life again, he would be damned but he would begin as agitator."

We hide this universality, if we can, but it appears at all points. We are as ungrateful as children. There is nothing we cherish and strive to draw to us, but in some hour we turn and rend it. We keep a running fire of sarcasm at ignorance and the life of the senses; then goes by, perchance, a fair girl, a piece of life, gay and happy, and making the commonest offices beautiful, by the energy and heart with which she does them, and seeing this, we admire and love her and them, and say, "Lo! a genuine creature of the fair earth, not dissipated, or too early ripened by books, philosophy, religion, society, or care!" insinuating a treachery and contempt for all we had so long loved and wrought in ourselves and others.

If we could have any security against moods! If the profoundest prophet could be holden to his words, and the hearer who is ready to sell all and join the crusade, could have any certificate that tomorrow his prophet shall not unsay his testimony! But the Truth sits veiled there on the Bench, and never interposes an adamantine syllable; and the most sincere and revolutionary doctrine, put as if the ark of God were carried forward some furlongs, and planted there for the succor of the world, shall in a few weeks be coldly set aside by the same speaker, as morbid; "I thought I was right, but I was not,"—and the same immeasurable credulity demanded for new audacities. If we were not of all opinions! if we did not in any moment shift the platform on which we stand, and look and speak from another! if there could be any regulation, any 'one-hour-rule,' that a man should never leave his point of view, without sound of trumpet. I am always insincere, as always knowing there are other moods.

How sincere and confidential we can be, saying all that lies in the mind, and yet go away feeling that all is yet unsaid, from the incapacity of the parties to know each other, although they use the same words! My companion assumes to know my mood and habit of thought, and we go on from explanation to explanation, until all is said which words can, and we leave matters just as they were at first, because of that vicious assumption. Is it that every man believes every other to be an incurable partialist, and himself an universalist? I talked yesterday with a pair of philosophers: I endeavored to show my good men that I love everything by turns, and nothing long; that I loved the centre, but doated on the superficies; that I loved man, if men seemed to me mice and rats; that I revered saints, but woke up glad that the old pagan world stood its ground, and died hard; that I was glad of men of every gift and nobility, but would not live in their arms. Could they but once understand, that I loved to know that they existed, and heartily wished them Godspeed, yet, out of my poverty of life and thought, had no word or welcome for them when they came to see me, and could well consent to their living in Oregon, for any claim I felt on them, it would be a great satisfaction.

NEW ENGLAND REFORMERS

New England Reformers

A Lecture read before the Society in Amory Hall,
on Sunday, 3 March, 1844

WHOEVER has had opportunity of acquaintance with society in New England, during the last twenty-five
years, with those middle and with those leading sections that
may constitute any just representation of the character and
aim of the community, will have been struck with the great
activity of thought and experimenting. His attention must be
commanded by the signs that the Church, or religious party,
is falling from the church nominal, and is appearing in temperance and non-resistance societies, in movements of abolitionists and of socialists, and in very significant assemblies,
called Sabbath and Bible Conventions,—composed of ultra-
ists, of seekers, of all the soul of the soldiery of dissent, and
meeting to call in question the authority of the Sabbath, of
the priesthood, and of the church. In these movements, nothing was more remarkable than the discontent they begot in
the movers. The spirit of protest and of detachment, drove
the members of these Conventions to bear testimony against
the church, and immediately afterward, to declare their discontent with these Conventions, their independence of their
colleagues, and their impatience of the methods whereby they
were working. They defied each other, like a congress of
kings, each of whom had a realm to rule, and a way of his
own that made concert unprofitable. What a fertility of projects for the salvation of the world! One apostle thought all
men should go to farming; and another, that no man should
buy or sell: that the use of money was the cardinal evil; another, that the mischief was in our diet, that we eat and drink
damnation. These made unleavened bread, and were foes to
the death to fermentation. It was in vain urged by the housewife, that God made yeast, as well as dough, and loves
fermentation just as dearly as he loves vegetation; that
fermentation develops the saccharine element in the grain,
and makes it more palatable and more digestible. No; they
wish the pure wheat, and will die but it shall not ferment.

Stop, dear nature, these incessant advances of thine; let us scotch these ever-rolling wheels! Others attacked the system of agriculture, the use of animal manures in farming; and the tyranny of man over brute nature; these abuses polluted his food. The ox must be taken from the plough, and the horse from the cart, the hundred acres of the farm must be spaded, and the man must walk wherever boats and locomotives will not carry him. Even the insect world was to be defended,— that had been too long neglected, and a society for the protection of ground-worms, slugs, and mosquitos was to be incorporated without delay. With these appeared the adepts of homœopathy, of hydropathy, of mesmerism, of phrenology, and their wonderful theories of the Christian miracles! Others assailed particular vocations, as that of the lawyer, that of the merchant, of the manufacturer, of the clergyman, of the scholar. Others attacked the institution of marriage, as the fountain of social evils. Others devoted themselves to the worrying of churches and meetings for public worship; and the fertile forms of antinomianism among the elder puritans, seemed to have their match in the plenty of the new harvest of reform.

With this din of opinion and debate, there was a keener scrutiny of institutions and domestic life than any we had known, there was sincere protesting against existing evils, and there were changes of employment dictated by conscience. No doubt, there was plentiful vaporing, and cases of backsliding might occur. But in each of these movements emerged a good result, a tendency to the adoption of simpler methods, and an assertion of the sufficiency of the private man. Thus it was directly in the spirit and genius of the age, what happened in one instance, when a church censured and threatened to excommunicate one of its members, on account of the somewhat hostile part to the church, which his conscience led him to take in the anti-slavery business; the threatened individual immediately excommunicated the church in a public and formal process. This has been several times repeated: it was excellent when it was done the first time, but, of course, loses all value when it is copied. Every project in the history of reform, no matter how violent and surprising, is good, when it is the dictate of a man's genius and constitution, but very dull and suspicious when adopted from another. It is right and beautiful in any man to say, 'I will take this coat, or this book, or this measure of corn of yours,'—in whom we see the act to be original, and to flow from the whole spirit and faith of him; for then that taking will have a giving as free and divine: but we are very easily disposed to resist the same generosity of speech, when we miss originality and truth to character in it.

There was in all the practical activities of New England, for the last quarter of a century, a gradual withdrawal of tender consciences from the social organizations. There is observable throughout, the contest between mechanical and spiritual methods, but with a steady tendency of the thoughtful and virtuous to a deeper belief and reliance on spiritual facts.

In politics, for example, it is easy to see the progress of dissent. The country is full of rebellion; the country is full of kings. Hands off! let there be no control and no interference in the administration of the affairs of this kingdom of me. Hence the growth of the doctrine and of the party of Free Trade, and the willingness to try that experiment, in the face of what appear incontestable facts. I confess, the motto of the Globe newspaper is so attractive to me, that I can seldom find much appetite to read what is below it in its columns, "The world is governed too much." So the country is frequently affording solitary examples of resistance to the government, solitary nullifiers, who throw themselves on their reserved rights; nay, who have reserved all their rights; who reply to the assessor, and to the clerk of court, that they do not know the State; and embarrass the courts of law, by non-juring, and the commander-in-chief of the militia, by non-resistance.

The same disposition to scrutiny and dissent appeared in civil, festive, neighborly, and domestic society. A restless, prying, conscientious criticism broke out in unexpected quarters. Who gave me the money with which I bought my coat? Why should professional labor and that of the counting-house be paid so disproportionately to the labor of the porter, and woodsawyer? This whole business of Trade gives me to pause and think, as it constitutes false relations between men; inasmuch as I am prone to count myself relieved of any responsibility to behave well and nobly to that person whom I pay with money, whereas if I had not that commodity, I should be put on my good behavior in all companies, and man would be a benefactor to man, as being himself his only certificate that he had a right to those aids and services which each asked of the other. Am I not too protected a person? is there not a wide disparity between the lot of me and the lot of thee, my poor brother, my poor sister? Am I not defrauded of my best culture in the loss of those gymnastics which manual labor and the emergencies of poverty constitute? I find nothing healthful or exalting in the smooth conventions of society; I do not like the close air of saloons. I begin to suspect myself to be a prisoner, though treated with all this courtesy and luxury. I pay a destructive tax in my conformity.

The same insatiable criticism may be traced in the efforts for the reform of Education. The popular education has been taxed with a want of truth and nature. It was complained that an education to things was not given. We are students of words: we are shut up in schools, and colleges, and recitation-rooms, for ten or fifteen years, and come out at last with a bag of wind, a memory of words, and do not know a thing. We cannot use our hands, or our legs, or our eyes, or our arms. We do not know an edible root in the woods, we cannot tell our course by the stars, nor the hour of the day by the sun. It is well if we can swim and skate. We are afraid of a horse, of a cow, of a dog, of a snake, of a spider. The Roman rule was, to teach a boy nothing that he could not learn standing. The old English rule was, 'All summer in the field, and all winter in the study.' And it seems as if a man should learn to plant, or to fish, or to hunt, that he might secure his subsistence at all events, and not be painful to his friends and fellow men. The lessons of science should be experimental also. The sight of the planet through a telescope, is worth all the course on astronomy: the shock of the electric spark in the elbow, out-values all the theories; the taste of the nitrous oxide, the firing of an artificial volcano, are better than volumes of chemistry.

One of the traits of the new spirit, is the inquisition it fixed on our scholastic devotion to the dead languages. The ancient languages, with great beauty of structure, contain wonderful remains of genius, which draw, and always will draw, certain likeminded men,—Greek men, and Roman men, in all countries, to their study; but by a wonderful drowsiness of usage, they had exacted the study of *all* men. Once (say two centuries ago), Latin and Greek had a strict relation to all the science and culture there was in Europe, and the Mathematics had a momentary importance at some era of activity in physical science. These things became stereotyped as *education*, as the manner of men is. But the Good Spirit never cared for the colleges, and though all men and boys were now drilled in Latin, Greek, and Mathematics, it had quite left these shells high and dry on the beach, and was now creating and feeding other matters at other ends of the world. But in a hundred high schools and colleges, this warfare against common sense still goes on. Four, or six, or ten years, the pupil is parsing Greek and Latin, and as soon as he leaves the University, as it is ludicrously called, he shuts those books for the last time. Some thousands of young men are graduated at our colleges in this country every year, and the persons who, at forty years, still read Greek, can all be counted on your hand. I never met with ten. Four or five persons I have seen who read Plato.

But is not this absurd, that the whole liberal talent of this country should be directed in its best years on studies which lead to nothing? What was the consequence? Some intelligent persons said or thought; 'Is that Greek and Latin some spell to conjure with, and not words of reason? If the physician, the lawyer, the divine, never use it to come at their ends, I need never learn it to come at mine. Conjuring is gone out of fashion, and I will omit this conjugating, and go straight to affairs.' So they jumped the Greek and Latin, and read law, medicine, or sermons, without it. To the astonishment of all, the self-made men took even ground at once with the oldest of the regular graduates, and in a few months the most conservative circles of Boston and New York had quite forgotten who of their gownsmen was college-bred, and who was not.

One tendency appears alike in the philosophical speculation, and in the rudest democratical movements, through all the petulance and all the puerility, the wish, namely, to cast aside the superfluous, and arrive at short methods, urged, as I suppose, by an intuition that the human spirit is equal to all emergencies, alone, and that man is more often injured than helped by the means he uses.

I conceive this gradual casting off of material aids, and the indication of growing trust in the private, self-supplied powers of the individual, to be the affirmative principle of the recent philosophy: and that it is feeling its own profound truth, and is reaching forward at this very hour to the happiest conclusions. I readily concede that in this, as in every period of intellectual activity, there has been a noise of denial and protest; much was to be resisted, much was to be got rid of by those who were reared in the old, before they could begin to affirm and to construct. Many a reformer perishes in his removal of rubbish,—and that makes the offensiveness of the class. They are partial; they are not equal to the work they pretend. They lose their way; in the assault on the kingdom of darkness, they expend all their energy on some accidental evil, and lose their sanity and power of benefit. It is of little moment that one or two, or twenty errors of our social system be corrected, but of much that the man be in his senses.

The criticism and attack on institutions which we have witnessed, has made one thing plain, that society gains nothing whilst a man, not himself renovated, attempts to renovate things around him: he has become tediously good in some particular, but negligent or narrow in the rest; and hypocrisy and vanity are often the disgusting result.

It is handsomer to remain in the establishment better than the establishment, and conduct that in the best manner, than to make a sally against evil by some single improvement, without supporting it by a total regeneration. Do not be so vain of your one objection. Do you think there is only one? Alas! my good friend, there is no part of society or of life better than any other part. All our things are right and wrong together. The wave of evil washes all our institutions alike. Do you complain of our Marriage? Our marriage is no worse than our education, our diet, our trade, our social customs. Do you complain of the laws of Property? It is a pedantry to give such importance to them. Can we not play the game of life with these counters, as well as with those; in the institution of property, as well as out of it. Let into it the new and renewing principle of love, and property will be universality.

No one gives the impression of superiority to the institution, which he must give who will reform it. It makes no difference what you say: you must make me feel that you are aloof from it; by your natural and super-natural advantages, do easily see to the end of it,—do see how man can do without it. Now all men are on one side. No man deserves to be heard against property. Only Love, only an Idea, is against property, as we hold it.

I cannot afford to be irritable and captious, nor to waste all my time in attacks. If I should go out of church whenever I hear a false sentiment, I could never stay there five minutes. But why come out? the street is as false as the church, and when I get to my house, or to my manners, or to my speech, I have not got away from the lie. When we see an eager assailant of one of these wrongs, a special reformer, we feel like asking him, What right have you, sir, to your one virtue? Is virtue piecemeal? This is a jewel amidst the rags of a beggar.

In another way the right will be vindicated. In the midst of abuses, in the heart of cities, in the aisles of false churches, alike in one place and in another,—wherever, namely, a just and heroic soul finds itself, there it will do what is next at hand, and by the new quality of character it shall put forth, it shall abrogate that old condition, law or school in which it stands, before the law of its own mind.

If partiality was one fault of the movement party, the other defect was their reliance on Association. Doubts such as those I have intimated, drove many good persons to agitate the questions of social reform. But the revolt against the spirit of commerce, the spirit of aristocracy, and the inveterate abuses of cities, did not appear possible to individuals; and to do battle against numbers, they armed themselves with numbers, and against concert, they relied on new concert.

Following, or advancing beyond the ideas of St. Simon, of Fourier, and of Owen, three communities have already been formed in Massachusetts on kindred plans, and many more in the country at large. They aim to give every member a share in the manual labor, to give an equal reward to labor and to talent, and to unite a liberal culture with an education to labor. The scheme offers, by the economies of associated labor and expense, to make every member rich, on the same amount of property, that, in separate families, would leave every member poor. These new associations are composed of men and women of superior talents and sentiments: yet it may easily be questioned, whether such a community will draw, except in its beginnings, the able and the good; whether those who have energy, will not prefer their chance of superiority and power in the world, to the humble certainties of the association; whether such a retreat does not promise to become an assylum to those who have tried and failed, rather than a field to the strong; and whether the members will not necessarily be fractions of men, because each finds that he cannot enter it, without some compromise. Friendship and association are very fine things, and a grand phalanx of the best of the human race, banded for some catholic object: yes, excellent; but remember that no society can ever be so large as one man. He in his friendship, in his natural and momentary associations, doubles or multiplies himself; but in the hour in which he mortgages himself to two or ten or twenty, he dwarfs himself below the stature of one.

But the men of less faith could not thus believe, and to such, concert appears the sole specific of strength. I have failed, and you have failed, but perhaps together we shall not fail. Our housekeeping is not satisfactory to us, but perhaps a phalanx, a community, might be. Many of us have differed in opinion, and we could find no man who could make the truth plain, but possibly a college, or an ecclesiastical council might. I have not been able either to persuade my brother or to prevail on myself, to disuse the traffic or the potation of brandy, but perhaps a pledge of total abstinence might effectually restrain us. The candidate my party votes for is not to be trusted with a dollar, but he will be honest in the Senate, for we can bring public opinion to bear on him. Thus concert was the specific in all cases. But concert is neither better nor worse, neither more nor less potent than individual force. All the men in the world cannot make a statue walk and speak, cannot make a drop of blood, or a blade of grass, any more than one man can. But let there be one man, let there be truth in two men, in ten men, then is concert for the first time possible, because the force which moves the world is a new quality, and can never be furnished by adding whatever quantities of a different kind. What is the use of the concert of the false and the disunited? There can be no concert in two, where there is no concert in one. When the individual is not *individual*, but is dual; when his thoughts look one way, and his actions another; when his faith is traversed by his habits; when his will, enlightened by reason, is warped by his sense; when with one hand he rows, and with the other backs water, what concert can be?

I do not wonder at the interest these projects inspire. The world is awaking to the idea of union, and these experiments show what it is thinking of. It is and will be magic. Men will live and communicate, and plough, and reap, and govern, as by added ethereal power, when once they are united; as in a celebrated experiment, by expiration and respiration exactly together, four persons lift a heavy man from the ground by the little finger only, and without sense of weight. But this union must be inward, and not one of covenants, and is to be reached by a reverse of the methods they use. The union is only perfect, when all the uniters are isolated. It is the union of friends who live in different streets or towns. Each man, if he attempts to join himself to others, is on all sides cramped and diminished of his proportion; and the stricter the union, the smaller and the more pitiful he is. But leave him alone, to recognize in every hour and place the secret soul, he will go up and down doing the works of a true member, and, to the astonishment of all, the work will be done with concert, though no man spoke. Government will be adamantine without any governor. The union must be ideal in actual individualism.

I pass to the indication in some particulars of that faith in man, which the heart is preaching to us in these days, and which engages the more regard, from the consideration, that the speculations of one generation are the history of the next following.

In alluding just now to our system of education, I spoke of the deadness of its details. But it is open to graver criticism than the palsy of its members: it is a system of despair. The disease with which the human mind now labors, is want of faith. Men do not believe in a power of education. We do not think we can speak to divine sentiments in man, and we do not try. We renounce all high aims. We believe that the defects of so many perverse and so many frivolous people, who make up society, are organic, and society is a hospital of incurables. A man of good sense but of little faith, whose compassion seemed to lead him to church as often as he went there, said to me; "that he liked to have concerts, and fairs, and churches, and other public amusements go on." I am afraid the remark is too honest, and comes from the same origin as the maxim of the tyrant, "If you would rule the world quietly, you must keep it amused." I notice too, that the ground on which eminent public servants urge the claims of popular education is fear: 'This country is filling up with thousands and millions of voters, and you must educate them to keep them from our throats.' We do not believe that any education, any system of philosophy, any influence of genius, will ever give depth of insight to a superficial mind. Having settled ourselves into this infidelity, our skill is expended to procure alleviations, diversion, opiates. We adorn the victim with manual skill, his tongue with languages, his body with inoffensive and comely manners. So have we cunningly hid the tragedy of limitation and inner death we cannot avert. Is it strange that society should be devoured by a secret melancholy, which breaks through all its smiles, and all its gayety and games?

But even one step farther our infidelity has gone. It appears that some doubt is felt by good and wise men, whether really the happiness and probity of men is increased by the culture of the mind in those disciplines to which we give the name of education. Unhappily, too, the doubt comes from scholars, from persons who have tried these methods. In their experience, the scholar was not raised by the sacred thoughts amongst which he dwelt, but used them to selfish ends. He was a profane person, and became a showman, turning his gifts to a marketable use, and not to his own sustenance and growth. It was found that the intellect could be independently developed, that is, in separation from the man, as any single organ can be invigorated, and the result was monstrous. A canine appetite for knowledge was generated, which must still be fed, but was never satisfied, and this knowledge not being directed on action, never took the character of substantial, humane truth, blessing those whom it entered. It gave the scholar certain powers of expression, the power of speech, the power of poetry, of literary art, but it did not bring him to peace, or to beneficence.

When the literary class betray a destitution of faith, it is not strange that society should be disheartened and sensualized by unbelief. What remedy? Life must be lived on a higher plane. We must go up to a higher platform, to which we are always invited to ascend; there, the whole aspect of things changes. I resist the skepticism of our education, and of our educated men. I do not believe that the differences of opinion and character in men are organic. I do not recognize, beside the class of the good and the wise, a permanent class of skeptics, or a class of conservatives, or of malignants, or of materialists. I do not believe in two classes. You remember the story of the poor woman who importuned King Philip of Macedon to grant her justice, which Philip refused: the woman exclaimed, "I appeal": the king, astonished, asked to whom she appealed: the woman replied, "from Philip drunk to Philip sober." The text will suit me very well. I believe not in two classes of men, but in man in two moods, in Philip drunk and Philip sober. I think, according to the good-hearted word of Plato, "Unwillingly the soul is deprived of truth." Iron conservative, miser, or thief, no man is, but by a supposed necessity, which he tolerates by shortness or torpidity of sight. The soul lets no man go without some visitations and holy-days of a diviner presence. It would be easy to show, by a narrow scanning of any man's biography, that we are not so wedded to our paltry performances of every kind, but that every man has at intervals the grace to scorn his performances, in comparing them with his belief of what he should do, that he puts himself on the side of his enemies, listening gladly to what they say of him, and accusing himself of the same things.

What is it men love in Genius, but its infinite hope, which degrades all it has done? Genius counts all its miracles poor and short. Its own idea it never executed. The Iliad, the Hamlet, the Doric column, the Roman arch, the Gothic minster, the German anthem, when they are ended, the master casts behind him. How sinks the song in the waves of melody which the universe pours over his soul! Before that gracious

Infinite, out of which he drew these few strokes, how mean they look, though the praises of the world attend them. From the triumphs of his art, he turns with desire to this greater defeat. Let those admire who will. With silent joy he sees himself to be capable of a beauty that eclipses all which his hands have done, all which human hands have ever done.

Well, we are all the children of genius, the children of virtue,—and feel their inspirations in our happier hours. Is not every man sometimes a radical in politics? Men are conservatives when they are least vigorous, or when they are most luxurious. They are conservatives after dinner, or before taking their rest; when they are sick, or aged: in the morning, or when their intellect or their conscience have been aroused, when they hear music, or when they read poetry, they are radicals. In the circle of the rankest tories that could be collected in England, Old or New, let a powerful and stimulating intellect, a man of great heart and mind, act on them, and very quickly these frozen conservators will yield to the friendly influence, these hopeless will begin to hope, these haters will begin to love, these immovable statues will begin to spin and revolve. I cannot help recalling the fine anecdote which Warton relates of Bishop Berkeley, when he was preparing to leave England, with his plan of planting the gospel among the American savages. "Lord Bathurst told me, that the members of the Scriblerus club, being met at his house at dinner, they agreed to rally Berkeley, who was also his guest, on his scheme at Bermudas. Berkeley, having listened to the many lively things they had to say, begged to be heard in his turn, and displayed his plan with such an astonishing and animating force of eloquence and enthusiasm, that they were struck dumb, and, after some pause, rose up all together with earnestness, exclaiming, 'Let us set out with him immediately.' " Men in all ways are better than they seem. They like flattery for the moment, but they know the truth for their own. It is a foolish cowardice which keeps us from trusting them, and speaking to them rude truth. They resent your honesty for an instant, they will thank you for it always. What is it we heartily wish of each other? Is it to be pleased and flattered? No, but to be convicted and exposed, to be shamed out of our nonsense of all kinds, and made men of, instead of ghosts and phantoms. We are weary of gliding ghostlike through the world, which is itself so slight and unreal. We crave a sense of reality, though it come in strokes of pain. I explain so,—by this manlike love of truth,—those excesses and errors into which souls of great vigor, but not equal insight, often fall. They feel the poverty at the bottom of all the seeming affluence of the world. They know the speed with which they come straight through the thin masquerade, and conceive a disgust at the indigence of nature: Rousseau, Mirabeau, Charles Fox, Napoleon, Byron,—and I could easily add names nearer home, of raging riders, who drive their steeds so hard, in the violence of living to forget its illusion: they would know the worst, and tread the floors of hell. The heroes of ancient and modern fame, Cimon, Themistocles, Alcibiades, Alexander, Cæsar, have treated life and fortune as a game to be well and skilfully played, but the stake not to be so valued, but that any time, it could be held as a trifle light as air, and thrown up. Cæsar, just before the battle of Pharsalia, discourses with the Egyptian priest, concerning the fountains of the Nile, and offers to quit the army, the empire, and Cleopatra, if he will show him those mysterious sources.

The same magnanimity shows itself in our social relations, in the preference, namely, which each man gives to the society of superiors over that of his equals. All that a man has, will he give for right relations with his mates. All that he has, will he give for an erect demeanor in every company and on each occasion. He aims at such things as his neighbors prize, and gives his days and nights, his talents and his heart, to strike a good stroke, to acquit himself in all men's sight as a man. The consideration of an eminent citizen, of a noted merchant, of a man of mark in his profession; naval and military honor, a general's commission, a marshal's baton, a ducal coronet, the laurel of poets, and, anyhow procured, the acknowledgment of eminent merit, have this lustre for each candidate, that they enable him to walk erect and unashamed, in the presence of some persons, before whom he felt himself inferior. Having raised himself to this rank, having established his equality with class after class, of those with whom he would live well, he still finds certain others, before whom he cannot possess himself, because they have somewhat fairer, somewhat grander, somewhat purer, which extorts homage of him. Is his ambition pure? then, will his laurels and his possessions seem worthless: instead of avoiding these men who make his fine gold dim, he will cast all behind him, and seek their society only, woo and embrace this his humiliation and mortification, until he shall know why his eye sinks, his voice is husky, and his brilliant talents are paralyzed in this presence. He is sure that the soul which gives the lie to all things, will tell none. His constitution will not mislead him. If it cannot carry itself as it ought, high and unmatchable in the presence of any man, if the secret oracles whose whisper makes the sweetness and dignity of his life, do here withdraw and accompany him no longer, it is time to undervalue what he has valued, to dispossess himself of what he has acquired, and with Cæsar to take in his hand the army, the empire, and Cleopatra, and say, 'All these will I relinquish, if you will show me the fountains of the Nile.' Dear to us are those who love us, the swift moments we spend with them are a compensation for a great deal of misery; they enlarge our life;—but dearer are those who reject us as unworthy, for they add another life: they build a heaven before us, whereof we had not dreamed, and thereby supply to us new powers out of the recesses of the spirit, and urge us to new and unattempted performances.

As every man at heart wishes the best and not inferior society, wishes to be convicted of his error, and to come to himself, so he wishes that the same healing should not stop in his thought, but should penetrate his will or active power. The selfish man suffers more from his selfishness, than he from whom that selfishness withholds some important benefit. What he most wishes is to be lifted to some higher platform, that he may see beyond his present fear the transalpine good, so that his fear, his coldness, his custom may be broken up like fragments of ice, melted and carried away in the great stream of good will. Do you ask my aid? I also wish to be a benefactor. I wish more to be a benefactor and servant, than you wish to be served by me, and surely the greatest good fortune that could befall me, is precisely to be so moved by you that I should say, 'Take me and all mine, and use me and mine freely to your ends'! for, I could not say it, otherwise than because a great enlargement had come to my heart and mind, which made me superior to my fortunes. Here we are paralyzed with fear; we hold on to our little properties, house and land, office and money, for the bread which they have in our experience yielded us, although we confess, that our being does not flow through them. We desire to be made great, we desire to be touched with that fire which shall command this ice to stream, and make our existence a benefit. If therefore we start objections to your project, O friend of the slave, or friend of the poor, or of the race, understand well, that it is because we wish to drive you to drive us into your measures. We wish to hear ourselves confuted. We are haunted with a belief that you have a secret, which it would highliest advantage us to learn, and we would force you to impart it to us, though it should bring us to prison, or to worse extremity.

Nothing shall warp me from the belief, that every man is a lover of truth. There is no pure lie, no pure malignity in nature. The entertainment of the proposition of depravity is the last profligacy and profanation. There is no skepticism, no atheism but that. Could it be received into common belief, suicide would unpeople the planet. It has had a name to live in some dogmatic theology, but each man's innocence and his real liking of his neighbor, have kept it a dead letter. I remember standing at the polls one day, when the anger of the political contest gave a certain grimness to the faces of the independent electors, and a good man at my side looking on the people, remarked, "I am satisfied that the largest part of these men, on either side, mean to vote right." I suppose, considerate observers looking at the masses of men, in their blameless, and in their equivocal actions, will assent, that in spite of selfishness and frivolity, the general purpose in the great number of persons is fidelity. The reason why any one refuses his assent to your opinion, or his aid to your benevolent design, is in you: he refuses to accept you as a bringer of truth, because, though you think you have it, he feels that you have it not. You have not given him the authentic sign.

If it were worth while to run into details this general doctrine of the latent but ever soliciting Spirit, it would be easy to adduce illustration in particulars of a man's equality to the church, of his equality to the state, and of his equality to every other man. It is yet in all men's memory, that, a few years ago, the liberal churches complained, that the Calvinistic church denied to them the name of Christian. I think the complaint was confession: a religious church would not complain. A religious man like Behmen, Fox, or Swedenborg, is not irritated by wanting the sanction of the church, but the church feels the accusation of his presence and belief.

It only needs, that a just man should walk in our streets, to make it appear how pitiful and inartificial a contrivance is our legislation. The man whose part is taken, and who does not wait for society in anything, has a power which society cannot choose but feel. The familiar experiment, called the hydrostatic paradox, in which a capillary column of water balances the ocean, is a symbol of the relation of one man to the whole family of men. The wise Dandini, on hearing the lives of Socrates, Pythagoras, and Diogenes read, "judged them to be great men every way, excepting, that they were too much subjected to the reverence of the laws, which to second and authorize, true virtue must abate very much of its original vigor."

And as a man is equal to the church, and equal to the state, so he is equal to every other man. The disparities of power in men are superficial; and all frank and searching conversation, in which a man lays himself open to his brother, apprizes each of their radical unity. When two persons sit and converse in a thoroughly good understanding, the remark is sure to be made, See how we have disputed about words! Let a clear, apprehensive mind, such as every man knows among his friends, converse with the most commanding poetic genius, I think, it would appear that there was no inequality such as men fancy between them; that a perfect understanding, a like receiving, a like perceiving, abolished differences, and the poet would confess, that his creative imagination gave him no deep advantage, but only the superficial one, that he could express himself, and the other could not; that his advantage was a knack, which might impose on indolent men, but could not impose on lovers of truth; for they know the tax of talent, or, what a price of greatness the power of expression too often pays. I believe it is the conviction of the purest men, that the net amount of man and man does not much vary. Each is incomparably superior to his companion in some faculty. His want of skill in other directions, has added to his fitness for his own work. Each seems to have some compensation yielded to him by his infirmity, and every hindrance operates as a concentration of his force.

These and the like experiences intimate, that man stands in strict connexion with a higher fact never yet manifested. There is power over and behind us, and we are the channels of its communications. We seek to say thus and so, and over our head some spirit sits, which contradicts what we say. We would persuade our fellow to this or that; another self within our eyes dissuades him. That which we keep back, this reveals. In vain we compose our faces and our words; it holds uncontrollable communication with the enemy, and he answers civilly to us, but believes the spirit. We exclaim, 'There's a traitor in the house!' but at last it appears that he is the true man, and I am the traitor. This open channel to the highest life is the first and last reality, so subtle, so quiet, yet so tenacious, that although I have never expressed the truth, and although I have never heard the expression of it from any other, I know that the whole truth is here for me. What if I cannot answer your questions? I am not pained that I cannot frame a reply to the question, What is the operation we call Providence? There lies the unspoken thing, present, omnipresent. Every time we converse, we seek to translate it into speech, but whether we hit, or whether we miss, we have the fact. Every discourse is an approximate answer: but it is of small consequence, that we do not get it into verbs and nouns, whilst it abides for contemplation forever.

If the auguries of the prophesying heart shall make themselves good in time, the man who shall be born, whose advent men and events prepare and foreshow, is one who shall enjoy his connexion with a higher life, with the man within man; shall destroy distrust by his trust, shall use his native but forgotten methods, shall not take counsel of flesh and blood, but shall rely on the Law alive and beautiful, which works over our heads and under our feet. Pitiless, it avails itself of our success, when we obey it, and of our ruin, when we contravene it. Men are all secret believers in it, else, the word justice would have no meaning: they believe that the best is the true;

that right is done at last; or chaos would come. It rewards actions after their nature, and not after the design of the agent. 'Work,' it saith to man, 'in every hour, paid or unpaid, see only that thou work, and thou canst not escape the reward: whether thy work be fine or coarse, planting corn, or writing epics, so only it be honest work, done to thine own approbation, it shall earn a reward to the senses as well as to the thought: no matter, how often defeated, you are born to victory. The reward of a thing well done, is to have done it.'

As soon as a man is wonted to look beyond surfaces, and to see how this high will prevails without an exception or an interval, he settles himself into serenity. He can already rely on the laws of gravity, that every stone will fall where it is due; the good globe is faithful, and carries us securely through the celestial spaces, anxious or resigned: we need not interfere to help it on, and he will learn, one day, the mild lesson they teach, that our own orbit is all our task, and we need not assist the administration of the universe. Do not be so impatient to set the town right concerning the unfounded pretensions and the false reputation of certain men of standing. They are laboring harder to set the town right concerning themselves, and will certainly succeed. Suppress for a few days your criticism on the insufficiency of this or that teacher or experimenter, and he will have demonstrated his insufficiency to all men's eyes. In like manner, let a man fall into the divine circuits, and he is enlarged. Obedience to his genius is the only liberating influence. We wish to escape from subjection, and a sense of inferiority,—and we make self-denying ordinances, we drink water, we eat grass, we refuse the laws, we go to jail: it is all in vain; only by obedience to his genius; only by the freest activity in the way constitutional to him, does an angel seem to arise before a man, and lead him by the hand out of all the wards of the prison.

That which befits us, embosomed in beauty and wonder as we are, is cheerfulness and courage, and the endeavor to realize our aspirations. The life of man is the true romance, which, when it is valiantly conducted, will yield the imagination a higher joy than any fiction. All around us, what powers are wrapped up under the coarse mattings of custom, and all wonder prevented. It is so wonderful to our neurologists that a man can see without his eyes, that it does not occur to them, that it is just as wonderful, that he should see with them; and that is ever the difference between the wise and the unwise: the latter wonders at what is unusual, the wise man wonders at the usual. Shall not the heart which has received so much, trust the Power by which it lives? May it not quit other leadings, and listen to the Soul that has guided it so gently, and taught it so much, secure that the future will be worthy of the past?

REPRESENTATIVE MEN

Seven Lectures

Contents

I

Uses of Great Men

IT IS NATURAL to believe in great men. If the companions of our childhood should turn out to be heroes, and their condition regal, it would not surprise us. All mythology opens with demigods, and the circumstance is high and poetic; that is, their genius is paramount. In the legends of the Gautama, the first men ate the earth, and found it deliciously sweet.

Nature seems to exist for the excellent. The world is upheld by the veracity of good men: they make the earth wholesome. They who lived with them found life glad and nutritious. Life is sweet and tolerable only in our belief in such society; and actually, or ideally, we manage to live with superiors. We call our children and our lands by their names. Their names are wrought into the verbs of language, their works and effigies are in our houses, and every circumstance of the day recalls an anecdote of them.

The search after the great is the dream of youth, and the most serious occupation of manhood. We travel into foreign parts to find his works,—if possible, to get a glimpse of him. But we are put off with fortune instead. You say, the English are practical; the Germans are hospitable; in Valencia, the climate is delicious; and in the hills of the Sacramento, there is gold for the gathering. Yes, but I do not travel to find comfortable, rich, and hospitable people, or clear sky, or ingots that cost too much. But if there were any magnet that would point to the countries and houses where are the persons who are intrinsically rich and powerful, I would sell all, and buy it, and put myself on the road to-day.

The race goes with us on their credit. The knowledge, that in the city is a man who invented the railroad, raises the credit of all the citizens. But enormous populations, if they be beggars, are disgusting, like moving cheese, like hills of ants, or of fleas—the more, the worse.

Our religion is the love and cherishing of these patrons.

The gods of fable are the shining moments of great men. We run all our vessels into one mould. Our colossal theologies of Judaism, Christism, Buddhism, Mahometism, are the necessary and structural action of the human mind. The student of history is like a man going into a warehouse to buy cloths or carpets. He fancies he has a new article. If he go to the factory, he shall find that his new stuff still repeats the scrolls and rosettes which are found on the interior walls of the pyramids of Thebes. Our theism is the purification of the human mind. Man can paint, or make, or think nothing but man. He believes that the great material elements had their origin from his thought. And our philosophy finds one essence collected or distributed.

If now we proceed to inquire into the kinds of service we derive from others, let us be warned of the danger of modern studies, and begin low enough. We must not contend against love, or deny the substantial existence of other people. I know not what would happen to us. We have social strengths. Our affection towards others creates a sort of vantage or purchase which nothing will supply. I can do that by another which I cannot do alone. I can say to you what I cannot first say to myself. Other men are lenses through which we read our own minds. Each man seeks those of different quality from his own, and such as are good of their kind; that is, he seeks other men, and the *otherest*. The stronger the nature, the more it is reactive. Let us have the quality pure. A little genius let us leave alone. A main difference betwixt men is, whether they attend their own affair or not. Man is that noble endogenous plant which grows, like the palm, from within, outward. His own affair, though impossible to others, he can open with celerity and in sport. It is easy to sugar to be sweet, and to nitre to be salt. We take a great deal of pains to waylay and entrap that which of itself will fall into our hands. I count him a great man who inhabits a higher sphere of thought, into which other men rise with labor and difficulty; he has but to open his eyes to see things in a true light, and in large relations; whilst they must make painful corrections, and keep a vigilant eye on many sources of error. His service to us is of like sort. It costs a beautiful person no exertion to paint her image on our eyes; yet how splendid is that benefit! It costs no more for a wise soul to convey his quality to other men. And every one can do his best thing easiest. *"Peu de moyens, beaucoup d'effêt."* He is great who is what he is from nature, and who never reminds us of others.

But he must be related to us, and our life receive from him some promise of explanation. I cannot tell what I would know; but I have observed there are persons who, in their character and actions, answer questions which I have not skill to put. One man answers some question which none of his contemporaries put, and is isolated. The past and passing religions and philosophies answer some other question. Certain men affect us as rich possibilities, but helpless to themselves and to their times,—the sport, perhaps, of some instinct that rules in the air;—they do not speak to our want. But the great are near; we know them at sight. They satisfy expectation, and fall into place. What is good is effective, generative; makes for itself room, food, and allies. A sound apple produces seed,—a hybrid does not. Is a man in his place, he is constructive, fertile, magnetic, inundating armies with his purpose, which is thus executed. The river makes its own shores, and each legitimate idea makes its own channels and welcome,—harvests for food, institutions for expression, weapons to fight with, and disciples to explain it. The true artist has the planet for his pedestal; the adventurer, after years of strife, has nothing broader than his own shoes.

Our common discourse respects two kinds of use or service from superior men. Direct giving is agreeable to the early belief of men; direct giving of material or metaphysical aid, as of health, eternal youth, fine senses, arts of healing, magical power, and prophecy. The boy believes there is a teacher who can sell him wisdom. Churches believe in imputed merit. But, in strictness, we are not much cognizant of direct serving. Man is endogenous, and education is his unfolding. The aid we have from others is mechanical, compared with the discoveries of nature in us. What is thus learned is delightful in the doing, and the effect remains. Right ethics are central, and go from the soul outward. Gift is contrary to the law of the universe. Serving others is serving us. I must absolve me to myself. 'Mind thy affair,' says the spirit:—'coxcomb, would you

meddle with the skies, or with other people?' Indirect service
is left. Men have a pictorial or representative quality, and
serve us in the intellect. Behmen and Swedenborg saw that
things were representative. Men are also representative; first,
of things, and secondly, of ideas.

As plants convert the minerals into food for animals, so
each man converts some raw material in nature to human use.
The inventors of fire, electricity, magnetism, iron, lead, glass,
linen, silk, cotton; the makers of tools; the inventor of deci-
mal notation; the geometer; the engineer; the musician,—
severally make an easy way for all, through unknown and impossible confusions. Each man is, by secret liking, connected
with some district of nature, whose agent and interpreter he
is, as Linnæus, of plants; Huber, of bees; Fries, of lichens;
Van Mons, of pears; Dalton, of atomic forms; Euclid, of
lines; Newton, of fluxions.

A man is a centre for nature, running out threads of relation through every thing, fluid and solid, material and elemental. The earth rolls; every clod and stone comes to the
meridian: so every organ, function, acid, crystal, grain of
dust, has its relation to the brain. It waits long, but its turn
comes. Each plant has its parasite, and each created thing its
lover and poet. Justice has already been done to steam, to
iron, to wood, to coal, to loadstone, to iodine, to corn, and
cotton; but how few materials are yet used by our arts! The
mass of creatures and of qualities are still hid and expectant.
It would seem as if each waited, like the enchanted princess
in fairy tales, for a destined human deliverer. Each must be
disenchanted, and walk forth to the day in human shape. In
the history of discovery, the ripe and latent truth seems to
have fashioned a brain for itself. A magnet must be made
man, in some Gilbert, or Swedenborg, or Oersted, before the
general mind can come to entertain its powers.

If we limit ourselves to the first advantages;—a sober grace
adheres to the mineral and botanic kingdoms, which, in the
highest moments, comes up as the charm of nature,—the
glitter of the spar, the sureness of affinity, the veracity of angles. Light and darkness, heat and cold, hunger and food,
sweet and sour, solid, liquid, and gas, circle us round in a
wreath of pleasures, and, by their agreeable quarrel, beguile

the day of life. The eye repeats every day the first eulogy on things—"He saw that they were good." We know where to find them; and these performers are relished all the more, after a little experience of the pretending races. We are entitled, also, to higher advantages. Something is wanting to science, until it has been humanized. The table of logarithms is one thing, and its vital play, in botany, music, optics, and architecture, another. There are advancements to numbers, anatomy, architecture, astronomy, little suspected at first, when, by union with intellect and will, they ascend into the life, and reappear in conversation, character, and politics.

But this comes later. We speak now only of our acquaintance with them in their own sphere, and the way in which they seem to fascinate and draw to them some genius who occupies himself with one thing, all his life long. The possibility of interpretation lies in the identity of the observer with the observed. Each material thing has its celestial side; has its translation, through humanity, into the spiritual and necessary sphere, where it plays a part as indestructible as any other. And to these, their ends, all things continually ascend. The gases gather to the solid firmament: the chemic lump arrives at the plant, and grows; arrives at the quadruped, and walks; arrives at the man, and thinks. But also the constituency determines the vote of the representative. He is not only representative, but participant. Like can only be known by like. The reason why he knows about them is, that he is of them; he has just come out of nature, or from being a part of that thing. Animated chlorine knows of chlorine, and incarnate zinc, of zinc. Their quality makes his career; and he can variously publish their virtues, because they compose him. Man, made of the dust of the world, does not forget his origin; and all that is yet inanimate will one day speak and reason. Unpublished nature will have its whole secret told. Shall we say that quartz mountains will pulverize into innumerable Werners, Von Buchs, and Beaumonts; and the laboratory of the atmosphere holds in solution I know not what Berzeliuses and Davys?

Thus, we sit by the fire, and take hold on the poles of the earth. This *quasi* omnipresence supplies the imbecility of our condition. In one of those celestial days, when heaven and earth meet and adorn each other, it seems a poverty that we can only spend it once: we wish for a thousand heads, a thousand bodies, that we might celebrate its immense beauty in many ways and places. Is this fancy? Well, in good faith, we are multiplied by our proxies. How easily we adopt their labors! Every ship that comes to America got its chart from Columbus. Every novel is a debtor to Homer. Every carpenter who shaves with a foreplane borrows the genius of a forgotten inventor. Life is girt all round with a zodiac of sciences, the contributions of men who have perished to add their point of light to our sky. Engineer, broker, jurist, physician, moralist, theologian, and every man, inasmuch as he has any science, is a definer and map-maker of the latitudes and longitudes of our condition. These road-makers on every hand enrich us. We must extend the area of life, and multiply our relations. We are as much gainers by finding a new property in the old earth, as by acquiring a new planet.

We are too passive in the reception of these material or semi-material aids. We must not be sacks and stomachs. To ascend one step,—we are better served through our sympathy. Activity is contagious. Looking where others look, and conversing with the same things, we catch the charm which lured them. Napoleon said, "You must not fight too often with one enemy, or you will teach him all your art of war." Talk much with any man of vigorous mind, and we acquire very fast the habit of looking at things in the same light, and, on each occurrence, we anticipate his thought.

Men are helpful through the intellect and the affections. Other help, I find a false appearance. If you affect to give me bread and fire, I perceive that I pay for it the full price, and at last it leaves me as it found me, neither better nor worse: but all mental and moral force is a positive good. It goes out from you, whether you will or not, and profits me whom you never thought of. I cannot even hear of personal vigor of any kind, great power of performance, without fresh resolution. We are emulous of all that man can do. Cecil's saying of Sir Walter Raleigh, "I know that he can toil terribly," is an electric touch. So are Clarendon's portraits,—of Hampden; "who was of an industry and vigilance not to be tired out or wearied by the most laborious, and of parts not to be imposed on by the most subtle and sharp, and of a personal courage equal to his best parts,"—of Falkland; "who was so severe an adorer of truth, that he could as easily have given himself leave to steal, as to dissemble." We cannot read Plutarch, without a tingling of the blood; and I accept the saying of the Chinese Mencius: "A sage is the instructer of a hundred ages. When the manners of Loo are heard of, the stupid become intelligent, and the wavering, determined."

This is the moral of biography; yet it is hard for departed men to touch the quick like our own companions, whose names may not last as long. What is he whom I never think of? whilst in every solitude are those who succor our genius, and stimulate us in wonderful manners. There is a power in love to divine another's destiny better than that other can, and, by heroic encouragements, hold him to his task. What has friendship so signal as its sublime attraction to whatever virtue is in us? We will never more think cheaply of ourselves, or of life. We are piqued to some purpose, and the industry of the diggers on the railroad will not again shame us.

Under this head, too, falls that homage, very pure, as I think, which all ranks pay to the hero of the day, from Coriolanus and Gracchus, down to Pitt, Lafayette, Wellington, Webster, Lamartine. Hear the shouts in the street! The people cannot see him enough. They delight in a man. Here is a head and a trunk! What a front! what eyes! Atlantean shoulders, and the whole carriage heroic, with equal inward force to guide the great machine! This pleasure of full expression to that which, in their private experience, is usually cramped and obstructed, runs, also, much higher, and is the secret of the reader's joy in literary genius. Nothing is kept back. There is fire enough to fuse the mountain of ore. Shakspeare's principal merit may be conveyed, in saying that he, of all men, best understands the English language, and can say what he will. Yet these unchoked channels and floodgates of expression are only health or fortunate constitution. Shakspeare's name suggests other and purely intellectual benefits.

Senates and sovereigns have no compliment, with their medals, swords, and armorial coats, like the addressing to a human being thoughts out of a certain height, and presupposing his intelligence. This honor, which is possible in

personal intercourse scarcely twice in a lifetime, genius perpetually pays; contented, if now and then, in a century, the
proffer is accepted. The indicators of the values of matter are
degraded to a sort of cooks and confectioners, on the appearance of the indicators of ideas. Genius is the naturalist or
geographer of the supersensible regions, and draws their
map; and, by acquainting us with new fields of activity, cools
our affection for the old. These are at once accepted as the
reality, of which the world we have conversed with is the
show.

We go to the gymnasium and the swimming-school to see
the power and beauty of the body; there is the like pleasure,
and a higher benefit, from witnessing intellectual feats of all
kinds; as, feats of memory, of mathematical combination,
great power of abstraction, the transmutings of the imagination, even versatility, and concentration, as these acts expose
the invisible organs and members of the mind, which respond, member for member, to the parts of the body. For,
we thus enter a new gymnasium, and learn to choose men by
their truest marks, taught, with Plato, "to choose those who
can, without aid from the eyes, or any other sense, proceed
to truth and to being." Foremost among these activities, are
the summersaults, spells, and resurrections, wrought by the
imagination. When this wakes, a man seems to multiply ten
times or a thousand times his force. It opens the delicious
sense of indeterminate size, and inspires an audacious mental
habit. We are as elastic as the gas of gunpowder, and a sentence in a book, or a word dropped in conversation, sets free
our fancy, and instantly our heads are bathed with galaxies,
and our feet tread the floor of the Pit. And this benefit is real,
because we are entitled to these enlargements, and, once having passed the bounds, shall never again be quite the miserable pedants we were.

The high functions of the intellect are so allied, that some
imaginative power usually appears in all eminent minds, even
in arithmeticians of the first class, but especially in meditative
men of an intuitive habit of thought. This class serve us, so
that they have the perception of identity and the perception
of reaction. The eyes of Plato, Shakspeare, Swedenborg,
Goethe, never shut on either of these laws. The perception of

these laws is a kind of metre of the mind. Little minds are little, through failure to see them.

Even these feasts have their surfeit. Our delight in reason degenerates into idolatry of the herald. Especially when a mind of powerful method has instructed men, we find the examples of oppression. The dominion of Aristotle, the Ptolemaic astronomy, the credit of Luther, of Bacon, of Locke,—in religion, the history of hierarchies, of saints, and the sects which have taken the name of each founder, are in point. Alas! every man is such a victim. The imbecility of men is always inviting the impudence of power. It is the delight of vulgar talent to dazzle and to bind the beholder. But true genius seeks to defend us from itself. True genius will not impoverish, but will liberate, and add new senses. If a wise man should appear in our village, he would create, in those who conversed with him, a new consciousness of wealth, by opening their eyes to unobserved advantages; he would establish a sense of immovable equality, calm us with assurances that we could not be cheated; as every one would discern the checks and guarantees of condition. The rich would see their mistakes and poverty, the poor their escapes and their resources.

But nature brings all this about in due time. Rotation is her remedy. The soul is impatient of masters, and eager for change. Housekeepers say of a domestic who has been valuable, "She had lived with me long enough." We are tendencies, or rather, symptoms, and none of us complete. We touch and go, and sip the foam of many lives. Rotation is the law of nature. When nature removes a great man, people explore the horizon for a successor; but none comes, and none will. His class is extinguished with him. In some other and quite different field, the next man will appear; not Jefferson, not Franklin, but now a great salesman; then a road-contractor; then a student of fishes; then a buffalo-hunting explorer, or a semi-savage western general. Thus we make a stand against our rougher masters; but against the best there is a finer remedy. The power which they communicate is not theirs. When we are exalted by ideas, we do not owe this to Plato, but to the idea, to which, also, Plato was debtor.

I must not forget that we have a special debt to a single

class. Life is a scale of degrees. Between rank and rank of our great men are wide intervals. Mankind have, in all ages, attached themselves to a few persons, who, either by the quality of that idea they embodied, or by the largeness of their reception, were entitled to the position of leaders and law-givers. These teach us the qualities of primary nature,—admit us to the constitution of things. We swim, day by day, on a river of delusions, and are effectually amused with houses and towns in the air, of which the men about us are dupes. But life is a sincerity. In lucid intervals we say, 'Let there be an entrance opened for me into realities; I have worn the fool's cap too long.' We will know the meaning of our economies and politics. Give us the cipher, and, if persons and things are scores of a celestial music, let us read off the strains. We have been cheated of our reason; yet there have been sane men, who enjoyed a rich and related existence. What they know, they know for us. With each new mind, a new secret of nature transpires; nor can the Bible be closed, until the last great man is born. These men correct the delirium of the animal spirits, make us considerate, and engage us to new aims and powers. The veneration of mankind selects these for the highest place. Witness the multitude of statues, pictures, and memorials which recall their genius in every city, village, house, and ship:—

> "Ever their phantoms arise before us,
>   Our loftier brothers, but one in blood;
>   At bed and table they lord it o'er us,
>   With looks of beauty, and words of good."

How to illustrate the distinctive benefit of ideas, the service rendered by those who introduce moral truths into the general mind?—I am plagued, in all my living, with a perpetual tariff of prices. If I work in my garden, and prune an apple-tree, I am well enough entertained, and could continue indefinitely in the like occupation. But it comes to mind that a day is gone, and I have got this precious nothing done. I go to Boston or New York, and run up and down on my affairs: they are sped, but so is the day. I am vexed by the recollection of this price I have paid for a trifling advantage. I remember the *peau d'ane*, on which whoso sat should have his desire, but a piece of the skin was gone for every wish. I go to a convention of philanthropists. Do what I can, I cannot keep my eyes off the clock. But if there should appear in the company some gentle soul who knows little of persons or parties, of Carolina or Cuba, but who announces a law that disposes these particulars, and so certifies me of the equity which checkmates every false player, bankrupts every self-seeker, and apprises me of my independence on any conditions of country, or time, or human body, that man liberates me; I forget the clock. I pass out of the sore relation to persons. I am healed of my hurts. I am made immortal by apprehending my possession of incorruptible goods. Here is great competition of rich and poor. We live in a market, where is only so much wheat, or wool, or land; and if I have so much more, every other must have so much less. I seem to have no good, without breach of good manners. Nobody is glad in the gladness of another, and our system is one of war, of an injurious superiority. Every child of the Saxon race is educated to wish to be first. It is our system; and a man comes to measure his greatness by the regrets, envies, and hatreds of his competitors. But in these new fields there is room: here are no self-esteems, no exclusions.

I admire great men of all classes, those who stand for facts, and for thoughts; I like rough and smooth, "Scourges of God," and "Darlings of the human race." I like the first Cæsar; and Charles V., of Spain; and Charles XII., of Sweden; Richard Plantagenet; and Bonaparte, in France. I applaud a sufficient man, an officer equal to his office; captains, ministers, senators. I like a master standing firm on legs of iron, well-born, rich, handsome, eloquent, loaded with advantages, drawing all men by fascination into tributaries and supporters of his power. Sword and staff, or talents sword-like or staff-like, carry on the work of the world. But I find him greater, when he can abolish himself, and all heroes, by letting in this element of reason, irrespective of persons; this subtiliser, and irresistible upward force, into our thought, destroying individualism; the power so great, that the potentate is nothing. Then he is a monarch, who gives a constitution to his people; a pontiff, who preaches the equality of souls, and releases his servants from their barbarous homages; an emperor, who can spare his empire.

But I intended to specify, with a little minuteness, two or three points of service. Nature never spares the opium or nepenthe; but, wherever she mars her creature with some deformity or defect, lays her poppies plentifully on the bruise, and the sufferer goes joyfully through life, ignorant of the ruin, and incapable of seeing it, though all the world point their finger at it every day. The worthless and offensive members of society, whose existence is a social pest, invariably think themselves the most ill-used people alive, and never get over their astonishment at the ingratitude and selfishness of their contemporaries. Our globe discovers its hidden virtues, not only in heroes and archangels, but in gossips and nurses. Is it not a rare contrivance that lodged the due inertia in every creature, the conserving, resisting energy, the anger at being waked or changed? Altogether independent of the intellectual force in each, is the pride of opinion, the security that we are right. Not the feeblest grandame, not a mowing idiot, but uses what spark of perception and faculty is left, to chuckle and triumph in his or her opinion over the absurdities of all the rest. Difference from me is the measure of absurdity. Not one has a misgiving of being wrong. Was it not a bright thought that made things cohere with this bitumen, fastest of cements? But, in the midst of this chuckle of self-gratulation, some figure goes by, which Thersites too can love and admire. This is he that should marshal us the way we were going. There is no end to his aid. Without Plato, we should almost lose our faith in the possibility of a reasonable book. We seem to want but one, but we want one. We love to associate with heroic persons, since our receptivity is unlimited; and, with the great, our thoughts and manners easily become great. We are all wise in capacity, though so few in energy. There needs but one wise man in a company, and all are wise, so rapid is the contagion.

Great men are thus a collyrium to clear our eyes from egotism, and enable us to see other people and their works. But there are vices and follies incident to whole populations and ages. Men resemble their contemporaries, even more than their progenitors. It is observed in old couples, or in persons who have been housemates for a course of years, that they grow alike; and, if they should live long enough, we should not be able to know them apart. Nature abhors these complaisances, which threaten to melt the world into a lump, and hastens to break up such maudlin agglutinations. The like assimilation goes on between men of one town, of one sect, of one political party; and the ideas of the time are in the air, and infect all who breathe it. Viewed from any high point, this city of New York, yonder city of London, the western civilization, would seem a bundle of insanities. We keep each other in countenance, and exasperate by emulation the frenzy of the time. The shield against the stingings of conscience, is the universal practice, or our contemporaries. Again; it is very easy to be as wise and good as your companions. We learn of our contemporaries what they know, without effort, and almost through the pores of the skin. We catch it by sympathy, or, as a wife arrives at the intellectual and moral elevations of her husband. But we stop where they stop. Very hardly can we take another step. The great, or such as hold of nature, and transcend fashions, by their fidelity to universal ideas, are saviors from these federal errors, and defend us from our contemporaries. They are the exceptions which we want, where all grows alike. A foreign greatness is the antidote for cabalism.

Thus we feed on genius, and refresh ourselves from too much conversation with our mates, and exult in the depth of nature in that direction in which he leads us. What indemnification is one great man for populations of pigmies! Every mother wishes one son a genius, though all the rest should be mediocre. But a new danger appears in the excess of influence of the great man. His attractions warp us from our place. We have become underlings and intellectual suicides. Ah! yonder in the horizon is our help:—other great men, new qualities, counterweights and checks on each other. We cloy of the honey of each peculiar greatness. Every hero becomes a bore at last. Perhaps Voltaire was not bad-hearted, yet he said of the good Jesus, even, "I pray you, let me never hear that man's name again." They cry up the virtues of George Washington,—"Damn George Washington!" is the poor

Jacobin's whole speech and confutation. But it is human nature's indispensable defence. The centripetence augments the
centrifugence. We balance one man with his opposite, and the
health of the state depends on the see-saw.

There is, however, a speedy limit to the use of heroes.
Every genius is defended from approach by quantities of un-
availableness. They are very attractive, and seem at a distance
our own: but we are hindered on all sides from approach.
The more we are drawn, the more we are repelled. There is
something not solid in the good that is done for us. The best
discovery the discoverer makes for himself. It has something
unreal for his companion, until he too has substantiated it. It
seems as if the Deity dressed each soul which he sends into
nature in certain virtues and powers not communicable to
other men, and, sending it to perform one more turn through
the circle of beings, wrote *"Not transferable,"* and *"Good for
this trip only,"* on these garments of the soul. There is somewhat deceptive about the intercourse of minds. The boundaries are invisible, but they are never crossed. There is such
good will to impart, and such good will to receive, that each
threatens to become the other; but the law of individuality
collects its secret strength: you are you, and I am I, and so
we remain.

For nature wishes every thing to remain itself; and, whilst
every individual strives to grow and exclude, and to exclude
and grow, to the extremities of the universe, and to impose
the law of its being on every other creature, Nature steadily
aims to protect each against every other. Each is self-
defended. Nothing is more marked than the power by which
individuals are guarded from individuals, in a world where
every benefactor becomes so easily a malefactor, only by continuation of his activity into places where it is not due; where
children seem so much at the mercy of their foolish parents,
and where almost all men are too social and interfering. We
rightly speak of the guardian angels of children. How superior in their security from infusions of evil persons, from vulgarity and second thought! They shed their own abundant
beauty on the objects they behold. Therefore, they are not at
the mercy of such poor educators as we adults. If we huff and
chide them, they soon come not to mind it, and get a self-

reliance; and if we indulge them to folly, they learn the limitation elsewhere.

We need not fear excessive influence. A more generous trust is permitted. Serve the great. Stick at no humiliation. Grudge no office thou canst render. Be the limb of their body, the breath of their mouth. Compromise thy egotism. Who cares for that, so thou gain aught wider and nobler? Never mind the taunt of Boswellism: the devotion may easily be greater than the wretched pride which is guarding its own skirts. Be another: not thyself, but a Platonist; not a soul, but a Christian; not a naturalist, but a Cartesian; not a poet, but a Shaksperian. In vain, the wheels of tendency will not stop, nor will all the forces of inertia, fear, or of love itself, hold thee there. On, and forever onward! The microscope observes a monad or wheel-insect among the infusories circulating in water. Presently, a dot appears on the animal, which enlarges to a slit, and it becomes two perfect animals. The ever-proceeding detachment appears not less in all thought, and in society. Children think they cannot live without their parents. But, long before they are aware of it, the black dot has appeared, and the detachment taken place. Any accident will now reveal to them their independence.

But *great men*:—the word is injurious. Is there caste? is there fate? What becomes of the promise to virtue? The thoughtful youth laments the superfœtation of nature. 'Generous and handsome,' he says, 'is your hero; but look at yonder poor Paddy, whose country is his wheelbarrow; look at his whole nation of Paddies.' Why are the masses, from the dawn of history down, food for knives and powder? The idea dignifies a few leaders, who have sentiment, opinion, love, self-devotion; and they make war and death sacred;—but what for the wretches whom they hire and kill? The cheapness of man is every day's tragedy. It is as real a loss that others should be low, as that we should be low; for we must have society.

Is it a reply to these suggestions, to say, society is a Pestalozzian school: all are teachers and pupils in turn. We are equally served by receiving and by imparting. Men who know the same things, are not long the best company for each

other. But bring to each an intelligent person of another experience, and it is as if you let off water from a lake, by cutting a lower basin. It seems a mechanical advantage, and great
benefit it is to each speaker, as he can now paint out his
thought to himself. We pass very fast, in our personal moods,
from dignity to dependence. And if any appear never to assume the chair, but always to stand and serve, it is because
we do not see the company in a sufficiently long period for
the whole rotation of parts to come about. As to what we call
the masses, and common men;—there are no common men.
All men are at last of a size; and true art is only possible, on
the conviction that every talent has its apotheosis somewhere.
Fair play, and an open field, and freshest laurels to all who
have won them! But heaven reserves an equal scope for every
creature. Each is uneasy until he has produced his private ray
unto the concave sphere, and beheld his talent also in its last
nobility and exaltation.

The heroes of the hour are relatively great: of a faster
growth; or they are such, in whom, at the moment of success,
a quality is ripe which is then in request. Other days will demand other qualities. Some rays escape the common observer,
and want a finely adapted eye. Ask the great man if there be
none greater. His companions are; and not the less great, but
the more, that society cannot see them. Nature never sends a
great man onto the planet, without confiding the secret to
another soul.

One gracious fact emerges from these studies,—that there
is true ascension in our love. The reputations of the nineteenth century will one day be quoted, to prove its barbarism.
The genius of humanity is the real subject whose biography
is written in our annals. We must infer much, and supply
many chasms in the record. The history of the universe is
symptomatic, and life is mnemonical. No man, in all the
procession of famous men, is reason or illumination, or that
essence we were looking for; but is an exhibition, in some
quarter, of new possibilities. Could we one day complete the
immense figure which these flagrant points compose! The
study of many individuals leads us to an elemental region
wherein the individual is lost, or wherein all touch by their
summits. Thought and feeling, that break out there, cannot

be impounded by any fence of personality. This is the key to the power of the greatest men,—their spirit diffuses itself. A new quality of mind travels by night and by day, in concentric circles from its origin, and publishes itself by unknown methods: the union of all minds appears intimate: what gets admission to one, cannot be kept out of any other: the smallest acquisition of truth or of energy, in any quarter, is so much good to the commonwealth of souls. If the disparities of talent and position vanish, when the individuals are seen in the duration which is necessary to complete the career of each; even more swiftly the seeming injustice disappears, when we ascend to the central identity of all the individuals, and know that they are made of the substance which ordaineth and doeth.

The genius of humanity is the right point of view of history. The qualities abide; the men who exhibit them have now more, now less, and pass away; the qualities remain on another brow. No experience is more familiar. Once you saw phœnixes: they are gone; the world is not therefore disenchanted. The vessels on which you read sacred emblems turn out to be common pottery; but the sense of the pictures is sacred, and you may still read them transferred to the walls of the world. For a time, our teachers serve us personally, as metres or milestones of progress. Once they were angels of knowledge, and their figures touched the sky. Then we drew near, saw their means, culture, and limits; and they yielded their place to other geniuses. Happy, if a few names remain so high, that we have not been able to read them nearer, and age and comparison have not robbed them of a ray. But, at last, we shall cease to look in men for completeness, and shall content ourselves with their social and delegated quality. All that respects the individual is temporary and prospective, like the individual himself, who is ascending out of his limits, into a catholic existence. We have never come at the true and best benefit of any genius, so long as we believe him an original force. In the moment when he ceases to help us as a cause, he begins to help us more as an effect. Then he appears as an exponent of a vaster mind and will. The opaque self becomes transparent with the light of the First Cause.

Yet, within the limits of human education and agency, we

may say, great men exist that there may be greater men. The destiny of organized nature is amelioration, and who can tell its limits? It is for man to tame the chaos; on every side, whilst he lives, to scatter the seeds of science and of song, that climate, corn, animals, men, may be milder, and the germs of love and benefit may be multiplied.

II

Plato; or, the Philosopher

AMONG BOOKS, Plato only is entitled to Omar's fanatical compliment to the Koran, when he said, "Burn the libraries; for, their value is in this book." These sentences contain the culture of nations; these are the corner-stone of schools; these are the fountain-head of literatures. A discipline it is in logic, arithmetic, taste, symmetry, poetry, language, rhetoric, ontology, morals, or practical wisdom. There was never such range of speculation. Out of Plato come all things that are still written and debated among men of thought. Great havoc makes he among our originalities. We have reached the mountain from which all these drift boulders were detached. The Bible of the learned for twenty-two hundred years, every brisk young man, who says in succession fine things to each reluctant generation,—Boethius, Rabelais, Erasmus, Bruno, Locke, Rousseau, Alfieri, Coleridge,—is some reader of Plato, translating into the vernacular, wittily, his good things. Even the men of grander proportion suffer some deduction from the misfortune (shall I say?) of coming after this exhausting generalizer. St. Augustine, Copernicus, Newton, Behmen, Swedenborg, Goethe, are likewise his debtors, and must say after him. For it is fair to credit the broadest generalizer with all the particulars deducible from his thesis.

Plato is philosophy, and philosophy, Plato,—at once the glory and the shame of mankind, since neither Saxon nor Roman have availed to add any idea to his categories. No wife, no children had he, and the thinkers of all civilized nations are his posterity, and are tinged with his mind. How many great men Nature is incessantly sending up out of night, to be *his men*,—Platonists! the Alexandrians, a constellation of genius; the Elizabethans, not less; Sir Thomas More, Henry More, John Hales, John Smith, Lord Bacon, Jeremy Taylor, Ralph Cudworth, Sydenham, Thomas Taylor; Marcilius Ficinus, and Picus Mirandola. Calvinism is in his Phædo: Chris-

tianity is in it. Mahometanism draws all its philosophy, in its
handbook of morals, the Akhlak-y-Jalaly, from him. Mysticism finds in Plato all its texts. This citizen of a town in
Greece is no villager nor patriot. An Englishman reads and
says, 'how English!' a German, — 'how Teutonic!' an Italian, — 'how Roman and how Greek!' As they say that Helen
of Argos, had that universal beauty that every body felt related to her, so Plato seems, to a reader in New England, an
American genius. His broad humanity transcends all sectional
lines.

This range of Plato instructs us what to think of the vexed
question concerning his reputed works, — what are genuine,
what spurious. It is singular that wherever we find a man
higher, by a whole head, than any of his contemporaries, it is
sure to come into doubt, what are his real works. Thus, Homer, Plato, Raffaelle, Shakspeare. For these men magnetise
their contemporaries, so that their companions can do for
them what they can never do for themselves; and the great
man does thus live in several bodies, and write, or paint, or
act, by many hands: and, after some time, it is not easy to say
what is the authentic work of the master, and what is only of
his school.

Plato, too, like every great man, consumed his own times.
What is a great man, but one of great affinities, who takes up
into himself all arts, sciences, all knowables, as his food? He
can spare nothing; he can dispose of every thing. What is not
good for virtue, is good for knowledge. Hence his contemporaries tax him with plagiarism. But the inventor only
knows how to borrow; and society is glad to forget the innumerable laborers who ministered to this architect, and reserves all its gratitude for him. When we are praising Plato, it
seems we are praising quotations from Solon, and Sophron,
and Philolaus. Be it so. Every book is a quotation; and every
house is a quotation out of all forests, and mines, and stone
quarries; and every man is a quotation from all his ancestors. And this grasping inventor puts all nations under contribution.

Plato absorbed the learning of his times, — Philolaus,
Timæus, Heraclitus, Parmenides, and what else; then his master, Socrates; and, finding himself still capable of a larger syn-

thesis,—beyond all example then or since,—he travelled into Italy, to gain what Pythagoras had for him; then into Egypt, and perhaps still farther east, to import the other element, which Europe wanted, into the European mind. This breadth entitles him to stand as the representative of philosophy. He says, in the Republic, "Such a genius as philosophers must of necessity have, is wont but seldom, in all its parts, to meet in one man; but its different parts generally spring up in different persons." Every man, who would do any thing well, must come to it from a higher ground. A philosopher must be more than a philosopher. Plato is clothed with the powers of a poet, stands upon the highest place of the poet, and, (though I doubt he wanted the decisive gift of lyric expression,) mainly is not a poet, because he chose to use the poetic gift to an ulterior purpose.

Great geniuses have the shortest biographies. Their cousins can tell you nothing about them. They lived in their writings, and so their house and street life was trivial and commonplace. If you would know their tastes and complexions, the most admiring of their readers most resembles them. Plato, especially, has no external biography. If he had lover, wife, or children, we hear nothing of them. He ground them all into paint. As a good chimney burns its smoke, so a philosopher converts the value of all his fortunes into his intellectual performances.

He was born 430, A. C., about the time of the death of Pericles; was of patrician connection in his times and city; and is said to have had an early inclination for war; but, in his twentieth year, meeting with Socrates, was easily dissuaded from this pursuit, and remained for ten years his scholar, until the death of Socrates. He then went to Megara; accepted the invitations of Dion and of Dionysius, to the court of Sicily; and went thither three times, though very capriciously treated. He travelled into Italy; then into Egypt, where he stayed a long time; some say three,—some say thirteen years. It is said, he went farther, into Babylonia: this is uncertain. Returning to Athens, he gave lessons, in the Academy, to those whom his fame drew thither; and died, as we have received it, in the act of writing, at eighty-one years.

But the biography of Plato is interior. We are to account

for the supreme elevation of this man, in the intellectual history of our race,—how it happens that, in proportion to the culture of men, they become his scholars; that, as our Jewish Bible has implanted itself in the table-talk and household life of every man and woman in the European and American nations, so the writings of Plato have preoccupied every school of learning, every lover of thought, every church, every poet,—making it impossible to think, on certain levels, except through him. He stands between the truth and every man's mind, and has almost impressed language, and the primary forms of thought, with his name and seal. I am struck, in reading him, with the extreme modernness of his style and spirit. Here is the germ of that Europe we know so well, in its long history of arts and arms: here are all its traits, already discernible in the mind of Plato,—and in none before him. It has spread itself since into a hundred histories, but has added no new element. This perpetual modernness is the measure of merit, in every work of art; since the author of it was not misled by any thing short-lived or local, but abode by real and abiding traits. How Plato came thus to be Europe, and philosophy, and almost literature, is the problem for us to solve.

This could not have happened, without a sound, sincere, and catholic man, able to honor, at the same time, the ideal, or laws of the mind, and fate, or the order of nature. The first period of a nation, as of an individual, is the period of unconscious strength. Children cry, scream, and stamp with fury, unable to express their desires. As soon as they can speak and tell their want, and the reason of it, they become gentle. In adult life, whilst the perceptions are obtuse, men and women talk vehemently and superlatively, blunder and quarrel: their manners are full of desperation; their speech is full of oaths. As soon as, with culture, things have cleared up a little, and they see them no longer in lumps and masses, but accurately distributed, they desist from that weak vehemence, and explain their meaning in detail. If the tongue had not been framed for articulation, man would still be a beast in the forest. The same weakness and want, on a higher plane, occurs daily in the education of ardent young men and women. 'Ah! you don't understand me; I have never met with any one who comprehends me:' and they sigh and weep, write verses, and walk alone,—fault of power to express their precise meaning. In a month or two, through the favor of their good genius, they meet some one so related as to assist their volcanic estate; and, good communication being once established, they are thenceforward good citizens. It is ever thus. The progress is to accuracy, to skill, to truth, from blind force.

There is a moment, in the history of every nation, when, proceeding out of this brute youth, the perceptive powers reach their ripeness, and have not yet become microscopic: so that man, at that instant, extends across the entire scale; and, with his feet still planted on the immense forces of night, converses, by his eyes and brain, with solar and stellar creation. That is the moment of adult health, the culmination of power.

Such is the history of Europe, in all points; and such in philosophy. Its early records, almost perished, are of the immigrations from Asia, bringing with them the dreams of barbarians; a confusion of crude notions of morals, and of natural philosophy, gradually subsiding, through the partial insight of single teachers.

Before Pericles, came the Seven Wise Masters; and we have the beginnings of geometry, metaphysics, and ethics: then the partialists,—deducing the origin of things from flux or water, or from air, or from fire, or from mind. All mix with these causes mythologic pictures. At last, comes Plato, the distributor, who needs no barbaric paint, or tattoo, or whooping; for he can define. He leaves with Asia the vast and superlative; he is the arrival of accuracy and intelligence. "He shall be as a god to me, who can rightly divide and define."

This defining is philosophy. Philosophy is the account which the human mind gives to itself of the constitution of the world. Two cardinal facts lie forever at the base; the one, and the two.—1. Unity, or Identity; and, 2. Variety. We unite all things, by perceiving the law which pervades them; by perceiving the superficial differences, and the profound resemblances. But every mental act,—this very perception of identity or oneness, recognizes the difference of things. Oneness and otherness. It is impossible to speak, or to think, without embracing both.

The mind is urged to ask for one cause of many effects; then for the cause of that; and again the cause, diving still into the profound: self-assured that it shall arrive at an absolute and sufficient one,—a one that shall be all. "In the midst of the sun is the light, in the midst of the light is truth, and in the midst of truth is the imperishable being," say the Vedas. All philosophy, of east and west, has the same centripetence. Urged by an opposite necessity, the mind returns from the one, to that which is not one, but other or many; from cause to effect; and affirms the necessary existence of variety, the self-existence of both, as each is involved in the other. These strictly-blended elements it is the problem of thought to separate, and to reconcile. Their existence is mutually contradictory and exclusive; and each so fast slides into the other, that we can never say what is one, and what it is not. The Proteus is as nimble in the highest as in the lowest grounds, when we contemplate the one, the true, the good,—as in the surfaces and extremities of matter.

In all nations, there are minds which incline to dwell in the conception of the fundamental Unity. The raptures of prayer and ecstasy of devotion lose all being in one Being. This tendency finds its highest expression in the religious writings of the East, and chiefly, in the Indian Scriptures, in the Vedas, the Bhagavat Geeta, and the Vishnu Purana. Those writings contain little else than this idea, and they rise to pure and sublime strains in celebrating it.

The Same, the Same: friend and foe are of one stuff; the ploughman, the plough, and the furrow, are of one stuff; and the stuff is such, and so much, that the variations of form are unimportant. "You are fit," (says the supreme Krishna to a sage,) "to apprehend that you are not distinct from me. That which I am, thou art, and that also is this world, with its gods, and heroes, and mankind. Men contemplate distinctions, because they are stupefied with ignorance." "The words *I* and *mine* constitute ignorance. What is the great end of all, you shall now learn from me. It is soul,—one in all bodies, pervading, uniform, perfect, preëminent over nature, exempt from birth, growth, and decay, omnipresent, made up of true knowledge, independent, unconnected with unrealities, with name, species, and the rest, in time past, present, and to come. The knowledge that this spirit, which is essentially one, is in one's own, and in all other bodies, is the wisdom of one who knows the unity of things. As one diffusive air, passing through the perforations of a flute, is distinguished as the notes of a scale, so the nature of the Great Spirit is single, though its forms be manifold, arising from the consequences of acts. When the difference of the investing form, as that of god, or the rest, is destroyed, there is no distinction." "The whole world is but a manifestation of Vishnu, who is identical with all things, and is to be regarded by the wise, as not differing from, but as the same as themselves. I neither am going nor coming; nor is my dwelling in any one place; nor art thou, thou; nor are others, others; nor am I, I." As if he had said, 'All is for the soul, and the soul is Vishnu; and animals and stars are transient paintings; and light is whitewash; and durations are deceptive; and form is imprisonment; and heaven itself a decoy.' That which the soul seeks is resolution into being, above form, out of Tartarus, and out of heaven,—liberation from nature.

If speculation tends thus to a terrific unity, in which all things are absorbed, action tends directly backwards to diversity. The first is the course or gravitation of mind; the second is the power of nature. Nature is the manifold. The unity absorbs, and melts or reduces. Nature opens and creates. These two principles reappear and interpenetrate all things, all thought; the one, the many. One is being; the other, intellect: one is necessity; the other, freedom: one, rest; the other, motion: one, power; the other, distribution: one, strength; the other, pleasure: one, consciousness; the other, definition: one, genius; the other, talent: one, earnestness; the other, knowledge: one, possession; the other, trade: one, caste; the other, culture: one, king; the other, democracy: and, if we dare carry these generalizations a step higher, and name the last tendency of both, we might say, that the end of the one is escape from organization,—pure science; and the end of the other is the highest instrumentality, or use of means, or executive deity.

Each student adheres, by temperament and by habit, to the first or to the second of these gods of the mind. By religion, he tends to unity; by intellect, or by the senses, to the many.

A too rapid unification, and an excessive appliance to parts and particulars, are the twin dangers of speculation.

To this partiality the history of nations corresponded. The country of unity, of immovable institutions, the seat of a philosophy delighting in abstractions, of men faithful in doctrine and in practice to the idea of a deaf, unimplorable, immense fate, is Asia; and it realizes this faith in the social institution of caste. On the other side, the genius of Europe is active and creative: it resists caste by culture; its philosophy was a discipline; it is a land of arts, inventions, trade, freedom. If the East loved infinity, the West delighted in boundaries.

European civility is the triumph of talent, the extension of system, the sharpened understanding, adaptive skill, delight in forms, delight in manifestation, in comprehensible results. Pericles, Athens, Greece, had been working in this element with the joy of genius not yet chilled by any foresight of the detriment of an excess. They saw before them no sinister political economy; no ominous Malthus; no Paris or London; no pitiless subdivision of classes,—the doom of the pin-makers, the doom of the weavers, of dressers, of stockingers, of carders, of spinners, of colliers; no Ireland; no Indian caste, superinduced by the efforts of Europe to throw it off. The understanding was in its health and prime. Art was in its splendid novelty. They cut the Pentelican marble as if it were snow, and their perfect works in architecture and sculpture seemed things of course, not more difficult than the completion of a new ship at the Medford yards, or new mills at Lowell. These things are in course, and may be taken for granted. The Roman legion, Byzantine legislation, English trade, the saloons of Versailles, the cafés of Paris, the steam-mill, steamboat, steam-coach, may all be seen in perspective; the town-meeting, the ballot-box, the newspaper and cheap press.

Meantime, Plato, in Egypt and in eastern pilgrimages, imbibed the idea of one Deity, in which all things are absorbed. The unity of Asia, and the detail of Europe; the infinitude of the Asiatic soul, and the defining, result-loving, machine-making, surface-seeking, opera-going Europe,—Plato came to join, and by contact, to enhance the energy of each. The excellence of Europe and Asia are in his brain. Metaphysics and natural philosophy expressed the genius of Europe; he sub-structs the religion of Asia, as the base.

In short, a balanced soul was born, perceptive of the two elements. It is as easy to be great as to be small. The reason why we do not at once believe in admirable souls, is because they are not in our experience. In actual life, they are so rare, as to be incredible; but, primarily, there is not only no presumption against them, but the strongest presumption in favor of their appearance. But whether voices were heard in the sky, or not; whether his mother or his father dreamed that the infant man-child was the son of Apollo; whether a swarm of bees settled on his lips, or not; a man who could see two sides of a thing was born. The wonderful synthesis so familiar in nature; the upper and the under side of the medal of Jove; the union of impossibilities, which reappears in every object; its real and its ideal power,—was now, also, transferred entire to the consciousness of a man.

The balanced soul came. If he loved abstract truth, he saved himself by propounding the most popular of all principles, the absolute good, which rules rulers, and judges the judge. If he made transcendental distinctions, he fortified himself by drawing all his illustrations from sources disdained by orators and polite conversers; from mares and puppies; from pitchers and soup-ladles; from cooks and criers; the shops of potters, horse-doctors, butchers, and fishmongers. He cannot forgive in himself a partiality, but is resolved that the two poles of thought shall appear in his statement. His argument and his sentence are self-poised and spherical. The two poles appear; yes, and become two hands, to grasp and appropriate their own.

Every great artist has been such by synthesis. Our strength is transitional, alternating; or, shall I say, a thread of two strands. The sea-shore, sea seen from shore, shore seen from sea; the taste of two metals in contact; and our enlarged powers at the approach and at the departure of a friend; the experience of poetic creativeness, which is not found in staying at home, nor yet in travelling, but in transitions from one to the other, which must therefore be adroitly managed to present as much transitional surface as possible; this command of two elements must explain the power and the charm of

Plato. Art expresses the one, or the same by the different. Thought seeks to know unity in unity; poetry to show it by variety; that is, always by an object or symbol. Plato keeps the two vases, one of æther and one of pigment, at his side, and invariably uses both. Things added to things, as statistics, civil history, are inventories. Things used as language are inexhaustibly attractive. Plato turns incessantly the obverse and the reverse of the medal of Jove.

To take an example:—The physical philosophers had sketched each his theory of the world; the theory of atoms, of fire, of flux, of spirit; theories mechanical and chemical in their genius. Plato, a master of mathematics, studious of all natural laws and causes, feels these, as second causes, to be no theories of the world, but bare inventories and lists. To the study of nature he therefore prefixes the dogma,—"Let us declare the cause which led the Supreme Ordainer to produce and compose the universe. He was good; and he who is good has no kind of envy. Exempt from envy, he wished that all things should be as much as possible like himself. Whosoever, taught by wise men, shall admit this as the prime cause of the origin and foundation of the world, will be in the truth." "All things are for the sake of the good, and it is the cause of every thing beautiful." This dogma animates and impersonates his philosophy.

The synthesis which makes the character of his mind appears in all his talents. Where there is great compass of wit, we usually find excellencies that combine easily in the living man, but in description appear incompatible. The mind of Plato is not to be exhibited by a Chinese catalogue, but is to be apprehended by an original mind in the exercise of its original power. In him the freest abandonment is united with the precision of a geometer. His daring imagination gives him the more solid grasp of facts; as the birds of highest flight have the strongest alar bones. His patrician polish, his intrinsic elegance, edged by an irony so subtle that it stings and paralyses, adorn the soundest health and strength of frame. According to the old sentence, "If Jove should descend to the earth, he would speak in the style of Plato."

With this palatial air, there is, for the direct aim of several of his works, and running through the tenor of them all, a certain earnestness, which mounts, in the Republic, and in the Phædo, to piety. He has been charged with feigning sickness at the time of the death of Socrates. But the anecdotes that have come down from the times attest his manly interference before the people in his master's behalf, since even the savage cry of the assembly to Plato is preserved; and the indignation towards popular government, in many of his pieces, expresses a personal exasperation. He has a probity, a native reverence for justice and honor, and a humanity which makes him tender for the superstitions of the people. Add to this, he believes that poetry, prophecy, and the high insight, are from a wisdom of which man is not master; that the gods never philosophise; but, by a celestial mania, these miracles are accomplished. Horsed on these winged steeds, he sweeps the dim regions, visits worlds which flesh cannot enter: he saw the souls in pain; he hears the doom of the judge; he beholds the penal metempsychosis; the Fates, with the rock and shears; and hears the intoxicating hum of their spindle.

But his circumspection never forsook him. One would say, he had read the inscription on the gates of Busyrane,—"Be bold;" and on the second gate,—"Be bold, be bold, and evermore be bold:" and then again had paused well at the third gate,—"Be not too bold." His strength is like the momentum of a falling planet; and his discretion, the return of its due and perfect curve,—so excellent is his Greek love of boundary, and his skill in definition. In reading logarithms, one is not more secure, than in following Plato in his flights. Nothing can be colder than his head, when the lightnings of his imagination are playing in the sky. He has finished his thinking, before he brings it to the reader; and he abounds in the surprises of a literary master. He has that opulence which furnishes, at every turn, the precise weapon he needs. As the rich man wears no more garments, drives no more horses, sits in no more chambers, than the poor,—but has that one dress, or equipage, or instrument, which is fit for the hour and the need; so Plato, in his plenty, is never restricted, but has the fit word. There is, indeed, no weapon in all the armory of wit which he did not possess and use,—epic, analysis, mania, intuition, music, satire, and irony, down to the customary and polite. His illustrations are poetry, and his jests illustrations. Socrates' profession of obstetric art is good philosophy; and his finding that word "cookery," and "adulatory art," for rhetoric, in the Gorgias, does us a substantial service still. No orator can measure in effect with him who can give good nicknames.

What moderation, and understatement, and checking his thunder in mid volley! He has good-naturedly furnished the courtier and citizen with all that can be said against the schools. "For philosophy is an elegant thing, if any one modestly meddles with it; but, if he is conversant with it more than is becoming, it corrupts the man." He could well afford to be generous,—he, who from the sunlike centrality and reach of his vision, had a faith without cloud. Such as his perception, was his speech: he plays with the doubt, and makes the most of it: he paints and quibbles; and by and by comes a sentence that moves the sea and land. The admirable earnest comes not only at intervals, in the perfect yes and no of the dialogue, but in bursts of light. "I, therefore, Callicles, am persuaded by these accounts, and consider how I may exhibit my soul before the judge in a healthy condition. Wherefore, disregarding the honors that most men value, and looking to the truth, I shall endeavor in reality to live as virtuously as I can; and, when I die, to die so. And I invite all other men, to the utmost of my power; and you, too, I in turn invite to this contest, which, I affirm, surpasses all contests here."

He is a great average man; one who, to the best thinking, adds a proportion and equality in his faculties, so that men see in him their own dreams and glimpses made available, and made to pass for what they are. A great common sense is his warrant and qualification to be the world's interpreter. He has reason, as all the philosophic and poetic class have: but he has, also, what they have not,—this strong solving sense to reconcile his poetry with the appearances of the world, and build a bridge from the streets of cities to the Atlantis. He omits never this graduation, but slopes his thought, however picturesque the precipice on one side, to an access from the plain. He never writes in ecstasy, or catches us up into poetic raptures.

*　　　*　　　*

Plato apprehended the cardinal facts. He could prostrate himself on the earth, and cover his eyes, whilst he adored that which cannot be numbered, or gauged, or known, or named: that of which every thing can be affirmed and denied: that " which is entity and nonentity." He called it super-essential. He even stood ready, as in the Parmenides, to demonstrate that it was so,—that this Being exceeded the limits of intellect. No man ever more fully acknowledged the Ineffable. Having paid his homage, as for the human race, to the Illimitable, he then stood erect, and for the human race affirmed, 'And yet things are knowable!'—that is, the Asia in his mind was first heartily honored,—the ocean of love and power, before form, before will, before knowledge, the Same, the Good, the One; and now, refreshed and empowered by this worship, the instinct of Europe, namely, culture, returns; and he cries, Yet things are knowable! They are knowable, because, being from one, things correspond. There is a scale: and the correspondence of heaven to earth, of matter to mind, of the part to the whole, is our guide. As there is a science of stars, called astronomy; a science of quantities, called mathematics; a science of qualities, called chemistry; so there is a science of sciences,—I call it Dialectic,—which is the Intellect discriminating the false and the true. It rests on the observation of identity and diversity; for, to judge, is to unite to an object the notion which belongs to it. The sciences, even the best,—mathematics, and astronomy,—are like sportsmen, who seize whatever prey offers, even without being able to make any use of it. Dialectic must teach the use of them. "This is of that rank that no intellectual man will enter on any study for its own sake, but only with a view to advance himself in that one sole science which embraces all."

"The essence or peculiarity of man is to comprehend a whole; or that which, in the diversity of sensations, can be comprised under a rational unity." "The soul which has never perceived the truth, cannot pass into the human form." I announce to men the Intellect. I announce the good of being interpenetrated by the mind that made nature: this benefit, namely, that it can understand nature, which it made and maketh. Nature is good, but intellect is better: as the lawgiver is before the law-receiver. I give you joy, O sons of men! that truth is altogether wholesome; that we have hope to search out what might be the very self of every thing. The misery of man is to be baulked of the sight of essence, and to be stuffed with conjectures: but the supreme good is reality; the supreme beauty is reality; and all virtue and all felicity depend on this science of the real: for courage is nothing else than knowledge: the fairest fortune that can befall man, is to be guided by his dæmon to that which is truly his own. This also is the essence of justice,—to attend every one his own: nay, the notion of virtue is not to be arrived at, except through direct contemplation of the divine essence. Courage, then! for, "the persuasion that we must search that which we do not know, will render us, beyond comparison, better, braver, and more industrious, than if we thought it impossible to discover what we do not know, and useless to search for it." He secures a position not to be commanded, by his passion for reality; valuing philosophy only as it is the pleasure of conversing with real being.

Thus, full of the genius of Europe, he said, *Culture.* He saw the institutions of Sparta, and recognized more genially, one would say, than any since, the hope of education. He delighted in every accomplishment, in every graceful and useful and truthful performance; above all, in the splendors of genius and intellectual achievement. "The whole of life, O Socrates, said Glauco, is, with the wise, the measure of hearing such discourses as these." What a price he sets on the feats of talent, on the powers of Pericles, of Isocrates, of Parmenides! What price, above price, on the talents themselves! He called the several faculties, gods, in his beautiful personation. What value he gives to the art of gymnastic in education; what to geometry; what to music; what to astronomy, whose appeasing and medicinal power he celebrates! In the Timæus, he indicates the highest employment of the eyes. "By us it is asserted, that God invented and bestowed sight on us for this purpose,—that, on surveying the circles of intelligence in the heavens, we might properly employ those of our own minds, which, though disturbed when compared with the others that are uniform, are still allied to their circulations; and that, having thus learned, and being naturally possessed of a correct reasoning faculty, we might, by imitating the uniform revolutions of divinity, set right our own wanderings and blunders." And in the Republic,—"By each of these disciplines, a certain organ of the soul is both purified and reanimated, which is blinded and buried by studies of another kind; an organ better worth saving than ten thousand eyes, since truth is perceived by this alone."

He said, Culture; but he first admitted its basis, and gave immeasurably the first place to advantages of nature. His patrician tastes laid stress on the distinctions of birth. In the doctrine of the organic character and disposition is the origin of caste. "Such as were fit to govern, into their composition the informing Deity mingled gold: into the military, silver; iron and brass for husbandmen and artificers." The East confirms itself, in all ages, in this faith. The Koran is explicit on this point of caste. "Men have their metal, as of gold and silver. Those of you who were the worthy ones in the state of ignorance, will be the worthy ones in the state of faith, as soon as you embrace it." Plato was not less firm. "Of the five orders of things, only four can be taught to the generality of men." In the Republic, he insists on the temperaments of the youth, as first of the first.

A happier example of the stress laid on nature, is in the dialogue with the young Theages, who wishes to receive lessons from Socrates. Socrates declares that, if some have grown wise by associating with him, no thanks are due to him; but, simply, whilst they were with him, they grew wise, not because of him; he pretends not to know the way of it. "It is adverse to many, nor can those be benefited by associating with me, whom the Dæmon opposes; so that it is not possible for me to live with these. With many, however, he does not prevent me from conversing, who yet are not at all benefited by associating with me. Such, O Theages, is the association with me; for, if it pleases the God, you will make great and rapid proficiency: you will not, if he does not please. Judge whether it is not safer to be instructed by some one of those who have power over the benefit which they impart to men, than by me, who benefit or not, just as it may happen." As if he had said, 'I have no system. I cannot be answerable for you. You will be what you must. If there is love between us, inconceivably delicious and profitable will our intercourse be; if not, your time is lost, and you will only annoy me. I shall seem to you stupid, and the reputation I have, false. Quite above us, beyond the will of you or me, is this secret affinity or repulsion laid. All my good is magnetic, and I educate, not by lessons, but by going about my business.'

He said, Culture; he said, Nature: and he failed not to add, 'There is also the divine.' There is no thought in any mind, but it quickly tends to convert itself into a power, and organizes a huge instrumentality of means. Plato, lover of limits, loved the illimitable, saw the enlargement and nobility which come from truth itself and good itself, and attempted, as if on the part of the human intellect, once for all, to do it adequate homage,—homage fit for the immense soul to receive, and yet homage becoming the intellect to render. He said, then, 'Our faculties run out into infinity, and return to us thence. We can define but a little way; but here is a fact which will not be skipped, and which to shut our eyes upon is suicide. All things are in a scale; and, begin where we will, ascend and ascend. All things are symbolical; and what we call results are beginnings.'

A key to the method and completeness of Plato is his twice bisected line. After he has illustrated the relation between the absolute good and true, and the forms of the intelligible world, he says:—"Let there be a line cut in two unequal parts. Cut again each of these two parts,—one representing the visible, the other the intelligible world,—and these two new sections, representing the bright part and the dark part of these worlds, you will have, for one of the sections of the visible world,—images, that is, both shadows and reflections; for the other section, the objects of these images,—that is, plants, animals, and the works of art and nature. Then divide the intelligible world in like manner; the one section will be of opinions and hypotheses, and the other section, of truths." To these four sections, the four operations of the soul correspond,—conjecture, faith, understanding, reason. As every pool reflects the image of the sun, so every thought and thing restores us an image and creature of the supreme Good. The universe is perforated by a million channels for his activity. All things mount and mount.

All his thought has this ascension; in Phædrus, teaching that beauty is the most lovely of all things, exciting hilarity, and shedding desire and confidence through the universe, wherever it enters; and it enters, in some degree, into all things: but that there is another, which is as much more beautiful than beauty, as beauty is than chaos; namely, wisdom, which our wonderful organ of sight cannot reach unto, but which, could it be seen, would ravish us with its perfect reality. He has the same regard to it as the source of excellence in works of art. "When an artificer, in the fabrication of any work, looks to that which always subsists according *to the same*; and, employing a model of this kind, expresses its idea and power in his work; it must follow, that his production should be beautiful. But when he beholds that which is born and dies, it will be far from beautiful."

Thus ever: the Banquet is a teaching in the same spirit, familiar now to all the poetry, and to all the sermons of the world, that the love of the sexes is initial; and symbolizes, at a distance, the passion of the soul for that immense lake of beauty it exists to seek. This faith in the Divinity is never out of mind, and constitutes the limitation of all his dogmas. Body cannot teach wisdom;—God only. In the same mind, he constantly affirms that virtue cannot be taught; that it is not a science, but an inspiration; that the greatest goods are produced to us through mania, and are assigned to us by a divine gift.

This leads me to that central figure, which he has established in his Academy, as the organ through which every considered opinion shall be announced, and whose biography he has likewise so labored, that the historic facts are lost in the light of Plato's mind. Socrates and Plato are the double star, which the most powerful instruments will not entirely separate. Socrates, again, in his traits and genius, is the best example of that synthesis which constitutes Plato's extraordinary power. Socrates, a man of humble stem, but honest enough; of the commonest history; of a personal homeliness so remarkable, as to be a cause of wit in others,—the rather that his broad good nature and exquisite taste for a joke invited the sally, which was sure to be paid. The players personated him on the stage; the potters copied his ugly face on their stone jugs. He was a cool fellow, adding to his humor a perfect temper, and a knowledge of his man, be he who he might whom he talked with, which laid the companion open to certain defeat in any debate,—and in debate he immoderately delighted. The young men are prodigiously fond of him, and invite him to their feasts, whither he goes for conversation. He can drink, too; has the strongest head in Athens; and, after leaving the whole party under the table, goes away, as if nothing had happened, to begin new dialogues with somebody that is sober. In short, he was what our country-people call *an old one*.

He affected a good many citizen-like tastes, was monstrously fond of Athens, hated trees, never willingly went beyond the walls, knew the old characters, valued the bores and philistines, thought every thing in Athens a little better than any thing in any other place. He was plain as a Quaker in habit and speech, affected low phrases, and illustrations from cocks and quails, soup-pans and sycamore-spoons, grooms and farriers, and unnameable offices,—especially if he talked with any superfine person. He had a Franklin-like wisdom. Thus, he showed one who was afraid to go on foot to Olympia, that it was no more than his daily walk within doors, if continuously extended, would easily reach.

Plain old uncle as he was, with his great ears,—an immense talker,—the rumor ran, that, on one or two occasions, in the war with Bœotia, he had shown a determination which had covered the retreat of a troop; and there was some story that, under cover of folly, he had, in the city government, when one day he chanced to hold a seat there, evinced a courage in opposing singly the popular voice, which had well-nigh ruined him. He is very poor; but then he is hardy as a soldier, and can live on a few olives; usually, in the strictest sense, on bread and water, except when entertained by his friends. His necessary expenses were exceedingly small, and no one could live as he did. He wore no under garment; his upper garment was the same for summer and winter; and he went barefooted; and it is said that, to procure the pleasure, which he loves, of talking at his ease all day with the most elegant and cultivated young men, he will now and then return to his shop, and carve statues, good or bad, for sale. However that be, it is certain that he had grown to delight in nothing else than this conversation; and that, under his hypocritical pretence of knowing nothing, he attacks and brings down all the fine speakers, all the fine philosophers of Athens, whether natives, or strangers from Asia Minor and the islands. Nobody can refuse to talk with him, he is so honest, and really curious to know; a man who was willingly confuted, if he did not speak the truth, and who willingly confuted others, asserting what was false; and not less pleased when confuted than when confuting; for he thought not any evil happened to men, of such a magnitude as false opinion respecting the just and unjust. A pitiless disputant, who knows nothing, but the bounds of whose conquering intelligence no man had ever reached; whose temper was imperturbable; whose dreadful logic was always leisurely and sportive; so careless and ignorant, as to disarm the wariest, and draw them, in the pleasantest manner, into horrible doubts and confusion. But he always knew the way out; knew it, yet would not tell it. No escape; he drives them to terrible choices by his dilemmas, and tosses the Hippiases and Gorgiases, with their grand reputations, as a boy tosses his balls. The tyrannous realist!—Meno has discoursed a thousand times, at length, on virtue, before many companies, and very well, as it appeared to him; but, at this moment, he cannot even tell what it is,—this cramp-fish of a Socrates has so bewitched him.

This hard-headed humorist, whose strange conceits, drollery, and *bonhommie*, diverted the young patricians, whilst the rumor of his sayings and quibbles gets abroad every day, turns out, in the sequel, to have a probity as invincible as his logic, and to be either insane, or, at least, under cover of this play, enthusiastic in his religion. When accused before the judges of subverting the popular creed, he affirms the immortality of the soul, the future reward and punishment; and, refusing to recant, in a caprice of the popular government, was condemned to die, and sent to the prison. Socrates entered the prison, and took away all ignominy from the place, which could not be a prison, whilst he was there. Crito bribed the jailer; but Socrates would not go out by treachery. "Whatever inconvenience ensue, nothing is to be preferred before justice. These things I hear like pipes and drums, whose sound makes me deaf to every thing you say." The fame of this prison, the fame of the discourses there, and the drinking of the hemlock, are one of the most precious passages in the history of the world.

The rare coincidence, in one ugly body, of the droll and the martyr, the keen street and market debater with the sweetest saint known to any history at that time, had forcibly struck the mind of Plato, so capacious of these contrasts; and the figure of Socrates, by a necessity, placed itself in the foreground of the scene, as the fittest dispenser of the intellectual treasures he had to communicate. It was a rare fortune, that this Æsop of the mob, and this robed scholar, should meet, to make each other immortal in their mutual faculty. The strange synthesis, in the character of Socrates, capped the synthesis in the mind of Plato. Moreover, by this means, he was able, in the direct way, and without envy, to avail himself of the wit and weight of Socrates, to which unquestionably his own debt was great; and these derived again their principal advantage from the perfect art of Plato.

It remains to say, that the defect of Plato in power is only that which results inevitably from his quality. He is intellectual in his aim; and, therefore, in expression, literary. Mounting into heaven, diving into the pit, expounding the laws of the state, the passion of love, the remorse of crime, the hope of the parting soul,—he is literary, and never otherwise. It is almost the sole deduction from the merit of Plato, that his writings have not,—what is, no doubt, incident to this regnancy of intellect in his work,—the vital authority which the screams of prophets and the sermons of unlettered Arabs and Jews possess. There is an interval; and to cohesion, contact is necessary.

I know not what can be said in reply to this criticism, but that we have come to a fact in the nature of things: an oak is not an orange. The qualities of sugar remain with sugar, and those of salt, with salt.

In the second place, he has not a system. The dearest defenders and disciples are at fault. He attempted a theory of the universe, and his theory is not complete or self-evident. One man thinks he means this; and another, that: he has said one thing in one place, and the reverse of it in another place.

He is charged with having failed to make the transition from ideas to matter. Here is the world, sound as a nut, perfect, not the smallest piece of chaos left, never a stitch nor an end, not a mark of haste, or botching, or second thought; but the theory of the world is a thing of shreds and patches.

The longest wave is quickly lost in the sea. Plato would willingly have a Platonism, a known and accurate expression for the world, and it should be accurate. It shall be the world passed through the mind of Plato,—nothing less. Every atom shall have the Platonic tinge; every atom, every relation or quality you knew before, you shall know again, and find here, but now ordered; not nature, but art. And you shall feel that Alexander indeed overran, with men and horses, some countries of the planet; but countries, and things of which countries are made, elements, planet itself, laws of planet and of men, have passed through this man as bread into his body, and become no longer bread, but body: so all this mammoth morsel has become Plato. He has clapped copyright on the world. This is the ambition of individualism. But the mouthful proves too large. *Boa constrictor* has good will to eat it, but he is foiled. He falls abroad in the attempt; and biting, gets strangled: the bitten world holds the biter fast by his own teeth. There he perishes: unconquered nature lives on, and forgets him. So it fares with all: so must it fare with Plato. In view of eternal nature, Plato turns out to be philosophical exercitations. He argues on this side, and on that. The acutest German, the lovingest disciple, could never tell what Platonism was; indeed, admirable texts can be quoted on both sides of every great question from him.

These things we are forced to say, if we must consider the effort of Plato, or of any philosopher, to dispose of Nature,—which will not be disposed of. No power of genius has ever yet had the smallest success in explaining existence. The perfect enigma remains. But there is an injustice in assuming this ambition for Plato. Let us not seem to treat with flippancy his venerable name. Men, in proportion to their intellect, have admitted his transcendant claims. The way to know him, is to compare him, not with nature, but with other men. How many ages have gone by, and he remains unapproached! A chief structure of human wit, like Karnac, or the mediæval cathedrals, or the Etrurian remains, it requires all the breadth of human faculty to know it. I think it is trueliest seen, when seen with the most respect. His sense deepens, his merits multiply, with study. When we say, here is a fine collection of fables; or, when we praise the style; or the common sense; or arithmetic; we speak as boys, and much of our impatient criticism of the dialectic, I suspect, is no better. The criticism is like our impatience of miles, when we are in a hurry; but it is still best that a mile should have seventeen hundred and sixty yards. The great-eyed Plato proportioned the lights and shades after the genius of our life.

Plato: New Readings

THE PUBLICATION, in Mr. Bohn's "Serial Library," of the excellent translations of Plato, which we esteem one of the chief benefits the cheap press has yielded, gives us an occasion to take hastily a few more notes of the elevation and bearings of this fixed star; or, to add a bulletin, like the journals, of *Plato at the latest dates.*

Modern science, by the extent of its generalization, has learned to indemnify the student of man for the defects of individuals, by tracing growth and ascent in races; and, by the simple expedient of lighting up the vast background, generates a feeling of complacency and hope. The human being has the saurian and the plant in his rear. His arts and sciences, the easy issue of his brain, look glorious when prospectively beheld from the distant brain of ox, crocodile, and fish. It seems as if nature, in regarding the geologic night behind her, when, in five or six millenniums, she had turned out five or six men, as Homer, Phidias, Menu, and Columbus, was no wise discontented with the result. These samples attested the virtue of the tree. These were a clear amelioration of trilobite and saurus, and a good basis for further proceeding. With this artist, time and space are cheap, and she is insensible to what you say of tedious preparation. She waited tranquilly the flowing periods of paleontology, for the hour to be struck when man should arrive. Then periods must pass before the motion of the earth can be suspected; then before the map of the instincts and the cultivable powers can be drawn. But as of races, so the succession of individual men is fatal and beautiful, and Plato has the fortune, in the history of mankind, to mark an epoch.

Plato's fame does not stand on a syllogism, or on any masterpieces of the Socratic reasoning, or on any thesis, as, for example, the immortality of the soul. He is more than an expert, or a schoolman, or a geometer, or the prophet of a peculiar message. He represents the privilege of the intellect, the

power, namely, of carrying up every fact to successive platforms, and so disclosing, in every fact, a germ of expansion.
These expansions are in the essence of thought. The naturalist
would never help us to them by any discoveries of the extent
of the universe, but is as poor, when cataloguing the resolved
nebula of Orion, as when measuring the angles of an acre.
But the Republic of Plato, by these expansions, may be said
to require, and so to anticipate, the astronomy of Laplace.
The expansions are organic. The mind does not create what
it perceives, any more than the eye creates the rose. In ascribing to Plato the merit of announcing them, we only say, here
was a more complete man, who could apply to nature the
whole scale of the senses, the understanding, and the reason.
These expansions, or extensions, consist in continuing the
spiritual sight where the horizon falls on our natural vision,
and, by this second sight, discovering the long lines of law
which shoot in every direction. Everywhere he stands on a
path which has no end, but runs continuously round the universe. Therefore, every word becomes an exponent of nature.
Whatever he looks upon discloses a second sense, and ulterior
senses. His perception of the generation of contraries, of
death out of life, and life out of death,—that law by which,
in nature, decomposition is recomposition, and putrefaction
and cholera are only signals of a new creation; his discernment of the little in the large, and the large in the small;
studying the state in the citizen, and the citizen in the state;
and leaving it doubtful whether he exhibited the Republic as
an allegory on the education of the private soul; his beautiful
definitions of ideas, of time, of form, of figure, of the line,
sometimes hypothetically given, as his defining of virtue,
courage, justice, temperance; his love of the apologue, and his
apologues themselves; the cave of Trophonius; the ring of
Gyges; the charioteer and two horses; the golden, silver,
brass, and iron temperaments; Theuth and Thamus; and the
visions of Hades and the Fates,—fables which have imprinted
themselves in the human memory like the signs of the zodiac;
his soliform eye and his boniform soul; his doctrine of assimilation; his doctrine of reminiscence; his clear vision of the
laws of return, or reaction, which secure instant justice
throughout the universe, instanced every where, but specially

in the doctrine, "what comes from God to us, returns from us to God," and in Socrates' belief that the laws below are sisters of the laws above.

More striking examples are his moral conclusions. Plato affirms the coincidence of science and virtue; for vice can never know itself and virtue; but virtue knows both itself and vice. The eye attested that justice was best, as long as it was profitable; Plato affirms that it is profitable throughout; that the profit is intrinsic, though the just conceal his justice from gods and men; that it is better to suffer injustice, than to do it; that the sinner ought to covet punishment; that the lie was more hurtful than homicide; and that ignorance, or the involuntary lie, was more calamitous than involuntary homicide; that the soul is unwillingly deprived of true opinions; and that no man sins willingly; that the order or proceeding of nature was from the mind to the body; and, though a sound body cannot restore an unsound mind, yet a good soul can, by its virtue, render the body the best possible. The intelligent have a right over the ignorant, namely, the right of instructing them. The right punishment of one out of tune, is to make him play in tune; the fine which the good, refusing to govern, ought to pay, is, to be governed by a worse man; that his guards shall not handle gold and silver, but shall be instructed that there is gold and silver in their souls, which will make men willing to give them every thing which they need.

This second sight explains the stress laid on geometry. He saw that the globe of earth was not more lawful and precise than was the super-sensible; that a celestial geometry was in place there, as a logic of lines and angles here below; that the world was throughout mathematical; the proportions are constant of oxygen, azote, and lime; there is just so much water, and slate, and magnesia; not less are the proportions constant of the moral elements.

This eldest Goethe, hating varnish and falsehood, delighted in revealing the real at the base of the accidental; in discovering connection, continuity, and representation, everywhere; hating insulation; and appears like the god of wealth among the cabins of vagabonds, opening power and capability in every thing he touches. Ethical science was new and vacant,

when Plato could write thus:—"Of all whose arguments are
left to the men of the present time, no one has ever yet condemned injustice, or praised justice, otherwise than as respects the repute, honors, and emoluments arising therefrom;
while, as respects either of them in itself, and subsisting by its
own power in the soul of the possessor, and concealed both
from gods and men, no one has yet sufficiently investigated,
either in poetry or prose writings,—how, namely, that the
one is the greatest of all the evils that the soul has within it,
and justice the greatest good."

His definition of ideas, as what is simple, permanent, uniform, and self-existent, forever discriminating them from the
notions of the understanding, marks an era in the world. He
was born to behold the self-evolving power of spirit, endless
generator of new ends; a power which is the key at once to
the centrality and the evanescence of things. Plato is so
centred, that he can well spare all his dogmas. Thus the fact
of knowledge and ideas reveals to him the fact of eternity;
and the doctrine of reminiscence he offers as the most probable particular explication. Call that fanciful,—it matters not:
the connection between our knowledge and the abyss of
being is still real, and the explication must be not less magnificent.

He has indicated every eminent point in speculation. He
wrote on the scale of the mind itself, so that all things have
symmetry in his tablet. He put in all the past, without weariness, and descended into detail with a courage like that he
witnessed in nature. One would say, that his forerunners had
mapped out each a farm, or a district, or an island, in intellectual geography, but that Plato first drew the sphere. He do-
mesticates the soul in nature: man is the microcosm. All the
circles of the visible heaven represent as many circles in the
rational soul. There is no lawless particle, and there is nothing
casual in the action of the human mind. The names of things,
too, are fatal, following the nature of things. All the gods of
the Pantheon are, by their names, significant of a profound
sense. The gods are the ideas. Pan is speech, or manifestation;
Saturn, the contemplative; Jove, the regal soul; and Mars,
passion. Venus is proportion; Calliope, the soul of the world;
Aglaia, intellectual illustration.

*   *   *

These thoughts, in sparkles of light, had appeared often to pious and to poetic souls; but this well-bred, all-knowing Greek geometer comes with command, gathers them all up into rank and gradation, the Euclid of holiness, and marries the two parts of nature. Before all men, he saw the intellectual values of the moral sentiment. He describes his own ideal, when he paints in Timæus a god leading things from disorder into order. He kindled a fire so truly in the centre, that we see the sphere illuminated, and can distinguish poles, equator, and lines of latitude, every arc and node: a theory so averaged, so modulated, that you would say, the winds of ages had swept through this rhythmic structure, and not that it was the brief extempore blotting of one short-lived scribe. Hence it has happened that a very well-marked class of souls, namely, those who delight in giving a spiritual, that is, an ethico-intellectual expression to every truth, by exhibiting an ulterior end which is yet legitimate to it, are said to Platonise. Thus, Michel Angelo is a Platonist, in his sonnets. Shakspeare is a Platonist, when he writes, "Nature is made better by no mean, but nature makes that mean," or,

"He, that can endure
To follow with allegiance a fallen lord,
Does conquer him that did his master conquer,
And earns a place in the story."

Hamlet is a pure Platonist, and 'tis the magnitude only of Shakspeare's proper genius that hinders him from being classed as the most eminent of this school. Swedenborg, throughout his prose poem of "Conjugal Love," is a Platonist.

His subtlety commended him to men of thought. The secret of his popular success is the moral aim, which endeared him to mankind. "Intellect," he said, "is king of heaven and of earth;" but, in Plato, intellect is always moral. His writings have also the sempiternal youth of poetry. For their arguments, most of them, might have been couched in sonnets: and poetry has never soared higher than in the Timæus and the Phædrus. As the poet, too, he is only contemplative. He did not, like Pythagoras, break himself with an institution. All his painting in the Republic must be esteemed mythical, with intent to bring out, sometimes in violent colors, his thought. You cannot institute, without peril of charlatanism.

It was a high scheme, his absolute privilege for the best, (which, to make emphatic, he expressed by community of women,) as the premium which he would set on grandeur. There shall be exempts of two kinds: first, those who by demerit have put themselves below protection,—outlaws; and secondly, those who by eminence of nature and desert are out of the reach of your rewards: let such be free of the city, and above the law. We confide them to themselves; let them do with us as they will. Let none presume to measure the irregularities of Michel Angelo and Socrates by village scales.

In his eighth book of the Republic, he throws a little mathematical dust in our eyes. I am sorry to see him, after such noble superiorities, permitting the lie to governors. Plato plays Providence a little with the baser sort, as people allow themselves with their dogs and cats.

III

Swedenborg; or, the Mystic

Among eminent persons, those who are most dear to men are not of the class which the economist calls producers: they have nothing in their hands; they have not cultivated corn, nor made bread; they have not led out a colony, nor invented a loom. A higher class, in the estimation and love of this city-building, market-going race of mankind, are the poets, who, from the intellectual kingdom, feed the thought and imagination with ideas and pictures which raise men out of the world of corn and money, and console them for the short-comings of the day, and the meannesses of labor and traffic. Then, also, the philosopher has his value, who flatters the intellect of this laborer, by engaging him with subtleties which instruct him in new faculties. Others may build cities; he is to understand them, and keep them in awe. But there is a class who lead us into another region,—the world of morals, or of will. What is singular about this region of thought, is, its claim. Wherever the sentiment of right comes in, it takes precedence of every thing else. For other things, I make poetry of them; but the moral sentiment makes poetry of me.

I have sometimes thought that he would render the greatest service to modern criticism, who shall draw the line of relation that subsists between Shakspeare and Swedenborg. The human mind stands ever in perplexity, demanding intellect, demanding sanctity, impatient equally of each without the other. The reconciler has not yet appeared. If we tire of the saints, Shakspeare is our city of refuge. Yet the instincts presently teach, that the problem of essence must take precedence of all others,—the questions of Whence? What? and Whither? and the solution of these must be in a life, and not in a book. A drama or poem is a proximate or oblique reply; but Moses, Menu, Jesus, work directly on this problem. The atmosphere of moral sentiment is a region of grandeur which reduces all material magnificence to toys, yet opens to every wretch that has reason the doors of the universe. Almost with a fierce haste it lays its empire on the man. In the language of the Koran, "God said, the heaven and the earth, and all that is between them, think ye that we created them in jest, and that ye shall not return to us?" It is the kingdom of the will, and by inspiring the will, which is the seat of personality, seems to convert the universe into a person;—

> "The realms of being to no other bow,
>   Not only all are thine, but all are Thou."

All men are commanded by the saint. The Koran makes a distinct class of those who are by nature good, and whose goodness has an influence on others, and pronounces this class to be the aim of creation: the other classes are admitted to the feast of being, only as following in the train of this. And the Persian poet exclaims to a soul of this kind,—

> "Go boldly forth, and feast on being's banquet;
>   Thou art the called,—the rest admitted with thee."

The privilege of this caste is an access to the secrets and structure of nature, by some higher method than by experience. In common parlance, what one man is said to learn by experience, a man of extraordinary sagacity is said, without experience, to divine. The Arabians say, that Abul Khain, the mystic, and Abu Ali Seena, the philosopher, conferred together; and, on parting, the philosopher said, "All that he sees, I know;" and the mystic said, "All that he knows, I see." If one should ask the reason of this intuition, the solution would lead us into that property which Plato denoted as Reminiscence, and which is implied by the Bramins in the tenet of Transmigration. The soul having been often born, or, as the Hindoos say, "travelling the path of existence through thousands of births," having beheld the things which are here, those which are in heaven, and those which are beneath, there is nothing of which she has not gained the knowledge: no wonder that she is able to recollect, in regard to any one thing, what formerly she knew. "For, all things in nature being linked and related, and the soul having heretofore known all, nothing hinders but that any man who has re-called to mind, or, according to the common phrase, has learned one thing only, should of himself recover all his ancient knowledge, and find out again all the rest, if he have but courage, and faint not in the midst of his researches. For inquiry and learning is reminiscence all." How much more, if he that inquires be a holy and godlike soul! For, by being assimilated to the original soul, by whom, and after whom, all things subsist, the soul of man does then easily flow into all things, and all things flow into it: they mix; and he is present and sympathetic with their structure and law.

This path is difficult, secret, and beset with terror. The ancients called it *ecstacy* or absence,—a getting out of their bodies to think. All religious history contains traces of the trance of saints,—a beatitude, but without any sign of joy, earnest, solitary, even sad; "the flight," Plotinus called it, "of the alone to the alone;" Μνεσις, the closing of the eyes,—whence our word, *Mystic*. The trances of Socrates, Plotinus, Porphyry, Behmen, Bunyan, Fox, Pascal, Guion, Swedenborg, will readily come to mind. But what as readily comes to mind, is, the accompaniment of disease. This beatitude comes in terror, and with shocks to the mind of the receiver. "It o'erinforms the tenement of clay," and drives the man mad; or, gives a certain violent bias, which taints his judgment. In the chief examples of religious illumination, somewhat morbid has mingled, in spite of the unquestionable increase of mental power. Must the highest good drag after it a quality which neutralizes and discredits it?—

> "Indeed, it takes
> From our achievements, when performed at height,
> The pith and marrow of our attribute."

Shall we say, that the economical mother disburses so much earth and so much fire, by weight and metre, to make a man, and will not add a pennyweight, though a nation is perishing for a leader? Therefore, the men of God purchased their science by folly or pain. If you will have pure carbon, carbuncle, or diamond, to make the brain transparent, the trunk and organs shall be so much the grosser: instead of porcelain, they are potter's earth, clay, or mud.

In modern times, no such remarkable example of this introverted mind has occurred, as in Emanuel Swedenborg, born in Stockholm, in 1688. This man, who appeared to his contemporaries a visionary, and elixir of moonbeams, no doubt led the most real life of any man then in the world: and now, when the royal and ducal Frederics, Cristierns, and Brunswicks, of that day, have slid into oblivion, he begins to spread himself into the minds of thousands. As happens in great men, he seemed, by the variety and amount of his powers, to be a composition of several persons,—like the giant fruits which are matured in gardens by the union of four or five single blossoms. His frame is on a larger scale, and possesses the advantages of size. As it is easier to see the reflection of the great sphere in large globes, though defaced by some crack or blemish, than in drops of water, so men of large calibre, though with some eccentricity or madness, like Pascal or Newton, help us more than balanced mediocre minds.

His youth and training could not fail to be extraordinary. Such a boy could not whistle or dance, but goes grubbing into mines and mountains, prying into chemistry and optics, physiology, mathematics, and astronomy, to find images fit for the measure of his versatile and capacious brain. He was a scholar from a child, and was educated at Upsala. At the age of twenty-eight, he was made Assessor of the Board of Mines, by Charles XII. In 1716, he left home for four years, and visited the universities of England, Holland, France, and Germany. He performed a notable feat of engineering in 1718, at the siege of Fredericshall, by hauling two galleys, five boats, and a sloop, some fourteen English miles overland, for the royal service. In 1721, he journeyed over Europe, to examine mines and smelting works. He published, in 1716, his Dædalus Hyperboreus, and, from this time, for the next thirty years, was employed in the composition and publication of his scientific works. With the like force, he threw himself into theology. In 1743, when he was fifty-four years old, what is called his illumination began. All his metallurgy, and transportation of ships overland, was absorbed into this ecstasy. He ceased to publish any more scientific books, withdrew from his practical labors, and devoted himself to the writing and publication of his voluminous theological works, which were printed at his own expense, or at that of the Duke of Brunswick, or other prince, at Dresden, Leipsic, London, or Amsterdam. Later, he resigned his office of Assessor: the salary attached to this office continued to be paid to him during his life. His duties had brought him into intimate acquaintance with King Charles XII., by whom he was much consulted and honored. The like favor was continued to him by his successor. At the Diet of 1751, Count Hopken says, the most solid memorials on finance were from his pen. In Sweden, he appears to have attracted a marked regard. His rare science and practical skill, and the added fame of second sight and extraordinary religious knowledge and gifts, drew to him queens, nobles, clergy, shipmasters, and people about the ports through which he was wont to pass in his many voyages. The clergy interfered a little with the importation and publication of his religious works; but he seems to have kept the friendship of men in power. He was never married. He had great modesty and gentleness of bearing. His habits were simple; he lived on bread, milk, and vegetables; he lived in a house situated in a large garden: he went several times to England, where he does not seem to have attracted any attention whatever from the learned or the eminent; and died at London, March 29, 1772, of apoplexy, in his eighty-fifth year. He is described, when in London, as a man of a quiet, clerical habit, not averse to tea and coffee, and kind to children. He wore a sword when in full velvet dress, and, whenever he walked out, carried a gold-headed cane. There is a common portrait of him in antique coat and wig, but the face has a wandering or vacant air.

The genius which was to penetrate the science of the age with a far more subtle science; to pass the bounds of space and time; venture into the dim spirit-realm, and attempt to establish a new religion in the world,—began its lessons in quarries and forges, in the smelting-pot and crucible, in shipyards and dissecting-rooms. No one man is perhaps able to judge of the merits of his works on so many subjects. One is glad to learn that his books on mines and metals are held in the highest esteem by those who understand these matters. It seems that he anticipated much science of the nineteenth century; anticipated, in astronomy, the discovery of the seventh planet,—but, unhappily, not also of the eighth; anticipated the views of modern astronomy in regard to the generation of earths by the sun; in magnetism, some important experiments and conclusions of later students; in chemistry, the atomic theory; in anatomy, the discoveries of Schlichting, Monro, and Wilson; and first demonstrated the office of the lungs. His excellent English editor magnanimously lays no stress on his discoveries, since he was too great to care to be original; and we are to judge, by what he can spare, of what remains.

A colossal soul, he lies vast abroad on his times, uncomprehended by them, and requires a long focal distance to be seen; suggests, as Aristotle, Bacon, Selden, Humboldt, that a certain vastness of learning, or *quasi* omnipresence of the human soul in nature, is possible. His superb speculation, as from a tower, over nature and arts, without ever losing sight of the texture and sequence of things, almost realizes his own picture, in the "Principia," of the original integrity of man. Over and above the merit of his particular discoveries, is the capital merit of his self-equality. A drop of water has the properties of the sea, but cannot exhibit a storm. There is beauty of a concert, as well as of a flute; strength of a host, as well as of a hero; and, in Swedenborg, those who are best acquainted with modern books will most admire the merit of mass. One of the missouriums and mastodons of literature, he is not to be measured by whole colleges of ordinary scholars. His stalwart presence would flutter the gowns of an university. Our books are false by being fragmentary: their sentences are *bonmots*, and not parts of natural discourse; childish expressions of surprise or pleasure in nature; or, worse, owing a brief notoriety to their petulance, or aversion from the order of nature,—being some curiosity or oddity, designedly not in harmony with nature, and purposely framed to excite surprise, as jugglers do by concealing their means. But Swedenborg is systematic, and respective of the world in every sentence: all the means are orderly given; his faculties work with astronomic punctuality, and this admirable writing is pure from all pertness or egotism.

Swedenborg was born into an atmosphere of great ideas. 'Tis hard to say what was his own: yet his life was dignified by noblest pictures of the universe. The robust Aristotelian method, with its breadth and adequateness, shaming our sterile and linear logic by its genial radiation, conversant with series and degree, with effects and ends, skilful to discriminate power from form, essence from accident, and opening, by its terminology and definition, high roads into nature, had trained a race of athletic philosophers. Harvey had shown the circulation of the blood: Gilbert had shown that the earth was a magnet: Descartes, taught by Gilbert's magnet, with its vortex, spiral, and polarity, had filled Europe with the leading thought of vortical motion, as the secret of nature. Newton, in the year in which Swedenborg was born, published the "Principia," and established the universal gravity. Malpighi, following the high doctrines of Hippocrates, Leucippus, and Lucretius, had given emphasis to the dogma that nature works in leasts, — "tota in minimis existit natura." Unrivalled dissectors, Swammerdam, Leeuwenhoek, Winslow, Eustachius, Heister, Vesalius, Boerhaave, had left nothing for scalpel or microscope to reveal in human or comparative anatomy: Linnæus, his contemporary, was affirming, in his beautiful science, that "Nature is always like herself:" and, lastly, the nobility of method, the largest application of principles, had been exhibited by Leibnitz and Christian Wolff, in cosmology; whilst Locke and Grotius had drawn the moral argument. What was left for a genius of the largest calibre, but to go over their ground, and verify and unite? It is easy to see, in these minds, the origin of Swedenborg's studies, and the suggestion of his problems. He had a capacity to entertain and vivify these volumes of thought. Yet the proximity of these geniuses, one or other of whom had introduced all his leading ideas, makes Swedenborg another example of the difficulty, even in a highly fertile genius, of proving originality, the first birth and annunciation of one of the laws of nature.

He named his favorite views, the doctrine of Forms, the doctrine of Series and Degrees, the doctrine of Influx, the doctrine of Correspondence. His statement of these doctrines deserves to be studied in his books. Not every man can read them, but they will reward him who can. His theologic works

are valuable to illustrate these. His writings would be a sufficient library to a lonely and athletic student; and the "Economy of the Animal Kingdom" is one of those books which,
by the sustained dignity of thinking, is an honor to the human race. He had studied spars and metals to some purpose.
His varied and solid knowledge makes his style lustrous with
points and shooting spicula of thought, and resembling one
of those winter mornings when the air sparkles with crystals.
The grandeur of the topics makes the grandeur of the style.
He was apt for cosmology, because of that native perception
of identity which made mere size of no account to him. In
the atom of magnetic iron, he saw the quality which would
generate the spiral motion of sun and planet.

The thoughts in which he lived were, the universality of
each law in nature; the Platonic doctrine of the scale or degrees; the version or conversion of each into other, and so the
correspondence of all the parts; the fine secret that little explains large, and large, little; the centrality of man in nature,
and the connection that subsists throughout all things: he saw
that the human body was strictly universal, or an instrument
through which the soul feeds and is fed by the whole of matter: so that he held, in exact antagonism to the skeptics, that,
"the wiser a man is, the more will he be a worshipper of the
Deity." In short, he was a believer in the Identity-philosophy,
which he held not idly, as the dreamers of Berlin or Boston,
but which he experimented with and stablished through years
of labor, with the heart and strength of the rudest Viking that
his rough Sweden ever sent to battle.

This theory dates from the oldest philosophers, and derives
perhaps its best illustration from the newest. It is this: that
nature iterates her means perpetually on successive planes. In
the old aphorism, *nature is always self-similar*. In the plant, the
eye or germinative point opens to a leaf, then to another leaf,
with a power of transforming the leaf into radicle, stamen,
pistil, petal, bract, sepal, or seed. The whole art of the plant
is still to repeat leaf on leaf without end, the more or less of
heat, light, moisture, and food, determining the form it shall
assume. In the animal, nature makes a vertebra, or a spine of
vertebræ, and helps herself still by a new spine, with a limited
power of modifying its form,—spine on spine, to the end of

the world. A poetic anatomist, in our own day, teaches that a snake, being a horizontal line, and man, being an erect line, constitute a right angle; and, between the lines of this mystical quadrant, all animated beings find their place: and he assumes the hair-worm, the span-worm, or the snake, as the type or prediction of the spine. Manifestly, at the end of the spine, nature puts out smaller spines, as arms; at the end of the arms, new spines, as hands; at the other end, she repeats the process, as legs and feet. At the top of the column, she puts out another spine, which doubles or loops itself over, as a span-worm, into a ball, and forms the skull, with extremities again: the hands being now the upper jaw, the feet the lower jaw, the fingers and toes being represented this time by upper and lower teeth. This new spine is destined to high uses. It is a new man on the shoulders of the last. It can almost shed its trunk, and manage to live alone, according to the Platonic idea in the Timæus. Within it, on a higher plane, all that was done in the trunk repeats itself. Nature recites her lesson once more in a higher mood. The mind is a finer body, and resumes its functions of feeding, digesting, absorbing, excluding, and generating, in a new and ethereal element. Here, in the brain, is all the process of alimentation repeated, in the acquiring, comparing, digesting, and assimilating of experience. Here again is the mystery of generation repeated. In the brain are male and female faculties: here is marriage, here is fruit. And there is no limit to this ascending scale, but series on series. Every thing, at the end of one use, is taken up into the next, each series punctually repeating every organ and process of the last. We are adapted to infinity. We are hard to please, and love nothing which ends: and in nature is no end; but every thing, at the end of one use, is lifted into a superior, and the ascent of these things climbs into dæmonic and celestial natures. Creative force, like a musical composer, goes on unweariedly repeating a simple air or theme, now high, now low, in solo, in chorus, ten thousand times reverberated, till it fills earth and heaven with the chant.

Gravitation, as explained by Newton, is good, but grander, when we find chemistry only an extension of the law of masses into particles, and that the atomic theory shows the action of chemistry to be mechanical also. Metaphysics shows us a sort of gravitation, operative also in the mental phenomena; and the terrible tabulation of the French statists brings every piece of whim and humor to be reducible also to exact numerical ratios. If one man in twenty thousand, or in thirty thousand, eats shoes, or marries his grandmother, then, in every twenty thousand, or thirty thousand, is found one man who eats shoes, or marries his grandmother. What we call gravitation, and fancy ultimate, is one fork of a mightier stream, for which we have yet no name. Astronomy is excellent; but it must come up into life to have its full value, and not remain there in globes and spaces. The globule of blood gyrates around its own axis in the human veins, as the planet in the sky; and the circles of intellect relate to those of the heavens. Each law of nature has the like universality; eating, sleep or hybernation, rotation, generation, metamorphosis, vortical motion, which is seen in eggs as in planets. These grand rhymes or returns in nature,—the dear, best-known face startling us at every turn, under a mask so unexpected that we think it the face of a stranger, and, carrying up the semblance into divine forms,—delighted the prophetic eye of Swedenborg; and he must be reckoned a leader in that revolution, which, by giving to science an idea, has given to an aimless accumulation of experiments, guidance and form, and a beating heart.

I own, with some regret, that his printed works amount to about fifty stout octavos, his scientific works being about half of the whole number; and it appears that a mass of manuscript still unedited remains in the royal library at Stockholm. The scientific works have just now been translated into English, in an excellent edition.

Swedenborg printed these scientific books in the ten years from 1734 to 1744, and they remained from that time neglected: and now, after their century is complete, he has at last found a pupil in Mr. Wilkinson, in London, a philosophic critic, with a coequal vigor of understanding and imagination comparable only to Lord Bacon's, who has produced his master's buried books to the day, and transferred them, with every advantage, from their forgotten Latin into English, to go round the world in our commercial and conquering tongue. This startling reappearance of Swedenborg, after a hundred years, in his pupil, is not the least remarkable fact in his history. Aided, it is said, by the munificence of Mr. Clissold, and also by his literary skill, this piece of poetic justice is done. The admirable preliminary discourses with which Mr. Wilkinson has enriched these volumes, throw all the contemporary philosophy of England into shade, and leave me nothing to say on their proper grounds.

The "Animal Kingdom" is a book of wonderful merits. It was written with the highest end,—to put science and the soul, long estranged from each other, at one again. It was an anatomist's account of the human body, in the highest style of poetry. Nothing can exceed the bold and brilliant treatment of a subject usually so dry and repulsive. He saw nature "wreathing through an everlasting spiral, with wheels that never dry, on axes that never creak," and sometimes sought "to uncover those secret recesses where nature is sitting at the fires in the depths of her laboratory;" whilst the picture comes recommended by the hard fidelity with which it is based on practical anatomy. It is remarkable that this sublime genius decides, peremptorily for the analytic, against the synthetic method; and, in a book whose genius is a daring poetic synthesis, claims to confine himself to a rigid experience.

He knows, if he only, the flowing of nature, and how wise was that old answer of Amasis to him who bade him drink up the sea,—"Yes, willingly, if you will stop the rivers that flow in." Few knew as much about nature and her subtle manners, or expressed more subtly her goings. He thought as large a demand is made on our faith by nature, as by miracles. "He noted that in her proceeding from first principles through her several subordinations, there was no state through which she did not pass, as if her path lay through all things." "For as often as she betakes herself upward from visible phenomena, or, in other words, withdraws herself inward, she instantly, as it were, disappears, while no one knows what has become of her, or whither she is gone: so that it is necessary to take science as a guide in pursuing her steps."

The pursuing the inquiry under the light of an end or final cause, gives wonderful animation, a sort of personality to the whole writing. This book announces his favorite dogmas. The

ancient doctrine of Hippocrates, that the brain is a gland; and
of Leucippus, that the atom may be known by the mass; or,
in Plato, the macrocosm by the microcosm; and, in the verses
of Lucretius,—

> Ossa videlicet e pauxillis atque minutis
> Ossibus sic et de pauxillis atque minutis
> Visceribus viscus gigni, sanguenque creari
> Sanguinis inter se multis coeuntibus guttis;
> Ex aurique putat micis consistere posse
> Aurum, et de terris terram concrescere parvis;
> Ignibus ex igneis, humorem humoribus esse.
>
> LIB. I. 835.

> "The principle of all things; entrails made
> Of smallest entrails; bone, of smallest bone;
> Blood, of small sanguine drops reduced to one;
> Gold, of small grains; earth, of small sands compacted;
> Small drops to water, sparks to fire contracted:"

and which Malpighi had summed in his maxim, that "nature
exists entire in leasts,"—is a favorite thought of Swedenborg.
"It is a constant law of the organic body, that large, compound, or visible forms exist and subsist from smaller, simpler, and ultimately from invisible forms, which act similarly
to the larger ones, but more perfectly and more universally;
and the least forms so perfectly and universally, as to involve
an idea representative of their entire universe." The unities of
each organ are so many little organs, homogeneous with their
compound: the unities of the tongue are little tongues; those
of the stomach, little stomachs; those of the heart are little
hearts. This fruitful idea furnishes a key to every secret. What
was too small for the eye to detect was read by the aggre-
gates; what was too large, by the units. There is no end to
his application of the thought. "Hunger is an aggregate of
very many little hungers, or losses of blood by the little veins
all over the body." It is a key to his theology, also. "Man is a
kind of very minute heaven, corresponding to the world of
spirits and to heaven. Every particular idea of man, and every
affection, yea, every smallest part of his affection, is an image

and effigy of him. A spirit may be known from only a single thought. God is the grand man."

The hardihood and thoroughness of his study of nature required a theory of forms, also. "Forms ascend in order from the lowest to the highest. The lowest form is angular, or the terrestrial and corporeal. The second and next higher form is the circular, which is also called the perpetual-angular, because the circumference of a circle is a perpetual angle. The form above this is the spiral, parent and measure of circular forms: its diameters are not rectilinear, but variously circular, and have a spherical surface for centre; therefore it is called the perpetual-circular. The form above this is the vortical, or perpetual-spiral: next, the perpetual-vortical, or celestial: last, the perpetual-celestial, or spiritual."

Was it strange that a genius so bold should take the last step, also,—conceive that he might attain the science of all sciences, to unlock the meaning of the world? In the first volume of the "Animal Kingdom," he broaches the subject, in a remarkable note.—

"In our doctrine of Representations and Correspondences, we shall treat of both these symbolical and typical resemblances, and of the astonishing things which occur, I will not say, in the living body only, but throughout nature, and which correspond so entirely to supreme and spiritual things, that one would swear that the physical world was purely symbolical of the spiritual world; insomuch, that if we choose to express any natural truth in physical and definite vocal terms, and to convert these terms only into the corresponding and spiritual terms, we shall by this means elicit a spiritual truth, or theological dogma, in place of the physical truth or precept: although no mortal would have predicted that any thing of the kind could possibly arise by bare literal transposition; inasmuch as the one precept, considered separately from the other, appears to have absolutely no relation to it. I intend, hereafter, to communicate a number of examples of such correspondences, together with a vocabulary containing the terms of spiritual things, as well as of the physical things for which they are to be substituted. This symbolism pervades the living body."

The fact, thus explicitly stated, is implied in all poetry, in

allegory, in fable, in the use of emblems, and in the structure
of language. Plato knew of it, as is evident from his twice
bisected line, in the sixth book of the Republic. Lord Bacon
had found that truth and nature differed only as seal and
print; and he instanced some physical propositions, with their
translation into a moral or political sense. Behmen, and all
mystics, imply this law, in their dark riddle-writing. The
poets, in as far as they are poets, use it; but it is known to
them only, as the magnet was known for ages, as a toy. Swedenborg first put the fact into a detached and scientific statement, because it was habitually present to him, and never not
seen. It was involved, as we explained already, in the doctrine
of identity and iteration, because the mental series exactly tal-
lies with the material series. It required an insight that could
rank things in order and series; or, rather, it required such
rightness of position, that the poles of the eye should coincide
with the axis of the world. The earth had fed its mankind
through five or six milleniums, and they had sciences, religions, philosophies; and yet had failed to see the correspondence of meaning between every part and every other part.
And, down to this hour, literature has no book in which the
symbolism of things is scientifically opened. One would say,
that, as soon as men had the first hint that every sensible object,—animal, rock, river, air,—nay, space and time, subsists
not for itself, nor finally to a material end, but as a picture-
language, to tell another story of beings and duties, other science would be put by, and a science of such grand presage
would absorb all faculties: that each man would ask of all
objects, what they mean: Why does the horizon hold me fast,
with my joy and grief, in this centre? Why hear I the same
sense from countless differing voices, and read one never
quite expressed fact in endless picture-language? Yet, whether
it be, that these things will not be intellectually learned, or,
that many centuries must elaborate and compose so rare and
opulent a soul,—there is no comet, rock-stratum, fossil, fish,
quadruped, spider, or fungus, that, for itself, does not interest
more scholars and classifiers, than the meaning and upshot of
the frame of things.

But Swedenborg was not content with the culinary use of
the world. In his fifty-fourth year, these thoughts held him

fast, and his profound mind admitted the perilous opinion, too frequent in religious history, that he was an abnormal person, to whom was granted the privilege of conversing with angels and spirits; and this ecstasy connected itself with just this office of explaining the moral import of the sensible world. To a right perception, at once broad and minute, of the order of nature, he added the comprehension of the moral laws in their widest social aspects; but whatever he saw, through some excessive determination to form, in his constitution, he saw not abstractly, but in pictures, heard it in dialogues, constructed it in events. When he attempted to announce the law most sanely, he was forced to couch it in parable.

Modern psychology offers no similar example of a deranged balance. The principal powers continued to maintain a healthy action; and, to a reader who can make due allowance in the report for the reporter's peculiarities, the results are still instructive, and a more striking testimony to the sublime laws he announced, than any that balanced dulness could afford. He attempts to give some account of the *modus* of the new state, affirming that "his presence in the spiritual world is attended with a certain separation, but only as to the intellectual part of his mind, not as to the will part;" and he affirms that "he sees, with the internal sight, the things that are in another life, more clearly than he sees the things which are here in the world."

Having adopted the belief that certain books of the Old and New Testaments were exact allegories, or written in the angelic and ecstatic mode, he employed his remaining years in extricating from the literal, the universal sense. He had borrowed from Plato the fine fable of "a most ancient people, men better than we, and dwelling nigher to the gods;" and Swedenborg added, that they used the earth symbolically; that these, when they saw terrestrial objects, did not think at all about them, but only about those which they signified. The correspondence between thoughts and things henceforward occupied him. "The very organic form resembles the end inscribed on it." A man is in general, and in particular, an organized justice or injustice, selfishness or gratitude. And the cause of this harmony he assigned in the Arcana: "The reason why all and single things, in the heavens and on earth, are representative, is because they exist from an influx of the Lord, through heaven." This design of exhibiting such correspondences, which, if adequately executed, would be the poem of the world, in which all history and science would play an essential part, was narrowed and defeated by the exclusively theologic direction which his inquiries took. His perception of nature is not human and universal, but is mystical and Hebraic. He fastens each natural object to a theologic notion;—a horse signifies carnal understanding; a tree, perception; the moon, faith; a cat means this; an ostrich, that; an artichoke, this other; and poorly tethers every symbol to a several ecclesiastic sense. The slippery Proteus is not so easily caught. In nature, each individual symbol plays innumerable parts, as each particle of matter circulates in turn through every system. The central identity enables any one symbol to express successively all the qualities and shades of real being. In the transmission of the heavenly waters, every hose fits every hydrant. Nature avenges herself speedily on the hard pedantry that would chain her waves. She is no literalist. Every thing must be taken genially, and we must be at the top of our condition, to understand any thing rightly.

His theological bias thus fatally narrowed his interpretation of nature, and the dictionary of symbols is yet to be written. But the interpreter, whom mankind must still expect, will find no predecessor who has approached so near to the true problem.

Swedenborg styles himself, in the title-page of his books, "Servant of the Lord Jesus Christ;" and by force of intellect, and in effect, he is the last Father in the Church, and is not likely to have a successor. No wonder that his depth of ethical wisdom should give him influence as a teacher. To the withered traditional church yielding dry catechisms, he let in nature again, and the worshipper, escaping from the vestry of verbs and texts, is surprised to find himself a party to the whole of his religion. His religion thinks for him, and is of universal application. He turns it on every side; it fits every part of life, interprets and dignifies every circumstance. Instead of a religion which visited him diplomatically three or four times,—when he was born, when he married, when he fell sick, and when he died, and for the rest never interfered with him,—here was a teaching which accompanied him all day, accompanied him even into sleep and dreams; into his thinking, and showed him through what a long ancestry his thoughts descend; into society, and showed by what affinities he was girt to his equals and his counterparts; into natural objects, and showed their origin and meaning, what are friendly, and what are hurtful; and opened the future world, by indicating the continuity of the same laws. His disciples allege that their intellect is invigorated by the study of his books.

There is no such problem for criticism as his theological writings, their merits are so commanding; yet such grave deductions must be made. Their immense and sandy diffuseness is like the prairie, or the desert, and their incongruities are like the last deliration. He is superfluously explanatory, and his feeling of the ignorance of men, strangely exaggerated. Men take truths of this nature very fast. Yet he abounds in assertions: he is a rich discoverer, and of things which most import us to know. His thought dwells in essential resemblances, like the resemblance of a house to the man who built it. He saw things in their law, in likeness of function, not of structure. There is an invariable method and order in his delivery of his truth, the habitual proceeding of the mind from inmost to outmost. What earnestness and weightiness,—his eye never roving, without one swell of vanity, or one look to self, in any common form of literary pride! a theoretic or speculative man, but whom no practical man in the universe could affect to scorn. Plato is a gownsman: his garment, though of purple, and almost sky-woven, is an academic robe, and hinders action with its voluminous folds. But this mystic is awful to Cæsar. Lycurgus himself would bow.

The moral insight of Swedenborg, the correction of popular errors, the announcement of ethical laws, take him out of comparison with any other modern writer, and entitle him to a place, vacant for some ages, among the lawgivers of mankind. That slow but commanding influence which he has acquired, like that of other religious geniuses, must be excessive also, and have its tides, before it subsides into a permanent amount. Of course, what is real and universal cannot be confined to the circle of those who sympathize strictly with his genius, but will pass forth into the common stock of wise and just thinking. The world has a sure chemistry, by which it extracts what is excellent in its children, and lets fall the infirmities and limitations of the grandest mind.

That metempsychosis which is familiar in the old mythology of the Greeks, collected in Ovid, and in the Indian Transmigration, and is there *objective*, or really takes place in bodies by alien will,—in Swedenborg's mind, has a more philosophic character. It is subjective, or depends entirely upon the thought of the person. All things in the universe arrange themselves to each person anew, according to his ruling love. Man is such as his affection and thought are. Man is man by virtue of willing, not by virtue of knowing and understanding. As he is, so he sees. The marriages of the world are broken up. Interiors associate all in the spiritual world. Whatever the angels looked upon was to them celestial. Each Satan appears to himself a man; to those as bad as he, a comely man; to the purified, a heap of carrion. Nothing can resist states: every thing gravitates: like will to like: what we call poetic justice takes effect on the spot. We have come into a world which is a living poem. Every thing is as I am. Bird and beast is not bird and beast, but emanation and effluvia of the minds and wills of men there present. Every one makes his own house and state. The ghosts are tormented with the fear of death, and cannot remember that they have died. They who are in evil and falsehood are afraid of all others. Such as have deprived themselves of charity, wander and flee: the societies which they approach discover their quality, and drive them away. The covetous seem to themselves to be abiding in cells where their money is deposited, and these to be infested with mice. They who place merit in good works seem to themselves to cut wood. "I asked such, if they were not wearied? They replied, that they have not yet done work enough to merit heaven."

He delivers golden sayings, which express with singular beauty the ethical laws; as when he uttered that famed sentence, that, "in heaven the angels are advancing continually to the spring-time of their youth, so that the oldest angel appears the youngest:" "The more angels, the more room:"

"The perfection of man is the love of use:" "Man, in his perfect form, is heaven:" "What is from Him, is Him:" "Ends
always ascend as nature descends:" And the truly poetic account of the writing in the inmost heaven, which, as it consists of inflexions according to the form of heaven, can be
read without instruction. He almost justifies his claim to preternatural vision, by strange insights of the structure of the
human body and mind. "It is never permitted to any one, in
heaven, to stand behind another and look at the back of his
head: for then the influx which is from the Lord is disturbed." The angels, from the sound of the voice, know a
man's love; from the articulation of the sound, his wisdom;
and from the sense of the words, his science.

In the "Conjugal Love," he has unfolded the science of
marriage. Of this book, one would say, that, with the highest
elements, it has failed of success. It came near to be the Hymn
of Love, which Plato attempted in the "Banquet;" the love,
which, Dante says, Casella sang among the angels in Paradise;
and which, as rightly celebrated, in its genesis, fruition, and
effect, might well entrance the souls, as it would lay open the
genesis of all institutions, customs, and manners. The book
had been grand, if the Hebraism had been omitted, and the
law stated without Gothicism, as ethics, and with that scope
for ascension of state which the nature of things requires. It
is a fine Platonic development of the science of marriage;
teaching that sex is universal, and not local; virility in the
male qualifying every organ, act, and thought; and the feminine in woman. Therefore, in the real or spiritual world, the
nuptial union is not momentary, but incessant and total; and
chastity not a local, but a universal virtue; unchastity being
discovered as much in the trading, or planting, or speaking,
or philosophizing, as in generation; and that, though the vir-
gins he saw in heaven were beautiful, the wives were incomparably more beautiful, and went on increasing in beauty
evermore.

Yet Swedenborg, after his mode, pinned his theory to a
temporary form. He exaggerates the circumstance of marriage; and, though he finds false marriages on earth, fancies a
wiser choice in heaven. But of progressive souls, all loves and
friendships are momentary. *Do you love me?* means, Do you

see the same truth? If you do, we are happy with the same happiness: but presently one of us passes into the perception of new truth;—we are divorced, and no tension in nature can hold us to each other. I know how delicious is this cup of love,—I existing for you, you existing for me; but it is a child's clinging to his toy; an attempt to eternize the fireside and nuptial chamber; to keep the picture-alphabet through which our first lessons are prettily conveyed. The Eden of God is bare and grand: like the out-door landscape, remembered from the evening fireside, it seems cold and desolate, whilst you cower over the coals; but, once abroad again, we pity these who can forego the magnificence of nature, for candle-light and cards. Perhaps the true subject of the "Conjugal Love" is *Conversation*, whose laws are profoundly eliminated. It is false, if literally applied to marriage. For God is the bride or bridegroom of the soul. Heaven is not the pairing of two, but the communion of all souls. We meet, and dwell an instant under the temple of one thought, and part as though we parted not, to join another thought in other fellowships of joy. So far from there being any thing divine in the low and proprietary sense of *Do you love me?* it is only when you leave and lose me, by casting yourself on a sentiment which is higher than both of us, that I draw near, and find myself at your side; and I am repelled, if you fix your eye on me, and demand love. In fact, in the spiritual world, we change sexes every moment. You love the worth in me; then I am your husband: but it is not me, but the worth, that fixes the love; and that worth is a drop of the ocean of worth that is beyond me. Meantime, I adore the greater worth in another, and so become his wife. He aspires to a higher worth in another spirit, and is wife or receiver of that influence.

Whether a self-inquisitorial habit, that he grew into, from jealousy of the sins to which men of thought are liable, he has acquired, in disentangling and demonstrating that particular form of moral disease, an acumen which no conscience can resist. I refer to his feeling of the profanation of thinking to what is good "from scientifics." "To reason about faith, is to doubt and deny." He was painfully alive to the difference between knowing and doing, and this sensibility is incessantly expressed. Philosophers are, therefore, vipers, cockatrices, asps, hemorrhoids, presters, and flying serpents; literary men are conjurors and charlatans.

But this topic suggests a sad afterthought, that here we find the seat of his own pain. Possibly Swedenborg paid the penalty of introverted faculties. Success, or a fortunate genius, seems to depend on a happy adjustment of heart and brain; on a due proportion, hard to hit, of moral and mental power, which, perhaps, obeys the law of those chemical ratios which make a proportion in volumes necessary to combination, as when gases will combine in certain fixed rates, but not at any rate. It is hard to carry a full cup: and this man, profusely endowed in heart and mind, early fell into dangerous discord with himself. In his Animal Kingdom, he surprised us, by declaring that he loved analysis, and not synthesis; and now, after his fiftieth year, he falls into jealousy of his intellect; and, though aware that truth is not solitary, nor is goodness solitary, but both must ever mix and marry, he makes war on his mind, takes the part of the conscience against it, and, on all occasions, traduces and blasphemes it. The violence is instantly avenged. Beauty is disgraced, love is unlovely, when truth, the half part of heaven, is denied, as much as when a bitterness in men of talent leads to satire, and destroys the judgment. He is wise, but wise in his own despite. There is an air of infinite grief, and the sound of wailing, all over and through this lurid universe. A vampyre sits in the seat of the prophet, and turns with gloomy appetite to the images of pain. Indeed, a bird does not more readily weave its nest, or a mole bore into the ground, than this seer of the souls substructs a new hell and pit, each more abominable than the last, round every new crew of offenders. He was let down through a column that seemed of brass, but it was formed of angelic spirits, that he might descend safely amongst the unhappy, and witness the vastation of souls; and heard there, for a long continuance, their lamentations; he saw their tormentors, who increase and strain pangs to infinity; he saw the hell of the jugglers, the hell of the assassins, the hell of the lascivious; the hell of robbers, who kill and boil men; the infernal tun of the deceitful; the excrementitious hells; the hell of the revengeful, whose faces resembled a round, broad cake, and their arms rotate like a wheel. Except Rabelais and Dean Swift, nobody ever had such science of filth and corruption.

These books should be used with caution. It is dangerous to sculpture these evanescing images of thought. True in transition, they become false if fixed. It requires, for his just apprehension, almost a genius equal to his own. But when his visions become the stereotyped language of multitudes of persons, of all degrees of age and capacity, they are perverted. The wise people of the Greek race were accustomed to lead the most intelligent and virtuous young men, as part of their education, through the Eleusinian mysteries, wherein, with much pomp and graduation, the highest truths known to ancient wisdom were taught. An ardent and contemplative young man, at eighteen or twenty years, might read once these books of Swedenborg, these mysteries of love and conscience, and then throw them aside for ever. Genius is ever haunted by similar dreams, when the hells and the heavens are opened to it. But these pictures are to be held as mystical, that is, as a quite arbitrary and accidental picture of the truth,—not as the truth. Any other symbol would be as good: then this is safely seen.

Swedenborg's system of the world wants central spontaneity; it is dynamic, not vital, and lacks power to generate life. There is no individual in it. The universe is a gigantic crystal, all whose atoms and laminæ lie in uninterrupted order, and with unbroken unity, but cold and still. What seems an individual and a will, is none. There is an immense chain of intermediation, extending from centre to extremes, which bereaves every agency of all freedom and character. The universe, in his poem, suffers under a magnetic sleep, and only reflects the mind of the magnetizer. Every thought comes into each mind by influence from a society of spirits that surround it, and into these from a higher society, and so on. All his types mean the same few things. All his figures speak one speech. All his interlocutors Swedenborgise. Be they who they may, to this complexion must they come at last. This Charon ferries them all over in his boat; kings, counsellors, cavaliers, doctors, Sir Isaac Newton, Sir Hans Sloane, King

George II., Mahomet, or whosoever, and all gather one grimness of hue and style. Only when Cicero comes by, our gentle seer sticks a little at saying he talked with Cicero, and, with a touch of human relenting, remarks, "one whom it was given me to believe was Cicero;" and when the *soi disant* Roman opens his mouth, Rome and eloquence have ebbed away,—it is plain theologic Swedenborg, like the rest. His heavens and hells are dull; fault of want of individualism. The thousand-fold relation of men is not there. The interest that attaches in nature to each man, because he is right by his wrong, and wrong by his right, because he defies all dogmatising and classification, so many allowances, and contingences, and futurities, are to be taken into account, strong by his vices, often paralysed by his virtues,—sinks into entire sympathy with his society. This want reacts to the centre of the system. Though the agency of "the Lord" is in every line referred to by name, it never becomes alive. There is no lustre in that eye which gazes from the centre, and which should vivify the immense dependency of beings.

The vice of Swedenborg's mind is its theologic determination. Nothing with him has the liberality of universal wisdom, but we are always in a church. That Hebrew muse, which taught the lore of right and wrong to men, had the same excess of influence for him, it has had for the nations. The mode, as well as the essence, was sacred. Palestine is ever the more valuable as a chapter in universal history, and ever the less an available element in education. The genius of Swedenborg, largest of all modern souls in this department of thought, wasted itself in the endeavor to reanimate and conserve what had already arrived at its natural term, and, in the great secular Providence, was retiring from its prominence, before western modes of thought and expression. Swedenborg and Behmen both failed by attaching themselves to the Christian symbol, instead of to the moral sentiment, which carries innumerable christianities, humanities, divinities, in its bosom.

The excess of influence shows itself in the incongruous importation of a foreign rhetoric. 'What have I to do,' asks the impatient reader, ' with jasper and sardonyx, beryl and chalcedony; what with arks and passovers, ephahs and ephods;

what with lepers and emerods; what with heave-offerings and
unleavened bread; chariots of fire, dragons crowned and
horned, behemoth and unicorn? Good for orientals, these are
nothing to me. The more learning you bring to explain them,
the more glaring the impertinence. The more coherent and
elaborate the system, the less I like it. I say, with the Spartan,
"Why do you speak so much to the purpose, of that which is
nothing to the purpose?" My learning is such as God gave me
in my birth and habit, in the delight and study of my eyes,
and not of another man's. Of all absurdities, this of some foreigner, proposing to take away my rhetoric, and substitute his
own, and amuse me with pelican and stork, instead of thrush
and robin; palm-trees and shittim-wood, instead of sassafras
and hickory,—seems the most needless.'

Locke said, "God, when he makes the prophet, does not
unmake the man." Swedenborg's history points the remark.
The parish disputes, in the Swedish church, between the
friends and foes of Luther and Melancthon, concerning "faith
alone," and " works alone," intrude themselves into his speculations upon the economy of the universe, and of the celestial societies. The Lutheran bishop's son, for whom the
heavens are opened, so that he sees with eyes, and in the richest symbolic forms, the awful truth of things, and utters
again, in his books, as under a heavenly mandate, the indisputable secrets of moral nature,—with all these grandeurs
resting upon him, remains the Lutheran bishop's son; his
judgments are those of a Swedish polemic, and his vast enlargements purchased by adamantine limitations. He carries
his controversial memory with him, in his visits to the souls.
He is like Michel Angelo, who, in his frescoes, put the cardinal who had offended him to roast under a mountain of devils; or, like Dante, who avenged, in vindictive melodies, all
his private wrongs; or, perhaps still more like Montaigne's
parish priest, who, if a hail-storm passes over the village,
thinks the day of doom is come, and the cannibals already
have got the pip. Swedenborg confounds us not less with the
pains of Melancthon, and Luther, and Wolfius, and his own
books, which he advertises among the angels.

Under the same theologic cramp, many of his dogmas are
bound. His cardinal position in morals is, that evils should be

shunned as sins. But he does not know what evil is, or what good is, who thinks any ground remains to be occupied, after saying that evil is to be shunned as evil. I doubt not he was led by the desire to insert the element of personality of Deity. But nothing is added. One man, you say, dreads erysipelas,—show him that this dread is evil: or, one dreads hell,—show him that *dread* is evil. He who loves goodness, harbors angels, reveres reverence, and lives with God. The less we have to do with our sins, the better. No man can afford to waste his moments in compunctions. "That is active duty," say the Hindoos, " which is not for our bondage; that is knowledge, which is for our liberation: all other duty is good only unto weariness."

Another dogma, growing out of this pernicious theologic limitation, is this Inferno. Swedenborg has devils. Evil, according to old philosophers, is good in the making. That pure malignity can exist, is the extreme proposition of unbelief. It is not to be entertained by a rational agent; it is atheism; it is the last profanation. Euripides rightly said,—

> "Goodness and being in the gods are one;
> He who imputes ill to them makes them none."

To what a painful perversion had Gothic theology arrived, that Swedenborg admitted no conversion for evil spirits! But the divine effort is never relaxed; the carrion in the sun will convert itself to grass and flowers; and man, though in brothels, or jails, or on gibbets, is on his way to all that is good and true. Burns, with the wild humor of his apostrophe to "poor old Nickie Ben,"

> "O wad ye tak a thought, and mend!"

has the advantage of the vindictive theologian. Every thing is superficial, and perishes, but love and truth only. The largest is always the truest sentiment, and we feel the more generous spirit of the Indian Vishnu,—"I am the same to all mankind. There is not one who is worthy of my love or hatred. They who serve me with adoration,—I am in them, and they in me. If one whose ways are altogether evil, serve me alone, he is as respectable as the just man; he is altogether well employed; he soon becometh of a virtuous spirit, and obtaineth eternal happiness."

For the anomalous pretension of Revelations of the other world,—only his probity and genius can entitle it to any serious regard. His revelations destroy their credit by running into detail. If a man say, that the Holy Ghost has informed him that the Last Judgment, (or the last of the judgments,) took place in 1757; or, that the Dutch, in the other world, live in a heaven by themselves, and the English, in a heaven by themselves; I reply, that the Spirit which is holy, is reserved, taciturn, and deals in laws. The rumors of ghosts and hobgoblins gossip and tell fortunes. The teachings of the high Spirit are abstemious, and, in regard to particulars, negative. Socrates's Genius did not advise him to act or to find, but if he purposed to do somewhat not advantageous, it dissuaded him. "What God is," he said, "I know not; what he is not, I know." The Hindoos have denominated the Supreme Being, the "Internal Check." The illuminated Quakers explained their Light, not as somewhat which leads to any action, but it appears as an obstruction to any thing unfit. But the right examples are private experiences, which are absolutely at one on this point. Strictly speaking, Swedenborg's revelation is a confounding of planes,—a capital offence in so learned a categorist. This is to carry the law of surface into the plane of substance, to carry individualism and its fopperies into the realm of essences and generals, which is dislocation and chaos.

The secret of heaven is kept from age to age. No imprudent, no sociable angel ever dropt an early syllable to answer the longings of saints, the fears of mortals. We should have listened on our knees to any favorite, who, by stricter obedience, had brought his thoughts into parallelism with the celestial currents, and could hint to human ears the scenery and circumstance of the newly parted soul. But it is certain that it must tally with what is best in nature. It must not be inferior in tone to the already known works of the artist who sculptures the globes of the firmament, and writes the moral law. It must be fresher than rainbows, stabler than mountains, agreeing with flowers, with tides, and the rising and setting of autumnal stars. Melodious poets shall be hoarse as street ballads, when once the penetrating key-note of nature and spirit is sounded,—the earth-beat, sea-beat, heart-beat, which makes the tune to which the sun rolls, and the globule of blood, and the sap of trees.

In this mood, we hear the rumor that the seer has arrived, and his tale is told. But there is no beauty, no heaven: for angels, goblins. The sad muse loves night and death, and the pit. His Inferno is mesmeric. His spiritual world bears the same relation to the generosities and joys of truth, of which human souls have already made us cognisant, as a man's bad dreams bear to his ideal life. It is indeed very like, in its endless power of lurid pictures, to the phenomena of dreaming, which nightly turns many an honest gentleman, benevolent, but dyspeptic, into a wretch, skulking like a dog about the outer yards and kennels of creation. When he mounts into the heaven, I do not hear its language. A man should not tell me that he has walked among the angels; his proof is, that his eloquence makes me one. Shall the archangels be less majestic and sweet than the figures that have actually walked the earth? These angels that Swedenborg paints give us no very high idea of their discipline and culture: they are all country parsons: their heaven is a *fête champêtre*, an evangelical picnic, or French distribution of prizes to virtuous peasants. Strange, scholastic, didactic, passionless, bloodless man, who denotes classes of souls as a botanist disposes of a carex, and visits doleful hells as a stratum of chalk or hornblende! He has no sympathy. He goes up and down the world of men, a modern Rhadamanthus in gold-headed cane and peruke, and with nonchalance, and the air of a referee, distributes souls. The warm, many-weathered, passionate-peopled world is to him a grammar of hieroglyphs, or an emblematic freemason's procession. How different is Jacob Behmen! *he* is tremulous with emotion, and listens awe-struck, with the gentlest humanity, to the Teacher whose lessons he conveys; and when he asserts that, "in some sort, love is greater than God," his heart beats so high that the thumping against his leathern coat is audible across the centuries. 'Tis a great difference. Behmen is healthily and beautifully wise, notwithstanding the mystical narrowness and incommunicableness. Swedenborg is disagreeably wise, and, with all his accumulated gifts, paralyzes and repels.

It is the best sign of a great nature, that it opens a foreground, and, like the breath of morning landscapes, invites us onward. Swedenborg is retrospective, nor can we divest him of his mattock and shroud. Some minds are for ever restrained from descending into nature; others are for ever prevented from ascending out of it. With a force of many men, he could never break the umbilical cord which held him to nature, and he did not rise to the platform of pure genius.

It is remarkable that this man, who, by his perception of symbols, saw the poetic construction of things, and the primary relation of mind to matter, remained entirely devoid of the whole apparatus of poetic expression, which that perception creates. He knew the grammar and rudiments of the Mother-Tongue,—how could he not read off one strain into music? Was he like Saadi, who, in his vision, designed to fill his lap with the celestial flowers, as presents for his friends; but the fragrance of the roses so intoxicated him, that the skirt dropped from his hands? or, is reporting a breach of the manners of that heavenly society? or, was it that he saw the vision intellectually, and hence that chiding of the intellectual that pervades his books? Be it as it may, his books have no melody, no emotion, no humor, no relief to the dead prosaic level. In his profuse and accurate imagery is no pleasure, for there is no beauty. We wander forlorn in a lack-lustre landscape. No bird ever sang in all these gardens of the dead. The entire want of poetry in so transcendent a mind betokens the disease, and, like a hoarse voice in a beautiful person, is a kind of warning. I think, sometimes, he will not be read longer. His great name will turn a sentence. His books have become a monument. His laurel so largely mixed with cypress, a charnel-breath so mingles with the temple incense, that boys and maids will shun the spot.

Yet, in this immolation of genius and fame at the shrine of conscience, is a merit sublime beyond praise. He lived to purpose: he gave a verdict. He elected goodness as the clue to which the soul must cling in all this labyrinth of nature. Many opinions conflict as to the true centre. In the shipwreck, some cling to running rigging, some to cask and barrel, some to spars, some to mast; the pilot chooses with science,—I plant myself here; all will sink before this; "he comes to land who sails with me." Do not rely on heavenly favor, or on compassion to folly, or on prudence, on common sense, the old usage and main chance of men: nothing can keep you,—not fate, nor health, nor admirable intellect; none can keep you, but rectitude only, rectitude for ever and ever!—and, with a tenacity that never swerved in all his studies, inventions, dreams, he adheres to this brave choice. I think of him as of some transmigrating votary of Indian legend, who says, 'though I be dog, or jackal, or pismire, in the last rudiments of nature, under what integument or ferocity, I cleave to right, as the sure ladder that leads up to man and to God.'

Swedenborg has rendered a double service to mankind, which is now only beginning to be known. By the science of experiment and use, he made his first steps: he observed and published the laws of nature; and, ascending by just degrees, from events to their summits and causes, he was fired with piety at the harmonies he felt, and abandoned himself to his joy and worship. This was his first service. If the glory was too bright for his eyes to bear, if he staggered under the trance of delight, the more excellent is the spectacle he saw, the realities of being which beam and blaze through him, and which no infirmities of the prophet are suffered to obscure; and he renders a second passive service to men, not less than the first,—perhaps, in the great circle of being, and in the retributions of spiritual nature, not less glorious or less beautiful to himself.

IV

Montaigne; or, the Skeptic

EVERY FACT is related on one side to sensation, and, on the other, to morals. The game of thought is, on the appearance of one of these two sides, to find the other: given the upper, to find the under side. Nothing so thin, but has these two faces; and, when the observer has seen the obverse, he turns it over to see the reverse. Life is a pitching of this penny,—heads or tails. We never tire of this game, because there is still a slight shudder of astonishment at the exhibition of the other face, at the contrast of the two faces. A man is flushed with success, and bethinks himself what this good luck signifies. He drives his bargain in the street; but it occurs, that he also is bought and sold. He sees the beauty of a human face, and searches the cause of that beauty, which must be more beautiful. He builds his fortunes, maintains the laws, cherishes his children; but he asks himself, why? and whereto? This head and this tail are called, in the language of philosophy, Infinite and Finite; Relative and Absolute; Apparent and Real; and many fine names beside.

Each man is born with a predisposition to one or the other of these sides of nature; and, it will easily happen that men will be found devoted to one or the other. One class has the perception of difference, and is conversant with facts and surfaces; cities and persons; and the bringing certain things to pass;—the men of talent and action. Another class have the perception of identity, and are men of faith and philosophy, men of genius.

Each of these riders drives too fast. Plotinus believes only in philosophers; Fenelon, in saints; Pindar and Byron, in poets. Read the haughty language in which Plato and the Platonists speak of all men who are not devoted to their own shining abstractions: other men are rats and mice. The literary class is usually proud and exclusive. The correspondence of Pope and Swift describes mankind around them as monsters; and that of Goethe and Schiller, in our own time, is scarcely more kind.

It is easy to see how this arrogance comes. The genius is a genius by the first look he casts on any object. Is his eye creative? Does he not rest in angles and colors, but beholds the design,—he will presently undervalue the actual object. In powerful moments, his thought has dissolved the works of art and nature into their causes, so that the works appear heavy and faulty. He has a conception of beauty which the sculptor cannot embody. Picture, statue, temple, railroad, steam-engine, existed first in an artist's mind, without flaw, mistake, or friction, which impair the executed models. So did the church, the state, college, court, social circle, and all the institutions. It is not strange that these men, remembering what they have seen and hoped of ideas, should affirm disdainfully the superiority of ideas. Having at some time seen that the happy soul will carry all the arts in power, they say, Why cumber ourselves with superfluous realizations? and, like dreaming beggars, they assume to speak and act as if these values were already substantiated.

On the other part, the men of toil and trade and luxury,—the animal world, including the animal in the philosopher and poet also,—and the practical world, including the painful drudgeries which are never excused to philosopher or poet any more than to the rest,—weigh heavily on the other side. The trade in our streets believes in no metaphysical causes, thinks nothing of the force which necessitated traders and a trading planet to exist: no, but sticks to cotton, sugar, wool, and salt. The ward meetings, on election days, are not softened by any misgiving of the value of these ballotings. Hot life is streaming in a single direction. To the men of this world, to the animal strength and spirits, to the men of practical power, whilst immersed in it, the man of ideas appears out of his reason. They alone have reason.

Things always bring their own philosophy with them, that is, prudence. No man acquires property without acquiring with it a little arithmetic, also. In England, the richest country that ever existed, property stands for more, compared with personal ability, than in any other. After dinner, a man believes less, denies more: verities have lost some charm. After dinner, arithmetic is the only science: ideas are disturbing, incendiary, follies of young men, repudiated by the solid portion of society: and a man comes to be valued by his athletic and animal qualities. Spence relates, that Mr. Pope was with Sir Godfrey Kneller, one day, when his nephew, a Guinea trader, came in. "Nephew," said Sir Godfrey, "you have the honor of seeing the two greatest men in the world." "I don't know how great men you may be," said the Guinea man, "but I don't like your looks. I have often bought a man much better than both of you, all muscles and bones, for ten guineas." Thus, the men of the senses revenge themselves on the professors, and repay scorn for scorn. The first had leaped to conclusions not yet ripe, and say more than is true; the others make themselves merry with the philosopher, and weigh man by the pound.—They believe that mustard bites the tongue, that pepper is hot, friction-matches are incendiary, revolvers to be avoided, and suspenders hold up pantaloons; that there is much sentiment in a chest of tea; and a man will be eloquent, if you give him good wine. Are you tender and scrupulous,—you must eat more mince-pie. They hold that Luther had milk in him when he said,

"Wer nicht liebt Wein, Weib, und Gesang,
    Der bleibt ein Narr sein Leben lang;"

and when he advised a young scholar, perplexed with foreordination and free-will, to get well drunk. "The nerves," says Cabanis, "they are the man." My neighbor, a jolly farmer, in the tavern bar-room, thinks that the use of money is sure and speedy spending. "For his part," he says, "he puts his down his neck, and gets the good of it."

The inconvenience of this way of thinking is, that it runs into indifferentism, and then into disgust. Life is eating us up. We shall be fables presently. Keep cool: it will be all one a hundred years hence. Life's well enough; but we shall be glad to get out of it, and they will all be glad to have us. Why should we fret and drudge? Our meat will taste to-morrow as it did yesterday, and we may at last have had enough of it. "Ah," said my languid gentleman at Oxford, "there's nothing new or true,—and no matter."

With a little more bitterness, the cynic moans: our life is like an ass led to market by a bundle of hay being carried before him: he sees nothing but the bundle of hay. "There is so much trouble in coming into the world," said Lord Boling-broke, "and so much more, as well as meanness, in going out of it, that 'tis hardly worth while to be here at all." I knew a philosopher of this kidney, who was accustomed briefly to sum up his experience of human nature in saying, "Mankind is a damned rascal:" and the natural corollary is pretty sure to follow,—'The world lives by humbug, and so will I.'

The abstractionist and the materialist thus mutually exas-perating each other, and the scoffer expressing the worst of materialism, there arises a third party to occupy the middle ground between these two, the skeptic, namely. He finds both wrong by being in extremes. He labors to plant his feet, to be the beam of the balance. He will not go beyond his card. He sees the one-sidedness of these men of the street; he will not be a Gibeonite; he stands for the intellectual faculties, a cool head, and whatever serves to keep it cool: no unadvised industry, no unrewarded self-devotion, no loss of the brains in toil. Am I an ox, or a dray?—You are both in extremes, he says. You that will have all solid, and a world of pig-lead, deceive yourselves grossly. You believe yourselves rooted and grounded on adamant; and yet, if we uncover the last facts of our knowledge, you are spinning like bubbles in a river, you know not whither or whence, and you are bottomed and capped and wrapped in delusions.

Neither will he be betrayed to a book, and wrapped in a gown. The studious class are their own victims: they are thin and pale, their feet are cold, their heads are hot, the night is without sleep, the day a fear of interruption,—pallor, squa-lor, hunger, and egotism. If you come near them, and see what conceits they entertain,—they are abstractionists, and spend their days and nights in dreaming some dream; in ex-pecting the homage of society to some precious scheme built on a truth, but destitute of proportion in its presentment, of justness in its application, and of all energy of will in the schemer to embody and vitalize it.

But I see plainly, he says, that I cannot see. I know that human strength is not in extremes, but in avoiding extremes. I, at least, will shun the weakness of philosophizing beyond my depth. What is the use of pretending to powers we have not? What is the use of pretending to assurances we have not, respecting the other life? Why exaggerate the power of virtue? Why be an angel before your time? These strings, wound up too high, will snap. If there is a wish for immortality, and no evidence, why not say just that? If there are conflicting evidences, why not state them? If there is not ground for a candid thinker to make up his mind, yea or nay,—why not suspend the judgment? I weary of these dogmatizers. I tire of these hacks of routine, who deny the dogmas. I neither affirm nor deny. I stand here to try the case. I am here to consider, σχεπτειν, to consider how it is. I will try to keep the balance true. Of what use to take the chair, and glibly rattle off theories of society, religion, and nature, when I know that practical objections lie in the way, insurmountable by me and by my mates? Why so talkative in public, when each of my neighbors can pin me to my seat by arguments I cannot refute? Why pretend that life is so simple a game, when we know how subtle and elusive the Proteus is? Why think to shut up all things in your narrow coop, when we know there are not one or two only, but ten, twenty, a thousand things, and unlike? Why fancy that you have all the truth in your keeping? There is much to say on all sides.

Who shall forbid a wise skepticism, seeing that there is no practical question on which any thing more than an approximate solution can be had? Is not marriage an open question, when it is alleged, from the beginning of the world, that such as are in the institution wish to get out, and such as are out wish to get in? And the reply of Socrates, to him who asked whether he should choose a wife, still remains reasonable, "that, whether he should choose one or not, he would repent it." Is not the state a question? All society is divided in opinion on the subject of the state. Nobody loves it; great numbers dislike it, and suffer conscientious scruples to allegiance: and the only defence set up, is, the fear of doing worse in disorganizing. Is it otherwise with the church? Or, to put any of the questions which touch mankind nearest,—shall the young man aim at a leading part in law, in politics, in trade? It will not be pretended that a success in either of these kinds is quite coincident with what is best and inmost in his mind. Shall he, then, cutting the stays that hold him fast to the social state, put out to sea with no guidance but his genius? There is much to say on both sides. Remember the open question between the present order of "competition," and the friends of "attractive and associated labor." The generous minds embrace the proposition of labor shared by all; it is the only honesty; nothing else is safe. It is from the poor man's hut alone, that strength and virtue come: and yet, on the other side, it is alleged that labor impairs the form, and breaks the spirit of man, and the laborers cry unanimously, 'We have no thoughts.' Culture, how indispensable! I cannot forgive you the want of accomplishments; and yet, culture will instantly destroy that chiefest beauty of spontaneousness. Excellent is culture for a savage; but once let him read in the book, and he is no longer able not to think of Plutarch's heroes. In short, since true fortitude of understanding consists "in not letting what we know be embarrassed by what we do not know," we ought to secure those advantages which we can command, and not risk them by clutching after the airy and unattainable. Come, no chimeras! Let us go abroad; let us mix in affairs; let us learn, and get, and have, and climb. "Men are a sort of moving plants, and, like trees, receive a great part of their nourishment from the air. If they keep too much at home, they pine." Let us have a robust, manly life; let us know what we know, for certain; what we have, let it be solid, and seasonable, and our own. A world in the hand is worth two in the bush. Let us have to do with real men and women, and not with skipping ghosts.

This, then, is the right ground of the skeptic,—this of consideration, of self-containing; not at all of unbelief; not at all of universal denying, nor of universal doubting,—doubting even that he doubts; least of all, of scoffing and profligate jeering at all that is stable and good. These are no more his moods than are those of religion and philosophy. He is the considerer, the prudent, taking in sail, counting stock, husbanding his means, believing that a man has too many enemies, than that he can afford to be his own; that we can not give ourselves too many advantages, in this unequal conflict, with powers so vast and unweariable ranged on one side, and this little, conceited, vulnerable popinjay that a man is, bobbing up and down into every danger, on the other. It is a position taken up for better defence, as of more safety, and one that can be maintained; and it is one of more opportunity and range: as, when we build a house, the rule is, to set it not too high nor too low, under the wind, but out of the dirt.

The philosophy we want is one of fluxions and mobility. The Spartan and Stoic schemes are too stark and stiff for our occasion. A theory of Saint John, and of nonresistance, seems, on the other hand, too thin and aerial. We want some coat woven of elastic steel, stout as the first, and limber as the second. We want a ship in these billows we inhabit. An angular, dogmatic house would be rent to chips and splinters, in this storm of many elements. No, it must be tight, and fit to the form of man, to live at all; as a shell is the architecture of a house founded on the sea. The soul of man must be the type of our scheme, just as the body of man is the type after which a dwelling-house is built. Adaptiveness is the peculiarity of human nature. We are golden averages, volitant stabilities, compensated or periodic errors, houses founded on the sea. The wise skeptic wishes to have a near view of the best game, and the chief players; what is best in the planet; art and nature, places and events, but mainly men. Every thing that is excellent in mankind,—a form of grace, an arm of iron, lips of persuasion, a brain of resources, every one skilful to play and win,—he will see and judge.

The terms of admission to this spectacle, are, that he have a certain solid and intelligible way of living of his own; some method of answering the inevitable needs of human life; proof that he has played with skill and success; that he has evinced the temper, stoutness, and the range of qualities which, among his contemporaries and countrymen, entitle him to fellowship and trust. For, the secrets of life are not shown except to sympathy and likeness. Men do not confide themselves to boys, or coxcombs, or pedants, but to their peers. Some wise limitation, as the modern phrase is; some condition between the extremes, and having itself a positive quality; some stark and sufficient man, who is not salt or sugar, but sufficiently related to the world to do justice to Paris or London, and, at the same time, a vigorous and original thinker, whom cities can not overawe, but who uses them,—is the fit person to occupy this ground of speculation.

These qualities meet in the character of Montaigne. And yet, since the personal regard which I entertain for Montaigne may be unduly great, I will, under the shield of this prince of egotists, offer, as an apology for electing him as the representative of skepticism, a word or two to explain how my love began and grew for this admirable gossip.

A single odd volume of Cotton's translation of the Essays remained to me from my father's library, when a boy. It lay long neglected, until, after many years, when I was newly escaped from college, I read the book, and procured the remaining volumes. I remember the delight and wonder in which I lived with it. It seemed to me as if I had myself written the book, in some former life, so sincerely it spoke to my thought and experience. It happened, when in Paris, in 1833, that, in the cemetery of Pere le Chaise, I came to a tomb of Auguste Collignon, who died in 1830, aged sixty-eight years, and who, said the monument, "lived to do right, and had formed himself to virtue on the Essays of Montaigne." Some years later, I became acquainted with an accomplished English poet, John Sterling; and, in prosecuting my correspondence, I found that, from a love of Montaigne, he had made a pilgrimage to his chateau, still standing near Castellan, in Perigord, and, after two hundred and fifty years, had copied from the walls of his library the inscriptions which Montaigne had written there. That Journal of Mr. Sterling's, published in the Westminster Review, Mr. Hazlitt has reprinted in the *Prolegomena* to his edition of the Essays. I heard with pleasure that one of the newly-discovered autographs of William Shakspeare was in a copy of Florio's translation of Montaigne. It is the only book which we certainly know to have been in the poet's library. And, oddly enough, the duplicate copy of Florio, which the British Museum purchased, with a view of protecting the Shakspeare autograph, (as I was informed in the Museum,) turned out to have the autograph of Ben Jonson in the fly-leaf. Leigh Hunt relates of Lord Byron, that Montaigne was the only great writer of past times whom he read with avowed satisfaction. Other coincidences, not needful to be mentioned here, concurred to make this old Gascon still new and immortal for me.

In 1571, on the death of his father, Montaigne, then thirty-eight years old, retired from the practice of law, at Bordeaux, and settled himself on his estate. Though he had been a man of pleasure, and sometimes a courtier, his studious habits now grew on him, and he loved the compass, staidness, and independence, of the country gentleman's life. He took up his economy in good earnest, and made his farms yield the most. Downright and plain-dealing, and abhorring to be deceived or to deceive, he was esteemed in the country for his sense and probity. In the civil wars of the League, which converted every house into a fort, Montaigne kept his gates open, and his house without defence. All parties freely came and went, his courage and honor being universally esteemed. The neighboring lords and gentry brought jewels and papers to him for safe-keeping. Gibbon reckons, in these bigoted times, but two men of liberality in France,—Henry IV. and Montaigne.

Montaigne is the frankest and honestest of all writers. His French freedom runs into grossness; but he has anticipated all censure by the bounty of his own confessions. In his times, books were written to one sex only, and almost all were written in Latin; so that, in a humorist, a certain nakedness of statement was permitted, which our manners, of a literature addressed equally to both sexes, do not allow. But, though a biblical plainness, coupled with a most uncanonical levity, may shut his pages to many sensitive readers, yet the offence is superficial. He parades it: he makes the most of it: nobody can think or say worse of him than he does. He pretends to most of the vices; and, if there be any virtue in him, he says, it got in by stealth. There is no man, in his opinion, who has not deserved hanging five or six times; and he pretends no exception in his own behalf. "Five or six as ridiculous stories," too, he says, "can be told of me, as of any man living." But, with all this really superfluous frankness, the opinion of an invincible probity grows into every reader's mind.

"When I the most strictly and religiously confess myself, I find that the best virtue I have has in it some tincture of vice; and I am afraid that Plato, in his purest virtue, (I, who am as sincere and perfect a lover of virtue of that stamp as any other whatever,) if he had listened, and laid his ear close to himself, would have heard some jarring sound of human mixture; but faint and remote, and only to be perceived by himself."

Here is an impatience and fastidiousness at color or pretence of any kind. He has been in courts so long as to have conceived a furious disgust at appearances; he will indulge himself with a little cursing and swearing; he will talk with sailors and gipsies, use flash and street ballads: he has stayed in-doors till he is deadly sick; he will to the open air, though it rain bullets. He has seen too much of gentlemen of the long robe, until he wishes for cannibals; and is so nervous, by factitious life, that he thinks, the more barbarous man is, the better he is. He likes his saddle. You may read theology, and grammar, and metaphysics elsewhere. Whatever you get here, shall smack of the earth and of real life, sweet, or smart, or stinging. He makes no hesitation to entertain you with the records of his disease; and his journey to Italy is quite full of that matter. He took and kept this position of equilibrium. Over his name, he drew an emblematic pair of scales, and wrote *Que sçais je?* under it. As I look at his effigy opposite the title-page, I seem to hear him say, 'You may play old Poz, if you will; you may rail and exaggerate,—I stand here for truth, and will not, for all the states, and churches, and revenues, and personal reputations of Europe, overstate the dry fact, as I see it; I will rather mumble and prose about what I certainly know,—my house and barns; my father, my wife, and my tenants; my old lean bald pate; my knives and forks; what meats I eat, and what drinks I prefer; and a hundred straws just as ridiculous,—than I will write, with a fine crow-quill, a fine romance. I like gray days, and autumn and winter weather. I am gray and autumnal myself, and think an undress, and old shoes that do not pinch my feet, and old friends who do not constrain me, and plain topics where I do not need to strain myself and pump my brains, the most suitable. Our condition as men is risky and ticklish enough. One can not be sure of himself and his fortune an hour, but he may be whisked off into some pitiable or ridiculous plight. Why should I vapor and play the philosopher, instead of ballasting, the best I can, this dancing balloon? So, at least, I live within compass, keep myself ready for action, and can shoot the gulf, at last, with decency. If there be any thing farcical in such a life, the blame is not mine: let it lie at fate's and nature's door.'

The Essays, therefore, are an entertaining soliloquy on every random topic that comes into his head; treating every thing without ceremony, yet with masculine sense. There have been men with deeper insight; but, one would say, never a man with such abundance of thoughts: he is never dull, never insincere, and has the genius to make the reader care for all that he cares for.

The sincerity and marrow of the man reaches to his sentences. I know not any where the book that seems less written. It is the language of conversation transferred to a book. Cut these words, and they would bleed; they are vascular and alive. One has the same pleasure in it that we have in listening to the necessary speech of men about their work, when any unusual circumstance gives momentary importance to the dialogue. For blacksmiths and teamsters do not trip in their speech; it is a shower of bullets. It is Cambridge men who correct themselves, and begin again at every half sentence, and, moreover, will pun, and refine too much, and swerve from the matter to the expression. Montaigne talks with shrewdness, knows the world, and books, and himself, and uses the positive degree: never shrieks, or protests, or prays: no weakness, no convulsion, no superlative: does not wish to jump out of his skin, or play any antics, or annihilate space or time; but is stout and solid; tastes every moment of the day; likes pain, because it makes him feel himself, and realize things; as we pinch ourselves to know that we are awake. He keeps the plain; he rarely mounts or sinks; likes to feel solid ground, and the stones underneath. His writing has no enthusiasms, no aspiration; contented, self-respecting, and keeping the middle of the road. There is but one exception,—in his love for Socrates. In speaking of him, for once his cheek flushes, and his style rises to passion.

Montaigne died of a quinsy, at the age of sixty, in 1592. When he came to die, he caused the mass to be celebrated in his chamber. At the age of thirty-three, he had been married. "But," he says, "might I have had my own will, I would not have married Wisdom herself, if she would have had me: but 'tis to much purpose to evade it, the common custom and use of life will have it so. Most of my actions are guided by example, not choice." In the hour of death, he gave the same weight to custom. *Que sçais je?* What do I know?

This book of Montaigne the world has endorsed, by translating it into all tongues, and printing seventy-five editions of it in Europe: and that, too, a circulation somewhat chosen, namely, among courtiers, soldiers, princes, men of the world, and men of wit and generosity.

Shall we say that Montaigne has spoken wisely, and given the right and permanent expression of the human mind, on the conduct of life?

We are natural believers. Truth, or the connection between cause and effect, alone interests us. We are persuaded that a thread runs through all things: all worlds are strung on it, as beads: and men, and events, and life, come to us, only because of that thread: they pass and repass, only that we may know the direction and continuity of that line. A book or statement which goes to show that there is no line, but random and chaos, a calamity out of nothing, a prosperity and no account of it, a hero born from a fool, a fool from a hero,—dispirits us. Seen or unseen, we believe the tie exists. Talent makes counterfeit ties; genius finds the real ones. We hearken to the man of science, because we anticipate the sequence in natural phenomena which he uncovers. We love whatever affirms, connects, preserves; and dislike what scatters or pulls down. One man appears whose nature is to all men's eyes conserving and constructive: his presence supposes a well-ordered society, agriculture, trade, large institutions, and empire. If these did not exist, they would begin to exist through his endeavors. Therefore, he cheers and comforts men, who feel all this in him very readily. The nonconformist and the rebel say all manner of unanswerable things against the existing republic, but discover to our sense no plan of house or state of their own. Therefore, though the town, and state, and way of living, which our counsellor contemplated, might be a very modest or musty prosperity, yet men rightly go for him, and reject the reformer, so long as he comes only with axe and crowbar.

But though we are natural conservers and causationists, and

reject a sour, dumpish unbelief, the skeptical class, which Montaigne represents, have reason, and every man, at some time, belongs to it. Every superior mind will pass through this domain of equilibration,—I should rather say, will know how to avail himself of the checks and balances in nature, as a natural weapon against the exaggeration and formalism of bigots and blockheads.

Skepticism is the attitude assumed by the student in relation to the particulars which society adores, but which he sees to be reverend only in their tendency and spirit. The ground occupied by the skeptic is the vestibule of the temple. Society does not like to have any breath of question blown on the existing order. But the interrogation of custom at all points is an inevitable stage in the growth of every superior mind, and is the evidence of its perception of the flowing power which remains itself in all changes.

The superior mind will find itself equally at odds with the evils of society, and with the projects that are offered to relieve them. The wise skeptic is a bad citizen; no conservative; he sees the selfishness of property, and the drowsiness of institutions. But neither is he fit to work with any democratic party that ever was constituted; for parties wish every one committed, and he penetrates the popular patriotism. His politics are those of the "Soul's Errand" of Sir Walter Raleigh; or of Krishna, in the Bhagavat, "There is none who is worthy of my love or hatred;" whilst he sentences law, physic, divinity, commerce, and custom. He is a reformer: yet he is no better member of the philanthropic association. It turns out that he is not the champion of the operative, the pauper, the prisoner, the slave. It stands in his mind, that our life in this world is not of quite so easy interpretation as churches and school-books say. He does not wish to take ground against these benevolences, to play the part of devil's attorney, and blazon every doubt and sneer that darkens the sun for him. But he says, There are doubts.

I mean to use the occasion, and celebrate the calendar-day of our Saint Michel de Montaigne, by counting and describing these doubts or negations. I wish to ferret them out of their holes, and sun them a little. We must do with them as the police do with old rogues, who are shown up to the pub-

lic at the marshal's office. They will never be so formidable,
when once they have been identified and registered. But I
mean honestly by them,—that justice shall be done to their
terrors. I shall not take Sunday objections, made up on purpose to be put down. I shall take the worst I can find,
whether I can dispose of them, or they of me.

I do not press the skepticism of the materialist. I know, the
quadruped opinion will not prevail. 'Tis of no importance
what bats and oxen think. The first dangerous symptom I report, is, the levity of intellect; as if it were fatal to earnestness
to know much. Knowledge is the knowing that we can not
know. The dull pray; the geniuses are light mockers. How
respectable is earnestness on every platform! but intellect kills
it. Nay, San Carlo, my subtle and admirable friend, one of
the most penetrating of men, finds that all direct ascension,
even of lofty piety, leads to this ghastly insight, and sends
back the votary orphaned. My astonishing San Carlo thought
the lawgivers and saints infected. They found the ark empty;
saw, and would not tell; and tried to choke off their approaching followers, by saying, 'Action, action, my dear fellows, is for you!' Bad as was to me this detection by San
Carlo, this frost in July, this blow from a bride, there was still
a worse, namely, the cloy or satiety of the saints. In the
mount of vision, ere they have yet risen from their knees, they
say, 'We discover that this our homage and beatitude is partial
and deformed: we must fly for relief to the suspected and
reviled Intellect, to the Understanding, the Mephistopheles,
to the gymnastics of talent.'

This is hobgoblin the first; and, though it has been the
subject of much elegy, in our nineteenth century, from Byron,
Goethe, and other poets of less fame, not to mention many
distinguished private observers,—I confess it is not very affecting to my imagination; for it seems to concern the shat-
tering of baby-houses and crockery-shops. What flutters the
church of Rome, or of England, or of Geneva, or of Boston,
may yet be very far from touching any principle of faith. I
think that the intellect and moral sentiment are unanimous;
and that, though philosophy extirpates bugbears, yet it supplies the natural checks of vice, and polarity to the soul. I
think that the wiser a man is, the more stupendous he finds

the natural and moral economy, and lifts himself to a more absolute reliance.

There is the power of moods, each setting at nought all but its own tissue of facts and beliefs. There is the power of complexions, obviously modifying the dispositions and sentiments. The beliefs and unbeliefs appear to be structural; and, as soon as each man attains the poise and vivacity which allow the whole machinery to play, he will not need extreme examples, but will rapidly alternate all opinions in his own life. Our life is March weather, savage and serene in one hour. We go forth austere, dedicated, believing in the iron links of Destiny, and will not turn on our heel to save our life: but a book, or a bust, or only the sound of a name, shoots a spark through the nerves, and we suddenly believe in will: my finger-ring shall be the seal of Solomon: fate is for imbeciles: all is possible to the resolved mind. Presently, a new experience gives a new turn to our thoughts: common sense resumes its tyranny: we say, 'Well, the army, after all, is the gate to fame, manners, and poetry: and, look you,—on the whole, selfishness plants best, prunes best, makes the best commerce, and the best citizen.' Are the opinions of a man on right and wrong, on fate and causation, at the mercy of a broken sleep or an indigestion? Is his belief in God and Duty no deeper than a stomach evidence? And what guaranty for the permanence of his opinions? I like not the French celerity,—a new church and state once a week.—This is the second negation; and I shall let it pass for what it will. As far as it asserts rotation of states of mind, I suppose it suggests its own remedy, namely, in the record of larger periods. What is the mean of many states; of all the states? Does the general voice of ages affirm any principle, or is no community of sentiment discoverable in distant times and places? And when it shows the power of self-interest, I accept that as part of the divine law, and must reconcile it with aspiration the best I can.

The word Fate, or Destiny, expresses the sense of mankind, in all ages,—that the laws of the world do not always befriend, but often hurt and crush us. Fate, in the shape of *Kinde* or nature, grows over us like grass. We paint Time with a scythe; Love and Fortune, blind; and Destiny, deaf. We have too little power of resistance against this ferocity which champs us up. What front can we make against these unavoidable, victorious, maleficent forces? What can I do against the influence of Race, in my history? What can I do against hereditary and constitutional habits, against scrofula, lymph, impotence? against climate, against barbarism, in my country? I can reason down or deny every thing, except this perpetual Belly: feed he must and will, and I cannot make him respectable.

But the main resistance which the affirmative impulse finds, and one including all others, is in the doctrine of the Illusionists. There is a painful rumor in circulation, that we have been practised upon in all the principal performances of life, and free agency is the emptiest name. We have been sopped and drugged with the air, with food, with woman, with children, with sciences, with events, which leave us exactly where they found us. The mathematics, 'tis complained, leave the mind where they find it: so do all sciences; and so do all events and actions. I find a man who has passed through all the sciences, the churl he was; and, through all the offices, learned, civil, and social, can detect the child. We are not the less necessitated to dedicate life to them. In fact, we may come to accept it as the fixed rule and theory of our state of education, that God is a substance, and his method is illusion. The eastern sages owned the goddess Yoganidra, the great illusory energy of Vishnu, by whom, as utter ignorance, the whole world is beguiled.

Or, shall I state it thus?—The astonishment of life, is, the absence of any appearance of reconciliation between the theory and practice of life. Reason, the prized reality, the Law, is apprehended, now and then, for a serene and profound moment, amidst the hubbub of cares and works which have no direct bearing on it;—is then lost, for months or years, and again found, for an interval, to be lost again. If we compute it in time, we may, in fifty years, have half a dozen reasonable hours. But what are these cares and works the better? A method in the world we do not see, but this parallelism of great and little, which never react on each other, nor discover the smallest tendency to converge. Experiences, fortunes, governings, readings, writings, are nothing to the purpose; as when a man comes into the room, it does not appear whether he has been fed on yams or buffalo,—he has contrived to get so much bone and fibre as he wants, out of rice or out of snow. So vast is the disproportion between the sky of law and the pismire of performance under it, that, whether he is a man of worth or a sot, is not so great a matter as we say. Shall I add, as one juggle of this enchantment, the stunning non-intercourse law which makes coöperation impossible? The young spirit pants to enter society. But all the ways of culture and greatness lead to solitary imprisonment. He has been often baulked. He did not expect a sympathy with his thought from the village, but he went with it to the chosen and intelligent, and found no entertainment for it, but mere misapprehension, distaste, and scoffing. Men are strangely mistimed and misapplied; and the excellence of each is an inflamed individualism which separates him more.

There are these, and more than these diseases of thought, which our ordinary teachers do not attempt to remove. Now shall we, because a good nature inclines us to virtue's side, say, There are no doubts,—and lie for the right? Is life to be led in a brave or in a cowardly manner? and is not the satisfaction of the doubts essential to all manliness? Is the name of virtue to be a barrier to that which is virtue? Can you not believe that a man of earnest and burly habit may find small good in tea, essays, and catechism, and want a rougher instruction, want men, labor, trade, farming, war, hunger, plenty, love, hatred, doubt, and terror, to make things plain to him; and has he not a right to insist on being convinced in his own way? When he is convinced, he will be worth the pains.

Belief consists in accepting the affirmations of the soul; unbelief, in denying them. Some minds are incapable of skepticism. The doubts they profess to entertain are rather a civility or accommodation to the common discourse of their company. They may well give themselves leave to speculate, for they are secure of a return. Once admitted to the heaven of thought, they see no relapse into night, but infinite invitation on the other side. Heaven is within heaven, and sky over sky, and they are encompassed with divinities. Others there are, to whom the heaven is brass, and it shuts down to the surface of the earth. It is a question of temperament, or of more or less immersion in nature. The last class must needs have a reflex or parasite faith; not a sight of realities, but an instinctive reliance on the seers and believers of realities. The manners and thoughts of believers astonish them, and convince them that these have seen something which is hid from themselves. But their sensual habit would fix the believer to his last position, whilst he as inevitably advances; and presently the unbeliever, for love of belief, burns the believer.

Great believers are always reckoned infidels, impracticable, fantastic, atheistic, and really men of no account. The spiritualist finds himself driven to express his faith by a series of skepticisms. Charitable souls come with their projects, and ask his coöperation. How can he hesitate? It is the rule of mere comity and courtesy to agree where you can, and to turn your sentence with something auspicious, and not freezing and sinister. But he is forced to say, 'O, these things will be as they must be: what can you do? These particular griefs and crimes are the foliage and fruit of such trees as we see growing. It is vain to complain of the leaf or the berry: cut it off; it will bear another just as bad. You must begin your cure lower down.' The generosities of the day prove an intractable element for him. The people's questions are not his; their methods are not his; and, against all the dictates of good nature, he is driven to say, he has no pleasure in them.

Even the doctrines dear to the hope of man, of the divine Providence, and of the immortality of the soul, his neighbors can not put the statement so that he shall affirm it. But he denies out of more faith, and not less. He denies out of honesty. He had rather stand charged with the imbecility of skepticism, than with untruth. I believe, he says, in the moral design of the universe; it exists hospitably for the weal of souls; but your dogmas seem to me caricatures: why should I make believe them? Will any say, this is cold and infidel? The wise and magnanimous will not say so. They will exult in his far-sighted good-will, that can abandon to the adversary all the ground of tradition and common belief, without losing a jot of strength. It sees to the end of all transgression. George Fox saw "that there was an ocean of darkness and death; but withal, an infinite ocean of light and love which flowed over that of darkness."

The final solution in which skepticism is lost, is, in the moral sentiment, which never forfeits its supremacy. All moods may be safely tried, and their weight allowed to all objections: the moral sentiment as easily outweighs them all, as any one. This is the drop which balances the sea. I play with the miscellany of facts, and take those superficial views which we call skepticism; but I know that they will presently appear to me in that order which makes skepticism impossible. A man of thought must feel the thought that is parent of the universe: that the masses of nature do undulate and flow.

This faith avails to the whole emergency of life and objects. The world is saturated with deity and with law. He is content with just and unjust, with sots and fools, with the triumph of folly and fraud. He can behold with serenity the yawning gulf between the ambition of man and his power of performance, between the demand and supply of power, which makes the tragedy of all souls.

Charles Fourier announced that "the attractions of man are proportioned to his destinies;" in other words, that every desire predicts its own satisfaction. Yet, all experience exhibits the reverse of this; the incompetency of power is the universal grief of young and ardent minds. They accuse the divine providence of a certain parsimony. It has shown the heaven and earth to every child, and filled him with a desire for the whole; a desire raging, infinite; a hunger, as of space to be filled with planets; a cry of famine, as of devils for souls. Then for the satisfaction,—to each man is administered a single drop, a bead of dew of vital power, *per day*,—a cup as large as space, and one drop of the water of life in it. Each man woke in the morning, with an appetite that could eat the solar system like a cake; a spirit for action and passion without bounds; he could lay his hand on the morning star: he could try conclusions with gravitation or chemistry; but, on the first motion to prove his strength,—hands, feet, senses, gave way, and would not serve him. He was an emperor deserted by his states, and left to whistle by himself, or thrust into a mob of emperors, all whistling: and still the sirens sang, "The attractions are proportioned to the destinies." In every house, in the heart of each maiden, and of each boy, in the soul of the soaring saint, this chasm is found,—between the largest promise of ideal power, and the shabby experience.

The expansive nature of truth comes to our succor, elastic, not to be surrounded. Man helps himself by larger generalizations. The lesson of life is practically to generalize; to believe what the years and the centuries say against the hours; to resist the usurpation of particulars; to penetrate to their catholic sense. Things seem to say one thing, and say the reverse. The appearance is immoral; the result is moral. Things seem to tend downward, to justify despondency, to promote rogues, to defeat the just; and, by knaves, as by martyrs, the just cause is carried forward. Although knaves win in every political struggle, although society seems to be delivered over from the hands of one set of criminals into the hands of another set of criminals, as fast as the government is changed, and the march of civilization is a train of felonies, yet, general ends are somehow answered. We see, now, events forced on, which seem to retard or retrograde the civility of ages. But the world-spirit is a good swimmer, and storms and waves can not drown him. He snaps his finger at laws: and so, throughout history, heaven seems to affect low and poor means. Through the years and the centuries, through evil agents, through toys and atoms, a great and beneficent tendency irresistibly streams.

Let a man learn to look for the permanent in the mutable and fleeting; let him learn to bear the disappearance of things he was wont to reverence, without losing his reverence; let him learn that he is here, not to work, but to be worked upon; and that, though abyss open under abyss, and opinion displace opinion, all are at last contained in the Eternal Cause.—

"If my bark sink, 'tis to another sea."

V

Shakspeare; or, the Poet

GREAT MEN are more distinguished by range and extent, than by originality. If we require the originality which consists in weaving, like a spider, their web from their own bowels; in finding clay, and making bricks, and building the house; no great men are original. Nor does valuable originality consist in unlikeness to other men. The hero is in the press of knights, and the thick of events; and, seeing what men want, and sharing their desire, he adds the needful length of sight and of arm, to come at the desired point. The greatest genius is the most indebted man. A poet is no rattlebrain, saying what comes uppermost, and, because he says every thing, saying, at last, something good; but a heart in unison with his time and country. There is nothing whimsical and fantastic in his production, but sweet and sad earnest, freighted with the weightiest convictions, and pointed with the most determined aim which any man or class knows of in his times.

The Genius of our life is jealous of individuals, and will not have any individual great, except through the general. There is no choice to genius. A great man does not wake up on some fine morning, and say, 'I am full of life, I will go to sea, and find an Antarctic continent: to-day I will square the circle: I will ransack botany, and find a new food for man: I have a new architecture in my mind: I foresee a new mechanic power:' no, but he finds himself in the river of the thoughts and events, forced onward by the ideas and necessities of his contemporaries. He stands where all the eyes of men look one way, and their hands all point in the direction in which he should go. The church has reared him amidst rites and pomps, and he carries out the advice which her music gave him, and builds a cathedral needed by her chants and processions. He finds a war raging: it educates him, by trumpet, in barracks, and he betters the instruction. He finds two counties groping to bring coal, or flour, or fish, from the place of production to the place of consumption, and he hits on a railroad. Every master has found his materials collected, and his power lay in his sympathy with his people, and in his love of the materials he wrought in. What an economy of power! and what a compensation for the shortness of life! All is done to his hand. The world has brought him thus far on his way. The human race has gone out before him, sunk the hills, filled the hollows, and bridged the rivers. Men, nations, poets, artisans, women, all have worked for him, and he enters into their labors. Choose any other thing, out of the line of tendency, out of the national feeling and history, and he would have all to do for himself: his powers would be expended in the first preparations. Great genial power, one would almost say, consists in not being original at all; in being altogether receptive; in letting the world do all, and suffering the spirit of the hour to pass unobstructed through the mind.

Shakspeare's youth fell in a time when the English people were importunate for dramatic entertainments. The court took offence easily at political allusions, and attempted to suppress them. The Puritans, a growing and energetic party, and the religious among the Anglican church, would suppress them. But the people wanted them. Inn-yards, houses without roofs, and extemporaneous enclosures at country fairs, were the ready theatres of strolling players. The people had tasted this new joy; and, as we could not hope to suppress newspapers now,—no, not by the strongest party,—neither then could king, prelate, or puritan, alone or united, suppress an organ, which was ballad, epic, newspaper, caucus, lecture, punch, and library, at the same time. Probably king, prelate, and puritan, all found their own account in it. It had become, by all causes, a national interest,—by no means conspicuous, so that some great scholar would have thought of treating it in an English history,—but not a whit less considerable, because it was cheap, and of no account, like a baker's-shop. The best proof of its vitality is the crowd of writers which suddenly broke into this field; Kyd, Marlow, Greene, Jonson, Chapman, Dekker, Webster, Heywood, Middleton, Peele, Ford, Massinger, Beaumont, and Fletcher.

The secure possession, by the stage, of the public mind, is of the first importance to the poet who works for it. He loses no time in idle experiments. Here is audience and expectation prepared. In the case of Shakspeare there is much more. At the time when he left Stratford, and went up to London, a great body of stage-plays, of all dates and writers, existed in manuscript, and were in turn produced on the boards. Here is the Tale of Troy, which the audience will bear hearing some part of every week; the Death of Julius Cæsar, and other stories out of Plutarch, which they never tire of; a shelf full of English history, from the chronicles of Brut and Arthur, down to the royal Henries, which men hear eagerly; and a string of doleful tragedies, merry Italian tales, and Spanish voyages, which all the London prentices know. All the mass has been treated, with more or less skill, by every playwright, and the prompter has the soiled and tattered manuscripts. It is now no longer possible to say who wrote them first. They have been the property of the Theatre so long, and so many rising geniuses have enlarged or altered them, inserting a speech, or a whole scene, or adding a song, that no man can any longer claim copyright on this work of numbers. Happily, no man wishes to. They are not yet desired in that way. We have few readers, many spectators and hearers. They had best lie where they are.

Shakspeare, in common with his comrades, esteemed the mass of old plays, waste stock, in which any experiment could be freely tried. Had the *prestige* which hedges about a modern tragedy existed, nothing could have been done. The rude warm blood of the living England circulated in the play, as in street-ballads, and gave body which he wanted to his airy and majestic fancy. The poet needs a ground in popular tradition on which he may work, and which, again, may restrain his art within the due temperance. It holds him to the people, supplies a foundation for his edifice; and, in furnishing so much work done to his hand, leaves him at leisure, and in full strength for the audacities of his imagination. In short, the poet owes to his legend what sculpture owed to the temple. Sculpture in Egypt, and in Greece, grew up in subordination to architecture. It was the ornament of the temple wall: at first, a rude relief carved on pediments, then the relief became bolder, and a head or arm was projected from the wall, the groups being still arranged with reference to the building, which serves also as a frame to hold the figures; and when, at last, the greatest freedom of style and treatment was reached, the prevailing genius of architecture still enforced a certain calmness and continence in the statue. As soon as the statue was begun for itself, and with no reference to the temple or palace, the art began to decline: freak, extravagance, and exhibition, took the place of the old temperance. This balance-wheel, which the sculptor found in architecture, the perilous irritability of poetic talent found in the accumulated dramatic materials to which the people were already wonted, and which had a certain excellence which no single genius, however extraordinary, could hope to create.

In point of fact, it appears that Shakspeare did owe debts in all directions, and was able to use whatever he found; and the amount of indebtedness may be inferred from Malone's laborious computations in regard to the First, Second, and Third parts of Henry VI., in which, "out of 6043 lines, 1771 were written by some author preceding Shakspeare; 2373 by him, on the foundation laid by his predecessors; and 1899 were entirely his own." And the proceeding investigation hardly leaves a single drama of his absolute invention. Malone's sentence is an important piece of external history. In Henry VIII., I think I see plainly the cropping out of the original rock on which his own finer stratum was laid. The first play was written by a superior, thoughtful man, with a vicious ear. I can mark his lines, and know well their cadence. See Wolsey's soliloquy, and the following scene with Cromwell, where,—instead of the metre of Shakspeare, whose secret is, that the thought constructs the tune, so that reading for the sense will best bring out the rhythm,—here the lines are constructed on a given tune, and the verse has even a trace of pulpit eloquence. But the play contains, through all its length, unmistakable traits of Shakspeare's hand, and some passages, as the account of the coronation, are like autographs. What is odd, the compliment to Queen Elizabeth is in the bad rhythm.

Shakspeare knew that tradition supplies a better fable than any invention can. If he lost any credit of design, he augmented his resources; and, at that day, our petulant demand for originality was not so much pressed. There was no literature for the million. The universal reading, the cheap press, were unknown. A great poet, who appears in illiterate times, absorbs into his sphere all the light which is any where radiating. Every intellectual jewel, every flower of sentiment, it is his fine office to bring to his people; and he comes to value his memory equally with his invention. He is therefore little solicitous whence his thoughts have been derived; whether through translation, whether through tradition, whether by travel in distant countries, whether by inspiration; from whatever source, they are equally welcome to his uncritical audience. Nay, he borrows very near home. Other men say wise things as well as he; only they say a good many foolish things, and do not know when they have spoken wisely. He knows the sparkle of the true stone, and puts it in high place, wherever he finds it. Such is the happy position of Homer, perhaps; of Chaucer, of Saadi. They felt that all wit was their wit. And they are librarians and historiographers, as well as poets. Each romancer was heir and dispenser of all the hundred tales of the world,—

> "Presenting Thebes' and Pelops' line
> And the tale of Troy divine."

The influence of Chaucer is conspicuous in all our early literature; and, more recently, not only Pope and Dryden have been beholden to him, but, in the whole society of English writers, a large unacknowledged debt is easily traced. One is charmed with the opulence which feeds so many pensioners. But Chaucer is a huge borrower. Chaucer, it seems, drew continually, through Lydgate and Caxton, from Guido di Colonna, whose Latin romance of the Trojan war was in turn a compilation from Dares Phrygius, Ovid, and Statius. Then Petrarch, Boccaccio, and the Provençal poets, are his benefactors: the Romaunt of the Rose is only judicious translation from William of Lorris and John of Meun: Troilus and Creseide, from Lollius of Urbino: The Cock and the Fox, from the *Lais* of Marie: The House of Fame, from the French or Italian: and poor Gower he uses as if he were only a brick-kiln or stone-quarry, out of which to build his house. He steals by this apology,—that what he takes has no worth where he finds it, and the greatest where he leaves it. It has come to be practically a sort of rule in literature, that a man, having once shown himself capable of original writing, is entitled thenceforth to steal from the writings of others at discretion. Thought is the property of him who can entertain it; and of him who can adequately place it. A certain awkwardness marks the use of borrowed thoughts; but, as soon as we have learned what to do with them, they become our own.

Thus, all originality is relative. Every thinker is retrospective. The learned member of the legislature, at Westminster, or at Washington, speaks and votes for thousands. Show us the constituency, and the now invisible channels by which the senator is made aware of their wishes, the crowd of practical and knowing men, who, by correspondence or conversation, are feeding him with evidence, anecdotes, and estimates, and it will bereave his fine attitude and resistance of something of their impressiveness. As Sir Robert Peel and Mr. Webster vote, so Locke and Rousseau think for thousands; and so there were fountains all around Homer, Menu, Saadi, or Milton, from which they drew; friends, lovers, books, traditions, proverbs,—all perished,—which, if seen, would go to reduce the wonder. Did the bard speak with authority? Did he feel himself overmatched by any companion? The appeal is to the consciousness of the writer. Is there at last in his breast a Delphi whereof to ask concerning any thought or thing, whether it be verily so, yea or nay? and to have answer, and to rely on that? All the debts which such a man could contract to other wit, would never disturb his consciousness of originality: for the ministrations of books, and of other minds, are a whiff of smoke to that most private reality with which he has conversed.

It is easy to see that what is best written or done by genius, in the world, was no man's work, but came by wide social labor, when a thousand wrought like one, sharing the same impulse. Our English Bible is a wonderful specimen of the strength and music of the English language. But it was not made by one man, or at one time; but centuries and churches brought it to perfection. There never was a time when there was not some translation existing. The Liturgy, admired for its energy and pathos, is an anthology of the piety of ages and nations, a translation of the prayers and forms of the Catholic church,—these collected, too, in long periods, from the prayers and meditations of every saint and sacred writer, all over the world. Grotius makes the like remark in respect to the Lord's Prayer, that the single clauses of which it is composed were already in use, in the time of Christ, in the rabbinical forms. He picked out the grains of gold. The nervous language of the Common Law, the impressive forms of our courts, and the precision and substantial truth of the legal distinctions, are the contribution of all the sharp-sighted, strong-minded men who have lived in the countries where these laws govern. The translation of Plutarch gets its excellence by being translation on translation. There never was a time when there was none. All the truly idiomatic and national phrases are kept, and all others successively picked out, and thrown away. Something like the same process had gone on, long before, with the originals of these books. The world takes liberties with world-books. Vedas, Æsop's Fables, Pilpay, Arabian Nights, Cid, Iliad, Robin Hood, Scottish Minstrelsy, are not the work of single men. In the composition of such works, the time thinks, the market thinks, the mason, the carpenter, the merchant, the farmer, the fop, all think for us. Every book supplies its time with one good word; every municipal law, every trade, every folly of the day, and the generic catholic genius who is not afraid or ashamed to owe his originality to the originality of all, stands with the next age as the recorder and embodiment of his own.

We have to thank the researches of antiquaries, and the Shakspeare Society, for ascertaining the steps of the English drama, from the Mysteries celebrated in churches and by churchmen, and the final detachment from the church, and the completion of secular plays, from Ferrex and Porrex, and Gammer Gurton's Needle, down to the possession of the stage by the very pieces which Shakspeare altered, remodelled, and finally made his own. Elated with success, and piqued by the growing interest of the problem, they have left no book-stall unsearched, no chest in a garret unopened, no file of old yellow accounts to decompose in damp and worms, so keen was the hope to discover whether the boy Shakspeare poached or not, whether he held horses at the theatre door, whether he kept school, and why he left in his will only his second-best bed to Ann Hathaway, his wife.

There is somewhat touching in the madness with which the passing age mischooses the object on which all candles shine, and all eyes are turned; the care with which it registers every trifle touching Queen Elizabeth, and King James, and the Essexes, Leicesters, Burleighs, and Buckinghams; and lets pass without a single valuable note the founder of another dynasty, which alone will cause the Tudor dynasty to be remembered,—the man who carries the Saxon race in him by the inspiration which feeds him, and on whose thoughts the foremost people of the world are now for some ages to be nourished, and minds to receive this and not another bias. A popular player,—nobody suspected he was the poet of the human race; and the secret was kept as faithfully from poets and intellectual men, as from courtiers and frivolous people. Bacon, who took the inventory of the human understanding for his times, never mentioned his name. Ben Jonson, though we have strained his few words of regard and panegyric, had no suspicion of the elastic fame whose first vibrations he was attempting. He no doubt thought the praise he has conceded to him generous, and esteemed himself, out of all question, the better poet of the two.

If it need wit to know wit, according to the proverb, Shakspeare's time should be capable of recognizing it. Sir Henry Wotton was born four years after Shakspeare, and died twenty-three years after him; and I find, among his correspondents and acquaintances, the following persons: Theodore Beza, Isaac Casaubon, Sir Philip Sidney, Earl of Essex, Lord Bacon, Sir Walter Raleigh, John Milton, Sir Henry Vane, Isaac Walton, Dr. Donne, Abraham Cowley, Bellarmine, Charles Cotton, John Pym, John Hales, Kepler, Vieta, Albericus Gentilis, Paul Sarpi, Arminius; with all of whom exists some token of his having communicated, without enumerating many others, whom doubtless he saw,—Shakspeare, Spenser, Jonson, Beaumont, Massinger, two Herberts, Marlow, Chapman, and the rest. Since the constellation of great men who appeared in Greece in the time of Pericles, there was never any such society;—yet their genius failed them to find out the best head in the universe. Our poet's mask was impenetrable. You cannot see the mountain near. It took a century to make it suspected; and not until two centuries had passed, after his death, did any criticism which we think adequate begin to appear. It was not possible to write the history of Shakspeare till now; for he is the father of German literature: it was on the introduction of Shakspeare into German, by Lessing, and the translation of his works by Wieland and Schlegel, that the rapid burst of German literature was most intimately connected. It was not until the nineteenth century, whose speculative genius is a sort of living Hamlet, that the tragedy of Hamlet could find such wondering readers. Now, literature, philosophy, and thought, are Shakspearized. His mind is the horizon beyond which, at present, we do not see. Our ears are educated to music by his rhythm. Coleridge and Goethe are the only critics who have expressed our convictions with any adequate fidelity: but there is in all cultivated minds a silent appreciation of his superlative power and beauty, which, like Christianity, qualifies the period.

The Shakspeare Society have inquired in all directions, advertised the missing facts, offered money for any information that will lead to proof; and with what result? Beside some important illustration of the history of the English stage, to which I have adverted, they have gleaned a few facts touching the property, and dealings in regard to property, of the poet. It appears that, from year to year, he owned a larger share in the Blackfriars' Theatre: its wardrobe and other appurtenances were his: that he bought an estate in his native village, with his earnings, as writer and shareholder; that he lived in the best house in Stratford; was intrusted by his neighbors with their commissions in London, as of borrowing money, and the like; that he was a veritable farmer. About the time when he was writing Macbeth, he sues Philip Rogers, in the borough-court of Stratford, for thirty-five shillings, ten pence, for corn delivered to him at different times; and, in all respects, appears as a good husband, with no reputation for eccentricity or excess. He was a good-natured sort of man, an actor and shareholder in the theatre, not in any striking manner distinguished from other actors and managers. I admit the importance of this information. It was well worth the pains that have been taken to procure it.

But whatever scraps of information concerning his condition these researches may have rescued, they can shed no light upon that infinite invention which is the concealed magnet of his attraction for us. We are very clumsy writers of history. We tell the chronicle of parentage, birth, birth-place, schooling, school-mates, earning of money, marriage, publication of books, celebrity, death; and when we have come to an end of this gossip, no ray of relation appears between it and the goddess-born; and it seems as if, had we dipped at random into the "Modern Plutarch," and read any other life there, it would have fitted the poems as well. It is the essence of poetry to spring, like the rainbow daughter of Wonder, from the invisible, to abolish the past, and refuse all history. Malone, Warburton, Dyce, and Collier, have wasted their oil. The famed theatres, Covent Garden, Drury Lane, the Park, and Tremont, have vainly assisted. Betterton, Garrick, Kemble, Kean, and Macready, dedicate their lives to this genius; him they crown, elucidate, obey, and express. The genius knows them not. The recitation begins; one golden word leaps out immortal from all this painted pedantry, and sweetly torments us with invitations to its own inaccessible homes. I remember, I went once to see the Hamlet of a famed performer, the pride of the English stage; and all I then heard, and all I now remember, of the tragedian, was that in which the tragedian had no part; simply, Hamlet's question to the ghost,—

> "What may this mean,
> That thou, dead corse, again in complete steel
> Revisit'st thus the glimpses of the moon?"

That imagination which dilates the closet he writes in to the world's dimension, crowds it with agents in rank and order, as quickly reduces the big reality to be the glimpses of the moon. These tricks of his magic spoil for us the illusions of the green-room. Can any biography shed light on the localities into which the Midsummer Night's Dream admits me? Did Shakspeare confide to any notary or parish recorder, sacristan, or surrogate, in Stratford, the genesis of that delicate creation? The forest of Arden, the nimble air of Scone Castle, the moonlight of Portia's villa, "the antres vast and desarts idle," of Othello's captivity,—where is the third cousin, or grand-nephew, the chancellor's file of accounts, or private letter, that has kept one word of those transcendent secrets? In fine, in this drama, as in all great works of art,—in the Cyclopæan architecture of Egypt and India; in the Phidian sculpture; the Gothic ministers; the Italian painting; the Ballads of Spain and Scotland,—the Genius draws up the ladder after him, when the creative age goes up to heaven, and gives way to a new, who see the works, and ask in vain for a history.

Shakspeare is the only biographer of Shakspeare; and even he can tell nothing, except to the Shakspeare in us; that is, to our most apprehensive and sympathetic hour. He cannot step from off his tripod, and give us anecdotes of his inspirations. Read the antique documents extricated, analyzed, and compared, by the assiduous Dyce and Collier; and now read one of those skiey sentences,—aerolites,—which seem to have fallen out of heaven, and which, not your experience, but the man within the breast, has accepted as words of fate; and tell me if they match; if the former account in any manner for the latter; or, which gives the most historical insight into the man.

Hence, though our external history is so meagre, yet, with Shakspeare for biographer, instead of Aubrey and Rowe, we have really the information which is material, that which describes character and fortune, that which, if we were about to meet the man and deal with him, would most import us to know. We have his recorded convictions on those questions which knock for answer at every heart,—on life and death, on love, on wealth and poverty, on the prizes of life, and the ways whereby we come at them; on the characters of men, and the influences, occult and open, which affect their fortunes; and on those mysterious and demoniacal powers which defy our science, and which yet interweave their malice and their gift in our brightest hours. Who ever read the volume of the Sonnets, without finding that the poet had there revealed, under masks that are no masks to the intelligent, the

lore of friendship and of love; the confusion of sentiments in
the most susceptible, and, at the same time, the most intellectual of men? What trait of his private mind has he hidden in
his dramas? One can discern, in his ample pictures of the gentleman and the king, what forms and humanities pleased him;
his delight in troops of friends, in large hospitality, in cheerful
giving. Let Timon, let Warwick, let Antonio the merchant,
answer for his great heart. So far from Shakspeare's being the
least known, he is the one person, in all modern history,
known to us. What point of morals, of manners, of economy,
of philosophy, of religion, of taste, of the conduct of life, has
he not settled? What mystery has he not signified his knowledge of? What office, or function, or district of man's work,
has he not remembered? What king has he not taught state,
as Talma taught Napoleon? What maiden has not found him
finer than her delicacy? What lover has he not outloved? What
sage has he not outseen? What gentleman has he not instructed in the rudeness of his behavior?

Some able and appreciating critics think no criticism on
Shakspeare valuable, that does not rest purely on the dramatic
merit; that he is falsely judged as poet and philosopher. I
think as highly as these critics of his dramatic merit, but still
think it secondary. He was a full man, who liked to talk; a
brain exhaling thoughts and images, which, seeking vent,
found the drama next at hand. Had he been less, we should
have had to consider how well he filled his place, how good
a dramatist he was,—and he is the best in the world. But it
turns out, that what he has to say is of that weight, as to
withdraw some attention from the vehicle; and he is like some
saint whose history is to be rendered into all languages, into
verse and prose, into songs and pictures, and cut up into
proverbs; so that the occasion which gave the saint's meaning
the form of a conversation, or of a prayer, or of a code of
laws, is immaterial, compared with the universality of its application. So it fares with the wise Shakspeare and his book
of life. He wrote the airs for all our modern music: he wrote
the text of modern life; the text of manners: he drew the man
of England and Europe; the father of the man in America: he
drew the man, and described the day, and what is done in it:
he read the hearts of men and women, their probity, and their

second thought, and wiles; the wiles of innocence, and the transitions by which virtues and vices slide into their contraries: he could divide the mother's part from the father's part in the face of the child, or draw the fine demarcations of freedom and of fate: he knew the laws of repression which make the police of nature: and all the sweets and all the terrors of human lot lay in his mind as truly but as softly as the landscape lies on the eye. And the importance of this wisdom of life sinks the form, as of Drama or Epic, out of notice. 'Tis like making a question concerning the paper on which a king's message is written.

Shakspeare is as much out of the category of eminent authors, as he is out of the crowd. He is inconceivably wise; the others, conceivably. A good reader can, in a sort, nestle into Plato's brain, and think from thence; but not into Shakspeare's. We are still out of doors. For executive faculty, for creation, Shakspeare is unique. No man can imagine it better. He was the farthest reach of subtlety compatible with an individual self,—the subtilest of authors, and only just within the possibility of authorship. With this wisdom of life, is the equal endowment of imaginative and of lyric power. He clothed the creatures of his legend with form and sentiments, as if they were people who had lived under his roof; and few real men have left such distinct characters as these fictions. And they spoke in language as sweet as it was fit. Yet his talents never seduced him into an ostentation, nor did he harp on one string. An omnipresent humanity coördinates all his faculties. Give a man of talents a story to tell, and his partiality will presently appear. He has certain observations, opinions, topics, which have some accidental prominence, and which he disposes all to exhibit. He crams this part, and starves that other part, consulting not the fitness of the thing, but his fitness and strength. But Shakspeare has no peculiarity, no importunate topic; but all is duly given; no veins, no curiosities: no cow-painter, no bird-fancier, no mannerist is he: he has no discoverable egotism: the great he tells greatly; the small, subordinately. He is wise without emphasis or assertion; he is strong, as nature is strong, who lifts the land into mountain slopes without effort, and by the same rule as she floats a bubble in the air, and likes as well to do the one as the other. This makes that equality of power in farce, tragedy, narrative, and love-songs; a merit so incessant, that each reader is incredulous of the perception of other readers.

This power of expression, or of transferring the inmost truth of things into music and verse, makes him the type of the poet, and has added a new problem to metaphysics. This is that which throws him into natural history, as a main production of the globe, and as announcing new eras and ameliorations. Things were mirrored in his poetry without loss or blur: he could paint the fine with precision, the great with compass; the tragic and the comic indifferently, and without any distortion or favor. He carried his powerful execution into minute details, to a hair point; finishes an eyelash or a dimple as firmly as he draws a mountain; and yet these, like nature's, will bear the scrutiny of the solar microscope.

In short, he is the chief example to prove that more or less of production, more or fewer pictures, is a thing indifferent. He had the power to make one picture. Daguerre learned how to let one flower etch its image on his plate of iodine; and then proceeds at leisure to etch a million. There are always objects; but there was never representation. Here is perfect representation, at last; and now let the world of figures sit for their portraits. No recipe can be given for the making of a Shakspeare; but the possibility of the translation of things into song is demonstrated.

His lyric power lies in the genius of the piece. The sonnets, though their excellence is lost in the splendor of the dramas, are as inimitable as they: and it is not a merit of lines, but a total merit of the piece; like the tone of voice of some incomparable person, so is this a speech of poetic beings, and any clause as unproducible now as a whole poem.

Though the speeches in the plays, and single lines, have a beauty which tempts the ear to pause on them for their euphuism, yet the sentence is so loaded with meaning, and so linked with its foregoers and followers, that the logician is satisfied. His means are as admirable as his ends; every subordinate invention, by which he helps himself to connect some irreconcilable opposites, is a poem too. He is not reduced to dismount and walk, because his horses are running off with him in some distant direction: he always rides.

The finest poetry was first experience: but the thought has suffered a transformation since it was an experience. Cultivated men often attain a good degree of skill in writing verses; but it is easy to read, through their poems, their personal history: any one acquainted with parties can name every figure: this is Andrew, and that is Rachel. The sense thus remains prosaic. It is a caterpillar with wings, and not yet a butterfly. In the poet's mind, the fact has gone quite over into the new element of thought, and has lost all that is exuvial. This generosity abides with Shakspeare. We say, from the truth and closeness of his pictures, that he knows the lesson by heart. Yet there is not a trace of egotism.

One more royal trait properly belongs to the poet. I mean his cheerfulness, without which no man can be a poet,—for beauty is his aim. He loves virtue, not for its obligation, but for its grace: he delights in the world, in man, in woman, for the lovely light that sparkles from them. Beauty, the spirit of joy and hilarity, he sheds over the universe. Epicurus relates, that poetry hath such charms that a lover might forsake his mistress to partake of them. And the true bards have been noted for their firm and cheerful temper. Homer lies in sunshine; Chaucer is glad and erect; and Saadi says, "It was rumored abroad that I was penitent; but what had I to do with repentance?" Not less sovereign and cheerful,—much more sovereign and cheerful, is the tone of Shakspeare. His name suggests joy and emancipation to the heart of men. If he should appear in any company of human souls, who would not march in his troop? He touches nothing that does not borrow health and longevity from his festal style.

And now, how stands the account of man with this bard and benefactor, when in solitude, shutting our ears to the reverberations of his fame, we seek to strike the balance? Solitude has austere lessons; it can teach us to spare both heroes and poets; and it weighs Shakspeare also, and finds him to share the halfness and imperfection of humanity.

Shakspeare, Homer, Dante, Chaucer, saw the splendor of meaning that plays over the visible world; knew that a tree had another use than for apples, and corn another than for meal, and the ball of the earth, than for tillage and roads: that these things bore a second and finer harvest to the mind, being emblems of its thoughts, and conveying in all their natural history a certain mute commentary on human life. Shakspeare employed them as colors to compose his picture. He rested in their beauty; and never took the step which seemed inevitable to such genius, namely, to explore the virtue which resides in these symbols, and imparts this power,—what is that which they themselves say? He converted the elements, which waited on his command, into entertainments. He was master of the revels to mankind. Is it not as if one should have, through majestic powers of science, the comets given into his hand, or the planets and their moons, and should draw them from their orbits to glare with the municipal fireworks on a holiday night, and advertise in all towns, "very superior pyrotechny this evening!" Are the agents of nature, and the power to understand them, worth no more than a street serenade, or the breath of a cigar? One remembers again the trumpet-text in the Koran,—"The heavens and the earth, and all that is between them, think ye we have created them in jest?" As long as the question is of talent and mental power, the world of men has not his equal to show. But when the question is to life, and its materials, and its auxiliaries, how does he profit me? What does it signify? It is but a Twelfth Night, or Midsummer-Night's Dream, or a Winter Evening's Tale: what signifies another picture more or less? The Egyptian verdict of the Shakspeare Societies comes to mind, that he was a jovial actor and manager. I can not marry this fact to his verse. Other admirable men have led lives in some sort of keeping with their thought; but this man, in wide contrast. Had he been less, had he reached only the common measure of great authors, of Bacon, Milton, Tasso, Cervantes, we might leave the fact in the twilight of human fate: but, that this man of men, he who gave to the science of mind a new and larger subject than had ever existed, and planted the standard of humanity some furlongs forward into Chaos,—that he should not be wise for himself,—it must even go into the world's history, that the best poet led an obscure and profane life, using his genius for the public amusement.

Well, other men, priest and prophet, Israelite, German, and

Swede, beheld the same objects: they also saw through them that which was contained. And to what purpose? The beauty straightway vanished; they read commandments, all-excluding mountainous duty; an obligation, a sadness, as of piled mountains, fell on them, and life became ghastly, joyless, a pilgrim's progress, a probation, beleaguered round with doleful histories of Adam's fall and curse, behind us; with doomsdays and purgatorial and penal fires before us; and the heart of the seer and the heart of the listener sank in them.

It must be conceded that these are half-views of half-men. The world still wants its poet-priest, a reconciler, who shall not trifle with Shakspeare the player, nor shall grope in graves with Swedenborg the mourner; but who shall see, speak, and act, with equal inspiration. For knowledge will brighten the sunshine; right is more beautiful than private affection; and love is compatible with universal wisdom.

VI

Napoleon; or, the Man of the World

Among the eminent persons of the nineteenth century, Bonaparte is far the best known, and the most powerful; and owes his predominance to the fidelity with which he expresses the tone of thought and belief, the aims of the masses of active and cultivated men. It is Swedenborg's theory, that every organ is made up of homogeneous particles; or, as it is sometimes expressed, every whole is made of similars; that is, the lungs are composed of infinitely small lungs; the liver, of infinitely small livers; the kidney, of little kidneys, &c. Following this analogy, if any man is found to carry with him the power and affections of vast numbers, if Napoleon is France, if Napoleon is Europe, it is because the people whom he sways are little Napoleons.

In our society, there is a standing antagonism between the conservative and the democratic classes; between those who have made their fortunes, and the young and the poor who have fortunes to make; between the interests of dead labor,—that is, the labor of hands long ago still in the grave, which labor is now entombed in money stocks, or in land and buildings owned by idle capitalists,—and the interests of living labor, which seeks to possess itself of land, and buildings, and money stocks. The first class is timid, selfish, illiberal, hating innovation, and continually losing numbers by death. The second class is selfish also, encroaching, bold, self-relying, always outnumbering the other, and recruiting its numbers every hour by births. It desires to keep open every avenue to the competition of all, and to multiply avenues;—the class of business men in America, in England, in France, and throughout Europe; the class of industry and skill. Napoleon is its representative. The instinct of active, brave, able men, throughout the middle class every where, has pointed out Napoleon as the incarnate Democrat. He had their virtues and their vices; above all, he had their spirit or aim. That tendency is material, pointing at a sensual success, and employing the richest and most various means to that end; conversant with mechanical powers, highly intellectual, widely and accurately learned and skilful, but subordinating all intellectual and spiritual forces into means to a material success. To be the rich man, is the end. "God has granted," says the Koran, "to every people a prophet in its own tongue." Paris, and London, and New York, the spirit of commerce, of money, and material power, were also to have their prophet; and Bonaparte was qualified and sent.

Every one of the million readers of anecdotes, or memoirs, or lives of Napoleon, delights in the page, because he studies in it his own history. Napoleon is thoroughly modern, and, at the highest point of his fortunes, has the very spirit of the newspapers. He is no saint,—to use his own word, "no capuchin," and he is no hero, in the high sense. The man in the street finds in him the qualities and powers of other men in the street. He finds him, like himself, by birth a citizen, who, by very intelligible merits, arrived at such a commanding position, that he could indulge all those tastes which the common man possesses, but is obliged to conceal and deny: good society, good books, fast travelling, dress, dinners, servants without number, personal weight, the execution of his ideas, the standing in the attitude of a benefactor to all persons about him, the refined enjoyments of pictures, statues, music, palaces, and conventional honors,—precisely what is agreeable to the heart of every man in the nineteenth century,—this powerful man possessed.

It is true that a man of Napoleon's truth of adaptation to the mind of the masses around him, becomes not merely representative, but actually a monopolizer and usurper of other minds. Thus Mirabeau plagiarized every good thought, every good word, that was spoken in France. Dumont relates, that he sat in the gallery of the Convention, and heard Mirabeau make a speech. It struck Dumont that he could fit it with a peroration, which he wrote in pencil immediately, and showed it to Lord Elgin, who sat by him. Lord Elgin approved it, and Dumont, in the evening, showed it to Mirabeau. Mirabeau read it, pronounced it admirable, and declared he would incorporate it into his harangue, to-morrow, to the Assembly. "It is impossible," said Dumont, "as, unfortunately, I have shown it to Lord Elgin." "If you have shown it to Lord Elgin, and to fifty persons beside, I shall still speak it to-morrow:" and he did speak it, with much effect, at the next day's session. For Mirabeau, with his overpowering personality, felt that these things, which his presence inspired, were as much his own, as if he had said them, and that his adoption of them gave them their weight. Much more absolute and centralizing was the successor to Mirabeau's popularity, and to much more than his predominance in France. Indeed, a man of Napoleon's stamp almost ceases to have a private speech and opinion. He is so largely receptive, and is so placed, that he comes to be a bureau for all the intelligence, wit, and power, of the age and country. He gains the battle; he makes the code; he makes the system of weights and measures; he levels the Alps; he builds the road. All distinguished engineers, savans, statists, report to him: so, likewise, do all good heads in every kind: he adopts the best measures, sets his stamp on them, and not these alone, but on every happy and memorable expression. Every sentence spoken by Napoleon, and every line of his writing, deserves reading, as it is the sense of France.

Bonaparte was the idol of common men, because he had in transcendent degree the qualities and powers of common men. There is a certain satisfaction in coming down to the lowest ground of politics, for we get rid of cant and hypocrisy. Bonaparte wrought, in common with that great class he represented, for power and wealth,—but Bonaparte, specially, without any scruple as to the means. All the sentiments which embarrass men's pursuit of these objects, he set aside. The sentiments were for women and children. Fontanes, in 1804, expressed Napoleon's own sense, when, in behalf of the Senate, he addressed him,—"Sire, the desire of perfection is the worst disease that ever afflicted the human mind." The advocates of liberty, and of progress, are "ideologists;"—a word of contempt often in his mouth;—"Necker is an ideologist:" "Lafayette is an ideologist."

An Italian proverb, too well known, declares that, "if you would succeed, you must not be too good." It is an advantage, within certain limits, to have renounced the dominion of the sentiments of piety, gratitude, and generosity; since, what was an impassable bar to us, and still is to others, becomes a convenient weapon for our purposes; just as the river which was a formidable barrier, winter transforms into the smoothest of roads.

Napoleon renounced, once for all, sentiments and affections, and would help himself with his hands and his head. With him is no miracle, and no magic. He is a worker in brass, in iron, in wood, in earth, in roads, in buildings, in money, and in troops, and a very consistent and wise master-workman. He is never weak and literary, but acts with the solidity and the precision of natural agents. He has not lost his native sense and sympathy with things. Men give way before such a man, as before natural events. To be sure, there are men enough who are immersed in things, as farmers, smiths, sailors, and mechanics generally; and we know how real and solid such men appear in the presence of scholars and grammarians: but these men ordinarily lack the power of arrangement, and are like hands without a head. But Bonaparte superadded to this mineral and animal force, insight and generalization, so that men saw in him combined the natural and the intellectual power, as if the sea and land had taken flesh and begun to cipher. Therefore the land and sea seem to presuppose him. He came unto his own, and they received him. This ciphering operative knows what he is working with, and what is the product. He knew the properties of gold and iron, of wheels and ships, of troops and diplomatists, and required that each should do after its kind.

The art of war was the game in which he exerted his arithmetic. It consisted, according to him, in having always more forces than the enemy, on the point where the enemy is attacked, or where he attacks: and his whole talent is strained by endless manœuvre and evolution, to march always on the enemy at an angle, and destroy his forces in detail. It is obvious that a very small force, skilfully and rapidly manœuvring, so as always to bring two men against one at the point of engagement, will be an over-match for a much larger body of men.

The times, his constitution, and his early circumstances, combined to develop this pattern democrat. He had the virtues of his class, and the conditions for their activity. That common sense, which no sooner respects any end, than it finds the means to effect it; the delight in the use of means; in the choice, simplification, and combining of means; the directness and thoroughness of his work; the prudence with which all was seen, and the energy with which all was done, make him the natural organ and head of what I may almost call, from its extent, the *modern* party.

Nature must have far the greatest share in every success, and so in his. Such a man was wanted, and such a man was born; a man of stone and iron, capable of sitting on horseback sixteen or seventeen hours, of going many days together without rest or food, except by snatches, and with the speed and spring of a tiger in action; a man not embarrassed by any scruples; compact, instant, selfish, prudent, and of a perception which did not suffer itself to be baulked or misled by any pretences of others, or any superstition, or any heat or haste of his own. "My hand of iron," he said, " was not at the extremity of my arm; it was immediately connected with my head." He respected the power of nature and fortune, and ascribed to it his superiority, instead of valuing himself, like inferior men, on his opinionativeness, and waging war with nature. His favorite rhetoric lay in allusion to his star; and he pleased himself, as well as the people, when he styled himself the "Child of Destiny." "They charge me," he said, " with the commission of great crimes: men of my stamp do not commit crimes. Nothing has been more simple than my elevation: 'tis in vain to ascribe it to intrigue or crime: it was owing to the peculiarity of the times, and to my reputation of having fought well against the enemies of my country. I have always marched with the opinion of great masses, and with events. Of what use, then, would crimes be to me?" Again he said, speaking of his son, "My son can not replace me; I could not replace myself. I am the creature of circumstances."

He had a directness of action never before combined with so much comprehension. He is a realist, terrific to all talkers, and confused truth-obscuring persons. He sees where the matter hinges, throws himself on the precise point of resistance, and slights all other considerations. He is strong in the right manner, namely, by insight. He never blundered into victory, but won his battles in his head, before he won them on the field. His principal means are in himself. He asks counsel of no other. In 1796, he writes to the Directory; "I have conducted the campaign without consulting any one. I should have done no good, if I had been under the necessity of conforming to the notions of another person. I have gained some advantages over superior forces, and when totally destitute of every thing, because, in the persuasion that your confidence was reposed in me, my actions were as prompt as my thoughts."

History is full, down to this day, of the imbecility of kings and governors. They are a class of persons much to be pitied, for they know not what they should do. The weavers strike for bread; and the king and his ministers, not knowing what to do, meet them with bayonets. But Napoleon understood his business. Here was a man who, in each moment and emergency, knew what to do next. It is an immense comfort and refreshment to the spirits, not only of kings, but of citizens. Few men have any next; they live from hand to mouth, without plan, and are ever at the end of their line, and, after each action, wait for an impulse from abroad. Napoleon had been the first man of the world, if his ends had been purely public. As he is, he inspires confidence and vigor by the extraordinary unity of his action. He is firm, sure, self-denying, self-postponing, sacrificing every thing to his aim,—money, troops, generals, and his own safety also, to his aim; not misled, like common adventurers, by the splendor of his own means. "Incidents ought not to govern policy," he said, "but policy, incidents." "To be hurried away by every event, is to have no political system at all." His victories were only so many doors, and he never for a moment lost sight of his way onward, in the dazzle and uproar of the present circumstance. He knew what to do, and he flew to his mark. He would shorten a straight line to come at his object. Horrible anecdotes may, no doubt, be collected from his history, of the price at which he bought his successes; but he must not therefore be set down as cruel; but only as one who knew no impediment to his will; not bloodthirsty, not cruel,—but wo to what thing or person stood in his way! Not bloodthirsty, but not sparing of blood,—and pitiless. He saw only the object: the obstacle must give way. "Sire, General Clarke can not combine with General Junot, for the dreadful fire of the Austrian battery."—"Let him carry the battery."—"Sire, every regiment that approaches the heavy artillery is sacrificed: Sire, what orders?"—"Forward, forward!" Seruzier, a colonel of artillery, gives, in his *Military Memoirs*, the following sketch of a scene after the battle of Austerlitz.—"At the moment in which the Russian army was making its retreat, painfully, but in good order, on the ice of the lake, the Emperor Napoleon came riding at full speed toward the artillery. 'You are losing time,' he cried; 'fire upon those masses; they must be engulfed: fire upon the ice!' The order remained unexecuted for ten minutes. In vain several officers and myself were placed on the slope of a hill to produce the effect: their balls and mine rolled upon the ice, without breaking it up. Seeing that, I tried a simple method of elevating light howitzers. The almost perpendicular fall of the heavy projectiles produced the desired effect. My method was immediately followed by the adjoining batteries, and in less than no time we buried" some* "thousands of Russians and Austrians under the waters of the lake."

In the plentitude of his resources, every obstacle seemed to vanish. "There shall be no Alps," he said; and he built his perfect roads, climbing by graded galleries their steepest precipices, until Italy was as open to Paris as any town in France. He laid his bones to, and wrought for his crown. Having decided what was to be done, he did that with might and main. He put out all his strength. He risked every thing, and spared nothing, neither ammunition, nor money, nor troops, nor generals, nor himself.

We like to see every thing do its office after its kind, whether it be a milch-cow or a rattle-snake; and, if fighting be the best mode of adjusting national differences, (as large majorities of men seem to agree,) certainly Bonaparte was right in making it thorough. "The grand principle of war," he said, " was, that an army ought always to be ready, by day and by night, and at all hours, to make all the resistance it is capable of making." He never economized his ammunition, but, on a hostile position, rained a torrent of iron,—shells,

---

*As I quote at second hand, and cannot procure Seruzier, I dare not adopt the high figure I find.

balls, grape-shot,—to annihilate all defence. On any point of
resistance, he concentrated squadron on squadron in over-
whelming numbers, until it was swept out of existence. To a
regiment of horse-chasseurs at Lobenstein, two days before
the battle of Jena, Napoleon said, "My lads, you must not fear
death; when soldiers brave death, they drive him into the enemy's ranks." In the fury of assault, he no more spared himself. He went to the edge of his possibility. It is plain that in
Italy he did what he could, and all that he could. He came,
several times, within an inch of ruin; and his own person was
all but lost. He was flung into the marsh at Arcola. The Austrians were between him and his troops, in the melée, and he
was brought off with desperate efforts. At Lonato, and at
other places, he was on the point of being taken prisoner. He
fought sixty battles. He had never enough. Each victory was
a new weapon. "My power would fall, were I not to support
it by new achievements. Conquest has made me what I am,
and conquest must maintain me." He felt, with every wise
man, that as much life is needed for conservation, as for creation. We are always in peril, always in a bad plight, just on
the edge of destruction, and only to be saved by invention
and courage.

This vigor was guarded and tempered by the coldest prudence and punctuality. A thunderbolt in the attack, he was
found invulnerable in his intrenchments. His very attack was
never the inspiration of courage, but the result of calculation.
His idea of the best defence consists in being still the attacking party. "My ambition," he says, "was great, but was of a
cold nature." In one of his conversations with Las Casas, he
remarked, "As to moral courage, I have rarely met with the
two-o'clock-in-the-morning kind: I mean unprepared courage, that which is necessary on an unexpected occasion; and
which, in spite of the most unforeseen events, leaves full freedom of judgment and decision:" and he did not hesitate to
declare that he was himself eminently endowed with this
"two-o'clock-in-the-morning courage, and that he had met
with few persons equal to himself in this respect."

Every thing depended on the nicety of his combinations,
and the stars were not more punctual than his arithmetic. His
personal attention descended to the smallest particulars. "At

Montebello, I ordered Kellermann to attack with eight hundred horse, and with these he separated the six thousand Hungarian grenadiers, before the very eyes of the Austrian cavalry. This cavalry was half a league off, and required a quarter of an hour to arrive on the field of action; and I have observed, that it is always these quarters of an hour that decide the fate of a battle." "Before he fought a battle, Bonaparte thought little about what he should do in case of success, but a great deal about what he should do in case of a reverse of fortune." The same prudence and good sense mark all his behavior. His instructions to his secretary at the Tuilleries are worth remembering. "During the night, enter my chamber as seldom as possible. Do not awake me when you have any good news to communicate; with that there is no hurry. But when you bring bad news, rouse me instantly, for then there is not a moment to be lost." It was a whimsical economy of the same kind which dictated his practice, when general in Italy, in regard to his burdensome correspondence. He directed Bourrienne to leave all letters unopened for three weeks, and then observed with satisfaction how large a part of the correspondence had thus disposed of itself, and no longer required an answer. His achievement of business was immense, and enlarges the known powers of man. There have been many working kings, from Ulysses to William of Orange, but none who accomplished a tithe of this man's performance.

To these gifts of nature, Napoleon added the advantage of having been born to a private and humble fortune. In his later days, he had the weakness of wishing to add to his crowns and badges the prescription of aristocracy: but he knew his debt to his austere education, and made no secret of his contempt for the born kings, and for "the hereditary asses," as he coarsely styled the Bourbons. He said that, "in their exile, they had learned nothing, and forgot nothing." Bonaparte had passed through all the degrees of military service, but also was citizen before he was emperor, and so has the key to citizenship. His remarks and estimates discover the information and justness of measurement of the middle class. Those who had to deal with him, found that he was not to be imposed upon, but could cipher as well as another man. This appears in all parts of his Memoirs, dictated at St. Helena. When the expenses of the empress, of his household, of his palaces, had accumulated great debts, Napoleon examined the bills of the creditors himself, detected overcharges and errors, and reduced the claims by considerable sums.

His grand weapon, namely, the millions whom he directed, he owed to the representative character which clothed him. He interests us as he stands for France and for Europe; and he exists as captain and king, only as far as the Revolution, or the interest of the industrious masses, found an organ and a leader in him. In the social interests, he knew the meaning and value of labor, and threw himself naturally on that side. I like an incident mentioned by one of his biographers at St. Helena. "When walking with Mrs. Balcombe, some servants, carrying heavy boxes, passed by on the road, and Mrs. Balcombe desired them, in rather an angry tone, to keep back. Napoleon interfered, saying, 'Respect the burden, Madam.' " In the time of the empire, he directed attention to the improvement and embellishment of the markets of the capital. "The market-place," he said, "is the Louvre of the common people." The principal works that have survived him are his magnificent roads. He filled the troops with his spirit, and a sort of freedom and companionship grew up between him and them, which the forms of his court never permitted between the officers and himself. They performed, under his eye, that which no others could do. The best document of his relation to his troops is the order of the day on the morning of the battle of Austerlitz, in which Napoleon promises the troops that he will keep his person out of reach of fire. This declaration, which is the reverse of that ordinarily made by generals and sovereigns on the eve of a battle, sufficiently explains the devotion of the army to their leader.

But though there is in particulars this identity between Napoleon and the mass of the people, his real strength lay in their conviction that he was their representative in his genius and aims, not only when he courted, but when he controlled and even when he decimated them by his conscriptions. He knew, as well as any Jacobin in France, how to philosophize on liberty and equality; and, when allusion was made to the precious blood of centuries, which was spilled by the killing of the Duc d'Enghien, he suggested, "Neither is my blood ditch-water." The people felt that no longer the throne was occupied, and the land sucked of its nourishment, by a small class of legitimates, secluded from all community with the children of the soil, and holding the ideas and superstitions of a long-forgotten state of society. Instead of that vampyre, a man of themselves held, in the Tuilleries, knowledge and ideas like their own, opening, of course, to them and their children, all places of power and trust. The day of sleepy, self-ish policy, ever narrowing the means and opportunities of young men, was ended, and a day of expansion and demand was come. A market for all the powers and productions of man was opened; brilliant prizes glittered in the eyes of youth and talent. The old, iron-bound, feudal France was changed into a young Ohio or New York; and those who smarted under the immediate rigors of the new monarch, pardoned them, as the necessary severities of the military system which had driven out the oppressor. And even when the majority of the people had begun to ask, whether they had really gained any thing under the exhausting levies of men and money of the new master,—the whole talent of the country, in every rank and kindred, took his part, and defended him as its natural patron. In 1814, when advised to rely on the higher classes, Napoleon said to those around him, "Gentlemen, in the situation in which I stand, my only nobility is the rabble of the Faubourgs."

Napoleon met this natural expectation. The necessity of his position required a hospitality to every sort of talent, and its appointment to trusts; and his feeling went along with this policy. Like every superior person, he undoubtedly felt a desire for men and compeers, and a wish to measure his power with other masters, and an impatience of fools and underlings. In Italy, he sought for men, and found none. "Good God!" he said, "how rare men are! There are eighteen millions in Italy, and I have with difficulty found two,—Dandolo and Melzi." In later years, with larger experience, his respect for mankind was not increased. In a moment of bitterness, he said, to one of his oldest friends, "Men deserve the contempt with which they inspire me. I have only to put some gold lace on the coat of my virtuous republicans, and they immediately become just what I wish them." This impatience at levity was, however, an oblique tribute of respect to those able persons who commanded his regard, not only when he found them friends and coadjutors, but also when they resisted his will. He could not confound Fox and Pitt, Carnot, Lafayette, and Bernadotte, with the danglers of his court; and, in spite of the detraction which his systematic egotism dictated toward the great captains who conquered with and for him, ample acknowledgments are made by him to Lannes, Duroc, Kleber, Dessaix, Massena, Murat, Ney, and Augereau. If he felt himself their patron, and the founder of their fortunes, as when he said, "I made my generals out of mud," he could not hide his satisfaction in receiving from them a seconding and support commensurate with the grandeur of his enterprise. In the Russian campaign, he was so much impressed by the courage and resources of Marshal Ney, that he said, "I have two hundred millions in my coffers, and I would give them all for Ney." The characters which he has drawn of several of his marshals, are discriminating, and, though they did not content the insatiable vanity of French officers, are, no doubt, substantially just. And, in fact, every species of merit was sought and advanced under his government. "I know," he said, "the depth and draught of water of every one of my generals." Natural power was sure to be well received at his court. Seventeen men, in his time, were raised from common soldiers to the rank of king, marshal, duke, or general; and the crosses of his Legion of Honor were given to personal valor, and not to family connexion. "When soldiers have been baptized in the fire of a battle-field, they have all one rank in my eyes."

When a natural king becomes a titular king, every body is pleased and satisfied. The Revolution entitled the strong populace of the Faubourg St. Antoine, and every horse-boy and powder-monkey in the army, to look on Napoleon, as flesh of his flesh, and the creature of *his* party: but there is something in the success of grand talent which enlists an universal sympathy. For, in the prevalence of sense and spirit over stupidity and malversation, all reasonable men have an interest; and, as intellectual beings, we feel the air purified by the electric shock, when material force is overthrown by intellectual energies. As soon as we are removed out of the reach of local and accidental partialities, man feels that Napoleon fights for him; these are honest victories; this strong steam-engine does our work. Whatever appeals to the imagination, by transcending the ordinary limits of human ability, wonderfully encourages and liberates us. This capacious head, revolving and disposing sovereignly trains of affairs, and animating such multitudes of agents; this eye, which looked through Europe; this prompt invention; this inexhaustible resource;—what events! what romantic pictures! what strange situations!— when spying the Alps, by a sunset in the Sicilian sea; drawing up his army for battle, in sight of the Pyramids, and saying to his troops, "From the tops of those pyramids, forty centuries look down on you;" fording the Red Sea; wading in the gulf of the Isthmus of Suez. On the shore of Plotemais, gigantic projects agitated him. "Had Acre fallen, I should have changed the face of the world." His army, on the night of the battle of Austerlitz, which was the anniversary of his inauguration as Emperor, presented him with a bouquet of forty standards taken in the fight. Perhaps it is a little puerile, the pleasure he took in making these contrasts glaring; as when he pleased himself with making kings wait in his antechambers, at Tilsit, at Paris, and at Erfurt.

We cannot, in the universal imbecility, indecision, and indolence of men, sufficiently congratulate ourselves on this strong and ready actor, who took occasion by the beard, and showed us how much may be accomplished by the mere force of such virtues as all men possess in less degrees; namely, by punctuality, by personal attention, by courage, and thoroughness. "The Austrians," he said, "do not know the value of time." I should cite him, in his earlier years, as a model of prudence. His power does not consist in any wild or extravagant force; in any enthusiasm, like Mahomet's; or singular power of persuasion; but in the exercise of common sense on each emergency, instead of abiding by rules and customs. The lesson he teaches is that which vigor always teaches,—that there is always room for it. To what heaps of cowardly doubts is not that man's life an answer. When he appeared, it was the belief of all military men that there could be nothing new in war; as it is the belief of men to-day, that nothing new can be undertaken in politics, or in church, or in letters, or in trade, or in farming, or in our social manners and customs; and as it is, at all times, the belief of society that the world is used up. But Bonaparte knew better than society; and, moreover, knew that he knew better. I think all men know better than they do; know that the institutions we so volubly commend are go-carts and baubles; but they dare not trust their presentiments. Bonaparte relied on his own sense, and did not care a bean for other people's. The world treated his novelties just as it treats every body's novelties,—made infinite objection; mustered all the impediments: but he snapped his finger at their objections. "What creates great difficulty," he remarks, "in the profession of the land-commander, is the necessity of feeding so many men and animals. If he allows himself to be guided by the commissaries, he will never stir, and all his expeditions will fail." An example of his common sense is what he says of the passage of the Alps in winter, which, all writers, one repeating after the other, had described as impracticable. "The winter," says Napoleon, "is not the most unfavorable season for the passage of lofty mountains. The snow is then firm, the weather settled, and there is nothing to fear from avalanches, the real and only danger to be apprehended in the Alps. On those high mountains, there are often very fine days in December, of a dry cold, with extreme calmness in the air." Read his account, too, of the way in which battles are gained. "In all battles, a moment occurs, when the bravest troops, after having made the greatest efforts, feel inclined to run. That terror proceeds from a want of confidence in their own courage; and it only requires a slight opportunity, a pretence, to restore confidence to them. The art is to give rise to the opportunity, and to invent the pretence. At Arcola, I won the battle with twenty-five horsemen. I seized that moment of lassitude, gave every man a trumpet, and gained the day with this handful. You see that two armies are two bodies which meet, and endeavor to frighten each other: a moment of panic occurs, and that moment must be turned to advantage. When a man has been present in many actions, he distinguishes that moment without difficulty: it is as easy as casting up an addition."

This deputy of the nineteenth century added to his gifts a

capacity for speculation on general topics. He delighted in running through the range of practical, of literary, and of abstract questions. His opinion is always original, and to the purpose. On the voyage to Egypt, he liked, after dinner, to fix on three or four persons to support a proposition, and as many to oppose it. He gave a subject, and the discussions turned on questions of religion, the different kinds of government, and the art of war. One day, he asked, whether the planets were inhabited? On another, what was the age of the world? Then he proposed to consider the probability of the destruction of the globe, either by water or by fire: at another time, the truth or fallacy of presentiments, and the interpretation of dreams. He was very fond of talking of religion. In 1806, he conversed with Fournier, bishop of Montpellier, on matters of theology. There were two points on which they could not agree, viz., that of hell, and that of salvation out of the pale of the church. The Emperor told Josephine, that he disputed like a devil on these two points, on which the bishop was inexorable. To the philosophers he readily yielded all that was proved against religion as the work of men and time; but he would not hear of materialism. One fine night, on deck, amid a clatter of materialism, Bonaparte pointed to the stars, and said, "You may talk as long as you please, gentlemen, but who made all that?" He delighted in the conversation of men of science, particularly of Monge and Berthollet; but the men of letters he slighted; "they were manufacturers of phrases." Of medicine, too, he was fond of talking, and with those of its practitioners whom he most esteemed,—with Corvisart at Paris, and with Antonomarchi at St. Helena. "Believe me," he said to the last, "we had better leave off all these remedies: life is a fortress which neither you nor I know any thing about. Why throw obstacles in the way of its defence? Its own means are superior to all the apparatus of your laboratories. Corvisart candidly agreed with me, that all your filthy mixtures are good for nothing. Medicine is a collection of uncertain prescriptions, the results of which, taken collectively, are more fatal than useful to mankind. Water, air, and cleanliness, are the chief articles in my pharmacopeia."

His memoirs, dictated to Count Montholon and General Gourgaud, at St. Helena, have great value, after all the deduction that, it seems, is to be made from them, on account of his known disingenuousness. He has the good-nature of strength and conscious superiority. I admire his simple, clear narrative of his battles;—good as Cæsar's; his good-natured and sufficiently respectful account of Marshal Wurmser and his other antagonists, and his own equality as a writer to his varying subject. The most agreeable portion is the Campaign in Egypt.

He had hours of thought and wisdom. In intervals of leisure, either in the camp or the palace, Napoleon appears as a man of genius, directing on abstract questions the native appetite for truth, and the impatience of words, he was wont to show in war. He could enjoy every play of invention, a romance, a *bon mot*, as well as a stratagem in a campaign. He delighted to fascinate Josephine and her ladies, in a dim-lighted apartment, by the terrors of a fiction, to which his voice and dramatic power lent every addition.

I call Napoleon the agent or attorney of the middle class of modern society; of the throng who fill the markets, shops, counting-houses, manufactories, ships, of the modern world, aiming to be rich. He was the agitator, the destroyer of prescription, the internal improver, the liberal, the radical, the inventor of means, the opener of doors and markets, the subverter of monopoly and abuse. Of course, the rich and aristocratic did not like him. England, the centre of capital, and Rome and Austria, centres of tradition and genealogy, opposed him. The consternation of the dull and conservative classes, the terror of the foolish old men and old women of the Roman conclave,—who in their despair took hold of any thing, and would cling to red-hot iron,—the vain attempts of statists to amuse and deceive him, of the emperor of Austria to bribe him; and the instinct of the young, ardent, and active men, every where, which pointed him out as the giant of the middle class, make his history bright and commanding. He had the virtues of the masses of his constituents: he had also their vices. I am sorry that the brilliant picture has its reverse. But that is the fatal quality which we discover in our pursuit of wealth, that it is treacherous, and is bought by the breaking or weakening of the sentiments: and it is inevitable that we should find the same fact in the history of this champion, who proposed to himself simply a brilliant career, without any stipulation or scruple concerning the means.

Bonaparte was singularly destitute of generous sentiments. The highest-placed individual in the most cultivated age and population of the world,—he has not the merit of common truth and honesty. He is unjust to his generals; egotistic, and monopolizing; meanly stealing the credit of their great actions from Kellermann, from Bernadotte; intriguing to involve his faithful Junot in hopeless bankruptcy, in order to drive him to a distance from Paris, because the familiarity of his manners offends the new pride of his throne. He is a boundless liar. The official paper, his "Moniteurs," and all his bulletins, are proverbs for saying what he wished to be believed; and worse,—he sat, in his premature old age, in his lonely island, coldly falsifying facts, and dates, and characters, and giving to history a theatrical eclat. Like all Frenchmen, he has a passion for stage effect. Every action that breathes of generosity is poisoned by this calculation. His star, his love of glory, his doctrine of the immortality of the soul, are all French. "I must dazzle and astonish. If I were to give the liberty of the press, my power could not last three days." To make a great noise is his favorite design. "A great reputation is a great noise: the more there is made, the farther off it is heard. Laws, institutions, monuments, nations, all fall; but the noise continues, and resounds in after ages." His doctrine of immortality is simply fame. His theory of influence is not flattering. "There are two levers for moving men,—interest and fear. Love is a silly infatuation, depend upon it. Friendship is but a name. I love nobody. I do not even love my brothers: perhaps Joseph, a little, from habit, and because he is my elder; and Duroc, I love him too; but why?—because his character pleases me: he is stern and resolute, and, I believe, the fellow never shed a tear. For my part, I know very well that I have no true friends. As long as I continue to be what I am, I may have as many pretended friends as I please. Leave sensibility to women: but men should be firm in heart and purpose, or they should have nothing to do with war and government." He was thoroughly unscrupulous. He would steal, slander, assassinate, drown, and poison, as his interest dictated. He had no generosity; but mere vulgar hatred: he was intensely selfish: he was perfidious: he cheated at cards: he was a prodigious gossip; and opened letters; and delighted in his infamous police; and rubbed his hands with joy when he had intercepted some morsel of intelligence concerning the men and women about him, boasting that "he knew every thing;" and interfered with the cutting the dresses of the women; and listened after the hurrahs and the compliments of the street, incognito. His manners were coarse. He treated women with low familiarity. He had the habit of pulling their ears, and pinching their cheeks, when he was in good humor, and of pulling the ears and whiskers of men, and of striking and horse-play with them, to his last days. It does not appear that he listened at key-holes, or, at least, that he was caught at it. In short, when you have penetrated through all the circles of power and splendor, you were not dealing with a gentleman, at last; but with an impostor and a rogue: and he fully deserves the epithet of *Jupiter Scapin*, or a sort of Scamp Jupiter.

In describing the two parties into which modern society divides itself,—the democrat and the conservative,—I said, Bonaparte represents the Democrat, or the party of men of business, against the stationary or conservative party. I omitted then to say, what is material to the statement, namely, that these two parties differ only as young and old. The democrat is a young conservative; the conservative is an old democrat. The aristocrat is the democrat ripe, and gone to seed,— because both parties stand on the one ground of the supreme value of property, which one endeavors to get, and the other to keep. Bonaparte may be said to represent the whole history of this party, its youth and its age; yes, and with poetic justice, its fate, in his own. The counter-revolution, the counter-party, still waits for its organ and representative, in a lover and a man of truly public and universal aims.

Here was an experiment, under the most favorable conditions, of the powers of intellect without conscience. Never was such a leader so endowed, and so weaponed; never leader found such aids and followers. And what was the result of this vast talent and power, of these immense armies, burned cities, squandered treasures, immolated millions of men, of this demoralized Europe? It came to no result. All passed away, like the smoke of his artillery, and left no trace. He left France smaller, poorer, feebler, than he found it; and the whole contest for freedom was to be begun again. The attempt was, in principle, suicidal. France served him with life, and limb, and estate, as long as it could identify its interest with him; but when men saw that after victory was another war; after the destruction of armies, new conscriptions; and they who had toiled so desperately were never nearer to the reward,—they could not spend what they had earned, nor repose on their down-beds, nor strut in their chateaux,—they deserted him. Men found that his absorbing egotism was deadly to all other men. It resembled the torpedo, which inflicts a succession of shocks on any one who takes hold of it, producing spasms which contract the muscles of the hand, so that the man can not open his fingers; and the animal inflicts new and more violent shocks, until he paralyzes and kills his victim. So, this exorbitant egotist narrowed, impoverished, and absorbed the power and existence of those who served him; and the universal cry of France, and of Europe, in 1814, was, "enough of him;" "*assez de Bonaparte.*"

It was not Bonaparte's fault. He did all that in him lay, to live and thrive without moral principle. It was the nature of things, the eternal law of man and of the world, which baulked and ruined him; and the result, in a million experiments, will be the same. Every experiment, by multitudes or by individuals, that has a sensual and selfish aim, will fail. The pacific Fourier will be as inefficient as the pernicious Napoleon. As long as our civilization is essentially one of property, of fences, of exclusiveness, it will be mocked by delusions. Our riches will leave us sick; there will be bitterness in our laughter; and our wine will burn our mouth. Only that good profits, which we can taste with all doors open, and which serves all men.

VII

Goethe; or, the Writer

I FIND a provision, in the constitution of the world, for the
writer or secretary, who is to report the doings of the miraculous spirit of life that every where throbs and works. His
office is a reception of the facts into the mind, and then a
selection of the eminent and characteristic experiences.

Nature will be reported. All things are engaged in writing
their history. The planet, the pebble, goes attended by its
shadow. The rolling rock leaves its scratches on the mountain; the river, its channel in the soil; the animal, its bones in
the stratum; the fern and leaf, their modest epitaph in the
coal. The falling drop makes its sculpture in the sand or the
stone. Not a foot steps into the snow, or along the ground,
but prints, in characters more or less lasting, a map of its
march. Every act of the man inscribes itself in the memories
of his fellows, and in his own manners and face. The air is
full of sounds; the sky, of tokens; the ground is all memoranda and signatures; and every object covered over with
hints, which speak to the intelligent.

In nature, this self-registration is incessant, and the narrative is the print of the seal. It neither exceeds nor comes short
of the fact. But nature strives upward; and, in man, the report
is something more than print of the seal. It is a new and finer
form of the original. The record is alive, as that which it recorded is alive. In man, the memory is a kind of looking-glass,
which, having received the images of surrounding objects, is
touched with life, and disposes them in a new order. The facts
which transpired do not lie in it inert; but some subside, and
others shine; so that soon we have a new picture, composed
of the eminent experiences. The man coöperates. He loves to
communicate; and that which is for him to say lies as a load
on his heart until it is delivered. But, besides the universal joy
of conversation, some men are born with exalted powers for
this second creation. Men are born to write. The gardener
saves every slip, and seed, and peach-stone: his vocation is to

be a planter of plants. Not less does the writer attend his affair. Whatever he beholds or experiences, comes to him as a model, and sits for its picture. He counts it all nonsense that they say, that some things are undescribable. He believes that all that can be thought can be written, first or last; and he would report the Holy Ghost, or attempt it. Nothing so broad, so subtle, or so dear, but comes therefore commended to his pen,—and he will write. In his eyes, a man is the faculty of reporting, and the universe is the possibility of being reported. In conversation, in calamity, he finds new materials; as our German poet said, "some god gave me the power to paint what I suffer." He draws his rents from rage and pain. By acting rashly, he buys the power of talking wisely. Vexations, and a tempest of passion, only fill his sail; as the good Luther writes, "When I am angry, I can pray well, and preach well:" and, if we knew the genesis of fine strokes of eloquence, they might recall the complaisance of Sultan Amurath, who struck off some Persian heads, that his physician, Vesalius, might see the spasms in the muscles of the neck. His failures are the preparation of his victories. A new thought, or a crisis of passion, apprises him that all that he has yet learned and written is exoteric,—is not the fact, but some rumor of the fact. What then? Does he throw away the pen? No; he begins again to describe in the new light which has shined on him,—if, by some means, he may yet save some true word. Nature conspires. Whatever can be thought can be spoken, and still rises for utterance, though to rude and stammering organs. If they cannot compass it, it waits and works, until, at last, it moulds them to its perfect will, and is articulated.

This striving after imitative expression, which one meets every where, is significant of the aim of nature, but is mere stenography. There are higher degrees, and nature has more splendid endowments for those whom she elects to a superior office; for the class of scholars or writers, who see connection where the multitude see fragments, and who are impelled to exhibit the facts in order, and so to supply the axis on which the frame of things turns. Nature has dearly at heart the formation of the speculative man, or scholar. It is an end never lost sight of, and is prepared in the original casting of things.

He is no permissive or accidental appearance, but an organic agent, one of the estates of the realm, provided and prepared, from of old and from everlasting, in the knitting and contexture of things. Presentiments, impulses, cheer him. There is a certain heat in the breast, which attends the perception of a primary truth, which is the shining of the spiritual sun down into the shaft of the mine. Every thought which dawns on the mind, in the moment of its emergence announces its own rank,—whether it is some whimsy, or whether it is a power.

If he have his incitements, there is, on the other side, invitation and need enough of his gift. Society has, at all times, the same want, namely, of one sane man with adequate powers of expression to hold up each object of monomania in its right relations. The ambitious and mercenary bring their last new mumbo-jumbo, whether tariff, Texas, railroad, Romanism, mesmerism, or California; and, by detaching the object from its relations, easily succeed in making it seen in a glare; and a multitude go mad about it, and they are not to be reproved or cured by the opposite multitude, who are kept from this particular insanity by an equal frenzy on another crotchet. But let one man have the comprehensive eye that can replace this isolated prodigy in its right neighborhood and bearings,—the illusion vanishes, and the returning reason of the community thanks the reason of the monitor.

The scholar is the man of the ages, but he must also wish with other men to stand well with his contemporaries. But there is a certain ridicule, among superficial people, thrown on the scholars or clerisy, which is of no import, unless the scholar heed it. In this country, the emphasis of conversation, and of public opinion, commends the practical man; and the solid portion of the community is named with significant respect in every circle. Our people are of Bonaparte's opinion concerning ideologists. Ideas are subversive of social order and comfort, and at last make a fool of the possessor. It is believed, the ordering a cargo of goods from New York to Smyrna; or, the running up and down to procure a company of subscribers to set a-going five or ten thousand spindles; or, the negotiations of a caucus, and the practising on the prejudices and facility of country-people, to secure their votes in November,—is practical and commendable.

If I were to compare action of a much higher strain with a life of contemplation, I should not venture to pronounce with much confidence in favor of the former. Mankind have such a deep stake in inward illumination, that there is much to be said by the hermit or monk in defence of his life of thought and prayer. A certain partiality, a headiness, and loss of balance, is the tax which all action must pay. Act, if you like,— but you do it at your peril. Men's actions are too strong for them. Show me a man who has acted, and who has not been the victim and slave of his action. What they have done commits and enforces them to do the same again. The first act, which was to be an experiment, becomes a sacrament. The fiery reformer embodies his aspiration in some rite or covenant, and he and his friends cleave to the form, and lose the aspiration. The Quaker has established Quakerism, the Shaker has established his monastery and his dance; and, although each prates of spirit, there is no spirit, but repetition, which is anti-spiritual. But where are his new things of to-day? In actions of enthusiasm, this drawback appears: but in those lower activities, which have no higher aim than to make us more comfortable and more cowardly, in actions of cunning, actions that steal and lie, actions that divorce the speculative from the practical faculty, and put a ban on reason and sentiment, there is nothing else but drawback and negation. The Hindoos write in their sacred books, "Children only, and not the learned, speak of the speculative and the practical faculties as two. They are but one, for both obtain the selfsame end, and the place which is gained by the followers of the one, is gained by the followers of the other. That man seeth, who seeth that the speculative and the practical doctrines are one." For great action must draw on the spiritual nature. The measure of action is the sentiment from which it proceeds. The greatest action may easily be one of the most private circumstance.

This disparagement will not come from the leaders, but from inferior persons. The robust gentlemen who stand at the head of the practical class, share the ideas of the time, and have too much sympathy with the speculative class. It is not from men excellent in any kind, that disparagement of any other is to be looked for. With such, Talleyrand's question is

ever the main one; not, is he rich? is he committed? is he
well-meaning? has he this or that faculty? is he of the movement? is he of the establishment?—but, *Is he any body?* does
he stand for something? He must be good of his kind. That
is all that Talleyrand, all that State-street, all that the common
sense of mankind asks. Be real and admirable, not as we
know, but as you know. Able men do not care in what kind
a man is able, so only that he is able. A master likes a master,
and does not stipulate whether it be orator, artist, craftsman,
or king.

Society has really no graver interest than the well-being of
the literary class. And it is not to be denied that men are
cordial in their recognition and welcome of intellectual accomplishments. Still the writer does not stand with us on any
commanding ground. I think this to be his own fault. A
pound passes for a pound. There have been times when he
was a sacred person: he wrote Bibles; the first hymns; the
codes; the epics; tragic songs; Sibylline verses; Chaldean oracles; Laconian sentences, inscribed on temple walls. Every
word was true, and woke the nations to new life. He wrote
without levity, and without choice. Every word was carved
before his eyes, into the earth and the sky; and the sun and
stars were only letters of the same purport, and of no more
necessity. But how can he be honored, when he does not
honor himself; when he loses himself in the crowd; when he
is no longer the lawgiver, but the sycophant, ducking to the
giddy opinion of a reckless public; when he must sustain with
shameless advocacy some bad government, or must bark, all
the year round, in opposition; or write conventional criticism,
or profligate novels; or, at any rate, write without thought,
and without recurrence, by day and by night, to the sources
of inspiration?

Some reply to these questions may be furnished by looking
over the list of men of literary genius in our age. Among
these, no more instructive name occurs than that of Goethe,
to represent the powers and duties of the scholar or writer.

I described Bonaparte as a representative of the popular external life and aims of the nineteenth century. Its other half,
its poet, is Goethe, a man quite domesticated in the century,
breathing its air, enjoying its fruits, impossible at any earlier

time, and taking away, by his colossal parts, the reproach of weakness, which, but for him, would lie on the intellectual works of the period. He appears at a time when a general culture has spread itself, and has smoothed down all sharp individual traits; when, in the absence of heroic characters, a social comfort and coöperation have come in. There is no poet, but scores of poetic writers; no Columbus, but hundreds of post-captains, with transit-telescope, barometer, and concentrated soup and pemmican; no Demosthenes, no Chatham, but any number of clever parliamentary and forensic debaters; no prophet or saint, but colleges of divinity; no learned man, but learned societies, a cheap press, reading-rooms, and book-clubs, without number. There was never such a miscellany of facts. The world extends itself like American trade. We conceive Greek or Roman life,—life in the middle ages,—to be a simple and comprehensible affair; but modern life to respect a multitude of things, which is distracting.

Goethe was the philosopher of this multiplicity; hundred-handed, Argus-eyed, able and happy to cope with this rolling miscellany of facts and sciences, and, by his own versatility, to dispose of them with ease; a manly mind, unembarrassed by the variety of coats of convention with which life had got encrusted, easily able by his subtlety to pierce these, and to draw his strength from nature, with which he lived in full communion. What is strange, too, he lived in a small town, in a petty state, in a defeated state, and in a time when Germany played no such leading part in the world's affairs as to swell the bosom of her sons with any metropolitan pride, such as might have cheered a French, or English, or once, a Roman or Attic genius. Yet there is no trace of provincial limitation in his muse. He is not a debtor to his position, but was born with a free and controlling genius.

The Helena, or the second part of Faust, is a philosophy of literature set in poetry; the work of one who found himself the master of histories, mythologies, philosophies, sciences, and national literatures, in the encyclopædical manner in which modern erudition, with its international intercourse of the whole earth's population, researches into Indian, Etruscan, and all Cyclopæan arts, geology, chemistry, astronomy;

and every one of these kingdoms assuming a certain aerial and poetic character, by reason of the multitude. One looks at a king with reverence; but if one should chance to be at a congress of kings, the eye would take liberties with the peculiarities of each. These are not wild miraculous songs, but elaborate forms, to which the poet has confided the results of eighty years of observation. This reflective and critical wisdom makes the poem more truly the flower of this time. It dates itself. Still he is a poet,—poet of a prouder laurel than any contemporary, and, under this plague of microscopes, (for he seems to see out of every pore of his skin,) strikes the harp with a hero's strength and grace.

The wonder of the book is its superior intelligence. In the menstruum of this man's wit, the past and the present ages, and their religions, politics, and modes of thinking, are dissolved into archetypes and ideas. What new mythologies sail through his head! The Greeks said, that Alexander went as far as Chaos; Goethe went, only the other day, as far; and one step farther he hazarded, and brought himself safe back.

There is a heart-cheering freedom in his speculation. The immense horizon which journeys with us lends its majesty to trifles, and to matters of convenience and necessity, as to solemn and festal performances. He was the soul of his century. If that was learned, and had become, by population, compact organization, and drill of parts, one great Exploring Expedition, accumulating a glut of facts and fruits too fast for any hitherto-existing savans to classify, this man's mind had ample chambers for the distribution of all. He had a power to unite the detached atoms again by their own law. He has clothed our modern existence with poetry. Amid littleness and detail, he detected the Genius of life, the old cunning Proteus, nestling close beside us, and showed that the dulness and prose we ascribe to the age was only another of his masks:—

"His very flight is presence in disguise:"

that he had put off a gay uniform for a fatigue dress, and was not a whit less vivacious or rich in Liverpool or the Hague, than once in Rome or Antioch. He sought him in public squares and main streets, in boulevards and hotels; and, in the solidest kingdom of routine and the senses, he showed the lurking dæmonic power; that, in actions of routine, a thread of mythology and fable spins itself: and this, by tracing the pedigree of every usage and practice, every institution, utensil, and means, home to its origin in the structure of man. He had an extreme impatience of conjecture and of rhetoric. "I have guesses enough of my own; if a man write a book, let him set down only what he knows." He writes in the plainest and lowest tone, omitting a great deal more than he writes, and putting ever a thing for a word. He has explained the distinction between the antique and the modern spirit and art. He has defined art, its scope and laws. He has said the best things about nature that ever were said. He treats nature as the old philosophers, as the seven wise masters did,—and, with whatever loss of French tabulation and dissection, poetry and humanity remain to us; and they have some doctoral skill. Eyes are better, on the whole, than telescopes or microscopes. He has contributed a key to many parts of nature, through the rare turn for unity and simplicity in his mind. Thus Goethe suggested the leading idea of modern botany, that a leaf, or the eye of a leaf, is the unit of botany, and that every part of the plant is only a transformed leaf to meet a new condition; and, by varying the conditions, a leaf may be converted into any other organ, and any other organ into a leaf. In like manner, in osteology, he assumed that one vertebra of the spine might be considered the unit of the skeleton: the head was only the uppermost vertebra transformed. "The plant goes from knot to knot, closing, at last, with the flower and the seed. So the tape-worm, the caterpillar, goes from knot to knot, and closes with the head. Man and the higher animals are built up through the vertebræ, the powers being concentrated in the head." In optics, again, he rejected the artificial theory of seven colors, and considered that every color was the mixture of light and darkness in new proportions. It is really of very little consequence what topic he writes upon. He sees at every pore, and has a certain gravitation towards truth. He will realize what you say. He hates to be trifled with, and to be made to say over again some old wife's fable, that has had possession of men's faith these thousand years. He may as well see if it is true as another. He sifts it. I am here, he would say, to be the measure and judge of these things. Why should I take them on trust? And, therefore, what he says of religion, of passion, of marriage, of manners, of property, of paper money, of periods of belief, of omens, of luck, or whatever else, refuses to be forgotten.

Take the most remarkable example that could occur of this tendency to verify every term in popular use. The Devil had played an important part in mythology in all times. Goethe would have no word that does not cover a thing. The same measure will still serve: "I have never heard of any crime which I might not have committed." So he flies at the throat of this imp. He shall be real; he shall be modern; he shall be European; he shall dress like a gentleman, and accept the manners, and walk in the streets, and be well initiated in the life of Vienna, and of Heidelberg, in 1820,—or he shall not exist. Accordingly, he stripped him of mythologic gear, of horns, cloven foot, harpoon tail, brimstone, and blue-fire, and, instead of looking in books and pictures, looked for him in his own mind, in every shade of coldness, selfishness, and unbelief that, in crowds, or in solitude, darkens over the human thought,—and found that the portrait gained reality and terror by every thing he added, and by every thing he took away. He found that the essence of this hobgoblin, which had hovered in shadow about the habitations of men, ever since there were men, was pure intellect, applied,—as always there is a tendency,—to the service of the senses: and he flung into literature, in his Mephistopheles, the first organic figure that has been added for some ages, and which will remain as long as the Prometheus.

I have no design to enter into any analysis of his numerous works. They consist of translations, criticism, dramas, lyric and every other description of poems, literary journals, and portraits of distinguished men. Yet I cannot omit to specify the Wilhelm Meister.

Wilhelm Meister is a novel in every sense, the first of its kind, called by its admirers the only delineation of modern society,—as if other novels, those of Scott, for example, dealt with costume and condition, this with the spirit of life. It is a book over which some veil is still drawn. It is read by very intelligent persons with wonder and delight. It is preferred by some such to Hamlet, as a work of genius. I suppose, no book of this century can compare with it in its delicious sweetness, so new, so provoking to the mind, gratifying it with so many and so solid thoughts, just insights into life, and manners, and characters; so many good hints for the conduct of life, so many unexpected glimpses into a higher sphere, and never a trace of rhetoric or dulness. A very provoking book to the curiosity of young men of genius, but a very unsatisfactory one. Lovers of light reading, those who look in it for the entertainment they find in a romance, are disappointed. On the other hand, those who begin it with the higher hope to read in it a worthy history of genius, and the just award of the laurel to its toils and denials, have also reason to complain. We had an English romance here, not long ago, professing to embody the hope of a new age, and to unfold the political hope of the party called 'Young England,' in which the only reward of virtue is a seat in parliament, and a peerage. Goethe's romance has a conclusion as lame and immoral. George Sand, in Consuelo and its continuation, has sketched a truer and more dignified picture. In the progress of the story, the characters of the hero and heroine expand at a rate that shivers the porcelain chess-table of aristocratic convention: they quit the society and habits of their rank; they lose their wealth; they become the servants of great ideas, and of the most generous social ends; until, at last, the hero, who is the centre and fountain of an association for the rendering of the noblest benefits to the human race, no longer answers to his own titled name: it sounds foreign and remote in his ear. "I am only man," he says; "I breathe and work for man," and this in poverty and extreme sacrifices. Goethe's hero, on the contrary, has so many weaknesses and impurities, and keeps such bad company, that the sober English public, when the book was translated, were disgusted. And yet it is so crammed with wisdom, with knowledge of the world, and with knowledge of laws; the persons so truly and subtly drawn, and with such few strokes, and not a word too much, the book remains ever so new and unexhausted, that we must even let it go its way, and be willing to get what good from it we can, assured that it has only begun its office, and has millions of readers yet to serve.

The argument is the passage of a democrat to the aristoc-

racy, using both words in their best sense. And this passage
is not made in any mean or creeping way, but through the
hall door. Nature and character assist, and the rank is made
real by sense and probity in the nobles. No generous youth
can escape this charm of reality in the book, so that it is
highly stimulating to intellect and courage.

The ardent and holy Novalis characterized the book as
"thoroughly modern and prosaic; the romantic is completely
levelled in it; so is the poetry of nature; the wonderful. The
book treats only of the ordinary affairs of men: it is a poeti-
cized civic and domestic story. The wonderful in it is ex-
pressly treated as fiction and enthusiastic dreaming:"—and
yet, what is also characteristic, Novalis soon returned to this
book, and it remained his favorite reading to the end of his
life.

What distinguishes Goethe for French and English readers,
is a property which he shares with his nation,—a habitual
reference to interior truth. In England and in America, there
is a respect for talent; and, if it is exerted in support of any
ascertained or intelligible interest or party, or in regular opposition to any, the public is satisfied. In France, there is even
a greater delight in intellectual brilliancy, for its own sake.
And, in all these countries, men of talent write from talent. It
is enough if the understanding is occupied, the taste propi-
tiated,—so many columns, so many hours, filled in a lively
and creditable way. The German intellect wants the French
sprightliness, the fine practical understanding of the English,
and the American adventure; but it has a certain probity,
which never rests in a superficial performance, but asks steadily, *To what end?* A German public asks for a controlling sincerity. Here is activity of thought; but what is it for? What
does the man mean? Whence, whence all these thoughts?

Talent alone can not make a writer. There must be a man
behind the book; a personality which, by birth and quality, is
pledged to the doctrines there set forth, and which exists to
see and state things so, and not otherwise; holding things
because they are things. If he can not rightly express himself
to-day, the same things subsist, and will open themselves to-
morrow. There lies the burden on his mind,—the burden of
truth to be declared,—more or less understood; and it con-

stitutes his business and calling in the world, to see those facts through, and to make them known. What signifies that he trips and stammers; that his voice is harsh or hissing; that his method or his tropes are inadequate? That message will find method and imagery, articulation and melody. Though he were dumb, it would speak. If not,—if there be no such God's word in the man,—what care we how adroit, how fluent, how brilliant he is?

It makes a great difference to the force of any sentence, whether there be a man behind it, or no. In the learned journal, in the influential newspaper, I discern no form; only some irresponsible shadow; oftener some monied corporation, or some dangler, who hopes, in the mask and robes of his paragraph, to pass for somebody. But, through every clause and part of speech of a right book, I meet the eyes of the most determined of men: his force and terror inundate every word: the commas and dashes are alive; so that the writing is athletic and nimble,—can go far and live long.

In England and America, one may be an adept in the writing of a Greek or Latin poet, without any poetic taste or fire. That a man has spent years on Plato and Proclus, does not afford a presumption that he holds heroic opinions, or undervalues the fashions of his town. But the German nation have the most ridiculous good faith on these subjects: the student, out of the lecture-room, still broods on the lessons; and the professor can not divest himself of the fancy, that the truths of philosophy have some application to Berlin and Munich. This earnestness enables them to out-see men of much more talent. Hence, almost all the valuable distinctions which are current in higher conversation, have been derived to us from Germany. But, whilst men distinguished for wit and learning, in England and France, adopt their study and their side with a certain levity, and are not understood to be very deeply engaged, from grounds of character, to the topic or the part they espouse,—Goethe, the head and body of the German nation, does not speak from talent, but the truth shines through: he is very wise, though his talent often veils his wisdom. However excellent his sentence is, he has somewhat better in view. It awakens my curiosity. He has the formidable independence which converse with truth gives: hear you, or forbear, his fact abides; and your interest in the writer is not confined to his story, and he dismissed from memory, when he has performed his task creditably, as a baker when he has left his loaf; but his work is the least part of him. The old Eternal Genius who built the world has confided himself more to this man than to any other. I dare not say that Goethe ascended to the highest grounds from which genius has spoken. He has not worshipped the highest unity; he is incapable of a self-surrender to the moral sentiment. There are nobler strains in poetry than any he has sounded. There are writers poorer in talent, whose tone is purer, and more touches the heart. Goethe can never be dear to men. His is not even the devotion to pure truth; but to truth for the sake of culture. He has no aims less large than the conquest of universal nature, of universal truth, to be his portion: a man not to be bribed, nor deceived, nor overawed; of a stoical self-command and self-denial, and having one test for all men,— *What can you teach me?* All possessions are valued by him for that only; rank, privileges, health, time, being itself.

He is the type of culture, the amateur of all arts, and sciences, and events; artistic, but not artist; spiritual, but not spiritualist. There is nothing he had not right to know: there is no weapon in the armory of universal genius he did not take into his hand, but with peremptory heed that he should not be for a moment prejudiced by his instruments. He lays a ray of light under every fact, and between himself and his dearest property. From him nothing was hid, nothing withholden. The lurking dæmons sat to him, and the saint who saw the dæmons; and the metaphysical elements took form. "Piety itself is no aim, but only a means, whereby, through purest inward peace, we may attain to highest culture." And his penetration of every secret of the fine arts will make Goethe still more statuesque. His affections help him, like women employed by Cicero to worm out the secret of conspirators. Enmities he has none. Enemy of him you may be,—if so you shall teach him aught which your good-will can not,—were it only what experience will accrue from your ruin. Enemy and welcome, but enemy on high terms. He can not hate any body; his time is worth too much. Temperamental antagonisms may be suffered, but like feuds of emperors, who fight dignifiedly across kingdoms.

His autobiography, under the title of "Poetry and Truth out of my Life," is the expression of the idea,—now familiar to the world through the German mind, but a novelty to England, Old and New, when that book appeared,—that a man exists for culture; not for what he can accomplish, but for what can be accomplished in him. The reaction of things on the man is the only noteworthy result. An intellectual man can see himself as a third person; therefore his faults and delusions interest him equally with his successes. Though he wishes to prosper in affairs, he wishes more to know the history and destiny of man; whilst the clouds of egotists drifting about him are only interested in a low success.

This idea reigns in the *Dichtung und Wahrheit*, and directs the selection of the incidents; and nowise the external importance of events, the rank of the personages, or the bulk of incomes. Of course, the book affords slender materials for what would be reckoned with us a "Life of Goethe;"—few dates; no correspondence; no details of offices or employments; no light on his marriage; and, a period of ten years, that should be the most active in his life, after his settlement at Weimar, is sunk in silence. Meantime, certain love-affairs, that came to nothing, as people say, have the strangest importance: he crowds us with details:—certain whimsical opinions, cosmogonies, and religions of his own invention, and, especially his relations to remarkable minds, and to critical epochs of thought:—these he magnifies. His "Daily and Yearly Journal," his "Italian Travels," his "Campaign in France," and the historical part of his "Theory of Colors," have the same interest. In the last, he rapidly notices Kepler, Roger Bacon, Galileo, Newton, Voltaire, &c.; and the charm of this portion of the book consists in the simplest statement of the relation betwixt these grandees of European scientific history and himself; the mere drawing of the lines from Goethe to Kepler, from Goethe to Bacon, from Goethe to Newton. The drawing of the line is for the time and person, a solution of the formidable problem, and gives pleasure when Iphigenia and Faust do not, without any cost of invention comparable to that of Iphigenia and Faust.

This lawgiver of art is not an artist. Was it that he knew too much, that his sight was microscopic, and interfered with the just perspective, the seeing of the whole? He is fragmentary; a writer of occasional poems, and of an encyclopædia of sentences. When he sits down to write a drama or a tale, he collects and sorts his observations from a hundred sides, and combines them into the body as fitly as he can. A great deal refuses to incorporate: this he adds loosely, as letters of the parties, leaves from their journals, or the like. A great deal still is left that will not find any place. This the bookbinder alone can give any cohesion to: and hence, notwithstanding the looseness of many of his works, we have volumes of detached paragraphs, aphorisms, *xenien*, &c.

I suppose the worldly tone of his tales grew out of the calculations of self-culture. It was the infirmity of an admirable scholar, who loved the world out of gratitude; who knew where libraries, galleries, architecture, laboratories, savans, and leisure, were to be had, and who did not quite trust the compensations of poverty and nakedness. Socrates loved Athens; Montaigne, Paris; and Madame de Staël said, she was only vulnerable on that side; (namely, of Paris.) It has its favorable aspect. All the geniuses are usually so ill-assorted and sickly, that one is ever wishing them somewhere else. We seldom see any body who is not uneasy or afraid to live. There is a slight blush of shame on the cheek of good men and aspiring men, and a spice of caricature. But this man was entirely at home and happy in his century and the world. None was so fit to live, or more heartily enjoyed the game. In this aim of culture, which is the genius of his works, is their power. The idea of absolute, eternal truth, without reference to my own enlargement by it, is higher. The surrender to the torrent of poetic inspiration is higher; but, compared with any motives on which books are written in England and America, this is very truth, and has the power to inspire which belongs to truth. Thus has he brought back to a book some of its ancient might and dignity.

Goethe, coming into an over-civilized time and country, when original talent was oppressed under the load of books and mechanical auxiliaries, and the distracting variety of claims, taught men how to dispose of this mountainous miscellany, and make it subservient. I join Napoleon with him, as being both representatives of the impatience and reaction of nature against the *morgue* of conventions,—two stern realists, who, with their scholars, have severally set the axe at the root of the tree of cant and seeming, for this time, and for all time. This cheerful laborer, with no external popularity or provocation, drawing his motive and his plan from his own breast, tasked himself with stints for a giant, and, without relaxation or rest, except by alternating his pursuits, worked on for eighty years with the steadiness of his first zeal.

It is the last lesson of modern science, that the highest simplicity of structure is produced, not by few elements, but by the highest complexity. Man is the most composite of all creatures: the wheel-insect, *volvox globator*, is at the other extreme. We shall learn to draw rents and revenues from the immense patrimony of the old and the recent ages. Goethe teaches courage, and the equivalence of all times; that the disadvantages of any epoch exist only to the faint-hearted. Genius hovers with his sunshine and music close by the darkest and deafest eras. No mortgage, no attainder, will hold on men or hours. The world is young: the former great men call to us affectionately. We too must write Bibles, to unite again the heavens and the earthly world. The secret of genius is to suffer no fiction to exist for us; to realize all that we know; in the high refinement of modern life, in arts, in sciences, in books, in men, to exact good faith, reality, and a purpose; and first, last, midst, and without end, to honor every truth by use.

THE END

ENGLISH TRAITS

Contents

First Visit to England

I HAVE BEEN twice in England. In 1833, on my return from a short tour in Sicily, Italy, and France, I crossed from Boulogne, and landed in London at the Tower stairs. It was a dark Sunday morning; there were few people in the streets; and I remember the pleasure of that first walk on English ground, with my companion, an American artist, from the Tower up through Cheapside and the Strand, to a house in Russell Square, whither we had been recommended to good chambers. For the first time for many months we were forced to check the saucy habit of travellers' criticism, as we could no longer speak aloud in the streets without being understood. The shop-signs spoke our language; our country names were on the door-plates; and the public and private buildings wore a more native and wonted front.

Like most young men at that time, I was much indebted to the men of Edinburgh, and of the Edinburgh Review,—to Jeffrey, Mackintosh, Hallam, and to Scott, Playfair, and De Quincey; and my narrow and desultory reading had inspired the wish to see the faces of three or four writers,—Coleridge, Wordsworth, Landor, De Quincey, and the latest and strongest contributor to the critical journals, Carlyle; and I suppose if I had sifted the reasons that led me to Europe, when I was ill and was advised to travel, it was mainly the attraction of these persons. If Goethe had been still living, I might have wandered into Germany also. Besides those I have named, (for Scott was dead,) there was not in Britain the man living whom I cared to behold, unless it were the Duke of Wellington, whom I afterwards saw at Westminster Abbey, at the funeral of Wilberforce. The young scholar fancies it happiness enough to live with people who can give an inside to the world; without reflecting that they are prisoners, too, of their own thought, and cannot apply themselves to yours. The conditions of literary success are almost destructive of the best social power, as they do not leave that frolic liberty which only can encounter a companion on the best terms. It is probable you left some obscure comrade at a tavern, or in the farms, with right mother-wit, and equality to life, when you crossed sea and land to play bo-peep with celebrated scribes. I have, however, found writers superior to their books, and I cling to my first belief, that a strong head will dispose fast enough of these impediments, and give one the satisfaction of reality, the sense of having been met, and a larger horizon.

On looking over the diary of my journey in 1833, I find nothing to publish in my memoranda of visits to places. But I have copied the few notes I made of visits to persons, as they respect parties quite too good and too transparent to the whole world to make it needful to affect any prudery of suppression about a few hints of those bright personalities.

At Florence, chief among artists I found Horatio Greenough, the American sculptor. His face was so handsome, and his person so well formed, that he might be pardoned, if, as was alleged, the face of his Medora, and the figure of a colossal Achilles in clay, were idealizations of his own. Greenough was a superior man, ardent and eloquent, and all his opinions had elevation and magnanimity. He believed that the Greeks had wrought in schools or fraternities,—the genius of the master imparting his design to his friends, and inflaming them with it, and when his strength was spent, a new hand, with equal heat, continued the work; and so by relays, until it was finished in every part with equal fire. This was necessary in so refractory a material as stone; and he thought art would never prosper until we left our shy jealous ways, and worked in society as they. All his thoughts breathed the same generosity. He was an accurate and a deep man. He was a votary of the Greeks, and impatient of Gothic art. His paper on Architecture, published in 1843, announced in advance the leading thoughts of Mr. Ruskin on the *morality* in architecture, notwithstanding the antagonism in their views of the history of art. I have a private letter from him,— later, but respecting the same period,—in which he roughly sketches his own theory. "Here is my theory of structure: A scientific arrangement of spaces and forms to functions and to site; an emphasis of features proportioned to their *gradated* importance in function; color and ornament to be decided and arranged and varied by strictly organic laws, having a distinct reason for each decision; the entire and immediate banishment of all make-shift and make-believe."

Greenough brought me, through a common friend, an invitation from Mr. Landor, who lived at San Domenica di Fiesole. On the 15th May I dined with Mr. Landor. I found him noble and courteous, living in a cloud of pictures at his Villa Gherardesca, a fine house commanding a beautiful landscape. I had inferred from his books, or magnified from some anecdotes, an impression of Achillean wrath,—an untamable petulance. I do not know whether the imputation were just or not, but certainly on this May day his courtesy veiled that haughty mind, and he was the most patient and gentle of hosts. He praised the beautiful cyclamen which grows all about Florence; he admired Washington; talked of Wordsworth, Byron, Massinger, Beaumont and Fletcher. To be sure, he is decided in his opinions, likes to surprise, and is well content to impress, if possible, his English whim upon the immutable past. No great man ever had a great son, if Philip and Alexander be not an exception; and Philip he calls the greater man. In art, he loves the Greeks, and in sculpture, them only. He prefers the Venus to every thing else, and, after that, the head of Alexander, in the gallery here. He prefers John of Bologna to Michael Angelo; in painting, Raffaelle; and shares the growing taste for Perugino and the early masters. The Greek histories he thought the only good; and after them, Voltaire's. I could not make him praise Mackintosh, nor my more recent friends; Montaigne very cordially,—and Charron also, which seemed undiscriminating. He thought Degerando indebted to "Lucas on Happiness" and "Lucas on Holiness"! He pestered me with Southey; but who is Southey?

He invited me to breakfast on Friday. On Friday I did not fail to go, and this time with Greenough. He entertained us at once with reciting half a dozen hexameter lines of Julius Cæsar's!—from Donatus, he said. He glorified Lord Chesterfield more than was necessary, and undervalued Burke, and undervalued Socrates; designated as three of the greatest of men, Washington, Phocion, and Timoleon; much as our pomologists, in their lists, select the three or the six best pears "for a small orchard;" and did not even omit to remark the similar termination of their names. "A great man," he said, "should make great sacrifices, and kill his hundred oxen, without knowing whether they would be consumed by gods and heroes, or whether the flies would eat them." I had visited Professor Amici, who had shown me his microscopes, magnifying (it was said) two thousand diameters; and I spoke of the uses to which they were applied. Landor despised entomology, yet, in the same breath, said, "the sublime was in a grain of dust." I suppose I teased him about recent writers, but he professed never to have heard of Herschel, *not even by name.* One room was full of pictures, which he likes to show, especially one piece, standing before which, he said "he would give fifty guineas to the man that would swear it was a Domenichino." I was more curious to see his library, but Mr. H——, one of the guests, told me that Mr. Landor gives away his books, and has never more than a dozen at a time in his house.

Mr. Landor carries to its height the love of freak which the English delight to indulge, as if to signalize their commanding freedom. He has a wonderful brain, despotic, violent, and inexhaustible, meant for a soldier, by what chance converted to letters, in which there is not a style nor a tint not known to him, yet with an English appetite for action and heroes. The thing done avails, and not what is said about it. An original sentence, a step forward, is worth more than all the censures. Landor is strangely undervalued in England; usually ignored; and sometimes savagely attacked in the Reviews. The criticism may be right, or wrong, and is quickly forgotten; but year after year the scholar must still go back to Landor for a multitude of elegant sentences—for wisdom, wit, and indignation that are unforgetable.

From London, on the 5th August, I went to Highgate, and wrote a note to Mr. Coleridge, requesting leave to pay my respects to him. It was near noon. Mr. Coleridge sent a verbal message, that he was in bed, but if I would call after one o'clock, he would see me. I returned at one, and he appeared, a short, thick old man, with bright blue eyes and fine clear complexion, leaning on his cane. He took snuff freely, which presently soiled his cravat and neat black suit. He asked whether I knew Allston, and spoke warmly of his merits and doings when he knew him in Rome; what a master of the Titianesque he was, &c., &c. He spoke of Dr. Channing. It was an unspeakable misfortune that he should have turned out a Unitarian after all. On this, he burst into a declamation on the folly and ignorance of Unitarianism,—its high unreasonableness; and taking up Bishop Waterland's book, which lay on the table, he read with vehemence two or three pages written by himself in the fly-leaves,—passages, too, which, I believe, are printed in the "Aids to Reflection." When he stopped to take breath, I interposed, that, "whilst I highly valued all his explanations, I was bound to tell him that I was born and bred a Unitarian." "Yes," he said, "I supposed so;" and continued as before. 'It was a wonder, that after so many ages of unquestioning acquiescence in the doctrine of St. Paul,—the doctrine of the Trinity, which was also, according to Philo Judæus, the doctrine of the Jews before Christ,—this handful of Priestleians should take on themselves to deny it, &c., &c. He was very sorry that Dr. Channing,—a man to whom he looked up,—no, to say that he looked *up* to him would be to speak falsely; but a man whom he looked *at* with so much interest,—should embrace such views. When he saw Dr. Channing, he had hinted to him that he was afraid he loved Christianity for what was lovely and excellent,—he loved the good in it, and not the true; and I tell you, sir, that I have known ten persons who loved the good, for one person who loved the true; but it is a far greater virtue to love the true for itself alone, than to love the good for itself alone. He (Coleridge) knew all about Unitarianism perfectly well, because he had once been a Unitarian, and knew what quackery it was. He had been called "the rising star of Unitarianism." ' He went on defining, or rather refining: 'The Trinitarian doctrine was realism; the idea of God was not essential, but superessential;' talked of *trinism* and *tetrakism*, and much more, of which I only caught this, 'that the will was that by which a person is a person; because, if one should push me in the street, and so I should force the man next me into the kennel, I should at once exclaim, "I did not do it, sir," meaning it was not my will.' And this also, 'that if you should insist on your faith here in England, and I on mine, mine would be the hotter side of the fagot.'

I took advantage of a pause to say, that he had many readers of all religious opinions in America, and I proceeded to inquire if the "extract" from the Independent's pamphlet, in the third volume of the Friend, were a veritable quotation. He replied, that it was really taken from a pamphlet in his possession, entitled "A Protest of one of the Independents," or something to that effect. I told him how excellent I thought it, and how much I wished to see the entire work. "Yes," he said, "the man was a chaos of truths, but lacked the knowledge that God was a God of order. Yet the passage would no doubt strike you more in the quotation than in the original, for I have filtered it."

When I rose to go, he said, "I do not know whether you care about poetry, but I will repeat some verses I lately made on my baptismal anniversary," and he recited with strong emphasis, standing, ten or twelve lines, beginning,

"Born unto God in Christ——"

He inquired where I had been travelling; and on learning that I had been in Malta and Sicily, he compared one island with the other, 'repeating what he had said to the Bishop of London when he returned from that country, that Sicily was an excellent school of political economy; for, in any town there, it only needed to ask what the government enacted, and reverse that to know what ought to be done; it was the most felicitously opposite legislation to any thing good and wise. There were only three things which the government had brought into that garden of delights, namely, itch, pox, and famine. Whereas, in Malta, the force of law and mind was seen, in making that barren rock of semi-Saracen inhabitants the seat of population and plenty.' Going out, he showed me in the next apartment a picture of Allston's, and told me 'that Montague, a picture-dealer, once came to see him, and, glancing towards this, said, "Well, you have got a picture!" thinking it the work of an old master; afterwards, Montague, still talking with his back to the canvas, put up his hand and touched it, and exclaimed, "By Heaven! this picture is not ten years old:"—so delicate and skilful was that man's touch.'

I was in his company for about an hour, but find it impossible to recall the largest part of his discourse, which was often like so many printed paragraphs in his book,—perhaps the same,—so readily did he fall into certain commonplaces. As I might have foreseen, the visit was rather a spectacle than a conversation, of no use beyond the satisfaction of my curiosity. He was old and preoccupied, and could not bend to a new companion and think with him.

From Edinburgh I went to the Highlands. On my return, I came from Glasgow to Dumfries, and being intent on delivering a letter which I had brought from Rome, inquired for Craigenputtock. It was a farm in Nithsdale, in the parish of Dunscore, sixteen miles distant. No public coach passed near it, so I took a private carriage from the inn. I found the house amid desolate heathery hills, where the lonely scholar nourished his mighty heart. Carlyle was a man from his youth, an author who did not need to hide from his readers, and as absolute a man of the world, unknown and exiled on that hill-farm, as if holding on his own terms what is best in London. He was tall and gaunt, with a cliff-like brow, self-possessed, and holding his extraordinary powers of conversation in easy command; clinging to his northern accent with evident relish; full of lively anecdote, and with a streaming humor, which floated every thing he looked upon. His talk playfully exalting the familiar objects, put the companion at once into an acquaintance with his Lars and Lemurs, and it was very pleasant to learn what was predestined to be a pretty mythology. Few were the objects and lonely the man, "not a person to speak to within sixteen miles except the minister of Dunscore;" so that books inevitably made his topics.

He had names of his own for all the matters familiar to his discourse. "Blackwood's" was the "sand magazine;" "Fraser's" nearer approach to possibility of life was the "mud magazine;" a piece of road near by that marked some failed enterprise was the "grave of the last sixpence." When too much praise of any genius annoyed him, he professed hugely to admire the talent shown by his pig. He had spent much time and contrivance in confining the poor beast to one enclosure in his pen, but pig, by great strokes of judgment, had found out how to let a board down, and had foiled him. For all that, he still thought man the most plastic little fellow in the planet, and he liked Nero's death, *"Qualis artifex pereo!"* better than most history. He worships a man that will manifest any truth to him. At one time he had inquired and read a good deal about America. Landor's principle was mere rebellion, and *that* he feared was the American principle. The best thing he knew of that country was, that in it a man can have meat for his labor. He had read in Stewart's book, that when he inquired in a New York hotel for the Boots, he had been shown across the street and had found Mungo in his own house dining on roast turkey.

We talked of books. Plato he does not read, and he disparaged Socrates; and, when pressed, persisted in making Mirabeau a hero. Gibbon he called the splendid bridge from the old world to the new. His own reading had been multifarious. Tristram Shandy was one of his first books after Robinson Crusoe, and Robertson's America an early favorite. Rousseau's Confessions had discovered to him that he was not a dunce; and it was now ten years since he had learned German, by the advice of a man who told him he would find in that language what he wanted.

He took despairing or satirical views of literature at this moment; recounted the incredible sums paid in one year by the great booksellers for puffing. Hence it comes that no newspaper is trusted now, no books are bought, and the booksellers are on the eve of bankruptcy.

He still returned to English pauperism, the crowded country, the selfish abdication by public men of all that public persons should perform. 'Government should direct poor men what to do. Poor Irish folk come wandering over these moors. My dame makes it a rule to give to every son of Adam bread to eat, and supplies his wants to the next house. But here are thousands of acres which might give them all meat, and nobody to bid these poor Irish go to the moor and till it. They burned the stacks, and so found a way to force the rich people to attend to them.'

We went out to walk over long hills, and looked at Criffel,

then without his cap, and down into Wordsworth's country. There we sat down, and talked of the immortality of the soul. It was not Carlyle's fault that we talked on that topic, for he had the natural disinclination of every nimble spirit to bruise itself against walls, and did not like to place himself where no step can be taken. But he was honest and true, and cognizant of the subtile links that bind ages together, and saw how every event affects all the future. 'Christ died on the tree: that built Dunscore kirk yonder: that brought you and me together. Time has only a relative existence.'

He was already turning his eyes towards London with a scholar's appreciation. London is the heart of the world, he said, wonderful only from the mass of human beings. He liked the huge machine. Each keeps its own round. The baker's boy brings muffins to the window at a fixed hour every day, and that is all the Londoner knows or wishes to know on the subject. But it turned out good men. He named certain individuals, especially one man of letters, his friend, the best mind he knew, whom London had well served.

On the 28th August, I went to Rydal Mount, to pay my respects to Mr. Wordsworth. His daughters called in their father, a plain, elderly, white-haired man, not prepossessing, and disfigured by green goggles. He sat down, and talked with great simplicity. He had just returned from a journey. His health was good, but he had broken a tooth by a fall, when walking with two lawyers, and had said, that he was glad it did not happen forty years ago; whereupon they had praised his philosophy.

He had much to say of America, the more that it gave occasion for his favorite topic,—that society is being enlightened by a superficial tuition, out of all proportion to its being restrained by moral culture. Schools do no good. Tuition is not education. He thinks more of the education of circumstances than of tuition. 'Tis not question whether there are offences of which the law takes cognizance, but whether there are offences of which the law does not take cognizance. Sin is what he fears, and how society is to escape without gravest mischiefs from this source—? He has even said, what seemed a paradox, that they needed a civil war in America, to teach the necessity of knitting the social ties stronger. 'There may be,' he said, 'in America some vulgarity in manner, but that's not important. That comes of the pioneer state of things. But I fear they are too much given to the making of money; and secondly, to politics; that they make political distinction the end, and not the means. And I fear they lack a class of men of leisure,—in short, of gentlemen,—to give a tone of honor to the community. I am told that things are boasted of in the second class of society there, which, in England,—God knows, are done in England every day,—but would never be spoken of. In America I wish to know not how many churches or schools, but what newspapers? My friend, Colonel Hamilton, at the foot of the hill, who was a year in America, assures me that the newspapers are atrocious, and accuse members of Congress of stealing spoons!' He was against taking off the tax on newspapers in England, which the reformers represent as a tax upon knowledge, for this reason, that they would be inundated with base prints. He said, he talked on political aspects, for he wished to impress on me and all good Americans to cultivate the moral, the conservative, &c., &c., and never to call into action the physical strength of the people, as had just now been done in England in the Reform Bill,—a thing prophesied by Delolme. He alluded once or twice to his conversation with Dr. Channing, who had recently visited him, (laying his hand on a particular chair in which the Doctor had sat.)

The conversation turned on books. Lucretius he esteems a far higher poet than Virgil: not in his system, which is nothing, but in his power of illustration. Faith is necessary to explain any thing, and to reconcile the foreknowledge of God with human evil. Of Cousin, (whose lectures we had all been reading in Boston,) he knew only the name.

I inquired if he had read Carlyle's critical articles and translations. He said, he thought him sometimes insane. He proceeded to abuse Goethe's Wilhelm Meister heartily. It was full of all manner of fornication. It was like the crossing of flies in the air. He had never gone farther than the first part; so disgusted was he that he threw the book across the room. I deprecated this wrath, and said what I could for the better parts of the book; and he courteously promised to look at it again. Carlyle, he said, wrote most obscurely. He was clever and deep, but he defied the sympathies of every body. Even Mr. Coleridge wrote more clearly, though he had always wished Coleridge would write more to be understood. He led me out into his garden, and showed me the gravel walk in which thousands of his lines were composed. His eyes are much inflamed. This is no loss, except for reading, because he never writes prose, and of poetry he carries even hundreds of lines in his head before writing them. He had just returned from a visit to Staffa, and within three days had made three sonnets on Fingal's Cave, and was composing a fourth, when he was called in to see me. He said, "If you are interested in my verses, perhaps you will like to hear these lines." I gladly assented; and he recollected himself for a few moments, and then stood forth and repeated, one after the other, the three entire sonnets with great animation. I fancied the second and third more beautiful than his poems are wont to be. The third is addressed to the flowers, which, he said, especially the ox-eye daisy, are very abundant on the top of the rock. The second alludes to the name of the cave, which is "Cave of Music;" the first to the circumstance of its being visited by the promiscuous company of the steamboat.

This recitation was so unlooked for and surprising,—he, the old Wordsworth, standing apart, and reciting to me in a garden-walk, like a schoolboy declaiming,—that I at first was near to laugh; but recollecting myself, that I had come thus far to see a poet, and he was chanting poems to me, I saw that he was right and I was wrong, and gladly gave myself up to hear. I told him how much the few printed extracts had quickened the desire to possess his unpublished poems. He replied, he never was in haste to publish; partly, because he corrected a good deal, and every alteration is ungraciously received after printing; but what he had written would be printed, whether he lived or died. I said, "Tintern Abbey" appeared to be the favorite poem with the public, but more contemplative readers preferred the first books of the "Excursion," and the Sonnets. He said, "Yes, they are better." He preferred such of his poems as touched the affections, to any others; for whatever is didactic,—what theories of society, and so on,—might perish quickly; but whatever combined a truth with an affection was κτημα ες αει, good to-day and good forever. He cited the sonnet "On the feelings of a high-minded Spaniard," which he preferred to any other, (I so understood him,) and the "Two Voices;" and quoted, with evident pleasure, the verses addressed "To the Skylark." In this connection, he said of the Newtonian theory, that it might yet be superseded and forgotten; and Dalton's atomic theory.

When I prepared to depart, he said he wished to show me what a common person in England could do, and he led me into the enclosure of his clerk, a young man, to whom he had given this slip of ground, which was laid out, or its natural capabilities shown, with much taste. He then said he would show me a better way towards the inn; and he walked a good part of a mile, talking, and ever and anon stopping short to impress the word or the verse, and finally parted from me with great kindness, and returned across the fields.

Wordsworth honored himself by his simple adherence to truth, and was very willing not to shine; but he surprised by the hard limits of his thought. To judge from a single conversation, he made the impression of a narrow and very English mind; of one who paid for his rare elevation by general tameness and conformity. Off his own beat, his opinions were of no value. It is not very rare to find persons loving sympathy and ease, who expiate their departure from the common, in one direction, by their conformity in every other.

CHAPTER II

Voyage to England

THE OCCASION of my second visit to England was an invitation from some Mechanics' Institutes in Lancashire and Yorkshire, which separately are organized much in the same way as our New England Lyceums, but, in 1847, had been linked into a "Union," which embraced twenty or thirty towns and cities, and presently extended into the middle counties, and northward into Scotland. I was invited, on liberal terms, to read a series of lectures in them all. The request was urged with every kind suggestion, and every assurance of aid and comfort, by friendliest parties in Manchester, who, in the sequel, amply redeemed their word. The remuneration was equivalent to the fees at that time paid in this country for the like services. At all events, it was sufficient to cover any travelling expenses, and the proposal offered an excellent opportunity of seeing the interior of England and Scotland, by means of a home, and a committee of intelligent friends, awaiting me in every town.

I did not go very willingly. I am not a good traveller, nor have I found that long journeys yield a fair share of reasonable hours. But the invitation was repeated and pressed at a moment of more leisure, and when I was a little spent by some unusual studies. I wanted a change and a tonic, and England was proposed to me. Besides, there were, at least, the dread attraction and salutary influences of the sea. So I took my berth in the packet-ship Washington Irving, and sailed from Boston on Tuesday, 5th October, 1847.

On Friday at noon, we had only made one hundred and thirty-four miles. A nimble Indian would have swum as far; but the captain affirmed that the ship would show us in time all her paces, and we crept along through the floating drift of boards, logs, and chips, which the rivers of Maine and New Brunswick pour into the sea after a freshet.

At last, on Sunday night, after doing one day's work in four, the storm came, the winds blew, and we flew before a north-wester, which strained every rope and sail. The good ship darts through the water all day, all night, like a fish, quivering with speed, gliding through liquid leagues, sliding from horizon to horizon. She has passed Cape Sable; she has reached the Banks; the land-birds are left; gulls, haglets, ducks, petrels, swim, dive, and hover around; no fishermen; she has passed the Banks; left five sail behind her, far on the edge of the west at sundown, which were far east of us at morn,—though they say at sea a stern chase is a long race,—and still we fly for our lives. The shortest sea-line from Boston to Liverpool is 2850 miles. This a steamer keeps, and saves 150 miles. A sailing ship can never go in a shorter line than 3000, and usually it is much longer. Our good master keeps his kites up to the last moment, studding-sails alow and aloft, and, by incessant straight steering, never loses a rod of way. Watchfulness is the law of the ship,—watch on watch, for advantage and for life. Since the ship was built, it seems, the master never slept but in his day-clothes whilst on board. "There are many advantages," says Saadi, "in sea-voyaging, but security is not one of them." Yet in hurrying over these abysses, whatever dangers we are running into, we are certainly running out of the risks of hundreds of miles every day, which have their own chances of squall, collision, sea-stroke, piracy, cold, and thunder. Hour for hour, the risk on a steamboat is greater; but the speed is safety, or, twelve days of danger, instead of twenty-four.

Our ship was registered 750 tons, and weighed perhaps, with all her freight, 1500 tons. The mainmast, from the deck to the top-button, measured 115 feet; the length of the deck, from stem to stern, 155. It is impossible not to personify a ship; every body does, in every thing they say:—she behaves well; she minds her rudder; she swims like a duck; she runs her nose into the water; she looks into a port. Then that wonderful *esprit du corps*, by which we adopt into our self-love every thing we touch, makes us all champions of her sailing qualities.

The conscious ship hears all the praise. In one week she has made 1467 miles, and now, at night, seems to hear the steamer behind her, which left Boston to-day at two, has mended her speed, and is flying before the gray south wind eleven and a half knots the hour. The sea-fire shines in her wake, and far around wherever a wave breaks. I read the hour, 9h. 45′, on my watch by this light. Near the equator, you can read small print by it; and the mate describes the phosphoric insects, when taken up in a pail, as shaped like a Carolina potato.

I find the sea-life an acquired taste, like that for tomatoes and olives. The confinement, cold, motion, noise, and odor are not to be dispensed with. The floor of your room is sloped at an angle of twenty or thirty degrees, and I waked every morning with the belief that some one was tipping up my berth. Nobody likes to be treated ignominiously, upset, shoved against the side of the house, rolled over, suffocated with bilge, mephitis, and stewing oil. We get used to these annoyances at last, but the dread of the sea remains longer. The sea is masculine, the type of active strength. Look, what egg-shells are drifting all over it, each one, like ours, filled with men in ecstasies of terror, alternating with cockney conceit, as the sea is rough or smooth. Is this sad-colored circle an eternal cemetery? In our graveyards we scoop a pit, but this aggressive water opens mile-wide pits and chasms, and makes a mouthful of a fleet. To the geologist, the sea is the only firmament; the land is in perpetual flux and change, now blown up like a tumor, now sunk in a chasm, and the registered observations of a few hundred years find it in a perpetual tilt, rising and falling. The sea keeps its old level; and 'tis no wonder that the history of our race is so recent, if the roar of the ocean is silencing our traditions. A rising of the sea, such as has been observed, say an inch in a century, from east to west on the land, will bury all the towns, monuments, bones, and knowledge of mankind, steadily and insensibly. If it is capable of these great and secular mischiefs, it is quite as ready at private and local damage; and of this no landsman seems so fearful as the seaman. Such discomfort and such danger as the narratives of the captain and mate disclose are bad enough as the costly fee we pay for entrance to Europe; but the wonder is always new that any sane man can be a sailor. And here, on the second day of our voyage, stepped out a little boy in his shirt-sleeves, who had hid himself, whilst the ship was in port, in the bread-closet, having no money, and wishing to go to England. The sailors have dressed him in Guernsey frock, with a knife in his belt, and he is climbing nimbly about after them, "likes the work first-rate, and, if the captain will take him, means now to come back again in the ship." The mate avers that this is the history of all sailors; nine out of ten are runaway boys; and adds, that all of them are sick of the sea, but stay in it out of pride. Jack has a life of risks, incessant abuse, and the worst pay. It is a little better with the mate, and not very much better with the captain. A hundred dollars a month is reckoned high pay. If sailors were contented, if they had not resolved again and again not to go to sea any more, I should respect them.

Of course, the inconveniences and terrors of the sea are not of any account to those whose minds are preoccupied. The water-laws, arctic frost, the mountain, the mine, only shatter cockneyism; every noble activity makes room for itself. A great mind is a good sailor, as a great heart is. And the sea is not slow in disclosing inestimable secrets to a good naturalist.

'Tis a good rule in every journey to provide some piece of liberal study to rescue the hours which bad weather, bad company, and taverns steal from the best economist. Classics which at home are drowsily read have a strange charm in a country inn, or in the transom of a merchant brig. I remember that some of the happiest and most valuable hours I have owed to books, passed, many years ago, on shipboard. The worst impediment I have found at sea is the want of light in the cabin.

We found on board the usual cabin library; Basil Hall, Dumas, Dickens, Bulwer, Balzac, and Sand were our sea-gods. Among the passengers, there was some variety of talent and profession; we exchanged our experiences, and all learned something. The busiest talk with leisure and convenience at sea, and sometimes a memorable fact turns up, which you have long had a vacant niche for, and seize with the joy of a collector. But, under the best conditions, a voyage is one of the severest tests to try a man. A college examination is nothing to it. Sea-days are long,—these lack-lustre, joyless days which whistled over us; but they were few,—only fifteen, as the captain counted, sixteen according to me. Reckoned from the time when we left soundings, our speed was such that the captain drew the line of his course in red ink on his chart, for the encouragement or envy of future navigators.

It has been said that the King of England would consult his dignity by giving audience to foreign ambassadors in the cabin of a man-of-war. And I think the white path of an Atlantic ship the right avenue to the palace front of this seafaring people, who for hundreds of years claimed the strict sovereignty of the sea, and exacted toll and the striking sail from the ships of all other peoples. When their privilege was disputed by the Dutch and other junior marines, on the plea that you could never anchor on the same wave, or hold property in what was always flowing, the English did not stick to claim the channel, or bottom of all the main. "As if," said they, "we contended for the drops of the sea, and not for its situation, or the bed of those waters. The sea is bounded by his majesty's empire."

As we neared the land, its genius was felt. This was inevitably the British side. In every man's thought arises now a new system, English sentiments, English loves and fears, English history and social modes. Yesterday, every passenger had measured the speed of the ship by watching the bubbles over the ship's bulwarks. To-day, instead of bubbles, we measure by Kinsale, Cork, Waterford, and Ardmore. There lay the green shore of Ireland, like some coast of plenty. We could see towns, towers, churches, harvests; but the curse of eight hundred years we could not discern.

CHAPTER III

Land

ALFIERI THOUGHT Italy and England the only countries worth living in; the former, because there nature vindicates her rights, and triumphs over the evils inflicted by the governments; the latter, because art conquers nature, and transforms a rude, ungenial land into a paradise of comfort and plenty. England is a garden. Under an ash-colored sky, the fields have been combed and rolled till they appear to have been finished with a pencil instead of a plough. The solidity of the structures that compose the towns speaks the industry of ages. Nothing is left as it was made. Rivers, hills, valleys, the sea itself feel the hand of a master. The long habitation of a powerful and ingenious race has turned every rood of land to its best use, has found all the capabilities, the arable soil, the quarriable rock, the highways, the byways, the fords, the navigable waters; and the new arts of intercourse meet you every where; so that England is a huge phalanstery, where all that man wants is provided within the precinct. Cushioned and comforted in every manner, the traveller rides as on a cannon-ball, high and low, over rivers and towns, through mountains, in tunnels of three or four miles, at near twice the speed of our trains; and reads quietly the Times newspaper, which, by its immense correspondence and reporting, seems to have machinized the rest of the world for his occasion.

The problem of the traveller landing at Liverpool is, Why England is England? What are the elements of that power which the English hold over other nations? If there be one test of national genius universally accepted, it is success; and if there be one successful country in the universe for the last millennium, that country is England.

A wise traveller will naturally choose to visit the best of actual nations; and an American has more reasons than another to draw him to Britain. In all that is done or begun by the Americans towards right thinking or practice, we are met by a civilization already settled and overpowering. The culture of the day, the thoughts and aims of men, are English thoughts and aims. A nation considerable for a thousand years since Egbert, it has, in the last centuries, obtained the ascendant, and stamped the knowledge, activity, and power of mankind with its impress. Those who resist it do not feel it or obey it less. The Russian in his snows is aiming to be English. The Turk and Chinese also are making awkward efforts to be English. The practical common-sense of modern society, the utilitarian direction which labor, laws, opinion, religion take, is the natural genius of the British mind. The influence of France is a constituent of modern civility, but not enough opposed to the English for the most wholesome effect. The American is only the continuation of the English genius into new conditions, more or less propitious.

See what books fill our libraries. Every book we read, every biography, play, romance, in whatever form, is still English history and manners. So that a sensible Englishman once said to me, "As long as you do not grant us copyright, we shall have the teaching of you."

But we have the same difficulty in making a social or moral estimate of England, as the sheriff finds in drawing a jury to try some cause which has agitated the whole community, and on which every body finds himself an interested party. Officers, jurors, judges have all taken sides. England has inoculated all nations with her civilization, intelligence, and tastes; and, to resist the tyranny and prepossession of the British element, a serious man must aid himself, by comparing with it the civilizations of the farthest east and west, the old Greek, the Oriental, and, much more, the ideal standard, if only by means of the very impatience which English forms are sure to awaken in independent minds.

Besides, if we will visit London, the present time is the best time, as some signs portend that it has reached its highest point. It is observed that the English interest us a little less within a few years; and hence the impression that the British power has culminated, is in solstice, or already declining.

As soon as you enter England, which, with Wales, is no larger than the State of Georgia,* this little land stretches by

*Add South Carolina, and you have more than an equivalent for the area of Scotland.

an illusion to the dimensions of an empire. The innumerable details, the crowded succession of towns, cities, cathedrals, castles, and great and decorated estates, the number and power of the trades and guilds, the military strength and splendor, the multitudes of rich and of remarkable people, the servants and equipages,—all these catching the eye, and never allowing it to pause, hide all boundaries, by the impression of magnificence and endless wealth.

I reply to all the urgencies that refer me to this and that object indispensably to be seen,—Yes, to see England well needs a hundred years; for, what they told me was the merit of Sir John Soane's Museum, in London,—that it was well packed and well saved,—is the merit of England;—it is stuffed full, in all corners and crevices, with towns, towers, churches, villas, palaces, hospitals, and charity-houses. In the history of art, it is a long way from a cromlech to York minster; yet all the intermediate steps may still be traced in this all-preserving island.

The territory has a singular perfection. The climate is warmer by many degrees than it is entitled to by latitude. Neither hot nor cold, there is no hour in the whole year when one cannot work. Here is no winter, but such days as we have in Massachusetts in November, a temperature which makes no exhausting demand on human strength, but allows the attainment of the largest stature. Charles the Second said, "it invited men abroad more days in the year and more hours in the day than another country." Then England has all the materials of a working country except wood. The constant rain,—a rain with every tide, in some parts of the island,— keeps its multitude of rivers full, and brings agricultural production up to the highest point. It has plenty of water, of stone, of potter's clay, of coal, of salt, and of iron. The land naturally abounds with game, immense heaths and downs are paved with quails, grouse, and woodcock, and the shores are animated by water birds. The rivers and the surrounding sea spawn with fish; there are salmon for the rich, and sprats and herrings for the poor. In the northern lochs, the herring are in innumerable shoals; at one season, the country people say, the lakes contain one part water and two parts fish.

The only drawback on this industrial conveniency, is the

darkness of its sky. The night and day are too nearly of a color. It strains the eyes to read and to write. Add the coal smoke. In the manufacturing towns, the fine soot or *blacks* darken the day, give white sheep the color of black sheep, discolor the human saliva, contaminate the air, poison many plants, and corrode the monuments and buildings.

The London fog aggravates the distempers of the sky, and sometimes justifies the epigram on the climate by an English wit, "in a fine day, looking up a chimney; in a foul day, looking down one." A gentleman in Liverpool told me that he found he could do without a fire in his parlor about one day in the year. It is however pretended, that the enormous consumption of coal in the island is also felt in modifying the general climate.

Factitious climate, factitious position. England resembles a ship in its shape, and, if it were one, its best admiral could not have worked it, or anchored it in a more judicious or effective position. Sir John Herschel said, "London was the centre of the terrene globe." The shopkeeping nation, to use a shop word, has a *good stand*. The old Venetians pleased themselves with the flattery, that Venice was in 45°, midway between the poles and the line; as if that were an imperial centrality. Long of old, the Greeks fancied Delphi the navel of the earth, in their favorite mode of fabling the earth to be an animal. The Jews believed Jerusalem to be the centre. I have seen a kratometric chart designed to show that the city of Philadelphia was in the same thermic belt, and, by inference, in the same belt of empire, as the cities of Athens, Rome, and London. It was drawn by a patriotic Philadelphian, and was examined with pleasure, under his showing, by the inhabitants of Chestnut Street. But, when carried to Charleston, to New Orleans, and to Boston, it somehow failed to convince the ingenious scholars of all those capitals.

But England is anchored at the side of Europe, and right in the heart of the modern world. The sea, which, according to Virgil's famous line, divided the poor Britons utterly from the world, proved to be the ring of marriage with all nations. It is not down in the books,—it is written only in the geologic strata,—that fortunate day when a wave of the German Ocean burst the old isthmus which joined Kent and Cornwall to France, and gave to this fragment of Europe its impregnable sea wall, cutting off an island of eight hundred miles in length, with an irregular breadth reaching to three hundred miles; a territory large enough for independence enriched with every seed of national power, so near, that it can see the harvests of the continent; and so far, that who would cross the strait must be an expert mariner, ready for tempests. As America, Europe, and Asia lie, these Britons have precisely the best commercial position in the whole planet, and are sure of a market for all the goods they can manufacture. And to make these advantages avail, the River Thames must dig its spacious outlet to the sea from the heart of the kingdom, giving road and landing to innumerable ships, and all the conveniency to trade, that a people so skilful and sufficient in economizing water-front by docks, warehouses, and lighters required. When James the First declared his purpose of punishing London by removing his Court, the Lord Mayor replied, "that, in removing his royal presence from his lieges, they hoped he would leave them the Thames."

In the variety of surface, Britain is a miniature of Europe, having plain, forest, marsh, river, sea-shore; mines in Cornwall; caves in Matlock and Derbyshire; delicious landscape in Dovedale, delicious sea-view at Tor Bay, Highlands in Scotland, Snowdon in Wales; and, in Westmoreland and Cumberland, a pocket Switzerland, in which the lakes and mountains are on a sufficient scale to fill the eye and touch the imagination. It is a nation conveniently small. Fontenelle thought, that nature had sometimes a little affectation; and there is such an artificial completeness in this nation of artificers, as if there were a design from the beginning to elaborate a bigger Birmingham. Nature held counsel with herself, and said, 'My Romans are gone. To build my new empire, I will choose a rude race, all masculine, with brutish strength. I will not grudge a competition of the roughest males. Let buffalo gore buffalo, and the pasture to the strongest! For I have work that requires the best will and sinew. Sharp and temperate northern breezes shall blow, to keep that will alive and alert. The sea shall disjoin the people from others, and knit them to a fierce nationality. It shall give them markets on every side. Long time I will keep them on their feet, by poverty, border-wars, seafaring, sea-risks, and the stimulus of gain. An island,—but not so large, the people not so many as to glut the great markets and depress one another, but proportioned to the size of Europe and the continents.'

With its fruits, and wares, and money, must its civil influence radiate. It is a singular coincidence to this geographic centrality, the spiritual centrality, which Emanuel Swedenborg ascribes to the people. "For the English nation, the best of them are in the centre of all Christians, because they have interior intellectual light. This appears conspicuously in the spiritual world. This light they derive from the liberty of speaking and writing, and thereby of thinking."

CHAPTER IV

Race

AN INGENIOUS anatomist has written a book* to prove
that races are imperishable, but nations are pliant political constructions, easily changed or destroyed. But this writer
did not found his assumed races on any necessary law, disclosing their ideal or metaphysical necessity; nor did he, on
the other hand, count with precision the existing races, and
settle the true bounds; a point of nicety, and the popular test
of the theory. The individuals at the extremes of divergence
in one race of men are as unlike as the wolf to the lapdog.
Yet each variety shades down imperceptibly into the next, and
you cannot draw the line where a race begins or ends. Hence
every writer makes a different count. Blumenbach reckons five
races; Humboldt three; and Mr. Pickering, who lately, in our
Exploring Expedition, thinks he saw all the kinds of men that
can be on the planet, makes eleven.

The British Empire is reckoned to contain 222,000,000
souls,—perhaps a fifth of the population of the globe; and to
comprise a territory of 5,000,000 square miles. So far have
British people predominated. Perhaps forty of these millions
are of British stock. Add the United States of America, which
reckon, exclusive of slaves, 20,000,000 of people, on a territory of 3,000,000 square miles, and in which the foreign element, however considerable, is rapidly assimilated, and you
have a population of English descent and language, of
60,000,000, and governing a population of 245,000,000
souls.

The British census proper reckons twenty-seven and a half
millions in the home countries. What makes this census important is the quality of the units that compose it. They are
free forcible men, in a country where life is safe, and has
reached the greatest value. They give the bias to the current
age; and that, not by chance or by mass, but by their character, and by the number of individuals among them of personal ability. It has been denied that the English have genius.

*The Races, a Fragment. By Robert Knox. London: 1850.

790

Be it as it may, men of vast intellect have been born on their soil, and they have made or applied the principal inventions. They have sound bodies, and supreme endurance in war and in labor. The spawning force of the race has sufficed to the colonization of great parts of the world; yet it remains to be seen whether they can make good the exodus of millions from Great Britain, amounting, in 1852, to more than a thousand a day. They have assimilating force, since they are imitated by their foreign subjects; and they are still aggressive and propagandist, enlarging the dominion of their arts and liberty. Their laws are hospitable, and slavery does not exist under them. What oppression exists is incidental and temporary; their success is not sudden or fortunate, but they have maintained constancy and self-equality for many ages.

Is this power due to their race, or to some other cause? Men hear gladly of the power of blood or race. Every body likes to know that his advantages cannot be attributed to air, soil, sea, or to local wealth, as mines and quarries, nor to laws and traditions, nor to fortune, but to superior brain, as it makes the praise more personal to him.

We anticipate in the doctrine of race something like that law of physiology, that, whatever bone, muscle, or essential organ is found in one healthy individual, the same part or organ may be found in or near the same place in its congener; and we look to find in the son every mental and moral property that existed in the ancestor. In race, it is not the broad shoulders, or litheness, or stature that give advantage, but a symmetry that reaches as far as to the wit. Then the miracle and renown begin. Then first we care to examine the pedigree, and copy heedfully the training,—what food they ate, what nursing, school, and exercises they had, which resulted in this mother-wit, delicacy of thought, and robust wisdom. How came such men as King Alfred, and Roger Bacon, William of Wykeham, Walter Raleigh, Philip Sidney, Isaac Newton, William Shakspeare, George Chapman, Francis Bacon, George Herbert, Henry Vane, to exist here? What made these delicate natures? was it the air? was it the sea? was it the parentage? For it is certain that these men are samples of their contemporaries. The hearing ear is always found close to the speaking tongue; and no genius can long or often utter any thing which is not invited and gladly entertained by men around him.

It is race, is it not? that puts the hundred millions of India under the dominion of a remote island in the north of Europe. Race avails much, if that be true, which is alleged, that all Celts are Catholics, and all Saxons are Protestants; that Celts love unity of power, and Saxons the representative principle. Race is a controlling influence in the Jew, who, for two millenniums, under every climate, has preserved the same character and employments. Race in the negro is of appalling importance. The French in Canada, cut off from all intercourse with the parent people, have held their national traits. I chanced to read Tacitus "on the Manners of the Germans," not long since, in Missouri, and the heart of Illinois, and I found abundant points of resemblance between the Germans of the Hercynian forest, and our *Hoosiers*, *Suckers*, and *Badgers* of the American woods.

But whilst race works immortally to keep its own, it is resisted by other forces. Civilization is a re-agent, and eats away the old traits. The Arabs of to-day are the Arabs of Pharaoh; but the Briton of to-day is a very different person from Cassibelaunus or Ossian. Each religious sect has its physiognomy. The Methodists have acquired a face; the Quakers, a face; the nuns, a face. An Englishman will pick out a dissenter by his manners. Trades and professions carve their own lines on face and form. Certain circumstances of English life are not less effective; as, personal liberty; plenty of food; good ale and mutton; open market, or good wages for every kind of labor; high bribes to talent and skill; the island life, or the million opportunities and outlets for expanding and misplaced talent; readiness of combination among themselves for politics or for business; strikes; and sense of superiority founded on habit of victory in labor and in war; and the appetite for superiority grows by feeding.

It is easy to add to the counteracting forces to race. Credence is a main element. 'Tis said, that the views of nature held by any people determine all their institutions. Whatever influences add to mental or moral faculty, take men out of nationality, as out of other conditions, and make the national life a culpable compromise.

These limitations of the formidable doctrine of race suggest others which threaten to undermine it, as not sufficiently based. The fixity or inconvertibleness of races as we see them, is a weak argument for the eternity of these frail boundaries, since all our historical period is a point to the duration in which nature has wrought. Any the least and solitariest fact in our natural history, such as the melioration of fruits and of animal stocks, has the worth of a *power* in the opportunity of geologic periods. Moreover, though we flatter the self-love of men and nations by the legend of pure races, all our experience is of the gradation and resolution of races, and strange resemblances meet us every where. It need not puzzle us that Malay and Papuan, Celt and Roman, Saxon and Tartar should mix, when we see the rudiments of tiger and baboon in our human form, and know that the barriers of races are not so firm, but that some spray sprinkles us from the antediluvian seas.

The low organizations are simplest; a mere mouth, a jelly, or a straight worm. As the scale mounts, the organizations become complex. We are piqued with pure descent, but nature loves inoculation. A child blends in his face the faces of both parents, and some feature from every ancestor whose face hangs on the wall. The best nations are those most widely related; and navigation, as effecting a world-wide mixture, is the most potent advancer of nations.

The English composite character betrays a mixed origin. Every thing English is a fusion of distant and antagonistic elements. The language is mixed; the names of men are of different nations,—three languages, three or four nations;— the currents of thought are counter: contemplation and practical skill; active intellect and dead conservatism; world-wide enterprise, and devoted use and wont; aggressive freedom and hospitable law, with bitter class-legislation; a people scattered by their wars and affairs over the face of the whole earth, and homesick to a man; a country of extremes,—dukes and chartists, Bishops of Durham and naked heathen colliers;—nothing can be praised in it without damning exceptions, and nothing denounced without salvos of cordial praise.

Neither do this people appear to be of one stem; but col-

lectively a better race than any from which they are derived.
Nor is it easy to trace it home to its original seats. Who can
call by right names what races are in Britain? Who can trace
them historically? Who can discriminate them anatomically,
or metaphysically?

In the impossibility of arriving at satisfaction on the historical question of race, and,—come of whatever disputable
ancestry,—the indisputable Englishman before me, himself
very well marked, and nowhere else to be found,—I fancied
I could leave quite aside the choice of a tribe as his lineal
progenitors. Defoe said in his wrath, "the Englishman was
the mud of all races." I incline to the belief, that, as water,
lime, and sand make mortar, so certain temperaments marry
well, and, by well-managed contrarieties, develop as drastic a
character as the English. On the whole, it is not so much a
history of one or of certain tribes of Saxons, Jutes, or Frisians,
coming from one place, and genetically identical, as it is an
anthology of temperaments out of them all. Certain
temperaments suit the sky and soil of England, say eight or
ten or twenty varieties, as, out of a hundred pear-trees, eight
or ten suit the soil of an orchard, and thrive, whilst all the
unadapted temperaments die out.

The English derive their pedigree from such a range of nationalities, that there needs sea-room and land-room to unfold the varieties of talent and character. Perhaps the ocean
serves as a galvanic battery to distribute acids at one pole, and
alkalies at the other. So England tends to accumulate her lib-
erals in America, and her conservatives at London. The Scandinavians in her race still hear in every age the murmurs of
their mother, the ocean; the Briton in the blood hugs the
homestead still.

Again, as if to intensate the influences that are not of race,
what we think of when we talk of English traits really nar-
rows itself to a small district. It excludes Ireland, and Scotland, and Wales, and reduces itself at last to London, that is,
to those who come and go thither. The portraits that hang
on the walls in the Academy Exhibition at London, the figures in Punch's drawings of the public men, or of the clubhouses, the prints in the shop-windows, are distinctive English, and not American, no, nor Scotch, nor Irish: but 'tis a

very restricted nationality. As you go north into the manufacturing and agricultural districts, and to the population that
never travels, as you go into Yorkshire, as you enter Scotland,
the world's Englishman is no longer found. In Scotland, there
is a rapid loss of all grandeur of mien and manners; a provincial eagerness and acuteness appear; the poverty of the country makes itself remarked, and a coarseness of manners; and,
among the intellectual, is the insanity of dialectics. In Ireland,
are the same climate and soil as in England, but less food, no
right relation to the land, political dependence, small tenantry, and an inferior or misplaced race.

These queries concerning ancestry and blood may be well
allowed, for there is no prosperity that seems more to depend
on the kind of man than British prosperity. Only a hardy and
wise people could have made this small territory great. We
say, in a regatta or yacht-race, that if the boats are anywhere
nearly matched, it is the man that wins. Put the best sailing
master into either boat, and he will win.

Yet it is fine for us to speculate in face of unbroken traditions, though vague, and losing themselves in fable. The traditions have got footing, and refuse to be disturbed. The
kitchen-clock is more convenient than sidereal time. We must
use the popular category, as we do by the Linnæan classification, for convenience, and not as exact and final. Otherwise,
we are presently confounded, when the best settled traits of
one race are claimed by some new ethnologist as precisely
characteristic of the rival tribe.

I found plenty of well-marked English types, the ruddy
complexion fair and plump, robust men, with faces cut like a
die, and a strong island speech and accent; a Norman type,
with the complacency that belongs to that constitution. Others, who might be Americans, for any thing that appeared in
their complexion or form: and their speech was much less
marked, and their thought much less bound. We will call
them Saxons. Then the Roman has implanted his dark complexion in the trinity or quaternity of bloods.

1. The sources from which tradition derives their stock are
mainly three. And, first, they are of the oldest blood of the
world,—the Celtic. Some peoples are deciduous or transi-

tory. Where are the Greeks? where the Etrurians? where the Romans? But the Celts or Sidonides are an old family, of whose beginning there is no memory, and their end is likely to be still more remote in the future; for they have endurance and productiveness. They planted Britain, and gave to the seas and mountains names which are poems, and imitate the pure voices of nature. They are favorably remembered in the oldest records of Europe. They had no violent feudal tenure, but the husbandman owned the land. They had an alphabet, astronomy, priestly culture, and a sublime creed. They have a hidden and precarious genius. They made the best popular literature of the middle ages in the songs of Merlin, and the tender and delicious mythology of Arthur.

2. The English come mainly from the Germans, whom the Romans found hard to conquer in two hundred and ten years,—say, impossible to conquer,—when one remembers the long sequel; a people about whom, in the old empire, the rumor ran, there was never any that meddled with them that repented it not.

3. Charlemagne, halting one day in a town of Narbonnese Gaul, looked out of a window, and saw a fleet of Northmen cruising in the Mediterranean. They even entered the port of the town where he was, causing no small alarm and sudden manning and arming of his galleys. As they put out to sea again, the emperor gazed long after them, his eyes bathed in tears. "I am tormented with sorrow," he said, "when I foresee the evils they will bring on my posterity." There was reason for these Xerxes' tears. The men who have built a ship and invented the rig,—cordage, sail, compass, and pump,—the working in and out of port, have acquired much more than a ship. Now arm them, and every shore is at their mercy. For, if they have not numerical superiority where they anchor, they have only to sail a mile or two to find it. Bonaparte's art of war, namely of concentrating force on the point of attack, must always be theirs who have the choice of the battle-ground. Of course they come into the fight from a higher ground of power than the land-nations; and can engage them on shore with a victorious advantage in the retreat. As soon as the shores are sufficiently peopled to make piracy a losing

business, the same skill and courage are ready for the service of trade.

The *Heimskringla*,* or Sagas of the Kings of Norway, collected by Snorro Sturleson, is the Iliad and Odyssey of English history. Its portraits, like Homer's, are strongly individualized. The Sagas describe a monarchical republic like Sparta. The government disappears before the importance of citizens. In Norway, no Persian masses fight and perish to aggrandize a king, but the actors are bonders or landholders, every one of whom is named and personally and patronymically described, as the king's friend and companion. A sparse population gives this high worth to every man. Individuals are often noticed as very handsome persons, which trait only brings the story nearer to the English race. Then the solid material interest predominates, so dear to English understanding, wherein the association is logical, between merit and land. The heroes of the Sagas are not the knights of South Europe. No vaporing of France and Spain has corrupted them. They are substantial farmers, whom the rough times have forced to defend their properties. They have weapons which they use in a determined manner, by no means for chivalry, but for their acres. They are people considerably advanced in rural arts, living amphibiously on a rough coast, and drawing half their food from the sea, and half from the land. They have herds of cows, and malt, wheat, bacon, butter, and cheese. They fish in the fiord, and hunt the deer. A king among these farmers has a varying power, sometimes not exceeding the authority of a sheriff. A king was maintained much as, in some of our country districts, a winter-schoolmaster is quartered, a week here, a week there, and a fortnight on the next farm, — on all the farmers in rotation. This the king calls going into guest-quarters; and it was the only way in which, in a poor country, a poor king, with many retainers, could be kept alive, when he leaves his own farm to collect his dues through the kingdom.

These Norsemen are excellent persons in the main, with good sense, steadiness, wise speech, and prompt action. But they have a singular turn for homicide; their chief end of man

*Heimskringla. Translated by Samuel Laing, Esq. London. 1844.

is to murder, or to be murdered; oars, scythes, harpoons, crowbars, peatknives, and hayforks, are tools valued by them all the more for their charming aptitude for assassinations. A pair of kings, after dinner, will divert themselves by thrusting each his sword through the other's body, as did Yngve and Alf. Another pair ride out on a morning for a frolic, and, finding no weapon near, will take the bits out of their horses' mouths, and crush each other's heads with them, as did Alric and Eric. The sight of a tent-cord or a cloak-string puts them on hanging somebody, a wife, or a husband, or, best of all, a king. If a farmer has so much as a hayfork, he sticks it into a King Dag. King Ingiald finds it vastly amusing to burn up half a dozen kings in a hall, after getting them drunk. Never was poor gentleman so surfeited with life, so furious to be rid of it, as the Northman. If he cannot pick any other quarrel, he will get himself comfortably gored by a bull's horns, like Egil, or slain by a land-slide, like the agricultural King Onund. Odin died in his bed, in Sweden; but it was a proverb of ill condition, to die the death of old age. King Hake of Sweden cuts and slashes in battle, as long as he can stand, then orders his war-ship, loaded with his dead men and their weapons, to be taken out to sea, the tiller shipped, and the sails spread; being left alone, he sets fire to some tar-wood, and lies down contented on deck. The wind blew off the land, the ship flew burning in clear flame, out between the islets into the ocean, and there was the right end of King Hake.

The early Sagas are sanguinary and piratical; the later are of a noble strain. History rarely yields us better passages than the conversation between King Sigurd the Crusader, and King Eystein, his brother, on their respective merits,—one, the soldier, and the other, a lover of the arts of peace.

But the reader of the Norman history must steel himself by holding fast the remote compensations which result from animal vigor. As the old fossil world shows that the first steps of reducing the chaos were confided to saurians and other huge and horrible animals, so the foundations of the new civility were to be laid by the most savage men.

The Normans came out of France into England worse men than they went into it, one hundred and sixty years before. They had lost their own language, and learned the Romance or barbarous Latin of the Gauls; and had acquired, with the language, all the vices it had names for. The conquest has obtained in the chronicles, the name of the "memory of sorrow." Twenty thousand thieves landed at Hastings. These founders of the House of Lords were greedy and ferocious dragoons, sons of greedy and ferocious pirates. They were all alike, they took every thing they could carry, they burned, harried, violated, tortured, and killed, until every thing English was brought to the verge of ruin. Such, however, is the illusion of antiquity and wealth, that decent and dignified men now existing boast their descent from these filthy thieves, who showed a far juster conviction of their own merits, by assuming for their types the swine, goat, jackal, leopard, wolf, and snake, which they severally resembled.

England yielded to the Danes and Northmen in the tenth and eleventh centuries, and was the receptacle into which all the mettle of that strenuous population was poured. The continued draught of the best men in Norway, Sweden, and Denmark, to these piratical expeditions, exhausted those countries, like a tree which bears much fruit when young, and these have been second-rate powers ever since. The power of the race migrated, and left Norway void. King Olaf said, "When King Harold, my father, went westward to England, the chosen men in Norway followed him: but Norway was so emptied then, that such men have not since been to find in the country, nor especially such a leader as King Harold was for wisdom and bravery."

It was a tardy recoil of these invasions, when, in 1801, the British government sent Nelson to bombard the Danish forts in the Sound; and, in 1807, Lord Cathcart, at Copenhagen, took the entire Danish fleet, as it lay in the basins, and all the equipments from the Arsenal, and carried them to England. Konghelle, the town where the kings of Norway, Sweden, and Denmark were wont to meet, is now rented to a private English gentleman for a hunting ground.

It took many generations to trim, and comb, and perfume the first boat-load of Norse pirates into royal highnesses and most noble Knights of the Garter: but every sparkle of ornament dates back to the Norse boat. There will be time enough to mellow this strength into civility and religion. It is a med-

ical fact, that the children of the blind see; the children of
felons have a healthy conscience. Many a mean, dastardly boy
is, at the age of puberty, transformed into a serious and generous youth.

The mildness of the following ages has not quite effaced
these traits of Odin; as the rudiment of a structure matured
in the tiger is said to be still found unabsorbed in the Caucasian man. The nation has a tough, acrid, animal nature,
which centuries of churching and civilizing have not been
able to sweeten. Alfieri said, "the crimes of Italy were the
proof of the superiority of the stock;" and one may say of
England, that this watch moves on a splinter of adamant. The
English uncultured are a brutal nation. The crimes recorded
in their calendars leave nothing to be desired in the way of
cold malignity. Dear to the English heart is a fair stand-up
fight. The brutality of the manners in the lower class appears
in the boxing, bear-baiting, cock-fighting, love of executions,
and in the readiness for a set-to in the streets, delightful to
the English of all classes. The costermongers of London
streets hold cowardice in loathing: — " we must work our fists
well; we are all handy with our fists." The public schools are
charged with being bear-gardens of brutal strength, and are
liked by the people for that cause. The fagging is a trait of
the same quality. Medwin, in the Life of Shelley, relates, that,
at a military school, they rolled up a young man in a snowball, and left him so in his room, while the other cadets went
to church; — and crippled him for life. They have retained impressment, deck-flogging, army-flogging, and school-flog-
ging. Such is the ferocity of the army discipline, that a soldier
sentenced to flogging, sometimes prays that his sentence may
be commuted to death. Flogging banished from the armies of
Western Europe, remains here by the sanction of the Duke of
Wellington. The right of the husband to sell the wife has been
retained down to our times. The Jews have been the favorite
victims of royal and popular persecution. Henry III. mortgaged all the Jews in the kingdom to his brother, the Earl of
Cornwall, as security for money which he borrowed. The torture of criminals, and the rack for extorting evidence, were
slowly disused. Of the criminal statutes, Sir Samuel Romilly
said, "I have examined the codes of all nations, and ours is

the worst, and worthy of the Anthropophagi." In the last session, the House of Commons was listening to details of flogging and torture practised in the jails.

As soon as this land, thus geographically posted, got a hardy people into it, they could not help becoming the sailors and factors of the globe. From childhood, they dabbled in water, they swum like fishes, their playthings were boats. In the case of the ship-money, the judges delivered it for law, that "England being an island, the very midland shires therein are all to be accounted maritime:" and Fuller adds, "the genius even of landlocked counties driving the natives with a maritime dexterity." As early as the conquest, it is remarked in explanation of the wealth of England, that its merchants trade to all countries.

The English, at the present day, have great vigor of body and endurance. Other countrymen look slight and undersized beside them, and invalids. They are bigger men than the Americans. I suppose a hundred English taken at random out of the street, would weigh a fourth more, than so many Americans. Yet, I am told, the skeleton is not larger. They are round, ruddy, and handsome; at least, the whole bust is well formed; and there is a tendency to stout and powerful frames. I remarked the stoutness, on my first landing at Liverpool; porter, drayman, coachman, guard,—what substantial, respectable, grandfatherly figures, with costume and manners to suit. The American has arrived at the old mansion-house, and finds himself among uncles, aunts, and grandsires. The pictures on the chimney-tiles of his nursery were pictures of these people. Here they are in the identical costumes and air, which so took him.

It is the fault of their forms that they grow stocky, and the women have that disadvantage,—few tall, slender figures of flowing shape, but stunted and thickset persons. The French say, that the Englishwomen have two left hands. But, in all ages, they are a handsome race. The bronze monuments of crusaders lying cross-legged, in the Temple Church at London, and those in Worcester and in Salisbury Cathedrals, which are seven hundred years old, are of the same type as the best youthful heads of men now in England;—please by beauty of the same character, an expression blending good-nature, valor, and refinement, and, mainly, by that uncorrupt youth in the face of manhood, which is daily seen in the streets of London.

Both branches of the Scandinavian race are distinguished for beauty. The anecdote of the handsome captives which Saint Gregory found at Rome, A. D. 600, is matched by the testimony of the Norman chroniclers, five centuries later, who wondered at the beauty and long flowing hair of the young English captives. Meantime, the Heimskringla has frequent occasion to speak of the personal beauty of its heroes. When it is considered what humanity, what resources of mental and moral power, the traits of the blonde race betoken,—its accession to empire marks a new and finer epoch, wherein the old mineral force shall be subjugated at last by humanity, and shall plough in its furrow henceforward. It is not a final race, once a crab always crab, but a race with a future.

On the English face are combined decision and nerve, with the fair complexion, blue eyes, and open and florid aspect. Hence the love of truth, hence the sensibility, the fine perception, and poetic construction. The fair Saxon man, with open front, and honest meaning, domestic, affectionate, is not the wood out of which cannibal, or inquisitor, or assassin is made, but he is moulded for law, lawful trade, civility, marriage, the nurture of children, for colleges, churches, charities, and colonies.

They are rather manly than warlike. When the war is over, the mask falls from the affectionate and domestic tastes, which make them women in kindness. This union of qualities is fabled in their national legend of *Beauty and the Beast*, or, long before, in the Greek legend of *Hermaphrodite*. The two sexes are co-present in the English mind. I apply to Britannia, queen of seas and colonies, the words in which her latest novelist portrays his heroine: "she is as mild as she is game, and as game as she is mild." The English delight in the antagonism which combines in one person the extremes of courage and tenderness. Nelson, dying at Trafalgar, sends his love to Lord Collingwood, and, like an innocent schoolboy that goes to bed, says, "Kiss me, Hardy," and turns to sleep. Lord Collingwood, his comrade, was of a nature the most affectionate and domestic. Admiral Rodney's figure approached to delicacy and effeminacy, and he declared himself very sensible to fear, which he surmounted only by considerations of honor and public duty. Clarendon says, the Duke of Buckingham was so modest and gentle, that some courtiers attempted to put affronts on him, until they found that this modesty and effeminacy was only a mask for the most terrible determination. And Sir James Parry said, the other day, of Sir John Franklin, that, "if he found Wellington Sound open, he explored it; for he was a man who never turned his back on a danger, yet of that tenderness, that he would not brush away a mosquito." Even for their highwaymen the same virtue is claimed, and Robin Hood comes described to us as *mitissimus prædonum*, the gentlest thief. But they know where their war-dogs lie. Cromwell, Blake, Marlborough, Chatham, Nelson, and Wellington, are not to be trifled with, and the brutal strength which lies at the bottom of society, the animal ferocity of the quays and cockpits, the bullies of the costermongers of Shoreditch, Seven Dials, and Spitalfields, they know how to wake up.

They have a vigorous health, and last well into middle and old age. The old men are as red as roses, and still handsome. A clear skin, a peach-bloom complexion, and good teeth, are found all over the island. They use a plentiful and nutritious diet. The operative cannot subsist on watercresses. Beef, mutton, wheatbread, and malt-liquors, are universal among the first-class laborers. Good feeding is a chief point of national pride among the vulgar, and, in their caricatures, they represent the Frenchman as a poor, starved body. It is curious that Tacitus found the English beer already in use among the Germans: "they make from barley or wheat a drink corrupted into some resemblance to wine." Lord Chief Justice Fortescue in Henry VI.'s time, says, "The inhabitants of England drink no water, unless at certain times, on a religious score, and by way of penance." The extremes of poverty and ascetic penance, it would seem, never reach cold water in England. Wood, the antiquary, in describing the poverty and maceration of Father Lacey, an English Jesuit, does not deny him beer. He says, "his bed was under a thatching, and the way to it up a ladder; his fare was coarse; his drink, of a penny a gawn, or gallon."

They have more constitutional energy than any other people. They think, with Henri Quatre, that manly exercises are the foundation of that elevation of mind which gives one nature ascendant over another; or, with the Arabs, that the days spent in the chase are not counted in the length of life. They box, run, shoot, ride, row, and sail from pole to pole. They eat, and drink, and live jolly in the open air, putting a bar of solid sleep between day and day. They walk and ride as fast as they can, their head bent forward, as if urged on some pressing affair. The French say, that Englishmen in the street always walk straight before them like mad dogs. Men and women walk with infatuation. As soon as he can handle a gun, hunting is the fine art of every Englishman of condition. They are the most voracious people of prey that ever existed. Every season turns out the aristocracy into the country, to shoot and fish. The more vigorous run out of the island to Europe, to America, to Asia, to Africa, and Australia, to hunt with fury by gun, by trap, by harpoon, by lasso, with dog, with horse, with elephant, or with dromedary, all the game that is in nature. These men have written the game-books of all countries, as Hawker, Scrope, Murray, Herbert, Maxwell, Cumming, and a host of travellers. The people at home are addicted to boxing, running, leaping, and rowing matches.

I suppose, the dogs and horses must be thanked for the fact, that the men have muscles almost as tough and supple as their own. If in every efficient man, there is first a fine animal, in the English race it is of the best breed, a wealthy, juicy, broad-chested creature, steeped in ale and good cheer, and a little overloaded by his flesh. Men of animal nature rely, like animals, on their instincts. The Englishman associates well with dogs and horses. His attachment to the horse arises from the courage and address required to manage it. The horse finds out who is afraid of it, and does not disguise its opinion. Their young boiling clerks and lusty collegians like the company of horses better than the company of professors. I suppose, the horses are better company for them. The horse has more uses than Buffon noted. If you go into the streets, every driver in bus or dray is a bully, and, if I wanted a good troop of soldiers, I should recruit among the stables. Add a certain degree of refinement to the vivacity of these riders, and you obtain the precise quality which makes the men and women of polite society formidable.

They come honestly by their horsemanship, with *Hengst* and *Horsa* for their Saxon founders. The other branch of their race had been Tartar nomads. The horse was all their wealth. The children were fed on mares' milk. The pastures of Tartary were still remembered by the tenacious practice of the Norsemen to eat horseflesh at religious feasts. In the Danish invasions, the marauders seized upon horses where they landed, and were at once converted into a body of expert cavalry.

At one time, this skill seems to have declined. Two centuries ago, the English horse never performed any eminent service beyond the seas; and the reason assigned, was, that the genius of the English hath always more inclined them to foot-service, as pure and proper manhood, without any mixture; whilst, in a victory on horseback, the credit ought to be divided betwixt the man and his horse. But in two hundred years, a change has taken place. Now, they boast that they understand horses better than any other people in the world, and that their horses are become their second selves.

"William the Conqueror being," says Camden, "better affected to beasts than to men, imposed heavy fines and punishments on those that should meddle with his game." The Saxon Chronicle says, "he loved the tall deer as if he were their father." And rich Englishmen have followed his example, according to their ability, ever since, in encroaching on the tillage and commons with their game-preserves. It is a proverb in England, that it is safer to shoot a man, than a hare. The severity of the game-laws certainly indicates an extravagant sympathy of the nation with horses and hunters. The gentlemen are always on horseback, and have brought horses to an ideal perfection,—the English racer is a factitious breed. A score or two of mounted gentlemen may frequently be seen running like centaurs down a hill nearly as steep as the roof of a house. Every inn-room is lined with pictures of races; telegraphs communicate, every hour, tidings of the heats from Newmarket and Ascot: and the House of Commons adjourns over the 'Derby Day.'

CHAPTER V

Ability

THE SAXON and the Northman are both Scandinavians. History does not allow us to fix the limits of the application of these names with any accuracy; but from the residence of a portion of these people in France, and from some effect of that powerful soil on their blood and manners, the Norman has come popularly to represent in England the aristocratic,—and the Saxon the democratic principle. And though, I doubt not, the nobles are of both tribes, and the workers of both, yet we are forced to use the names a little mythically, one to represent the worker, and the other the enjoyer.

The island was a prize for the best race. Each of the dominant races tried its fortune in turn. The Phœnician, the Celt, and the Goth, had already got in. The Roman came, but in the very day when his fortune culminated. He looked in the eyes of a new people that was to supplant his own. He disembarked his legions, erected his camps and towers,—presently he heard bad news from Italy, and worse and worse, every year; at last, he made a handsome compliment of roads and walls, and departed. But the Saxon seriously settled in the land, builded, tilled, fished, and traded, with German truth and adhesiveness. The Dane came, and divided with him. Last of all, the Norman, or French-Dane, arrived, and formally conquered, harried and ruled the kingdom. A century later, it came out, that the Saxon had the most bottom and longevity, had managed to make the victor speak the language and accept the law and usage of the victim; forced the baron to dictate Saxon terms to Norman kings; and, step by step, got all the essential securities of civil liberty invented and confirmed. The genius of the race and the genius of the place conspired to this effect. The island is lucrative to free labor, but not worth possession on other terms. The race was so intellectual, that a feudal or military tenure could not last longer than the war. The power of the Saxon-Danes, so thoroughly beaten in the war, that the name of English and villein were synonymous, yet so vivacious as to extort charters from the kings, stood on the strong personality of these people. Sense and economy must rule in a world which is made of sense and economy, and the banker, with his seven *per cent*, drives the earl out of his castle. A nobility of soldiers cannot keep down a commonalty of shrewd scientific persons. What signifies a pedigree of a hundred links, against a cotton-spinner with steam in his mill; or, against a company of broad-shouldered Liverpool merchants, for whom Stephenson and Brunel are contriving locomotives and a tubular bridge?

These Saxons are the hands of mankind. They have the taste for toil, a distaste for pleasure or repose, and the telescopic appreciation of distant gain. They are the wealth-makers,—and by dint of mental faculty, which has its own conditions. The Saxon works after liking, or, only for himself; and to set him at work, and to begin to draw his monstrous values out of barren Britain, all dishonor, fret, and barrier must be removed, and then his energies begin to play.

The Scandinavian fancied himself surrounded by Trolls,—a kind of goblin men, with vast power of work and skilful production,—divine stevedores, carpenters, reapers, smiths, and masons, swift to reward every kindness done them, with gifts of gold and silver. In all English history, this dream comes to pass. Certain Trolls or working brains, under the names of Alfred, Bede, Caxton, Bracton, Camden, Drake, Selden, Dugdale, Newton, Gibbon, Brindley, Watt, Wedgwood, dwell in the troll-mounts of Britain, and turn the sweat of their face to power and renown.

If the race is good, so is the place. Nobody landed on this spellbound island with impunity. The enchantments of barren shingle and rough weather, transformed every adventurer into a laborer. Each vagabond that arrived bent his neck to the yoke of gain, or found the air too tense for him. The strong survived, the weaker went to the ground. Even the pleasure-hunters and sots of England are of a tougher texture. A hard temperament had been formed by Saxon and Saxon-Dane, and such of these French or Normans as could reach it, were naturalized in every sense.

All the admirable expedients or means hit upon in England,

must be looked at as growths or irresistible offshoots of the expanding mind of the race. A man of that brain thinks and acts thus; and his neighbor, being afflicted with the same kind of brain, though he is rich, and called a baron, or a duke, thinks the same thing, and is ready to allow the justice of the thought and act in his retainer or tenant, though sorely against his baronial or ducal will.

The island was renowned in antiquity for its breed of mastiffs, so fierce, that, when their teeth were set, you must cut their heads off to part them. The man was like his dog. The people have that nervous bilious temperament, which is known by medical men to resist every means employed to make its possessor subservient to the will of others. The English game is main force to main force, the planting of foot to foot, fair play and open field,—a rough tug without trick or dodging, till one or both come to pieces. King Ethelwald spoke the language of his race, when he planted himself at Wimborne, and said, 'he would do one of two things, or there live, or there lie.' They hate craft and subtlety. They neither poison, nor waylay, nor assassinate; and, when they have pounded each other to a poultice, they will shake hands and be friends for the remainder of their lives.

You shall trace these Gothic touches at school, at country fairs, at the hustings, and in parliament. No artifice, no breach of truth and plain dealing,—not so much as secret ballot, is suffered in the island. In parliament, the tactics of the opposition is to resist every step of the government, by a pitiless attack: and in a bargain, no prospect of advantage is so dear to the merchant, as the thought of being tricked is mortifying.

Sir Kenelm Digby, a courtier of Charles and James, who won the sea-fight of Scanderoon, was a model Englishman in his day. "His person was handsome and gigantic, he had so graceful elocution and noble address, that, had he been dropt out of the clouds in any part of the world, he would have made himself respected: he was skilled in six tongues, and master of arts and arms."* Sir Kenelm wrote a book, "Of Bodies and of Souls," in which he propounds, that "syllo-

*Antony Wood.

gisms do breed or rather are all the variety of man's life. They are the steps by which we walk in all our businesses. Man, as he is man, doth nothing else but weave such chains. Whatsoever he doth, swarving from this work, he doth as deficient from the nature of man: and, if he do aught beyond this, by breaking out into divers sorts of exterior actions, he findeth, nevertheless, in this linked sequel of simple discourses, the art, the cause, the rule, the bounds, and the model of it."*

There spoke the genius of the English people. There is a necessity on them to be logical. They would hardly greet the good that did not logically fall,—as if it excluded their own merit, or shook their understandings. They are jealous of minds that have much facility of association, from an instinctive fear that the seeing many relations to their thought might impair this serial continuity and lucrative concentration. They are impatient of genius, or of minds addicted to contemplation, and cannot conceal their contempt for sallies of thought, however lawful, whose steps they cannot count by their wonted rule. Neither do they reckon better a syllogism that ends in syllogism. For they have a supreme eye to facts, and theirs is a logic that brings salt to soup, hammer to nail, oar to boat, the logic of cooks, carpenters, and chemists, following the sequence of nature, and one on which words make no impression. Their mind is not dazzled by its own means, but locked and bolted to results. They love men, who, like Samuel Johnson, a doctor in the schools, would jump out of his syllogism the instant his major proposition was in danger, to save that, at all hazards. Their practical vision is spacious, and they can hold many threads without entangling them. All the steps they orderly take; but with the high logic of never confounding the minor and major proposition; keeping their eye on their aim, in all the complicity and delay incident to the several series of means they employ. There is room in their minds for this and that,—a science of degrees. In the courts, the independence of the judges and the loyalty of the suitors are equally excellent. In Parliament, they have hit on that capital invention of freedom, a constitutional opposition. And when courts and parliament are both deaf, the plaintiff is not

*Man's Soule, p. 29.

silenced. Calm, patient, his weapon of defence from year to year is the obstinate reproduction of the grievance, with calculations and estimates. But, meantime, he is drawing numbers and money to his opinion, resolved that if all remedy fails, right of revolution is at the bottom of his charter-box. They are bound to see their measure carried, and stick to it through ages of defeat.

Into this English logic, however, an infusion of justice enters, not so apparent in other races,—a belief in the existence of two sides, and the resolution to see fair play. There is on every question, an appeal from the assertion of the parties, to the proof of what is asserted. They are impious in their scepticism of a theory, but kiss the dust before a fact. Is it a machine, is it a charter, is it a boxer in the ring, is it a candidate on the hustings,—the universe of Englishmen will suspend their judgment, until the trial can be had. They are not to be led by a phrase, they want a working plan, a working machine, a working constitution, and will sit out the trial, and abide by the issue, and reject all preconceived theories. In politics they put blunt questions, which must be answered; who is to pay the taxes? what will you do for trade? what for corn? what for the spinner?

This singular fairness and its results strike the French with surprise. Philip de Commines says, "Now, in my opinion, among all the sovereignties I know in the world, that in which the public good is best attended to, and the least violence exercised on the people, is that of England." Life is safe, and personal rights; and what is freedom, without security? whilst, in France, 'fraternity,' 'equality,' and 'indivisible unity,' are names for assassination. Montesquieu said, "England is the freest country in the world. If a man in England had as many enemies as hairs on his head, no harm would happen to him."

Their self-respect, their faith in causation, and their realistic logic or coupling of means to ends, have given them the leadership of the modern world. Montesquieu said, "No people have true common sense but those who are born in England." This common sense is a perception of all the conditions of our earthly existence, of laws that can be stated, and of laws that cannot be stated, or that are learned only by practice, in which allowance for friction is made. They are impious in their scepticism of theory, and in high departments they are cramped and sterile. But the unconditional surrender to facts, and the choice of means to reach their ends, are as admirable as with ants and bees.

The bias of the nation is a passion for utility. They love the lever, the screw, and pulley, the Flanders draught-horse, the waterfall, wind-mills, tide-mills; the sea and the wind to bear their freight ships. More than the diamond Koh-i-noor, which glitters among their crown jewels, they prize that dull pebble which is wiser than a man, whose poles turn themselves to the poles of the world, and whose axis is parallel to the axis of the world. Now, their toys are steam and galvanism. They are heavy at the fine arts, but adroit at the coarse; not good in jewelry or mosaics, but the best iron-masters, colliers, wool-combers, and tanners, in Europe. They apply themselves to agriculture, to draining, to resisting encroachments of sea, wind, travelling sands, cold and wet sub-soil; to fishery, to manufacture of indispensable staples,—salt, plumbago, leather, wool, glass, pottery, and brick,—to bees and silkworms;—and by their steady combinations they succeed. A manufacturer sits down to dinner in a suit of clothes which was wool on a sheep's back at sunrise. You dine with a gentleman on venison, pheasant, quail, pigeons, poultry, mushrooms, and pine-apples, all the growth of his estate. They are neat husbands for ordering all their tools pertaining to house and field. All are well kept. There is no want and no waste. They study use and fitness in their building, in the order of their dwellings, and in their dress. The Frenchman invented the ruffle, the Englishman added the shirt. The Englishman wears a sensible coat buttoned to the chin, of rough but solid and lasting texture. If he is a lord, he dresses a little worse than a commoner. They have diffused the taste for plain substantial hats, shoes, and coats through Europe. They think him the best dressed man, whose dress is so fit for his use that you cannot notice or remember to describe it.

They secure the essentials in their diet, in their arts, and manufactures. Every article of cutlery shows, in its shape, thought and long experience of workmen. They put the expense in the right place, as, in their sea-steamers, in the solidity of the machinery and the strength of the boat. The admirable equipment of their arctic ships carries London to the pole. They build roads, aqueducts, warm and ventilate houses. And they have impressed their directness and practical habit on modern civilization.

In trade, the Englishman believes that nobody breaks who ought not to break; and, that, if he do not make trade every thing, it will make him nothing; and acts on this belief. The spirit of system, attention to details, and the subordination of details, or, the not driving things too finely, (which is charged on the Germans,) constitute that despatch of business, which makes the mercantile power of England.

In war, the Englishman looks to his means. He is of the opinion of Civilis, his German ancestor, whom Tacitus reports as holding "that the gods are on the side of the strongest;" —a sentence which Bonaparte unconsciously translated, when he said, "that he had noticed, that Providence always favored the heaviest battalion." Their military science propounds that if the weight of the advancing column is greater than that of the resisting, the latter is destroyed. Therefore Wellington, when he came to the army in Spain, had every man weighed, first with accoutrements, and then without; believing that the force of an army depended on the weight and power of the individual soldiers, in spite of cannon. Lord Palmerston told the House of Commons, that more care is taken of the health and comfort of English troops than of any other troops in the world; and that, hence the English can put more men into the rank, on the day of action, on the field of battle, than any other army. Before the bombardment of the Danish forts in the Baltic, Nelson spent day after day, himself in the boats, on the exhausting service of sounding the channel. Clerk of Eldin's celebrated manœuvre of breaking the line of sea-battle, and Nelson's feat of *doubling,* or stationing his ships one on the outer bow, and another on the outer quarter of each of the enemy's were only translations into naval tactics of Bonaparte's rule of concentration. Lord Collingwood was accustomed to tell his men, that, if they could fire three well-directed broadsides in five minutes, no vessel could resist them; and, from constant practice, they came to do it in three minutes and a half.

But conscious that no race of better men exists, they rely most on the simplest means; and do not like ponderous and difficult tactics, but delight to bring the affair hand to hand, where the victory lies with the strength, courage, and endurance of the individual combatants. They adopt every improvement in rig, in motor, in weapons, but they fundamentally believe that the best stratagem in naval war, is to lay your ship close alongside of the enemy's ship, and bring all your guns to bear on him, until you or he go to the bottom. This is the old fashion, which never goes out of fashion, neither in nor out of England.

It is not usually a point of honor, nor a religious sentiment, and never any whim that they will shed their blood for; but usually property, and right measured by property, that breeds revolution. They have no Indian taste for a tomahawk-dance, no French taste for a badge or a proclamation. The Englishman is peaceably minding his business, and earning his day's wages. But if you offer to lay hand on his day's wages, on his cow, or his right in common, or his shop, he will fight to the Judgment. Magna-charta, jury-trial, *habeas-corpus*, star-chamber, ship-money, Popery, Plymouth-colony, American Revolution, are all questions involving a yeoman's right to his dinner, and, except as touching that, would not have lashed the British nation to rage and revolt.

Whilst they are thus instinct with a spirit of order, and of calculation, it must be owned they are capable of larger views; but the indulgence is expensive to them, costs great crises, or accumulations of mental power. In common, the horse works best with blinders. Nothing is more in the line of English thought, than our unvarnished Connecticut question, "Pray, sir, how do you get your living when you are at home?" The questions of freedom, of taxation, of privilege, are money questions. Heavy fellows, steeped in beer and fleshpots, they are hard of hearing and dim of sight. Their drowsy minds need to be flagellated by war and trade and politics and persecution. They cannot well read a principle, except by the light of fagots and of burning towns.

Tacitus says of the Germans, "powerful only in sudden efforts, they are impatient of toil and labor." This highly-destined race, if it had not somewhere added the chamber of patience to its brain, would not have built London. I know not from which of the tribes and temperaments that went to the composition of the people this tenacity was supplied, but they clinch every nail they drive. They have no running for luck, and no immoderate speed. They spend largely on their fabric, and await the slow return. Their leather lies tanning seven years in the vat. At Rogers's mills, in Sheffield, where I was shown the process of making a razor and a penknife, I was told there is no luck in making good steel; that they make no mistakes, every blade in the hundred and in the thousand is good. And that is characteristic of all their work,—no more is attempted than is done.

When Thor and his companions arrive at Utgard, he is told that "nobody is permitted to remain here, unless he understand some art, and excel in it all other men." The same question is still put to the posterity of Thor. A nation of laborers, every man is trained to some one art or detail, and aims at perfection in that; not content unless he has something in which he thinks he surpasses all other men. He would rather not do any thing at all, than not do it well. I suppose no people have such thoroughness;—from the highest to the lowest, every man meaning to be master of his art.

"To show capacity," a Frenchman described as the end of a speech in debate: "no," said an Englishman, "but to set your shoulder at the wheel,—to advance the business." Sir Samuel Romilly refused to speak in popular assemblies, confining himself to the House of Commons, where a measure can be carried by a speech. The business of the House of Commons is conducted by a few persons, but these are hard-worked. Sir Robert Peel "knew the Blue Books by heart." His colleagues and rivals carry Hansard in their heads. The high civil and legal offices are not beds of ease, but posts which exact frightful amounts of mental labor. Many of the great leaders, like Pitt, Canning, Castlereagh, Romilly, are soon worked to death. They are excellent judges in England of a good worker, and when they find one, like Clarendon, Sir Philip Warwick, Sir William Coventry, Ashley, Burke, Thurlow, Mansfield, Pitt, Eldon, Peel, or Russell, there is nothing too good or too high for him.

They have a wonderful heat in the pursuit of a public aim.

Private persons exhibit, in scientific and antiquarian researches, the same pertinacity as the nation showed in the coalitions in which it yoked Europe against the empire of Bonaparte, one after the other defeated, and still renewed, until the sixth hurled him from his seat.

Sir John Herschel, in completion of the work of his father, who had made the catalogue of the stars of the northern hemisphere, expatriated himself for years at the Cape of Good Hope, finished his inventory of the southern heaven, came home, and redacted it in eight years more;—a work whose value does not begin until thirty years have elapsed, and thenceforward a record to all ages of the highest import. The Admiralty sent out the Arctic expeditions year after year, in search of Sir John Franklin, until, at last, they have threaded their way through polar pack and Behring's Straits, and solved the geographical problem. Lord Elgin, at Athens, saw the imminent ruin of the Greek remains, set up his scaffoldings, in spite of epigrams, and, after five years' labor to collect them, got his marbles on shipboard. The ship struck a rock, and went to the bottom. He had them all fished up, by divers, at a vast expense, and brought to London; not knowing that Haydon, Fuseli, and Canova, and all good heads in all the world, were to be his applauders. In the same spirit, were the excavation and research by Sir Charles Fellowes, for the Xanthian monument; and of Layard, for his Nineveh sculptures.

The nation sits in the immense city they have builded, a London extended into every man's mind, though he live in Van Dieman's Land or Capetown. Faithful performance of what is undertaken to be performed, they honor in themselves, and exact in others, as certificate of equality with themselves. The modern world is theirs. They have made and make it day by day. The commercial relations of the world are so intimately drawn to London, that every dollar on earth contributes to the strength of the English government. And if all the wealth in the planet should perish by war or deluge, they know themselves competent to replace it.

They have approved their Saxon blood, by their sea-going qualities; their descent from Odin's smiths, by their hereditary skill in working in iron; their British birth, by husbandry and immense wheat harvests; and justified their occupancy of the centre of habitable land, by their supreme ability and cosmopolitan spirit. They have tilled, builded, forged, spun, and woven. They have made the island a thoroughfare; and London a shop, a law-court, a record-office, and scientific bureau, inviting to strangers; a sanctuary to refugees of every political and religious opinion; and such a city, that almost every active man, in any nation, finds himself, at one time or other, forced to visit it.

In every path of practical activity, they have gone even with the best. There is no secret of war, in which they have not shown mastery. The steam-chamber of Watt, the locomotive of Stephenson, the cotton-mule of Roberts, perform the labor of the world. There is no department of literature, of science, or of useful art, in which they have not produced a first-rate book. It is England, whose opinion is waited for on the merit of a new invention, an improved science. And in the complications of the trade and politics of their vast empire, they have been equal to every exigency, with counsel and with conduct. Is it their luck, or is it in the chambers of their brain, — it is their commercial advantage, that whatever light appears in better method or happy invention, breaks out *in their race*. They are a family to which a destiny attaches, and the Banshee has sworn that a male heir shall never be wanting. They have a wealth of men to fill important posts, and the vigilance of party criticism insures the selection of a competent person.

A proof of the energy of the British people, is the highly artificial construction of the whole fabric. The climate and geography, I said, were factitious, as if the hands of man had arranged the conditions. The same character pervades the whole kingdom. Bacon said, "Rome was a state not subject to paradoxes;" but England subsists by antagonisms and contradictions. The foundations of its greatness are the rolling waves; and, from first to last, it is a museum of anomalies. This foggy and rainy country furnishes the world with astronomical observations. Its short rivers do not afford water-power, but the land shakes under the thunder of the mills. There is no gold mine of any importance, but there is more gold in England than in all other countries. It is too far north for the culture of the vine, but the wines of all countries are in its docks. The French Comte de Lauraguais said, "no fruit ripens in England but a baked apple"; but oranges and pine-apples are as cheap in London as in the Mediterranean. The Mark-Lane Express, or the Custom House Returns bear out to the letter the vaunt of Pope,

> "Let India boast her palms, nor envy we
>   The weeping amber, nor the spicy tree,
>   While, by our oaks, those precious loads are borne,
>   And realms commanded which those trees adorn."

The native cattle are extinct, but the island is full of artificial breeds. The agriculturist Bakewell, created sheep and cows and horses to order, and breeds in which every thing was omitted but what is economical. The cow is sacrificed to her bag, the ox to his surloin. Stall-feeding makes sperm-mills of the cattle, and converts the stable to a chemical factory. The rivers, lakes and ponds, too much fished, or obstructed by factories, are artificially filled with the eggs of salmon, turbot and herring.

Chat Moss and the fens of Lincolnshire and Cambridge-shire are unhealthy and too barren to pay rent. By cylindrical tiles, and guttapercha tubes, five millions of acres of bad land have been drained and put on equality with the best, for rape-culture and grass. The climate too, which was already believed to have become milder and drier by the enormous consump-tion of coal, is so far reached by this new action, that fogs and storms are said to disappear. In due course, all England will be drained, and rise a second time out of the waters. The latest step was to call in the aid of steam to agriculture. Steam is almost an Englishman. I do not know but they will send him to Parliament, next, to make laws. He weaves, forges, saws, pounds, fans, and now he must pump, grind, dig, and plough for the farmer. The markets created by the manufac-turing population have erected agriculture into a great thriv-ing and spending industry. The value of the houses in Britain is equal to the value of the soil. Artificial aids of all kinds are cheaper than the natural resources. No man can afford to walk, when the parliamentary-train carries him for a penny a mile. Gas-burners are cheaper than daylight in numberless floors in the cities. All the houses in London buy their water. The English trade does not exist for the exportation of native products, but on its manufactures, or the making well every thing which is ill made elsewhere. They make ponchos for the Mexican, bandannas for the Hindoo, ginseng for the Chinese, beads for the Indian, laces for the Flemings, telescopes for astronomers, cannons for kings.

The Board of Trade caused the best models of Greece and Italy to be placed within the reach of every manufacturing population. They caused to be translated from foreign languages and illustrated by elaborate drawings, the most approved works of Munich, Berlin, and Paris. They have ransacked Italy to find new forms, to add a grace to the products of their looms, their potteries, and their foundries.*

The nearer we look, the more artificial is their social system. Their law is a network of fictions. Their property, a scrip or certificate of right to interest on money that no man ever saw. Their social classes are made by statute. Their ratios of power and representation are historical and legal. The last Reform-bill took away political power from a mound, a ruin, and a stone-wall, whilst Birmingham and Manchester, whose mills paid for the wars of Europe, had no representative. Purity in the elective Parliament is secured by the purchase of seats.† Foreign power is kept by armed colonies; power at home, by a standing army of police. The pauper lives better than the free laborer; the thief better than the pauper; and the transported felon better than the one under imprisonment. The crimes are factitious, as smuggling, poaching, nonconformity, heresy and treason. Better, they say in England, kill a man than a hare. The sovereignty of the seas is maintained by the impressment of seamen. "The impressment of seamen," said Lord Eldon, "is the life of our navy." Solvency is maintained by means of a national debt, on the principle, "if you will not lend me the money, how can I pay you?" For the administration of justice, Sir Samuel Romilly's expedient for clearing the arrears of business in Chancery, was, the

---

*See Memorial of H. Greenough, p. 66, New York, 1853.

†Sir S. Romilly, purest of English patriots, decided that the only independent mode of entering Parliament was to buy a seat, and he bought Horsham.

Chancellor's staying away entirely from his court. Their system of education is factitious. The Universities galvanize dead
languages into a semblance of life. Their church is artificial.
The manners and customs of society are artificial;—made up
men with made up manners;—and thus the whole is Bir-
minghamized, and we have a nation whose existence is a
work of art;—a cold, barren, almost arctic isle, being made
the most fruitful, luxurious and imperial land in the whole
earth.

Man in England submits to be a product of political economy. On a bleak moor, a mill is built, a banking-house is
opened, and men come in, as water in a sluice-way, and
towns and cities rise. Man is made as a Birmingham button.
The rapid doubling of the population dates from Watt's
steam-engine. A landlord, who owns a province, says, "the
tenantry are unprofitable; let me have sheep." He unroofs the
houses, and ships the population to America. The nation is
accustomed to the instantaneous creation of wealth. It is the
maxim of their economists, "that the greater part in value of
the wealth now existing in England, has been produced by
human hands within the last twelve months." Meantime,
three or four days' rain will reduce hundreds to starving in
London.

One secret of their power is their mutual good understanding. Not only good minds are born among them, but all the
people have good minds. Every nation has yielded some good
wit, if, as has chanced to many tribes, only one. But the intellectual organization of the English admits a communicable-
ness of knowledge and ideas among them all. An electric
touch by any of their national ideas, melts them into one family, and brings the hoards of power which their individuality
is always hiving, into use and play for all. Is it the smallness
of the country, or is it the pride and affection of race,—they
have solidarity, or responsibleness, and trust in each other.

Their minds, like wool, admit of a dye which is more lasting than the cloth. They embrace their cause with more tenacity than their life. Though not military, yet every common
subject by the poll is fit to make a soldier of. These private
reserved mute family-men can adopt a public end with all

their heat, and this strength of affection makes the romance of their heroes. The difference of rank does not divide the national heart. The Danish poet Ohlenschlager complains, that who writes in Danish, writes to two hundred readers. In Germany, there is one speech for the learned, and another for the masses, to that extent, that, it is said, no sentiment or phrase from the works of any great German writer is ever heard among the lower classes. But in England, the language of the noble is the language of the poor. In Parliament, in pulpits, in theatres, when the speakers rise to thought and passion, the language becomes idiomatic; the people in the street best understand the best words. And their language seems drawn from the Bible, the common law, and the works of Shakspeare, Bacon, Milton, Pope, Young, Cowper, Burns, and Scott. The island has produced two or three of the greatest men that ever existed, but they were not solitary in their own time. Men quickly embodied what Newton found out, in Greenwich observatories, and practical navigation. The boys know all that Hutton knew of strata, or Dalton of atoms, or Harvey of blood-vessels; and these studies, once dangerous, are in fashion. So what is invented or known in agriculture, or in trade, or in war, or in art, or in literature, and antiquities. A great ability, not amassed on a few giants, but poured into the general mind, so that each of them could at a pinch stand in the shoes of the other; and they are more bound in character, than differenced in ability or in rank. The laborer is a possible lord. The lord is a possible basket-maker. Every man carries the English system in his brain, knows what is confided to him, and does therein the best he can. The chancellor carries England on his mace, the midshipman at the point of his dirk, the smith on his hammer, the cook in the bowl of his spoon; the postilion cracks his whip for England, and the sailor times his oars to "God save the King!" The very felons have their pride in each other's English stanchness. In politics and in war, they hold together as by hooks of steel. The charm in Nelson's history, is, the unselfish greatness; the assurance of being supported to the uttermost by those whom he supports to the uttermost. Whilst they are some ages ahead of the rest of the world in the art of living; whilst in some directions they do not represent the modern spirit, but constitute it,—this vanguard of civility and power they coldly hold, marching in phalanx, lockstep, foot after foot, file after file of heroes, ten thousand deep.

CHAPTER VI

Manners

I FIND the Englishman to be him of all men who stands firmest in his shoes. They have in themselves what they value in their horses, mettle and bottom. On the day of my arrival at Liverpool, a gentleman, in describing to me the Lord Lieutenant of Ireland, happened to say, "Lord Clarendon has pluck like a cock, and will fight till he dies;" and, what I heard first I heard last, and the one thing the English value, is pluck. The cabmen have it; the merchants have it; the bishops have it; the women have it; the journals have it; the Times newspaper, they say, is the pluckiest thing in England, and Sydney Smith had made it a proverb, that little Lord John Russell, the minister, would take the command of the Channel fleet to-morrow.

They require you to dare to be of your own opinion, and they hate the practical cowards who cannot in affairs answer directly yes or no. They dare to displease, nay, they will let you break all the commandments, if you do it natively, and with spirit. You must be somebody; then you may do this or that, as you will.

Machinery has been applied to all work, and carried to such perfection, that little is left for the men but to mind the engines and feed the furnaces. But the machines require punctual service, and, as they never tire, they prove too much for their tenders. Mines, forges, mills, breweries, railroads, steam-pump, steamplough, drill of regiments, drill of police, rule of court, and shop-rule, have operated to give a mechanical regularity to all the habit and action of men. A terrible machine has possessed itself of the ground, the air, the men and women, and hardly even thought is free.

The mechanical might and organization requires in the people constitution and answering spirits: and he who goes among them must have some weight of metal. At last, you take your hint from the fury of life you find, and say, one thing is plain, this is no country for fainthearted people: don't creep about diffidently; make up your mind; take your own course, and you shall find respect and furtherance.

It requires, men say, a good constitution to travel in Spain. I say as much of England, for other cause, simply on account of the vigor and brawn of the people. Nothing but the most serious business, could give one any counterweight to these Baresarks, though they were only to order eggs and muffins for their breakfast. The Englishman speaks with all his body. His elocution is stomachic,—as the American's is labial. The Englishman is very petulant and precise about his accommodation at inns, and on the roads; a quiddle about his toast and his chop, and every species of convenience, and loud and pungent in his expressions of impatience at any neglect. His vivacity betrays itself, at all points, in his manners, in his respiration, and the inarticulate noises he makes in clearing the throat;—all significant of burly strength. He has stamina; he can take the initiative in emergencies. He has that *aplomb*, which results from a good adjustment of the moral and physical nature, and the obedience of all the powers to the will; as if the axes of his eyes were united to his backbone, and only moved with the trunk.

This vigor appears in the incuriosity, and stony neglect, each of every other. Each man walks, eats, drinks, shaves, dresses, gesticulates, and, in every manner, acts, and suffers without reference to the bystanders, in his own fashion, only careful not to interfere with them, or annoy them; not that he is trained to neglect the eyes of his neighbors,—he is really occupied with his own affair, and does not think of them. Every man in this polished country consults only his convenience, as much as a solitary pioneer in Wisconsin. I know not where any personal eccentricity is so freely allowed, and no man gives himself any concern with it. An Englishman walks in a pouring rain, swinging his closed umbrella like a walking-stick; wears a wig, or a shawl, or a saddle, or stands on his head, and no remark is made. And as he has been doing this for several generations, it is now in the blood.

In short, every one of these islanders is an island himself, safe, tranquil, incommunicable. In a company of strangers, you would think him deaf; his eyes never wander from his table and newspaper. He is never betrayed into any curiosity or unbecoming emotion. They have all been trained in one severe school of manners, and never put off the harness. He does not give his hand. He does not let you meet his eye. It is almost an affront to look a man in the face, without being introduced. In mixed or in select companies they do not introduce persons; so that a presentation is a circumstance as valid as a contract. Introductions are sacraments. He withholds his name. At the hotel, he is hardly willing to whisper it to the clerk at the book-office. If he give you his private address on a card, it is like an avowal of friendship; and his bearing, on being introduced, is cold, even though he is seeking your acquaintance, and is studying how he shall serve you.

It was an odd proof of this impressive energy, that, in my lectures, I hesitated to read and threw out for its impertinence many a disparaging phrase, which I had been accustomed to spin, about poor, thin, unable mortals;—so much had the fine physique and the personal vigor of this robust race worked on my imagination.

I happened to arrive in England, at the moment of a commercial crisis. But it was evident, that, let who will fail, England will not. These people have sat here a thousand years, and here will continue to sit. They will not break up, or arrive at any desperate revolution, like their neighbors; for they have as much energy, as much continence of character as they ever had. The power and possession which surround them are their own creation, and they exert the same commanding industry at this moment.

They are positive, methodical, cleanly, and formal, loving routine, and conventional ways; loving truth and religion, to be sure, but inexorable on points of form. All the world praises the comfort and private appointments of an English inn, and of English households. You are sure of neatness and of personal decorum. A Frenchman may possibly be clean; an Englishman is conscientiously clean. A certain order and complete propriety is found in his dress and in his belongings.

Born in a harsh and wet climate, which keeps him in doors whenever he is at rest, and being of an affectionate and loyal temper, he dearly loves his house. If he is rich, he buys a demesne, and builds a hall; if he is in middle condition, he spares no expense on his house. Without, it is all planted: within, it is wainscoted, carved, curtained, hung with pictures, and filled with good furniture. 'Tis a passion which survives all others, to deck and improve it. Hither he brings all that is rare and costly, and with the national tendency to sit fast in the same spot for many generations, it comes to be, in the course of time, a museum of heirlooms, gifts, and trophies of the adventures and exploits of the family. He is very fond of silver plate, and, though he have no gallery of portraits of his ancestors, he has of their punch-bowls and porringers. Incredible amounts of plate are found in good houses, and the poorest have some spoon or saucepan, gift of a godmother, saved out of better times.

An English family consists of a few persons, who, from youth to age, are found revolving within a few feet of each other, as if tied by some invisible ligature, tense as that cartilage which we have seen attaching the two Siamese. England produces under favorable conditions of ease and culture the finest women in the world. And, as the men are affectionate and true-hearted, the women inspire and refine them. Nothing can be more delicate without being fantastical, nothing more firm and based in nature and sentiment, than the courtship and mutual carriage of the sexes. The song of 1596 says, "The wife of every Englishman is counted blest." The sentiment of Imogen in Cymbeline is copied from English nature; and not less the Portia of Brutus, the Kate Percy, and the Desdemona. The romance does not exceed the height of noble passion in Mrs. Lucy Hutchinson, or in Lady Russell, or even as one discerns through the plain prose of Pepys's Diary, the sacred habit of an English wife. Sir Samuel Romilly could not bear the death of his wife. Every class has its noble and tender examples.

Domesticity is the taproot which enables the nation to branch wide and high. The motive and end of their trade and empire is to guard the independence and privacy of their homes. Nothing so much marks their manners as the concentration on their household ties. This domesticity is carried into court and camp. Wellington governed India and Spain and his own troops, and fought battles like a good family-man, paid his debts, and, though general of an army in Spain, could not stir abroad for fear of public creditors. This taste for house and parish merits has of course its doting and foolish side. Mr. Cobbett attributes the huge popularity of Perceval, prime minister in 1810, to the fact that he was wont to go to church, every Sunday, with a large quarto gilt prayerbook under one arm, his wife hanging on the other, and followed by a long brood of children.

They keep their old customs, costumes, and pomps, their wig and mace, sceptre and crown. The middle ages still lurk in the streets of London. The Knights of the Bath take oath to defend injured ladies; the gold-stick-in-waiting survives. They repeated the ceremonies of the eleventh century in the coronation of the present Queen. A hereditary tenure is natural to them. Offices, farms, trades, and traditions descend so. Their leases run for a hundred and a thousand years. Terms of service and partnership are lifelong, or are inherited. "Holdship has been with me," said Lord Eldon, "eight-and-twenty years, knows all my business and books." Antiquity of usage is sanction enough. Wordsworth says of the small freeholders of Westmoreland, "Many of these humble sons of the hills had a consciousness that the land which they tilled had for more than five hundred years been possessed by men of the same name and blood." The ship-carpenter in the public yards, my lord's gardener and porter, have been there for more than a hundred years, grandfather, father, and son.

The English power resides also in their dislike of change. They have difficulty in bringing their reason to act, and on all occasions use their memory first. As soon as they have rid themselves of some grievance, and settled the better practice, they make haste to fix it as a finality, and never wish to hear of alteration more.

Every Englishman is an embryonic chancellor: His instinct is to search for a precedent. The favorite phrase of their law, is, "a custom whereof the memory of man runneth not back to the contrary." The barons say, "*Nolumus mutari*;" and the cockneys stifle the curiosity of the foreigner on the reason of any practice, with "Lord, sir, it was always so." They hate innovation. Bacon told them, Time was the right reformer; Chatham, that "confidence was a plant of slow growth;" Canning, to "advance with the times;" and Wellington, that "habit was ten times nature." All their statesmen learn the irresistibility of the tide of custom, and have invented many fine phrases to cover this slowness of perception, and prehensility of tail.

A seashell should be the crest of England, not only because it represents a power built on the waves, but also the hard finish of the men. The Englishman is finished like a cowry or a murex. After the spire and the spines are formed, or, with the formation, a juice exudes, and a hard enamel varnishes every part. The keeping of the proprieties is as indispensable as clean linen. No merit quite countervails the want of this, whilst this sometimes stands in lieu of all. " 'Tis in bad taste," is the most formidable word an Englishman can pronounce. But this japan costs them dear. There is a prose in certain Englishmen, which exceeds in wooden deadness all rivalry with other countrymen. There is a knell in the conceit and externality of their voice, which seems to say, *Leave all hope behind*. In this Gibraltar of propriety, mediocrity gets intrenched, and consolidated, and founded in adamant. An Englishman of fashion is like one of those souvenirs, bound in gold vellum, enriched with delicate engravings, on thick hot-pressed paper, fit for the hands of ladies and princes, but with nothing in it worth reading or remembering.

A severe decorum rules the court and the cottage. When Thalberg, the pianist, was one evening performing before the Queen, at Windsor, in a private party, the Queen accompanied him with her voice. The circumstance took air, and all England shuddered from sea to sea. The indecorum was never repeated. Cold, repressive manners prevail. No enthusiasm is permitted except at the opera. They avoid every thing marked. They require a tone of voice that excites no attention in the room. Sir Philip Sydney is one of the patron saints of England, of whom Wotton said, "His wit was the measure of congruity."

Pretension and vaporing are once for all distasteful. They keep to the other extreme of low tone in dress and manners. They avoid pretension and go right to the heart of the thing. They hate nonsense, sentimentalism, and highflown expression; they use a studied plainness. Even Brummel their fop was marked by the severest simplicity in dress. They value themselves on the absence of every thing theatrical in the public business, and on conciseness and going to the point, in private affairs.

In an aristocratical country, like England, not the Trial by Jury, but the dinner is the capital institution. It is the mode of doing honor to a stranger, to invite him to eat,—and has been for many hundred years. "And they think," says the Venetian traveller of 1500, "no greater honor can be conferred or received, than to invite others to eat with them, or to be invited themselves, and they would sooner give five or six ducats to provide an entertainment for a person, than a groat to assist him in any distress."* It is reserved to the end of the day, the family-hour being generally six, in London, and, if any company is expected, one or two hours later. Every one dresses for dinner, in his own house, or in another man's. The guests are expected to arrive within half an hour of the time fixed by card of invitation, and nothing but death or mutilation is permitted to detain them. The English dinner is precisely the model on which our own are constructed in the Atlantic cities. The company sit one or two hours, before the ladies leave the table. The gentlemen remain over their wine an hour longer, and rejoin the ladies in the drawing-room, and take coffee. The dress-dinner generates a talent of table-talk, which reaches great perfection: the stories are so good, that one is sure they must have been often told before, to have got such happy turns. Hither come all manner of clever projects, bits of popular science, of practical invention, of miscellaneous humor; political, literary, and personal news; railroads, horses, diamonds, agriculture, horticulture, pisciculture, and wine.

English stories, bon-mots, and the recorded table-talk of their wits, are as good as the best of the French. In America, we are apt scholars, but have not yet attained the same perfection: for the range of nations from which London draws, and the steep contrasts of condition create the picturesque in society, as broken country makes picturesque landscape, whilst our prevailing equality makes a prairie tameness: and secondly, because the usage of a dress-dinner every day at

---

*"Relation of England."   Printed by the Camden Society.

dark, has a tendency to hive and produce to advantage every thing good. Much attrition has worn every sentence into a bullet. Also one meets now and then with polished men, who know every thing, have tried every thing, can do every thing, and are quite superior to letters and science. What could they not, if only they would?

CHAPTER VII
Truth

THE TEUTONIC TRIBES have a national singleness of heart, which contrasts with the Latin races. The German name has a proverbial significance of sincerity and honest meaning. The arts bear testimony to it. The faces of clergy and laity in old sculptures and illuminated missals are charged with earnest belief. Add to this hereditary rectitude, the punctuality and precise dealing which commerce creates, and you have the English truth and credit. The government strictly performs its engagements. The subjects do not understand trifling on its part. When any breach of promise occurred, in the old days of prerogative, it was resented by the people as an intolerable grievance. And, in modern times, any slipperiness in the government in political faith, or any repudiation or crookedness in matters of finance, would bring the whole nation to a committee of inquiry and reform. Private men keep their promises, never so trivial. Down goes the flying word on the tablets, and is indelible as Domesday Book.

Their practical power rests on their national sincerity. Veracity derives from instinct, and marks superiority in organization. Nature has endowed some animals with cunning, as a compensation for strength withheld; but it has provoked the malice of all others, as if avengers of public wrong. In the nobler kinds, where strength could be afforded, her races are loyal to truth, as truth is the foundation of the social state. Beasts that make no truce with man, do not break faith with each other. 'Tis said, that the wolf, who makes a *cache* of his prey, and brings his fellows with him to the spot, if, on digging, it is not found, is instantly and unresistingly torn in pieces. English veracity seems to result on a sounder animal structure, as if they could afford it. They are blunt in saying what they think, sparing of promises, and they require plaindealing of others. We will not have to do with a man in a mask. Let us know the truth. Draw a straight line, hit whom and where it will. Alfred, whom the affection of the nation makes the type of their race, is called by his friend Asser, the *truth-speaker*; *Alueredus veridicus*. Geoffrey of Monmouth says of King Aurelius, uncle of Arthur, that "above all things he hated a lie." The Northman Guttorm said to King Olaf, "it is royal work to fulfil royal words." The mottoes of their families are monitory proverbs, as, *Fare fac,*—Say, do,—of the Fairfaxes; *Say and seal*, of the house of Fiennes; *Vero nil verius*, of the DeVeres. To be king of their word, is their pride. When they unmask cant, they say, "the English of this is," &c.; and to give the lie is the extreme insult. The phrase of the lowest of the people is "honor-bright," and their vulgar praise, "his word is as good as his bond." They hate shuffling and equivocation, and the cause is damaged in the public opinion, on which any paltering can be fixed. Even Lord Chesterfield, with his French breeding, when he came to define a gentleman, declared that truth made his distinction: and nothing ever spoken by him would find so hearty a suffrage from his nation. The Duke of Wellington, who had the best right to say so, advises the French General Kellermann, that he may rely on the parole of an English officer. The English, of all classes, value themselves on this trait, as distinguishing them from the French, who, in the popular belief, are more polite than true. An Englishman understates, avoids the superlative, checks himself in compliments, alleging, that in the French language, one cannot speak without lying.

They love reality in wealth, power, hospitality, and do not easily learn to make a show, and take the world as it goes. They are not fond of ornaments, and if they wear them, they must be gems. They read gladly in old Fuller, that a lady, in the reign of Elizabeth, " would have as patiently digested a lie, as the wearing of false stones or pendants of counterfeit pearl." They have the earth-hunger, or preference for property in land, which is said to mark the Teutonic nations. They build of stone: public and private buildings are massive and durable: In comparing their ships' houses, and public offices with the American, it is commonly said, that they spend a pound, where we spend a dollar. Plain rich clothes, plain rich equipage, plain rich finish throughout their house and belongings, mark the English truth.

They confide in each other,—English believes in English.

The French feel the superiority of this probity. The English-man is not springing a trap for his admiration, but is honestly minding his business. The Frenchman is vain. Madame de Stael says, that the English irritated Napoleon, mainly, be-cause they have found out how to unite success with honesty. She was not aware how wide an application her foreign read-ers would give to the remark. Wellington discovered the ruin of Bonaparte's affairs, by his own probity. He augured ill of the empire, as soon as he saw that it was mendacious, and lived by war. If war do not bring in its sequel new trade, better agriculture and manufactures, but only games, fire-works, and spectacles,—no prosperity could support it; much less, a nation decimated for conscripts, and out of pocket, like France. So he drudged for years on his military works at Lis-bon, and from this base at last extended his gigantic lines to Waterloo, believing in his countrymen and their syllogisms above all the rhodomontade of Europe.

At a St. George's festival, in Montreal, where I happened to be a guest, since my return home, I observed that the chairman complimented his compatriots, by saying, "they confided that wherever they met an Englishman, they found a man who would speak the truth." And one cannot think this festival fruitless, if, all over the world, on the 23d of April, wherever two or three English are found, they meet to en-courage each other in the nationality of veracity.

In the power of saying rude truth, sometimes in the lion's mouth, no men surpass them. On the king's birthday, when each bishop was expected to offer the king a purse of gold, Latimer gave Henry VIII. a copy of the Vulgate, with a mark at the passage, "Whoremongers and adulterers God will judge;" and they so honor stoutness in each other, that the king passed it over. They are tenacious of their belief, and cannot easily change their opinions to suit the hour. They are like ships with too much head on to come quickly about, nor will prosperity or even adversity be allowed to shake their habitual view of conduct. Whilst I was in London, M. Guizot arrived there on his escape from Paris, in February, 1848. Many private friends called on him. His name was immedi-ately proposed as an honorary member of the Athenæum. M.

Guizot was blackballed. Certainly, they knew the distinction
of his name. But the Englishman is not fickle. He had really
made up his mind, now for years as he read his newspaper,
to hate and despise M. Guizot; and the altered position of
the man as an illustrious exile, and a guest in the country,
make no difference to him, as they would instantly, to an
American.

They require the same adherence, thorough conviction and
reality in public men. It is the want of character which makes
the low reputation of the Irish members. "See them," they
said, "one hundred and twenty-seven all voting like sheep,
never proposing any thing, and all but four voting the income
tax,"—which was an ill-judged concession of the Government, relieving Irish property from the burdens charged on
English.

They have a horror of adventurers in or out of Parliament.
The ruling passion of Englishmen, in these days, is, a terror
of humbug. In the same proportion, they value honesty,
stoutness, and adherence to your own. They like a man committed to his objects. They hate the French, as frivolous; they
hate the Irish, as aimless; they hate the Germans, as professors. In February, 1848, they said, Look, the French king and
his party fell for want of a shot; they had not conscience to
shoot, so entirely was the pith and heart of monarchy eaten
out.

They attack their own politicians every day, on the same
grounds, as adventurers. They love stoutness in standing for
your right, in declining money or promotion that costs any
concession. The barrister refuses the silk gown of Queen's
Counsel, if his junior have it one day earlier. Lord Collingwood would not accept his medal for victory on 14th February, 1797, if he did not receive one for victory on 1st June,
1794; and the long withholden medal was accorded. When
Castlereagh dissuaded Lord Wellington from going to the
king's levee, until the unpopular Cintra business had been explained, he replied, "You furnish me a reason for going. I will
go to this, or I will never go to a king's levee." The radical
mob at Oxford cried after the tory lord Eldon, "There's old
Eldon; cheer him; he never ratted." They have given the par-

liamentary nickname of *Trimmers* to the timeservers, whom English character does not love.*

They are very liable in their politics to extraordinary delusions, thus, to believe what stands recorded in the gravest books, that the movement of 10 April, 1848, was urged or assisted by foreigners: which, to be sure, is paralleled by the democratic whimsy in this country, which I have noticed to be shared by men sane on other points, that the English are at the bottom of the agitation of slavery, in American politics: and then again to the French popular legends on the subject of *perfidious Albion*. But suspicion will make fools of nations as of citizens.

A slow temperament makes them less rapid and ready than other countrymen, and has given occasion to the observation, that English wit comes afterwards,—which the French denote as *esprit d'escalier*. This dulness makes their attachment to home, and their adherence in all foreign countries to home habits. The Englishman who visits Mount Etna, will carry his teakettle to the top. The old Italian author of the "Relation of England" (in 1500), says, "I have it on the best information, that, when the war is actually raging most furiously, they will seek for good eating, and all their other comforts, without thinking what harm might befall them." Then their eyes seem to be set at the bottom of a tunnel, and they affirm the one small fact they know, with the best faith in the world that nothing else exists. And, as their own belief in guineas is perfect, they readily, on all occasions, apply the pecuniary argument as final. Thus when the Rochester rappings began to be heard of in England, a man deposited £100 in a sealed box in the Dublin Bank, and then advertised in the newspapers to all somnambulists, mesmerizers, and others, that whoever could tell him the number of his note, should have the money. He let it lie there six months, the newspapers now

---

*It is an unlucky moment to remember these sparkles of solitary virtue in the face of the honors lately paid in England to the Emperor Louis Napoleon. I am sure that no Englishman whom I had the happiness to know, consented, when the aristocracy and the commons of London cringed like a Neapolitan rabble, before a successful thief. But—how to resist one step, though odious, in a linked series of state necessities?—Governments must always learn too late, that the use of dishonest agents is as ruinous for nations as for single men.

and then, at his instance, stimulating the attention of the adepts; but none could ever tell him; and he said, "now let me never be bothered more with this proven lie." It is told of a good Sir John, that he heard a case stated by counsel, and made up his mind; then the counsel for the other side taking their turn to speak, he found himself so unsettled and perplexed, that he exclaimed, "So help me God! I will never listen to evidence again." Any number of delightful examples of this English stolidity are the anecdotes of Europe. I knew a very worthy man,—a magistrate, I believe he was, in the town of Derby,—who went to the opera, to see Malibran. In one scene, the heroine was to rush across a ruined bridge. Mr. B. arose, and mildly yet firmly called the attention of the audience and the performers to the fact, that, in his judgment, the bridge was unsafe! This English stolidity contrasts with French wit and tact. The French, it is commonly said, have greatly more influence in Europe than the English. What influence the English have is by brute force of wealth and power; that of the French by affinity and talent. The Italian is subtle, the Spaniard treacherous: tortures, it was said, could never wrest from an Egyptian the confession of a secret. None of these traits belong to the Englishman. His choler and conceit force every thing out. Defoe, who knew his countrymen well, says of them,

> "In close intrigue, their faculty's but weak,
> For generally whate'er they know, they speak,
> And often their own counsels undermine
> By mere infirmity without design;
> From whence, the learned say, it doth proceed,
> That English treasons never can succeed;
> For they're so open-hearted, you may know
> Their own most secret thoughts, and others' too."

CHAPTER VIII

Character

THE ENGLISH RACE are reputed morose. I do not know that they have sadder brows than their neighbors of northern climates. They are sad by comparison with the singing and dancing nations: not sadder, but slow and staid, as finding their joys at home. They, too, believe that where there is no enjoyment of life, there can be no vigor and art in speech or thought: that your merry heart goes all the way, your sad one tires in a mile. This trait of gloom has been fixed on them by French travellers, who, from Froissart, Voltaire, Le Sage, Mirabeau, down to the lively journalists of the *feuilletons*, have spent their wit on the solemnity of their neighbors. The French say, gay conversation is unknown in their island. The Englishman finds no relief from reflection, except in reflection. When he wishes for amusement, he goes to work. His hilarity is like an attack of fever. Religion, the theatre, and the reading the books of his country, all feed and increase his natural melancholy. The police does not interfere with public diversions. It thinks itself bound in duty to respect the pleasures and rare gayety of this inconsolable nation; and their well-known courage is entirely attributable to their disgust of life.

I suppose, their gravity of demeanor and their few words have obtained this reputation. As compared with the Americans, I think them cheerful and contented. Young people, in this country, are much more prone to melancholy. The English have a mild aspect, and a ringing cheerful voice. They are large-natured, and not so easily amused as the southerners, and are among them as grown people among children, requiring war, or trade, or engineering, or science, instead of frivolous games. They are proud and private, and, even if disposed to recreation, will avoid an open garden. They sported sadly; *ils s'amusaient tristement, selon la coutume de leur pays*, said Froissart; and, I suppose, never nation built their party-walls so thick, or their garden-fences so high. Meat and wine produce no effect on them: they are just as cold, quiet, and composed, at the end, as at the beginning of dinner.

The reputation of taciturnity they have enjoyed for six or seven hundred years; and a kind of pride in bad public speaking is noted in the House of Commons, as if they were willing to show that they did not live by their tongues, or thought they spoke well enough if they had the tone of gentlemen. In mixed company, they shut their mouths. A Yorkshire mill-owner told me, he had ridden more than once all the way from London to Leeds, in the first-class carriage, with the same persons, and no word exchanged. The clubhouses were established to cultivate social habits, and it is rare that more than two eat together, and oftenest one eats alone. Was it then a stroke of humor in the serious Swedenborg, or was it only his pitiless logic, that made him shut up the English souls in a heaven by themselves?

They are contradictorily described as sour, splenetic, and stubborn,—and as mild, sweet, and sensible. The truth is, they have great range and variety of character. Commerce sends abroad multitudes of different classes. The choleric Welshman, the fervid Scot, the bilious resident in the East or West Indies, are wide of the perfect behavior of the educated and dignified man of family. So is the burly farmer; so is the country 'squire, with his narrow and violent life. In every inn, is the Commercial-Room, in which 'travellers,' or bagmen who carry patterns, and solicit orders, for the manufacturers, are wont to be entertained. It easily happens that this class should characterize England to the foreigner, who meets them on the road, and at every public house, whilst the gentry avoid the taverns, or seclude themselves whilst in them.

But these classes are the right English stock, and may fairly show the national qualities, before yet art and education have dealt with them. They are good lovers, good haters, slow but obstinate admirers, and, in all things, very much steeped in their temperament, like men hardly awaked from deep sleep, which they enjoy. Their habits and instincts cleave to nature. They are of the earth, earthy; and of the sea, as the sea-kinds, attached to it for what it yields them, and not from any sentiment. They are full of coarse strength, rude exercise, butcher's

meat, and sound sleep; and suspect any poetic insinuation or
any hint for the conduct of life which reflects on this animal
existence, as if somebody were fumbling at the umbilical cord
and might stop their supplies. They doubt a man's sound
judgment, if he does not eat with appetite, and shake their
heads if he is particularly chaste. Take them as they come, you
shall find in the common people a surly indifference, sometimes gruffness and ill temper; and, in minds of more power,
magazines of inexhaustible war, challenging

"The ruggedest hour that time and spite dare bring
To frown upon the enraged Northumberland."

They are headstrong believers and defenders of their opinion,
and not less resolute in maintaining their whim and perversity. Hezekiah Woodward wrote a book against the Lord's
Prayer. And one can believe that Burton the Anatomist of
Melancholy, having predicted from the stars the hour of his
death, slipped the knot himself round his own neck, not to
falsify his horoscope.

Their looks bespeak an invincible stoutness: they have extreme difficulty to run away, and will die game. Wellington
said of the young coxcombs of the Life-Guards delicately
brought up, "but the puppies fight well;" and Nelson said of
his sailors, "they really mind shot no more than peas." Of
absolute stoutness no nation has more or better examples.
They are good at storming redoubts, at boarding frigates, at
dying in the last ditch, or any desperate service which has
daylight and honor in it; but not, I think, at enduring the
rack, or any passive obedience, like jumping off a castle-roof
at the word of a czar. Being both vascular and highly organized, so as to be very sensible of pain; and intellectual, so as
to see reason and glory in a matter.

Of that constitutional force, which yields the supplies of
the day, they have the more than enough, the excess which
creates courage on fortitude, genius in poetry, invention in
mechanics, enterprise in trade, magnificence in wealth, splendor in ceremonies, petulance and projects in youth. The
young men have a rude health which runs into peccant humors. They drink brandy like water, cannot expend their

quantities of waste strength on riding, hunting, swimming, and fencing, and run into absurd frolics with the gravity of the Eumenides. They stoutly carry into every nook and corner of the earth their turbulent sense; leaving no lie uncontradicted; no pretension unexamined. They chew hasheesh; cut themselves with poisoned creases; swing their hammock in the boughs of the Bohon Upas; taste every poison; buy every secret; at Naples, they put St. Januarius's blood in an alembic; they saw a hole into the head of the "winking Virgin," to know why she winks; measure with an English footrule every cell of the Inquisition, every Turkish caaba, every Holy of holies; translate and send to Bentley the arcanum bribed and bullied away from shuddering Bramins; and measure their own strength by the terror they cause. These travellers are of every class, the best and the worst; and it may easily happen that those of rudest behavior are taken notice of and remembered. The Saxon melancholy in the vulgar rich and poor appears as gushes of ill-humor, which every check exasperates into sarcasm and vituperation. There are multitudes of rude young English who have the self-sufficiency and bluntness of their nation, and who, with their disdain of the rest of mankind, and with this indigestion and choler, have made the English traveller a proverb for uncomfortable and offensive manners. It was no bad description of the Briton generically, what was said two hundred years ago, of one particular Oxford scholar: "He was a very bold man, uttered any thing that came into his mind, not only among his companions, but in public coffee-houses, and would often speak his mind of particular persons then accidentally present, without examining the company he was in; for which he was often reprimanded, and several times threatened to be kicked and beaten."

The common Englishman is prone to forget a cardinal article in the bill of social rights, that every man has a right to his own ears. No man can claim to usurp more than a few cubic feet of the audibilities of a public room, or to put upon the company with the loud statement of his crotchets or personalities.

But it is in the deep traits of race that the fortunes of nations are written, and however derived, whether a happier tribe or mixture of tribes, the air, or what circumstance, that mixed for them the golden mean of temperament,—here exists the best stock in the world, broad-fronted, broad-bottomed, best for depth, range, and equability, men of aplomb and reserves, great range and many moods, strong instincts, yet apt for culture; war-class as well as clerks; earls and tradesmen; wise minority, as well as foolish majority; abysmal temperament, hiding wells of wrath, and glooms on which no sunshine settles; alternated with a common sense and humanity which hold them fast to every piece of cheerful duty; making this temperament a sea to which all storms are superficial; a race to which their fortunes flow, as if they alone had the elastic organization at once fine and robust enough for dominion; as if the burly inexpressive, now mute and contumacious, now fierce and sharp-tongued dragon, which once made the island light with his fiery breath, had bequeathed his ferocity to his conqueror. They hide virtues under vices, or the semblance of them. It is the misshapen hairy Scandinavian troll again, who lifts the cart out of the mire, or "threshes the corn that ten day-laborers could not end," but it is done in the dark, and with muttered maledictions. He is a churl with a soft place in his heart, whose speech is a brash of bitter waters, but who loves to help you at a pinch. He says no, and serves you, and your thanks disgust him. Here was lately a cross-grained miser, odd and ugly, resembling in countenance the portrait of Punch, with the laugh left out; rich by his own industry; sulking in a lonely house; who never gave a dinner to any man, and disdained all courtesies; yet as true a worshipper of beauty in form and color as ever existed, and profusely pouring over the cold mind of his countrymen creations of grace and truth, removing the reproach of sterility from English art, catching from their savage climate every fine hint, and importing into their galleries every tint and trait of sunnier cities and skies; making an era in painting; and, when he saw that the splendor of one of his pictures in the Exhibition dimmed his rival's that hung next it, secretly took a brush and blackened his own.

They do not wear their heart in their sleeve for daws to peck at. They have that phlegm or staidness, which it is a compliment to disturb. "Great men," said Aristotle, "are always of a nature originally melancholy." 'Tis the habit of a mind which attaches to abstractions with a passion which gives vast results. They dare to displease, they do not speak to expectation. They like the sayers of No, better than the sayers of Yes. Each of them has an opinion which he feels it becomes him to express all the more that it differs from yours. They are meditating opposition. This gravity is inseparable from minds of great resources.

There is an English hero superior to the French, the German, the Italian, or the Greek. When he is brought to the strife with fate, he sacrifices a richer material possession, and on more purely metaphysical grounds. He is there with his own consent, face to face with fortune, which he defies. On deliberate choice, and from grounds of character, he has elected his part to live and die for, and dies with grandeur. This race has added new elements to humanity, and has a deeper root in the world.

They have great range of scale, from ferocity to exquisite refinement. With larger scale, they have great retrieving power. After running each tendency to an extreme, they try another tack with equal heat. More intellectual than other races, when they live with other races, they do not take their language, but bestow their own. They subsidize other nations, and are not subsidized. They proselyte, and are not proselyted. They assimilate other races to themselves, and are not assimilated. The English did not calculate the conquest of the Indies. It fell to their character. So they administer in different parts of the world, the codes of every empire and race; in Canada, old French law; in the Mauritius, the Code Napoleon; in the West Indies, the edicts of the Spanish Cortes; in the East Indies, the Laws of Menu; in the Isle of Man, of the Scandinavian Thing; at the Cape of Good Hope, of the old Netherlands; and in the Ionian Islands, the Pandects of Justinian.

They are very conscious of their advantageous position in history. England is the lawgiver, the patron, the instructor, the ally. Compare the tone of the French and of the English press: the first querulous, captious, sensitive about English opinion; the English press is never timorous about French opinion, but arrogant and contemptuous.

They are testy and headstrong through an excess of will and

bias; churlish as men sometimes please to be who do not forget a debt, who ask no favors, and who will do what they like with their own. With education and intercourse, these asperities wear off, and leave the good will pure. If anatomy is reformed according to national tendencies, I suppose, the spleen will hereafter be found in the Englishman, not found in the American, and differencing the one from the other. I anticipate another anatomical discovery, that this organ will be found to be cortical and caducous, that they are superficially morose, but at last tender-hearted, herein differing from Rome and the Latin nations. Nothing savage, nothing mean resides in the English heart. They are subject to panics of credulity and of rage, but the temper of the nation, however disturbed, settles itself soon and easily, as, in this temperate zone, the sky after whatever storms clears again, and serenity is its normal condition.

A saving stupidity masks and protects their perception as the curtain of the eagle's eye. Our swifter Americans, when they first deal with English, pronounce them stupid; but, later, do them justice as people who wear well, or hide their strength. To understand the power of performance that is in their finest wits, in the patient Newton, or in the versatile transcendent poets, or in the Dugdales, Gibbons, Hallams, Eldons, and Peels, one should see how English day-laborers hold out. High and low, they are of an unctuous texture. There is an adipocere in their constitution, as if they had oil also for their mental wheels, and could perform vast amounts of work without damaging themselves.

Even the scale of expense on which people live, and to which scholars and professional men conform, proves the tension of their muscle, when vast numbers are found who can each lift this enormous load. I might even add, their daily feasts argue a savage vigor of body.

No nation was ever so rich in able men; "gentlemen," as Charles I. said of Strafford, "whose abilities might make a prince rather afraid than ashamed in the greatest affairs of state;" men of such temper, that, like Baron Vere, "had one seen him returning from a victory, he would by his silence have suspected that he had lost the day; and, had he beheld him in a retreat, he would have collected him a conqueror by the cheerfulness of his spirit."*

The following passage from the Heimskringla might almost stand as a portrait of the modern Englishman: — "Haldor was very stout and strong, and remarkably handsome in appearances. King Harold gave him this testimony, that he, among all his men, cared least about doubtful circumstances, whether they betokened danger or pleasure; for, whatever turned up, he was never in higher nor in lower spirits, never slept less nor more on account of them, nor ate nor drank but according to his custom. Haldor was not a man of many words, but short in conversation, told his opinion bluntly, and was obstinate and hard: and this could not please the king, who had many clever people about him, zealous in his service. Haldor remained a short time with the king, and then came to Iceland, where he took up his abode in Hiardaholt, and dwelt in that farm to a very advanced age."†

The national temper, in the civil history, is not flashy or whiffling. The slow, deep English mass smoulders with fire, which at last sets all its borders in flame. The wrath of London is not French wrath, but has a long memory, and, in its hottest heat, a register and rule.

Half their strength they put not forth. They are capable of a sublime resolution, and if hereafter the war of races, often predicted, and making itself a war of opinions also (a question of despotism and liberty coming from Eastern Europe), should menace the English civilization, these sea-kings may take once again to their floating castles, and find a new home and a second millennium of power in their colonies.

The stability of England is the security of the modern world. If the English race were as mutable as the French, what reliance? But the English stand for liberty. The conservative, money-loving, lord-loving English are yet liberty-loving; and so freedom is safe: for they have more personal force than any other people. The nation always resist the immoral action of their government. They think humanely on

*Fuller. Worthies of England.
†Heimskringla, Laing's translation, vol. iii. p. 37.

the affairs of France, of Turkey, of Poland, of Hungary, of Schleswig Holstein, though overborne by the statecraft of the rulers at last.

Does the early history of each tribe show the permanent bias, which, though not less potent, is masked, as the tribe spreads its activity into colonies, commerce, codes, arts, letters? The early history shows it, as the musician plays the air which he proceeds to conceal in a tempest of variations. In Alfred, in the Northmen, one may read the genius of the English society, namely, that private life is the place of honor. Glory, a career, and ambition, words familiar to the longitude of Paris, are seldom heard in English speech. Nelson wrote from their hearts his homely telegraph, "England expects every man to do his duty."

For actual service, for the dignity of a profession, or to appease diseased or inflamed talent, the army and navy may be entered (the worst boys doing well in the navy); and the civil service, in departments where serious official work is done; and they hold in esteem the barrister engaged in the severer studies of the law. But the calm, sound, and most British Briton shrinks from public life, as charlatanism, and respects an economy founded on agriculture, coal-mines, manufactures, or trade, which secures an independence through the creation of real values.

They wish neither to command or obey, but to be kings in their own houses. They are intellectual and deeply enjoy literature; they like well to have the world served up to them in books, maps, models, and every mode of exact information, and, though not creators in art, they value its refinement. They are ready for leisure, can direct and fill their own day, nor need so much as others the constraint of a necessity. But the history of the nation discloses, at every turn, this original predilection for private independence, and, however this inclination may have been disturbed by the bribes with which their vast colonial power has warped men out of orbit, the inclination endures, and forms and reforms the laws, letters, manners, and occupations. They choose that welfare which is compatible with the commonwealth, knowing that such alone is stable; as wise merchants prefer investments in the three per cents.

CHAPTER IX

Cockayne

THE ENGLISH are a nation of humorists. Individual right is pushed to the uttermost bound compatible with public order. Property is so perfect, that it seems the craft of that race, and not to exist elsewhere. The king cannot step on an acre which the peasant refuses to sell. A testator endows a dog or a rookery, and Europe cannot interfere with his absurdity. Every individual has his particular way of living, which he pushes to folly, and the decided sympathy of his compatriots is engaged to back up Mr. Crump's whim by statutes, and chancellors, and horse-guards. There is no freak so ridiculous but some Englishman has attempted to immortalize by money and law. British citizenship is as omnipotent as Roman was. Mr. Cockayne is very sensible of this. The pursy man means by freedom the right to do as he pleases, and does wrong in order to feel his freedom, and makes a conscience of persisting in it.

He is intensely patriotic, for his country is so small. His confidence in the power and performance of his nation makes him provokingly incurious about other nations. He dislikes foreigners. Swedenborg, who lived much in England, notes "the similitude of minds among the English, in consequence of which they contract familiarity with friends who are of that nation, and seldom with others: and they regard foreigners, as one looking through a telescope from the top of a palace regards those who dwell or wander about out of the city." A much older traveller, the Venetian who wrote the "Relation of England,"* in 1500, says:—"The English are great lovers of themselves, and of every thing belonging to them. They think that there are no other men than themselves, and no other world but England; and, whenever they see a handsome foreigner, they say that he looks like an Englishman, and it is a great pity he should not be an Englishman; and whenever they partake of any delicacy with a foreigner, they ask him whether such a thing is made in his country." When he adds

*Printed by the Camden Society.

epithets of praise, his climax is "so English;" and when he wishes to pay you the highest compliment, he says, I should not know you from an Englishman. France is, by its natural contrast, a kind of blackboard on which English character draws its own traits in chalk. This arrogance habitually exhibits itself in allusions to the French. I suppose that all men of English blood in America, Europe, or Asia, have a secret feeling of joy that they are not French natives. Mr. Coleridge is said to have given public thanks to God, at the close of a lecture, that he had defended him from being able to utter a single sentence in the French language. I have found that Englishmen have such a good opinion of England, that the ordinary phrases, in all good society, of postponing or disparaging one's own things in talking with a stranger, are seriously mistaken by them for an insuppressible homage to the merits of their nation; and the New Yorker or Pennsylvanian who modestly laments the disadvantage of a new country, log-huts, and savages, is surprised by the instant and unfeigned commiseration of the whole company, who plainly account all the world out of England a heap of rubbish.

The same insular limitation pinches his foreign politics. He sticks to his traditions and usages, and, so help him God! he will force his island by-laws down the throat of great countries, like India, China, Canada, Australia, and not only so, but impose Wapping on the Congress of Vienna, and trample down all nationalities with his taxed boots. Lord Chatham goes for liberty, and no taxation without representation;—for that is British law; but not a hobnail shall they dare make in America, but buy their nails in England,—for that also is British law; and the fact that British commerce was to be recreated by the independence of America, took them all by surprise.

In short, I am afraid that English nature is so rank and aggressive as to be a little incompatible with every other. The world is not wide enough for two.

But, beyond this nationality, it must be admitted, the island offers a daily worship to the old Norse god Brage, celebrated among our Scandinavian forefathers, for his eloquence and majestic air. The English have a steady courage, that fits them for great attempts and endurance: they have also a petty courage, through which every man delights in showing himself for what he is, and in doing what he can; so that, in all companies, each of them has too good an opinion of himself to imitate any body. He hides no defect of his form, features, dress, connection, or birthplace, for he thinks every circumstance belonging to him comes recommended to you. If one of them have a bald, or a red, or a green head, or bow legs, or a scar, or mark, or a paunch, or a squeaking or a raven voice, he has persuaded himself that there is something modish and becoming in it, and that it sits well on him.

But nature makes nothing in vain, and this little superfluity of self-regard in the English brain, is one of the secrets of their power and history. For, it sets every man on being and doing what he really is and can. It takes away a dodging, skulking, secondary air, and encourages a frank and manly bearing, so that each man makes the most of himself, and loses no opportunity for want of pushing. A man's personal defects will commonly have with the rest of the world, precisely that importance which they have to himself. If he makes light of them, so will other men. We all find in these a convenient meter of character, since a little man would be ruined by the vexation. I remember a shrewd politician, in one of our western cities, told me, "that he had known several successful statesmen made by their foible." And another, an ex-governor of Illinois, said to me, "If a man knew any thing, he would sit in a corner and be modest; but he is such an ignorant peacock, that he goes bustling up and down, and hits on extraordinary discoveries."

There is also this benefit in brag, that the speaker is unconsciously expressing his own ideal. Humor him by all means, draw it all out, and hold him to it. Their culture generally enables the travelled English to avoid any ridiculous extremes of this self-pleasing, and to give it an agreeable air. Then the natural disposition is fostered by the respect which they find entertained in the world for English ability. It was said of Louis XIV., that his gait and air were becoming enough in so great a monarch, yet would have been ridiculous in another man; so the prestige of the English name warrants a certain confident bearing, which a Frenchman or Belgian could not carry. At all events, they feel themselves at liberty to assume the most extraordinary tone on the subject of English merits.

An English lady on the Rhine hearing a German speaking of her party as foreigners, exclaimed, "No, we are not foreigners; we are English; it is you that are foreigners." They tell you daily, in London, the story of the Frenchman and Englishman who quarrelled. Both were unwilling to fight, but their companions put them up to it: at last, it was agreed, that they should fight alone, in the dark, and with pistols: the candles were put out, and the Englishman, to make sure not to hit any body, fired up the chimney, and brought down the Frenchman. They have no curiosity about foreigners, and answer any information you may volunteer with "Oh, Oh!" until the informant makes up his mind, that they shall die in their ignorance, for any help he will offer. There are really no limits to this conceit, though brighter men among them make painful efforts to be candid.

The habit of brag runs through all classes, from the Times newspaper through politicians and poets, through Wordsworth, Carlyle, Mill, and Sydney Smith, down to the boys of Eton. In the gravest treatise on political economy, in a philosophical essay, in books of science, one is surprised by the most innocent exhibition of unflinching nationality. In a tract on Corn, a most amiable and accomplished gentleman writes thus: — "Though Britain, according to Bishop Berkeley's idea, were surrounded by a wall of brass ten thousand cubits in height, still she would as far excel the rest of the globe in riches, as she now does, both in this secondary quality, and in the more important ones of freedom, virtue, and science."*

The English dislike the American structure of society, whilst yet trade, mills, public education, and chartism are doing what they can to create in England the same social condition. America is the paradise of the economists; is the favorable exception invariably quoted to the rules of ruin; but when he speaks directly of the Americans, the islander forgets his philosophy, and remembers his disparaging anecdotes.

But this childish patriotism costs something, like all narrowness. The English sway of their colonies has no root of

*William Spence.

kindness. They govern by their arts and ability; they are more just than kind; and, whenever an abatement of their power is felt, they have not conciliated the affection on which to rely.

Coarse local distinctions, as those of nation, province, or town, are useful in the absence of real ones; but we must not insist on these accidental lines. Individual traits are always triumphing over national ones. There is no fence in metaphysics discriminating Greek, or English, or Spanish science. Æsop, and Montaigne, Cervantes, and Saadi are men of the world; and to wave our own flag at the dinner table or in the University, is to carry the boisterous dulness of a fire-club into a polite circle. Nature and destiny are always on the watch for our follies. Nature trips us up when we strut; and there are curious examples in history on this very point of national pride.

George of Cappadocia, born at Epiphania in Cilicia, was a low parasite, who got a lucrative contract to supply the army with bacon. A rogue and informer, he got rich, and was forced to run from justice. He saved his money, embraced Arianism, collected a library, and got promoted by a faction to the episcopal throne of Alexandria. When Julian came, A. D. 361, George was dragged to prison; the prison was burst open by the mob, and George was lynched, as he deserved. And this precious knave became, in good time, Saint George of England, patron of chivalry, emblem of victory and civility, and the pride of the best blood of the modern world.

Strange, that the solid truth-speaking Briton should derive from an impostor. Strange, that the New World should have no better luck,—that broad America must wear the name of a thief. Amerigo Vespucci, the pickledealer at Seville, who went out, in 1499, a subaltern with Hojeda, and whose highest naval rank was boatswain's mate in an expedition that never sailed, managed in this lying world to supplant Columbus, and baptize half the earth with his own dishonest name. Thus nobody can throw stones. We are equally badly off in our founders; and the false pickledealer is an offset to the false bacon-seller.

CHAPTER X

Wealth

THERE IS NO COUNTRY in which so absolute a homage is paid to wealth. In America, there is a touch of shame when a man exhibits the evidences of large property, as if, after all, it needed apology. But the Englishman has pure pride in his wealth, and esteems it a final certificate. A coarse logic rules throughout all English souls;—if you have merit, can you not show it by your good clothes, and coach, and horses? How can a man be a gentleman without a pipe of wine? Haydon says, "there is a fierce resolution to make every man live according to the means he possesses." There is a mixture of religion in it. They are under the Jewish law, and read with sonorous emphasis that their days shall be long in the land, they shall have sons and daughters, flocks and herds, wine and oil. In exact proportion, is the reproach of poverty. They do not wish to be represented except by opulent men. An Englishman who has lost his fortune, is said to have died of a broken heart. The last term of insult is, "a beggar." Nelson said, "the want of fortune is a crime which I can never get over." Sydney Smith said, "poverty is infamous in England." And one of their recent writers speaks, in reference to a private and scholastic life, of "the grave moral deterioration which follows an empty exchequer." You shall find this sentiment, if not so frankly put, yet deeply implied, in the novels and romances of the present century, and not only in these, but in biography, and in the votes of public assemblies, in the tone of the preaching, and in the table-talk.

I was lately turning over Wood's *Athenæ Oxonienses*, and looking naturally for another standard in a chronicle of the scholars of Oxford for two hundred years. But I found the two disgraces in that, as in most English books, are, first, disloyalty to Church and State, and, second, to be born poor, or to come to poverty. A natural fruit of England is the brutal political economy. Malthus finds no cover laid at nature's table for the laborer's son. In 1809, the majority in Parliament expressed itself by the language of Mr. Fuller in the House of

Commons, "if you do not like the country, damn you, you can leave it." When Sir S. Romilly proposed his bill forbidding parish officers to bind children apprentices at a greater distance than forty miles from their home, Peel opposed, and Mr. Wortley said, "though, in the higher ranks, to cultivate family affections was a good thing, 'twas not so among the lower orders. Better take them away from those who might deprave them. And it was highly injurious to trade to stop binding to manufacturers, as it must raise the price of labor, and of manufactured goods."

The respect for truth of facts in England, is equalled only by the respect for wealth. It is at once the pride of art of the Saxon, as he is a wealth-maker, and his passion for independence. The Englishman believes that every man must take care of himself, and has himself to thank, if he do not mend his condition. To pay their debts is their national point of honor. From the Exchequer and the East India House to the huckster's shop, every thing prospers, because it is solvent. The British armies are solvent, and pay for what they take. The British empire is solvent; for, in spite of the huge national debt, the valuation mounts. During the war from 1789 to 1815, whilst they complained that they were taxed within an inch of their lives, and, by dint of enormous taxes, were subsidizing all the continent against France, the English were growing rich every year faster than any people ever grew before. It is their maxim, that the weight of taxes must be calculated not by what is taken, but by what is left. Solvency is in the ideas and mechanism of an Englishman. The Crystal Palace is not considered honest until it pays;—no matter how much convenience, beauty, or eclat, it must be self-supporting. They are contented with slower steamers, as long as they know that swifter boats lose money. They proceed logically by the double method of labor and thrift. Every household exhibits an exact economy, and nothing of that uncalculated headlong expenditure which families use in America. If they cannot pay, they do not buy; for they have no presumption of better fortunes next year, as our people have; and they say without shame, I cannot afford it. Gentlemen do not hesitate to ride in the second-class cars, or in the second cabin. An economist, or a man who can proportion his means and his ambition, or bring the year round with expenditure which expresses his character, without embarrassing one day of his future, is already a master of life, and a freeman. Lord Burleigh writes to his son, "that one ought never to devote more than two thirds of his income to the ordinary expenses of life, since the extraordinary will be certain to absorb the other third."

The ambition to create value evokes every kind of ability, government becomes a manufacturing corporation, and every house a mill. The headlong bias to utility will let no talent lie in a napkin,—if possible, will teach spiders to weave silk stockings. An Englishman, while he eats and drinks no more, or not much more than another man, labors three times as many hours in the course of a year, as any other European; or, his life as a workman is three lives. He works fast. Every thing in England is at a quick pace. They have reinforced their own productivity, by the creation of that marvellous machinery which differences this age from any other age.

'Tis a curious chapter in modern history, the growth of the machine-shop. Six hundred years ago, Roger Bacon explained the precession of the equinoxes, the consequent necessity of the reform of the calendar; measured the length of the year, invented gunpowder; and announced, (as if looking from his lofty cell, over five centuries, into ours,) "that machines can be constructed to drive ships more rapidly than a whole galley of rowers could do; nor would they need any thing but a pilot to steer them. Carriages also might be constructed to move with an incredible speed, without the aid of any animal. Finally, it would not be impossible to make machines, which, by means of a suit of wings, should fly in the air in the manner of birds." But the secret slept with Bacon. The six hundred years have not yet fulfilled his words. Two centuries ago, the sawing of timber was done by hand; the carriage wheels ran on wooden axles; the land was tilled by wooden ploughs. And it was to little purpose, that they had pit-coal, or that looms were improved, unless Watt and Stephenson had taught them to work force-pumps and power-looms, by steam. The great strides were all taken within the last hundred years. The Life of Sir Robert Peel, who died, the other day, the model Englishman, very properly has, for a frontispiece, a drawing of the spinning-jenny, which wove the web of his fortunes. Hargreaves invented the spinning-jenny, and died in a workhouse. Arkwright improved the invention; and the machine dispensed with the work of ninety-nine men: that is, one spinner could do as much work as one hundred had done before. The loom was improved further. But the men would sometimes strike for wages, and combine against the masters, and, about 1829-30, much fear was felt, lest the trade would be drawn away by these interruptions, and the emigration of the spinners, to Belgium and the United States. Iron and steel are very obedient. Whether it were not possible to make a spinner that would not rebel, nor mutter, nor scowl, nor strike for wages, nor emigrate? At the solicitation of the masters, after a mob and riot at Staley Bridge, Mr. Roberts of Manchester undertook to create this peaceful fellow, instead of the quarrelsome fellow God had made. After a few trials, he succeeded, and, in 1830, procured a patent for his self-acting mule; a creation, the delight of mill-owners, and "destined," they said, "to restore order among the industrious classes"; a machine requiring only a child's hand to piece the broken yarns. As Arkwright had destroyed domestic spinning, so Roberts destroyed the factory spinner. The power of machinery in Great Britain, in mills, has been computed to be equal to 600,000,000 men, one man being able by the aid of steam to do the work which required two hundred and fifty men to accomplish fifty years ago. The production has been commensurate. England already had this laborious race, rich soil, water, wood, coal, iron, and favorable climate. Eight hundred years ago, commerce had made it rich, and it was recorded, "England is the richest of all the northern nations." The Norman historians recite, that "in 1067, William carried with him into Normandy, from England, more gold and silver than had ever before been seen in Gaul." But when, to this labor and trade, and these native resources was added this goblin of steam, with his myriad arms, never tired, working night and day everlastingly, the amassing of property has run out of all figures. It makes the motor of the last ninety years. The steampipe has added to her population and wealth the equivalent of four or five Englands. Forty thousand ships are entered in Lloyd's lists. The yield of wheat has gone on from

2,000,000 quarters in the time of the Stuarts, to 13,000,000 in 1854. A thousand million of pounds sterling are said to compose the floating money of commerce. In 1848, Lord John Russell stated that the people of this country had laid out £300,000,000 of capital in railways, in the last four years. But a better measure than these sounding figures, is the estimate, that there is wealth enough in England to support the entire population in idleness for one year.

The wise, versatile, all-giving machinery makes chisels, roads, locomotives, telegraphs. Whitworth divides a bar to a millionth of an inch. Steam twines huge cannon into wreaths, as easily as it braids straw, and vies with the volcanic forces which twisted the strata. It can clothe shingle mountains with ship-oaks, make sword-blades that will cut gun-barrels in two. In Egypt, it can plant forests, and bring rain after three thousand years. Already it is ruddering the balloon, and the next war will be fought in the air. But another machine more potent in England than steam, is the Bank. It votes an issue of bills, population is stimulated, and cities rise; it refuses loans, and emigration empties the country; trade sinks; revolutions break out; kings are dethroned. By these new agents our social system is moulded. By dint of steam and of money, war and commerce are changed. Nations have lost their old omnipotence; the patriotic tie does not hold. Nations are getting obsolete, we go and live where we will. Steam has enabled men to choose what law they will live under. Money makes place for them. The telegraph is a limp-band that will hold the Fenris-wolf of war. For now, that a telegraph line runs through France and Europe, from London, every message it transmits makes stronger by one thread, the band which war will have to cut.

The introduction of these elements gives new resources to existing proprietors. A sporting duke may fancy that the state depends on the House of Lords, but the engineer sees, that every stroke of the steam-piston gives value to the duke's land, fills it with tenants; doubles, quadruples, centuples the duke's capital, and creates new measures and new necessities for the culture of his children. Of course, it draws the nobility into the competition as stockholders in the mine, the canal, the railway, in the application of steam to agriculture, and sometimes into trade. But it also introduces large classes into the same competition; the old energy of the Norse race arms itself with these magnificent powers; new men prove an over-match for the land-owner, and the mill buys out the castle. Scandinavian Thor, who once forged his bolts in icy Hecla, and built galleys by lonely fiords; in England, has advanced with the times, has shorn his beard, enters Parliament, sits down at a desk in the India House, and lends Miollnir to Birmingham for a steam-hammer.

The creation of wealth in England in the last ninety years, is a main fact in modern history. The wealth of London determines prices all over the globe. All things precious, or useful, or amusing, or intoxicating, are sucked into this commerce and floated to London. Some English private fortunes reach, and some exceed a million of dollars a year. A hundred thousand palaces adorn the island. All that can feed the senses and passions, all that can succor the talent, or arm the hands of the intelligent middle class, who never spare in what they buy for their own consumption; all that can aid science, gratify taste, or soothe comfort, is in open market. Whatever is excellent and beautiful in civil, rural, or ecclesiastic architecture; in fountain, garden, or grounds; the English noble crosses sea and land to see and to copy at home. The taste and science of thirty peaceful generations; the gardens which Evelyn planted; the temples and pleasure-houses which Inigo Jones and Christopher Wren built; the wood that Gibbons carved; the taste of foreign and domestic artists, Shenstone, Pope, Brown, Loudon, Paxton, are in the vast auction, and the hereditary principle heaps on the owner of to-day the benefit of ages of owners. The present possessors are to the full as absolute as any of their fathers, in choosing and procuring what they like. This comfort and splendor, the breadth of lake and mountain, tillage, pasture, and park, sumptuous castle and modern villa,—all consist with perfect order. They have no revolutions; no horse-guards dictating to the crown; no Parisian *poissardes* and barricades; no mob: but drowsy habitude, daily dress-dinners, wine, and ale, and beer, and gin, and sleep.

With this power of creation, and this passion for independence, property has reached an ideal perfection. It is felt and treated as the national life-blood. The laws are framed to give property the securest possible basis, and the provisions to lock and transmit it have exercised the cunningest heads in a profession which never admits a fool. The rights of property nothing but felony and treason can override. The house is a castle which the king cannot enter. The Bank is a strong box to which the king has no key. Whatever surly sweetness possession can give, is tested in England to the dregs. Vested rights are awful things, and absolute possession gives the smallest freeholder identity of interest with the duke. High stone fences, and padlocked garden-gates announce the absolute will of the owner to be alone. Every whim of exaggerated egotism is put into stone and iron, into silver and gold, with costly deliberation and detail.

An Englishman hears that the Queen Dowager wishes to establish some claim to put her park paling a rod forward into his grounds, so as to get a coachway, and save her a mile to the avenue. Instantly he transforms his paling into stone-masonry, solid as the walls of Cuma, and all Europe cannot prevail on him to sell or compound for an inch of the land. They delight in a freak as the proof of their sovereign freedom. Sir Edward Boynton, at Spic Park, at Cadenham, on a precipice of incomparable prospect, built a house like a long barn, which had not a window on the prospect side. Strawberry Hill of Horace Walpole, Fonthill Abbey of Mr. Beckford, were freaks; and Newstead Abbey became one in the hands of Lord Byron.

But the proudest result of this creation has been the great and refined forces it has put at the disposal of the private citizen. In the social world, an Englishman to-day has the best lot. He is a king in a plain coat. He goes with the most powerful protection, keeps the best company, is armed by the best education, is seconded by wealth; and his English name and accidents are like a flourish of trumpets announcing him. This, with his quiet style of manners, gives him the power of a sovereign, without the inconveniences which belong to that rank. I much prefer the condition of an English gentleman of the better class, to that of any potentate in Europe,—whether for travel, or for opportunity of society, or for access to means of science or study, or for mere comfort and easy healthy relation to people at home.

Such as we have seen is the wealth of England, a mighty mass, and made good in whatever details we care to explore. The cause and spring of it is the wealth of temperament in the people. The wonder of Britain is this plenteous nature. Her worthies are ever surrounded by as good men as themselves; each is a captain a hundred strong, and that wealth of men is represented again in the faculty of each individual, — that he has waste strength, power to spare. The English are so rich, and seem to have established a tap-root in the bowels of the planet, because they are constitutionally fertile and creative.

But a man must keep an eye on his servants, if he would not have them rule him. Man is a shrewd inventor, and is ever taking the hint of a new machine from his own structure, adapting some secret of his own anatomy in iron, wood, and leather, to some required function in the work of the world. But it is found that the machine unmans the user. What he gains in making cloth, he loses in general power. There should be temperance in making cloth, as well as in eating. A man should not be a silk-worm; nor a nation a tent of caterpillars. The robust rural Saxon degenerates in the mills to the Leicester stockinger, to the imbecile Manchester spinner, — far on the way to be spiders and needles. The incessant repetition of the same hand-work dwarfs the man, robs him of his strength, wit, and versatility, to make a pin-polisher, a buckle-maker, or any other specialty; and presently, in a change of industry, whole towns are sacrificed like ant-hills, when the fashion of shoe-strings supersedes buckles, when cotton takes the place of linen, or railways of turnpikes, or when commons are inclosed by landlords. Then society is admonished of the mischief of the division of labor, and that the best political economy is care and culture of men; for, in these crises, all are ruined except such as are proper individuals, capable of thought, and of new choice and the application of their talent to new labor. Then again come in new calamities. England is aghast at the disclosure of her fraud in the adulteration of food, of drugs, and of almost every fabric in her mills and shops; finding that milk will not nourish, nor sugar sweeten, nor bread satisfy, nor pepper bite the tongue, nor glue stick. In true England all is false and forged. This too is the reaction of machinery, but of the larger machinery of commerce. 'Tis not, I suppose, want of probity, so much as the tyranny of trade, which necessitates a perpetual competition of underselling, and that again a perpetual deterioration of the fabric.

The machinery has proved, like the balloon, unmanageable, and flies away with the aeronaut. Steam, from the first, hissed and screamed to warn him; it was dreadful with its explosion, and crushed the engineer. The machinist has wrought and watched, engineers and firemen without number have been sacrificed in learning to tame and guide the monster. But harder still it has proved to resist and rule the dragon Money, with his paper wings. Chancellors and Boards of Trade, Pitt, Peel, and Robinson, and their Parliaments, and their whole generation, adopted false principles, and went to their graves in the belief that they were enriching the country which they were impoverishing. They congratulated each other on ruinous expedients. It is rare to find a merchant who knows why a crisis occurs in trade, why prices rise or fall, or who knows the mischief of paper money. In the culmination of national prosperity, in the annexation of countries; building of ships, depots, towns; in the influx of tons of gold and silver; amid the chuckle of chancellors and financiers, it was found that bread rose to famine prices, that the yeoman was forced to sell his cow and pig, his tools, and his acre of land; and the dreadful barometer of the poor-rates was touching the point of ruin. The poor-rate was sucking in the solvent classes, and forcing an exodus of farmers and mechanics. What befals from the violence of financial crises, befals daily in the violence of artificial legislation.

Such a wealth has England earned, ever new, bounteous, and augmenting. But the question recurs, does she take the step beyond, namely, to the wise use, in view of the supreme wealth of nations? We estimate the wisdom of nations by seeing what they did with their surplus capital. And, in view of these injuries, some compensation has been attempted in England. A part of the money earned returns to the brain to buy schools, libraries, bishops, astronomers, chemists, and artists with; and a part to repair the wrongs of this intemperate weaving, by hospitals, savings-banks, Mechanics' Institutes, public grounds, and other charities and amenities. But the antidotes are frightfully inadequate, and the evil requires a deeper cure, which time and a simpler social organization must supply. At present, she does not rule her wealth. She is simply a good England, but no divinity, or wise and instructed soul. She too is in the stream of fate, one victim more in a common catastrophe.

But being in the fault, she has the misfortune of greatness to be held as the chief offender. England must be held responsible for the despotism of expense. Her prosperity, the splendor which so much manhood and talent and perseverance has thrown upon vulgar aims, is the very argument of materialism. Her success strengthens the hands of base wealth. Who can propose to youth poverty and wisdom, when mean gain has arrived at the conquest of letters and arts; when English success has grown out of the very renunciation of principles, and the dedication to outsides? A civility of trifles, of money and expense, an erudition of sensation takes place, and the putting as many impediments as we can, between the man and his objects. Hardly the bravest among them have the manliness to resist it successfully. Hence, it has come, that not the aims of a manly life, but the means of meeting a certain ponderous expense, is that which is to be considered by a youth in England, emerging from his minority. A large family is reckoned a misfortune. And it is a consolation in the death of the young, that a source of expense is closed.

CHAPTER XI

Aristocracy

THE FEUDAL character of the English state, now that it is getting obsolete, glares a little, in contrast with the democratic tendencies. The inequality of power and property shocks republican nerves. Palaces, halls, villas, walled parks, all over England, rival the splendor of royal seats. Many of the halls, like Haddon, or Kedleston, are beautiful desolations. The proprietor never saw them, or never lived in them. Primogeniture built these sumptuous piles, and, I suppose, it is the sentiment of every traveller, as it was mine, 'Twas well to come ere these were gone. Primogeniture is a cardinal rule of English property and institutions. Laws, customs, manners, the very persons and faces, affirm it.

The frame of society is aristocratic, the taste of the people is loyal. The estates, names, and manners of the nobles flatter the fancy of the people, and conciliate the necessary support. In spite of broken faith, stolen charters, and the devastation of society by the profligacy of the court, we take sides as we read for the loyal England and King Charles's "return to his right" with his Cavaliers,—knowing what a heartless trifler he is, and what a crew of God-forsaken robbers they are. The people of England knew as much. But the fair idea of a settled government connecting itself with heraldic names, with the written and oral history of Europe, and, at last, with the Hebrew religion, and the oldest traditions of the world, was too pleasing a vision to be shattered by a few offensive realities, and the politics of shoemakers and costermongers. The hopes of the commoners take the same direction with the interest of the patricians. Every man who becomes rich buys land, and does what he can to fortify the nobility, into which he hopes to rise. The Anglican clergy are identified with the aristocracy. Time and law have made the joining and moulding perfect in every part. The Cathedrals, the Universities, the national music, the popular romances, conspire to uphold the heraldry, which the current politics of the day are sapping. The taste of the people is conservative. They are proud of the castles, and of the language and symbol of chivalry. Even the word lord is the luckiest style that is used in any language to designate a patrician. The superior education and manners of the nobles recommend them to the country.

The Norwegian pirate got what he could, and held it for his eldest son. The Norman noble, who was the Norwegian pirate baptized, did likewise. There was this advantage of western over oriental nobility, that this was recruited from below. English history is aristocracy with the doors open. Who has courage and faculty, let him come in. Of course, the terms of admission to this club are hard and high. The selfishness of the nobles comes in aid of the interest of the nation to require signal merit. Piracy and war gave place to trade, politics, and letters; the war-lord to the law-lord; the law-lord to the merchant and the mill-owner; but the privilege was kept, whilst the means of obtaining it were changed.

The foundations of these families lie deep in Norwegian exploits by sea, and Saxon sturdiness on land. All nobility in its beginnings was somebody's natural superiority. The things these English have done were not done without peril of life, nor without wisdom and conduct; and the first hands, it may be presumed, were often challenged to show their right to their honors, or yield them to better men. "He that will be a head, let him be a bridge," said the Welsh chief Benegridran, when he carried all his men over the river on his back. "He shall have the book," said the mother of Alfred, "who can read it;" and Alfred won it by that title: and I make no doubt that feudal tenure was no sinecure, but baron, knight, and tenant, often had their memories refreshed, in regard to the service by which they held their lands. The De Veres, Bohuns, Mowbrays, and Plantagenets were not addicted to contemplation. The middle age adorned itself with proofs of manhood and devotion. Of Richard Beauchamp, Earl of Warwick, the Emperor told Henry V. that no Christian king had such another knight for wisdom, nurture, and manhood, and caused him to be named, "Father of curtesie." "Our success in France," says the historian, "lived and died with him."*

The war-lord earned his honors, and no donation of land

*Fuller's Worthies. II. p. 472.

was large, as long as it brought the duty of protecting it, hour by hour, against a terrible enemy. In France and in England, the nobles were, down to a late day, born and bred to war: and the duel, which in peace still held them to the risks of war, diminished the envy that, in trading and studious nations, would else have pried into their title. They were looked on as men who played high for a great stake.

Great estates are not sinecures, if they are to be kept great. A creative economy is the fuel of magnificence. In the same line of Warwick, the successor next but one to Beauchamp, was the stout earl of Henry VI. and Edward IV. Few esteemed themselves in the mode, whose heads were not adorned with the black ragged staff, his badge. At his house in London, six oxen were daily eaten at a breakfast; and every tavern was full of his meat; and who had any acquaintance in his family, should have as much boiled and roast as he could carry on a long dagger.

The new age brings new qualities into request, the virtues of pirates gave way to those of planters, merchants, senators, and scholars. Comity, social talent, and fine manners, no doubt, have had their part also. I have met somewhere with a historiette, which, whether more or less true in its particulars, carries a general truth. "How came the Duke of Bedford by his great landed estates? His ancestor having travelled on the continent, a lively, pleasant man, became the companion of a foreign prince wrecked on the Dorsetshire coast, where Mr. Russell lived. The prince recommended him to Henry VIII., who, liking his company, gave him a large share of the plundered church lands."

The pretence is that the noble is of unbroken descent from the Norman, and has never worked for eight hundred years. But the fact is otherwise. Where is Bohun? where is De Vere? The lawyer, the farmer, the silkmercer lies *perdu* under the coronet, and winks to the antiquary to say nothing; especially skilful lawyers, nobody's sons, who did some piece of work at a nice moment for government, and were rewarded with ermine.

The national tastes of the English do not lead them to the life of the courtier, but to secure the comfort and independence of their homes. The aristocracy are marked by their predilection for country-life. They are called the county-families. They have often no residence in London, and only go thither a short time, during the season, to see the opera; but they concentrate the love and labor of many generations on the building, planting and decoration of their homesteads. Some of them are too old and too proud to wear titles, or, as Sheridan said of Coke, "disdain to hide their head in a coronet;" and some curious examples are cited to show the stability of English families. Their proverb is, that, fifty miles from London, a family will last a hundred years; at a hundred miles, two hundred years; and so on; but I doubt that steam, the enemy of time, as well as of space, will disturb these ancient rules. Sir Henry Wotton says of the first Duke of Buckingham, "He was born at Brookeby in Leicestershire, where his ancestors had chiefly continued about the space of four hundred years, rather without obscurity, than with any great lustre."* Wraxall says, that, in 1781, Lord Surrey, afterwards Duke of Norfolk, told him, that when the year 1783 should arrive, he meant to give a grand festival to all the descendants of the body of Jockey of Norfolk, to mark the day when the dukedom should have remained three hundred years in their house, since its creation by Richard III. Pepys tells us, in writing of an Earl Oxford, in 1666, that the honor had now remained in that name and blood six hundred years.

This long descent of families and this cleaving through ages to the same spot of ground captivates the imagination. It has too a connection with the names of the towns and districts of the country.

The names are excellent,—an atmosphere of legendary melody spread over the land. Older than all epics and histories, which clothe a nation, this undershirt sits close to the body. What history too, and what stores of primitive and savage observation it infolds! Cambridge is the bridge of the Cam; Sheffield the field of the river Sheaf; Leicester the *castra* or camp of the Lear or Leir (now Soar); Rochdale, of the Roch; Exeter or Excester, the *castra* of the Ex; Exmouth, Dartmouth, Sidmouth, Teignmouth, the mouths of the Ex, Dart, Sid, and Teign rivers. Waltham is strong town; Radcliffe is

*Reliquiæ Wottonianæ, p. 208.

red cliff; and so on:—a sincerity and use in naming very striking to an American, whose country is whitewashed all over by unmeaning names, the cast-off clothes of the country from which its emigrants came; or, named at a pinch from a psalm-tune. But the English are those "barbarians" of Jamblichus, who "are stable in their manners, and firmly continue to employ the same words, which also are dear to the gods."

'Tis an old sneer, that the Irish peerage drew their names from playbooks. The English lords do not call their lands after their own names, but call themselves after their lands; as if the man represented the country that bred him; and they rightly wear the token of the glebe that gave them birth; suggesting that the tie is not cut, but that there in London,— the crags of Argyle, the kail of Cornwall, the downs of Devon, the iron of Wales, the clays of Stafford, are neither forgetting nor forgotten, but know the man who was born by them, and who, like the long line of his fathers, has carried that crag, that shore, dale, fen, or woodland, in his blood and manners. It has, too, the advantage of suggesting responsibleness. A susceptible man could not wear a name which represented in a strict sense a city or a county of England, without hearing in it a challenge to duty and honor.

The predilection of the patricians for residence in the country, combined with the degree of liberty possessed by the peasant, makes the safety of the English hall. Mirabeau wrote prophetically from England, in 1784, "If revolution break out in France, I tremble for the aristocracy: their chateaux will be reduced to ashes, and their blood spilt in torrents. The English tenant would defend his lord to the last extremity." The English go to their estates for grandeur. The French live at court, and exile themselves to their estates for economy. As they do not mean to live with their tenants, they do not conciliate them, but wring from them the last sous. Evelyn writes from Blois, in 1644, "The wolves are here in such numbers, that they often come and take children out of the streets: yet will not the Duke, who is sovereign here, permit them to be destroyed."

In evidence of the wealth amassed by ancient families, the traveller is shown the palaces in Piccadilly, Burlington House, Devonshire House, Lansdowne House in Berkshire

Square, and, lower down in the city, a few noble houses which still withstand in all their amplitude the encroachment of streets. The Duke of Bedford includes or included a mile square in the heart of London, where the British Museum, once Montague House, now stands, and the land occupied by Woburn Square, Bedford Square, Russell Square. The Marquis of Westminster built within a few years the series of squares called Belgravia. Stafford House is the noblest palace in London. Northumberland House holds its place by Charing Cross. Chesterfield House remains in Audley Street. Sion House and Holland House are in the suburbs. But most of the historical houses are masked or lost in the modern uses to which trade or charity has converted them. A multitude of town palaces contain inestimable galleries of art.

In the country, the size of private estates is more impressive. From Barnard Castle I rode on the highway twenty-three miles from High Force, a fall of the Tees, towards Darlington, past Raby Castle, through the estate of the Duke of Cleveland. The Marquis of Breadalbane rides out of his house a hundred miles in a straight line to the sea, on his own property. The Duke of Sutherland owns the county of Sutherland, stretching across Scotland from sea to sea. The Duke of Devonshire, besides his other estates, owns 96,000 acres in the County of Derby. The Duke of Richmond has 40,000 acres at Goodwood, and 300,000 at Gordon Castle. The Duke of Norfolk's park in Sussex is fifteen miles in circuit. An agriculturist bought lately the island of Lewes, in Hebrides, containing 500,000 acres. The possessions of the Earl of Lonsdale gave him eight seats in Parliament. This is the Heptarchy again: and before the Reform of 1832, one hundred and fifty-four persons sent three hundred and seven members to Parliament. The borough-mongers governed England.

These large domains are growing larger. The great estates are absorbing the small freeholds. In 1786, the soil of England was owned by 250,000 corporations and proprietors; and, in 1822, by 32,000. These broad estates find room in this narrow island. All over England, scattered at short intervals among ship-yards, mills, mines, and forges, are the paradises of the nobles, where the livelong repose and refinement are heightened by the contrast with the roar of industry and necessity, out of which you have stepped aside.

I was surprised to observe the very small attendance usually in the House of Lords. Out of 573 peers, on ordinary days, only twenty or thirty. Where are they? I asked. "At home on their estates, devoured by *ennui*, or in the Alps, or up the Rhine, in the Harz Mountains, or in Egypt, or in India, on the Ghauts." But, with such interests at stake, how can these men afford to neglect them? "O," replied my friend, "why should they work for themselves, when every man in England works for them, and will suffer before they come to harm?" The hardest radical instantly uncovers, and changes his tone to a lord. It was remarked, on the 10th April, 1848, (the day of the Chartist demonstration,) that the upper classes were, for the first time, actively interesting themselves in their own defence, and men of rank were sworn special constables, with the rest. "Besides, why need they sit out the debate? Has not the Duke of Wellington, at this moment, their proxies,—the proxies of fifty peers in his pocket, to vote for them, if there be an emergency?"

It is however true, that the existence of the House of Peers as a branch of the government entitles them to fill half the Cabinet; and their weight of property and station give them a virtual nomination of the other half; whilst they have their share in the subordinate offices, as a school of training. This monopoly of political power has given them their intellectual and social eminence in Europe. A few law lords and a few political lords take the brunt of public business. In the army, the nobility fill a large part of the high commissions, and give to these a tone of expense and splendor, and also of exclusiveness. They have borne their full share of duty and danger in this service; and there are few noble families which have not paid in some of their members, the debt of life or limb, in the sacrifices of the Russian war. For the rest, the nobility have the lead in matters of state, and of expense; in questions of taste, in social usages, in convivial and domestic hospitalities. In general, all that is required of them is to sit securely, to preside at public meetings, to countenance charities, and to give the example of that decorum so dear to the British heart.

If one asks, in the critical spirit of the day, what service this class have rendered?—uses appear, or they would have perished long ago. Some of these are easily enumerated, others more subtle make a part of unconscious history. Their institution is one step in the progress of society. For a race yields a nobility in some form, however we name the lords, as surely as it yields women.

The English nobles are high-spirited, active, educated men, born to wealth and power, who have run through every country, and kept in every country the best company, have seen every secret of art and nature, and, when men of any ability or ambition, have been consulted in the conduct of every important action. You cannot wield great agencies without lending yourself to them, and, when it happens that the spirit of the earl meets his rank and duties, we have the best examples of behavior. Power of any kind readily appears in the manners; and beneficent power, *le talent de bien faire*, gives a majesty which cannot be concealed or resisted.

These people seem to gain as much as they lose by their position. They survey society, as from the top of St. Paul's, and, if they never hear plain truth from men, they see the best of every thing, in every kind, and they see things so grouped and amassed as to infer easily the sum and genius, instead of tedious particularities. Their good behavior deserves all its fame, and they have that simplicity, and that air of repose, which are the finest ornament of greatness.

The upper classes have only birth, say the people here, and not thoughts. Yes, but they have manners, and, 'tis wonderful, how much talent runs into manners:—nowhere and never so much as in England. They have the sense of superiority, the absence of all the ambitious effort which disgusts in the aspiring classes, a pure tone of thought and feeling, and the power to command, among their other luxuries, the presence of the most accomplished men in their festive meetings.

Loyalty is in the English a sub-religion. They wear the laws as ornaments, and walk by their faith in their painted May-Fair, as if among the forms of gods. The economist of 1855 who asks, of what use are the lords? may learn of Franklin to ask, of what use is a baby? They have been a social church proper to inspire sentiments mutually honoring the lover and the loved. Politeness is the ritual of society, as prayers are of the church; a school of manners, and a gentle blessing to the age in which it grew. 'Tis a romance adorning English life with a larger horizon; a midway heaven, fulfilling to their sense their fairy tales and poetry. This, just as far as the breeding of the nobleman really made him brave, handsome, accomplished, and great-hearted.

On general grounds, whatever tends to form manners, or to finish men, has a great value. Every one who has tasted the delight of friendship, will respect every social guard which our manners can establish, tending to secure from the intrusion of frivolous and distasteful people. The jealousy of every class to guard itself, is a testimony to the reality they have found in life. When a man once knows that he has done justice to himself, let him dismiss all terrors of aristocracy as superstitions, so far as he is concerned. He who keeps the door of a mine, whether of cobalt, or mercury, or nickel, or plumbago, securely knows that the world cannot do without him. Every body who is real is open and ready for that which is also real.

Besides, these are they who make England that strongbox and museum it is; who gather and protect works of art, dragged from amidst burning cities and revolutionary countries, and brought hither out of all the world. I look with respect at houses six, seven, eight hundred, or, like Warwick Castle, nine hundred years old. I pardoned high park-fences, when I saw, that, besides does and pheasants, these have preserved Arundel marbles, Townley galleries, Howard and Spenserian libraries, Warwick and Portland vases, Saxon manuscripts, monastic architectures, millennial trees, and breeds of cattle elsewhere extinct. In these manors, after the frenzy of war and destruction subsides a little, the antiquary finds the frailest Roman jar, or crumbling Egyptian mummy-case, without so much as a new layer of dust, keeping the series of history unbroken, and waiting for its interpreter, who is sure to arrive. These lords are the treasurers and librarians of mankind, engaged by their pride and wealth to this function.

Yet there were other works for British dukes to do. George Loudon, Quintinye, Evelyn, had taught them to make gardens. Arthur Young, Bakewell, and Mechi, have made them agricultural. Scotland was a camp until the day of Culloden. The Dukes of Athol, Sutherland, Buccleugh, and the Marquis of Breadalbane have introduced the rape-culture, the sheep-farm, wheat, drainage, the plantation of forests, the artificial replenishment of lakes and ponds with fish, the renting of game-preserves. Against the cry of the old tenantry, and the sympathetic cry of the English press, they have rooted out and planted anew, and now six millions of people live, and live better on the same land that fed three millions.

The English barons, in every period, have been brave and great, after the estimate and opinion of their times. The grand old halls scattered up and down in England, are dumb vouchers to the state and broad hospitality of their ancient lords. Shakspeare's portraits of good duke Humphrey, of Warwick, of Northumberland, of Talbot, were drawn in strict consonance with the traditions. A sketch of the Earl of Shrewsbury, from the pen of Queen Elizabeth's archbishop Parker;* Lord Herbert of Cherbury's autobiography; the letters and essays of Sir Philip Sidney; the anecdotes preserved by the antiquaries Fuller and Collins; some glimpses at the interiors of noble houses, which we owe to Pepys and Evelyn; the details which Ben Jonson's masques (performed at Kenilworth, Althorpe, Belvoir, and other noble houses,) record or suggest; down to Aubrey's passages of the life of Hobbes in the house of the Earl of Devon, are favorable pictures of a romantic style of manners. Penshurst still shines for us, and its Christmas revels, "where logs not burn, but men." At Wilton House, the "Arcadia" was written, amidst conversations with Fulke Greville, Lord Brooke, a man of no vulgar mind, as his own poems declare him. I must hold Ludlow Castle an honest house, for which Milton's "Comus" was written, and the company nobly bred which performed it with knowledge and sympathy. In the roll of nobles, are found poets, philosophers, chemists, astronomers, also men of solid virtues and of lofty sentiments; often they have been the friends and patrons of genius and learning, and especially of the fine arts; and at this moment, almost every great house has its sumptuous picture-gallery.

*Dibdin's Literary Reminiscences, vol. i, xii.

Of course, there is another side to this gorgeous show. Every victory was the defect of a party only less worthy. Castles are proud things, but 'tis safest to be outside of them. War is a foul game, and yet war is not the worst part of aristocratic history. In later times, when the baron, educated only for war, with his brains paralyzed by his stomach, found himself idle at home, he grew fat and wanton, and a sorry brute. Grammont, Pepys, and Evelyn, show the kennels to which the king and court went in quest of pleasure. Prostitutes taken from the theatres, were made duchesses, their bastards dukes and earls. "The young men sat uppermost, the old serious lords were out of favor." The discourse that the king's companions had with him was "poor and frothy." No man who valued his head might do what these pot-companions familiarly did with the king. In logical sequence of these dignified revels, Pepys can tell the beggarly shifts to which the king was reduced, who could not find paper at his council table, and "no handkerchers" in his wardrobe, "and but three bands to his neck," and the linen-draper and the stationer were out of pocket, and refusing to trust him, and the baker will not bring bread any longer. Meantime, the English Channel was swept, and London threatened by the Dutch fleet, manned too by English sailors, who, having been cheated of their pay for years by the king, enlisted with the enemy.

The Selwyn correspondence in the reign of George III., discloses a rottenness in the aristocracy, which threatened to decompose the state. The sycophancy and sale of votes and honor, for place and title; lewdness, gaming, smuggling, bribery, and cheating; the sneer at the childish indiscretion of quarrelling with ten thousand a year; the want of ideas; the splendor of the titles, and the apathy of the nation, are instructive, and make the reader pause and explore the firm bounds which confined these vices to a handful of rich men. In the reign of the Fourth George, things do not seem to have mended, and the rotten debauchee let down from a window by an inclined plane into his coach to take the air, was a scandal to Europe which the ill fame of his queen and of his family did nothing to retrieve.

Under the present reign, the perfect decorum of the Court is thought to have put a check on the gross vices of the aristocracy; yet gaming, racing, drinking, and mistresses, bring them down, and the democrat can still gather scandals, if he will. Dismal anecdotes abound, verifying the gossip of the last generation of dukes served by bailiffs, with all their plate in pawn; of great lords living by the showing of their houses; and of an old man wheeled in his chair from room to room, whilst his chambers are exhibited to the visitor for money; of ruined dukes and earls living in exile for debt. The historic names of the Buckinghams, Beauforts, Marlboroughs, and Hertfords, have gained no new lustre, and now and then darker scandals break out, ominous as the new chapters added under the Orleans dynasty to the *"Causes Célèbres"* in France. Even peers, who are men of worth and public spirit, are over-taken and embarrassed by their vast expense. The respectable Duke of Devonshire, willing to be the Mecænas and Lucullus of his island, is reported to have said, that he cannot live at Chatsworth but one month in the year. Their many houses eat them up. They cannot sell them, because they are entailed. They will not let them, for pride's sake, but keep them empty, aired, and the grounds mown and dressed, at a cost of four or five thousand pounds a year. The spending is for a great part in servants, in many houses exceeding a hundred.

Most of them are only chargeable with idleness, which, because it squanders such vast power of benefit, has the mischief of crime. "They might be little Providences on earth," said my friend, "and they are, for the most part, jockeys and fops." Campbell says, "acquaintance with the nobility, I could never keep up. It requires a life of idleness, dressing, and attendance on their parties." I suppose, too, that a feeling of self-respect is driving cultivated men out of this society, as if the noble were slow to receive the lessons of the times, and had not learned to disguise his pride of place. A man of wit, who is also one of the celebrities of wealth and fashion, confessed to his friend, that he could not enter their houses without being made to feel that they were great lords, and he a low plebeian. With the tribe of *artistes*, including the musical tribe, the patrician morgue keeps no terms, but excludes them. When Julia Grisi and Mario sang at the houses of the Duke of Wellington and other grandees, a cord was stretched between the singer and the company.

When every noble was a soldier, they were carefully bred to great personal prowess. The education of a soldier is a simpler affair than that of an earl in the nineteenth century. And this was very seriously pursued; they were expert in every species of equitation, to the most dangerous practices, and this down to the accession of William of Orange. But graver men appear to have trained their sons for civil affairs. Elizabeth extended her thought to the future; and Sir Philip Sidney in his letter to his brother, and Milton and Evelyn, gave plain and hearty counsel. Already too, the English noble and squire were preparing for the career of the country-gentleman, and his peaceable expense. They went from city to city, learning receipts to make perfumes, sweet powders, pomanders, antidotes, gathering seeds, gems, coins, and divers curiosities, preparing for a private life thereafter, in which they should take pleasure in these recreations.

All advantages given to absolve the young patrician from intellectual labor are of course mistaken. "In the university, noblemen are exempted from the public exercises for the degree, &c., by which they attain a degree called *honorary*. At the same time, the fees they have to pay for matriculation, and on all other occasions, are much higher."* Fuller records "the observation of foreigners, that Englishmen, by making their children gentlemen, before they are men, cause they are so seldom wise men." This cockering justifies Dr. Johnson's bitter apology for primogeniture, "that it makes but one fool in a family."

The revolution in society has reached this class. The great powers of industrial art have no exclusion of name or blood. The tools of our time, namely, steam, ships, printing, money, and popular education, belong to those who can handle them: and their effect has been, that advantages once confined to men of family, are now open to the whole middle class. The road that grandeur levels for his coach, toil can travel in his cart.

This is more manifest every day, but I think it is true throughout English history. English history, wisely read, is the vindication of the brain of that people. Here, at last, were

*Huber. History of English Universities.

climate and condition friendly to the working faculty. Who now will work and dare, shall rule. This is the charter, or the chartism, which fogs, and seas, and rains proclaimed,—that intellect and personal force should make the law; that industry and administrative talent should administer; that work should wear the crown. I know that not this, but something else is pretended. The fiction with which the noble and the bystander equally please themselves is, that the former is of unbroken descent from the Norman, and so has never worked for eight hundred years. All the families are new, but the name is old, and they have made a covenant with their memories not to disturb it. But the analysis of the peerage and gentry shows the rapid decay and extinction of old families, the continual recruiting of these from new blood. The doors, though ostentatiously guarded, are really open, and hence the power of the bribe. All the barriers to rank only whet the thirst, and enhance the prize. "Now," said Nelson, when clearing for battle, "a peerage, or Westminster Abbey!" "I have no illusion left," said Sydney Smith, "but the Archbishop of Canterbury." "The lawyers," said Burke, "are only birds of passage in this House of Commons," and then added, with a new figure, "they have their best bower anchor in the House of Lords."

Another stride that has been taken, appears in the perishing of heraldry. Whilst the privileges of nobility are passing to the middle class, the badge is discredited, and the titles of lordship are getting musty and cumbersome. I wonder that sensible men have not been already impatient of them. They belong, with wigs, powder, and scarlet coats, to an earlier age, and may be advantageously consigned, with paint and tattoo, to the dignitaries of Australia and Polynesia.

A multitude of English, educated at the universities, bred into their society with manners, ability, and the gifts of fortune, are every day confronting the peers on a footing of equality, and outstripping them, as often, in the race of honor and influence. That cultivated class is large and ever enlarging. It is computed that, with titles and without, there are seventy thousand of these people coming and going in London, who make up what is called high society. They cannot shut their eyes to the fact that an untitled nobility possess all the power without the inconveniences that belong to rank, and the rich Englishman goes over the world at the present day, drawing more than all the advantages which the strongest of his kings could command.

CHAPTER XII

Universities

O F BRITISH universities, Cambridge has the most illustrious names on its list. At the present day, too, it has
the advantage of Oxford, counting in its *alumni* a greater
number of distinguished scholars. I regret that I had but a
single day wherein to see King's College Chapel, the beautiful
lawns and gardens of the colleges, and a few of its gownsmen.

But I availed myself of some repeated invitations to Oxford, where I had introductions to Dr. Daubeny, Professor of
Botany, and to the Regius Professor of Divinity, as well as to
a valued friend, a Fellow of Oriel, and went thither on the
last day of March, 1848. I was the guest of my friend in Oriel,
was housed close upon that college, and I lived on college
hospitalities.

My new friends showed me their cloisters, the Bodleian Library, the Randolph Gallery, Merton Hall, and the rest. I saw
several faithful, high-minded young men, some of them in the
mood of making sacrifices for peace of mind,—a topic, of
course, on which I had no counsel to offer. Their affectionate
and gregarious ways reminded me at once of the habits of *our*
Cambridge men, though I imputed to these English an advantage in their secure and polished manners. The halls are
rich with oaken wainscoting and ceiling. The pictures of the
founders hang from the walls; the tables glitter with plate. A
youth came forward to the upper table, and pronounced the
ancient form of grace before meals, which, I suppose, has
been in use here for ages, *Benedictus benedicat; benedicitur,
benedicatur.*

It is a curious proof of the English use and wont, or of
their good nature, that these young men are locked up every
night at nine o'clock, and the porter at each hall is required
to give the name of any belated student who is admitted after
that hour. Still more descriptive is the fact, that out of twelve
hundred young men, comprising the most spirited of the aristocracy, a duel has never occurred.

Oxford is old, even in England, and conservative. Its foundations date from Alfred, and even from Arthur, if, as is alleged, the Pheryllt of the Druids had a seminary here. In the reign of Edward I., it is pretended, here were thirty thousand students; and nineteen most noble foundations were then established. Chaucer found it as firm as if it had always stood; and it is, in British story, rich with great names, the school of the island, and the link of England to the learned of Europe. Hither came Erasmus, with delight, in 1497. Albericus Gentilis, in 1580, was relieved and maintained by the university. Albert Alaskie, a noble Polonian, Prince of Sirad, who visited England to admire the wisdom of Queen Elizabeth, was entertained with stage-plays in the Refectory of Christchurch, in 1583. Isaac Casaubon, coming from Henri Quatre of France, by invitation of James I., was admitted to Christ's College, in July, 1613. I saw the Ashmolean Museum, whither Elias Ashmole, in 1682, sent twelve cart-loads of rarities. Here indeed was the Olympia of all Antony Wood's and Aubrey's games and heroes, and every inch of ground has its lustre. For Wood's *Athenæ Oxonienses*, or calendar of the writers of Oxford for two hundred years, is a lively record of English manners and merits, and as much a national monument as Purchas's Pilgrims or Hansard's Register. On every side, Oxford is redolent of age and authority. Its gates shut of themselves against modern innovation. It is still governed by the statutes of Archbishop Laud. The books in Merton Library are still chained to the wall. Here, on August 27, 1660, John Milton's *Pro Populo Anglicano Defensio*, and *Iconoclastes* were committed to the flames. I saw the school-court or quadrangle, where, in 1683, the Convocation caused the Leviathan of Thomas Hobbes to be publicly burnt. I do not know whether this learned body have yet heard of the Declaration of American Independence, or whether the Ptolemaic astronomy does not still hold its ground against the novelties of Copernicus.

As many sons, almost so many benefactors. It is usual for a nobleman, or indeed for almost every wealthy student, on quitting college, to leave behind him some article of plate; and gifts of all values, from a hall, or a fellowship, or a library, down to a picture or a spoon, are continually accruing, in the course of a century. My friend Doctor J., gave me the following anecdote. In Sir Thomas Lawrence's collection at London, were the cartoons of Raphael and Michel Angelo. This inestimable prize was offered to Oxford University for seven thousand pounds. The offer was accepted, and the committee charged with the affair had collected three thousand pounds, when among other friends, they called on Lord Eldon. Instead of a hundred pounds, he surprised them by putting down his name for three thousand pounds. They told him, they should now very easily raise the remainder. "No," he said, "your men have probably already contributed all they can spare; I can as well give the rest": and he withdrew his cheque for three thousand, and wrote four thousand pounds. I saw the whole collection in April, 1848.

In the Bodleian Library, Dr. Bandinel showed me the manuscript Plato, of the date of A. D. 896, brought by Dr. Clarke from Egypt; a manuscript Virgil, of the same century; the first Bible printed at Mentz, (I believe in 1450); and a duplicate of the same, which had been deficient in about twenty leaves at the end. But, one day, being in Venice, he bought a room full of books and manuscripts,—every scrap and fragment,—for four thousand louis d'ors, and had the doors locked and sealed by the consul. On proceeding, afterwards, to examine his purchase, he found the twenty deficient pages of his Mentz Bible, in perfect order; brought them to Oxford, with the rest of his purchase, and placed them in the volume; but has too much awe for the Providence that appears in bibliography also, to suffer the reunited parts to be re-bound. The oldest building here is two hundred years younger than the frail manuscript brought by Dr. Clarke from Egypt. No candle or fire is ever lighted in the Bodleian. Its catalogue is the standard catalogue on the desk of every library in Oxford. In each several college, they underscore in red ink on this catalogue the titles of books contained in the library of that college,—the theory being that the Bodleian has all books. This rich library spent during the last year (1847) for the purchase of books £1668.

The logical English train a scholar as they train an engineer. Oxford is a Greek factory, as Wilton mills weave carpet, and Sheffield grinds steel. They know the use of a tutor, as they know the use of a horse; and they draw the greatest amount of benefit out of both. The reading men are kept by hard

walking, hard riding, and measured eating and drinking, at
the top of their condition, and two days before the examination, do not work, but lounge, ride, or run, to be fresh on
the college doomsday. Seven years' residence is the theoretic
period for a master's degree. In point of fact, it has long been
three years' residence, and four years more of standing. This
"three years" is about twenty-one months in all.*

"The whole expense," says Professor Sewel, "of ordinary
college tuition at Oxford, is about sixteen guineas a year." But
this plausible statement may deceive a reader unacquainted
with the fact, that the principal teaching relied on is private
tuition. And the expenses of private tuition are reckoned at
from £50 to £70 a year, or, $1000 for the whole course of
three years and a half. At Cambridge $750 a year is economi-
cal, and $1500 not extravagant.†

The number of students and of residents, the dignity of the
authorities, the value of the foundations, the history and the
architecture, the known sympathy of entire Britain in what is
done there, justify a dedication to study in the undergraduate,
such as cannot easily be in America, where his college is half
suspected by the Freshman to be insignificant in the scale beside trade and politics. Oxford is a little aristocracy in itself,
numerous and dignified enough to rank with other estates in
the realm; and where fame and secular promotion are to be
had for study, and in a direction which has the unanimous
respect of all cultivated nations.

This aristocracy, of course, repairs its own losses; fills
places, as they fall vacant, from the body of students. The
number of fellowships at Oxford is 540, averaging £200 a
year, with lodging and diet at the college. If a young American, loving learning, and hindered by poverty, were offered a
home, a table, the walks, and the library, in one of these academical palaces, and a thousand dollars a year as long as he
chose to remain a bachelor, he would dance for joy. Yet these
young men thus happily placed, and paid to read, are impatient of their few checks, and many of them preparing to resign their fellowships. They shuddered at the prospect of
dying a Fellow, and they pointed out to me a paralytic old

*Huber, ii. p. 304.
†Bristed. Five Years at an English University.

man, who was assisted into the hall. As the number of under-graduates at Oxford is only about 1200 or 1300, and many of these are never competitors, the chance of a fellowship is very great. The income of the nineteen colleges is conjectured at £150,000 a year.

The effect of this drill is the radical knowledge of Greek and Latin, and of mathematics, and the solidity and taste of English criticism. Whatever luck there may be in this or that award, an Eton captain can write Latin longs and shorts, can turn the Court-Guide into hexameters, and it is certain that a Senior Classic can quote correctly from the *Corpus Poetarum*, and is critically learned in all the humanities. Greek erudition exists on the Isis and Cam, whether the Maud man or the Brazen Nose man be properly ranked or not; the atmosphere is loaded with Greek learning; the whole river has reached a certain height, and kills all that growth of weeds, which this Castalian water kills. The English nature takes culture kindly. So Milton thought. It refines the Norseman. Access to the Greek mind lifts his standard of taste. He has enough to think of, and, unless of an impulsive nature, is indisposed from writing or speaking, by the fulness of his mind, and the new severity of his taste. The great silent crowd of thorough-bred Grecians always known to be around him, the English writer cannot ignore. They prune his orations, and point his pen. Hence, the style and tone of English journalism. The men have learned accuracy and comprehension, logic, and pace, or speed of working. They have bottom, endurance, wind. When born with good constitutions, they make those eupeptic studying-mills, the cast-iron men, the *dura ilia*, whose powers of performance compare with ours, as the steam-hammer with the music-box;—Cokes, Mansfields, Seldens, and Bentleys, and when it happens that a superior brain puts a rider on this admirable horse, we obtain those masters of the world who combine the highest energy in affairs, with a supreme culture.

It is contended by those who have been bred at Eton, Harrow, Rugby, and Westminster, that the public sentiment within each of those schools is high-toned and manly; that, in their playgrounds, courage is universally admired, mean-ness despised, manly feelings and generous conduct are encouraged: that an unwritten code of honor deals to the spoiled child of rank, and to the child of upstart wealth an even-handed justice, purges their nonsense out of both, and does all that can be done to make them gentlemen.

Again, at the universities, it is urged, that all goes to form what England values as the flower of its national life,—a well-educated gentleman. The German Huber, in describing to his countrymen the attributes of an English gentleman, frankly admits, that, "in Germany, we have nothing of the kind. A gentleman must possess a political character, an independent and public position, or, at least, the right of assuming it. He must have average opulence, either of his own, or in his family. He should also have bodily activity and strength, unattainable by our sedentary life in public offices. The race of English gentlemen presents an appearance of manly vigor and form, not elsewhere to be found among an equal number of persons. No other nation produces the stock. And, in England, it has deteriorated. The university is a decided presumption in any man's favor. And so eminent are the members that a glance at the calendars will show that in all the world one cannot be in better company than on the books of one of the larger Oxford or Cambridge colleges."*

These seminaries are finishing schools for the upper classes, and not for the poor. The useful is exploded. The definition of a public school is "a school which excludes all that could fit a man for standing behind a counter."†

No doubt, the foundations have been perverted. Oxford, which equals in wealth several of the smaller European states, shuts up the lectureships which were made "public for all men thereunto to have concourse;" mis-spends the revenues bestowed for such youths "as should be most meet for towardness, poverty, and painfulness;" there is gross favoritism; many chairs and many fellowships are made beds of ease; and 'tis likely that the university will know how to resist and make inoperative the terrors of parliamentary inquiry; no doubt, their learning is grown obsolete;—but Oxford also has its merits, and I found here also proof of the national fidelity and thoroughness. Such knowledge as they prize they possess and

*Huber: History of the English Universities.   Newman's Translation.
†See Bristed.   Five Years in an English University.   New York. 1852.

impart. Whether in course or by indirection, whether by a cramming tutor or by examiners with prizes and foundation scholarships, education according to the English notion of it is arrived at. I looked over the Examination Papers of the year 1848, for the various scholarships and fellowships, the Lusby, the Hertford, the Dean-Ireland, and the University, (copies of which were kindly given me by a Greek professor,) containing the tasks which many competitors had victoriously performed, and I believed they would prove too severe tests for the candidates for a Bachelor's degree in Yale or Harvard. And, in general, here was proof of a more searching study in the appointed directions, and the knowledge pretended to be conveyed was conveyed. Oxford sends out yearly twenty or thirty very able men, and three or four hundred well-educated men.

The diet and rough exercise secure a certain amount of old Norse power. A fop will fight, and, in exigent circumstances, will play the manly part. In seeing these youths, I believed I saw already an advantage in vigor and color and general habit, over their contemporaries in the American colleges. No doubt much of the power and brilliancy of the reading-men is merely constitutional or hygienic. With a hardier habit and resolute gymnastics, with five miles more walking, or five ounces less eating, or with a saddle and gallop of twenty miles a day, with skating and rowing-matches, the American would arrive at as robust exegesis, and cheery and hilarious tone. I should readily concede these advantages, which it would be easy to acquire, if I did not find also that they read better than we, and write better.

English wealth falling on their school and university training, makes a systematic reading of the best authors, and to the end of a knowledge how the things whereof they treat really stand: whilst pamphleteer or journalist reading for an argument for a party, or reading to write, or, at all events, for some by-end imposed on them, must read meanly and fragmentarily. Charles I. said, that he understood English law as well as a gentleman ought to understand it.

Then they have access to books; the rich libraries collected at every one of many thousands of houses, give an advantage not to be attained by a youth in this country, when one thinks how much more and better may be learned by a scholar, who, immediately on hearing of a book, can consult it, than by one who is on the quest, for years, and reads inferior books, because he cannot find the best.

Again, the great number of cultivated men keep each other up to a high standard. The habit of meeting well-read and knowing men teaches the art of omission and selection.

Universities are, of course, hostile to geniuses, which seeing and using ways of their own, discredit the routine: as churches and monasteries persecute youthful saints. Yet we all send our sons to college, and, though he be a genius, he must take his chance. The university must be retrospective. The gale that gives direction to the vanes on all its towers blows out of antiquity. Oxford is a library, and the professors must be librarians. And I should as soon think of quarrelling with the janitor for not magnifying his office by hostile sallies into the street, like the Governor of Kertch or Kinburn, as of quarrelling with the professors for not admiring the young neologists who pluck the beards of Euclid and Aristotle, or for not attempting themselves to fill their vacant shelves as original writers.

It is easy to carp at colleges, and the college, if we will wait for it, will have its own turn. Genius exists there also, but will not answer a call of a committee of the House of Commons. It is rare, precarious, eccentric, and darkling. England is the land of mixture and surprise, and when you have settled it that the universities are moribund, out comes a poetic influence from the heart of Oxford, to mould the opinions of cities, to build their houses as simply as birds their nests, to give veracity to art, and charm mankind, as an appeal to moral order always must. But besides this restorative genius, the best poetry of England of this age, in the old forms, comes from two graduates of Cambridge.

CHAPTER XIII

Religion

N O PEOPLE, at the present day, can be explained by their national religion. They do not feel responsible for it; it lies far outside of them. Their loyalty to truth, and their labor and expenditure rest on real foundations, and not on a national church. And English life, it is evident, does not grow out of the Athanasian creed, or the Articles, or the Eucharist. It is with religion as with marriage. A youth marries in haste; afterwards, when his mind is opened to the reason of the conduct of life, he is asked, what he thinks of the institution of marriage, and of the right relations of the sexes? 'I should have much to say,' he might reply, 'if the question were open, but I have a wife and children, and all question is closed for me.' In the barbarous days of a nation, some *cultus* is formed or imported; altars are built, tithes are paid, priests ordained. The education and expenditure of the country take that direction, and when wealth, refinement, great men, and ties to the world, supervene, its prudent men say, why fight against Fate, or lift these absurdities which are now mountainous? Better find some niche or crevice in this mountain of stone which religious ages have quarried and carved, wherein to bestow yourself, than attempt any thing ridiculously and dangerously above your strength, like removing it.

In seeing old castles and cathedrals, I sometimes say, as to-day, in front of Dundee Church tower, which is eight hundred years old, 'this was built by another and a better race than any that now look on it.' And, plainly, there has been great power of sentiment at work in this island, of which these buildings are the proofs: as volcanic basalts show the work of fire which has been extinguished for ages. England felt the full heat of the Christianity which fermented Europe, and drew, like the chemistry of fire, a firm line between barbarism and culture. The power of the religious sentiment put an end to human sacrifices, checked appetite, inspired the crusades, inspired resistance to tyrants, inspired self-respect, set bounds to serfdom and slavery, founded liberty, created the

religious architecture,—York, Newstead, Westminster, Fountains Abbey, Ripon, Beverley, and Dundee,—works to which
the key is lost, with the sentiment which created them; inspired the English Bible, the liturgy, the monkish histories,
the chronicle of Richard of Devizes. The priest translated the
Vulgate, and translated the sanctities of old hagiology into
English virtues on English ground. It was a certain affirmative
or aggressive state of the Caucasian races. Man awoke refreshed by the sleep of ages. The violence of the northern
savages exasperated Christianity into power. It lived by the
love of the people. Bishop Wilfrid manumitted two hundred
and fifty serfs, whom he found attached to the soil. The clergy
obtained respite from labor for the boor on the Sabbath, and
on church festivals. "The lord who compelled his boor to labor between sunset on Saturday and sunset on Sunday, forfeited him altogether." The priest came out of the people, and
sympathized with his class. The church was the mediator,
check, and democratic principle, in Europe. Latimer, Wicliffe,
Arundel, Cobham, Antony Parsons, Sir Harry Vane, George
Fox, Penn, Bunyan are the democrats, as well as the saints of
their times. The Catholic church, thrown on this toiling, serious people, has made in fourteen centuries a massive system,
close fitted to the manners and genius of the country, at once
domestical and stately. In the long time, it has blended with
every thing in heaven above and the earth beneath. It moves
through a zodiac of feasts and fasts, names every day of the
year, every town and market and headland and monument,
and has coupled itself with the almanac, that no court can be
held, no field ploughed, no horse shod, without some leave
from the church. All maxims of prudence or shop or farm are
fixed and dated by the church. Hence, its strength in the agricultural districts. The distribution of land into parishes enforces a church sanction to every civil privilege; and the
gradation of the clergy,—prelates for the rich, and curates for
the poor,—with the fact that a classical education has been
secured to the clergyman, makes them "the link which unites
the sequestered peasantry with the intellectual advancement
of the age."*

*Wordsworth.

The English church has many certificates to show, of humble effective service in humanizing the people, in cheering and refining men, feeding, healing, and educating. It has the seal of martyrs and confessors; the noblest books; a sublime architecture; a ritual marked by the same secular merits, nothing cheap or purchasable.

From this slow-grown church important reactions proceed; much for culture, much for giving a direction to the nation's affection and will to-day. The carved and pictured chapel,—its entire surface animated with image and emblem,—made the parish-church a sort of book and Bible to the people's eye.

Then, when the Saxon instinct had secured a service in the vernacular tongue, it was the tutor and university of the people. In York minster, on the day of the enthronization of the new archbishop, I heard the service of evening prayer read and chanted in the choir. It was strange to hear the pretty pastoral of the betrothal of Rebecca and Isaac, in the morning of the world, read with circumstantiality in York minster, on the 13th January, 1848, to the decorous English audience, just fresh from the Times newspaper and their wine; and listening with all the devotion of national pride. That was binding old and new to some purpose. The reverence for the Scriptures is an element of civilization, for thus has the history of the world been preserved, and is preserved. Here in England every day a chapter of Genesis, and a leader in the Times.

Another part of the same service on this occasion was not insignificant. Handel's coronation anthem, *God save the King*, was played by Dr. Camidge on the organ, with sublime effect. The minster and the music were made for each other. It was a hint of the part the church plays as a political engine. From his infancy, every Englishman is accustomed to hear daily prayers for the queen, for the royal family and the Parliament, by name; and this lifelong consecration of these personages cannot be without influence on his opinions.

The universities, also, are parcel of the ecclesiastical system, and their first design is to form the clergy. Thus the clergy for a thousand years have been the scholars of the nation.

The national temperament deeply enjoys the unbroken order and tradition of its church; the liturgy, ceremony, architecture; the sober grace, the good company, the connection with the throne, and with history, which adorn it. And whilst it endears itself thus to men of more taste than activity, the stability of the English nation is passionately enlisted to its support, from its inextricable connection with the cause of public order, with politics and with the funds.

Good churches are not built by bad men; at least, there must be probity and enthusiasm somewhere in the society. These minsters were neither built nor filled by atheists. No church has had more learned, industrious or devoted men; plenty of "clerks and bishops, who, out of their gowns, would turn their backs on no man."* Their architecture still glows with faith in immortality. Heats and genial periods arrive in history, or, shall we say, plentitudes of Divine Presence, by which high tides are caused in the human spirit, and great virtues and talents appear, as in the eleventh, twelfth, thir-teenth, and again in the sixteenth and seventeenth centuries, when the nation was full of genius and piety.

But the age of the Wicliffes, Cobhams, Arundels, Beckets; of the Latimers, Mores, Cranmers; of the Taylors, Leightons, Herberts; of the Sherlocks, and Butlers, is gone. Silent revolutions in opinion have made it impossible that men like these should return, or find a place in their once sacred stalls. The spirit that dwelt in this church has glided away to animate other activities; and they who come to the old shrines find apes and players rustling the old garments.

The religion of England is part of good-breeding. When you see on the continent the well-dressed Englishman come into his ambassador's chapel, and put his face for silent prayer into his smooth-brushed hat, one cannot help feeling how much national pride prays with him, and the religion of a gentleman. So far is he from attaching any meaning to the words, that he believes himself to have done almost the generous thing, and that it is very condescending in him to pray to God. A great duke said, on the occasion of a victory, in the House of Lords, that he thought the Almighty God had not been well used by them, and that it would become their magnanimity, after so great successes, to take order that a

*Fuller.

proper acknowledgment be made. It is the church of the gentry; but it is not the church of the poor. The operatives do not own it, and gentlemen lately testified in the House of Commons that in their lives they never saw a poor man in a ragged coat inside a church.

The torpidity on the side of religion of the vigorous English understanding, shows how much wit and folly can agree in one brain. Their religion is a quotation; their church is a doll; and any examination is interdicted with screams of terror. In good company, you expect them to laugh at the fanaticism of the vulgar; but they do not: they are the vulgar.

The English, in common perhaps with Christendom in the nineteenth century, do not respect power, but only performance; value ideas only for an economic result. Wellington esteems a saint only as far as he can be an army chaplain: — "Mr. Briscoll, by his admirable conduct and good sense, got the better of Methodism, which had appeared among the soldiers, and once among the officers." They value a philosopher as they value an apothecary who brings bark or a drench; and inspiration is only some blowpipe, or a finer mechanical aid.

I suspect that there is in an Englishman's brain a valve that can be closed at pleasure, as an engineer shuts off steam. The most sensible and well-informed men possess the power of thinking just so far as the bishop in religious matters, and as the chancellor of the exchequer in politics. They talk with courage and logic, and show you magnificent results, but the same men who have brought free trade or geology to their present standing, look grave and lofty, and shut down their valve, as soon as the conversation approaches the English church. After that, you talk with a box-turtle.

The action of the university, both in what is taught, and in the spirit of the place, is directed more on producing an English gentleman, than a saint or a psychologist. It ripens a bishop, and extrudes a philosopher. I do not know that there is more cabalism in the Anglican, than in other churches, but the Anglican clergy are identified with the aristocracy. They say, here, that, if you talk with a clergyman, you are sure to find him well-bred, informed, and candid. He entertains your thought or your project with sympathy and praise. But if a second clergyman come in, the sympathy is at an end: two together are inaccessible to your thought, and, whenever it comes to action, the clergyman invariably sides with his church.

The Anglican church is marked by the grace and good sense of its forms, by the manly grace of its clergy. The gospel it preaches, is, 'By taste are ye saved.' It keeps the old structures in repair, spends a world of money in music and building; and in buying Pugin, and architectural literature. It has a general good name for amenity and mildness. It is not in ordinary a persecuting church; it is not inquisitorial, not even inquisitive, is perfectly well-bred, and can shut its eyes on all proper occasions. If you let it alone, it will let you alone. But its instinct is hostile to all change in politics, literature, or social arts. The church has not been the founder of the London University, of the Mechanics' Institutes, of the Free School, or whatever aims at diffusion of knowledge. The Platonists of Oxford are as bitter against this heresy, as Thomas Taylor.

The doctrine of the Old Testament is the religion of England. The first leaf of the New Testament it does not open. It believes in a Providence which does not treat with levity a pound sterling. They are neither transcendentalists nor christians. They put up no Socratic prayer, much less any saintly prayer for the queen's mind; ask neither for light nor right, but say bluntly, "grant her in health and wealth long to live." And one traces this Jewish prayer in all English private history, from the prayers of King Richard, in Richard of Devizes' Chronicle, to those in the diaries of Sir Samuel Romilly, and of Haydon the painter. "Abroad with my wife," writes Pepys piously, "the first time that ever I rode in my own coach; which do make my heart rejoice and praise God, and pray him to bless it to me, and continue it." The bill for the naturalization of the Jews (in 1753) was resisted by petitions from all parts of the kingdom, and by petition from the city of London, reprobating this bill, as "tending extremely to the dishonor of the Christian religion, and extremely injurious to the interests and commerce of the kingdom in general, and of the city of London in particular."

But they have not been able to congeal humanity by act of Parliament. "The heavens journey still and sojourn not," and arts, wars, discoveries, and opinion, go onward at their own pace. The new age has new desires, new enemies, new trades, new charities, and reads the Scriptures with new eyes. The chatter of French politics, the steam-whistle, the hum of the mill, and the noise of embarking emigrants, had quite put most of the old legends out of mind; so that when you came to read the liturgy to a modern congregation, it was almost absurd in its unfitness, and suggested a masquerade of old costumes.

No chemist has prospered in the attempt to crystallize a religion. It is endogenous, like the skin, and other vital organs. A new statement every day. The prophet and apostle knew this, and the nonconformist confutes the conformists, by quoting the texts they must allow. It is the condition of a religion, to require religion for its expositor. Prophet and apostle can only be rightly understood by prophet and apostle. The statesman knows that the religious element will not fail, any more than the supply of fibrine and chyle; but it is in its nature constructive, and will organize such a church as it wants. The wise legislator will spend on temples, schools, libraries, colleges, but will shun the enriching of priests. If, in any manner, he can leave the election and paying of the priest to the people, he will do well. Like the Quakers, he may resist the separation of a class of priests, and create opportunity and expectation in the society, to run to meet natural endowment, in this kind. But, when wealth accrues to a chaplaincy, a bishopric, or rectorship, it requires moneyed men for its stewards, who will give it another direction than to the mystics of their day. Of course, money will do after its kind, and will steadily work to unspiritualize and unchurch the people to whom it was bequeathed. The class certain to be excluded from all preferment are the religious,—and driven to other churches;— which is nature's *vis medicatrix*.

The curates are ill paid, and the prelates are overpaid. This abuse draws into the church the children of the nobility, and other unfit persons, who have a taste for expense. Thus a bishop is only a surpliced merchant. Through his lawn, I can see the bright buttons of the shopman's coat glitter. A wealth like that of Durham makes almost a premium on felony. Brougham, in a speech in the House of Commons on the

Irish elective franchise, said, "How will the reverend bishops of the other house be able to express their due abhorrence of the crime of perjury, who solemnly declare in the presence of God, that when they are called upon to accept a living, perhaps of £4000 a year, at that very instant, they are moved by the Holy Ghost to accept the office and administration thereof, and for no other reason whatever?" The modes of initiation are more damaging than custom-house oaths. The Bishop is elected by the Dean and Prebends of the cathedral. The Queen sends these gentlemen a *congé d'élire*, or leave to elect; but also sends them the name of the person whom they are to elect. They go into the cathedral, chant and pray, and beseech the Holy Ghost to assist them in their choice; and, after these invocations, invariably find that the dictates of the Holy Ghost agree with the recommendations of the Queen.

But you must pay for conformity. All goes well as long as you run with conformists. But you, who are honest men in other particulars, know, that there is alive somewhere a man whose honesty reaches to this point also, that he shall not kneel to false gods, and, on the day when you meet him, you sink into the class of counterfeits. Besides, this succumbing has grave penalties. If you take in a lie, you must take in all that belongs to it. England accepts this ornamented national church, and it glazes the eyes, bloats the flesh, gives the voice a stertorous clang, and clouds the understanding of the receivers.

The English church, undermined by German criticism, had nothing left but tradition, and was led logically back to Romanism. But that was an element which only hot heads could breathe: in view of the educated class, generally, it was not a fact to front the sun; and the alienation of such men from the church became complete.

Nature, to be sure, had her remedy. Religious persons are driven out of the Established Church into sects, which instantly rise to credit, and hold the Establishment in check. Nature has sharper remedies, also. The English, abhorring change in all things, abhorring it most in matters of religion, cling to the last rag of form, and are dreadfully given to cant. The English, (and I wish it were confined to them, but 'tis a taint in the Anglo-Saxon blood in both hemispheres,) the English and the Americans cant beyond all other nations. The French relinquish all that industry to them. What is so odious as the polite bows to God, in our books and newspapers? The popular press is flagitious in the exact measure of its sanctimony, and the religion of the day is a theatrical Sinai, where the thunders are supplied by the property-man. The fanaticism and hypocrisy create satire. Punch finds an inexhaustible material. Dickens writes novels on Exeter-Hall humanity. Thackeray exposes the heartless high life. Nature revenges herself more summarily by the heathenism of the lower classes. Lord Shaftesbury calls the poor thieves together, and reads sermons to them, and they call it 'gas.' George Borrow summons the Gypsies to hear his discourse on the Hebrews in Egypt, and reads to them the Apostles' Creed in Rommany. "When I had concluded," he says, "I looked around me. The features of the assembly were twisted, and the eyes of all turned upon me with a frightful squint: not an individual present but squinted; the genteel Pepa, the good-humored Chicharona, the Cosdami, all squinted: the Gypsy jockey squinted worst of all."

The church at this moment is much to be pitied. She has nothing left but possession. If a bishop meets an intelligent gentleman, and reads fatal interrogations in his eyes, he has no resource but to take wine with him. False position introduces cant, perjury, simony, and ever a lower class of mind and character into the clergy: and, when the hierarchy is afraid of science and education, afraid of piety, afraid of tradition, and afraid of theology, there is nothing left but to quit a church which is no longer one.

But the religion of England, — is it the Established Church? no; is it the sects? no; they are only perpetuations of some private man's dissent, and are to the Established Church as cabs are to a coach, cheaper and more convenient, but really the same thing. Where dwells the religion? Tell me first where dwells electricity, or motion, or thought or gesture. They do not dwell or stay at all. Electricity cannot be made fast, mortared up and ended, like London Monument, or the Tower, so that you shall know where to find it, and keep it fixed, as the English do with their things, forevermore; it is passing, glancing, gesticular; it is a traveller, a newness, a surprise, a secret, which perplexes them, and puts them out. Yet, if religion be the doing of all good, and for its sake the suffering of all evil, *souffrir de tout le monde et ne faire souffrir personne*, that divine secret has existed in England from the days of Alfred to those of Romilly, of Clarkson, and of Florence Nightingale, and in thousands who have no fame.

CHAPTER XIV

Literature

A STRONG common sense, which it is not easy to unseat or disturb, marks the English mind for a thousand years: a rude strength newly applied to thought, as of sailors and soldiers who had lately learned to read. They have no fancy, and never are surprised into a covert or witty word, such as pleased the Athenians and Italians, and was convertible into a fable not long after; but they delight in strong earthy expression, not mistakable, coarsely true to the human body, and, though spoken among princes, equally fit and welcome to the mob. This homeliness, veracity, and plain style, appear in the earliest extant works, and in the latest. It imports into songs and ballads the smell of the earth, the breath of cattle, and, like a Dutch painter, seeks a household charm, though by pails and pans. They ask their constitutional utility in verse. The kail and herrings are never out of sight. The poet nimbly recovers himself from every sally of the imagination. The English muse loves the farmyard, the lane, and market. She says, with De Stael, "I tramp in the mire with wooden shoes, whenever they would force me into the clouds." For, the Englishman has accurate perceptions; takes hold of things by the right end, and there is no slipperiness in his grasp. He loves the axe, the spade, the oar, the gun, the steampipe: he has built the engine he uses. He is materialist, economical, mercantile. He must be treated with sincerity and reality, with muffins, and not the promise of muffins; and prefers his hot chop, with perfect security and convenience in the eating of it, to the chances of the amplest and Frenchiest bill of fare, engraved on embossed paper. When he is intellectual, and a poet or a philosopher, he carries the same hard truth and the same keen machinery into the mental sphere. His mind must stand on a fact. He will not be baffled, or catch at clouds, but the mind must have a symbol palpable and resisting. What he relishes in Dante, is the vice-like tenacity with which he holds a mental image before the eyes, as if it were a scutcheon painted on a shield. Byron "liked something craggy to break his mind upon." A taste for plain strong speech, what is called a biblical style, marks the English. It is in Alfred, and the Saxon Chronicle, and in the Sagas of the Northmen. Latimer was homely. Hobbes was perfect in the "noble vulgar speech." Donne, Bunyan, Milton, Taylor, Evelyn, Pepys, Hooker, Cotton, and the translators, wrote it. How realistic or materialistic in treatment of his subject, is Swift. He describes his fictitious persons, as if for the police. Defoe has no insecurity or choice. Hudibras has the same hard mentality,—keeping the truth at once to the senses, and to the intellect.

It is not less seen in poetry. Chaucer's hard painting of his Canterbury pilgrims satisfies the senses. Shakspeare, Spenser, and Milton, in their loftiest ascents, have this national grip and exactitude of mind. This mental materialism makes the value of English transcendental genius; in these writers, and in Herbert, Henry More, Donne, and Sir Thomas Browne. The Saxon materialism and narrowness, exalted into the sphere of intellect, makes the very genius of Shakspeare and Milton. When it reaches the pure element, it treads the clouds as securely as the adamant. Even in its elevations, materialistic, its poetry is common sense inspired; or iron raised to white heat.

The marriage of the two qualities is in their speech. It is a tacit rule of the language to make the frame or skeleton, of Saxon words, and, when elevation or ornament is sought, to interweave Roman; but sparingly; nor is a sentence made of Roman words alone, without loss of strength. The children and laborers use the Saxon unmixed. The Latin unmixed is abandoned to the colleges and Parliament. Mixture is a secret of the English island; and, in their dialect, the male principle is the Saxon; the female, the Latin; and they are combined in every discourse. A good writer, if he has indulged in a Roman roundness, makes haste to chasten and nerve his period by English monosyllables.

When the Gothic nations came into Europe, they found it lighted with the sun and moon of Hebrew and of Greek genius. The tablets of their brain, long kept in the dark, were finely sensible to the double glory. To the images from this twin source (of Christianity and art), the mind became fruitful as by the incubation of the Holy Ghost. The English mind flowered in every faculty. The common-sense was surprised and inspired. For two centuries, England was philosophic, religious, poetic. The mental furniture seemed of larger scale; the memory capacious like the storehouse of the rains; the ardor and endurance of study; the boldness and facility of their mental construction; their fancy, and imagination, and easy spanning of vast distances of thought; the enterprise or accosting of new subjects; and, generally, the easy exertion of power, astonish, like the legendary feats of Guy of Warwick. The union of Saxon precision and oriental soaring, of which Shakspeare is the perfect example, is shared in less degree by the writers of two centuries. I find not only the great masters out of all rivalry and reach, but the whole writing of the time charged with a masculine force and freedom.

There is a hygienic simpleness, rough vigor, and closeness to the matter in hand, even in the second and third class of writers; and, I think, in the common style of the people, as one finds it in the citation of wills, letters, and public documents, in proverbs, and forms of speech. The more hearty and sturdy expression may indicate that the savageness of the Norseman was not all gone. Their dynamic brains hurled off their words, as the revolving stone hurls off scraps of grit. I could cite from the seventeenth century sentences and phrases of edge not to be matched in the nineteenth. Their poets by simple force of mind equalized themselves with the accumulated science of ours. The country gentlemen had a posset or drink they called October; and the poets, as if by this hint, knew how to distil the whole season into their autumnal verses: and, as nature, to pique the more, sometimes works up deformities into beauty, in some rare Aspasia, or Cleopatra; and, as the Greek art wrought many a vase or column, in which too long, or too lithe, or nodes, or pits and flaws, are made a beauty of; so these were so quick and vital, that they could charm and enrich by mean and vulgar objects.

A man must think that age well taught and thoughtful, by which masques and poems, like those of Ben Jonson, full of heroic sentiment in a manly style, were received with favor. The unique fact in literary history, the unsurprised reception of Shakspeare;—the reception proved by his making his fortune; and the apathy proved by the absence of all contemporary panegyric,—seems to demonstrate an elevation in the mind of the people. Judge of the splendor of a nation, by the insignificance of great individuals in it. The manner in which they learned Greek and Latin, before our modern facilities were yet ready, without dictionaries, grammars, or indexes, by lectures of a professor, followed by their own searchings,—required a more robust memory, and coöperation of all the faculties; and their scholars, Camden, Usher, Selden, Mede, Gataker, Hooker, Taylor, Burton, Bentley, Brian Walton, acquired the solidity and method of engineers.

The influence of Plato tinges the British genius. Their minds loved analogy; were cognisant of resemblances, and climbers on the staircase of unity. 'Tis a very old strife between those who elect to see identity, and those who elect to see discrepances; and it renews itself in Britain. The poets, of course, are of one part; the men of the world, of the other. But Britain had many disciples of Plato;—More, Hooker, Bacon, Sidney, Lord Brooke, Herbert, Browne, Donne, Spenser, Chapman, Milton, Crashaw, Norris, Cudworth, Berkeley, Jeremy Taylor.

Lord Bacon has the English duality. His centuries of observations, on useful science, and his experiments, I suppose, were worth nothing. One hint of Franklin, or Watt, or Dalton, or Davy, or any one who had a talent for experiment, was worth all his lifetime of exquisite trifles. But he drinks of a diviner stream, and marks the influx of idealism into England. Where that goes, is poetry, health, and progress. The rules of its genesis or its diffusion are not known. That knowledge, if we had it, would supersede all that we call science of the mind. It seems an affair of race, or of meta-chemistry;—the vital point being,—how far the sense of unity, or instinct of seeking resemblances, predominated. For, wherever the mind takes a step, it is, to put itself at one with a larger class, discerned beyond the lesser class with which it has been conversant. Hence, all poetry, and all affirmative action comes.

Bacon, in the structure of his mind, held of the analogists, of the idealists, or (as we popularly say, naming from the best example) Platonists. Whoever discredits analogy, and requires heaps of facts, before any theories can be attempted, has no poetic power, and nothing original or beautiful will be produced by him. Locke is as surely the influx of decomposition and of prose, as Bacon and the Platonists, of growth. The Platonic is the poetic tendency; the so-called scientific is the negative and poisonous. 'Tis quite certain, that Spenser, Burns, Byron, and Wordsworth will be Platonists; and that the dull men will be Lockists. Then politics and commerce will absorb from the educated class men of talents without genius, precisely because such have no resistance.

Bacon, capable of ideas, yet devoted to ends, required in his map of the mind, first of all, universality, or *prima philosophia*, the receptacle for all such profitable observations and axioms as fall not within the compass of any of the special parts of philosophy, but are more common, and of a higher stage. He held this element essential: it is never out of mind: he never spares rebukes for such as neglect it; believing that no perfect discovery can be made in a flat or level, but you must ascend to a higher science. "If any man thinketh philosophy and universality to be idle studies, he doth not consider that all professions are from thence served and supplied, and this I take to be a great cause that has hindered the progression of learning, because these fundamental knowledges have been studied but in passage." He explained himself by giving various quaint examples of the summary or common laws, of which each science has its own illustration. He complains, that "he finds this part of learning very deficient, the profounder sort of wits drawing a bucket now and then for their own use, but the spring-head unvisited. This was the *dry light* which did scorch and offend most men's watery natures." Plato had signified the same sense, when he said, "All the great arts require a subtle and speculative research into the law of nature, since loftiness of thought and perfect mastery over every subject seem to be derived from some such source as this. This Pericles had, in addition to a great natural genius. For, meeting with Anaxagoras, who was a person of this kind, he attached himself to him, and nourished himself with sublime speculations on the absolute intelligence; and imported thence into the oratorical art, whatever could be useful to it."

A few generalizations always circulate in the world, whose authors we do not rightly know, which astonish, and appear to be avenues to vast kingdoms of thought, and these are in the world *constants*, like the Copernican and Newtonian theories in physics. In England, these may be traced usually to Shakspeare, Bacon, Milton, or Hooker, even to Van Helmont and Behmen, and do all have a kind of filial retrospect to Plato and the Greeks. Of this kind is Lord Bacon's sentence, that "nature is commanded by obeying her;" his doctrine of poetry, which "accommodates the shows of things to the desires of the mind," or the Zoroastrian definition of poetry, mystical, yet exact, "apparent pictures of unapparent natures;" Spenser's creed, that "soul is form, and doth the body make;" the theory of Berkeley, that we have no certain assurance of the existence of matter; Doctor Samuel Clarke's argument for theism from the nature of space and time; Harrington's political rule, that power must rest on land,—a rule which requires to be liberally interpreted; the theory of Swedenborg, so cosmically applied by him, that the man makes his heaven and hell; Hegel's study of civil history, as the conflict of ideas and the victory of the deeper thought; the identity-philosophy of Schelling, couched in the statement that "all difference is quantitative." So the very announcement of the theory of gravitation, of Kepler's three harmonic laws, and even of Dalton's doctrine of definite proportions, finds a sudden response in the mind, which remains a superior evidence to empirical demonstrations. I cite these generalizations, some of which are more recent, merely to indicate a class. Not these particulars, but the mental plane or the atmosphere from which they emanate, was the home and elements of the writers and readers in what we loosely call the Elizabethan age, (say, in literary history, the period from 1575 to 1625,) yet a period almost short enough to justify Ben Jonson's remark on Lord Bacon; "about his time, and within his view, were born all the wits that could honor a nation, or help study."

Such richness of genius had not existed more than once before. These heights could not be maintained. As we find stumps of vast trees in our exhausted soils, and have received traditions of their ancient fertility to tillage, so history reckons epochs in which the intellect of famed races became effete. So it fared with English genius. These heights were followed by a meanness, and a descent of the mind into lower levels; the loss of wings; no high speculation. Locke, to whom the meaning of ideas was unknown, became the type of philosophy, and his "understanding" the measure, in all nations, of the English intellect. His countrymen forsook the lofty sides of Parnassus, on which they had once walked with echoing steps, and disused the studies once so beloved; the powers of thought fell into neglect. The later English want the faculty of Plato and Aristotle, of grouping men in natural classes by an insight of general laws, so deep, that the rule is deduced with equal precision from few subjects or from one, as from multitudes of lives. Shakspeare is supreme in that, as in all the great mental energies. The Germans generalize: the English cannot interpret the German mind. German science comprehends the English. The absence of the faculty in England is shown by the timidity which accumulates mountains of facts, as a bad general wants myriads of men and miles of redoubts, to compensate the inspirations of courage and conduct.

The English shrink from a generalization. "They do not look abroad into universality, or they draw only a bucket-full at the fountain of the First Philosophy for their occasion, and do not go to the spring-head." Bacon, who said this, is almost unique among his countrymen in that faculty, at least among the prose-writers. Milton, who was the stair or high table-land to let down the English genius from the summits of Shakspeare, used this privilege sometimes in poetry, more rarely in prose. For a long interval afterwards, it is not found. Burke was addicted to generalizing, but his was a shorter line; as his thoughts have less depth, they have less compass. Hume's abstractions are not deep or wise. He owes his fame to one keen observation, that no copula had been detected between any cause and effect, either in physics or in thought; that the term cause and effect was loosely or gratuitously applied to what we know only as consecutive, not at all as causal. Doctor Johnson's written abstractions have little value: the tone of feeling in them makes their chief worth.

Mr. Hallam, a learned and elegant scholar, has written the history of European literature for three centuries,—a performance of great ambition, inasmuch as a judgment was to be attempted on every book. But his eye does not reach to the ideal standards: the verdicts are all dated from London: all new thought must be cast into the old moulds. The expansive element which creates literature is steadily denied. Plato is resisted, and his school. Hallam is uniformly polite, but with deficient sympathy; writes with resolute generosity, but is unconscious of the deep worth which lies in the mystics, and which often outvalues as a seed of power and a source of revolution all the correct writers and shining reputations of their day. He passes in silence, or dismisses with a kind of contempt, the profounder masters: a lover of ideas is not only uncongenial, but unintelligible. Hallam inspires respect by his knowledge and fidelity, by his manifest love of good books, and he lifts himself to own better than almost any the greatness of Shakspeare, and better than Johnson he appreciates Milton. But in Hallam, or in the firmer intellectual nerve of Mackintosh, one still finds the same type of English genius. It is wise and rich, but it lives on its capital. It is retrospective. How can it discern and hail the new forms that are looming up on the horizon,—new and gigantic thoughts which cannot dress themselves out of any old wardrobe of the past?

The essays, the fiction, and the poetry of the day have the like municipal limits. Dickens, with preternatural apprehension of the language of manners, and the varieties of street life, with pathos and laughter, with patriotic and still enlarging generosity, writes London tracts. He is a painter of English details, like Hogarth; local and temporary in his tints and style, and local in his aims. Bulwer, an industrious writer, with occasional ability, is distinguished for his reverence of intellect as a temporality, and appeals to the worldly ambition of the student. His romances tend to fan these low flames. Their novelists despair of the heart. Thackeray finds that God has made no allowance for the poor thing in his universe;— more's the pity, he thinks;—but 'tis not for us to be wiser: we must renounce ideals, and accept London.

The brilliant Macaulay, who expresses the tone of the English governing classes of the day, explicitly teaches, that *good* means good to eat, good to wear, material commodity; that the glory of modern philosophy is its direction on "fruit;" to yield economical inventions; and that its merit is to avoid

ideas, and avoid morals. He thinks it the distinctive merit of
the Baconian philosophy, in its triumph over the old Platonic,
its disentangling the intellect from theories of the all-Fair and
all-Good, and pinning it down to the making a better sick
chair and a better wine-whey for an invalid;—this not ironi-
cally, but in good faith;—that, "solid advantage," as he calls
it, meaning always sensual benefit, is the only good. The eminent benefit of astronomy is the better navigation it creates
to enable the fruit-ships to bring home their lemons and wine
to the London grocer. It was a curious result, in which the
civility and religion of England for a thousand years, ends, in
denying morals, and reducing the intellect to a sauce-pan. The
critic hides his skepticism under the English cant of practical.
To convince the reason, to touch the conscience, is romantic
pretension. The fine arts fall to the ground. Beauty, except as
luxurious commodity, does not exist. It is very certain, I may
say in passing, that if Lord Bacon had been only the sensualist
his critic pretends, he would never have acquired the fame
which now entitles him to this patronage. It is because he had
imagination, the leisures of the spirit, and basked in an element of contemplation out of all modern English atmospheric
gauges, that he is impressive to the imaginations of men, and
has become a potentate not to be ignored. Sir David Brewster
sees the high place of Bacon, without finding Newton indebted to him, and thinks it a mistake. Bacon occupies it by
specific gravity or levity, not by any feat he did, or by any
tutoring more or less of Newton &c., but an effect of the
same cause which showed itself more pronounced afterwards
in Hooke, Boyle, and Halley.

Coleridge, a catholic mind, with a hunger for ideas, with
eyes looking before and after to the highest bards and sages,
and who wrote and spoke the only high criticism in his
time,—is one of those who save England from the reproach
of no longer possessing the capacity to appreciate what rarest
wit the island has yielded. Yet the misfortune of his life, his
vast attempts but most inadequate performings, failing to accomplish any one masterpiece, seems to mark the closing of
an era. Even in him, the traditional Englishman was too
strong for the philosopher, and he fell into *accommodations*:
and, as Burke had striven to idealize the English State, so

Coleridge 'narrowed his mind' in the attempt to reconcile the gothic rule and dogma of the Anglican Church, with eternal ideas. But for Coleridge, and a lurking taciturn minority, uttering itself in occasional criticism, oftener in private discourse, one would say, that in Germany and in America, is the best mind in England rightly respected. It is the surest sign of national decay, when the Bramins can no longer read or understand the Braminical philosophy.

In the decomposition and asphyxia that followed all this materialism, Carlyle was driven by his disgust at the pettiness and the cant, into the preaching of Fate. In comparison with all this rottenness, any check, any cleansing, though by fire, seemed desirable and beautiful. He saw little difference in the gladiators, or the "causes" for which they combated; the one comfort was, that they were all going speedily into the abyss together: And his imagination, finding no nutriment in any creation, avenged itself by celebrating the majestic beauty of the laws of decay. The necessities of mental structure force all minds into a few categories, and where impatience of the tricks of men makes Nemesis amiable, and builds altars to the negative Deity, the inevitable recoil is to heroism or the gallantry of the private heart, which decks its immolation with glory, in the unequal combat of will against fate.

Wilkinson, the editor of Swedenborg, the annotator of Fourier, and the champion of Hahnemann, has brought to metaphysics and to physiology a native vigor, with a catholic perception of relations, equal to the highest attempts, and a rhetoric like the armory of the invincible knights of old. There is in the action of his mind a long Atlantic roll not known except in deepest waters, and only lacking what ought to accompany such powers, a manifest centrality. If his mind does not rest in immovable biases, perhaps the orbit is larger, and the return is not yet: but a master should inspire a confidence that he will adhere to his convictions, and give his present studies always the same high place.

It would be easy to add exceptions to the limitary tone of English thought, and much more easy to adduce examples of excellence in particular veins: and if, going out of the region of dogma, we pass into that of general culture, there is no end to the graces and amenities, wit, sensibility and erudition, of the learned class. But the artificial succor which marks all English performance, appears in letters also: much of their æsthetic production is antiquarian and manufactured, and literary reputations have been achieved by forcible men, whose relation to literature was purely accidental, but who were driven by tastes and modes they found in vogue into their several careers. So, at this moment, every ambitious young man studies geology: so members of Parliament are made, and churchmen.

The bias of Englishmen to practical skill has reacted on the national mind. They are incapable of an inutility, and respect the five mechanic powers even in their song. The voice of their modern muse has a slight hint of the steam-whistle, and the poem is created as an ornament and finish of their monarchy, and by no means as the bird of a new morning which forgets the past world in the full enjoyment of that which is forming. They are with difficulty ideal; they are the most conditioned men, as if, having the best conditions, they could not bring themselves to forfeit them. Every one of them is a thousand years old, and lives by his memory: and when you say this, they accept it as praise.

Nothing comes to the book-shops but politics, travels, statistics, tabulation, and engineering, and even what is called philosophy and letters is mechanical in its structure, as if inspiration had ceased, as if no vast hope, no religion, no song of joy, no wisdom, no analogy, existed any more. The tone of colleges, and of scholars and of literary society has this mortal air. I seem to walk on a marble floor, where nothing will grow. They exert every variety of talent on a lower ground, and may be said to live and act in a sub-mind. They have lost all commanding views in literature, philosophy, and science. A good Englishman shuts himself out of three fourths of his mind, and confines himself to one fourth. He has learning, good sense, power of labor, and logic: but a faith in the laws of the mind like that of Archimedes; a belief like that of Euler and Kepler, that experience must follow and not lead the laws of the mind; a devotion to the theory of politics, like that of Hooker, and Milton, and Harrington, the modern English mind repudiates.

I fear the same fault lies in their science, since they have known how to make it repulsive, and bereave nature of its charm;—though perhaps the complaint flies wider, and the vice attaches to many more than to British physicists. The eye of the naturalist must have a scope like nature itself, a susceptibility to all impressions, alive to the heart as well as to the logic of creation. But English science puts humanity to the door. It wants the connection which is the test of genius. The science is false by not being poetic. It isolates the reptile or mollusk it assumes to explain; whilst reptile or mollusk only exists in system, in relation. The poet only sees it as an inevitable step in the path of the Creator. But, in England, one hermit finds this fact, and another finds that, and lives and dies ignorant of its value. There are great exceptions, of John Hunter, a man of ideas; perhaps of Robert Brown, the botanist; and of Richard Owen, who has imported into Britain the German homologies, and enriched science with contributions of his own, adding sometimes the divination of the old masters to the unbroken power of labor in the English mind. But for the most part, the natural science in England is out of its loyal alliance with morals, and is as void of imagination and free play of thought, as conveyancing. It stands in strong contrast with the genius of the Germans, those semi-Greeks, who love analogy, and, by means of their height of view, preserve their enthusiasm, and think for Europe.

No hope, no sublime augury cheers the student, no secure striding from experiment onward to a foreseen law, but only a casual dipping here and there, like diggers in California "prospecting for a placer" that will pay. A horizon of brass of the diameter of his umbrella shuts down around his senses. Squalid contentment with conventions, satire at the names of philosophy and religion, parochial and shop-till politics, and idolatry of usage, betray the ebb of life and spirit. As they trample on nationalities to reproduce London and Londoners in Europe and Asia, so they fear the hostility of ideas, of poetry, of religion,—ghosts which they cannot lay;—and, having attempted to domesticate and dress the Blessed Soul itself in English broadcloth and gaiters, they are tormented with fear that herein lurks a force that will sweep their system away. The artists say, "Nature puts them out;" the scholars have become un-ideal. They parry earnest speech with banter and levity; they laugh you down, or they change the subject. "The fact is," say they over their wine, "all that about liberty, and so forth, is gone by; it won't do any longer." The practical and comfortable oppress them with inexorable claims, and the smallest fraction of power remains for heroism and poetry. No poet dares murmur of beauty out of the precinct of his rhymes. No priest dares hint at a Providence which does not respect English utility. The island is a roaring volcano of fate, of material values, of tariffs, and laws of repression, glutted markets and low prices.

In the absence of the highest aims, of the pure love of knowledge, and the surrender to nature, there is the suppression of the imagination, the priapism of the senses and the understanding; we have the factitious instead of the natural; tasteless expense, arts of comfort, and the rewarding as an illustrious inventor whosoever will contrive one impediment more to interpose between the man and his objects.

Thus poetry is degraded, and made ornamental. Pope and his school wrote poetry fit to put round frosted cake. What did Walter Scott write without stint? a rhymed traveller's guide to Scotland. And the libraries of verses they print have this Birmingham character. How many volumes of well-bred metre we must gingle through, before we can be filled, taught, renewed! We want the miraculous; the beauty which we can manufacture at no mill,—can give no account of; the beauty of which Chaucer and Chapman had the secret. The poetry of course is low and prosaic; only now and then, as in Wordsworth, conscientious; or in Byron, passional; or in Tennyson, factitious. But if I should count the poets who have contributed to the bible of existing England sentences of guidance and consolation which are still glowing and effective,—how few! Shall I find my heavenly bread in the reigning poets? Where is great design in modern English poetry? The English have lost sight of the fact that poetry exists to speak the spiritual law, and that no wealth of description or of fancy is yet essentially new, and out of the limits of prose, until this condition is reached. Therefore the grave old poets, like the Greek artists, heeded their designs, and less considered the finish. It was their office to lead to the divine sources, out of which all this, and much more, readily springs; and, if this religion is in the poetry, it raises us to some purpose, and we can well afford some staidness, or hardness, or want of popular tune in the verses.

The exceptional fact of the period is the genius of Wordsworth. He had no master but nature and solitude. "He wrote a poem," says Landor, " without the aid of war." His verse is the voice of sanity in a worldly and ambitious age. One regrets that his temperament was not more liquid and musical. He has written longer than he was inspired. But for the rest, he has no competitor.

Tennyson is endowed precisely in points where Wordsworth wanted. There is no finer ear, nor more command of the keys of language. Color, like the dawn, flows over the horizon from his pencil, in waves so rich that we do not miss the central form. Through all his refinements, too, he has reached the public,—a certificate of good sense and general power, since he who aspires to be the English poet must be as large as London, not in the same kind as London, but in his own kind. But he wants a subject, and climbs no mount of vision to bring its secrets to the people. He contents himself with describing the Englishman as he is, and proposes no better. There are all degrees in poetry, and we must be thankful for every beautiful talent. But it is only a first success, when the ear is gained. The best office of the best poets has been to show how low and uninspired was their general style, and that only once or twice they have struck the high chord.

That expansiveness which is the essence of the poetic element, they have not. It was no Oxonian, but Hafiz, who said, "Let us be crowned with roses, let us drink wine, and break up the tiresome old roof of heaven into new forms." A stanza of the song of nature the Oxonian has no ear for, and he does not value the salient and curative influence of intellectual action, studious of truth, without a by-end.

By the law of contraries, I look for an irresistible taste for Orientalism in Britain. For a self-conceited modish life, made up of trifles, clinging to a corporeal civilization, hating ideas, there is no remedy like the Oriental largeness. That astonishes and disconcerts English decorum. For once there is thunder it never heard, light it never saw, and power which trifles with time and space. I am not surprised, then, to find an Englishman like Warren Hastings, who had been struck with the grand style of thinking in the Indian writings, deprecating the prejudices of his countrymen, while offering them a translation of the Bhagvat. "Might I, an unlettered man, venture to prescribe bounds to the latitude of criticism, I should exclude, in estimating the merit of such a production, all rules drawn from the ancient or modern literature of Europe, all references to such sentiments or manners as are become the standards of propriety for opinion and action in our own modes, and, equally, all appeals to our revealed tenets of religion and moral duty."* He goes on to bespeak indulgence to "ornaments of fancy unsuited to our taste, and passages elevated to a tract of sublimity into which our habits of judgment will find it difficult to pursue them."

Meantime, I know that a retrieving power lies in the English race, which seems to make any recoil possible; in other words, there is at all times a minority of profound minds existing in the nation, capable of appreciating every soaring of intellect and every hint of tendency. While the constructive talent seems dwarfed and superficial, the criticism is often in the noblest tone, and suggests the presence of the invisible gods. I can well believe what I have often heard, that there are two nations in England; but it is not the Poor and the Rich; nor is it the Normans and Saxons; nor the Celt and the Goth. These are each always becoming the other; for Robert Owen does not exaggerate the power of circumstance. But the two complexions, or two styles of mind,—the perceptive class, and the practical finality class,—are ever in counterpoise, interacting mutually; one, in hopeless minorities; the other, in huge masses; one studious, contemplative, experimenting; the other, the ungrateful pupil, scornful of the source, whilst availing itself of the knowledge for gain; these two nations, of genius and of animal force, though the first consist of only a dozen souls, and the second of twenty millions, forever by their discord and their accord yield the power of the English State.

*Preface to Wilkins's Translation of the Bhagvat Geeta.

CHAPTER XV

The "Times"

THE POWER of the newspaper is familiar in America, and in accordance with our political system. In England, it stands in antagonism with the feudal institutions, and it is all the more beneficent succor against the secretive tendencies of a monarchy. The celebrated Lord Somers "knew of no good law proposed and passed in his time, to which the public papers had not directed his attention." There is no corner and no night. A relentless inquisition drags every secret to the day, turns the glare of this solar microscope on every malfaisance, so as to make the public a more terrible spy than any foreigner; and no weakness can be taken advantage of by an enemy, since the whole people are already forewarned. Thus England rids herself of those incrustations which have been the ruin of old states. Of course, this inspection is feared. No antique privilege, no comfortable monopoly, but sees surely that its days are counted; the people are familiarized with the reason of reform, and, one by one, take away every argument of the obstructives. "So your grace likes the comfort of reading the newspapers," said Lord Mansfield to the Duke of Northumberland; "mark my words; you and I shall not live to see it, but this young gentleman (Lord Eldon) may, or it may be a little later; but a little sooner or later, these newspapers will most assuredly write the dukes of Northumberland out of their titles and possessions, and the country out of its king." The tendency in England towards social and political institutions like those of America, is inevitable, and the ability of its journals is the driving force.

England is full of manly, clever, well-bred men who possess the talent of writing off-hand pungent paragraphs, expressing with clearness and courage their opinion on any person or performance. Valuable or not, it is a skill that is rarely found, out of the English journals. The English do this, as they write poetry, as they ride and box, by being educated to it. Hundreds of clever Praeds, and Freres, and Froudes, and Hoods, and Hooks, and Maginns, and Mills, and Macaulays, make poems, or short essays for a journal, as they make speeches in Parliament and on the hustings, or, as they shoot and ride. It is a quite accidental and arbitrary direction of their general ability. Rude health and spirits, an Oxford education, and the habits of society are implied, but not a ray of genius. It comes of the crowded state of the professions, the violent interest which all men take in politics, the facility of experimenting in the journals, and high pay.

The most conspicuous result of this talent is the "Times" newspaper. No power in England is more felt, more feared, or more obeyed. What you read in the morning in that journal, you shall hear in the evening in all society. It has ears every where, and its information is earliest, completest, and surest. It has risen, year by year, and victory by victory, to its present authority. I asked one of its old contributors, whether it had once been abler than it is now? "Never," he said; "these are its palmiest days." It has shown those qualities which are dear to Englishmen, unflinching adherence to its objects, prodigal intellectual ability, and a towering assurance, backed by the perfect organization in its printing-house, and its world-wide net-work of correspondence and reports. It has its own history and famous trophies. In 1820, it adopted the cause of Queen Caroline, and carried it against the king. It adopted a poor-law system, and almost alone lifted it through. When Lord Brougham was in power, it decided against him, and pulled him down. It declared war against Ireland, and conquered it. It adopted the League against the Corn Laws, and, when Cobden had begun to despair, it announced his triumph. It denounced and discredited the French Republic of 1848, and checked every sympathy with it in England, until it had enrolled 200,000 special constables to watch the Chartists, and make them ridiculous on the 10th April. It first denounced and then adopted the new French Empire, and urged the French Alliance and its results. It has entered into each municipal, literary, and social question, almost with a controlling voice. It has done bold and seasonable service in exposing frauds which threatened the commercial community. Meantime, it attacks its rivals by perfecting its printing machinery, and will drive them out of circulation: for the only limit to the circulation of the "Times" is the impossibility of printing copies fast enough; since a daily paper can only be new and seasonable for a few hours. It will kill all but that paper which is diametrically in opposition; since many papers, first and last, have lived by their attacks on the leading journal.

The late Mr. Walter was printer of the "Times," and had gradually arranged the whole *materiel* of it in perfect system. It is told, that when he demanded a small share in the proprietary, and was refused, he said, "As you please, gentlemen; and you may take away the 'Times' from this office, when you will; I shall publish the 'New Times,' next Monday morning." The proprietors, who had already complained that his charges for printing were excessive, found that they were in his power, and gave him whatever he wished.

I went one day with a good friend to the "Times" office, which was entered through a pretty garden-yard, in Printing-House Square. We walked with some circumspection, as if we were entering a powder-mill; but the door was opened by a mild old woman, and, by dint of some transmission of cards, we were at last conducted into the parlor of Mr. Morris, a very gentle person, with no hostile appearances. The statistics are now quite out of date, but I remember he told us that the daily printing was then 35,000 copies; that on the 1st March, 1848, the greatest number ever printed,—54,000 were issued; that, since February, the daily circulation had increased by 8000 copies. The old press they were then using printed five or six thousand sheets per hour; the new machine, for which they were then building an engine, would print twelve thousand per hour. Our entertainer confided us to a courteous assistant to show us the establishment, in which, I think, they employed a hundred and twenty men. I remember, I saw the reporters' room, in which they redact their hasty stenographs, but the editor's room, and who is in it, I did not see, though I shared the curiosity of mankind respecting it.

The staff of the "Times" has always been made up of able men. Old Walter, Sterling, Bacon, Barnes, Alsiger, Horace Twiss, Jones Loyd, John Oxenford, Mr. Mosely, Mr. Bailey, have contributed to its renown in their special departments. But it has never wanted the first pens for occasional assistance. Its private information is inexplicable, and recalls the stories of Fouché's police, whose omniscience made it believed that the Empress Josephine must be in his pay. It has mercantile and political correspondents in every foreign city; and its expresses outrun the despatches of the government. One hears anecdotes of the rise of its servants, as of the functionaries of the India House. I was told of the dexterity of one of its reporters, who, finding himself, on one occasion, where the magistrates had strictly forbidden reporters, put his hands into his coat-pocket, and with pencil in one hand, and tablet in the other, did his work.

The influence of this journal is a recognized power in Europe, and, of course, none is more conscious of it than its conductors. The tone of its articles has often been the occasion of comment from the official organs of the continental courts, and sometimes the ground of diplomatic complaint. What would the "Times" say? is a terror in Paris, in Berlin, in Vienna, in Copenhagen, and in Nepaul. Its consummate discretion and success exhibit the English skill of combination. The daily paper is the work of many hands, chiefly, it is said, of young men recently from the University, and perhaps reading law in chambers in London. Hence the academic elegance, and classic allusion, which adorn its columns. Hence, too, the heat and gallantry of its onset. But the steadiness of the aim suggests the belief that this fire is directed and fed by older engineers; as if persons of exact information, and with settled views of policy, supplied the writers with the basis of fact, and the object to be attained, and availed themselves of their younger energy and eloquence to plead the cause. Both the council and the executive departments gain by this division. Of two men of equal ability, the one who does not write, but keeps his eye on the course of public affairs, will have the higher judicial wisdom. But the parts are kept in concert; all the articles appear to proceed from a single will. The "Times" never disapproves of what itself has said, or cripples itself by apology for the absence of the editor, or the indiscretion of him who held the pen. It speaks out bluff and bold, and sticks to what it says. It draws from any number of learned and skilful contributors; but a more learned and skilful person supervises, corrects, and coördinates. Of this closet, the secret does not transpire. No writer is suffered to claim the authorship of any paper; every thing good, from whatever quarter, comes out editorially; and thus, by making the paper every thing, and those who write it nothing, the character and the awe of the journal gain.

The English like it for its complete information. A statement of fact in the "Times" is as reliable as a citation from Hansard. Then, they like its independence; they do not know, when they take it up, what their paper is going to say: but, above all, for the nationality and confidence of its tone. It thinks for them all; it is their understanding and day's ideal daguerreotyped. When I see them reading its columns, they seem to me becoming every moment more British. It has the national courage, not rash and petulant, but considerate and determined. No dignity or wealth is a shield from its assault. It attacks a duke as readily as a policeman, and with the most provoking airs of condescension. It makes rude work with the Board of Admiralty. The Bench of Bishops is still less safe. One bishop fares badly for his rapacity, and another for his bigotry, and a third for his courtliness. It addresses occasionally a hint to Majesty itself, and sometimes a hint which is taken. There is an air of freedom even in their advertising columns, which speaks well for England to a foreigner. On the days when I arrived in London in 1847, I read among the daily announcements, one offering a reward of fifty pounds to any person who would put a nobleman, described by name and title, late a member of Parliament, into any county jail in England, he having been convicted of obtaining money under false pretences.

Was never such arrogancy as the tone of this paper. Every slip of an Oxonian or Cantabrigian who writes his first leader, assumes that we subdued the earth before we sat down to write this particular "Times." One would think, the world was on its knees to the "Times" Office, for its daily breakfast. But this arrogance is calculated. Who would care for it, if it "surmised," or "dared to confess," or "ventured to predict," &c. No; *it is so*, and so it shall be.

The morality and patriotism of the "Times" claims only to be representative, and by no means ideal. It gives the argument, not of the majority, but of the commanding class. Its editors know better than to defend Russia, or Austria, or English vested rights, on abstract grounds. But they give a voice to the class who, at the moment, take the lead; and they have an instinct for finding where the power now lies, which is eternally shifting its banks. Sympathizing with, and speaking for the class that rules the hour, yet, being apprised of every ground-swell, every Chartist resolution, every Church squabble, every strike in the mills, they detect the first tremblings of change. They watch the hard and bitter struggles of the authors of each liberal movement, year by year,—watching them only to taunt and obstruct them,—until, at last, when they see that these have established their fact, that power is on the point of passing to them,—they strike in, with the voice of a monarch, astonish those whom they succor, as much as those whom they desert, and make victory sure. Of course, the aspirants see that the "Times" is one of the goods of fortune, not to be won but by winning their cause.

"Punch" is equally an expression of English good sense, as the "London Times." It is the comic version of the same sense. Many of its caricatures are equal to the best pamphlets, and will convey to the eye in an instant the popular view which was taken of each turn of public affairs. Its sketches are usually made by masterly hands, and sometimes with genius; the delight of every class, because uniformly guided by that taste which is tyrannical in England. It is a new trait of the nineteenth century, that the wit and humor of England, as in Punch, so in the humorists, Jerrold, Dickens, Thackeray, Hood, have taken the direction of humanity and freedom.

The "Times," like every important institution, shows the way to a better. It is a living index of the colossal British power. Its existence honors the people who dare to print all they know, dare to know all the facts, and do not wish to be flattered by hiding the extent of the public disaster. There is always safety in valor. I wish I could add, that this journal aspired to deserve the power it wields, by guidance of the public sentiment to the right. It is usually pretended, in Parliament and elsewhere, that the English press has a high tone,—which it has not. It has an imperial tone, as of a powerful and independent nation. But as with other empires, its tone is prone to be official, and even officinal. The "Times" shares all the limitations of the governing classes, and wishes never to be in a minority. If only it dared to cleave to the right, to show the right to be the only expedient, and feed its batteries from the central heart of humanity, it might not have so many men of rank among its contributors, but genius would be its cordial and invincible ally; it might now and then bear the brunt of formidable combinations, but no journal is ruined by wise courage. It would be the natural leader of British reform; its proud function, that of being the voice of Europe, the defender of the exile and patriot against despots, would be more effectually discharged; it would have the authority which is claimed for that dream of good men not yet come to pass, an International Congress; and the least of its victories would be to give to England a new millennium of beneficent power.

CHAPTER XVI

Stonehenge

I T HAD BEEN agreed between my friend Mr. C. and me, that before I left England, we should make an excursion together to Stonehenge, which neither of us had seen; and the project pleased my fancy with the double attraction of the monument and the companion. It seemed a bringing together of extreme points, to visit the oldest religious monument in Britain, in company with her latest thinker, and one whose influence may be traced in every contemporary book. I was glad to sum up a little my experiences, and to exchange a few reasonable words on the aspects of England, with a man on whose genius I set a very high value, and who had as much penetration, and as severe a theory of duty, as any person in it. On Friday, 7th July, we took the South Western Railway through Hampshire to Salisbury, where we found a carriage to convey us to Amesbury. The fine weather and my friend's local knowledge of Hampshire, in which he is wont to spend a part of every summer, made the way short. There was much to say, too, of the travelling Americans, and their usual objects in London. I thought it natural, that they should give some time to works of art collected here, which they cannot find at home, and a little to scientific clubs and museums, which, at this moment, make London very attractive. But my philosopher was not contented. Art and 'high art' is a favorite target for his wit. "Yes, *Kunst* is a great delusion, and Goethe and Schiller wasted a great deal of good time on it:"—and he thinks he discovers that old Goethe found this out, and, in his later writings, changed his tone. As soon as men begin to talk of art, architecture, and antiquities, nothing good comes of it. He wishes to go through the British Museum in silence, and thinks a sincere man will see something, and say nothing. In these days, he thought, it would become an architect to consult only the grim necessity, and say, 'I can build you a coffin for such dead persons as you are, and for such dead purposes as you have, but you shall have no ornament.' For the science, he had, if possible, even less tolerance, and compared the savans of Somerset House to the boy who asked Confucius "how many stars in the sky?" Confucius replied, "he minded things near him:" then said the boy, "how many hairs are there in your eyebrows?" Confucius said, "he didn't know and didn't care."

Still speaking of the Americans, C. complained that they dislike the coldness and exclusiveness of the English, and run away to France, and go with their countrymen, and are amused, instead of manfully staying in London, and confronting Englishmen, and acquiring their culture, who really have much to teach them.

I told C. that I was easily dazzled, and was accustomed to concede readily all that an Englishman would ask; I saw everywhere in the country proofs of sense and spirit, and success of every sort: I like the people: they are as good as they are handsome; they have everything, and can do everything: but meantime, I surely know, that, as soon as I return to Massachusetts, I shall lapse at once into the feeling, which the geography of America inevitably inspires, that we play the game with immense advantage; that there and not here is the seat and centre of the British race; and that no skill or activity can long compete with the prodigious natural advantages of that country, in the hands of the same race; and that England, an old and exhausted island, must one day be contented, like other parents, to be strong only in her children. But this was a proposition which no Englishman of whatever condition can easily entertain.

We left the train at Salisbury, and took a carriage to Amesbury, passing by Old Sarum, a bare, treeless hill, once containing the town which sent two members to Parliament,—now, not a hut;—and, arriving at Amesbury, stopped at the George Inn. After dinner, we walked to Salisbury Plain. On the broad downs, under the gray sky, not a house was visible, nothing but Stonehenge, which looked like a group of brown dwarfs in the wide expanse,—Stonehenge and the barrows,—which rose like green bosses about the plain, and a few hayricks. On the top of a mountain, the old temple would not be more impressive. Far and wide a few shepherds with their flocks sprinkled the plain, and a bagman drove along the road. It looked as if the wide margin given in this crowded isle to this primeval temple were accorded by the veneration of the British race to the old egg out of which all their ecclesiastical structures and history had proceeded. Stonehenge is a circular colonnade with a diameter of a hundred feet, and enclosing a second and a third colonnade within. We walked round the stones, and clambered over them, to wont ourselves with their strange aspect and groupings, and found a nook sheltered from the wind among them, where C. lighted his cigar. It was pleasant to see, that, just this simplest of all simple structures,—two upright stones and a lintel laid across,—had long outstood all later churches, and all history, and were like what is most permanent on the face of the planet: these, and the barrows,—mere mounds, (of which there are a hundred and sixty within a circle of three miles about Stonehenge,) like the same mound on the plain of Troy, which still makes good to the passing mariner on Hellespont, the vaunt of Homer and the fame of Achilles. Within the enclosure, grow buttercups, nettles, and, all around, wild thyme, daisy, meadowsweet, goldenrod, thistle, and the carpeting grass. Over us, larks were soaring and singing,—as my friend said, "the larks which were hatched last year, and the wind which was hatched many thousand years ago." We counted and measured by paces the biggest stones, and soon knew as much as any man can suddenly know of the inscrutable temple. There are ninety-four stones, and there were once probably one hundred and sixty. The temple is circular, and uncovered, and the situation fixed astronomically,—the grand entrances here, and at Abury, being placed exactly northeast, "as all the gates of the old cavern temples are." How came the stones here? for these *sarsens* or Druidical sandstones, are not found in this neighborhood. The *sacrificial stone*, as it is called, is the only one in all these blocks, that can resist the action of fire, and as I read in the books, must have been brought one hundred and fifty miles.

On almost every stone we found the marks of the mineralogist's hammer and chisel. The nineteen smaller stones of the inner circle are of granite. I, who had just come from Professor Sedgwick's Cambridge Museum of megatheria and mastodons, was ready to maintain that some cleverer elephants or mylodonta had borne off and laid these rocks one on another.

Only the good beasts must have known how to cut a well-wrought tenon and mortise, and to smooth the surface of some of the stones. The chief mystery is, that any mystery should have been allowed to settle on so remarkable a monument, in a country on which all the muses have kept their eyes now for eighteen hundred years. We are not yet too late to learn much more than is known of this structure. Some diligent Fellowes or Layard will arrive, stone by stone, at the whole history, by that exhaustive British sense and perseverance, so whimsical in its choice of objects, which leaves its own Stonehenge or Choir Gaur to the rabbits, whilst it opens pyramids, and uncovers Nineveh. Stonehenge, in virtue of the simplicity of its plan, and its good preservation, is as if new and recent; and, a thousand years hence, men will thank this age for the accurate history it will yet eliminate. We walked in and out, and took again and again a fresh look at the uncanny stones. The old sphinx put our petty differences of nationality out of sight. To these conscious stones we two pilgrims were alike known and near. We could equally well revere their old British meaning. My philosopher was subdued and gentle. In this quiet house of destiny, he happened to say, "I plant cypresses wherever I go, and if I am in search of pain, I cannot go wrong." The spot, the gray blocks, and their rude order, which refuses to be disposed of, suggested to him the flight of ages, and the succession of religions. The old times of England impress C. much: he reads little, he says, in these last years, but "*Acta Sanctorum*," the fifty-three volumes of which are in the "London Library." He finds all English history therein. He can see, as he reads, the old saint of Iona sitting there, and writing, a man to men. The *Acta Sanctorum* show plainly that the men of those times believed in God, and in the immortality of the soul, as their abbeys and cathedrals testify: now, even the puritanism is all gone. London is pagan. He fancied that greater men had lived in England, than any of her writers; and, in fact, about the time when those writers appeared, the last of these were already gone.

We left the mound in the twilight, with the design to return the next morning, and coming back two miles to our inn, we were met by little showers, and late as it was, men and women were out attempting to protect their spread windrows. The grass grows rank and dark in the showery England. At the inn, there was only milk for one cup of tea. When we called for more, the girl brought us three drops. My friend was annoyed who stood for the credit of an English inn, and still more, the next morning, by the dog-cart, sole procurable vehicle, in which we were to be sent to Wilton. I engaged the local antiquary, Mr. Brown, to go with us to Stonehenge, on our way, and show us what he knew of the "astronomical" and "sacrificial" stones. I stood on the last, and he pointed to the upright, or rather, inclined stone, called the "astronomical," and bade me notice that its top ranged with the sky-line. "Yes." Very well. Now, at the summer solstice, the sun rises exactly over the top of that stone, and, at the Druidical temple at Abury, there is also an astronomical stone, in the same relative positions.

In the silence of tradition, this one relation to science becomes an important clue; but we were content to leave the problem, with the rocks. Was this the "Giants' Dance" which Merlin brought from Killaraus, in Ireland, to be Uther Pendragon's monument to the British nobles whom Hengist slaughtered here, as Geoffrey of Monmouth relates? or was it a Roman work, as Inigo Jones explained to King James; or identical in design and style with the East Indian temples of the sun; as Davies in the Celtic Researches maintains? Of all the writers, Stukeley is the best. The heroic antiquary, charmed with the geometric perfections of his ruin, connects it with the oldest monuments and religion of the world, and with the courage of his tribe, does not stick to say, "the Deity who made the world by the scheme of Stonehenge." He finds that the *cursus** on Salisbury Plain stretches across the downs, like a line of latitude upon the globe, and the meridian line of Stonehenge passes exactly through the middle of this *cursus*. But here is the high point of the theory: the Druids had the magnet; laid their courses by it; their cardinal points in

---

*Connected with Stonehenge are an avenue and a *cursus*. The avenue is a narrow road of raised earth, extending 594 yards in a straight line from the grand entrance, then dividing into two branches, which lead, severally, to a row of barrows; and to the *cursus*,—an artificially formed flat tract of ground. This is half a mile northeast from Stonehenge, bounded by banks and ditches, 3036 yards long, by 110 broad.

Stonehenge, Ambresbury, and elsewhere, which vary a little
from true east and west, followed the variations of the compass. The Druids were Phœnicians. The name of the magnet
is *lapis Heracleus*, and Hercules was the god of the Phœnicians. Hercules, in the legend, drew his bow at the sun, and
the sun-god gave him a golden cup, with which he sailed over
the ocean. What was this, but a compass-box? This cup or
little boat, in which the magnet was made to float on water,
and so show the north, was probably its first form, before it
was suspended on a pin. But science was an *arcanum*, and, as
Britain was a Phœnician secret, so they kept their compass a
secret, and it was lost with the Tyrian commerce. The golden
fleece, again, of Jason, was the compass,—a bit of loadstone,
easily supposed to be the only one in the world, and therefore
naturally awakening the cupidity and ambition of the young heroes of a maritime nation to join in an expedition to obtain possession of this wise stone. Hence the fable that the ship Argo was
loquacious and oracular. There is also some curious coincidence
in the names. Apollodorus makes *Magnes* the son of *Æolus*, who
married *Nais*. On hints like these, Stukeley builds again the
grand colonnade into historic harmony, and computing backward by the known variations of the compass, bravely assigns
the year 406 before Christ, for the date of the temple.

For the difficulty of handling and carrying stones of this
size, the like is done in all cities, every day, with no other aid
than horse power. I chanced to see a year ago men at work
on the substructure of a house in Bowdoin Square, in Boston,
swinging a block of granite of the size of the largest of the
Stonehenge columns with an ordinary derrick. The men were
common masons, with paddies to help, nor did they think
they were doing anything remarkable. I suppose, there were
as good men a thousand years ago. And we wonder how
Stonehenge was built and forgotten. After spending half an
hour on the spot, we set forth in our dog-cart over the downs
for Wilton, C. not suppressing some threats and evil omens
on the proprietors, for keeping these broad plains a wretched
sheep-walk, when so many thousands of English men were
hungry and wanted labor. But I heard afterwards that it is
not an economy to cultivate this land, which only yields one
crop on being broken up and is then spoiled.

We came to Wilton and to Wilton Hall,—the renowned seat of the Earls of Pembroke, a house known to Shakspeare and Massinger, the frequent home of Sir Philip Sidney where he wrote the Arcadia; where he conversed with Lord Brooke, a man of deep thought, and a poet, who caused to be engraved on his tombstone, "Here lies Fulke Greville Lord Brooke, the friend of Sir Philip Sidney." It is now the property of the Earl of Pembroke, and the residence of his brother, Sidney Herbert, Esq., and is esteemed a noble specimen of the English manor-hall. My friend had a letter from Mr. Herbert to his housekeeper, and the house was shown. The state drawing-room is a double cube, 30 feet high, by 30 feet wide, by 60 feet long: the adjoining room is a single cube, of 30 feet every way. Although these apartments and the long library were full of good family portraits, Vandykes and other; and though there were some good pictures, and a quadrangle cloister full of antique and modern statuary,—to which C., catalogue in hand, did all too much justice,—yet the eye was still drawn to the windows, to a magnificent lawn, on which grew the finest cedars in England. I had not seen more charming grounds. We went out, and walked over the estate. We crossed a bridge built by Inigo Jones over a stream, of which the gardener did not know the name, (*Qu.* Alph?) watched the deer; climbed to the lonely sculptured summer house, on a hill backed by a wood; came down into the Italian garden, and into a French pavilion, garnished with French busts; and so again, to the house, where we found a table laid for us with bread, meats, peaches, grapes, and wine.

On leaving Wilton House, we took the coach for Salisbury. The Cathedral, which was finished 600 years ago, has even a spruce and modern air, and its spire is the highest in England. I know not why, but I had been more struck with one of no fame at Coventry, which rises 300 feet from the ground, with the lightness of a mullein-plant, and not at all implicated with the church. Salisbury is now esteemed the culmination of the Gothic art in England, as the buttresses are fully unmasked, and honestly detailed from the sides of the pile. The interior of the Cathedral is obstructed by the organ in the middle, acting like a screen. I know not why in real architecture the hunger of the eye for length of line is so rarely gratified. The rule of art is that a colonnade is more beautiful the longer it is, and that *ad infinitum*. And the nave of a church is seldom so long that it need be divided by a screen.

We loitered in the church, outside the choir, whilst service was said. Whilst we listened to the organ, my friend remarked, the music is good, and yet not quite religious, but somewhat as if a monk were panting to some fine Queen of Heaven. C. was unwilling, and we did not ask to have the choir shown us, but returned to our inn, after seeing another old church of the place. We passed in the train Clarendon Park, but could see little but the edge of a wood, though C. had wished to pay closer attention to the birthplace of the Decrees of Clarendon. At Bishopstoke we stopped, and found Mr. H., who received us in his carriage, and took us to his house at Bishops Waltham.

On Sunday, we had much discourse on a very rainy day. My friends asked, whether there were any Americans?—any with an American idea,—any theory of the right future of that country? Thus challenged, I bethought myself neither of caucuses nor congress, neither of presidents nor of cabinet-ministers, nor of such as would make of America another Europe. I thought only of the simplest and purest minds; I said, 'Certainly yes;—but those who hold it are fanatics of a dream which I should hardly care to relate to your English ears, to which it might be only ridiculous,—and yet it is the only true.' So I opened the dogma of no-government and non-resistance, and anticipated the objections and the fun, and procured a kind of hearing for it. I said, it is true that I have never seen in any country a man of sufficient valor to stand for this truth, and yet it is plain to me, that no less valor than this can command my respect. I can easily see the bankruptcy of the vulgar musket-worship,—though great men be musket-worshippers;—and 'tis certain, as God liveth, the gun that does not need another gun, the law of love and justice alone, can effect a clean revolution. I fancied that one or two of my anecdotes made some impression on C., and I insisted, that the manifest absurdity of the view to English feasibility could make no difference to a gentleman; that as to our secure tenure of our mutton-chop and spinage in London or in Boston, the soul might quote Talleyrand, *"Monsieur, je n'en* *vois pas la nécessité.*"* As I had thus taken in the conversation the saint's part, when dinner was announced, C. refused to go out before me,—"he was altogether too wicked." I planted my back against the wall, and our host wittily rescued us from the dilemma, by saying, he was the wickedest, and would walk out first, then C. followed, and I went last.

On the way to Winchester, whither our host accompanied us in the afternoon, my friends asked many questions respecting American landscape, forests, houses,—my house, for example. It is not easy to answer these queries well. There I thought, in America, lies nature sleeping, over-growing, almost conscious, too much by half for man in the picture, and so giving a certain *tristesse*, like the rank vegetation of swamps and forests seen at night, steeped in dews and rains, which it loves; and on it man seems not able to make much impression. There, in that great sloven continent, in high Alleghany pastures, in the sea-wide, sky-skirted prairie, still sleeps and murmurs and hides the great mother, long since driven away from the trim hedge-rows and over-cultivated garden of England. And, in England, I am quite too sensible of this. Every one is on his good behavior, and must be dressed for dinner at six. So I put off my friends with very inadequate details, as best I could.

Just before entering Winchester, we stopped at the Church of Saint Cross, and, after looking through the quaint antiquity, we demanded a piece of bread and a draught of beer, which the founder, Henry de Blois, in 1136, commanded should be given to every one who should ask it at the gate. We had both, from the old couple who take care of the church. Some twenty people, every day, they said, make the same demand. This hospitality of seven hundred years' standing did not hinder C. from pronouncing a malediction on the priest who receives £2000 a year, that were meant for the poor, and spends a pittance on this small beer and crumbs.

In the Cathedral, I was gratified, at least by the ample dimensions. The length of line exceeds that of any other English church; being 556 feet by 250 in breadth of transept. I think I prefer this church to all I have seen, except Westmin-

---

*"*Mais, Monseigneur, il faut que j'existe.*"

ster and York. Here was Canute buried, and here Alfred the Great was crowned and buried, and here the Saxon kings: and, later, in his own church, William of Wykeham. It is very old: part of the crypt into which we went down and saw the Saxon and Norman arches of the old church on which the present stands, was built fourteen or fifteen hundred years ago. Sharon Turner says, "Alfred was buried at Winchester, in the Abbey he had founded there, but his remains were removed by Henry I. to the new Abbey in the meadows at Hyde, on the northern quarter of the city, and laid under the high altar. The building was destroyed at the Reformation, and what is left of Alfred's body now lies covered by modern buildings, or buried in the ruins of the old."* William of Wykeham's shrine tomb was unlocked for us, and C. took hold of the recumbent statue's marble hands, and patted them affectionately, for he rightly values the brave man who built Windsor, and this Cathedral, and the School here, and New College at Oxford. But it was growing late in the afternoon. Slowly we left the old house, and parting with our host, we took the train for London.

*History of the Anglo-Saxons, I. 599.

CHAPTER XVII

Personal

I N THESE COMMENTS on an old journey now revised after seven busy years have much changed men and things in England, I have abstained from reference to persons, except in the last chapter, and in one or two cases where the fame of the parties seemed to have given the public a property in all that concerned them. I must further allow myself a few notices, if only as an acknowledgment of debts that cannot be paid. My journeys were cheered by so much kindness from new friends, that my impression of the island is bright with agreeable memories both of public societies and of households: and, what is nowhere better found than in England, a cultivated person fitly surrounded by a happy home, " with honor, love, obedience, troops of friends," is of all institutions the best. At the landing in Liverpool, I found my Manchester correspondent awaiting me, a gentleman whose kind reception was followed by a train of friendly and effective attentions which never rested whilst I remained in the country. A man of sense and of letters, the editor of a powerful local journal, he added to solid virtues an infinite sweetness and *bonhommie*. There seemed a pool of honey about his heart which lubricated all his speech and action with fine jets of mead. An equal good fortune attended many later accidents of my journey, until the sincerity of English kindness ceased to surprise. My visit fell in the fortunate days when Mr. Bancroft was the American Minister in London, and at his house, or through his good offices, I had easy access to excellent persons and to privileged places. At the house of Mr. Carlyle, I met persons eminent in society and in letters. The privileges of the Athenæum and of the Reform Clubs were hospitably opened to me, and I found much advantage in the circles of the "Geologic," the "Antiquarian," and the "Royal Societies." Every day in London gave me new opportunities of meeting men and women who give splendor to society. I saw Rogers, Hallam, Macaulay, Milnes, Milman, Barry Cornwall, Dickens, Thackeray, Tennyson, Leigh Hunt, D'Israeli, Helps, Wilkinson, Bailey, Kenyon, and Forster: the younger poets, Clough, Arnold, and Patmore; and, among the men of science, Robert Brown, Owen, Sedgwick, Faraday, Buckland, Lyell, De la Beche, Hooker, Carpenter, Babbage, and Edward Forbes. It was my privilege also to converse with Miss Baillie, with Lady Morgan, with Mrs. Jameson, and Mrs. Somerville. A finer hospitality made many private houses not less known and dear. It is not in distinguished circles that wisdom and elevated characters are usually found, or, if found, not confined thereto; and my recollections of the best hours go back to private conversations in different parts of the kingdom, with persons little known. Nor am I insensible to the courtesy which frankly opened to me some noble mansions, if I do not adorn my page with their names. Among the privileges of London, I recall with pleasure two or three signal days, one at Kew, where Sir William Hooker showed me all the riches of the vast botanic garden; one at the Museum, where Sir Charles Fellowes explained in detail the history of his Ionic trophy-monument; and still another, on which Mr. Owen accompanied my countryman Mr. H. and myself through the Hunterian Museum.

The like frank hospitality, bent on real service, I found among the great and the humble, wherever I went; in Birmingham, in Oxford, in Leicester, in Nottingham, in Sheffield, in Manchester, in Liverpool. At Edinburgh, through the kindness of Dr. Samuel Brown, I made the acquaintance of De Quincey, of Lord Jeffrey, of Wilson, of Mrs. Crowe, of the Messrs. Chambers, and of a man of high character and genius, the short lived painter, David Scott.

At Ambleside in March, 1848, I was for a couple of days the guest of Miss Martineau, then newly returned from her Egyptian tour. On Sunday afternoon, I accompanied her to Rydal Mount. And as I have recorded a visit to Wordsworth, many years before, I must not forget this second interview. We found Mr. Wordsworth asleep on the sofa. He was at first silent and indisposed, as an old man suddenly waked, before he had ended his nap; but soon became full of talk on the French news. He was nationally bitter on the French: bitter on Scotchmen, too. No Scotchman, he said, can write English. He detailed the two models, on one or the other of which all the sentences of the historian Robertson are framed. Nor could Jeffrey, nor the Edinburgh Reviewers write English, nor can * * *, who is a pest to the English tongue. Incidentally he added, Gibbon cannot write English. The Edinburgh Review wrote what would tell and what would sell. It had however changed the tone of its literary criticism from the time when a certain letter was written to the editor by Coleridge. Mrs. W. had the Editor's answer in her possession. Tennyson he thinks a right poetic genius, though with some affectation. He had thought an elder brother of Tennyson at first the better poet, but must now reckon Alfred the true one. . . . In speaking of I know not what style, he said, "to be sure, it was the manner, but then you know the matter always comes out of the manner." . . . He thought Rio Janeiro the best place in the world for a great capital city. . . . We talked of English national character. I told him, it was not creditable that no one in all the country knew anything of Thomas Taylor, the Platonist, whilst in every American library his translations are found. I said, if Plato's Republic were published in England as a new book to-day, do you think it would find any readers?—he confessed, it would not: "and yet," he added after a pause, with that complacency which never deserts a true-born Englishman, "and yet we have embodied it all."

His opinions of French, English, Irish, and Scotch, seemed rashly formulized from little anecdotes of what had befallen himself and members of his family, in a diligence or stagecoach. His face sometimes lighted up, but his conversation was not marked by special force or elevation. Yet perhaps it is a high compliment to the cultivation of the English generally, when we find such a man not distinguished. He had a healthy look, with a weather-beaten face, his face corrugated, especially the large nose.

Miss Martineau, who lived near him, praised him to me not for his poetry, but for thrift and economy; for having afforded to his country-neighbors an example of a modest household, where comfort and culture were secured without any display. She said, that, in his early housekeeping at the cottage where he first lived, he was accustomed to offer his friends bread and plainest fare: if they wanted any thing more, they must pay him for their board. It was the rule of the house. I replied, that it evinced English pluck more than any anecdote I knew. A gentleman in the neighborhood told the story of Walter Scott's staying once for a week with Wordsworth, and slipping out every day under pretence of a walk, to the Swan Inn, for a cold cut and porter; and one day passing with Wordsworth the inn, he was betrayed by the landlord's asking him if he had come for his porter. Of course, this trait would have another look in London, and there you will hear from different literary men, that Wordsworth had no personal friend, that he was not amiable, that he was parsimonious, &c. Landor, always generous, says, that he never praised any body. A gentleman in London showed me a watch that once belonged to Milton, whose initials are engraved on its face. He said, he once showed this to Wordsworth, who took it in one hand, then drew out his own watch, and held it up with the other, before the company, but no one making the expected remark, he put back his own in silence. I do not attach much importance to the disparagement of Wordsworth among London scholars. Who reads him well will know, that in following the strong bent of his genius, he was careless of the many, careless also of the few, self-assured that he should "create the taste by which he is to be enjoyed." He lived long enough to witness the revolution he had wrought, and "to see what he foresaw." There are torpid places in his mind, there is something hard and sterile in his poetry, want of grace and variety, want of due catholicity and cosmopolitan scope: he had conformities to English politics and traditions; he had egotistic puerilities in the choice and treatment of his subjects; but let us say of him, that, alone in his time he treated the human mind well, and with an absolute trust. His adherence to his poetic creed rested on real inspirations. The Ode on Immortality is the high-water-mark which the intellect has reached in this age. New means were employed, and new realms added to the empire of the muse, by his courage.

CHAPTER XVIII

Result

ENGLAND is the best of actual nations. It is no ideal framework, it is an old pile built in different ages, with repairs, additions, and makeshifts; but you see the poor best you have got. London is the epitome of our times, and the Rome of to-day. Broad-fronted broad-bottomed Teutons, they stand in solid phalanx foursquare to the points of compass; they constitute the modern world, they have earned their vantage-ground, and held it through ages of adverse possession. They are well marked and differing from other leading races. England is tender-hearted. Rome was not. England is not so public in its bias; private life is its place of honor. Truth in private life, untruth in public, marks these home-loving men. Their political conduct is not decided by general views, but by internal intrigues and personal and family interest. They cannot readily see beyond England. The history of Rome and Greece, when written by their scholars, degenerates into English party pamphlets. They cannot see beyond England, nor in England can they transcend the interests of the governing classes. "English principles" mean a primary regard to the interests of property. England, Scotland, and Ireland combine to check the colonies. England and Scotland combine to check Irish manufactures and trade. England rallies at home to check Scotland. In England, the strong classes check the weaker. In the home population of near thirty millions, there are but one million voters. The Church punishes dissent, punishes education. Down to a late day, marriages performed by dissenters were illegal. A bitter class-legislation gives power to those who are rich enough to buy a law. The game-laws are a proverb of oppression. Pauperism incrusts and clogs the state, and in hard times becomes hideous. In bad seasons, the porridge was diluted. Multitudes lived miserably by shell-fish and sea-ware. In cities, the children are trained to beg, until they shall be old enough to rob. Men and women were convicted of poisoning scores of children for burial-fees. In Irish districts, men deteriorated in size

and shape, the nose sunk, the gums were exposed, with diminished brain and brutal form. During the Australian emigration, multitudes were rejected by the commissioners as
being too emaciated for useful colonists. During the Russian
war, few of those that offered as recruits were found up to
the medical standard, though it had been reduced.

The foreign policy of England, though ambitious and lavish of money, has not often been generous or just. It has a
principal regard to the interest of trade, checked however by
the aristocratic bias of the ambassador, which usually puts
him in sympathy with the continental Courts. It sanctioned
the partition of Poland, it betrayed Genoa, Sicily, Parga,
Greece, Turkey, Rome, and Hungary.

Some public regards they have. They have abolished slavery
in the West Indies, and put an end to human sacrifices in the
East. At home they have a certain statute hospitality. England
keeps open doors, as a trading country must, to all nations. It
is one of their fixed ideas, and wrathfully supported by their
laws in unbroken sequence for a thousand years. In *Magna
Charta* it was ordained, that all "merchants shall have safe and
secure conduct to go out and come into England, and to stay
there, and to pass as well by land as by water, to buy and sell
by the ancient allowed customs, without any evil toll, except
in time of war, or when they shall be of any nation at war
with us." It is a statute and obliged hospitality, and peremptorily maintained. But this shop-rule had one magnificent effect. It extends its cold unalterable courtesy to political exiles
of every opinion, and is a fact which might give additional
light to that portion of the planet seen from the farthest star.
But this perfunctory hospitality puts no sweetness into their
unaccommodating manners, no check on that puissant nationality which makes their existence incompatible with all
that is not English.

What we must say about a nation is a superficial dealing
with symptoms. We cannot go deep enough into the biography of the spirit who never throws himself entire into one
hero, but delegates his energy in parts or spasms to vicious
and defective individuals. But the wealth of the source is seen
in the plenitude of English nature. What variety of power and
talent; what facility and plenteousness of knighthood, lord-

ship, ladyship, royalty, loyalty; what a proud chivalry is indicated in "Collins's Peerage," through eight hundred years! What dignity resting on what reality and stoutness! What courage in war, what sinew in labor, what cunning workmen, what inventors and engineers, what seamen and pilots, what clerks and scholars! No one man and no few men can represent them. It is a people of myriad personalities. Their many-headedness is owing to the advantageous position of the middle class, who are always the source of letters and science. Hence the vast plenty of their æsthetic production. As they are many-headed, so they are many-nationed: their colonization annexes archipelagoes and continents, and their speech seems destined to be the universal language of men. I have noted the reserve of power in the English temperament. In the island, they never let out all the length of all the reins, there is no Berserkir rage, no abandonment or ecstasy of will or intellect, like that of the Arabs in the time of Mahomet, or like that which intoxicated France in 1789. But who would see the uncoiling of that tremendous spring, the explosion of their well-husbanded forces, must follow the swarms which pouring now for two hundred years from the British islands, have sailed, and rode, and traded, and planted, through all climates, mainly following the belt of empire, the temperate zones, carrying the Saxon seed, with its instinct for liberty and law, for arts and for thought,—acquiring under some skies a more electric energy than the native air allows,—to the conquest of the globe. Their colonial policy, obeying the necessities of a vast empire, has become liberal. Canada and Australia have been contented with substantial independence. They are expiating the wrongs of India, by benefits; first, in works for the irrigation of the peninsula, and roads and telegraphs; and secondly, in the instruction of the people, to qualify them for self-government, when the British power shall be finally called home.

Their mind is in a state of arrested development,—a divine cripple like Vulcan; a blind *savant* like Huber and Sanderson. They do not occupy themselves on matters of general and lasting import, but on a corporeal civilization, on goods that perish in the using. But they read with good intent, and what they learn they incarnate. The English mind turns every abstraction it can receive into a portable utensil, or a working institution. Such is their tenacity, and such their practical turn, that they hold all they gain. Hence we say, that only the English race can be trusted with freedom,—freedom which is double-edged and dangerous to any but the wise and robust. The English designate the kingdoms emulous of free institutions, as the sentimental nations. Their culture is not an outside varnish, but is thorough and secular in families and the race. They are oppressive with their temperament, and all the more that they are refined. I have sometimes seen them walk with my countrymen when I was forced to allow them every advantage, and their companions seemed bags of bones.

There is cramp limitation in their habit of thought, sleepy routine, and a tortoise's instinct to hold hard to the ground with his claws, lest he should be thrown on his back. There is a drag of inertia which resists reform in every shape;—law-reform, army-reform, extension of suffrage, Jewish franchise, Catholic emancipation,—the abolition of slavery, of impressment, penal code, and entails. They praise this drag, under the formula, that it is the excellence of the British constitution, that no law can anticipate the public opinion. These poor tortoises must hold hard, for they feel no wings sprouting at their shoulders. Yet somewhat divine warms at their heart, and waits a happier hour. It hides in their sturdy will. "Will," said the old philosophy, "is the measure of power," and personality is the token of this race. *Quid vult valde vult.* What they do they do with a will. You cannot account for their success by their Christianity, commerce, charter, common law, Parliament, or letters, but by the contumacious sharptongued energy of English *naturel*, with a poise impossible to disturb, which makes all these its instruments. They are slow and reticent, and are like a dull good horse which lets every nag pass him, but with whip and spur will run down every racer in the field. They are right in their feeling, though wrong in their speculation.

The feudal system survives in the steep inequality of property and privilege, in the limited franchise, in the social barriers which confine patronage and promotion to a caste, and still more in the submissive ideas pervading these people. The fagging of the schools is repeated in the social classes. An

Englishman shows no mercy to those below him in the social scale, as he looks for none from those above him: any forbearance from his superiors surprises him, and they suffer in his good opinion. But the feudal system can be seen with less pain on large historical grounds. It was pleaded in mitigation of the rotten borough, that it worked well, that substantial justice was done. Fox, Burke, Pitt, Erskine, Wilberforce, Sheridan, Romilly, or whatever national man, were by this means sent to Parliament, when their return by large constituencies would have been doubtful. So now we say, that the right measures of England are the men it bred; that it has yielded more able men in five hundred years than any other nation; and, though we must not play Providence, and balance the chances of producing ten great men against the comfort of ten thousand mean men, yet retrospectively we may strike the balance, and prefer one Alfred, one Shakspeare, one Milton, one Sidney, one Raleigh, one Wellington, to a million foolish democrats.

The American system is more democratic, more humane; yet the American people do not yield better or more able men, or more inventions or books or benefits, than the English. Congress is not wiser or better than Parliament. France has abolished its suffocating old *régime*, but is not recently marked by any more wisdom or virtue.

The power of performance has not been exceeded,—the creation of value. The English have given importance to individuals, a principal end and fruit of every society. Every man is allowed and encouraged to be what he is, and is guarded in the indulgence of his whim. "Magna Charta," said Rushworth, "is such a fellow that he will have no sovereign." By this general activity, and by this sacredness of individuals, they have in seven hundred years evolved the principles of freedom. It is the land of patriots, martyrs, sages, and bards, and if the ocean out of which it emerged should wash it away, it will be remembered as an island famous for immortal laws, for the announcements of original right which make the stone tables of liberty.

CHAPTER XIX

Speech at Manchester

A FEW DAYS after my arrival at Manchester, in November, 1847, the Manchester Athenæum gave its annual Banquet in the Free-Trade Hall. With other guests, I was invited to be present, and to address the company. In looking over recently a newspaper-report of my remarks, I incline to reprint it, as fitly expressing the feeling with which I entered England, and which agrees well enough with the more deliberate results of better acquaintance recorded in the foregoing pages. Sir Archibald Alison, the historian, presided, and opened the meeting with a speech. He was followed by Mr. Cobden, Lord Brackley, and others, among whom was Mr. Cruikshank, one of the contributors to "Punch." Mr. Dickens's letter of apology for his absence was read. Mr. Jerrold, who had been announced, did not appear. On being introduced to the meeting I said,—

Mr. Chairman and Gentlemen: It is pleasant to me to meet this great and brilliant company, and doubly pleasant to see the faces of so many distinguished persons on this platform. But I have known all these persons already. When I was at home, they were as near to me as they are to you. The arguments of the League and its leader are known to all the friends of free trade. The gayeties and genius, the political, the social, the parietal wit of "Punch" go duly every fortnight to every boy and girl in Boston and New York. Sir, when I came to sea, I found the "History of Europe"* on the ship's cabin table, the property of the captain;—a sort of programme or play-bill to tell the seafaring New Englander what he shall find on his landing here. And as for Dombey, sir, there is no land where paper exists to print on, where it is not found; no man who can read, that does not read it, and, if he cannot, he finds some charitable pair of eyes that can, and hears it.

But these things are not for me to say; these compliments, though true, would better come from one who felt and un-

*By Sir A. Alison.

derstood these merits more. I am not here to exchange civilities with you, but rather to speak of that which I am sure interests these gentlemen more than their own praises; of that which is good in holidays and working-days, the same in one century and in another century. That which lures a solitary American in the woods with the wish to see England, is the moral peculiarity of the Saxon race,—its commanding sense of right and wrong,—the love and devotion to that,—this is the imperial trait, which arms them with the sceptre of the globe. It is this which lies at the foundation of that aristocratic character, which certainly wanders into strange vagaries, so that its origin is often lost sight of, but which, if it should lose this, would find itself paralyzed; and in trade, and in the mechanic's shop, gives that honesty in performance, that thoroughness and solidity of work, which is a national characteristic. This conscience is one element, and the other is that loyal adhesion, that habit of friendship, that homage of man to man, running through all classes,—the electing of worthy persons to a certain fraternity, to acts of kindness and warm and staunch support, from year to year, from youth to age,—which is alike lovely and honorable to those who render and those who receive it;—which stands in strong contrast with the superficial attachments of other races, their excessive courtesy, and short-lived connection.

You will think me very pedantic, gentlemen, but holiday though it be, I have not the smallest interest in any holiday, except as it celebrates real and not pretended joys; and I think it just, in this time of gloom and commercial disaster, of affliction and beggary in these districts, that, on these very accounts I speak of, you should not fail to keep your literary anniversary. I seem to hear you say, that, for all that is come and gone yet, we will not reduce by one chaplet or one oak leaf the braveries of our annual feast. For I must tell you, I was given to understand in my childhood, that the British island from which my forefathers came, was no lotus-garden, no paradise of serene sky and roses and music and merriment all the year round, no, but a cold foggy mournful country, where nothing grew well in the open air, but robust men and virtuous women, and these of a wonderful fibre and endurance; that their best parts were slowly revealed; their virtues did not come out until they quarrelled: they did not strike twelve the first time; good lovers, good haters, and you could know little about them till you had seen them long, and little good of them till you had seen them in action; that in prosperity they were moody and dumpish, but in adversity they were grand. Is it not true, sir, that the wise ancients did not praise the ship parting with flying colors from the port, but only that brave sailer which came back with torn sheets and battered sides, stript of her banners, but having ridden out the storm? And so, gentlemen, I feel in regard to this aged England, with the possessions, honors and trophies, and also with the infirmities of a thousand years gathering around her, irretrievably committed as she now is to many old customs which cannot be suddenly changed; pressed upon by the transitions of trade, and new and all incalculable modes, fabrics, arts, machines, and competing populations,—I see her not dispirited, not weak, but well remembering that she has seen dark days before;—indeed with a kind of instinct that she sees a little better in a cloudy day, and that in storm of battle and calamity, she has a secret vigor and a pulse like a cannon. I see her in her old age, not decrepit, but young, and still daring to believe in her power of endurance and expansion. Seeing this, I say, All hail! mother of nations, mother of heroes, with strength still equal to the time; still wise to entertain and swift to execute the policy which the mind and heart of mankind requires in the present hour, and thus only hospitable to the foreigner, and truly a home to the thoughtful and generous who are born in the soil. So be it! so let it be! If it be not so, if the courage of England goes with the chances of a commercial crisis, I will go back to the capes of Massachusetts, and my own Indian stream, and say to my countrymen, the old race are all gone, and the elasticity and hope of mankind must henceforth remain on the Alleghany ranges, or nowhere.

THE CONDUCT OF LIFE

Contents

I

FATE

———

DELICATE omens traced in air
To the lone bard true witness bare;
Birds with auguries on their wings
Chanted undeceiving things
Him to beckon, him to warn;
Well might then the poet scorn
To learn of scribe or courier
Hints writ in vaster character;
And on his mind, at dawn of day,
Soft shadows of the evening lay.
For the prevision is allied
Unto the thing so signified;
Or say, the foresight that awaits
Is the same Genius that creates.

Fate

I<small>T</small> <small>CHANCED</small> during one winter, a few years ago, that our cities were bent on discussing the theory of the Age. By an odd coincidence, four or five noted men were each reading a discourse to the citizens of Boston or New York, on the Spirit of the Times. It so happened that the subject had the same prominence in some remarkable pamphlets and journals issued in London in the same season. To me, however, the question of the times resolved itself into a practical question of the conduct of life. How shall I live? We are incompetent to solve the times. Our geometry cannot span the huge orbits of the prevailing ideas, behold their return, and reconcile their opposition. We can only obey our own polarity. 'Tis fine for us to speculate and elect our course, if we must accept an irresistible dictation.

In our first steps to gain our wishes, we come upon immovable limitations. We are fired with the hope to reform men. After many experiments, we find that we must begin earlier,—at school. But the boys and girls are not docile; we can make nothing of them. We decide that they are not of good stock. We must begin our reform earlier still,—at generation: that is to say, there is Fate, or laws of the world.

But if there be irresistible dictation, this dictation understands itself. If we must accept Fate, we are not less compelled to affirm liberty, the significance of the individual, the grandeur of duty, the power of character. This is true, and that other is true. But our geometry cannot span these extreme points, and reconcile them. What to do? By obeying each thought frankly, by harping, or, if you will, pounding on each string, we learn at last its power. By the same obedience to other thoughts, we learn theirs, and then comes some reasonable hope of harmonizing them. We are sure, that, though we know not how, necessity does comport with liberty, the individual with the world, my polarity with the spirit of the times. The riddle of the age has for each a private solution. If one would study his own time, it must be by this method of taking up in turn each of the leading topics which belong to our scheme of human life, and, by firmly stating all that is agreeable to experience on one, and doing the same justice to the opposing facts in the others, the true limitations will appear. Any excess of emphasis, on one part, would be corrected, and a just balance would be made.

But let us honestly state the facts. Our America has a bad name for superficialness. Great men, great nations, have not been boasters and buffoons, but perceivers of the terror of life, and have manned themselves to face it. The Spartan, embodying his religion in his country, dies before its majesty without a question. The Turk, who believes his doom is written on the iron leaf in the moment when he entered the world, rushes on the enemy's sabre with undivided will. The Turk, the Arab, the Persian, accepts the foreordained fate.

> "On two days, it steads not to run from thy grave,
>   The appointed, and the unappointed day;
> On the first, neither balm nor physician can save,
>   Nor thee, on the second, the Universe slay."

The Hindoo, under the wheel, is as firm. Our Calvinists, in the last generation, had something of the same dignity. They felt that the weight of the Universe held them down to their place. What could *they* do? Wise men feel that there is something which cannot be talked or voted away,—a strap or belt which girds the world.

> "The Destiny, minister general,
>   That executeth in the world o'er all,
>   The purveyance which God hath seen beforne,
>   So strong it is, that tho' the world had sworn
>   The contrary of a thing by yea or nay,
>   Yet sometime it shall fallen on a day
>   That falleth not oft in a thousand year;
>   For, certainly, our appetités here,
>   Be it of war, or peace, or hate, or love,
>   All this is ruled by the sight above."
>   CHAUCER: *The Knighte's Tale.*

The Greek Tragedy expressed the same sense: "Whatever is fated, that will take place. The great immense mind of Jove is not to be transgressed."

Savages cling to a local god of one tribe or town. The broad ethics of Jesus were quickly narrowed to village theologies, which preach an election or favoritism. And, now and then, an amiable parson, like Jung Stilling, or Robert Huntington, believes in a pistareen-Providence, which, whenever the good man wants a dinner, makes that somebody shall knock at his door, and leave a half-dollar. But Nature is no sentimentalist,—does not cosset or pamper us. We must see that the world is rough and surly, and will not mind drowning a man or a woman; but swallows your ship like a grain of dust. The cold, inconsiderate of persons, tingles your blood, benumbs your feet, freezes a man like an apple. The diseases, the elements, fortune, gravity, lightning, respect no persons. The way of Providence is a little rude. The habit of snake and spider, the snap of the tiger and other leapers and bloody jumpers, the crackle of the bones of his prey in the coil of the anaconda,—these are in the system, and our habits are like theirs. You have just dined, and, however scrupulously the slaughter-house is concealed in the graceful distance of miles, there is complicity,—expensive races,—race living at the expense of race. The planet is liable to shocks from comets, perturbations from planets, rendings from earthquake and volcano, alterations of climate, precessions of equinoxes. Rivers dry up by opening of the forest. The sea changes its bed. Towns and counties fall into it. At Lisbon, an earthquake killed men like flies. At Naples, three years ago, ten thousand persons were crushed in a few minutes. The scurvy at sea; the sword of the climate in the west of Africa, at Cayenne, at Panama, at New Orleans, cut off men like a massacre. Our western prairie shakes with fever and ague. The cholera, the small-pox, have proved as mortal to some tribes, as a frost to the crickets, which, having filled the summer with noise, are silenced by a fall of the temperature of one night. Without uncovering what does not concern us, or counting how many species of parasites hang on a bombyx; or groping after intestinal parasites, or infusory biters, or the obscurities of alternate generation;—the forms of the shark, the *labrus*, the jaw of the sea-wolf paved with crushing teeth, the weapons of the grampus, and other warriors hidden in the sea,—are hints of ferocity in the interiors of nature. Let us not deny it up and

down. Providence has a wild, rough, incalculable road to its
end, and it is of no use to try to whitewash its huge, mixed
instrumentalities, or to dress up that terrific benefactor in a
clean shirt and white neckcloth of a student in divinity.

Will you say, the disasters which threaten mankind are exceptional, and one need not lay his account for cataclysms
every day? Aye, but what happens once, may happen again,
and so long as these strokes are not to be parried by us, they
must be feared.

But these shocks and ruins are less destructive to us, than
the stealthy power of other laws which act on us daily. An
expense of ends to means is fate;—organization tyrannizing
over character. The menagerie, or forms and powers of the
spine, is a book of fate: the bill of the bird, the skull of the
snake, determines tyrannically its limits. So is the scale of
races, of temperaments; so is sex; so is climate; so is the reaction of talents imprisoning the vital power in certain directions. Every spirit makes its house; but afterwards the house
confines the spirit.

The gross lines are legible to the dull: the cabman is
phrenologist so far: he looks in your face to see if his shilling
is sure. A dome of brow denotes one thing; a pot-belly another; a squint, a pug-nose, mats of hair, the pigment of the
epidermis, betray character. People seem sheathed in their
tough organization. Ask Spurzheim, ask the doctors, ask
Quetelet, if temperaments decide nothing? or if there be anything they do not decide? Read the description in medical
books of the four temperaments, and you will think you are
reading your own thoughts which you had not yet told. Find
the part which black eyes, and which blue eyes, play severally
in the company. How shall a man escape from his ancestors,
or draw off from his veins the black drop which he drew from
his father's or his mother's life? It often appears in a family,
as if all the qualities of the progenitors were potted in several
jars,—some ruling quality in each son or daughter of the
house,—and sometimes the unmixed temperament, the rank
unmitigated elixir, the family vice, is drawn off in a separate
individual, and the others are proportionally relieved. We
sometimes see a change of expression in our companion, and
say, his father, or his mother, comes to the windows of his

eyes, and sometimes a remote relative. In different hours, a man represents each of several of his ancestors, as if there were seven or eight of us rolled up in each man's skin,— seven or eight ancestors at least,—and they constitute the variety of notes for that new piece of music which his life is. At the corner of the street, you read the possibility of each passenger, in the facial angle, in the complexion, in the depth of his eye. His parentage determines it. Men are what their mothers made them. You may as well ask a loom which weaves huckaback, why it does not make cashmere, as expect poetry from this engineer, or a chemical discovery from that jobber. Ask the digger in the ditch to explain Newton's laws: the fine organs of his brain have been pinched by overwork and squalid poverty from father to son, for a hundred years. When each comes forth from his mother's womb, the gate of gifts closes behind him. Let him value his hands and feet, he has but one pair. So he has but one future, and that is already predetermined in his lobes, and described in that little fatty face, pig-eye, and squat form. All the privilege and all the legislation of the world cannot meddle or help to make a poet or a prince of him.

Jesus said, "When he looketh on her, he hath committed adultery." But he is an adulterer before he has yet looked on the woman, by the superfluity of animal, and the defect of thought, in his constitution. Who meets him, or who meets her, in the street, sees that they are ripe to be each other's victim.

In certain men, digestion and sex absorb the vital force, and the stronger these are, the individual is so much weaker. The more of these drones perish, the better for the hive. If, later, they give birth to some superior individual, with force enough to add to this animal a new aim, and a complete apparatus to work it out, all the ancestors are gladly forgotten. Most men and most women are merely one couple more. Now and then, one has a new cell or camarilla opened in his brain,—an architectural, a musical, or a philological knack, some stray taste or talent for flowers, or chemistry, or pigments, or story-telling, a good hand for drawing, a good foot for dancing, an athletic frame for wide journeying, &c.— which skill nowise alters rank in the scale of nature, but serves to pass the time, the life of sensation going on as before. At last, these hints and tendencies are fixed in one, or in a succession. Each absorbs so much food and force, as to become itself a new centre. The new talent draws off so rapidly the vital force, that not enough remains for the animal functions, hardly enough for health; so that, in the second generation, if the like genius appear, the health is visibly deteriorated, and the generative force impaired.

People are born with the moral or with the material bias;— uterine brothers with this diverging destination: and I suppose, with high magnifiers, Mr. Frauenhofer or Dr. Carpenter might come to distinguish in the embryo at the fourth day, this is a Whig, and that a Free-soiler.

It was a poetic attempt to lift this mountain of Fate, to reconcile this despotism of race with liberty, which led the Hindoos to say, "Fate is nothing but the deeds committed in a prior state of existence." I find the coincidence of the extremes of eastern and western speculation in the daring statement of Schelling, "there is in every man a certain feeling, that he has been what he is from all eternity, and by no means became such in time." To say it less sublimely,—in the history of the individual is always an account of his condition, and he knows himself to be a party to his present estate.

A good deal of our politics is physiological. Now and then, a man of wealth in the heyday of youth adopts the tenet of broadest freedom. In England, there is always some man of wealth and large connection planting himself, during all his years of health, on the side of progress, who, as soon as he begins to die, checks his forward play, calls in his troops, and becomes conservative. All conservatives are such from personal defects. They have been effeminated by position or nature, born halt and blind, through luxury of their parents, and can only, like invalids, act on the defensive. But strong natures, backwoodsmen, New Hampshire giants, Napoleons, Burkes, Broughams, Websters, Kossuths, are inevitable patriots, until their life ebbs, and their defects and gout, palsy and money, warp them.

The strongest idea incarnates itself in majorities and nations, in the healthiest and strongest. Probably, the election goes by avoirdupois weight, and, if you could weigh bodily the tonnage of any hundred of the Whig and the Democratic party in a town, on the Dearborn balance, as they passed the hayscales, you could predict with certainty which party would carry it. On the whole, it would be rather the speediest way of deciding the vote, to put the selectmen or the mayor and aldermen at the hayscales.

In science, we have to consider two things: power and circumstance. All we know of the egg, from each successive discovery, is, *another vesicle*; and if, after five hundred years, you get a better observer, or a better glass, he finds within the last observed another. In vegetable and animal tissue, it is just alike, and all that the primary power or spasm operates, is, still, vesicles, vesicles. Yes,—but the tyrannical Circumstance! A vesicle in new circumstances, a vesicle lodged in darkness, Oken thought, became animal; in light, a plant. Lodged in the parent animal, it suffers changes, which end in unsheathing miraculous capability in the unaltered vesicle, and it unlocks itself to fish, bird, or quadruped, head and foot, eye and claw. The Circumstance is Nature. Nature is, what you may do. There is much you may not. We have two things,—the circumstance, and the life. Once we thought, positive power was all. Now we learn, that negative power, or circumstance, is half. Nature is the tyrannous circumstance, the thick skull, the sheathed snake, the ponderous, rock-like jaw; necessitated activity; violent direction; the conditions of a tool, like the locomotive, strong enough on its track, but which can do nothing but mischief off of it; or skates, which are wings on the ice, but fetters on the ground.

The book of Nature is the book of Fate. She turns the gigantic pages,—leaf after leaf,—never re-turning one. One leaf she lays down, a floor of granite; then a thousand ages, and a bed of slate; a thousand ages, and a measure of coal; a thousand ages, and a layer of marl and mud: vegetable forms appear; her first misshapen animals, zoophyte, trilobium, fish; then, saurians,—rude forms, in which she has only blocked her future statue, concealing under these unwieldly monsters the fine type of her coming king. The face of the planet cools and dries, the races meliorate, and man is born. But when a race has lived its term, it comes no more again.

The population of the world is a conditional population;

not the best, but the best that could live now; and the scale
of tribes, and the steadiness with which victory adheres to one
tribe, and defeat to another, is as uniform as the superposition of strata. We know in history what weight belongs to
race. We see the English, French, and Germans planting
themselves on every shore and market of America and Australia, and monopolizing the commerce of these countries. We
like the nervous and victorious habit of our own branch of
the family. We follow the step of the Jew, of the Indian, of
the Negro. We see how much will has been expended to ex-
tinguish the Jew, in vain. Look at the unpalatable conclusions
of Knox, in his "Fragment of Races,"—a rash and unsatisfactory writer, but charged with pungent and unforgetable
truths. "Nature respects race, and not hybrids." "Every race
has its own *habitat*." "Detach a colony from the race, and it
deteriorates to the crab." See the shades of the picture. The
German and Irish millions, like the Negro, have a great deal
of guano in their destiny. They are ferried over the Atlantic,
and carted over America, to ditch and to drudge, to make
corn cheap, and then to lie down prematurely to make a spot
of green grass on the prairie.

One more fagot of these adamantine bandages, is, the new
science of Statistics. It is a rule, that the most casual and extraordinary events—if the basis of population is broad
enough—become matter of fixed calculation. It would not be
safe to say when a captain like Bonaparte, a singer like Jenny
Lind, or a navigator like Bowditch, would be born in Boston:
but, on a population of twenty or two hundred millions,
something like accuracy may be had.*

'Tis frivolous to fix pedantically the date of particular inventions. They have all been invented over and over fifty
times. Man is the arch machine, of which all these shifts
drawn from himself are toy models. He helps himself on each
emergency by copying or duplicating his own structure, just
so far as the need is. 'Tis hard to find the right Homer,

---

*"Everything which pertains to the human species, considered as a whole,
belongs to the order of physical facts. The greater the number of individuals,
the more does the influence of the individual will disappear, leaving predominance to a series of general facts dependent on causes by which society exists,
and is preserved."—QUETELET.

Zoroaster, or Menu; harder still to find the Tubal Cain, or Vulcan, or Cadmus, or Copernicus, or Fust, or Fulton, the indisputable inventor. There are scores and centuries of them. "The air is full of men." This kind of talent so abounds, this constructive tool-making efficiency, as if it adhered to the chemic atoms, as if the air he breathes were made of Vaucansons, Franklins, and Watts.

Doubtless, in every million there will be an astronomer, a mathematician, a comic poet, a mystic. No one can read the history of astronomy, without perceiving that Copernicus, Newton, Laplace, are not new men, or a new kind of men, but that Thales, Anaximenes, Hipparchus, Empedocles, Aristarchus, Pythagoras, Œnopides, had anticipated them; each had the same tense geometrical brain, apt for the same vigorous computation and logic, a mind parallel to the movement of the world. The Roman mile probably rested on a measure of a degree of the meridian. Mahometan and Chinese know what we know of leap-year, of the Gregorian calendar, and of the precession of the equinoxes. As, in every barrel of cowries, brought to New Bedford, there shall be one *orangia*, so there will, in a dozen millions of Malays and Mahometans, be one or two astronomical skulls. In a large city, the most casual things, and things whose beauty lies in their casualty, are produced as punctually and to order as the baker's muffin for breakfast. Punch makes exactly one capital joke a week; and the journals contrive to furnish one good piece of news every day.

And not less work the laws of repression, the penalties of violated functions. Famine, typhus, frost, war, suicide, and effete races, must be reckoned calculable parts of the system of the world.

These are pebbles from the mountain, hints of the terms by which our life is walled up, and which show a kind of mechanical exactness, as of a loom or mill, in what we call casual or fortuitous events.

The force with which we resist these torrents of tendency looks so ridiculously inadequate, that it amounts to little more than a criticism or a protest made by a minority of one, under compulsion of millions. I seemed, in the height of a tempest, to see men overboard struggling in the waves, and

driven about here and there. They glanced intelligently at
each other, but 'twas little they could do for one another;
'twas much if each could keep afloat alone. Well, they had a
right to their eye-beams, and all the rest was Fate.

We cannot trifle with this reality, this cropping-out in our
planted gardens of the core of the world. No picture of life
can have any veracity that does not admit the odious facts. A
man's power is hooped in by a necessity, which, by many
experiments, he touches on every side, until he learns its arc.

The element running through entire nature, which we popularly call Fate, is known to us as limitation. Whatever limits
us, we call Fate. If we are brute and barbarous, the fate takes
a brute and dreadful shape. As we refine, our checks become
finer. If we rise to spiritual culture, the antagonism takes a
spiritual form. In the Hindoo fables, Vishnu follows Maya
through all her ascending changes, from insect and crawfish
up to elephant; whatever form she took, he took the male
form of that kind, until she became at last woman and goddess, and he a man and a god. The limitations refine as the
soul purifies, but the ring of necessity is always perched at
the top.

When the gods in the Norse heaven were unable to bind
the Fenris Wolf with steel or with weight of mountains,—the
one he snapped and the other he spurned with his heel,—
they put round his foot a limp band softer than silk or cobweb, and this held him: the more he spurned it, the stiffer it
drew. So soft and so stanch is the ring of Fate. Neither
brandy, nor nectar, nor sulphuric ether, nor hell-fire, nor
ichor, nor poetry, nor genius, can get rid of this limp band.
For if we give it the high sense in which the poets use it, even
thought itself is not above Fate: that too must act according
to eternal laws, and all that is wilful and fantastic in it is in
opposition to its fundamental essence.

And, last of all, high over thought, in the world of morals,
Fate appears as vindicator, levelling the high, lifting the low,
requiring justice in man, and always striking soon or late,
when justice is not done. What is useful will last; what is
hurtful will sink. "The doer must suffer," said the Greeks:
"you would soothe a Deity not to be soothed." "God himself

cannot procure good for the wicked," said the Welsh triad. "God may consent, but only for a time," said the bard of Spain. The limitation is impassable by any insight of man. In its last and loftiest ascensions, insight itself, and the freedom of the will, is one of its obedient members. But we must not run into generalizations too large, but show the natural bounds or essential distinctions, and seek to do justice to the other elements as well.

Thus we trace Fate, in matter, mind, and morals,—in race, in retardations of strata, and in thought and character as well. It is everywhere bound or limitation. But Fate has its lord; limitation its limits; is different seen from above and from below; from within and from without. For, though Fate is immense, so is power, which is the other fact in the dual world, immense. If Fate follows and limits power, power attends and antagonizes Fate. We must respect Fate as natural history, but there is more than natural history. For who and what is this criticism that pries into the matter? Man is not order of nature, sack and sack, belly and members, link in a chain, nor any ignominious baggage, but a stupendous antagonism, a dragging together of the poles of the Universe. He betrays his relation to what is below him,—thick-skulled, small-brained, fishy, quadrumanous,—quadruped ill-disguised, hardly escaped into biped, and has paid for the new powers by loss of some of the old ones. But the lightning which explodes and fashions planets, maker of planets and suns, is in him. On one side, elemental order, sandstone and granite, rock-ledges, peat-bog, forest, sea and shore; and, on the other part, thought, the spirit which composes and decomposes nature,—here they are, side by side, god and devil, mind and matter, king and conspirator, belt and spasm, riding peacefully together in the eye and brain of every man.

Nor can he blink the freewill. To hazard the contradiction,—freedom is necessary. If you please to plant yourself on the side of Fate, and say, Fate is all; then we say, a part of Fate is the freedom of man. Forever wells up the impulse of choosing and acting in the soul. Intellect annuls Fate. So far as a man thinks, he is free. And though nothing is more disgusting than the crowing about liberty by slaves, as most men are, and the flippant mistaking for freedom of some paper preamble like a "Declaration of Independence," or the statute right to vote, by those who have never dared to think or to act, yet it is wholesome to man to look not at Fate, but the other way: the practical view is the other. His sound relation to these facts is to use and command, not to cringe to them. "Look not on nature, for her name is fatal," said the oracle. The too much contemplation of these limits induces meanness. They who talk much of destiny, their birth-star, &c., are in a lower dangerous plane, and invite the evils they fear.

I cited the instinctive and heroic races as proud believers in Destiny. They conspire with it; a loving resignation is with the event. But the dogma makes a different impression, when it is held by the weak and lazy. 'Tis weak and vicious people who cast the blame on Fate. The right use of Fate is to bring up our conduct to the loftiness of nature. Rude and invincible except by themselves are the elements. So let man be. Let him empty his breast of his windy conceits, and show his lordship by manners and deeds on the scale of nature. Let him hold his purpose as with the tug of gravitation. No power, no persuasion, no bribe shall make him give up his point. A man ought to compare advantageously with a river, an oak, or a mountain. He shall have not less the flow, the expansion, and the resistance of these.

'Tis the best use of Fate to teach a fatal courage. Go face the fire at sea, or the cholera in your friend's house, or the burglar in your own, or what danger lies in the way of duty, knowing you are guarded by the cherubim of Destiny. If you believe in Fate to your harm, believe it, at least, for your good.

For, if Fate is so prevailing, man also is part of it, and can confront fate with fate. If the Universe have these savage accidents, our atoms are as savage in resistance. We should be crushed by the atmosphere, but for the reaction of the air within the body. A tube made of a film of glass can resist the shock of the ocean, if filled with the same water. If there be omnipotence in the stroke, there is omnipotence of recoil.

1. But Fate against Fate is only parrying and defence: there are, also, the noble creative forces. The revelation of Thought

takes man out of servitude into freedom. We rightl
ourselves, we were born, and afterward we were bor
and many times. We have successive experiences so important, that the new forgets the old, and hence the mythology
of the seven or the nine heavens. The day of days, the great
day of the feast of life, is that in which the inward eye
opens to the Unity in things, to the omnipresence of
law;—sees that what is must be, and ought to be, or is the
best. This beatitude dips from on high down on us, and we
see. It is not in us so much as we are in it. If the air come
to our lungs, we breathe and live; if not, we die. If the
light come to our eyes, we see; else not. And if truth come
to our mind, we suddenly expand to its dimensions, as if
we grew to worlds. We are as lawgivers; we speak for Nature; we prophesy and divine.

This insight throws us on the party and interest of the Universe, against all and sundry; against ourselves, as much as
others. A man speaking from insight affirms of himself what
is true of the mind: seeing its immortality, he says, I am immortal; seeing its invincibility, he says, I am strong. It is not
in us, but we are in it. It is of the maker, not of what is made.
All things are touched and changed by it. This uses, and is
not used. It distances those who share it, from those who
share it not. Those who share it not are flocks and herds. It
dates from itself;—not from former men or better men,—
gospel, or constitution, or college, or custom. Where it
shines, Nature is no longer intrusive, but all things make a
musical or pictorial impression. The world of men show like
a comedy without laughter:—populations, interests, government, history;—'tis all toy figures in a toy house. It does not
overvalue particular truths. We hear eagerly every thought
and word quoted from an intellectual man. But, in his presence, our own mind is roused to activity, and we forget very
fast what he says, much more interested in the new play of
our own thought, than in any thought of his. 'Tis the majesty
into which we have suddenly mounted, the impersonality, the
scorn of egotisms, the sphere of laws, that engage us. Once
we were stepping a little this way, and a little that way; now,
we are as men in a balloon, and do not think so much of the

point we have left, or the point we would make, as of the liberty and glory of the way.

Just as much intellect as you add, so much organic power. He who sees through the design, presides over it, and must will that which must be. We sit and rule, and, though we sleep, our dream will come to pass. Our thought, though it were only an hour old, affirms an oldest necessity, not to be separated from thought, and not to be separated from will. They must always have coëxisted. It apprises us of its sovereignty and godhead, which refuse to be severed from it. It is not mine or thine, but the will of all mind. It is poured into the souls of all men, as the soul itself which constitutes them men. I know not whether there be, as is alleged, in the upper region of our atmosphere, a permanent westerly current, which carries with it all atoms which rise to that height, but I see, that when souls reach a certain clearness of perception, they accept a knowledge and motive above selfishness. A breath of will blows eternally through the universe of souls in the direction of the Right and Necessary. It is the air which all intellects inhale and exhale, and it is the wind which blows the worlds into order and orbit.

Thought dissolves the material universe, by carrying the mind up into a sphere where all is plastic. Of two men, each obeying his own thought, he whose thought is deepest will be the strongest character. Always one man more than another represents the will of Divine Providence to the period.

2. If thought makes free, so does the moral sentiment. The mixtures of spiritual chemistry refuse to be analyzed. Yet we can see that with the perception of truth is joined the desire that it shall prevail. That affection is essential to will. Moreover, when a strong will appears, it usually results from a certain unity of organization, as if the whole energy of body and mind flowed in one direction. All great force is real and elemental. There is no manufacturing a strong will. There must be a pound to balance a pound. Where power is shown in will, it must rest on the universal force. Alaric and Bonaparte must believe they rest on a truth, or their will can be bought or bent. There is a bribe possible for any finite will. But the pure sympathy with universal ends is an infinite force, and cannot be bribed or bent. Whoever has had ex-

perience of the moral sentiment cannot choose but believe in unlimited power. Each pulse from that heart is an oath from the Most High. I know not what the word *sublime* means, if it be not the intimations in this infant of a terrific force. A text of heroism, a name and anecdote of courage, are not arguments, but sallies of freedom. One of these is the verse of the Persian Hafiz, " 'Tis written on the gate of Heaven, 'Wo unto him who suffers himself to be betrayed by Fate!' " Does the reading of history make us fatalists? What courage does not the opposite opinion show! A little whim of will to be free gallantly contending against the universe of chemistry.

But insight is not will, nor is affection will. Perception is cold, and goodness dies in wishes; as Voltaire said, 'tis the misfortune of worthy people that they are cowards; *"un des plus grands malheurs des honnêtes gens c'est qu'ils sont des lâches."* There must be a fusion of these two to generate the energy of will. There can be no driving force, except through the conversion of the man into his will, making him the will, and the will him. And one may say boldly, that no man has a right perception of any truth, who has not been reacted on by it, so as to be ready to be its martyr.

The one serious and formidable thing in nature is a will. Society is servile from want of will, and therefore the world wants saviours and religions. One way is right to go: the hero sees it, and moves on that aim, and has the world under him for root and support. He is to others as the world. His approbation is honor; his dissent, infamy. The glance of his eye has the force of sunbeams. A personal influence towers up in memory only worthy, and we gladly forget numbers, money, climate, gravitation, and the rest of Fate.

We can afford to allow the limitation, if we know it is the meter of the growing man. We stand against Fate, as children stand up against the wall in their father's house, and notch their height from year to year. But when the boy grows to man, and is master of the house, he pulls down that wall, and builds a new and bigger. 'Tis only a question of time. Every brave youth is in training to ride and rule this dragon. His science is to make weapons and wings of these passions and retarding forces. Now whether, seeing these two things, fate and power, we are permitted to believe in unity? The bulk of mankind believe in two gods. They are under one dominion here in the house, as friend and parent, in social circles, in letters, in art, in love, in religion: but in mechanics, in dealing with steam and climate, in trade, in politics, they think they come under another; and that it would be a practical blunder to transfer the method and way of working of one sphere, into the other. What good, honest, generous men at home, will be wolves and foxes on change! What pious men in the parlor will vote for what reprobates at the polls! To a certain point, they believe themselves the care of a Providence. But, in a steamboat, in an epidemic, in war, they believe a malignant energy rules.

But relation and connection are not somewhere and sometimes, but everywhere and always. The divine order does not stop where their sight stops. The friendly power works on the same rules, in the next farm, and the next planet. But, where they have not experience, they run against it, and hurt themselves. Fate, then, is a name for facts not yet passed under the fire of thought;—for causes which are unpenetrated.

But every jet of chaos which threatens to exterminate us, is convertible by intellect into wholesome force. Fate is unpenetrated causes. The water drowns ship and sailor, like a grain of dust. But learn to swim, trim your bark, and the wave which drowned it, will be cloven by it, and carry it, like its own foam, a plume and a power. The cold is inconsiderate of persons, tingles your blood, freezes a man like a dew-drop. But learn to skate, and the ice will give you a graceful, sweet, and poetic motion. The cold will brace your limbs and brain to genius, and make you foremost men of time. Cold and sea will train an imperial Saxon race, which nature cannot bear to lose, and, after cooping it up for a thousand years in yonder England, gives a hundred Englands, a hundred Mexicos. All the bloods it shall absorb and domineer: and more than Mexicos,—the secrets of water and steam, the spasms of electricity, the ductility of metals, the chariot of the air, the ruddered balloon are awaiting you.

The annual slaughter from typhus far exceeds that of war; but right drainage destroys typhus. The plague in the sea-service from scurvy is healed by lemon juice and other diets portable or procurable: the depopulation by cholera and small-pox is ended by drainage and vaccination; and every other pest is not less in the chain of cause and effect, and may be fought off. And, whilst art draws out the venom, it commonly extorts some benefit from the vanquished enemy. The mischievous torrent is taught to drudge for man: the wild beasts he makes useful for food, or dress, or labor; the chemic explosions are controlled like his watch. These are now the steeds on which he rides. Man moves in all modes, by legs of horses, by wings of wind, by steam, by gas of balloon, by electricity, and stands on tiptoe threatening to hunt the eagle in his own element. There's nothing he will not make his carrier.

Steam was, till the other day, the devil which we dreaded. Every pot made by any human potter or brazier had a hole in its cover, to let off the enemy, lest he should lift pot and roof, and carry the house away. But the Marquis of Worcester, Watt, and Fulton bethought themselves, that, where was power, was not devil, but was God; that it must be availed of, and not by any means let off and wasted. Could he lift pots and roofs and houses so handily? he was the workman they were in search of. He could be used to lift away, chain, and compel other devils, far more reluctant and dangerous, namely, cubic miles of earth, mountains, weight or resistance of water, machinery, and the labors of all men in the world; and time he shall lengthen, and shorten space.

It has not fared much otherwise with higher kinds of steam. The opinion of the million was the terror of the world, and it was attempted, either to dissipate it, by amusing nations, or to pile it over with strata of society,—a layer of soldiers; over that, a layer of lords; and a king on the top; with clamps and hoops of castles, garrisons, and police. But, sometimes, the religious principle would get in, and burst the hoops, and rive every mountain laid on top of it. The Fultons and Watts of politics, believing in unity, saw that it was a power, and, by satisfying it, (as justice satisfies everybody,) through a different disposition of society,—grouping it on a level, instead of piling it into a mountain,—they have contrived to make of his terror the most harmless and energetic form of a State.

Very odious, I confess, are the lessons of Fate. Who likes to have a dapper phrenologist pronouncing on his fortunes? Who likes to believe that he has hidden in his skull, spine, and pelvis, all the vices of a Saxon or Celtic race, which will be sure to pull him down,—with what grandeur of hope and resolve he is fired,—into a selfish, huckstering, servile, dodging animal? A learned physician tells us, the fact is invariable with the Neapolitan, that, when mature, he assumes the forms of the unmistakable scoundrel. That is a little overstated,—but may pass.

But these are magazines and arsenals. A man must thank his defects, and stand in some terror of his talents. A transcendent talent draws so largely on his forces, as to lame him; a defect pays him revenues on the other side. The sufferance, which is the badge of the Jew, has made him, in these days, the ruler of the rulers of the earth. If Fate is ore and quarry, if evil is good in the making, if limitation is power that shall be, if calamities, oppositions, and weights are wings and means,—we are reconciled.

Fate involves the melioration. No statement of the Universe can have any soundness, which does not admit its ascending effort. The direction of the whole, and of the parts, is toward benefit, and in proportion to the health. Behind every individual, closes organization: before him, opens liberty,—the Better, the Best. The first and worst races are dead. The second and imperfect races are dying out, or remain for the maturing of higher. In the latest race, in man, every generosity, every new perception, the love and praise he extorts from his fellows, are certificates of advance out of fate into freedom. Liberation of the will from the sheaths and clogs of organization which he has outgrown, is the end and aim of this world. Every calamity is a spur and valuable hint; and where his endeavors do not yet fully avail, they tell as tendency. The whole circle of animal life,—tooth against tooth,—devouring war, war for food, a yelp of pain and a grunt of triumph, until, at last, the whole menagerie, the whole chemical mass is mellowed and refined for higher use,—pleases at a sufficient perspective.

But to see how fate slides into freedom, and freedom into fate, observe how far the roots of every creature run, or find, if you can, a point where there is no thread of connection. Our life is consentaneous and far-related. This knot of nature is so well tied, that nobody was ever cunning enough to find the two ends. Nature is intricate, overlapped, interweaved, and endless. Christopher Wren said of the beautiful King's College chapel, "that, if anybody would tell him where to lay the first stone, he would build such another." But where shall we find the first atom in this house of man, which is all consent, inosculation, and balance of parts?

The web of relation is shown in *habitat*, shown in hybernation. When hybernation was observed, it was found, that, whilst some animals became torpid in winter, others were torpid in summer: hybernation then was a false name. The *long sleep* is not an effect of cold, but is regulated by the supply of food proper to the animal. It becomes torpid when the fruit or prey it lives on is not in season, and regains its activity when its food is ready.

Eyes are found in light; ears in auricular air; feet on land; fins in water; wings in air; and, each creature where it was meant to be, with a mutual fitness. Every zone has its own *Fauna*. There is adjustment between the animal and its food, its parasite, its enemy. Balances are kept. It is not allowed to diminish in numbers, nor to exceed. The like adjustments exist for man. His food is cooked, when he arrives; his coal in the pit; the house ventilated; the mud of the deluge dried; his companions arrived at the same hour, and awaiting him with love, concert, laughter, and tears. These are coarse adjustments, but the invisible are not less. There are more belongings to every creature than his air and his food. His instincts must be met, and he has predisposing power that bends and fits what is near him to his use. He is not possible until the invisible things are right for him, as well as the visible. Of what changes, then, in sky and earth, and in finer skies and earths, does the appearance of some Dante or Columbus apprise us!

How is this effected? Nature is no spendthrift, but takes

the shortest way to her ends. As the general says to his soldiers, "if you want a fort, build a fort," so nature makes every creature do its own work and get its living,—is it planet, animal, or tree. The planet makes itself. The animal cell makes itself;—then, what it wants. Every creature,—wren or dragon,—shall make its own lair. As soon as there is life, there is self-direction, and absorbing and using of material. Life is freedom,—life in the direct ratio of its amount. You may be sure, the new-born man is not inert. Life works both voluntarily and supernaturally in its neighborhood. Do you suppose, he can be estimated by his weight in pounds, or, that he is contained in his skin,—this reaching, radiating, jaculating fellow? The smallest candle fills a mile with its rays, and the papillæ of a man run out to every star.

When there is something to be done, the world knows how to get it done. The vegetable eye makes leaf, pericarp, root, bark, or thorn, as the need is; the first cell converts itself into stomach, mouth, nose, or nail, according to the want: the world throws its life into a hero or a shepherd; and puts him where he is wanted. Dante and Columbus were Italians, in their time: they would be Russians or Americans to-day. Things ripen, new men come. The adaptation is not capricious. The ulterior aim, the purpose beyond itself, the correlation by which planets subside and crystallize, then animate beasts and men, will not stop, but will work into finer particulars, and from finer to finest.

The secret of the world is, the tie between person and event. Person makes event, and event person. The "times," "the age," what is that, but a few profound persons and a few active persons who epitomize the times?—Goethe, Hegel, Metternich, Adams, Calhoun, Guizot, Peel, Cobden, Kossuth, Rothschild, Astor, Brunel, and the rest. The same fitness must be presumed between a man and the time and event, as between the sexes, or between a race of animals and the food it eats, or the inferior races it uses. He thinks his fate alien, because the copula is hidden. But the soul contains the event that shall befall it, for the event is only the actualization of its thoughts; and what we pray to ourselves for is always granted. The event is the print of your form. It fits you like your skin. What each does is proper to him. Events are the children of his body and mind. We learn that the soul of Fate is the soul of us, as Hafiz sings,

> Alas! till now I had not known,
> My guide and fortune's guide are one.

All the toys that infatuate men, and which they play for,—houses, land, money, luxury, power, fame, are the selfsame thing, with a new gauze or two of illusion overlaid. And of all the drums and rattles by which men are made willing to have their heads broke, and are led out solemnly every morning to parade,—the most admirable is this by which we are brought to believe that events are arbitrary, and independent of actions. At the conjuror's, we detect the hair by which he moves his puppet, but we have not eyes sharp enough to descry the thread that ties cause and effect.

Nature magically suits the man to his fortunes, by making these the fruit of his character. Ducks take to the water, eagles to the sky, waders to the sea margin, hunters to the forest, clerks to counting-rooms, soldiers to the frontier. Thus events grow on the same stem with persons; are sub-persons. The pleasure of life is according to the man that lives it, and not according to the work or the place. Life is an ecstasy. We know what madness belongs to love,—what power to paint a vile object in hues of heaven. As insane persons are indifferent to their dress, diet, and other accommodations, and, as we do in dreams, with equanimity, the most absurd acts, so, a drop more of wine in our cup of life will reconcile us to strange company and work. Each creature puts forth from itself its own condition and sphere, as the slug sweats out its slimy house on the pear-leaf, and the woolly aphides on the apple perspire their own bed, and the fish its shell. In youth, we clothe ourselves with rainbows, and go as brave as the zodiac. In age, we put out another sort of perspiration,—gout, fever, rheumatism, caprice, doubt, fretting, and avarice.

A man's fortunes are the fruit of his character. A man's friends are his magnetisms. We go to Herodotus and Plutarch for examples of Fate; but we are examples. "*Quisque suos patimur manes.*" The tendency of every man to enact all that is in his constitution is expressed in the old belief, that the efforts which we make to escape from our destiny only serve to lead us into it: and I have noticed, a man likes better to be complimented on his position, as the proof of the last or total excellence, than on his merits.

A man will see his character emitted in the events that seem to meet, but which exude from and accompany him. Events expand with the character. As once he found himself among toys, so now he plays a part in colossal systems, and his growth is declared in his ambition, his companions, and his performance. He looks like a piece of luck, but is a piece of causation;—the mosaic, angulated and ground to fit into the gap he fills. Hence in each town there is some man who is, in his brain and performance, an explanation of the tillage, production, factories, banks, churches, ways of living, and society, of that town. If you do not chance to meet him, all that you see will leave you a little puzzled: if you see him, it will become plain. We know in Massachusetts who built New Bedford, who built Lynn, Lowell, Lawrence, Clinton, Fitchburg, Holyoke, Portland, and many another noisy mart. Each of these men, if they were transparent, would seem to you not so much men, as walking cities, and, wherever you put them, they would build one.

History is the action and reaction of these two,—Nature and Thought;—two boys pushing each other on the curbstone of the pavement. Everything is pusher or pushed: and matter and mind are in perpetual tilt and balance, so. Whilst the man is weak, the earth takes up him. He plants his brain and affections. By and by he will take up the earth, and have his gardens and vineyards in the beautiful order and productiveness of his thought. Every solid in the universe is ready to become fluid on the approach of the mind, and the power to flux it is the measure of the mind. If the wall remain adamant, it accuses the want of thought. To a subtler force, it will stream into new forms, expressive of the character of the mind. What is the city in which we sit here, but an aggregate of incongruous materials, which have obeyed the will of some man? The granite was reluctant, but his hands were stronger, and it came. Iron was deep in the ground, and well combined with stone; but could not hide from his fires. Wood, lime, stuffs, fruits, gums, were dispersed over the earth and sea, in

vain. Here they are, within reach of every man's day-labor,—
what he wants of them. The whole world is the flux of matter
over the wires of thought to the poles or points where it
would build. The races of men rise out of the ground preoccupied with a thought which rules them, and divided into
parties ready armed and angry to fight for this metaphysical
abstraction. The quality of the thought differences the Egyptian and the Roman, the Austrian and the American. The
men who come on the stage at one period are all found to be
related to each other. Certain ideas are in the air. We are all
impressionable, for we are made of them; all impressionable,
but some more than others, and these first express them. This
explains the curious contemporaneousness of inventions and
discoveries. The truth is in the air, and the most impressionable brain will announce it first, but all will announce it a few
minutes later. So women, as most susceptible, are the best
index of the coming hour. So the great man, that is, the man
most imbued with the spirit of the time, is the impressionable
man,—of a fibre irritable and delicate, like iodine to light. He
feels the infinitesimal attractions. His mind is righter than
others, because he yields to a current so feeble as can be felt
only by a needle delicately poised.

The correlation is shown in defects. Möller, in his Essay on
Architecture, taught that the building which was fitted accurately to answer its end, would turn out to be beautiful,
though beauty had not been intended. I find the like unity in
human structures rather virulent and pervasive; that a crudity
in the blood will appear in the argument; a hump in the
shoulder will appear in the speech and handiwork. If his mind
could be seen, the hump would be seen. If a man has a seesaw
in his voice, it will run into his sentences, into his poem, into
the structure of his fable, into his speculation, into his charity.
And, as every man is hunted by his own dæmon, vexed by his
own disease, this checks all his activity.

So each man, like each plant, has his parasites. A strong,
astringent, bilious nature has more truculent enemies than the
slugs and moths that fret my leaves. Such an one has curcu-
lios, borers, knife-worms: a swindler ate him first, then a
client, then a quack, then smooth, plausible gentlemen, bitter
and selfish as Moloch.

This correlation really existing can be divined. If the threads are there, thought can follow and show them. Especially when a soul is quick and docile; as Chaucer sings,

> "Or if the soul of proper kind
>   Be so perfect as men find,
>   That it wot what is to come,
>   And that he warneth all and some
>   Of every of their aventures,
>   By previsions or figures;
>   But that our flesh hath not might
>   It to understand aright
>   For it is warned too darkly."—

Some people are made up of rhyme, coincidence, omen, periodicity, and presage: they meet the person they seek; what their companion prepares to say to them, they first say to him; and a hundred signs apprise them of what is about to befall.

Wonderful intricacy in the web, wonderful constancy in the design this vagabond life admits. We wonder how the fly finds its mate, and yet year after year we find two men, two women, without legal or carnal tie, spend a great part of their best time within a few feet of each other. And the moral is, that what we seek we shall find; what we flee from flees from us; as Goethe said, "what we wish for in youth, comes in heaps on us in old age," too often cursed with the granting of our prayer: and hence the high caution, that, since we are sure of having what we wish, we beware to ask only for high things.

One key, one solution to the mysteries of human condition, one solution to the old knots of fate, freedom, and foreknowledge, exists, the propounding, namely, of the double consciousness. A man must ride alternately on the horses of his private and his public nature, as the equestrians in the circus throw themselves nimbly from horse to horse, or plant one foot on the back of one, and the other foot on the back of the other. So when a man is the victim of his fate, has sciatica in his loins, and cramp in his mind; a club-foot and a club in his wit; a sour face, and a selfish temper; a strut in his gait, and a conceit in his affection; or is ground to powder by the vice of his race; he is to rally on his relation to the Universe, which his ruin benefits. Leaving the dæmon who suffers, he is to take sides with the Deity who secures universal benefit by his pain.

To offset the drag of temperament and race, which pulls down, learn this lesson, namely, that by the cunning co-presence of two elements, which is throughout nature, whatever lames or paralyzes you, draws in with it the divinity, in some form, to repay. A good intention clothes itself with sudden power. When a god wishes to ride, any chip or pebble will bud and shoot out winged feet, and serve him for a horse.

Let us build altars to the Blessed Unity which holds nature and souls in perfect solution, and compels every atom to serve an universal end. I do not wonder at a snow-flake, a shell, a summer landscape, or the glory of the stars; but at the necessity of beauty under which the universe lies; that all is and must be pictorial; that the rainbow, and the curve of the horizon, and the arch of the blue vault are only results from the organism of the eye. There is no need for foolish amateurs to fetch me to admire a garden of flowers, or a sun-gilt cloud, or a waterfall, when I cannot look without seeing splendor and grace. How idle to choose a random sparkle here or there, when the indwelling necessity plants the rose of beauty on the brow of chaos, and discloses the central intention of Nature to be harmony and joy.

Let us build altars to the Beautiful Necessity. If we thought men were free in the sense, that, in a single exception one fantastical will could prevail over the law of things, it were all one as if a child's hand could pull down the sun. If, in the least particular, one could derange the order of nature,—who would accept the gift of life?

Let us build altars to the Beautiful Necessity, which secures that all is made of one piece; that plaintiff and defendant, friend and enemy, animal and planet, food and eater, are of one kind. In astronomy, is vast space, but no foreign system; in geology, vast time, but the same laws as to-day. Why should we be afraid of Nature, which is no other than "philosophy and theology embodied"? Why should we fear to be crushed by savage elements, we who are made up of the same elements? Let us build to the Beautiful Necessity, which makes man brave in believing that he cannot shun a danger that is appointed, nor incur one that is not; to the Necessity which rudely or softly educates him to the perception that there are no contingencies; that Law rules throughout existence, a Law which is not intelligent but intelligence,—not personal nor impersonal,—it disdains words and passes understanding; it dissolves persons; it vivifies nature; yet solicits the pure in heart to draw on all its omnipotence.

II

POWER

———

His tongue was framed to music,
And his hand was armed with skill,
His face was the mould of beauty,
And his heart the throne of will.

Power

THERE is not yet any inventory of a man's faculties, any more than a bible of his opinions. Who shall set a limit to the influence of a human being? There are men, who, by their sympathetic attractions, carry nations with them, and lead the activity of the human race. And if there be such a tie, that, wherever the mind of man goes, nature will accompany him, perhaps there are men whose magnetisms are of that force to draw material and elemental powers, and, where they appear, immense instrumentalities organize around them. Life is a search after power; and this is an element with which the world is so saturated,—there is no chink or crevice in which it is not lodged,—that no honest seeking goes unrewarded. A man should prize events and possessions as the ore in which this fine mineral is found; and he can well afford to let events and possessions, and the breath of the body go, if their value has been added to him in the shape of power. If he have secured the elixir, he can spare the wide gardens from which it was distilled. A cultivated man, wise to know and bold to perform, is the end to which nature works, and the education of the will is the flowering and result of all this geology and astronomy.

All successful men have agreed in one thing,—they were *causationists*. They believed that things went not by luck, but by law; that there was not a weak or a cracked link in the chain that joins the first and last of things. A belief in causality, or strict connection between every trifle and the principle of being, and, in consequence, belief in compensation, or, that nothing is got for nothing,—characterizes all valuable minds, and must control every effort that is made by an industrious one. The most valiant men are the best believers in the tension of the laws. "All the great captains," said Bonaparte, "have performed vast achievements by conforming with the rules of the art,—by adjusting efforts to obstacles."

The key to the age may be this, or that, or the other, as the young orators describe;—the key to all ages is—Imbecility; imbecility in the vast majority of men, at all times, and, even in heroes, in all but certain eminent moments; victims of gravity, custom, and fear. This gives force to the strong,—that the multitude have no habit of self-reliance or original action.

We must reckon success a constitutional trait. Courage,—the old physicians taught, (and their meaning holds, if their physiology is a little mythical,)—courage, or the degree of life, is as the degree of circulation of the blood in the arteries. "During passion, anger, fury, trials of strength, wrestling, fighting, a large amount of blood is collected in the arteries, the maintenance of bodily strength requiring it, and but little is sent into the veins. This condition is constant with intrepid persons." Where the arteries hold their blood, is courage and adventure possible. Where they pour it unrestrained into the veins, the spirit is low and feeble. For performance of great mark, it needs extraordinary health. If Eric is in robust health, and has slept well, and is at the top of his condition, and thirty years old, at his departure from Greenland, he will steer west, and his ships will reach Newfoundland. But take out Eric, and put in a stronger and bolder man,—Biorn, or Thorfin,—and the ships will, with just as much ease, sail six hundred, one thousand, fifteen hundred miles further, and reach Labrador and New England. There is no chance in results. With adults, as with children, one class enter cordially into the game, and whirl with the whirling world; the others have cold hands, and remain bystanders; or are only dragged in by the humor and vivacity of those who can carry a dead weight. The first wealth is health. Sickness is poor-spirited, and cannot serve any one: it must husband its resources to live. But health or fulness answers its own ends, and has to spare, runs over, and inundates the neighborhoods and creeks of other men's necessities.

All power is of one kind, a sharing of the nature of the world. The mind that is parallel with the laws of nature will be in the current of events, and strong with their strength. One man is made of the same stuff of which events are made; is in sympathy with the course of things; can predict it. Whatever befalls, befalls him first; so that he is equal to whatever shall happen. A man who knows men, can talk well on politics, trade, law, war, religion. For, everywhere, men are led in the same manners.

The advantage of a strong pulse is not to be supplied by any labor, art, or concert. It is like the climate, which easily rears a crop, which no glass, or irrigation, or tillage, or manures, can elsewhere rival. It is like the opportunity of a city like New York, or Constantinople, which needs no diplomacy to force capital or genius or labor to it. They come of themselves, as the waters flow to it. So a broad, healthy, massive understanding seems to lie on the shore of unseen rivers, of unseen oceans, which are covered with barks, that, night and day, are drifted to this point. That is poured into its lap, which other men lie plotting for. It is in everybody's secret; anticipates everybody's discovery; and if it do not command every fact of the genius and the scholar, it is because it is large and sluggish, and does not think them worth the exertion which you do.

This affirmative force is in one, and is not in another, as one horse has the spring in him, and another in the whip. "On the neck of the young man," said Hafiz, "sparkles no gem so gracious as enterprise." Import into any stationary district, as into an old Dutch population in New York or Pennsylvania, or among the planters of Virginia, a colony of hardy Yankees, with seething brains, heads full of steam-hammer, pulley, crank, and toothed wheel,—and everything begins to shine with values. What enhancement to all the water and land in England, is the arrival of James Watt or Brunel! In every company, there is not only the active and passive sex, but, in both men and women, a deeper and more important *sex of mind*, namely, the inventive or creative class of both men and women, and the uninventive or accepting class. Each *plus* man represents his set, and, if he have the accidental advantage of personal ascendency,—which implies neither more nor less of talent, but merely the temperamental or taming eye of a soldier or a schoolmaster, (which one has, and one has not, as one has a black moustache and one a blond,) then quite easily and without envy or resistance, all his coadjutors and feeders will admit his right to absorb them. The merchant works by book-keeper and cashier; the lawyer's authorities are hunted up by clerks; the geologist reports the surveys of his subalterns; Commander Wilkes appropriates the results of all the naturalists attached to the Expedition; Thorwaldsen's statue is finished by stone-cutters; Dumas has journeymen; and Shakspeare was theatre-manager, and used the labor of many young men, as well as the playbooks.

There is always room for a man of force, and he makes room for many. Society is a troop of thinkers, and the best heads among them take the best places. A feeble man can see the farms that are fenced and tilled, the houses that are built. The strong man sees the possible houses and farms. His eye makes estates, as fast as the sun breeds clouds.

When a new boy comes into school, when a man travels, and encounters strangers every day, or, when into any old club a new comer is domesticated, that happens which befalls, when a strange ox is driven into a pen or pasture where cattle are kept; there is at once a trial of strength between the best pair of horns and the new comer, and it is settled thenceforth which is the leader. So now, there is a measuring of strength, very courteous, but decisive, and an acquiescence thenceforward when these two meet. Each reads his fate in the other's eyes. The weaker party finds, that none of his information or wit quite fits the occasion. He thought he knew this or that: he finds that he omitted to learn the end of it. Nothing that he knows will quite hit the mark, whilst all the rival's arrows are good, and well thrown. But if he knew all the facts in the encyclopædia, it would not help him: for this is an affair of presence of mind, of attitude, of aplomb: the opponent has the sun and wind, and, in every cast, the choice of weapon and mark; and, when he himself is matched with some other antagonist, his own shafts fly well and hit. 'Tis a question of stomach and constitution. The second man is as good as the first,—perhaps better; but has not stoutness or stomach, as the first has, and so his wit seems over-fine or under-fine.

Health is good,—power, life, that resists disease, poison, and all enemies, and is conservative, as well as creative. Here is question, every spring, whether to graft with wax, or whether with clay; whether to whitewash or to potash, or to prune; but the one point is the thrifty tree. A good tree, that agrees with the soil, will grow in spite of blight, or bug, or pruning, or neglect, by night and by day, in all weathers and all treatments. Vivacity, leadership, must be had, and we are not allowed to be nice in choosing. We must fetch the pump with dirty water, if clean cannot be had. If we will make bread, we must have contagion, yeast, emptyings, or what not, to induce fermentation into the dough: as the torpid artist seeks inspiration at any cost, by virtue or by vice, by friend or by fiend, by prayer or by wine. And we have a certain instinct, that where is great amount of life, though gross and peccant, it has its own checks and purifications, and will be found at last in harmony with moral laws.

We watch in children with pathetic interest, the degree in which they possess recuperative force. When they are hurt by us, or by each other, or go to the bottom of the class, or miss the annual prizes, or are beaten in the game,—if they lose heart, and remember the mischance in their chamber at home, they have a serious check. But if they have the buoyancy and resistance that preoccupies them with new interest in the new moment,—the wounds cicatrize, and the fibre is the tougher for the hurt.

One comes to value this *plus* health, when he sees that all difficulties vanish before it. A timid man listening to the alarmists in Congress, and in the newspapers, and observing the profligacy of party,—sectional interests urged with a fury which shuts its eyes to consequences, with a mind made up to desperate extremities, ballot in one hand, and rifle in the other,—might easily believe that he and his country have seen their best days, and he hardens himself the best he can against the coming ruin. But, after this has been foretold with equal confidence fifty times, and government six per cents have not declined a quarter of a mill, he discovers that the enormous elements of strength which are here in play, make our politics unimportant. Personal power, freedom, and the resources of nature strain every faculty of every citizen. We prosper with such vigor, that, like thrifty trees, which grow in spite of ice, lice, mice, and borers, so we do not suffer from the profligate swarms that fatten on the national treasury. The huge animals nourish huge parasites, and the rancor of the disease attests the strength of the constitution. The same energy in the Greek *Demos* drew the remark, that the evils of popular government appear greater than they are; there is compensation for them in the spirit and energy it awakens. The rough and ready style which belongs to a people of sailors, foresters, farmers, and mechanics, has its advantages. Power educates the potentate. As long as our people quote English standards they dwarf their own proportions. A Western lawyer of eminence said to me he wished it were a penal offence to bring an English law-book into a court in this country, so pernicious had he found in his experience our deference to English precedent. The very word 'commerce' has only an English meaning, and is pinched to the cramp exigencies of English experience. The commerce of rivers, the commerce of railroads, and who knows but the commerce of air-balloons, must add an American extension to the pond-hole of admiralty. As long as our people quote English standards, they will miss the sovereignty of power; but let these rough riders,—legislators in shirt-sleeves,—Hoosier, Sucker, Wolverine, Badger,—or whatever hard head Arkansas, Oregon, or Utah sends,—half orator, half assassin, to represent its wrath and cupidity at Washington,—let these drive as they may; and the disposition of territories and public lands, the necessity of balancing and keeping at bay the snarling majorities of German, Irish, and of native millions, will bestow promptness, address, and reason, at last, on our buffalo-hunter, and authority and majesty of manners. The instinct of the people is right. Men expect from good whigs, put into office by the respectability of the country, much less skill to deal with Mexico, Spain, Britain, or with our own malcontent members, than from some strong transgressor, like Jefferson, or Jackson, who first conquers his own government, and then uses the same genius to conquer the foreigner. The senators who dissented from Mr. Polk's Mexican war, were not those who knew better, but those who, from political position, could afford it; not Webster, but Benton and Calhoun.

This power, to be sure, is not clothed in satin. 'Tis the power of Lynch law, of soldiers and pirates; and it bullies the peaceable and loyal. But it brings its own antidote; and here is my point,—that all kinds of power usually emerge at the same time; good energy, and bad; power of mind, with physical health; the ecstasies of devotion, with the exasperations of debauchery. The same elements are always present, only sometimes these conspicuous, and sometimes those; what was yesterday foreground, being to-day background,—what was surface, playing now a not less effective part as basis. The longer the drought lasts, the more is the atmosphere surcharged with water. The faster the ball falls to the sun, the force to fly off is by so much augmented. And, in morals, wild liberty breeds iron conscience; natures with great impulses have great resources, and return from far. In politics, the sons of democrats will be whigs; whilst red republicanism, in the father, is a spasm of nature to engender an intolerable tyrant in the next age. On the other hand, conservatism, ever more timorous and narrow, disgusts the children, and drives them for a mouthful of fresh air into radicalism.

Those who have most of this coarse energy,—the 'bruisers,' who have run the gauntlet of caucus and tavern through the county or the state, have their own vices, but they have the good nature of strength and courage. Fierce and unscrupulous, they are usually frank and direct, and above falsehood. Our politics fall into bad hands, and churchmen and men of refinement, it seems agreed, are not fit persons to send to Congress. Politics is a deleterious profession, like some poisonous handicrafts. Men in power have no opinions, but may be had cheap for any opinion, for any purpose,—and if it be only a question between the most civil and the most forcible, I lean to the last. These Hoosiers and Suckers are really better than the snivelling opposition. Their wrath is at least of a bold and manly cast. They see, against the unanimous declarations of the people, how much crime the people will bear; they proceed from step to step, and they have calculated but too justly upon their Excellencies, the New England governors, and upon their Honors, the New England legislators. The messages of the governors and the resolutions of the legislatures, are a proverb for expressing a sham virtuous indignation, which, in the course of events, is sure to be belied.

In trade, also, this energy usually carries a trace of ferocity. Philanthropic and religious bodies do not commonly make their executive officers out of saints. The communities hitherto founded by Socialists,—the Jesuits, the Port-Royalists, the American communities at New Harmony, at Brook Farm, at Zoar, are only possible, by installing Judas as steward. The rest of the offices may be filled by good burgesses. The pious and charitable proprietor has a foreman not quite so pious and charitable. The most amiable of country gentlemen has a certain pleasure in the teeth of the bull-dog which guards his orchard. Of the Shaker society, it was formerly a sort of proverb in the country, that they always sent the devil to market. And in representations of the Deity, painting, poetry, and popular religion have ever drawn the wrath from Hell. It is an esoteric doctrine of society, that a little wickedness is good to make muscle; as if conscience were not good for hands and legs, as if poor decayed formalists of law and order cannot run like wild goats, wolves, and conies; that, as there is a use in medicine for poisons, so the world cannot move without rogues; that public spirit and the ready hand are as well found among the malignants. 'Tis not very rare, the coincidence of sharp private and political practice, with public spirit, and good neighborhood.

I knew a burly Boniface who for many years kept a public-house in one of our rural capitals. He was a knave whom the town could ill spare. He was a social, vascular creature, grasping and selfish. There was no crime which he did not or could not commit. But he made good friends of the selectmen, served them with his best chop, when they supped at his house, and also with his honor the Judge, he was very cordial, grasping his hand. He introduced all the fiends, male and female, into the town, and united in his person the functions of bully, incendiary, swindler, barkeeper, and burglar. He girdled the trees, and cut off the horses' tails of the temperance people, in the night. He led the 'rummies' and radicals in town-meeting with a speech. Meantime, he was civil, fat, and easy, in his house, and precisely the most public-spirited citizen. He was active in getting the roads repaired and planted with shade-trees; he subscribed for the fountains, the gas, and the telegraph; he introduced the new horse-rake, the new scraper, the baby-jumper, and what not, that Connecticut sends to the admiring citizens. He did this the easier, that the peddler stopped at his house, and paid his keeping, by setting up his new trap on the landlord's premises.

Whilst thus the energy for originating and executing work, deforms itself by excess, and so our axe chops off our own fingers,—this evil is not without remedy. All the elements whose aid man calls in, will sometimes become his masters, especially those of most subtle force. Shall he, then, renounce steam, fire, and electricity, or, shall he learn to deal with them? The rule for this whole class of agencies is,—all *plus* is good; only put it in the right place.

Men of this surcharge of arterial blood cannot live on nuts, herb-tea, and elegies; cannot read novels, and play whist; cannot satisfy all their wants at the Thursday Lecture, or the Boston Athenæum. They pine for adventure, and must go to Pike's Peak; had rather die by the hatchet of a Pawnee, than sit all day and every day at a counting-room desk. They are made for war, for the sea, for mining, hunting, and clearing; for hair-breadth adventures, huge risks, and the joy of eventful living. Some men cannot endure an hour of calm at sea. I remember a poor Malay cook, on board a Liverpool packet, who, when the wind blew a gale, could not contain his joy; "Blow!" he cried, "me do tell you, blow!" Their friends and governors must see that some vent for their explosive complexion is provided. The roisters who are destined for infamy at home, if sent to Mexico, will "cover you with glory," and come back heroes and generals. There are Oregons, Californias, and Exploring Expeditions enough appertaining to America, to find them in files to gnaw, and in crocodiles to eat. The young English are fine animals, full of blood, and when they have no wars to breathe their riotous valors in, they seek for travels as dangerous as war, diving into Maelstroms; swimming Hellesponts; wading up the snowy Himmaleh; hunting lion, rhinoceros, elephant, in South Africa; gypsying with Borrow in Spain and Algiers; riding alligators in South America with Waterton; utilizing Bedouin, Sheik, and Pacha, with Layard; yachting among the icebergs of Lancaster Sound; peeping into craters on the equator; or running on the creases of Malays in Borneo.

The excess of virility has the same importance in general history, as in private and industrial life. Strong race or strong individual rests at last on natural forces, which are best in the savage, who, like the beasts around him, is still in reception of the milk from the teats of Nature. Cut off the connection between any of our works, and this aboriginal source, and the work is shallow. The people lean on this, and the mob is not quite so bad an argument as we sometimes say, for it has this good side. "March without the people," said a French deputy from the tribune, "and you march into night: their instincts are a finger-pointing of Providence, always turned toward real benefit. But when you espouse an Orleans party, or a Bourbon, or a Montalembert party, or any other but an organic party, though you mean well, you have a personality instead of a principle, which will inevitably drag you into a corner."

The best anecdotes of this force are to be had from savage life, in explorers, soldiers, and buccaneers. But who cares for fallings-out of assassins, and fights of bears, or grindings of icebergs? Physical force has no value, where there is nothing else. Snow in snow-banks, fire in volcanoes and solfataras is cheap. The luxury of ice is in tropical countries, and midsummer days. The luxury of fire is, to have a little on our hearth: and of electricity, not volleys of the charged cloud, but the manageable stream on the battery-wires. So of spirit, or energy; the rests or remains of it in the civil and moral man, are worth all the cannibals in the Pacific.

In history, the great moment is, when the savage is just ceasing to be a savage, with all his hairy Pelasgic strength directed on his opening sense of beauty:—and you have Pericles and Phidias,—not yet passed over into the Corinthian civility. Everything good in nature and the world is in that moment of transition, when the swarthy juices still flow plentifully from nature, but their astringency or acridity is got out by ethics and humanity.

The triumphs of peace have been in some proximity to war. Whilst the hand was still familiar with the sword-hilt, whilst the habits of the camp were still visible in the port and complexion of the gentleman, his intellectual power culminated: the compression and tension of these stern conditions is a training for the finest and softest arts, and can rarely be compensated in tranquil times, except by some analogous vigor drawn from occupations as hardy as war.

We say that success is constitutional; depends on a *plus* condition of mind and body, on power of work, on courage; that it is of main efficacy in carrying on the world, and, though rarely found in the right state for an article of commerce, but oftener in the supersaturate or excess, which makes it dangerous and destructive, yet it cannot be spared, and must be had in that form, and absorbents provided to take off its edge.

The affirmative class monopolize the homage of mankind. They originate and execute all the great feats. What a force was coiled up in the skull of Napoleon! Of the sixty thousand men making his army at Eylau, it seems some thirty thousand were thieves and burglars. The men whom, in peaceful communities, we hold if we can, with iron at their legs, in prisons, under the muskets of sentinels, this man dealt with, hand to hand, dragged them to their duty, and won his victories by their bayonets.

This aboriginal might gives a surprising pleasure when it appears under conditions of supreme refinement, as in the proficients in high art. When Michel Angelo was forced to paint the Sistine Chapel in fresco, of which art he knew nothing, he went down into the Pope's gardens behind the Vatican, and with a shovel dug out ochres, red and yellow, mixed them with glue and water with his own hands, and having, after many trials, at last suited himself, climbed his ladders, and painted away, week after week, month after month, the sibyls and prophets. He surpassed his successors in rough vigor, as much as in purity of intellect and refinement. He was not crushed by his one picture left unfinished at last. Michel was wont to draw his figures first in skeleton, then to clothe them with flesh, and lastly to drape them. "Ah!" said a brave painter to me, thinking on these things, "if a man has failed, you will find he has dreamed instead of working. There is no way to success in our art, but to take off your coat, grind paint, and work like a digger on the railroad, all day and every day."

Success goes thus invariably with a certain *plus* or positive power: an ounce of power must balance an ounce of weight. And, though a man cannot return into his mother's womb, and be born with new amounts of vivacity, yet there are two economies, which are the best *succedanea* which the case admits. The first is, the stopping off decisively our miscellaneous activity, and concentrating our force on one or a few points; as the gardener, by severe pruning, forces the sap of the tree into one or two vigorous limbs, instead of suffering it to spindle into a sheaf of twigs.

"Enlarge not thy destiny," said the oracle: "endeavor not to do more than is given thee in charge." The one prudence in life is concentration; the one evil is dissipation: and it makes no difference whether our dissipations are coarse or fine; property and its cares, friends, and a social habit, or politics, or music, or feasting. Everything is good which takes away one plaything and delusion more, and drives us home to add one stroke of faithful work. Friends, books, pictures, lower duties, talents, flatteries, hopes,—all are distractions which cause oscillations in our giddy balloon, and make a good poise and a straight course impossible. You must elect your work; you shall take what your brain can, and drop all the rest. Only so, can that amount of vital force accumulate, which can make the step from knowing to doing. No matter how much faculty of idle seeing a man has, the step from knowing to doing is rarely taken. 'Tis a step out of a chalk circle of imbecility into fruitfulness. Many an artist lacking this, lacks all: he sees the masculine Angelo or Cellini with despair. He, too, is up to Nature and the First Cause in his thought. But the spasm to collect and swing his whole being into one act, he has not. The poet Campbell said, that "a man accustomed to work was equal to any achievement he resolved on, and, that, for himself, necessity not inspiration was the prompter of his muse."

Concentration is the secret of strength in politics, in war, in trade, in short, in all management of human affairs. One of the high anecdotes of the world is the reply of Newton to the inquiry, "how he had been able to achieve his discoveries?"—"By always intending my mind." Or if you will have a text from politics, take this from Plutarch: "There was, in the whole city, but one street in which Pericles was ever seen, the street which led to the market-place and the council house. He declined all invitations to banquets, and all gay assemblies and company. During the whole period of his administration, he never dined at the table of a friend." Or if we seek an example from trade,—"I hope," said a good man to Rothschild, "your children are not too fond of money and business: I am sure you would not wish that."—"I am sure I should wish that: I wish them to give mind, soul, heart, and body to business,—that is the way to be happy. It requires a great deal of boldness and a great deal of caution, to make a great fortune, and when you have got it, it requires ten times as much wit to keep it. If I were to listen to all the projects proposed to me, I should ruin myself very soon. Stick to one business, young man. Stick to your brewery, (he said this to young Buxton,) and you will be the great brewer of London. Be brewer, and banker, and merchant, and manufacturer, and you will soon be in the Gazette."

Many men are knowing, many are apprehensive and tenacious, but they do not rush to a decision. But in our flowing affairs a decision must be made,—the best, if you can; but any is better than none. There are twenty ways of going to a point, and one is the shortest; but set out at once on one. A man who has that presence of mind which can bring to him on the instant all he knows, is worth for action a dozen men who know as much, but can only bring it to light slowly. The good Speaker in the House is not the man who knows the theory of parliamentary tactics, but the man who decides off-hand. The good judge is not he who does hair-splitting justice to every allegation, but who, aiming at substantial justice, rules something intelligible for the guidance of suitors. The good lawyer is not the man who has an eye to every side and angle of contingency, and qualifies all his qualifications, but who throws himself on your part so heartily, that he can get you out of a scrape. Dr. Johnson said, in one of his flowing sentences, "Miserable beyond all names of wretchedness is that unhappy pair, who are doomed to reduce beforehand to the principles of abstract reason all the details of each domestic day. There are cases where little can be said, and much must be done."

The second substitute for temperament is drill, the power of use and routine. The hack is a better roadster than the Arab barb. In chemistry, the galvanic stream, slow, but continuous, is equal in power to the electric spark, and is, in our arts, a better agent. So in human action, against the spasm of energy, we offset the continuity of drill. We spread the same amount of force over much time, instead of condensing it into a moment. 'Tis the same ounce of gold here in a ball, and there in a leaf. At West Point, Col. Buford, the chief engineer, pounded with a hammer on the trunnions of a cannon, until he broke them off. He fired a piece of ordnance some hundred times in swift succession, until it burst. Now which stroke broke the trunnion? Every stroke. Which blast burst the piece? Every blast. *"Diligence passe sens,"* Henry VIII. was wont to say, or, great is drill. John Kemble said, that the worst provincial company of actors would go through a play better than the best amateur company. Basil Hall likes to show that the worst regular troops will beat the best volunteers. Practice is nine tenths. A course of mobs is good practice for orators. All the great speakers were bad speakers at first. Stumping it through England for seven years, made Cobden a consummate debater. Stumping it through New England for twice seven, trained Wendell Phillips. The way to learn German, is, to read the same dozen pages over and over a hundred times, till you know every word and particle in them, and can pronounce and repeat them by heart. No genius can recite a ballad at first reading, so well as mediocrity can at the fifteenth or twentieth reading. The rule for hospitality and Irish 'help,' is, to have the same dinner every day throughout the year. At last, Mrs. O'Shaughnessy learns to cook it to a nicety, the host learns to carve it, and the guests are well served. A humorous friend of mine thinks, that the reason why Nature is so perfect in her art, and gets up such inconceivably fine sunsets, is, that she has learned how, at last, by dint of doing the same thing so very often. Cannot one converse better on a topic on which he has experience, than on one which is new? Men whose opinion is valued on 'Change, are only such as have a special experience, and off that ground their opinion is not valuable. "More are made good by exercitation, than by nature," said Democritus. The friction in nature is so enormous that we cannot spare any power. It is not question to express our thought, to elect our way, but to overcome resistances of the medium and material in everything we do. Hence the use of drill, and the worthlessness of amateurs to cope with practitioners. Six hours every day at the piano, only to give facility of touch; six hours a day at painting, only to give command of the odious materials, oil, ochres, and brushes. The masters say, that they know a master in music, only by seeing the pose of the hands on the keys;—so difficult and vital an act is the command of the instrument. To have learned the use of the tools, by thousands of manipulations; to have learned the arts of reckoning, by endless adding and dividing, is the power of the mechanic and the clerk.

I remarked in England, in confirmation of a frequent experience at home, that, in literary circles, the men of trust and consideration, bookmakers, editors, university deans and professors, bishops, too, were by no means men of the largest literary talent, but usually of a low and ordinary intellectuality, with a sort of mercantile activity and working talent. Indifferent hacks and mediocrities tower, by pushing their forces to a lucrative point, or by working power, over multitudes of superior men, in Old as in New England.

I have not forgotten that there are sublime considerations which limit the value of talent and superficial success. We can easily overpraise the vulgar hero. There are sources on which we have not drawn. I know what I abstain from. I adjourn what I have to say on this topic to the chapters on Culture and Worship. But this force or spirit, being the means relied on by Nature for bringing the work of the day about,—as far as we attach importance to household life, and the prizes of the world, we must respect that. And I hold, that an economy may be applied to it; it is as much a subject of exact law and arithmetic as fluids and gases are; it may be husbanded, or wasted; every man is efficient only as he is a container or vessel of this force, and never was any signal act or achievement in history, but by this expenditure. This is not gold, but the gold-maker; not the fame, but the exploit.

If these forces and this husbandry are within reach of our will, and the laws of them can be read, we infer that all success, and all conceivable benefit for man, is also, first or last, within his reach, and has its own sublime economies by which it may be attained. The world is mathematical, and has no casualty, in all its vast and flowing curve. Success has no more eccentricity, than the gingham and muslin we weave in our mills. I know no more affecting lesson to our busy, plotting New England brains, than to go into one of the factories with which we have lined all the watercourses in the States. A man hardly knows how much he is a machine, until he begins to make telegraph, loom, press, and locomotive, in his own image. But in these, he is forced to leave out his follies and hindrances, so that when we go to the mill, the machine is more moral than we. Let a man dare go to a loom, and see if he be equal to it. Let machine confront machine, and see how they come out. The world-mill is more complex than the calico-mill, and the architect stooped less. In the gingham-mill, a broken thread or a shred spoils the web through a piece of a hundred yards, and is traced back to the girl that wove it, and lessens her wages. The stockholder, on being shown this, rubs his hands with delight. Are you so cunning, Mr. Profitloss, and do you expect to swindle your master and employer, in the web you weave? A day is a more magnificent cloth than any muslin, the mechanism that makes it is infi-nitely cunninger, and you shall not conceal the sleezy, fraud-ulent, rotten hours you have slipped into the piece, nor fear that any honest thread, or straighter steel, or more inflexible shaft, will not testify in the web.

III

WEALTH

———

Who shall tell what did befall,
Far away in time, when once,
Over the lifeless ball,
Hung idle stars and suns?
What god the element obeyed?
Wings of what wind the lichen bore,
Wafting the puny seeds of power,
Which, lodged in rock, the rock abrade?
And well the primal pioneer
Knew the strong task to it assigned
Patient through Heaven's enormous year
To build in matter home for mind.
From air the creeping centuries drew
The matted thicket low and wide,
This must the leaves of ages strew
The granite slab to clothe and hide,
Ere wheat can wave its golden pride.
What smiths, and in what furnace, rolled
(In dizzy æons dim and mute
The reeling brain can ill compute)
Copper and iron, lead, and gold?
What oldest star the fame can save
Of races perishing to pave
The planet with a floor of lime?
Dust is their pyramid and mole:
Who saw what ferns and palms were pressed
Under the tumbling mountain's breast,

In the safe herbal of the coal?
But when the quarried means were piled,
All is waste and worthless, till
Arrives the wise selecting will,
And, out of slime and chaos, Wit
Draws the threads of fair and fit.
Then temples rose, and towns, and marts,
The shop of toil, the hall of arts;
Then flew the sail across the seas
To feed the North from tropic trees;
The storm-wind wove, the torrent span,
Where they were bid the rivers ran;
New slaves fulfilled the poet's dream,
Galvanic wire, strong-shouldered steam.
Then docks were built, and crops were stored,
And ingots added to the hoard.
But, though light-headed man forget,
Remembering Matter pays her debt:
Still, through her motes and masses, draw
Electric thrills and ties of Law,
Which bind the strengths of Nature wild
To the conscience of a child.

Wealth

As soon as a stranger is introduced into any company, one of the first questions which all wish to have answered, is, How does that man get his living? And with reason. He is no whole man until he knows how to earn a blameless livelihood. Society is barbarous, until every industrious man can get his living without dishonest customs.

Every man is a consumer, and ought to be a producer. He fails to make his place good in the world, unless he not only pays his debt, but also adds something to the common wealth. Nor can he do justice to his genius, without making some larger demand on the world than a bare subsistence. He is by constitution expensive, and needs to be rich.

Wealth has its source in applications of the mind to nature, from the rudest strokes of spade and axe, up to the last secrets of art. Intimate ties subsist between thought and all production; because a better order is equivalent to vast amounts of brute labor. The forces and the resistances are Nature's, but the mind acts in bringing things from where they abound to where they are wanted; in wise combining; in directing the practice of the useful arts, and in the creation of finer values, by fine art, by eloquence, by song, or the reproductions of memory. Wealth is in applications of mind to nature; and the art of getting rich consists not in industry, much less in saving, but in a better order, in timeliness, in being at the right spot. One man has stronger arms, or longer legs; another sees by the course of streams, and growth of markets, where land will be wanted, makes a clearing to the river, goes to sleep, and wakes up rich. Steam is no stronger now, than it was a hundred years ago; but is put to better use. A clever fellow was acquainted with the expansive force of steam; he also saw the wealth of wheat and grass rotting in Michigan. Then he cunningly screws on the steam-pipe to the wheat-crop. Puff now, O Steam! The steam puffs and expands as before, but this time it is dragging all Michigan at its back to hungry New York and hungry England. Coal lay in ledges under the ground since the Flood, until a laborer with pick and windlass brings it to the surface. We may well call it black diamonds.

Every basket is power and civilization. For coal is a portable climate. It carries the heat of the tropics to Labrador and the polar circle: and it is the means of transporting itself whithersoever it is wanted. Watt and Stephenson whispered in the ear of mankind their secret, that *a half-ounce of coal will draw two tons a mile*, and coal carries coal, by rail and by boat, to make Canada as warm as Calcutta, and with its comfort brings its industrial power.

When the farmer's peaches are taken from under the tree, and carried into town, they have a new look, and a hundredfold value over the fruit which grew on the same bough, and lies fulsomely on the ground. The craft of the merchant is this bringing a thing from where it abounds, to where it is costly.

Wealth begins in a tight roof that keeps the rain and wind out; in a good pump that yields you plenty of sweet water; in two suits of clothes, so to change your dress when you are wet; in dry sticks to burn; in a good double-wick lamp; and three meals; in a horse, or a locomotive, to cross the land; in a boat to cross the sea; in tools to work with; in books to read; and so, in giving, on all sides, by tools and auxiliaries, the greatest possible extension to our powers, as if it added feet, and hands, and eyes, and blood, length to the day, and knowledge, and good-will.

Wealth begins with these articles of necessity. And here we must recite the iron law which Nature thunders in these northern climates. First, she requires that each man should feed himself. If, happily, his fathers have left him no inheritance, he must go to work, and by making his wants less, or his gains more, he must draw himself out of that state of pain and insult in which she forces the beggar to lie. She gives him no rest until this is done: she starves, taunts, and torments him, takes away warmth, laughter, sleep, friends, and daylight, until he has fought his way to his own loaf. Then, less peremptorily, but still with sting enough, she urges him to the acquisition of such things as belong to him. Every warehouse and shop-window, every fruit-tree, every thought of every hour, opens a new want to him, which it concerns his power and dignity to gratify. It is of no use to argue the wants down: the philosophers have laid the greatness of man in making his wants few; but will a man content himself with a hut and a handful of dried pease? He is born to be rich. He is thoroughly related; and is tempted out by his appetites and fancies to the conquest of this and that piece of nature, until he finds his well-being in the use of his planet, and of more planets than his own. Wealth requires, besides the crust of bread and the roof,—the freedom of the city, the freedom of the earth, travelling, machinery, the benefits of science, music, and fine arts, the best culture, and the best company. He is the rich man who can avail himself of all men's faculties. He is the richest man who knows how to draw a benefit from the labors of the greatest number of men, of men in distant countries, and in past times. The same correspondence that is between thirst in the stomach, and water in the spring, exists between the whole of man and the whole of nature. The elements offer their service to him. The sea, washing the equator and the poles, offers its perilous aid, and the power and empire that follow it,—day by day to his craft and audacity. "Beware of me," it says, "but if you can hold me, I am the key to all the lands." Fire offers, on its side, an equal power. Fire, steam, lightning, gravity, ledges of rock, mines of iron, lead, quicksilver, tin, and gold; forests of all woods; fruits of all climates; animals of all habits; the powers of tillage; the fabrics of his chemic laboratory; the webs of his loom; the masculine draught of his locomotive, the talismans of the machine-shop; all grand and subtile things, minerals, gases, ethers, passions, war, trade, government, are his natural playmates, and, according to the excellence of the machinery in each human being, is his attraction for the instruments he is to employ. The world is his tool-chest, and he is successful, or his education is carried on just so far, as is the marriage of his faculties with nature, or, the degree in which he takes up things into himself.

The strong race is strong on these terms. The Saxons are the merchants of the world; now, for a thousand years, the leading race, and by nothing more than their quality of personal independence, and, in its special modification, pecuniary independence. No reliance for bread and games on the government, no clanship, no patriarchal style of living by the revenues of a chief, no marrying-on,—no system of clientship suits them; but every man must pay his scot. The English are prosperous and peaceable, with their habit of considering that every man must take care of himself, and has himself to thank, if he do not maintain and improve his position in society.

The subject of economy mixes itself with morals, inasmuch as it is a peremptory point of virtue that a man's independence be secured. Poverty demoralizes. A man in debt is so far a slave; and Wall-street thinks it easy for a *millionaire* to be a man of his word, a man of honor, but, that, in failing circumstances, no man can be relied on to keep his integrity. And when one observes in the hotels and palaces of our Atlantic capitals, the habit of expense, the riot of the senses, the absence of bonds, clanship, fellow-feeling of any kind, he feels, that, when a man or a woman is driven to the wall, the chances of integrity are frightfully diminished, as if virtue were coming to be a luxury which few could afford, or, as Burke said, "at a market almost too high for humanity." He may fix his inventory of necessities and of enjoyments on what scale he pleases, but if he wishes the power and privilege of thought, the chalking out his own career, and having society on his own terms, he must bring his wants within his proper power to satisfy.

The manly part is to do with might and main what you can do. The world is full of fops who never did anything, and who have persuaded beauties and men of genius to wear their fop livery, and these will deliver the fop opinion, that it is not respectable to be seen earning a living; that it is much more respectable to spend without earning; and this doctrine of the snake will come also from the elect sons of light; for wise men are not wise at all hours, and will speak five times from their taste or their humor, to once from their reason. The brave workman, who might betray his feeling of it in his manners, if he do not succumb in his practice, must replace the grace or elegance forfeited, by the merit of the work done. No matter whether he make shoes, or statues, or laws. It is the privilege of any human work which is well done to invest the doer with a certain haughtiness. He can well afford not to conciliate, whose faithful work will answer for him. The mechanic at his bench carries a quiet heart and assured manners, and deals on even terms with men of any condition. The artist has made his picture so true, that it disconcerts criticism. The statue is so beautiful, that it contracts no stain from the market, but makes the market a silent gallery for itself. The case of the young lawyer was pitiful to disgust,—a paltry matter of buttons or tweezer-cases; but the determined youth saw in it an aperture to insert his dangerous wedges, made the insignificance of the thing forgotten, and gave fame by his sense and energy to the name and affairs of the Tittleton snuffbox factory.

Society in large towns is babyish, and wealth is made a toy. The life of pleasure is so ostentatious, that a shallow observer must believe that this is the agreed best use of wealth, and, whatever is pretended, it ends in cosseting. But, if this were the main use of surplus capital, it would bring us to barricades, burned towns, and tomahawks, presently. Men of sense esteem wealth to be the assimilation of nature to themselves, the converting of the sap and juices of the planet to the incarnation and nutriment of their design. Power is what they want,—not candy;—power to execute their design, power to give legs and feet, form and actuality to their thought, which, to a clear-sighted man, appears the end for which the Universe exists, and all its resources might be well applied. Columbus thinks that the sphere is a problem for practical navigation, as well as for closet geometry, and looks on all kings and peoples as cowardly landsmen, until they dare fit him out. Few men on the planet have more truly belonged to it. But he was forced to leave much of his map blank. His successors inherited his map, and inherited his fury to complete it.

So the men of the mine, telegraph, mill, map, and survey, —the monomaniacs, who talk up their project in marts, and offices, and entreat men to subscribe:—how did our factories get built? how did North America get netted with iron rails, except by the importunity of these orators, who dragged all the prudent men in? Is party the madness of many for the gain of a few? This *speculative* genius is the madness of few for the gain of the world. The projectors are sacrificed, but the public is the gainer. Each of these idealists, working after his thought, would make it tyrannical, if he could. He is met and antagonized by other speculators, as hot as he. The equilibrium is preserved by these counteractions, as one tree keeps

down another in the forest, that it may not absorb all the sap
in the ground. And the supply in nature of railroad presidents, copper-miners, grand-junctioners, smoke-burners, fire-
annihilators, &c., is limited by the same law which keeps
the proportion in the supply of carbon, of alum, and of
hydrogen.

To be rich is to have a ticket of admission to the master-
works and chief men of each race. It is to have the sea, by
voyaging; to visit the mountains, Niagara, the Nile, the desert, Rome, Paris, Constantinople; to see galleries, libraries,
arsenals, manufactories. The reader of Humboldt's "Cosmos"
follows the marches of a man whose eyes, ears, and mind are
armed by all the science, arts, and implements which mankind
have anywhere accumulated, and who is using these to add to
the stock. So is it with Denon, Beckford, Belzoni, Wilkinson,
Layard, Kane, Lepsius, and Livingston. "The rich man," says
Saadi, "is everywhere expected and at home." The rich take
up something more of the world into man's life. They include
the country as well as the town, the ocean-side, the White
Hills, the Far West, and the old European homesteads of
man, in their notion of available material. The world is his,
who has money to go over it. He arrives at the sea-shore, and
a sumptuous ship has floored and carpeted for him the stormy
Atlantic, and made it a luxurious hotel, amid the horrors of
tempests. The Persians say, " 'Tis the same to him who wears
a shoe, as if the whole earth were covered with leather."

Kings are said to have long arms, but every man should
have long arms, and should pluck his living, his instruments,
his power, and his knowing, from the sun, moon, and stars.
Is not then the demand to be rich legitimate? Yet, I have
never seen a rich man. I have never seen a man as rich as all
men ought to be, or, with an adequate command of nature.
The pulpit and the press have many commonplaces denouncing the thirst for wealth; but if men should take these moralists at their word, and leave off aiming to be rich, the
moralists would rush to rekindle at all hazards this love of
power in the people, lest civilization should be undone. Men
are urged by their ideas to acquire the command over nature.
Ages derive a culture from the wealth of Roman Cæsars, Leo
Tenths, magnificent Kings of France, Grand Dukes of Tus-

cany, Dukes of Devonshire, Townleys, Vernons, and Peels, in England; or whatever great proprietors. It is the interest of all men, that there should be Vaticans and Louvres full of noble works of art; British Museums, and French Gardens of Plants, Philadelphia Academies of Natural History, Bodleian, Ambrosian, Royal, Congressional Libraries. It is the interest of all that there should be Exploring Expeditions; Captain Cooks to voyage round the world, Rosses, Franklins, Richardsons, and Kanes, to find the magnetic and the geographic poles. We are all richer for the measurement of a degree of latitude on the earth's surface. Our navigation is safer for the chart. How intimately our knowledge of the system of the Universe rests on that!—and a true economy in a state or an individual will forget its frugality in behalf of claims like these.

Whilst it is each man's interest, that, not only ease and convenience of living, but also wealth or surplus product should exist somewhere, it need not be in his hands. Often it is very undesirable to him. Goethe said well, "nobody should be rich but those who understand it." Some men are born to own, and can animate all their possessions. Others cannot: their owning is not graceful; seems to be a compromise of their character: they seem to steal their own dividends. They should own who can administer; not they who hoard and conceal; not they who, the greater proprietors they are, are only the greater beggars, but they whose work carves out work for more, opens a path for all. For he is the rich man in whom the people are rich, and he is the poor man in whom the people are poor: and how to give all access to the masterpieces of art and nature, is the problem of civilization. The socialism of our day has done good service in setting men on thinking how certain civilizing benefits, now only enjoyed by the opulent, can be enjoyed by all. For example, the providing to each man the means and apparatus of science, and of the arts. There are many articles good for occasional use, which few men are able to own. Every man wishes to see the ring of Saturn, the satellites and belts of Jupiter and Mars; the mountains and craters in the moon: yet how few can buy a telescope! and of those, scarcely one would like the trouble of keeping it in order, and exhibiting it. So of electrical and chemical apparatus, and many the like things. Every man may have occasion to consult books which he does not care to possess, such as cyclopædias, dictionaries, tables, charts, maps, and public documents: pictures also of birds, beasts, fishes, shells, trees, flowers, whose names he desires to know.

There is a refining influence from the arts of Design on a prepared mind, which is as positive as that of music, and not to be supplied from any other source. But pictures, engravings, statues, and casts, beside their first cost, entail expenses, as of galleries and keepers for the exhibition; and the use which any man can make of them is rare, and their value, too, is much enhanced by the numbers of men who can share their enjoyment. In the Greek cities, it was reckoned profane, that any person should pretend a property in a work of art, which belonged to all who could behold it. I think sometimes,— could I only have music on my own terms;—could I live in a great city, and know where I could go whenever I wished the ablution and inundation of musical waves,—that were a bath and a medicine.

If properties of this kind were owned by states, towns, and lyceums, they would draw the bonds of neighborhood closer. A town would exist to an intellectual purpose. In Europe, where the feudal forms secure the permanence of wealth in certain families, those families buy and preserve these things, and lay them open to the public. But in America, where democratic institutions divide every estate into small portions, after a few years, the public should step into the place of these proprietors, and provide this culture and inspiration for the citizen.

Man was born to be rich, or, inevitably grows rich by the use of his faculties; by the union of thought with nature. Property is an intellectual production. The game requires coolness, right reasoning, promptness, and patience in the players. Cultivated labor drives out brute labor. An infinite number of shrewd men, in infinite years, have arrived at certain best and shortest ways of doing, and this accumulated skill in arts, cultures, harvestings, curings, manufactures, navigations, exchanges, constitutes the worth of our world to-day.

Commerce is a game of skill, which every man cannot play, which few men can play well. The right merchant is one who has the just average of faculties we call *common sense*; a man of a strong affinity for facts, who makes up his decision on what he has seen. He is thoroughly persuaded of the truths of arithmetic. There is always a reason, *in the man*, for his good or bad fortune, and so, in making money. Men talk as if there were some magic about this, and believe in magic, in all parts of life. He knows, that all goes on the old road, pound for pound, cent for cent,—for every effect a perfect cause,—and that good luck is another name for tenacity of purpose. He insures himself in every transaction, and likes small and sure gains. Probity and closeness to the facts are the basis, but the masters of the art add a certain long arithmetic. The problem is, to combine many and remote operations, with the accuracy and adherence to the facts, which is easy in near and small transactions; so to arrive at gigantic results, without any compromise of safety. Napoleon was fond of telling the story of the Marseilles banker, who said to his visitor, surprised at the contrast between the splendor of the banker's chateau and hospitality, and the meanness of the counting-room in which he had seen him,—"Young man, you are too young to understand how masses are formed,—the true and only power,—whether composed of money, water, or men, it is all alike,—a mass is an immense centre of motion, but it must be begun, it must be kept up:"—and he might have added, that the way in which it must be begun and kept up, is, by obedience to the law of particles.

Success consists in close appliance to the laws of the world, and, since those laws are intellectual and moral, an intellectual and moral obedience. Political Economy is as good a book wherein to read the life of man, and the ascendency of laws over all private and hostile influences, as any Bible which has come down to us.

Money is representative, and follows the nature and fortunes of the owner. The coin is a delicate meter of civil, social, and moral changes. The farmer is covetous of his dollar, and with reason. It is no waif to him. He knows how many strokes of labor it represents. His bones ache with the day's work that earned it. He knows how much land it represents;—how much rain, frost, and sunshine. He knows that, in the dollar, he gives you so much discretion and patience, so much hoeing, and threshing. Try to lift his dollar; you must lift all that weight. In the city, where money follows the skit of a pen, or a lucky rise in exchange, it comes to be looked on as light. I wish the farmer held it dearer, and would spend it only for real bread; force for force.

The farmer's dollar is heavy, and the clerk's is light and nimble; leaps out of his pocket; jumps on to cards and faro-tables: but still more curious is its susceptibility to metaphysical changes. It is the finest barometer of social storms, and announces revolutions.

Every step of civil advancement makes every man's dollar worth more. In California, the country where it grew,—what would it buy? A few years since, it would buy a shanty, dysentery, hunger, bad company, and crime. There are wide countries, like Siberia, where it would buy little else to-day, than some petty mitigation of suffering. In Rome, it will buy beauty and magnificence. Forty years ago, a dollar would not buy much in Boston. Now it will buy a great deal more in our old town, thanks to railroads, telegraphs, steamers, and the contemporaneous growth of New York, and the whole country. Yet there are many goods appertaining to a capital city, which are not yet purchasable here, no, not with a mountain of dollars. A dollar in Florida is not worth a dollar in Massachusetts. A dollar is not value, but representative of value, and, at last, of moral values. A dollar is rated for the corn it will buy, or to speak strictly, not for the corn or house-room, but for Athenian corn, and Roman house-room,—for the wit, probity, and power, which we eat bread and dwell in houses to share and exert. Wealth is mental; wealth is moral. The value of a dollar is, to buy just things: a dollar goes on increasing in value with all the genius, and all the virtue of the world. A dollar in a university, is worth more than a dollar in a jail; in a temperate, schooled, law-abiding community, than in some sink of crime, where dice, knives, and arsenic, are in constant play.

The "Bank-Note Detector" is a useful publication. But the current dollar, silver or paper, is itself the detector of the right and wrong where it circulates. Is it not instantly enhanced by the increase of equity? If a trader refuses to sell his vote, or adheres to some odious right, he makes so much more equity in Massachusetts; and every acre in the State is more worth, in the hour of his action. If you take out of State-street the ten honestest merchants, and put in ten roguish persons, controlling the same amount of capital,—the rates of insurance will indicate it; the soundness of banks will show it: the highways will be less secure: the schools will feel it; the children will bring home their little dose of the poison: the judge will sit less firmly on the bench, and his decisions be less upright; he has lost so much support and constraint,—which all need; and the pulpit will betray it, in a laxer rule of life. An apple-tree, if you take out every day for a number of days, a load of loam, and put in a load of sand about its roots,—will find it out. An apple-tree is a stupid kind of creature, but if this treatment be pursued for a short time, I think it would begin to mistrust something. And if you should take out of the powerful class engaged in trade a hundred good men, and put in a hundred bad, or, what is just the same thing, introduce a demoralizing institution, would not the dollar, which is not much stupider than an apple-tree, presently find it out? The value of a dollar is social, as it is created by society. Every man who removes into this city, with any purchasable talent or skill in him, gives to every man's labor in the city, a new worth. If a talent is anywhere born into the world, the community of nations is enriched; and, much more, with a new degree of probity. The expense of crime, one of the principal charges of every nation, is so far stopped. In Europe, crime is observed to increase or abate with the price of bread. If the Rothschilds at Paris do not accept bills, the people at Manchester, at Paisley, at Birmingham, are forced into the highway, and landlords are shot down in Ireland. The police records attest it. The vibrations are presently felt in New York, New Orleans, and Chicago. Not much otherwise, the economical power touches the masses through the political lords. Rothschild refuses the Russian loan, and there is peace, and the harvests are saved. He takes it, and there is war, and an agitation through a large portion of mankind, with every hideous result, ending in revolution, and a new order.

Wealth brings with it its own checks and balances. The basis of political economy is non-interference. The only safe rule is found in the self-adjusting meter of demand and supply.

Do not legislate. Meddle, and you snap the sinews with your
sumptuary laws. Give no bounties: make equal laws: secure
life and property, and you need not give alms. Open the
doors of opportunity to talent and virtue, and they will do
themselves justice, and property will not be in bad hands. In
a free and just commonwealth, property rushes from the idle
and imbecile, to the industrious, brave, and persevering.

The laws of nature play through trade, as a toy-battery exhibits the effects of electricity. The level of the sea is not more
surely kept, than is the equilibrium of value in society, by the
demand and supply: and artifice or legislation punishes itself,
by reactions, gluts, and bankruptcies. The sublime laws play
indifferently through atoms and galaxies. Whoever knows
what happens in the getting and spending of a loaf of bread
and a pint of beer; that no wishing will change the rigorous
limits of pints and penny loaves; that, for all that is consumed, so much less remains in the basket and pot; but what
is gone out of these is not wasted, but well spent, if it nourish
his body, and enable him to finish his task;—knows all of
political economy that the budgets of empires can teach him.
The interest of petty economy is this symbolization of the
great economy; the way in which a house, and a private man's
methods, tally with the solar system, and the laws of give and
take, throughout nature; and, however wary we are of the
falsehoods and petty tricks which we suicidally play off on
each other, every man has a certain satisfaction, whenever his
dealing touches on the inevitable facts; when he sees that
things themselves dictate the price, as they always tend to do,
and, in large manufactures, are seen to do. Your paper is not
fine or coarse enough,—is too heavy, or too thin. The manufacturer says, he will furnish you with just that thickness or
thinness you want; the pattern is quite indifferent to him;
here is his schedule;—any variety of paper, as cheaper or
dearer, with the prices annexed. A pound of paper costs so
much, and you may have it made up in any pattern you fancy.

There is in all our dealings a self-regulation that supersedes
chaffering. You will rent a house, but must have it cheap. The
owner can reduce the rent, but so he incapacitates himself
from making proper repairs, and the tenant gets not the
house he would have, but a worse one; besides, that a relation

a little injurious is established between land-lord and tenant. You dismiss your laborer, saying, "Patrick, I shall send for you as soon as I cannot do without you." Patrick goes off contented, for he knows that the weeds will grow with the potatoes, the vines must be planted, next week, and, however unwilling you may be, the cantelopes, crook-necks, and cucumbers will send for him. Who but must wish that all labor and value should stand on the same simple and surly market? If it is the best of its kind, it will. We must have joiner, locksmith, planter, priest, poet, doctor, cook, weaver, ostler; each in turn, through the year.

If a St. Michael's pear sells for a shilling, it costs a shilling to raise it. If, in Boston, the best securities offer twelve *per cent.* for money, they have just six *per cent.* of insecurity. You may not see that the fine pear costs you a shilling, but it costs the community so much. The shilling represents the number of enemies the pear has, and the amount of risk in ripening it. The price of coal shows the narrowness of the coal-field, and a compulsory confinement of the miners to a certain district. All salaries are reckoned on contingent, as well as on actual services. "If the wind were always southwest by west," said the skipper, "women might take ships to sea." One might say, that all things are of one price; that nothing is cheap or dear; and that the apparent disparities that strike us, are only a shopman's trick of concealing the damage in your bargain. A youth coming into the city from his native New Hampshire farm, with its hard fare still fresh in his remembrance, boards at a first-class hotel, and believes he must somehow have outwitted Dr. Franklin and Malthus, for luxuries are cheap. But he pays for the one convenience of a better dinner, by the loss of some of the richest social and educational advantages. He has lost what guards! what incentives! He will perhaps find by and by, that he left the Muses at the door of the hotel, and found the Furies inside. Money often costs too much, and power and pleasure are not cheap. The ancient poet said, "the gods sell all things at a fair price."

There is an example of the compensations in the commercial history of this country. When the European wars threw the carrying-trade of the world, from 1800 to 1812, into American bottoms, a seizure was now and then made of an American ship. Of course, the loss was serious to the owner, but the country was indemnified; for we charged threepence a pound for carrying cotton, sixpence for tobacco, and so on; which paid for the risk and loss, and brought into the country an immense prosperity, early marriages, private wealth, the building of cities, and of states: and, after the war was over, we received compensation over and above, by treaty, for all the seizures. Well, the Americans grew rich and great. But the pay-day comes round. Britain, France, and Germany, which our extraordinary profits had impoverished, send out, attracted by the fame of our advantages, first their thousands, then their millions, of poor people, to share the crop. At first, we employ them, and increase our prosperity: but, in the artificial system of society and of protected labor, which we also have adopted and enlarged, there come presently checks and stoppages. Then we refuse to employ these poor men. But they will not so be answered. They go into the poor rates, and, though we refuse wages, we must now pay the same amount in the form of taxes. Again, it turns out that the largest proportion of crimes are committed by foreigners. The cost of the crime, and the expense of courts, and of prisons, we must bear, and the standing army of preventive police we must pay. The cost of education of the posterity of this great colony, I will not compute. But the gross amount of these costs will begin to pay back what we thought was a net gain from our transatlantic customers of 1800. It is vain to refuse this payment. We cannot get rid of these people, and we cannot get rid of their will to be supported. That has become an inevitable element of our politics; and, for their votes, each of the dominant parties courts and assists them to get it executed. Moreover, we have to pay, not what would have contented them at home, but what they have learned to think necessary here; so that opinion, fancy, and all manner of moral considerations complicate the problem.

There are a few measures of economy which will bear to be named without disgust; for the subject is tender, and we may easily have too much of it; and therein resembles the hideous animalcules of which our bodies are built up,—which, offensive in the particular, yet compose valuable and effective masses. Our nature and genius force us to respect ends, whilst we use means. We must use the means, and yet, in our most accurate using, somehow screen and cloak them, as we can only give them any beauty, by a reflection of the glory of the end. That is the good head, which serves the end, and commands the means. The rabble are corrupted by their means: the means are too strong for them, and they desert their end.

1. The first of these measures is that each man's expense must proceed from his character. As long as your genius buys, the investment is safe, though you spend like a monarch. Nature arms each man with some faculty which enables him to do easily some feat impossible to any other, and thus makes him necessary to society. This native determination guides his labor and his spending. He wants an equipment of means and tools proper to his talent. And to save on this point, were to neutralize the special strength and helpfulness of each mind. Do your work, respecting the excellence of the work, and not its acceptableness. This is so much economy, that, rightly read, it is the sum of economy. Profligacy consists not in spending years of time or chests of money,—but in spending them off the line of your career. The crime which bankrupts men and states, is, job-work;—declining from your main design, to serve a turn here or there. Nothing is beneath you, if it is in the direction of your life: nothing is great or desirable, if it is off from that. I think we are entitled here to draw a straight line, and say, that society can never prosper, but must always be bankrupt, until every man does that which he was created to do.

Spend for your expense, and retrench the expense which is not yours. Allston, the painter, was wont to say, that he built a plain house, and filled it with plain furniture, because he would hold out no bribe to any to visit him, who had not similar tastes to his own. We are sympathetic, and, like children, want everything we see. But it is a large stride to independence,—when a man, in the discovery of his proper talent, has sunk the necessity for false expenses. As the betrothed maiden, by one secure affection, is relieved from a system of slaveries,—the daily inculcated necessity of pleasing all,—so the man who has found what he can do, can spend on that, and leave all other spending. Montaigne said, "When

he was a younger brother, he went brave in dress and equipage, but afterward his chateau and farms might answer for
him." Let a man who belongs to the class of nobles, those,
namely, who have found out that they can do something, relieve himself of all vague squandering on objects not his. Let
the realist not mind appearances. Let him delegate to others
the costly courtesies and decorations of social life. The virtues
are economists, but some of the vices are also. Thus, next to
humility, I have noticed that pride is a pretty good husband.
A good pride is, as I reckon it, worth from five hundred to
fifteen hundred a year. Pride is handsome, economical: pride
eradicates so many vices, letting none subsist but itself, that it
seems as if it were a great gain to exchange vanity for pride.
Pride can go without domestics, without fine clothes, can live
in a house with two rooms, can eat potato, purslain, beans,
lyed corn, can work on the soil, can travel afoot, can talk with
poor men, or sit silent well-contented in fine saloons. But
vanity costs money, labor, horses, men, women, health, and
peace, and is still nothing at last, a long way leading nowhere.—Only one drawback; proud people are intolerably
selfish, and the vain are gentle and giving.

Art is a jealous mistress, and, if a man have a genius for
painting, poetry, music, architecture, or philosophy, he makes
a bad husband, and an ill provider, and should be wise in
season, and not fetter himself with duties which will embitter
his days, and spoil him for his proper work. We had in this
region, twenty years ago, among our educated men, a sort of
Arcadian fanaticism, a passionate desire to go upon the land,
and unite farming to intellectual pursuits. Many effected their
purpose, and made the experiment, and some became downright ploughmen; but all were cured of their faith that scholarship and practical farming, (I mean, with one's own hands,)
could be united.

With brow bent, with firm intent, the pale scholar leaves
his desk to draw a freer breath, and get a juster statement of
his thought, in the garden-walk. He stoops to pull up a purslain, or a dock, that is choking the young corn, and finds
there are two: close behind the last, is a third; he reaches out
his hand to a fourth; behind that, are four thousand and one.
He is heated and untuned, and, by and by, wakes up from his

idiot dream of chickweed and red-root, to remember his morning thought, and to find, that, with his adamantine purposes, he has been duped by a dandelion. A garden is like those pernicious machineries we read of, every month, in the newspapers, which catch a man's coat-skirt or his hand, and draw in his arm, his leg, and his whole body to irresistible destruction. In an evil hour he pulled down his wall, and added a field to his homestead. No land is bad, but land is worse. If a man own land, the land owns him. Now let him leave home, if he dare. Every tree and graft, every hill of melons, row of corn, or quickset hedge, all he has done, and all he means to do, stand in his way, like duns, when he would go out of his gate. The devotion to these vines and trees he finds poisonous. Long free walks, a circuit of miles, free his brain, and serve his body. Long marches are no hardship to him. He believes he composes easily on the hills. But this pottering in a few square yards of garden is dispiriting and drivelling. The smell of the plants has drugged him, and robbed him of energy. He finds a catalepsy in his bones. He grows peevish and poor-spirited. The genius of reading and of gardening are antagonistic, like resinous and vitreous electricity. One is concentrative in sparks and shocks: the other is diffuse strength; so that each disqualifies its workman for the other's duties.

An engraver whose hands must be of an exquisite delicacy of stroke, should not lay stone walls. Sir David Brewster gives exact instructions for microscopic observation:—"Lie down on your back, and hold the single lens and object over your eye," &c. &c. How much more the seeker of abstract truth, who needs periods of isolation, and rapt concentration, and almost a going out of the body to think!

2. Spend after your genius, *and by system*. Nature goes by rule, not by sallies and saltations. There must be system in the economies. Saving and unexpensiveness will not keep the most pathetic family from ruin, nor will bigger incomes make free spending safe. The secret of success lies never in the amount of money, but in the relation of income to outgo; as if, after expense has been fixed at a certain point, then new and steady rills of income, though never so small, being added, wealth begins. But in ordinary, as means increase,

spending increases faster, so that, large incomes, in England
and elsewhere, are found not to help matters;—the eating
quality of debt does not relax its voracity. When the cholera
is in the potato, what is the use of planting larger crops? In
England, the richest country in the universe, I was assured by
shrewd observers, that great lords and ladies had no more
guineas to give away than other people; that liberality with
money is as rare, and as immediately famous a virtue as it is
here. Want is a growing giant whom the coat of Have was
never large enough to cover. I remember in Warwickshire, to
have been shown a fair manor, still in the same name as in
Shakspeare's time. The rent-roll, I was told, is some fourteen
thousand pounds a year: but, when the second son of the late
proprietor was born, the father was perplexed how to provide
for him. The eldest son must inherit the manor; what to do
with this supernumerary? He was advised to breed him for
the Church, and to settle him in the rectorship, which was in
the gift of the family; which was done. It is a general rule in
that country, that bigger incomes do not help anybody. It is
commonly observed, that a sudden wealth, like a prize drawn
in a lottery, or a large bequest to a poor family, does not
permanently enrich. They have served no apprenticeship to
wealth, and, with the rapid wealth, come rapid claims: which
they do not know how to deny, and the treasure is quickly
dissipated.

A system must be in every economy, or the best single expedients are of no avail. A farm is a good thing, when it
begins and ends with itself, and does not need a salary, or a
shop, to eke it out. Thus, the cattle are a main link in the
chain-ring. If the non-conformist or æsthetic farmer leaves
out the cattle, and does not also leave out the want which the
cattle must supply, he must fill the gap by begging or stealing.
When men now alive were born, the farm yielded everything
that was consumed on it. The farm yielded no money, and
the farmer got on without. If he fell sick, his neighbors came
in to his aid: each gave a day's work; or a half day; or lent
his yoke of oxen, or his horse, and kept his work even: hoed
his potatoes, mowed his hay, reaped his rye; well knowing
that no man could afford to hire labor, without selling his
land. In autumn, a farmer could sell an ox or a hog, and get

a little money to pay taxes withal. Now, the farmer buys almost all he consumes,—tin-ware, cloth, sugar, tea, coffee,
fish, coal, railroad-tickets, and newspapers.

A master in each art is required, because the practice is
never with still or dead subjects, but they change in your
hands. You think farm-buildings and broad acres a solid property: but its value is flowing like water. It requires as much
watching as if you were decanting wine from a cask. The
farmer knows what to do with it, stops every leak, turns all
the streamlets to one reservoir, and decants wine: but a blun-
derhead comes out of Cornhill, tries his hand, and it all leaks
away. So is it with granite streets, or timber townships, as
with fruit or flowers. Nor is any investment so permanent,
that it can be allowed to remain without incessant watching,
as the history of each attempt to lock up an inheritance
through two generations for an unborn inheritor may show.

When Mr. Cockayne takes a cottage in the country, and
will keep his cow, he thinks a cow is a creature that is fed on
hay, and gives a pail of milk twice a day. But the cow that he
buys gives milk for three months; then her bag dries up.
What to do with a dry cow? who will buy her? Perhaps he
bought also a yoke of oxen to do his work; but they get
blown and lame. What to do with blown and lame oxen? The
farmer fats his, after the spring-work is done, and kills them
in the fall. But how can Cockayne, who has no pastures, and
leaves his cottage daily in the cars, at business hours, be poth-
ered with fatting and killing oxen? He plants trees; but there
must be crops, to keep the trees in ploughed land. What shall
be the crops? He will have nothing to do with trees, but will
have grass. After a year or two, the grass must be turned up
and ploughed: now what crops? Credulous Cockayne!

3. Help comes in the custom of the country, and the rule
of *Impera parendo*. The rule is not to dictate, nor to insist on
carrying out each of your schemes by ignorant wilfulness, but
to learn practically the secret spoken from all nature, that
things themselves refuse to be mismanaged, and will show to
the watchful their own law. Nobody need stir hand or foot.
The custom of the country will do it all. I know not how to
build or to plant; neither how to buy wood, nor what to do
with the house-lot, the field, or the wood-lot, when bought.

Never fear: it is all settled how it shall be, long beforehand, in the custom of the country, whether to sand, or whether to clay it, when to plough, and how to dress, whether to grass, or to corn; and you cannot help or hinder it. Nature has her own best mode of doing each thing, and she has somewhere told it plainly, if we will keep our eyes and ears open. If not, she will not be slow in undeceiving us, when we prefer our own way to hers. How often we must remember the art of the surgeon, which, in replacing the broken bone, contents itself with releasing the parts from false position; they fly into place by the action of the muscles. On this art of nature all our arts rely.

Of the two eminent engineers in the recent construction of railways in England, Mr. Brunel went straight from terminus to terminus, through mountains, over streams, crossing highways, cutting ducal estates in two, and shooting through this man's cellar, and that man's attic window, and so arriving at his end, at great pleasure to geometers, but with cost to his company. Mr. Stephenson, on the contrary, believing that the river knows the way, followed his valley, as implicitly as our Western Railroad follows the Westfield River, and turned out to be the safest and cheapest engineer. We say the cows laid out Boston. Well, there are worse surveyors. Every pedestrian in our pastures has frequent occasion to thank the cows for cutting the best path through the thicket, and over the hills: and travellers and Indians know the value of a buffalo-trail, which is sure to be the easiest possible pass through the ridge.

When a citizen, fresh from Dock-square, or Milk-street, comes out and buys land in the country, his first thought is to a fine outlook from his windows: his library must command a western view: a sunset every day, bathing the shoulder of Blue Hills, Wachusett, and the peaks of Monadnoc and Uncanoonuc. What, thirty acres, and all this magnificence for fifteen hundred dollars! It would be cheap at fifty thousand. He proceeds at once, his eyes dim with tears of joy, to fix the spot for his corner-stone. But the man who is to level the ground, thinks it will take many hundred loads of gravel to fill the hollow to the road. The stone-mason who should build the well thinks he shall have to dig forty feet: the baker doubts he shall never like to drive up to the door: the practi-

cal neighbor cavils at the position of the barn; and the citizen
comes to know that his predecessor the farmer built the house
in the right spot for the sun and wind, the spring, and water-
drainage, and the convenience to the pasture, the garden, the
field, and the road. So Dock-square yields the point, and
things have their own way. Use has made the farmer wise,
and the foolish citizen learns to take his counsel. From step
to step he comes at last to surrender at discretion. The farmer
affects to take his orders; but the citizen says, You may ask
me as often as you will, and in what ingenious forms, for an
opinion concerning the mode of building my wall, or sinking
my well, or laying out my acre, but the ball will rebound to
you. These are matters on which I neither know, nor need to
know anything. These are questions which you and not I shall
answer.

Not less, within doors, a system settles itself paramount
and tyrannical over master and mistress, servant and child,
cousin and acquaintance. 'Tis in vain that genius or virtue or
energy of character strive and cry against it. This is fate. And
'tis very well that the poor husband reads in a book of a new
way of living, and resolves to adopt it at home: let him go
home and try it, if he dare.

4. Another point of economy is to look for seed of the
same kind as you sow: and not to hope to buy one kind with
another kind. Friendship buys friendship; justice, justice; military merit, military success. Good husbandry finds wife, children, and household. The good merchant large gains, ships,
stocks, and money. The good poet fame, and literary credit;
but not either, the other. Yet there is commonly a confusion
of expectations on these points. Hotspur lives for the moment; praises himself for it; and despises Furlong, that he
does not. Hotspur, of course, is poor; and Furlong a good
provider. The odd circumstance is, that Hotspur thinks it a
superiority in himself, this improvidence, which ought to be
rewarded with Furlong's lands.

I have not at all completed my design. But we must not
leave the topic, without casting one glance into the interior
recesses. It is a doctrine of philosophy, that man is a being of
degrees; that there is nothing in the world, which is not repeated in his body; his body being a sort of miniature or

summary of the world: then that there is nothing in his body, which is not repeated as in a celestial sphere in his mind: then, there is nothing in his brain, which is not repeated in a higher sphere, in his moral system.

5. Now these things are so in Nature. All things ascend, and the royal rule of economy is, that it should ascend also, or, whatever we do must always have a higher aim. Thus it is a maxim, that money is another kind of blood. *Pecunia alter sanguis*: or, the estate of a man is only a larger kind of body, and admits of regimen analogous to his bodily circulations. So there is no maxim of the merchant, *e. g.*, "Best use of money is to pay debts;" "Every business by itself;" "Best time is present time;" "The right investment is in tools of your trade;" or the like, which does not admit of an extended sense. The counting-room maxims liberally expounded are laws of the Universe. The merchant's economy is a coarse symbol of the soul's economy. It is, to spend for power, and not for pleasure. It is to invest income; that is to say, to take up particulars into generals; days into integral eras,—literary, emotive, practical, of its life, and still to ascend in its investment. The merchant has but one rule, *absorb and invest*: he is to be capitalist: the scraps and filings must be gathered back into the crucible; the gas and smoke must be burned, and earnings must not go to increase expense, but to capital again. Well, the man must be capitalist. Will he spend his income, or will he invest? His body and every organ is under the same law. His body is a jar, in which the liquor of life is stored. Will he spend for pleasure? The way to ruin is short and facile. Will he not spend, but hoard for power? It passes through the sacred fermentations, by that law of Nature whereby everything climbs to higher platforms, and bodily vigor becomes mental and moral vigor. The bread he eats is first strength and animal spirits: it becomes, in higher laboratories, imagery and thought; and in still higher results, courage and endurance. This is the right compound interest; this is capital doubled, quadrupled, centupled; man raised to his highest power.

The true thrift is always to spend on the higher plane; to invest and invest, with keener avarice, that he may spend in spiritual creation, and not in augmenting animal existence.

Nor is the man enriched, in repeating the old experiments of animal sensation, nor unless through new powers and ascending pleasures, he knows himself by the actual experience of higher good, to be already on the way to the highest.

IV

CULTURE

———

Can rules or tutors educate
The semigod whom we await?
He must be musical,
Tremulous, impressional,
Alive to gentle influence
Of landscape and of sky,
And tender to the spirit-touch
Of man's or maiden's eye:
But, to his native centre fast,
Shall into Future fuse the Past,
And the world's flowing fates in
    his own mould recast.

Culture

THE WORD of ambition at the present day is Culture. Whilst all the world is in pursuit of power, and of wealth as a means of power, culture corrects the theory of success. A man is the prisoner of his power. A topical memory makes him an almanac; a talent for debate, a disputant; skill to get money makes him a miser, that is, a beggar. Culture reduces these inflammations by invoking the aid of other powers against the dominant talent, and by appealing to the rank of powers. It watches success. For performance, Nature has no mercy, and sacrifices the performer to get it done; makes a dropsy or a tympany of him. If she wants a thumb, she makes one at the cost of arms and legs, and any excess of power in one part is usually paid for at once by some defect in a contiguous part.

Our efficiency depends so much on our concentration, that Nature usually in the instances where a marked man is sent into the world, overloads him with bias, sacrificing his symmetry to his working power. It is said, no man can write but one book; and if a man have a defect, it is apt to leave its impression on all his performances. If she creates a policeman like Fouché, he is made up of suspicions and of plots to circumvent them. "The air," said Fouché, "is full of poniards." The physician Sanctorius spent his life in a pair of scales, weighing his food. Lord Coke valued Chaucer highly, because the Canon Yeman's Tale illustrates the statute *Hen. V. Chap. 4*, against alchemy. I saw a man who believed the principal mischiefs in the English state were derived from the devotion to musical concerts. A freemason, not long since, set out to explain to this country, that the principal cause of the success of General Washington, was, the aid he derived from the freemasons.

But worse than the harping on one string, Nature has secured individualism, by giving the private person a high conceit of his weight in the system. The pest of society is egotists. There are dull and bright, sacred and profane, coarse and fine egotists. 'Tis a disease that, like influenza, falls on all constitutions. In the distemper known to physicians as *chorea*, the patient sometimes turns round, and continues to spin slowly on one spot. Is egotism a metaphysical varioloid of this malady? The man runs round a ring formed by his own talent, falls into an admiration of it, and loses relation to the world. It is a tendency in all minds. One of its annoying forms, is a craving for sympathy. The sufferers parade their miseries, tear the lint from their bruises, reveal their indictable crimes, that you may pity them. They like sickness, because physical pain will extort some show of interest from the bystanders, as we have seen children, who, finding themselves of no account when grown people come in, will cough till they choke, to draw attention.

This distemper is the scourge of talent,—of artists, inventors, and philosophers. Eminent spiritualists shall have an incapacity of putting their act or word aloof from them, and seeing it bravely for the nothing it is. Beware of the man who says, "I am on the eve of a revelation." It is speedily punished, inasmuch as this habit invites men to humor it, and by treating the patient tenderly, to shut him up in a narrower selfism, and exclude him from the great world of God's cheerful fallible men and women. Let us rather be insulted, whilst we are insultable. Religious literature has eminent examples, and if we run over our private list of poets, critics, philanthropists, and philosophers, we shall find them infected with this dropsy and elephantiasis, which we ought to have tapped.

This goitre of egotism is so frequent among notable persons, that we must infer some strong necessity in nature which it subserves; such as we see in the sexual attraction. The preservation of the species was a point of such necessity, that Nature has secured it at all hazards by immensely overloading the passion, at the risk of perpetual crime and disorder. So egotism has its root in the cardinal necessity by which each individual persists to be what he is.

This individuality is not only not inconsistent with culture, but is the basis of it. Every valuable nature is there in its own right, and the student we speak to must have a motherwit invincible by his culture, which uses all books, arts, facilities, and elegancies of intercourse, but is never subdued and lost in them. He only is a well-made man who has a good determination. And the end of culture is not to destroy this, God forbid! but to train away all impediment and mixture, and leave nothing but pure power. Our student must have a style and determination, and be a master in his own specialty. But, having this, he must put it behind him. He must have a catholicity, a power to see with a free and disengaged look every object. Yet is this private interest and self so overcharged, that, if a man seeks a companion who can look at objects for their own sake, and without affection or self-reference, he will find the fewest who will give him that satisfaction; whilst most men are afflicted with a coldness, an incuriosity, as soon as any object does not connect with their self-love. Though they talk of the object before them, they are thinking of themselves, and their vanity is laying little traps for your admiration.

But after a man has discovered that there are limits to the interest which his private history has for mankind, he still converses with his family, or a few companions,—perhaps with half a dozen personalities that are famous in his neighborhood. In Boston, the question of life is the names of some eight or ten men. Have you seen Mr. Allston, Doctor Channing, Mr. Adams, Mr. Webster, Mr. Greenough? Have you heard Everett, Garrison, Father Taylor, Theodore Parker? Have you talked with Messieurs Turbinewheel, Summitlevel, and Lacofrupees? Then you may as well die. In New York, the question is of some other eight, or ten, or twenty. Have you seen a few lawyers, merchants, and brokers,—two or three scholars, two or three capitalists, two or three editors of newspapers? New York is a sucked orange. All conversation is at an end, when we have discharged ourselves of a dozen personalities, domestic or imported, which make up our American existence. Nor do we expect anybody to be other than a faint copy of these heroes.

Life is very narrow. Bring any club or company of intelligent men together again after ten years, and if the presence of some penetrating and calming genius could dispose them to frankness, what a confession of insanities would come up! The "causes" to which we have sacrificed, Tariff or Democracy, Whigism or Abolition, Temperance or Socialism, would show like roots of bitterness and dragons of wrath: and our talents are as mischievous as if each had been seized upon by some bird of prey, which had whisked him away from fortune, from truth, from the dear society of the poets, some zeal, some bias, and only when he was now gray and nerveless, was it relaxing its claws, and he awaking to sober perceptions.

Culture is the suggestion from certain best thoughts, that a man has a range of affinities, through which he can modulate the violence of any master-tones that have a droning preponderance in his scale, and succor him against himself. Culture redresses his balance, puts him among his equals and superiors, revives the delicious sense of sympathy, and warns him of the dangers of solitude and repulsion.

'Tis not a compliment but a disparagement to consult a man only on horses, or on steam, or on theatres, or on eating, or on books, and, whenever he appears, considerately to turn the conversation to the bantling he is known to fondle. In the Norse heaven of our forefathers, Thor's house had five hundred and forty floors; and man's house has five hundred and forty floors. His excellence is facility of adaptation and of transition through many related points, to wide contrasts and extremes. Culture kills his exaggeration, his conceit of his village or his city. We must leave our pets at home, when we go into the street, and meet men on broad grounds of good meaning and good sense. No performance is worth loss of geniality. 'Tis a cruel price we pay for certain fancy goods called fine arts and philosophy. In the Norse legend, Allfadir did not get a drink of Mimir's spring, (the fountain of wisdom,) until he left his eye in pledge. And here is a pedant that cannot unfold his wrinkles, nor conceal his wrath at interruption by the best, if their conversation do not fit his impertinency,—here is he to afflict us with his personalities. 'Tis incident to scholars, that each of them fancies he is pointedly odious in his community. Draw him out of this limbo of irritability. Cleanse with healthy blood his parchment skin. You restore to him his eyes which he left in pledge at Mimir's spring. If you are the victim of your doing, who cares what you do? We can spare your opera, your gazetteer, your chemic analysis, your history, your syllogisms. Your man of genius pays dear for his distinction. His head runs up into a spire, and instead of a healthy man, merry and wise, he is some mad dominie. Nature is reckless of the individual. When she has points to carry, she carries them. To wade in marshes and sea-margins is the destiny of certain birds, and they are so accurately made for this, that they are imprisoned in those places. Each animal out of its *habitat* would starve. To the physician, each man, each woman, is an amplification of one organ. A soldier, a locksmith, a bank-clerk, and a dancer could not exchange functions. And thus we are victims of adaptation.

The antidotes against this organic egotism, are, the range and variety of attractions, as gained by acquaintance with the world, with men of merit, with classes of society, with travel, with eminent persons, and with the high resources of philosophy, art, and religion: books, travel, society, solitude.

The hardiest skeptic who has seen a horse broken, a pointer trained, or, who has visited a menagerie, or the exhibition of the Industrious Fleas, will not deny the validity of education. "A boy," says Plato, "is the most vicious of all wild beasts;" and, in the same spirit, the old English poet Gascoigne says, "a boy is better unborn than untaught." The city breeds one kind of speech and manners; the back-country a different style; the sea, another; the army, a fourth. We know that an army which can be confided in, may be formed by discipline; that, by systematic discipline all men may be made heroes: Marshal Lannes said to a French officer, "Know, Colonel, that none but a poltroon will boast that he never was afraid." A great part of courage is the courage of having done the thing before. And, in all human action, those faculties will be strong which are used. Robert Owen said, "Give me a tiger, and I will educate him." 'Tis inhuman to want faith in the power of education, since to meliorate, is the law of nature; and men are valued precisely as they exert onward or meliorating force. On the other hand, poltroonery is the acknowledging an inferiority to be incurable.

Incapacity of melioration is the only mortal distemper. There are people who can never understand a trope, or any second or expanded sense given to your words, or any humor; but remain literalists, after hearing the music, and poetry, and rhetoric, and wit, of seventy or eighty years. They are past the help of surgeon or clergy. But even these can understand pitchforks and the cry of fire! and I have noticed in some of this class a marked dislike of earthquakes.

Let us make our education brave and preventive. Politics is an after-work, a poor patching. We are always a little late. The evil is done, the law is passed, and we begin the up-hill agitation for repeal of that of which we ought to have prevented the enacting. We shall one day learn to supersede politics by education. What we call our root-and-branch reforms of slavery, war, gambling, intemperance, is only medicating the symptoms. We must begin higher up, namely, in Education.

Our arts and tools give to him who can handle them much the same advantage over the novice, as if you extended his life, ten, fifty, or a hundred years. And I think it the part of good sense to provide every fine soul with such culture, that it shall not, at thirty or forty years, have to say, 'This which I might do is made hopeless through my want of weapons.'

But it is conceded that much of our training fails of effect; that all success is hazardous and rare; that a large part of our cost and pains is thrown away. Nature takes the matter into her own hands, and, though we must not omit any jot of our system, we can seldom be sure that it has availed much, or, that as much good would not have accrued from a different system.

Books, as containing the finest records of human wit, must always enter into our notion of culture. The best heads that ever existed, Pericles, Plato, Julius Cæsar, Shakspeare, Goethe, Milton, were well-read, universally educated men, and quite too wise to undervalue letters. Their opinion has weight, because they had means of knowing the opposite opinion. We look that a great man should be a good reader, or, in proportion to the spontaneous power should be the assimilating power. Good criticism is very rare, and always precious. I am always happy to meet persons who perceive the transcendent superiority of Shakspeare over all other writers. I like people who like Plato. Because this love does not consist with self-conceit.

But books are good only as far as a boy is ready for them. He sometimes gets ready very slowly. You send your child to the schoolmaster, but 'tis the schoolboys who educate him. You send him to the Latin class, but much of his tuition comes, on his way to school, from the shop-windows. You like the strict rules and the long terms; and he finds his best leading in a by-way of his own, and refuses any companions but of his choosing. He hates the grammar and *Gradus*, and loves guns, fishing-rods, horses, and boats. Well, the boy is right; and you are not fit to direct his bringing up, if your theory leaves out his gymnastic training. Archery, cricket, gun and fishing-rod, horse and boat, are all educators, liberalizers; and so are dancing, dress, and the street-talk; and,— provided only the boy has resources, and is of a noble and ingenuous strain,— these will not serve him less than the books. He learns chess, whist, dancing, and theatricals. The father observes that another boy has learned algebra and geometry in the same time. But the first boy has acquired much more than these poor games along with them. He is infatuated for weeks with whist and chess; but presently will find out, as you did, that when he rises from the game too long played, he is vacant and forlorn, and despises himself. Thenceforward it takes place with other things, and has its due weight in his experience. These minor skills and accomplishments, for example, dancing, are tickets of admission to the dress-circle of mankind, and the being master of them enables the youth to judge intelligently of much, on which, otherwise, he would give a pedantic squint. Landor said, "I have suffered more from my bad dancing, than from all the misfortunes and miseries of my life put together." Provided always the boy is teachable, (for we are not proposing to make a statue out of punk,) football, cricket, archery, swimming, skating, climbing, fencing, riding, are lessons in the art of power, which it is his main business to learn;— riding, specially, of which Lord Herbert of Cherbury said, "a good rider on a good horse is as much above himself and others as the world can make him." Besides, the gun, fishing-rod, boat, and horse, constitute, among all who use them, secret freemasonries. They are as if they belonged to one club.

There is also a negative value in these arts. Their chief use to the youth, is, not amusement, but to be known for what they are, and not to remain to him occasions of heart-burn. We are full of superstitions. Each class fixes its eyes on the advantages it has not; the refined, on rude strength; the democrat, on birth and breeding. One of the benefits of a college education is, to show the boy its little avail. I knew a leading man in a leading city, who, having set his heart on an education at the university, and missed it, could never quite feel himself the equal of his own brothers who had gone thither. His easy superiority to multitudes of professional men could never quite countervail to him this imaginary defect. Balls, riding, wine-parties, and billiards, pass to a poor boy for something fine and romantic, which they are not; and a free admission to them on an equal footing, if it were possible, only once or twice, would be worth ten times its cost, by undeceiving him.

I am not much an advocate for travelling, and I observe that men run away to other countries, because they are not good in their own, and run back to their own, because they pass for nothing in the new places. For the most part, only the light characters travel. Who are you that have no task to keep you at home? I have been quoted as saying captious things about travel; but I mean to do justice. I think, there is a restlessness in our people, which argues want of character. All educated Americans, first or last, go to Europe;—perhaps, because it is their mental home, as the invalid habits of this country might suggest. An eminent teacher of girls said, "the idea of a girl's education, is, whatever qualifies them for going to Europe." Can we never extract this tape-worm of Europe from the brain of our countrymen? One sees very well what their fate must be. He that does not fill a place at home, cannot abroad. He only goes there to hide his insignificance in a larger crowd. You do not think you will find anything there which you have not seen at home? The stuff of all countries is just the same. Do you suppose, there is any country where they do not scald milkpans, and swaddle the infants, and burn the brushwood, and broil the fish? What is true anywhere is true everywhere. And let him go where he will, he can only find so much beauty or worth as he carries.

Of course, for some men, travel may be useful. Naturalists, discoverers, and sailors are born. Some men are made for couriers, exchangers, envoys, missionaries, bearers of despatches, as others are for farmers and working-men. And if the man is of a light and social turn, and Nature has aimed to make a legged and winged creature, framed for locomotion, we must follow her hint, and furnish him with that breeding which gives currency, as sedulously as with that which gives worth. But let us not be pedantic, but allow to travel its full effect. The boy grown up on the farm, which he has never left, is said in the country to have had *no chance*, and boys and men of that condition look upon work on a railroad, or drudgery in a city, as opportunity. Poor country boys of Vermont and Connecticut formerly owed what knowledge they had, to their peddling trips to the Southern States. California and the Pacific Coast is now the university of this class, as Virginia was in old times. 'To have *some chance*' is their word. And the phrase 'to know the world,' or to travel, is synonymous with all men's ideas of advantage and superiority. No doubt, to a man of sense, travel offers advantages. As many languages as he has, as many friends, as many arts and trades, so many times is he a man. A foreign country is a point of comparison, wherefrom to judge his own. One use of travel, is, to recommend the books and works of home; [we go to Europe to be Americanized;] and another, to find men. For, as Nature has put fruits apart in latitudes, a new fruit in every degree, so knowledge and fine moral quality she lodges in distant men. And thus, of the six or seven teachers whom each man wants among his contemporaries, it often happens, that one or two of them live on the other side of the world.

Moreover, there is in every constitution a certain solstice, when the stars stand still in our inward firmament, and when there is required some foreign force, some diversion or alterative to prevent stagnation. And, as a medical remedy, travel seems one of the best. Just as a man witnessing the admirable effect of ether to lull pain, and meditating on the contingencies of wounds, cancers, lockjaws, rejoices in Dr. Jackson's benign discovery, so a man who looks at Paris, at Naples, or at London, says, 'If I should be driven from my own home, here, at least, my thoughts can be consoled by the most prodigal amusement and occupation which the human race in ages could contrive and accumulate.'

Akin to the benefit of foreign travel, the æsthetic value of railroads is to unite the advantages of town and country life, neither of which we can spare. A man should live in or near a large town, because, let his own genius be what it may, it will repel quite as much of agreeable and valuable talent as it draws, and, in a city, the total attraction of all the citizens is sure to conquer, first or last, every repulsion, and drag the most improbable hermit within its walls some day in the year. In town, he can find the swimming-school, the gymnasium, the dancing-master, the shooting-gallery, opera, theatre, and panorama; the chemist's shop, the museum of natural history; the gallery of fine arts; the national orators, in their turn; foreign travellers, the libraries, and his club. In the country, he can find solitude and reading, manly labor, cheap living, and his old shoes; moors for game, hills for geology, and groves for devotion. Aubrey writes, "I have heard Thomas Hobbes say, that, in the Earl of Devon's house, in Derbyshire, there was a good library and books enough for him, and his lordship stored the library with what books he thought fit to be bought. But the want of good conversation was a very great inconvenience, and, though he conceived he could order his thinking as well as another, yet he found a great defect. In the country, in long time, for want of good conversation, one's understanding and invention contract a moss on them, like an old paling in an orchard."

Cities give us collision. 'Tis said, London and New York take the nonsense out of a man. A great part of our education is sympathetic and social. Boys and girls who have been brought up with well-informed and superior people, show in their manners an inestimable grace. Fuller says, that "William, Earl of Nassau, won a subject from the King of Spain, every time he put off his hat." You cannot have one well-bred man, without a whole society of such. They keep each other up to any high point. Especially women;—it requires a great many cultivated women,—saloons of bright, elegant, reading women, accustomed to ease and refinement, to spectacles, pictures, sculpture, poetry, and to elegant society, in order that you should have one Madame de Staël. The head of a commercial house, or a leading lawyer or politician is brought into daily contact with troops of men from all parts of the country, and those too the driving-wheels, the business men of each section, and one can hardly suggest for an apprehensive man a more searching culture. Besides, we must remember the high social possibilities of a million of men. The best bribe which London offers to-day to the imagination, is, that, in such a vast variety of people and conditions, one can believe there is room for persons of romantic character to exist, and that the poet, the mystic, and the hero may hope to confront their counterparts.

I wish cities could teach their best lesson,—of quiet manners. It is the foible especially of American youth,—pretension. The mark of the man of the world is absence of pretension. He does not make a speech; he takes a low business-tone, avoids all brag, is nobody, dresses plainly, promises not at all, performs much, speaks in monosyllables, hugs his fact. He calls his employment by its lowest name, and so takes from evil tongues their sharpest weapon. His conversation clings to the weather and the news, yet he allows himself to be surprised into thought, and the unlocking of his learning and philosophy. How the imagination is piqued by anecdotes of some great man passing incognito, as a king in gray clothes,—of Napoleon affecting a plain suit at his glittering levee; of Burns, or Scott, or Beethoven, or Wellington, or Goethe, or any container of transcendent power, passing for nobody; of Epaminondas, "who never says anything, but will listen eternally;" of Goethe, who preferred trifling subjects and common expressions in intercourse with strangers, worse rather than better clothes, and to appear a little more capricious than he was. There are advantages in the old hat and box-coat. I have heard, that, throughout this country, a certain respect is paid to good broadcloth; but dress makes a little restraint: men will not commit themselves. But the box-coat is like wine; it unlocks the tongue, and men say what they think. An old poet says,

> "Go far and go sparing,
> For you'll find it certain,
> The poorer and the baser you appear,
> The more you'll look through still."*

---

*Beaumont and Fletcher: *The Tamer Tamed.*

Not much otherwise Milnes writes, in the "Lay of the Humble,"

"To me men are for what they are,
They wear no masks with me."

'Tis odd that our people should have—not water on the brain,—but a little gas there. A shrewd foreigner said of the Americans, that, "whatever they say has a little the air of a speech." Yet one of the traits down in the books as distinguishing the Anglo-Saxon, is, a trick of self-disparagement. To be sure, in old, dense countries, among a million of good coats, a fine coat comes to be no distinction, and you find humorists. In an English party, a man with no marked manners or features, with a face like red dough, unexpectedly discloses wit, learning, a wide range of topics, and personal familiarity with good men in all parts of the world, until you think you have fallen upon some illustrious personage. Can it be that the American forest has refreshed some weeds of old Pietish barbarism just ready to die out,—the love of the scarlet feather, of beads, and tinsel? The Italians are fond of red clothes, peacock plumes, and embroidery; and I remember one rainy morning in the city of Palermo, the street was in a blaze with scarlet umbrellas. The English have a plain taste. The equipages of the grandees are plain. A gorgeous livery indicates new and awkward city wealth. Mr. Pitt, like Mr. Pym, thought the title of *Mister* good against any king in Europe. They have piqued themselves on governing the whole world in the poor, plain, dark Committee-room which the House of Commons sat in, before the fire.

Whilst we want cities as the centres where the best things are found, cities degrade us by magnifying trifles. The countryman finds the town a chop-house, a barber's shop. He has lost the lines of grandeur of the horizon, hills and plains, and with them, sobriety and elevation. He has come among a supple, glib-tongued tribe, who live for show, servile to public opinion. Life is dragged down to a fracas of pitiful cares and disasters. You say the gods ought to respect a life whose objects are their own; but in cities they have betrayed you to a cloud of insignificant annoyances:

"Mirmidons, race féconde,
 Mirmidons,
 Enfin nous commandons;
 Jupiter livre le monde
 Aux mirmidons, aux mirmidons."*

'Tis heavy odds
Against the gods,
When they will match with myrmidons.
We spawning, spawning myrmidons,
Our turn to-day! we take command,
Jove gives the globe into the hand
Of myrmidons, of myrmidons.

What is odious but noise, and people who scream and be-wail? people whose vane points always east, who live to dine, who send for the doctor, who coddle themselves, who toast their feet on the register, who intrigue to secure a padded chair, and a corner out of the draught. Suffer them once to begin the enumeration of their infirmities, and the sun will go down on the unfinished tale. Let these triflers put us out of conceit with petty comforts. To a man at work, the frost is but a color: the rain, the wind, he forgot them when he came in. Let us learn to live coarsely, dress plainly, and lie hard. The least habit of dominion over the palate has certain good effects not easily estimated. Neither will we be driven into a quiddling abstemiousness. 'Tis a superstition to insist on a special diet. All is made at last of the same chemical atoms.

A man in pursuit of greatness feels no little wants. How can you mind diet, bed, dress, or salutes or compliments, or the figure you make in company, or wealth, or even the bringing things to pass, when you think how paltry are the machinery and the workers? Wordsworth was praised to me, in Westmoreland, for having afforded to his country neighbors an example of a modest household where comfort and culture were secured, without display. And a tender boy who wears his rusty cap and outgrown coat, that he may secure the coveted place in college, and the right in the library, is

*Béranger.

educated to some purpose. There is a great deal of self-denial and manliness in poor and middle-class houses, in town and country, that has not got into literature, and never will, but that keeps the earth sweet; that saves on superfluities, and spends on essentials; that goes rusty, and educates the boy; that sells the horse, but builds the school; works early and late, takes two looms in the factory, three looms, six looms, but pays off the mortgage on the paternal farm, and then goes back cheerfully to work again.

We can ill spare the commanding social benefits of cities; they must be used; yet cautiously, and haughtily,—and will yield their best values to him who best can do without them. Keep the town for occasions, but the habits should be formed to retirement. Solitude, the safeguard of mediocrity, is to genius the stern friend, the cold, obscure shelter where moult the wings which will bear it farther than suns and stars. He who should inspire and lead his race must be defended from travelling with the souls of other men, from living, breathing, reading, and writing in the daily, time-worn yoke of their opinions. "In the morning,—solitude;" said Pythagoras; that Nature may speak to the imagination, as she does never in company, and that her favorite may make acquaintance with those divine strengths which disclose themselves to serious and abstracted thought. 'Tis very certain that Plato, Plotinus, Archimedes, Hermes, Newton, Milton, Wordsworth, did not live in a crowd, but descended into it from time to time as benefactors: and the wise instructor will press this point of securing to the young soul in the disposition of time and the arrangements of living, periods and habits of solitude. The high advantage of university-life is often the mere mechanical one, I may call it, of a separate chamber and fire,—which parents will allow the boy without hesitation at Cambridge, but do not think needful at home. We say solitude, to mark the character of the tone of thought; but if it can be shared between two or more than two, it is happier, and not less noble. "We four," wrote Neander to his sacred friends, " will enjoy at Halle the inward blessedness of a *civitas Dei*, whose foundations are forever friendship. The more I know you, the more I dissatisfy and must dissatisfy all my wonted companions. Their very presence stupefies me. The common understanding withdraws itself from the one centre of all existence."

Solitude takes off the pressure of present importunities that more catholic and humane relations may appear. The saint and poet seek privacy to ends the most public and universal: and it is the secret of culture, to interest the man more in his public, than in his private quality. Here is a new poem, which elicits a good many comments in the journals, and in conversation. From these it is easy, at last, to eliminate the verdict which readers passed upon it; and that is, in the main, unfavorable. The poet, as a craftsman, is only interested in the praise accorded to him, and not in the censure, though it be just. And the poor little poet hearkens only to that, and rejects the censure, as proving incapacity in the critic. But the poet *cultivated* becomes a stockholder in both companies,— say Mr. Curfew,—in the Curfew stock, and in the *humanity* stock; and, in the last, exults as much in the demonstration of the unsoundness of Curfew, as his interest in the former gives him pleasure in the currency of Curfew. For, the depreciation of his Curfew stock only shows the immense values of the humanity stock. As soon as he sides with his critic against himself, with joy, he is a cultivated man.

We must have an intellectual quality in all property and in all action, or they are nought. I must have children, I must have events, I must have a social state and history, or my thinking and speaking want body or basis. But to give these accessories any value, I must know them as contingent and rather showy possessions, which pass for more to the people than to me. We see this abstraction in scholars, as a matter of course: but what a charm it adds when observed in practical men. Bonaparte, like Cæsar, was intellectual, and could look at every object for itself, without affection. Though an egotist *à l'outrance*, he could criticize a play, a building, a character, on universal grounds, and give a just opinion. A man known to us only as a celebrity in politics or in trade, gains largely in our esteem if we discover that he has some intellectual taste or skill; as when we learn of Lord Fairfax, the Long Parliament's general, his passion for antiquarian studies; or of the French regicide Carnot, his sublime genius in mathematics; or of a living banker, his success in poetry; or of a partisan journalist, his devotion to ornithology. So, if in travelling in the dreary wildernesses of Arkansas or Texas, we should observe on the next seat a man reading Horace, or Martial, or Calderon, we should wish to hug him. In callings that require roughest energy, soldiers, sea-captains, and civil engineers sometimes betray a fine insight, if only through a certain gentleness when off duty; a good-natured admission that there are illusions, and who shall say that he is not their sport? We only vary the phrase, not the doctrine, when we say, that culture opens the sense of beauty. A man is a beggar who only lives to the useful, and, however he may serve as a pin or rivet in the social machine, cannot be said to have arrived at self-possession. I suffer, every day, from the want of perception of beauty in people. They do not know the charm with which all moments and objects can be embellished, the charm of manners, of self-command, of benevolence. Repose and cheerfulness are the badge of the gentleman,—repose in energy. The Greek battle-pieces are calm; the heroes, in whatever violent actions engaged, retain a serene aspect; as we say of Niagara, that it falls without speed. A cheerful, intelligent face is the end of culture, and success enough. For it indicates the purpose of Nature and wisdom attained.

When our higher faculties are in activity, we are domesticated, and awkwardness and discomfort give place to natural and agreeable movements. It is noticed, that the consideration of the great periods and spaces of astronomy induces a dignity of mind, and an indifference to death. The influence of fine scenery, the presence of mountains, appeases our irritations and elevates our friendships. Even a high dome, and the expansive interior of a cathedral, have a sensible effect on manners. I have heard that stiff people lose something of their awkwardness under high ceilings, and in spacious halls. I think, sculpture and painting have an effect to teach us manners, and abolish hurry.

But, over all, culture must reinforce from higher influx the empirical skills of eloquence, or of politics, or of trade, and the useful arts. There is a certain loftiness of thought and power to marshal and adjust particulars, which can only come from an insight of their whole connection. The orator who has once seen things in their divine order, will never quite lose sight of this, and will come to affairs as from a higher ground, and, though he will say nothing of philosophy, he will have a certain mastery in dealing with them, and an incapableness of being dazzled or frighted, which will distinguish his handling from that of attorneys and factors. A man who stands on a good footing with the heads of parties at Washington, reads the rumors of the newspapers, and the guesses of provincial politicians, with a key to the right and wrong in each statement, and sees well enough where all this will end. Archimedes will look through your Connecticut machine, at a glance, and judge of its fitness. And much more, a wise man who knows not only what Plato, but what Saint John can show him, can easily raise the affair he deals with, to a certain majesty. Plato says, Pericles owed this elevation to the lessons of Anaxagoras. Burke descended from a higher sphere when he would influence human affairs. Franklin, Adams, Jefferson, Washington, stood on a fine humanity, before which the brawls of modern senates are but pot-house politics.

But there are higher secrets of culture, which are not for the apprentices, but for proficients. These are lessons only for the brave. We must know our friends under ugly masks. The calamities are our friends. Ben Jonson specifies in his address to the Muse:—

> "Get him the time's long grudge, the court's ill-will,
> And, reconciled, keep him suspected still,
> Make him lose all his friends, and, what is worse,
> Almost all ways to any better course;
> With me thou leav'st a better Muse than thee,
> And which thou brought'st me, blessed Poverty."

We wish to learn philosophy by rote, and play at heroism. But the wiser God says, Take the shame, the poverty, and the penal solitude, that belong to truth-speaking. Try the rough water as well as the smooth. Rough water can teach lessons worth knowing. When the state is unquiet, personal qualities are more than ever decisive. Fear not a revolution which will constrain you to live five years in one. Don't be so tender at making an enemy now and then. Be willing to go to Coventry sometimes, and let the populace bestow on you their coldest contempts. The finished man of the world must eat of every apple once. He must hold his hatreds also at arm's length, and not remember spite. He has neither friends nor enemies, but values men only as channels of power.

He who aims high, must dread an easy home and popular manners. Heaven sometimes hedges a rare character about with ungainliness and odium, as the burr that protects the fruit. If there is any great and good thing in store for you, it will not come at the first or the second call, nor in the shape of fashion, ease, and city drawing-rooms. Popularity is for dolls. "Steep and craggy," said Porphyry, "is the path of the gods." Open your Marcus Antoninus. In the opinion of the ancients, he was the great man who scorned to shine, and who contested the frowns of fortune. They preferred the noble vessel too late for the tide, contending with winds and waves, dismantled and unrigged, to her companion borne into harbor with colors flying and guns firing. There is none of the social goods that may not be purchased too dear, and mere amiableness must not take rank with high aims and self-subsistency.

Bettine replies to Goethe's mother, who chides her disregard of dress,—"If I cannot do as I have a mind, in our poor Frankfort, I shall not carry things far." And the youth must rate at its true mark the inconceivable levity of local opinion. The longer we live, the more we must endure the elementary existence of men and women; and every brave heart must treat society as a child, and never allow it to dictate.

"All that class of the severe and restrictive virtues," said Burke, "are almost too costly for humanity." Who wishes to be severe? Who wishes to resist the eminent and polite, in behalf of the poor, and low, and impolite? and who that dares do it, can keep his temper sweet, his frolic spirits? The high virtues are not debonair, but have their redress in being illustrious at last. What forests of laurel we bring, and the tears of mankind, to those who stood firm against the opinion of their contemporaries! The measure of a master is his success in bringing all men round to his opinion twenty years later.

Let me say here, that culture cannot begin too early. In talking with scholars, I observe that they lost on ruder companions those years of boyhood which alone could give imaginative literature a religious and infinite quality in their esteem. I find, too, that the chance for appreciation is much increased by being the son of an appreciator, and that these boys who now grow up are caught not only years too late, but two or three births too late, to make the best scholars of. And I think it a presentable motive to a scholar, that, as, in an old community, a well-born proprietor is usually found, after the first heats of youth, to be a careful husband, and to feel a habitual desire that the estate shall suffer no harm by his administration, but shall be delivered down to the next heir in as good condition as he received it;—so, a considerate man will reckon himself a subject of that secular melioration by which mankind is mollified, cured, and refined, and will shun every expenditure of his forces on pleasure or gain, which will jeopardize this social and secular accumulation.

The fossil strata show us that Nature began with rudimental forms, and rose to the more complex, as fast as the earth was fit for their dwelling-place; and that the lower perish, as the higher appear. Very few of our race can be said to be yet finished men. We still carry sticking to us some remains of the preceding inferior quadruped organization. We call these millions men; but they are not yet men. Half-engaged in the soil, pawing to get free, man needs all the music that can be brought to disengage him. If Love, red Love, with tears and joy; if Want with his scourge; if War with his cannonade; if Christianity with its charity; if Trade with its money; if Art with its portfolios; if Science with her telegraphs through the deeps of space and time; can set his dull nerves throbbing, and by loud taps on the tough chrysalis, can break its walls, and let the new creature emerge erect and free,—make way, and sing pæan! The age of the quadruped is to go out,—the age of the brain and of the heart is to come in. The time will come when the evil forms we have known can no more be organized. Man's culture can spare nothing, wants all the material. He is to convert all impediments into instruments, all enemies into power. The formidable mischief will only make the more useful slave. And if one shall read the future of the race hinted in the organic effort of Nature to mount and meliorate, and the corresponding impulse to the Better in the human being, we shall dare affirm that there is nothing he will not overcome and convert, until at last culture shall absorb the chaos and gehenna. He will convert the Furies into Muses, and the hells into benefit.

V

BEHAVIOR

———

GRACE, Beauty, and Caprice
Build this golden portal;
Graceful women, chosen men
Dazzle every mortal:
Their sweet and lofty countenance
His enchanting food;
He need not go to them, their forms
Beset his solitude.
He looketh seldom in their face,
His eyes explore the ground,
The green grass is a looking-glass
Whereon their traits are found.
Little he says to them,
So dances his heart in his breast,
Their tranquil mien bereaveth him
Of wit, of words, of rest.
Too weak to win, too fond to shun
The tyrants of his doom,
The much deceived Endymion
Slips behind a tomb.

Behavior

THE SOUL which animates Nature is not less significantly
published in the figure, movement, and gesture of animated bodies, than in its last vehicle of articulate speech. This
silent and subtile language is Manners; not *what*, but *how*.
Life expresses. A statue has no tongue, and needs none. Good
tableaux do not need declamation. Nature tells every secret
once. Yes, but in man she tells it all the time, by form, attitude, gesture, mien, face, and parts of the face, and by the
whole action of the machine. The visible carriage or action of
the individual, as resulting from his organization and his will
combined, we call manners. What are they but thought entering the hands and feet, controlling the movements of the
body, the speech and behavior?

There is always a best way of doing everything, if it be to
boil an egg. Manners are the happy ways of doing things;
each once a stroke of genius or of love,—now repeated and
hardened into usage. They form at last a rich varnish, with
which the routine of life is washed, and its details adorned. If
they are superficial, so are the dew-drops which give such a
depth to the morning meadows. Manners are very communicable: men catch them from each other. Consuelo, in the romance, boasts of the lessons she had given the nobles in
manners, on the stage; and, in real life, Talma taught Napoleon the arts of behavior. Genius invents fine manners, which
the baron and the baroness copy very fast, and, by the advantage of a palace, better the instruction. They stereotype the
lesson they have learned into a mode.

The power of manners is incessant,—an element as uncon-
cealable as fire. The nobility cannot in any country be disguised, and no more in a republic or a democracy, than in a
kingdom. No man can resist their influence. There are certain
manners which are learned in good society, of that force, that,
if a person have them, he or she must be considered, and is
everywhere welcome, though without beauty, or wealth, or
genius. Give a boy address and accomplishments, and you
give him the mastery of palaces and fortunes where he goes.
He has not the trouble of earning or owning them: they

solicit him to enter and possess. We send girls of a timid, retreating disposition to the boarding-school, to the riding-school, to the ballroom, or wheresoever they can come into acquaintance and nearness of leading persons of their own sex; where they might learn address, and see it near at hand. The power of a woman of fashion to lead, and also to daunt and repel, derives from their belief that she knows resources and behaviors not known to them; but when these have mastered her secret, they learn to confront her, and recover their self-possession.

Every day bears witness to their gentle rule. People who would obtrude, now do not obtrude. The mediocre circle learns to demand that which belongs to a high state of nature or of culture. Your manners are always under examination, and by committees little suspected,—a police in citizens' clothes,—but are awarding or denying you very high prizes when you least think of it.

We talk much of utilities,—but 'tis our manners that associate us. In hours of business, we go to him who knows, or has, or does this or that which we want, and we do not let our taste or feeling stand in the way. But this activity over, we return to the indolent state, and wish for those we can be at ease with; those who will go where we go, whose manners do not offend us, whose social tone chimes with ours. When we reflect on their persuasive and cheering force; how they recommend, prepare, and draw people together; how, in all clubs, manners make the members; how manners make the fortune of the ambitious youth; that, for the most part, his manners marry him, and, for the most part, he marries manners; when we think what keys they are, and to what secrets; what high lessons and inspiring tokens of character they convey; and what divination is required in us, for the reading of this fine telegraph, we see what range the subject has, and what relations to convenience, power, and beauty.

Their first service is very low,—when they are the minor morals: but 'tis the beginning of civility,—to make us, I mean, endurable to each other. We prize them for their rough-plastic, abstergent force; to get people out of the quadruped state; to get them washed, clothed, and set up on end; to slough their animal husks and habits; compel them to be clean; overawe their spite and meanness, teach them to stifle the base, and choose the generous expression, and make them know how much happier the generous behaviors are.

Bad behavior the laws cannot reach. Society is infested with rude, cynical, restless, and frivolous persons who prey upon the rest, and whom, a public opinion concentrated into good manners, forms accepted by the sense of all, can reach:—the contradictors and railers at public and private tables, who are like terriers, who conceive it the duty of a dog of honor to growl at any passer-by, and do the honors of the house by barking him out of sight:—I have seen men who neigh like a horse when you contradict them, or say something which they do not understand:—then the overbold, who make their own invitation to your hearth; the persevering talker, who gives you his society in large, saturating doses; the pitiers of themselves,—a perilous class; the frivolous Asmodeus, who relies on you to find him in ropes of sand to twist; the monotones; in short, every stripe of absurdity;—these are social inflictions which the magistrate cannot cure or defend you from, and which must be intrusted to the restraining force of custom, and proverbs, and familiar rules of behavior impressed on young people in their school-days.

In the hotels on the banks of the Mississippi, they print, or used to print, among the rules of the house, that "no gentleman can be permitted to come to the public table without his coat;" and in the same country, in the pews of the churches, little placards plead with the worshipper against the fury of expectoration. Charles Dickens self-sacrificingly undertook the reformation of our American manners in unspeakable particulars. I think the lesson was not quite lost; that it held bad manners up, so that the churls could see the deformity. Unhappily, the book had its own deformities. It ought not to need to print in a reading-room a caution to strangers not to speak loud; nor to persons who look over fine engravings, that they should be handled like cobwebs and butterflies' wings; nor to persons who look at marble statues, that they shall not smite them with canes. But, even in the perfect civilization of this city, such cautions are not quite needless in the Athenæum and City Library.

Manners are factitious, and grow out of circumstance as

well as out of character. If you look at the pictures of patricians and of peasants, of different periods and countries, you will see how well they match the same classes in our towns. The modern aristocrat not only is well drawn in Titian's Venetian doges, and in Roman coins and statues, but also in the pictures which Commodore Perry brought home of dignitaries in Japan. Broad lands and great interests not only arrive to such heads as can manage them, but form manners of power. A keen eye, too, will see nice gradations of rank, or see in the manners the degree of homage the party is wont to receive. A prince who is accustomed every day to be courted and deferred to by the highest grandees, acquires a corresponding expectation, and a becoming mode of receiving and replying to this homage.

There are always exceptional people and modes. English grandees affect to be farmers. Claverhouse is a fop, and, under the finish of dress, and levity of behavior, hides the terror of his war. But Nature and Destiny are honest, and never fail to leave their mark, to hang out a sign for each and for every quality. It is much to conquer one's face, and perhaps the ambitious youth thinks he has got the whole secret when he has learned, that disengaged manners are commanding. Don't be deceived by a facile exterior. Tender men sometimes have strong wills. We had, in Massachusetts, an old statesman, who had sat all his life in courts and in chairs of state, without overcoming an extreme irritability of face, voice, and bearing: when he spoke, his voice would not serve him; it cracked, it broke, it wheezed, it piped;—little cared he; he knew that it had got to pipe, or wheeze, or screech his argument and his indignation. When he sat down, after speaking, he seemed in a sort of fit, and held on to his chair with both hands: but underneath all this irritability, was a puissant will, firm, and advancing, and a memory in which lay in order and method like geologic strata every fact of his history, and under the control of his will.

Manners are partly factitious, but, mainly, there must be capacity for culture in the blood. Else all culture is vain. The obstinate prejudice in favor of blood, which lies at the base of the feudal and monarchical fabrics of the old world, has some reason in common experience. Every man,—mathematician, artist, soldier, or merchant,—looks with confidence for some traits and talents in his own child, which he would not dare to presume in the child of a stranger. The Orientalists are very orthodox on this point. "Take a thorn-bush," said the emir Abdel-Kader, "and sprinkle it for a whole year with water;—it will yield nothing but thorns. Take a date-tree, leave it without culture, and it will always produce dates. Nobility is the date-tree, and the Arab populace is a bush of thorns."

A main fact in the history of manners is the wonderful expressiveness of the human body. If it were made of glass, or of air, and the thoughts were written on steel tablets within, it could not publish more truly its meaning than now. Wise men read very sharply all your private history in your look and gait and behavior. The whole economy of nature is bent on expression. The tell-tale body is all tongues. Men are like Geneva watches with crystal faces which expose the whole movement. They carry the liquor of life flowing up and down in these beautiful bottles, and announcing to the curious how it is with them. The face and eyes reveal what the spirit is doing, how old it is, what aims it has. The eyes indicate the antiquity of the soul, or, through how many forms it has already ascended. It almost violates the proprieties, if we say above the breath here, what the confessing eyes do not hesitate to utter to every street passenger.

Man cannot fix his eye on the sun, and so far seems imperfect. In Siberia, a late traveller found men who could see the satellites of Jupiter with their unarmed eye. In some respects the animals excel us. The birds have a longer sight, beside the advantage by their wings of a higher observatory. A cow can bid her calf, by secret signal, probably of the eye, to run away, or to lie down and hide itself. The jockeys say of certain horses, that "they look over the whole ground." The out-door life, and hunting, and labor, give equal vigor to the human eye. A farmer looks out at you as strong as the horse; his eye-beam is like the stroke of a staff. An eye can threaten like a loaded and levelled gun, or can insult like hissing or kicking; or, in its altered mood, by beams of kindness, it can make the heart dance with joy.

The eye obeys exactly the action of the mind. When a thought strikes us, the eyes fix, and remain gazing at a distance; in enumerating the names of persons or of countries, as France, Germany, Spain, Turkey, the eyes wink at each new name. There is no nicety of learning sought by the mind, which the eyes do not vie in acquiring. "An artist," said Michel Angelo, "must have his measuring tools not in the hand, but in the eye;" and there is no end to the catalogue of its performances, whether in indolent vision, (that of health and beauty,) or in strained vision, (that of art and labor.)

Eyes are bold as lions,—roving, running, leaping, here and there, far and near. They speak all languages. They wait for no introduction; they are no Englishmen; ask no leave of age, or rank; they respect neither poverty nor riches, neither learning nor power, nor virtue, nor sex, but intrude, and come again, and go through and through you, in a moment of time. What inundation of life and thought is discharged from one soul into another, through them! The glance is natural magic. The mysterious communication established across a house between two entire strangers, moves all the springs of wonder. The communication by the glance is in the greatest part not subject to the control of the will. It is the bodily symbol of identity of nature. We look into the eyes to know if this other form is another self, and the eyes will not lie, but make a faithful confession what inhabitant is there. The revelations are sometimes terrific. The confession of a low, usurping devil is there made, and the observer shall seem to feel the stirring of owls, and bats, and horned hoofs, where he looked for innocence and simplicity. 'Tis remarkable, too, that the spirit that appears at the windows of the house does at once invest himself in a new form of his own, to the mind of the beholder.

The eyes of men converse as much as their tongues, with the advantage, that the ocular dialect needs no dictionary, but is understood all the world over. When the eyes say one thing, and the tongue another, a practised man relies on the language of the first. If the man is off his centre, the eyes show it. You can read in the eyes of your companion, whether your argument hits him, though his tongue will not confess it. There is a look by which a man shows he is going to say a good thing, and a look when he has said it. Vain and forgotten are all the fine offers and offices of hospitality, if there is no holiday in the eye. How many furtive inclinations avowed by the eye, though dissembled by the lips! One comes away from a company, in which, it may easily happen, he has said nothing, and no important remark has been addressed to him, and yet, if in sympathy with the society, he shall not have a sense of this fact, such a stream of life has been flowing into him, and out from him, through the eyes. There are eyes, to be sure, that give no more admission into the man than blueberries. Others are liquid and deep,—wells that a man might fall into;—others are aggressive and devouring, seem to call out the police, take all too much notice, and require crowded Broadways, and the security of millions, to protect individuals against them. The military eye I meet, now darkly sparkling under clerical, now under rustic brows. 'Tis the city of Lacedæmon; 'tis a stack of bayonets. There are asking eyes, asserting eyes, prowling eyes; and eyes full of fate,—some of good, and some of sinister omen. The alleged power to charm down insanity, or ferocity in beasts, is a power behind the eye. It must be a victory achieved in the will, before it can be signified in the eye. 'Tis very certain that each man carries in his eye the exact indication of his rank in the immense scale of men, and we are always learning to read it. A complete man should need no auxiliaries to his personal presence. Whoever looked on him would consent to his will, being certified that his aims were generous and universal. The reason why men do not obey us, is because they see the mud at the bottom of our eye.

If the organ of sight is such a vehicle of power, the other features have their own. A man finds room in the few square inches of the face for the traits of all his ancestors; for the expression of all his history, and his wants. The sculptor, and Winckelmann, and Lavater, will tell you how significant a feature is the nose; how its forms express strength or weakness of will, and good or bad temper. The nose of Julius Cæsar, of Dante, and of Pitt, suggest "the terrors of the beak." What refinement, and what limitations, the teeth betray! "Beware you don't laugh," said the wise mother, "for then you show all your faults."

Balzac left in manuscript a chapter, which he called "*Théorie de la démarche*," in which he says: "The look, the voice, the respiration, and the attitude or walk, are identical. But, as it has not been given to man, the power to stand guard, at once, over these four different simultaneous expressions of his thought, watch that one which speaks out the truth, and you will know the whole man."

Palaces interest us mainly in the exhibition of manners, which, in the idle and expensive society dwelling in them, are raised to a high art. The maxim of courts is, that manner is power. A calm and resolute bearing, a polished speech, an embellishment of trifles, and the art of hiding all uncomfortable feeling, are essential to the courtier: and Saint Simon, and Cardinal de Retz, and Rœderer, and an encyclopædia of *Mémoires*, will instruct you, if you wish, in those potent secrets. Thus, it is a point of pride with kings, to remember faces and names. It is reported of one prince, that his head had the air of leaning downwards, in order not to humble the crowd. There are people who come in ever like a child with a piece of good news. It was said of the late Lord Holland, that he always came down to breakfast with the air of a man who had just met with some signal good-fortune. In "*Notre Dame*," the grandee took his place on the dais, with the look of one who is thinking of something else. But we must not peep and eavesdrop at palace-doors.

Fine manners need the support of fine manners in others. A scholar may be a well-bred man, or he may not. The enthusiast is introduced to polished scholars in society, and is chilled and silenced by finding himself not in their element. They all have somewhat which he has not, and, it seems, ought to have. But if he finds the scholar apart from his companions, it is then the enthusiast's turn, and the scholar has no defence, but must deal on his terms. Now they must fight the battle out on their private strengths. What is the talent of that character so common,—the successful man of the world,—in all marts, senates, and drawing-rooms? Manners: manners of power; sense to see his advantage, and manners up to it. See him approach his man. He knows that troops behave as they are handled at first;—that is his cheap secret; just what happens to every two persons who meet on any affair,—one instantly perceives that he has the key of the situation, that his will comprehends the other's will, as the cat does the mouse; and he has only to use courtesy, and furnish good-natured reasons to his victim to cover up the chain, lest he be shamed into resistance.

The theatre in which this science of manners has a formal importance is not with us a court, but dress-circles, wherein, after the close of the day's business, men and women meet at leisure, for mutual entertainment, in ornamented drawing-rooms. Of course, it has every variety of attraction and merit; but, to earnest persons, to youths or maidens who have great objects at heart, we cannot extol it highly. A well-dressed, talkative company, where each is bent to amuse the other,— yet the high-born Turk who came hither fancied that every woman seemed to be suffering for a chair; that all the talkers were brained and exhausted by the deoxygenated air: it spoiled the best persons: it put all on stilts. Yet here are the secret biographies written and read. The aspect of that man is repulsive; I do not wish to deal with him. The other is irritable, shy, and on his guard. The youth looks humble and manly: I choose him. Look on this woman. There is not beauty, nor brilliant sayings, nor distinguished power to serve you; but all see her gladly; her whole air and impression are healthful. Here come the sentimentalists, and the invalids. Here is Elise, who caught cold in coming into the world, and has always increased it since. Here are creep-mouse manners; and thievish manners. "Look at Northcote," said Fuseli; "he looks like a rat that has seen a cat." In the shallow company, easily excited, easily tired, here is the columnar Bernard: the Alleghanies do not express more repose than his behavior. Here are the sweet following eyes of Cecile: it seemed always that she demanded the heart. Nothing can be more excellent in kind than the Corinthian grace of Gertrude's manners, and yet Blanche, who has no manners, has better manners than she; for the movements of Blanche are the sallies of a spirit which is sufficient for the moment, and she can afford to express every thought by instant action.

Manners have been somewhat cynically defined to be a contrivance of wise men to keep fools at a distance. Fashion is shrewd to detect those who do not belong to her train, and seldom wastes her attentions. Society is very swift in its instincts, and, if you do not belong to it, resists and sneers at you; or quietly drops you. The first weapon enrages the party attacked; the second is still more effective, but is not to be resisted, as the date of the transaction is not easily found. People grow up and grow old under this infliction, and never suspect the truth, ascribing the solitude which acts on them very injuriously, to any cause but the right one.

The basis of good manners is self-reliance. Necessity is the law of all who are not self-possessed. Those who are not self-possessed, obtrude, and pain us. Some men appear to feel that they belong to a Pariah caste. They fear to offend, they bend and apologize, and walk through life with a timid step. As we sometimes dream that we are in a well-dressed company without any coat, so Godfrey acts ever as if he suffered from some mortifying circumstance. The hero should find himself at home, wherever he is: should impart comfort by his own security and good-nature to all beholders. The hero is suffered to be himself. A person of strong mind comes to perceive that for him an immunity is secured so long as he renders to society that service which is native and proper to him,—an immunity from all the observances, yea, and duties, which society so tyrannically imposes on the rank and file of its members. "Euripides," says Aspasia, "has not the fine manners of Sophocles; but,"—she adds good-humoredly, "the movers and masters of our souls have surely a right to throw out their limbs as carelessly as they please, on the world that belongs to them, and before the creatures they have animated."*

Manners require time, as nothing is more vulgar than haste. Friendship should be surrounded with ceremonies and respects, and not crushed into corners. Friendship requires more time than poor busy men can usually command. Here comes to me Roland, with a delicacy of sentiment leading and inwrapping him like a divine cloud or holy ghost. 'Tis a great destitution to both that this should not be entertained with large leisures, but contrariwise should be balked by importunate affairs.

But through this lustrous varnish, the reality is ever shining. 'Tis hard to keep the *what* from breaking through this

*Landor: *Pericles and Aspasia.*

pretty painting of the *how*. The core will come to the surface.
Strong will and keen perception overpower old manners, and
create new; and the thought of the present moment has a
greater value than all the past. In persons of character, we do
not remark manners, because of their instantaneousness. We
are surprised by the thing done, out of all power to watch
the way of it. Yet nothing is more charming than to recognize
the great style which runs through the actions of such. People
masquerade before us in their fortunes, titles, offices, and connections, as academic or civil presidents, or senators, or professors, or great lawyers, and impose on the frivolous, and a
good deal on each other, by these fames. At least, it is a point
of prudent good manners to treat these reputations tenderly,
as if they were merited. But the sad realist knows these fellows at a glance, and they know him; as when in Paris the
chief of the police enters a ballroom, so many diamonded pretenders shrink and make themselves as inconspicuous as they
can, or give him a supplicating look as they pass. "I had received," said a sibyl, "I had received at birth the fatal gift of
penetration:"—and these Cassandras are always born.

Manners impress as they indicate real power. A man who
is sure of his point, carries a broad and contented expression,
which everybody reads. And you cannot rightly train one to
an air and manner, except by making him the kind of man of
whom that manner is the natural expression. Nature forever
puts a premium on reality. What is done for effect, is seen to
be done for effect; what is done for love, is felt to be done
for love. A man inspires affection and honor, because he was
not lying in wait for these. The things of a man for which we
visit him, were done in the dark and the cold. A little integrity
is better than any career. So deep are the sources of this sur-
face-action, that even the size of your companion seems to
vary with his freedom of thought. Not only is he larger, when
at ease, and his thoughts generous, but everything around
him becomes variable with expression. No carpenter's rule,
no rod and chain, will measure the dimensions of any house
or house-lot: go into the house: if the proprietor is constrained and deferring, 'tis of no importance how large his
house, how beautiful his grounds,—you quickly come to the
end of all: but if the man is self-possessed, happy, and at

home, his house is deep-founded, indefinitely large and interesting, the roof and dome buoyant as the sky. Under the humblest roof, the commonest person in plain clothes sits there massive, cheerful, yet formidable like the Egyptian colossi.

Neither Aristotle, nor Leibnitz, nor Junius, nor Champollion has set down the grammar-rules of this dialect, older than Sanscrit; but they who cannot yet read English, can read this. Men take each other's measure, when they meet for the first time,—and every time they meet. How do they get this rapid knowledge, even before they speak, of each other's power and dispositions? One would say, that the persuasion of their speech is not in what they say,—or, that men do not convince by their argument,—but by their personality, by who they are, and what they said and did heretofore. A man already strong is listened to, and everything he says is applauded. Another opposes him with sound argument, but the argument is scouted, until by and by it gets into the mind of some weighty person; then it begins to tell on the community.

Self-reliance is the basis of behavior, as it is the guaranty that the powers are not squandered in too much demonstration. In this country, where school education is universal, we have a superficial culture, and a profusion of reading and writing and expression. We parade our nobilities in poems and orations, instead of working them up into happiness. There is a whisper out of the ages to him who can understand it,—'whatever is known to thyself alone, has always very great value.' There is some reason to believe, that, when a man does not write his poetry, it escapes by other vents through him, instead of the one vent of writing; clings to his form and manners, whilst poets have often nothing poetical about them except their verses. Jacobi said, that "when a man has fully expressed his thought, he has somewhat less possession of it." One would say, the rule is,—What a man is irresistibly urged to say, helps him and us. In explaining his thought to others, he explains it to himself: but when he opens it for show, it corrupts him.

Society is the stage on which manners are shown; novels are their literature. Novels are the journal or record of manners; and the new importance of these books derives from the fact, that the novelist begins to penetrate the surface, and treat this part of life more worthily. The novels used to be all alike, and had a quite vulgar tone. The novels used to lead us on to a foolish interest in the fortunes of the boy and girl they described. The boy was to be raised from a humble to a high position. He was in want of a wife and a castle, and the object of the story was to supply him with one or both. We watched sympathetically, step by step, his climbing, until, at last, the point is gained, the wedding day is fixed, and we follow the gala procession home to the castle, when the doors are slammed in our face, and the poor reader is left outside in the cold, not enriched by so much as an idea, or a virtuous impulse.

But the victories of character are instant, and victories for all. Its greatness enlarges all. We are fortified by every heroic anecdote. The novels are as useful as Bibles, if they teach you the secret, that the best of life is conversation, and the greatest success is confidence, or perfect understanding between sincere people. 'Tis a French definition of friendship, *rien que s'entendre*, good understanding. The highest compact we can make with our fellow, is,—'Let there be truth between us two forevermore.' That is the charm in all good novels, as it is the charm in all good histories, that the heroes mutually understand, from the first, and deal loyally, and with a profound trust in each other. It is sublime to feel and say of another, I need never meet, or speak, or write to him: we need not reinforce ourselves, or send tokens of remembrance: I rely on him as on myself: if he did thus or thus, I know it was right.

In all the superior people I have met, I notice directness, truth spoken more truly, as if everything of obstruction, of malformation, had been trained away. What have they to conceal? What have they to exhibit? Between simple and noble persons, there is always a quick intelligence: they recognize at sight, and meet on a better ground than the talents and skills they may chance to possess, namely, on sincerity and uprightness. For, it is not what talents or genius a man has, but how he is to his talents, that constitutes friendship and character. The man that stands by himself, the universe stands by him also. It is related of the monk Basle, that, being excommunicated by the Pope, he was, at his death, sent in charge of an angel to find a fit place of suffering in hell: but, such was the eloquence and good-humor of the monk, that, wherever he went he was received gladly, and civilly treated, even by the most uncivil angels: and, when he came to discourse with them, instead of contradicting or forcing him, they took his part, and adopted his manners: and even good angels came from far, to see him, and take up their abode with him. The angel that was sent to find a place of torment for him, attempted to remove him to a worse pit, but with no better success; for such was the contented spirit of the monk, that he found something to praise in every place and company, though in hell, and made a kind of heaven of it. At last the escorting angel returned with his prisoner to them that sent him, saying, that no phlegethon could be found that would burn him; for that, in whatever condition, Basle remained incorrigibly Basle. The legend says, his sentence was remitted, and he was allowed to go into heaven, and was canonized as a saint.

There is a stroke of magnanimity in the correspondence of Bonaparte with his brother Joseph, when the latter was King of Spain, and complained that he missed in Napoleon's letters the affectionate tone which had marked their childish correspondence. "I am sorry," replies Napoleon, "you think you shall find your brother again only in the Elysian Fields. It is natural, that at forty, he should not feel towards you as he did at twelve. But his feelings towards you have greater truth and strength. His friendship has the features of his mind."

How much we forgive to those who yield us the rare spectacle of heroic manners! We will pardon them the want of books, of arts, and even of the gentler virtues. How tenaciously we remember them! Here is a lesson which I brought along with me in boyhood from the Latin School, and which ranks with the best of Roman anecdotes. Marcus Scaurus was accused by Quintus Varius Hispanus, that he had excited the allies to take arms against the Republic. But he, full of firmness and gravity, defended himself in this manner: "Quintus Varius Hispanus alleges that Marcus Scaurus, President of the Senate, excited the allies to arms: Marcus Scaurus, President of the Senate, denies it. There is no witness. Which do you believe, Romans?" *"Utri creditis, Quirites?"* When he had said these words, he was absolved by the assembly of the people.

I have seen manners that make a similar impression with personal beauty; that give the like exhilaration, and refine us like that; and, in memorable experiences, they are suddenly better than beauty, and make that superfluous and ugly. But they must be marked by fine perception, the acquaintance with real beauty. They must always show self-control: you shall not be facile, apologetic, or leaky, but king over your word; and every gesture and action shall indicate power at rest. Then they must be inspired by the good heart. There is no beautifier of complexion, or form, or behavior, like the wish to scatter joy and not pain around us. 'Tis good to give a stranger a meal, or a night's lodging. 'Tis better to be hospitable to his good meaning and thought, and give courage to a companion. We must be as courteous to a man as we are to a picture, which we are willing to give the advantage of a good light. Special precepts are not to be thought of: the talent of well-doing contains them all. Every hour will show a duty as paramount as that of my whim just now; and yet I will write it,—that there is one topic peremptorily forbidden to all well-bred, to all rational mortals, namely, their distempers. If you have not slept, or if you have slept, or if you have headache, or sciatica, or leprosy, or thunder-stroke, I beseech you, by all angels, to hold your peace, and not pollute the morning, to which all the housemates bring serene and pleasant thoughts, by corruption and groans. Come out of the azure. Love the day. Do not leave the sky out of your landscape. The oldest and the most deserving person should come very modestly into any newly awaked company, respecting the divine communications, out of which all must be presumed to have newly come. An old man who added an elevating culture to a large experience of life, said to me, "When you come into the room, I think I will study how to make humanity beautiful to you."

As respects the delicate question of culture, I do not think that any other than negative rules can be laid down. For positive rules, for suggestion, Nature alone inspires it. Who dare assume to guide a youth, a maid, to perfect manners?—the golden mean is so delicate, difficult,—say frankly, unattainable. What finest hands would not be clumsy to sketch the genial precepts of the young girl's demeanor? The chances seem infinite against success; and yet success is continually attained. There must not be secondariness, and 'tis a thousand to one that her air and manner will at once betray that she is not primary, but that there is some other one or many of her class, to whom she habitually postpones herself. But Nature lifts her easily, and without knowing it, over these impossibilities, and we are continually surprised with graces and felicities not only unteachable, but undescribable.

VI

WORSHIP

———

THIS is he, who, felled by foes,
Sprung harmless up, refreshed by blows:
He to captivity was sold,
But him no prison-bars would hold:
Though they sealed him in a rock,
Mountain chains he can unlock:
Thrown to lions for their meat,
The crouching lion kissed his feet:
Bound to the stake, no flames appalled,
But arched o'er him an honoring vault.
This is he men miscall Fate,
Threading dark ways, arriving late,
But ever coming in time to crown
The truth, and hurl wrongdoers down.
He is the oldest, and best known,
More near than aught thou call'st thy own,
Yet, greeted in another's eyes,
Disconcerts with glad surprise.
This is Jove, who, deaf to prayers,
Floods with blessings unawares.
Draw, if thou canst, the mystic line,
Severing rightly his from thine,
Which is human, which divine.

Worship

S OME of my friends have complained, when the preceding
papers were read, that we discussed Fate, Power, and
Wealth, on too low a platform; gave too much line to the evil
spirit of the times; too many cakes to Cerberus; that we ran
Cudworth's risk of making, by excess of candor, the argument
of atheism so strong, that he could not answer it. I have no
fears of being forced in my own despite to play, as we say,
the devil's attorney. I have no infirmity of faith; no belief that
it is of much importance what I or any man may say: I am
sure that a certain truth will be said through me, though
I should be dumb, or though I should try to say the reverse. Nor do I fear skepticism for any good soul. A just
thinker will allow full swing to his skepticism. I dip my pen
in the blackest ink, because I am not afraid of falling into
my inkpot. I have no sympathy with a poor man I knew,
who, when suicides abounded, told me he dared not look
at his razor. We are of different opinions at different hours,
but we always may be said to be at heart on the side of
truth.

I see not why we should give ourselves such sanctified airs.
If the Divine Providence has hid from men neither disease,
nor deformity, nor corrupt society, but has stated itself out in
passions, in war, in trade, in the love of power and pleasure,
in hunger and need, in tyrannies, literatures, and arts,—let us
not be so nice that we cannot write these facts down coarsely
as they stand, or doubt but there is a counter-statement as
ponderous, which we can arrive at, and which, being put, will
make all square. The solar system has no anxiety about its
reputation, and the credit of truth and honesty is as safe; nor
have I any fear that a skeptical bias can be given by leaning
hard on the sides of fate, of practical power, or of trade,
which the doctrine of Faith cannot down-weigh. The strength
of that principle is not measured in ounces and pounds: it
tyrannizes at the centre of Nature. We may well give skepticism as much line as we can. The spirit will return, and fill
us. It drives the drivers. It counterbalances any accumulations
of power.

"Heaven kindly gave our blood a moral flow."

We are born loyal. The whole creation is made of hooks and eyes, of bitumen, of sticking-plaster, and whether your community is made in Jerusalem or in California, of saints or of wreckers, it coheres in a perfect ball. Men as naturally make a state, or a church, as caterpillars a web. If they were more refined, it would be less formal, it would be nervous, like that of the Shakers, who, from long habit of thinking and feeling together, it is said, are affected in the same way, at the same time, to work and to play, and as they go with perfect sympathy to their tasks in the field or shop, so are they inclined for a ride or a journey at the same instant, and the horses come up with the family carriage unbespoken to the door.

We are born believing. A man bears beliefs, as a tree bears apples. A self-poise belongs to every particle; and a rectitude to every mind, and is the Nemesis and protector of every society. I and my neighbors have been bred in the notion, that, unless we came soon to some good church,—Calvinism, or Behmenism, or Romanism, or Mormonism,—there would be a universal thaw and dissolution. No Isaiah or Jeremy has arrived. Nothing can exceed the anarchy that has followed in our skies. The stern old faiths have all pulverized. 'Tis a whole population of gentlemen and ladies out in search of religions. 'Tis as flat anarchy in our ecclesiastic realms, as that which existed in Massachusetts, in the Revolution, or which prevails now on the slope of the Rocky Mountains or Pike's Peak. Yet we make shift to live. Men are loyal. Nature has self-poise in all her works; certain proportions in which oxygen and azote combine, and, not less a harmony in faculties, a fitness in the spring and the regulator.

The decline of the influence of Calvin, or Fenelon, or Wesley, or Channing, need give us no uneasiness. The builder of heaven has not so ill constructed his creature as that the religion, that is, the public nature, should fall out: the public and the private element, like north and south, like inside and outside, like centrifugal and centripetal, adhere to every soul, and cannot be subdued, except the soul is dissipated. God builds his temple in the heart on the ruins of churches and religions.

In the last chapters, we treated some particulars of the question of culture. But the whole state of man is a state of culture; and its flowering and completion may be described as Religion, or Worship. There is always some religion, some hope and fear extended into the invisible,—from the blind boding which nails a horseshoe to the mast or the threshold, up to the song of the Elders in the Apocalypse. But the religion cannot rise above the state of the votary. Heaven always bears some proportion to earth. The god of the cannibals will be a cannibal, of the crusaders a crusader, and of the merchants a merchant. In all ages, souls out of time, extraordinary, prophetic, are born, who are rather related to the system of the world, than to their particular age and locality. These announce absolute truths, which, with whatever reverence received, are speedily dragged down into a savage interpretation. The interior tribes of our Indians, and some of the Pacific islanders, flog their gods, when things take an unfavorable turn. The Greek poets did not hesitate to let loose their petulant wit on their deities also. Laomedon, in his anger at Neptune and Apollo, who had built Troy for him, and demanded their price, does not hesitate to menace them that he will cut their ears off.* Among our Norse forefathers, King Olaf's mode of converting Eyvind to Christianity was to put a pan of glowing coals on his belly, which burst asunder. "Wilt thou now, Eyvind, believe in Christ?" asks Olaf, in excellent faith. Another argument was an adder put into the mouth of the reluctant disciple Rand, who refused to believe.

Christianity, in the romantic ages, signified European culture,—the grafted or meliorated tree in a crab forest. And to marry a pagan wife or husband, was to marry Beast, and voluntarily to take a step backwards towards the baboon.

> "Hengist had verament
> A daughter both fair and gent,
> But she was heathen Sarazine,
> And Vortigern for love fine
> Her took to fere and to wife,
> And was cursed in all his life;
> For he let Christian wed heathen,

*Iliad, Book xxi. l. 455.

And mixed our blood as flesh and mathen."*

What Gothic mixtures the Christian creed drew from the pagan sources, Richard of Devizes's chronicle of Richard I.'s crusade, in the twelfth century, may show. King Richard taunts God with forsaking him: "O fie! O how unwilling should I be to forsake thee, in so forlorn and dreadful a position, were I thy lord and advocate, as thou art mine. In sooth, my standards will in future be despised, not through my fault, but through thine: in sooth, not through any cowardice of my warfare, art thou thyself, my king and my God conquered, this day, and not Richard thy vassal." The religion of the early English poets is anomalous, so devout and so blasphemous, in the same breath. Such is Chaucer's extraordinary confusion of heaven and earth in the picture of Dido.

> "She was so fair,
> So young, so lusty, with her eyen glad,
> That if that God that heaven and earthe made
> Would have a love for beauty and goodness,
> And womanhede, truth, and seemliness,
> Whom should he loven but this lady sweet?
> There n' is no woman to him half so meet."

With these grossnesses, we complacently compare our own taste and decorum. We think and speak with more temperance and gradation,—but is not indifferentism as bad as superstition?

We live in a transition period, when the old faiths which comforted nations, and not only so, but made nations, seem to have spent their force. I do not find the religions of men at this moment very creditable to them, but either childish and insignificant, or unmanly and effeminating. The fatal trait is the divorce between religion and morality. Here are know-nothing religions, or churches that proscribe intellect; scortatory religions; slave-holding and slave-trading religions; and, even in the decent populations, idolatries wherein the whiteness of the ritual covers scarlet indulgence. The lover of the old religion complains that our contemporaries, scholars as well as merchants, succumb to a great despair,—have cor-

*Moths or worms.

rupted into a timorous conservatism, and believe in nothing. In our large cities, the population is godless, materialized,—no bond, no fellow-feeling, no enthusiasm. These are not men, but hungers, thirsts, fevers, and appetites walking. How is it people manage to live on,—so aimless as they are? After their peppercorn aims are gained, it seems as if the lime in their bones alone held them together, and not any worthy purpose. There is no faith in the intellectual, none in the moral universe. There is faith in chemistry, in meat, and wine, in wealth, in machinery, in the steam-engine, galvanic battery, turbine-wheels, sewing machines, and in public opinion, but not in divine causes. A silent revolution has loosed the tension of the old religious sects, and, in place of the gravity and permanence of those societies of opinion, they run into freak and extravagance. In creeds never was such levity; witness the heathenisms in Christianity, the periodic "revivals," the Millennium mathematics, the peacock ritualism, the retrogression to Popery, the maundering of Mormons, the squalor of Mesmerism, the deliration of rappings, the rat and mouse revelation, thumps in table-drawers, and black art. The architecture, the music, the prayer, partake of the madness: the arts sink into shift and make-believe. Not knowing what to do, we ape our ancestors; the churches stagger backward to the mummeries of the dark ages. By the irresistible maturing of the general mind, the Christian traditions have lost their hold. The dogma of the mystic offices of Christ being dropped, and he standing on his genius as a moral teacher, 'tis impossible to maintain the old emphasis of his personality; and it recedes, as all persons must, before the sublimity of the moral laws. From this change, and in the momentary absence of any religious genius that could offset the immense material activity, there is a feeling that religion is gone. When Paul Leroux offered his article *"Dieu"* to the conductor of a leading French journal, he replied, *"La question de Dieu manque d'actualité."* In Italy, Mr. Gladstone said of the late King of Naples, "it has been a proverb, that he has erected the negation of God into a system of government." In this country, the like stupefaction was in the air, and the phrase "higher law" became a political jibe. What proof of infidelity, like the toleration and propagandism of slavery? What, like the direction of education? What, like the facility of conversion? What, like the externality of churches that once sucked the roots of right and wrong, and now have perished away till they are a speck of whitewash on the wall? What proof of skepticism like the base rate at which the highest mental and moral gifts are held? Let a man attain the highest and broadest culture that any American has possessed, then let him die by sea-storm, railroad collision, or other accident, and all America will acquiesce that the best thing has happened to him; that, after the education has gone far, such is the expensiveness of America, that the best use to put a fine person to, is, to drown him to save his board.

Another scar of this skepticism is the distrust in human virtue. It is believed by well-dressed proprietors that there is no more virtue than they possess; that the solid portion of society exist for the arts of comfort: that life is an affair to put somewhat between the upper and lower mandibles. How prompt the suggestion of a low motive! Certain patriots in England devoted themselves for years to creating a public opinion that should break down the corn-laws and establish free trade. 'Well,' says the man in the street, 'Cobden got a stipend out of it.' Kossuth fled hither across the ocean to try if he could rouse the New World to a sympathy with European liberty. 'Aye,' says New York, 'he made a handsome thing of it, enough to make him comfortable for life.'

See what allowance vice finds in the respectable and well-conditioned class. If a pickpocket intrude into the society of gentlemen, they exert what moral force they have, and he finds himself uncomfortable, and glad to get away. But if an adventurer go through all the forms, procure himself to be elected to a post of trust, as of senator, or president,—though by the same arts as we detest in the house-thief,—the same gentlemen who agree to discountenance the private rogue, will be forward to show civilities and marks of respect to the public one: and no amount of evidence of his crimes will prevent them giving him ovations, complimentary dinners, opening their own houses to him, and priding themselves on his acquaintance. We were not deceived by the professions of the private adventurer,—the louder he talked of his honor, the faster we counted our spoons; but we appeal to the sanctified preamble of the messages and proclamations of the public sinner, as the proof of sincerity. It must be that they who pay this homage have said to themselves, On the whole, we don't know about this that you call honesty; a bird in the hand is better.

Even well-disposed, good sort of people are touched with the same infidelity, and for brave, straightforward action, use half-measures and compromises. Forgetful that a little measure is a great error, forgetful that a wise mechanic uses a sharp tool, they go on choosing the dead men of routine. But the official men can in nowise help you in any question of to-day, they deriving entirely from the old dead things. Only those can help in counsel or conduct who did not make a party pledge to defend this or that, but who were appointed by God Almighty, before they came into the world, to stand for this which they uphold.

It has been charged that a want of sincerity in the leading men is a vice general throughout American society. But the multitude of the sick shall not make us deny the existence of health. In spite of our imbecility and terrors, and "universal decay of religion," &c. &c., the moral sense reappears to-day with the same morning newness that has been from of old the fountain of beauty and strength. You say, there is no religion now. 'Tis like saying in rainy weather, there is no sun, when at that moment we are witnessing one of his superlative effects. The religion of the cultivated class now, to be sure, consists in an avoidance of acts and engagements which it was once their religion to assume. But this avoidance will yield spontaneous forms in their due hour. There is a principle which is the basis of things, which all speech aims to say, and all action to evolve, a simple, quiet, undescribed, undescribable presence, dwelling very peacefully in us, our rightful lord: we are not to do, but to let do; not to work, but to be worked upon; and to this homage there is a consent of all thoughtful and just men in all ages and conditions. To this sentiment belong vast and sudden enlargements of power. 'Tis remarkable that our faith in ecstasy consists with total inexperience of it. It is the order of the world to educate with accuracy the senses and the understanding; and the enginery at work to draw out these powers in priority, no doubt, has its office. But we are never without a hint that these powers are mediate and servile, and that we are one day to deal with real being,—essences with essences. Even the fury of material activity has some results friendly to moral health. The energetic action of the times develops individualism, and the religious appear isolated. I esteem this a step in the right direction. Heaven deals with us on no representative system. Souls are not saved in bundles. The Spirit saith to the man, 'How is it with thee? thee personally? is it well? is it ill?' For a great nature, it is a happiness to escape a religious training,—religion of character is so apt to be invaded. Religion must always be a crab fruit: it cannot be grafted and keep its wild beauty. "I have seen," said a traveller who had known the extremes of society, "I have seen human nature in all its forms, it is everywhere the same, but the wilder it is, the more virtuous."

We say, the old forms of religion decay, and that a skepticism devastates the community. I do not think it can be cured or stayed by any modification of theologic creeds, much less by theologic discipline. The cure for false theology is mother-wit. Forget your books and traditions, and obey your moral perceptions at this hour. That which is signified by the words "moral" and "spiritual," is a lasting essence, and, with whatever illusions we have loaded them, will certainly bring back the words, age after age, to their ancient meaning. I know no words that mean so much. In our definitions, we grope after the *spiritual* by describing it as invisible. The true meaning of *spiritual* is *real*; that law which executes itself, which works without means, and which cannot be conceived as not existing. Men talk of "mere morality,"—which is much as if one should say, 'poor God, with nobody to help him.' I find the omnipresence and the almightiness in the reaction of every atom in Nature. I can best indicate by examples those reactions by which every part of Nature replies to the purpose of the actor,—beneficently to the good, penally to the bad. Let us replace sentimentalism by realism, and dare to uncover those simple and terrible laws which, be they seen or unseen, pervade and govern.

Every man takes care that his neighbor shall not cheat him. But a day comes when he begins to care that he do not cheat his neighbor. Then all goes well. He has changed his market-cart into a chariot of the sun. What a day dawns, when we have taken to heart the doctrine of faith! to prefer, as a better investment, being to doing; being to seeming; logic to rhythm and to display; the year to the day; the life to the year; character to performance;—and have come to know, that justice will be done us; and, if our genius is slow, the term will be long.

'Tis certain that worship stands in some commanding relation to the health of man, and to his highest powers, so as to be, in some manner, the source of intellect. All the great ages have been ages of belief. I mean, when there was any extraordinary power of performance, when great national movements began, when arts appeared, when heroes existed, when poems were made, the human soul was in earnest, and had fixed its thoughts on spiritual verities, with as strict a grasp as that of the hands on the sword, or the pencil, or the trowel. It is true that genius takes its rise out of the mountains of rectitude; that all beauty and power which men covet, are somehow born out of that Alpine district; that any extraordinary degree of beauty in man or woman involves a moral charm. Thus, I think, we very slowly admit in another man a higher degree of moral sentiment than our own,—a finer conscience, more impressionable, or, which marks minuter degrees; an ear to hear acuter notes of right and wrong, than we can. I think we listen suspiciously and very slowly to any evidence to that point. But, once satisfied of such superiority, we set no limit to our expectation of his genius. For such persons are nearer to the secret of God than others; are bathed by sweeter waters; they hear notices, they see visions, where others are vacant. We believe that holiness confers a certain insight, because not by our private, but by our public force, can we share and know the nature of things.

There is an intimate interdependence of intellect and morals. Given the equality of two intellects,—which will form the most reliable judgments, the good, or the bad hearted? "The heart has its arguments, with which the understanding is not acquainted." For the heart is at once aware of the state of health or disease, which is the controlling state, that is, of sanity or of insanity, prior, of course, to all question of the

ingenuity of arguments, the amount of facts, or the elegance
of rhetoric. So intimate is this alliance of mind and heart, that
talent uniformly sinks with character. The bias of errors of
principle carries away men into perilous courses, as soon as
their will does not control their passion or talent. Hence the
extraordinary blunders, and final wrong head, into which men
spoiled by ambition usually fall. Hence the remedy for all
blunders, the cure of blindness, the cure of crime, is love. "As
much love, so much mind," said the Latin proverb. The superiority that has no superior; the redeemer and instructor of
souls, as it is their primal essence, is love.

The moral must be the measure of health. If your eye is on
the eternal, your intellect will grow, and your opinions and
actions will have a beauty which no learning or combined
advantages of other men can rival. The moment of your loss
of faith, and acceptance of the lucrative standard, will be
marked in the pause, or solstice of genius, the sequent retrogression, and the inevitable loss of attraction to other minds.
The vulgar are sensible of the change in you, and of your
descent, though they clap you on the back, and congratulate
you on your increased common sense.

Our recent culture has been in natural science. We have
learned the manners of the sun and of the moon, of the rivers
and the rains, of the mineral and elemental kingdoms, of
plants and animals. Man has learned to weigh the sun, and its
weight neither loses nor gains. The path of a star, the moment of an eclipse, can be determined to the fraction of a
second. Well, to him the book of history, the book of love,
the lures of passion, and the commandments of duty are
opened: and the next lesson taught, is, the continuation of
the inflexible law of matter into the subtile kingdom of will,
and of thought; that, if, in sidereal ages, gravity and projection keep their craft, and the ball never loses its way in its
wild path through space,—a secreter gravitation, a secreter
projection, rule not less tyrannically in human history, and
keep the balance of power from age to age unbroken. For,
though the new element of freedom and an individual has
been admitted, yet the primordial atoms are prefigured and
predetermined to moral issues, are in search of justice, and
ultimate right is done. Religion or worship is the attitude of

those who see this unity, intimacy, and sincerity; who see that, against all appearances, the nature of things works for truth and right forever.

'Tis a short sight to limit our faith in laws to those of gravity, of chemistry, of botany, and so forth. Those laws do not stop where our eyes lose them, but push the same geometry and chemistry up into the invisible plane of social and rational life, so that, look where we will, in a boy's game, or in the strifes of races, a perfect reaction, a perpetual judgment keeps watch and ward. And this appears in a class of facts which concerns all men, within and above their creeds.

Shallow men believe in luck, believe in circumstances: It was somebody's name, or he happened to be there at the time, or, it was so then, and another day it would have been otherwise. Strong men believe in cause and effect. The man was born to do it, and his father was born to be the father of him and of this deed, and, by looking narrowly, you shall see there was no luck in the matter, but it was all a problem in arithmetic, or an experiment in chemistry. The curve of the flight of the moth is preordained, and all things go by number, rule, and weight.

Skepticism is unbelief in cause and effect. A man does not see, that, as he eats, so he thinks: as he deals, so he is, and so he appears; he does not see, that his son is the son of his thoughts and of his actions; that fortunes are not exceptions but fruits; that relation and connection are not somewhere and sometimes, but everywhere and always; no miscellany, no exemption, no anomaly,—but method, and an even web; and what comes out, that was put in. As we are, so we do; and as we do, so is it done to us; we are the builders of our fortunes; cant and lying and the attempt to secure a good which does not belong to us, are, once for all, balked and vain. But, in the human mind, this tie of fate is made alive. The law is the basis of the human mind. In us, it is inspiration; out there in Nature, we see its fatal strength. We call it the moral sentiment.

We owe to the Hindoo Scriptures a definition of Law, which compares well with any in our Western books. "Law it is, which is without name, or color, or hands, or feet; which is smallest of the least, and largest of the large; all, and knowing all things; which hears without ears, sees without eyes, moves without feet, and seizes without hands."

If any reader tax me with using vague and traditional phrases, let me suggest to him, by a few examples, what kind of a trust this is, and how real. Let me show him that the dice are loaded; that the colors are fast, because they are the native colors of the fleece; that the globe is a battery, because every atom is a magnet; and that the police and sincerity of the Universe are secured by God's delegating his divinity to every particle; that there is no room for hypocrisy, no margin for choice.

The countryman leaving his native village, for the first time, and going abroad, finds all his habits broken up. In a new nation and language, his sect, as Quaker, or Lutheran, is lost. What! it is not then necessary to the order and existence of society? He misses this, and the commanding eye of his neighborhood, which held him to decorum. This is the peril of New York, of New Orleans, of London, of Paris, to young men. But after a little experience, he makes the discovery that there are no large cities,—none large enough to hide in; that the censors of action are as numerous and as near in Paris, as in Littleton or Portland; that the gossip is as prompt and vengeful. There is no concealment, and, for each offence, a several vengeance; that, reaction, or *nothing for nothing*, or, *things are as broad as they are long*, is not a rule for Littleton or Portland, but for the Universe.

We cannot spare the coarsest muniment of virtue. We are disgusted by gossip; yet it is of importance to keep the angels in their proprieties. The smallest fly will draw blood, and gossip is a weapon impossible to exclude from the privatest, highest, selectest. Nature created a police of many ranks. God has delegated himself to a million deputies. From these low external penalties, the scale ascends. Next come the resentments, the fears, which injustice calls out; then, the false relations in which the offender is put to other men; and the reaction of his fault on himself, in the solitude and devastation of his mind.

You cannot hide any secret. If the artist succor his flagging spirits by opium or wine, his work will characterize itself as the effect of opium or wine. If you make a picture or a statue, it sets the beholder in that state of mind you had, when you made it. If you spend for show, on building, or gardening, or on pictures, or on equipages, it will so appear. We are all physiognomists and penetrators of character, and things themselves are detective. If you follow the suburban fashion in building a sumptuous-looking house for a little money, it will appear to all eyes as a cheap dear house. There is no privacy that cannot be penetrated. No secret can be kept in the civilized world. Society is a masked ball, where every one hides his real character, and reveals it by hiding. If a man wish to conceal anything he carries, those whom he meets know that he conceals somewhat, and usually know what he conceals. Is it otherwise if there be some belief or some purpose he would bury in his breast? 'Tis as hard to hide as fire. He is a strong man who can hold down his opinion. A man cannot utter two or three sentences, without disclosing to intelligent ears precisely where he stands in life and thought, namely, whether in the kingdom of the senses and the understanding, or, in that of ideas and imagination, in the realm of intuitions and duty. People seem not to see that their opinion of the world is also a confession of character. We can only see what we are, and if we misbehave we suspect others. The fame of Shakspeare or of Voltaire, of Thomas à Kempis, or of Bonaparte, characterizes those who give it. As gas-light is found to be the best nocturnal police, so the universe protects itself by pitiless publicity.

Each must be armed—not necessarily with musket and pike. Happy, if, seeing these, he can feel that he has better muskets and pikes in his energy and constancy. To every creature is his own weapon, however skilfully concealed from himself, a good while. His work is sword and shield. Let him accuse none, let him injure none. The way to mend the bad world, is to create the right world. Here is a low political economy plotting to cut the throat of foreign competition, and establish our own;—excluding others by force, or making war on them; or, by cunning tariffs, giving preference to worse wares of ours. But the real and lasting victories are those of peace, and not of war. The way to conquer the foreign artisan, is, not to kill him, but to beat his work. And the Crystal Palaces and World Fairs, with their committees and prizes on all kinds of industry, are the result of this feeling. The American workman who strikes ten blows with his hammer, whilst the foreign workman only strikes one, is as really vanquishing that foreigner, as if the blows were aimed at and told on his person. I look on that man as happy, who, when there is question of success, looks into his work for a reply, not into the market, not into opinion, not into patronage. In every variety of human employment, in the mechanical and in the fine arts, in navigation, in farming, in legislating, there are among the numbers who do their task perfunctorily, as we say, or just to pass, and as badly as they dare,—there are the working-men, on whom the burden of the business falls,—those who love work, and love to see it rightly done, who finish their task for its own sake; and the state and the world is happy, that has the most of such finishers. The world will always do justice at last to such finishers: it cannot otherwise. He who has acquired the ability, may wait securely the occasion of making it felt and appreciated, and know that it will not loiter. Men talk as if victory were something fortunate. Work is victory. Wherever work is done, victory is obtained. There is no chance, and no blanks. You want but one verdict: if you have your own, you are secure of the rest. And yet, if witnesses are wanted, witnesses are near. There was never a man born so wise or good, but one or more companions came into the world with him, who delight in his faculty, and report it. I cannot see without awe, that no man thinks alone, and no man acts alone, but the divine assessors who came up with him into life,—now under one disguise, now under another,—like a police in citizens' clothes, walk with him, step for step, through all the kingdom of time.

This reaction, this sincerity is the property of all things. To make our word or act sublime, we must make it real. It is our system that counts, not the single word or unsupported action. Use what language you will, you can never say anything but what you are. What I am, and what I think, is conveyed to you, in spite of my efforts to hold it back. What I am has been secretly conveyed from me to another, whilst I was vainly making up my mind to tell him it. He has heard from me what I never spoke.

As men get on in life, they acquire a love for sincerity, and somewhat less solicitude to be lulled or amused. In the progress of the character, there is an increasing faith in the moral sentiment, and a decreasing faith in propositions. Young people admire talents, and particular excellences. As we grow older, we value total powers and effects, as the spirit, or quality of the man. We have another sight, and a new standard; an insight which disregards what is done *for* the eye, and pierces to the doer; an ear which hears not what men say, but hears what they do not say.

There was a wise, devout man who is called, in the Catholic Church, St. Philip Neri, of whom many anecdotes touching his discernment and benevolence are told at Naples and Rome. Among the nuns in a convent not far from Rome, one had appeared, who laid claim to certain rare gifts of inspiration and prophecy, and the abbess advised the Holy Father, at Rome, of the wonderful powers shown by her novice. The Pope did not well know what to make of these new claims, and Philip coming in from a journey, one day, he consulted him. Philip undertook to visit the nun, and ascertain her character. He threw himself on his mule, all travel-soiled as he was, and hastened through the mud and mire to the distant convent. He told the abbess the wishes of his Holiness, and begged her to summon the nun without delay. The nun was sent for, and, as soon as she came into the apartment, Philip stretched out his leg all bespattered with mud, and desired her to draw off his boots. The young nun, who had become the object of much attention and respect, drew back with anger, and refused the office: Philip ran out of doors, mounted his mule, and returned instantly to the Pope; "Give yourself no uneasiness, Holy Father, any longer: here is no miracle, for here is no humility."

We need not much mind what people please to say, but what they must say; what their natures say, though their busy, artful, Yankee understandings try to hold back, and choke that word, and to articulate something different. If we will sit quietly,—what they ought to say is said, with their will, or against their will. We do not care for you, let us pretend what we will:—we are always looking through you to the dim dictator behind you. Whilst your habit or whim chatters, we civilly and impatiently wait until that wise superior shall speak again. Even children are not deceived by the false reasons which their parents give in answer to their questions, whether touching natural facts, or religion, or persons. When the parent, instead of thinking how it really is, puts them off with a traditional or a hypocritical answer, the children perceive that it is traditional or hypocritical. To a sound constitution the defect of another is at once manifest: and the marks of it are only concealed from us by our own dislocation. An anatomical observer remarks, that the sympathies of the chest, abdomen, and pelvis, tell at last on the face, and on all its features. Not only does our beauty waste, but it leaves word how it went to waste. Physiognomy and phrenology are not new sciences, but declarations of the soul that it is aware of certain new sources of information. And now sciences of broader scope are starting up behind these. And so for ourselves, it is really of little importance what blunders in statement we make, so only we make no wilful departures from the truth. How a man's truth comes to mind, long after we have forgotten all his words! How it comes to us in silent hours, that truth is our only armor in all passages of life and death! Wit is cheap, and anger is cheap; but if you cannot argue or explain yourself to the other party, cleave to the truth against me, against thee, and you gain a station from which you cannot be dislodged. The other party will forget the words that you spoke, but the part you took continues to plead for you.

Why should I hasten to solve every riddle which life offers me? I am well assured that the Questioner, who brings me so many problems, will bring the answers also in due time. Very rich, very potent, very cheerful Giver that he is, he shall have it all his own way, for me. Why should I give up my thought, because I cannot answer an objection to it? Consider only, whether it remains in my life the same it was. That only which we have within, can we see without. If we meet no gods, it is because we harbor none. If there is grandeur in you, you will find grandeur in porters and sweeps. He only is rightly immortal, to whom all things are immortal. I have read somewhere, that none is accomplished, so long as any are incomplete; that the happiness of one cannot consist with the misery of any other.

The Buddhists say, "No seed will die:" every seed will

grow. Where is the service which can escape its remuneration? What is vulgar, and the essence of all vulgarity, but the avarice of reward? 'Tis the difference of artisan and artist, of talent and genius, of sinner and saint. The man whose eyes are nailed not on the nature of his act, but on the wages, whether it be money, or office, or fame,—is almost equally low. He is great, whose eyes are opened to see that the reward of actions cannot be escaped, because he is transformed into his action, and taketh its nature, which bears its own fruit, like every other tree. A great man cannot be hindered of the effect of his act, because it is immediate. The genius of life is friendly to the noble, and in the dark brings them friends from far. Fear God, and where you go, men shall think they walk in hallowed cathedrals.

And so I look on those sentiments which make the glory of the human being, love, humility, faith, as being also the intimacy of Divinity in the atoms; and, that, as soon as the man is right, assurances and previsions emanate from the interior of his body and his mind; as, when flowers reach their ripeness, incense exhales from them, and, as a beautiful atmosphere is generated from the planet by the averaged emanations from all its rocks and soils.

Thus man is made equal to every event. He can face danger for the right. A poor, tender, painful body, he can run into flame or bullets or pestilence, with duty for his guide. He feels the insurance of a just employment. I am not afraid of accident, as long as I am in my place. It is strange that superior persons should not feel that they have some better resistance against cholera, than avoiding green peas and salads. Life is hardly respectable,—is it? if it has no generous, guaranteeing task, no duties or affections, that constitute a necessity of existing. Every man's task is his life-preserver. The conviction that his work is dear to God and cannot be spared, defends him. The lightning-rod that disarms the cloud of its threat is his body in its duty. A high aim reacts on the means, on the days, on the organs of the body. A high aim is curative, as well as arnica. "Napoleon," says Goethe, "visited those sick of the plague, in order to prove that the man who could vanquish fear, could vanquish the plague also; and he was right. 'Tis incredible what force the will has in such cases: it penetrates the body, and puts it in a state of activity, which repels all hurtful influences; whilst fear invites them."

It is related of William of Orange, that, whilst he was besieging a town on the continent, a gentleman sent to him on public business came to his camp, and, learning that the King was before the walls, he ventured to go where he was. He found him directing the operation of his gunners, and, having explained his errand, and received his answer, the King said, "Do you not know, sir, that every moment you spend here is at the risk of your life?" "I run no more risk," replied the gentleman, "than your Majesty." "Yes," said the King, "but my duty brings me here, and yours does not." In a few minutes, a cannon-ball fell on the spot, and the gentleman was killed.

Thus can the faithful student reverse all the warnings of his early instinct, under the guidance of a deeper instinct. He learns to welcome misfortune, learns that adversity is the prosperity of the great. He learns the greatness of humility. He shall work in the dark, work against failure, pain, and ill-will. If he is insulted, he can be insulted; all his affair is not to insult. Hafiz writes,

> At the last day, men shall wear
> On their heads the dust,
> As ensign and as ornament
> Of their lowly trust.

The moral equalizes all; enriches, empowers all. It is the coin which buys all, and which all find in their pocket. Under the whip of the driver, the slave shall feel his equality with saints and heroes. In the greatest destitution and calamity, it surprises man with a feeling of elasticity which makes nothing of loss.

I recall some traits of a remarkable person whose life and discourse betrayed many inspirations of this sentiment. Benedict was always great in the present time. He had hoarded nothing from the past, neither in his cabinets, neither in his memory. He had no designs on the future, neither for what he should do to men, nor for what men should do for him. He said, 'I am never beaten until I know that I am beaten. I meet powerful brutal people to whom I have no skill to reply.

They think they have defeated me. It is so published in society, in the journals; I am defeated in this fashion, in all men's sight, perhaps on a dozen different lines. My leger may show that I am in debt, cannot yet make my ends meet, and vanquish the enemy so. My race may not be prospering: we are sick, ugly, obscure, unpopular. My children may be worsted. I seem to fail in my friends and clients, too. That is to say, in all the encounters that have yet chanced, I have not been weaponed for that particular occasion, and have been historically beaten; and yet, I know, all the time, that I have never been beaten; have never yet fought, shall certainly fight, when my hour comes, and shall beat.' "A man," says the Vishnu Sarma, "who having well compared his own strength or weakness with that of others, after all doth not know the difference, is easily overcome by his enemies."

'I spent,' he said, 'ten months in the country. Thick-starred Orion was my only companion. Wherever a squirrel or a bee can go with security, I can go. I ate whatever was set before me; I touched ivy and dogwood. When I went abroad, I kept company with every man on the road, for I knew that my evil and my good did not come from these, but from the Spirit, whose servant I was. For I could not stoop to be a circumstance, as they did, who put their life into their fortune and their company. I would not degrade myself by casting about in my memory for a thought, nor by waiting for one. If the thought come, I would give it entertainment. It should, as it ought, go into my hands and feet; but if it come not spontaneously, it comes not rightly at all. If it can spare me, I am sure I can spare it. It shall be the same with my friends. I will never woo the loveliest. I will not ask any friendship or favor. When I come to my own, we shall both know it. Nothing will be to be asked or to be granted.' Benedict went out to seek his friend, and met him on the way; but he expressed no surprise at any coincidences. On the other hand, if he called at the door of his friend, and he was not at home, he did not go again; concluding that he had misinterpreted the intimations.

He had the whim not to make an apology to the same individual whom he had wronged. For this, he said, was a piece of personal vanity; but he would correct his conduct in that respect in which he had faulted, to the next person he should meet. Thus, he said, universal justice was satisfied.

Mira came to ask what she should do with the poor Genesee woman who had hired herself to work for her, at a shilling a day, and, now sickening, was like to be bedridden on her hands. Should she keep her, or should she dismiss her? But Benedict said, 'Why ask? One thing will clear itself as the thing to be done, and not another, when the hour comes. Is it a question, whether to put her into the street? Just as much whether to thrust the little Jenny on your arm into the street. The milk and meal you give the beggar, will fatten Jenny. Thrust the woman out, and you thrust your babe out of doors, whether it so seem to you or not.'

In the Shakers, so called, I find one piece of belief, in the doctrine which they faithfully hold, that encourages them to open their doors to every wayfaring man who proposes to come among them; for, they say, the Spirit will presently manifest to the man himself, and to the society, what manner of person he is, and whether he belongs among them. They do not receive him, they do not reject him. And not in vain have they worn their clay coat, and drudged in their fields, and shuffled in their Bruin dance, from year to year, if they have truly learned thus much wisdom.

Honor him whose life is perpetual victory; him, who, by sympathy with the invisible and real, finds support in labor, instead of praise; who does not shine, and would rather not. With eyes open, he makes the choice of virtue, which outrages the virtuous; of religion, which churches stop their discords to burn and exterminate; for the highest virtue is always against the law.

Miracle comes to the miraculous, not to the arithmetician. Talent and success interest me but moderately. The great class, they who affect our imagination, the men who could not make their hands meet around their objects, the rapt, the lost, the fools of ideas,—they suggest what they cannot execute. They speak to the ages, and are heard from afar. The Spirit does not love cripples and malformations. If there ever was a good man, be certain, there was another, and will be more.

And so in relation to that future hour, that spectre clothed with beauty at our curtain by night, at our table by day,—

the apprehension, the assurance of a coming change. The race of mankind have always offered at least this implied thanks for the gift of existence,—namely, the terror of its being taken away; the insatiable curiosity and appetite for its continuation. The whole revelation that is vouchsafed us, is, the gentle trust, which, in our experience we find, will cover also with flowers the slopes of this chasm.

Of immortality, the soul, when well employed, is incurious. It is so well, that it is sure it will be well. It asks no questions of the Supreme Power. The son of Antiochus asked his father, when he would join battle? "Dost thou fear," replied the King, "that thou only in all the army wilt not hear the trumpet?" 'Tis a higher thing to confide, that, if it is best we should live, we shall live,—'tis higher to have this conviction, than to have the lease of indefinite centuries and millenniums and æons. Higher than the question of our duration is the question of our deserving. Immortality will come to such as are fit for it, and he who would be a great soul in future, must be a great soul now. It is a doctrine too great to rest on any legend, that is, on any man's experience but our own. It must be proved, if at all, from our own activity and designs, which imply an interminable future for their play.

What is called religion effeminates and demoralizes. Such as you are, the gods themselves could not help you. Men are too often unfit to live, from their obvious inequality to their own necessities, or, they suffer from politics, or bad neighbors, or from sickness, and they would gladly know that they were to be dismissed from the duties of life. But the wise instinct asks, 'How will death help them?' These are not dismissed when they die. You shall not wish for death out of pusillanimity. The weight of the Universe is pressed down on the shoulders of each moral agent to hold him to his task. The only path of escape known in all the worlds of God is performance. You must do your work, before you shall be released. And as far as it is a question of fact respecting the government of the Universe, Marcus Antoninus summed the whole in a word, "It is pleasant to die, if there be gods; and sad to live, if there be none."

And so I think that the last lesson of life, the choral song which rises from all elements and all angels, is, a voluntary obedience, a necessitated freedom. Man is made of the same atoms as the world is, he shares the same impressions, predispositions, and destiny. When his mind is illuminated, when his heart is kind, he throws himself joyfully into the sublime order, and does, with knowledge, what the stones do by structure.

The religion which is to guide and fulfil the present and coming ages, whatever else it be, must be intellectual. The scientific mind must have a faith which is science. "There are two things," said Mahomet, "which I abhor, the learned in his infidelities, and the fool in his devotions." Our times are impatient of both, and specially of the last. Let us have nothing now which is not its own evidence. There is surely enough for the heart and imagination in the religion itself. Let us not be pestered with assertions and half-truths, with emotions and snuffle.

There will be a new church founded on moral science, at first cold and naked, a babe in a manger again, the algebra and mathematics of ethical law, the church of men to come, without shawms, or psaltery, or sackbut; but it will have heaven and earth for its beams and rafters; science for symbol and illustration; it will fast enough gather beauty, music, picture, poetry. Was never stoicism so stern and exigent as this shall be. It shall send man home to his central solitude, shame these social, supplicating manners, and make him know that much of the time he must have himself to his friend. He shall expect no coöperation, he shall walk with no companion. The nameless Thought, the nameless Power, the superpersonal Heart,—he shall repose alone on that. He needs only his own verdict. No good fame can help, no bad fame can hurt him. The Laws are his consolers, the good Laws themselves are alive, they know if he have kept them, they animate him with the leading of great duty, and an endless horizon. Honor and fortune exist to him who always recognizes the neighborhood of the great, always feels himself in the presence of high causes.

VII

CONSIDERATIONS
BY THE WAY

———

HEAR what British Merlin sung,
Of keenest eye and truest tongue.
Say not, the chiefs who first arrive
Usurp the seats for which all strive;
The forefathers this land who found
Failed to plant the vantage-ground;
Ever from one who comes to-morrow
Men wait their good and truth to borrow.
But wilt thou measure all thy road,
See thou lift the lightest load.
Who has little, to him who has less, can spare,
And thou, Cyndyllan's son! beware
Ponderous gold and stuffs to bear,
To falter ere thou thy task fulfil,—
Only the light-armed climb the hill.
The richest of all lords is Use,
And ruddy Health the loftiest Muse.
Live in the sunshine, swim the sea,
Drink the wild air's salubrity:
Where the star Canope shines in May,
Shepherds are thankful, and nations gay.
The music that can deepest reach,
And cure all ill, is cordial speech:

Mask thy wisdom with delight,
Toy with the bow, yet hit the white.
Of all wit's uses, the main one
Is to live well with who has none.
Cleave to thine acre; the round year
Will fetch all fruits and virtues here:
Fool and foe may harmless roam,
Loved and lovers bide at home.
A day for toil, an hour for sport,
But for a friend is life too short.

Considerations by the Way

ALTHOUGH this garrulity of advising is born with us, I confess that life is rather a subject of wonder, than of didactics. So much fate, so much irresistible dictation from temperament and unknown inspiration enters into it, that we doubt we can say anything out of our own experience whereby to help each other. All the professions are timid and expectant agencies. The priest is glad if his prayers or his sermon meet the condition of any soul; if of two, if of ten, 'tis a signal success. But he walked to the church without any assurance that he knew the distemper, or could heal it. The physician prescribes hesitatingly out of his few resources, the same tonic or sedative to this new and peculiar constitution, which he has applied with various success to a hundred men before. If the patient mends, he is glad and surprised. The lawyer advises the client, and tells his story to the jury, and leaves it with them, and is as gay and as much relieved as the client, if it turns out that he has a verdict. The judge weighs the arguments, and puts a brave face on the matter, and, since there must be a decision, decides as he can, and hopes he has done justice, and given satisfaction to the community; but is only an advocate after all. And so is all life a timid and unskilful spectator. We do what we must, and call it by the best names. We like very well to be praised for our action, but our conscience says, "Not unto us." 'Tis little we can do for each other. We accompany the youth with sympathy, and manifold old sayings of the wise, to the gate of the arena, but 'tis certain that not by strength of ours, or of the old sayings, but only on strength of his own, unknown to us or to any, he must stand or fall. That by which a man conquers in any passage, is a profound secret to every other being in the world, and it is only as he turns his back on us and on all men, and draws on this most private wisdom, that any good can come to him. What we have, therefore, to say of life, is rather description, or, if you please, celebration, than available rules.

Yet vigor is contagious, and whatever makes us either think or feel strongly, adds to our power, and enlarges our field of action. We have a debt to every great heart, to every fine genius; to those who have put life and fortune on the cast of an act of justice; to those who have added new sciences; to those who have refined life by elegant pursuits. 'Tis the fine souls who serve us, and not what is called fine society. Fine society is only a self-protection against the vulgarities of the street and the tavern. Fine society, in the common acceptation, has neither ideas nor aims. It renders the service of a perfumery, or a laundry, not of a farm or factory. 'Tis an exclusion and a precinct. Sidney Smith said, "A few yards in London cement or dissolve friendship." It is an unprincipled decorum; an affair of clean linen and coaches, of gloves, cards, and elegance in trifles. There are other measures of self-respect for a man, than the number of clean shirts he puts on every day. Society wishes to be amused. I do not wish to be amused. I wish that life should not be cheap, but sacred. I wish the days to be as centuries, loaded, fragrant. Now we reckon them as bank-days, by some debt which is to be paid us, or which we are to pay, or some pleasure we are to taste. Is all we have to do to draw the breath in, and blow it out again? Porphyry's definition is better; "Life is that which holds matter together." The babe in arms is a channel through which the energies we call fate, love, and reason, visibly stream. See what a cometary train of auxiliaries man carries with him, of animals, plants, stones, gases, and imponderable elements. Let us infer his ends from this pomp of means. Mirabeau said, "Why should we feel ourselves to be men, unless it be to succeed in everything, everywhere. You must say of nothing, *That is beneath me*, nor feel that anything can be out of your power. Nothing is impossible to the man who can will. *Is that necessary? That shall be:*—this is the only law of success." Whoever said it, this is in the right key. But this is not the tone and genius of the men in the street. In the streets, we grow cynical. The men we meet are coarse and torpid. The finest wits have their sediment. What quantities of fribbles, paupers, invalids, epicures, antiquaries, politicians, thieves, and triflers of both sexes, might be advantageously spared! Mankind divides itself into two classes,—benefactors and malefactors. The second class is vast, the first a handful. A person seldom falls sick, but the bystanders are animated with a faint hope that he will die:—quantities of poor lives; of distressing invalids; of cases for a gun. Franklin said, "Mankind are very superficial and dastardly: they begin upon a thing, but, meeting with a difficulty, they fly from it discouraged: but they have capacities, if they would employ them." Shall we then judge a country by the majority, or by the minority? By the minority, surely. 'Tis pedantry to estimate nations by the census, or by square miles of land, or other than by their importance to the mind of the time.

Leave this hypocritical prating about the masses. Masses are rude, lame, unmade, pernicious in their demands and influence, and need not to be flattered but to be schooled. I wish not to concede anything to them, but to tame, drill, divide, and break them up, and draw individuals out of them. The worst of charity is, that the lives you are asked to preserve are not worth preserving. Masses! the calamity is the masses. I do not wish any mass at all, but honest men only, lovely, sweet, accomplished women only, and no shovel-handed, narrow-brained, gin-drinking million stockingers or lazzaroni at all. If government knew how, I should like to see it check, not multiply the population. When it reaches its true law of action, every man that is born will be hailed as essential. Away with this hurrah of masses, and let us have the considerate vote of single men spoken on their honor and their conscience. In old Egypt, it was established law, that the vote of a prophet be reckoned equal to a hundred hands. I think it was much under-estimated. "Clay and clay differ in dignity," as we discover by our preferences every day. What a vicious practice is this of our politicians at Washington pairing off! as if one man who votes wrong, going away, could excuse you, who mean to vote right, for going away; or, as if your presence did not tell in more ways than in your vote. Suppose the three hundred heroes at Thermopylæ had paired off with three hundred Persians: would it have been all the same to Greece, and to history? Napoleon was called by his men *Cent Mille*. Add honesty to him, and they might have called him Hundred Million.

Nature makes fifty poor melons for one that is good, and shakes down a tree full of gnarled, wormy, unripe crabs, before you can find a dozen dessert apples; and she scatters nations of naked Indians, and nations of clothed Christians,

with two or three good heads among them. Nature works
very hard, and only hits the white once in a million throws.
In mankind, she is contented if she yields one master in a
century. The more difficulty there is in creating good men,
the more they are used when they come. I once counted in a
little neighborhood, and found that every able-bodied man
had, say from twelve to fifteen persons dependent on him for
material aid,—to whom he is to be for spoon and jug, for
backer and sponsor, for nursery and hospital, and many functions beside: nor does it seem to make much difference
whether he is bachelor or patriarch; if he do not violently
decline the duties that fall to him, this amount of helpfulness
will in one way or another be brought home to him. This is
the tax which his abilities pay. The good men are employed
for private centres of use, and for larger influence. All revelations, whether of mechanical or intellectual or moral science,
are made not to communities, but to single persons. All the
marked events of our day, all the cities, all the colonizations,
may be traced back to their origin in a private brain. All the
feats which make our civility were the thoughts of a few good
heads.

Meantime, this spawning productivity is not noxious or
needless. You would say, this rabble of nations might be
spared. But no, they are all counted and depended on. Fate
keeps everything alive so long as the smallest thread of public
necessity holds it on to the tree. The coxcomb and bully and
thief class are allowed as proletaries, every one of their vices
being the excess or acridity of a virtue. The mass are animal,
in pupilage, and near chimpanzee. But the units, whereof this
mass is composed are neuters, every one of which may be
grown to a queen-bee. The rule is, we are used as brute atoms, until we think: then, we use all the rest. Nature turns all
malfaisance to good. Nature provided for real needs. No sane
man at last distrusts himself. His existence is a perfect answer
to all sentimental cavils. If he is, he is wanted, and has the
precise properties that are required. That we are here, is proof
we ought to be here. We have as good right, and the same
sort of right to be here, as Cape Cod or Sandy Hook have to
be there.

To say then, the majority are wicked, means no malice, no

bad heart in the observer, but, simply, that the majority are unripe, and have not yet come to themselves, do not yet know their opinion. *That*, if they knew it, is an oracle for them and for all. But in the passing moment, the quadruped interest is very prone to prevail: and this beast-force, whilst it makes the discipline of the world, the school of heroes, the glory of martyrs, has provoked, in every age, the satire of wits, and the tears of good men. They find the journals, the clubs, the governments, the churches, to be in the interest, and the pay of the devil. And wise men have met this obstruction in their times, like Socrates, with his famous irony; like Bacon, with life-long dissimulation; like Erasmus, with his book "The Praise of Folly;" like Rabelais, with his satire rending the nations. "They were the fools who cried against me, you will say," wrote the Chevalier de Boufflers to Grimm; "aye, but the fools have the advantage of numbers, and 'tis that which decides. 'Tis of no use for us to make war with them; we shall not weaken them; they will always be the masters. There will not be a practice or an usage introduced, of which they are not the authors."

In front of these sinister facts, the first lesson of history is the good of evil. Good is a good doctor, but Bad is sometimes a better. 'Tis the oppressions of William the Norman, savage forest-laws, and crushing despotism, that made possible the inspirations of *Magna Charta* under John. Edward I. wanted money, armies, castles, and as much as he could get. It was necessary to call the people together by shorter, swifter ways,—and the House of Commons arose. To obtain subsidies, he paid in privileges. In the twenty-fourth year of his reign, he decreed, "that no tax should be levied without consent of Lords and Commons;"—which is the basis of the English Constitution. Plutarch affirms that the cruel wars which followed the march of Alexander, introduced the civility, language, and arts of Greece into the savage East; introduced marriage; built seventy cities; and united hostile nations under one government. The barbarians who broke up the Roman empire did not arrive a day too soon. Schiller says, the Thirty Years' War made Germany a nation. Rough, selfish despots serve men immensely, as Henry VIII. in the contest with the Pope; as the infatuations no less than the wisdom of

Cromwell; as the ferocity of the Russian czars; as the fanaticism of the French regicides of 1789. The frost which kills the harvest of a year, saves the harvests of a century, by destroying the weevil or the locust. Wars, fires, plagues, break up immovable routine, clear the ground of rotten races and dens of distemper, and open a fair field to new men. There is a tendency in things to right themselves, and the war or revolution or bankruptcy that shatters a rotten system, allows things to take a new and natural order. The sharpest evils are bent into that periodicity which makes the errors of planets, and the fevers and distempers of men, self-limiting. Nature is upheld by antagonism. Passions, resistance, danger, are educators. We acquire the strength we have overcome. Without war, no soldier; without enemies, no hero. The sun were insipid, if the universe were not opaque. And the glory of character is in affronting the horrors of depravity, to draw thence new nobilities of power: as Art lives and thrills in new use and combining of contrasts, and mining into the dark evermore for blacker pits of night. What would painter do, or what would poet or saint, but for crucifixions and hells? And evermore in the world is this marvellous balance of beauty and disgust, magnificence and rats. Not Antoninus, but a poor washer-woman said, "The more trouble, the more lion; that's my principle."

I do not think very respectfully of the designs or the doings of the people who went to California, in 1849. It was a rush and a scramble of needy adventurers, and, in the western country, a general jail-delivery of all the rowdies of the rivers. Some of them went with honest purposes, some with very bad ones, and all of them with the very commonplace wish to find a short way to wealth. But Nature watches over all, and turns this malfaisance to good. California gets peopled and subdued,—civilized in this immoral way,—and, on this fiction, a real prosperity is rooted and grown. 'Tis a decoy-duck; 'tis tubs thrown to amuse the whale: but real ducks, and whales that yield oil, are caught. And, out of Sabine rapes, and out of robbers' forays, real Romes and their heroisms come in fulness of time.

In America, the geography is sublime, but the men are not: the inventions are excellent, but the inventors one is sometimes ashamed of. The agencies by which events so grand as the opening of California, of Texas, of Oregon, and the junction of the two oceans, are effected, are paltry,—coarse selfishness, fraud, and conspiracy: and most of the great results of history are brought about by discreditable means.

The benefaction derived in Illinois, and the great West, from railroads is inestimable, and vastly exceeding any intentional philanthropy on record. What is the benefit done by a good King Alfred, or by a Howard, or Pestalozzi, or Elizabeth Fry, or Florence Nightingale, or any lover, less or larger, compared with the involuntary blessing wrought on nations by the selfish capitalists who built the Illinois, Michigan, and the network of the Mississippi valley roads, which have evoked not only all the wealth of the soil, but the energy of millions of men. 'Tis a sentence of ancient wisdom, "that God hangs the greatest weights on the smallest wires."

What happens thus to nations, befalls every day in private houses. When the friends of a gentleman brought to his notice the follies of his sons, with many hints of their danger, he replied, that he knew so much mischief when he was a boy, and had turned out on the whole so successfully, that he was not alarmed by the dissipation of boys; 'twas dangerous water, but, he thought, they would soon touch bottom, and then swim to the top. This is bold practice, and there are many failures to a good escape. Yet one would say, that a good understanding would suffice as well as moral sensibility to keep one erect; the gratifications of the passions are so quickly seen to be damaging, and,—what men like least,— seriously lowering them in social rank. Then all talent sinks with character.

"Croyez moi, l'erreur aussi a son mérite," said Voltaire. We see those who surmount, by dint of some egotism or infatuation, obstacles from which the prudent recoil. The right partisan is a heady narrow man, who, because he does not see many things, sees some one thing with heat and exaggeration, and, if he falls among other narrow men, or on objects which have a brief importance, as some trade or politics of the hour, he prefers it to the universe, and seems inspired, and a godsend to those who wish to magnify the matter, and carry a point. Better, certainly, if we could secure the strength and

fire which rude, passionate men bring into society, quite clear
of their vices. But who dares draw out the linchpin from the
wagon-wheel? 'Tis so manifest, that there is no moral deformity, but is a good passion out of place; that there is no man
who is not indebted to his foibles; that, according to the old
oracle, "the Furies are the bonds of men;" that the poisons
are our principal medicines, which kill the disease, and save
the life. In the high prophetic phrase, *He causes the wrath of
man to praise him*, and twists and wrenches our evil to our
good. Shakspeare wrote,—

> " 'Tis said, best men are moulded of their faults;"

and great educators and lawgivers, and especially generals,
and leaders of colonies, mainly rely on this stuff, and esteem
men of irregular and passional force the best timber. A man
of sense and energy, the late head of the Farm School in Boston harbor, said to me, "I want none of your good boys,—
give me the bad ones." And this is the reason, I suppose,
why, as soon as the children are good, the mothers are scared,
and think they are going to die. Mirabeau said, "There are
none but men of strong passions capable of going to greatness; none but such capable of meriting the public gratitude."
Passion, though a bad regulator, is a powerful spring. Any
absorbing passion has the effect to deliver from the little coils
and cares of every day: 'tis the heat which sets our human
atoms spinning, overcomes the friction of crossing thresholds,
and first addresses in society, and gives us a good start and
speed, easy to continue, when once it is begun. In short, there
is no man who is not at some time indebted to his vices, as
no plant that is not fed from manures. We only insist that the
man meliorate, and that the plant grow upward, and convert
the base into the better nature.

The wise workman will not regret the poverty or the solitude which brought out his working talents. The youth is
charmed with the fine air and accomplishments of the children of fortune. But all great men come out of the middle
classes. 'Tis better for the head; 'tis better for the heart. Marcus Antoninus says, that Fronto told him, "that the so-called
high-born are for the most part heartless;" whilst nothing is
so indicative of deepest culture as a tender consideration of

the ignorant. Charles James Fox said of England, "The history of this country proves, that we are not to expect from men in affluent circumstances the vigilance, energy, and exertion without which the House of Commons would lose its greatest force and weight. Human nature is prone to indulgence, and the most meritorious public services have always been performed by persons in a condition of life removed from opulence." And yet what we ask daily, is to be conventional. Supply, most kind gods! this defect in my address, in my form, in my fortunes, which puts me a little out of the ring: supply it, and let me be like the rest whom I admire, and on good terms with them. But the wise gods say, No, we have better things for thee. By humiliations, by defeats, by loss of sympathy, by gulfs of disparity, learn a wider truth and humanity than that of a fine gentleman. A Fifth-Avenue landlord, a West-End householder, is not the highest style of man: and, though good hearts and sound minds are of no condition, yet he who is to be wise for many, must not be protected. He must know the huts where poor men lie, and the chores which poor men do. The first-class minds, Æsop, Socrates, Cervantes, Shakspeare, Franklin, had the poor man's feeling and mortification. A rich man was never insulted in his life: but this man must be stung. A rich man was never in danger from cold, or hunger, or war, or ruffians, and you can see he was not, from the moderation of his ideas. 'Tis a fatal disadvantage to be cockered, and to eat too much cake. What tests of manhood could he stand? Take him out of his protections. He is a good book-keeper; or he is a shrewd adviser in the insurance office: perhaps he could pass a college examination, and take his degrees: perhaps he can give wise counsel in a court of law. Now plant him down among farmers, firemen, Indians, and emigrants. Set a dog on him: set a highwayman on him: try him with a course of mobs: send him to Kansas, to Pike's Peak, to Oregon: and, if he have true faculty, this may be the element he wants, and he will come out of it with broader wisdom and manly power. Æsop, Saadi, Cervantes, Regnard, have been taken by corsairs, left for dead, sold for slaves, and know the realities of human life.

Bad times have a scientific value. These are occasions a good learner would not miss. As we go gladly to Faneuil

Hall, to be played upon by the stormy winds and strong fingers of enraged patriotism, so is a fanatical persecution, civil war, national bankruptcy, or revolution, more rich in the central tones than languid years of prosperity. What had been, ever since our memory, solid continent, yawns apart, and discloses its composition and genesis. We learn geology the morning after the earthquake, on ghastly diagrams of cloven mountains, upheaved plains, and the dry bed of the sea.

In our life and culture, everything is worked up, and comes in use,—passion, war, revolt, bankruptcy, and not less, folly and blunders, insult, ennui, and bad company. Nature is a rag-merchant, who works up every shred and ort and end into new creations; like a good chemist, whom I found, the other day, in his laboratory, converting his old shirts into pure white sugar. Life is a boundless privilege, and when you pay for your ticket, and get into the car, you have no guess what good company you shall find there. You buy much that is not rendered in the bill. Men achieve a certain greatness unawares, when working to another aim.

If now in this connection of discourse, we should venture on laying down the first obvious rules of life, I will not here repeat the first rule of economy, already propounded once and again, that every man shall maintain himself,—but I will say, get health. No labor, pains, temperance, poverty, nor exercise, that can gain it, must be grudged. For sickness is a cannibal which eats up all the life and youth it can lay hold of, and absorbs its own sons and daughters. I figure it as a pale, wailing, distracted phantom, absolutely selfish, heedless of what is good and great, attentive to its sensations, losing its soul, and afflicting other souls with meanness and mopings, and with ministration to its voracity of trifles. Dr. Johnson said severely, "Every man is a rascal as soon as he is sick." Drop the cant, and treat it sanely. In dealing with the drunken, we do not affect to be drunk. We must treat the sick with the same firmness, giving them, of course, every aid,—but withholding ourselves. I once asked a clergyman in a retired town, who were his companions? what men of ability he saw? he replied, that he spent his time with the sick and the dying. I said, he seemed to me to need quite other company, and all the more that he had this: for if people were sick and dying to any purpose, we would leave all and go to them, but, as far as I had observed, they were as frivolous as the rest, and sometimes much more frivolous. Let us engage our companions not to spare us. I knew a wise woman who said to her friends, "When I am old, rule me." And the best part of health is fine disposition. It is more essential than talent, even in the works of talent. Nothing will supply the want of sunshine to peaches, and, to make knowledge valuable, you must have the cheerfulness of wisdom. Whenever you are sincerely pleased, you are nourished. The joy of the spirit indicates its strength. All healthy things are sweet-tempered. Genius works in sport, and goodness smiles to the last; and, for the reason, that whoever sees the law which distributes things, does not despond, but is animated to great desires and endeavors. He who desponds betrays that he has not seen it.

'Tis a Dutch proverb, that "paint costs nothing," such are its preserving qualities in damp climates. Well, sunshine costs less, yet is finer pigment. And so of cheerfulness, or a good temper, the more it is spent, the more of it remains. The latent heat of an ounce of wood or stone is inexhaustible. You may rub the same chip of pine to the point of kindling, a hundred times; and the power of happiness of any soul is not to be computed or drained. It is observed that a depression of spirits develops the germs of a plague in individuals and nations.

It is an old commendation of right behavior, "*Aliis lætus, sapiens sibi*," which our English proverb translates, "Be merry *and* wise." I know how easy it is to men of the world to look grave and sneer at your sanguine youth, and its glittering dreams. But I find the gayest castles in the air that were ever piled, far better for comfort and for use, than the dungeons in the air that are daily dug and caverned out by grumbling, discontented people. I know those miserable fellows, and I hate them, who see a black star always riding through the light and colored clouds in the sky overhead: waves of light pass over and hide it for a moment, but the black star keeps fast in the zenith. But power dwells with cheerfulness; hope puts us in a working mood, whilst despair is no muse, and untunes the active powers. A man should make life and Nature happier to us, or he had better never been born. When the political economist reckons up the unproductive classes, he should put at the head this class of pitiers of themselves, cravers of sympathy, bewailing imaginary disasters. An old French verse runs, in my translation:—

> Some of your griefs you have cured,
> 　And the sharpest you still have survived;
> But what torments of pain you endured
> 　From evils that never arrived!

There are three wants which never can be satisfied: that of the rich, who wants something more; that of the sick, who wants something different; and that of the traveller, who says, 'Anywhere but here.' The Turkish cadi said to Layard, "After the fashion of thy people, thou hast wandered from one place to another, until thou art happy and content in none." My countrymen are not less infatuated with the *rococo* toy of Italy. All America seems on the point of embarking for Europe. But we shall not always traverse seas and lands with light purposes, and for pleasure, as we say. One day we shall cast out the passion for Europe, by the passion for America. Culture will give gravity and domestic rest to those who now travel only as not knowing how else to spend money. Already, who provoke pity like that excellent family party just arriving in their well-appointed carriage, as far from home and any honest end as ever? Each nation has asked successively, 'What are they here for?' until at last the party are shamefaced, and anticipate the question at the gates of each town.

Genial manners are good, and power of accommodation to any circumstance, but the high prize of life, the crowning fortune of a man is to be born with a bias to some pursuit, which finds him in employment and happiness,—whether it be to make baskets, or broadswords, or canals, or statutes, or songs. I doubt not this was the meaning of Socrates, when he pronounced artists the only truly wise, as being actually, not apparently so.

In childhood, we fancied ourselves walled in by the horizon, as by a glass bell, and doubted not, by distant travel, we should reach the baths of the descending sun and stars. On experiment, the horizon flies before us, and leaves us on an endless common, sheltered by no glass bell. Yet 'tis strange how tenaciously we cling to that bell-astronomy, of a protecting domestic horizon. I find the same illusion in the search after happiness, which I observe, every summer, recommenced in this neighborhood, soon after the pairing of the birds. The young people do not like the town, do not like the sea-shore, they will go inland; find a dear cottage deep in the mountains, secret as their hearts. They set forth on their travels in search of a home: they reach Berkshire; they reach Vermont; they look at the farms;—good farms, high mountain-sides: but where is the seclusion? The farm is near this; 'tis near that; they have got far from Boston, but 'tis near Albany, or near Burlington, or near Montreal. They explore a farm, but the house is small, old, thin; discontented people lived there, and are gone:—there's too much sky, too much out-doors; too public. The youth aches for solitude. When he comes to the house, he passes through the house. That does not make the deep recess he sought. 'Ah! now, I perceive,' he says, 'it must be deep with persons; friends only can give depth.' Yes, but there is a great dearth, this year, of friends; hard to find, and hard to have when found: they are just going away: they too are in the whirl of the flitting world, and have engagements and necessities. They are just starting for Wisconsin; have letters from Bremen:—see you again, soon. Slow, slow to learn the lesson, that there is but one depth, but one interior, and that is—his purpose. When joy or calamity or genius shall show him it, then woods, then farms, then city shopmen and cab-drivers, indifferently with prophet or friend, will mirror back to him its unfathomable heaven, its populous solitude.

The uses of travel are occasional, and short; but the best fruit it finds, when it finds it, is conversation; and this is a main function of life. What a difference in the hospitality of minds! Inestimable is he to whom we can say what we cannot say to ourselves. Others are involuntarily hurtful to us, and bereave us of the power of thought, impound and imprison us. As, when there is sympathy, there needs but one wise man in a company, and all are wise,—so, a blockhead makes a blockhead of his companion. Wonderful power to benumb possesses this brother. When he comes into the office or public room, the society dissolves; one after another slips out, and the apartment is at his disposal. What is incurable but a frivolous habit? A fly is as untamable as a hyena. Yet folly in the sense of fun, fooling, or dawdling can easily be borne; as Talleyrand said, "I find nonsense singularly refreshing;" but a virulent, aggressive fool taints the reason of a household. I have seen a whole family of quiet, sensible people unhinged and beside themselves, victims of such a rogue. For the steady wrongheadedness of one perverse person irritates the best: since we must withstand absurdity. But resistance only exasperates the acrid fool, who believes that Nature and gravitation are quite wrong, and he only is right. Hence all the dozen inmates are soon perverted, with whatever virtues and industries they have, into contradictors, accusers, explainers, and repairers of this one malefactor; like a boat about to be overset, or a carriage run away with,—not only the foolish pilot or driver, but everybody on board is forced to assume strange and ridiculous attitudes, to balance the vehicle and prevent the upsetting. For remedy, whilst the case is yet mild, I recommend phlegm and truth: let all the truth that is spoken or done be at the zero of indifference, or truth itself will be folly. But, when the case is seated and malignant, the only safety is in amputation; as seamen say, you shall cut and run. How to live with unfit companions?—for, with such, life is for the most part spent: and experience teaches little better than our earliest instinct of self-defence, namely, not to engage, not to mix yourself in any manner with them; but let their madness spend itself unopposed;—you are you, and I am I.

Conversation is an art in which a man has all mankind for his competitors, for it is that which all are practising every day while they live. Our habit of thought,—take men as they rise,—is not satisfying; in the common experience, I fear, it is poor and squalid. The success which will content them, is, a bargain, a lucrative employment, an advantage gained over a competitor, a marriage, a patrimony, a legacy, and the like. With these objects, their conversation deals with surfaces: politics, trade, personal defects, exaggerated bad news, and the rain. This is forlorn, and they feel sore and sensitive. Now, if one comes who can illuminate this dark house with thoughts, show them their native riches, what gifts they have, how indispensable each is, what magical powers over nature and men; what access to poetry, religion, and the powers which constitute character; he wakes in them the feeling of worth, his suggestions require new ways of living, new books, new men, new arts and sciences,—then we come out of our egg-shell existence into the great dome, and see the zenith over and the nadir under us. Instead of the tanks and buckets of knowledge to which we are daily confined, we come down to the shore of the sea, and dip our hands in its miraculous waves. 'Tis wonderful the effect on the company. They are not the men they were. They have all been to California, and all have come back millionnaires. There is no book and no pleasure in life comparable to it. Ask what is best in our experience, and we shall say, a few pieces of plain-dealing with wise people. Our conversation once and again has apprised us that we belong to better circles than we have yet beheld; that a mental power invites us, whose generalizations are more worth for joy and for effect than anything that is now called philosophy or literature. In excited conversation, we have glimpses of the Universe, hints of power native to the soul, far-darting lights and shadows of an Andes landscape, such as we can hardly attain in lone meditation. Here are oracles sometimes profusely given, to which the memory goes back in barren hours.

Add the consent of will and temperament, and there exists the covenant of friendship. Our chief want in life, is, somebody who shall make us do what we can. This is the service of a friend. With him we are easily great. There is a sublime attraction in him to whatever virtue is in us. How he flings wide the doors of existence! What questions we ask of him! what an understanding we have! how few words are needed! It is the only real society. An Eastern poet, Ali Ben Abu Taleb, writes with sad truth,—

"He who has a thousand friends has not a friend to spare,
  And he who has one enemy shall meet him everywhere."

But few writers have said anything better to this point than Hafiz, who indicates this relation as the test of mental health: "Thou learnest no secret until thou knowest friendship, since to the unsound no heavenly knowledge enters." Neither is life long enough for friendship. That is a serious and majestic affair, like a royal presence, or a religion, and not a postilion's dinner to be eaten on the run. There is a pudency about friendship, as about love, and though fine souls never lose sight of it, yet they do not name it. With the first class of men our friendship or good understanding goes quite behind all accidents of estrangement, of condition, of reputation. And yet we do not provide for the greatest good of life. We take care of our health; we lay up money; we make our roof tight, and our clothing sufficient; but who provides wisely that he shall not be wanting in the best property of all,—friends? We know that all our training is to fit us for this, and we do not take the step towards it. How long shall we sit and wait for these benefactors?

It makes no difference, in looking back five years, how you have been dieted or dressed; whether you have been lodged on the first floor or the attic; whether you have had gardens and baths, good cattle and horses, have been carried in a neat equipage, or in a ridiculous truck: these things are forgotten so quickly, and leave no effect. But it counts much whether we have had good companions, in that time;—almost as much as what we have been doing. And see the overpowering importance of neighborhood in all association. As it is marriage, fit or unfit, that makes our home, so it is who lives near us of equal social degree,—a few people at convenient distance, no matter how bad company,—these, and these only, shall be your life's companions: and all those who are native, congenial, and by many an oath of the heart, sacramented to you, are gradually and totally lost. You cannot deal systematically with this fine element of society, and one may take a good deal of pains to bring people together, and to organize clubs and debating societies, and yet no result come of it. But it is certain that there is a great deal of good in us that does not know itself, and that a habit of union and competition brings people up and keeps them up to their highest point; that life would be twice or ten times life, if spent with wise and fruitful companions. The obvious inference is, a little useful deliberation and preconcert, when one goes to buy house and land.

But we live with people on other platforms; we live with

dependents, not only with the young whom we are to teach all we know, and clothe with the advantages we have earned, but also with those who serve us directly, and for money. Yet the old rules hold good. Let not the tie be mercenary, though the service is measured by money. Make yourself necessary to somebody. Do not make life hard to any. This point is acquiring new importance in American social life. Our domestic service is usually a foolish fracas of unreasonable demand on one side, and shirking on the other. A man of wit was asked, in the train, what was his errand in the city? He replied, "I have been sent to procure an angel to do cooking." A lady complained to me, that, of her two maidens, one was absent-minded, and the other was absent-bodied. And the evil increases from the ignorance and hostility of every ship-load of the immigrant population swarming into houses and farms. Few people discern that it rests with the master or the mistress what service comes from the man or the maid; that this identical hussy was a tutelar spirit in one house, and a haridan in the other. All sensible people are selfish, and nature is tugging at every contract to make the terms of it fair. If you are proposing only your own, the other party must deal a little hardly by you. If you deal generously, the other, though selfish and unjust, will make an exception in your favor, and deal truly with you. When I asked an iron-master about the slag and cinder in railroad iron,—"O," he said, "there's always good iron to be had: if there's cinder in the iron, 'tis because there was cinder in the pay."

But why multiply these topics, and their illustrations, which are endless? Life brings to each his task, and, whatever art you select, algebra, planting, architecture, poems, commerce, politics,—all are attainable, even to the miraculous triumphs, on the same terms, of selecting that for which you are apt;—begin at the beginning, proceed in order, step by step. 'Tis as easy to twist iron anchors, and braid cannons, as to braid straw, to boil granite as to boil water, if you take all the steps in order. Wherever there is failure, there is some giddiness, some superstition about luck, some step omitted, which Nature never pardons. The happy conditions of life may be had on the same terms. Their attraction for you is the pledge that they are within your reach. Our prayers are

prophets. There must be fidelity, and there must be adherence. How respectable the life that clings to its objects!
Youthful aspirations are fine things, your theories and plans
of life are fair and commendable:—but will you stick? Not
one, I fear, in that Common full of people, or, in a thousand,
but one: and, when you tax them with treachery, and remind
them of their high resolutions, they have forgotten that they
made a vow. The individuals are fugitive, and in the act of
becoming something else, and irresponsible. The race is great,
the ideal fair, but the men whiffling and unsure. The hero is
he who is immovably centred. The main difference between
people seems to be, that one man can come under obligations
on which you can rely,—is obligable; and another is not. As
he has not a law within him, there's nothing to tie him to.

'Tis inevitable to name particulars of virtue, and of condition, and to exaggerate them. But all rests at last on that integrity which dwarfs talent, and can spare it. Sanity consists
in not being subdued by your means. Fancy prices are paid
for position, and for the culture of talent, but to the grand
interests, superficial success is of no account. The man,—it is
his attitude,—not feats, but forces,—not on set days and
public occasions, but, at all hours, and in repose alike as in
energy, still formidable, and not to be disposed of. The populace says, with Horne Tooke, "If you would be powerful,
pretend to be powerful." I prefer to say, with the old prophet,
"Seekest thou great things? seek them not:"—or, what was
said of a Spanish prince, "The more you took from him, the
greater he looked." *Plus on lui ôte, plus il est grand.*

The secret of culture is to learn, that a few great points
steadily reappear, alike in the poverty of the obscurest farm,
and in the miscellany of metropolitan life, and that these few
are alone to be regarded,—the escape from all false ties; courage to be what we are; and love of what is simple and beautiful; independence, and cheerful relation, these are the
essentials,—these, and the wish to serve,—to add somewhat
to the well-being of men.

VIII

BEAUTY

———

WAS never form and never face
So sweet to SEYD as only grace
Which did not slumber like a stone
But hovered gleaming and was gone.
Beauty chased he everywhere,
In flame, in storm, in clouds of air.
He smote the lake to feed his eye
   With the beryl beam of the broken wave;
He flung in pebbles well to hear
   The moment's music which they gave.
Oft pealed for him a lofty tone
From nodding pole and belting zone.
He heard a voice none else could hear
From centred and from errant sphere.
The quaking earth did quake in rhyme,
Seas ebbed and flowed in epic chime.
In dens of passion, and pits of wo,
He saw strong Eros struggling through,
To sun the dark and solve the curse,
And beam to the bounds of the universe.
While thus to love he gave his days
In loyal worship, scorning praise,
How spread their lures for him, in vain,
Thieving Ambition and paltering Gain!
He thought it happier to be dead,
To die for Beauty, than live for bread.

Beauty

THE SPIRAL TENDENCY of vegetation infects education also. Our books approach very slowly the things we most wish to know. What a parade we make of our science, and how far off, and at arm's length, it is from its objects! Our botany is all names, not powers: poets and romancers talk of herbs of grace and healing; but what does the botanist know of the virtues of his weeds? The geologist lays bare the strata, and can tell them all on his fingers: but does he know what effect passes into the man who builds his house in them? what effect on the race that inhabits a granite shelf? what on the inhabitants of marl and of alluvium?

We should go to the ornithologist with a new feeling, if he could teach us what the social birds say, when they sit in the autumn council, talking together in the trees. The want of sympathy makes his record a dull dictionary. His result is a dead bird. The bird is not in its ounces and inches, but in its relations to Nature; and the skin or skeleton you show me, is no more a heron, than a heap of ashes or a bottle of gases into which his body has been reduced, is Dante or Washington. The naturalist is led *from* the road by the whole distance of his fancied advance. The boy had juster views when he gazed at the shells on the beach, or the flowers in the meadow, unable to call them by their names, than the man in the pride of his nomenclature. Astrology interested us, for it tied man to the system. Instead of an isolated beggar, the farthest star felt him, and he felt the star. However rash and however falsified by pretenders and traders in it, the hint was true and divine, the soul's avowal of its large relations, and, that climate, century, remote natures, as well as near, are part of its biography. Chemistry takes to pieces, but it does not construct. Alchemy which sought to transmute one element into another, to prolong life, to arm with power,—that was in the right direction. All our science lacks a human side. The tenant is more than the house. Bugs and stamens and spores, on which we lavish so many years, are not finalities, and man, when his powers unfold in order, will take Nature along with him, and emit light into all her recesses. The human heart concerns us more than the poring into microscopes, and is larger than can be measured by the pompous figures of the astronomer.

We are just so frivolous and skeptical. Men hold themselves cheap and vile: and yet a man is a fagot of thunderbolts. All the elements pour through his system: he is the flood of the flood, and fire of the fire; he feels the antipodes and the pole, as drops of his blood: they are the extension of his personality. His duties are measured by that instrument he is; and a right and perfect man would be felt to the centre of the Copernican system. 'Tis curious that we only believe as deep as we live. We do not think heroes can exert any more awful power than that surface-play which amuses us. A deep man believes in miracles, waits for them, believes in magic, believes that the orator will decompose his adversary; believes that the evil eye can wither, that the heart's blessing can heal; that love can exalt talent; can overcome all odds. From a great heart secret magnetisms flow incessantly to draw great events. But we prize very humble utilities, a prudent husband, a good son, a voter, a citizen, and deprecate any romance of character; and perhaps reckon only his money value,—his intellect, his affection, as a sort of bill of exchange, easily convertible into fine chambers, pictures, music, and wine.

The motive of science was the extension of man, on all sides, into Nature, till his hands should touch the stars, his eyes see through the earth, his ears understand the language of beast and bird, and the sense of the wind; and, through his sympathy, heaven and earth should talk with him. But that is not our science. These geologies, chemistries, astronomies, seem to make wise, but they leave us where they found us. The invention is of use to the inventor, of questionable help to any other. The formulas of science are like the papers in your pocket-book, of no value to any but the owner. Science in England, in America, is jealous of theory, hates the name of love and moral purpose. There's a revenge for this inhumanity. What manner of man does science make? The boy is not attracted. He says, I do not wish to be such a kind of man as my professor is. The collector has dried all the plants in his herbal, but he has lost weight and humor. He has got all snakes and lizards in his phials, but science has done for him also, and has put the man into a bottle. Our reliance on the physician is a kind of despair of ourselves. The clergy have bronchitis, which does not seem a certificate of spiritual health. Macready thought it came of the *falsetto* of their voicing. An Indian prince, Tisso, one day riding in the forest, saw a herd of elk sporting. "See how happy," he said, "these browsing elks are! Why should not priests, lodged and fed comfortably in the temples, also amuse themselves?" Returning home, he imparted this reflection to the king. The king, on the next day, conferred the sovereignty on him, saying, "Prince, administer this empire for seven days: at the termination of that period, I shall put thee to death." At the end of the seventh day, the king inquired, "From what cause hast thou become so emaciated?" He answered, "From the horror of death." The monarch rejoined: "Live, my child, and be wise. Thou hast ceased to take recreation, saying to thyself, in seven days I shall be put to death. These priests in the temple incessantly meditate on death; how can they enter into healthful diversions?" But the men of science or the doctors or the clergy are not victims of their pursuits, more than others. The miller, the lawyer, and the merchant, dedicate themselves to their own details, and do not come out men of more force. Have they divination, grand aims, hospitality of soul, and the equality to any event, which we demand in man, or only the reactions of the mill, of the wares, of the chicane?

No object really interests us but man, and in man only his superiorities; and, though we are aware of a perfect law in Nature, it has fascination for us only through its relation to him, or, as it is rooted in the mind. At the birth of Winckelmann, more than a hundred years ago, side by side with this arid, departmental, *post mortem* science, rose an enthusiasm in the study of Beauty; and perhaps some sparks from it may yet light a conflagration in the other. Knowledge of men, knowledge of manners, the power of form, and our sensibility to personal influence, never go out of fashion. These are facts of a science which we study without book, whose teachers and subjects are always near us.

So inveterate is our habit of criticism, that much of our knowledge in this direction belongs to the chapter of pathology. The crowd in the street oftener furnishes degradations

than angels or redeemers: but they all prove the transparency.
Every spirit makes its house; and we can give a shrewd guess
from the house to the inhabitant. But not less does Nature
furnish us with every sign of grace and goodness. The delicious faces of children, the beauty of school-girls, "the sweet
seriousness of sixteen," the lofty air of well-born, well-bred
boys, the passionate histories in the looks and manners of
youth and early manhood, and the varied power in all that
well-known company that escort us through life,—we know
how these forms thrill, paralyze, provoke, inspire, and enlarge us.

Beauty is the form under which the intellect prefers to
study the world. All privilege is that of beauty; for there are
many beauties; as, of general nature, of the human face and
form, of manners, of brain, or method, moral beauty, or
beauty of the soul.

The ancients believed that a genius or demon took possession at birth of each mortal, to guide him; that these genii
were sometimes seen as a flame of fire partly immersed in the
bodies which they governed;—on an evil man, resting on his
head; in a good man, mixed with his substance. They thought
the same genius, at the death of its ward, entered a new-born
child, and they pretended to guess the pilot, by the sailing of
the ship. We recognize obscurely the same fact, though we
give it our own names. We say, that every man is entitled to
be valued by his best moment. We measure our friends so. We
know, they have intervals of folly, whereof we take no heed,
but wait the reappearings of the genius, which are sure and
beautiful. On the other side, everybody knows people who
appear beridden, and who, with all degrees of ability, never
impress us with the air of free agency. They know it too, and
peep with their eyes to see if you detect their sad plight. We
fancy, could we pronounce the solving word, and disenchant
them, the cloud would roll up, the little rider would be discovered and unseated, and they would regain their freedom.
The remedy seems never to be far off, since the first step into
thought lifts this mountain of necessity. Thought is the pent
air-ball which can rive the planet, and the beauty which certain objects have for him, is the friendly fire which expands

the thought, and acquaints the prisoner that liberty and power await him.

The question of Beauty takes us out of surfaces, to thinking of the foundations of things. Goethe said, "The beautiful is a manifestation of secret laws of Nature, which, but for this appearance, had been forever concealed from us." And the working of this deep instinct makes all the excitement—much of it superficial and absurd enough—about works of art, which leads armies of vain travellers every year to Italy, Greece, and Egypt. Every man values every acquisition he makes in the science of beauty, above his possessions. The most useful man in the most useful world, so long as only commodity was served, would remain unsatisfied. But, as fast as he sees beauty, life acquires a very high value.

I am warned by the ill fate of many philosophers not to attempt a definition of Beauty. I will rather enumerate a few of its qualities. We ascribe beauty to that which is simple; which has no superfluous parts; which exactly answers its end; which stands related to all things; which is the mean of many extremes. It is the most enduring quality, and the most ascending quality. We say, love is blind, and the figure of Cupid is drawn with a bandage round his eyes. Blind:—yes, because he does not see what he does not like; but the sharpest-sighted hunter in the universe is Love, for finding what he seeks, and only that; and the mythologists tell us, that Vulcan was painted lame, and Cupid blind, to call attention to the fact, that one was all limbs, and the other, all eyes. In the true mythology, Love is an immortal child, and Beauty leads him as a guide: nor can we express a deeper sense than when we say, Beauty is the pilot of the young soul.

Beyond their sensuous delight, the forms and colors of Nature have a new charm for us in our perception, that not one ornament was added for ornament, but is a sign of some better health, or more excellent action. Elegance of form in bird or beast, or in the human figure, marks some excellence of structure: or beauty is only an invitation from what belongs to us. 'Tis a law of botany, that in plants, the same virtues follow the same forms. It is a rule of largest application, true in a plant, true in a loaf of bread, that in the construction of any fabric or organism, any real increase of fitness to its end, is an increase of beauty.

The lesson taught by the study of Greek and of Gothic art, of antique and of Pre-Raphaelite painting, was worth all the research,—namely, that all beauty must be organic; that outside embellishment is deformity. It is the soundness of the bones that ultimates itself in a peach-bloom complexion: health of constitution that makes the sparkle and the power of the eye. 'Tis the adjustment of the size and of the joining of the sockets of the skeleton, that gives grace of outline and the finer grace of movement. The cat and the deer cannot move or sit inelegantly. The dancing-master can never teach a badly built man to walk well. The tint of the flower proceeds from its root, and the lustres of the sea-shell begin with its existence. Hence our taste in building rejects paint, and all shifts, and shows the original grain of the wood: refuses pilasters and columns that support nothing, and allows the real supporters of the house honestly to show themselves. Every necessary or organic action pleases the beholder. A man leading a horse to water, a farmer sowing seed, the labors of haymakers in the field, the carpenter building a ship, the smith at his forge, or, whatever useful labor, is becoming to the wise eye. But if it is done to be seen, it is mean. How beautiful are ships on the sea! but ships in the theatre,—or ships kept for picturesque effect on Virginia Water, by George IV., and men hired to stand in fitting costumes at a penny an hour!—What a difference in effect between a battalion of troops marching to action, and one of our independent companies on a holiday! In the midst of a military show, and a festal procession gay with banners, I saw a boy seize an old tin pan that lay rusting under a wall, and poising it on the top of a stick, he set it turning, and made it describe the most elegant imaginable curves, and drew away attention from the decorated procession by this startling beauty.

Another text from the mythologists. The Greeks fabled that Venus was born of the foam of the sea. Nothing interests us which is stark or bounded, but only what streams with life, what is in act or endeavor to reach somewhat beyond. The pleasure a palace or a temple gives the eye, is, that an order and method has been communicated to stones, so that they speak and geometrize, become tender or sublime with expression. Beauty is the moment of transition, as if the form were just ready to flow into other forms. Any fixedness, heaping, or concentration on one feature,—a long nose, a sharp chin, a hump-back,—is the reverse of the flowing, and therefore deformed. Beautiful as is the symmetry of any form, if the form can move, we seek a more excellent symmetry. The interruption of equilibrium stimulates the eye to desire the restoration of symmetry, and to watch the steps through which it is attained. This is the charm of running water, sea-waves, the flight of birds, and the locomotion of animals. This is the theory of dancing, to recover continually in changes the lost equilibrium, not by abrupt and angular, but by gradual and curving movements. I have been told by persons of experience in matters of taste, that the fashions follow a law of gradation, and are never arbitrary. The new mode is always only a step onward in the same direction as the last mode; and a cultivated eye is prepared for and predicts the new fashion. This fact suggests the reason of all mistakes and offence in our own modes. It is necessary in music, when you strike a discord, to let down the ear by an intermediate note or two to the accord again: and many a good experiment, born of good sense, and destined to succeed, fails, only because it is offensively sudden. I suppose, the Parisian milliner who dresses the world from her imperious boudoir will know how to reconcile the Bloomer costume to the eye of mankind, and make it triumphant over Punch himself, by interposing the just gradations. I need not say, how wide the same law ranges; and how much it can be hoped to effect. All that is a little harshly claimed by progressive parties, may easily come to be conceded without question, if this rule be observed. Thus the circumstances may be easily imagined, in which woman may speak, vote, argue causes, legislate, and drive a coach, and all the most naturally in the world, if only it come by degrees. To this streaming or flowing belongs the beauty that all circular movement has; as, the circulation of waters, the circulation of the blood, the periodical motion of planets, the annual wave of vegetation, the action and reaction of Nature: and, if we follow it out, this demand in our thought for an ever-onward action, is the argument for the immortality.

One more text from the mythologists is to the same purpose,—*Beauty rides on a lion.* Beauty rests on necessities. The line of beauty is the result of perfect economy. The cell of the bee is built at that angle which gives the most strength with the least wax; the bone or the quill of the bird gives the most alar strength, with the least weight. "It is the purgation of superfluities," said Michel Angelo. There is not a particle to spare in natural structures. There is a compelling reason in the uses of the plant, for every novelty of color or form: and our art saves material, by more skilful arrangement, and reaches beauty by taking every superfluous ounce that can be spared from a wall, and keeping all its strength in the poetry of columns. In rhetoric, this art of omission is a chief secret of power, and, in general, it is proof of high culture, to say the greatest matters in the simplest way.

Veracity first of all, and forever. *Rien de beau que le vrai.* In all design, art lies in making your object prominent, but there is a prior art in choosing objects that are prominent. The fine arts have nothing casual, but spring from the instincts of the nations that created them.

Beauty is the quality which makes to endure. In a house that I know, I have noticed a block of spermaceti lying about closets and mantel-pieces, for twenty years together, simply because the tallow-man gave it the form of a rabbit; and, I suppose, it may continue to be lugged about unchanged for a century. Let an artist scrawl a few lines or figures on the back of a letter, and that scrap of paper is rescued from danger, is put in portfolio, is framed and glazed, and, in proportion to the beauty of the lines drawn, will be kept for centuries. Burns writes a copy of verses, and sends them to a newspaper, and the human race take charge of them that they shall not perish.

As the flute is heard farther than the cart, see how surely a beautiful form strikes the fancy of men, and is copied and reproduced without end. How many copies are there of the Belvedere Apollo, the Venus, the Psyche, the Warwick Vase, the Parthenon, and the Temple of Vesta? These are objects of tenderness to all. In our cities, an ugly building is soon removed, and is never repeated, but any beautiful building is copied and improved upon, so that all masons and carpenters work to repeat and preserve the agreeable forms, whilst the ugly ones die out.

The felicities of design in art, or in works of Nature, are shadows or forerunners of that beauty which reaches its perfection in the human form. All men are its lovers. Wherever it goes, it creates joy and hilarity, and everything is permitted to it. It reaches its height in woman. "To Eve," say the Mahometans, "God gave two thirds of all beauty." A beautiful woman is a practical poet, taming her savage mate, planting tenderness, hope, and eloquence, in all whom she approaches. Some favors of condition must go with it, since a certain serenity is essential, but we love its reproofs and superiorities. Nature wishes that woman should attract man, yet she often cunningly moulds into her face a little sarcasm, which seems to say, 'Yes, I am willing to attract, but to attract a little better kind of a man than any I yet behold.' French *mémoires* of the fifteenth century celebrate the name of Pauline de Viguiere, a virtuous and accomplished maiden, who so fired the enthusiasm of her contemporaries, by her enchanting form, that the citizens of her native city of Toulouse obtained the aid of the civil authorities to compel her to appear publicly on the balcony at least twice a week, and, as often as she showed herself, the crowd was dangerous to life. Not less, in England, in the last century, was the fame of the Gunnings, of whom, Elizabeth married the Duke of Hamilton; and Maria, the Earl of Coventry. Walpole says, "the concourse was so great, when the Duchess of Hamilton was presented at court, on Friday, that even the noble crowd in the drawing-room clambered on chairs and tables to look at her. There are mobs at their doors to see them get into their chairs, and people go early to get places at the theatres, when it is known they will be there." "Such crowds," he adds, elsewhere, "flock to see the Duchess of Hamilton, that seven hundred people sat up all night, in and about an inn, in Yorkshire, to see her get into her post-chaise next morning."

But why need we console ourselves with the fames of Helen of Argos, or Corinna, or Pauline of Toulouse, or the Duchess of Hamilton? We all know this magic very well, or can divine it. It does not hurt weak eyes to look into beautiful eyes never so long. Women stand related to beautiful Nature around us, and the enamored youth mixes their form with moon and stars, with woods and waters, and the pomp of summer. They heal us of awkwardness by their words and looks. We observe their intellectual influence on the most serious student. They refine and clear his mind; teach him to put a pleasing method into what is dry and difficult. We talk to them, and wish to be listened to; we fear to fatigue them, and acquire a facility of expression which passes from conversation into habit of style.

That Beauty is the normal state, is shown by the perpetual effort of Nature to attain it. Mirabeau had an ugly face on a handsome ground; and we see faces every day which have a good type, but have been marred in the casting: a proof that we are all entitled to beauty, should have been beautiful, if our ancestors had kept the laws,—as every lily and every rose is well. But our bodies do not fit us, but caricature and satirize us. Thus, short legs, which constrain us to short, mincing steps, are a kind of personal insult and contumely to the owner; and long stilts, again, put him at perpetual disadvantage, and force him to stoop to the general level of mankind. Martial ridicules a gentleman of his day whose countenance resembled the face of a swimmer seen under water. Saadi describes a schoolmaster "so ugly and crabbed, that a sight of him would derange the ecstasies of the orthodox." Faces are rarely true to any ideal type, but are a record in sculpture of a thousand anecdotes of whim and folly. Portrait painters say that most faces and forms are irregular and unsymmetrical; have one eye blue, and one gray; the nose not straight; and one shoulder higher than another; the hair unequally distributed, etc. The man is physically as well as metaphysically a thing of shreds and patches, borrowed unequally from good and bad ancestors, and a misfit from the start.

A beautiful person, among the Greeks, was thought to betray by this sign some secret favor of the immortal gods: and we can pardon pride, when a woman possesses such a figure, that wherever she stands, or moves, or leaves a shadow on the wall, or sits for a portrait to the artist, she confers a favor on the world. And yet—it is not beauty that inspires the deepest passion. Beauty without grace is the hook without the bait. Beauty, without expression, tires. Abbé Ménage said of the

President Le Bailleul, "that he was fit for nothing but to sit for his portrait." A Greek epigram intimates that the force of love is not shown by the courting of beauty, but when the like desire is inflamed for one who is ill-favored. And petulant old gentlemen, who have chanced to suffer some intolerable weariness from pretty people, or who have seen cut flowers to some profusion, or who see, after a world of pains have been successfully taken for the costume, how the least mistake in sentiment takes all the beauty out of your clothes,—affirm, that the secret of ugliness consists not in irregularity, but in being uninteresting.

We love any forms, however ugly, from which great qualities shine. If command, eloquence, art, or invention, exist in the most deformed person, all the accidents that usually displease, please, and raise esteem and wonder higher. The great orator was an emaciated, insignificant person, but he was all brain. Cardinal De Retz says of De Bouillon, "With the physiognomy of an ox, he had the perspicacity of an eagle." It was said of Hooke, the friend of Newton, "he is the most, and promises the least, of any man in England." "Since I am so ugly," said Du Guesclin, "it behooves that I be bold." Sir Philip Sidney, the darling of mankind, Ben Jonson tells us, "was no pleasant man in countenance, his face being spoiled with pimples, and of high blood, and long." Those who have ruled human destinies, like planets, for thousands of years, were not handsome men. If a man can raise a small city to be a great kingdom, can make bread cheap, can irrigate deserts, can join oceans by canals, can subdue steam, can organize victory, can lead the opinions of mankind, can enlarge knowledge, 'tis no matter whether his nose is parallel to his spine, as it ought to be, or whether he has a nose at all; whether his legs are straight, or whether his legs are amputated; his deformities will come to be reckoned ornamental, and advantageous on the whole. This is the triumph of expression, degrading beauty, charming us with a power so fine and friendly and intoxicating, that it makes admired persons insipid, and the thought of passing our lives with them insupportable. There are faces so fluid with expression, so flushed and rippled by the play of thought, that we can hardly find what the mere features really are. When the delicious beauty

of lineaments loses its power, it is because a more delicious
beauty has appeared; that an interior and durable form has
been disclosed. Still, Beauty rides on her lion, as before. Still,
"it was for beauty that the world was made." The lives of the
Italian artists, who established a despotism of genius amidst
the dukes and kings and mobs of their stormy epoch, prove
how loyal men in all times are to a finer brain, a finer method,
than their own. If a man can cut such a head on his stone
gate-post as shall draw and keep a crowd about it all day, by
its beauty, good nature, and inscrutable meaning;—if a man
can build a plain cottage with such symmetry, as to make all
the fine palaces look cheap and vulgar; can take such advantage of Nature, that all her powers serve him; making use of
geometry, instead of expense; tapping a mountain for his
water-jet; causing the sun and moon to seem only the decorations of his estate; this is still the legitimate dominion of
beauty.

The radiance of the human form, though sometimes astonishing, is only a burst of beauty for a few years or a few
months, at the perfection of youth, and in most, rapidly declines. But we remain lovers of it, only transferring our interest to interior excellence. And it is not only admirable in
singular and salient talents, but also in the world of manners.

But the sovereign attribute remains to be noted. Things are
pretty, graceful, rich, elegant, handsome, but, until they speak
to the imagination, not yet beautiful. This is the reason why
beauty is still escaping out of all analysis. It is not yet possessed, it cannot be handled. Proclus says, "it swims on the
light of forms." It is properly not in the form, but in the
mind. It instantly deserts possession, and flies to an object in
the horizon. If I could put my hand on the north star, would
it be as beautiful? The sea is lovely, but when we bathe in it,
the beauty forsakes all the near water. For the imagination
and senses cannot be gratified at the same time. Wordsworth
rightly speaks of "a light that never was on sea or land,"
meaning, that it was supplied by the observer, and the Welsh
bard warns his countrywomen, that

—"half of their charms with Cadwallon shall die."

The new virtue which constitutes a thing beautiful, is a certain cosmical quality, or, a power to suggest relation to the whole world, and so lift the object out of a pitiful individuality. Every natural feature,—sea, sky, rainbow, flowers, musical tone,—has in it somewhat which is not private, but universal, speaks of that central benefit which is the soul of Nature, and thereby is beautiful. And, in chosen men and women, I find somewhat in form, speech, and manners, which is not of their person and family, but of a humane, catholic, and spiritual character, and we love them as the sky. They have a largeness of suggestion, and their face and manners carry a certain grandeur, like time and justice.

The feat of the imagination is in showing the convertibility of every thing into every other thing. Facts which had never before left their stark common sense, suddenly figure as Eleusinian mysteries. My boots and chair and candlestick are fairies in disguise, meteors and constellations. All the facts in Nature are nouns of the intellect, and make the grammar of the eternal language. Every word has a double, treble, or centuple use and meaning. What! has my stove and pepper-pot a false bottom! I cry you mercy, good shoe-box! I did not know you were a jewel-case. Chaff and dust begin to sparkle, and are clothed about with immortality. And there is a joy in perceiving the representative or symbolic character of a fact, which no bare fact or event can ever give. There are no days in life so memorable as those which vibrated to some stroke of the imagination.

The poets are quite right in decking their mistresses with the spoils of the landscape, flower-gardens, gems, rainbows, flushes of morning, and stars of night, since all beauty points at identity, and whatsoever thing does not express to me the sea and sky, day and night, is somewhat forbidden and wrong. Into every beautiful object, there enters somewhat immeasurable and divine, and just as much into form bounded by outlines, like mountains on the horizon, as into tones of music, or depths of space. Polarized light showed the secret architecture of bodies; and when the *second-sight* of the mind is opened, now one color or form or gesture, and now another, has a pungency, as if a more interior ray had been emitted, disclosing its deep holdings in the frame of things.

The laws of this translation we do not know, or why one

feature or gesture enchants, why one word or syllable intoxicates, but the fact is familiar that the fine touch of the eye, or a grace of manners, or a phrase of poetry, plants wings at our shoulders; as if the Divinity, in his approaches, lifts away mountains of obstruction, and deigns to draw a truer line, which the mind knows and owns. This is that haughty force of beauty, "*vis superba formæ*," which the poets praise,—under calm and precise outline, the immeasurable and divine: Beauty hiding all wisdom and power in its calm sky.

All high beauty has a moral element in it, and I find the antique sculpture as ethical as Marcus Antoninus: and the beauty ever in proportion to the depth of thought. Gross and obscure natures, however decorated, seem impure shambles; but character gives splendor to youth, and awe to wrinkled skin and gray hairs. An adorer of truth we cannot choose but obey, and the woman who has shared with us the moral sentiment,—her locks must appear to us sublime. Thus there is a climbing scale of culture, from the first agreeable sensation which a sparkling gem or a scarlet stain affords the eye, up through fair outlines and details of the landscape, features of the human face and form, signs and tokens of thought and character in manners, up to the ineffable mysteries of the intellect. Wherever we begin, thither our steps tend: an ascent from the joy of a horse in his trappings, up to the perception of Newton, that the globe on which we ride is only a larger apple falling from a larger tree; up to the perception of Plato, that globe and universe are rude and early expressions of an all-dissolving Unity,—the first stair on the scale to the temple of the Mind.

IX

ILLUSIONS

———

FLOW, flow the waves hated,
Accursed, adored,
The waves of mutation:
No anchorage is.
Sleep is not, death is not;
Who seem to die live.
House you were born in,
Friends of your spring-time,
Old man and young maid,
Day's toil and its guerdon,
They are all vanishing,
Fleeing to fables,
Cannot be moored.
See the stars through them,
Through treacherous marbles.
Know, the stars yonder,
The stars everlasting,
Are fugitive also,
And emulate, vaulted,
The lambent heat-lightning,
And fire-fly's flight.

When thou dost return
On the wave's circulation,
Beholding the shimmer,
The wild dissipation,

And, out of endeavor
To change and to flow,
The gas become solid,
And phantoms and nothings
Return to be things,
And endless imbroglio
Is law and the world,—
Then first shalt thou know,
That in the wild turmoil,
Horsed on the Proteus,
Thou ridest to power,
And to endurance.

Illusions

SOME YEARS AGO, in company with an agreeable party, I spent a long summer day in exploring the Mammoth Cave in Kentucky. We traversed, through spacious galleries affording a solid masonry foundation for the town and county overhead, the six or eight black miles from the mouth of the cavern to the innermost recess which tourists visit, — a niche or grotto made of one seamless stalactite, and called, I believe, Serena's Bower. I lost the light of one day. I saw high domes, and bottomless pits; heard the voice of unseen waterfalls; paddled three quarters of a mile in the deep Echo River, whose waters are peopled with the blind fish; crossed the streams "Lethe" and "Styx;" plied with music and guns the echoes in these alarming galleries; saw every form of stalagmite and stalactite in the sculptured and fretted chambers, — icicle, orange-flower, acanthus, grapes, and snowball. We shot Bengal lights into the vaults and groins of the sparry cathedrals, and examined all the masterpieces which the four combined engineers, water, limestone, gravitation, and time, could make in the dark.

The mysteries and scenery of the cave had the same dignity that belongs to all natural objects, and which shames the fine things to which we foppishly compare them. I remarked, especially, the mimetic habit, with which Nature, on new instruments, hums her old tunes, making night to mimic day, and chemistry to ape vegetation. But I then took notice, and still chiefly remember, that the best thing which the cave had to offer was an illusion. On arriving at what is called the "Star-Chamber," our lamps were taken from us by the guide, and extinguished or put aside, and, on looking upwards, I saw or seemed to see the night heaven thick with stars glimmering more or less brightly over our heads, and even what seemed a comet flaming among them. All the party were touched with astonishment and pleasure. Our musical friends sung with much feeling a pretty song, "The stars are in the quiet sky," &c., and I sat down on the rocky floor to enjoy the serene picture. Some crystal specks in the black ceiling high overhead, reflecting the light of a half-hid lamp, yielded this magnificent effect.

I own, I did not like the cave so well for eking out its sublimities with this theatrical trick. But I have had many experiences like it, before and since; and we must be content to be pleased without too curiously analyzing the occasions. Our conversation with Nature is not just what it seems. The cloud-rack, the sunrise and sunset glories, rainbows, and northern lights are not quite so spheral as our childhood thought them; and the part our organization plays in them is too large. The senses interfere everywhere, and mix their own structure with all they report of. Once, we fancied the earth a plane, and stationary. In admiring the sunset, we do not yet deduct the rounding, coördinating, pictorial powers of the eye.

The same interference from our organization creates the most of our pleasure and pain. Our first mistake is the belief that the circumstance gives the joy which we give to the circumstance. Life is an ecstasy. Life is sweet as nitrous oxide; and the fisherman dripping all day over a cold pond, the switchman at the railway intersection, the farmer in the field, the negro in the rice-swamp, the fop in the street, the hunter in the woods, the barrister with the jury, the belle at the ball, all ascribe a certain pleasure to their employment, which they themselves give it. Health and appetite impart the sweetness to sugar, bread, and meat. We fancy that our civilization has got on far, but we still come back to our primers.

We live by our imaginations, by our admirations, by our sentiments. The child walks amid heaps of illusions, which he does not like to have disturbed. The boy, how sweet to him is his fancy! how dear the story of barons and battles! What a hero he is, whilst he feeds on his heroes! What a debt is his to imaginative books! He has no better friend or influence, than Scott, Shakspeare, Plutarch, and Homer. The man lives to other objects, but who dare affirm that they are more real? Even the prose of the streets is full of refractions. In the life of the dreariest alderman, fancy enters into all details, and colors them with rosy hue. He imitates the air and actions of people whom he admires, and is raised in his own eyes. He pays a debt quicker to a rich man than to a poor man. He wishes the bow and compliment of some leader in the state, or in society; weighs what he says; perhaps he never comes nearer to him for that, but dies at last better contented for this amusement of his eyes and his fancy.

The world rolls, the din of life is never hushed. In London, in Paris, in Boston, in San Francisco, the carnival, the masquerade is at its height. Nobody drops his domino. The unities, the fictions of the piece it would be an impertinence to break. The chapter of fascinations is very long. Great is paint; nay, God is the painter; and we rightly accuse the critic who destroys too many illusions. Society does not love its unmaskers. It was wittily, if somewhat bitterly, said by D'Alembert, "*qu'un état de vapeur était un état très fâcheux, parcequ'il nous faisait voir les choses comme elles sont.*" I find men victims of illusion in all parts of life. Children, youths, adults, and old men, all are led by one bawble or another. Yoganidra, the goddess of illusion, Proteus, or Momus, or Gylfi's Mocking,—for the Power has many names,—is stronger than the Titans, stronger than Apollo. Few have overheard the gods, or surprised their secret. Life is a succession of lessons which must be lived to be understood. All is riddle, and the key to a riddle is another riddle. There are as many pillows of illusion as flakes in a snow-storm. We wake from one dream into another dream. The toys, to be sure, are various, and are graduated in refinement to the quality of the dupe. The intellectual man requires a fine bait; the sots are easily amused. But everybody is drugged with his own frenzy, and the pageant marches at all hours, with music and banner and badge.

Amid the joyous troop who give in to the charivari, comes now and then a sad-eyed boy, whose eyes lack the requisite refractions to clothe the show in due glory, and who is afflicted with a tendency to trace home the glittering miscellany of fruits and flowers to one root. Science is a search after identity, and the scientific whim is lurking in all corners. At the State Fair, a friend of mine complained that all the varieties of fancy pears in our orchards seem to have been selected by somebody who had a whim for a particular kind of pear, and only cultivated such as had that perfume; they were all alike. And I remember the quarrel of another youth with the confectioners, that, when he racked his wit to choose the best comfits in the shops, in all the endless varieties of sweetmeat he could only find three flavors, or two. What then? Pears and cakes are good for something; and because you, unluckily, have an eye or nose too keen, why need you spoil the comfort which the rest of us find in them? I knew a humorist, who, in a good deal of rattle, had a grain or two of sense. He shocked the company by maintaining that the attributes of God were two,—power and risibility; and that it was the duty of every pious man to keep up the comedy. And I have known gentlemen of great stake in the community, but whose sympathies were cold,—presidents of colleges, and governors, and senators,—who held themselves bound to sign every temperance pledge, and act with Bible societies, and missions, and peace-makers, and cry *Hist-a-boy!* to every good dog. We must not carry comity too far, but we all have kind impulses in this direction. When the boys come into my yard for leave to gather horse-chestnuts, I own I enter into Nature's game, and affect to grant the permission reluctantly, fearing that any moment they will find out the imposture of that showy chaff. But this tenderness is quite unnecessary; the enchantments are laid on very thick. Their young life is thatched with them. Bare and grim to tears is the lot of the children in the hovel I saw yesterday; yet not the less they hung it round with frippery romance, like the children of the happiest fortune, and talked of "the dear cottage where so many joyful hours had flown." Well, this thatching of hovels is the custom of the country. Women, more than all, are the element and kingdom of illusion. Being fascinated, they fascinate. They see through Claude-Lorraines. And how dare any one, if he could, pluck away the *coulisses*, stage effects, and ceremonies, by which they live? Too pathetic, too pitiable, is the region of affection, and its atmosphere always liable to *mirage*.

We are not very much to blame for our bad marriages. We live amid hallucinations; and this especial trap is laid to trip up our feet with, and all are tripped up first or last. But the mighty Mother who had been so sly with us, as if she felt that she owed us some indemnity, insinuates into the Pandora-box of marriage some deep and serious benefits, and some great joys. We find a delight in the beauty and happiness of children, that makes the heart too big for the body. In the worst-assorted connections there is ever some mixture of true marriage. Teague and his jade get some just relations of mutual respect, kindly observation, and fostering of each other, learn something, and would carry themselves wiselier, if they were now to begin.

'Tis fine for us to point at one or another fine madman, as if there were any exempts. The scholar in his library is none. I, who have all my life heard any number of orations and debates, read poems and miscellaneous books, conversed with many geniuses, am still the victim of any new page; and, if Marmaduke, or Hugh, or Moosehead, or any other, invent a new style or mythology, I fancy that the world will be all brave and right, if dressed in these colors, which I had not thought of. Then at once I will daub with this new paint; but it will not stick. 'Tis like the cement which the peddler sells at the door; he makes broken crockery hold with it, but you can never buy of him a bit of the cement which will make it hold when he is gone.

Men who make themselves felt in the world avail themselves of a certain fate in their constitution, which they know how to use. But they never deeply interest us, unless they lift a corner of the curtain, or betray never so slightly their penetration of what is behind it. 'Tis the charm of practical men, that outside of their practicality are a certain poetry and play, as if they led the good horse Power by the bridle, and preferred to walk, though they can ride so fiercely. Bonaparte is intellectual, as well as Cæsar; and the best soldiers, sea-captains, and railway men have a gentleness, when off duty; a good-natured admission that there are illusions, and who shall say that he is not their sport? We stigmatize the cast-iron fellows, who cannot so detach themselves, as "dragon-ridden," "thunder-stricken," and fools of fate, with whatever powers endowed.

Since our tuition is through emblems and indirections, 'tis well to know that there is method in it, a fixed scale, and rank above rank in the phantasms. We begin low with coarse masks, and rise to the most subtle and beautiful. The red men told Columbus, "they had an herb which took away fatigue;"

but he found the illusion of "arriving from the east at the Indies" more composing to his lofty spirit than any tobacco. Is not our faith in the impenetrability of matter more sedative than narcotics? You play with jackstraws, balls, bowls, horse and gun, estates and politics; but there are finer games before you. Is not time a pretty toy? Life will show you masks that are worth all your carnivals. Yonder mountain must migrate into your mind. The fine star-dust and nebulous blur in Orion, "the portentous year of Mizar and Alcor," must come down and be dealt with in your household thought. What if you shall come to discern that the play and playground of all this pompous history are radiations from yourself, and that the sun borrows his beams? What terrible questions we are learning to ask! The former men believed in magic, by which temples, cities, and men were swallowed up, and all trace of them gone. We are coming on the secret of a magic which sweeps out of men's minds all vestige of theism and beliefs which they and their fathers held and were framed upon.

There are deceptions of the senses, deceptions of the passions, and the structural, beneficent illusions of sentiment and of the intellect. There is the illusion of love, which attributes to the beloved person all which that person shares with his or her family, sex, age, or condition, nay, with the human mind itself. 'Tis these which the lover loves, and Anna Matilda gets the credit of them. As if one shut up always in a tower, with one window, through which the face of heaven and earth could be seen, should fancy that all the marvels he beheld belonged to that window. There is the illusion of time, which is very deep; who has disposed of it? or come to the conviction that what seems the *succession* of thought is only the distribution of wholes into causal series? The intellect sees that every atom carries the whole of Nature; that the mind opens to omnipotence; that, in the endless striving and ascents, the metamorphosis is entire, so that the soul doth not know itself in its own act, when that act is perfected. There is illusion that shall deceive even the elect. There is illusion that shall deceive even the performer of the miracle. Though he make his body, he denies that he makes it. Though the world exist from thought, thought is daunted in presence of the world. One after the other we accept the mental laws, still resisting those which follow, which however must be accepted. But all our concessions only compel us to new profusion. And what avails it that science has come to treat space and time as simply forms of thought, and the material world as hypothetical, and withal our pretension of *property* and even of self-hood are fading with the rest, if, at last, even our thoughts are not finalities; but the incessant flowing and ascension reach these also, and each thought which yesterday was a finality, to-day is yielding to a larger generalization?

With such volatile elements to work in, 'tis no wonder if our estimates are loose and floating. We must work and affirm, but we have no guess of the value of what we say or do. The cloud is now as big as your hand, and now it covers a county. That story of Thor, who was set to drain the drinking-horn in Asgard, and to wrestle with the old woman, and to run with the runner Lok, and presently found that he had been drinking up the sea, and wrestling with Time, and racing with Thought, describes us who are contending, amid these seeming trifles, with the supreme energies of Nature. We fancy we have fallen into bad company and squalid condition, low debts, shoe-bills, broken glass to pay for, pots to buy, butcher's meat, sugar, milk, and coal. 'Set me some great task, ye gods! and I will show my spirit.' 'Not so,' says the good Heaven; 'plod and plough, vamp your old coats and hats, weave a shoestring; great affairs and the best wine by and by.' Well, 'tis all phantasm; and if we weave a yard of tape in all humility, and as well as we can, long hereafter we shall see it was no cotton tape at all, but some galaxy which we braided, and that the threads were Time and Nature.

We cannot write the order of the variable winds. How can we penetrate the law of our shifting moods and susceptibility? Yet they differ as all and nothing. Instead of the firmament of yesterday, which our eyes require, it is to-day an eggshell which coops us in; we cannot even see what or where our stars of destiny are. From day to day, the capital facts of human life are hidden from our eyes. Suddenly the mist rolls up, and reveals them, and we think how much good time is gone, that might have been saved, had any hint of these things been shown. A sudden rise in the road shows us the system of mountains, and all the summits, which have been just as near us all the year, but quite out of mind. But these alternations are not without their order, and we are parties to our various fortune. If life seem a succession of dreams, yet poetic justice is done in dreams also. The visions of good men are good; it is the undisciplined will that is whipped with bad thoughts and bad fortunes. When we break the laws, we lose our hold on the central reality. Like sick men in hospitals, we change only from bed to bed, from one folly to another; and it cannot signify much what becomes of such castaways,—wailing, stupid, comatose creatures,—lifted from bed to bed, from the nothing of life to the nothing of death.

In this kingdom of illusions we grope eagerly for stays and foundations. There is none but a strict and faithful dealing at home, and a severe barring out of all duplicity or illusion there. Whatever games are played with us, we must play no games with ourselves, but deal in our privacy with the last honesty and truth. I look upon the simple and childish virtues of veracity and honesty as the root of all that is sublime in character. Speak as you think, be what you are, pay your debts of all kinds. I prefer to be owned as sound and solvent, and my word as good as my bond, and to be what cannot be skipped, or dissipated, or undermined, to all the *éclat* in the universe. This reality is the foundation of friendship, religion, poetry, and art. At the top or at the bottom of all illusions, I set the cheat which still leads us to work and live for appearances, in spite of our conviction, in all sane hours, that it is what we really are that avails with friends, with strangers, and with fate or fortune.

One would think from the talk of men, that riches and poverty were a great matter; and our civilization mainly respects it. But the Indians say, that they do not think the white man with his brow of care, always toiling, afraid of heat and cold, and keeping within doors, has any advantage of them. The permanent interest of every man is, never to be in a false position, but to have the weight of Nature to back him in all that he does. Riches and poverty are a thick or thin costume; and our life—the life of all of us—identical. For we transcend the circumstance continually, and taste the real quality of existence; as in our employments, which only differ in the manipulations, but express the same laws; or in our thoughts, which wear no silks, and taste no ice-creams. We see God face to face every hour, and know the savor of Nature.

The early Greek philosophers Heraclitus and Xenophanes measured their force on this problem of identity. Diogenes of Apollonia said, that unless the atoms were made of one stuff, they could never blend and act with one another. But the Hindoos, in their sacred writings, express the liveliest feeling, both of the essential identity, and of that illusion which they conceive variety to be. "The notions, '*I am*,' and '*This is mine*,' which influence mankind, are but delusions of the mother of the world. Dispel, O Lord of all creatures! the conceit of knowledge which proceeds from ignorance." And the beatitude of man they hold to lie in being freed from fascination.

The intellect is stimulated by the statement of truth in a trope, and the will by clothing the laws of life in illusions. But the unities of Truth and of Right are not broken by the disguise. There need never be any confusion in these. In a crowded life of many parts and performers, on a stage of nations, or in the obscurest hamlet in Maine or California, the same elements offer the same choices to each new comer, and, according to his election, he fixes his fortune in absolute Nature. It would be hard to put more mental and moral philosophy than the Persians have thrown into a sentence:—

> "Fooled thou must be, though wisest of the wise:
> Then be the fool of virtue, not of vice."

There is no chance, and no anarchy, in the universe. All is system and gradation. Every god is there sitting in his sphere. The young mortal enters the hall of the firmament: there is he alone with them alone, they pouring on him benedictions and gifts, and beckoning him up to their thrones. On the instant, and incessantly, fall snow-storms of illusions. He fancies himself in a vast crowd which sways this way and that, and whose movement and doings he must obey: he fancies himself poor, orphaned, insignificant. The mad crowd drives hither and thither, now furiously commanding this thing to be done, now that. What is he that he should resist their will, and think or act for himself? Every moment, new changes, and new showers of deceptions, to baffle and distract him.

And when, by and by, for an instant, the air clears, and the cloud lifts a little, there are the gods still sitting around him on their thrones,—they alone with him alone.

THE END

UNCOLLECTED PROSE

Contents

The Lord's Supper

The Kingdom of God is not meat and drink, but righteousness, and peace, and joy in the Holy Ghost.—ROMANS XIV. 17.

IN THE HISTORY of the Church no subject has been more fruitful of controversy than the Lord's Supper. There never has been any unanimity in the understanding of its nature, nor any uniformity in the mode of celebrating it. Without considering the frivolous questions which have been lately debated as to the posture in which men should partake of it; whether mixed or unmixed wine should be served; whether leavened or unleavened bread should be broken; the questions have been settled differently in every church, who should be admitted to the feast, and how often it should be prepared. In the Catholic Church, infants were at one time permitted and then forbidden to partake; and, since the ninth century, the laity receive the bread only, the cup being reserved to the priesthood. So, as to the time of the solemnity. In the fourth Lateran Council, it was decreed that any believer should communicate at least once in a year—at Easter. Afterwards it was determined that this Sacrament should be received three times in the year—at Easter, Whitsuntide, and Christmas. But more important controversies have arisen respecting its nature. The famous question of the Real Presence was the main controversy between the Church of England and the Church of Rome. The doctrine of the Consubstantiation taught by Luther was denied by Calvin. In the Church of England, Archbishops Laud and Wake maintained that the elements were an Eucharist or sacrifice of Thanksgiving to God; Cudworth and Warburton, that this was not a sacrifice, but a sacrificial feast; and Bishop Hoadley, that it was neither a sacrifice nor a feast after sacrifice, but a simple commemoration. And finally, it is now near two hundred years since the Society of Quakers denied the authority of the rite altogether, and gave good reasons for disusing it.

I allude to these facts only to show that, so far from the supper being a tradition in which men are fully agreed, there has always been the widest room for difference of opinion upon this particular.

Having recently given particular attention to this subject, I was led to the conclusion that Jesus did not intend to establish an institution for perpetual observance when he ate the Passover with his disciples; and, further, to the opinion, that it is not expedient to celebrate it as we do. I shall now endeavor to state distinctly my reasons for these two opinions.

I. The authority of the rite.

An account of the last supper of Christ with his disciples is given by the four Evangelists, Matthew, Mark, Luke, and John.

In St. Matthew's Gospel (Matt. XXVI. 26–30) are recorded the words of Jesus in giving bread and wine on that occasion to his disciples, but no expression occurs intimating that this feast was hereafter to be commemorated.

In St. Mark (Mark XIV. 23) the same words are recorded, and still with no intimation that the occasion was to be remembered.

St. Luke (Luke XXII. 15), after relating the breaking of the bread, has these words: This do in remembrance of me.

In St. John, although other occurrences of the same evening are related, this whole transaction is passed over without notice.

Now observe the facts. Two of the Evangelists, namely, Matthew and John, were of the twelve disciples, and were present on that occasion. Neither of them drops the slightest intimation of any intention on the part of Jesus to set up anything permanent. John, especially, the beloved disciple, who has recorded with minuteness the conversation and the transactions of that memorable evening, has quite omitted such a notice. Neither does it appear to have come to the knowledge of Mark who, though not an eye-witness, relates the other facts. This material fact, that the occasion was to be remembered, is found in Luke alone, who was not present. There is no reason, however, that we know, for rejecting the account of Luke. I doubt not, the expression was used by Jesus. I shall presently consider its meaning. I have only brought these accounts together, that you may judge whether it is likely that a solemn institution, to be continued to the end of time by all mankind, as they should come, nation after nation, within the influence of the Christian religion, would have been established in this slight manner—in a manner so slight, that the intention of commemorating it should not appear, from their narrative, to have caught the ear or dwelt in the mind of the only two among the twelve who wrote down what happened.

Still we must suppose that the expression, *"This do in remembrance of me,"* had come to the ear of Luke from some disciple who was present. What did it really signify? It is a prophetic and an affectionate expression. Jesus is a Jew, sitting with his countrymen, celebrating their national feast. He thinks of his own impending death, and wishes the minds of his disciples to be prepared for it. "When hereafter," he says to them, "you shall keep the Passover, it will have an altered aspect to your eyes. It is now a historical covenant of God with the Jewish nation. Hereafter, it will remind you of a new covenant sealed with my blood. In years to come, as long as your people shall come up to Jerusalem to keep this feast, the connection which has subsisted between us will give a new meaning in your eyes to the national festival, as the anniversary of my death." I see natural feeling and beauty in the use of such language from Jesus, a friend to his friends; I can readily imagine that he was willing and desirous, when his disciples met, his memory should hallow their intercourse; but I cannot bring myself to believe that in the use of such an expression he looked beyond the living generation, beyond the abolition of the festival he was celebrating, and the scattering of the nation, and meant to impose a memorial feast upon the whole world.

Without presuming to fix precisely the purpose in the mind of Jesus, you will see that many opinions may be entertained of his intention, all consistent with the opinion that he did not design a perpetual ordinance. He may have foreseen that his disciples would meet to remember him, and that with good effect. It may have crossed his mind that this would be easily continued a hundred or a thousand years—as men more easily transmit a form than a virtue—and yet have been altogether out of his purpose to fasten it upon men in all times and all countries.

But though the words, *Do this in remembrance of me*, do

not occur in Matthew, Mark, or John, and although it should be granted us that, taken alone, they do not necessarily import so much as is usually thought, yet many persons are apt to imagine that the very striking and personal manner in which this eating and drinking is described, indicates a striking and formal purpose to found a festival. And I admit that this impression might probably be left upon the mind of one who read only the passages under consideration in the New Testament. But this impression is removed by reading any narrative of the mode in which the ancient or the modern Jews have kept the Passover. It is then perceived that the leading circumstances in the Gospels are only a faithful account of that ceremony. Jesus did not celebrate the Passover, and afterwards the Supper, but the Supper *was* the Passover. He did with his disciples exactly what every master of a family in Jerusalem was doing at the same hour with his household. It appears that the Jews ate the lamb and the unleavened bread, and drank wine after a prescribed manner. It was the custom for the master of the feast to break the bread and to bless it, using this formula, which the Talmudists have preserved to us, "Blessed be Thou, O Lord our God, the King of the world, who hast produced this food from the earth,"—and to give it to every one at the table. It was the custom of the master of the family to take the cup which contained the wine, and to bless it, saying, "Blessed be Thou, O Lord, who givest us the fruit of the vine,"—and then to give the cup to all. Among the modern Jews who in their dispersion retain the Passover, a hymn is also sung after this ceremony, specifying the twelve great works done by God for the deliverance of their fathers out of Egypt.

But still it may be asked, why did Jesus make expressions so extraordinary and emphatic as these—"This is my body which is broken for you. Take; eat. This is my blood which is shed for you. Drink it."—I reply they are not extraordinary expressions from him. They were familiar in his mouth. He always taught by parables and symbols. It was the national way of teaching and was largely used by him. Remember the readiness which he always showed to spiritualize every occurrence. He stooped and wrote on the sand. He admonished his disciples respecting the leaven of the Pharisees. He instructed the woman of Samaria respecting living water. He permitted himself to be anointed, declaring that it was for his interment. He washed the feet of his disciples. These are admitted to be symbolical actions and expressions. Here, in like manner, he calls the bread his body, and bids the disciples eat. He had used the same expression repeatedly before. The reason why St. John does not repeat his words on this occasion, seems to be that he had reported a similar discourse of Jesus to the people of Capernaum more at length already (John VI. 27). He there tells the Jews, "Except ye eat the flesh of the Son of Man and drink His blood, ye have no life in you." And when the Jews on that occasion complained that they did not comprehend what he meant, he added for their better understanding, and as if for our understanding, that we might not think his body was to be actually eaten, that he only meant, *we should live by his commandment*. He closed his discourse with these explanatory expressions: "The flesh profiteth nothing; the *words* that I speak to you, they are spirit and they are life."

Whilst I am upon this topic, I cannot help remarking that it is not a little singular that we should have preserved this rite and insisted upon perpetuating one symbolical act of Christ whilst we have totally neglected all others—particularly one other which had at least an equal claim to our observance. Jesus washed the feet of his disciples and told them that, as he had washed their feet, they ought to wash one another's feet; for he had given them an example, that they should do as he had done to them. I ask any person who believes the Supper to have been designed by Jesus to be commemorated forever, to go and read the account of it in the other Gospels, and then compare with it the account of this transaction in St. John, and tell me if this be not much more explicitly authorized than the Supper. It only differs in this, that we have found the Supper used in New England and the washing of the feet not. But if we had found it an established rite in our churches, on grounds of mere authority, it would have been impossible to have argued against it. That rite is used by the Church of Rome, and by the Sandemanians. It has been very properly dropped by other Christians. Why? For two reasons: (1) because it was a local custom, and unsuitable in western countries; and (2) because it was typical, and all understand that humility is the thing signified. But the Passover was local too, and does not concern us, and its bread and wine were typical, and do not help us to understand the redemption which they signified.

These views of the original account of the Lord's Supper lead me to esteem it an occasion full of solemn and prophetic interest, but never intended by Jesus to be the foundation of a perpetual institution.

It appears however in Christian history that the disciples had very early taken advantage of these impressive words of Christ to hold religious meetings, where they broke bread and drank wine as symbols.

I look upon this fact as very natural in the circumstances of the church. The disciples lived together; they threw all their property into a common stock; they were bound together by the memory of Christ, and nothing could be more natural than that this eventful evening should be affectionately remembered by them; that they, Jews like Jesus, should adopt his expressions and his types, and furthermore, that what was done with peculiar propriety by them, his personal friends, with less propriety should come to be extended to their companions also. In this way religious feasts grew up among the early Christians. They were readily adopted by the Jewish converts who were familiar with religious feasts, and also by the Pagan converts whose idolatrous worship had been made up of sacred festivals, and who very readily abused these to gross riot, as appears from the censures of St. Paul. Many persons consider this fact, the observance of such a memorial feast by the early disciples, decisive of the question whether it ought to be observed by us. For my part I see nothing to wonder at in its originating with them; all that is surprising is that it should exist among us. There was good reason for his personal friends to remember their friend and repeat his words. It was only too probable that among the half converted Pagans and Jews, any rite, any form, would find favor, whilst yet unable to comprehend the spiritual character of Christianity.

The circumstance, however, that St. Paul adopts these views, has seemed to many persons conclusive in favor of the institution. I am of opinion that it is wholly upon the epistle to the Corinthians, and not upon the Gospels, that the ordinance stands. Upon this matter of St. Paul's view of the Supper, a few important considerations must be stated.

The end which he has in view, in the eleventh chapter of the first epistle is, not to enjoin upon his friends to observe the Supper, but to censure their abuse of it. We quote the passage now-a-days as if it enjoined attendance upon the Supper; but he wrote it merely to chide them for drunkenness. To make their enormity plainer he goes back to the origin of this religious feast to show what sort of feast that was, out of which this riot of theirs came, and so relates the transactions of the Last Supper. *"I have received of the Lord,"* he says, *"that which I delivered to you."* By this expression it is often thought that a miraculous communication is implied; but certainly without good reason, if it is remembered that St. Paul was living in the lifetime of all the apostles who could give him an account of the transaction; and it is contrary to all reason to suppose that God should work a miracle to convey information that could so easily be got by natural means. So that the import of the expression is that he had received the story of an eye-witness such as we also possess.

But there is a material circumstance which diminishes our confidence in the correctness of the Apostle's view; and that is, the observation that his mind had not escaped the prevalent error of the primitive church, the belief, namely, that the second coming of Christ would shortly occur, until which time, he tells them, this feast was to be kept. Elsewhere he tells them, that, at that time the world would be burnt up with fire, and a new government established, in which the Saints would sit on thrones; so slow were the disciples during the life, and after the ascension of Christ, to receive the idea which we receive, that his second coming was a spiritual kingdom, the dominion of his religion in the hearts of men, to be extended gradually over the whole world.

In this manner we may see clearly enough how this ancient ordinance got its footing among the early Christians, and this single expectation of a speedy reappearance of a temporal Messiah, which kept its influence even over so spiritual a man as St. Paul, would naturally tend to preserve the use of the rite when once established.

We arrive then at this conclusion, *first*, that it does not appear, from a careful examination of the account of the Last Supper in the Evangelists, that it was designed by Jesus to be perpetual; *secondly*, that it does not appear that the opinion of St. Paul, all things considered, ought to alter our opinion derived from the evangelists.

One general remark before quitting this branch of the subject. We ought to be cautious in taking even the best ascertained opinions and practices of the primitive church, for our own. If it could be satisfactorily shown that they esteemed it authorized and to be transmitted forever, that does not settle the question for us. We know how inveterately they were attached to their Jewish prejudices, and how often even the influence of Christ failed to enlarge their views. On every other subject succeeding times have learned to form a judgment more in accordance with the spirit of Christianity than was the practice of the early ages.

But it is said: "Admit that the rite was not designed to be perpetual. What harm doth it? Here it stands, generally accepted, under some form, by the Christian world, the undoubted occasion of much good; is it not better it should remain?"

II. This is the question of expediency.

I proceed to state a few objections that in my judgment lie against its use in its present form.

1. If the view which I have taken of the history of the institution be correct, then the claim of authority should be dropped in administering it. You say, every time you celebrate the rite, that Jesus enjoined it; and the whole language you use conveys that impression. But if you read the New Testament as I do, you do not believe he did.

2. It has seemed to me that the use of this ordinance tends to produce confusion in our views of the relation of the soul to God. It is the old objection to the doctrine of the Trinity,—that the true worship was transferred from God to Christ, or that such confusion was introduced into the soul, that an undivided worship was given nowhere. Is not that the effect of the Lord's Supper? I appeal now to the convictions of communicants—and ask such persons whether they have not been occasionally conscious of a painful confusion of thought between the worship due to God and the commem-

oration due to Christ. For, the service does not stand upon the basis of a voluntary act, but is imposed by authority. It is an expression of gratitude to Christ, enjoined by Christ. There is an endeavor to keep Jesus in mind, whilst yet the prayers are addressed to God. I fear it is the effect of this ordinance to clothe Jesus with an authority which he never claimed and which distracts the mind of the worshipper. I know our opinions differ much respecting the nature and offices of Christ, and the degree of veneration to which he is entitled. I am so much a Unitarian as this: that I believe the human mind cannot admit but one God, and that every effort to pay religious homage to more than one being, goes to take away all right ideas. I appeal, brethren, to your individual experience. In the moment when you make the least petition to God, though it be but a silent wish that he may approve you, or add one moment to your life,—do you not, in the very act, necessarily exclude all other beings from your thought? In that act, the soul stands alone with God, and Jesus is no more present to the mind than your brother or your child.

But is not Jesus called in Scripture the Mediator? He is the mediator in that only sense in which possibly any being can mediate between God and man—that is an Instructor of man. He teaches us how to become like God. And a true disciple of Jesus will receive the light he gives most thankfully; but the thanks he offers, and which an exalted being will accept, are not *compliments*—commemorations,—but the use of that instruction.

3. Passing other objections, I come to this, that the *use of the elements*, however suitable to the people and the modes of thought in the East, where it originated, is foreign and unsuited to affect us. Whatever long usage and strong association may have done in some individuals to deaden this repulsion, I apprehend that their use is rather tolerated than loved by any of us. We are not accustomed to express our thoughts or emotions by symbolical actions. Most men find the bread and wine no aid to devotion and to some, it is a painful impediment. To eat bread is one thing; to love the precepts of Christ and resolve to obey them is quite another.

The statement of this objection leads me to say that I think this difficulty, wherever it is felt, to be entitled to the greatest weight. It is alone a sufficient objection to the ordinance. It is my own objection. This mode of commemorating Christ is not suitable to me. That is reason enough why I should abandon it. If I believed that it was enjoined by Jesus on his disciples, and that he even contemplated making permanent this mode of commemoration, every way agreeable to an eastern mind, and yet, on trial, it was disagreeable to my own feelings, I should not adopt it. I should choose other ways which, as more effectual upon me, he would approve more. For I choose that my remembrances of him should be pleasing, affecting, religious. I will love him as a glorified friend, after the free way of friendship, and not pay him a stiff sign of respect, as men do to those whom they fear. A passage read from his discourses, a moving provocation to works like his, any act or meeting which tends to awaken a pure thought, a flow of love, an original design of virtue, I call a worthy, a true commemoration.

4. Fourthly, the importance ascribed to this particular ordinance is not consistent with the spirit of Christianity. The general object and effect of this ordinance is unexceptionable. It has been, and is, I doubt not, the occasion of indefinite good; but an importance is given by Christians to it which never can belong to any form. My friends, the apostle well assures us that "the kingdom of God is not meat and drink, but righteousness and peace and joy, in the Holy Ghost." I am not so foolish as to declaim against forms. Forms are as essential as bodies; but to exalt particular forms, to adhere to one form a moment after it is out-grown, is unreasonable, and it is alien to the spirit of Christ. If I understand the distinction of Christianity, the reason why it is to be preferred over all other systems and is divine is this, that it is a moral system; that it presents men with truths which are their own reason, and enjoins practices that are their own justification; that if miracles may be said to have been its evidence to the first Christians, they are not its evidence to us, but the doctrines themselves; that every practice is Christian which praises itself, and every practice unchristian which condemns itself. I am not engaged to Christianity by decent forms, or saving ordinances; it is not usage, it is not what I do not understand, that binds me to it—let these be the sandy foun-

dations of falsehoods. What I revere and obey in it is its reality, its boundless charity, its deep interior life, the rest it gives to my mind, the echo it returns to my thoughts, the perfect accord it makes with my reason through all its representation of God and His Providence; and the persuasion and courage that come out thence to lead me upward and onward. Freedom is the essence of this faith. It has for its object simply to make men good and wise. Its institutions, then, should be as flexible as the wants of men. That form out of which the life and suitableness have departed, should be as worthless in its eyes as the dead leaves that are falling around us.

And therefore, although for the satisfaction of others, I have labored to show by the history that this rite was not intended to be perpetual; although I have gone back to weigh the expressions of Paul, I feel that here is the true point of view. In the midst of considerations as to what Paul thought, and why he so thought, I cannot help feeling that it is time misspent to argue to or from his convictions, or those of Luke and John, respecting any form. I seem to lose the substance in seeking the shadow. That for which Paul lived and died so gloriously; that for which Jesus gave himself to be crucified; the end that animated the thousand martyrs and heroes who have followed his steps, was to redeem us from a formal religion, and teach us to seek our well-being in the formation of the soul. The whole world was full of idols and ordinances. The Jewish was a religion of forms. The Pagan was a religion of forms; it was all body—it had no life—and the Almighty God was pleased to qualify and send forth a man to teach men that they must serve him with the heart; that only that life was religious which was thoroughly good; that sacrifice was smoke, and forms were shadows. This man lived and died true to this purpose; and now, with his blessed word and life before us, Christians must contend that it is a matter of vital importance—really a duty, to commemorate him by a certain form, whether that form be agreeable to their understandings or not.

Is not this to make vain the gift of God? Is not this to turn back the hand on the dial? Is not this to make men—to make ourselves—forget that not forms, but duties; not names, but righteousness and love are enjoined; and that in the eye of

God there is no other measure of the value of any one form than the measure of its use?

There remain some practical objections to the ordinance into which I shall not now enter. There is one on which I had intended to say a few words; I mean the unfavorable relation in which it places that numerous class of persons who abstain from it merely from disinclination to the rite.

Influenced by these considerations, I have proposed to the brethren of the Church to drop the use of the elements and the claim of authority in the administration of this ordinance, and have suggested a mode in which a meeting for the same purpose might be held free of objection.

My brethren have considered my views with patience and candor, and have recommended unanimously an adherence to the present form. I have, therefore, been compelled to consider whether it becomes me to administer it. I am clearly of opinion I ought not. This discourse has already been so far extended, that I can only say that the reason of my determination is shortly this:—It is my desire, in the office of a Christian minister, to do nothing which I cannot do with my whole heart. Having said this, I have said all. I have no hostility to this institution; I am only stating my want of sympathy with it. Neither should I ever have obtruded this opinion upon other people, had I not been called by my office to administer it. That is the end of my opposition, that I am not interested in it. I am content that it stand to the end of the world, if it please men and please heaven, and I shall rejoice in all the good it produces.

As it is the prevailing opinion and feeling in our religious community, that it is an indispensable part of the pastoral office to administer this ordinance, I am about to resign into your hands that office which you have confided to me. It has many duties for which I am feebly qualified. It has some which it will always be my delight to discharge, according to my ability, wherever I exist. And whilst the recollection of its claims oppresses me with a sense of my unworthiness, I am consoled by the hope that no time and no change can deprive me of the satisfaction of pursuing and exercising its highest functions.

September 9, 1832.

ESSAYS FROM "THE DIAL"

The Editors to the Reader

W E INVITE the attention of our countrymen to a new design. Probably not quite unexpected or unannounced will our Journal appear, though small pains have been taken to secure its welcome. Those, who have immediately acted in editing the present Number, cannot accuse themselves of any unbecoming forwardness in their undertaking, but rather of a backwardness, when they remember how often in many private circles the work was projected, how eagerly desired, and only postponed because no individual volunteered to combine and concentrate the free-will offerings of many coöperators. With some reluctance the present conductors of this work have yielded themselves to the wishes of their friends, finding something sacred and not to be withstood in the importunity which urged the production of a Journal in a new spirit.

As they have not proposed themselves to the work, neither can they lay any the least claim to an option or determination of the spirit in which it is conceived, or to what is peculiar in the design. In that respect, they have obeyed, though with great joy, the strong current of thought and feeling, which, for a few years past, has led many sincere persons in New England to make new demands on literature, and to reprobate that rigor of our conventions of religion and education which is turning us to stone, which renounces hope, which looks only backward, which asks only such a future as the past, which suspects improvement, and holds nothing so much in horror as new views and the dreams of youth.

With these terrors the conductors of the present Journal have nothing to do,—not even so much as a word of reproach to waste. They know that there is a portion of the youth and of the adult population of this country, who have not shared them; who have in secret or in public paid their vows to truth and freedom; who love reality too well to care for names, and who live by a Faith too earnest and profound to suffer them to doubt the eternity of its object, or to shake themselves free from its authority. Under the fictions and customs which occupied others, these have explored the Necessary, the Plain, the True, the Human,—and so gained a vantage ground, which commands the history of the past and the present.

No one can converse much with different classes of society in New England, without remarking the progress of a revolution. Those who share in it have no external organization, no badge, no creed, no name. They do not vote, or print, or even meet together. They do not know each other's faces or names. They are united only in a common love of truth, and love of its work. They are of all conditions and constitutions. Of these acolytes, if some are happily born and well bred, many are no doubt ill dressed, ill placed, ill made—with as many scars of hereditary vice as other men. Without pomp, without trumpet, in lonely and obscure places, in solitude, in servitude, in compunctions and privations, trudging beside the team in the dusty road, or drudging a hireling in other men's cornfields, schoolmasters, who teach a few children rudiments for a pittance, ministers of small parishes of the obscurer sects, lone women in dependent condition, matrons and young maidens, rich and poor, beautiful and hard-favored, without concert or proclamation of any kind, they have silently given in their several adherence to a new hope, and in all companies do signify a greater trust in the nature and resources of man, than the laws or the popular opinions will well allow.

This spirit of the time is felt by every individual with some difference,—to each one casting its light upon the objects nearest to his temper and habits of thought;—to one, coming in the shape of special reforms in the state; to another, in modifications of the various callings of men, and the customs of business; to a third, opening a new scope for literature and art; to a fourth, in philosophical insight; to a fifth, in the vast solitudes of prayer. It is in every form a protest against usage, and a search for principles. In all its movements, it is peaceable, and in the very lowest marked with a triumphant success. Of course, it rouses the opposition of all which it judges and condemns, but it is too confident in its tone to comprehend an objection, and so builds no outworks for possible defence against contingent enemies. It has the step of Fate, and goes on existing like an oak or a river, because it must.

In literature, this influence appears not yet in new books so much as in the higher tone of criticism. The antidote to all narrowness is the comparison of the record with nature, which at once shames the record and stimulates to new attempts. Whilst we look at this, we wonder how any book has been thought worthy to be preserved. There is somewhat in all life untranslatable into language. He who keeps his eye on that will write better than others, and think less of his writing, and of all writing. Every thought has a certain imprisoning as well as uplifting quality, and, in proportion to its energy on the will, refuses to become an object of intellectual contemplation. Thus what is great usually slips through our fingers, and it seems wonderful how a lifelike word ever comes to be written. If our Journal share the impulses of the time, it cannot now prescribe its own course. It cannot foretell in orderly propositions what it shall attempt. All criticism should be poetic; unpredictable; superseding, as every new thought does, all foregone thoughts, and making a new light on the whole world. Its brow is not wrinkled with circumspection, but serene, cheerful, adoring. It has all things to say, and no less than all the world for its final audience.

Our plan embraces much more than criticism; were it not so, our criticism would be naught. Everything noble is directed on life, and this is. We do not wish to say pretty or curious things, or to reiterate a few propositions in varied forms, but, if we can, to give expression to that spirit which lifts men to a higher platform, restores to them the religious sentiment, brings them worthy aims and pure pleasures, purges the inward eye, makes life less desultory, and, through raising man to the level of nature, takes away its melancholy from the landscape, and reconciles the practical with the speculative powers.

But perhaps we are telling our little story too gravely. There are always great arguments at hand for a true action, even for the writing of a few pages. There is nothing but seems near it and prompts it,—the sphere in the ecliptic, the sap in the apple tree,—every fact, every appearance seem to persuade to it.

Our means correspond with the ends we have indicated. As we wish not to multiply books, but to report life, our resources are therefore not so much the pens of practised writers, as the discourse of the living, and the portfolios which friendship has opened to us. From the beautiful recesses of private thought; from the experience and hope of spirits which are withdrawing from all old forms, and seeking in all that is new somewhat to meet their inappeasable longings; from the secret confession of genius afraid to trust itself to aught but sympathy; from the conversation of fervid and mystical pietists; from tear-stained diaries of sorrow and passion; from the manuscripts of young poets; and from the records of youthful taste commenting on old works of art; we hope to draw thoughts and feelings, which being alive can impart life.

And so with diligent hands and good intent we set down our Dial on the earth. We wish it may resemble that instrument in its celebrated happiness, that of measuring no hours but those of sunshine. Let it be one cheerful rational voice amidst the din of mourners and polemics. Or to abide by our chosen image, let it be such a Dial, not as the dead face of a clock, hardly even such as the Gnomon in a garden, but rather such a Dial as is the Garden itself, in whose leaves and flowers and fruits the suddenly awakened sleeper is instantly apprised not what part of dead time, but what state of life and growth is now arrived and arriving.

Thoughts on Modern Literature

THERE IS no better illustration of the laws by which the world is governed than Literature. There is no luck in it. It proceeds by Fate. Every scripture is given by the inspiration of God. Every composition proceeds out of a greater or less depth of thought, and this is the measure of its effect. The highest class of books are those which express the moral element; the next, works of imagination; and the next, works of science;—all dealing in realities,—what ought to be, what is, and what appears. These, in proportion to the truth and beauty they involve, remain; the rest perish. They proceed out of the silent living mind to be heard again by the living mind. Of the best books it is hardest to write the history. Those books which are for all time are written indifferently at any time. For high genius is a day without night, a Caspian Ocean which hath no tides. And yet is literature in some sort a creature of time. Always the oracular soul is the source of thought, but always the occasion is administered by the low mediations of circumstance. Religion, Love, Ambition, War, some fierce antagonism, or it may be, some petty annoyance must break the round of perfect circulation, or no spark, no joy, no event can be. The poet rambling through the fields or the forest, absorbed in contemplation to that degree, that his walk is but a pretty dream, would never awake to precise thought, if the scream of an eagle, the cries of a crow or curlew near his head did not break the sweet continuity. Nay the finest lyrics of the poet come of this unequal parentage; the imps of matter beget such child on the soul, fair daughter of God. Nature mixes facts with thoughts to yield a poem. But the gift of immortality is of the mother's side. In the spirit in which they are written is the date of their duration, and never in the magnitude of the facts. Everything lasts in proportion to its beauty. In proportion as it was not polluted by any wilfulness of the writer, but flowed from his mind after the divine order of cause and effect, it was not his but nature's, and shared the sublimity of the sea and sky. That which is truly told, nature herself takes in charge against the whims and injustice of men. For ages, Herodotus was reckoned a credulous gossip in his descriptions of Africa, and now the sublime silent desert testifies through the mouths of Bruce, Lyons, Caillaud, Burckhardt, Belzoni, to the truth of the calumniated historian.

And yet men imagine that books are dice, and have no merit in their fortune; that the trade and the favor of a few critics can get one book into circulation, and defeat another; and that in the production of these things the author has chosen and may choose to do thus and so. Society also wishes to assign subjects and methods to its writers. But neither reader nor author may intermeddle. You cannot reason at will in this and that other vein, but only as you must. You cannot make quaint combinations, and bring to the crucible and alembic of truth things far fetched or fantastic or popular, but your method and your subject are foreordained in all your nature, and in all nature, or ever the earth was, or it has no worth. All that gives currency still to any book, advertised in the morning's newspaper in London or Boston, is the remains of faith in the breast of men that not adroit book makers, but the inextinguishable soul of the universe reports of itself in articulate discourse to-day as of old. The ancients strongly expressed their sense of the unmanageableness of these words of the spirit by saying, that the God made his priest insane, took him hither and thither as leaves are whirled by the tempest. But we sing as we are bid. Our inspirations are very manageable and tame. Death and sin have whispered in the ear of the wild horse of Heaven, and he has become a dray and a hack. And step by step with the entrance of this era of ease and convenience, the belief in the proper Inspiration of man has departed.

Literary accomplishments, skill in grammar and rhetoric, knowledge of books, can never atone for the want of things which demand voice. Literature is a poor trick when it busies itself to make words pass for things. The most original book in the world is the Bible. This old collection of the ejaculations of love and dread, of the supreme desires and contritions of men proceeding out of the region of the grand and eternal, by whatsoever different mouths spoken, and through a wide extent of times and countries, seems, especially if you add to our canon the kindred sacred writings of the Hindoos, Persians, and Greeks, the alphabet of the nations,—and all posterior literature either the chronicle of facts under very inferior ideas, or, when it rises to sentiment, the combinations, analogies, or degradations of this. The elevation of this book may be measured by observing, how certainly all elevation of thought clothes itself in the words and forms of speech of that book. For the human mind is not now sufficiently erect to judge and correct that scripture. Whatever is majestically thought in a great moral element, instantly approaches this old Sanscrit. It is in the nature of things that the highest originality must be moral. The only person, who can be entirely independent of this fountain of literature and equal to it, must be a prophet in his own proper person. Shakspeare, the first literary genius of the world, the highest in whom the moral is not the predominating element, leans on the Bible: his poetry supposes it. If we examine this brilliant influence— Shakspeare—as it lies in our minds, we shall find it reverent not only of the letter of this book, but of the whole frame of society which stood in Europe upon it, deeply indebted to the traditional morality, in short, compared with the tone of the Prophets, *secondary*. On the other hand, the Prophets do not imply the existence of Shakspeare or Homer,—advert to no books or arts, only to dread ideas and emotions. People imagine that the place, which the Bible holds in the world, it owes to miracles. It owes it simply to the fact that it came out of a profounder depth of thought than any other book, and the effect must be precisely proportionate. Gibbon fancied that it was combinations of circumstances that gave Christianity its place in history. But in nature it takes an ounce to balance an ounce.

All just criticism will not only behold in literature the action of necessary laws, but must also oversee literature itself. The erect mind disparages all books. What are books? it saith: they can have no permanent value. How obviously initial they are to their authors. The books of the nations, the universal books, are long ago forgotten by those who wrote them, and one day we shall forget this primer learning. Literature is made up of a few ideas and a few fables. It is a heap of nouns and verbs enclosing an intuition or two. We must learn to judge books by absolute standards. When we are aroused to a life in ourselves, these traditional splendors of letters grow very pale and cold. Men seem to forget that all literature is ephemeral, and unwillingly entertain the supposition of its utter disappearance. They deem not only letters in general, but the best books in particular, parts of a preëstablished harmony, fatal, unalterable, and do not go behind Virgil and Dante, much less behind Moses, Ezekiel, and St. John. But no man can be a good critic of any book, who does not read it in a wisdom which transcends the instructions of any book, and treats the whole extant product of the human intellect as only one age revisable and reversible by him.

In our fidelity to the higher truth, we need not disown our debt in our actual state of culture, in the twilights of experience to these rude helpers. They keep alive the memory and the hope of a better day. When we flout all particular books as initial merely, we truly express the privilege of spiritual nature; but, alas, not the fact and fortune of this low Massachusetts and Boston, of these humble Junes and Decembers of mortal life. Our souls are not self-fed, but do eat and drink of chemical water and wheat. Let us not forget the genial miraculous force we have known to proceed from a book. We go musing into the vault of day and night; no constellation shines, no muse descends, the stars are white points, the roses brick-colored leaves, and frogs pipe, mice cheep, and wagons creak along the road. We return to the house and take up Plutarch or Augustine, and read a few sentences or pages, and lo! the air swarms with life; the front of heaven is full of fiery shapes; secrets of magnanimity and grandeur invite us on every hand; life is made up of them. Such is our debt to a book. Observe, moreover, that we ought to credit literature with much more than the bare word it gives us. I have just been reading poems which now in my memory shine with a certain steady, warm, autumnal light. That is not in their grammatical construction which they give me. If I analyze the sentences, it eludes me, but is the genius and suggestion of the whole. Over every true poem lingers a certain wild beauty, immeasurable; a happiness lightsome and delicious fills the heart and brain,—as they say, every man walks environed by his proper atmosphere, extending to some distance around him. This beautiful result must be credited to literature also in casting its account.

In looking at the library of the Present Age we are first struck with the fact of the immense miscellany. It can hardly be characterized by any species of book, for every opinion old and new, every hope and fear, every whim and folly has an organ. It prints a vast carcass of tradition every year, with as much solemnity as a new revelation. Along with these it vents books that breathe of new morning, that seem to heave with the life of millions, books for which men and women peak and pine; books which take the rose out of the cheek of him that wrote them, and give him to the midnight a sad, solitary, diseased man; which leave no man where they found him, but make him better or worse; and which work dubiously on society, and seem to inoculate it with a venom before any healthy result appears.

In order to any complete view of the literature of the present age, an inquiry should include what it quotes, what it writes, and what it wishes to write. In our present attempt to enumerate some traits of the recent literature, we shall have somewhat to offer on each of these topics, but we cannot promise to set in very exact order what we have to say.

In the first place, it has all books. It reprints the wisdom of the world. How can the age be a bad one, which gives me Plato and Paul and Plutarch, St. Augustine, Spinoza, Chapman, Beaumont and Fletcher, Donne and Sir Thomas Browne, beside its own riches? Our presses groan every year with new editions of all the select pieces of the first of mankind,—meditations, history, classifications, opinions, epics, lyrics, which the age adopts by quoting them. If we should designate favorite studies in which the age delights more than in the rest of this great mass of the permanent literature of the human race, one or two instances would be conspicuous. First; the prodigious growth and influence of the genius of Shakspeare, in the last one hundred and fifty years, is itself a fact of the first importance. It almost alone has called out the genius of the German nation into an activity, which spreading from the poetic into the scientific, religious, and philosophical domains, has made theirs now at last the paramount intellectual influence of the world, reacting with great energy on England and America. And thus, and not by mechanical diffusion, does an original genius work and spread himself. Society becomes an immense Shakspeare. Not otherwise could the poet be admired, nay, not even seen;—not until his living, conversing, and writing had diffused his spirit into the young and acquiring class, so that he had multiplied himself into a thousand sons, a thousand Shakspeares, and so understands himself.

Secondly; the history of freedom it studies with eagerness in civil, in religious, in philosophic history. It has explored every monument of Anglo-Saxon history and law, and mainly every scrap of printed or written paper remaining from the period of the English Commonwealth. It has, out of England, devoted much thought and pains to the history of philosophy. It has groped in all nations where was any literature for the early poetry not only the dramatic, but the rudest lyric; for songs and ballads, the Nibelungen Lied, the poems of Hans Sachs and Henry of Alckmaer in Germany, for the Cid in Spain, for the rough-cast verse of the interior nations of Europe, and in Britain for the ballads of Scotland and of Robinhood.

In its own books also, our age celebrates its wants, achievements, and hopes. A wide superficial cultivation, often a mere clearing and whitewashing, indicate the new taste in the hitherto neglected savage, whether of the cities or the fields, to know the arts and share the spiritual efforts of the refined. The time is marked by the multitude of writers. Soldiers, sailors, servants, nobles, princes, women, write books. The progress of trade and the facilities for locomotion have made the world nomadic again. Of course it is well informed. All facts are exposed. The age is not to be trifled with: it wishes to know who is who, and what is what. Let there be no ghost stories more. Send Humboldt and Bonpland to explore Mexico, Guiana, and the Cordilleras. Let Captain Parry learn if there be a northwest passage to America, and Mr. Lander learn the true course of the Niger. Pückler Muskau will go to Algiers, and Sir Francis Head to the Pampas, to the Brünnens of Nassau, and to Canada. Then let us have charts true and Gazeteers correct. We will know where Babylon stood, and settle the topography of the Roman Forum. We will know whatever is to be known of Australasia, of Japan, of Persia, of Egypt, of Timbuctoo, of Palestine.

Thus Christendom has become a great reading-room; and its books have the convenient merits of the newspaper, its eminent propriety, and its superficial exactness of information. The age is well bred, knows the world, has no nonsense, and herein is well distinguished from the learned ages that preceded ours. That there is no fool like your learned fool, is a proverb plentifully illustrated in the history and writings of the English and European scholars for the half millenium that preceded the beginning of the eighteenth century. The best heads of their time build or occupy such card-house theories of religion, politics, and natural science, as a clever boy would now blow away. What stuff in Kepler, in Cardan, in Lord Bacon. Montaigne, with all his French wit and downright sense, is little better: a sophomore would wind him round his finger. Some of the Medical Remains of Lord Bacon in the book for his own use, "Of the Prolongation of Life," will move a smile in the unpoetical practitioner of the Medical College. They remind us of the drugs and practice of the leeches and enchanters of Eastern romance. Thus we find in his whimsical collection of astringents:

"A stomacher of scarlet cloth; whelps or young healthy boys applied to the stomach; hippocratic wines, so they be made of austere materials.

"8. To remember masticatories for the mouth.

"9. And orange flower water to be smelled or snuffed up.

"10. In the third hour after the sun is risen to take in air from some high and open place with a ventilation of *rosæ moschatæ* and fresh violets, and to stir the earth with infusion of wine and mint.

"17. To use once during supper time wine in which gold is quenched.

"26. Heroic desires.

"28. To provide always an apt breakfast.

"29. To do nothing against a man's genius."

To the substance of some of these specifics we have no objection. We think we should get no better at the Medical College to-day: and of all astringents we should reckon the best,

"heroic desires," and "doing nothing against one's genius."
Yet the principle of modern classification is different. In the
same place, it is curious to find a good deal of pretty nonsense
concerning the virtues of the ashes of a hedgehog, the heart
of an ape, the moss that groweth upon the skull of a dead
man unburied, and the comfort that proceeds to the system
from wearing beads of amber, coral, and hartshorn;—or
from rings of sea horse teeth worn for cramp;—to find all
these masses of moonshine side by side with the gravest and
most valuable observations.

The good Sir Thomas Browne recommends as empirical
cures for the gout:

"To wear shoes made of a lion's skin.

"Try transplantation: Give poultices taken from the part to
dogs.

"Try the magnified amulet of Muffetus, of spiders' legs
worn in a deer's skin, or of tortoises' legs cut off from the
living tortoise and wrapped up in the skin of a kid."

Burton's Anatomy of Melancholy is an encyclopædia of
authors and of opinions, where one who should forage for
exploded theories might easily load his panniers. In
dæmonology, for example; "The air," he says, "is not so full
of flies in summer as it is at all times of invisible devils. They
counterfeit suns and moons, and sit on ships' masts. They
cause whirlwinds on a sudden and tempestuous storms, which
though our meteorologists generally refer to natural causes,
yet I am of Bodine's mind, they are more often caused by
those aerial devils in their several quarters. Cardan gives much
information concerning them. His father had one of them, an
aerial devil, bound to him for eight and twenty years; as Ag-
grippa's dog had a devil tied to his collar. Some think that
Paracelsus had one confined in his sword pommel. Others
wear them in rings. At Hammel in Saxony, the devil in the
likeness of a pied piper carried away 130 children that were
never after seen."

All this sky-full of cobwebs is now forever swept clean
away. Another race is born. Humboldt and Herschel, Davy
and Arago, Malthus and Bentham have arrived. If Robert
Burton should be quoted to represent the army of scholars,
who have furnished a contribution to his moody pages, Hor-

ace Walpole, whose letters circulate in the libraries, might be taken with some fitness to represent the spirit of much recent literature. He has taste, common sense, love of facts, impatience of humbug, love of history, love of splendor, love of justice, and the sentiment of honor among gentlemen; but no life whatever of the higher faculties, no faith, no hope, no aspiration, no question touching the secret of nature.

The favorable side of this research and love of facts is the bold and systematic criticism, which has appeared in every department of literature. From Wolf's attack upon the authenticity of the Homeric Poems, dates a new epoch in learning. Ancient history has been found to be not yet settled. It is to be subjected to common sense. It is to be cross examined. It is to be seen, whether its traditions will consist not with universal belief, but with universal experience. Niebuhr has sifted Roman history by the like methods. Heeren has made good essays towards ascertaining the necessary facts in the Grecian, Persian, Assyrian, Egyptian, Ethiopic, Carthaginian nations. English history has been analyzed by Turner, Hallam, Brodie, Lingard, Palgrave. Goethe has gone the circuit of human knowledge, as Lord Bacon did before him, writing True or False on every article. Bentham has attempted the same scrutiny in reference to Civil Law. Pestalozzi out of a deep love undertook the reform of education. The ambition of Coleridge in England embraced the whole problem of philosophy; to find, that is, a foundation in thought for everything that existed in fact. The German philosophers, Schelling, Kant, Fichte, have applied their analysis to nature and thought with an antique boldness. There can be no honest inquiry, which is not better than acquiescence. Inquiries, which once looked grave and vital no doubt, change their appearance very fast, and come to look frivolous beside the later queries to which they gave occasion.

This skeptical activity, at first directed on circumstances and historical views deemed of great importance, soon penetrated deeper than Rome or Egypt, than history or institutions, or the vocabulary of metaphysics, namely, into the thinker himself, and into every function he exercises. The poetry and the speculation of the age are marked by a certain philosophic turn, which discriminates them from the works of earlier times. The poet is not content to see how "fair hangs the apple from the rock," "what music a sunbeam awoke in the groves," nor of Hardiknute, how "stately steppes he east the way, and stately steppes he west," but he now revolves, What is the apple to me? and what the birds to me? and what is Hardiknute to me? and what am I? And this is called *subjectiveness*, as the eye is withdrawn from the object and fixed on the subject or mind.

We can easily concede that a steadfast tendency of this sort appears in modern literature. It is the new consciousness of the one mind which predominates in criticism. It is the uprise of the soul and not the decline. It is founded on that insatiable demand for unity—the need to recognise one nature in all the variety of objects,—which always characterizes a genius of the first order. Accustomed always to behold the presence of the universe in every part, the soul will not condescend to look at any new part as a stranger, but saith,— "I know all already, and what art thou? Show me thy relations to me, to all, and I will entertain thee also."

There is a pernicious ambiguity in the use of the term *subjective*. We say, in accordance with the general view I have stated, that the single soul feels its right to be no longer confounded with numbers, but itself to sit in judgment on history and literature, and to summon all facts and parties before its tribunal. And in this sense the age is subjective.

But, in all ages, and now more, the narrow-minded have no interest in anything but its relation to their personality. What will help them to be delivered from some burden, eased in some circumstance, flattered, or pardoned, or enriched, what will help to marry or to divorce them, to prolong or to sweeten life, is sure of their interest, and nothing else. Every form under the whole heaven they behold in this most partial light or darkness of intense selfishness, until we hate their being. And this habit of intellectual selfishness has acquired in our day the fine name of subjectiveness.

Nor is the distinction between these two habits to be found in the circumstance of using the first person singular, or reciting facts and feelings of personal history. A man may say *I*, and never refer to himself as an individual; and a man may recite passages of his life with no feeling of egotism. Nor need a man have a vicious subjectiveness because he deals in abstract propositions.

But the criterion, which discriminates these two habits in the poet's mind, is the tendency of his composition; namely, whether it leads us to nature, or to the person of the writer. The great always introduce us to facts; small men introduce us always to themselves. The great man, even whilst he relates a private fact personal to him, is really leading us away from him to an universal experience. His own affection is in nature, in *What is*, and, of course, all his communication leads outward to it, starting from whatsoever point. The great never with their own consent become a load on the minds they instruct. The more they draw us to them, the farther from them or more independent of them we are, because they have brought us to the knowledge of somewhat deeper than both them and us. The great never hinder us; for, as the Jews had a custom of laying their beds north and south, founded on an opinion that the path of God was east and west, and they would not desecrate by the infirmities of sleep the Divine circuits, so the activity of the good is coincident with the axle of the world, with the sun and moon, with the course of the rivers and of the winds, with the stream of laborers in the street, and with all the activity and well being of the race. The great lead us to nature, and, in our age, to metaphysical nature, to the invisible awful facts, to moral abstractions, which are not less nature than is a river or a coal mine; nay, they are far more nature, but its essence and soul.

But the weak and evil, led also to analyze, saw nothing in thought but luxury. Thought for the selfish became selfish. They invited us to contemplate nature, and showed us an abominable self. Would you know the genius of the writer? Do not enumerate his talents or his feats, but ask thyself, What spirit is he of? Do gladness and hope and fortitude flow from his page into thy heart? Has he led thee to nature because his own soul was too happy in beholding her power and love; or is his passion for the wilderness only the sensibility of the sick, the exhibition of a talent, which only shines whilst you praise it; which has no root in the character, and can thus minister to the vanity but not to the happiness of the possessor; and which derives all its eclat from our conventional education, but would not make itself intelligible to the wise man of another age or country? The water we wash with never speaks of itself, nor does fire, or wind, or tree. Neither does the noble natural man: he yields himself to your occasion and use; but his act expresses a reference to universal good.

Another element of the modern poetry akin to this subjective tendency, or rather the direction of that same on the question of resources, is, the Feeling of the Infinite. Of the perception now fast becoming a conscious fact,—that there is One Mind, and that all the powers and privileges which lie in any, lie in all; that I as a man may claim and appropriate whatever of true or fair or good or strong has anywhere been exhibited; that Moses and Confucius, Montaigne and Leibnitz are not so much individuals as they are parts of man and parts of me, and my intelligence proves them my own,—literature is far the best expression. It is true, this is not the only nor the obvious lesson it teaches. A selfish commerce and government have caught the eye and usurped the hand of the masses. It is not to be contested that selfishness and the senses write the laws under which we live, and that the street seems to be built, and the men and women in it moving not in reference to pure and grand ends, but rather to very short and sordid ones. Perhaps no considerable minority, perhaps no one man leads a quite clean and lofty life. What then? We concede in sadness the fact. But we say that these low customary ways are not all that survives in human beings. There is that in us which mutters, and that which groans, and that which triumphs, and that which aspires. There are facts on which men of the world superciliously smile, which are worth all their trade and politics, the impulses, namely, which drive young men into gardens and solitary places, and cause extravagant gestures, starts, distortions of the countenance, and passionate exclamations; sentiments, which find no aliment or language for themselves on the wharves, in court, or market, but which are soothed by silence, by darkness, by the pale stars, and the presence of nature. All over the modern world the educated and susceptible have betrayed their discontent with the limits of our municipal life, and with the poverty of our dogmas of religion and philosophy. They betray this impatience by fleeing for resource to a conversation with nature—which is courted in a certain moody and exploring spirit, as if they anticipated a more intimate union of man with the world than has been known in recent ages. Those who cannot tell what they desire or expect, still sigh and struggle with indefinite thoughts and vast wishes. The very child in the nursery prattles mysticism, and doubts and philosophizes. A wild striving to express a more inward and infinite sense characterizes the works of every art. The music of Beethoven is said by those who understand it, to labor with vaster conceptions and aspirations than music has attempted before. This Feeling of the Infinite has deeply colored the poetry of the period. This new love of the vast, always native in Germany, was imported into France by De Staël, appeared in England in Coleridge, Wordsworth, Byron, Shelley, Felicia Hemans, and finds a most genial climate in the American mind. Scott and Crabbe, who formed themselves on the past, had none of this tendency; their poetry is objective. In Byron, on the other hand, it predominates; but in Byron it is blind, it sees not its true end—an infinite good, alive and beautiful, a life nourished on absolute beatitudes, descending into nature to behold itself reflected there. His will is perverted, he worships the accidents of society, and his praise of nature is thieving and selfish.

Nothing certifies the prevalence of this taste in the people more than the circulation of the poems,—one would say, most incongruously united by some bookseller,—of Coleridge, Shelley, and Keats. The only unity is in the subjectiveness and the aspiration common to the three writers. Shelley, though a poetic mind, is never a poet. His muse is uniformly imitative; all his poems composite. A good English scholar he is, with ear, taste, and memory, much more, he is a character full of noble and prophetic traits; but imagination, the original, authentic fire of the bard, he has not. He is clearly modern, and shares with Richter, Chateaubriand, Manzoni, and Wordsworth, the feeling of the infinite, which so labors for expression in their different genius. But all his lines are arbitrary, not necessary. When we read poetry, the mind asks,— Was this verse one of twenty which the author might have written as well; or is this what that man was created to say?

But, whilst every line of the true poet will be genuine, he is in a boundless power and freedom to say a million things. And the reason why he can say one thing well, is because his vision extends to the sight of all things, and so he describes each as one who knows many and all.

The fame of Wordsworth is a leading fact in modern literature, when it is considered how hostile his genius at first seemed to the reigning taste, and with what feeble poetic talents his great and steadily growing dominion has been established. More than any other poet his success has been not his own, but that of the idea which he shared with his coevals, and which he has rarely succeeded in adequately expressing. The Excursion awakened in every lover of nature the right feeling. We saw stars shine, we felt the awe of mountains, we heard the rustle of the wind in the grass, and knew again the ineffable secret of solitude. It was a great joy. It was nearer to nature than anything we had before. But the interest of the poem ended almost with the narrative of the influences of nature on the mind of the Boy, in the first book. Obviously for that passage the poem was written, and with the exception of this and of a few strains of the like character in the sequel, the whole poem was dull. Here was no poem, but here was poetry, and a sure index where the subtle muse was about to pitch her tent and find the argument of her song. It was the human soul in these last ages striving for a just publication of itself. Add to this, however, the great praise of Wordsworth, that more than any other contemporary bard he is pervaded with a reverence of somewhat higher than (conscious) thought. There is in him that property common to all great poets, a wisdom of humanity, which is superior to any talents which they exert. It is the wisest part of Shakspeare and of Milton. For they are poets by the free course which they allow to the informing soul, which through their eyes beholdeth again and blesseth the things which it hath made. The soul is superior to its knowledge, wiser than any of its works.

With the name of Wordsworth rises to our recollection the name of his contemporary and friend, Walter Savage Landor—a man working in a very different and peculiar spirit, yet one whose genius and accomplishments deserve a wiser criticism than we have yet seen applied to them, and the rather that his name does not readily associate itself with any school of writers. Of Thomas Carlyle, also we shall say nothing at this time, since the quality and the energy of his influence on the youth of this country will require at our hands ere long a distinct and faithful acknowledgment.

But of all men he, who has united in himself and that in the most extraordinary degree the tendencies of the era, is the German poet, naturalist, and philosopher, Goethe. Whatever the age inherited or invented, he made his own. He has owed to Commerce and to the victories of the Understanding, all their spoils. Such was his capacity, that the magazines of the world's ancient or modern wealth, which arts and intercourse and skepticism could command—he wanted them all. Had there been twice so much, he could have used it as well. Geologist, mechanic, merchant, chemist, king, radical, painter, composer,—all worked for him, and a thousand men seemed to look through his eyes. He learned as readily as other men breathe. Of all the men of this time, not one has seemed so much at home in it as he. He was not afraid to live. And in him this encyclopædia of facts, which it has been the boast of the age to compile, wrought an equal effect. He was knowing; he was brave; he was clean from all narrowness; he has a perfect propriety and taste,—a quality by no means common to the German writers. Nay, since the earth, as we said, had become a reading-room, the new opportunities seem to have aided him to be that resolute realist he is, and seconded his sturdy determination to see things for what they are. To look at him, one would say, there was never an observer before. What sagacity, what industry of observation! to read his record is a frugality of time, for you shall find no word that does not stand for a thing, and he is of that comprehension, which can see the value of truth. His love of nature has seemed to give a new meaning to that word. There was never man more domesticated in this world than he. And he is an apology for the analytic spirit of the period, because, of his analysis, always wholes were the result. All conventions, all traditions he rejected. And yet he felt his entire right and duty to stand before and try and judge every fact in nature. He thought it necessary to dot round with his own pen the entire sphere of knowables; and for many of his stories, this seems the only reason: Here is a piece of humanity I had hitherto omitted to sketch;—take this. He does not say so in syllables,—yet a sort of conscientious feeling he had to be *up* to the universe, is the best account and apology for many of them. He shared also the subjectiveness of the age, and that too in both the senses I have discriminated. With the sharpest eye for form, color, botany, engraving, medals, persons, and manners, he never stopped at surface, but pierced the purpose of a thing, and studied to reconcile that purpose with his own being. What he could so reconcile was good; what he could not, was false. Hence a certain greatness encircles every fact he treats; for to him it has a soul, an eternal reason why it was so, and not otherwise. This is the secret of that deep realism, which went about among all objects he beheld, to find the cause why they must be what they are. It was with him a favorite task to find a theory of every institution, custom, art, work of art, which he observes. Witness his explanation of the Italian mode of reckoning the hours of the day, as growing out of the Italian climate; of the obelisk of Egypt, as growing out of a common natural fracture in the granite parallelopiped in Upper Egypt; of the Doric architecture, and the Gothic; of the Venetian music of the gondolier originating in the habit of the fishers' wives of the Lido singing to their husbands on the sea; of the Amphitheatre, which is the enclosure of the natural cup of heads that arranges itself round every spectacle in the street; of the coloring of Titian and Paul Veronese, which one may verify in the common daylight in Venice every afternoon; of the Carnival at Rome; of the domestic rural architecture in Italy; and many the like examples.

But also that other vicious subjectiveness, that vice of the time, infected him also. We are provoked with his Olympian self-complacency, the patronizing air with which he vouchsafes to tolerate the genius and performances of other mortals, "the good Hiller," "our excellent Kant," "the friendly Wieland," &c. &c. There is a good letter from Wieland to Merck, in which Wieland relates that Goethe read to a select party his journal of a tour in Switzerland with the Grand Duke, and their passage through Valois and over the St. Gothard. "It was," says Wieland, "as good as Xenophon's Anabasis. The piece is one of his most masterly productions, and is thought and written with the greatness peculiar to him. The fair hearers were enthusiastic at the nature in this piece; I liked the sly art in the composition, whereof they saw nothing, still better. It is a true poem, so concealed is the art too. But what most remarkably in this as in all his other works distinguishes him from Homer and Shakspeare, is, that the Me, the *Ille ego*, everywhere glimmers through, although without any boasting and with an infinite fineness." This subtle element of egotism in Goethe certainly does not seem to deform his compositions, but to lower the moral influence of the man. He differs from all the great in the total want of frankness. Whoso saw Milton, whoso saw Shakspeare, saw them do their best, and utter their whole heart manlike among their brethren. No man was permitted to call Goethe brother. He hid himself, and worked always to astonish, which is an egotism, and therefore little.

If we try Goethe by the ordinary canons of criticism, we should say that his thinking is of great altitude, and all level; — not a succession of summits, but a high Asiatic table land. Dramatic power, the rarest talent in literature, he has very little. He has an eye constant to the fact of life, and that never pauses in its advance. But the great felicities, the miracles of poetry, he has never. It is all design with him, just thought and instructed expression, analogies, allusion, illustration, which knowledge and correct thinking supply; but of Shakspeare and the transcendant muse, no syllable. Yet in the court and law to which we ordinarily speak, and without adverting to absolute standards, we claim for him the praise of truth, of fidelity to his intellectual nature. He is the king of all scholars. In these days and in this country, where the scholars are few and idle, where men read easy books and sleep after dinner, it seems as if no book could so safely be put in the hands of young men as the letters of Goethe, which attest the incessant activity of this man to eighty years, in an endless variety of studies with uniform cheerfulness and greatness of mind. They cannot be read without shaming us into an emulating industry. Let him have the praise of the love of truth. We think, when we contemplate the stupendous glory of the world, that it were life enough for one man merely to lift his hands and cry with St. Augustine, "Wrangle who pleases, I will wonder." Well, this he did. Here was a man, who, in the feeling that the thing itself was so admirable as to leave all comment behind, went up and down from object to object, lifting the veil from everyone, and did no more. What he said of Lavater, may trulier be said of him, that "it was fearful to stand in the presence of one, before whom all the boundaries within which nature has circumscribed our being were laid flat." His are the bright and terrible eyes, which meet the modern student in every sacred chapel of thought, in every public enclosure.

But now, that we may not seem to dodge the question which all men ask, nor pay a great man so ill a compliment as to praise him only in the conventional and comparative speech, let us honestly record our thought upon the total worth and influence of this genius. Does he represent not only the achievement of that age in which he lived, but that which it would be and is now becoming? And what shall we think of that absence of the moral sentiment, that singular equivalence to him of good and evil in action, which discredits his compositions to the pure? The spirit of his biography, of his poems, of his tales, is identical, and we may here set down by way of comment on his genius the impressions recently awakened in us by the story of Wilhelm Meister.

All great men have written proudly, nor cared to explain. They knew that the intelligent reader would come at last, and would thank them. So did Dante, so did Machiavel. Goethe has done this in Meister. We can fancy him saying to himself;—There are poets enough of the ideal; let me paint the Actual, as, after years of dreams, it will still appear and reappear to wise men. That all shall right itself in the long Morrow, I may well allow, and my novel may easily wait for the same regeneration. The age, that can damn it as false and falsifying, will see that it is deeply one with the genius and history of all the centuries. I have given my characters a bias to error. Men have the same. I have let mischances befall instead of good fortune. They do so daily. And out of many vices and misfortunes, I have let a great success grow, as I had known in my own and many other examples. Fierce churchmen and effeminate aspirants will chide and hate my name, but every keen beholder of life will justify my truth, and will acquit me of prejudging the cause of humanity by painting it with this morose fidelity. To a profound soul is not austere truth the sweetest flattery?

Yes, O Goethe! but the ideal is truer than the actual. That is ephemeral, but this changes not. Moreover, because nature is moral, that mind only can see, in which the same order entirely obtains. An interchangeable Truth, Beauty, and Goodness, each wholly interfused in the other, must make the humors of that eye, which would see causes reaching to their last effect and reproducing the world forever. The least inequality of mixture, the excess of one element over the other, in that degree diminishes the transparency of things, makes the world opaque to the observer, and destroys so far the value of his experience. No particular gifts can countervail this defect. In reading Meister, I am charmed with the insight; to use a phrase of Ben Jonson's, "it is rammed with life." I find there actual men and women even too faithfully painted. I am, moreover, instructed in the possibility of a highly accomplished society, and taught to look for great talent and culture under a grey coat. But this is all. The limits of artificial society are never quite out of sight. The vicious conventions, which hem us in like prison walls, and which the poet should explode at his touch, stand for all they are worth in the newspaper. I am never lifted above myself. I am not transported out of the dominion of the senses, or cheered with an infinite tenderness, or armed with a grand trust.

Goethe, then, must be set down as the poet of the Actual, not of the Ideal; the poet of limitation, not of possibility; of this world, and not of religion and hope; in short, if I may say so, the poet of prose, and not of poetry. He accepts the base doctrine of Fate, and gleans what straggling joys may yet remain out of its ban. He is like a banker or a weaver with a passion for the country, he steals out of the hot streets before sunrise, or after sunset, or on a rare holiday, to get a draught of sweet air, and a gaze at the magnificence of summer, but dares not break from his slavery and lead a man's life in a man's relation to nature. In that which should be his own place, he feels like a truant, and is scourged back presently to his task and his cell. Poetry is with Goethe thus external, the gilding of the chain, the mitigation of his fate; but the muse never essays those thunder-tones, which cause to vibrate the sun and the moon, which dissipate by dreadful melody all this iron network of circumstance, and abolish the old heavens and the old earth before the free-will or Godhead of man. That Goethe had not a moral perception proportionate to his other powers, is not then merely a circumstance, as we might relate of a man that he had or had not the sense of tune or an eye for colors; but it is the cardinal fact of health or disease; since, lacking this, he failed in the high sense to be a creator, and with divine endowments drops by irreversible decree into the common history of genius. He was content to fall into the track of vulgar poets, and spend on common aims his splendid endowments, and has declined the office proffered to now and then a man in many centuries in the power of his genius—of a Redeemer of the human mind. He has written better than other poets, only as his talent was subtler, but the ambition of creation he refused. Life for him is prettier, easier, wiser, decenter, has a gem or two more on its robe, but its old eternal burden is not relieved; no drop of healthier blood flows yet in its veins. Let him pass. Humanity must wait for its physician still at the side of the road, and confess as this man goes out that they have served it better, who assured it out of the innocent hope in their hearts that a Physician will come, than this majestic Artist, with all the treasuries of wit, of science, and of power at his command.

The criticism, which is not so much spoken as felt in reference to Goethe, instructs us directly in the hope of literature. We feel that a man gifted like him should not leave the world as he found it. It is true, though somewhat sad, that every fine genius teaches us how to blame himself. Being so much, we cannot forgive him for not being more. When one of these grand monads is incarnated, whom nature seems to design for eternal men and draw to her bosom, we think that the old wearinesses of Europe and Asia, the trivial forms of daily life will now end, and a new morning break on us all. What is Austria? What is England? What is our graduated and petrified social scale of ranks and employments? Shall not a poet redeem us from these idolatries, and pale their legendary lustre before the fires of the Divine Wisdom which burn in his heart? All that in our sovereign moments each of us has

divined of the powers of thought, all the hints of omnipresence and energy which we have caught, this man should unfold and constitute facts.

And this is the insatiable craving which alternately saddens
and gladdens men at this day. The Doctrine of the Life of
Man established after the truth through all his faculties; — this
is the thought which the literature of this hour meditates and
labors to say. This is that which tunes the tongue and fires
the eye and sits in the silence of the youth. Verily it will not
long want articulate and melodious expression. There is nothing in the heart but comes presently to the lips. The very
depth of the sentiment, which is the author of all the cuta-
neous life we see, is guarantee for the riches of science and of
song in the age to come. He, who doubts whether this age
or this country can yield any contribution to the literature of
the world, only betrays his own blindness to the necessities of
the human soul. Has the power of poetry ceased, or the need?
Have the eyes ceased to see that which they would have, and
which they have not? Have they ceased to see other eyes? Are
there no lonely, anxious, wondering children, who must tell
their tale? Are we not evermore whipped by thoughts;

> "In sorrow steeped and steeped in love
> Of thoughts not yet incarnated?"

The heart beats in this age as of old, and the passions are busy
as ever. Nature has not lost one ringlet of her beauty, one
impulse of resistance and valor. From the necessity of loving
none are exempt, and he that loves must utter his desires. A
charm as radiant as beauty ever beamed, a love that fainteth
at the sight of its object, is new to-day.

> "The world does not run smoother than of old,
> There are sad haps that must be told."

Man is not so far lost but that he suffers ever the great Discontent, which is the elegy of his loss and the prediction of
his recovery. In the gay saloon he laments that these figures
are not what Raphael and Guercino painted. Withered
though he stand and trifler though he be, the august spirit of
the world looks out from his eyes. In his heart he knows the
ache of spiritual pain, and his thought can animate the sea

and land. What then shall hinder the Genius of the time from speaking its thought? It cannot be silent, if it would. It will write in a higher spirit, and a wider knowledge, and with a grander practical aim, than ever yet guided the pen of poet. It will write the annals of a changed world, and record the descent of principles into practice, of love into Government, of love into Trade. It will describe the new heroic life of man, the now unbelieved possibility of simple living and of clean and noble relations with men. Religion will bind again these that were sometime frivolous, customary, enemies, skeptics, self-seekers, into a joyful reverence for the circumambient Whole, and that which was ecstasy shall become daily bread.

New Poetry

THE TENDENCIES of the times are so democratical, that we shall soon have not so much as a pulpit or raised platform in any church or townhouse, but each person, who is moved to address any public assembly, will speak from the floor. The like revolution in literature is now giving importance to the portfolio over the book. Only one man in the thousand may print a book, but one in ten or one in five may inscribe his thoughts, or at least with short commentary his favorite readings in a private journal. The philosophy of the day has long since broached a more liberal doctrine of the poetic faculty than our fathers held, and reckons poetry the right and power of every man to whose culture justice is done. We own that, though we were trained in a stricter school of literary faith, and were in all our youth inclined to the enforcement of the straitest restrictions on the admission of candidates to the Parnassian fraternity, and denied the name of poetry to every composition in which the workmanship and the material were not equally excellent, in our middle age we have grown lax, and have learned to find pleasure in verses of a ruder strain,— to enjoy *verses of society*, or those effusions which in persons of a happy nature are the easy and unpremeditated translation of their thoughts and feelings into rhyme. This new taste for a certain private and household poetry, for somewhat less pretending than the festal and solemn verses which are written for the nations, really indicates, we suppose, that a new style of poetry exists. The number of writers has increased. Every child has been taught the tongues. The universal communication of the arts of reading and writing has brought the works of the great poets into every house, and made all ears familiar with the poetic forms. The progress of popular institutions has favored self-respect, and broken down that terror of the great, which once imposed awe and hesitation on the talent of the masses of society. A wider epistolary intercourse ministers to the ends of sentiment and reflection than ever existed before; the practice of writing diaries is becoming almost general; and every day witnesses new attempts to throw into verse the experiences of private life.

What better omen of true progress can we ask than an increasing intellectual and moral interest of men in each other? What can be better for the republic than that the Capitol, the White House, and the Court House are becoming of less importance than the farm-house and the book-closet? If we are losing our interest in public men, and finding that their spell lay in number and size only, and acquiring instead a taste for the depths of thought and emotion as they may be sounded in the soul of the citizen or the countryman, does it not replace man for the state, and character for official power? Men should be treated with solemnity; and when they come to chant their private griefs and doubts and joys, they have a new scale by which to compute magnitude and relation. Art is the noblest consolation of calamity. The poet is compensated for his defects in the street and in society, if in his chamber he has turned his mischance into noble numbers.

Is there not room then for a new department in poetry, namely, *Verses of the Portfolio*? We have fancied that we drew greater pleasure from some manuscript verses than from printed ones of equal talent. For there was herein the charm of character; they were confessions; and the faults, the imperfect parts, the fragmentary verses, the halting rhymes, had a worth beyond that of a high finish; for they testified that the writer was more man than artist, more earnest than vain; that the thought was too sweet and sacred to him, than that he should suffer his ears to hear or his eyes to see a superficial defect in the expression.

The characteristic of such verses is, that being not written for publication, they lack that finish which the conventions of literature require of authors. But if poetry of this kind has merit, we conceive that the prescription which demands a rhythmical polish may be easily set aside; and when a writer has outgrown the state of thought which produced the poem, the interest of letters is served by publishing it imperfect, as we preserve studies, torsos, and blocked statues of the great masters. For though we should be loath to see the wholesome conventions, to which we have alluded, broken down by a general incontinence of publication, and every man's and woman's diary flying into the bookstores, yet it is to be considered, on the other hand, that men of genius are often more incapable than others of that elaborate execution which criticism exacts. Men of genius in general are, more than others, incapable of any perfect exhibition, because however agreeable it may be to them to act on the public, it is always a secondary aim. They are humble, self-accusing, moody men, whose worship is toward the Ideal Beauty, which chooses to be courted not so often in perfect hymns, as in wild ear-piercing ejaculations, or in silent musings. Their face is forward, and their heart is in this heaven. By so much are they disqualified for a perfect success in any particular performance to which they can give only a divided affection. But the man of talents has every advantage in the competition. He can give that cool and commanding attention to the thing to be done, that shall secure its just performance. Yet are the failures of genius better than the victories of talent; and we are sure that some crude manuscript poems have yielded us a more sustaining and a more stimulating diet, than many elaborated and classic productions.

We have been led to these thoughts by reading some verses, which were lately put into our hands by a friend with the remark, that they were the production of a youth, who had long passed out of the mood in which he wrote them, so that they had become quite dead to him. Our first feeling on reading them was a lively joy. So then the Muse is neither dead nor dumb, but has found a voice in these cold Cisatlantic States. Here is poetry which asks no aid of magnitude or number, of blood or crime, but finds theatre enough in the first field or brookside, breadth and depth enough in the flow of its own thought. Here is self-repose, which to our mind is stabler than the Pyramids; here is self-respect which leads a man to date from his heart more proudly than from Rome. Here is love which sees through surface, and adores the gentle nature and not the costume. Here is religion, which is not of the Church of England, nor of the Church of Boston. Here is the good wise heart, which sees that the end of culture is strength and cheerfulness. In an age too which tends with so strong an inclination to the philosophical muse, here is poetry more purely intellectual than any American verses we have yet seen, distinguished from all competition by two merits; the fineness of perception; and the poet's trust in his own genius to that degree, that there is an absence of all conventional imagery, and a bold use of that which the moment's mood had made sacred to him, quite careless that it might be sacred to no other, and might even be slightly ludicrous to the first reader.

We proceed to give our readers some selections, taken without much order from this rich pile of manuscript. We first find the poet in his boat.

BOAT SONG.

THE RIVER calmly flows,
  Through shining banks, through lonely glen,
Where the owl shrieks, though ne'er the cheer of men
    Has stirred its mute repose,
Still if you should walk there, you would go there again.

    The stream is well alive;
  Another passive world you see,
Where downward grows the form of every tree;
    Like soft light clouds they thrive:
Like them let us in our pure loves reflected be.

    A yellow gleam is thrown
  Into the secrets of that maze
Of tangled trees, which late shut out our gaze,
    Refusing to be known;
It must its privacy unclose,—its glories blaze.

    Sweet falls the summer air
  Over her frame who sails with me:
Her way like that is beautifully free,
    Her nature far more rare,
And is her constant heart of virgin purity.

    A quivering star is seen
  Keeping his watch above the hill,
Though from the sun's retreat small light is still
    Poured on earth's saddening mien:—
We all are tranquilly obeying Evening's will.

Thus ever love the POWER;
To simplest thoughts dispose the mind;
In each obscure event a worship find
Like that of this dim hour,—
In lights, and airs, and trees, and in all human kind.

We smoothly glide below
The faintly glimmering worlds of light:
Day has a charm, and this deceptive night
Brings a mysterious show;—
He shadows our dear earth,—but his cool stars are white.

Two Years before the Mast

Two Years before the Mast. A Personal Narrative of Life at Sea. New York: Harper and Brothers. 12mo. pp. 483.

THIS IS a voice from the forecastle. Though a narrative of literal, prosaic truth, it possesses something of the romantic charm of Robinson Crusoe. Few more interesting chapters of the literature of the sea have ever fallen under our notice. The author left the halls of the University for the deck of a merchant vessel, exchanging "the tight dress coat, silk cap, and kid gloves of an undergraduate at Cambridge, for the loose duck trowsers, checked shirt, and tarpaulin hat of a sailor," and here presents us the fruits of his voyage. His book will have a wide circulation; it will be praised in the public prints; we shall be told that it does honor to his head and heart; but we trust that it will do much more than this; that it will open the eyes of many to the condition of the sailor, to the fearful waste of man, by which the luxuries of foreign climes are made to increase the amount of commercial wealth. This simple narrative, stamped with deep sincerity, and often displaying an unstudied, pathetic eloquence, may lead to reflections, which mere argument and sentimental appeals do not call forth. It will serve to hasten the day of reckoning between society and the sailor, which, though late, will not fail to come.

Social Destiny of Man

Social Destiny of Man: or Association and Reorganization of Indus-
try. By Albert Brisbane. Philadelphia. 12mo. pp. 480.

This work is designed to give a condensed view of the
system of M. Fourier, for the improvement and elevation
of productive industry. It will be read with deep interest by a
large class of our population. The name of Fourier may be
placed at the head of modern thinkers, whose attention has
been given to the practical evils of society and the means of
their removal. His general principles should be cautiously separated from the details which accompany their exposition,
many of which are so exclusively adapted to the French character, as to prejudice their reception with persons of opposite
habits and associations. The great question, which he brings
up for discussion, concerns the union of labor and capital in
the same individuals, by a system of combined and organized
industry. This question, it is more than probable, will not be
set aside at once, whenever its importance is fully perceived,
and those who are interested in its decision will find materials
of no small value in the writings of M. Fourier. They may be
regarded, in some sense, as the scientific analysis of the co-
öperative principle, which has, within a few years past, engaged the public attention in England, and in certain cases,
received a successful, practical application.

Michael Angelo,
Considered as a Philosophic Poet

Michael Angelo, considered as a Philosophic Poet, with Translations.
By JOHN EDWARD TAYLOR. London: Saunders & Otley, Conduit Street. 1840.

WE WELCOME this little book with joy, and a hope that
it may be republished in Boston. It would find, probably, but a small circle of readers, but that circle would be
more ready to receive and prize it than the English public for
whom it was intended, if we may judge by the way in which
Mr. Taylor, all through his prefatory essay, has considered it
necessary to apologize for, or, at least, explain views very
commonly received among ourselves.

The essay is interesting from the degree of acquaintance it
exhibits with some of those great ones, who have held up the
highest aims to the soul, and from the degree of insight
which reverence and delicacy of mind have given to the author. From every line comes the soft breath of green pastures
where " walk the good shepherds."

Of the sonnets, we doubt the possibility of making good
translations into English. No gift of the Muse is more injured
by change of form than the Italian sonnet. As those of Petrarch will not bear it, from their infinite grace, those of
Dante from their mystic and subtle majesty; so these of Angelo, from the rugged naiveté with which they are struck off
from the mind, as huge splinters of stone might be from some
vast block, can never be "done into English," as the old translators, with an intelligent modesty, were wont to write of
their work. The grand thought is not quite evaporated in the
process, but the image of the stern and stately writer is lost.
We do not know again such words as "concetto," "superna"
in their English representatives.

But since a knowledge of the Italian language is not so
common an attainment as could be wished, we ought to be
grateful for this attempt to extend the benefit of these noble
expressions of the faith which inspired one of the most full
and noble lives that has ever redeemed and encouraged man.

Fidelity must be the highest merit of these translations; for not even an Angelo could translate his peer. This, so far as we have looked at them, they seem to possess. And even in the English dress, we think none, to whom they are new, can read the sonnets,—

> "Veggio nel volto tuo col pensier mie."
> "S'un casto amor, s'una pietá superna."
> "La vita del mio amor non é cuor mio."

and others of the same pure religion, without a delight which shall

> "Cast a light upon the day,
> A light which will not go away,
> A sweet forewarning."

We hope they may have the opportunity. It is a very little book with a great deal in it, and five hundred copies will sell in two years.

We add Mr. Taylor's little preface, which happily expresses his design.

"The remarks on the poetry and philosophy of Michael Angelo, which are prefixed to these translations have been collected and are now published in the hope that they may invite the student of literature to trace the relation which unites the efforts of the pure intelligence and the desires of the heart to their highest earthly accomplishment under the complete forms of Art. For the example of so eminent a mind, watched and judged not only by its finished works, but, as it were, in its growth and from its inner source of Love and Knowledge cannot but enlarge the range of our sympathy for the best powers and productions of man. And if these pages should meet with any readers inclined, like their writer, to seek and to admire the veiled truth and solemn beauty of the eldertime, they will add their humble testimony to the fact, that whatever be the purpose and tendencies of the time we live in, we are not all unmindful of the better part of our inheritance in this world."

Essays and Poems

Essays and Poems. By JONES VERY. Boston: C. C. Little and James Brown.

THIS LITTLE VOLUME would have received an earlier notice, if we had been at all careful to proclaim our favorite books. The genius of this book is religious, and reaches an extraordinary depth of sentiment. The author, plainly a man of a pure and kindly temper, casts himself into the state of the high and transcendental obedience to the inward Spirit. He has apparently made up his mind to follow all its leadings, though he should be taxed with absurdity or even with insanity. In this enthusiasm he writes most of these verses, which rather flow through him than from him. There is no *composition*, no elaboration, no artifice in the structure of the rhyme, no variety in the imagery; in short, no pretension to literary merit, for this would be departure from his singleness, and followed by loss of insight. He is not at liberty even to correct these unpremeditated poems for the press; but if another will publish them, he offers no objection. In this way they have come into the world, and as yet have hardly begun to be known. With the exception of the few first poems, which appear to be of an earlier date, all these verses bear the unquestionable stamp of grandeur. They are the breathings of a certain entranced devotion, which one would say, should be received with affectionate and sympathizing curiosity by all men, as if no recent writer had so much to show them of what is most their own. They are as sincere a litany as the Hebrew songs of David or Isaiah, and only less than they, because indebted to the Hebrew muse for their tone and genius. This makes the singularity of the book, namely, that so pure an utterance of the most domestic and primitive of all sentiments should in this age of revolt and experiment use once more the popular religious language, and so show itself secondary and morbid. These sonnets have little range of topics, no extent of observation, no playfulness; there is even a certain torpidity in the concluding lines of some of them, which reminds one of church hymns; but, whilst they flow with great sweetness, they have the sublime unity of the Decalogue or the Code of Menu, and if as monotonous, yet are they almost as pure as the sounds of Surrounding Nature. We gladly insert from a newspaper the following sonnet, which appeared since the volume was printed.

THE BARBERRY BUSH.

The bush that has most briers and bitter fruit,
Wait till the frost has turned its green leaves red,
Its sweetened berries will thy palate suit,
And thou may'st find e'en there a homely bread.
Upon the hills of Salem scattered wide,
Their yellow blossoms gain the eye in Spring;
And straggling e'en upon the turnpike's side,
Their ripened branches to your hand they bring,
I 've plucked them oft in boyhood's early hour,
That then I gave such name, and thought it true;
But now I know that other fruit as sour
Grows on what now thou callest *Me* and *You*;
Yet, wilt thou wait the autumn that I see,
Will sweeter taste than these red berries be.

Walter Savage Landor

WE SOMETIMES meet in a stage coach in New England an erect muscular man, with fresh complexion and a smooth hat, whose nervous speech instantly betrays the English traveller;—a man nowise cautious to conceal his name or that of his native country, or his very slight esteem for the persons and the country that surround him. When Mr. Bull rides in an American coach, he speaks quick and strong, he is very ready to confess his ignorance of everything about him, persons, manners, customs, politics, geography. He wonders that the Americans should build with wood, whilst all this stone is lying in the roadside, and is astonished to learn that a wooden house may last a hundred years; nor will he remember the fact as many minutes after it has been told him; he wonders they do not make elder-wine and cherry-bounce, since here are cherries, and every mile is crammed with elder bushes. He has never seen a good horse in America, nor a good coach, nor a good inn. Here is very good earth and water, and plenty of them,—that he is free to allow,—to all others gifts of nature or man, his eyes are sealed by the inexorable demand for the precise conveniences to which he is accustomed in England. Add to this proud blindness the better quality of great downrightness in speaking the truth, and the love of fair play, on all occasions, and, moreover, the peculiarity which is alleged of the Englishman, that his virtues do not come out until he quarrels. Transfer these traits to a very elegant and accomplished mind, and we shall have no bad picture of Walter Savage Landor, who may stand as a favorable impersonation of the genius of his countrymen at the present day. A sharp dogmatic man with a great deal of knowledge, a great deal of worth, and a great deal of pride, with a profound contempt for all that he does not understand, a master of all elegant learning and capable of the utmost delicacy of sentiment, and yet prone to indulge a sort of ostentation of coarse imagery and language. His partialities and dislikes are by no means calculable, but are often whimsical and amusing; yet they are quite sincere, and, like those of Johnson and Coleridge, are easily separable from the man.

What he says of Wordsworth, is true of himself, that he delights to throw a clod of dirt on the table, and cry, "Gentlemen, there is a better man than all of you." Bolivar, Mina, and General Jackson will never be greater soldiers than Napoleon and Alexander, let Mr. Landor think as he will; nor will he persuade us to burn Plato and Xenophon, out of our admiration of Bishop Patrick, or "Lucas on Happiness," or "Lucas on Holiness," or even Barrow's Sermons. Yet a man may love a paradox, without losing either his wit or his honesty. A less pardonable eccentricity is the cold and gratuitous obtrusion of licentious images, not so much the suggestion of merriment as of bitterness. Montaigne assigns as a reason for his license of speech, that he is tired of seeing his Essays on the work-tables of ladies, and he is determined they shall for the future put them out of sight. In Mr. Landor's coarseness there is a certain air of defiance; and the rude word seems sometimes to arise from a disgust at niceness and over-refinement. Before a well-dressed company he plunges his fingers in a sess-pool, as if to expose the whiteness of his hands and the jewels of his ring. Afterward, he washes them in water, he washes them in wine; but you are never secure from his freaks. A sort of Earl Peterborough in literature, his eccentricity is too decided not to have diminished his greatness. He has capital enough to have furnished the brain of fifty stock authors, yet has written no good book.

But we have spoken all our discontent. Possibly his writings are open to harsher censure; but we love the man from sympathy, as well as for reasons to be assigned; and have no wish, if we were able, to put an argument in the mouth of his critics. Now for twenty years we have still found the "Imaginary Conversations" a sure resource in solitude, and it seems to us as original in its form as in its matter. Nay, when we remember his rich and ample page, wherein we are always sure to find free and sustained thought, a keen and precise understanding, an affluent and ready memory familiar with all chosen books, an industrious observation in every department of life, an experience to which nothing has occurred in vain, honor for every just and generous sentiment, and a scourge like that of the Furies for every oppressor, whether public or private, we feel how dignified is this perpetual Censor in his curule chair, and we wish to thank a benefactor of the reading world.

Mr. Landor is one of the foremost of that small class who make good in the nineteenth-century the claims of pure literature. In these busy days of avarice and ambition, when there is so little disposition to profound thought, or to any but the most superficial intellectual entertainments, a faithful scholar receiving from past ages the treasures of wit, and enlarging them by his own love, is a friend and consoler of mankind. When we pronounce the names of Homer and Æschylus,—Horace, Ovid, and Plutarch,—Erasmus, Scaliger, and Montaigne,—Ben Jonson and Isaak Walton,—Dryden and Pope,—we pass at once out of trivial associations, and enter into a region of the purest pleasure accessible to human nature. We have quitted all beneath the moon, and entered that crystal sphere in which everything in the world of matter reappears, but transfigured and immortal. Literature is the effort of man to indemnify himself for the wrongs of his condition. The existence of the poorest play-wright and the humblest scrivener is a good omen. A charm attaches to the most inferior names which have in any manner got themselves enrolled in the registers of the House of Fame, even as porters and grooms in the courts, to Creech and Fenton, Theobald and Dennis, Aubrey and Spence. From the moment of entering a library and opening a desired book, we cease to be citizens, creditors, debtors, housekeepers, and men of care and fear. What boundless leisure! what original jurisdiction! the old constellations have set, new and brighter have arisen; an elysian light tinges all objects.

> "In the afternoon we came unto a land
> In which it seemed always afternoon."

And this sweet asylum of an intellectual life must appear to have the sanction of nature, as long as so many men are born with so decided an aptitude for reading and writing. Let us thankfully allow every faculty and art which opens new scope to a life so confined as ours. There are vast spaces in a thought; a slave, to whom the religious sentiment is opened, has a freedom which makes his master's freedom a slavery. Let us not be so illiberal with our schemes for the renovation of society and nature, as to disesteem or deny the literary spirit. Certainly there are heights in nature which command this; there are many more which this commands. It is vain to call it a luxury, and as saints and reformers are apt to do, decry it as a species of day-dreaming. What else are sanctities, and reforms, and all other things? Whatever can make for itself an element, means, organs, servants, and the most profound and permanent existence in the hearts and heads of millions of men, must have a reason for its being. Its excellency is reason and vindication enough. If rhyme rejoices us, there should be rhyme, as much as if fire cheers us, we should bring wood and coals. Each kind of excellence takes place for its hour, and excludes everything else. Do not brag of your actions, as if they were better than Homer's verses or Raphael's pictures. Raphael and Homer feel that action is pitiful beside their enchantments. They could act too, if the stake was worthy of them; but now all that is good in the universe urges them to their task. Whoever writes for the love of truth and beauty, and not with ulterior ends, belongs to this sacred class, and among these, few men of the present age, have a better claim to be numbered than Mr. Landor. Wherever genius or taste has existed, wherever freedom and justice are threatened, which he values as the element in which genius may work, his interest is sure to be commanded. His love of beauty is passionate, and betrays itself in all petulant and contemptuous expressions.

But beyond his delight in genius, and his love of individual and civil liberty, Mr. Landor has a perception that is much more rare, the appreciation of character. This is the more remarkable considered with his intense nationality, to which we have already alluded. He is buttoned in English broadcloth to the chin. He hates the Austrians, the Italians, the French, the Scotch, and the Irish. He has the common prejudices of the English landholder; values his pedigree, his acres, and the syllables of his name; loves all his advantages, is not insensible to the beauty of his watchseal, or the Turk's head on his umbrella; yet with all this miscellaneous pride, there is a noble nature within him, which instructs him that he is so rich that he can well spare all his trappings, and, leaving to others the painting of circumstance, aspire to the office of delineating character. He draws his own portrait in the costume of a village schoolmaster, and a sailor, and serenely enjoys the victory of nature over fortune. Not only the elaborated story of Normanby, but the whimsical selection of his heads prove this taste. He draws with evident pleasure the portrait of a man, who never said anything right, and never did anything wrong. But in the character of Pericles, he has found full play for beauty and greatness of behavior, where the circumstances are in harmony with the man. These portraits, though mere sketches, must be valued as attempts in the very highest kind of narrative, which not only has very few examples to exhibit of any success, but very few competitors in the attempt. The word Character is in all mouths; it is a force which we all feel; yet who has analyzed it? What is the nature of that subtle, and majestic principle which attaches us to a few persons, not so much by personal as by the most spiritual ties? What is the quality of the persons who, without being public men, or literary men, or rich men, or active men, or (in the popular sense) religious men, have a certain salutary omnipresence in all our life's history, almost giving their own quality to the atmosphere and the landscape? A moral force, yet wholly unmindful of creed and catechism, intellectual, but scornful of books, it works directly and without means, and though it may be resisted at any time, yet resistance to it is a suicide. For the person who stands in this lofty relation to his fellow men is always the impersonation to them of their conscience. It is a sufficient proof of the extreme delicacy of this element, evanescing before any but the most sympathetic vision, that it has so seldom been employed in the drama and in novels. Mr. Landor, almost alone among living English writers, has indicated his perception of it.

These merits make Mr. Landor's position in the republic of letters one of great mark and dignity. He exercises with a grandeur of spirit the office of writer, and carries it with an air of old and unquestionable nobility. We do not recollect an example of more complete independence in literary history. He has no clanship, no friendships, that warp him. He was one of the first to pronounce Wordsworth the great poet of the age, yet he discriminates his faults with the greater freedom. He loves Pindar, Æschylus, Euripides, Aristophanes,

Demosthenes, Virgil, yet with open eyes. His position is by no means the highest in literature; he is not a poet or a philosopher. He is a man full of thoughts, but not, like Coleridge, a man of ideas. Only from a mind conversant with the First Philosophy can definitions be expected. Coleridge has contributed many valuable ones to modern literature. Mr. Landor's definitions are only enumerations of particulars; the generic law is not seized. But as it is not from the highest Alps or Andes, but from less elevated summits, that the most attractive landscape is commanded, so is Mr. Landor the most useful and agreeable of critics. He has commented on a wide variety of writers, with a closeness and an extent of view, which has enhanced the value of those authors to his readers. His Dialogue on the Epicurean philosophy is a theory of the genius of Epicurus. The Dialogue between Barrow and Newton is the best of all criticisms on the Essays of Bacon. His picture of Demosthenes in three several Dialogues is new and adequate. He has illustrated the genius of Homer, Æschylus, Pindar, Euripides, Thucydides. Then he has examined before he expatiated, and the minuteness of his verbal criticism gives a confidence in his fidelity, when he speaks the language of meditation or of passion. His acquaintance with the English tongue is unsurpassed. He "hates false words, and seeks with care, difficulty, and moroseness, those that fit the thing." He knows the value of his own words. "They are not," he says, " written on slate." He never stoops to explanation, nor uses seven words where one will do. He is a master of condensation and suppression, and that in no vulgar way. He knows the wide difference between compression and an obscure elliptical style. The dense writer has yet ample room and choice of phrase, and even a gamesome mood often between his valid words. There is no inadequacy or disagreeable contraction in his sentence, any more than in a human face, where in a square space of a few inches is found room for every possible variety of expression.

Yet it is not as an artist, that Mr. Landor commends himself to us. He is not epic or dramatic, he has not the high, overpowering method, by which the master gives unity and integrity to a work of many parts. He is too wilful, and never abandons himself to his genius. His books are a strange mixture of politics, etymology, allegory, sentiment, and personal history, and what skill of transition he may possess is superficial, not spiritual. His merit must rest at last, not on the spirit of the dialogue, or the symmetry of any of his historical portraits, but on the value of his sentences. Many of these will secure their own immortality in English literature; and this, rightly considered, is no mean merit. These are not plants and animals, but the genetical atoms, of which both are composed. All our great debt to the oriental world is of this kind, not utensils and statues of the precious metal, but bullion and gold dust. Of many of Mr. Landor's sentences we are fain to remember what was said of those of Socrates, that they are cubes, which will stand firm, place them how or where you will.

We will enrich our pages with a few paragraphs, which we hastily select from such of Mr. Landor's volumes as lie on our table.

———

"The great man is he who hath nothing to fear and nothing to hope from another. It is he, who while he demonstrates the iniquity of the laws, and is able to correct them, obeys them peaceably. It is he who looks on the ambitious, both as weak and fraudulent. It is he who hath no disposition or occasion for any kind of deceit, no reason for being or for appearing different from what he is. It is he who can call together the most select company when it pleases him. . . . . Him I would call the powerful man who controls the storms of his mind, and turns to good account the worst accidents of his fortune. The great man, I was going on to show thee, is somewhat more. He must be able to do this, and he must have that intellect which puts into motion the intellect of others."

"All titulars else must be produced by others; a knight by a knight, a peer by a King, while a gentleman is self-existent."

"Critics talk most about the *visible* in sublimity . . the Jupiter, the Neptune. Magnitude and power are sublime, but in the second degree, managed as they may be. Where the heart is not shaken, the gods thunder and stride in vain. True sublimity is the perfection of the pathetic, which has other sources than pity; generosity, for instance, and self-devotion. When the generous and self-devoted man suffers, there comes Pity; the basis of the sublime is then above the water, and the poet, with or without the gods, can elevate it above the skies. Terror is but the relic of a childish feeling; pity is not given to children. So said he; I know not whether rightly, for the wisest differ on poetry, the knowledge of which, like other most important truths, seems to be reserved for a purer state of sensation and existence."

"O Cyrus, I have observed that the authors of good make men very bad as often as they talk much about them."

"The habit of haranguing is in itself pernicious; I have known even the conscientious and pious, the humane and liberal dried up by it into egoism and vanity, and have watched the mind, growing black and rancid in its own smoke."

GLORY.

"Glory is a light which shines from us on others, not from others on us."

"If thou lovest Glory, thou must trust her truth. She followeth him who doth not turn and gaze after her."

RICHARD I.

"Let me now tell my story . . to confession another time. I sailed along the realms of my family; on the right was England, on the left was France; little else could I discover than sterile eminences and extensive shoals. They fled behind me; so pass away generations; so shift, and sink, and die away affections. In the wide ocean I was little of a monarch; old men guided me, boys instructed me; these taught me the names of my towns and harbors, those showed me the extent of my dominions; one cloud, that dissolved in one hour, half covered them.

"I debark in Sicily. I place my hand upon the throne of Tancred, and fix it. I sail again, and within a day or two I behold, as the sun is setting, the solitary majesty of Crete, mother of a religion, it is said, that lived two thousand years. Onward, and many specks bubble up along the blue Ægean; islands, every one of which, if the songs and stories of the pilots are true, is the monument of a greater man than I am. I leave them afar off . . . . and for whom? O, abbot, to join creatures of less import than the sea-mews on their cliffs; men praying to be heard, and fearing to be understood, ambitious of another's power in the midst of penitence, avaricious of another's wealth under vows of poverty, and jealous of another's glory in the service of their God. Is this Christianity? and is Saladin to be damned if he despises it?"

DEMOSTHENES.

"While I remember what I have been, I never can be less. External power can affect those only who have none intrinsically. I have seen the day, Eubulides, when the most august of cities had but one voice within her walls; and when the stranger, on entering them, stopped at the silence of the gateway, and said, 'Demosthenes is speaking in the assembly of the people.'"

"There are few who form their opinions of greatness from the individual. Ovid says, 'the girl is the least part of herself.' Of himself, certainly, the man is."

"No men are so facetious as those whose minds are somewhat perverted. Truth enjoys good air and clear light, but no playground."

"I found that the principal means (of gratifying the universal desire of happiness) lay in the avoidance of those very things, which had hitherto been taken up as the instruments of enjoyment and content; such as military commands, political offices, clients, adventures in commerce, and extensive landed property."

"Abstinence from low pleasures is the only means of meriting or of obtaining the higher."

"Praise keeps good men good."

"The highest price we can pay for a thing is to ask for it."

"There is a gloom in deep love as in deep water; there is a silence in it which suspends the foot; and the folded arms, and the dejected head are the images it reflects. No voice shakes its surface; the Muses themselves approach it with a tardy and a timid step, and with a low and tremulous and melancholy song."

"Anaxagoras is the true, firm, constant friend of Pericles; the golden lamp that shines perpetually on the image I adore."

[The Letter of Pericles to Aspasia in reply to her request to be permitted to visit Xeniades.]

"Do what your heart tells you; yes, Aspasia, do *all* it tells you. Remember how august it is. It contains the temple, not only of Love, but of Conscience; and a whisper is heard from the extremity of one to the extremity of the other.

"Bend in pensiveness, even in sorrow, on the flowery bank of youth, whereunder runs the stream that passes ir-reversibly! let the garland drop into it, let the hand be re-freshed by it—but—may the beautiful feet of Aspasia stand firm."

E.

The Senses and the Soul

WHAT we know is a point to what we do not know." The first questions are still to be asked. Let any man bestow a thought on himself, how he came hither, and whither he tends, and he will find that all the literature, all the philosophy that is on record, have done little to dull the edge of inquiry. The globe that swims so silently with us through the sea of space, has never a port, but with its little convoy of friendly orbs pursues its voyage through the signs of heaven, to renew its navigation again forever. The wonderful tidings our glasses and calendars give us concerning the hospitable lights that hang around us in the deep, do not appease but inflame our curiosity; and in like manner, our culture does not lead to any goal, but its richest results of thought and action are only new preparation.

Here on the surface of our swimming earth we come out of silence into society already formed, into language, customs, and traditions, ready made, and the multitude of our associates discountenance us from expressing any surprise at the somewhat agreeable novelty of Being, and frown down any intimation on our part of a disposition to assume our own vows, to preserve our independence, and to institute any inquiry into the sweet and sublime vision which surrounds us.

And yet there seems no need that any should fear we should grow too wise. The path of truth has obstacles enough of its own. We dwell on the surface of nature. We dwell amidst surfaces; and surface laps so closely on surface, that we cannot easily pierce to see the interior organism. Then the subtlety of things! Under every cause, another cause. Truth soars too high or dives too deep, for the most resolute inquirer. See of how much we know nothing. See the strange position of man. Our science neither comprehends him as a whole, nor any one of its particulars. See the action and reaction of Will and Necessity. See his passions, and their origin in the deeps of nature and circumstance. See the Fear that rides even the brave. See the omnipresent Hope, whose fountains in our consciousness no metaphysician can find. Consider the phenomenon of Laughter, and explore the elements of the Comic. What do we know of the mystery of Music? and what of Form? why this stroke, this outline should express beauty, and that other not? See the occult region of Demonology, with coincidence, foresight, dreams, and omens. Consider the appearance of Death, the formidable secret of our destiny, looming up as the barrier of nature.

Our ignorance is great enough, and yet the fact most surprising is not our ignorance, but the aversation of men from knowledge. That which, one would say, would unite all minds and join all hands, the ambition to push as far as fate would permit, the planted garden of man on every hand into the kingdom of Night, really fires the heart of few and solitary men. Tell men to study themselves, and for the most part, they find nothing less interesting. Whilst we walk environed before and behind with Will, Fate, Hope, Fear, Love, and Death, these phantoms or angels, whom we catch at but cannot embrace, it is droll to see the contentment and incuriosity of man. All take for granted,—the learned as well as the unlearned,—that a great deal, nay, almost all, is known and forever settled. But in truth all is now to be begun, and every new mind ought to take the attitude of Columbus, launch out from the gaping loiterers on the shore, and sail west for a new world.

This profound ignorance, this deep sleep of the higher faculties of man, coexists with a great abundance of what are called the means of learning, great activity of book-making, and of formal teaching. Go into one of our public libraries, when a new box of books and journals has arrived with the usual importation of the periodical literature of England. The best names of Britain are on the covers. What a mass of literary production for a single week or month! We speculate upon it before we read. We say, what an invention is the press and the journal, by which a hundred pale students, each a hive of distilled flowers of learning, of thought,—each a poet,—each an accomplished man whom the selectest influences have joined to breed and enrich, are made to unite their manifold streams for the information and delight of everybody who can read! How lame is speech, how imperfect the communication of the ancient Harper, wandering from castle to hamlet, to sing to a vagrant audience his melodious thoughts! These unopened books contain the chosen verses of a hundred minstrels, born, living, and singing in distant countries and different languages; for, the intellectual wealth of the world, like its commercial, rolls to London, and through that great heart is hurled again to the extremities. And here, too, is the result, not poetic, of how much thought, how much experience, and how much suffering of wise and cultivated men! How can we in America expect books of our own, whilst this bale of wisdom arrives once or twice in a month at our ports?

In this mind we open the books, and begin to read. We find they are books about books; and then perhaps the book criticized was itself a compilation or digest of others; so that the page we read is at third or fourth hand from the event or sentiment which it describes. Then we find that much the largest proportion of the pages relates exclusively to matter of fact—to the superficial fact, and, as if systematically, shuns any reference to a thought or law which the fact indicated. A large part again, both of the prose and verse, is gleanings from old compositions, and the oft repeated praise of such is repeated in the phrase of the present day. We have even the mortification to find one more deduction still from our anticipated prize, namely, that a large portion of ostentatious criticism is merely a hired advertisement of the great booksellers. In the course of our turning of leaves, we fall at last on an extraordinary passage—a record of thought and virtue, or a clarion strain of poetry, or perchance a traveller makes us acquainted with strange modes of life and some relic of primeval religion, or, rarer yet, a profound sentence is here printed—shines here new but eternal on these linen pages,—we wonder whence it came,—or perhaps trace it instantly home—*aut Erasmus aut Diabolus*—to the only head it could come from.

A few thoughts are all we glean from the best inspection of the paper pile; all the rest is combination and confectionary. A little part abides in our memory, and goes to exalt the sense of duty, and make us happier. For the rest, our heated expectation is chilled and disappointed. Some indirect benefit will no doubt accrue. If we read with braced and active mind, we learn this negative fact, itself a piece of human life. We contrast this mountain of dross with the grains of gold,—we oversee the writer, and learn somewhat of the laws of writing. But a lesson as good we might be learning elsewhere.

Now what is true of a month's or a year's issue of new books, seems to me with a little qualification true of the age. The *stock-writers*, (for the honesty of the literary class has given this population a name,) vastly out-number the thinking men. One man, two men,—possibly, three or four,— have cast behind them the long-descended costume of the academy, and the expectations of fashion, and have said, This world is too fair, this world comes home too near to me than that I should walk a stranger in it, and live at second-hand, fed by other men's doctrines, or treading only in their steps; I feel a higher right herein, and will hearken to the Oracle myself. Such have perceived the extreme poverty of literature, have seen that there was not and could not be help for the fervent soul, except through its own energy. But the great number of those who have voluminously ministered to the popular tastes were men of talents, who had some feat which each could do with words, but who have not added to wisdom or to virtue. Talent amuses; Wisdom instructs. Talent shows me what another man can do; Genius acquaints me with the spacious circuits of the common nature. One is carpentry; the other is growth. To make a step into the world of thought is now given to but few men; to make a second step beyond the first, only one in a country can do; but to carry the thought on to three steps, marks a great teacher. Aladdin's palace with its one unfinished window, which all the gems in the royal treasury cannot finish in the style of the meanest of the profusion of jewelled windows that were built by the Genie in a night, is but too true an image of the efforts of talent to add one verse to the copious text which inspiration writes by one or another scribe from age to age.

It is not that the literary class or those for whom they write, are not lovers of truth, and amenable to principles. All are so. The hunger of men for truth is immense; but they are not erect on their feet; the senses are too strong for the soul. Our senses barbarize us. When the ideal world recedes before the senses, we are on a retrograde march. The savage surrenders to his senses; he is subject to paroxysms of joy and fear;

he is lewd, and a drunkard. The Esquimaux in the exhilaration of the morning sun, when he is invigorated by sleep, will sell his bed. He is the fool of the moment's sensations to the degree of losing sight of the whole amount of his sensations in so many years. And there is an Esquimaux in every man which makes us believe in the permanence of this moment's state of our game more than our own experience will warrant. In the fine day we despise the house. At sea, the passengers always judge from the weather of the present moment of the probable length of the voyage. In a fresh breeze, they are sure of a good run; becalmed, they are equally sure of a long passage. In trade, the momentary state of the markets betrays continually the experienced and long-sighted. In politics, and in our opinion of the prospects of society, we are in like manner the slaves of the hour. Meet one or two malignant declaimers, and we are weary of life, and distrust the permanence of good institutions. A single man in a ragged coat at an election looks revolutionary. But ride in a stage-coach with one or two benevolent persons in good spirits, and the Republic seems to us safe.

It is but an extension of the despotism of sense,—shall I say, only a calculated sensuality,—a little more comprehensive devotion which subjugates the eminent and the reputed wise, and hinders an ideal culture. In the great stakes which the leaders of society esteem not at all fanciful but solid, in the best reputed professions and operations, what is there which will bear the scrutiny of reason? The most active lives have so much routine as to preclude progress almost equally with the most inactive. We defer to the noted merchants whose influence is felt not only in their native cities, but in most parts of the globe; but our respect does them and ourselves great injustice, for their trade is without system, their affairs unfold themselves after no law of the mind; but are bubble built on bubble without end; a work of arithmetic, not of commerce, much less of considerate humanity. They add voyage to voyage, and buy stocks that they may buy stocks, and no ulterior purpose is thought of. When you see their dexterity in particulars, you cannot overestimate the resources of good sense, and when you find how empty they are of all remote aims, you cannot underestimate their philosophy.

The men of letters and the professions we have charged with the like surrender to routine. It is no otherwise with the men of office. Statesmen are solitary. At no time do they form a class. Governments, for the most part, are carried on by political merchants quite without principle, and according to the maxims of trade and huckster; so that what is true of merchants is true of public officers. Why should we suffer ourselves to be cheated by sounding names and fair shows? The titles, the property, the notoriety, the brief consequence of our fellows are only the decoration of the sacrifice, and add to the melancholy of the observer.

"The earth goes on the earth glittering with gold,
The earth goes to the earth sooner than it should,
The earth builds on the earth castles and towers,
The earth says to the earth, all this is ours."

All this is covered up by the speedy succession of the particulars, which tread so close on each other's heel, as to allow no space for the man to question the whole thing. There is somewhat terrific in this mask of routine. Captain Franklin, after six weeks travelling on the ice to the North Pole, found himself two hundred miles south of the spot he had set out from. The ice had floated; and we sometimes start to think we are spelling out the same sentences, saying the same words, repeating the same acts as in former years. Our ice may float also.

This preponderance of the senses can we balance and redress? Can we give permanence to the lightnings of thought which lick up in a moment these combustible mountains of sensation and custom, and reveal the moral order after which the earth is to be rebuilt anew? Grave questions truly, but such as to leave us no option. To know the facts is already a choosing of sides, ranges us on the party of Light and Reason, sounds the signal for the strife, and prophesies an end to the insanity and a restoration of the balance and rectitude of man.

Transcendentalism

T HE MORE liberal thought of intelligent persons acquires
a new name in each period or community; and in ours,
by no very good luck, as it sometimes appears to us, has been
designated as Transcendentalism. We have every day occasion
to remark its perfect identity, under whatever new phraseology or application to new facts, with the liberal thought of
all men of a religious and contemplative habit in other times
and countries. We were lately so much struck with two independent testimonies to this fact, proceeding from persons,
one in sympathy with the Quakers, and the other with the
Calvinistic Church, that we have begged the privilege to tran-
scribe an extract from two private letters, in order that we
might bring them together.

The Calvinist writes to his Correspondent after this manner.

"All the peculiarities of the theology, denominated Trinitarian, are directly or indirectly transcendental. The sinful-
ness of man involves the supposition of a nature in man,
which transcends all limits of animal life and of social mo-
ralities. The reality of spirit, in the highest sense of that holy
word, as the essence of God and the inward ground and
law of man's being and doing, is supposed both in the fact
of sin, and the possibility of redemption of sin. The mystery of the Father revealed only in the Son as the Word of
Life, the Light which illumines every man, outwardly in
the incarnation and offering for sin, inwardly as the Christ
in us, energetic and quickening in the inspirations of the
Holy Spirit,—the great mystery wherein we find redemption, this, like the rest, is transcendental. So throughout, as
might be shown by the same induction suggested in relation to another aspect of the matter. Now here is my point.
Trinitarians, whose whole system from beginning to end is
transcendental, ideal,—an idea is the highest truth,—war
against the very foundations of whatever is transcendental,
ideal; all must be empiric, sensuous, inductive. A system,
which used to create and sustain the most fervid enthusiasm, as is its nature, for it makes God all in all, leads in

crusade against all even the purest and gentlest enthusiasm. It fights for the letter of Orthodoxy, for usage, for custom, for tradition, against the Spirit as it breathes like healing air through the damps and unwholesome swamps, or like strong wind throwing down rotten trees and rotten frameworks of men. It builds up with one hand the Temple of Truth on the outside; and with the other works as in a frenzy to tear up its very foundations. So has it seemed to me. The transcendentalists do not err in excess but in defect, if I understand the case. They do not hold wild dreams for realities; the vision is deeper, broader, more spiritual than they have seen. They do not believe with too strong faith; their faith is too dim of sight, too feeble of grasp, too wanting in certainty. I regret that they should ever seem to undervalue the Scriptures. For those scriptures have flowed out of the same spirit which is in every pure heart; and I would have the one spirit recognise and respond to itself under all the multiform shapes of word, of deed, of faith, of love, of thought, of affection, in which it is enrobed; just as that spirit in us recognises and responds to itself now in the gloom of winter, now in the cheer of summer, now in the bloom of spring, now in the maturity of autumn; and in all the endless varieties of each."

The Friend writes thus.

"Hold fast, I beseech you, to the resolution to wait for light from the Lord. Go not to men for a creed, faint not, but be of good courage. The darkness is only for a season. We must be willing to tarry the Lord's time in the wilderness, if we would enter the Promised Land. The purest saints that I have ever known were long, very long, in darkness and in doubt. Even when they had firm faith, they were long without *feeling* what they *believed in*. One told me he was two years in chaotic darkness, without an inch of firm ground to stand upon, watching for the dayspring from on high, and after this long probation it shone upon his path, and he has walked by its light for years. Do not fear or regret your isolation from men, your difference from all around you. It is often necessary to the enlargement of the soul that it should thus dwell alone for a season, and when the mystical union of God and man shall be completely developed, and you feel yourself newly born a child of light, one of the sons of God, you will also feel new ties to your fellow men; you will love them all in God, and each will be to you whatever their state will permit them to be.

"It is very interesting to me to see, as I do, all around me here, the essential doctrines of the Quakers revived, modified, stript of all that puritanism and sectarianism had heaped upon them, and made the foundation of an intellectual philosophy, that is illuminating the finest minds and reaches the wants of the least cultivated. The more I reflect upon the Quakers, the more I admire the early ones, and am surprised at their being so far in advance of their age, but they have educated the world till it is now able to go beyond those teachers.

"Spiritual growth, which they considered at variance with intellectual culture, is now wedded to it, and man's whole nature is advanced. The intellectual had so lorded it over the moral, that much onesided cultivation was requisite to make things even. I remember when your intellect was all in all, and the growth of the moral sense came after. It has now taken its proper place in your mind, and the intellect appears for a time prostrate, but in due season both will go on harmoniously, and you will be a perfect man. If you suffer more than many before coming into the light, it is because your character is deeper and your happy enlargement will be proportioned to it."

The identity, which the writer of this letter finds between the speculative opinions of serious persons at the present moment, and those entertained by the first Quakers, is indeed so striking as to have drawn a very general attention of late years to the history of that sect. Of course, in proportion to the depth of the experience, will be its independence on time and circumstances, yet one can hardly read George Fox's Journal, or Sewel's History of the Quakers, without many a rising of joyful surprise at the correspondence of facts and expressions to states of thought and feeling, with which we are very familiar. The writer justly remarks the equal adaptation of the philosophy in question "to the finest minds, and to the least cultivated." And so we add in regard to these works, that quite apart from the pleasure of reading modern history in old books, the reader will find another reward in the abundant illustration they furnish to the fact, that wherever the religious enthusiasm makes its appearance, it supplies the place of poetry and philosophy and of learned discipline, and inspires by itself the same vastness of thinking; so that in learning the religious experiences of a strong but untaught mind, you seem to have suggested in turn all the sects of the philosophers.

We seize the occasion to adorn our pages with the dying speech of James Naylor, one of the companions of Fox, who had previously been for eight years a common soldier in the army. Its least service will be to show how far the religious sentiment could exalt the thinking and purify the language of the most uneducated men.

"There is a spirit which I feel," said James Naylor a few hours before his death, "that delights to do no evil, nor to revenge any wrong, but delights to endure all things, in hope to enjoy its own in the end. Its hope is to outlive all wrath and contention, and to weary out all exultation and cruelty, or whatever is of a nature contrary to itself. It sees to the end of all temptations. As it bears no evil in itself, so it conceives none in thought to any other. If it be betrayed, it bears it; for its ground and spring is the mercies and forgiveness of God. Its crown is meekness, its life is everlasting love unfeigned, and it takes its kingdom with entreaty, and keeps it by lowliness of mind. In God alone it can rejoice, though none else regard it, or can own its life. It is conceived in sorrow, and brought forth without any to pity it; nor doth it murmur at grief and oppression. It never rejoiceth but through sufferings; for with the world's joy it is murdered. I found it alone being forsaken. I have fellowship therein with them who lived in dens and desolate places of the earth, who through death obtained this resurrection and eternal holy life."

Prayers

Not with fond shekels of the tested gold,
Nor gems whose rates are either rich or poor,
As fancy values them: but with true prayers,
That shall be up at heaven, and enter there
Ere sunrise; prayers from preserved souls,
From fasting maids, whose minds are dedicate
To nothing temporal.

SHAKSPEARE.

PYTHAGORAS said that the time when men are honestest, is when they present themselves before the gods. If we can overhear the prayer, we shall know the man. But prayers are not made to be overheard, or to be printed, so that we seldom have the prayer otherwise than it can be inferred from the man and his fortunes, which are the answer to the prayer, and always accord with it. Yet there are scattered about in the earth a few records of these devout hours which it would edify us to read, could they be collected in a more catholic spirit than the wretched and repulsive volumes which usurp that name. Let us not have the prayers of one sect, nor of the Christian Church, but of men in all ages and religions, who have prayed well. The prayer of Jesus is, as it deserves, become a form for the human race. Many men have contributed a single expression, a single word to the language of devotion, which is immediately caught and stereotyped in the prayers of their church and nation. Among the remains of Euripides, we have this prayer; "Thou God of all! infuse light into the souls of men, whereby they may be enabled to know what is the root from whence all their evils spring, and by what means they may avoid them." In the Phædrus of Plato, we find this petition in the mouth of Socrates; "O gracious Pan! and ye other gods who preside over this place! grant that I may be beautiful within; and that those external things, which I have, may be such as may best agree with a right internal disposition of mind; and that I may account him to be rich, who is wise and just." Wacic the Caliph, who died A. D. 845, ended his life, the Arabian historians tell us, with these words; "O thou whose kingdom never passes away, pity one whose dignity is so transient." But what led us to these remembrances was the happy accident which in this undevoutage lately brought us acquainted with two or three diaries which attest, if there be need of attestation, the eternity of the sentiment and its equality to itself through all the variety of expression. The first is the prayer of a deaf and dumb boy.

"When my long-attached friend comes to me, I have pleasure to converse with him, and I rejoice to pass my eyes over his countenance; but soon I am weary of spending my time causelessly and unimproved and I desire to leave him, (*but not in rudeness,*) because I wish to be engaged in my business. But thou, O my Father, knowest I always delight to commune with thee in my lone and silent heart; I am never full of thee; I am never weary of thee; I am always desiring thee. I hunger with strong hope and affection for thee, and I thirst for thy grace and spirit.

"When I go to visit my friends, I must put on my best garments, and I must think of my manner to please them. I am tired to stay long, because my mind is not free, and they sometimes talk gossip with me. But, Oh my Father, thou visitest me in my work, and I can lift up my desires to thee, and my heart is cheered and at rest with thy presence, and I am always alone with thee, *and thou dost not steal my time by foolishness.* I always ask in my heart, where can I find thee?"

The next is a voice out of a solitude as strict and sacred as that in which nature had isolated this eloquent mute.

"My Father, when I cannot be cheerful or happy, I can be true and obedient, and I will not forget that joy has been, and may still be. If there is no hour of solitude granted me, still I will commune with thee. If I may not search out and pierce my thought, so much the more may my living praise thee. At whatever price, I must be alone with thee; this must be the demand I make. These *duties* are not the life, but the means which enable us to show forth the life. So must I take up this cross, and bear it willingly. Why should I feel reproved when a busy one enters the room? I am not idle though I sit with folded hands; but instantly I must seek some cover. For that shame I reprove myself. Are they only the valuable members of society who labor to dress and feed it? Shall we never ask the aim of all this hurry and foam, of this aimless activity? Let the purpose for which I live be always before me; let every thought and word go to confirm and illuminate that end; namely, that I must become near and dear to thee; that now I am beyond the reach of all but thee.

"How can we not be reconciled to thy will? I will know the joy of giving to my friend the dearest treasure I have. I know that sorrow comes not at once only. We cannot meet it, and say, now it is overcome, but again, and yet again its flood pours over us, and as full as at first.

"If but this tedious battle could be fought,
    Like Sparta's heroes at one rocky pass,
'One day be spent in dying,' men had sought
    The spot and been cut down like mower's grass."

The next is in a metrical form. It is the aspiration of a different mind, in quite other regions of power and duty, yet they all accord at last.

"Great God, I ask thee for no meaner pelf
    Than that I may not disappoint myself,
That in my action I may soar as high,
    As I can now discern with this clear eye.

And next in value, which they kindness lends,
    That I may greatly disappoint my friends,
Howe'er they think or hope that it may be,
    They may not dream how thou 'st distinguished me.

That my weak hand may equal my firm faith,
    And my life practise more than my tongue saith;
That my low conduct may not show,
    Nor my relenting lines,
That I thy purpose did not know,
    Or overrated thy designs."

The last of the four orisons is written in a singularly calm and healthful spirit, and contains this petition.

"My Father! I now come to thee with a desire to thank thee for the continuance of our love, the one for the other. I feel that without thy love in me, I should be alone here in the flesh. I cannot express my gratitude for what thou hast been and continuest to be to me. But thou knowest what my feelings are. When nought on earth seemeth pleasant to me, thou dost make thyself known to me, and teach me that which is needful for me, and dost cheer my travels on. I know that thou hast not created me and placed me here on earth, amidst its toils and troubles, and the follies of those around me, and told me to be like thyself, when I see so little of thee here to profit by; thou hast not done this, and then left me to myself, a poor, weak man, scarcely able to earn my bread. No; thou art my Father, and I will love thee, for thou didst first love me, and lovest me still. We will ever be parent and child. Wilt thou give me strength to persevere in this great work of redemption. Wilt thou show me the true means of accomplishing it. . . . I thank thee for the knowledge that I have attained of thee by thy sons who have been before me, and especially for him who brought me so perfect a type of thy goodness and love to men. . . . . I know that thou wilt deal with me as I deserve. I place myself therefore in thy hand, knowing that thou wilt keep me from all harm so long as I consent to live under thy protecting care."

Let these few scattered leaves, which a chance, (as men say, but which to us shall be holy,) brought under our eye nearly at the same moment, stand as an example of innumerable similar expressions which no mortal witness has reported, and be a sign of the times. Might they be suggestion to many a heart of yet higher secret experiences which are ineffable! But we must not tie up the rosary on which we have strung these few white beads, without adding a pearl of great price from that book of prayer, the "Confessions of Saint Augustine."

"And being admonished to reflect upon myself, I entered into the very inward parts of my soul, by thy conduct; and

I was able to do it, because now thou wert become my helper. I entered and discerned with the eye of my soul, (such as it was,) even beyond my soul and mind itself the Light unchangeable. Not this vulgar light which all flesh may look upon, nor as it were a greater of the same kind, as though the brightness of this should be manifold greater and with its greatness take up all space. Not such was this light, but other, yea, far other from all these. Neither was it so above my understanding, as oil swims above water, or as the heaven is above the earth. But it is above me, because it made me; and I am under it, because I was made by it. He that knows truth or verity, knows what that Light is, and he that knows it knows eternity, and it is known by charity. O eternal Verity! and true Charity! and dear Eternity! thou art my God, to thee do I sigh day and night. Thee when I first knew, thou liftedst me up that I might see there was what I might see, and that I was not yet such as to see. And thou didst beat back my weak sight upon myself, shooting out beams upon me after a vehement manner, and I even trembled between love and horror, and I found myself to be far off, and even in the very region of dissimilitude from thee."

Fourierism and the Socialists

THE INCREASING ZEAL and numbers of the disciples of Fourier, in America and in Europe, entitle them to an attention which their theory and practical projects will justify and reward. In London, a good weekly newspaper (lately changed into a monthly journal) called "The Phalanx," devoted to the social doctrines of Charles Fourier and bearing for its motto, "Association and Colonization," is edited by Hugh Doherty. Mr. Etzler's inventions, as described in the Phalanx, promise to cultivate twenty thousand acres with the aid of four men only and cheap machinery. Thus the laborers are threatened with starvation if they do not organize themselves into corporations, so that machinery may labor *for* instead of working *against* them. It appears that Mr. Young, an Englishman of large property, has purchased the Benedictine Abbey of Citeaux, in the Mont d'Or, in France, with its ample domains, for the purpose of establishing a colony there. We also learn that some members of the sect have bought an estate at Santa Catharina, fifty miles from Rio Janeiro, in a good situation for an agricultural experiment, and one hundred laborers have sailed from Havre to that port, and nineteen hundred more are to follow. On the anniversary of the birthday of Fourier, which occurred in April, public festivals were kept by the Socialists in London, in Paris, and in New York. In the city of New York, the disciples of Fourier have bought a column in the Daily Tribune, Horace Greeley's excellent newspaper, whose daily and weekly circulation exceeds twenty thousand copies, and through that organ are now diffusing their opinions.

We had lately an opportunity of learning something of these Socialists and their theory from the indefatigable apostle of the sect in New York, Albert Brisbane. Mr. Brisbane pushes his doctrine with all the force of memory, talent, honest faith, and importunacy. As we listened to his exposition, it appeared to us the sublime of mechanical philosophy; for the system was the perfection of arrangement and contrivance. The force of arrangement could no farther go. The merit of the plan was that it was a system; that it had not the partiality and hint-and-fragment character of most popular schemes, but was coherent and comprehensive of facts to a wonderful degree. It was not daunted by distance, or magnitude, or remoteness of any sort, but strode about nature with a giant's step, and skipped no fact, but wove its large Ptolemaic web of cycle and epicycle, of phalanx and phalanstery, with laudable assiduity. Mechanics were pushed so far as fairly to meet spiritualism. One could not but be struck with strange coincidences betwixt Fourier and Swedenborg. Genius hitherto has been shamefully misapplied, a mere trifler. It must now set itself to raise the social condition of man, and to redress the disorders of the planet he inhabits. The Desert of Sahara, the Campagna di Roma, the frozen polar circles, which by their pestilential or hot or cold airs poison the temperate regions, accuse man. Society, concert, cooperation, is the secret of the coming Paradise. By reason of the isolation of men at the present day, all work is drudgery. By concert, and the allowing each laborer to choose his own work, it becomes pleasure. "Attractive Industry" would speedily subdue, by adventurous, scientific, and persistent tillage, the pestilential tracts; would equalize temperature; give health to the globe, and cause the earth to yield 'healthy imponderable fluids' to the solar system, as now it yields noxious fluids. The hyæna, the jackal, the gnat, the bug, the flea, were all beneficent parts of the system; the good Fourier knew what those creatures should have been, had not the mould slipped, through the bad state of the atmosphere, caused, no doubt, by these same vicious imponderable fluids. All these shall be redressed by human culture, and the useful goat, and dog, and innocent poetical moth, or the wood-tick to consume decomposing wood, shall take their place. It takes 1680 men to make one Man, complete in all the faculties; that is, to be sure that you have got a good joiner, a good cook, a barber, a poet, a judge, an umbrella-maker, a mayor and aldermen, and so on. Your community should consist of 2000 persons, to prevent accidents of omission; and each community should take up 6000 acres of land. Now fancy the earth planted with fifties and hundreds of these phalanxes side by side,—what tillage, what architecture, what refectories, what dormitories, what reading rooms, what concerts, what lectures, what gardens, what baths! What is not in one, will be in another, and

many will be within easy distance. Then know you and all,
that Constantinople is the natural capital of the globe. There,
in the Golden Horn, will be the Arch-Phalanx established,
there will the Omniarch reside. Aladdin and his magician, or
the beautiful Scheherzarade, can alone in these prosaic times,
before the sight, describe the material splendors collected
there. Poverty shall be abolished; deformity, stupidity, and
crime shall be no more. Genius, grace, art, shall abound, and
it is not to be doubted but that, in the reign of "Attractive
Industry," all men will speak in blank verse.

Certainly we listened with great pleasure to such gay and
magnificent pictures. The ability and earnestness of the advocate and his friends, the comprehensiveness of their theory,
its apparent directness of proceeding to the end they would
secure, the indignation they felt and uttered at all other speculation in the presence of so much social misery, commanded
our attention and respect. It contained so much truth, and
promised in the attempts that shall be made to realize it so
much valuable instruction, that we are engaged to observe
every step of its progress. Yet in spite of the assurances of its
friends, that it was new and widely discriminated from all
other plans for the regeneration of society, we could not exempt it from the criticism which we apply to so many projects
for reform with which the brain of the age teems. Our feeling
was, that Fourier had skipped no fact but one, namely, Life.
He treats man as a plastic thing, something that may be put
up or down, ripened or retarded, moulded, polished, made
into solid, or fluid, or gas, at the will of the leader; or, perhaps, as a vegetable, from which, though now a poor crab, a
very good peach can by manure and exposure be in time produced, but skips the faculty of life, which spawns and scorns
system and system-makers, which eludes all conditions, which
makes or supplants a thousand phalanxes and New-Harmo-
nies with each pulsation. There is an order in which in a
sound mind the faculties always appear, and which, according
to the strength of the individual, they seek to realize in the
surrounding world. The value of Fourier's system is that it is
a statement of such an order externized, or carried outward
into its correspondence in facts. The mistake is, that this particular order and series is to be imposed by force of preaching

and votes on all men, and carried into rigid execution. But what is true and good must not only be begun by life, but must be conducted to its issues by life. Could not the conceiver of this design have also believed that a similar model lay in every mind, and that the method of each associate might be trusted, as well as that of his particular Committee and General Office, No. 200 Broadway? nay, that it would be better to say, let us be lovers and servants of that which is just; and straightway every man becomes a centre of a holy and beneficent republic, which he sees to include all men in its law, like that of Plato, and of Christ. Before such a man the whole world becomes Fourierized or Christized or humanized, and in the obedience to his most private being, he finds himself, according to his presentiment, though against all sensuous probability, acting in strict concert with all others who followed their private light.

Yet in a day of small, sour, and fierce schemes, one is admonished and cheered by a project of such friendly aims, and of such bold and generous proportion; there is an intellectual courage and strength in it, which is superior and commanding: it certifies the presence of so much truth in the theory, and in so far is destined to be fact.

But now, whilst we write these sentences, comes to us a paper from Mr. Brisbane himself. We are glad of the opportunity of letting him speak for himself. He has much more to say than we have hinted, and here has treated a general topic. We have not room for quite all the matter which he has sent us, but persuade ourselves that we have retained every material statement, in spite of the omissions which we find it necessary to make, to contract his paper to so much room as we offered him.

Mr. Brisbane, in a prefatory note to his article, announces himself as an advocate of the Social Laws discovered by CHARLES FOURIER, and intimates that he wishes to connect whatever value attaches to any statement of his, with the work in which he is exclusively engaged, that of Social Reform. He adds the following broad and generous declaration.

"It seems to me that, with the spectacle of the present misery and degradation of the human race before us, all scientific researches and speculations, to be of any real value, should have a bearing upon the means of their social elevation and happiness. The mass of scientific speculations, which are every day offered to the world by men, who are not animated by a deep interest in the elevation of their race, and who exercise their talents merely to build up systems, or to satisfy a spirit of controversy, or personal ambition, are perfectly valueless. What is more futile than barren philosophical speculation, that leads to no great practical results?"

Chardon Street and Bible Conventions

IN THE MONTH of November, 1840, a Convention of Friends of Universal Reform assembled in the Chardon Street Chapel, in Boston, in obedience to a call in the newspapers signed by a few individuals, inviting all persons to a public discussion of the institutions of the Sabbath, the Church and the Ministry. The Convention organized itself by the choice of Edmund Quincy, as Moderator, spent three days in the consideration of the Sabbath, and adjourned to a day in March, of the following year, for the discussion of the second topic. In March, accordingly, a three-days' session was holden, in the same place, on the subject of the Church, and a third meeting fixed for the following November, which was accordingly holden, and the Convention, debated, for three days again, the remaining subject of the Priesthood. This Convention never printed any report of its deliberations, nor pretended to arrive at any *Result*, by the expression of its sense in formal resolutions,—the professed object of those persons who felt the greatest interest in its meetings being simply the elucidation of truth through free discussion. The daily newspapers reported, at the time, brief sketches of the course of proceedings, and the remarks of the principal speakers. These meetings attracted a good deal of public attention, and were spoken of in different circles in every note of hope, of sympathy, of joy, of alarm, of abhorrence, and of merriment. The composition of the assembly was rich and various. The singularity and latitude of the summons drew together, from all parts of New England, and also from the Middle States, men of every shade of opinion, from the straitest orthodoxy to the wildest heresy, and many persons whose church was a church of one member only. A great variety of dialect and of costume was noticed; a great deal of confusion, eccentricity, and freak appeared, as well as of zeal and enthusiasm. If the assembly was disorderly, it was picturesque. Madmen, madwomen, men with beards, Dunkers, Muggletonians, Come-outers, Groaners, Agrarians, Seventh-day-Baptists, Quakers, Abolitionists, Calvinists, Unitarians, and Philosophers,—all came successively to the top, and seized their moment, if not their *hour*, wherein to chide, or pray, or preach, or protest. The faces were a study. The most daring innovators, and the champions-until-death of the old cause, sat side by side. The still living merit of the oldest New England families, glowing yet, after several generations, encountered the founders of families, fresh merit, emerging, and expanding the brows to a new breadth, and lighting a clownish face with sacred fire. The assembly was characterized by the predominance of a certain plain, sylvan strength and earnestness, whilst many of the most intellectual and cultivated persons attended its councils. Dr. Channing, Edward Taylor, Bronson Alcott, Mr. Garrison, Mr. May, Theodore Parker, H. C. Wright, Dr. Osgood, William Adams, Edward Palmer, Jones Very, Maria W. Chapman, and many other persons of a mystical, or sectarian, or philanthropic renown, were present, and some of them participant. And there was no want of female speakers; Mrs. Little and Mrs. Lucy Sessions took a pleasing and memorable part in the debate, and that flea of Conventions, Mrs. Abigail Folsom, was but too ready with her interminable scroll. If there was not parliamentary order, there was life, and the assurance of that constitutional love for religion and religious liberty, which, in all periods, characterizes the inhabitants of this part of America.

There was a great deal of wearisome speaking in each of those three days' sessions, but relieved by signal passages of pure eloquence, by much vigor of thought, and especially by the exhibition of character, and by the victories of character. These men and women were in search of something better and more satisfying than a vote or a definition, and they found what they sought, or the pledge of it, in the attitude taken by individuals of their number, of resistance to the insane routine of parliamentary usage, in the lofty reliance on principles, and the prophetic dignity and transfiguration which accompanies, even amidst opposition and ridicule, a man whose mind is made up to obey the great inward Commander, and who does not anticipate his own action, but awaits confidently the new emergency for the new counsel. By no means the least value of this Convention, in our eye, was the scope it gave to the genius of Mr. Alcott, and not its least instructive lesson was the gradual but sure ascendency of his spirit, in spite of the incredulity and derision with which he is at first received, and in spite, we might add, of his own failures. Moreover, although no decision was had, and no action taken on all the great points mooted in the discussion, yet the Convention brought together many remarkable persons, face to face, and gave occasion to memorable interviews and conversations, in the hall, in the lobbies, or around the doors.

Before this body broke up in November last, a short adjournment was carried, for the purpose of appointing a Committee to summon a new Convention, to be styled 'the Bible Convention,' for the discussion of the credibility and authority of the Scriptures of the Old and New Testaments. A Committee was agreed upon, and, by their invitation, the new Association met in the Masonic Temple, in Boston, on the 29th of March, of the present year. This meeting was less numerously attended, and did not exhibit at its birth the same vigor as its predecessors. Many persons who had been conspicuous in the former meetings were either out of the country, or hindered from early attendance. Several who wished to be present at its deliberations deferred their journey until the second day, believing that, like the former Convention, it would sit three days. Possibly from the greater unpopularity of its object, out of doors, some faintness or coldness surprised the members. At all events, it was hurried to a conclusion on the first day to the great disappointment of many. Mr. Brownson, Mr. Alcott, Mr. West, and among others a Mormon preacher took part in the conversation. But according to the general testimony of those present, as far as we can collect it, the best speech made on that occasion was that of Nathaniel H. Whiting, of South Marshfield. Mr. Whiting had already distinguished himself in the Chardon Street meetings. Himself a plain unlettered man, leaving for the day a mechanical employment to address his fellows, he possesses eminent gifts for success in assemblies so constituted. He has fluency, self-command, an easy, natural method, and very considerable power of statement. No one had more entirely the ear of this audience, for it is not to be forgotten that, though, as we have said there were scholars and highly intellectual persons in this company, the bulk of the assemblage was made up of

quite other materials, namely, of those whom religion and
solitary thought have educated, and not books or society,—
young farmers and mechanics from the country, whose best
training has been in the Anti-slavery, and Temperance, and
Non-resistance Clubs.

Agriculture of Massachusetts

IN AN AFTERNOON in April, after a long walk, I traversed an orchard where two boys were grafting apple trees, and found the Farmer in his corn field. He was holding the plough, and his son driving the oxen. This man always impresses me with respect, he is so manly, so sweet-tempered, so faithful, so disdainful of all appearances, excellent and reverable in his old weather-worn cap and blue frock bedaubed with the soil of the field, so honest withal, that he always needs to be watched lest he should cheat himself. I still remember with some shame, that in some dealing we had together a long time ago, I found that he had been looking to my interest in the affair, and I had been looking to my interest, and nobody had looked to his part. As I drew near this brave laborer in the midst of his own acres, I could not help feeling for him the highest respect. Here is the Cæsar, the Alexander of the soil, conquering and to conquer, after how many and many a hard-fought summer's day and winter's day, not like Napoleon hero of sixty battles only, but of six thousand, and out of every one he has come victor; and here he stands, with Atlantic strength and cheer, invincible still. These slight and useless city-limbs of ours will come to shame before this strong soldier, for his have done their own work and ours too. What good this man has, or has had, he has earned. No rich father or father-in-law left him any inheritance of land or money. He borrowed the money with which he bought his farm, and has bred up a large family, given them a good education, and improved his land in every way year by year, and this without prejudice to himself the landlord, for here he is, a man every inch of him, and reminds us of the hero of the Robinhood ballad,

> "Much, the miller's son,
> There was no inch of his body
> But it was worth a groom."

Innocence and justice have written their names on his brow. Toil has not broken his spirit. His laugh rings with the sweetness and hilarity of a child; yet he is a man of a strongly intellectual taste, of much reading, and of an erect good sense and independent spirit which can neither brook usurpation nor falsehood in any shape. I walked up and down, the field, as he ploughed his furrow, and we talked as we walked. Our conversation naturally turned on the season and its new labors. He had been reading the Report of the Agricultural Survey of the Commonwealth, and had found good things in it; but it was easy to see that he felt towards the author much as soldiers do towards the historiographer who follows the camp, more good nature than reverence for the gownsman.

The First Report, he said, is better than the last, as I observe the first sermon of a minister is often his best, for every man has one thing which he specially wishes to say, and that comes out at first. But who is this book written for? Not for farmers; no pains are taken to send it to them; it was by accident that this copy came into my hands for a few days. And it is not for them. They could not afford to follow such advice as is given here; they have sterner teachers; their own business teaches them better. No; this was written for the literary men. But in that case, the State should not be taxed to pay for it. Let us see. The account of the maple sugar,—that is very good and entertaining, and, I suppose, true. The story of the farmer's daughter, whom education had spoiled for everything useful on a farm,—that is good too, and we have much that is like it in Thomas's Almanack. But why this recommendation of stone houses? They are not so cheap, not so dry, and not so fit for us. Our roads are always changing their direction, and after a man has built at great cost a stone house, a new road is opened, and he finds himself a mile or two from the highway. Then our people are not stationary, like those of old countries, but always alert to better themselves, and will remove from town to town as a new market opens, or a better farm is to be had, and do not wish to spend too much on their buildings.

The Commissioner advises the farmers to sell their cattle and their hay in the fall, and buy again in the spring. But we farmers always know what our interest dictates, and do accordingly. We have no choice in this matter; our way is but too plain. Down below, where manure is cheap, and hay dear, they will sell their oxen in November; but for me to sell

my cattle and my produce in the fall, would be to sell my
farm, for I should have no manure to renew a crop in the
spring. And thus Necessity farms it, necessity finds out when
to go to Brighton, and when to feed in the stall, better than
Mr. Colman can tell us.

But especially observe what is said throughout these Reports of the model farms and model farmers. One would
think that Mr. D. and Major S. were the pillars of the Commonwealth. The good Commissioner takes off his hat when
he approaches them, distrusts the value of "his feeble praise,"
and repeats his compliments as often as their names are introduced. And yet, in my opinion, Mr. D. with all his knowledge and present skill, would starve in two years on any one
of fifty poor farms in this neighborhood, on each of which
now a farmer manages to get a good living. Mr. D. inherited
a farm, and spends on it every year from other resources; otherwise his farm had ruined him long since;—and as for the
Major he never got rich by his skill in making land produce,
but by his skill in making men produce. The truth is, a farm
will not make an honest man rich in money. I do not know
of a single instance, in which a man has honestly got rich by
farming alone. It cannot be done. The way in which men who
have farms grow rich, is either by other resources; or by
trade; or by getting their labor for nothing; or by other methods of which I could tell you many sad anecdotes. What does
the Agricultural Surveyor know of all this? What can he
know? He is the victim of the "Reports," that are sent him of
particular farms. He cannot go behind the estimates to know
how the contracts were made, and how the sales were effected. The true men of skill, the poor farmers who by the
sweat of their face, without an inheritance, and without offence to their conscience, have reared a family of valuable citizens and matrons to the state, reduced a stubborn soil to a
good farm, although their buildings are many of them
shabby, are the only right subjects of this Report; yet these
make no figure in it. These should be holden up to imitation,
and their methods detailed; yet their houses are very uninvit-
ing and unconspicuous to State Commissioners. So with
these premiums to Farms, and premiums to Cattle Shows.
The class that I describe, must pay the premium which is

awarded to the rich. Yet the premium obviously ought to be given for the good management of a poor farm.

In this strain the Farmer proceeded, adding many special criticisms. He had a good opinion of the Surveyor, and acquitted him of any blame in the matter, but was incorrigible in his skepticism concerning the benefits conferred by legislatures on the agriculture of Massachusetts. I believe that my friend is a little stiff and inconvertible in his own opinions, and that there is another side to be heard; but so much wisdom seemed to lie under his statement, that it deserved a record.

The Zincali

The Zincali: or an Account of the Gypsies of Spain; with an Original Collection of their Songs and Poetry. By GEORGE BORROW. Two Volumes in one. New York: Wiley & Putnam.

OUR LIST of tribes in America indigenous and imported wants the Gypsies, as the Flora of the western hemisphere wants the race of heaths. But as it is all one to the urchin of six years, whether the fine toys are to be found in his father's house or across the road at his grandfather's, so we have always domesticated the Gypsy in school-boy literature from the English tales and traditions. This reprinted London book is equally sure of being read here as in England, and is a most acceptable gift to the lovers of the wild and wonderful. There are twenty or thirty pages in it of fascinating romantic attraction, and the whole book, though somewhat rudely and miscellaneously put together, is animated, and tells us what we wish to know. Mr. Borrow visited the Gypsies in Spain and elsewhere, as an agent of the British and Foreign Bible Society, and seems to have been commended to this employment by the rare accomplishment of a good acquaintance with the language of this singular people. How he acquired his knowledge of their speech, which seems to have opened their hearts to him, he does not inform us; and he appears to have prospered very indifferently in the religious objects of his mission; but to have really had that in his nature or education which gave him access to the gypsy gang, so that he has seen them, talked confidentially with them, and brought away something distinct enough from them.

He has given us sketches of their past and present manner of life and employments, in the different European states, collected a strange little magazine of their poetry, and added a vocabulary of their language. He has interspersed some anecdotes of life and manners, which are told with great spirit.

This book is very entertaining, and yet, out of mere love and respect to human nature, we must add that this account of the Gypsy race must be imperfect and very partial, and that the author never sees his object quite near enough. For, on the whole, the impression made by the book is dismal; the poverty, the employments, conversations, mutual behavior of the Gypsies, are dismal; the poetry is dismal. Men do not love to be dismal, and always have their own reliefs. If we take Mr. Borrow's story as final, here is a great people subsisting for centuries unmixed with the surrounding population, like a bare and blasted heath in the midst of smiling plenty, yet cherishing their wretchedness, by rigorous usage and tradition, as if they loved it. It is an aristocracy of rags, and suffering, and vice, yet as exclusive as the patricians of wealth and power. We infer that the picture is false; that resources and compensation exist, which are not shown us. If Gypsies are pricked, we believe they will bleed; if wretched, they will jump at the first opportunity of bettering their condition. What unmakes man is essentially incredible. The air may be loaded with fogs or with fetid gases, and continue respirable; but if it be decomposed, it can no longer sustain life. The condition of the Gypsy may be bad enough, tried by the scale of English comfort, and yet appear tolerable and pleasant to the Gypsy, who finds attractions in his out-door way of living, his freedom, and sociability, which the Agent of the Bible Society does not reckon. And we think that a traveler of another way of thinking would not find the Gypsy so void of conscience as Mr. Borrow paints him, as the differences in that particular are universally exaggerated in daily conversation. And lastly, we suspect the walls of separation between the Gypsy and the surrounding population are less firm than we are here given to understand.

Ancient Spanish Ballads

Ancient Spanish Ballads, Historical and Romantic. Translated, with Notes. By J. G. LOCKHART. New York: Wiley & Putnam.

T HE ENTERPRISING publishers, Messrs. Wiley & Putnam, who have reprinted, in a plain but very neat form, Mr. Lockhart's gorgeously illustrated work, have judiciously prefixed to it, by way of introduction, a critique on the book from the Edinburgh Review, and have added at the end of the volume an analytical account, with specimens of the Romance of the Cid, from the Penny Magazine. This is done with the greatest propriety, for the Cid seems to be the proper centre of Spanish legendary poetry. The Iliad, the Nibelungen, the Cid, the Robin Hood Ballads, Frithiof's Saga, (for the last also depends for its merit on its fidelity to the legend,) are five admirable collections of early popular poetry of so many nations; and with whatever difference of form, they possess strong mutual resemblances, chiefly apparent in the spirit which they communicate to the reader, of health, vigor, cheerfulness, and good hope. In this day of reprinting and of restoration, we hope that Southey's Chronicle of the Cid, which is a kind of "Harmony of the Gospels" of the Spanish Romance, may be republished in a volume of convenient size. That is a strong book, and makes lovers and admirers of "My Cid, the Perfect one, who was born in a fortunate hour." Its traits of heroism and bursts of simple emotion, once read, can never be forgotten; "I am not a man to be besieged;" and "God! What a glad man was the Cid on that day," and many the like words still ring in our ears. The Cortes at Toledo, where judgment was given between the Cid and his sons-in-law, is one of the strongest dramatic scenes in literature. Several of the best ballads in Mr. Lockhart's collection recite incidents of the Cid's history. The best ballad in the book is the "Count Alarcos and the Infanta Solisa," which is a meet companion for Chaucer's Griselda. The "Count Garci Perez de Vargas" is one of our favorites; and there is one called the "Bridal of Andalla," which we have long lost all power to read as a poem, since we have heard it sung by a voice so rich, and sweet, and penetrating, as to make the ballad the inalienable property of the singer.

Tecumseh

Tecumseh; a Poem. By GEORGE H. COLTON. New York: Wiley & Putnam.

THIS PLEASING summer-day story is the work of a well read, cultivated writer, with a skillful ear, and an evident admirer of Scott and Campbell. There is a metrical sweetness and calm perception of beauty spread over the poem, which declare that the poet enjoyed his own work; and the smoothness and literary finish of the cantos seem to indicate more years than it appears our author has numbered. Yet the perusal suggested that the author had written this poem in the feeling, that the delight he has experienced from Scott's effective lists of names might be reproduced in America by the enumeration of the sweet and sonorous Indian names of our waters. The success is exactly correspondent. The verses are tuneful, but are secondary; and remind the ear so much of the model, as to show that the noble aboriginal names were not suffered to make their own measures in the poet's ear, but must modulate their wild beauty to a foreign metre. They deserved better at the author's hands. We felt, also, the objection that is apt to lie against poems on new subjects by persons versed in old books, that the costume is exaggerated at the expense of the man. The most Indian thing about the Indian is surely not his moccasins, or his calumet, his wampum, or his stone hatchet, but traits of character and sagacity, skill or passion; which would be intelligible at Paris or at Pekin, and which Scipio or Sidney, Lord Clive or Colonel Crockett would be as likely to exhibit as Osceola and Black Hawk.

Intelligence

EXPLORING EXPEDITION. The United States Corvette Vincennes, Captain Charles Wilkes, the flag ship of the Exploring Expedition, arrived at New York on Friday, June 10th, from a cruise of nearly four years. The Brigs Porpoise and Oregon may shortly be expected. The Expedition has executed every part of the duties confided to it by the Government. A long list of ports, harbors, islands, reefs, and shoals, named in the list, have been visited and examined or surveyed. The positions assigned on the charts to several vigias, reefs, shoals, and islands, have been carefully looked for, run over, and found to have no existence in or near the places assigned them. Several of the principal groups and islands in the Pacific Ocean have been visited, examined, and surveyed; and friendly intercourse, and protective commercial regulations, established with the chiefs and natives. The discoveries in the Antarctic Ocean (Antarctic continent,—Observations for fixing the Southern Magnetic pole, &c.) *preceded* those of the French and English expeditions. The Expedition, during its absence, has also examined and surveyed a large portion of the Oregon Territory, a part of Upper California, including the Columbia and Sacramento Rivers, with their various tributaries. Several exploring parties from the Squadron have explored, examined, and fixed those portions of the Oregon Territory least known. A map of the Territory, embracing its Rivers, Sounds, Harbors, Coasts, Forts, &c., has been prepared, which will furnish the information relative to our possessions on the Northwest Coast, and the whole of Oregon. Experiments have been made with the pendulum, magnetic apparatus, and various other instruments, on all occasions,— the temperature of the ocean, at various depths ascertained in the different seas traversed, and full meteorological and other observations kept up during the cruise. Charts of all the surveys have been made, with views and sketches of headlands, towns or villages, &c., with descriptions of all that appertains to the localities, productions, language, customs, and manners. At some of the islands, this duty has been attended with much labor, exposure, and risk of life,—the treacherous character of the natives rendering it absolutely necessary that the officers and men should be armed, while on duty, and at all times prepared against their murderous attacks. On several occasions, boats have been absent from the different vessels of the Squadron on surveying duty, (the greater part of which has been performed in boats,) among islands, reefs, &c., for a period of ten, twenty, and thirty days at one time. On one of these occasions, two of the officers were killed at the Fiji group, while defending their boat's crew from an attack by the Natives.

Harvard University. On the subject of the University we cannot help wishing that a change will one day be adopted which will put an end to the foolish bickering between the government and the students, which almost every year breaks out into those uncomfortable fracases which are called 'Rebellions.' Cambridge is so well endowed, and offers such large means of education, that it can easily assume the position of an University, and leave to the numerous younger Colleges the charge of pupils too young to be trusted from home. This is instantly effected by the Faculty's confining itself to the office of Instruction, and omitting to assume the office of Parietal Government. Let the College provide the best teachers in each department, and for a stipulated price receive the pupil to its lecture-rooms and libraries; but in the matter of morals and manners, leave the student to his own conscience, and if he is a bad subject to the ordinary police. This course would have the effect of keeping back pupils from College, a year or two, or, in some cases, of bringing the parents or guardians of the pupil to reside in Cambridge; but it would instantly destroy the root of endless grievances between the student and teacher, put both parties on the best footing,— indispensable one would say, to good teaching,— and relieve the professors of an odious guardianship, always degenerating into espionage, which must naturally indispose men of genius and honorable mind from accepting the professor's chair.

English Reformers

WHILST Mr. Sparks visits England to explore the manuscripts of the Colonial Office, and Dr. Waagen on a mission of Art, Mr. Alcott, whose genius and efforts in the great art of Education have been more appreciated in England than in America, has now been spending some months in that country, with the aim to confer with the most eminent Educators and philanthropists, in the hope to exchange intelligence, and import into this country whatever hints have been struck out there, on the subject of literature and the First Philosophy. The design was worthy, and its first results have already reached us. Mr. Alcott was received with great cordiality of joy and respect by his friends in London, and presently found himself domesticated at an institution, managed on his own methods and called after his name, the School of Mr. Wright at Alcott House, Ham, Surrey. He was introduced to many men of literary and philanthropic distinction, and his arrival was made the occasion of meetings for public conversation on the great ethical questions of the day.

Mr. Alcott's mission, beside making us acquainted with the character and labors of some excellent persons, has loaded our table with a pile of English books, pamphlets, periodicals, flying prospectuses, and advertisements, proceeding from a class very little known in this country, and on many accounts important, the party, namely, who represent Social Reform. Here are Educational Circulars, and Communist Apostles; Alists; Plans for Syncretic Associations, and Pestalozzian Societies, Self-supporting Institutions, Experimental Normal Schools, Hydropathic and Philosophical Associations, Health Unions and Phalansterian Gazettes, Paradises within the reach of all men, Appeals of Man to Woman, and Necessities of Internal Marriage illustrated by Phrenological Diagrams. These papers have many sins to answer for. There is an abundance of superficialness, of pedantry, of inflation, and of want of thought. It seems as if these sanguine schemers rushed to the press with every notion that danced before their brain, and clothed it in the most clumsily compounded and terminated words, for want of time to find the right one. But although these men sometimes use a swollen and vicious diction, yet they write to ends which raise them out of the jurisdiction of ordinary criticism. They speak to the conscience, and have that superiority over the crowd of their contemporaries, which belongs to men who entertain a good hope. Moreover, these pamphlets may well engage the attention of the politician, as straws of no mean significance to show the tendencies of the time.

Mr. Alcott's visit has brought us nearer to a class of Englishmen, with whom we had already some slight but friendly correspondence, who possess points of so much attraction for us, that we shall proceed to give a short account both of what we already knew, and what we have lately learned, concerning them. The central figure in the group is a very remarkable person, who for many years, though living in great retirement, has made himself felt by many of the best and ablest men in England and in Europe, we mean James Pierrepont Greaves, who died at Alcott-House in the month of March of this year. Mr. Greaves was formerly a wealthy merchant in the city of London, but was deprived of his property by French spoliations in Napoleon's time. Quitting business, he travelled and resided for some time in Germany. His leisure was given to books of the deepest character; and in Switzerland he found a brother in Pestalozzi. With him he remained ten years, living abstemiously, almost on biscuit and water; and though they never learned each the other's language, their daily intercourse appears to have been of the deepest and happiest kind. Mr. Greaves there made himself useful in a variety of ways. Pestalozzi declared that Mr. Greaves understood his aim and methods better than any other observer. And he there became acquainted with some eminent persons. Mr. Greaves on his return to England introduced as much as he could of the method and life, whose beautiful and successful operations he had witnessed; and although almost all that he did was misunderstood, or dragged downwards, he has been a chief instrument in the regeneration in the British schools. For a single and unknown individual his influence has been extensive. He set on foot Infant Schools, and was for many years Secretary to the Infant School Society, which office brought him in contact with many parties, and he has

connected himself with almost every effort for human emancipation. In this work he was engaged up to the time of his
death. His long and active career developed his own faculties
and powers in a wonderful manner. At his house, No. 49
Burton Street, London, he was surrounded by men of open
and accomplished minds, and his doors were thrown open
weekly for meetings for the discussion of universal subjects.
In the last years he has resided at Cheltenham, and visited
Stockport for the sake of acquainting himself with the Socialists and their methods.

His active and happy career continued nearly to the seven-
tieth year, with heart and head unimpaired and undaunted,
his eyes and other faculties sound, except his lower limbs,
which suffered from his sedentary occupation of writing. For
nearly thirty-six years he abstained from all fermented drinks,
and all animal food. In the last years he dieted almost wholly
on fruit. The private correspondent, from whose account,
written two years ago, we have derived our sketch, proceeds
in these words. "Through evil reports, revilings, seductions,
and temptations many and severe, the Spirit has not let him
go, but has strongly and securely held him, in a manner not
often witnessed. New consciousness opens to him every day.
His literary abilities would not be by critics entitled to praise,
nor does he speak with what is called eloquence; but as he is
so much the 'lived word,' I have described, there is found a
potency in all he writes and all he says, which belongs not to
beings less devoted to the Spirit. Supplies of money have
come to him as fast, or nearly as fast as required, and at all
events his serenity was never disturbed on this account, unless
when it has happened that, having more than his expenses
required, he has volunteered extraneous expenditures. He has
been, I consider, a great apostle of the Newness to many,
even when neither he nor they knew very clearly what was
going forward. Thus inwardly married, he has remained outwardly a bachelor."

Mr. Greaves is described to us by another correspondent as
being "the soul of his circle, a prophet of whom the world
heard nothing, but who has quickened much of the thought
now current in the most intellectual circles of the kingdom.
He was acquainted with every man of deep character in En-

gland, and many both in Germany and Switzerland; and Strauss, the author of the 'Life of Christ,' was a pupil of Mr. Greaves, when he held conversations in one of the Colleges of Germany, after leaving Pestalozzi. A most remarkable man; nobody remained the same after leaving him. He was the prophet of the deepest affirmative truths, and no man ever sounded his depths. The best of the thought in the London Monthly Magazine was the transcript of his Idea. He read and wrote much, chiefly in the manner of Coleridge, with pen in hand, in the form of notes on the text of his author. But, like Boehmen and Swedenborg, neither his thoughts nor his writings were for the popular mind. His favorites were the chosen illuminated minds of all time, and with them he was familiar. His library is the most select and rare which I have seen, including most of the books which we have sought with so ill success on our side of the water."*

His favorite dogma was the superiority of Being to all knowing and doing. Association on a high basis was his ideal for the present conjuncture. "I hear every one crying out for association," said he; "I join in the cry; but then I say, associate first with the Spirit,—educate for this spirit-association, and far more will follow than we have as yet any idea of. Nothing good can be done without association; but then we must associate with goodness; and this goodness is the spirit-nature, without which all our societarian efforts will be turned to corruption. Education has hitherto been all outward; it must now be inward. The educator must keep in view that which elevates man, and not the visible exterior

*The following notice of Mr. Greaves occurs in Mr. Morgan's "Hampden in the Nineteenth Century." "The gentleman whom he met at the school was Mr. J. P. Greaves, at that time Honorary Secretary to the Infant School Society, and a most active and disinterested promoter of the system. He had resided for three (?) years with Pestalozzi, who set greater value upon right feelings and rectitude of conduct, than upon the acquisition of languages. A collection of highly interesting letters, addressed to this gentleman by Pestalozzi on the subject of education, has been published. Among the numerous advocates for various improvements, there was not one who exceeded him in personal sacrifices to what he esteemed a duty. At the same time he had some peculiar opinions, resembling the German mystical and metaphysical speculations, hard to be understood, and to which few in general are willing to listen, and still fewer to subscribe; but his sincerity, and the kindness of his disposition always secured for him a patient hearing."—Vol. II. p. 22.

world." We have the promise of some extracts from the writings of this great man, which we hope shortly to offer to the readers of this Journal. His friend, Mr. Lane, is engaged in arranging and editing his manuscript remains.

Mr. Heraud, a poet and journalist, chiefly known in this country as the editor for two years of the (London) Monthly Magazine, a disciple, in earlier years, of Coleridge, and by nature and taste contemplative and inclined to a mystical philosophy, was a friend and associate of Mr. Greaves; and for the last years has been more conspicuous than any other writer in that connexion of opinion. The Monthly Magazine, during his editorship, really was conducted in a bolder and more creative spirit than any other British Journal; and though papers on the highest transcendental themes were found in odd vicinity with the lowest class of flash and so-called comic tales, yet a necessity, we suppose, of British taste made these strange bed-fellows acquainted, and Mr. Heraud had done what he could. His papers called "Foreign Aids to Self Intelligence," were of signal merit, especially the papers on Boehmen and Swedenborg. The last is, we think, the very first adequate attempt to do justice to this mystic, by an analysis of his total works; and, though avowedly imperfect, is, as far as it goes, a faithful piece of criticism. We hope that Mr. Heraud, who announces a work in three volumes, called "Foreign Aids to Self Intelligence, designed for an Historical Introduction to the Study of Ontological Science, preparatory to a Critique of Pure Being," as now in preparation for the press, and of which, we understand, the Essays in the Monthly Magazine were a part, will be enabled to fulfil his design. Mr. Heraud is described by his friends as the most amiable of men, and a fluent and popular lecturer on the affirmative philosophy. He has recently intimated a wish to cross the Atlantic, and read in Boston, a course of six lectures on the subject of Christism as distinct from Christianity.

One of the best contributors to Mr. Heraud's Magazine was Mr. J. Westland Marston. The papers marked with his initials are the most eloquent in the book. We have greatly regretted their discontinuance, and have hailed him again in his new appearance as a dramatic author. Mr. Marston is a writer of singular purity of taste, with a heart very open to the moral impulses, and in his settled conviction, like all persons of a high poetic nature, the friend of a universal reform, beginning in education. His thought on that subject is, that "it is only by teachers becoming men of genius, that a nobler position can be secured to them." At the same time he seems to share that disgust, which men of fine taste so quickly entertain in regard to the language and methods of that class with which their theory throws them into correspondence, and to be continually attracted through his taste to the manners and persons of the aristocracy, whose selfishness and frivolity displease and repel him again. Mr. Marston has lately written a Tragedy, called "The Patrician's Daughter," which we have read with great pleasure, barring always the fatal prescription, which in England seems to mislead every fine poet to attempt the drama. It must be the reading of tragedies that fills them with this superstition for the buskin and the pall, and not a sympathy with existing nature and the spirit of the age. The Patrician's Daughter is modern in its plot and characters, perfectly simple in its style; the dialogue is full of spirit, and the story extremely well told. We confess, as we drew out this bright pamphlet from amid the heap of crude declamation on Marriage and Education, on Dietetics and Hydropathy, on Chartism and Socialism, grim tracts on flesh-eating and dram-drinking, we felt the glad refreshment of its sense and melody, and thanked the fine office which speaks to the imagination, and paints with electric pencil a new form,— new forms on the lurid cloud. Although the vengeance of Mordaunt strikes us as overstrained, yet his character, and the growth of his fortunes is very natural, and is familiar to English experience in the Thurlows, Burkes, Foxes, and Cannings. The Lady Mabel is finely drawn. Pity that the catastrophe should be wrought by the deliberate lie of Lady Lydia; for beside that lovers, as they of all men speak the most direct speech, easily pierce the cobwebs of fraud, it is a weak way of making a play, to hinge the crisis on a lie, instead of letting it grow, as in life, out of the faults and conditions of the parties, as, for example, in Goethe's Tasso. On all accounts but one, namely, the lapse of five years between two acts, the play seems to be eminently fit for representation.

Mr. Marston is also the author of two tracts on Poetry and Poetic Culture.

Another member of this circle is Francis Barham, the dramatic poet, author of "The Death of Socrates," a tragedy, and other pieces; also a contributor to the Monthly Magazine. To this gentleman we are under special obligations, as he has sent us, with other pamphlets, a manuscript paper "On American Literature," written with such flowing good will, and with an aim so high, that we must submit some portion of it to our readers.

Intensely sympathizing, as I have ever done, with the great community of truth-seekers, I glory in the rapid progress of that Alistic,* or divine literature, which they develop and cultivate. To me this Alistic literature is so catholic and universal, that it has spread its energies and influences through every age and nation, in brighter or obscurer manifestations. It forms the intellectual patrimony of the universe, delivered down from kindling sire to kindling son, through all nations, peoples, and languages. Like the God from whom it springs, on whom it lives, and to whom it returns, this divine literature is ever young, ever old, ever

---

*In explanation of this term, we quote a few sentences from a printed prospectus issued by Mr. Barham. "*The Alist*; *a Monthly Magazine of Divinity and Universal Literature*. I have adopted the title of 'the Alist, or Divine,' for this periodical, because the extension of Divinity and divine truth is its main object. It appears to me, that by a firm adherence to the το Θειον, or divine principle of things, a Magazine may assume a specific character, far more elevated, catholic, and attractive, than the majority of periodicals attain. This Magazine is therefore specially written for those persons who may, without impropriety, be termed Alists, or Divines; those who endeavor to develop Divinity as the grand primary essence of all existence,—the element which forms the all in all,—the element in which we live, and move, and have our being. Such Alists, (deriving their name from Alah—the Hebrew title of God,) are Divines in the highest sense of the word; for they cultivate Alism, or the Divinity of Divinities, as exhibited in all Scripture and nature, and they extend religious and philanthropical influences through all churches, states, and systems of education. This doctrine of Alism, or the life of God in the soul of man, affords the only prothetic point of union, sufficiently intense and authoritative to unite men in absolute catholicity. In proportion as they cultivate one and the same God in their minds, will their minds necessarily unite and harmonize; but without this is done, permanent harmony is impossible."

present, ever remote. Like heaven's own sunshine, it adorns all it touches, and it touches all. It is a perfect cosmopolite in essence and in action; it has nothing local or limitary in its nature; it participates the character of the soul from which it emanated. It subsists whole in itself, it is its own place, its own time, nor seeks abroad the life it grants at home; aye, it is an eternal now, an eternal present, at once beginning, middle, and end of every past and every future.

It is, I conceive, salutary for us to take this enlarged view of literature. We should seek after literary perfection in this cosmopolite spirit, and embrace it wherever we find it, as a divine gift; for, in the words of Pope,

> "both precepts and example tell
> That nature's masterpiece is writing well."

So was it with the august and prophetic Milton. To him literature was a universal presence. He regarded it as the common delight and glory of gods and men. He felt that its *moral beauty* lived and flourished in the large heart of humanity itself, and could never be monopolized by times or places. Most deeply do I think and feel with Milton, when he utters the following words. "What God may have determined for me, I know not; but this I know, that if ever he instilled an intense love of moral beauty into the breast of any man, he has instilled it into mine. Hence wherever I find a man despising the false estimates of the vulgar, and daring to aspire in sentiment and language and conduct to what the highest wisdom through every age has taught us, as most excellent, to him I unite myself by a kind of necessary attachment. And if I am so influenced by nature, or destiny, that by no exertions or labors of my own I may exalt myself to this summit of worth and honor, yet no power in heaven or earth will hinder me from looking with reverence and affection upon those, who have thoroughly attained this glory, or appeared engaged in the successful pursuit of it."

Mr. Barham proceeds to apply this sentiment as analogous to his own sentiment, in respect to the literatures of other nations, but specially to that of America.

The unity of language unites the literature of Britain and America, in an essential and imperishable marriage, which no Atlantic Ocean can divide. Yes; I as an Englishman say this, and maintain it. United in language, in literature, in interest, and in blood, I regard the English in England and the English in America as one and the same people, the same magnificent brotherhood. The fact is owned in the common names by which they are noted; John and Jonathan, Angles and Yankees, all reëcho the fact.

Mr. Barham proceeds to exhibit the manifold reasons that enjoin union on the two countries, deprecates the divisions that have sometimes suspended the peace, and continues;

Let us rather maintain the generous policy of Milton, and with full acclamation of concord recite his inspiring words;

"Go on both hand in hand, O nations, never to be disunited. Be the praise and the heroic song of all posterity. Merit this, but seek only virtue, not the extension of your limits. For what needs to win a fading triumphal laurel out of the tears of wretched men, but to settle the true worship of God and justice in the commonwealth. Then shall the hardest difficulties smooth themselves out before you, envy shall sink to hell, and craft and malice shall be confounded, whether it be homebred mischief or outlandish cunning. Yea, other nations will then covet to serve you; for lordship and victory are but the pages of justice and virtue. Commit securely to true wisdom the vanquishing and uncaging of craft and subtlety, which are but her two runagates. Join your invincible might to do worthy and godlike deeds, and then he that seeks to break your union, a cleaving curse be his inheritance throughout all generations."

Mr. Barham then proceeds to express his conviction, that the specific character, which the literature of these countries should aim at, is the Alistic or Divine. It is only by an aim so high, that an author can reach any excellence.

"He builds too low who builds beneath the skies."

But our limits forbid any more extracts from this friendly manuscript at present.

Another eminent member of this circle is Mr. Charles Lane, for many years manager of the London Mercantile Price Current; a man of a fine intellectual nature, inspired and hallowed by a profounder faith. Mr. Lane is the author of some pieces marked with his initials, in the Monthly Magazine, and of some remarkable tracts. Those which we have seen are, "The Old, the New-Old, and the New;" "Tone in Speech;" some papers in a Journal of Health; and last and best, a piece called "The Third Dispensation," prefixed by way of preface to an English translation of Mme. Gatti de Gamond's "Phalansterian," a French book of the Fourier School. In this Essay Mr. Lane considers that History has exhibited two dispensations, namely, *first*, the Family Union, or connexion by tribes, which soon appeared to be a disunion or a dispersive principle; *second*, the National Union. Both these, though better than the barbarism which they displaced, are themselves barbarism, in contrast with the *third*, or Universal Union.

"As man is the uniter in all arrangements which stand *below* him, and in which the objects could not unite themselves, so man needs a uniter *above* him, to whom he submits, in the certain incapability of self-union. This uniter, unity, or One, is the premonitor whence exists the premonition Unity, which so recurrently becomes conscious in man. By a neglect of interior submission, man fails of this antecedent, Unity; and as a consequence his attempts at union by exterior mastery have no success." Certain conditions are necessary to this, namely, the external arrangements indispensable *for* the evolution of the Uniting Spirit can alone be provided *by* the Uniting Spirit.

"We seem to be in an endless circle, of which both halves have lost their centre connexion; for it is an operation no less difficult than the junction of two such discs that is requisite to unity. These segments also being in motion, each upon a false centre of its own, the obstacles to union are incalculably multiplied.

"The spiritual or theoretic world in man revolves upon one set of principles, and the practical or actual world upon another. In ideality man recognizes the purest truths, the highest notions of justice; in actuality he departs from all these, and his entire career is confessedly a life of self-falseness and clever injustice. This barren ideality, and this actuality replete with bitter fruits, are the two hemispheres to be united for their mutual completion, and their common central point is the reality antecedent to them both. This point is not to be discovered by the rubbing of these two half globes together, by their curved sides, nor even as a school boy would attempt to unite his severed marble by the flat sides. The circle must be drawn anew from reality as a central point, the new radius embracing equally the new ideality and the new actuality.

"With this newness of love in men there would resplendently shine forth in them a newness of light, and a newness of life, charming the steadiest beholder."—*Introduction*, p. 4.

The remedy, which Mr. Lane proposes for the existing evils, is his "True Harmonic Association." But he more justly confides in "ceasing from doing" than in exhausting efforts at inadequate remedies. "From medicine to medicine is a change from disease to disease; and man must cease from self-activity, ere the spirit can fill him with truth in mind or health in body. The Civilization is become intensely false, and thrusts the human being into false predicaments. The antagonism of business to all that is high and good and generic is hourly declared by the successful, as well as by the failing. The mercantile system, based on individual aggrandizement, draws men from unity; its swelling columns of figures describe, in pounds, shillings, and pence, the degrees of man's departure from love, from wisdom, from power. The idle are as unhappy as the busy. Whether the dread factory-bell, or the foxhunter's horn calls to a pursuit more fatal to man's best interests, is an inquiry which appears more likely to terminate in the cessation of both, than in a preference of either."

Mr. Lane does not confound society with sociableness. "On the contrary, it is when the sympathy with man is the stronger and the truer, that the sympathy with men grows weaker, and the sympathy with their actions weakest."

We must content ourselves with these few sentences from Mr. Lane's book, but we shall shortly hear from him again. This is no man of letters, but a man of ideas. Deep opens below deep in his thought, and for the solution of each new problem he recurs, with new success, to the highest truth, to that which is most generous, most simple, and most powerful; to that which cannot be comprehended, or overseen, or exhausted. His words come to us like the voices of home out of a far country.

With Mr. Lane is associated in the editorship of a monthly tract, called "The Healthian," and in other kindred enterprises, Mr. Henry G. Wright, who is the teacher of the School at Ham Common, near Richmond, and the author of several tracts on moral and social topics.

This school is founded on a faith in the presence of the Divine Spirit in man. The teachers say, "that in their first experiments they found they had to deal with a higher nature than the mere mechanical. They found themselves in contact with an essence indefinably delicate. The great difficulty with relation to the children, with which they were first called to wrestle, was an unwillingness to admit access to their spiritual natures. The teachers felt this keenly. They sought for the cause. They found it in their own hearts. Pure spirit would not, could not hold communion with their corrupted modes. These must be surrendered, and love substituted in lieu of them. The experience was soon made that the primal duty of the educator is entire self-surrender to love. Not partial, not of the individual, but pure, unlimited, universal. It is impossible to speak to natures deeper than those from which you speak. Reason cries to Reason, Love to Love. Hence the personal elevation of the teacher is of supreme importance." Mr. Alcott, who may easily be a little partial to an instructor who has adopted cordially his own methods, writes thus of his friend.

"Mr. Wright is a younger disciple of the same eternal verity, which I have loved and served so long. You have never seen his like, so deep serene, so clear, so true, and so good. His school is a most refreshing and happy place. The children are mostly under twelve years of age, of both sexes; and his art and method of education simple and natural. It seemed like being again in my own school, save that a wiser wisdom directs, and a lovelier love presides over its order and teachings. He is not yet thirty years of age, but he has more genius for education than any man I have seen, and not of children alone, but he possesses the rare art of teaching men and women. What I have dreamed and stammered, and preached, and prayed about so long, is in him clear and definite. It is life, influence, reality. I flatter myself that I shall bring him with me on my return. He cherishes hopes of making our land the place of his experiment on human culture, and of proving to others the worth of the divine idea that now fills and exalts him."

In consequence of Mr. Greaves's persuasion, which seems to be shared by his friends, that the special remedy for the evils of society at the present moment is association; perhaps from a more universal tendency, which has drawn in many of the best minds in this country also to accuse the idealism, which contents itself with the history of the private mind, and to demand of every thinker the warmest dedication to the race, this class of which we speak are obviously inclined to favor the plans of the Socialists. They appear to be in active literary and practical connexion with Mr. Doherty, the intelligent and catholic editor of the London Phalanx, who is described to us as having been a personal friend of Fourier, and himself a man of sanguine temper, but a friend of temperate measures, and willing to carry his points with wise moderation, on one side; and in friendly relations with Robert Owen, "the philanthropist, 'who writes in brick and clay, in gardens and green fields,' who is a believer in the comforts and humanities of life, and would give these in abundance to all men," although they are widely distinguished from this last in their devout spiritualism. Many of the papers on our table contain schemes and hints for a better social organization, especially the plan of what they call "a Concordium, or a Primitive Home, which is about to be commenced by united individuals, who are desirous, under industrial and progressive education, with simplicity in diet, dress, lodging, &c., to retain the means for the harmonic development of their physical, intellectual, and moral natures." The institution is to be in the country, the inmates are to be of both sexes, they are to labor on the land, their drink is to be water, and their food chiefly uncooked by fire, and the habits of the members throughout of the same simplicity. Their unity is to be based on their education in a religious love, which subordinates all persons, and perpetually invokes the presence of the spirit in every transaction. It is through this tendency that these gentlemen have been drawn into fellowship with a humbler, but far larger class of their countrymen, of whom Goodwyn Barmby may stand for the representative.

Mr. Barmby is the editor of a penny magazine, called "The Promethean, or Communitarian Apostle," published monthly, and, as the covers inform us, "the cheapest of all magazines, and the paper the most devoted of any to the cause of the people; consecrated to Pantheism in Religion, and Communism in Politics." Mr. Barmby is a sort of Camille Desmoulins of British Revolution, a radical poet, with too little fear of grammar and rhetoric before his eyes, with as little fear of the Church or the State, writing often with as much fire, though not with as much correctness, as Ebenezer Elliott. He is the author of a poem called "The European Pariah," which will compare favorably with the Corn-law Rhymes. His paper is of great interest, as it details the conventions, the counsels, the measures of Barmby and his friends, for the organization of a new order of things, totally at war with the establishment. Its importance arises from the fact, that it comes obviously from the heart of the people. It is a cry of the miner and weaver for bread, for daylight, and fresh air, for space to exist in, and time to catch their breath and rest themselves in; a demand for political suffrage, and the power to tax as a counterpart to the liability of being taxed; a demand for leisure, for learning, for arts and sciences, for the higher social enjoyments. It is one of a cloud of pamphlets in the same temper and from the same quarter, which show a wholly new state of feeling in the body of the British people. In a time of distress among the manufacturing classes, severe beyond any precedent, when, according to the statements vouched by Lord Brougham in the House of Peers, and Mr. O'Connell and others in the Commons, wages are reduced in some of the manufacturing villages to six pence a week, so that men are forced to sustain themselves and their families at less than a penny a day; when the most revolting expedients are resorted to for food; when families attempt by a recumbent posture to diminish the pangs of hunger; in the midst of this exasperation the voice of the people is temperate and wise beyond all former example. They are intent on personal as well as on national reforms. Jack Cade leaves behind him his bludgeon and torch, and is grown amiable, literary, philosophical, and mystical. He reads Fourier, he reads Shelley, he reads Milton. He goes for temperance, for non-resistance, for education, and for the love-marriage, with the two poets above named; and for association, after the doctrines either of Owen or of Fourier. One of the most remarkable of the tracts before us is "A Plan for the Education and Improvement of the People, addressed to the Working Classes of the United Kingdom; written in Warwick Gaol, by William Lovett, cabinet-maker, and John Collins, tool-maker," which is a calm, intelligent, and earnest plea for a new organization of the people, for the highest social and personal benefits, urging the claims of general education, of the Infant School, the Normal School, and so forth; announcing rights, but with equal emphasis admitting duties. And Mr. Barmby, whilst he attacks with great spirit and great contempt the conventions of society, is a worshipper of love and of beauty, and vindicates the arts. "The apostleship of veritable doctrine," he says, "in the fine arts is a really religious Apostolate, as the fine arts in their perfect manifestation tend to make mankind virtuous and happy."

It will give the reader some precise information of the views of the most devout and intelligent persons in the company we have described, if we add an account of a public conversation which occurred during the last summer. In the (London) Morning Chronicle, of 5 July, we find the following advertisement. "Public Invitation. An open meeting of the friends to human progress will be held to-morrow, July 6, at Mr. Wright's Alcott-House School, Ham Common, near Richmond, Surrey, for the purpose of considering and adopting means for the promotion of the great end, when all who are interested in human destiny are earnestly urged to attend.

The chair taken at Three o'clock and again at Seven, by A. Bronson Alcott, Esq., now on a visit from America. Omnibuses travel to and fro, and the Richmond steam-boat reaches at a convenient hour."

Of this conference a private correspondent has furnished us with the following report.

A very pleasant day to us was Wednesday, the sixth of July. On that day an open meeting was held at Mr. Wright's, Alcott-House School, Ham, Surrey, to define the aims and initiate the means of human culture. There were some sixteen or twenty of us assembled on the lawn at the back of the house. We came from many places; one 150 miles; another a hundred; others from various distances; and our brother Bronson Alcott from Concord, North America. We found it not easy to propose a question sufficiently comprehensive to unfold the whole of the fact with which our bosoms labored. We aimed at nothing less than to speak of the instauration of Spirit and its incarnation in a beautiful form. We had no chairman, and needed none. We came not to dispute, but to hear and to speak. And when a word failed in extent of meaning, we loaded the word with new meaning. The word did not confine our experience, but from our own being we gave significance to the word. Into one body we infused many lives, and it shone as the image of divine or angelic or human thought. For a word is a Proteus that means to a man what the man is. Three papers were successively presented.

Tennyson

Poems. By ALFRED TENNYSON. Two Volumes. Boston: W. D. Ticknor.

TENNYSON is more simply the songster than any poet of our time. With him the delight of musical expression is first, the thought second. It was well observed by one of our companions, that he has described just what we should suppose to be his method of composition in this verse from "The Miller's Daughter."

> "A love-song I had somewhere read,
> An echo from a measured strain,
> Beat time to nothing in my head
> From some odd corner of the brain.
> It haunted me the morning long,
> With weary sameness in the rhymes,
> *The phantom of a silent song,*
> *That went and came a thousand times.*"

So large a proportion of even the good poetry of our time is ever over-ethical or over-passionate, and the stock poetry is so deeply tainted with a sentimental egotism, that this, whose chief merits lay in its melody and picturesque power, was most refreshing. What a relief, after sermonizing and wailing had dulled the sense with such a weight of cold abstraction, to be soothed by this ivory lute!

Not that he wanted nobleness and individuality in his thoughts, or a due sense of the poet's vocation; but he won us to truths, not forced them upon us; as we listened, the cope

> "Of the self-attained futurity
> Was cloven with the million stars which tremble
> O'er the deep mind of dauntless infamy."

And he seemed worthy thus to address his friend,

> "Weak truth a-leaning on her crutch,
> Wan, wasted truth in her utmost need,

> Thy kingly intellect shall feed,
> Until she be an athlete bold."

Unless thus sustained, the luxurious sweetness of his verse must have wearied. Yet it was not of aim or meaning we thought most, but of his exquisite sense for sounds and melodies, as marked by himself in the description of Cleopatra.

> "Her warbling voice, a lyre of widest range,
> Touched by all passion, did fall down and glance
> From tone to tone, and glided through all change
> Of liveliest utterance."

Or in the fine passage in the Vision of Sin, where

> "Then the music touched the gates and died;
> Rose again from where it seemed to fail,
> Stormed in orbs of song, a growing gale;" &c.

Or where the Talking Oak composes its serenade for the pretty Alice; but indeed his descriptions of melody are almost as abundant as his melodies, though the central music of the poet's mind is, he says, as that of the

> "fountain
> Like sheet lightning,
> Ever brightening
> With a low melodious thunder;
> All day and all night it is ever drawn
> From the brain of the purple mountain
> Which stands in the distance yonder:
> It springs on a level of bowery lawn,
> And the mountain draws it from heaven above,
> And it sings a song of undying love."

Next to his music, his delicate, various, gorgeous music, stands his power of picturesque representation. And his, unlike those of most poets, are eye-pictures, not mind-pictures. And yet there is no hard or tame fidelity, but a simplicity and ease at representation (which is quite another thing from reproduction) rarely to be paralleled. How, in the Palace of Art, for instance, they are unrolled slowly and gracefully, as if painted one after another on the same canvass. The touch is calm and masterly, though the result is looked at with a sweet, self-pleasing eye. Who can forget such as this, and of such there are many, painted with as few strokes and with as complete a success?

> "A still salt pool, locked in with bars of sand;
>   Left on the shore; that hears all night
>   The plunging seas draw backward from the land
>   Their moon-led waters white."

Tennyson delights in a garden. Its groups, and walks, and mingled bloom intoxicate him, and us through him. So high is his organization, and so powerfully stimulated by color and perfume, that it heightens all our senses too, and the rose is glorious, not from detecting its ideal beauty, but from a perfection of hue and scent, we never felt before. All the earlier poems are flower-like, and this tendency is so strong in him, that a friend observed, he could not keep up the character of the tree in his Oak of Summer Chase, but made it talk like an "enormous flower." The song,

> "A spirit haunts the year's last hours,"

is not to be surpassed for its picture of the autumnal garden.

The new poems, found in the present edition, show us our friend of ten years since much altered, yet the same. The light he sheds on the world is mellowed and tempered. If the charm he threw around us before was somewhat too sensuous, it is not so now; he is deeply thoughtful; the dignified and graceful man has displaced the Antinous beauty of the youth. His melody is less rich, less intoxicating, but deeper; a sweetness from the soul, sweetness as of the hived honey of fine experiences, replaces the sweetness which captivated the ear only, in many of his earlier verses. His range of subjects was great before, and is now such that he would seem too merely the amateur, but for the success in each, which says that the same fluent and apprehensive nature, which threw itself with such ease into the forms of outward beauty, has now been intent rather on the secrets of the shaping spirit. In 'Locksley Hall,' 'St. Simeon Stylites,' 'Ulysses,' 'Love and Duty,' 'The Two Voices,' are deep tones, that bespeak that acquaintance with realities, of which, in the 'Palace of Art,' he had expressed his need. The keen sense of outward beauty, the ready shaping fancy, had not been suffered to degrade the poet into that basest of beings, an intellectual voluptuary, and a pensive but serene wisdom hallows all his song.

His opinions on subjects, that now divide the world, are stated in two or three of these pieces, with that temperance and candor of thought, now more rare even than usual, and with a simplicity bordering on homeliness of diction, which is peculiarly pleasing, from the sense of plastic power and refined good sense it imparts.

A gentle and gradual style of narration, without prolixity or tameness, is seldom to be found in the degree in which such pieces as 'Dora' and 'Godiva' display it. The grace of the light ballad pieces is as remarkable in its way, as was his grasp and force in 'Oriana,' 'The Lord of Burleigh,' 'Edward Gray,' and 'Lady Clare,' are distinguished for different shades of this light grace, tender, and speaking more to the soul than the sense, like the different hues in the landscape, when the sun is hid in clouds, so gently shaded that they seem but the echoes of themselves.

I know not whether most to admire the bursts of passion in 'Locksley Hall,' the playful sweetness of the 'Talking Oak,' or the mere catching of a cadence in such slight things as

"Break, break, break
On thy cold gray stones, O sea," &c.

Nothing is more uncommon than the lightness of touch, which gives a charm to such little pieces as the 'Skipping Rope.'

We regret much to miss from this edition 'The Mystic,' 'The Deserted House,' and 'Elegiacs,' all favorites for years past, and not to be disparaged in favor of any in the present collection. England, we believe, has not shown a due sense of the merits of this poet, and to us is given the honor of rendering homage more readily to an accurate and elegant intellect, a musical reception of nature, a high tendency in thought, and a talent of singular fineness, flexibility, and scope.

Letter to W. E. Channing

A Letter to Rev. Wm. E. Channing, D. D. By O. A. BROWNSON. Boston: Charles C. Little and James Brown. 1842.

THAT THERE is no knowledge of God possible to man but a subjective knowledge,—no revelation but the development of the individual within himself, and to himself,—are prevalent statements, which Mr. Brownson opposes by a single formula, that *life is relative in its very nature*. God alone is; all creatures live by virtue of what is not themselves, no less than by virtue of what is themselves, the prerogative of man being to do consciously, that is, more or less intelligently. Mr. Brownson carefully discriminates between Essence and Life. Essence, being object to itself, alone has freedom, which is what the old theologians named sovereignty;—a noble word for the thing intended, were it not desecrated in our associations, in being usurped by creatures that are slaves to time and circumstance. But life implies a causative object, as well as causative subject; wherefore *creatures* are only free by Grace of God.

That men should live, with God for predominating object, is the Ideal of Humanity, or the Law of Holiness, in the highest sense; for this object alone can emancipate them from what is below themselves. But a nice discrimination must be made here. The Ideal of Humanity, as used by Mr. Brownson, does not mean the highest idea of himself, which a man can form by induction on himself as an individual; it means God's idea of man, which shines into every man from the beginning; "Enlighteneth every man that cometh into the world," though his darkness comprehendeth it not, until it is "made flesh." It is by virtue of that freedom which is God's alone, and which is the issue of absolute love, that is, "because God so loved the world," he takes up the subject, Jesus, and makes himself objective to him without measure, thereby rendering his life as divine as it is human, though it remains also as human,—strictly speaking,—as it is divine.

To all men's consciousness it is true that God is objective in a degree, or they were not distinctively human. His glory is refracted, as it were, to their eyes, through the universe. But only in a man, to whom he has made himself the imperative object, does he approach men, in all points, in such degree as to make them divine. He is no less free (sovereign) in coming to each man in Christ, than, in the first instance, in making Jesus of Nazareth the Christ. Men are only free inasmuch as they are open to this majestic access, and are able to pray with St. Augustine, "What art thou to me, oh Lord? *Have mercy on me that I may ask.* The house of my soul is too strait for thee to come into; but let it, oh Lord, be enlarged by thee. It is ruinous, but let it be repaired by thee," &c.

The Unitarian Church, as Mr. Brownson thinks, indicates truth, in so far as it insists on the life of Jesus as being that wherein we find grace; but in so far as it does not perceive that this life is something more than a series of good actions, which others may reproduce, it leans on an arm of flesh, and puts an idol in the place of Christ. The Trinitarian Church, he thinks, therefore, has come nearer the truth, by its formulas of doctrine; and especially the Roman Catholic Church, by the Eucharist. The error of both Churches has been to predicate of the being, Jesus, what is only true of his life. The being, Jesus, was a man; his life is God. It is the doctrine of John the Evangelist throughout, that the soul lives by the real presence of Jesus Christ, as literally as the body lives by bread. The unchristianized live only partially, by so much of the word as shines in the darkness which may not hinder it quite. This partial life repeats in all time the prophecies of antiquity, and is another witness to Jesus Christ, "the same yesterday, to-day, and forever."

Mr. Brownson thinks that he has thus discovered a formula of "the faith once delivered to the saints," which goes behind and annihilates the controversy between Unitarians and Trinitarians, and may lead them both to a deeper comprehension and clearer expression of the secret of life.

Literary Intelligence

THE DEATH of Dr. Channing at Bennington in Vermont, on the 2d October, is an event of great note to the whole country. The great loss of the community is mitigated by the new interest which intellectual power always acquires by the death of the possessor. Dr. Channing was a man of so much rectitude, and such power to express his sense of right, that his value to this country, of which he was a kind of public *Conscience*, can hardly be overestimated. Not only his merits, but his limitations also, which made all his virtues and talents intelligible and available for the correction and elevation of society, made our Cato dear, and his loss not to be repaired. His interest in the times, and the fidelity and independence, with which, for so many years, he had exercised that censorship on commercial, political, and literary morals, which was the spontaneous dictate of his character, had earned for him an accumulated capital of veneration, which caused his opinion to be waited for in each emergency, as that of the wisest and most upright of judges. We shall probably soon have an opportunity to give an extended account of his character and genius. In most parts of this country notice has been taken of this event, and in London also. Beside the published discourses of Messrs. Gannett, Hedge, Clarke, Parker, Pierpont, and Bellows, Mr. Bancroft made Dr. Channing's genius the topic of a just tribute in a lecture before the Diffusion Society at the Masonic Temple. We regret that the city has not yet felt the propriety of paying a public honor to the memory of one of the truest and noblest of its citizens.

Augustine's Confessions

Confessions of St. Augustine. Boston: E. P. Peabody.

WE HEARTILY WELCOME this reprint from the recent London edition, which was a revision, by the Oxford divines, of an old English translation. It is a rare addition to our religious library. The great Augustine,—one of the truest, richest, subtlest, eloquentest of authors, comes now in this American dress, to stand on the same shelf with his far-famed disciples, with A-Kempis, Herbert, Taylor, Scougal, and Fenelon. The Confessions have also a high interest as one of the honestest autobiographies ever written. In this view it takes even rank with Montaigne's Essays, with Luther's Table Talk, the Life of John Bunyan, with Rousseau's Confessions, and the Life of Dr. Franklin. In opening the book at random, we have fallen on his reflections on the death of an early friend.

"O madness, which knowest not how to love men like men! I fretted, sighed, wept, was distracted, had neither rest nor counsel. For I bore about a shattered and bleeding soul, impatient of being borne by me, yet where to repose it I found not. All things looked ghastly; yea the very light; whatsoever was not what he was, was revolting and hateful, except groaning and tears. In those alone found I a little refreshment. I fled out of my country; for so should mine eyes look less for him where they were not wont to see him. And thus from Thagaste I came to Carthage. Times lose no time; nor do they roll idly by; through our senses they work strange operations on the mind. Behold, they went and came day by day, and by coming and going introduced into my mind other imaginations and other remembrances; and little by little patched me up again with my old kind of delights unto which that my sorrow gave way. And yet there succeeded not indeed other griefs, yet the causes of other griefs. For whence had that former grief so easily reached my inmost soul but that I had poured out my soul upon the dust in loving one, that must die, as if he would never die. For what restored and refreshed me chiefly, was the solaces of other friends with whom I did love what instead of thee I loved: and this was a great fable and protracted lie, by whose adulterous stimulus our soul, which lay itching in our ears, was defiled. But that fable would not die to me so oft as any of my friends died. There were other things which in them did more take my mind; to talk and jest together; to do kind offices by turns; to read together honied books; to play the fool or be earnest together; to dissent at times without discontent, as a man might with his ownself; and even with the seldomness of those dissentings, to season our more frequent consentings; sometimes to teach, and sometimes learn; long for the absent with impatience, and welcome the coming with joy."

—BOOK 4.

Europe and European Books

THE American Academy, the Historical Society, and Harvard University, would do well to make the Cunard steamers the subject of examination in regard to their literary and ethical influence. These rapid sailers must be arraigned as the conspicuous agents in the immense and increasing intercourse between the old and the new continents. We go to school to Europe. We imbibe an European taste. Our education, so called,—our drilling at college, and our reading since,—has been European, and we write on the English culture and to an English public, in America and in Europe. This powerful star, it is thought, will soon culminate and descend, and the impending reduction of the transatlantic excess of influence on the American education is already a matter of easy and frequent computation. Our eyes will be turned westward, and a new and stronger tone in literature will be the result. The Kentucky stump-oratory, the exploits of Boone and David Crockett, the journals of western pioneers, agriculturalists, and socialists, and the letters of Jack Downing, are genuine growths, which are sought with avidity in Europe, where our European-like books are of no value. It is easy to see that soon the centre of population and property of the English race, which long ago began its travels, and which is still on the eastern shore, will shortly hover midway over the Atlantic main, and then as certainly fall within the American coast, so that the writers of the English tongue shall write to the American and not to the island public, and then will the great Yankee be born.

But at present we have our culture from Europe and Europeans. Let us be content and thankful for these good gifts for a while yet. The collections of art, at Dresden, Paris, Rome, and the British Museum and libraries offer their splendid hospitalities to the American. And beyond this, amid the dense population of that continent, lifts itself ever and anon some eminent head, a prophet to his own people, and their interpreter to the people of other countries. The attraction of these individuals is not to be resisted by theoretic statements. It is true there is always something deceptive, self-deceptive, in our travel. We go to France, to Germany, to see men, and find but what we carry. A man is a man, one as good as another, many doors to one open court, and that open court as entirely accessible from our private door, or through John or Peter, as through Humboldt or Laplace. But we cannot speak to ourselves. We brood on our riches but remain dumb; that makes us unhappy; and we take ship and go man-hunting in order to place ourselves *en rapport*, according to laws of personal magnetism, to acquire speech or expression. Seeing Herschel or Schelling, or Swede or Dane, satisfies the conditions, and we can express ourselves happily.

But Europe has lost weight lately. Our young men go thither in every ship, but not as in the golden days, when the same tour would show the traveler the noble heads of Scott, of Mackintosh, Coleridge, Wordsworth, Goethe, Cuvier, and Humboldt. We remember when arriving in Paris, we crossed the river on a brilliant morning, and at the bookshop of Papinot, in the Rue de Sorbonne, at the gates of the University, purchased for two sous a Programme, which announced that every Monday we might attend the lecture of Dumas on Chemistry at noon; at a half hour later either Villemain or Ampère on French literature; at other hours, Guizot on Modern History; Cousin on the Philosophy of Ancient History; Fauriel on Foreign Literature; Prevost on Geology; Lacroix on the Differential Calculus: Jouffroy on the History of Modern Philosophy; Lacretelle on Ancient History; Desfontaines or Mirbel on Botany.

Hard by, at the Place du Panthéon, Dégérando, Royer Collard, and their colleagues were giving courses on Law, on the law of nations, the Pandects and commercial equity. For two magical sous more, we bought the Programme of the College Royal de France, on which we still read with admiring memory, that every Monday, Silvestre de Sacy lectures on the Persian language; at other hours, Lacroix on the Integral Mathematics; Jouffroy on Greek Philosophy; Biot on Physics; Lerminier on the History of Legislation; Elie de Beaumont on Natural History; Magendie on Medicine; Thénard on Chemistry; Binet on Astronomy; and so on, to the end of the week. On the same wonderful ticket, as if royal munificence had not yet sufficed, we learned that at the Museum of Natural History, at the Garden of Plants, three days in the week, Brongniart would teach Vegetable Physiology, and Gay-Lussac Chemistry, and Flourent Anatomy. With joy we read these splendid news in the Café Procope, and straightway joined the troop of students of all nations, kindreds, and tongues, whom this great institution drew together to listen to the first *savans* of the world without fee or reward. The professors are changed, but the liberal doors still stand open at this hour. This royal liberality, which seems to atone for so many possible abuses of power, could not exist without important consequences to the student on his return home.

The University of Gottingen has sunk from its high place by the loss of its brightest stars. The last was Heeren, whose learning was really useful, and who has made ingenious attempts at the solution of ancient historical problems. Ethiopia, Assyria, Carthage, and the Theban Desert are still revealing secrets, latent for three millenniums, under the powerful night glass of the Teutonic scholars, who make astronomy, geology, chemistry, trade, statistics, medals, tributary to their inquisitions. In the last year also died Sismondi, who by his History of the Italian Republics reminded mankind of the prodigious wealth of life and event, which Time, devouring his children as fast as they are born, is giving to oblivion in Italy, the piazza and forum of History, and for a time made Italian subjects of the middle age popular for poets, and romancers, and by his kindling chronicles of Milan and Lombardy perhaps awoke the great genius of Manzoni. That history is full of events, yet, as Ottilia writes in Goethe's novel, that she never can bring away from history anything but a few anecdotes, so the "Italian Republics" lies in the memory like a confused *melée*, a confused noise of slaughter, and rapine, and garments rolled in blood. The method, if method there be, is so slight and artificial, that it is quite overlaid and lost in the unvaried details of treachery and violence. Hallam's sketches of the same history were greatly more luminous and memorable, partly from the advantage of his design, which compelled him to draw outlines, and not bury the grand lines of destiny in municipal details. Italy furnished in that age no man of genius to its political arena, though many of talent, and this want degrades the history.

We still remember with great pleasure, Mr. Hallam's fine sketch of the external history of the rise and establishment of the Papacy, which Mr. Ranke's voluminous researches, though they have great value for their individual portraits, have not superseded.

It was a brighter day than we have often known in our literary calendar, when within the twelvemonth a single London advertisement announced a new volume of poems by Wordsworth, poems by Tennyson, and a play by Henry Taylor. Wordsworth's nature or character has had all the time it needed, in order to make its mark, and supply the want of talent. We have learned how to read him. We have ceased to expect that which he cannot give. He has the merit of just moral perception, but not that of deft poetic execution. How would Milton curl his lip at such slipshod newspaper style! Many of his poems, as, for example, the Rylstone Doe, might be all improvised. Nothing of Milton, nothing of Marvell, of Herbert, of Dryden, could be. These are such verses as in a just state of culture should be *vers de Société*, such as every gentleman could write, but none would think of printing or of claiming the poet's laurel on their merit. The Pindar, the Shakspeare, the Dante, whilst they have the just and open soul, have also the eye to see the dimmest star that glimmers in the Milky Way, the serratures of every leaf, the test objects of the microscope, and then the tongue to utter the same things in words that engrave them on all the ears of mankind. The poet demands all gifts and not one or two only.

The poet, like the electric rod, must reach from a point nearer to the sky than all surrounding objects down to the earth, and down to the dark wet soil, or neither is of use. The poet must not only converse with pure thought, but he must demonstrate it almost to the senses. His words must be pictures, his verses must be spheres and cubes, to be seen, and smelled and handled. His fable must be a good story, and its meaning must hold as pure truth. In the debates on the Copyright Bill, in the English Parliament, Mr. Sergeant Wakley, the coroner, quoted Wordsworth's poetry in derision, and asked the roaring House of Commons, what that meant, and whether a man should have a public reward for writing such stuff. Homer, Horace, Milton, and Chaucer would defy the coroner. Whilst they have wisdom to the wise, he would see, that to the external, they have external meaning. Coleridge excellently said of poetry, that poetry must first be good sense, as a palace might well be magnificent, but first it must be a house.

Wordsworth is open to ridicule of this kind. And yet Wordsworth, though satisfied if he can suggest to a sympathetic mind his own mood, and though setting a private and exaggerated value on his compositions, though confounding his accidental with the universal consciousness, and taking the public to task for not admiring his poetry,—is really a superior master of the English language, and his poems evince a power of diction that is no more rivalled by his contemporaries, than is his poetic insight. But the capital merit of Wordsworth is, that he has done more for the sanity of this generation than any other writer. Early in life, at a crisis, it is said, in his private affairs, he made his election between assuming and defending some legal rights with the chances of wealth and a position in the world—and the inward promptings of his heavenly genius; he took his part; he accepted the call to be a poet, and sat down, far from cities, with coarse clothing and plain fare to obey the heavenly vision. The choice he had made in his will, manifested itself in every line to be real. We have poets who write the poetry of society, of the patrician and conventional Europe, as Scott and Moore, and others who, like Byron or Bulwer, write the poetry of vice and disease. But Wordsworth threw himself into his place, made no reserves or stipulations; man and writer were not to be divided. He sat at the foot of Helvellyn and on the margin of Winandermere, and took their lustrous mornings and their sublime midnights for his theme, and not Marlow, nor Massinger, not Horace, nor Milton, nor Dante. He once for all forsook the styles, and standards, and modes of thinking of London and Paris, and the books read there, and the aims pursued, and wrote Helvellyn and Winandermere, and the dim spirits which these haunts harbored. There was not the least attempt to reconcile these with the spirit of fashion and selfishness, nor to show with great deference to the superior judgment of dukes and earls, that although London was the home for men of great parts, yet Westmoreland had these consolations for such as fate had condemned to the country life; but with a complete satisfaction, he pitied and rebuked their false lives, and celebrated his own with the religion of a true priest. Hence the antagonism which was immediately felt between his poetry and the spirit of the age, that here not only criticism but conscience and will were parties; the spirit of literature, and the modes of living, and the conventional theories of the conduct of life were called in question on wholly new grounds, not from Platonism, nor from Christianity, but from the lessons which the country muse taught a stout pedestrian climbing a mountain, and in following a river from its parent rill down to the sea. The Cannings and Jeffreys of the capital, the Court Journals and Literary Gazettes were not well pleased, and voted the poet a bore. But that which rose in him so high as to the lips, rose in many others as high as to the heart. What he said, they were prepared to hear and confirm. The influence was in the air, and was wafted up and down into lone and into populous places, resisting the popular taste, modifying opinions which it did not change, and soon came to be felt in poetry, in criticism, in plans of life, and at last in legislation. In this country, it very early found a strong hold, and its effect may be traced on all the poetry both of England and America.

But notwithstanding all Wordsworth's grand merits, it was a great pleasure to know that Alfred Tennyson's two volumes were coming out in the same ship; it was a great pleasure to receive them. The elegance, the wit, and subtlety of this writer, his rich fancy, his power of language, his metrical skill, his independence on any living masters, his peculiar topics, his taste for the costly and gorgeous, discriminate the musky poet of gardens and conservatories of parks and palaces. Perhaps we felt the popular objection that he wants rude truth, he is too fine. In these boudoirs of damask and alabaster, one is farther off from stern nature and human life than in Lallah Rookh and "the Loves of the Angels." Amid swinging censers and perfumed lamps, amidst velvet and glory we long for rain and frost. Otto of roses is good, but wild air is better. A critical friend of ours affirms that the vice, which bereaved modern painters of their power, is the ambition to begin where their fathers ended; to equal the masters in their ex-

quisite finish, instead of in their religious purpose. The painters are not willing to paint ill enough: they will not paint for
their times, agitated by the spirit which agitates their country;
so should their picture picture us and draw all men after
them; but they copy the technics of their predecessors, and
paint for their predecessors' public. It seems as if the same
vice had worked in poetry. Tennyson's compositions are not
so much poems as studies in poetry, or sketches after the
styles of sundry old masters. He is not the husband who
builds the homestead after his own necessity, from foundation stone to chimney-top and turret, but a tasteful bachelor
who collects quaint stair cases and groined ceilings. We have
no right to such superfineness. We must not make our bread
of pure sugar. These delicacies and splendors are then legitimate when they are the excess of substantial and necessary
expenditure. The best songs in English poetry are by that
heavy, hard, pedantic poet, Ben Jonson. Jonson is rude, and
only on rare occasions gay. Tennyson is always fine; but Jonson's beauty is more grateful than Tennyson's. It is a natural
manly grace of a robust workman. Ben's flowers are not in
pots, at a city florist's ranged on a flower stand, but he is a
countryman at a harvest-home, attending his ox-cart from the
fields, loaded with potatoes and apples, with grapes and
plums, with nuts and berries, and stuck with boughs of hemlock and sweet briar, with ferns and pond lilies which the
children have gathered. But let us not quarrel with our benefactors. Perhaps Tennyson is too quaint and elegant. What
then? It is long since we have as good a lyrist; it will be long
before we have his superior. "Godiva" is a noble poem that
will tell the legend a thousand years. The poem of all the
poetry of the present age, for which we predict the longest
term, is "Abou ben Adhem" of Leigh Hunt. Fortune will still
have her part in every victory, and it is strange that one of
the best poems should be written by a man who has hardly
written any other. And "Godiva" is a parable which belongs
to the same gospel. "Locksley Hall" and "the Two Voices" are
meditative poems, which were slowly written to be slowly
read. "The Talking Oak," though a little hurt by its wit and
ingenuity, is beautiful, and the most poetic of the volume.
"Ulysses" belongs to a high class of poetry, destined to be the

highest, and to be more cultivated in the next generation. "Œnone" was a sketch of the same kind. One of the best specimens we have of the class is Wordsworth's "Laodamia," of which no special merit it can possess equals the total merit of having selected such a subject in such a spirit.

Next to the poetry the novels, which come to us in every ship from England, have an importance increased by the immense extension of their circulation through the new cheap press, which sends them to so many willing thousands. So much novel reading ought not to leave the readers quite unaffected, and undoubtedly gives some tinge of romance to the daily life of young merchants and maidens. We have heard it alleged, with some evidence, that the prominence given to intellectual power in Bulwer's romances had proved a main stimulus to mental culture in thousands of young men in England and America. The effect on manners cannot be less sensible, and we can easily believe that the behavior of the ball room, and of the hotel has not failed to draw some addition of dignity and grace from the fair ideals, with which the imagination of a novelist has filled the heads of the most imitative class.

We are not very well versed in these books, yet we have read Mr. Bulwer enough to see that the story is rapid and interesting; he has really seen London society, and does not draw ignorant caricatures. He is not a genius, but his novels are marked with great energy, and with a courage of experiment which in each instance had its degree of success. The story of Zanoni was one of those world-fables which is so agreeable to the human imagination, that it is found in some form in the language of every country, and is always reappearing in literature. Many of the details of this novel preserve a poetic truth. We read Zanoni with pleasure, because magic is natural. It is implied in all superior culture that a complete man would need no auxiliaries to his personal presence. The eye and the word are certainly subtler and stronger weapons than either money or knives. Whoever looked on the hero, would consent to his will, being certified that his aims were universal, not selfish; and he would be obeyed as naturally as the rain and the sunshine are. For this reason, children delight in fairy tales. Nature is described in them as the ser-

vant of man, which they feel ought to be true. But Zanoni
pains us, and the author loses our respect, because he speedily
betrays that he does not see the true limitations of the charm;
because the power with which his hero is armed, is a toy,
inasmuch as the power does not flow from its legitimate
fountains in the mind; is a power for London; a divine power
converted into a burglar's false key or a highwayman's pistol
to rob and kill with.

But Mr. Bulwer's recent stories have given us, who do not
read novels, occasion to think of this department of literature,
supposed to be the natural fruit and expression of the age. We
conceive that the obvious division of modern romance is into
two kinds; first, the novels *of costume* or *of circumstance*, which
is the old style, and vastly the most numerous. In this class, the
hero, without any particular character, is in a very particular circumstance; he is greatly in want of a fortune or of a wife, and
usually of both, and the business of the piece is to provide him
suitably. This is the problem to be solved in thousands of
English romances, including the Porter novels and the more
splendid examples of the Edgeworth and Scott romances.

It is curious how sleepy and foolish we are, that these tales
will so take us. Again and again we have been caught in that
old foolish trap;—then, as before, to feel indignant to have
been duped and dragged after a foolish boy and girl, to see
them at last married and portioned, and the reader instantly
turned out of doors, like a beggar that has followed a gay
procession into a castle. Had one noble thought opening the
chambers of the intellect, one sentiment from the heart of
God been spoken by them, the reader had been made a par-
ticipator of their triumph; he too had been an invited and
eternal guest; but this reward granted them is property, all-
excluding property, a little cake baked for them to eat and for
none other, nay, a preference and cosseting which is rude and
insulting to all but the minion.

Excepting in the stories of Edgeworth and Scott, whose
talent knew how to give to the book a thousand adventitious
graces, the novels of costume are all one, and there is but one
standard English novel, like the one orthodox sermon, which
with slight variation is repeated every Sunday from so many
pulpits.

But the other novel, of which Wilhelm Meister is the best specimen, the novel *of character*, treats the reader with more respect; a castle and a wife are not the indispensable conclusion, but the development of character being the problem, the reader is made a partaker of the whole prosperity. Every thing good in such a story remains with the reader, when the book is closed.

A noble book was Wilhelm Meister. It gave the hint of a cultivated society which we found nowhere else. It was founded on power to do what was necessary, each person finding it an indispensable qualification of membership, that he could do something useful, as in mechanics or agriculture or other indispensable art; then a probity, a justice, was to be its element, symbolized by the insisting that each property should be cleared of privilege, and should pay its full tax to the State. Then, a perception of beauty was the equally indispensable element of the association, by which each was so dignified and all were so dignified; then each was to obey his genius to the length of abandonment. They watched each candidate vigilantly, without his knowing that he was observed, and when he had given proof that he was a faithful man, then all doors, all houses, all relations were open to him; high behavior fraternized with high behavior, without question of heraldry and the only power recognised is the force of character.

The novels of Fashion of D'Israeli, Mrs. Gore, Mr. Ward, belong to the class of novels of costume, because the aim is a purely external success.

Of the tales of fashionable life, by far the most agreeable and the most efficient, was Vivian Grey. Young men were and still are the readers and victims. Byron ruled for a time, but Vivian, with no tithe of Byron's genius, rules longer. One can distinguish at sight the Vivians in all companies. They would quiz their father, and mother, and lover, and friend. They discuss sun and planets, liberty and fate, love and death, over the soup. They never sleep, go nowhere, stay nowhere, eat nothing, and know nobody, but are up to anything, though it were the Genesis of nature, or the last Cataclasm,—Festus-like, Faust-like, Jove-like; and could write an Iliad any rainy morning, if fame were not such a bore. Men, women, though the greatest and fairest, are stupid things; but a rifle, and a mild pleasant gunpowder, a spaniel, and a cheroot, are themes for Olympus. I fear it was in part the influence of such pictures on living society, which made the style of manners, of which we have so many pictures, as for example, in the following account of the English fashionist. "His highest triumph is to appear with the most wooden manners, as little polished as will suffice to avoid castigation, nay, to contrive even his civilities, so that they may appear as near as may be to affronts; instead of a noble high-bred ease, to have the courage to offend against every restraint of decorum, to invert the relation in which our sex stand to women, so that they appear the attacking, and he the passive or defensive party."

We must here check our gossip in mid volley, and adjourn the rest of our critical chapter to a more convenient season.

The Bible in Spain

The Bible in Spain, or the Journeys, Adventures, and Imprisonments of an Englishman in an attempt to circulate the Scriptures in the Peninsula. By GEORGE BORROW. Author of "The Gipsies in Spain."

THIS IS a charming book, full of free breezes, and mountain torrents, and pictures of romantic interest. Mr. Borrow is a self-sufficing man of free nature, his mind is always in the fresh air; he is not unworthy to climb the sierras and rest beneath the cork trees where we have so often enjoyed the company of Don Quixote. And he has the merit, almost miraculous to-day, of leaving us almost always to draw our own inferences from what he gives us. We can wander on in peace, secure against being forced back upon ourselves, or forced sideways to himself. It is as good to read through this book of pictures, as to stay in a house hung with Gobelin tapestry. The Gipsies are introduced here with even more spirit than in his other book. He sketches men and nature with the same bold and clear, though careless touch. Cape Finisterre and the entrance into Gallicia are as good parts as any to look at.

Paracelsus

M R. BROWNING was known to us before, by a little book
called "Pippa Passes," full of bold openings, motley
with talent like this, and rich in touches of personal experience. A version of the thought of the day so much less penetrating than Faust and Festus cannot detain us long; yet we
are pleased to see each man in his kind bearing witness, that
neither sight nor thought will enable to attain that golden
crown which is the reward of life, of profound experiences
and gradual processes, the golden crown of wisdom. The artist nature is painted with great vigor in Aprile. The author
has come nearer that, than to the philosophic nature. There
is music in the love of Festus for his friend, especially in the
last scene, the thought of his taking sides with him against
the divine judgment is true as poesy.

Past and Present*

H ERE is Carlyle's new poem, his Iliad of English woes, to
follow his poem on France, entitled the History of the
French Revolution. In its first aspect it is a political tract, and
since Burke, since Milton, we have had nothing to compare
with it. It grapples honestly with the facts lying before all
men, groups and disposes them with a master's mind, — and
with a heart full of manly tenderness, offers his best counsel
to his brothers. Obviously it is the book of a powerful and
accomplished thinker, who has looked with naked eyes at the
dreadful political signs in England for the last few years, has
conversed much on these topics with such wise men of all
ranks and parties as are drawn to a scholar's house, until such
daily and nightly meditation has grown into a great connexion, if not a system of thoughts, and the topic of English
politics becomes the best vehicle for the expression of his recent thinking, recommended to him by the desire to give
some timely counsels, and to strip the worst mischiefs of their
plausibility. It is a brave and just book, and not a semblance.
"No new truth," say the critics on all sides. Is it so? truth is
very old; but the merit of seers is not to invent, but to dispose
objects in their right places, and he is the commander who is
always in the mount, whose eye not only sees details, but
throws crowds of details into their right arrangement and a
larger and juster totality than any other. The book makes
great approaches to true contemporary history, a very rare
success, and firmly holds up to daylight the absurdities still
tolerated in the English and European system. It is such an
appeal to the conscience and honor of England as cannot be
forgotten, or be feigned to be forgotten. It has the merit
which belongs to every honest book, that it was self-examin-
ing before it was eloquent, and so hits all other men, and, as
the country people say of good preaching, "comes bounce
down into every pew." Every reader shall carry away something. The scholar shall read and write, the farmer and me-

*Past and Present. By THOMAS CARLYLE. Boston: Charles C. Little and
James Brown.

chanic shall toil with new resolution, nor forget the book when they resume their labor.

Though no theocrat, and more than most philosophers a believer in political systems, Mr. Carlyle very fairly finds the calamity of the times not in bad bills of Parliament, nor the remedy in good bills, but the vice in false and superficial aims of the people, and the remedy in honesty and insight. Like every work of genius, its great value is in telling such simple truths. As we recall the topics, we are struck with the force given to the plain truths; the picture of the English nation all sitting enchanted, the poor enchanted so they cannot work, the rich enchanted so that they cannot enjoy, and are rich in vain; the exposure of the progress of fraud into all arts and social activities; the proposition, that the laborer must have a greater share in his earnings; that the principle of permanence shall be admitted into all contracts of mutual service; that the state shall provide at least school-master's education for all the citizens; the exhortation to the workman, that he shall respect the work and not the wages; to the scholar, that he shall be there for light; to the idle, that no man shall sit idle; the picture of Abbot Samson, the true governor, who "is not there to expect reason and nobleness of others, he is there to give them of his own reason and nobleness;" and the assumption throughout the book, that a new chivalry and nobility, namely the dynasty of labor is replacing the old nobilities. These things strike us with a force, which reminds us of the morals of the Oriental or early Greek masters, and of no modern book. Truly in these things there is great reward. It is not by sitting still at a grand distance, and calling the human race *larvæ*, that men are to be helped, nor by helping the depraved after their own foolish fashion, but by doing unweariedly the particular work we were born to do. Let no man think himself absolved because he does a generous action and befriends the poor, but let him see whether he so holds his property that a benefit goes from it to all. A man's diet should be what is simplest and readiest to be had, because it is so private a good. His house should be better, because that is for the use of hundreds, perhaps of thousands, and is the property of the traveler. But his speech is a perpetual and public instrument; let that always side with the race, and yield neither a lie nor a sneer. His manners,—let them be hospitable and civilizing, so that no Phidias or Raphael shall have taught anything better in canvass or stone; and his acts should be representative of the human race, as one who makes them rich in his having and poor in his want.

It requires great courage in a man of letters to handle the contemporary practical questions; not because he then has all men for his rivals, but because of the infinite entanglements of the problem, and the waste of strength in gathering unripe fruits. The task is superhuman; and the poet knows well, that a little time will do more than the most puissant genius. Time stills the loud noise of opinions, sinks the small, raises the great, so that the true emerges without effort and in perfect harmony to all eyes; but the truth of the present hour, except in particulars and single relations, is unattainable. Each man can very well know his own part of duty, if he will; but to bring out the truth for beauty and as literature, surmounts the powers of art. The most elaborate history of to-day will have the oddest dislocated look in the next generation. The historian of to-day is yet three ages off. The poet cannot descend into the turbid present without injury to his rarest gifts. Hence that necessity of isolation which genius has always felt. He must stand on his glass tripod, if he would keep his electricity.

But when the political aspects are so calamitous, that the sympathies of the man overpower the habits of the poet, a higher than literary inspiration may succor him. It is a costly proof of character, that the most renowned scholar of England should take his reputation in his hand, and should descend into the ring, and he has added to his love whatever honor his opinions may forfeit. To atone for this departure from the vows of the scholar and his eternal duties, to this secular charity, we have at least this gain, that here is a message which those to whom it was addressed cannot choose but hear. Though they die, they must listen. It is plain that whether by hope or by fear, or were it only by delight in this panorama of brilliant images, all the great classes of English society must read, even those whose existence it proscribes. Poor Queen Victoria,—poor Sir Robert Peel,—poor Primate and Bishops,—poor Dukes and Lords! there is no help in place or pride, or in looking another way; a grain of wit is more penetrating than the lightning of the night-storm, which no curtains or shutters will keep out. Here is a book which will be read, no thanks to anybody but itself. What pains, what hopes, what vows, shall come of the reading! Here is a book as full of treason as an egg is full of meat, and every lordship and worship and high form and ceremony of English conservatism tossed like a foot-ball into the air, and kept in the air with merciless kicks and rebounds, and yet not a word is punishable by statute. The wit has eluded all official zeal; and yet these dire jokes, these cunning thrusts, this flaming sword of Cherubim waved high in air illuminates the whole horizon, and shows to the eyes of the universe every wound it inflicts. Worst of all for the party attacked, it bereaves them beforehand of all sympathy, by anticipating the plea of poetic and humane conservatism, and impressing the reader with the conviction, that the satirist himself has the truest love for everything old and excellent in English land and institutions, and a genuine respect for the basis of truth in those whom he exposes.

We are at some loss how to state what strikes us as the fault of this remarkable book, for the variety and excellence of the talent displayed in it is pretty sure to leave all special criticism in the wrong. And we may easily fail in expressing the general objection which we feel. It appears to us as a certain disproportion in the picture, caused by the obtrusion of the whims of the painter. In this work, as in his former labors, Mr. Carlyle reminds us of a sick giant. His humors, are expressed with so much force of constitution, that his fancies are more attractive and more credible than the sanity of duller men. But the habitual exaggeration of the tone wearies whilst it stimulates. It is felt to be so much deduction from the universality of the picture. It is not serene sunshine, but everything is seen in lurid stormlights. Every object attitudinizes, to the very mountains and stars almost, under the refractions of this wonderful humorist, and instead of the common earth and sky, we have a Martin's Creation or Judgment Day. A crisis has always arrived which requires a *deus ex machinâ*. One can hardly credit, whilst under the spell of this magician, that the world always had the same bankrupt look, to foregoing ages as to us,—as of a failed world just recollecting its old withered forces to begin again and try and do a little business. It was perhaps inseparable from the attempt to write a book of wit and imagination on English politics that a certain local emphasis and of effect, such as is the vice of preaching, should appear, producing on the reader a feeling of forlornness by the excess of value attributed to circumstances. But the splendor of wit cannot outdazzle the calm daylight, which always shows every individual man in balance with his age, and able to work out his own salvation from all the follies of that, and no such glaring contrasts or severalties in that or this. Each age has its own follies, as its majority is made up of foolish young people; its superstitions appear no superstitions to itself; and if you should ask the contemporary, he would tell you with pride or with regret (according as he was practical or poetic) that it had none. But after a short time, down go its follies and weakness, and the memory of them; its virtues alone remain, and its limitation assumes the poetic form of a beautiful superstition, as the dimness of our sight clothes the objects in the horizon with mist and color. The revelation of Reason is this of the unchangeableness of the fact of humanity under all its subjective aspects, that to the cowering it always cowers, to the daring it opens great avenues. The ancients are only venerable to us, because distance has destroyed what was trivial; as the sun and stars affect us only grandly, because we cannot reach to their smoke and surfaces, and say, Is that all?

And yet the gravity of the times, the manifold and increasing dangers of the English state, may easily excuse some overcoloring of the picture, and we at this distance are not so far removed from any of the specific evils, and are deeply participant in too many, not to share the gloom, and thank the love and the courage of the counsellor. This book is full of humanity, and nothing is more excellent in this, as in all Mr. Carlyle's works, than the attitude of the writer. He has the dignity of a man of letters who knows what belongs to him, and never deviates from his sphere; a continuer of the great line of scholars, and sustains their office in the highest credit and honor. If the good heaven have any word to impart to this unworthy generation, here is one scribe qualified and clothed for its occasion. One excellence he has in an age of Mammon and of criticism, that he never suffers the eye of his wonder to close. Let who will be the dupe of trifles, he cannot keep his eye off from that gracious Infinite which embosoms us. As a literary artist, he has great merits, beginning with the main one, that he never wrote one dull line. How well read, how adroit, what thousand arts in his one art of writing; with his expedient for expressing those unproven opinions, which he entertains but will not endorse, by summoning one of his men of straw from the cell, and the respectable Sauerteig, or Teufelsdrock, or Dryasdust, or Picturesque Traveller says what is put into his mouth and disappears. That morbid temperament has given his rhetoric a somewhat bloated character, a luxury to many imaginative and learned persons, like a showery south wind with its sunbursts and rapid chasing of lights and glooms over the landscape, and yet its offensiveness to multitudes of reluctant lovers makes us often wish some concession were possible on the part of the humorist. Yet it must not be forgotten that in all his fun of castanets, or playing of tunes with a whiplash like some renowned charioteers,—in all this glad and needful vending of his redundant spirits,—he does yet ever and anon, as if catching the glance of one wise man in the crowd, quit his tempestuous key, and lance at him in clear level tone the very word, and then with new glee returns to his game. He is like a lover or an outlaw who wraps up his message in a serenade, which is nonsense to the sentinel, but salvation to the ear for which it is meant. He does not dodge the question, but gives sincerity where it is due.

One word more respecting this remarkable style. We have in literature few specimens of magnificence. Plato is the purple ancient, and Bacon and Milton the moderns of the richest strains. Burke sometimes reaches to that exuberant fulness, though deficient in depth. Carlyle in his strange half mad way, has entered the Field of the Cloth of Gold, and shown a vigor and wealth of resource, which has no rival in the tourney play of these times;—the indubitable champion of England. Carlyle is the first domestication of the modern system with its infinity of details into style. We have been civilizing very fast, building London and Paris, and now planting New

England and India, New Holland and Oregon,—and it has not appeared in literature,—there has been no analogous expansion and recomposition in books. Carlyle's style is the first emergence of all this wealth and labor, with which the world has gone with child so long. London and Europe tunnelled, graded, corn-lawed, with trade-nobility, and east and west Indies for dependencies, and America, with the Rocky Hills in the horizon, have never before been conquered in literature. This is the first invasion and conquest. How like an air-balloon or bird of Jove does he seem to float over the continent, and stooping here and there pounce on a fact as a symbol which was never a symbol before. This is the first experiment; and something of rudeness and haste must be pardoned to so great an achievement. It will be done again and again, sharper, simpler, but fortunate is he who did it first, though never so giant-like and fabulous. This grandiose character pervades his wit and his imagination. We have never had anything in literature so like earthquakes, as the laughter of Carlyle. He "shakes with his mountain mirth." It is like the laughter of the genii in the horizon. These jokes shake down Parliament-house and Windsor Castle, Temple, and Tower, and the future shall echo the dangerous peals. The other particular of magnificence is in his rhymes. Carlyle is a poet who is altogether too burly in his frame and habit to submit to the limits of metre. Yet he is full of rhythm not only in the perpetual melody of his periods, but in the burdens, refrains, and grand returns of his sense and music. Whatever thought or motto has once appeared to him fraught with meaning, becomes an omen to him henceforward, and is sure to return with deeper tones and weightier import, now as promise, now as threat, now as confirmation, in gigantic reverberation, as if the hills, the horizon, and the next ages returned the sound.

Antislavery Poems

Antislavery Poems. By JOHN PIERPONT. Boston: Oliver Johnson. 1843.

THESE POEMS are much the most readable of all the metrical pieces we have met with on the subject; indeed, it is strange how little poetry this old outrage of negro slavery has produced. Cowper's lines in the Task are still the best we have. Mr. Pierpont has a good deal of talent, and writes very spirited verses, full of point. He has no continuous meaning which enables him to write a long and equal poem, but every poem is a series of detached epigrams, some better, some worse. His taste is not always correct, and from the boldest flight he shall suddenly alight in very low places. Neither is the motive of the poem ever very high, so that they seem to be rather squibs than prophecies or imprecations: but for political satire, we think the "Word from a Petitioner" very strong, and the "Gag" the best piece of poetical indignation in America.

Sonnets

Sonnets and other Poems. By WILLIAM LLOYD GARRISON.
Boston. 1843. pp. 96.

MR. GARRISON has won his palms in quite other fields than those of the lyric muse, and he is far more likely to be the subject than the author of good poems. He is rich enough in the earnestness and the success of his character to be patient with the very rapid withering of the poetic garlands he has snatched in passing. Yet though this volume contains little poetry, both the subjects and the sentiments will everywhere command respect. That piece in the volume, which pleased us most, was the address to his first-born child.

America—an Ode

America— an Ode; and other Poems. By N. W. COFFIN. Boston: S. G. SIMPKINS.

OUR Mæcenas shakes his head very doubtfully at this well-printed Ode, and only says, "An ode nowadays needs to be admirable to carry sail at all. Mr. Sprague's Centennial Ode, and Ode at the Shakspeare Jubilee, are the only American lyrics that we have prospered in reading,—if we dare still remember them." Yet he adds mercifully, "The good verses run like golden brooks through the dark forests of toil, rippling and musical, and undermine the heavy banks till they fall in and are borne away. Thirty-five pieces follow the Ode, of which everything is neat, pretty, harmonious, tasteful, the sentiment pleasing, manful, if not inspired. If the poet have nothing else, he has a good ear."

Channing's Poems

Poems by WILLIAM ELLERY CHANNING. Boston. 1843.

WE have already expressed our faith in Mr. Channing's genius, which in some of the finest and rarest traits of the poet is without a rival in this country. This little volume has already become a sign of great hope and encouragement to the lovers of the muse. The refinement and the sincerity of his mind, not less than the originality and delicacy of the diction, are not merits to be suddenly apprehended, but are sure to find a cordial appreciation. Yet we would willingly invite any lover of poetry to read "The Earth-Spirit," "Reverence," "The Lover's Song," "Death," and "The Poet's Hope."

A Letter

As we are very liable in common with the letter-writing world, to fall behindhand in our correspondence, and a little more liable because, in consequence of our editorial function, we receive more epistles than our individual share, we have thought that we might clear our account by writing a quarterly catholic letter to all and several who have honored us in verse, or prose, with their confidence, and expressed a curiosity to know our opinion. We shall be compelled to dispose very rapidly of quite miscellaneous topics.

And first, in regard to the writer who has given us his speculations on Rail-roads and Air-roads, our correspondent shall have his own way. To the rail-way, we must say, like the courageous lord mayor at his first hunting, when told the hare was coming, "Let it come, in Heaven's name, I am not afraid on 't." Very unlooked for political and social effects of the iron road are fast appearing. It will require an expansion of the police of the old world. When a rail-road train shoots through Europe every day from Brussels to Vienna, from Vienna to Constantinople, it cannot stop every twenty or thirty miles, at a German customhouse, for examination of property and passports. But when our correspondent proceeds to Flying-machines, we have no longer the smallest taper light of credible information and experience left, and must speak on *a priori* grounds. Shortly then, we think the population is not yet quite fit for them, and therefore there will be none. Our friend suggests so many inconveniences from piracy out of the high air to orchards and lone houses, and also to other high fliers, and the total inadequacy of the present system of defence, that we have not the heart to break the sleep of the good public by the repetition of these details. When children come into the library, we put the inkstand and the watch on the high shelf, until they be a little older; and nature has set the sun and moon in plain sight and use, but laid them on the high shelf, where her roystering boys may not in some mad Saturday afternoon pull them down or burn their fingers. The sea and the iron road are safer toys for such ungrown people; we are not yet ripe to be birds.

In the next place, to fifteen letters on Communities, and the Prospects of Culture, and the destinies of the cultivated class,—what answer? Excellent reasons have been shown us why the writers, obviously persons of sincerity and of elegance, should be dissatisfied with the life they lead, and with their company. They have exhausted all its benefit, and will not bear it much longer. Excellent reasons they have shown why something better should be tried. They want a friend to whom they can speak and from whom they may hear now and then a reasonable word. They are willing to work, so it be with friends. They do not entertain anything absurd or even difficult. They do not wish to force society into hated reforms, nor to break with society. They do not wish a township, or any large expenditure, or incorporated association, but simply a concentration of chosen people. By the slightest possible concert persevered in through four or five years, they think that a neighborhood might be formed of friends who would provoke each other to the best activity.

They believe that this society would fill up the terrific chasm of ennui, and would give their genius that inspiration which it seems to wait in vain. But 'the selfishness!' One of the writers relentingly says, What shall my uncles and aunts do without me? and desires to be distinctly understood not to propose the Indian mode of giving decrepit relatives as much of the mud of holy Ganges as they can swallow, and more, but to begin the enterprise of concentration, by concentrating all uncles and aunts in one delightful village by themselves!—so heedless is our correspondent of putting all the dough into one pan, and all the leaven into another. Another objection seems to have occurred to a subtle but ardent advocate. Is it, he writes, a too great wilfulness and intermeddling with life,—with life, which is better accepted than calculated? Perhaps so; but let us not be too curiously good; the Buddhist is a practical Necessitarian; the Yankee is not. We do a good many selfish things every day; among them all let us do one thing of enlightened selfishness. It were fit to forbid concert and calculation in this particular, if that were our system, if we were up to the mark of self-denial and faith in our general activity. But to be prudent in all the particulars of life, and in this one thing alone religiously forbearing; prudent to

secure to ourselves an injurious society, temptations to folly
and despair, degrading examples and enemies; and only ab-
stinent when it is proposed to provide ourselves with guides,
examples, lovers!——

We shall hardly trust ourselves to reply to arguments by
which we would too gladly be persuaded. The more discontent, the better we like it. It is not for nothing, we assure
ourselves, that our people are busied with these projects of a
better social state, and that sincere persons of all parties are
demanding somewhat vital and poetic of our stagnant society.
How fantastic and unpresentable soever the theory has hitherto seemed, how swiftly shrinking from the examination of
practical men, let us not lose the warning of that most significant dream. How joyfully we have felt the admonition of
larger natures which despised our aims and pursuits, conscious that a voice out of heaven spoke to us in that scorn.
But it would be unjust not to remind our younger friends
that, whilst this aspiration has always made its mark in the
lives of men of thought, in vigorous individuals it does not
remain a detached object, but is satisfied along with the satisfaction of other aims. To live solitary and unexpressed, is
painful,—painful in proportion to one's consciousness of
we are never quite forsaken by the Divine Providence. The
loneliest man after twenty years discovers that he stood in a
circle of friends, who will then show like a close fraternity
held by some masonic tie. But we are impatient of the tedious introductions of Destiny, and a little faithless, and
would venture something to accelerate them. One thing is
plain, that discontent and the luxury of tears will bring
nothing to pass. Regrets and Bohemian castles and æsthetic
villages are not a very self-helping class of productions, but
are the voices of debility. Especially to one importunate correspondent we must say, that there is no chance for the
æsthetic village. Every one of the villagers has committed
his several blunder; his genius was good, his stars consent-
ing, but he was a marplot. And though the recuperative
force in every man may be relied on infinitely, it must be
relied on, before it will exert itself. As long as he sleeps in
the shade of the present error, the after-nature does not be-

tray its resources. Whilst he dwells in the old sin, he will pay the old fine.

More letters we have on the subject of the position of young men, which accord well enough with what we see and hear. There is an American disease, a paralysis of the active faculties, which falls on young men in this country, as soon as they have finished their college education, which strips them of all manly aims and bereaves them of animal spirits, so that the noblest youths are in a few years converted into pale Caryatides to uphold the temple of conventions. They are in the state of the young Persians, when "that mighty Yezdam prophet" addressed them and said, "Behold the signs of evil days are come; there is now no longer any right course of action, nor any self-devotion left among the Iranis." As soon as they have arrived at this term, there are no employments to satisfy them, they are educated above the work of their times and country, and disdain it. Many of the more acute minds pass into a lofty criticism of these things, which only embitters their sensibility to the evil, and widens the feeling of hostility between them and the citizens at large. From this cause, companies of the best educated young men in the Atlantic states every week take their departure for Europe; for no business that they have in that country, but simply because they shall so be hid from the reproachful eyes of their countrymen, and agreeably entertained for one or two years, with some lurking hope, no doubt, that something may turn up to give them a decided direction. It is easy to see that this is only a postponement of their proper work, with the additional disadvantage of a two years' vacation. Add that this class is rapidly increasing by the infatuation of the active class, who, whilst they regard these young Athenians with suspicion and dislike, educate their own children in the same courses, and use all possible endeavors to secure to them the same result.

Certainly we are not insensible to this calamity, as described by the observers or witnessed by ourselves. It is not quite new and peculiar, though we should not know where to find in literature any record of so much unbalanced intellectuality; such undeniable apprehension without talent, so much power without equal applicability, as our young men pretend to. Yet in Theodore Mundt's* account of Frederic Holderlin's "Hyperion," we were not a little struck with the following Jeremiad of the despair of Germany, whose tone is still so familiar, that we were somewhat mortified to find that it was written in 1799.

"Then came I to the Germans. I cannot conceive of a people more disjoined than the Germans. Mechanics you shall see, but no man; priests, but no man; thinkers, but no man. Is it not like some battlefield, where hands and arms and all members lie scattered about, whilst the life-blood runs away into the sand? Let every man mind his own, you say, and I say the same. Only let him mind it with all his heart, and not with this cold study, literally, hypocritically to appear that which he passes for, but in good earnest, and in all love, let him be that which he is; then there is a soul in his deed. And is he driven into a circumstance where the spirit must not live, let him thrust it from him with scorn, and learn to dig and plough. There is nothing holy which is not desecrated, which is not degraded to a mean end among this people. It is heartrending to see your poet, your artist, and all who still revere genius, who love and foster the Beautiful. The Good! They live in the world as strangers in their own house; they are like the patient Ulysses whilst he sat in the guise of a beggar at his own door, whilst shameless rioters shouted in the hall and ask, who brought the raggamuffin here? Full of love, talent and hope, spring up the darlings of the muse among the Germans; come seven years later, and they flit about like ghosts, cold and silent; they are like a soil which an enemy has sown with poison, that it will not bear a blade of grass. On earth all is imperfect! is the old proverb of the German. Aye, but if one should say to these Godforsaken, that with them all is imperfect, only because they leave nothing pure which they do not pollute, nothing holy which they do not defile with their fumbling hands; that with them nothing prospers; because the godlike nature which is the root of all prosperity, they do not revere; that with them, truly, life is shallow and anxious and full of discord, because they de-

*Geschichte der Literatur der Gegenwart. 1842. p. 86.

spise genius, which brings power and nobleness into manly action, cheerfulness into endurance, and love and brotherhood into towns and houses. Where a people honors genius in its artists, there breathes like an atmosphere a universal soul, to which the shy sensibility opens, which melts self-conceit,—all hearts become pious and great, and it adds fire to heroes. The home of all men is with such a people, and there will the stranger gladly abide. But where the divine nature and the artist is crushed, the sweetness of life is gone, and every other planet is better than the earth. Men deteriorate, folly increases, and a gross mind with it; drunkenness comes with disaster; with the wantonness of the tongue and with the anxiety for a livelihood, the blessing of every year becomes a curse, and all the gods depart."

The steep antagonism between the money-getting and the academic class must be freely admitted, and perhaps is the more violent, that whilst our work is imposed by the soil and the sea, our culture is the tradition of Europe. But we cannot share the desperation of our contemporaries, least of all should we think a preternatural enlargement of the intellect a calamity. A new perception, the smallest new activity given to the perceptive power, is a victory won to the living universe from chaos and old night, and cheaply bought by any amounts of hard-fare and false social position. The balance of mind and body will redress itself fast enough. Superficialness is the real distemper. In all the cases we have ever seen where people were supposed to suffer from too much wit, or as men said, from a blade too sharp for the scabbard, it turned out that they had not wit enough. It may easily happen that we are grown very idle and must go to work, and that the times must be worse before they are better. It is very certain, that speculation is no succedaneum for life. What we would know, we must do. As if any taste or imagination could take the place of fidelity! The old Duty is the old God. And we may come to this by the rudest teaching. A friend of ours went five years ago to Illinois to buy a farm for his son. Though there were crowds of emigrants in the roads, the country was open on both sides, and long intervals between hamlets and houses. Now after five years he has just been to visit the young farmer and see how he prospered, and reports that a miracle has been wrought. From Massachusetts to Illinois, the land is fenced in and builded over, almost like New England itself, and the proofs of thrifty cultivation everywhere abound;—a result not so much owing to the natural increase of population, as to the hard times, which, driving men out of cities and trade, forced them to take off their coats and go to work on the land, which has rewarded them not only with wheat but with habits of labor. Perhaps the adversities of our commerce have not yet been pushed to the wholesomest degree of severity. Apathies and total want of work and reflection on the imaginative character of American life, &c. &c., are like seasickness, which never will obtain any sympathy, if there is a woodpile in the yard, or an unweeded patch in the garden; not to mention the graver absurdity of a youth of noble aims, who can find no field for his energies, whilst the colossal wrongs of the Indian, of the Negro, of the emigrant, remain unmitigated, and the religious, civil, and judicial forms of the country are confessedly effete and offensive. We must refer our clients back to themselves, believing that every man knows in his heart the cure for the disease he so ostentatiously bewails.

As far as our correspondents have entangled their private griefs with the cause of American Literature, we counsel them to disengage themselves as fast as possible. In Cambridge orations, and elsewhere, there is much inquiry for that great absentee American Literature. What can have become of it? The least said is best. A literature is no man's private concern, but a secular and generic result, and is the affair of a power which works by a prodigality of life and force very dismaying to behold,—the race never dying, the individual never spared, and every trait of beauty purchased by hecatombs of private tragedy. The pruning in the wild gardens of nature is never forborne. Many of the best must die of consumption, many of despair, and many be stupid and insane, before the one great and fortunate life, which they each predicted, can shoot up into a thrifty and beneficent existence.

But passing to a letter which is a generous and a just tribute to Bettina von Arnim, we have it in our power to furnish

our correspondent and all sympathizing readers with a
sketch,* though plainly from no very friendly hand, of the
new work of that eminent lady, who in the silence of Tieck
and Schelling, seems to hold a monopoly of genius in Germany.

"At last has the long expected work of the Frau von Arnim
here appeared. It is true her name is not prefixed; more properly is the dedication, *This Book belongs to the King*, also the
title; but partly because her genius shines so unmistakeably
out of every line, partly because this work refers so directly to
her earlier writings, and appears only as an enlargement of
them, none can doubt who the author is. We know not how
we should characterize to the reader this most original work.
Bettina, or we should say, the Frau von Arnim, exhibits her
eccentric wisdom under the person of Goethe's Mother, the
Frau Rath, whilst she herself is still a child, who, (1807) sits
upon 'the shawl' at the foot of the Frau Rath, and listens
devoutly to the gifted mother of the great poet. Moreover,
Bettina does not conceal that she solely, or at any rate prin-
cipally, propounds *her* views from the Frau Rath. And in fact,
it could not be otherwise, since we come to hear the newest
philosophical wisdom which makes a strange enough figure
in the mouth of Goethe's mother. If we mistake not, the intimate intercourse with Bruno Bauer is also an essential impulse for Frau von Arnim, and we must not therefore wonder
if the Frau Rath loses her way in pure philosophical hypotheses, wherein she avails herself of the known phrases of
the school. It is true, she quickly recovers herself again,
clothes her perceptions in poetical garb, mounts bravely to
the boldest visions, or, (and this oftenest happens,) becomes
a humorist, spices her discourses in Frankfort dialect by idiomatic expressions, and hits off in her merriest humors capital
sketches. For the most part, the whole humoristic dress seems
only assumed in order to make the matter, which is in the last
degree radical, less injurious. As to the object of these 'sayings
and narratives reported from memory' of the Frau Rath,
(since she leads the conversation throughout,) our sketch

*We translate the following extract from the Berlin Correspondence of the
Deutsche Schnellpost of September.

must be short. 'It is Freedom which constitutes the truest being' of man. Man should be free from all traditions, from all prejudices, since every holding on somewhat traditional, is unbelief, spiritual selfmurder. The God's impulse to truth is the only right belief. Man himself should handle and prove, 'since whoever reflects on a matter, has always a better right to truth, than who lets himself be slapped on the cheek by an article-of-Faith.' By Sin she understands that which derogates from the soul, since every hindrance and constraint interrupts the Becoming of the soul. In general, art and science have only the destination to make free what is bound. But the human spirit can rule all, and, in that sense, 'man is God, only we are not arrived so far as to describe the true pure Man in us.' If, in the department of religion, this principle leads to the overthrow of the whole historical Christendom, so, in the political world, it leads to the ruin of all our actual governments. Therefore she wishes for a strong reformer, as Napoleon promised for a time to be, who, however, already in 1807, when these conversations are ascribed to the Frau Rath, had shown that instead of a world's liberator, he would be a world's oppressor. Bettina makes variations on the verse, 'and wake an avenger, a hero awake!' and in this sense is also her dedication to read. It were noble if a stronger one should come, who in more beautiful moderation, in perfecter clearness of soul and freedom of thought, should plant the tree of equity. Where remains the Regent, if it is not the genius of humanity? that is the Executive principle, in her system. The state has the same will, the same conscience-voice for good and evil as the Christ; yet it crumbles itself away into dogmaticalness of civil officers against one another. The transgressor is the state's own transgression! the proof that it, as man, has trespassed against humanity. The old state's doctors, who excite it to a will, are also its disease. But they who do not agree in this will, and cannot struggle through soul-narrowing relations, are the demagogues, against whom the unsound state trespasses, so long as it knows not how to bring their sound strength into harmony. And precisely to those must it dedicate itself, since they are its integration and restoration, whilst the others who conform to it, make it more sunken and stagnant. If it be objected, that this her truth is only a poetic dream which in the actual world has no place, she answers; 'even were the truth a dream, it is not therefore to be denied; let us dedicate our genius to this dream, let us form an Ideal Paradise, which the spiritual system of Nature requires at our hands.' 'Is the whole fabric of state, she asks, only a worse arranged hospital, where the selfish or the ambitious would fasten on the poor human race the foolish fantastic malversations of their roguery for beneficent coöperation? and with it the political economy, so destitute of all genius to bind the useful with the beautiful, on which these state's doctors plume themselves so much, and so with their triviality exhibit as a pattern to us, a wretched picture of ignorance, of selfishness, and of iniquity; when I come on that, I feel my veins swell with wrath. If I come on the belied nature, or how should I call this spectre of actuality! Yea justly! No! with these men armed in mail against every poetic truth, we must not parley; the great fools' conspiracy of that actuality-spectre defends with mock reasoning its Turkish states'-conduct, before which certainly the revelation of the Ideal withdraws into a poetic dream-region.' But whilst the existing state in itself is merely null, whilst the transgressor against this state is not incorporated with its authorizations with its directions and tendencies, so is the transgressor ever the accuser of the state itself. In general, must the state draw up to itself at least the lowest class, and not let it sink in mire; and Bettina lets the Frau Rath make the proposal, instead of shutting up the felon in penitentiaries, to instruct him in the sciences, as from his native energies, from his unbroken powers, great performances might be looked for. But in order also to show practically the truth of her assertions, that the present state does not fulfil its duties especially to the poorest class, at the close of the book are inserted, 'Experiences of a young Swiss in Voigtland.' This person visited the so-called Family-houses, which compose a colony of extremest poverty. There he went into many chambers, listened to the history of the life, still oftener to the history of the day, of the inhabitants; informed himself of their merit and their wants, and comes to the gloomiest results. The hard reproaches, which were made against the Overseers of the Poor, appear unhappily only too well founded. We have hastily sketched, with a few literal

quotations, the contents of this remarkable book of this remarkable woman, and there remains no space further to elaborate judgment. The highflying idealism, which the Frau von
Arnim cherishes, founders and must founder against the actuality which, as opposed to her imagination, she holds for
absolute nothing. So reality, with her, always converts itself
to spectres, whilst these dreams are to her the only reality. In
our opinion an energetic thorough experiment for the realization of her ideas would plunge us in a deeper misery than we
at present have to deplore."

The Huguenots in France and America

THE HUGUENOTS is a very entertaining book, drawn from excellent sources, rich in its topics, describing many admirable persons and events, and supplies an old defect in our popular literature. The editor's part is performed with great assiduity and conscience. Yet amidst this enumeration of all the geniuses, and beauties, and sanctities of France, what has the greatest man in France, at that period, Michael de Montaigne, done, or left undone, that his name should be quite omitted?

The Spanish Student

The Spanish Student. A Play in Three Acts. By H. W. Longfellow.

A PLEASING TALE, but Cervantes shall speak for us out of *La Gitanilla*.

"You must know, Preciosa, that as to this name of *Poet*, few are they who deserve it,—and I am no *Poet*, but only a lover of Poesy, so that I have no need to beg or borrow the verses of others. The verses, I gave you the other day, are mine, and those of to-day as well;—but, for all that, I am no poet, neither is it my prayer to be so."

"Is it then so bad a thing to be a poet?" asked Preciosa.

"Not bad," replied the Page, "but to be a poet and nought else, I do not hold to be very good. For poetry should be like a precious jewel, whose owner does not put it on every day, nor show it to the world at every step; but only when it is fitting, and when there is a reason for showing it. Poetry is a most lovely damsel; chaste, modest, and discreet; spirited, but yet retiring, and ever holding itself within the strictest rule of honor. She is the friend of Solitude. She finds in the fountains her delight, in the fields her counsellor, in the trees and flowers enjoyment and repose; and lastly, she charms and instructs all that approach her."

The Dream of a Day

The Dream of a Day, and other Poems. By JAMES G. PERCIVAL. New Haven. 1843.

Mr. PERCIVAL printed his last book of poems sixteen years ago, and every school-boy learned to declaim his "Bunker Hill," since which time, he informs us, his studies have been for the most part very adverse to poetic inspirations. Yet here we have specimens of no less than one hundred and fifty different forms of stanza. Such thorough workmanship in the poetical art is without example or approach in this country, and deserves all honor. We have imitations of four of the leading classes of ancient measures,—the Dactylic, Iambic, Anapestic, and Trochaic, to say nothing of rarer measures, now never known out of colleges. Then come songs for national airs, formed on the rhythm of the music, including Norwegian, German, Russian, Bohemian, Gaelic, and Welsh,—Teutonian and Slavonian. But unhappily this diligence is not without its dangers. It has prejudiced the creative power,

> "And made that art, which was a rage."

Neatness, terseness, objectivity, or at any rate the absence of subjectivity, characterize these poems. Our bard has not quite so much fire as we had looked for, grows warm but does not ignite; those sixteen years of "adverse" studies have had their effect on Pegasus, who now trots soundly and resolutely on, but forbears rash motions, and never runs away with us. The old critics of England were hardly steadier to their triad of "Gower, Lydgate, and Chaucer," than our American magazines to the trinity of "Bryant, Dana, and Percival." A gentle constellation truly, all of the established religion, having the good of their country and their species at heart. Percival has not written anything quite as good on the whole as his two fast associates, but surpasses them both in labor, in his mimetic skill, and in his objectiveness. He is the most objective of the American poets. Bryant has a superb propriety of feeling, has plainly always been in good society, but his sweet oaten pipe discourses only pastoral music. Dana has the most established religion, more sentiment, more reverence, more of England; whilst Mr. Percival is an upright, soldierly, free-spoken man, very much of a patriot, hates cant, and does his best.

The Tragic

He has seen but half the universe who never has been shown the House of Pain. As the salt sea covers more than two thirds of the surface of the globe, so sorrow encroaches in man on felicity. The conversation of men is a mixture of regrets and apprehensions. I do not know but the prevalent hue of things to the eye of leisure is melancholy. In the dark hours, our existence seems to be a defensive war, a struggle against the encroaching All, which threatens surely to engulf us soon, and is impatient of our short reprieve. How slender the possession that yet remains to us; how faint the animation! how the spirit seems already to contract its domain, retiring within narrower walls by the loss of memory, leaving its planted fields to erasure and annihilation. Already our own thoughts and words have an alien sound. There is a simultaneous diminution of memory and hope. Projects that once we laughed and leaped to execute, find us, now sleepy and preparing to lie down in the snow. And in the serene hours we have no courage to spare. We cannot afford to let go any advantages. The riches of body or of mind which we do not need today, are the reserved fund against the calamity that may arrive tomorrow. It is usually agreed that some nations have a more sombre temperament, and one would say that history gave no record of any society in which despondency came so readily to heart as we see it and feel it in ours. Melancholy cleaves to the English mind in both hemispheres as closely as to the strings of an Æolian harp. Men and women at thirty years, and even earlier, have lost all spring and vivacity, and if they fail in their first enterprizes, they throw up the game. But whether we, and those who are next to us, are more or less vulnerable, no theory of life can have any right, which leaves out of account the values of vice, pain, disease, poverty, insecurity, disunion, fear, and death.

What are the conspicuous tragic elements in human nature?

The bitterest tragic element in life to be derived from an intellectual source is the belief in a brute Fate or Destiny; the belief that the order of nature and events is controlled by a law not adapted to man, nor man to that, but which holds on its way to the end, serving him if his wishes chance to lie in the same course,—crushing him if his wishes lie contrary to it,—and heedless whether it serves or crushes him. This is the terrible idea that lies at the foundation of the old Greek tragedy, and makes the Œdipus and Antigone and Orestes objects of such hopeless commiseration. They must perish, and there is no over-god to stop or to mollify this hideous enginery that grinds and thunders, and takes them up into its terrific system. The same idea makes the paralyzing terror with which the East Indian mythology haunts the imagination. The same thought is the predestination of the Turk. And universally in uneducated and unreflecting persons, on whom too the religious sentiment exerts little force, we discover traits of the same superstition; 'if you baulk water, you will be drowned the next time:' 'if you count ten stars, you will fall down dead:' 'if you spill the salt;' 'if your fork sticks upright in the floor;' 'if you say the Lord's prayer backwards;'— and so on, a several penalty, nowise grounded in the nature of the thing, but on an arbitrary will. But this terror of contravening an unascertained and unascertainable will, cannot coexist with reflection: it disappears with civilization, and can no more be reproduced than the fear of ghosts after childhood. It is discriminated from the doctrine of Philosophical Necessity herein: that the last is an Optimism, and therefore the suffering individual finds his good consulted in the good of all, of which he is a part. But in Destiny, it is not the good of the whole or the *best will* that is enacted, but only *one particular will*. Destiny properly is not a will at all, but an immense whim; and this is the only ground of terror and despair in the rational mind, and of tragedy in literature. Hence the antique tragedy, which was founded on this faith, can never be reproduced.

But after the reason and faith have introduced a better public and private tradition, the tragic element is somewhat circumscribed. There must always remain, however, the hindrance of our private satisfaction by the laws of the world. The law which establishes nature and the human race, continually thwarts the will of ignorant individuals, and this in the particulars of disease, want, insecurity, and disunion.

But the essence of tragedy does not seem to me to lie in any list of particular evils. After we have enumerated famine, fever, inaptitude, mutilation, rack, madness, and loss of friends, we have not yet included the proper tragic element, which is Terror, and which does not respect definite evils but indefinite; an ominous spirit which haunts the afternoon and the night, idleness and solitude. A low haggard sprite sits by our side "casting the fashion of uncertain evils,"—a sinister presentiment, a power of the imagination to dislocate things orderly and cheerful, and show them in startling disarray. Hark! what sounds on the night wind, the cry of Murder in that friendly house: see these marks of stamping feet, of hidden riot. The whisper overheard, the detected glance, the glare of malignity, ungrounded fears, suspicions, half-knowledge, and mistakes darken the brow and chill the heart of men. And accordingly it is natures not clear, not of quick and steady perceptions, but imperfect characters from which somewhat is hidden that all others see, who suffer most from these causes. In those persons who move the profoundest pity, tragedy seems to consist in temperament, not in events. There are people who have an appetite for grief, pleasure is not strong enough and they crave pain, mithridatic stomachs which must be fed on poisoned bread, natures so doomed that no prosperity can soothe their ragged and dishevelled desolation. They mis-hear and mis-behold, they suspect and dread. They handle every nettle and ivy in the hedge, and tread on every snake in the meadow.

"Come bad chance,
And we add to it our strength,
And we teach it art and length,
Itself o'er us to advance."

Frankly then it is necessary to say that all sorrow dwells in a low region. It is superficial; for the most part fantastic, or in the appearance and not in things. Tragedy is in the eye of the observer, and not in the heart of the sufferer. It looks like an insupportable load under which earth moans aloud, but analyze it; it is not I, it is not you, it is always another person who is tormented. If a man says, lo I suffer,—it is apparent that he suffers not, for grief is dumb. It is so distributed as not to destroy. That which would rend you, falls on tougher textures. That which seems intolerable reproach or bereavement, does not take from the accused or bereaved man or woman appetite or sleep. Some men are above grief, and some below it. Few are capable of love. In phlegmatic natures calamity is unaffecting, in shallow natures it is rhetorical. Tragedy must be somewhat which I can respect. A querulous habit is not tragedy. A panic such as frequently in ancient or savage nations put a troop or an army to flight without an enemy; a fear of ghosts; a terror of freezing to death that seizes a man in a winter midnight on the moors; a fright at uncertain sounds heard by a family at night in the cellar or on the stairs; are terrors that make the knees knock and the teeth chatter, but are no tragedy, any more than sea-sickness, which may also destroy life. It is full of illusion. As it comes, it has its support. The most exposed classes, soldiers, sailors, paupers, are nowise destitute of animal spirits. The spirit is true to itself, and finds its own support in any condition, learns to live in what is called calamity, as easily as in what is called felicity, as the frailest glass-bell will support a weight of a thousand pounds of water at the bottom of a river or sea, if filled with the same.

A man should not commit his tranquillity to things, but should keep as much as possible the reins in his own hands, rarely giving way to extreme emotion of joy or grief. It is observed that the earliest works of the art of sculpture are countenances of sublime tranquillity. The Egyptian sphinxes, which sit today as they sat when the Greek came and saw them and departed, and when the Roman came and saw them and departed, and as they will still sit when the Turk, the Frenchman, and the Englishman, who visit them now, shall have passed by, " with their stony eyes fixed on the East and on the Nile," have countenances expressive of complacency and repose, an expression of health, deserving their longevity, and verifying the primeval sentence of history on the permanency of that people; "Their strength is to sit still." To this architectural stability of the human form, the Greek genius added an ideal beauty, without disturbing the seals of serenity; permitting no violence of mirth, or wrath, or suffering. This was true to human nature. For, in life, actions are few, opinions even few, prayers few; loves, hatreds, or any emissions of the soul. All that life demands of us through the greater part of the day, is an equilibrium, a readiness, open eyes and ears, and free hands. Society asks this, and truth, and love, and the genius of our life. There is a fire in some men which demands an outlet in some rude action; they betray their impatience of quiet by an irregular Catalinarian gait; by irregular, faltering, disturbed speech, too emphatic for the occasion. They treat trifles with a tragic air. This is not beautiful. Could they not lay a rod or two of stone wall, and work off this superabundant irritability. When two strangers meet in the highway, what each demands of the other is, that the aspect should show a firm mind, ready for any event of good or ill, prepared alike to give death or to give life, as the emergency of the next moment may require. We must walk as guests in nature,—not impassioned, but cool and disengaged. A man should try time, and his face should wear the expression of a just judge, who has nowise made up his opinion, who fears nothing and even hopes nothing, but who puts nature and fortune on their merits: he will hear the case out, and then decide. For all melancholy, as all passion, belongs to the exterior life. Whilst a man is not grounded in the divine life by his proper roots, he clings by some tendrils of affection to society,—mayhap to what is best and greatest in it, and in calm times it will not appear that he is adrift and not moored; but let any shock take place in society, any revolution of custom, of law, of opinion, and at once his type of permanence is shaken. The disorder of his neighbors appears to him universal disorder; chaos is come again. But in truth he was already a driving wreck, before the wind arose which only revealed to him his vagabond state. If a man is centred, men and events appear to him a fair image or reflection of that which he knoweth beforehand in himself. If any perversity or profligacy break out in society, he will join with others to avert the mischief, but it will not arouse resentment or fear, because he discerns its impassable limits. He sees already in the ebullition of sin, the simultaneous redress.

Particular reliefs, also, fit themselves to human calamities, for the world will be in equilibrium, and hates all manner of exaggeration. Time, the consoler, time, the rich carrier of all

changes, dries the freshest tears by obtruding new figures,
new costumes, new roads, on our eye, new voices on our ear.
As the west wind lifts up again the heads of the wheat which
were bent down and lodged in the storm, and combs out the
matted and dishevelled grass as it lay in night-locks on the
ground, so we let in time as a drying wind into the seed-field
of thoughts which are dank and wet, and low-bent. Time restores to them temper and elasticity. How fast we forget the
blow that threatened to cripple us. Nature will not sit still;
the faculties will do somewhat; new hopes spring, new affections twine, and the broken is whole again.

Time consoles, but Temperament resists the impression of
pain. Nature proportions her defence to the assault. Our human being is wonderfully plastic, if it cannot win this satisfaction here, it makes itself amends by running out there and
winning that. It is like a stream of water, which, if dammed
up on one bank, over-runs the other, and flows equally at its
own convenience over sand, or mud, or marble. Most suffering is only apparent. We fancy it is torture: the patient has his
own compensations. A tender American girl doubts of Divine
Providence whilst she reads the horrors of "the middle passage:" and they are bad enough at the mildest; but to such as
she these crucifixions do not come: they come to the obtuse
and barbarous, to whom they are not horrid, but only a little
worse than the old sufferings. They exchange a cannibal war
for the stench of the hold. They have gratifications which
would be none to the civilized girl. The market-man never
damned the lady because she had not paid her bill, but the
stout Irish woman has to take that once a month. She, however, never feels weakness in her back because of the slave-
trade. This self-adapting strength is especially seen in disease.
"It is my duty," says Sir Charles Bell, "to visit certain wards
of the hospital where there is no patient admitted but with
that complaint which most fills the imagination with the idea
of insupportable pain and certain death. Yet these wards are
not the least remarkable for the composure and cheerfulness
of their inmates. The individual who suffers has a mysterious
counterbalance to that condition, which, to us who look
upon her, appears to be attended with no alleviating circumstance." Analogous supplies are made to those individuals

whose character leads them to vast exertions of body and mind. Napoleon said to one of his friends at St. Helena, "Nature seems to have calculated that I should have great reverses to endure, for she has given me a temperament like a block of marble. Thunder cannot move it; the shaft merely glides along. The great events of my life have slipped over me without making any impression on my moral or physical nature."

The intellect is a consoler, which delights in detaching, or putting an interval between a man and his fortune, and so converts the sufferer into a spectator, and his pain into poetry. It yields the joys of conversation, of letters, and of science. Hence also the torments of life become tuneful tragedy, solemn and soft with music, and garnished with rich dark pictures. But higher still than the activities of art, the intellect in its purity, and the moral sense in its purity, are not distinguished from each other, and both ravish us into a region whereinto these passionate clouds of sorrow cannot rise.

Chronology

1803   Born May 25, Election Day, in Boston, Massachusetts, the fourth child of William (pastor of Boston's First Church) and Ruth Haskins Emerson, both of English descent. Described by father at age two as "rather a dull scholar." From age three attends nursery and then grammar school.

1811   Father dies May 12 of stomach tumor at age forty-two, leaving children to be raised by his widow with help from his sister, Mary Moody Emerson, whose idiosyncratic religious orthodoxy and acute critical intelligence were a lifelong influence. Of eight children, only Ralph Waldo and four brothers survive childhood: William (b. 1801), Edward Bliss (b. 1805), Charles Chauncy (b. 1808), and the retarded Robert Bulkeley (b. 1807), named for illustrious ancestor Peter Bulkeley, first-generation Puritan minister and a founder of Concord, Massachusetts.

1812   Enters Boston Public Latin School; begins writing poetry.

1817–21   Attends Harvard College and lives in President Kirkland's lodgings as his "freshman" or orderly; waits on table and teaches during vacations to pay costs. Begins keeping a journal to record his "luckless ragamuffin ideas." By junior year prefers the name Waldo. Wins prizes for oratory and for essays on Socrates and ethical philosophy; graduates thirtieth in a class of fifty-nine and delivers class poem at graduation after six others decline the honor. Following graduation teaches in brother William's school for young ladies in Boston.

1822   Continues to teach. Dedicates his seventh "Wideworld" journal to "the Spirit of America." Publishes essay on "The Religion of the Middle Ages" in *The Christian Disciple*, a leading Unitarian religious review.

1823   Takes walking trip to the Connecticut Valley. Runs school alone when William departs to study theology in Germany. Childhood dreams, he complains, "are all fading away & giving place to some very sober & very disgusting views of a quiet mediocrity of talents and condition."

1824   Dedicates himself to the study of divinity; complains in
            journal of his lack of warmth and self-confidence, but
            hopes "to put on eloquence as a robe."

1825   Closes school. Notes in journal that his "unpleasing boy-
            hood is past" and enters middle class at Harvard Divinity
            School. When studies are interrupted by eye trouble, re-
            sumes teaching, this time in Chelmsford, Massachusetts.
            Edward sails for Europe for his health; William, back
            from Germany, decides against ministerial career because
            of religious doubts.

1826   Begins year with "mended eyes," but afflicted by rheuma-
            tism of the hip. Teaches in Roxbury, then opens school in
            Cambridge (a student later describes him as "not inclined
            to win boys by a surface amiability, but kindly in expla-
            nation or advice"). William and Edward study law, the
            former on Wall Street and the latter in Daniel Webster's
            office. Impressed by Sampson Reed's *Observations on the
            Growth of the Mind*, a treatise that discusses "correspon-
            dences" between nature and spirit. Approbated to preach
            in October, but with onset of lung trouble, voyages to
            Charleston, South Carolina, financed by uncle Samuel
            Ripley.

1827   "I am not sick; I am not well; but luke-sick," he writes
            William in January, complaining of "a certain stricture" in
            his lungs. Sails for St. Augustine, Florida; establishes
            friendship with Napoleon's nephew Achille Murat, and is
            intrigued by this "consistent Atheist." Returns to Boston
            in spring and continues to preach. In December, while
            preaching in Concord, New Hampshire, meets Ellen
            Louisa Tucker.

1828   Edward becomes deranged; Waldo links this collapse to
            his brother's "preternatural energy" and assures himself
            that he is protected from a similar fate by the "mixture of
            silliness" in his character. Made honorary member of Phi
            Beta Kappa. Engaged to Ellen Tucker in December.

1829–30   Invited in January to become junior pastor of Boston's
            Second Church—the church of the Mathers. Becomes
            chaplain of state senate, as his late father had been. Al-

though Ellen is ill with tuberculosis, they marry in September. Elected to Boston School Committee in December. In November 1830, Edward, his health failing, sails for Puerto Rico.

1831   Ellen dies on February 8 at age nineteen. Waldo notes the religious resignation of her last hours and writes, "My angel is gone to heaven this morning & I am alone in the world & strangely happy"; five days later he prays, "God be merciful to me a sinner & repair this miserable debility in which her death has left my soul." Begins walking to her tomb every morning. Charles' health begins to fail, and he sails for Puerto Rico where Edward is employed at the American consulate.

1832   Uneasy with role as minister; feels "the profession is antiquated" and "in an altered age we worship in the dead forms of our forefathers." Writes Second Church governing board requesting changes in communion service and, when denied, decides to resign. Suffers from persistent diarrhea. In September delivers sermon "The Lord's Supper" explaining his objections to the rite and concludes he is "not interested in it." In poor health, sails for Europe on December 25.

1833   Lands in Malta in February much improved in health. Enthusiastically travels north through Italy, spending Easter week in Rome and meeting Walter Savage Landor in Florence; describes religious pomp at Sistine Chapel as "millinery & imbecility," but finds Pope's Easter benediction at St. Peter's "a sublime spectacle." Arrives in Paris in June. Complains it is "a loud modern New York of a place" but enjoys cafés and liveliness; visits Jardin des Plantes and decides to become "a naturalist." In London in July; meets John Stuart Mill, Coleridge, and Wordsworth, and begins lifelong friendship with Carlyle, whom he visits in Craigenputtock, Scotland. Sails for home in September and notes, "I like my book about nature & wish I knew where & how I ought to live." Preaches at Boston Second Church in October and in November lectures on "The Uses of Natural History."

1834   Lectures in Boston on natural history and continues to preach nearly every Sunday; begins to correspond with

Carlyle. In spring receives first half of Ellen's estate (about $11,600). In October moves with mother to Emerson family home in Concord (later named by Hawthorne the Old Manse). Decides "not to utter any speech, poem, or book that is not entirely & peculiarly my work." Edward dies in Puerto Rico.

1835   Lectures in Boston on lives of great men. In January feels "very sober joy" on being engaged to Lydia Jackson of Plymouth; buys house in Concord for $3,500 and then marries Lydia in September. Declines pastorate in East Lexington, Massachusetts, but agrees to preach there every Sunday or procure a substitute. Delivers address on Concord history for the town's second centennial; begins winter lecture series on "English Literature" in Boston.

1836   Pronounces it a "gloomy epoch" when Charles dies of tuberculosis in May. Margaret Fuller visits the Emerson home for three weeks in July. Informal group (later dubbed Transcendental Club)—including Fuller, Orestes Brownson, Theodore Parker, Bronson Alcott, James Freeman Clarke, among others—organized for discussions and continues to meet until 1843. His "little azure-coloured *Nature*" published anonymously, a common practice, in September. Sees American edition of Carlyle's *Sartor Resartus* through press at own expense. (Although advances for this and future American editions of Carlyle's works are a financial hardship, Emerson will eventually recover his investment and send Carlyle nearly $3,000 in profits.) Son Waldo born October 30. Gives lecture series on "Philosophy of History" in winter.

1837   Notes in journal that "the land stinks with suicide" as American economy slides into severe depression. Receives final portion of Ellen's estate, bringing total to about $23,000, yielding an annual income of some $1,200. "Concord Hymn" sung July 4 at unveiling of monument to Revolutionary soldiers. Delivers "The American Scholar" as Harvard's Phi Beta Kappa oration in August and is toasted as "the Spirit of Concord" who "makes us all of One Mind." Lectures in winter on "Human Culture," defined as "educating the eye to the true harmony of the unshorn landscape."

1838   Finding the pulpit a constraint, asks East Lexington church committee to relieve him of responsibilities in February. In April writes open letter to President Van Buren protesting displacement of Cherokee Indians from their ancestral lands. Delivers address at Harvard Divinity School (July 15), subsequently attacked as "the latest form of infidelity." Though defended by George Ripley, Orestes Brownson, J. F. Clarke, and Theodore Parker, he is not invited back to Harvard for nearly thirty years. Dartmouth Oration ("Literary Ethics") delivered July 24. Meets Jones Very and develops close friendship with Thoreau, with whom he takes walks in the woods. Winter lecture series on "Human Life" includes such topics as "Head," "Home," "Love," "Duty," "Genius," "Demonology," and "Animal Magnetism."

1839   Preaches his last sermon in January. Daughter Ellen born February 24, with Thoreau's mother serving as midwife. Visits from Very, Fuller, Alcott, and Carolyn Sturgis lead Emerson to note his "porcupine impossibility of contact with men," although of Alcott and Fuller he writes, "Cold as I am, they are almost dear." Edits and finds publisher for Very's poems and essays. Lectures on "The Present Age" in winter on a widening circuit.

1840   With Margaret Fuller, brings out first issue of *The Dial* in July, hoping it will be "one cheerful rational voice amidst the din of mourners and polemics." Strives to write " with some pains Essays on various matters as a sort of apology to my country for my apparent idleness." Attends reformers' Chardon Street Convention, but when invited to join Brook Farm community declines "to remove from my present prison to a prison a little larger."

1841   First series of *Essays* published in March, and aunt, Mary Moody Emerson, pronounces it a "strange medly of atheism and false independence"; favorable reviews in London and Paris lay basis for international reputation. Invites Thoreau to join household in spring, offering room and board in exchange for gardening and household chores. In summer delivers "The Method of Nature" at Waterville College in Maine. Daughter Edith born November 22. Lectures on "The Times" in winter.

1842   Devastated by death of five-year-old Waldo from scarlet
        fever in January, avers that he comprehends "nothing of
        this fact but its bitterness." Succeeds Margaret Fuller as
        editor of *The Dial* when she resigns. Raises money to send
        Bronson Alcott to England. Takes walking trip in Septem-
        ber with Hawthorne, now living at the Old Manse, to
        visit Shaker community in village of Harvard, Massachu-
        setts. On lecture tour in New York City—the lecture
        "Poetry of the Times" is reviewed by young editor Walter
        Whitman—dines with Horace Greeley and Albert Bris-
        bane and visits between lectures at home of Henry
        James, Sr.

1843   In spring, finds Thoreau employment in Staten Island as
        tutor to children of his brother William, now a New York
        State district judge. Completes a translation of Dante's
        Vita Nuova. Summer, entertains Daniel Webster at his
        home and pronounces him "no saint . . . but according
        to his lights a very true & admirable man."

1844   Last issue of *The Dial* appears in April. Son Edward
        Waldo born July 10. Purchases land on shore of Walden
        Pond. Contributes $500 toward land for the Alcott family
        when they purchase a house in Concord (later Haw-
        thorne's Wayside). Opposes annexation of Texas and war
        with Mexico: "Mexico will poison us." Delivers address
        attacking slavery in the West Indies. *Essays: Second Series*
        published in October.

1845   Gives Thoreau permission to build hut on Walden prop-
        erty. His discourse at Middlebury College provokes a local
        minister to ask God "to deliver us from ever hearing any
        more such transcendental nonsense." Refuses to lecture at
        the New Bedford Lyceum when informed that Negroes
        are excluded from membership. In winter delivers "The
        Representative Men" lecture series.

1846   April, hears Edward Everett's inaugural discourse as pres-
        ident of Harvard and decries "the corpse-cold Unitarian-
        ism & Immortality of Brattle street & Boston." In July
        feels limited sympathy for Thoreau's night in jail ("this
        prison is one step to suicide"). *Poems* published in Decem-
        ber, including "Threnody," an elegy for his son Waldo.

1847–48 Sails for Liverpool in October, having been invited to lecture in various British industrial cities; Thoreau leaves Walden Pond to take charge of the Emerson household. November to February, lectures extensively on various topics, including "Natural Aristocracy," in an England and Scotland disturbed by political unrest. Sees Carlyle, Wordsworth, Harriet Martineau, Dickens, and Tennyson. May, visits Paris during attempted revolution, where he meets Alexis de Tocqueville. Returns to England in June, dines with Chopin, and visits Stonehenge with Carlyle. Disembarks in Boston in late July.

1849 Offers winter lecture series on "Mind and Manners in the Nineteenth Century," drawing on English experiences, and a spring series on "Laws of the Intellect." Begins smoking cigars. *Nature; Addresses, and Lectures* published in September.

1850 January, *Representative Men* published. Winter–spring, extensive lecturing in New England, New York, Philadelphia, Cleveland, and Cincinnati. July, mourns death of Margaret Fuller Ossoli in shipwreck ("I have lost in her my audience") and sends Thoreau to Fire Island beach to search for her effects. Winter, lectures on "The Conduct of Life."

1851 Outraged by Webster's March 7 speech defending Fugitive Slave Law, fills journal with passionate condemnation of this former hero ("all the drops of his blood have eyes that look downward") and speaks against the law.

1852 Contributes to *Memoirs of Margaret Fuller Ossoli*. Praises *Uncle Tom's Cabin*. During winter, 1852–53, lectures to enthusiastic crowds from Boston to St. Louis, Philadelphia to Maine and Montreal.

1853 Mother dies at age eighty-four.

1854 Demanding lecture schedule throughout country includes attack on Fugitive Slave Law in New York City.

1855 Anti-slavery lectures in Boston, New York, and Philadelphia. Writes Whitman praising *Leaves of Grass* ("I give you joy of your free & brave thought. . . . I greet you at the beginning of a great career"). Helps F. B. Sanborn establish the Concord Academy, whose pupils will include the children of Emerson, Hawthorne, and Henry James, Sr. Saturday Club founded, with Emerson as a charter member, for informal literary discussions. Addresses Woman's Rights Convention in Boston.

1856   Lecture schedule ranges from New England to the Middle West. *English Traits* published in August. Speaks in favor of Kansas Relief, a fund raised to help Kansans impoverished by marauding pro-slavery advocates.

1857   Listens approvingly to Captain John Brown's speech in Concord. Moves remains of mother and Waldo ("I ventured to look into the coffin") to Sleepy Hollow Cemetery.

1858   Declares himself an abolitionist "of the most absolute abolition." Spends two weeks in August camping in the Adirondacks with Louis Agassiz, Oliver Wendell Holmes, and others. Calculates his income for the year at $4,162.11.

1859   His feeble-minded brother Bulkeley dies at age fifty-two. Records in journal his fear that he has "no new thoughts, and that [his] life is quite at an end." Much agitated by capture and execution of John Brown, and predicts that his hanging will make the gallows "sacred as the cross."

1860   Lectures throughout New York, New England, the Middle West, and at Toronto. Walks on Boston Common with Whitman for two hours on a March day trying to persuade him to tone down the "sex element" in *Leaves of Grass*. William Dean Howells visits in August as part of the itinerary of his literary pilgrimage. Declares in November that news of Lincoln's election is "sublime." *Conduct of Life* published in December.

1861   Told to "dry up" by unruly pro-Union crowd while attempting to speak at Massachusetts Anti-Slavery Society ("the mob roared . . . and after several beginnings, I withdrew"). Roused by unity and patriotism of New

England following attack on Fort Sumter, visits Charlestown Navy Yard and declares "sometimes gunpowder smells good." Says of war that "amputation is better than cancer."

1862   Lectures on "American Civilization" in Washington and meets Lincoln. Reads address at Thoreau's funeral averring that "the country knows not yet, or in the least part, how great a son it has lost." Celebrates Emancipation Proclamation in an address printed in the *Atlantic Monthly*.

1863   Aunt Mary dies at age eighty-nine. Appointed to committee to review standards of U.S. Military Academy at West Point. Lectures throughout Midwest.

1864   Attends Hawthorne's funeral and laments "the painful solitude of the man—which, I suppose, could not longer be endured, & he died of it." Lectures on "American Life" and the "Fortune of the Republic," exhorting Americans to " wake" and correct the injustices of the political system " with energy"; declares "this country, the last found, is the great charity of God to the human race." Elected to newly formed American Academy of Arts and Sciences.

1865   Eulogizes martyred Lincoln as "the true representative of this continent." Thinks Grant's terms for Lee's surrender too lenient. Daughter Edith engaged to Col. William Forbes, later president of Bell Telephone Co., son of railroad magnate John Murray Forbes. Lectures seventy-seven times.

1866   Receives honorary Doctor of Laws degree from Harvard. Reads to son Edward Waldo his poem "Terminus" ("It is time to be old,/ To take in sail.").

1867   *May-Day and Other Pieces* published in April. Delivers Phi Beta Kappa oration at Harvard, ending twenty-nine-year exile. Named an overseer of Harvard College. Lectures eighty times, the peak of his platform career, traveling west twice as far as Minnesota and Iowa.

1868   William dies in New York in September.

1870   *Society and Solitude* published in March; writes preface for
            edition of *Plutarch's Morals*. Lectures at Harvard on "Nat-
            ural History of Intellect" and is much occupied with uni-
            versity affairs.

1871   Repetition of Harvard course cut short due to fatigue;
            April–May, travels to West Coast, in a private Pullman car
            leased by John Forbes, for relaxation and relief with family
            and friends. Meets naturalist John Muir and notes that
            California "has better days, & more of them" than any
            other place. Back in Concord, visited by Bret Harte.

1872   Health declines; suffers lapses of memory while lecturing.
            House in Concord badly damaged by fire in July; James
            Russell Lowell and other friends raise $17,000 to repair
            house and send Emerson abroad for a vacation. Travels to
            Egypt and Europe with daughter Ellen in October. In
            Paris, Henry James, Jr., guides them through the Louvre;
            sees Carlyle for last time. Meets Hermann Grimm, Hip-
            polyte Taine, Ivan Turgenev, Robert Browning, Friedrich
            Max Müller, Benjamin Jowett, and John Ruskin.

1873   Returns in May to cheering crowd in Concord and dis-
            covers house has been restored by friends.

1874   Publishes *Parnassus*, an anthology of his favorite poetry
            (Whitman and Poe are not included).

1875   Ceases writing in his private journals; *Letters and Social
            Aims* published in December with editorial assistance of
            Ellen and James Elliot Cabot.

1876   Emma Lazarus visits, and this "real unconverted Jew" cre-
            ates much interest in household. *Selected Poems* published.

1877–82   Lives last years serenely in mental twilight (at Long-
            fellow's funeral in his own last year, Emerson is reported
            to have said, "That gentleman was a sweet, beautiful soul,
            but I have entirely forgotten his name"). Dies of pneu-
            monia on April 27, 1882, in Concord.

Note on the Texts

Emerson was a meticulous editor of his own work, and his care produced books which were generally error-free in their first printings and which remained largely unchanged through various reissues. Two important exceptions, however, were the heavily revised 1849 edition of *Nature*, prepared for the volume of *Nature; Addresses, and Lectures*, and the second edition of *Essays: First Series*, published in 1847. With these two exceptions, the texts in this volume reproduce the first printings in book form of Emerson's major works, 1832–1860.

Nature; Addresses, and Lectures was published in 1849, although each of the pieces in the book had been published previously. *Nature*, which appeared in a slim volume in 1836, had been Emerson's first published book. The addresses—"The American Scholar," the "Address" at the Harvard Divinity School, "Literary Ethics," and "The Method of Nature"—were all published as separate pamphlets in the years in which they were delivered. The lectures had appeared originally in *The Dial* between 1841 and 1844. *Nature; Addresses, and Lectures* appears in this volume as Emerson prepared it for publication in 1849. Although other revised editions appeared in later years, these were neither as carefully nor as thoroughly reworked. The late editions, moreover, represent an older, more conservative Emerson, while the 1849 edition of *Nature; Addresses, and Lectures* presents Emerson at the height of his creative powers.

Essays: First Series was originally published in 1841 as simply *Essays*, although Emerson toyed briefly with the title "Forest Essays." Always the most conscientious of self-editors, Emerson spend a period of months in 1841 correcting proofs for the first edition. Six years later, he again found himself tinkering with his "lilliputian" book. By 1845 the original edition of 1500 copies had been sold, and a number of English pirated editions had appeared. Emerson, who calculated the timeliness of such decisions carefully, yielded to the urgings of his publisher, James Munroe and Company, and in 1847 undertook the extensive revision of his first volume of essays. The extended title, *Essays: First Series*, was introduced then to distinguish it from the second book of essays which had been published three years earlier. Apart from the correction of one misprint, no further changes were introduced into this 1847 edition, which was reprinted almost every two years until 1878. Three later editions were supervised by Emerson but none was extensively revised, and despite the existence of these newer editions, printings of the 1847 edition, from stereotype plates, continued to appear. This revised edition of 1847 provides the text of the *Essays: First Series* reprinted in this volume.

Essays: Second Series was published by James Munroe and Company in October 1844. As he had done with his first series of essays, Emerson published the second series at his "own risk," and his publishers received thirty percent of the profits as their commission. Emerson wrote in a letter of October 14, 1845: "I do not well carry figures in my head, but I believe I have received or am to receive between 5 & 600 dollars for each edition of my 'Essays.'" A second edition (without major changes) of *Essays: Second Series* was published in 1850 by Phillips, Sampson & Co. and reprinted in 1855. A "New and Revised Edition" appeared in July 1876. These versions of the text are further removed from the work Emerson so meticulously saw through the press in 1844, and this volume therefore reproduces the text of *Essays: Second Series* from its first edition.

Representative Men first appeared in January 1850. The edition sold steadily and was reprinted in 1857 from the 1850 plates. Emerson made fourteen changes, mostly correcting errors in wording and punctuation, for this reprint. A "New and Revised Edition" appeared in 1876, published by Houghton, Osgood & Co., and was reproduced in 1879 for the Riverside Press Edition. This volume reproduces the text of the first edition.

English Traits originally appeared in August 1856 and became an instant popular success. The book went through a second printing later that same year, bringing the edition to 5,000, and a third printing the following year of an additional 2,000. Seven minor variations appeared by the third printing, but no major revision of the work was ever undertaken. The 1856 plates, with these seven changes, remained unaltered in subsequent printings through 1883. In 1870 the work was re-published for the *Prose Works* edition and in 1876 for the Little Classics edition, each of which introduced some evidently non-authorial changes. The first edition of 1856 provides the text reproduced in this volume.

The Conduct of Life, which was printed from stereotype plates in 1860, also sold well and underwent several reprint-ings within the next few years. Emerson's extensive proof-reading labors appear to have been successful because only one substantive change (correcting the spelling of Œnipodes to Œnopides) appeared in the "seventh thousand" printing of 1861. A "New and Revised Edition" of *The Conduct of Life* appeared in April 1876 and was reprinted in 1879. The book was also published in 1883 in the Riverside Press Edition. This volume takes the text of *The Conduct of Life* from the 1860 first edition, which Emerson edited and corrected himself.

The sermon entitled "The Lord's Supper" was delivered before the Second Church and Society on September 19, 1832, but, despite the notoriety surrounding Emerson's resignation from the ministry, the sermon apparently was not printed un-til 1876, when it appeared in Octavius Brooks Frothingham's *Transcendentalism in New England*. Evidently, Emerson chose to allow only his actual letter of resignation, "Letter to the Second Church and Society" (1832), to be printed at the time. This document contained no hint of Emerson's radical views on the celebration of communion and referred only to family matters and problems of health to account for his early retire-ment from the ministry. Two years after Emerson's death, "The Lord's Supper" was published in the Riverside edition of his *Miscellanies* (1884). This edition contained a number of variations from the version published by Frothingham in 1876, including extensive changes of commas and one substan-tive change—"stopped" for "stooped" (1132.39). In addition, the Riverside edition dropped several lines at two separate places, at least one of which appears to have been a printer's error, and corrected two biblical verse references from the ear-lier edition, where they were misassigned, possibly by Emer-son himself. This volume reproduces the text of "The Lord's Supper" from its first appearance in Frothingham's volume (1876) rather than from the posthumous Riverside edition.

The remaining pieces of uncollected prose were originally printed in *The Dial*, July 1840 through April 1844, the journal with which Emerson was closely associated even before he assumed the editorship (or "rotation in martyrdom" as he called it) in the spring of 1842. The texts in this volume are taken from their original appearance in *The Dial*.

Preparation of the textual and other notes has been aided by Edward Waldo Emerson's annotations in the Centenary Edition of Ralph Waldo Emerson's *Works*, by material drawn from the Harvard University Press Edition of Emerson's collected works, and by the generous assistance of Colonel Douglas Emory Wilson.

The standards for American English in some ways were conspicuously different in earlier periods from what they are now. In nineteenth-century writings, for example, a word might be spelled in more than one way, even in the same work, and such variations might be carried into print. Commas were sometimes used expressively to suggest the movements of voice, and capitals were sometimes meant to give significances to a word beyond those it might have in its uncapitalized form. Since modernization would remove such effects, this volume preserves the spelling, punctuation, capitalization, and wording of those first revised editions, which of the available texts, appear most faithful to Emerson's intentions at each stage of his career. The present volume represents the *texts* of these editions; it does not attempt to reproduce the features of their typographic design—such as the display capitalization of chapter openings. The table of contents for *Nature; Addresses, and Lectures* has been expanded to list individual chapter titles in *Nature*, and separate heads have been added for "Addresses" and "Lectures." A table of contents is provided for the section "Uncollected Prose." Obvious typographical errors have been corrected, and the following is a list of those errors by page and line number: 14.5, χοσμος; 27.34, than; 40.28, back back; 42.11 pressent; 47.1, achievments; 62.39, Skakspeare; 64.23 satify; 90.4, display; 93.3, *1839*; 116.28, has; 122.29, things; 123.34, incarnation?; 124.24, runs; 136.35, prophecy; 137.30, abominatious; 144.23, worship,; 145.39, -by; 158.16, harvest o; 183.38, books, they said, and; 191.3, *1841*; 193.11, 1841; 208.16, rainguages; 208.18, guages; 213.38, yard-stick, stick,; 246.5, barrenness; 270.33, tit-poe; 332.38, plastie; 359.25, stringing; 375.36, Hankal; 448.1, when; 465.30, boats; 468.4, Whereve; 504.26, ot; 542.38, and and; 645.3, guaged; 649.9, reality."; 660.2, charlatan; 672.13, things; 683.37–38, inportation; 712.40 arrayed; 729.24, satifaction; 734.17, achievments; 736.8, for, Europe; 803.17–18, costarmongers; 807.37, temperature; 812.23, dpended; 890.17, men; 951.13, Œnipodes; 1144.37, comdemns; 1147.9, realites; 1156.15, alway; 1169.24, poetry; 1205.20, laborer; 1205.26, nawspaper; 1206.8, Swendenborg; 1290.31, depair; 1293.3, readness; 1293.25, willnot.

Notes

In the notes below, numbers refer to page and line of this volume (the line count includes chapter headings). No note is made for material found in a standard desk-reference book. Notes at the foot of the page in the text are Emerson's own.

NATURE; ADDRESSES, AND LECTURES

4.4   *January, 1842*] This lecture was given in December, 1841. See note 191.3.

5.2–7   A subtle . . . form.] In the 1849 edition these verses by Emerson replaced the 1836 epigraph, attributed to Plotinus: "Nature is but an image or imitation of wisdom, the last thing of the soul; nature being a thing which doth only do, but not know."

10.20   I am . . . fear] In the 1836 edition Emerson wrote: "Almost I fear to think how glad I am."

12.22–23   "More . . . of."] See 44.17 ff.

17.2   Leonidas] King of Sparta who died with his men in 480 B.C. defending the mountain pass at Thermopylae against an invading Persian army.

17.4–5   Winkelried] Swiss patriot whose sacrifice enabled his countrymen to win the Battle of Sempach in 1386.

17.15–16   Sir Harry Vane] Governor of Massachusetts in 1636–37, Vane was also a leader of the Puritan movement in England and was executed by order of Charles II in 1662.

17.20   Lord Russel] William Russell (b. 1639) was a Whig parliamentarian executed for treason in 1683.

21.36–37   "It is . . . body."] I Cor. 15:44.

24.12–13   "The visible . . . invisible."] From Emanuel Swedenborg (1688–1772).

24.37–39   "Can . . . wonder?"] Cf. *Macbeth*, III, iv, 110–12.

35.10–11   The ornament . . . air.] From Sonnet lxx.

35.14–19   No . . . politic.] From Sonnet cxxiv.

35.23–26   Take . . . morn.] Cf. *Measure for Measure*, IV, i, 1–4.

37.22–27   "These . . . counsel."] Cf. Prov. 8:23 ff.

38.11–12 "The things . . . eternal."] II Cor. 4:18.

38.14 Berkeley and Viasa] George Berkeley (1685–1753) was a philosophical idealist and an opponent of Locke; Viasa was said to have been the author of the Vedas.

42.1–2 "The golden . . . eternity,"] Cf. Milton's "Comus," 13–14.

47.4 Hohenlohe] A nineteenth-century German priest famous for miraculous cures.

49.7–8 The kingdom . . . observation] Cf. Luke 17:20–21. See also 483.22–23.

75.6 balm-of-Gilead] A poplar tree with fragrant leaves; cf. Jer. 8:22.

81.21 'A pagan . . . outworn,'] Wordsworth's sonnet, "The world is too much with us."

82.26 Epaminondas] Theban military hero, died 362 B.C.

85.36 Denderah] Egyptian temple decorated with the signs of the zodiac.

90.39 Massena] André Masséna was one of Napoleon's marshals.

95.17–18 Eyes . . . lame.] Cf. Job 29:15.

97.36–37 "God . . . away."] This is a version of Napoleon's words upon crowning himself king of Italy in 1805.

98.24 squeak and gibber] Cf. *Hamlet*, I, i, 116.

101.37 screaming] Later changed by Emerson to "honking."

102.40 Agiocochook] Indian name of Mount Washington.

103.24 Cousin] Victor Cousin (1792–1867) was professor of philosophy at the Sorbonne. Emerson read with interest his *Introduction to the History of Philosophy* (1832). See also 776.31.

105.11 into public] Emerson entered the revision "to the public" in his wife's copy of *Nature; Addresses, and Lectures*.

106.15 secular] Of long duration. See also 404.18, 546.31, 683.31, 781.30, 885.5, 932.8, 1033.16.

115.6–7 Where . . . perish.] Prov. 29:18.

119.5 Empedocles] The story relates that this Greek philosopher of the fifth century B.C. threw himself into Mount Etna to demonstrate his divinity, but that his sandal was expelled by the volcano.

124.38 fool] Emerson noted that "fool" should read "prophet" in his wife's copy, but he later changed the word to "drinker."

160.18   best tract] Emerson alludes to *Areopagitica*.

161.35   Perfectionist or "Comer out,"] Nineteenth-century religious reformers.

191.3   *January, 1842*] The edition originally read "January, 1841," with an erratum added on the contents page correcting it to "January, 1842." The lecture was actually delivered in December, 1841.

211.1   THE YOUNG AMERICAN] This lecture, originally published in *The Dial* (April 1844), was heavily revised by Emerson in 1849—mainly by excision of passages concerning American dependence on European culture and European critics, the growth of Boston and of railroads, and the exploitation of Irish labor.

222.18   three Communities] Probably Brook Farm, Fruitlands, and Hopedale.

223.8   Etzlers] J. A. Etzler was a utopian writer and speculator whose book, *The Paradise within the Reach of All Men, Without Labor, by Powers of Machinery*, was criticized by Thoreau in a review titled "Paradise (To Be) Regained."

225.7   Harnden] William Frederick Harnden established a messenger service between New York and Boston in 1839.

227.3   Repudiation] Emerson evidently refers to the refusal by several states, most particularly Pennsylvania, to redeem bonds sold abroad to finance public works. Carlyle and Sterling, two of Emerson's closest English friends, had each lost large sums of money as a result of this practice.

ESSAYS: FIRST SERIES

237.23–24   are merely the] Emerson marked "merely" for excision in a friend's copy of *Essays*.

241.2–3   Sidney . . . Robinson] Probably Algernon Sidney (1622–83), one of the regicide judges executed for treason by Charles II. In "Marmaduke Robinson," Emerson seems to have conflated the names of two Quakers executed by the Puritans in 1659—Marmaduke Stevenson and William Robinson.

242.32–33   Io . . . Isis] Io, a priestess of Hera, was beloved of Zeus, who changed her into a heifer to conceal her from his wife. She was restored to her original form in Egypt after long wandering. Isis was identified with Hathor, bovine-headed goddess of beauty.

243.39   Rospigliosi Aurora] A print of Guido Reni's "Aurora," a gift from Thomas Carlyle, which hung in Emerson's parlor.

246.5   bareness] The 1847 reading, "barrenness" appears to be a typographical error; the 1841 reading (followed here) seems more correct in context.

247.4   Astaboras]   The Atbara, a river flowing into the Nile from Ethiopia.

249.10   Philoctetes]   Eponymous hero of Sophocles' play.

250.2   Menu]   Or Manu, son of Brahma, who dictated a book of laws.

250.20   Belus]   Presumably Baal.

252.3   agent or patient]   From the Latin roots for acting and suffering.

257.2   "Ne te . . . extra."]   Do not seek yourself outside yourself.

262.27   father and mother]   Cf. Matthew 10:37.

262.29   lintels . . . door-post]   Cf. Deuteronomy 6:9 and Exodus 12:23.

264.1   But . . . work,]   In the 1841 edition the sentence reads, "But do your thing, . . ."

267.2   gazetted]   Retired from use.

276.33–34 'Let . . . obey.']   Cf. Exodus 20:19.

280.29   Parry and Franklin]   Sir William Edward Parry (1790–1855), and Sir John Franklin (1786–1847), English Arctic explorers.

289.37   "It is . . . by it."]   Cf. John 1:10.

292.9–11   "Of all . . . sleep."]   Aeschylus, *The Furies*, 894–96.

295.8   Polycrates]   The Tyrant of Samos, fearing Nemesis because of his good fortune, threw an emerald into the sea, but it returned in the belly of a fish.

297.25–27 "Winds . . . nothing."]   Wordsworth, "September, 1802, near Dover."

306.5   "A few . . . rules"]   Wordsworth, "Alas! What Boots the Long Laborious Quest."

306.35–36 'Not . . . with us.']   Cf. Psalm 115:1.

313.30–31 "Earth . . . splendors"]   Cf. Wordsworth, "Ode: Intimations of Immortality," line 77.

318.18–19 Doth . . . voice?]   Prov. 8:1.

320.6   a Chiffinch, an Iachimo]   Rascally characters in, respectively, Scott's *Peveril of the Peak* and Shakespeare's *Cymbeline*.

320.17   I AM]   Exodus 3:14.

321.14   thorough lights]   Windows.

327.3   Every promise]   In 1841 the essay began: "Every soul is a celestial Venus to every other soul. The heart has its sabbaths and jubilees, in which the world appears as a hymeneal feast, and all natural sounds and the circle of the seasons are erotic odes and dances. Love is omnipresent in nature as motive and reward. Love is our highest word, and the synonym of God. Every promise . . ."

327.18   heyday . . . blood]   Cf. *Hamlet*, III, iv, 68–70.

330.26–28   "Thou . . . heart."]   John Donne, "Epithalamion," 202–03.

331.13–18   "Fountain-heads . . . upon."]   From John Fletcher's *The Nice Valour; or, The Passionate Mad-Man*, Act III.

335.21–23   "Her . . . thought."]   John Donne, "The Second Anniversarie," 244–48.

336.25–26   "The person . . . it."]   Abraham Cowley, "Resolved to be Beloved," 23–24.

343.18–19   "crush . . . wine"]   Cf. *Comus*, line 47.

343.37   We doubt]   Meaning "we suspect."

346.1–4   "The valiant . . . toiled."]   Shakespeare, sonnet XXV.

346.9   *naturlangsamkeit*]   Slow natural process.

348.19   My author]   Montaigne.

361.13   "afternoon men"]   Wastrels or idlers.

375.25–30   "Indeed, . . . use!"]   Cf. *Henry IV, Part II*, II, ii, 13–19.

376.26   precision]   Rigid observance of rules. See also 506.13.

377.13–14   Prytaneum]   See Plato's *Apology*, 36. Socrates suggests that he deserves not death but free maintenance by the state.

380.30   Lovejoy]   Elijah Lovejoy, an Abolitionist publisher, was killed by a pro-slavery mob in 1837.

381.12–13   "Let . . . grave."]   Cf. Tennyson's "A Dirge."

388.3–4   "Can . . . eternity."]   Byron, *Cain*, I, i, 536–37.

389.16   Zeno and Arrian]   Stoic philosophers of the third century B.C. and second century A.D., respectively.

398.13–14   "highest praising . . . praising."]   Cf. *Areopagitica*, paragraph 4.

400.33   shreds and patches]   Cf. *Hamlet*, III, iv, 102.

403.15   dawn . . . mid-noon,]   Cf. *Paradise Lost*, V, 310–11.

408.28–29   circumspection]   The first-edition reading, "circumscription," was preferred in the Riverside edition.

409.29–30   "Then . . . all."]   I Cor. 15:28.

411.23–24   "Forgive . . . right."]   Edward Young, *The Complaint; or, Night Thoughts*, IX, 2316–17.

436.31–32   "What, . . . fast?"]   Cf. *Hamlet*, I, v, 162.

ESSAYS: SECOND SERIES

450.19–20   under the line]   Beneath the equator.

452.37–453.4   "So . . . make."]   "An Hymne in Honour of Beautie," stanza xix.

454.12–13   See . . . ball]   To celebrate the nomination of William Henry Harrison in 1840, the Whigs thus symbolized their slogan, "Keep the ball rolling."

462.6–7   "So . . . top;"]   From the dedication of George Chapman's translation of Homer, 1612–15.

465.30   boasts]   "Boasts" is the common correction of the first-edition "boats."

473.16   The Indian]   In Robert Southey's "The Curse of Kehama," 1810.

476.19   *Pero si muove*]   Facing ecclesiastical persecution, Galileo denied his observation that the earth turns round the sun, but then added: "And yet it does move."

478.9   Education-Farm]   Emerson is undoubtedly alluding to Brook Farm, the utopian community in West Roxbury, Massachusetts, founded by George Ripley and others in 1841.

481.5–6   Grahamites]   Followers of Sylvester Graham (1794–1851), reformist physician and inventor of "Graham flour."

491.36   Adrastia]   Nemesis or destiny.

520.24   "If you . . . on!——"]   Emerson loosely quotes Scott's *Waverly*; the reference is to the clan chief and his retinue.

527.37–528.7   "As . . . might."]   From Keats's *Hyperion*, II, 206 ff.

581.13   Nick Bottom]   The weaver in *A Midsummer Night's Dream* who, with his fellow tradesmen, performs "Pyramus and Thisbe" for the Duke Theseus.

REPRESENTATIVE MEN

659.19–20   "Nature . . . that mean,"] *The Winter's Tale*, IV, iv, 88–90.

659.21–24   "He, . . . story."] *Antony and Cleopatra*, III, xiii, 43–46.

663.30–32   "Indeed, . . . attribute."] *Hamlet*, I, iv, 20–22.

679.18   Casella sang] Cf. *Purgatorio*, II, 112.

680.14   eliminated] Brought out. See also 918.15, 1029.9.

692.20–21   "Wer nicht . . . lang;"] He who does not love wine, woman and song, remains a fool his whole life long.

699.18   old Poz] A character in the writings of Irish novelist Maria Edgeworth (1767-1849) who is always sure of his knowledge.

714.20–21   "Presenting . . . divine."] Milton's "Il Penseroso," 99–100.

720.12   who see . . . and ask] Emended to "which sees . . . and asks" in the Centenary edition.

ENGLISH TRAITS

771.2   Allston] The American artist Washington Allston (1779–1843) settled in Cambridge, Massachusetts, after long residence in Italy and England. His first wife, Ann, was the sister of the noted Unitarian divine, William Ellery Channing (1780–1842).

774.5   *"Qualis artifex pereo!"*] "What an artist perishes in me!"

803.7   Sir James Parry] Changed in second printing to Sir Edward Parry.

817.7–10   "Let . . . adorn."] "Windsor Forest," 28–32.

831.1   by . . . Asser] Changed in second printing to "by a writer at the Norman Conquest."

833.6   make . . . instantly] "Makes no difference . . . it would" appears in the third printing.

833.35   Cintra business] Lord Wellington defeated the French in Portugal in 1808, but at a convention held at Cintra the English commissioner agreed to allow the French to leave Portugal with their arms and property.

834.5   10 April, 1848,] Date of mass procession and demonstration of Chartists; see 866.13–14.

834.11   *perfidious Albion*] Napoleon called England *Albion perfide*.

834.28   Rochester rappings] Spiritualist manifestations in Rochester, N.Y.

835.25–32   "In . . . too."]   "The True-born Englishman," (1701), II, 15–22.

838.10–11   "The ruggedest . . . Northumberland."]   *Henry IV, Part II*, I, i, 151.

839.6   creases]   Daggers with wavy blades. See 979.33.

854.28   Fenris-wolf]   In Scandinavian mythology, the wolf Fenris, son of Loki, was bound by a slim chain, Gleipnir, specially fashioned by the gods. See 952.23.

863.11   I doubt]   Meaning "I fear."

875.28–29   *Benedictus . . . benedicatur.*]   May the blessed one bless; he is blessed, let him be blessed.

882.17   Kertch or Kinburn]   Emerson evidently alludes to actions taken by governors of these Russian posts captured by the allies in the Crimean War.

884.5   Richard of Devizes]   Chronicler (fl. later twelfth century) of the deeds of Richard Coeur de Lion in Palestine. See 888.27–28.

888.8   Pugin]   Augustus Charles Pugin (1762–1832) was an architectural historian.

915.3   Mr. C.]   Thomas Carlyle.

921.23   (*Qu.* Alph?)]   Emerson playfully alludes to the sacred river in Coleridge's "Kubla Khan."

THE CONDUCT OF LIFE

946.25   Spurzheim]   Johann Caspar Spurzheim was a phrenologist who lectured in Boston in 1832.

946.26   Quetelet]   L. A. J. Quetelet (1796–1874) was a Belgian statistician who applied probability theory to social and political questions.

948.11–12   Mr. Frauenhofer or Dr. Carpenter]   The former was a distinguished astronomer and optician, the latter a student of the microscope.

949.15   Oken]   Lorenz Oken (1779–1851) was an early propounder of cellular theory.

951.2   Fust]   Johann Fust was associated with Gutenberg in the development of printing.

951.13   Œnopides]   Œnopides of Chios was an astronomer and mathematician of the fifth century B.C.

963.37–38   "*Quisque . . . manes.*"]   "The spirits who haunt us are ourselves." Virgil, *Aeneid*, IV, 743.

1007.33   *Impera parendo*]   Command by obeying.

1031.25–30   "Get . . . Poverty."]   Epigram LXV, "To My Muse."

1043.32   Winckelmann, and Lavater]   Eighteenth-century art historian and physiognomist, respectively.

1056.1   "Heaven . . . flow."]   From Edward Young's poem *The Complaint; or, Night Thoughts* (1742–45), VII, 347.

1086.11   " 'Tis . . . faults;"]   Cf. *Measure for Measure*, V, i, 439.

1118.30   Claude-Lorraines]   Colored optical devices for viewing landscapes, named after the seventeenth-century painter.

UNCOLLECTED PROSE

1130.16   Mark XIV. 23]   Corrected to Mark 24:22–25 in the 1884 Riverside edition.

1130.19   Luke XXII. 15]   Corrected to Luke 22:19 in the 1884 Riverside edition.

1172.6   some selections]   Only one of Emerson's selections is included here; the others have been omitted.

1213.5   Non-resistance Clubs.]   Emerson concludes with a long quotation from Mr. Whiting, here omitted.

1224.11   On the . . . University]   Emerson had already devoted a paragraph, here omitted, to details about the faculty and bequests at Harvard.

1266.37   Martin's Creation]   Emerson undoubtedly refers to the British painter John Martin (1789–1854), who specialized in sublime treatments of biblical subjects.

Library of Congress Cataloging in Publication Data

Emerson, Ralph Waldo, 1803–1882.
 Essays and lectures.

 (The Library of America; 15)
 Edited by Joel Porte.
 Contents: Nature; addresses, and lectures—Essays: first and
second series—Representative men—English traits—The conduct
of life—Uncollected prose.
 I. Porte, Joel. II. Title. III. Series.
PS1605   1983   814'.3   83–5447
ISBN 0–940450–15–1

This book is set in 10 point Linotron Galliard, a face designed for photocomposition by Matthew Carter and based on the sixteenth-century face Granjon. The paper is Olin Nyalite and conforms to guidelines adopted by the Committee on Book Longevity of the Council on Library Resources. The binding material is Brillianta, a 100% rayon cloth made by Van Heek-Scholco Textielfabrieken, Holland. Composition by Haddon Craftsmen, Inc. and The Clarinda Company. Printing and binding by R. R. Donnelley & Sons Company. Designed by Bruce Campbell.

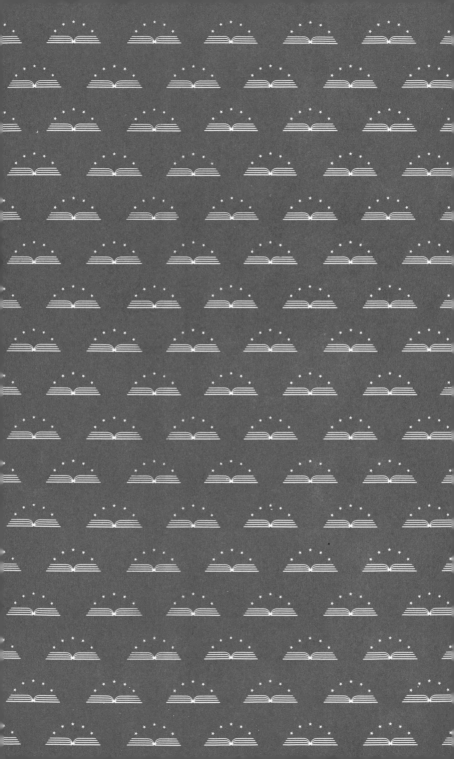